# CCIE Routing and Switching v5.0 Official Cert Guide, Volume 1

## Fifth Edition

Narbik Kocharians, CCIE No. 12410
Peter Palúch, CCIE No. 23527

**Cisco Press**

800 East 96th Street

Indianapolis, IN 46240

# CCIE Routing and Switching v5.0 Official Cert Guide, Volume 1, Fifth Edition

Narbik Kocharians, CCIE No. 12410

Peter Palúch, CCIE No. 23527

Copyright© 2015 Pearson Education, Inc.

Published by:
Cisco Press
800 East 96th Street
Indianapolis, IN 46240 USA

Printed in the United States of America

Second Printing February 2015

Library of Congress Control Number: 2014944345

ISBN-13: 978-1-58714-396-0

ISBN-10: 1-58714-396-8

## Warning and Disclaimer

## Trademark Acknowledgments

All terms mentioned in this book that are known to be trademarks or service marks have been appropriately capitalized. Cisco Press or Cisco Systems, Inc., cannot attest to the accuracy of this information. Use of a term in this book should not be regarded as affecting the validity of any trademark or service mark.

## Special Sales

For information about buying this title in bulk quantities, or for special sales opportunities (which may include electronic versions; custom cover designs; and content particular to your business, training goals, marketing focus, or branding interests), please contact our corporate sales department at corpsales@pearsoned.com or (800) 382-3419.

For government sales inquiries, please contact governmentsales@pearsoned.com.

For questions about sales outside the U.S., please contact international@pearsoned.com.

## Feedback Information

At Cisco Press, our goal is to create in-depth technical books of the highest quality and value. Each book is crafted with care and precision, undergoing rigorous development that involves the unique expertise of members from the professional technical community.

Readers' feedback is a natural continuation of this process. If you have any comments regarding how we could improve the quality of this book, or otherwise alter it to better suit your needs, you can contact us through email at feedback@ciscopress.com. Please make sure to include the book title and ISBN in your message.

We greatly appreciate your assistance.

**Publisher:** Paul Boger

**Associate Publisher:** Dave Dusthimer

**Business Operation Manager, Cisco Press:** Jan Cornelssen

**Executive Editor:** Brett Bartow

**Managing Editor:** Sandra Schroeder

**Senior Development Editor:** Christopher Cleveland

**Senior Project Editor:** Tonya Simpson

**Copy Editor:** John Edwards

**Technical Editors:** Paul Negron, Sean Wilkins

**Editorial Assistant:** Vanessa Evans

**Cover Designer:** Mark Shirar

**Composition:** Tricia Bronkella

**Indexer:** Tim Wright

**Proofreader:** Chuck Hutchinson

**Americas Headquarters**
Cisco Systems, Inc.
170 West Tasman Drive
San Jose, CA 95134-1706
USA
www.cisco.com
Tel: 408 526-4000
800 553-NETS (6387)
Fax: 408 527-0883

**Asia Pacific Headquarters**
Cisco Systems, Inc.
168 Robinson Road
#28-01 Capital Tower
Singapore 068912
www.cisco.com
Tel: +65 6317 7777
Fax: +65 6317 7799

**Europe Headquarters**
Cisco Systems International BV
Haarlerbergpark
Haarlerbergweg 13-19
1101 CH Amsterdam
The Netherlands
www.europe.cisco.com
Tel: +31 0 800 020 0791
Fax: +31 0 20 357 1100

Cisco has more than 200 offices worldwide. Addresses, phone numbers, and fax numbers are listed on the Cisco Website at **www.cisco.com/go/offices**.

©2007 Cisco Systems, Inc. All rights reserved. CCVP, the Cisco logo, and the Cisco Square Bridge logo are trademarks of Cisco Systems, Inc.; Changing the Way We Work, Live, Play, and Learn is a service mark of Cisco Systems, Inc.; and Access Registrar, Aironet, BPX, Catalyst, CCDA, CCDP, CCIE, CCIP, CCNA, CCNP, CCSP, Cisco, the Cisco Certified Internetwork Expert logo, Cisco IOS, Cisco Press, Cisco Systems, Cisco Systems Capital, the Cisco Systems logo, Cisco Unity, Enterprise/Solver, EtherChannel, EtherFast, EtherSwitch, Fast Step, Follow Me Browsing, FormShare, GigaDrive, GigaStack, HomeLink, Internet Quotient, IOS, IP/TV, iQ Expertise, the iQ logo, iQ Net Readiness Scorecard, iQuick Study, LightStream, Linksys, MeetingPlace, MGX, Networking Academy, Network Registrar, Packet, PIX, ProConnect, RateMUX, ScriptShare, SlideCast, SMARTnet, StackWise, The Fastest Way to Increase Your Internet Quotient, and TransPath are registered trademarks of Cisco Systems, Inc. and/or its affiliates in the United States and certain other countries.

All other trademarks mentioned in this document or Website are the property of their respective owners. The use of the word partner does not imply a partnership relationship between Cisco and any other company. (0609R)

## About the Authors

**Narbik Kocharians**, CCIE No. 12410 (Routing and Switching, Security, SP), is a Triple CCIE with more than 32 years of experience in the IT industry. He has designed, implemented, and supported numerous enterprise networks. Narbik is the president of Micronics Training Inc. (www.micronicstraining.com), where he teaches CCIE R&S and SP boot camps.

**Peter Palúch**, CCIE No. 23527 (Routing and Switching), is an assistant professor, Cisco Networking Academy instructor, and instructor trainer at the Faculty of Management Science and Informatics, University of Zilina, Slovakia. Peter has cooperated in various educational activities in Slovakia and abroad, focusing on networking and Linux-based network server systems. He is also active at the Cisco Support Community, holding the Cisco Designated VIP award in LAN & WAN Routing and Switching areas since the award program inception in 2011. Upon invitation by Cisco in 2012, Peter joined two Job Task Analysis groups that assisted defining the upcoming CCIE R&S and CCNP R&S certification exam topics. Peter holds an M.Sc. degree in Applied Informatics and a doctoral degree in the area of VoIP quality degradation factors. Together with his students, Peter has started the project of implementing the EIGRP routing protocol into the Quagga open-source routing software suite, and has been driving the effort since its inception in 2013.

## About the Technical Reviewers

**Paul Negron**, CCIE No. 14856, CCSI No. 22752, has been affiliated with networking technologies for 17 years and has been involved with the design of core network services for a number of service providers, such as Comcast, Qwest, British Telecom, and Savvis to name a few. He currently instructs all the CCNP Service Provider–level courses, including Advanced BGP, MPLS, and the QoS course. Paul has six years of experience with satellite communications as well as ten years of experience with Cisco platforms.

**Sean Wilkins** is an accomplished networking consultant for SR-W Consulting (www.sr-wconsulting.com) and has been in the field of IT since the mid 1990s, working with companies such as Cisco, Lucent, Verizon, and AT&T as well as several other private companies. Sean currently holds certifications with Cisco (CCNP/CCDP), Microsoft (MCSE), and CompTIA (A+ and Network+). He also has a Master of Science in information technology with a focus in network architecture and design, a Master of Science in organizational management, a Master's Certificate in network security, a Bachelor of Science in computer networking, and Associates of Applied Science in computer information systems. In addition to working as a consultant, Sean spends most of his time as a technical writer and editor for various companies; check out this work at his author website: www.infodispersion.com.

# Dedications

**From Narbik Kocharians:**

I would like to dedicate this book to my wife, Janet, for her love, encouragement, and continuous support, and to my dad for his words of wisdom.

**From Peter Palúch:**

To my family, students, colleagues, and friends.

# Acknowledgments

**From Narbik Kocharians:**

First, I would like to thank God for giving me the opportunity and ability to write, teach, and do what I truly enjoy doing. Also, I would like to thank my family, especially my wife of 29 years, Janet, for her constant encouragement and help. She does such an amazing job of interacting with students and handling all the logistics of organizing classes as I focus on teaching. I also would like to thank my children, Chris, Patrick, Alexandra, and my little one, Daniel, for their patience.

A special thanks goes to Mr. Brett Bartow for his patience and our constant changing of the deadlines. It goes without saying that the technical editors and reviewers did a phenomenal job; thank you very much. Finally, I would like to thank all my students who inspire me every day, and you, for reading this book.

**From Peter Palúch:**

The opportunity to cooperate on the new edition of this book has been an honor and privilege beyond words for me. Wendell Odom, who has so gracefully and generously passed the torch to us, was the key person in introducing me to the Cisco Press representatives as a possible author, and I will be forever indebted to him for all the trust he has blessed us with. I have strived very much to live up to the unparalelled high level of content all previous authors have maintained throughout all editions of this book, and I would like to sincerely thank all of them for authoring such a great book that has significantly helped me achieve my certification in the first place.

My next immense thank you goes to Brett Bartow, the executive editor for this book. Brett's inviting and forthcoming attitude throughout the time of editing the book, compounded with his patience and understanding for my ever-moving (and constantly missed) deadlines, is second to none. He has done all in his power to help us, the authors, without compromising the quality of the work.

I would not have been able to complete my work on this volume without the endless support of my family. They have encouraged me, supported me, and gone out of their way to accommodate my needs. Words are not enough to express my gratitude.

Psalm 127, whose musical setting in works of Monteverdi, Handel, or Vivaldi I have come to admire, begins with words "Unless the Lord build the house, they labor in vain who build." Indeed, if it was not first and foremost the Lord's blessing and help throughout, this work would not have been finished successfully. To my Lord and Savior, Jesus Christ—thank you!

# Contents at a Glance

# Contents

# Icons Used in This Book

# Command Syntax Conventions

The conventions used to present command syntax in this book are the same conventions used in the IOS Command Reference. The Command Reference describes these conventions as follows:

- **Boldface** indicates commands and keywords that are entered literally as shown. In actual configuration examples and output (not general command syntax), boldface indicates commands that are manually input by the user (such as a **show** command).

- *Italic* indicates arguments for which you supply actual values.

- Vertical bars (|) separate alternative, mutually exclusive elements.

- Square brackets ([ ]) indicate an optional element.

- Braces ({ }) indicate a required choice.

- Braces within brackets ([{ }]) indicate a required choice within an optional element.

# Introduction

The Cisco Certified Internetwork Expert (CCIE) certification might be the most challenging and prestigious of all networking certifications. It has received numerous awards and certainly has built a reputation as one of the most difficult certifications to earn in all of the technology world. Having a CCIE certification opens doors professionally and typically results in higher pay and looks great on a resume.

Cisco currently offers several CCIE certifications. This book covers the version 5.0 exam blueprint topics of the written exam for the CCIE Routing and Switching certification. The following list details the currently available CCIE certifications at the time of this book's publication; check www.cisco.com/go/ccie for the latest information. The certifications are listed in the order in which they appear on the web page:

- CCDE
- CCIE Collaboration
- CCIE Data Center
- CCIE Routing & Switching
- CCIE Security
- CCIE Service Provider
- CCIE Service Provider Operations
- CCIE Wireless

Each of the CCDE and CCIE certifications requires the candidate to pass both a written exam and a one-day, hands-on lab exam. The written exam is intended to test your knowledge of theory, protocols, and configuration concepts that follow good design practices. The lab exam proves that you can configure and troubleshoot actual gear.

## Why Should I Take the CCIE Routing and Switching Written Exam?

The first and most obvious reason to take the CCIE Routing and Switching written exam is that it is the first step toward obtaining the CCIE Routing and Switching certification. Also, you cannot schedule a CCIE lab exam until you pass the corresponding written exam. In short, if you want all the professional benefits of a CCIE Routing and Switching certification, you start by passing the written exam.

The benefits of getting a CCIE certification are varied and include the following:

- Better pay
- Career-advancement opportunities

- Applies to certain minimum requirements for Cisco Silver and Gold Channel Partners, as well as those seeking Master Specialization, making you more valuable to Channel Partners

- Better movement through the problem-resolution process when calling the Cisco TAC

- Prestige

- Credibility for consultants and customer engineers, including the use of the Cisco CCIE logo

The other big reason to take the CCIE Routing and Switching written exam is that it recertifies an individual's associate-, professional-, and expert-level Cisco certifications, regardless of his or her technology track. Recertification requirements do change, so please verify the requirements at www.cisco.com/go/certifications.

## CCIE Routing and Switching Written Exam 400-101

The CCIE Routing and Switching written exam, at the time of this writing, consists of a two-hour exam administered at a proctored exam facility affiliated with Pearson VUE (www.vue.com/cisco). The exam typically includes approximately 100 multiple-choice questions. No simulation questions are currently part of the written exam.

As with most exams, everyone wants to know what is on the exam. Cisco provides general guidance as to topics on the exam in the CCIE Routing and Switching written exam blueprint, the most recent copy of which can be accessed from www.cisco.com/go/ccie.

Cisco changes both the CCIE written and lab blueprints over time, but Cisco seldom, if ever, changes the exam numbers. However, exactly this change occurred when the CCIE Routing and Switching blueprint was refreshed for v5.0. The previous written exam for v4.0 was numbered 350-001; the v5.0 written exam is identified by 400-101.

Table I-1 lists the CCIE Routing and Switching written exam blueprint 5.0 at press time. Table I-1 also lists the chapters that cover each topic.

**Table I-1**   *CCIE Routing and Switching Written Exam Blueprint*

| Topics | Book Volume | Book Chapter |
|---|---|---|
| **1.0 Network Principles** | | |
| *1.1 Network theory* | | |
| 1.1.a Describe basic software architecture differences between IOS and IOS XE | | |
| 1.1.a (i) Control plane and Forwarding plane | 1 | 1 |
| 1.1.a (ii) Impact on troubleshooting and performance | 1 | 1 |
| 1.1.a (iii) Excluding a specific platform's architecture | 1 | 1 |

| Topics | Book Volume | Book Chapter |
|---|---|---|
| **1.1.b Identify Cisco Express Forwarding concepts** | | |
| 1.1.b (i) RIB, FIB, LFIB, Adjacency table | 1 | 6 |
| 1.1.b (ii) Load-balancing hash | 1 | 6 |
| 1.1.b (iii) Polarization concept and avoidance | 1 | 6 |
| **1.1.c Explain general network challenges** | | |
| 1.1.c (i) Unicast flooding | 1 | 4 |
| 1.1.c (ii) Out-of-order packets | 1 | 4 |
| 1.1.c (iii) Asymmetric routing | 1 | 4 |
| 1.1.c (iv) Impact of micro burst | 1 | 4 |
| **1.1.d Explain IP operations** | | |
| 1.1.d (i) ICMP unreachable, redirect | 1 | 4 |
| 1.1.d (ii) IPv4 options, IPv6 extension headers | 1 | 4 |
| 1.1.d (iii) IPv4 and IPv6 fragmentation | 1 | 4 |
| 1.1.d (iv) TTL | 1 | 4 |
| 1.1.d (v) IP MTU | 1 | 4 |
| **1.1.e Explain TCP operations** | | |
| 1.1.e (i) IPv4 and IPv6 PMTU | 1 | 4 |
| 1.1.e (ii) MSS | 1 | 4 |
| 1.1.e (iii) Latency | 1 | 4 |
| 1.1.e (iv) Windowing | 1 | 4 |
| 1.1.e (v) Bandwidth delay product | 1 | 4 |
| 1.1.e (vi) Global synchronization | 1 | 4 |
| 1.1.e (vii) Options | 1 | 4 |
| **1.1.f Explain UDP operations** | | |
| 1.1.f (i) Starvation | 1 | 4 |
| 1.1.f (ii) Latency | 1 | 4 |
| 1.1.f (iii) RTP/RTCP concepts | 1 | 4 |
| *1.2 Network implementation and operation* | | |
| **1.2.a Evaluate proposed changes to a network** | | |
| 1.2.a (i) Changes to routing protocol parameters | 1 | 7–10 |
| 1.2.a (ii) Migrate parts of a network to IPv6 | 1 | 4 |

| Topics | Book Volume | Book Chapter |
|---|---|---|
| 1.2.a (iii) Routing protocol migration | 1 | 6 |
| 1.2.a (iv) Adding multicast support | 2 | 8 |
| 1.2.a (v) Migrate Spanning Tree Protocol | 1 | 3 |
| 1.2.a (vi) Evaluate impact of new traffic on existing QoS design | 2 | 3, 4, 5 |
| *1.3 Network troubleshooting* | | |
| 1.3.a Use IOS troubleshooting tools | | |
| 1.3.a (i) debug, conditional debug | 1 | 4 |
| 1.3.a (ii) ping, traceroute with extended options | 1 | 4 |
| 1.3.a (iii) Embedded packet capture | 2 | 9 |
| 1.3.a (iv) Performance monitor | 1 | 5 |
| 1.3.b Apply troubleshooting methodologies | | |
| 1.3.b (i) Diagnose the root cause of networking issues (analyze symptoms, identify and describe root cause) | 1 | 11 |
| 1.3.b (ii) Design and implement valid solutions according to constraints | 1 | 11 |
| 1.3.b (iii) Verify and monitor resolution | 1 | 11 |
| 1.3.c Interpret packet capture | | |
| 1.3.c (i) Using Wireshark trace analyzer | 2 | 9 |
| 1.3.c (ii) Using IOS embedded packet capture | 2 | 9 |
| **2.0 Layer 2 Technologies** | | |
| *2.1 LAN switching technologies* | | |
| 2.1.a Implement and troubleshoot switch administration | | |
| 2.1.a (i) Managing the MAC address table | 1 | 1 |
| 2.1.a (ii) errdisable recovery | 1 | 3 |
| 2.1.a (iii) L2 MTU | 1 | 1 |
| 2.1.b Implement and troubleshoot Layer 2 protocols | | |
| 2.1.b (i) CDP, LLDP | 1 | 3 |
| 2.1.b (ii) UDLD | 1 | 3 |
| 2.1.c Implement and troubleshoot VLAN | | |
| 2.1.c (i) Access ports | 1 | 2 |
| 2.1.c (ii) VLAN database | 1 | 2 |
| 2.1.c (iii) Normal, extended VLAN, voice VLAN | 1 | 2 |

| Topics | Book Volume | Book Chapter |
| --- | --- | --- |
| 2.1.d Implement and troubleshoot trunking | | |
| 2.1.d (i) VTPv1, VTPv2, VTPv3, VTP pruning | 1 | 2 |
| 2.1.d (ii) dot1Q | 1 | 2 |
| 2.1.d (iii) Native VLAN | 1 | 2 |
| 2.1.d (iv) Manual pruning | 1 | 2 |
| 2.1.e Implement and troubleshoot EtherChannel | | |
| 2.1.e (i) LACP, PAgP, manual | 1 | 3 |
| 2.1.e (ii) Layer 2, Layer 3 | 1 | 3 |
| 2.1.e (iii) Load balancing | 1 | 3 |
| 2.1.e (iv) EtherChannel misconfiguration guard | 1 | 3 |
| 2.1.f Implement and troubleshoot spanning tree | | |
| 2.1.f (i) PVST+/RPVST+/MST | 1 | 3 |
| 2.1.f (ii) Switch priority, port priority, path cost, STP timers | 1 | 3 |
| 2.1.f (iii) PortFast, BPDU Guard, BPDU Filter | 1 | 3 |
| 2.1.f (iv) Loop Guard, Root Guard | 1 | 3 |
| 2.1.g Implement and troubleshoot other LAN switching technologies | | |
| 2.1.g (i) SPAN, RSPAN, ERSPAN | 1 | 1 |
| 2.1.h Describe chassis virtualization and aggregation technologies | | |
| 2.1.h (i) Multichassis | 1 | 1 |
| 2.1.h (ii) VSS concepts | 1 | 1 |
| 2.1.h (iii) Alternatives to STP | 1 | 1 |
| 2.1.h (iv) Stackwise | 1 | 1 |
| 2.1.h (v) Excluding specific platform implementation | 1 | 1 |
| 2.1.i Describe spanning-tree concepts | | |
| 2.1.i (i) Compatibility between MST and RSTP | 1 | 3 |
| 2.1.i (ii) STP dispute, STP Bridge Assurance | 1 | 3 |
| 2.2 Layer 2 multicast | | |
| 2.2.a Implement and troubleshoot IGMP | | |
| 2.2.a (i) IGMPv1, IGMPv2, IGMPv3 | 2 | 7 |
| 2.2.a (ii) IGMP snooping | 2 | 7 |
| 2.2.a (iii) IGMP querier | 2 | 7 |

| Topics | Book Volume | Book Chapter |
| --- | --- | --- |
| 2.2.a (iv) IGMP filter | 2 | 7 |
| 2.2.a (v) IGMP proxy | 2 | 7 |
| 2.2.b Explain MLD | 2 | 8 |
| 2.2.c Explain PIM snooping | 2 | 8 |
| *2.3 Layer 2 WAN circuit technologies* | | |
| 2.3.a Implement and troubleshoot HDLC | 2 | 6 |
| 2.3.b Implement and troubleshoot PPP | | |
| 2.3.b (i) Authentication (PAP, CHAP) | 2 | 6 |
| 2.3.b (ii) PPPoE | 2 | 6 |
| 2.3.b (iii) MLPPP | 2 | 6 |
| 2.3.c Describe WAN rate-based Ethernet circuits | | |
| 2.3.c (i) Metro and WAN Ethernet topologies | 2 | 6 |
| 2.3.c (ii) Use of rate-limited WAN Ethernet services | 2 | 6 |
| **3.0 Layer 3 Technologies** | | |
| *3.1 Addressing technologies* | | |
| 3.1.a Identify, implement, and troubleshoot IPv4 addressing and subnetting | | |
| 3.1.a (i) Address types, VLSM | 1 | 4 |
| 3.1.a (ii) ARP | 1 | 4 |
| 3.1.b Identify, implement, and troubleshoot IPv6 addressing and subnetting | | |
| 3.1.b (i) Unicast, multicast | 1 | 4 |
| 3.1.b (ii) EUI-64 | 1 | 4 |
| 3.1.b (iii) ND, RS/RA | 1 | 4 |
| 3.1.b (iv) Autoconfig/SLAAC, temporary addresses (RFC 4941) | 1 | 4 |
| 3.1.b (v) Global prefix configuration feature | 1 | 4 |
| 3.1.b (vi) DHCP protocol operations | 1 | 4 |
| 3.1.b (vii) SLAAC/DHCPv6 interaction | 2 | 10 |
| 3.1.b (viii) Stateful, stateless DHCPv6 | 1 | 4 |
| 3.1.b (ix) DHCPv6 prefix delegation | 1 | 4 |
| *3.2 Layer 3 multicast* | | |
| 3.2.a Troubleshoot reverse path forwarding | | |

| Topics | Book Volume | Book Chapter |
|---|---|---|
| 3.2.a (i) RPF failure | 2 | 8 |
| 3.2.a (ii) RPF failure with tunnel interface | 2 | 8 |
| 3.2.b Implement and troubleshoot IPv4 protocol independent multicast | | |
| 3.2.b (i) PIM dense mode, sparse mode, sparse-dense mode | 2 | 8 |
| 3.2.b (ii) Static RP, auto-RP, BSR | 2 | 8 |
| 3.2.b (iii) Bidirectional PIM | 2 | 8 |
| 3.2.b (iv) Source-specific multicast | 2 | 8 |
| 3.2.b (v) Group-to-RP mapping | 2 | 8 |
| 3.2.b (vi) Multicast boundary | 2 | 8 |
| 3.2.c Implement and troubleshoot multicast source discovery protocol | | |
| 3.2.c (i) Intra-domain MSDP (anycast RP) | 2 | 8 |
| 3.2.c (ii) SA filter | 2 | 8 |
| 3.2.d Describe IPv6 multicast | | |
| 3.2.d (i) IPv6 multicast addresses | 2 | 7 |
| 3.2.d (ii) PIMv6 | 2 | 8 |
| 3.3 Fundamental routing concepts | | |
| 3.3.a Implement and troubleshoot static routing | 1 | 6 |
| 3.3.b Implement and troubleshoot default routing | 1 | 7–11 |
| 3.3.c Compare routing protocol types | | |
| 3.3.c (i) Distance vector | 1 | 7 |
| 3.3.c (ii) Link state | 1 | 7 |
| 3.3.c (iii) Path vector | 1 | 7 |
| 3.3.d Implement, optimize, and troubleshoot administrative distance | 1 | 11 |
| 3.3.e Implement and troubleshoot passive interface | 1 | 7–10 |
| 3.3.f Implement and troubleshoot VRF lite | 2 | 11 |
| 3.3.g Implement, optimize, and troubleshoot filtering with any routing protocol | 1 | 11 |
| 3.3.h Implement, optimize, and troubleshoot redistribution between any routing protocols | 1 | 11 |
| 3.3.i Implement, optimize, and troubleshoot manual and auto summarization with any routing protocol | 1 | 7–10 |

| Topics | Book Volume | Book Chapter |
|---|---|---|
| 3.5.d (ii) Topology table, update, query, active, passive | 1 | 8 |
| 3.5.d (iii) Stuck in active | 1 | 8 |
| 3.5.d (iv) Graceful shutdown | 1 | 8 |
| 3.5.e Implement and troubleshoot EIGRP stub | | |
| 3.5.e (i) Stub | 1 | 8 |
| 3.5.e (ii) Leak-map | 1 | 8 |
| 3.5.f Implement and troubleshoot load balancing | | |
| 3.5.f (i) equal-cost | 1 | 8 |
| 3.5.f (ii) unequal-cost | 1 | 8 |
| 3.5.f (iii) add-path | 1 | 8 |
| 3.5.g Implement EIGRP (multiaddress) named mode | | |
| 3.5.g (i) Types of families | 1 | 8 |
| 3.5.g (ii) IPv4 address-family | 1 | 8 |
| 3.5.g (iii) IPv6 address-family | 1 | 8 |
| 3.5.h Implement, troubleshoot, and optimize EIGRP convergence and scalability | | |
| 3.5.h (i) Describe fast convergence requirements | 1 | 8 |
| 3.5.h (ii) Control query boundaries | 1 | 8 |
| 3.5.h (iii) IP FRR/fast reroute (single hop) | 1 | 8 |
| 3.5.h (iv) Summary leak-map | 1 | 8 |
| 3.5.h (v) Summary metric | 1 | 8 |
| 3.6 OSPF (v2 and v3) | | |
| 3.6.a Describe packet types | | |
| 3.6.a (i) LSA types (1, 2, 3, 4, 5, 7, 9) | 1 | 9 |
| 3.6.a (ii) Route types (N1, N2, E1, E2) | 1 | 9 |
| 3.6.b Implement and troubleshoot neighbor relationship | 1 | 9 |
| 3.6.c Implement and troubleshoot OSPFv3 address-family support | | |
| 3.6.c (i) IPv4 address-family | 1 | 9 |
| 3.6.c (ii) IPv6 address-family | 1 | 9 |
| 3.6.d Implement and troubleshoot network types, area types, and router types | | |
| 3.6.d (i) Point-to-point, multipoint, broadcast, nonbroadcast | 1 | 9 |

| Topics | Book Volume | Book Chapter |
|---|---|---|
| 3.6.d (ii) LSA types, area type: backbone, normal, transit, stub, NSSA, totally stub | 1 | 9 |
| 3.6.d (iii) Internal router, ABR, ASBR | 1 | 9 |
| 3.6.d (iv) Virtual link | 1 | 9 |
| 3.6.e Implement and troubleshoot path preference | 1 | 9 |
| 3.6.f Implement and troubleshoot operations | | |
| 3.6.f (i) General operations | 1 | 9 |
| 3.6.f (ii) Graceful shutdown | 1 | 9 |
| 3.6.f (iii) GTSM (Generic TTL Security Mechanism) | 1 | 9 |
| 3.6.g Implement, troubleshoot, and optimize OSPF convergence and scalability | | |
| 3.6.g (i) Metrics | 1 | 9 |
| 3.6.g (ii) LSA throttling, SPF tuning, fast hello | 1 | 9 |
| 3.6.g (iii) LSA propagation control (area types, ISPF) | 1 | 9 |
| 3.6.g (iv) IP FRR/fast reroute (single hop) | 1 | 9 |
| 3.6.g (v) LFA/loop-free alternative (multihop) | 1 | 9 |
| 3.6.g (vi) OSPFv3 prefix suppression | 1 | 9 |
| 3.7 BGP | | |
| 3.7.a Describe, implement, and troubleshoot peer relationships | | |
| 3.7.a (i) Peer-group, template | 2 | 1 |
| 3.7.a (ii) Active, passive | 2 | 1 |
| 3.7.a (iii) States, timers | 2 | 1 |
| 3.7.a (iv) Dynamic neighbors | 2 | 1 |
| 3.7.b Implement and troubleshoot IBGP and EBGP | | |
| 3.7.b (i) EBGP, IBGP | 2 | 1 |
| 3.7.b (ii) 4-byte AS number | 2 | 1 |
| 3.7.b (iii) Private AS | 2 | 1 |
| 3.7.c Explain attributes and best-path selection | 2 | 1 |
| 3.7.d Implement, optimize, and troubleshoot routing policies | | |
| 3.7.d (i) Attribute manipulation | 2 | 2 |
| 3.7.d (ii) Conditional advertisement | 2 | 2 |
| 3.7.d (iii) Outbound route filtering | 2 | 2 |

| Topics | Book Volume | Book Chapter |
|---|---|---|
| 3.7.d (iv) Communities, extended communities | 2 | 2 |
| 3.7.d (v) Multihoming | 2 | 2 |
| 3.7.e Implement and troubleshoot scalability | | |
| 3.7.e (i) Route-reflector, cluster | 2 | 2 |
| 3.7.e (ii) Confederations | 2 | 2 |
| 3.7.e (iii) Aggregation, AS set | 2 | 2 |
| 3.7.f Implement and troubleshoot multiprotocol BGP | | |
| 3.7.f (i) IPv4, IPv6, VPN address-family | 2 | 2 |
| 3.7.g Implement and troubleshoot AS path manipulations | | |
| 3.7.g (i) Local AS, allow AS in, remove private AS | 2 | 2 |
| 3.7.g (ii) Prepend | 2 | 2 |
| 3.7.g (iii) Regexp | 2 | 2 |
| 3.7.h Implement and troubleshoot other features | | |
| 3.7.h (i) Multipath | 2 | 2 |
| 3.7.h (ii) BGP synchronization | 2 | 2 |
| 3.7.h (iii) Soft reconfiguration, route refresh | 2 | 2 |
| 3.7.i Describe BGP fast convergence features | | |
| 3.7.i (i) Prefix independent convergence | 2 | 2 |
| 3.7.i (ii) Add-path | 2 | 2 |
| 3.7.i (iii) Next-hop address tracking | 2 | 2 |
| 3.8 IS-IS (for IPv4 and IPv6) | | |
| 3.8.a Describe basic IS-IS network | | |
| 3.8.a (i) Single area, single topology | 1 | 10 |
| 3.8.b Describe neighbor relationship | 1 | 10 |
| 3.8.c Describe network types, levels, and router types | | |
| 3.8.c (i) NSAP addressing | 1 | 10 |
| 3.8.c (ii) Point-to-point, broadcast | 1 | 10 |
| 3.8.d Describe operations | 1 | 10 |
| 3.8.e Describe optimization features | | |
| 3.8.e (i) Metrics, wide metric | 1 | 10 |
| 4.0 VPN Technologies | | |

| Topics | Book Volume | Book Chapter |
|---|---|---|
| *4.1 Tunneling* | | |
| 4.1.a Implement and troubleshoot MPLS operations | | |
| 4.1.a (i) Label stack, LSR, LSP | 2 | 11 |
| 4.1.a (ii) LDP | 2 | 11 |
| 4.1.a (iii) MPLS ping, MPLS traceroute | 2 | 11 |
| 4.1.b Implement and troubleshoot basic MPLS L3VPN | | |
| 4.1.b (i) L3VPN, CE, PE, P | 2 | 11 |
| 4.1.b (ii) Extranet (route leaking) | 2 | 11 |
| 4.1.c Implement and troubleshoot encapsulation | | |
| 4.1.c (i) GRE | 2 | 10 |
| 4.1.c (ii) Dynamic GRE | 2 | 10 |
| 4.1.c (iii) LISP encapsulation principles supporting EIGRP OTP | 1 | 8 |
| 4.1.d Implement and troubleshoot DMVPN (single hub) | | |
| 4.1.d (i) NHRP | 2 | 10 |
| 4.1.d (ii) DMVPN with IPsec using preshared key | 2 | 10 |
| 4.1.d (iii) QoS profile | 2 | 10 |
| 4.1.d (iv) Pre-classify | 2 | 10 |
| 4.1.e Describe IPv6 tunneling techniques | | |
| 4.1.e (i) 6in4, 6to4 | 2 | 8 |
| 4.1.e (ii) ISATAP | 2 | 8 |
| 4.1.e (iii) 6RD | 2 | 8 |
| 4.1.e (iv) 6PE/6VPE | 2 | 8 |
| 4.1.g Describe basic Layer 2 VPN—wireline | | |
| 4.1.g (i) L2TPv3 general principles | 2 | 10 |
| 4.1.g (ii) ATOM general principles | 2 | 11 |
| 4.1.h Describe basic L2VPN—LAN services | | |
| 4.1.h (i) MPLS-VPLS general principles | 2 | 10 |
| 4.1.h (ii) OTV general principles | 2 | 10 |
| *4.2 Encryption* | | |
| 4.2.a Implement and troubleshoot IPsec with preshared key | | |
| 4.2.a (i) IPv4 site to IPv4 site | 2 | 10 |

| Topics | Book Volume | Book Chapter |
|---|---|---|
| 4.2.a (ii) IPv6 in IPv4 tunnels | 2 | 10 |
| 4.2.a (iii) Virtual tunneling Interface (VTI) | 2 | 10 |
| 4.2.b Describe GET VPN | 2 | 10 |
| **5.0 Infrastructure Security** | | |
| *5.1 Device security* | | |
| 5.1.a Implement and troubleshoot IOS AAA using local database | 2 | 9 |
| 5.1.b Implement and troubleshoot device access control | | |
| 5.1.b (i) Lines (VTY, AUX, console) | 1 | 5 |
| 5.1.b (ii) SNMP | 1 | 5 |
| 5.1.b (iii) Management plane protection | 2 | 9 |
| 5.1.b (iv) Password encryption | 1 | 5 |
| 5.1.c Implement and troubleshoot control plane policing | 2 | 9 |
| 5.1.d Describe device security using IOS AAA with TACACS+ and RADIUS | | |
| 5.1.d (i) AAA with TACACS+ and RADIUS | 2 | 9 |
| 5.1.d (ii) Local privilege authorization fallback | 2 | 9 |
| *5.2 Network security* | | |
| 5.2.a Implement and troubleshoot switch security features | | |
| 5.2.a (i) VACL, PACL | 2 | 9 |
| 5.2.a (ii) Stormcontrol | 2 | 9 |
| 5.2.a (iii) DHCP snooping | 2 | 9 |
| 5.2.a (iv) IP source-guard | 2 | 9 |
| 5.2.a (v) Dynamic ARP inspection | 2 | 9 |
| 5.2.a (vi) port-security | 2 | 9 |
| 5.2.a (vii) Private VLAN | 1 | 2 |
| 5.2.b Implement and troubleshoot router security features | | |
| 5.2.b (i) IPv4 access control lists (standard, extended, time-based) | 2 | 9 |
| 5.2.b (ii) IPv6 traffic filter | 2 | 9 |
| 5.2.b (iii) Unicast reverse path forwarding | 2 | 9 |
| 5.2.c Implement and troubleshoot IPv6 first-hop security | | |
| 5.2.c (i) RA guard | 2 | 9 |

| Topics | Book Volume | Book Chapter |
|---|---|---|
| 5.2.c (ii) DHCP guard | 2 | 9 |
| 5.2.c (iii) Binding table | 2 | 9 |
| 5.2.c (iv) Device tracking | 2 | 9 |
| 5.2.c (v) ND inspection/snooping | 2 | 9 |
| 5.2.c (vii) Source guard | 2 | 9 |
| 5.2.c (viii) PACL | 2 | 9 |
| 5.2.d Describe 802.1x | | |
| 5.2.d (i) 802.1x, EAP, RADIUS | 2 | 9 |
| 5.2.d (ii) MAC authentication bypass | 2 | 9 |
| 6.0 Infrastructure Services | | |
| 6.1 System management | | |
| 6.1.a Implement and troubleshoot device management | | |
| 6.1.a (i) Console and VTY | 1 | 5 |
| 6.1.a (ii) Telnet, HTTP, HTTPS, SSH, SCP | 1 | 5 |
| 6.1.a (iii) (T)FTP | 1 | 5 |
| 6.1.b Implement and troubleshoot SNMP | | |
| 6.1.b (i) v2c, v3 | 1 | 5 |
| 6.1.c Implement and troubleshoot logging | | |
| 6.1.c (i) Local logging, syslog, debug, conditional debug | 1 | 5 |
| 6.1.c (ii) Timestamp | 2 | 6 |
| 6.2 Quality of service | | |
| 6.2.a Implement and troubleshoot end-to-end QoS | | |
| 6.2.a (i) CoS and DSCP mapping | 2 | 3 |
| 6.2.b Implement, optimize, and troubleshoot QoS using MQC | | |
| 6.2.b (i) Classification | 2 | 3 |
| 6.2.b (ii) Network-based application recognition (NBAR) | 2 | 3 |
| 6.2.b (iii) Marking using IP precedence, DSCP, CoS, ECN | 2 | 3 |
| 6.2.b (iv) Policing, shaping | 2 | 5 |
| 6.2.b (v) Congestion management (queuing) | 2 | 4 |
| 6.2.b (vi) HQoS, subrate Ethernet link | 2 | 3, 4, 5 |
| 6.2.b (vii) Congestion avoidance (WRED) | 2 | 4 |

| Topics | Book Volume | Book Chapter |
|---|---|---|
| 6.2.c Describe Layer 2 QoS | | |
| 6.2.c (i) Queuing, scheduling | 2 | 4 |
| 6.2.c (ii) Classification, marking | 2 | 2 |
| *6.3 Network services* | | |
| 6.3.a Implement and troubleshoot first-hop redundancy protocols | | |
| 6.3.a (i) HSRP, GLBP, VRRP | 1 | 5 |
| 6.3.a (ii) Redundancy using IPv6 RS/RA | 1 | 5 |
| 6.3.b Implement and troubleshoot Network Time Protocol | | |
| 6.3.b (i) NTP master, client, version 3, version 4 | 1 | 5 |
| 6.3.b (ii) NTP Authentication | 1 | 5 |
| 6.3.c Implement and troubleshoot IPv4 and IPv6 DHCP | | |
| 6.3.c (i) DHCP client, IOS DHCP server, DHCP relay | 1 | 5 |
| 6.3.c (ii) DHCP options | 1 | 5 |
| 6.3.c (iii) DHCP protocol operations | 1 | 5 |
| 6.3.c (iv) SLAAC/DHCPv6 interaction | 1 | 4 |
| 6.3.c (v) Stateful, stateless DHCPv6 | 1 | 4 |
| 6.3.c (vi) DHCPv6 prefix delegation | 1 | 4 |
| 6.3.d Implement and troubleshoot IPv4 Network Address Translation | | |
| 6.3.d (i) Static NAT, dynamic NAT, policy-based NAT, PAT | 1 | 5 |
| 6.3.d (ii) NAT ALG | 2 | 10 |
| 6.3.e Describe IPv6 Network Address Translation | | |
| 6.3.e (i) NAT64 | 2 | 10 |
| 6.3.e (ii) NPTv6 | 2 | 10 |
| *6.4 Network optimization* | | |
| 6.4.a Implement and troubleshoot IP SLA | | |
| 6.4.a (i) ICMP, UDP, jitter, VoIP | 1 | 5 |
| 6.4.b Implement and troubleshoot tracking object | | |
| 6.4.b (i) Tracking object, tracking list | 1 | 5 |
| 6.4.b (ii) Tracking different entities (for example, interfaces, routes, IPSLA, and so on) | 1 | 5 |
| 6.4.c Implement and troubleshoot NetFlow | | |

| Topics | Book Volume | Book Chapter |
|---|---|---|
| 6.4.c (i) NetFlow v5, v9 | 1 | 5 |
| 6.4.c (ii) Local retrieval | 1 | 5 |
| 6.4.c (iii) Export (configuration only) | 1 | 5 |
| 6.4.d Implement and troubleshoot embedded event manager | | |
| 6.4.d (i) EEM policy using applet | 1 | 5 |
| 6.4.e Identify performance routing (PfR) | | |
| 6.4.e (i) Basic load balancing | 1 | 11 |
| 6.4.e (ii) Voice optimization | 1 | 11 |

To give you practice on these topics, and pull the topics together, Edition 5 of the *CCIE Routing and Switching v5.0 Official Cert Guide, Volume 1* includes a large set of CD questions that mirror the types of questions expected for the Version 5.0 blueprint. By their very nature, these topics require the application of the knowledge listed throughout the book. This special section of questions provides a means to learn and practice these skills with a proportionally larger set of questions added specifically for this purpose.

These questions will be available to you in the practice test engine database, whether you take full exams or choose questions by category.

## About the *CCIE Routing and Switching v5.0 Official Cert Guide, Volume 1*, Fifth Edition

This section provides a brief insight into the contents of the book, the major goals, and some of the book features that you will encounter when using this book.

## Book Organization

This volume contains four major parts. Beyond the chapters in these parts of the book, you will find several useful appendixes gathered in Part V.

Following is a description of each part's coverage:

- Part I, "LAN Switching" (Chapters 1–3)

  This part focuses on LAN Layer 2 features, specifically Ethernet (Chapter 1), VLANs and trunking (Chapter 2), and Spanning Tree Protocol (Chapter 3).

- Part II, "IP Networking" (Chapters 4–5)

  This part covers details across the spectrum of the TCP/IP protocol stack. It includes Layer 3 basics (Chapter 4) and IP services such as DHCP and ARP (Chapter 5).

- **Part III, "IP IGP Routing" (Chapters 6–11)**

  This part covers some of the more important topics on the exam and is easily the largest part of this volume. It covers Layer 3 forwarding concepts (Chapter 6), followed by three routing protocol chapters, one each about RIPv2, EIGRP, OSPF, and IS-IS (Chapters 7 through 10, respectively), and concludes with a discussion of IGP redistribution and routing information optimization (Chapter 11).

- **Part IV, "Final Preparation"**

  Chapter 12, "Final Preparation," contains instructions about using the testing software on the CD to verify your knowledge, presents suggestions on approaching your studies, and includes hints about further expanding your knowledge by participating in the Cisco Learning Network.

- **Part V, "Appendixes"**

  - Appendix A, "Answers to the 'Do I Know This Already?' Quizzes"—This appendix lists answers and explanations for the questions at the beginning of each chapter.

  - Appendix B, "Exam Updates"—As of the first printing of the book, this appendix contains only a few words that reference the web page for this book, at www.ciscopress.com/title/9781587143960. As the blueprint evolves over time, the authors will post new materials at the website. Any future printings of the book will include the latest newly added materials in printed form in Appendix B. If Cisco releases a major exam update, changes to the book will be available only in a new edition of the book and not on this site.

**Note**  Appendixes C, D, E, F, and G and the Glossary are in printable, PDF format on the CD.

  - Appendix C, "Decimal to Binary Conversion Table" (CD-only)—This appendix lists the decimal values 0 through 255, with their binary equivalents.

  - Appendix D, "IP Addressing Practice" (CD-only)—This appendix lists several practice problems for IP subnetting and finding summary routes. The explanations to the answers use the shortcuts described in the book.

  - Appendix E, "Key Tables for CCIE Study" (CD-only)—This appendix lists the most important tables from the core chapters of the book. The tables have much of the content removed so that you can use them as an exercise. You can print the PDF file and then fill in the table from memory, checking your answers against the completed tables in Appendix F.

  - Appendix G, "Study Planner" (CD-only)—This appendix is a spreadsheet with major study milestones, where you can track your progress through your study.

  - Glossary (CD-only)—The Glossary contains the key terms listed in the book.

# Book Features

The core chapters of this book have several features that help you make the best use of your time:

■ **"Do I Know This Already?" Quizzes:** Each chapter begins with a quiz that helps you to determine the amount of time you need to spend studying that chapter. If you score yourself strictly, and you miss only one question, you might want to skip the core of the chapter and move on to the "Foundation Summary" section at the end of the chapter, which lets you review facts and spend time on other topics. If you miss more than one, you might want to spend some time reading the chapter or at least reading sections that cover topics about which you know you are weaker.

■ **Foundation Topics:** These are the core sections of each chapter. They explain the protocols, concepts, and configuration for the topics in that chapter.

■ **Foundation Summary:** The "Foundation Summary" section of this book departs from the typical features of the "Foundation Summary" section of other Cisco Press Exam Certification Guides. This section does not repeat any details from the "Foundation Topics" section; instead, it simply summarizes and lists facts related to the chapter but for which a longer or more detailed explanation is not warranted.

■ **Key topics:** Throughout the "Foundation Topics" section, a Key Topic icon has been placed beside the most important areas for review. After reading a chapter, when doing your final preparation for the exam, take the time to flip through the chapters, looking for the Key Topic icons, and review those paragraphs, tables, figures, and lists.

■ **Fill In Key Tables from Memory:** The more important tables from the chapters have been copied to PDF files available on the CD as Appendix E. The tables have most of the information removed. After printing these mostly empty tables, you can use them to improve your memory of the facts in the table by trying to fill them out. This tool should be useful for memorizing key facts. That same CD-only appendix contains the completed tables so that you can check your work.

■ **CD-based practice exam:** The companion CD contains multiple-choice questions and a testing engine. The CD includes 200 questions unique to the CD. As part of your final preparation, you should practice with these questions to help you get used to the exam-taking process, as well as to help refine and prove your knowledge of the exam topics.

■ **Key terms and Glossary:** The more important terms mentioned in each chapter are listed at the end of each chapter under the heading "Definitions." The Glossary, found on the CD that comes with this book, lists all the terms from the chapters. When studying each chapter, you should review the key terms, and for those terms about which you are unsure of the definition, you can review the short definitions from the Glossary.

■ **Further Reading:** Most chapters include a suggested set of books and websites for additional study on the same topics covered in that chapter. Often, these references will be useful tools for preparation for the CCIE Routing and Switching lab exam.

**Blueprint topics covered in this chapter:**

This chapter covers the following subtopics from the Cisco CCIE Routing and Switching written exam blueprint. Refer to the full blueprint in Table I-1 in the Introduction for more details on the topics covered in each chapter and their context within the blueprint.

- Ethernet

- Speed

- Duplex

- Fast Ethernet

- Gigabit Ethernet

- SPAN, RSPAN, and ERSPAN

- Virtual Switch System (VSS)

- IOS-XE

## CHAPTER 1

# Ethernet Basics

Ethernet has been the mainstay LAN protocol for years, and that is not anticipated to change anytime soon. More often than not, most people studying network and network fundamentals are very familiar with the protocol operations, its limitations, and its strengths. This level of familiarity often makes us complacent when it comes to determining a solid starting point for teaching technology. But when we consider how many technologies owe their capacity and capabilities to Ethernet, it becomes clear that this is the best place to start any discussion about networking. Ethernet is so established and useful that its role is expanding constantly. In fact, today it has even found its way into the WAN. Ethernet WAN technologies like Metro-Ethernet have changed the way we build geographically dispersed infrastructure and have paved the way for greater throughput in what was traditionally a slow and restrictive mode of transport.

So with the understanding that the majority of readers are probably very familiar with Ethernet based on working with it on a day-to-day basis, we still need to ensure that we pay proper due diligence to the technology simply because it is so fundamental to the creation of both the most basic and the most complex network environments, and even though we are for the most part very knowledgeable about its operation, we might have forgotten some of the nuisances of its operation. So in this chapter, the intention is to outline those operations as clearly and succinctly as possible.

For exam preparation, it is typically useful to use all the refresher tools: Take the "Do I Know This Already?" quiz, complete the definitions of the terms listed at the end of the chapter, print and complete the tables in Appendix E, "Key Tables for CCIE Study," and certainly answer all the CD-ROM questions concerning Ethernet.

## "Do I Know This Already?" Quiz

Table 1-1 outlines the major headings in this chapter and the corresponding "Do I Know This Already?" quiz questions.

**Table 1-1**    *"Do I Know This Already?" Foundation Topics Section-to-Question Mapping*

| Foundation Topics Section | Questions Covered in This Section | Score |
|---|---|---|
| Ethernet Layer 1: Wiring, Speed, and Duplex | 1–4 | |
| Ethernet Layer 2: Framing and Addressing | 5–6 | |
| Switching and Bridging Logic | 7 | |
| SPAN, RSPAN, and ERSPAN | 8–9 | |
| Virtual Switch System | 10–11 | |
| IOS Modernization | 12 | |
| **Total Score** | | |

To best use this pre-chapter assessment, remember to score yourself strictly. You can find the answers in Appendix A, "Answers to the 'Do I Know This Already?' Quizzes."

1.  Which of the following denotes the correct usage of pins on the RJ-45 connectors at the opposite ends of an Ethernet crossover cable?

    a.  1 to 1

    b.  1 to 2

    c.  1 to 3

    d.  6 to 1

    e.  6 to 2

    f.  6 to 3

2.  Which of the following denotes the correct usage of pins on the RJ-45 connectors at the opposite ends of an Ethernet straight-through cable?

    a.  1 to 1

    b.  1 to 2

    c.  1 to 3

    d.  6 to 1

    e.  6 to 2

    f.  6 to 3

**3.** Which of the following commands must be configured on a Cisco IOS switch interface to disable Ethernet autonegotiation?

   **a.** no auto-negotiate

   **b.** no auto

   **c.** Both **speed** and **duplex**

   **d.** duplex

   **e.** speed

**4.** Consider an Ethernet crossover cable between two 10/100 ports on Cisco switches. One switch has been configured for 100-Mbps full duplex. Which of the following is true about the other switch?

   **a.** It will use a speed of 10 Mbps.

   **b.** It will use a speed of 100 Mbps.

   **c.** It will use a duplex setting of half duplex.

   **d.** It will use a duplex setting of full duplex.

**5.** Which of the following Ethernet header type fields is a 2-byte field?

   **a.** DSAP

   **b.** Type (in SNAP header)

   **c.** Type (in Ethernet V2 header)

   **d.** LLC Control

**6.** Which of the following standards defines a Fast Ethernet standard?

   **a.** IEEE 802.1Q

   **b.** IEEE 802.3U

   **c.** IEEE 802.1X

   **d.** IEEE 802.3Z

   **e.** IEEE 802.3AB

   **f.** IEEE 802.1AD

**7.** Suppose a brand-new Cisco IOS–based switch has just been taken out of the box and cabled to several devices. One of the devices sends a frame. For which of the following destinations would a switch flood the frames out all ports (except the port upon which the frame was received)?

   **a.** Broadcasts

   **b.** Unknown unicasts

   **c.** Known unicasts

   **d.** Multicasts

**8.** Which of the following configuration issues will keep a SPAN session from becoming active?

   **a.** Misconfigured destination port

   **b.** Destination port configured as a trunk

   **c.** Destination port shutdown

   **d.** Source port configured as a trunk

**9.** Which of the following are rules for SPAN configuration?

   **a.** SPAN source and destination ports must be configured for the same speed and duplex.

   **b.** If the SPAN source port is configured for 100 Mbps, the destination port must be configured for 100 Mbps or more.

   **c.** In a SPAN session, sources must consist of either physical interfaces or VLANs, but not a mix of these.

   **d.** Remote SPAN VLANs must be in the range of VLAN 1–66.

   **e.** Only three SPAN sessions can be configured on one switch.

**10.** What tool is available to reduce the complexity of a modern network infrastructure that has direct impact on both Layer 2 and Layer 3 design?

   **a.** Spanning Tree Protocol

   **b.** Bridge Assurance

   **c.** Virtual Switch Design

   **d.** Virtual Switching System

   **e.** IOS-XR

**11.** In a Virtual Switch System configuration, what operational component is used to transport Control, Management, and Data Plane traffic between peers?

   **a.** VPC-Link

   **b.** Sham-Link

   **c.** Virtual Switch Link

   **d.** Port-Channel

   **e.** Ether-Channel

**12.** Cisco IOS was expanded so that it could support modern enterprise deployments by moving away from a monolithic architecture to a more modular design model. What is this current version of IOS?

    **a.** CUOS

    **b.** IOS-NG

    **c.** LINUX

    **d.** IOS-XE

    **e.** IOS-version 2.0

## Foundation Topics

## Ethernet Layer 1: Wiring, Speed, and Duplex

Before you make an Ethernet LAN functional, end-user devices, routers, and switches must be cabled correctly. To run with fewer transmission errors at higher speeds, and to support longer cable distances, variations of copper and optical cabling can be used. The different Ethernet specifications, cable types, and cable lengths per the various specifications are important for the exam, and are listed in the "Foundation Summary" section, later in this chapter.

### RJ-45 Pinouts and Category 5 Wiring

You should know the details of crossover and straight-through Category 5 (Cat 5), Cat 5e, or Cat 6 cabling for almost any networking job. The EIA/TIA defines the cabling specifications for Ethernet LANs (www.eia.org and http://www.tiaonline.org), including the pinouts for the RJ-45 connects, as shown in Figure 1-1.

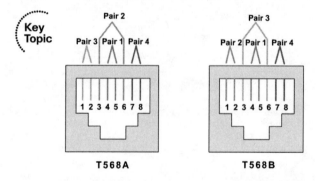

**Figure 1-1** *RJ-45 Pinouts with Four-Pair UTP Cabling*

The most popular Ethernet standards (10BASE-T and 100BASE-TX) each use two twisted pairs (specifically pairs 2 and 3 shown in Figure 1-1), with one pair used for transmission in each direction. Depending on which pair a device uses to transmit and receive, either a straight-through or crossover cable is required. Table 1-2 summarizes how the cabling and pinouts work.

**Table 1-2** *Ethernet Cabling Types*

| Type of Cable | Pinouts | Key Pins Connected |
|---|---|---|
| Straight-through | T568A (both ends) or T568B (both ends) | 1–1; 2–2; 3–3; 6–6 |
| Crossover | T568A on one end, and T568B on the other | 1–3; 2–6; 3–1; 6–2 |

Many Ethernet standards use two twisted pairs, with one pair being used for transmission in each direction. For example, a PC network interface card (NIC) transmits on pair 1,2 and receives on pair 3,6; switch ports do the opposite. So, a straight-through cable works well, connecting pair 1,2 on the PC (PC transmit pair) to the switch port's pair 1,2, on which the switch receives. When the two devices on the ends of the cable both transmit using the same pins, a crossover cable is required. For example, if two connected switches send using the pair at pins 3,6 and receive on pins 1,2, the cable needs to connect the pair at 3,6 on one end to pins 1,2 at the other end, and vice versa.

**Note**   Crossover cables can also be used between a pair of PCs, swapping the transmit pair on one end (1,2) with the receive pins at the other end (3,6).

Cisco also supports a switch feature that lets the switch figure out whether the wrong cable is installed: *Auto-MDIX* (automatic medium-dependent interface crossover) detects the wrong cable and causes the switch to swap the pair it uses for transmitting and receiving, which solves the cabling problem. (As of publication, this feature is not supported on all Cisco switch models.)

## Autonegotiation, Speed, and Duplex

By default, each Cisco switch port uses *Ethernet autonegotiation* to determine the speed and duplex setting (half or full). The switches can also set their duplex setting with the **duplex interface** subcommand, and their speed with—you guessed it—the **speed interface** subcommand.

Switches can dynamically detect the speed setting on a particular Ethernet segment by using a few different methods. Cisco switches (and many other devices) can sense the speed using the *Fast Link Pulses (FLP)* of the autonegotiation process. However, if autonegotiation is disabled on either end of the cable, the switch detects the speed anyway based on the incoming electrical signal. You can force a speed mismatch by statically configuring different speeds on both ends of the cable, causing the link to no longer function.

Switches detect duplex settings through autonegotiation only. If both ends have autonegotiation enabled, the duplex is negotiated. However, if either device on the cable disables autonegotiation, the devices without a configured duplex setting must assume a default. Cisco switches use a default duplex setting of half duplex (HDX) (for 10-Mbps and 100-Mbps interfaces) or full duplex (FDX) (for 1000-Mbps interfaces). To disable autonegotiation on a Cisco switch port, you simply need to statically configure the speed and the duplex settings.

Ethernet devices can use FDX only when collisions cannot occur on the attached cable; a collision-free link can be guaranteed only when a shared hub is not in use. The next few topics review how Ethernet deals with collisions when they do occur, as well as what is different with Ethernet logic in cases where collisions cannot occur and FDX is allowed.

## CSMA/CD

The original Ethernet specifications expected collisions to occur on the LAN. The media were shared, creating a literal electrical bus. Any electrical signal induced onto the wire could collide with a signal induced by another device. When two or more Ethernet frames overlap on the transmission medium at the same instant in time, a collision occurs; the collision results in bit errors and lost frames.

The original Ethernet specifications defined the *Carrier Sense Multiple Access with Collision Detection (CSMA/CD)* algorithm to deal with the inevitable collisions. CSMA/CD minimizes the number of collisions, but when they occur, CSMA/CD defines how the sending stations can recognize the collisions and retransmit the frame. The following list outlines the steps in the CSMA/CD process:

1. A device with a frame to send listens until the Ethernet is not busy (in other words, the device cannot sense a carrier signal on the Ethernet segment).

2. When the Ethernet is not busy, the sender begins sending the frame.

3. The sender listens to make sure that no collision occurred.

4. If there was a collision, all stations that sent a frame send a jamming signal to ensure that all stations recognize the collision.

5. After the jamming is complete, each sender of one of the original collided frames randomizes a timer and waits that long before resending. (Other stations that did not create the collision do not have to wait to send.)

6. After all timers expire, the original senders can begin again with Step 1.

### Collision Domains and Switch Buffering

A *collision domain* is a set of devices that can send frames that collide with frames sent by another device in that same set of devices. Before the advent of LAN switches, Ethernets were either physically shared (10BASE2 and 10BASE5) or shared by virtue of shared hubs and their Layer 1 "repeat out all other ports" logic. Ethernet switches greatly reduce the number of possible collisions, both through frame buffering and through their more complete Layer 2 logic.

By definition of the term, Ethernet hubs

■ Operate solely at Ethernet Layer 1

■ Repeat (regenerate) electrical signals to improve cabling distances

■ Forward signals received on a port out all other ports (no buffering)

As a result of a hub's logic, a hub creates a single *collision domain*. Switches, however, create a different collision domain per switch port, as shown in Figure 1-2.

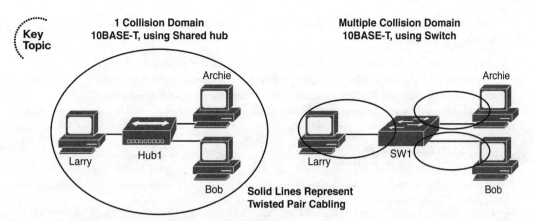

**Figure 1-2**  *Collision Domains with Hubs and Switches*

Switches have the same cabling and signal regeneration benefits as hubs, but switches do a lot more—including sometimes reducing or even eliminating collisions by buffering frames. When switches receive multiple frames on different switch ports, they store the frames in memory buffers to prevent collisions.

For example, imagine that a switch receives three frames at the same time, entering three different ports, and they all must exit the same switch port. The switch simply stores two of the frames in memory, forwarding the frames sequentially. As a result, in Figure 1-2, the switch prevents any frame sent by Larry from colliding with a frame sent by Archie or Bob—which by definition puts each of the PCs attached to the switch in Figure 1-2 in different collision domains.

When a switch port connects through cable to a single other nonhub device—for example, like the three PCs in Figure 1-2—no collisions can possibly occur. The only devices that could create a collision are the switch port and the one connected device—and they each have a separate twisted pair on which to transmit. Because collisions cannot occur, such segments can use full-duplex logic.

**Note**  NICs operating in HDX mode use *loopback circuitry* when transmitting a frame. This circuitry loops the transmitted frame back to the receive side of the NIC so that when the NIC receives a frame over the cable, the combined looped-back signal and received signal allows the NIC to notice that a collision has occurred.

## Basic Switch Port Configuration

The three key configuration elements on a Cisco switch port are autonegotiation, speed, and duplex. Cisco switches use autonegotiation by default; it is then disabled if both the speed and duplex are manually configured. You can set the speed using the **speed** {auto | 10 | 100 | 1000} interface subcommand, assuming that the interface supports multiple speeds. You configure the duplex setting using the **duplex** {**auto** | **half** | **full**} interface sub-command.

Example 1-1 shows the manual configuration of the speed and duplex on the link between Switch1 and Switch4 from Figure 1-3, and the results of having mismatched duplex settings. (The book refers to specific switch commands used on IOS-based switches, referred to as "Catalyst IOS" by the Cisco CCIE blueprint.)

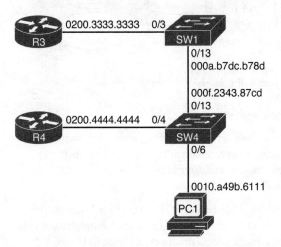

**Figure 1-3** *Simple Switched Network with Trunk*

**Example 1-1** *Manual Setting for Duplex and Speed, with Mismatched Duplex*

```
switch1# show interface fa 0/13
FastEthernet0/13 is up, line protocol is up
  Hardware is Fast Ethernet, address is 000a.b7dc.b78d (bia 000a.b7dc.b78d)
  MTU 1500 bytes, BW 100000 Kbit, DLY 100 usec,
     reliability 255/255, txload 1/255, rxload 1/255
  Encapsulation ARPA, loopback not set
  Keepalive set (10 sec)
  Full-duplex, 100Mb/s
! remaining lines omitted for brevity
! Below, Switch1's interface connecting to Switch4 is configured for 100 Mbps,
! HDX. Note that IOS rejects the first duplex command; you cannot set duplex until
! the speed is manually configured.
switch1# conf t
Enter configuration commands, one per line.  End with CNTL/Z.
switch1(config)# int fa 0/13
switch1(config-if)# duplex half
Duplex will not be set until speed is set to non-auto value
switch1(config-if)# speed 100
05:08:41: %LINEPROTO-5-UPDOWN: Line protocol on Interface FastEthernet0/13, changed
  state þto down
```

```
05:08:46: %LINEPROTO-5-UPDOWN: Line protocol on Interface FastEthernet0/13, changed
   state þto up
switch1(config-if)# duplex half
!!!!!!!!!!!!!!!!!!!!!!!!!!!!!!!!!!!!!!!!!!!!!!!!!!!!!!!!!!!!!!!!!!!!!!!!!!!!!!!!!!!!!
! NOT SHOWN: Configuration for 100/half on Switch4's int·fa 0/13.
!!!!!!!!!!!!!!!!!!!!!!!!!!!!!!!!!!!!!!!!!!!!!!!!!!!!!!!!!!!!!!!!!!!!!!!!!!!!!!!!!!!!!!
! Now with both switches manually configured for speed and duplex, neither will be
! using Ethernet auto-negotiation. As a result, below the duplex setting on Switch1
! can be changed to FDX with Switch4 remaining configured to use HDX.
switch1# conf t
Enter configuration commands, one per line.  End with CNTL/Z.
switch1(config)# int fa 0/13
switch1(config-if)# duplex full
05:13:03: %LINEPROTO-5-UPDOWN: Line protocol on Interface FastEthernet0/13, changed
   state to down
05:13:08: %LINEPROTO-5-UPDOWN: Line protocol on Interface FastEthernet0/13, changed
   state to up
switch1(config-if)#^Z
switch1# sh int fa 0/13
FastEthernet0/13 is up, line protocol is up
! Lines omitted for brevity
   Full-duplex, 100Mb/s
! remaining lines omitted for brevity
! Below, Switch4 is shown to be HDX. Note
! the collisions counters at the end of the show interface command.
switch4# sh int fa 0/13
FastEthernet0/13 is up, line protocol is up (connected)
   Hardware is Fast Ethernet, address is 000f.2343.87cd (bia 000f.2343.87cd)
   MTU 1500 bytes, BW 100000 Kbit, DLY 1000 usec,
      reliability 255/255, txload 1/255, rxload 1/255
   Encapsulation ARPA, loopback not set
   Keepalive set (10 sec)
   Half-duplex, 100Mb/s
! Lines omitted for brevity
   5 minute output rate 583000 bits/sec, 117 packets/sec
      25654 packets input, 19935915 bytes, 0 no buffer
      Received 173 broadcasts (0 multicast)
      0 runts, 0 giants, 0 throttles
      0 input errors, 0 CRC, 0 frame, 0 overrun, 0 ignored
      0 watchdog, 173 multicast, 0 pause input
      0 input packets with dribble condition detected
      26151 packets output, 19608901 bytes, 0 underruns
      54 output errors, 5 collisions, 0 interface resets
      0 babbles, 54 late collision, 59 deferred
      0 lost carrier, 0 no carrier, 0 PAUSE output
      0 output buffer failures, 0 output buffers swapped out
```

```
02:40:49: %CDP-4-DUPLEX_MISMATCH: duplex mismatch discovered on FastEthernet0/13
(not full duplex), with Switch1 FastEthernet0/13 (full duplex).
! Above, CDP messages have been exchanged over the link between switches. CDP
! exchanges information about Duplex on the link, and can notice (but not fix)
! the mismatch.
```

The statistics on Switch4 near the end of the example show collisions (detected in the time during which the first 64 bytes were being transmitted) and late collisions (after the first 64 bytes were transmitted). In an Ethernet that follows cabling length restrictions, collisions should be detected while the first 64 bytes are being transmitted. In this case, Switch1 is using FDX logic, meaning that it sends frames anytime—including when Switch4 is sending frames. As a result, Switch4 receives frames anytime, and if sending at the time, it believes a collision has occurred. Switch4 has deferred 59 frames, meaning that it chose to wait before sending frames because it was currently receiving a frame. Also, the retransmission of the frames that Switch4 thought were destroyed because of a collision, but might not have been, causes duplicate frames to be received, occasionally causing application connections to fail and routers to lose neighbor relationships.

## Ethernet Layer 2: Framing and Addressing

In this book, as in many Cisco courses and documents, the word *frame* refers to the bits and bytes that include the Layer 2 header and trailer, along with the data encapsulated by that header and trailer. The term *packet* is most often used to describe the Layer 3 header and data, without a Layer 2 header or trailer. Ethernet's Layer 2 specifications relate to the creation, forwarding, reception, and interpretation of Ethernet frames.

The original Ethernet specifications were owned by the combination of Digital Equipment Corp., Intel, and Xerox—hence the name "Ethernet (DIX)." Later, in the early 1980s, the IEEE standardized Ethernet, defining parts (Layer 1 and some of Layer 2) in the 802.3 *Media Access Control (MAC)* standard, and other parts of Layer 2 in the 802.2 *Logical Link Control (LLC)* standard. Later, the IEEE realized that the 1-byte Destination Service Access Point (DSAP) field in the 802.2 LLC header was too small. As a result, the IEEE introduced a new frame format with a *Sub-Network Access Protocol (SNAP)* header after the 802.2 header, as shown in the third style of header in Figure 1-4. Finally, in 1997, the IEEE added the original DIX V2 framing to the 802.3 standard as well, as shown in the top frame in Figure 1-4.

Table 1-3 lists the header fields, along with a brief explanation. The more important fields are explained in more detail after the table.

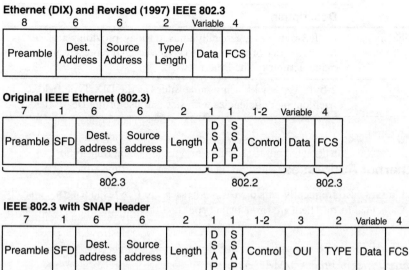

**Figure 1-4**  *Ethernet Framing Options*

**Table 1-3**  *Ethernet Header Fields*

| Field | Description |
|---|---|
| Preamble (DIX) | Provides synchronization and signal transitions to allow proper clocking of the transmitted signal. Consists of 62 alternating 1s and 0s, and ends with a pair of 1s. |
| Preamble and Start of Frame Delimiter (802.3) | Same purpose and binary value as DIX preamble; 802.3 simply renames the 8-byte DIX preamble as a 7-byte preamble and a 1-byte Start of Frame Delimiter (SFD). |
| Type (or Protocol Type) (DIX) | 2-byte field that identifies the type of protocol or protocol header that follows the header. Allows the receiver of the frame to know how to process a received frame. |
| Length (802.3) | Describes the length, in bytes, of the data following the Length field, up to the Ethernet trailer. Allows an Ethernet receiver to predict the end of the received frame. |
| Destination Service Access Point (802.2) | DSAP; 1-byte protocol type field. The size limitations, along with other uses of the low-order bits, required the later addition of SNAP headers. |
| Source Service Access Point (802.2) | SSAP; 1-byte protocol type field that describes the upper-layer protocol that created the frame. |
| Control (802.2) | 1- or 2-byte field that provides mechanisms for both connectionless and connection-oriented operation. Generally used only for connectionless operation by modern protocols, with a 1-byte value of 0x03. |

| Field | Description |
|---|---|
| Organizationally Unique Identifier (SNAP) | OUI; 3-byte field, generally unused today, providing a place for the sender of the frame to code the OUI representing the manufacturer of the Ethernet NIC. |
| Type (SNAP) | 2-byte Type field, using same values as the DIX Type field, overcoming deficiencies with size and use of the DSAP field. |

## Types of Ethernet Addresses

Ethernet addresses, also frequently called MAC addresses, are 6 bytes in length, typically listed in hexadecimal form. There are three main types of Ethernet address, as listed in Table 1-4.

**Table 1-4**   *Three Types of Ethernet/MAC Address*

| Type of Ethernet/ MAC Address | Description and Notes |
|---|---|
| Unicast | Fancy term for an address that represents a single LAN interface. The I/G bit, the least significant bit in the most significant byte, is set to 0. |
| Broadcast | An address that means "all devices that reside on this LAN right now." Always a value of hex FFFFFFFFFFFF. |
| Multicast | A MAC address that implies some subset of all devices currently on the LAN. By definition, the I/G bit is set to 1. |

Most engineers instinctively know how unicast and broadcast addresses are used in a typical network. When an Ethernet NIC needs to send a frame, it puts its own unicast address in the Source Address field of the header. If it wants to send the frame to a particular device on the LAN, the sender puts the other device's MAC address in the Ethernet header's Destination Address field. If the sender wants to send the frame to every device on the LAN, it sends the frame to the FFFF.FFFF.FFFF broadcast destination address. (A frame sent to the broadcast address is named a *broadcast* or *broadcast frame*, and frames sent to unicast MAC addresses are called *unicasts* or *unicast frames*.)

Multicast Ethernet frames are used to communicate with a possibly dynamic subset of the devices on a LAN. The most common use for Ethernet multicast addresses involves the use of IP multicast. For example, if only 3 of 100 users on a LAN want to watch the same video stream using an IP multicast–based video application, the application can send a single multicast frame. The three interested devices prepare by listening for frames sent to a particular multicast Ethernet address, processing frames destined for that address. Other devices might receive the frame, but they ignore its contents. Because the concept of Ethernet multicast is most often used today with IP multicast, most of the rest of the details of Ethernet multicast are covered in Volume 2, Chapter 7, "Introduction to IP Multicasting."

## Ethernet Address Formats

The IEEE intends for unicast addresses to be unique in the universe by administering the assignment of MAC addresses. The IEEE assigns each vendor a code to use as the first 3 bytes of its MAC addresses; that first half of the addresses is called the *Organizationally Unique Identifier (OUI)*. The IEEE expects each manufacturer to use its OUI for the first 3 bytes of the MAC assigned to any Ethernet product created by that vendor. The vendor then assigns a unique value in the low-order 3 bytes for each Ethernet card that it manufactures—thereby ensuring global uniqueness of MAC addresses. Figure 1-5 shows the basic Ethernet address format, along with some additional details.

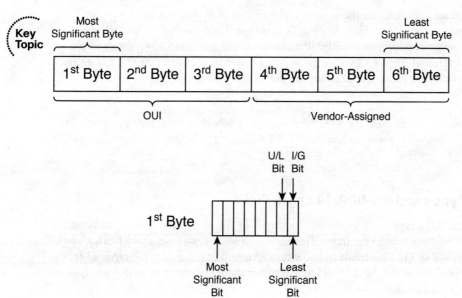

**Figure 1-5**  *Ethernet Address Format*

According to Figure 1-5, within each byte of a MAC address, the most and least significant bits are the leftmost and rightmost bits, respectively. When an Ethernet frame is transmitted, its bytes are sent in their usual order but the bits in individual bytes are transmitted *in the reverse order*, least significant bit first. The FCS field is the only exception to this rule. Many documents refer to this reversed bit order as *canonical*. The two least significant bits in the first byte of a MAC address are of special significance:

■   The Individual/Group (I/G) bit, the first address bit received by a NIC

■   The Universal/Local (U/L) bit

Table 1-5 summarizes the meaning of each bit.

**Table 1-5**   *I/G and U/L Bits*

| Field | Meaning |
|-------|---------|
| I/G | Binary 0 means that the address is a unicast; Binary 1 means that the address is a multicast or broadcast. |
| U/L | Binary 0 means that the address is vendor assigned; Binary 1 means that the address has been administratively assigned, overriding the vendor-assigned address. |

The I/G bit signifies whether the address represents an individual device or a group of devices, and the U/L bit identifies locally configured addresses. For example, the Ethernet multicast addresses used by IP multicast implementations always start with 0x01005E. Hex 01 (the first byte of the address) converts to binary 00000001, with the least significant bit being 1, confirming the use of the I/G bit.

**Note**   Often, when overriding the MAC address to use a local address, the device or device driver does not enforce the setting of the U/L bit to a value of 1.

## Protocol Types and the 802.3 Length Field

Each of the three types of Ethernet header shown in Figure 1-4 has a field identifying the format of the Data field in the frame. Generically called a *Type* field, these fields allow the receiver of an Ethernet frame to know how to interpret the data in the received frame. For example, a router might want to know whether the frame contains an IP packet, an IPX packet, and so on.

DIX and the revised IEEE framing use the Type field, also called the Protocol Type field. The originally defined IEEE framing uses those same 2 bytes as a Length field. To distinguish the style of Ethernet header, the Ethernet Type field values begin at 1536, and the length of the Data field in an IEEE frame is limited to decimal 1500 or less. That way, an Ethernet NIC can easily determine whether the frame follows the DIX or original IEEE format.

The original IEEE frame used a 1-byte Protocol Type field (DSAP) for the 802.2 LLC standard type field. It also reserved the high-order 2 bits for other uses, similar to the I/G and U/L bits in MAC addresses. As a result, there were not enough possible combinations in the DSAP field for the needs of the market—so the IEEE had to define yet another type field, this one inside an additional IEEE SNAP header. Table 1-6 summarizes the meaning of the three main Type field options with Ethernet.

**Table 1-6**  *Ethernet Type Fields*

| Type Field | Description |
|---|---|
| Protocol Type | DIX V2 Type field; 2 bytes; registered values now administered by the IEEE |
| DSAP | 802.2 LLC; 1 byte, with 2 high-order bits reserved for other purposes; registered values now administered by the IEEE |
| SNAP | SNAP header; 2 bytes; uses same values as Ethernet Protocol Type; signified by an 802.2 DSAP of 0xAA |

## Switching and Bridging Logic

In this chapter so far, you have been reminded about the cabling details for Ethernet along with the formats and meanings of the fields inside Ethernet frames. A switch's ultimate goal is to deliver those frames to the appropriate destination(s) based on the destination MAC address in the frame header. Table 1-7 summarizes the logic used by switches when forwarding frames, which differs based on the type of destination Ethernet address and on whether the destination address has been added to its MAC address table.

**Table 1-7**  *LAN Switch Forwarding Behavior*

| Type of Address | Switch Action |
|---|---|
| Known unicast | Forwards frame out the single interface associated with the destination address |
| Unknown unicast | Floods frame out all interfaces, except the interface on which the frame was received |
| Broadcast | Floods frame identically to unknown unicasts |
| Multicast | Floods frame identically to unknown unicasts, unless multicast optimizations are configured |

For unicast forwarding to work most efficiently, switches need to know about all the unicast MAC addresses and out which interface the switch should forward frames sent to each MAC address. Switches learn MAC addresses, and the port to associate with them, by reading the source MAC address of received frames. You can see the learning process in Example 1-2, along with several other details of switch operation. Figure 1-6 lists the devices in the network associated with Example 1-2, along with their MAC addresses.

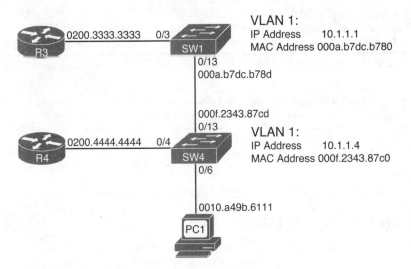

**Figure 1-6**  *Sample Network with MAC Addresses Shown*

**Example 1-2**  *Command Output Showing MAC Address Table Learning (Continued)*

```
Switch1# show mac-address-table dynamic
          Mac Address Table
-------------------------------------------


Vlan    Mac Address      Type        Ports
----    -----------      ----        -----
  1     000f.2343.87cd   DYNAMIC     Fa0/13
  1     0200.3333.3333   DYNAMIC     Fa0/3
  1     0200.4444.4444   DYNAMIC     Fa0/13
Total Mac Addresses for this criterion: 3
! Above, Switch1's MAC address table lists three dynamically learned addresses,
! including Switch4's FA 0/13 MAC.
! Below, Switch1 pings Switch4's management IP address.
Switch1# ping 10.1.1.4

Type escape sequence to abort.
Sending 5, 100-byte ICMP Echos to 10.1.1.4, timeout is 2 seconds:
!!!!!
Success rate is 100 percent (5/5), round-trip min/avg/max = 1/2/4 ms
! Below Switch1 now knows the MAC address associated with Switch4's management IP
! address. Each switch has a range of reserved MAC addresses, with the first MAC
! being used by the switch IP address, and the rest being assigned in sequence to
! the switch interfaces – note 0xcd (last byte of 2nd address in the table below)
! is for Switch4's FA 0/13 interface, and is 13 (decimal) larger than Switch4's
! base MAC address.
```

```
Switch1# show mac-address-table dynamic
          Mac Address Table
-------------------------------------------


Vlan    Mac Address       Type       Ports
----    -----------       ----       -----
  1     000f.2343.87c0    DYNAMIC    Fa0/13
  1     000f.2343.87cd    DYNAMIC    Fa0/13
  1     0200.3333.3333    DYNAMIC    Fa0/3
  1     0200.4444.4444    DYNAMIC    Fa0/13
Total Mac Addresses for this criterion: 4
! Not shown: PC1 ping 10.1.1.23 (R3) PC1's MAC in its MAC address table
-------------------------------------------


Vlan    Mac Address       Type       Ports
----    -----------       ----       -----
  1     000f.2343.87c0    DYNAMIC    Fa0/13
  1     000f.2343.87cd    DYNAMIC    Fa0/13
  1     0010.a49b.6111    DYNAMIC    Fa0/13
  1     0200.3333.3333    DYNAMIC    Fa0/3
  1     0200.4444.4444    DYNAMIC    Fa0/13
Total Mac Addresses for this criterion: 5
! Above, Switch1 learned the PC's MAC address, associated with FA 0/13,
! because the frames sent by the PC came into Switch1 over its FA 0/13.
! Below, Switch4's MAC address table shows PC1's MAC off its FA 0/6
switch4# show mac-address-table dynamic
          Mac Address Table
-------------------------------------------


Vlan    Mac Address       Type       Ports
----    -----------       --------   -----
  1     000a.b7dc.b780    DYNAMIC    Fa0/13
  1     000a.b7dc.b78d    DYNAMIC    Fa0/13
  1     0010.a49b.6111    DYNAMIC    Fa0/6
  1     0200.3333.3333    DYNAMIC    Fa0/13
  1     0200.4444.4444    DYNAMIC    Fa0/4
Total Mac Addresses for this criterion: 5
! Below, for example, the aging timeout (default 300 seconds) is shown, followed
! by a command just listing the mac address table entry for a single address.
switch4# show mac-address-table aging-time
Vlan    Aging Time
----    ----------
  1     300
switch4# show mac-address-table address 0200.3333.3333
          Mac Address Table
```

```
-------------------------------------------

Vlan    Mac Address      Type      Ports
----    -----------      --------  -----
   1    0200.3333.3333   DYNAMIC   Fa0/13
Total Mac Addresses for this criterion: 1
```

## SPAN, RSPAN, and ERSPAN

Cisco Catalyst switches support a method of directing all traffic from a source port or source VLAN to a single port. This feature, called SPAN (for Switch Port Analyzer) in the Cisco documentation and sometimes referred to as session monitoring because of the commands used to configure it, is useful for many applications. These include monitoring traffic for compliance reasons, for data collection purposes, or to support a particular application. For example, all traffic from a voice VLAN can be delivered to a single switch port to facilitate call recording in a VoIP network. Another common use of this feature is to support intrusion detection/prevention system (IDS/IPS) security solutions.

SPAN sessions can be sourced from a port or ports, or from a VLAN. This provides great flexibility in collecting or monitoring traffic from a particular source device or an entire VLAN.

The destination port for a SPAN session can be on the local switch, as in SPAN operation. Or it can be a port on another switch in the network. This mode is known as Remote SPAN, or RSPAN. In RSPAN, a specific VLAN must be configured across the entire switching path from the source port or VLAN to the RSPAN destination port. This requires that the RSPAN VLAN be included in any trunks in that path, too. See Figure 1-7 for the topology of SPAN, Figure 1-8 for that of RSPAN, and Figure 1-9 for that of Encapsulated Remote SPAN (ERSPAN).

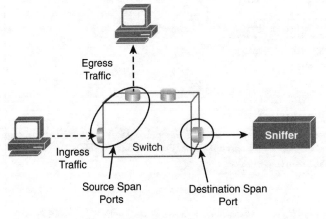

**Figure 1-7**   *SPAN Topology*

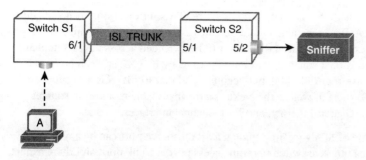

**Figure 1-8** *RSPAN Topology*

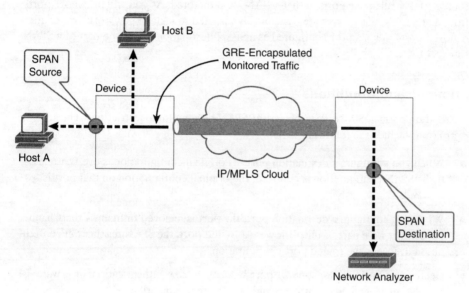

**Figure 1-9** *ERSPAN Topology*

The information in this section applies specifically to the Cisco 3560 switching platform; the Cisco 3750 and many other platforms use identical or similar rules and configuration commands.

## Core Concepts of SPAN, RSPAN, and ERSPAN

To understand SPAN, RSPAN, and ERSPAN, it helps to break them down into their fundamental elements. This also helps you understand how to configure these features.

In SPAN, you create a SPAN source that consists of at least one port or at least one VLAN on a switch. On the same switch, you configure a destination port. The SPAN source data is then gathered and delivered to the SPAN destination.

In RSPAN, you create the same source type—at least one port or at least one VLAN. The destination for this session is the RSPAN VLAN, rather than a single port on the switch. At the switch that contains an RSPAN destination port, the RSPAN VLAN data is delivered to the RSPAN port.

In ERSPAN, we are actually encapsulating the Remote SPAN information. Encapsulated Remote SPAN (ERSPAN), as the name implies, creates a generic routing encapsulation (GRE) tunnel for all captured traffic and allows it to be extended across Layer 3 domains. This feature is an operational enhancement brought to us by IOS-XE and can be found in current platforms like the ASR 1000, but keep in mind that ERSPAN is also supported by the Catalyst 6500, 7600, as well as the Nexus platforms. Viable monitoring sources include Fast Ethernet, Gigabit Ethernet, and Port-Channel interfaces.

Regardless of the type of SPAN we are running, a SPAN source port can be any type of port—a routed port, a physical switch port, an access port, a trunk port, an EtherChannel port (either one physical port or the entire port-channel interface), and so on. On a SPAN source VLAN, all active ports in that VLAN are monitored. As you add or remove ports from that VLAN, the sources are dynamically updated to include new ports or exclude removed ports. Also, a port configured as a SPAN destination cannot be part of a SPAN source VLAN.

## Restrictions and Conditions

Destination ports in SPAN, RSPAN, and ERSPAN have multiple restrictions. The key restrictions include the following:

- When you configure a destination port, its original configuration is overwritten. If the SPAN configuration is removed, the original configuration on that port is restored.

- When you configure a destination port, the port is removed from any EtherChannel bundle if it were part of one. If it were a routed port, the SPAN destination configuration overrides the routed port configuration.

- Destination ports do not support port security, 802.1x authentication, or private VLANs. In general, SPAN/RSPAN and 802.1x are incompatible.

- Destination ports do not support any Layer 2 protocols, including CDP, Spanning Tree, VTP, DTP, and so on.

A set of similar restrictions for RSPAN destination VLANs also exists. See the references in the "Further Reading" section at the end of this chapter for more information about those restrictions.

SPAN, RSPAN, and ERSPAN require compliance with a number of specific conditions to work. For SPAN, the key restrictions include the following:

- The source can be either one or more ports or a VLAN, but not a mix of these.

- Up to 64 SPAN destination ports can be configured on a switch.

- Switched or routed ports can be configured as SPAN source ports or SPAN destination ports.

- Be careful to avoid overloading the SPAN destination port. A 100-Mbps source port can easily overload a 10-Mbps destination port; it's even easier to overload a 100-Mbps destination port when the source is a VLAN.

- Within a single SPAN session, you cannot deliver traffic to a destination port when it is sourced by a mix of SPAN, RSPAN, or ERSPAN source ports or VLANs. This restriction comes into play when you want to mirror traffic to both a local port on a switch (in SPAN) and a remote port on another switch (in RSPAN or ERSPAN mode).

- A SPAN destination port cannot be a source port, and a source port cannot be a destination port.

- Only one SPAN/RSPAN/ERSPAN session can send traffic to a single destination port.

- A SPAN destination port ceases to act as a normal switch port. That is, it passes only SPAN-related traffic.

- It's possible to configure a trunk port as the source of a SPAN or RSPAN session. In this case, all VLANs on the trunk are monitored by default; the **filter vlan** command option can be configured to limit the VLANs being monitored in this situation.

- Traffic that is routed from another VLAN to a source VLAN cannot be monitored with SPAN. An easy way to understand this concept is that only traffic that enters or exits the switch in a source port or VLAN is forwarded in a SPAN session. In other words, if the traffic comes from another source within the switch (by routing from another VLAN, for example), that traffic isn't forwarded through SPAN.

SPAN, RSPAN, and ERSPAN support three types of traffic: transmitted, received, and both. By default, SPAN is enabled for traffic both entering and exiting the source port or VLAN. However, SPAN can be configured to monitor just transmitted traffic or just received traffic. Some additional conditions apply to these traffic types, as detailed in this list:

**Key Topic**

- For Receive (RX) SPAN, the goal is to deliver all traffic received to the SPAN destination. As a result, each frame to be transported across a SPAN connection is copied and sent before any modification (for example, VACL or ACL filtering, QoS modification, or even ingress or egress policing).

- For Transmit (TX) SPAN, all relevant filtering or modification by ACLs, VACLs, QoS, or policing actions are taken before the switch forwards the traffic to the SPAN/RSPAN destination. As a result, not all transmit traffic necessarily makes it to a SPAN destination. Also, the frames that are delivered do not necessarily match the original frames exactly, depending on policies applied before they are forwarded to the SPAN destination.

- A special case applies to certain types of Layer 2 frames. SPAN/RSPAN usually ignores CDP, spanning-tree BPDUs, VTP, DTP, and PAgP frames. However, these traffic types can be forwarded along with the normal SPAN traffic if the **encapsulation replicate** command is configured.

## Basic SPAN Configuration

The goal for the configuration in Example 1-3 is to mirror traffic sent to or received from interface fa0/12 to interface fa0/24. All traffic sent or received on fa0/12 is sent to fa0/24. This configuration is typical of a basic traffic-monitoring application.

**Example 1-3**  *Basic SPAN Configuration Example*

```
MDF-ROC1# configure terminal
MDF-ROC1(config)# monitor session 1 source interface fa0/12
MDF-ROC1(config)# monitor session 1 destination interface fa0/24
```

## Complex SPAN Configuration

In Example 1-4, we configure a switch to send the following traffic to interface fa0/24, preserving the encapsulation from the sources:

- Received on interface fa0/18

- Sent on interface fa0/9

- Sent and received on interface fa0/19 (which is a trunk)

We also filter (remove) VLANs 1, 2, 3, and 229 from the traffic coming from the fa0/19 trunk port.

**Example 1-4**  *Complex SPAN Configuration Example*

```
MDF-ROC3# config term
MDF-ROC3(config)# monitor session 11 source interface fa0/18 rx
MDF-ROC3(config)# monitor session 11 source interface fa0/9 tx
MDF-ROC3(config)# monitor session 11 source interface fa0/19
MDF-ROC3(config)# monitor session 11 filter vlan 1 - 3 , 229
MDF-ROC3(config)# monitor session 11 destination interface fa0/24 encapsulation
  replicate
```

## RSPAN Configuration

In Example 1-5, we configure two switches, IDF-SYR1 and IDF-SYR2, to send traffic to RSPAN VLAN 199, which is delivered to port fa0/24 on switch MDF-SYR9 as follows:

- From IDF-SYR1, all traffic received on VLANs 66–68

- From IDF-SYR2, all traffic received on VLAN 9

- From IDF-SYR2, all traffic sent and received on VLAN 11

Note that all three switches use a different session ID, which is permissible in RSPAN. The only limitation on session numbering is that the session number must be 1 to 66.

**Example 1-5**  *RSPAN Configuration Example*

```
IDF-SYR1# config term
IDF-SYR1(config)# vlan 199
IDF-SYR1(config-vlan)# remote span
IDF-SYR1(config-vlan)# exit
IDF-SYR1(config)# monitor session 3 source vlan 66 - 68 rx
IDF-SYR1(config)# monitor session 3 destination remote vlan 199
!Now moving to IDF-SYR2:
IDF-SYR2# config term
IDF-SYR2(config)# vlan 199
IDF-SYR2(config-vlan)# remote span
IDF-SYR2(config-vlan)# exit
IDF-SYR2(config)# monitor session 23 source vlan 9 rx
IDF-SYR2(config)# monitor session 23 source vlan 11
IDF-SYR2(config)# monitor session 23 destination remote vlan 199
!Now moving to MDF-SYR9
MDF-SYR9# config term
MDF-SYR9(config)# vlan 199
MDF-SYR9(config-vlan)# remote span
MDF-SYR9(config-vlan)# exit
MDF-SYR9(config)# monitor session 63 source remote vlan 199
MDF-SYR9(config)# monitor session 63 destination interface fa0/24
MDF-SYR9(config)# end
```

## ERSPAN Configuration

In Example 1-6, we will configure ASR 1002 to capture received traffic and send to it to Catalyst 6509 Gig2/2/1. This traffic will simply be captured, encapsulated in GRE by ASR 1002 natively, and routed over to the Catalyst 6509. A sniffing station on the 6500 attached to GE2/2/1 will see the complete Ethernet frame (L2 to L7) information.

**Example 1-6**  *ERSPAN Configuration Example*

```
ASR1002(config)# monitor session 1 type erspan-source
ASR1002(config-mon-erspan-src)# source interface gig0/1/0 rx
ASR1002(config-mon-erspan-src)# no shutdown
ASR1002(config-mon-erspan-src)# destination
ASR1002(config-mon-erspan-src-dst)# erspan-id 101
ASR1002(config-mon-erspan-src-dst)# ip address 10.1.1.1
ASR1002(config-mon-erspan-src-dst)# origin ip address 172.16.1.1
!Now for the configuration of the Catalyst 6500
SW6509(config)# monitor session 2 type erspan-destination
SW6509(config-mon-erspan-dst)# destination interface gigabitEthernet2/2/1
SW6509(config-mon-erspan-dst)# no shutdown
SW6509(config-mon-erspan-dst)# source
SW6509(config-mon-erspan-dst-src)# erspan-id 101
SW6509(config-mon-erspan-dst-src)# ip address 10.1.1.1
```

You can verify SPAN, RSPAN, or ERSPAN operation using the **show monitor session** command, as illustrated in Example 1-7.

**Example 1-7**  *ERSPAN Verification Example*

```
ASR1002# show monitor session 1
Session 1
---------
Type                  : ERSPAN Source Session
Status                : Admin Enabled
Source Ports          :
  RX Only        : Gi0/1/0
Destination IP Address : 10.1.1.1
MTU                   : 1464
Destination ERSPAN ID : 101
Origin IP Address     : 172.16.1.1
```

From a troubleshooting standpoint, it's important to note that if the destination port is shut down, the SPAN instance won't come up. When you bring the port up, the SPAN session will follow.

## Virtual Switch System

In any modern network, we find it essential to create topologies that support high availability and reliability of devices, connections, and services. The typical approach employed by network operators is to configure these features and capabilities by creating redundant Layer 2 switch fabric such that it will support multipathing through the use of redundant pairs or links. Figure 1-10 shows a typical switch network configuration.

Observe that the application and configuration of these redundant network elements and links we are describing can very quickly increase the complexity of our network design and operation. One method of overcoming this complication is to employ virtual switching. This technology actually simplifies the network by reducing the number of network elements, and this eliminates or masks the complexity of managing redundant switches and links. This feature exists in Cisco Catalyst 6500 and 4500 Series switches running IOS-XE (discussed in further detail in the section, "IOS-XE," later in this chapter).

For the purposes of our discussions, we will look at a Virtual Switch System (VSS) that combines a pair of Catalyst 4500 or 4500-X Series switches into a single network element. The VSS manages the redundant links in such a fashion that they will be seen by external devices as a single Port-channel.

This approach simplifies network configuration and operation by reducing the total number of Layer 3 routing neighbors and by simultaneously providing a loop-free Layer 2 topology.

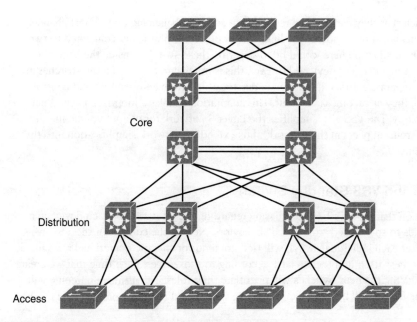

**Figure 1-10**    *Typical Switch Network Design*

## Virtual Switching System

The fundamental reason for employing a VSS is to logically combine a pair of switches into a single network element, as already described. To better understand this process, we need to look closely at what this feature does for the logical topology. For example, a VSS in the distribution layer of the network interacts with the access and core networks above and below it as if it were a single switch, as illustrated in Figure 1-11.

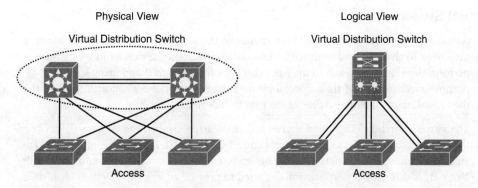

**Figure 1-11**    *VSS in the Distribution Network*

Notice that a switch in the access layer connects to both switches of the VSS using one logical port channel because the VSS is perceived as being a single switch to external devices—a logical switch if you will. Special adaptations are incorporated into the VSS devices such that they can manage redundancy and load balancing on the port channel to ensure managed operation of the link, even though it is physically connected to two devices. The inclination here would be to describe these switches inside the VSS configuration as independent devices; however, this is not accurate. Though the switches are physically separate entities, it must be understood that from an operation and control plane level, they are acting as one unit. This adaptation enables a loop-free Layer 2 network topology. The VSS also simplifies the Layer 3 network topology by reducing the number of routing peers in the network, thus extending network simplification into the data plane itself.

## VSS Active and VSS Standby Switch

The adoption that we have been discussing regarding the operation of each device in a VSS extends to specialized "role based" behaviors. Now in the context of the VSS, we will find that each individual switch will first contend for specific operational roles inside the VSS process itself and then behave according to those roles. Each time that we create or restart a VSS, the peer switches will negotiate their roles. The ultimate outcome will be that one device will become the VSS active switch, and the other will become the VSS standby.

The VSS active switch controls the VSS, running the Layer 2 and Layer 3 control protocols for the switching modules on both switches. The VSS active switch also provides management functions for the VSS, such as module online insertion and removal (OIR) and the console interface.

The VSS active and standby switches perform packet forwarding for ingress data traffic on their locally hosted interfaces. However, the VSS standby switch sends all control traffic to the VSS active switch for processing.

## Virtual Switch Link

As mentioned previously, for the two switches of the VSS to act as one network element, they need to share control information and data traffic, and the manner in which they perform this sharing extends to the roles that they have assumed and many special-purpose mechanisms. Of these special-purpose constructs, none are more important that the virtual switch link that connects the two VSS devices.

The virtual switch link (VSL) is a special link that carries control and data traffic between the two switches of a VSS, as shown in Figure 1-12. The VSL is typically implemented as an EtherChannel, and as such, can support up to eight links incorporated into the bundle. Not only is this special-purpose link designed to provide an avenue of communication between the VSS peers, but it is also optimized to provide control and management plane traffic higher priority than data traffic in an effort to ensure that control and management messages are never discarded. Data traffic is load balanced among the VSL links by either the default or the configured EtherChannel load-balancing algorithm.

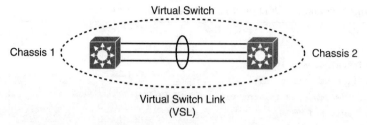

**Figure 1-12**  *Virtual Switch Link*

## Multichassis EtherChannel (MEC)

Note that we have been speaking significantly about the idea of EtherChannel.
EtherChannel (also known as a port channel) is a collection of two or more physical links
that combine to form one logical link. Layer 2 protocols operate on the EtherChannel
as a single logical entity. This extends to protocols like Spanning Tree Protocol, which
would normally serve to block redundant links between devices in an effort to prevent
the formation of switching loops. But the notion that we are describing is a special
kind of Port-channel that can exist not between two physical devices, but between
multiple chassis. This affords us a hardware or device failover capability that does not
exist in normal EtherChannel deployments. This is because VSS enables the creation of
Multichassis EtherChannel (MEC), which is an EtherChannel whose member ports can be
distributed across the member switches in a VSS. Because non-VSS switches connected
to a VSS view the MEC as a standard EtherChannel, non-VSS switches can connect in
a dual-homed manner. Traffic traversing the MEC can be load balanced locally within
a VSS member switch much like that of standard EtherChannels. Cisco MEC supports
dynamic EtherChannel protocols, to include the industry-standard Link Aggregation
Control Protocol (LACP) and the Cisco-proprietary Port Aggregation Protocol (PAgP),
as well as static EtherChannel configuration. In total, a VSS can support a maximum of
256 EtherChannels. This limit applies to the total number of regular EtherChannels and
MECs.

## Basic VSS Configuration

To create the most basic configuration needed to support VSS, first you have to create
the same virtual switch domain on both sides of the VSS. This switch domain will be referenced as a number used on both switches of the VSS; this number must fall between 1
and 255. After assigning the domain number, you must configure one switch to be switch
number 1 and the other switch to be switch number 2, as illustrated in Example 1-8.

**Example 1-8**   *Assigning Virtual Switch Domain and Switch Numbers*

```
SW1# conf t
Enter configuration commands, one per line. End with CNTL/Z.
SW1(config)# switch virtual domain 10
Domain ID 10 config will take effect only
after the exec command 'switch convert mode virtual' is issued
SW1(config-vs-domain)# switch 1
SW1(config-vs-domain)# exit
SW1(config)#


SW2# conf t
Enter configuration commands, one per line. End with CNTL/Z.
SW2(config)# switch virtual domain 10
Domain ID 10 config will take effect only
after the exec command 'switch convert mode virtual' is issued
SW2(config-vs-domain)# switch 2
SW2(config-vs-domain)# exit
SW2(config)#
```

Next, we will need to create the VSL, which requires a unique port channel on each
switch, as shown in Example 1-9. During the configuration, both port channels are set up
on the VSS active switch. If the VSS standby switch VSL port channel number has been
configured previously for another use, the VSS will come up in route processor redundancy mode. To avoid this situation, check that both port channel numbers are available
on both of the peer switches.

**Example 1-9**   *Configuring VSL Port Channel*

```
SW1(config)# int port-channel 5
SW1(config-if)# switchport
SW1(config-if)# switch virtual link 1
SW1(config-if)# no shut
SW1(config-if)# exit
*Jan 24 05:19:57.092: %SPANTREE-6-PORTDEL_ALL_VLANS: Port-channel5 deleted from all
  Vlans


SW2(config)# int port-channel 10
SW2(config-if)# switchport
SW2(config-if)# switch virtual link 2
SW2(config-if)# no shut
SW2(config-if)# exit
SW2(config)#
*Jan 24 05:14:17.273: %SPANTREE-6-PORTDEL_ALL_VLANS: Port-channel10 deleted from
  all Vlans
```

Now that we have created the Port-channel interfaces, it is necessary to add VSL physical member ports to the appropriate Port-channel. In Example 1-10, interfaces Gigabit Ethernet 7/3 and 7/4 on Switch 1 are going to be connected to interfaces Gigabit Ethernet 4/45 and 4/46 on Switch 2.

**Example 1-10**  *Configuring VSL Ports*

```
SW1(config)# int range gig7/3 - 4
SW1(config-if-range)# switchport mode trunk
SW1(config-if-range)# channel-group 5 mode on
WARNING: Interface GigabitEthernet7/3 placed in restricted config mode. All
  extraneous configs removed!
WARNING: Interface GigabitEthernet7/4 placed in restricted config mode. All
  extraneous configs removed!
SW1(config-if-range)# exit


SW2(config)# int range gig4/45 - 46
SW2(config-if-range)# switchport mode trunk
SW2(config-if-range)# channel-group 10 mode on
WARNING: Interface GigabitEthernet4/45 placed in restricted config mode. All
  extraneous configs removed!
WARNING: Interface GigabitEthernet4/46 placed in restricted config mode. All
  extraneous configs removed!
SW2(config-if-range)# exit
```

**Note**  After the interfaces are put into a VSL Port-channel with the **channel-group** command, the interfaces go into "notconnect" status. Interface status will show "up," but the line protocol will be "down." The interface will be in up/down (not connect) status until the switch is rebooted.

Now we will need to complete the switch conversion process by implementing the **switch convert mode virtual** command on Switch 1. The system will prompt to confirm the action. Enter yes, as illustrated in Example 1-11. This will allow the system to create a converted configuration file that will be stored in the system bootflash.

**Example 1-11**  *Converting the Switch to Virtual Switch Mode*

```
SW1# switch convert mode virtual

This command will convert all interface names
to naming convention "interface-type switch-number/slot/port",
save the running config to startup-config and

reload the switch.
Do you want to proceed? [yes/no]: yes
Converting interface names
```

```
Building configuration...
Compressed configuration from 6551 bytes to 2893 bytes[OK]
Saving converted configuration to bootflash: ...
Destination filename [startup-config.converted_vs-20130124-062921]?
Please stand by while rebooting the system...
Restarting system.


Rommon (G) Signature verification PASSED
Rommon (P) Signature verification PASSED
FPGA   (P) Signature verification PASSED


Similarly you need to enter the "switch convert mode virtual" command on Switch 2
   for converting to Virtual Switch Mode.


SW2# switch convert mode virtual


This command will convert all interface names
to naming convention "interface-type switch-number/slot/port",
save the running config to startup-config and
reload the switch.
Do you want to proceed? [yes/no]: yes
Converting interface names
Building configuration...
Compressed configuration from 6027 bytes to 2774 bytes[OK]
Saving converted configuration to bootflash: ...
Destination filename [startup-config.converted_vs-20130124-052526]?
Please stand by while rebooting the system...
Restarting system.


Rommon (G) Signature verification PASSED
Rommon (P) Signature verification PASSED
FPGA   (P) Signature verification PASSED




***********************************************************
*                                                         *
* Welcome to Rom Monitor for   WS-X45-SUP7-E System.      *
* Copyright (c) 2008-2012 by Cisco Systems, Inc.          *
* All rights reserved.                                    *
*                                                         *
***********************************************************
```

After confirmation is completed on each switch, the running configuration will be saved as the startup configuration and the switch will reboot. After the reboot, the switch will be in virtual switch mode.

## VSS Verification Procedures

A handful of simple **show** commands can be used to display specifics associated with the VSS configuration of a particular VSS pair. The virtual switch domain number, and the switch number and role for each of the switches, can be found through the **show switch virtual** command, as illustrated in Example 1-12.

**Example 1-12**  *Display the Virtual Switch Domain Number*

```
SW1# sh switch virtual

Executing the command on VSS member switch role = VSS Active, id = 1

Switch mode               : Virtual Switch
Virtual switch domain number : 10
Local switch number       : 1
Local switch operational role: Virtual Switch Active
Peer switch number        : 2
Peer switch operational role : Virtual Switch Standby


Executing the command on VSS member switch role = VSS Standby, id = 2

Switch mode               : Virtual Switch
Virtual switch domain number : 10
Local switch number       : 2
Local switch operational role: Virtual Switch Standby
Peer switch number        : 1
Peer switch operational role : Virtual Switch Active
```

One of the most important operational requirements of a VSS is to ensure that one switch in the cluster is the active switch and the other is the standby. The console of the standby switch should appear as illustrated in Example 1-13.

**Example 1-13**  *Console of the Standby Switch*

```
SW2-standby>
Standby console disabled
```

As we described in the theoretical portion of our discussion, there are a number of roles and configurational requirements associated with VSS. To see these variables for each of the switches in the VSS, use the **show switch virtual role** command. Example 1-14 shows the type and detail that this command can generate.

**Example 1-14**   *Virtual Role Assignment and Priority*

```
SW1# sh switch virtual role
Executinq the command on VSS member switch role = VSS Active, id = 1
RRP information for Instance 1
----------------------------------------------------------------------
Valid Flags   Peer       Preferred Reserved
                  Count      Peer      Peer
----------------------------------------------------------------------
TRUE   V       1           1           1
Switch Switch Status Preempt          Priority Role    Local   Remote
       Number         Oper(Conf)      Oper(Conf)        SID     SID
----------------------------------------------------------------------
LOCAL   1     UP    FALSE(N )       100(100) ACTIVE   0       0
REMOTE  2     UP    FALSE(N )       100(100) STANDBY 6834    6152


Peer 0 represents the local switch


Flags : V - Valid
In dual-active recovery mode: No


Executing the command on VSS member switch role = VSS Standby, id = 2


RRP information for Instance 2


----------------------------------------------------------------------
Valid Flags   Peer       Preferred Reserved
                  Count      Peer      Peer


----------------------------------------------------------------------
TRUE    V      1           1           1


Switch Switch Status Preempt          Priority Role    Local   Remote
       Number         Oper(Conf)      Oper(Conf)        SID     SID
----------------------------------------------------------------------
LOCAL   2     UP    FALSE(N )       100(100) STANDBY 0       0
REMOTE  1     UP    FALSE(N )       100(100) ACTIVE   6152    6834


Peer 0 represents the local switch


Flags : V - Valid
In dual-active recovery mode: No
```

To display information about the VSL, use the **show switch virtual link** command, as shown in Example 1-15.

**Example 1-15** *Virtual Switch Link Details*

```
SW1# sh switch virtual link

Executing the command on VSS member switch role = VSS Active, id = 1

VSL Status : UP
VSL Uptime : 3 minutes
VSL Control Link : Gi1/7/4

Executing the command on VSS member switch role = VSS Standby, id = 2

VSL Status : UP
VSL Uptime : 3 minutes
VSL Control Link : Gi2/4/45
```

Additionally, Example 1-16 illustrates how to verify information about the VSL port channel configuration using the **show switch virtual link port-channel** command.

**Example 1-16** *Display the Virtual Switch Domain Number*

```
SW1# sh switch virtual link port-channel

Executing the command on VSS member switch role = VSS Active, id = 1

Flags: D - down        P - bundled in port-channel
       I - stand-alone s - suspended
       H - Hot-standby (LACP only)
       R - Layer3      S - Layer2
       U - in use      N - not in use, no aggregation
       f - failed to allocate aggregator

       M - not in use, no aggregation due to minimum links not met
       m - not in use, port not aggregated due to minimum links not met
       u - unsuitable for bundling
       d - default port

       w - waiting to be aggregated

Group Port-channel Protocol   Ports
------+-------------+-----------+--------------------
5     Po5(SU)           -        Gi1/7/3(P) Gi1/7/4(P)
10    Po10(SU)          -        Gi2/4/45(P) Gi2/4/46(P)

Executing the command on VSS member switch role = VSS Standby, id = 2

Flags: D - down        P - bundled in port-channel
```

```
            I - stand-alone s - suspended
            H - Hot-standby (LACP only)
            R - Layer3      S - Layer2
            U - in use      N - not in use, no aggregation
            f - failed to allocate aggregator

            M - not in use, no aggregation due to minimum links not met
            m - not in use, port not aggregated due to minimum links not met
            u - unsuitable for bundling
            d - default port

            w - waiting to be aggregated

Group Port-channel Protocol    Ports
------+-------------+-----------+-------------------
5     Po5(SU)           -        Gi1/7/3(P) Gi1/7/4(P)
10    Po10(SU)          -        Gi2/4/45(P) Gi2/4/46(P)

SW1#
```

# IOS-XE

In the twenty-first century, we find ourselves dealing with the ever-evolving needs of a modern network, meaning a network with the capacity to support varied and intelligent management tools as well as software-defined network mechanisms that rapidly exceed the capacity of the traditional Internetworking Operating System (IOS). This has resulted largely because of the monolithic nature of IOS itself.

We first have to recognize that IOS has served us well over the years, but now the demands of networks have forced us to relook at how we support the operational process of typical protocols like OSPF, EIGRP, MPLS, BGP, and IPv6, to name a few. So it should come as no surprise that in an effort to expand the serviceability and survivability of IOS, it was necessary for it to evolve as well. In fact, IOS has evolved into three primary operating systems that each service and fulfill different purposes in the grand scheme of the network. These operation systems include variants like NX-OS, IOS-XR, and IOS-XE. Of these, the one we will concern ourselves with is IOS-XE.

It should go without saying that IOS-XE was designed for routers, switches, and appliances, and as such, it embraces all the field-tested capabilities and features of IOS, while adding new functionality and benefits traditionally found in a portable operating system interface (POSIX) environment. This was the most logical approach available to integrate network-aware applications into modern routing devices. As a result, IOS-XE seamlessly integrates a generic approach to network management into every function, borrowing heavily from the equally reliable POSIX operating system. Furthermore, through the incorporation of a series of well-defined application programming interfaces (API), Cisco has improved IOS portability. Specifically, we are making reference to the operation of

IOS across platforms as well as extending capabilities outside of IOS. This final component to IOS-XE creates a future where application integration will be simplified, integral, and commonplace.

IOS has been the center point for network expansion, configuration, and operation for decades, and this same functionality is now integrated into IOS-XE, thus preserving all the advantages of traditional IOS and its unparalleled history for delivering functionality for business-critical applications. All of this is done while retaining the same look and feel of IOS, but doing it while ensuring enhanced "future-proof" functionality.

How is all this possible? IOS-XE runs a modern Linux operating system that employs a single daemon; the additional functionality we have been discussing will be run as isolated processes within the OS of the host. This means that we have all the capabilities we had in IOS with enhanced operations and functionality that will not require retraining.

At first glance, this might not seem to be that big of an improvement, but if we keep in mind that running IOS and these other applications as separate processes, it becomes apparent that we can now leverage symmetrical multiprocessing. This in itself means that we can garner the benefits of load balancing across multiple-core CPUs by binding processes to different cores. Thus, we create an operational environment where it is possible to support multithreading and multicore CPUs. This capability, coupled with how IOS-XE separates the control plane from the forwarding plane, ensures a level of management and control that could not possibly exist in the context of the traditional monolithic IOS.

Today, the IOS that runs on routers runs all the necessary modules to perform network operations in the same memory space. This is problematic if something were to happen to the routing engine because the result would be that the entire IOS kernel could crash. As early as five years ago, this might have been a tenable situation, but in the modern enterprise this is catastrophic, because today's business networks running virtualization-enabled infrastructures consolidated on single platforms cannot allow a single process to bring down an entire assembly.

By moving the software architecture to a system daemon running on a "Linux platform," we now have the multiple levels of abstraction. The overall result is now inside of IOS-XE individual system functions that have been isolated from the primary operation kernel by placing them into separate processes. This means that should one of these isolated processes fail, it will not affect the kernel. So the idea of symmetrical multiprocessing gets taken one step further now by creating individual threads for each underlying process we have on our routing devices.

It is through this isolated operation model that application designers will have the ability to build drivers for new data plane ASICs and have them interoperate with sets of standard APIs. It is these APIs that will then create control plane and data plane processing separation.

It has been customary for some time to describe the operation mechanism of a router as falling into one or more different categories. Specifically, we are referring to the control plane, the data plane, and the input/output plane. The capability of an operating system to isolate the operation mechanisms of these three planes has a direct impact on device uptime as it relates to planned or unplanned outages.

As a result of the modular architecture that we have attributed to IOS-XE, we see both a logical and a physical isolation of the control and data planes themselves. This at first might seem to be a subtle difference, but in fact, this has far-reaching benefits. Now we have physical separation of the three planes through modular blades that are installed into the chassis, each having dedicated hardware resources. IOS-XE also maintains logical separation as an abstraction layer. We get even more capabilities to reduce failure domains within the routing system, as well as the capability to isolate operation loads between planes. An example of this would be heavy stress caused by forwarding massive amounts of traffic in the data plane, which would have no impact on the control plane running on the same chassis. This is made possible by the fact that IOS-XE runs a separate driver instance for each bay or blade slot in the chassis; therefore, one drive failing will have no impact on the other bays or the chassis as a whole. The outcome is that all the other processes will continue to forward traffic. In addition to this, we can actually patch individual drivers without bringing down the entire chassis.

This separation is achieved through the Forwarding and Feature Manager (FFM) and the Forwarding Engine Driver (FED).

The FFM provides a set of APIs used to manage the control plane processes. The resulting outcome is that the FFM programs the data plane through the FED and maintains all forwarding states for the system. It is the FED that allows the drivers to affect the data plane, and it is provided by the platform.

# Foundation Summary

This section lists additional details and facts to round out the coverage of the topics in this chapter. Unlike most of the Cisco Press Exam Certification Guides, this "Foundation Summary" does not repeat information presented in the "Foundation Topics" section of the chapter. Please take the time to read and study the details in the "Foundation Topics" section of the chapter, as well as review items noted with a Key Topic icon.

Table 1-8 lists the different types of Ethernet and some distinguishing characteristics of each type.

**Table 1-8**  *Ethernet Standards*

| Type of Ethernet | General Description |
|---|---|
| 10BASE5 | Commonly called "Thicknet"; uses coaxial cabling |
| 10BASE2 | Commonly called "Thinnet"; uses coaxial cabling |
| 10BASE-T | First type of Ethernet to use twisted-pair cabling |
| DIX Ethernet Version 2 | Layer 1 and Layer 2 specifications for original Ethernet, from Digital/Intel/Xerox; typically called DIX V2 |
| IEEE 802.3 | Called MAC because of the name of the IEEE committee (Media Access Control); original Layer 1 and 2 specifications, standardized using DIX V2 as a basis |
| IEEE 802.2 | Called LLC because of the name of the IEEE committee (Logical Link Control); Layer 2 specification for headers common to multiple IEEE LAN specifications |
| IEEE 802.3u | IEEE standard for Fast Ethernet (100 Mbps) over copper and optical cabling; typically called FastE |
| IEEE 802.3z | Gigabit Ethernet over optical cabling; typically called GigE |
| IEEE 802.3ab | Gigabit Ethernet over copper cabling |

Switches forward frames when necessary, and do not forward when there is no need to do so, thus reducing overhead. To accomplish this, switches perform three actions:

■ Learn MAC addresses by examining the source MAC address of each received frame

■ Decide when to forward a frame or when to filter (not forward) a frame, based on the destination MAC address

■ Create a loop-free environment with other bridges by using the Spanning Tree Protocol

The internal processing algorithms used by switches vary among models and vendors; regardless, the internal processing can be categorized as one of the methods listed in Table 1-9.

**Table 1-9**  *Switch Internal Processing*

| Switching Method | Description |
|---|---|
| Store-and-forward | The switch fully receives all bits in the frame (store) before forwarding the frame (forward). This allows the switch to check the frame check sequence (FCS) before forwarding the frame, thus ensuring that errored frames are not forwarded. |
| Cut-through | The switch performs the address table lookup as soon as the Destination Address field in the header is received. The first bits in the frame can be sent out the outbound port before the final bits in the incoming frame are received. This does not allow the switch to discard frames that fail the FCS check, but the forwarding action is faster, resulting in lower latency. |
| Fragment-free | This performs like cut-through switching, but the switch waits for 64 bytes to be received before forwarding the first bytes of the outgoing frame. According to Ethernet specifications, collisions should be detected during the first 64 bytes of the frame, so frames that are in error because of a collision will not be forwarded. |

Table 1-10 lists some of the most popular Cisco IOS commands related to the topics in this chapter.

**Table 1-10**  *Catalyst IOS Commands for Catalyst Switch Configuration*

| Command | Description |
|---|---|
| interface vlan 1 | Global command; moves user to interface configuration mode for a VLAN interface |
| interface fastethernet 0/*x* | Puts user in interface configuration mode for that interface |
| duplex {auto \| full \| half} | Used in interface configuration mode; sets duplex mode for the interface |
| speed {10 \| 100 \| 1000 \| auto \| nonegotiate} | Used in interface configuration mode; sets speed for the interface |
| show mac address-table [aging-time \| count \| dynamic \| static] [address *hw-addr*] [interface *interface-id*] [vlan *vlan-id*] | Displays the MAC address table; the security option displays information about the restricted or static settings |
| show interface fastethernet 0/*x* | Displays interface status for a physical 10/100 interface |
| show interface vlan 1 | Displays IP address configuration for a VLAN |
| remote span | In VLAN configuration mode, specifies that the VLAN is configured as a remote SPAN destination VLAN |

| Command | Description |
|---|---|
| monitor session *1-66* source [vlan *vlan-id* \| interface *interface-id*] [rx \| tx \| both] | Configures a SPAN or RSPAN source, which can include one or more physical interfaces or one or more VLANs; optionally specifies traffic entering (Rx) or leaving (Tx), or both, with respect to the specified source |
| monitor session 1-66 destination [remote vlan *vlan-id*] \| interface *interface-id*] | Configures the destination of a SPAN or RSPAN session to be either a physical interface or a remote VLAN |
| monitor session *1-66* filter vlan [*vlan* \| *vlan-range*] | Removes traffic from the specified VLAN or VLAN range from the monitored traffic stream |
| show monitor session *session-id* | Displays the status of a SPAN session |

Table 1-11 outlines the types of UTP cabling.

**Table 1-11**  *UTP Cabling Reference*

| UTP Category | Max Speed Rating | Description |
|---|---|---|
| 1 | — | Used for telephones and not for data |
| 2 | 4 Mbps | Originally intended to support Token Ring over UTP |
| 3 | 10 Mbps | Can be used for telephones as well; popular option for Ethernet in years past, if Cat 3 cabling for phones was already in place |
| 4 | 16 Mbps | Intended for the fast Token Ring speed option |
| 5 | 1 Gbps | Very popular for cabling to the desktop |
| 5e | 1 Gbps | Added mainly for the support of copper cabling for Gigabit Ethernet |
| 6 | 1 Gbps+ | Intended as a replacement for Cat 5e, with capabilities to support multigigabit speeds |

Table 1-12 lists the pertinent details of the Ethernet standards and the related cabling.

**Table 1-12**   *Ethernet Types and Cabling Standards*

| Standard | Cabling | Maximum Single Cable Length |
|---|---|---|
| 10BASE5 | Thick coaxial | 500 m |
| 10BASE2 | Thin coaxial | 185 m |
| 10BASE-T | UTP Cat 3, 4, 5, 5e, 6 | 100 m |
| 100BASE-FX | Two strands, multimode | 400 m |
| 100BASE-T | UTP Cat 3, 4, 5, 5e, 6, 2 pair | 100 m |
| 100BASE-T4 | UTP Cat 3, 4, 5, 5e, 6, 4 pair | 100 m |
| 100BASE-TX | UTP Cat 3, 4, 5, 5e, 6, or STP, 2 pair | 100 m |
| 1000BASE-LX | Long-wavelength laser, MM or SM fiber | 10 km (SM)<br>3 km (MM) |
| 1000BASE-SX | Short-wavelength laser, MM fiber | 220 m with 62.5-micron fiber;<br>550 m with 50-micron fiber |
| 1000BASE-ZX | Extended wavelength, SM fiber | 100 km |
| 1000BASE-CS | STP, 2 pair | 25 m |
| 1000BASE-T | UTP Cat 5, 5e, 6, 4 pair | 100 m |

# Memory Builders

The CCIE Routing and Switching written exam, like all Cisco CCIE written exams, covers a fairly broad set of topics. This section provides some basic tools to help you exercise your memory about some of the broader topics covered in this chapter.

## Fill In Key Tables from Memory

Appendix E, "Key Tables for CCIE Study," on the CD in the back of this book, contains empty sets of some of the key summary tables in each chapter. Print Appendix E, refer to this chapter's tables in it, and fill in the tables from memory. Refer to Appendix F, "Solutions for Key Tables for CCIE Study," on the CD to check your answers.

## Definitions

Next, take a few moments to write down the definitions for the following terms:

Autonegotiation, half duplex, full duplex, crossover cable, straight-through cable, unicast address, multicast address, broadcast address, loopback circuitry, I/G bit, U/L bit, CSMA/CD, SPAN, RSPAN, ERSPAN, remote VLAN, monitor session, VLAN filtering, encapsulation replication, VSS, VSL, FED, FFM

Refer to the glossary to check your answers.

## Further Reading

For a good reference for more information on the actual FLPs used by autonegotiation, refer to the Fast Ethernet web page of the University of New Hampshire Research Computing Center's InterOperability Laboratory, at www.iol.unh.edu/services/testing/fe/training/.

For information about configuring SPAN and RSPAN, and for a full set of restrictions (specific to the 3560 and 3750), see www.ciscosystems.com/en/US/docs/switches/lan/catalyst3560/software/release/12.2_50_se/configuration/guide/swspan.html.

**Blueprint topics covered in this chapter:**

This chapter covers the following subtopics from the Cisco CCIE Routing and Switching written exam blueprint. Refer to the full blueprint in Table I-1 in the Introduction for more details on the topics covered in each chapter and their context within the blueprint.

- VLANs

- VLAN Trunking

- VLAN Trunking Protocol (VTP)

- PPP over Ethernet (PPPoE)

## CHAPTER 2

# Virtual LANs and VLAN Trunking

This chapter continues with the coverage of some of the most fundamental and important LAN topics with coverage of VLANs and VLAN trunking. As usual, for those of you current in your knowledge of the topics in this chapter, review the items next to the Key Topic icons spread throughout the chapter, plus the "Foundation Summary" and "Memory Builders" sections at the end of the chapter.

## "Do I Know This Already?" Quiz

Table 2-1 outlines the major headings in this chapter and the corresponding "Do I Know This Already?" quiz questions.

**Table 2-1**  *"Do I Know This Already?" Foundation Topics Section-to-Question Mapping*

| Foundation Topics Section | Questions Covered in This Section | Score |
|---|---|---|
| Virtual LANs | 1–2 | |
| VLAN Trunking Protocol | 3–5 | |
| VLAN Trunking: ISL and 802.1Q | 6–9 | |
| Configuring PPPoE | 10 | |
| **Total Score** | | |

To best use this pre-chapter assessment, remember to score yourself strictly. You can find the answers in Appendix A, "Answers to the 'Do I Know This Already?' Quizzes."

1. Assume that VLAN 28 does not yet exist on Switch1. Which of the following commands, issued in the global configuration mode (reached with the **configure terminal** command) or any of its submodes would cause the VLAN to be created?

   a.  **vlan 28**

   b.  **vlan 28 name fred**

   c.  **switchport vlan 28**

   d.  **switchport access vlan 28**

   e.  **switchport access 28**

**2.** Which of the following are advantages of using Private VLANs?

    **a.** Better LAN security

    **b.** IP subnet conservation

    **c.** Better consistency in VLAN configuration details

    **d.** Reducing the impact of broadcasts on end-user devices

    **e.** Reducing the unnecessary flow of frames to switches that do not have any ports in the VLAN to which the frame belongs

**3.** Which of the following VLANs can be pruned by VTP on an 802.1Q trunk?

    **a.** 1–1023

    **b.** 1–1001

    **c.** 2–1001

    **d.** 1–1005

    **e.** 2–1005

**4.** An existing switched network has ten switches, with Switch1 and Switch2 being the only VTPv2 servers in the network. The other switches are all VTPv2 clients and have successfully learned about the VLANs from the VTPv2 servers. The only configured VTP parameter on all switches is the VTP domain name (Larry). The VTP revision number is 201. What happens when a new, already-running VTPv2 client switch, named Switch11, with domain name Larry and revision number 301, connects through a trunk to any of the other ten switches?

    **a.** No VLAN information changes; Switch11 ignores the VTP updates sent from the two existing VTP servers until the revision number reaches 302.

    **b.** The original ten switches replace their old VLAN configuration with the configuration in Switch11.

    **c.** Switch11 replaces its own VLAN configuration with the configuration sent to it by one of the original VTP servers.

    **d.** Switch11 merges its existing VLAN database with the database learned from the VTP servers, because Switch11 had a higher revision number.

5. An existing switched network has ten switches, with Switch1 and Switch2 being the only VTPv3 servers in the network, and Switch1 being the primary server. The other switches are all VTPv3 clients, and have successfully learned about the VLANs from the VTP server. The only configured VTP parameter is the VTP domain name (Larry). The VTP revision number is 201. What happens when an already-running VTPv3 server switch, named Switch11, with domain name Larry and revision number 301, connects through a trunk to any of the other ten switches?

   a. No VLAN information changes; all VTP updates between the original VTP domain and the new switch are ignored.

   b. The original ten switches replace their old VLAN configuration with the configuration in Switch11.

   c. Switch11 replaces its old VLAN configuration with the configuration sent to it by one of the original VTP servers.

   d. Switch11 merges its existing VLAN database with the database learned from the VTP servers, because Switch11 had a higher revision number.

   e. None of the other answers is correct.

6. Assume that two brand-new Cisco switches were removed from their cardboard boxes. PC1 was attached to one switch, PC2 was attached to the other, and the two switches were connected with a cross-over cable. The switch connection dynamically formed an 802.1Q trunk. When PC1 sends a frame to PC2, how many additional bytes of header are added to the frame before it passes over the trunk?

   a. 0

   b. 4

   c. 8

   d. 26

7. Assume that two brand-new Cisco Catalyst 3560 switches were connected with a cross-over cable. Before the cable was attached, one switch interface was configured with the **switchport trunk encapsulation dot1q**, **switchport mode trunk**, and **switchport nonegotiate** subcommands. Which of the following must be configured on the other switch before trunking will work between the switches?

   a. **switchport trunk encapsulation dot1q**

   b. **switchport mode trunk**

   c. **switchport nonegotiate**

   d. No configuration is required.

**8.** When configuring trunking on a Cisco router Fa0/1 interface, under which configuration modes could the IP address associated with the native VLAN (VLAN 1 in this case) be configured?

   **a.** Interface Fa0/1 configuration mode

   **b.** Interface Fa0/1.1 configuration mode

   **c.** Interface Fa0/1.2 configuration mode

   **d.** None of the other answers is correct.

**9.** Which of the following about 802.1Q are false?

   **a.** Encapsulates the entire frame inside an 802.1Q header and trailer

   **b.** Has a concept of a native VLAN

   **c.** Allows VTP to operate only on extended-range VLANs

   **d.** Is chosen over ISL by DTP

**10.** Which command enables PPPoE client functionality on the outside Ethernet interface on a Cisco router?

   **a.** pppoe enable

   **b.** pppoe-client enable

   **c.** pppoe-client dialer-pool-number

   **d.** pppoe-client dialer-number

# Foundation Topics

## Virtual LANs

In an Ethernet LAN, a set of devices that receive a broadcast sent by any one of the devices in the same set is called a *broadcast domain*. On switches that have no concept of virtual LANs (VLAN), a switch simply forwards all broadcasts out all interfaces, except the interface on which it received the frame. As a result, all the interfaces on an individual switch are in the same broadcast domain. Also, if the switch connects to other switches and hubs, the interfaces on those switches and hubs are also in the same broadcast domain.

A *VLAN* is simply an administratively defined subset of switch ports that are in the same broadcast domain. Ports can be grouped into different VLANs on a single switch, and on multiple interconnected switches as well. By creating multiple VLANs, the switches create multiple, yet contained, broadcast domains. By doing so, a broadcast sent by a device in one VLAN is forwarded to the other devices in that same VLAN; however, the broadcast is not forwarded to devices in the other VLANs.

Key
Topic

With VLANs and IP, best practices dictate a one-to-one relationship between VLANs and IP subnets. Simply put, the devices in a single VLAN are typically also in the same single IP subnet. Alternately, it is possible to put multiple subnets in one VLAN, and use secondary IP addresses on routers to route between the VLANs and subnets. Ultimately, the CCIE written exams tend to focus more on the best use of technologies, so this book will assume that one subnet sits on one VLAN, unless otherwise stated.

Layer 2 switches forward frames between devices in the same VLAN, but they do not forward frames between two devices in different VLANs. To forward data between two VLANs, a multilayer switch (MLS) or router is needed. Chapter 6, "IP Forwarding (Routing)," covers the details of MLS.

## VLAN Configuration

On Cisco IOS–based switches, a VLAN is primarily identified by its numerical ID, which is the only mandatory argument when creating, modifying, or deleting a VLAN. A VLAN can be assigned a verbal name for better orientation, but only a very few places in the CLI allow substituting the VLAN name for its ID. Also, a VLAN has an operational state: It can either be *active*, which is the default state, or it can be *suspended*. A suspended VLAN is hibernated—while it exists, it does not operate. Access ports in a suspended VLAN are unable to communicate and drop all frames, similar to ports put into a nonexistent VLAN. Putting a suspended VLAN back into the active state also reinstates normal communication on all ports in that VLAN.

Configuring VLANs in a network of Cisco switches requires just a few simple steps:

**Step 1.**   Create the VLAN itself, optionally configuring its name and state.

**Step 2.**   Associate the correct ports with that VLAN.

The challenge relates to how some background tasks differ depending on how the Cisco *VLAN Trunking Protocol (VTP)* is configured, and whether normal-range or extended-range VLANs are being used. We will discuss VTP and VLAN ranges in more detail later in this chapter.

## Using VLAN Database Mode to Create VLANs

To begin, consider Example 2-1, which shows some of the basic mechanics of VLAN creation in *VLAN database configuration mode.* While this configuration mode is considered obsolete on recent switches and might not be supported at all, it might still be used on older Catalyst platforms and on ISR and ISR G2 routers with switching modules installed. VLAN database configuration mode allows the creation of VLANs, basic administrative settings for each VLAN, and verification of VTP configuration information. Only normal-range (VLANs 1–1005) VLANs can be configured in this mode, and the VLAN configuration is stored in a Flash file called vlan.dat. In general, the *VLAN database configuration mode* should be avoided if possible, and hopefully you will not need to use it anymore; however, there are still switches and even relatively recent routers deployed in networks that do not support the newer way of configuring VLANs in global configuration mode.

Example 2-1 demonstrates VLAN database configuration mode, showing the configuration on Switch3 from Figure 2-1. The example shows VLANs 21 and 22 being created.

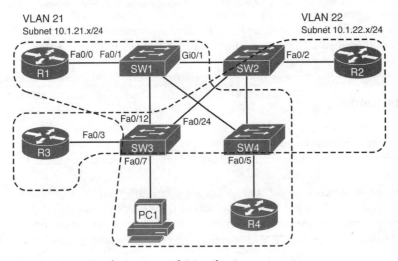

**Figure 2-1**   *Simple Access and Distribution*

**Example 2-1**   *VLAN Creation in VLAN Database Mode – Switch3*

```
! Below, note that Fa0/12 and Fa0/24 are missing from the list, because they have
! dynamically become trunks, supporting multiple VLANs.


Switch3# show vlan brief
VLAN Name                             Status    Ports
---- -------------------------------- --------- -------------------------------
1    default                          active    Fa0/1, Fa0/2, Fa0/3, Fa0/4
                                                Fa0/5, Fa0/6, Fa0/7, Fa0/8
                                                Fa0/9, Fa0/10, Fa0/11, Fa0/13
                                                Fa0/14, Fa0/15, Fa0/16, Fa0/17
                                                Fa0/18, Fa0/19, Fa0/20, Fa0/21
                                                Fa0/22, Fa0/23


! Below, "unsup" means that this 2950 switch does not support FDDI and TR


1002 fddi-default                     act/unsup
1003 token-ring-default               act/unsup
1004 fddinet-default                  act/unsup
1005 trnet-default                    act/unsup


! Below, vlan database moves user to VLAN database configuration mode.
! The vlan 21 command defines the VLAN, as seen in the next command output
! (show current), VLAN 21 is not in the "current" VLAN list.


Switch3# vlan database
Switch3(vlan)# vlan 21
VLAN 21 added:
    Name: VLAN0021


! The show current command lists the VLANs available to the IOS when the switch
! is in VTP Server mode. The command lists the VLANs in numeric order, with
! VLAN 21 missing.


Switch3(vlan)# show current
  VLAN ISL Id: 1
    Name: default
    Media Type: Ethernet
    VLAN 802.10 Id: 100001
    State: Operational
    MTU: 1500
    Backup CRF Mode: Disabled
    Remote SPAN VLAN: No
```

```
! Lines omitted for brevity
! Next, note that show proposed lists VLAN 21. The vlan 21 command
! creates the definition, but it must be "applied" before it is "current".

Switch3(vlan)# show proposed
  VLAN ISL Id: 1
    Name: default
    Media Type: Ethernet
    VLAN 802.10 Id: 100001
    State: Operational
    MTU: 1500
    Backup CRF Mode: Disabled
    Remote SPAN VLAN: No

  VLAN ISL Id: 21
    Name: VLAN0021
    Media Type: Ethernet
    VLAN 802.10 Id: 100021
    State: Operational
    MTU: 1500
    Backup CRF Mode: Disabled
    Remote SPAN VLAN: No

! Lines omitted for brevity
! Next, you could apply to complete the addition of VLAN 21,
! abort to not make the changes and exit VLAN database mode, or
! reset to not make the changes but stay in VLAN database mode.

Switch3(vlan)# ?
VLAN database editing buffer manipulation commands:
  abort  Exit mode without applying the changes
  apply  Apply current changes and bump revision number
  exit   Apply changes, bump revision number, and exit mode
  no     Negate a command or set its defaults
  reset  Abandon current changes and reread current database
  show   Show database information
  vlan   Add, delete, or modify values associated with a single VLAN
  vtp    Perform VTP administrative functions.

! The apply command was used, making the addition of VLAN 21 complete.

Switch3(vlan)# apply
APPLY completed.
```

```
! A show current now would list VLAN 21.


Switch3(vlan)# vlan 22 name ccie-vlan-22
VLAN 22 added:
    Name: ccie-vlan-22


! Above and below, some variations on commands are shown, along with the
! creation of VLAN 22, with name ccie-vlan-22.
! Below, the vlan 22 option is used on show current and show proposed
! detailing the fact that the apply has not been done yet.


Switch3(vlan)# show current 22
VLAN 22 does not exist in current database
Switch3(vlan)# show proposed 22
  VLAN ISL Id: 22


! Lines omitted for brevity
! Finally, the user exits VLAN database mode using CTRL-Z, which does
! not inherently apply the change. CTRL-Z actually executes an abort.


Switch3(vlan)# ^Z
```

## Using Configuration Mode to Put Interfaces into VLANs

To put a VLAN to use, the VLAN must be created, and then switch ports must be
assigned to the VLAN. Example 2-2 shows how to associate the interfaces with the correct VLANs, once again on Switch3.

**Note**    At the end of Example 2-1, VLAN 22 had not been successfully created. The
assumption for Example 2-2, however, is that VLAN 22 has been successfully created.

**Example 2-2**    *Assigning Interfaces to VLANs – Switch3*

```
! First, the switchport mode access command configures respective interfaces for
! static access mode, and the switchport access vlan command assigns them into
! respective VLANs.

Switch3# conf t
Enter configuration commands, one per line.  End with CNTL/Z.
Switch3(config)# int fa 0/3
Switch3(config-if)# switchport mode access
Switch3(config-if)# switchport access vlan 22
```

```
Switch3(config-if)# int fa 0/7
Switch3(config-if)# switchport mode access
Switch3(config-if)# switchport access vlan 21
Switch3(config-if)# ^Z

! Below, show vlan brief lists these same two interfaces as now being in
! VLANs 21 and 22, respectively.

Switch3# show vlan brief

VLAN Name                             Status    Ports
---- -------------------------------- --------- -------------------------------
1    default                          active    Fa0/1, Fa0/2, Fa0/4, Fa0/5
                                                Fa0/6, Fa0/8, Fa0/9, Fa0/10
                                                Fa0/11, Fa0/13, Fa0/14, Fa0/15
                                                Fa0/16, Fa0/17, Fa0/18, Fa0/19
                                                Fa0/20, Fa0/21, Fa0/22, Fa0/23
21   VLAN0021                         active    Fa0/7
22   ccie-vlan-22                     active    Fa0/3

! Lines omitted for brevity
! While the VLAN configuration is not shown in the running-config at this point,
! the switchport access command that assigns the VLAN for the interface is in the
! configuration, as seen with the show run int fa 0/3 command.

Switch3# show run int fa 0/3
interface FastEthernet0/3
 switchport access vlan 22
 switchport mode access
```

## Using Configuration Mode to Create VLANs

At this point, the two new VLANs (21 and 22) have been created on Switch3, and the two interfaces are now in the correct VLANs. However, all recent Cisco IOS–based switches support a different way to create VLANs, using configuration mode, as shown in Example 2-3. This is the preferred mode for configuring VLANs whenever supported, and is the only mode that can be used to configure extended-range and Private VLANs. All VLAN settings are performed in the **vlan** *vlan-id* mode accessed from global configuration level. Configuration changes apply only after exiting the **vlan** mode; this is one of the few IOS CLI contexts in which changes are not applied immediately after entering individual commands.

**Example 2-3**    *Creating VLANs in Configuration Mode – Switch3*

```
! First, VLAN 31 did not exist when the switchport access vlan 31 command was
! issued. As a result, the switch both created the VLAN and put interface fa0/8
! into that VLAN. Then, the vlan 32 global command was used to create a
! VLAN from configuration mode, and the name subcommand was used to assign a
! non-default name.

Switch3# conf t
Enter configuration commands, one per line.  End with CNTL/Z.
Switch3(config)# int fa 0/8
Switch3(config-if)# switchport mode access
Switch3(config-if)# switchport access vlan 31
% Access VLAN does not exist. Creating vlan 31
Switch3(config-if)# exit
Switch3(config)# vlan 32
Switch3(config-vlan)# name ccie-vlan-32
Switch3(config-vlan)# ^Z
Switch3# show vlan brief


VLAN Name                             Status    Ports
---- -------------------------------- --------- -------------------------------
1    default                          active    Fa0/1, Fa0/2, Fa0/4, Fa0/5
                                                Fa0/6, Fa0/9, Fa0/10, Fa0/11
                                                Fa0/13, Fa0/14, Fa0/15, Fa0/16
                                                Fa0/17, Fa0/18, Fa0/19, Fa0/20
                                                Fa0/21, Fa0/22, Fa0/23
21   VLAN0021                         active    Fa0/7
22   ccie-vlan-22                     active    Fa0/3
31   VLAN0031                         active    Fa0/8
32   ccie-vlan-32                     active

! Portions omitted for brevity
```

Example 2-3 shows how the **switchport access vlan** subcommand creates the VLAN, as needed, and assigns the interface to that VLAN. Note that in Example 2-3, the **show vlan brief** output lists Fa0/8 as being in VLAN 31. Because no ports have been assigned to VLAN 32 as of yet, the final line in Example 2-3 simply does not list any interfaces.

## Modifying the Operational State of VLANs

The state of a VLAN—active or suspended—can be manipulated both in **vlan database** and in configuration mode. A VLAN can be suspended in two ways: *globally* in the entire VTP domain and *locally* on a single switch without influencing its state through

VTP on other switches. The **state suspend** command, valid both in **vlan database** and in configuration mode, is used to globally suspend a VLAN. Suspending a VLAN locally, also called "locally shutting down the VLAN," is accomplished using the **shutdown** command, and is supported only in the configuration mode in the VLAN context. Do not confuse the **shutdown** command in the VLAN context with the same command available under **interface Vlan** mode, which has a different and unrelated meaning (shutting down an SVI without further impairing the operation of the corresponding VLAN itself). Global and local VLAN states can be configured independently, but for a VLAN to be operational on a switch, it must be both globally and locally activated. Manipulating the operational state of VLANs and the use of corresponding commands are shown in greater detail in Example 2-4.

**Example 2-4**  *Modifying the Operational State of VLANs*

```
! First, put the VLAN 21 to global suspended state in vlan database mode. The state
! will be propagated by VTP to all switches in the VTP domain if VTP is used.

Switch3# vlan database
Switch3(vlan)# vlan 21 state ?
  active   VLAN Active State
  suspend  VLAN Suspended State
Switch3(vlan)# vlan 21 state suspend
VLAN 31 modified:
    State SUSPENDED
Switch3(vlan)# exit
APPLY completed.
Exiting....

! VLAN 21 will now be listed as suspended

Switch3# show vlan brief
VLAN Name                             Status    Ports
---- -------------------------------- --------- -------------------------------
1    default                          active    Fa0/1, Fa0/2, Fa0/4, Fa0/5
                                                 Fa0/6, Fa0/9, Fa0/10, Fa0/11
                                                 Fa0/13, Fa0/14, Fa0/15, Fa0/16
                                                 Fa0/17, Fa0/18, Fa0/19, Fa0/20
                                                 Fa0/21, Fa0/22, Fa0/23
21   VLAN0021                         suspended Fa0/7

! Portions omitted for brevity


! Now use the configuration mode to reactivate the VLAN
```

```
Switch3# conf t
Enter configuration commands, one per line.  End with CNTL/Z.
Switch3(config)# vlan 21
Switch3(config-vlan)# state active
Switch3(config-vlan)# exit
Switch3(config)# do show vlan brief
VLAN Name                             Status    Ports
---- -------------------------------- --------- -------------------------------
1    default                          active    Fa0/1, Fa0/2, Fa0/4, Fa0/5
                                                Fa0/6, Fa0/9, Fa0/10, Fa0/11
                                                Fa0/13, Fa0/14, Fa0/15, Fa0/16
                                                Fa0/17, Fa0/18, Fa0/19, Fa0/20
                                                Fa0/21, Fa0/22, Fa0/23
21   VLAN0021                         active    Fa0/7

! Portions omitted for brevity

! To locally suspend a VLAN, enter its configuration context and issue
! the shutdown command, then exit. Alternatively, you may also use the
! shutdown vlan global level configuration command that has exactly
! the same effect. In the VLAN listing, the VLAN 21 will be reported as
! active in the VTP domain on other switches, yet locally shutdown.
! It is also possible to both use the state suspend to suspend the VLAN
! via VTP globally, and shutdown to also have it locally shut down.

Switch3(config)# vlan 21
Switch3(config-vlan)# shutdown
Switch3(config-vlan)# exit
Switch3(config)# do show vlan brief
VLAN Name                             Status    Ports
---- -------------------------------- --------- -------------------------------
1    default                          active    Fa0/1, Fa0/2, Fa0/4, Fa0/5
                                                Fa0/6, Fa0/9, Fa0/10, Fa0/11
                                                Fa0/13, Fa0/14, Fa0/15, Fa0/16
                                                Fa0/17, Fa0/18, Fa0/19, Fa0/20
                                                Fa0/21, Fa0/22, Fa0/23
21   VLAN0021                         act/lshut Fa0/7

! Portions omitted for brevity

! To reactivate the locally shut VLAN, enter the no shutdown command in vlan 21
! context, or more straightforward, enter the no shutdown vlan 21 command

Switch3(config)# no shutdown vlan 21
Switch3(config)# do show vlan brief
```

```
VLAN Name                             Status    Ports
---- --------------------------------  --------- -------------------------------
1    default                          active    Fa0/1, Fa0/2, Fa0/4, Fa0/5
                                                Fa0/6, Fa0/9, Fa0/10, Fa0/11
                                                Fa0/13, Fa0/14, Fa0/15, Fa0/16
                                                Fa0/17, Fa0/18, Fa0/19, Fa0/20
                                                Fa0/21, Fa0/22, Fa0/23
21   VLAN0021                         active    Fa0/7

! Portions omitted for brevity
```

The VLAN creation process is simple but laborious in a large network. If many VLANs exist, and they exist on multiple switches, instead of manually configuring the VLANs on each switch, you can use VTP to distribute the VLAN configuration of a VLAN to the rest of the switches. VTP will be discussed later in the chapter.

## Private VLANs

Engineers can design VLANs with many goals in mind. In many cases today, devices end up in the same VLAN just based on the physical locations of the wiring drops. Security is another motivating factor in VLAN design: Devices in different VLANs do not overhear each other's broadcasts and possibly other communication. Additionally, the separation of hosts into different VLANs and subnets requires an intervening router or multilayer switch between the subnets, and these types of devices typically provide more robust security features.

Regardless of the design motivations behind grouping devices into VLANs, good design practices typically call for the use of a single IP subnet per VLAN. In some cases, however, the need to increase security by separating devices into many small VLANs conflicts with the design goal of conserving the use of the available IP subnets. The Cisco Private VLAN feature described in RFC 5517 addresses this issue. Private VLANs allow a switch to separate ports as if they were on different VLANs, while consuming only a single subnet.

A common place to implement Private VLANs is in the multitenant offerings of a service provider (SP). The SP can install a single router and a single switch. Then, the SP attaches devices from multiple customers to the switch. Private VLANs then allow the SP to use only a single subnet for the entire building, separating different customers' switch ports so that they cannot communicate directly, while supporting all customers with a single router and switch.

Conceptually, a Private VLAN is a mechanism that partitions a given VLAN into an arbitrary number of nonoverlapping sub-VLANs, or *secondary VLANs*. This partitioning is invisible to the outside world that continues to see only the original VLAN, in this context called the *primary VLAN*. An important consequence of this private partitioning is that from outside, the primary VLAN continues to use the same VLAN ID and IP subnet as the original VLAN. Internally, all secondary VLANs will share this common IP subnet, although each of them has a different, unique VLAN ID that is associated with the primary VLAN. Hence, a Private VLAN can be described as a cluster of one or more secondary VLANs, represented to the outside by a single primary VLAN, not unlike a BGP confederation, where multiple internal sub-ASes are represented to external peers as a single AS. Consider the topology in Figure 2-2 for an overview.

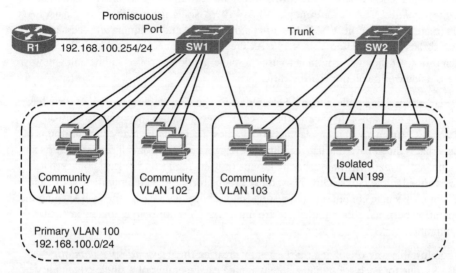

**Figure 2-2**    *Switched Network Utilizing Private VLANs*

Let us first consider the behavior of Private VLANs on a single switch. We will later discuss how the Private VLAN functionality extends to multiple switches over trunks.

Secondary VLANs can be of two types: *community* VLANs and *isolated* VLANs. Ports assigned to the same community VLAN can communicate with each other directly, but they are not allowed to communicate with ports in any other VLAN. This behavior is similar to ordinary VLANs. A single primary VLAN can be associated with multiple community VLANs, each of them representing a group of devices that can talk directly to each other but that are separated from any other similar groups.

On the other hand, ports assigned to an isolated VLAN can neither communicate with each other nor with ports in any other VLAN. A single primary VLAN can be associated with at most one isolated VLAN, as having multiple isolated VLANs under a single primary VLAN would make no sense.

A single primary VLAN can be associated with zero or more community VLANs and with at most one isolated VLAN. A secondary VLAN, either a community or an isolated VLAN, must be associated with exactly one primary VLAN.

As an example, consider a block of flats that needs to be fully networked, with you being the person responsible for configuring the networking equipment. A simple approach would be to connect all flats to a switch and assign all ports to a single VLAN, say, VLAN 100 utilizing the IP subnet 192.168.100.0/24. All stations in this VLAN share this IP space and can communicate with each other directly, and use a gateway IP address from the same subnet, for example, 192.168.100.254, to reach other networks. However, this network has an obvious security issue—users in individual flats are not controlled and cannot be trusted. A single misbehaving or infected computer in one flat can wreak havoc throughout the entire VLAN. Therefore, it is natural to require that individual flats be isolated from each other but still continue to use the former VLAN 100, the same IP subnet, and the same default gateway. This can be accomplished by creating a new *secondary isolated* VLAN, for example, VLAN 199, associating it with the original VLAN 100 (thereby making the VLAN 100 a *primary* VLAN) and assigning all access ports toward flats to the isolated VLAN 199. As a result, individual flats will be isolated from each other, yet they will continue to use the same IP address space and default gateway. The outside world will not see any difference.

Life is seldom that simple, though. Selected users can start coming to you after a while and request direct visibility with other selected users because they want to mutually share files, stream a video, or play network games. There can be many similar groups of users that want to have mutual visibility, yet remain isolated from all other users. As an example, consider that three separate groups of users requesting mutual connectivity have formed in the block. Obviously, these groups form three communities, with members of each single community requesting full visibility with each other, yet keeping the separation between communities and from users that do not belong to any particular community.

A comfortable way of solving this task is by creating three *secondary community* VLANs, one for each community, and assigning each member of a single community to the same community VLAN. In this example, the first group can be assigned to community VLAN 101, the second group can be assigned to community VLAN 102, and the remaining group can be put into community VLAN 103. These secondary community VLANs 101–103 will be associated with the primary VLAN 100, again sharing its IP address space and default gateway. All other flats will remain in isolated VLAN 199 and will keep their total isolation.

Depending on what secondary VLAN type a switch port is assigned to, we call these ports either *community ports* or *isolated ports*. In the preceding example, switch ports configured with VLANs 101–103 would be called community ports, while switch ports configured with VLAN 199 would be called isolated ports. Note that none of the ports mentioned so far is assigned to the primary VLAN 100. Both community and isolated ports behave as normal access ports—they technically belong to a single VLAN and they do not tag frames.

**Key Topic**

According to communication rules described so far, hosts in a particular community VLAN can only talk to other hosts in the same community VLAN and no one else; hosts in a particular isolated VLAN can talk to no one at all. There is, so far, no possibility of communicating with the world outside the given Private VLAN, nor a way of accessing common shared resources, such as network printers, storage, or servers. Clearly, the usefulness of such VLANs would be questionable at best. Therefore, there must be a way of defining a special port that is allowed to communicate with any member of any secondary VLAN under a particular primary VLAN. A device attached to such a port—a router, server, NAS, printer, and so on—would then be accessible by any host in any secondary VLAN under a particular primary VLAN, regardless of the type of the secondary VLAN.

In Private VLAN terminology, such ports are called *promiscuous* ports. A promiscuous port is not associated with any particular secondary VLAN. Instead, it is associated with the corresponding primary VLAN itself. A device connected to a promiscuous port can communicate with devices in all secondary VLANs associated with this primary VLAN and vice versa. A device in a secondary VLAN that is associated with a particular primary VLAN can communicate with any promiscuous port in that primary VLAN. If there are multiple promiscuous ports in the primary VLAN, they can also communicate with each other. Promiscuous ports also behave as access ports in the sense they do not use tagging.

In the preceding example, if the default gateway 192.168.100.254 is an external router, it would be connected to a promiscuous port on the switch that implements the Private VLAN. This setup would allow hosts in VLANs 101–103 and 199 to communicate with other networks through this router.

If Private VLANs are in use, the rules of communication on a single switch can be summarized as follows:

- A port in a particular community VLAN (that is, a community port) can communicate with all other ports in the same community VLAN and with all promiscuous ports in the corresponding primary VLAN.

- A port in a particular isolated VLAN (that is, an isolated port) can communicate with all promiscuous ports in the corresponding primary VLAN.

- A port in a particular primary VLAN (that is, a promiscuous port) can communicate with all other promiscuous ports in the same primary VLAN and with all ports in all secondary VLANs associated with this primary VLAN.

Extending the operation of Private VLANs over a set of switches is fairly simple. The basic goal is to increase the span of Private VLANs while keeping their defined behavior and containment. A port in a particular community VLAN shall be able to communicate with other ports in the same community VLAN and with all promiscuous ports in the corresponding primary VLAN on any switch. Similarly, a port in a particular isolated VLAN shall be able to communicate with all promiscuous ports in the corresponding primary VLAN on any switch. A promiscuous port in a particular primary VLAN shall be able to communicate with all other promiscuous ports in that primary VLAN and with all ports in all associated secondary VLANs on all switches. Because these requirements implicitly assume that a frame received on a port in a primary or secondary VLAN can be forwarded through trunk ports to other switches, yet another communication rule is hereby established: A frame received on a promiscuous, community, or isolated port can always be forwarded through a trunk port.

Obviously, if all primary/secondary VLANs, their IDs, types, and associations are configured identically on all switches (provided they support the Private VLAN feature), each switch will give frames the same consistent treatment as soon as their membership in a particular VLAN is established. As frames between switches are carried by trunk ports, it is important to see how the tagging of frames received on a Private VLAN port is performed.

If a frame is received on a community or isolated port and is forwarded through a trunk, the switch will tag the frame using the VLAN ID of the corresponding *secondary* VLAN. The receiving switch will then forward the received frame further according to the type of the secondary VLAN.

If a frame is received on a promiscuous port and is forwarded through a trunk, the switch will tag the frame using the VLAN ID of the corresponding *primary* VLAN. The receiving switch will then forward the frame further as a frame coming from a promiscuous port.

**Key Topic**

To summarize the communication and tagging rules in Private VLANs:

- A port in a particular community VLAN (that is, a community port) can communicate with all other ports in the same community VLAN, with all promiscuous ports in the corresponding primary VLAN, and with all trunks.

- A port in a particular isolated VLAN (that is, an isolated port) can communicate with all promiscuous ports in the corresponding primary VLAN, and with all trunks.

- A port in a particular primary VLAN (that is, a promiscuous port) can communicate with all other promiscuous ports in the same primary VLAN, with all ports in all secondary VLANs associated with this primary VLAN, and with all trunks.

- A frame received on a community or isolated port will be tagged with the ID of the corresponding secondary VLAN when forwarded out a trunk.

- A frame received on a promiscuous port will be tagged with the ID of the corresponding primary VLAN when forwarded out a trunk.

- A frame received on a trunk tagged with a community or isolated VLAN ID will be forwarded as if it was received on a local community or isolated port in the corresponding secondary VLAN.

- A frame received on a trunk tagged with a primary VLAN ID will be forwarded as if it was received on a local promiscuous port in the corresponding primary VLAN.

- Community VLANs can be seen as VLANs carrying "upstream" traffic from a host to other hosts of the same community VLAN and to promiscuous ports in the corresponding primary VLAN. Isolated VLANs can be seen as VLANs carrying "upstream" traffic from hosts to promiscuous ports in the corresponding primary VLAN. A Primary VLAN can be seen as a VLAN carrying "downstream" traffic from promiscuous ports to other promiscuous ports and hosts in all associated secondary VLANs.

Table 2-2 summarizes the communication rules between various ports.

**Table 2-2**   *Private VLAN Communications Between Ports*

| Description of Who Can Talk to Whom | Primary VLAN Ports | Community VLAN Ports[1] | Isolated VLAN Ports[1] |
|---|---|---|---|
| Talk to ports in primary VLAN (promiscuous ports) | Yes | Yes | Yes |
| Talk to ports in the same secondary VLAN (host ports) | N/A[2] | Yes | No |
| Talk to ports in another secondary VLAN | N/A[2] | No | No |
| Talk to trunks | Yes | Yes | Yes |

1 Community and isolated VLANs are secondary VLANs.

2 Promiscuous ports, by definition in the primary VLAN, can talk to all other ports.

There are two common misconceptions regarding the Private VLAN operation on trunks. The first misconception relates to the tagging. It is often incorrectly believed that Private VLANs use double tagging on trunks. This belief is supported by the apparent nesting of secondary VLANs inside their associated primary VLAN. In reality, secondary VLANs do not exist "inside" their primary VLAN; rather, they are only *associated* with it. This association merely indicates that a frame received in a secondary VLAN can be forwarded out promiscuous ports in the associated primary VLAN and vice versa.

The second misconception is related to trunk port types. We have so far described normal trunks (**switchport mode trunk**) that can be used both for ordinary and Private VLANs. There are, however, two special types of trunk ports with respect to Private VLANs. These special trunk port types are called Promiscuous PVLAN Trunk and Isolated PVLAN Trunk ports. Both these types *shall not be used* in ordinary Private VLAN deployments between switches supporting Private VLANs; rather, their usage is limited to a set of special scenarios. To understand better, consider Figure 2-3, which contains a slightly modified topology, with VLAN 100 being the primary VLAN, VLANs 101 and 102 being community VLANs, and VLAN 199 being an isolated VLAN. In addition, there is VLAN 999, which spans the router and both switches and serves the purpose of a management VLAN. The SW1 switch is assumed to support Private VLANs while SW2 does not support them.

The first special trunk type is the *Promiscuous PVLAN Trunk*. Whenever a frame from a secondary VLAN is going to be sent out such a trunk, its VLAN tag will be rewritten with the appropriate primary VLAN ID. This rewriting is necessary when a trunk carrying a set of VLANs including Private VLANs is to be connected to an external device that does not support Private VLANs, yet which shall be reachable from the Private VLANs as if connected to a promiscuous port. If, for example, a router-on-stick like R1 in Figure 2-3 is used to route between several VLANs including a primary VLAN, the external router does not understand that multiple secondary VLANs actually map to a single primary VLAN. The Promiscuous PVLAN Trunk port will translate all secondary VLAN IDs into the corresponding primary VLAN ID so that the external router always sees only the primary VLAN.

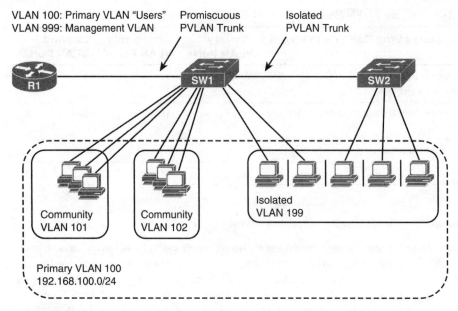

**Figure 2-3**  *Switched Topology Utilizing Special Trunk Types*

The second special type of a trunk is the *Isolated PVLAN Trunk*. This trunk type translates a primary VLAN ID into the ID of the isolated VLAN that is associated with the primary VLAN. This is used to extend the isolated VLAN over a trunk carrying multiple VLANs to a switch that does not support Private VLANs but is capable of isolating its own ports. To illustrate, entry-level Catalyst switches do not support Private VLANs but they support so-called *protected* ports (this feature is sometimes called the Private VLAN Edge). On these switches, a protected port can be configured using the **switch-port protected** command. Protected ports configured with this command are prohibited from ever communicating with each other—in essence, they act just like isolated ports. If a frame is received on a promiscuous port in the primary PVLAN and is about to be sent out the Isolated PVLAN Trunk port, its VLAN tag currently carrying the primary VLAN ID will be rewritten to the isolated VLAN ID. If the neighboring switch has its protected ports assigned to the isolated VLAN (although the VLAN is not configured as isolated on that switch because it does not support Private VLANs), it will be able to forward the frame to the appropriate host. In Figure 2-3, the Isolated PVLAN Trunk is used to extend the isolated PVLAN 199 from SW1 to SW2 that does not support PVLANs, yet is capable of locally isolating its ports in VLAN 199. SW2 will not allow these ports to communicate together while allowing them to communicate with the trunk toward SW1. SW1 will make sure that a frame received on another isolated port in VLAN 199 will not be forwarded out the isolated PVLAN trunk toward SW2, and that a frame tagged with VLAN 199 coming through the isolated PVLAN trunk from SW2 will not be forwarded out any other isolated port in the same secondary VLAN. This way, the isolated secondary VLAN is extended to SW2 without losing any of its isolated properties. Should, however, R1 or any other device on a promiscuous port send a packet to a station on SW2, this packet would ordinarily be tagged with primary VLAN 100. On the isolated PVLAN trunk on SW1, however, the tag 100 will be rewritten to 199 and forwarded to SW2, allowing the R1 on the promiscuous trunk to communicate with stations on SW2.

So, in essence, the special nature of these trunks lies in the tag rewriting they perform:

■ A Promiscuous PVLAN Trunk port rewrites the secondary VLAN ID into the primary PVLAN ID upon sending a frame. When a frame is received, no tag manipulation is performed. Also, no tag manipulation is performed for frames in ordinary VLANs.

■ An Isolated PVLAN Trunk port rewrites the primary VLAN ID into the isolated secondary VLAN ID upon sending a frame. When a frame is received, no tag manipulation is performed. Also, no tag manipulation is performed for frames in ordinary VLANs.

Special Private VLAN Trunk types are supported only on selected higher-level Catalyst switches.

Example 2-5 shows the configuration of a switch with Private VLANs. Configuration of ordinary trunks is not shown, as there is nothing specific regarding it.

**Example 2-5**  *Configuring Private VLANs*

```
! If not running VTPv3, a switch must be put into VTP Transparent mode before
! configuring Private VLANs

AccessSw(config)# vtp mode transparent
Setting device to VTP Transparent mode for VLANS.

! One isolated secondary VLAN and three community secondary VLANs will now be
! created. Afterwards, they will be associated with the primary VLAN 100.

AccessSw(config)# vlan 199
AccessSw(config-vlan)# name Isolated
AccessSw(config-vlan)# private-vlan isolated
AccessSw(config-vlan)# vlan 101
AccessSw(config-vlan)# name Community1
AccessSw(config-vlan)# private-vlan community
AccessSw(config-vlan)# vlan 102
AccessSw(config-vlan)# name Community2
AccessSw(config-vlan)# private-vlan community
AccessSw(config-vlan)# vlan 103
AccessSw(config-vlan)# name Community3
AccessSw(config-vlan)# private-vlan community
AccessSw(config-vlan)# vlan 100
AccessSw(config-vlan)# name Primary1
AccessSw(config-vlan)# private-vlan primary
AccessSw(config-vlan)# private-vlan association 101-103,199
AccessSw(config-vlan)# exit
```

```
! The show vlan private-vlan command is useful to verify the types and associations
! of private VLANs and their member ports. At this moment, there are no ports
! assigned to these VLANs yet.

AccessSw(config)# do show vlan private-vlan

Primary Secondary Type            Ports
------- --------- --------------- -------------------------------------------
100     101       community
100     102       community
100     103       community
100     199       isolated


! Now, ports will be assigned to these VLANs:
! Fa0/1 - 3:  Secondary community VLAN 101
! Fa0/4 - 5:  Secondary community VLAN 102
! Fa0/6 - 8:  Secondary community VLAN 103
! Fa0/9 - 12: Secondary isolated  VLAN 199
! Fa0/13:     Promiscuous port in primary VLAN 100
! For brevity purposes, only the configuration of Fa0/1 - 3 will be shown, as all
! other ports in secondary VLANs, isolated or community, are configured similarly
! Afterwards, show vlan private-vlan is issued to verify the port assignment.
! As Fa0/13 is a promiscuous port, it will be shown in all associated secondary
! VLANs

AccessSw(config)# interface range fa0/1 - 3
AccessSw(config-if-range)# switchport mode private-vlan host
AccessSw(config-if-range)# switchport private-vlan host-association 100 101
AccessSw(config-if-range)# interface fa0/13
AccessSw(config-if)# switchport mode private-vlan promiscuous
AccessSw(config-if)# switchport private-vlan mapping 100 101-103,199
AccessSw(config-if)# do show vlan private-vlan

Primary Secondary Type            Ports
------- --------- --------------- -------------------------------------------
100     101       community       Fa0/1, Fa0/2, Fa0/3, Fa0/13
100     102       community       Fa0/4, Fa0/5, Fa0/13
100     103       community       Fa0/6, Fa0/7, Fa0/8, Fa0/13
100     199       isolated        Fa0/9, Fa0/10, Fa0/11, Fa0/12, Fa0/13


! If a SVI is used as a gateway for devices associated with the primary VLAN 100,
! it must also be configured as promiscuous

AccessSw(config-if)# interface Vlan100
AccessSw(config-if)# private-vlan mapping 101-103,199
AccessSw(config-if)# ip address 192.168.100.254 255.255.255.0
```

# VLAN Trunking: ISL and 802.1Q

VLAN trunking allows switches, routers, and even PCs with the appropriate network interface cards (NIC) and/or software drivers to send traffic for multiple VLANs across a single link. To know to which VLAN a frame belongs, the sending switch, router, or PC adds a header to the original Ethernet frame, with that header having a field in which to place the VLAN ID of the associated VLAN. This section describes the protocol details for the two trunking protocols, followed by the details of how to configure trunking.

## ISL and 802.1Q Concepts

If two devices are to perform trunking, they must agree to use either Inter-Switch Link (ISL) or 802.1Q, because there are several differences between the two, as summarized in Table 2-3.

Key Topic

**Table 2-3**   *Comparing ISL and 802.1Q*

| Feature | ISL | 802.1Q |
|---|---|---|
| VLANs supported | Normal and extended range[1] | Normal and extended range |
| Protocol defined by | Cisco | IEEE |
| Encapsulates original frame or inserts tag | Encapsulates | Inserts tag |
| Has a concept of native VLAN | No | Yes |

1 ISL originally supported only normal-range VLANs, but was later improved to support extended-range VLANs as well.

ISL and 802.1Q differ in how they add a header to the Ethernet frame before sending it over a trunk. ISL adds a new 26-byte header, plus a new trailer (to allow for the new FCS value), encapsulating the entire original frame. This encapsulating header uses the source address (listed as SA in Figure 2-4) of the device doing the trunking, instead of the source MAC of the original frame. ISL uses a multicast destination address (listed as DA in Figure 2-4) of either 0100.0C00.0000 or 0300.0C00.0000. Overall, though, an ISL frame is technically a SNAP-encapsulated frame.

802.1Q inserts a 4-byte header, called a tag, into the original frame (right after the Source Address field). The original frame's addresses are left intact. Normally, an Ethernet controller would expect to find either an Ethernet Type field or 802.3 Length field right after the Source Address field. With an 802.1Q tag, the first 2 bytes after the Address fields hold a registered Ethernet type value of 0x8100, which implies that the frame includes an 802.1Q header. Because 802.1Q does not actually encapsulate the original frame, it is often called *frame tagging*. Figure 2-4 shows the contents of the headers used by both ISL and 802.1Q.

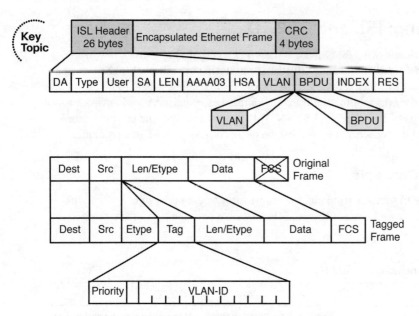

**Figure 2-4**   *ISL and 802.1Q Frame Marking Methods*

Finally, the last row from Table 2-3 refers to the *native VLAN*. On trunks, 802.1Q does not tag frames sent inside the native VLAN, and assigns all received untagged frames to the native VLAN. The native VLAN feature allows a switch to attempt to use 802.1Q trunking on an interface, but if the other device does not support trunking, the traffic for that one native VLAN can still be sent over the link. By default, the native VLAN is VLAN 1, which is also the default access VLAN. It is absolutely necessary that the native VLANs on both ends of a trunk link match; otherwise a native VLAN mismatch occurs, causing the two VLANs to effectively merge. To detect and possibly avoid any ill effects of a native VLAN mismatch, Cisco switches implement a proprietary extension to PVST+ and Rapid PVST+ that allows them to detect and block the mismatched native VLANs on the trunk. This extension is described in more detail in Chapter 3, "Spanning Tree Protocol." Also, Cisco Discovery Protocol (CDP) will detect and report a native VLAN mismatch. As a best practice, on each trunk, its native VLAN should be changed from VLAN 1 to a different VLAN, and this VLAN should not be used for any other purpose except being configured as a native VLAN. This prevents users from attempting a VLAN hopping attack by sending double-tagged frames that would be detagged on trunks if the top tag matches the trunk's native VLAN.

Detailed information about the ISL and 802.1Q tagging as implemented by Cisco can be found at Cisco.com published as a technote document called "Inter-Switch Link and IEEE 802.1Q Frame Format," Document ID: 17056.

## ISL and 802.1Q Configuration

Cisco switches use the *Dynamic Trunk Protocol (DTP)* to dynamically learn whether the device on the other end of the cable wants to perform trunking and, if so, which trunking protocol to use. It is meant both to ease the initial deployment of a switched network and to minimize configuration errors that result from mismatched port configuration on an interconnection between two switches.

DTP learns whether to trunk based on the DTP mode defined for an interface. The individual DTP modes are

- **dynamic auto:** The port will negotiate the mode automatically; however, it prefers to be an access port.

- **dynamic desirable:** The port will negotiate the mode automatically; however, it prefers to be a trunk port.

Out of these modes, **dynamic desirable** has a higher priority—if both ports are dynamic but one is configured as auto and the other as desirable, the resulting operating mode will be trunk. DTP also negotiates the type of encapsulation on the trunk should either of the two devices support both ISL and 802.1Q. If both devices support both trunk types, they will choose ISL. Should the DTP negotiation fail, any port in dynamic mode, either desirable or auto, will be operating as an access port. An upcoming section, "Trunk Configuration Compatibility," covers the different DTP modes and their combinations in closer detail.

Different types of Cisco switches have different default DTP modes. For example, earlier Catalyst 2950 and 3550 models default to dynamic desirable mode. Later Catalyst models, such as 2960, 3560 or 3750, default to dynamic auto mode. Authoritative information pertaining to the particular switch platform and IOS version can be found in the appropriate Command Reference.

While DTP and VTP are independent protocols, DTP carries the VTP domain name in its messages. Switches will successfully negotiate the link operating mode only if the VTP domain name on both switches is the same, or one switch has no VTP domain name configured yet (that is, it uses a NULL domain name). The reason behind tying the DTP negotiation to the VTP domain name is that in different VTP domains, there might be different sets of VLANs, and identically numbered VLANs might be used for different purposes (that is why the network was split into several VTP domains in the first place—to keep the VLAN databases separate and independent). As a result, switches should not try to bring up the link as a trunk, as extending VLANs from one VTP domain to another can have undesired consequences.

With the DTP mode set to desirable, switches can simply be connected, and they should dynamically form a trunk. You can, however, configure trunking details and verify the results with **show** commands. Table 2-4 lists some of the key Catalyst IOS commands related to trunking.

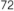

**Table 2-4**   *VLAN Trunking–Related Commands*

| Command | Function |
|---|---|
| **switchport \| no switchport** | Toggle defining whether to treat the interface as a switch interface (**switchport**) or as a routed interface (**no switchport**) |
| **switchport mode ...** | Sets DTP negotiation parameters |
| **switchport trunk ...** | Sets trunking parameters if the interface is trunking |
| **switchport access ...** | Sets nontrunking-related parameters if the interface is not trunking |
| **show interfaces trunk** | Summary of trunk-related information |
| **show interfaces** *type number* **trunk** | Lists trunking details for a particular interface |
| **show interfaces** *type number* **switchport** | Lists both trunking and nontrunking details for a particular interface |

Figure 2-5 lists several details regarding Switch1's trunking configuration and status, as shown in Example 2-6. R1 is not configured to trunk, so Switch1 will fail to negotiate trunking. Switch2 is a Catalyst 3550, which supports both ISL and 802.1Q, so they will negotiate trunking and use ISL. Switch3 and Switch4 are Catalyst 2950s, which support only 802.1Q; as a result, Switch1 negotiates trunking, but picks 802.1Q as the trunking protocol. While both Catalyst 3550 and 2950 are End-of-Life at the time of writing, their default port settings of dynamic desirable serve a useful example of how simply interconnecting them results in links dynamically becoming trunks. With recent Catalyst models, such as 2960, 3560, 3750, or 3850 Series, the default setting is **dynamic auto**, so the same topology in Figure 2-5 equipped with any of these platforms would negotiate all connected ports to operate in access mode.

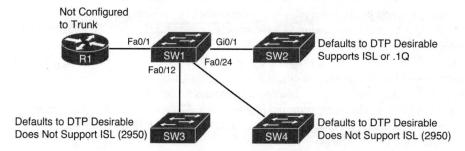

**Figure 2-5**   *Trunking Configuration Reference for Example 2-6*

**Example 2-6**  *Trunking Configuration and* **show** *Command Example – Switch1*

```
! The administrative mode of dynamic desirable (trunking) and negotiate (trunking
! encapsulation) means that Switch1 attempted to negotiate to trunk, but the
! operational mode of static access means that trunking negotiation failed.
! The reference to "operational trunking encapsulation" of native means that
! no tagging occurs.

Switch1# show int fa 0/1 switchport
Name: Fa0/1
Switchport: Enabled
Administrative Mode: dynamic desirable
Operational Mode: static access
Administrative Trunking Encapsulation: negotiate
Operational Trunking Encapsulation: native
Negotiation of Trunking: On
Access Mode VLAN: 1 (default)
Trunking Native Mode VLAN: 1 (default)
Administrative private-vlan host-association: none
Administrative private-vlan mapping: none
Operational private-vlan: none
Trunking VLANs Enabled: ALL
Pruning VLANs Enabled: 2-1001

Protected: false
Unknown unicast blocked: disabled
Unknown multicast blocked: disabled

Voice VLAN: none (Inactive)
Appliance trust: none

! Next, the show int gig 0/1 trunk command shows the configured mode
! (desirable), and the current status (n-isl), meaning negotiated ISL. Note
! that the trunk supports the extended VLAN range as well.

Switch1# show int gig 0/1 trunk
Port        Mode        Encapsulation Status       Native vlan
Gi0/1       desirable   n-isl         trunking     1


Port     Vlans allowed on trunk
Gi0/1    1-4094


Port     Vlans allowed and active in management domain
Gi0/1    1,21-22
```

```
Port         Vlans in spanning tree forwarding state and not pruned
Gi0/1        1,21-22


! Next, Switch1 lists all three trunks - the segments connecting to the other
! three switches - along with the type of encapsulation.


Switch1# show int trunk
Port         Mode         Encapsulation   Status        Native vlan
Fa0/12       desirable    n-802.1q        trunking      1
Fa0/24       desirable    n-802.1q        trunking      1
Gi0/1        desirable    n-isl           trunking      1


Port         Vlans allowed on trunk
Fa0/12       1-4094
Fa0/24       1-4094
Gi0/1        1-4094


Port         Vlans allowed and active in management domain
Fa0/12       1,21-22
Fa0/24       1,21-22
Gi0/1        1,21-22


Port         Vlans in spanning tree forwarding state and not pruned
Fa0/12       1,21-22
Fa0/24       1,21-22
Gi0/1        1,21-22
```

The possibility to configure the port to negotiate its operating mode dynamically also explains why there can be both **switchport access** and **switchport trunk** commands present on a single interface. Though confusing at first sight, these commands merely define how a port would behave *if* it was operating either as an access or a trunk port. Commands related to a currently unused operating mode of a port might be present but they are ignored.

As shown in Example 2-7, on newer Catalyst platforms, the **show dtp** commands display the operating state of DTP globally and on individual ports.

**Example 2-7**    show dtp *Command Output on SW1*

```
SW1# show dtp
Global DTP information
        Sending DTP Hello packets every 30 seconds
        Dynamic Trunk timeout is 300 seconds
        12 interfaces using DTP
```

```
! The TOS/TAS/TNS stand for Trunk Operating/Administrative/Negotiation Status
! The TOT/TAT/TNT stand for Trunk Operating/Administrative/Negotiation Type
! In the following output, Fa0/12 is configured as dynamic desirable

SW1# show dtp interface fa0/12
DTP information for FastEthernet0/12:
  TOS/TAS/TNS:                               TRUNK/DESIRABLE/TRUNK
  TOT/TAT/TNT:                               ISL/NEGOTIATE/ISL
  Neighbor address 1:                        00179446B30E
  Neighbor address 2:                        000000000000
  Hello timer expiration (sec/state):        19/RUNNING
  Access timer expiration (sec/state):       289/RUNNING
  Negotiation timer expiration (sec/state):  never/STOPPED
  Multidrop timer expiration (sec/state):    never/STOPPED
  FSM state:                                 S6:TRUNK
  # times multi & trunk                      0
  Enabled:                                   yes
  In STP:                                    no

Statistics
----------
3 packets received (3 good)
0 packets dropped
    0 nonegotiate, 0 bad version, 0 domain mismatches,
    0 bad TLVs, 0 bad TAS, 0 bad TAT, 0 bad TOT, 0 other
6 packets output (6 good)
    3 native, 3 software encap isl, 0 isl hardware native
0 output errors
0 trunk timeouts
2 link ups, last link up on Mon Mar 01 1993, 00:14:09
2 link downs, last link down on Mon Mar 01 1993, 00:14:02
```

**Note**    Without any configuration, the default port settings on recent Catalyst switch series such as 2960, 3560, 3750, 3650, and 3850 are as follows: mode set to dynamic auto, native VLAN set to 1, access VLAN set to 1, trunk encapsulation set to auto (if both ISL and dot1q supported) or dot1q, all VLANs allowed, and VLANs 2–1001 eligible for pruning. On older 2950 and 3550 models, the default mode was dynamic desirable.

### Allowed, Active, and Pruned VLANs

Although a trunk can support VLANs 1–4094, several mechanisms reduce the actual number of VLANs whose traffic flows over the trunk. First, VLANs can be administratively forbidden from existing over the trunk using the **switchport trunk allowed** interface subcommand. Also, any allowed VLANs must be configured on the switch before they are considered active on the trunk. Finally, VTP can prune VLANs from the trunk, with the switch simply ceasing to forward frames from that VLAN over the trunk.

The **show interface trunk** command lists the VLANs that fall into each category, as shown in the last command in Example 2-6. The categories are summarized as follows:

- **Allowed VLANs:** Each trunk allows all VLANs by default. However, VLANs can be removed or added to the list of allowed VLANs by using the **switchport trunk allowed** command.

- **Allowed and active:** To be active, a VLAN must be in the allowed list for the trunk (based on trunk configuration), the VLAN must exist in the VLAN configuration on the switch, and it must be in the active state (not suspended or locally shutdown). With PVST+, an STP instance is actively running on this trunk for the VLANs in this list.

- **Active and not pruned:** This list is a subset of the "allowed and active" list, with any VTP-pruned VLANs and VLANs for which PVST+ considers the port Blocking removed.

### Trunk Configuration Compatibility

In most production networks, switch trunks are configured using the same standard throughout the network. For example, rather than allow DTP to negotiate trunking, many engineers configure trunk interfaces to always trunk (**switchport mode trunk**) and disable DTP on ports that should not trunk. IOS includes several commands that impact whether a particular segment becomes a trunk. Because many enterprises use a typical standard, it is easy to forget the nuances of how the related commands work. This section covers those small details.

Two IOS configuration commands impact if and when two switches form a trunk. The **switchport mode** and **switchport nonegotiate** interface subcommands define whether DTP even attempts to negotiate a trunk, and what rules it uses when the attempt is made. Additionally, the settings on the switch ports on either side of the segment dictate whether a trunk forms or not.

Table 2-5 summarizes the trunk configuration options. The first column suggests the configuration on one switch, with the last column listing the configuration options on the other switch that would result in a working trunk between the two switches.

Key
Topic

**Table 2-5**   *Trunking Configuration Options That Lead to a Working Trunk*

| Configuration Command on One Side[1] | Short Name | Meaning | To Trunk, Other Side Must Be |
|---|---|---|---|
| switchport mode trunk | Trunk | Always trunks on this end; sends DTP to help other side choose to trunk | On, desirable, auto |
| switchport mode trunk; switchport nonegotiate | Nonegotiate | Always trunks on this end; does not send nor process DTP messages (good when other switch is a non-Cisco switch) | On |
| switchport mode dynamic desirable | Desirable | Sends DTP messages indicating dynamic mode with preferred trunking, and trunks if negotiation succeeds | On, desirable, auto |
| switchport mode dynamic auto | Auto | Sends DTP messages indicating dynamic mode with preferred access, and trunks if negotiation succeeds | On, desirable |
| switchport mode access | Access | Never trunks; can send a single DTP message when entering the access mode to help other side reach same conclusion, ceases to send and process DTP messages afterward | (Never trunks) |
| switchport mode access; switchport nonegotiate | Access (with nonegotiate) | Never trunks; does not send or process DTP messages | (Never trunks) |

1 When the **switchport nonegotiate** command is not listed in the first column, the default (DTP negotiation is active) is assumed.

**Note**   If an interface trunks, the type of trunking (ISL or 802.1Q) is controlled by the setting on the **switchport trunk encapsulation** command if the switch supports multiple trunk encapsulations. This command includes an option for dynamically negotiating the type (using DTP) or configuring one of the two types.

Also, for DTP negotiation to succeed, both switches must either be configured with the same VTP domain name, or at least one switch must have its VTP domain name unconfigured (that is, NULL).

## Configuring Trunking on Routers

VLAN trunking can be used on routers and hosts as well as on switches. However, routers do not support DTP, so you must manually configure them to support trunking. Additionally, you must manually configure a switch on the other end of the segment to trunk, because the router does not participate in DTP.

The majority of router trunking configurations use subinterfaces, with each subinterface being associated with one VLAN. The subinterface number does not have to match the VLAN ID; rather, the **encapsulation** command sits under each subinterface, with the associated VLAN ID being part of the **encapsulation** command. Use subinterface numbers starting with 1; the subinterface number 0 is the physical interface itself (for example, interface Fa0/0.0 is the Fa0/0 itself). Also, because good design calls for one IP subnet per VLAN, if the router wants to forward IP packets between the VLANs, the router needs to have an IP address associated with each trunking subinterface.

You can configure 802.1Q native VLANs under a subinterface or under the physical interface on a router. If they are configured under a subinterface, you use the **encapsulation dot1q** *vlan-id* **native** subcommand, with the inclusion of the **native** keyword meaning that frames exiting this subinterface should not be tagged, and incoming untagged frames shall be processed by this subinterface. As with other router trunking configurations, the associated IP address would be configured on that same subinterface. Alternately, if not configured on a subinterface, the router assumes that the native VLAN is associated with the physical interface. In this case, the **encapsulation** command is not needed nor supported under the physical interface; the associated IP address, however, would need to be configured under the physical interface. Configuring an (understandably distinct) IP address on both physical interface and a subinterface under the same physical interface using **encapsulation dot1q** *vlan-id* **native**, thereby technically resulting in two different interfaces for the native VLAN, is not supported. All incoming untagged frames will be processed by the subinterface configuration only. A notable exception to this rule can be seen on ISR G1 routers equipped with 10-Mbps Ethernet built-in interfaces. On these router platforms, settings for the native VLAN shall be configured on the physical Ethernet interface directly. While the router will accept the configuration of a subinterface with the **encapsulation dot1q** *vlan-id* **native** command, incoming untagged frames will be processed by the configuration of the physical interface. This exception applies only to ISR platforms with 10-Mbps Ethernet interfaces, and is not present on platforms with Fast Ethernet or faster interfaces.

If the router supports native VLAN configuration on a subinterface, it is recommended to use subinterfaces instead of putting the native VLAN configuration on a physical port. Aside from keeping the configuration more consistent (all configuration being placed on subinterfaces), this configuration allows the router to correctly process frames that, despite being originated in the native VLAN, carry an 802.1Q tag. Tagging such frames is done when using the CoS field inside an 802.1Q tag. If the native VLAN configuration was done on a physical interface, the router would not be able to recognize that a frame carrying an 802.1Q tag with a nonzero VLAN ID is really a CoS-marked frame in the native VLAN. When using subinterfaces, the **encapsulation dot1q** *vlan-id* **native** command allows the router to recognize that both untagged frames and CoS-marked frames tagged with the particular *vlan-id* should be processed as frames in the native VLAN.

Example 2-8 shows an example configuration for Router1 in Figure 2-1, both for ISL and 802.1Q. In this case, Router1 needs to forward packets between the subnets on VLANs 21 and 22. The first part of the example shows ISL configuration, with no native VLANs, and therefore only a subinterface being used for each VLAN. The second part of the example shows an alternative 802.1Q configuration, using the option of placing the native VLAN (VLAN 21) configuration on the physical interface.

Key
Topic

**Example 2-8**  *Trunking Configuration on Router1*

```
! Note the subinterface on the Fa0/0 interface, with the encapsulation
! command noting the type of trunking, as well as the VLAN number. The subinterface
! number does not have to match the VLAN ID. Also note the IP addresses for
! each interface, allowing Router1 to route between VLANs.
! The encapsulation command must be entered on a subinterface before entering any
! other IP-related commands, such as configuring an IP address.

Router1(config)# interface fa0/0
Router1(config-if)# no shutdown
Router1(config-if)# interface fa0/0.1
Router1(config-subif)# encapsulation isl 21
Router1(config-subif)# ip address 10.1.21.1 255.255.255.0
Router1(config-subif)# interface fa0/0.2
Router1(config-subif)# encapsulation isl 22
Router1(config-subif)# ip address 10.1.22.1 255.255.255.0

! Next, an alternative 802.1Q configuration is shown. Note that this configuration
! places the IP address for VLAN 21 on the physical interface; the router simply
! associates the physical interface with the native VLAN. Alternatively,
! a subinterface could be used, with the encapsulation dot1q 21 native command
! specifying that the router should treat this VLAN as the native VLAN.

Router1(config)# interface fa0/0
Router1(config-if)# ip address 10.1.21.1 255.255.255.0
Router1(config-if)# no shutdown
Router1(config-if)# interface fa0/0.2
Router1(config-subif)# encapsulation dot1q 22
Router1(config-subif)# ip address 10.1.22.1 255.255.255.0
```

Note also that the router does not have an explicitly defined allowed VLAN list on an interface. However, the allowed VLAN list is implied based on the configured VLANs. For example, in this example, when using ISL, Router1 allows VLANs 21 and 22, while when using 802.1Q, it allows the native VLAN and VLAN 22.

## 802.1Q-in-Q Tunneling

Traditionally, VLANs have not extended beyond the WAN boundary. VLANs in one campus extend to a WAN edge router, but VLAN protocols are not used on the WAN.

Today, several emerging alternatives exist for the passage of VLAN traffic across a WAN, including 802.1Q-in-Q, its standardized version 802.1ad called Provider Bridges, another standard 802.1ah called Provider Backbone Bridges, Layer2 Tunneling Protocol (L2TPv3),

Ethernet over MPLS (EoMPLS), and VLAN Private LAN Services (VPLS). While these topics are more applicable to the CCIE Service Provider certification, you should at least know the concept of 802.1 Q-in-Q tunneling.

Also known as Q-in-Q on Catalyst switches, 802.1Q-in-Q allows an SP to preserve 802.1Q VLAN tags across a WAN service. By doing so, VLANs actually span multiple geographically dispersed sites. Figure 2-6 shows the basic idea.

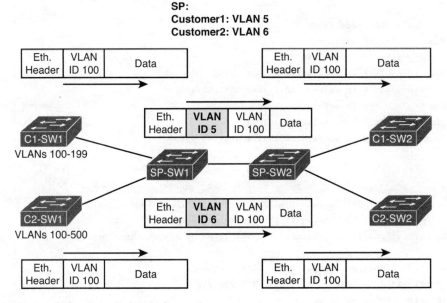

**Figure 2-6**   *Q-in-Q: Basic Operation*

The ingress SP switch takes the 802.1Q frame, and then tags each frame entering the interface with an additional 802.1Q header, called the S-tag (the original customer tags are called C-tags and are not modified nor processed). In this case, all of Customer1's frames are tagged as VLAN 5 as they pass over the WAN; Customer2's frames are tagged with VLAN 6. After removing the S-tag at egress, the customer switch sees the original 802.1Q frame with the C-tag intact, and can interpret the VLAN ID correctly. The receiving SP switch (SP-SW2 in this case) can keep the various customers' traffic separate based on the additional VLAN S-tags.

Notice that if the trunk between SP-SW1 and SP-SW2 used VLAN 5 as the native VLAN, frames coming from Customer1 would not have an S-tag added on this trunk. As a result, they would be received by SP-SW2 tagged only with the C-tag, and would be processed in the VLAN indicated in the C-tag instead of VLAN 5. This could result in Customer1's traffic leaking out to another customer, or to be otherwise misforwarded or blackholed. To prevent this, SP's switches are usually configured with **vlan dot1q tag native** command to essentially deactivate the concept of native VLAN, and to tag all frames on trunks regardless of the native VLAN setting.

Using Q-in-Q, an SP can offer VLAN services, even when the customers use overlapping VLAN IDs. Customers get more flexibility for network design options, particularly with metro Ethernet services. Plus, CDP and VTP traffic can be configured to pass transparently over the Q-in-Q service.

On Catalyst switches, the Q-in-Q is supported on 3550 and higher platforms. Example 2-9 shows the configuration, which is relatively straightforward.

**Key Topic**

**Example 2-9**  *Q-in-Q Configuration Example on a Catalyst 3560*

```
! It is assumed that C1-SW1 and C1-SW2 have their ports towards SP-SW1 configured
! as ordinary 802.1Q trunks. On SP-SW1, the vlan dot1q tag native is used to
! force tagging on all VLANs including native VLAN on trunks. Also, because
! a customer's C-tagged frame may already contain 1500 bytes in its payload, this
! payload including the C-tag is considered a new payload in the S-tagged frame,
! and thus may grow up to 1504 bytes. Therefore, the MTU of the resulting frames
! is increased to 1504 bytes using the system mtu commands. Their use must also
! be carefully matched by neighboring devices.

SP-SW1(config)# vlan dot1q tag native
SP-SW1(config)# system mtu 1504 ! Applies to 100Mbps interfaces
SP-SW1(config)# system mtu jumbo 1504 ! Applies to 1Gbps and 10Gbps interfaces
!
SP-SW1(config)# vlan 5
SP-SW1(config-vlan)# name Customer1
SP-SW1(config-vlan)# exit
SP-SW1(config)# vlan 6
SP-SW1(config-vlan)# name Customer2
SP-SW1(config-vlan)# exit


! The Fa0/24 interface connects to SP-SW2. This interface is configured as an
! ordinary trunk port

SP-SW1(config)# interface FastEthernet0/24
SP-SW1(config-if)# switchport trunk encapsulation dot1q
SP-SW1(config-if)# switchport mode trunk


! The Fa0/1 interface connects to C1-SW1. Here, apart from 802.1Q-in-Q tunneling,
! the switch is also configured to tunnel selected Layer2 management protocols.
! To assign all Customer1's traffic to SP's VLAN 5, switchport access vlan 5 is
! used.

SP-SW1(config)# interface FastEthernet0/1
SP-SW1(config-if)# switchport mode dot1q-tunnel
SP-SW1(config-if)# switchport access vlan 5
```

```
SP-SW1(config-if)# l2protocol-tunnel cdp
SP-SW1(config-if)# l2protocol-tunnel lldp
SP-SW1(config-if)# l2protocol-tunnel stp
SP-SW1(config-if)# l2protocol-tunnel vtp

! The Fa0/2 interface connects to C2-SW1. This is the basic 802.1Q-in-Q tunneling
! configuration without any Layer2 management protocol tunneling

SP-SW1(config)# interface FastEthernet0/2
SP-SW1(config-if)# switchport mode dot1q-tunnel
SP-SW1(config-if)# switchport access vlan 6

! The show interfaces Fa0/1 switchport shows that the interface is operating
! in QinQ tunneling mode. The show vlan (not shown here for brevity) would display
! the Fa0/1 in the Customer1 VLAN just like an ordinary access port.

SP-SW1# show interfaces fa0/1 switchport
Name: Fa0/1
Switchport: Enabled
Administrative Mode: tunnel
Operational Mode: tunnel
Administrative Trunking Encapsulation: negotiate
Operational Trunking Encapsulation: native
Negotiation of Trunking: Off
Access Mode VLAN: 5 (Customer1)
Trunking Native Mode VLAN: 1 (default)
Administrative Native VLAN tagging: enabled
Voice VLAN: none
Administrative private-vlan host-association: none
Administrative private-vlan mapping: none
Administrative private-vlan trunk native VLAN: none
Administrative private-vlan trunk Native VLAN tagging: enabled
Administrative private-vlan trunk encapsulation: dot1q
Administrative private-vlan trunk normal VLANs: none
Administrative private-vlan trunk associations: none
Administrative private-vlan trunk mappings: none
Operational private-vlan: none
Trunking VLANs Enabled: ALL
Pruning VLANs Enabled: 2-1001
Capture Mode Disabled
Capture VLANs Allowed: ALL

Protected: false
Unknown unicast blocked: disabled
```

```
Unknown multicast blocked: disabled
Appliance trust: none
SP-SW1#
```

## VLAN Trunking Protocol

VTP advertises VLAN configuration information to neighboring switches so that the VLAN configuration can be made on one switch, with all the other switches in the domain learning the VLAN information dynamically. VTP advertises the VLAN ID, VLAN name, and VLAN type and state for each VLAN. However, VTP does not advertise any information about which ports (interfaces) should be in each VLAN, so the configuration to associate a switch interface with a particular VLAN (using the **switchport access vlan** command) must still be configured on each individual switch.

The VTP protocol exists in three versions. VTPv1 and VTPv2 are widely supported across the CatOS and IOS-based switching platforms. VTPv3 support on IOS-based switches is, at the time of writing, relatively new. On entry-level Catalyst switches, VTPv3 is supported starting with IOS Release 12.2(52)SE.

VTPv1 is the default VTP version supported and active on enterprise IOS-based switches. It supports disseminating of normal-range VLANs only.

VTPv2 enhancements include the following:

- **Support for Token Ring Concentrator Relay Function and Bridge Relay Function (TrCRF and TrBRF) type VLANs:** These VLANs were used to segment a Token Ring network into multiple logical rings and interconnecting bridges. There is no use for them in Ethernet-based networks.

- **Support for unknown Type-Length-Value (TLV) records:** VTP messages can contain additional information elements stored as TLV records. A switch running VTPv1 would drop all unrecognized TLVs from received messages, not propagating them farther to neighboring switches. VTPv2-enabled switches keep all TLVs in propagated messages even if they are not recognized.

- **Optimized VLAN database consistency checking:** In VTPv1, VLAN database consistency checks are performed whenever the VLAN database is modified, either through CLI, SNMP, or VTP. In VTPv2, these consistency checks are skipped if the change was caused by a received VTP message, as the message itself was originated as a result of a CLI or SNMP action that must already have been sanitized. This is really just an implementation optimization.

There is ongoing confusion regarding the VTP transparent mode. The IOS documentation for earlier Catalyst series appeared to suggest that VTPv1 switches in transparent mode forward VTP messages only if their version and domain match the settings on the transparent switch, while VTPv2 transparent switches allegedly forward VTP messages regardless of their domain and version. Documentation to recent Catalyst switches is less clear, but it states that both VTPv1 and VTPv2 transparent switches check the domain and only forward the message if its domain matches the domain configured on the transparent switch.

In reality, experiments performed on multiple Catalyst switch types that supported both VTPv1 and VTPv2 show that, regardless of the activated VTP version, a transparent switch whose VTP domain was NULL (that is, unconfigured) forwarded all VTP messages happily. A transparent switch with a configured domain forwarded VTP messages only if their domain matched.

VTPv3 differs from VTPv2 in the following aspects:

- **The server role has been modified:** There are two server types in VTPv3: primary and secondary. A primary server is allowed to modify VTP domain contents, and there can be at most one primary server per VTP domain at any time. A secondary server (often called just a server) is not allowed to modify VTP domain contents, but it can be promoted to the role of primary server, retaking the role from the existing primary server if it exists. Ownership of the primary server role is a runtime state that is not stored in the configuration; instead, it is requested in the privileged EXEC mode if necessary. This modification significantly reduces the probability of unintended modification of the VLAN database, as it is not possible to modify the database contents without the concerted effort of making a switch the primary server.

- **VTPv3 password storage and usage has been improved:** The VTP password can be stored in an encrypted form that cannot be displayed back as plaintext. While this encrypted string can be carried over to a different switch to make it a valid member of the domain, the promotion of a secondary server into the primary server role will require entering the password in its plaintext form.

- **VTPv3 is capable of distributing information about the full range of VLANs including Private VLANs:** With VTPv3, it is not necessary to use Transparent mode when using extended-range VLANs and Private VLANs. Pruning, however, still applies only to normal-range VLANs, even in VTPv3.

- **VTPv3 supports the off mode in which the switch does not participate in VTPv3 operations and drops all received VTP messages:** It is also possible to deactivate VTP on a per-trunk basis.

- **VTPv3 is a generalized mechanism for distributing contents of an arbitrary database, and is not limited to synchronizing VLAN information over a set of switches:** As an example, VTPv3 is also capable of distributing and synchronizing the MST region configuration among all switches in a VTP domain.

Each Cisco switch uses one of four VTP modes, as outlined in Table 2-6.

**Table 2-6**   *VTP Modes and Features*

| Function | Server Mode | Client Mode | Transparent Mode | Off Mode* |
|---|---|---|---|---|
| Originates VTP advertisements | Yes | Yes | No | No |
| Processes received advertisements to update its VLAN configuration | Yes | Yes | No | No |
| Forwards received VTP advertisements | Yes | Yes | Yes | No |
| Saves VLAN configuration in NVRAM or vlan.dat | Yes | Yes | Yes | Yes |
| Can create, modify, or delete VLANs using configuration commands | Yes | No | Yes | Yes |

* The Off mode is supported only with VTPv3.

VTPv1 and VTPv2 use four types of messages:

■ **Summary Advertisement:** This message is originated by VTP Server and Client switches every 5 minutes and, in addition, after each modification to the VLAN database. This message carries information about VTP domain name, revision number, identity of the last updater, time stamp of the last update, MD5 sum computed over the contents of the VLAN database and the VTP password (if configured), and the number of Subset Advertisement messages that optionally follow this Summary Advertisement. Summary Advertisement messages do not carry VLAN database contents.

■ **Subset Advertisement:** This message is originated by VTP Server and Client switches after modifying the VLAN database. Subset Advertisements carry full contents of the VLAN database. One Subset Advertisement can hold multiple VLAN database entries. However, multiple Subset Advertisements might be required if the VLAN database is large.

■ **Advertisement Request:** This message is originated by VTP Server and Client switches to request their neighbors send the complete VLAN database or a part of it. Advertisement requests are sent when a VTP Client switch is restarted, when a switch enters the Client mode, or when a Server or Client switch receives a Summary Advertisement with a higher revision number than its own.

■ **Join:** This message is originated by each VTP Server and Client switch periodically every 6 seconds if VTP Pruning is active. Join messages contain a bit field that, for each VLAN in the normal range, indicates whether it is active or unused (that is, pruned).

At press time, the details about VTPv3 message types were not made public.

**Note**   In any VTP version, VTP messages are transmitted and accepted only on trunk ports. Access ports neither send nor accept VTP messages. For two switches to communicate in VTP, they must first be interconnected through a working trunk link.

## VTP Process and Revision Numbers

Let us first have a look at the VTPv1 and VTPv2 update process. Differences in VTPv3 will be explained later.

In VTPv1 and VTPv2, the update process begins when a switch administrator, from a VTP server switch, adds, deletes, or updates the configuration for a VLAN. When the new configuration occurs, the VTP server increments the old VTP *revision number* by 1 and advertises the entire VLAN configuration database along with the new revision number.

The VTP revision number concept allows switches to know when VLAN database changes have occurred. Upon receiving a VTP update, if the revision number in a received VTP update is larger than a switch's current revision number, it believes that there is a new version of the VLAN database. Figure 2-7 shows an example in which the old VTP revision number was 3; the server adds a new VLAN (incrementing the revision number to 4), and then propagates the VTP database to the other switches.

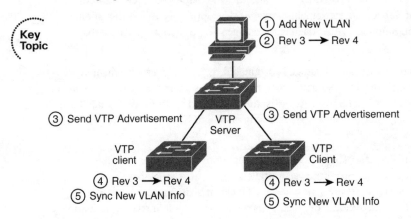

**Figure 2-7**  *VTP Revision Number Basic Operation*

Cisco switches default to use VTP server mode, but they do not start sending VTP updates until the switch has been configured with a VTP domain name. At that point, the server begins to send its VTP updates, with an updated database and revision number each time its VLAN configuration changes. However, the VTP clients in Figure 2-7 actually do not have to have the VTP domain name configured. If not configured yet, the client will assume that it should use the VTP domain name in the first received VTP update. However, the client does need one small bit of configuration, namely, the VTP mode, as configured with the **vtp mode** global configuration command. As a side note, switches must of course be interconnected with trunk links, as VTP messages are exchanged only over trunks.

VTP clients and servers alike will accept VTP updates from other VTP server and client switches. For better availability, a switched network using VTP needs at least two VTP server switches. Under normal operations, a VLAN change could be made on one server switch, and the other VTP server (plus all the clients) would learn about the changes to the VLAN database. Once learned, both VTP servers and clients store the VLAN configuration in their respective vlan.dat files in flash memory; they do not store the VLAN configuration in NVRAM.

With multiple VTP servers installed in a LAN, it is possible to accidentally overwrite the VTP configuration in the network. If trunks fail and then changes are made on more than one VTP server, the VTP configuration databases could differ, with different configuration revision numbers. When the formerly separated parts of the LAN reconnect using trunks, the VTP database with a higher revision number is propagated throughout the VTP domain, replacing some switches' VTP databases. Note also that because VTP clients can actually originate VTP updates, under the right circumstances, a VTP client can update the VTP database on another VTP client or server. In summary, for a newly connected VTP server or client to change another switch's VTP database, the following must be true:

- The new link connecting the new switch is trunking.

- The new switch has the same VTP domain name as the other switches.

- The new switch's revision number is higher than that of the existing switches.

- The new switch must have the same password, if configured on the existing switches.

To protect a VTP domain from being joined by unauthorized switches, use VTP passwords. VTP Summary Advertisements carry an MD5 hash computed over the VLAN database contents and the VTP password if configured. After receiving an update to the VLAN database in the form of a Summary Advertisement and at least one Subset Advertisement, the receiving switch computes its own MD5 hash over the contents of the VLAN database reconstituted from these messages and its own VTP password, and compares it to the MD5 hash value indicated in the Summary Advertisement. For these MD5 hash values to match, the sending and receiving switch must be using the same VTP password and the messages must be genuine (that is, not changed or tampered with during transit). Contrary to the popular belief, the MD5 hash present in Summary Advertisements is not computed from the VTP password alone. Also, the MD5 hash—being present only in Summary Advertisements—is not used to protect VTP messages themselves. Some installations simply use VTP transparent or off mode on all switches, which prevents switches from ever listening to other switches' VTP updates and erroneously modifying their VLAN configuration databases.

VTPv3 addresses the problem of inadvertent (or intentional) rewrite of a VLAN database by introducing the concept of a *primary server*. A primary server is the only switch in a VTPv3 domain whose VLAN database can be propagated throughout the domain. VTPv3 servers and clients will share their VLAN database only if they agree both on the domain name and on the identity of a primary server (given by its base MAC address). Also, a primary server is the only switch that allows an administrator to perform modifications to the VLAN database.

Other VTPv3 switches configured as servers are called *secondary servers*. Unlike VTPv1/VTPv2 servers, secondary servers in VTPv3 do not permit an administrator to modify the VLAN database; rather, they are only eligible to be promoted to the role of a primary server, taking over this role from the existing primary server if present. Clients in VTPv3 neither allow an administrator to modify the VLAN database nor are eligible to be promoted to the primary server role. Both secondary servers and clients store a copy of the primary server's VLAN database and will share it with their neighboring servers and clients that agree on the identity of the primary server. This means that even in VTPv3, a secondary server or a client switch with a higher revision number can overwrite a neighbor's VLAN database, but for this to occur, these switches must first match on the domain name, primary server's identity, and VTP password.

The state of two or more server or client switches in a VTPv3 domain having different opinions about the identity of a primary server is called a *conflict*. Conflicting switches do not synchronize their VLAN databases even if all other VTP parameters match. This concept of a conflict is at the core of VTPv3's improved resiliency against inadvertent VLAN database overwrites. Because changes to the VLAN database can only be performed on a primary server, switches that agree on the primary server's identity also immediately share the primary server's database. If a switch is disconnected from the network, unless it is the primary server itself, its VLAN database can be modified only if that switch is promoted to a primary server while disconnected. After this switch is connected back to the network, its idea of the primary server's identity does not match its neighbors' knowledge about the primary server; that is, a conflict exists. Therefore, even if its revision number is higher, its VLAN database will not be accepted by its neighbors. This way, the possibility of inadvertent VLAN database overwrites is greatly reduced, though not completely avoided.

There can be at most one primary server in a VTPv3 domain. Only switches configured as VTPv3 servers can be promoted to the role of a primary server, and the promotion is always performed in the privileged EXEC mode by invoking the **vtp primary** command. The state of a primary server is therefore a volatile runtime state that cannot be permanently stored in the configuration. After a primary server is reloaded, it comes back only as a secondary server again. A switch newly promoted to the role of a primary server using the **vtp primary** command will flood its VLAN database to its neighbors, and they will install and flood it further even if the new primary server's revision number is lower. This way, the new primary server's database is asserted over the VTP domain.

With VTPv3, it is no longer possible to reset the configuration revision number to 0 by setting the switch to the transparent mode and back. The revision number will be reset to 0 only by modifying the VTP domain name or by configuring a VTP password.

If a VTPv3 switch detects an older switch running VTPv1 or VTPv2 on its port, it will revert to VTPv2 operation on that port, forcing the older switch to operate in VTPv2 mode. Cooperation between VTPv3 and VTPv1-only switches is not supported.

## VTP Configuration

VTP sends updates out all active trunk interfaces (ISL or 802.1Q) by default. However, with all default settings from Cisco, switches are in server mode, with no VTP domain name configured, and they do not send any VTP updates. Before any switches can learn VLAN information from another switch, a working trunk must interconnect them, and at least one switch must have a bare-minimum VTP server configuration—specifically, a domain name.

Example 2-10 shows Switch3 configuring a VTP domain name to become a VTP server and advertise the VLANs it has configured. The example also lists several key VTP **show** commands. (Note that the example begins with VLANs 21 and 22 configured on Switch3, and all default settings for VTP on all four switches. Also keep in mind that the output of various **show** commands can differ from this example depending on your IOS version and VTP version supported/activated.)

**Example 2-10** *VTP Configuration and* **show** *Command Example*

```
! First, Switch3 is configured with a VTP domain ID of CCIE-domain.

Switch3# conf t
Enter configuration commands, one per line.  End with CNTL/Z.
Switch3(config)# vtp domain CCIE-domain
Changing VTP domain name from NULL to CCIE-domain


! Next, on Switch1, the VTP status shows the same revision as Switch3, and it
! learned the VTP domain name CCIE-domain. Note that Switch1 has no VTP-related
! configuration, so it is a VTP server; it learned the VTP domain name from
! Switch3.

Switch1# show vtp status
VTP Version capable             : 1 to 3
VTP version running             : 1
VTP Domain Name                 : CCIE-domain
VTP Pruning Mode                : Disabled
VTP Traps Generation            : Disabled
Device ID                       : 0023.ea41.ca00
Configuration last modified by 10.1.1.3 at 9-9-13 13:31:46
Local updater ID is 10.1.1.1 on interface Vl1 (lowest numbered VLAN interface
  found)
```

```
Feature VLAN:
--------------
VTP Operating Mode              : Server
Maximum VLANs supported locally : 1005
Number of existing VLANs        : 7
Configuration Revision          : 2
MD5 digest                      : 0x0E 0x07 0x9D 0x9A 0x27 0x10 0x6C 0x0B
                                  0x0E 0x35 0x98 0x1E 0x2F 0xEE 0x88 0x88


! The show vlan brief command lists the VLANs learned from Switch3.


Switch1# show vlan brief
VLAN Name                             Status    Ports
---- -------------------------------- --------- ------------------------------
1    default                          active    Fa0/1, Fa0/2, Fa0/3, Fa0/4
                                                Fa0/5, Fa0/6, Fa0/7, Fa0/10
                                                Fa0/11, Fa0/13, Fa0/14, Fa0/15
                                                Fa0/16, Fa0/17, Fa0/18, Fa0/19
                                                Fa0/20, Fa0/21, Fa0/22, Fa0/23
                                                Gi0/2
21   VLAN0021                         active
22   ccie-vlan-22                     active
1002 fddi-default                     act/unsup
1003 token-ring-default               act/unsup
1004 fddinet-default                  act/unsup
1005 trnet-default                    act/unsup
```

Example 2-11 shows examples of a few VTP configuration options. Table 2-7 provides a list of the most used options, along with explanations.

**Table 2-7**   *VTP Global Configuration Options*

| Option | Meaning |
|--------|---------|
| domain | Sets the name of the VTP domain. Received VTP messages are ignored if the domain name indicated in these messages does not match the receiving switch's domain name. A switch can be a member of a single domain only. |
| password | Sets the password to prevent unauthorized switches from joining the domain. The password is taken into account when generating the MD5 hash of the VLAN database. Received VTP updates are ignored if the passwords on the sending and receiving switch do not match. If VTPv3 is used, the password can also be specified as **hidden**, meaning that the password will never be displayed in plaintext in the **show vtp password** output. The **secret** keyword is used when entering the password in an already encrypted form. |

| Option | Meaning |
|---|---|
| mode | Sets server, client, or transparent mode on the switch. If VTPv3 is supported, it is also possible to set the off mode, effectively disabling VTP on the switch. |
| version | Sets VTP version. Configuring the version 1 or 2 on a server switch applies to all switches in the domain. VTPv3 has to be configured manually on each switch. Prior to activating version 3, the switch must use a non-NULL domain name. |
| pruning | Enables VTP pruning, which prevents flooding on a per-VLAN basis to switches that do not have any ports configured as members of that VLAN. Regardless of the VTP version, the pruning applies only to normal-range VLANs. |
| interface | Specifies the interface whose IP address is used to identify this switch as an updater in VTP updates. By default, a configured IP address from the lowest numbered VLAN SVI interface will be used. |

Example 2-11 shows the use of VTPv3. Differences in running VTPv3 are most visible in the need of designating a selected switch as the primary server using the **vtp primary** command before changes to the VLAN database can be performed on it, and in the way VTP passwords are used. While not shown in the following example, VTPv3 can also be deactivated either globally on the switch using the **vtp mode off** command, or on a per-interface basis using the simple **no vtp** command (the status of VTP on individual interfaces can be conveniently verified using the **show vtp interface** command). It is worth noting that after changing the VTP mode from **off** to any other mode, all existing VLANs except those hardwired into IOS (1, 1002–1005) will be deleted.

**Example 2-11**   *Use of VTPv3 Example*

```
! To use VTPv3, each switch has to be configured individually for version 3 opera-
! tion. It is assumed that all four switches have been converted to VTPv3. Switches
! 1 and 2 are configured as VTP servers, switches 3 and 4 are configured as VTP
! clients. Only the Switch3 configuration is shown here for brevity purposes.

Switch3(config)# vtp version 3
Switch3(config)#
Sep  9 15:49:34.493: %SW_VLAN-6-OLD_CONFIG_FILE_READ: Old version 2 VLAN configura-
  tion file detected and read OK.  Version 3
    files will be written in the future.
Switch3(config)# vtp mode client
Setting device to VTP Client mode for VLANS.

! An attempt to create a new VLAN on Switch1 will fail, as the Switch1 has not yet
! been promoted to the role of primary server. The example also shows how to
! promote it, and subsequently create the VLAN without further obstacles. The "No
```

```
! conflicting VTP3 devices found." statement means that all switches in the VTP
! domain agree on the identity of the current primary server and thus share its
! VLAN database.


Switch1# conf t
Enter configuration commands, one per line.  End with CNTL/Z.
Switch1(config)# vlan 23
VTP VLAN configuration not allowed when device is not the primary server for vlan
   database.
Switch1(config)# do vtp primary
This system is becoming primary server for feature vlan
No conflicting VTP3 devices found.
Do you want to continue? [confirm]
Switch1(config)#
Sep  9 17:06:59.332: %SW_VLAN-4-VTP_PRIMARY_SERVER_CHG: 0023.ea41.ca00 has become
   the primary server for the VLAN VTP feature
Switch1(config)# vlan 23
Switch1(config-vlan)# name ccie-vlan-23
Switch1(config-vlan)# exit


! On Switch3, the show vtp status shows:


Switch3(config)# do show vtp status
VTP Version capable            : 1 to 3
VTP version running            : 3
VTP Domain Name                : CCIE-domain
VTP Pruning Mode               : Disabled
VTP Traps Generation           : Disabled
Device ID                      : 0023.ea93.8e80


Feature VLAN:
--------------
VTP Operating Mode             : Client
Number of existing VLANs       : 8
Number of existing extended VLANs : 0
Maximum VLANs supported locally : 255
Configuration Revision         : 2
Primary ID                     : 0023.ea41.ca00
Primary Description            : Switch1
MD5 digest                     : 0x2A 0x42 0xC5 0x50 0x4B 0x9C 0xB6 0xDE
                                 0x17 0x8E 0xE0 0xB6 0x2E 0x67 0xA4 0x9C


Feature MST:
--------------
VTP Operating Mode             : Transparent
```

```
Feature UNKNOWN:
--------------
VTP Operating Mode              : Transparent


! Trying to promote the Switch3 to the role of primary server would fail, as it is
! configured to operate as a client:

Switch3(config)# do vtp primary
System can become primary server for Vlan feature only when configured as a server


! The password handling in VTPv3 has been improved. The password can be configured
! as being hidden, in which case it will never be displayed again in plaintext:

Switch1(config)# vtp password S3cr3tP4ssw0rd hidden
Setting device VTP password
Switch1(config)# do show vtp password
VTP Password: 8C70EFBABDD6EC0300A57BE402409C48


! This string can be used to populate the password setting on other switches
! without ever knowing the plaintext form, e.g.:

Switch2(config)# vtp password 8C70EFBABDD6EC0300A57BE402409C48 secret
Setting device VTP password


! After the password is configured in the secret form (or originally configured in
! the plain form and marked hidden), any attempt to promote a switch to the primary
! server role will require entering the password in the plaintext form into the
! CLI. Without knowing the plaintext form of the password, it is not possible to
! designate a switch as a primary server:

Switch2(config)# do vtp primary
This system is becoming primary server for feature vlan
Enter VTP Password: <entering 8C70EFBABDD6EC0300A57BE402409C48>
Password mismatch
Switch2(config)# do vtp primary
This system is becoming primary server for feature vlan
Enter VTP Password: <entering S3cr3tP4ssw0rd>
No conflicting VTP3 devices found.
Do you want to continue? [confirm]
Switch2(config)#
Sep  9 17:10:42.215: %SW_VLAN-4-VTP_PRIMARY_SERVER_CHG: 0017.9446.b300 has become
  the primary server for the VLAN VTP feature
```

### Normal-Range and Extended-Range VLANs

Because of historical reasons, some VLAN numbers are considered to be *normal*, whereas some others are considered to be *extended*. Normal-range VLANs are VLANs 1–1005, and can be advertised through VTP versions 1 and 2. These VLANs can be configured both in VLAN database mode and in global configuration mode, with the details being stored in the vlan.dat file in Flash.

Extended-range VLANs range from 1006–4094, inclusive. However, if using VTPv1 or VTPv2, these additional VLANs cannot be configured in VLAN database mode, nor stored in the vlan.dat file, nor advertised through VTP. In fact, to configure them, the switch must be in VTP transparent mode. (Also, you should take care to avoid using VLANs 1006–1024 for compatibility with CatOS-based switches.) VTPv3 removes these limitations: Both normal- and extended-range VLANs can be advertised by VTPv3. Also, with VTPv3, information about all VLANs is again stored in the vlan.dat file in Flash.

Both ISL and 802.1Q support extended-range VLANs today. Originally, ISL began life only supporting normal-range VLANs, using only 10 of the 15 bits reserved in the ISL header to identify the VLAN ID. The later-defined 802.1Q used a 12-bit VLAN ID field, thereby allowing support of the extended range. Following that, Cisco changed ISL to use 12 of its reserved 15 bits in the VLAN ID field, thereby supporting the extended range.

Table 2-8 summarizes VLAN numbers and provides some additional notes.

**Table 2-8**    *Valid VLAN Numbers, Normal and Extended*

| VLAN Number | Normal or Extended? | Can Be Advertised and Pruned by VTP Versions 1 and 2? | Comments |
|---|---|---|---|
| 0 | Reserved | — | Not available for use |
| 1 | Normal | No | On Cisco switches, the default VLAN for all access ports; cannot be deleted or changed |
| 2–1001 | Normal | Yes | — |
| 1002–1005 | Normal | No | Defined specifically for use with FDDI and TR translational bridging |
| 1006–4094 | Extended | No | — |
| 4095 | Reserved | No | Not available for use |

## Storing VLAN Configuration

Catalyst IOS stores VLAN and VTP configuration in one of two places—either in a Flash file called vlan.dat or in the running configuration. (Remember that the term "Catalyst

IOS" refers to a switch that uses IOS, not the Catalyst OS, which is often called CatOS.) IOS chooses the storage location in part based on the VTP version and mode, and in part based on whether the VLANs are normal-range VLANs or extended-range VLANs. Table 2-9 describes what happens based on what configuration mode is used to configure the VLANs, the VTP mode, and the VLAN range. (Note that VTPv1/VTPv2 clients also store the VLAN configuration in vlan.dat, and they do not understand extended-range VLANs.)

**Key Topic**

**Table 2-9**  *VLAN Configuration and Storage for VTPv1 and VTPv2*

| Function | When in VTP Server Mode | When in VTP Transparent Mode |
|---|---|---|
| Normal-range VLANs can be configured from | Both VLAN database and configuration modes | Both VLAN database and configuration modes |
| Extended-range VLANs can be configured from | Nowhere—cannot be configured | Configuration mode only |
| VTP and normal-range VLAN configuration commands are stored in | vlan.dat in Flash | Both vlan.dat in Flash and running configuration[1] |
| Extended-range VLAN configuration commands are stored in | Nowhere—extended range not allowed in VTP server mode | Running configuration only |

1 When a switch reloads, if the VTP mode or domain name in the vlan.dat file and the startup config file differs, the switch uses only the vlan.dat file's contents for VLAN configuration.

**Note**   The configuration characteristics referenced in Table 2-9 do not include the interface configuration command **switchport access vlan**; they include the commands that create a VLAN (**vlan** command) and VTP configuration commands.

For VTPv3, the situation is greatly simplified: Regardless of the mode (server, client, transparent, or off), both normal- and extended-range VLANs are stored in the vlan.dat file. If transparent or off mode is selected, VLANs are also present in the running-config.

Of particular interest for those of you stronger with CatOS configuration skills is that when you erase the startup-config file and reload the Cisco IOS switch, you do not actually erase the normal-range VLAN and VTP configuration information. To erase the VLAN and VTP configuration, you must use the **delete flash:vlan.dat** EXEC command. Also note that if multiple switches are in VTP server mode, if you delete vlan.dat on one switch and then reload it, as soon as the switch comes back up and brings up a trunk, it learns the old VLAN database through a VTP update from the other VTP server.

## Configuring PPPoE

Although it might seem out of place in this chapter on VLANs and VLAN trunking, Point to Point Protocol over Ethernet (PPPoE) fits best here. Somewhat similar to VLANs that virtualize Ethernet switched infrastructure into multiple isolated multiaccess switched environments, PPPoE virtualizes Ethernet into multiple point-to-point sessions between client hosts and an access concentrator, turning the broadcast Ethernet into a point-to-multipoint environment. PPP itself is a great Layer2 protocol for point-to-point links, with capabilities very well suited to a service provider's needs, such as per-user authentication (and resulting billing), negotiation of allowed higher protocols carried over the PPP link including their settings (such as endpoint IP addresses), negotiation of compression, link bundling (also called multilink), and so on. PPPoE described in RFC 2516 was originally conceived as a method for carrying PPP-based sessions over Ethernet access networks often used in service provider networks, with the PPPoE software client running on a PC equipped with an ordinary Ethernet card. With the advent of Digital Subscriber Line (DSL) technology, the use of PPPoE with DSL allowed for a simple deployment. Client PCs continued to run PPPoE software clients, while a DSL modem connected to a common LAN with the client PCs simply took the Ethernet frames containing PPP datagrams and transmitted them inside a series of ATM cells over the DSL interface, essentially bridging them over the ATM-based DSL network to the Broadband Remote Access Server (BRAS). In the opposite direction, the modem received Ethernet frames encapsulated in series of ATM cells, reconstructed them and forwarded them onto the LAN. As the features of routers improved, the PPPoE client functionality moved from PCs to the router connected to the DSL network itself.

The PPPoE client feature permits a Cisco IOS router, rather than an endpoint host, to serve as the client in a network. This permits entire LANs to connect to the Internet over a single PPPoE connection terminated at the single router.

In a DSL environment, PPP interface IP addresses are derived from an upstream DHCP server using IP Configuration Protocol (IPCP), a subprotocol of PPP. Therefore, IP address negotiation must be enabled on the router's dialer interface. This is done using the **ip address negotiated** command in the dialer interface configuration.

Because PPPoE introduces an 8-byte overhead (2 bytes for the PPP header and 6 bytes for PPPoE), the MTU for PPPoE is usually decreased to 1492 bytes so that the entire encapsulated frame fits within the 1500-byte Ethernet frame. Additionally, for TCP sessions, the negotiated Maximum Segment Size is clamped down to 1452 bytes, allowing for 40 bytes in TCP and IP headers and 8 bytes in the PPPoE, totaling 1500 bytes that must fit into an ordinary Ethernet frame. A maximum transmission unit (MTU) mismatch can prevent a PPPoE connection from coming up or from properly carrying large datagrams. Checking the MTU setting is a good first step when troubleshooting PPPoE connections.

Those familiar with ISDN BRI configuration will recognize the dialer interface configuration and related commands in Example 2-11. The key difference between ISDN BRI configuration and PPPoE is the **pppoe-client dial-pool-number** command.

Configuring an Ethernet edge router for PPPoE Client mode is the focus of this section. This task requires configuring the Ethernet interface (physical or subinterface) and a corresponding dialer interface.

Figure 2-8 shows the topology. Example 2-12 shows the configuration steps. The first step is to configure the outside Ethernet interface as a PPPoE client and assign it to a dialer interface. The second step is to configure the corresponding dialer interface. Additional steps, including Network Address Translation (NAT) configuration, are also shown.

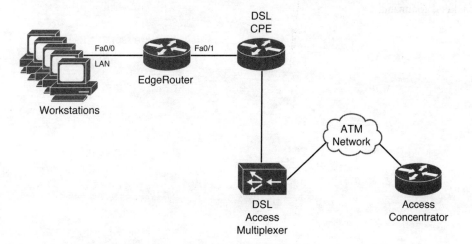

**Figure 2-8**    *PPPoE Topology for Example 2-12*

**Example 2-12**    *Configuring PPPoE on EdgeRouter*

```
EdgeRouter# conf t
EdgeRouter(config)# interface fa0/0
EdgeRouter(config-if)# no shutdown
EdgeRouter(config-if)# ip address 192.168.100.1 255.255.255.0
EdgeRouter(config-if)# ip nat inside
EdgeRouter(config)# interface fa0/1
EdgeRouter(config-if)# no shutdown
EdgeRouter(config-if)# pppoe-client dial-pool-number 1
EdgeRouter(config-if)# exit
EdgeRouter(config)# interface dialer1
EdgeRouter(config-if)# mtu 1492
EdgeRouter(config-if)# ip tcp adjust-mss 1452
EdgeRouter(config-if)# encapsulation ppp
EdgeRouter(config-if)# ip address negotiated
EdgeRouter(config-if)# ppp chap hostname Username@ISP
EdgeRouter(config-if)# ppp chap password Password4ISP
EdgeRouter(config-if)# ip nat outside
```

```
EdgeRouter(config-if)# dialer pool 1
EdgeRouter(config-if)# exit
EdgeRouter(config)# ip nat inside source list 1 interface dialer1 overload
EdgeRouter(config)# access-list 1 permit 192.168.100.0 0.0.0.255
EdgeRouter(config)# ip route 0.0.0.0 0.0.0.0 dialer1
```

You can verify PPPoE connectivity using the **show pppoe session** command. Cisco IOS includes debug functionality for PPPoE through the **debug pppoe [data | errors | events | packets]** command.

# Foundation Summary

This section lists additional details and facts to round out the coverage of the topics in this chapter. Unlike most of the Cisco Press Exam Certification Guides, this "Foundation Summary" does not repeat information presented in the "Foundation Topics" section of the chapter. Please take the time to read and study the details in the "Foundation Topics" section of the chapter as well as review items noted with a Key Topic icon.

Table 2-10 lists some of the most popular IOS commands related to the topics in this chapter. (The command syntax was retaken from the *Catalyst 3560 Multilayer Switch Command Reference, 15.0(2)SE*. Note that some switch platforms might have differences in the command syntax.)

**Table 2-10**   *Catalyst IOS Commands Related to Chapter 2*

| Command | Description |
|---|---|
| **show mac address-table [aging-time \| count \| dynamic \| static] [address** *hw-addr*] **[interface** *interface-id*] **[vlan** *vlan-id*] | Displays the MAC address table; the security option displays information about the restricted or static settings |
| **show interfaces [***interface-id*] **switchport \| trunk]** | Displays detailed information about an interface operating as an access port or a trunk |
| **show vlan [brief \| id** *vlan-id* **\| internal usage \| name** *vlan-name* **\| private-vlan \| summary]** | EXEC command that lists information about the VLAN |
| **show vtp status** | Lists VTP configuration and status information |
| **switchport mode {access \| dot1q-tunnel \| dynamic {auto \| desirable} \| private-vlan {host \| promiscuous} \| trunk}** | Configuration command setting nontrunking (**access**, **private-vlan**), tunneling (**dot1q-tunnel**) trunking (**trunk**), and dynamic trunking (**auto** and **desirable**) parameters |
| **switchport nonegotiate** | Interface subcommand that disables DTP messages; interface must not be configured as a dynamic port |
| **switchport trunk {allowed vlan** *vlan-list*} **\| {encapsulation {dot1q \| isl \| negotiate}} \| {native vlan** *vlan-id*} **\| {pruning vlan** *vlan-list*} | Interface subcommand used to set parameters used when the port is trunking |
| **switchport access vlan** *vlan-id* | Interface subcommand that statically configures the interface as a member of that one VLAN |

Table 2-11 lists the commands related to VLAN creation—both the VLAN database mode configuration commands (reached with the **vlan database** privileged mode command) and the normal configuration mode commands.

> **Note** Some command parameters might not be listed in Table 2-11.

**Table 2-11** *VLAN Database and Configuration Mode Command List and Comparison*

| VLAN Database | Configuration |
| --- | --- |
| vtp {domain *domain-name* | password *password* | pruning | v2-mode | {server | client | transparent}} | vtp {domain *domain-name* | file *filename* | interface *name* | mode {client | server | transparent | off } | password *password* [ hidden | secret] | pruning | version *number*} |
| vlan *vlan-id* [name *vlan-name*] [state {active | suspend}] | vlan *vlan-id* |
| show {current | proposed | difference} | No equivalent |
| apply | abort | reset | No equivalent |

**Table 2-12** *Cisco IOS PPPoE Client Commands*

| Command | Description |
| --- | --- |
| pppoe-client dial-pool-number *number* | Configures the outside Ethernet interface on a router for PPPoE operation and assigns the PPPoE client into a dialer pool to be used later by a dialer interface |
| debug pppoe [data | errors | events | packets] | Enables debugging for PPPoE troubleshooting |

# Memory Builders

The CCIE Routing and Switching written exam, like all Cisco CCIE written exams, covers a fairly broad set of topics. This section provides some basic tools to help you exercise your memory about some of the broader topics covered in this chapter.

## Fill In Key Tables from Memory

Appendix E, "Key Tables for CCIE Study," on the CD in the back of this book, contains empty sets of some of the key summary tables in each chapter. Print Appendix E, refer to this chapter's tables in it, and fill in the tables from memory. Refer to Appendix F, "Solutions for Key Tables for CCIE Study," on the CD to check your answers.

## Definitions

Next, take a few moments to write down the definitions for the following terms:

VLAN, broadcast domain, DTP, VTP pruning, 802.1Q, ISL, native VLAN, encapsulation, Private VLAN, promiscuous port, community VLAN, isolated VLAN, promiscuous port, community port, isolated port, 802.1Q-in-Q, Layer 2 protocol tunneling, PPPoE, DSL.

Refer to the glossary to check your answers.

## Further Reading

The topics in this chapter tend to be covered in slightly more detail in CCNP Switching exam preparation books. For more details on these topics, refer to the Cisco Press CCNP preparation books found at www.ciscopress.com/ccnp.

*Cisco LAN Switching*, by Kennedy Clark and Kevin Hamilton, is an excellent reference for LAN-related topics in general, and certainly very useful for CCIE written and lab exam preparation.

DTP protocol details are not covered in official Cisco documentation; however, DTP has been filed as U.S. Patent No. 6,445,715, which is publicly available at www.google.com/?tbm=pts.

**Blueprint topics covered in this chapter:**

This chapter covers the following subtopics from the Cisco CCIE Routing and Switching written exam blueprint. Refer to the full blueprint in Table I-1 in the Introduction for more details on the topics covered in each chapter and their context within the blueprint.

- Spanning Tree Protocol
    - 802.1D STP
    - 802.1w RSTP
    - 802.1s MST
    - Loop Guard
    - Root Guard
    - EtherChannel Misconfiguration Guard
    - BPDU Guard and BPDU Filter
    - UDLD
    - Bridge Assurance
- EtherChannel
- Troubleshooting Complex Layer 2 Issues

## CHAPTER 3

# Spanning Tree Protocol

Spanning Tree Protocol (STP) is probably one of the most widely known protocols covered on the CCIE Routing and Switching written exam. STP has been around for a long time, is used in most every campus network today, and is covered extensively on the CCNP SWITCH exam. This chapter covers a broad range of topics related to STP.

## "Do I Know This Already?" Quiz

Table 3-1 outlines the major headings in this chapter and the corresponding "Do I Know This Already?" quiz questions.

**Table 3-1** *"Do I Know This Already?" Foundation Topics Section-to-Question Mapping*

| Foundation Topics Section | Questions Covered in This Section | Score |
| --- | --- | --- |
| 802.1D Spanning Tree Protocol and Improvements | 1–8 | |
| Protecting and Optimizing Spanning Tree | 9 | |
| Configuring and Troubleshooting EtherChannels | 10 | |
| Troubleshooting Complex Layer 2 Issues | 11 | |
| Total Score | | |

To best use this pre-chapter assessment, remember to score yourself strictly. You can find the answers in Appendix A, "Answers to the 'Do I Know This Already?' Quizzes."

1. Assume that a nonroot 802.1D switch has ceased to receive Hello BPDUs. Which STP setting determines how long a nonroot switch waits before trying to choose a new Root Port?

   a. Hello timer setting on the Root

   b. MaxAge timer setting on the Root

   c. ForwardDelay timer setting on the Root

   d. Hello timer setting on the nonroot switch

   e. MaxAge timer setting on the nonroot switch

   f. ForwardDelay timer setting on the nonroot switch

**2.** Assume that a nonroot 802.1D switch receives a Hello BPDU with the TCN flag set. Which STP setting determines how long the nonroot switch waits before timing out inactive CAM entries?

   **a.** Hello timer setting on the Root

   **b.** MaxAge timer setting on the Root

   **c.** ForwardDelay timer setting on the Root

   **d.** Hello timer setting on the nonroot switch

   **e.** MaxAge timer setting on the nonroot switch

   **f.** ForwardDelay timer setting on the nonroot switch

**3.** Assume that a nonroot Switch1 (SW1) is Discarding on an 802.1Q trunk connected to Switch2 (SW2). Both switches are in the same MST region. SW1 ceases to receive Hellos from SW2. What timers have an impact on how long Switch1 takes to both become the Designated Port on that link and reach the Forwarding state?

   **a.** Hello timer setting on the Root

   **b.** MaxAge timer setting on the Root

   **c.** ForwardDelay timer on the Root

   **d.** Hello timer setting on SW1

   **e.** MaxAge timer setting on SW1

   **f.** ForwardDelay timer on SW1

**4.** Which of the following statements are true regarding support of multiple spanning trees over an 802.1Q trunk?

   **a.** Only one common spanning tree can be supported.

   **b.** Cisco PVST+ supports multiple spanning trees if the switches are Cisco switches.

   **c.** 802.1Q supports multiple spanning trees when using IEEE 802.1s MST.

   **d.** Two PVST+ domains can pass over a region of non-Cisco switches using 802.1Q trunks by encapsulating non-native VLAN Hellos inside the native VLAN Hellos.

**5.** When a switch notices a failure, and the failure requires STP convergence, it notifies the Root by sending a TCN BPDU. Which of the following best describes why the notification is needed?

   **a.** To speed STP convergence by having the Root converge quickly.

   **b.** To allow the Root to keep accurate count of the number of topology changes.

   **c.** To trigger the process that causes all switches to use a short timer to help flush the CAM.

   **d.** There is no need for TCN today; it is a holdover from DEC's STP specification.

6. Two switches have four parallel Ethernet segments, none of which forms into an EtherChannel. Assuming that 802.1D is in use, what is the maximum number of the eight ports (four on each switch) that stabilize into a Forwarding state?

   a. 1

   b. 3

   c. 4

   d. 5

   e. 7

7. IEEE 802.1w does not use the exact same port states as does 802.1D. Which of the following are valid 802.1w port states?

   a. Blocking

   b. Listening

   c. Learning

   d. Forwarding

   e. Disabled

   f. Discarding

8. What STP tools or protocols supply a "MaxAge optimization," allowing a switch to bypass the wait for MaxAge to expire when its Root Port stops receiving Hellos?

   a. Loop Guard

   b. UDLD

   c. BPDU Guard

   d. Bridge Assurance

   e. IEEE 802.1w

9. A trunk between switches lost its physical transmit path in one direction only. Which of the following features protect against the STP problems caused by such an event?

   a. Loop Guard

   b. UDLD

   c. Dispute

   d. PortFast

**10.** A switch has four Ethernet segments toward its neighbor, with the intention of using them in an EtherChannel. Some settings on the physical ports on this switch might be different and yet these ports will be allowed to be bundled in a single EtherChannel. Which settings do not have to match?

    **a.** DTP negotiation settings (auto/desirable/on)

    **b.** Allowed VLAN list

    **c.** STP per-VLAN port cost on the ports on a single switch

    **d.** If 802.1Q, native VLAN

**11.** A computer's NIC is hardcoded to 1000 Mbps and full-duplex, and it is connected to a switch whose Fast Ethernet interface is set to autonegotiate speed and duplex. What speed and duplex will the switch use if the autonegotiation on the computer's NIC is deactivated as a result of hardcoding the speed and duplex?

    **a.** 100 Mbps and full-duplex

    **b.** 100 Mbps and half-duplex

    **c.** 1000 Mbps and full-duplex

    **d.** 1000 Mbps and half-duplex

    **e.** The link will be inactive.

# Foundation Topics

## 802.1D Spanning Tree Protocol and Improvements

Although many CCIE candidates already know STP well, the details are easily forgotten. For example, you can install a campus LAN, possibly turn on a few STP optimizations and security features out of habit, and have a working LAN using STP—without ever really contemplating how STP does what it does. And in a network that makes good use of Layer 3 switching, each STP instance might span only three to four switches, making the STP issues much more manageable—but more forgettable in terms of helping you remember things you need to know for the exam. This chapter reviews the details of IEEE 802.1D STP, and then goes on to related topics—802.1w RSTP, multiple spanning trees, STP optimizations, and STP security features. STP terminology refers to bridges in many places; in the following sections, the words *bridge* and *switch* will be used interchangeably with respect to STP. While the upcoming sections about various STP versions might appear lengthy and reiterate on many known facts, be sure to read them very carefully in their entirety. It is always tiresome to read an in-depth discussion about a protocol as notorious as STP—but as we know, it's details that matter, especially for a CCIE. This chapter tries to put several details about STP straight, cleaning up numerous misconceptions that have crept in the common understanding of STP over the years of its existence.

Before diving into STP internals, it is worthwhile to comment on a possible naming confusion regarding various STP versions. The first IEEE-standardized STP, also often called the "legacy" STP, was originally described in 802.1D. Its improvements were subsequently published in so-called amendments: The Rapid STP (RSTP) was standardized in amendment 802.1w, while Multiple STP (MSTP) was covered in amendment 802.1s. Since then, the amendments have been integrated into existing standards. The latest 802.1D-2004 standard no longer includes the legacy STP at all (which is considered obsolete), and instead, it covers the RSTP originally found in 802.1w. The 802.1s MSTP is integrated into 802.1Q-2005 and later revisions. With current standards, therefore, RSTP is covered in 802.1D while MSTP is covered in 802.1Q, and legacy STP has been dropped. Still, many people are used to the old naming, with 802.1D referring to STP, 802.1w referring to RSTP, and 802.1s referring to MSTP.

STP uses messaging between switches to stabilize the network into a logical loop-free topology. To do so, STP causes some interfaces (popularly called *ports* when discussing STP) to simply not forward or receive traffic—in other words, the ports are in a *Blocking* state. The remaining ports, in an STP *Forwarding* state, together provide a loop-free path to every Ethernet segment in the network.

STP protocol messages are called Bridge Protocol Data Units (BPDU), the basic structure for which is shown in Figure 3-1.

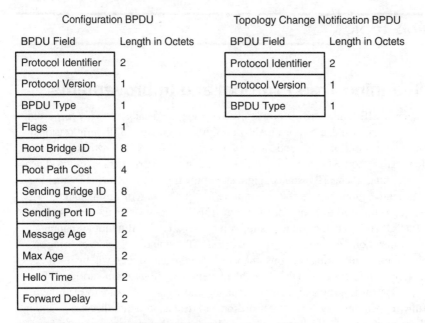

**Figure 3-1**   *Format of STP Bridge Protocol Data Units*

For STP, the Protocol Identifier value is set to 0x0000 and the Protocol Version is also set to 0x00. The BPDU Type field identifies two kinds of STP BPDUs: Configuration BPDUs (type 0x00) and Topology Change Notification BPDUs (type 0x80). The Flags field uses 2 bits out of 8 to handle topology change events: the Topology Change Acknowledgment flag and the Topology Change flag. Following the Flags, there is a series of fields identifying the root bridge, distance of the BPDU's sender from the root bridge, the sender bridge's own identifier, and the identifier of the port on the sender bridge that forwarded this BPDU. The MessageAge field is an estimation of the BPDU's age since it was originated by the root bridge. At the root bridge, it is set to 0. Any other switch will increment this value, usually by 1, before forwarding the BPDU further. The remaining lifetime of a BPDU after being received by a switch is MaxAge-MessageAge. Finally, the remaining fields carry the values of STP timers: MaxAge, HelloTime, ForwardDelay. These timer values always reflect the timer settings on the root switch. Timers configured on a nonroot switch are not used and would become effective only if the switch itself became the root switch.

Bridges and ports are identified by their IDs in BPDUs. Without discussing the exact format at this point, an object in STP that is called "identifier," or ID, always has a configurable part called the *priority*, and a fixed part that cannot be modified by management. Both bridges and ports have IDs with configurable priorities.

**Key Topic**

STP operation is based on the ability to compare any two arbitrary Configuration BPDUs and determine which one of them is better, or *superior*. The other BPDU is called *inferior*. To determine which BPDU out of a pair of BPDUs is superior, they are compared in the following sequence of values, looking for the first occurrence of a lower value:

- Root Bridge ID (RBID)

- Root Path Cost (RPC)

- Sender Bridge ID (SBID)

- Sender Port ID (SPID)

- Receiver Port ID (RPID; not included in the BPDU, evaluated locally)

First, the RBID value in both BPDUs is compared. If one of the BPDUs contains a lower RBID value, this BPDU is declared superior and the comparison process stops. Otherwise, both BPDUs carry the same RBID value and the RPC is compared. Again, if one of the BPDUs carries a lower RPC value, this BPDU is declared superior. In case both BPDUs carry an identical RPC value, the comparison process moves to the SBID. Should the SBID value be also found identical, the SPID will be compared. If even the SPID values in both BPDUs are the same, RPIDs of ports that received the same BPDU are compared. This very last step is very uncommon and would be seen in situations where a single BPDU was received by multiple ports of a single switch, possibly because of multiple connections to a hub or a non-STP switch being placed somewhere in between. In any case, precisely this capability of selecting a single superior BPDU out of a set of BPDUs is at the core of STP's capability to choose exactly one root bridge per a switched environment, exactly one Root Port on a nonroot bridge, and exactly one Designated Port for each connected network segment, as each of these roles is derived from the concept of a superior BPDU. Only Configuration BPDUs are compared; Topology Change Notification BPDUs do not convey information used to build a loop-free topology and are not compared. Therefore, whenever a comparison of BPDUs is discussed, it is implied that the BPDUs in question are Configuration BPDUs.

Additionally, an important fact to remember is that each port in STP stores (that is, remembers) the superior BPDU it has either sent or received. As you will see later, Root Ports and Blocking ports store the received BPDU sent by the "upstream" designated switch (because that BPDU is superior to the one that would be sent out from this port), while Designated Ports store their own sent BPDU (because that one is superior to any received BPDU). Essentially, each port stores the Designated Port's BPDU—whether it is the port itself that is Designated or it is a neighbor's port. Should a port store a received BPDU, it must be received again within a time interval of MaxAge-MessageAge seconds; otherwise it will expire after this period. This expiry is always driven by the timers in the BPDU, that is, according to timers of the root switch.

In the following sections, Configuration BPDUs will also be called simply Hello BPDUs or Hellos, as their origination is driven by the Hello timer.

## Choosing Which Ports Forward: Choosing Root Ports and Designated Ports

To determine which ports forward and block, STP follows a three-step process, as listed in Table 3-2. Following the table, each of the three steps is explained in more detail.

**Table 3-2** *Three Major 802.1D STP Process Steps*

| Major Step | Description |
|---|---|
| Elect the root switch | The switch with the lowest bridge ID; the standard bridge ID is 2-byte priority followed by a MAC address unique to that switch. |
| Determine each switch's Root Port | The one port on each nonroot switch that receives the superior resulting BPDU from among all received BPDUs on all its ports. |
| Determine the Designated Port for each segment | When multiple switches connect to the same segment, this is the switch that forwards the superior BPDU from among all forwarded BPDUs onto that segment. |

### Electing a Root Switch

Only one switch can be the *root* of the spanning tree; to select the root, the switches hold an *election*. Each switch begins its STP logic by creating and sending an STP Hello bridge protocol data unit (BPDU) message, claiming itself to be the root switch. If a switch hears a *superior Hello* to its own Hello—namely, a Hello with a lower bridge ID—it stops claiming to be root by ceasing to originate and send Hellos. Instead, the switch starts forwarding the superior Hellos received from the superior candidate. Eventually, all switches except the switch with the lowest bridge ID cease to originate Hellos; that one switch wins the election and becomes the root switch.

The original IEEE 802.1D bridge ID held two fields:

- The 2-byte Priority field, which was designed to be configured on the various switches to affect the results of the STP election process.

- A 6-byte MAC Address field, which was included as a tiebreaker, because each switch's bridge ID includes a MAC address value that should be unique to each switch. As a result, some switch must win the root election.

The format of the original 802.1D bridge ID has been redefined in amendment 802.1t and since then integrated into 802.1D-2004. Figure 3-2 shows the original and new format of the bridge IDs.

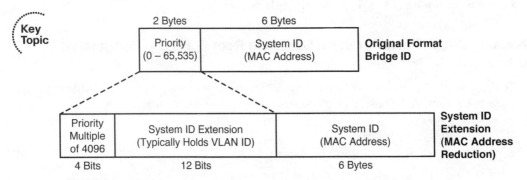

**Figure 3-2** *IEEE 802.1D STP Bridge ID Formats*

The format was changed mainly because of the advent of multiple spanning trees as supported by Per VLAN Spanning Tree Plus (PVST+) and IEEE 802.1s Multiple Spanning Trees (MST). With the old-style bridge ID format, a switch's bridge ID for each STP instance (possibly one per VLAN) was identical if the switch used a single MAC address when building the bridge ID. Because VLANs cause a single physical switch to behave as multiple logical switches, having multiple STP instances with the same bridge ID was in violation of the 802.1D that required a distinct bridge ID for each switch. Vendors such as Cisco used a different MAC address for each VLAN when creating the old-style bridge IDs. This provided a different bridge ID per VLAN, but it consumed a large number of reserved MAC addresses in each switch.

The System ID Extension, originally described in IEEE 802.1t, allows a network to use multiple instances of STP, even one per VLAN, but without the need to consume a separate MAC address on each switch for each STP instance. The System ID Extension field allows the VLAN ID to be placed into what was formerly the last 12 bits of the Priority field. A switch can use a single MAC address to build bridge IDs and, with the VLAN number in the System ID Extension field, still have a unique bridge ID in each VLAN. The use of the System ID Extension field is also called *MAC address reduction*, because of the need for many fewer reserved MAC addresses on each switch. The use of the System ID Extension on a switch is indicated by the presence of the **spanning-tree extend system-id** command in global configuration mode. Older switches equipped with a larger reserve of MAC addresses allow this command to be removed, reverting to the old-style bridge IDs. Recent switches, however, do not allow this command to be removed even though it is displayed in the running config, and always use the System ID Extension.

## Determining the Root Port

After the root switch is elected, the rest of the switches now need to determine their *Root Port (RP)*. The process proceeds as described in the following list:

1.  The root switch creates and sends a Hello every Hello timer (2 seconds by default). This Hello contains the RBID and SBID fields set to the ID of the root, RPC set to 0, and SPID set to the identifier of the egress port.

2.  Each nonroot switch receiving a BPDU on a particular port adds that port's cost to the RPC value in the received BPDU, yielding a *resulting* BPDU. Subsequently, the switch declares the port receiving the superior resulting BPDU as its Root Port.

3.  Hellos received on the Root Port of a nonroot switch are forwarded through its remaining designated ports after updating the RPC, SBID, SPID, and MessageAge fields accordingly. Hellos received on other ports of a nonroot switch are processed but they are not forwarded.

4.  Switches do not forward Hellos out Root Ports and ports that stabilize into a Blocking state. Hellos forwarded out these ports would be inferior (and therefore uninteresting) to Hellos originated by some neighboring switch's Designated Port on those segments.

The result of this process is that each nonroot switch chooses exactly one port as its Root Port, as there is always only a single received Hello that is superior over all other received Hellos. According to the sequence of compared fields in received Hellos when selecting a superior BPDU, a Root Port always provides the least-cost path toward the switch with the lowest Bridge ID (that is, the root switch). If there are multiple equal-cost paths, additional tiebreakers (SBID, SPID, RPID) will allow the receiving switch to always choose exactly one path in a deterministic fashion: first, port toward the neighbor with the lowest Bridge ID; then, if there are multiple links toward that neighbor, port connected to the neighbor's port with the lowest Port ID; and finally, if the same BPDU is received on multiple ports at once, the receiving port with the lowest Port ID.

In this sense, the STP operation is quite similar to the operation of the Routing Information Protocol (RIP), the simplest distance-vector routing protocol. Just like RIP, STP tries to find the least-cost path toward a particular destination, in this case, the root bridge, and has additional criteria to select a single path if there are multiple least-cost paths available. Hellos can be likened to RIP Update messages with RBID identifying the *destination*, RPC expressing the next hop's *metric* to the destination, SBID being the *next-hop identifier*, and SPID identifying the *next hop's interface*. Each time a Hello is received, the receiving switch can be thought to reevaluate its choice of a Root Port and updates the choice if necessary, just like a RIP router receives updates every 30 seconds and reevaluates its choice of least-cost paths to individual destinations. In fact, STP can be seen as a special case of a timer-driven distance-vector routing protocol, selecting exactly one path to exactly one particular destination, the root bridge. This makes STP similar to, though of course not entirely analogous to, RIP.

A switch must examine the RPC value in each Hello, plus the switch's STP port costs, to determine its least-cost path to reach the root. To do so, the switch adds the cost listed in the Hello message to the switch's port cost of the port on which the Hello was received. For example, Figure 3-3 shows the loop network design and details several STP cost calculations.

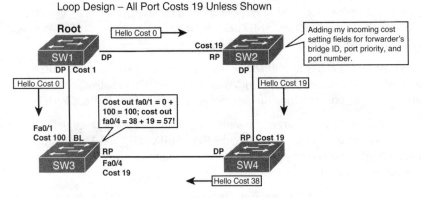

**Figure 3-3**  *Calculating STP Costs to Determine RPs*

In Figure 3-3, SW1 happened to become root, and is originating Hellos of cost 0. SW3 receives two Hellos, one with cost 0 and one with cost 38. However, SW3 must then calculate its cost to reach the root, which is the advertised cost (0 and 38, respectively) plus SW3's port costs (100 and 19, respectively). As a result, although SW3 has a direct link to SW1, the calculated cost is lower out interface Fa0/4 (cost 57) than it is out interface Fa0/1 (cost 100), so SW3 chooses its Fa0/4 interface as its RP.

**Note**   Many people think of STP costs as being associated with a segment; however, the cost is actually associated with interfaces. Good design practices dictate using the same STP cost on each end of a point-to-point Ethernet segment, but the values can be different.

**Key Topic**

While the costs shown in Figure 3-3 might seem a bit contrived, the same result would happen with default port costs if the link from SW1 to SW3 were Fast Ethernet (default cost 19), and the other links were Gigabit Ethernet (default cost 4). Table 3-3 lists the default port costs according to various revisions of the IEEE 802.1D standard. Before 802.1D-1998, IEEE did not specify any recommended STP port cost values for different link speeds in their standard. Speeds shown in Table 3-3 were chosen by Cisco and used in its STP implementations of that time. The 802.1D-1998 revision of the standard provided a table of recommended values, but as the speeds of Ethernet links continued to increase dramatically, IEEE revised these recommended values again in its 802.1D-2004 revision of the standard. On recent Catalyst switches, the default costs correspond to the 802.1D-1998 version of the standard if PVST or Rapid PVST is used, and to the 802.1D-2004 version if MSTP is used. With PVST and Rapid PVST, the 802.1D-2004 costs can be activated using the **spanning-tree pathcost method long** global configuration command. By default, **spanning-tree pathcost method short** is configured, causing the switch to use the older revision of the costs.

**Table 3-3**   *Default Port Costs*

| Port speed | Pre-802.1D-1998 Cost | 802.1D-1998 Cost | 802.1D-2004 Cost |
|---|---|---|---|
| 10 Mbps | 100 | 100 | 2000000 |
| 100 Mbps | 10 | 19 | 200000 |
| 1 Gbps | 1 | 4 | 20000 |
| 10 Gbps | 1 | 2 | 2000 |

## Determining the Designated Port

A converged STP topology results in only one switch forwarding Hellos onto each LAN segment. The switch that forwards Hellos onto a LAN segment is called the *designated switch* for that segment, and the port that it uses to forward frames onto that segment is called the *Designated Port (DP)*. All remaining ports on a switch that have been determined as neither Root nor Designated will be moved to Blocking state. In the following text, they will be labeled as Non-Designated ports.

**Key Topic**

To win the right to be the DP, a switch must send superior Hellos onto the segment. For example, consider the segment between SW3 and SW4 in Figure 3-3 before the DP has been determined on that segment. SW3 would get Hellos directly from SW1, compute its cost to the root over that path, and then forward the Hello out its Fa0/4 interface to SW4, with RPC set to 100. Similarly, SW4 will forward a Hello with RPC of 38, as shown in Figure 3-3. SW4's port on this segment becomes the DP, as it sends superior Hellos because of their lower RPC value. Even after SW3 selects its Fa0/4 as the Root Port (as it receives superior resulting BPDUs from among all ports on SW3), any Hellos sent from SW3's Fa0/4 port would indicate the RPC of 57, still being inferior to SW4's Hellos.

Only the DP forwards Hellos onto a LAN segment. In the same example, SW4 keeps sending the Hellos with an RPC of 38 out the port, but SW3 stops sending its inferior Hellos. There would be no harm if SW3 continued to send its inferior BPDUs out its Fa0/1 and Fa0/4 ports, but because STP always cares only for superior BPDUs, this would be a waste of effort. Therefore, neither Root Ports nor ports in the Blocking state send BPDUs.

The tiebreakers during DP selection are the same as before: first, the switch with the least-cost path to the root identified by the lowest Bridge ID; then the neighboring switch with the lowest Bridge ID; and finally the port on the neighbor with the lowest Bridge ID with the lowest Port ID.

**Key Topic**

To sum up the rules:

■   The root switch is the switch that has the lowest Bridge ID in the topology.

■   On each nonroot switch, a Root Port is the port receiving the best (that is, superior) resulting BPDUs from all received BPDUs on all ports. The adjective "resulting" refers to the addition of the port's cost to the BPDU's RPC value before comparing the received BPDUs.

■   On each connected segment, a Designated Port is the port sending the best (that is, superior) BPDUs on the segment. No modifications to the BPDUs are performed; BPDUs are compared immediately.

■   All ports that are neither Root Ports nor Designated Ports are superfluous in an active topology and will be put into the Blocking state.

■   Configuration BPDUs are sent out only from Designated Ports. Root and Non-Designated ports do not emit Configuration BPDUs because they would be inferior to BPDUs of a Designated Port on this segment and hence ignored.

- Each port stores the best (that is, superior) BPDU it has received or sent itself. Designated Ports store the BPDU they send; Root and Blocking ports store the best BPDU they receive. The stored BPDU determines the role of the port and is used for comparisons.

- Received superior stored BPDUs will expire in MaxAge-MessageAge seconds if not received within this time period.

## Converging to a New STP Topology

Although STP is very illustratively described in the three steps discussed earlier, this approach also gives an impression that after the three steps are completed, STP effectively goes dormant until a topology change occurs. Such impression would be incorrect, though. In reality, STP never stops working. With each received BPDU, a switch reevaluates its own choice of the root switch, Root Port, and Designated/Non-Designated Ports, effectively performing all three steps all over again. In a stable topology, received BPDUs do not change, and therefore, processing them yields the same results again and again. This is similar to the operation of the RIP that also never stops running—it's just that in a stable network which has converged, processing periodic received updates produces the same set of best paths, which gives off an impression that the protocol has done its job and has stopped. In reality, both STP and RIP continue running indefinitely, only in a stable and converged topology, each run produces the same results.

Of course, a topology in which STP runs can change over time, and STP has to react appropriately. In precise terms, for STP, a *topology change* is an event that occurs when

- A Topology Change Notification BPDU is received by a Designated Port of a switch

- A port moves to the Forwarding state and the switch has at least one Designated Port (meaning that it is not a standalone switch with just a Root Port connected to an upstream switch and no other connected ports)

- A port moves from Learning or Forwarding to Blocking

- A switch becomes the root switch

When a change to the topology occurs, the elementary reaction of switches that detect the topology change is to start originating BPDUs with appropriately updated contents, propagating the information to their neighbors. These neighbors will process the updated BPDUs, reevaluating their choice of the root switch, Root Port, and Designated/Non-Designated Ports with each received BPDU as usual, and forwarding the BPDU farther according to usual STP rules.

For an example, consider Figure 3-4, which shows the same loop network as in Figure 3-3. In this case, however, the link from SW1 to SW2 has just failed.

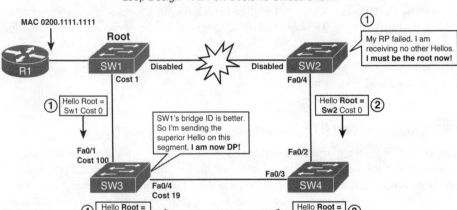

**Figure 3-4** *Reacting to the Loss of Link Between SW1 and SW2*

The following list describes some of the key steps from Figure 3-4:

1. SW2's Root Port goes down. On SW2, the loss of a Root Port causes it to reelect its Root Port by choosing the port receiving superior resulting BPDUs. However, as the only remaining port is Fa0/4 connected to SW4, and SW4 did not send any BPDUs to SW2 from its Root Port Fa0/2, SW2 has no received BPDUs to choose from, and it will start considering itself a root switch, flooding its own Hellos through all its connected ports.

2. SW4 notices that the latest Hellos indicate a new root switch. However, these Hellos from SW2 received on SW4's Fa0/2 port, its current Root Port, are inferior to the BPDU stored on that port. When the link between SW1 and SW2 still worked, BPDU arriving at SW4's Fa0/2 contained the SW1's Bridge ID as the RBID. After the link between SW1 and SW2 went down and SW2 started considering itself as the root bridge, its BPDUs arriving at SW4's Fa0/2 port contained SW2's Bridge ID as the RBID. However, SW2 has a higher Bridge ID than SW1; otherwise, it would be the root switch right away. Therefore, BPDUs claiming that SW2 is the root bridge are inferior to the BPDU stored on SW4's Fa0/2 that claims SW1 is the root bridge, and as a result, they are ignored until the BPDU stored on SW4's Fa0/2 expires. This expiry will take MaxAge-MessageAge, or 20–1=19 seconds. Until then, SW4 does not forward any BPDUs to SW3.

3. During the time SW4 receives inferior BPDUs from SW2 on its Fa0/2 port, it does not forward any BPDUs to SW3. As a result, SW3 ceases to receive BPDUs on its Fa0/4 port, which is its current Root Port. The BPDU stored on SW3's Fa0/4 port expires in MaxAge-MessageAge, or 20–2=18 seconds. After it expires, Fa0/4 becomes a Designated Port and moves to the Listening state. SW3 then searches for a new Root Port by looking for the superior received resulting BPDU, ultimately choosing Fa0/1 as its new port. Afterward, it will forward SW1's Hello out its Fa0/4 port after updating the necessary fields.

4. In the meantime, SW4 might have the BPDU expired from its Fa0/2, started accepting BPDUs from SW2, declared the Fa0/2 as its Root Port toward SW2, and started relaying the Hellos from SW2 to SW3. Even if that was the case, SW3 would treat these Hellos from SW4 as inferior because Hellos sent out from SW3's Fa0/4 claim that the root switch is SW1 having a lower Bridge ID than SW2. After SW4 receives the relayed Hello from SW3, it will learn about a better root switch than SW2, namely, SW1, and will choose its Fa0/3 as the Root Port. Afterward, it will forward the Hello out its Fa0/2 port.

5. After SW2 receives the forwarded Hello from SW4, it will also learn about SW1 being a better root switch than itself. Therefore, SW2 will stop considering itself as a root switch and will instead declare its Fa0/4 port as the Root Port, finally converging on the new loop-free topology.

## Topology Change Notification and Updating the CAM

Simply updating the active topology by processing new BPDUs is not sufficient. When STP reconverges on a new active topology, some Content Addressable Memory (CAM) entries might be invalid (CAM is the Cisco term for what is more generically called the MAC address table, switching table, or bridging table on a switch). For example, before the link failure shown in Figure 3-4, SW3's CAM might have had an entry for 0200.1111.1111 (Router1's MAC address) pointing out Fa0/4 to SW4. Remember, at the beginning of the scenario described in Figure 3-4, SW3 was Blocking on its Fa0/1 interface back to SW1. When the link between SW1 and SW2 failed, SW3 would need to change its CAM entry for 0200.1111.111 to point out port Fa0/1.

STP is not a protocol that tries to find shortest paths toward individual MAC addresses, so it cannot be expected to fill the CAM tables with new correct entries. All STP can do is to instruct switches to age out unused entries prematurely, assuming that the unused entries are exactly those that need updating. Even if good entries are flushed from CAM tables, this does not impair basic connectivity—switches will flood frames to unknown destinations rather than dropping them.

To update the CAMs, two things need to occur:

■ All switches need to be notified to time out their apparently unused CAM entries.

■ Each switch needs to use a short timer, equivalent to the Forward Delay timer (default 15 seconds), to time out the CAM entries.

A topology change can start as a highly localized event—a port becoming Forwarding or transitioning from Learning or Forwarding to Blocking on a particular single switch. The information about this change must nevertheless be propagated to all switches in the topology. Therefore, a switch that detects a topology change must notify the root switch, and the root switch in turn can notify all switches in the topology. (Recall that it is the root switch's Hello that is propagated throughout the network to all switches; a nonroot switch has no way of sending its own Configuration BPDU to all remaining switches in a topology because that BPDU would be inferior, and thus ignored, by possibly many switches.) To do so, a switch detecting a topology change notifies the root switch using a *Topology Change Notification (TCN)* BPDU. The TCN goes up the tree to the root. After that, the root notifies all the rest of the switches. The process is illustrated in Figure 3-5 and runs as follows:

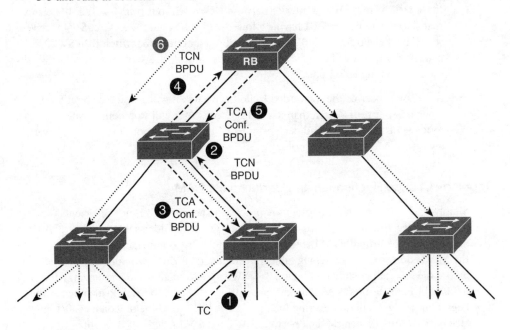

**Figure 3-5**   *Propagating Information About Topology Change*

1. A topology change event occurs on a port of a switch.

2. After detecting the event, the switch sends a TCN BPDU out its Root Port; it repeats this message every Hello time until it is acknowledged.

3. The next designated switch receiving that TCN BPDU sends back an acknowledgment through its next forwarded Hello BPDU by marking the Topology Change Acknowledgment (TCA) bit in the Flags field of the Hello.

4. The designated switch on the segment in the second step repeats the first two steps, sending a TCN BPDU out its Root Port, and awaits acknowledgment from the designated switch on that segment.

5. After the TCN arrives at the root switch, it also acknowledges its arrival through sending a BPDU with the Topology Change Acknowledgment bit set through the port through which the TCN BPDU came in. At this point, the root switch has been informed about a topology change that occurred somewhere in the network.

6. For the next MaxAge+ForwardDelay seconds, the root switch will originate BPDUs with the Topology Change (TC) bit set, instructing all switches to shorten the aging time for CAM entries to ForwardDelay seconds.

By each successive switch repeating Steps 2 and 3, eventually the root receives a TCN BPDU. After it is received, the root sets the *Topology Change (TC)* flag on the next several Hellos (during the next MaxAge+ForwardDelay seconds), which are forwarded to all switches in the network, notifying them that a change has occurred. A switch receiving a Hello BPDU with the TC flag set uses the short (ForwardDelay time derived from the value in the received BPDU, set by the root switch) timer to time out unused entries in the CAM.

### Transitioning from Blocking to Forwarding

When STP reconverges to a new, stable topology, some ports that were Blocking might have been designated as DP or RP, so these ports need to be in a Forwarding state. However, the transition from Blocking to Forwarding state cannot be made immediately without the risk of causing loops.

To transition to Forwarding state but also prevent temporary loops, a switch first puts a formerly Blocking port into *Listening* state, and then into *Learning* state, with each state lasting for the length of time defined by the ForwardDelay timer (by default, 15 seconds). Table 3-4 summarizes the key points about all the 802.1D STP port states.

**Key Topic**

**Table 3-4**  *IEEE 802.1D Spanning Tree Interface States*

| State | Forwards Data Frames? | Learns Source MACs of Received Frames? | Transitory or Stable State? |
|---|---|---|---|
| Blocking | No | No | Stable |
| Listening | No | No | Transitory |
| Learning | No | Yes | Transitory |
| Forwarding | Yes | Yes | Stable |
| Disabled | No | No | Stable |

In summary, when STP logic senses a change in the topology, it converges, possibly picking different ports as RP, DP, or neither. Any switch changing its RPs or DPs sends a TCN BPDU to the root at this point. For the ports newly designated as RP or DP, 802.1D STP first uses the Listening and Learning states before reaching the Forwarding state. (The transition from Forwarding to Blocking can be made immediately.)

## Per-VLAN Spanning Tree and STP over Trunks

If only one instance of STP was used for a switched network with redundant links but with multiple VLANs, several ports would be in a Blocking state, unused under stable conditions. The redundant links would essentially be used for backup purposes.

The Cisco Per VLAN Spanning Tree Plus (PVST+) feature creates an STP instance for each VLAN. By tuning STP configuration per VLAN, each STP instance can use a different root switch and have different interfaces block. As a result, the traffic load can be balanced across the available links. For example, in the common building design with distribution and access links in Figure 3-6, focus on the left side of the figure. In this case, the access layer switches block on different ports on VLANs 1 and 2, with different root switches. Support for PVST+ implies the capability of trunk ports to be selectively blocked or forwarding for individual VLANs.

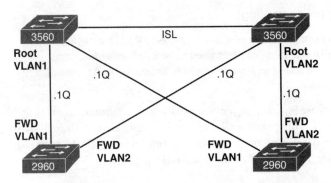

**Figure 3-6**   *Operation of PVST+ for Better Load Balancing*

With different root switches and with default port costs, the access layer switches end up sending VLAN1 traffic over one uplink and VLAN2 traffic over another uplink.

Using 802.1Q VLANs with IEEE 802.1D STP requires some extra thought as to how it works. Non-Cisco switches that follow exclusively the IEEE standard support only a so-called *Common Spanning Tree (CST)*. Here, only one instance of STP runs in the network (not even being tied to a specific VLAN because basic STP does not know anything about VLANs), and that one STP topology is used for all VLANs, hence being called as "common." Although using only one STP instance reduces the STP messaging overhead, it does not allow load balancing by using multiple STP instances, as was shown with PVST+ in Figure 3-6.

When building networks using a mix of Cisco and non-Cisco switches, along with 802.1Q trunking, you can still take advantage of multiple STP instances in the Cisco portion of the network, but we need to look closer at the rules that govern the interoperation between the 802.1D STP and PVST+, and the cooperation of PVST+ regions interconnected by CST regions.

Cisco PVST+ running on trunks uses a VLAN 1 STP instance to communicate with non-Cisco switches and their STP. VLAN 1's STP instance in PVST+ regions interoperates and merges with the STP in CST regions. As a result, the entire switched network computes a single loop-free topology. In CST regions, the active loop-free topology is binding for all VLANs; inside PVST+ regions, the active loop-free topology applies to VLAN 1 only. Other VLANs inside PVST+ regions have their own PVST+ instances.

PVST+ instances for VLANs other that VLAN 1 in PVST+ regions treat CST regions simply as loop-free shared segments. This is done by encapsulating the PVST+ BPDUs on trunks differently than ordinary BPDUs: Their destination MAC address is set to the multicast address 0100.0CCC.CCCD (ordinary STP BPDUs are destined to 0180.C200.0000), they are tagged with the corresponding VLAN (ordinary STP BPDUs are untagged), and by using SNAP encapsulation (ordinary STP BPDUs use LLC encapsulation without SNAP). In addition, each PVST+ BPDU has a special TLV record placed at its end that carries the VLAN number in which the PVST+ BPDU was originated. We will call this TLV the Port VLAN ID TLV, or a PVID TLV. This TLV is analyzed by PVST+ switches and compared to the VLAN in which the BPDU is received to detect native VLAN mismatches. As a result, PVST+ BPDUs are tunneled across CST regions, with CST switches flooding them as ordinary multicasts without processing them. To non-VLAN 1 PVST+ instances, the entire switched network appears as PVST+ regions interconnected by shared segments. By tunneling PVST+ BPDUs across CST regions, PVST+ STP instances for VLANs 2–4094 in individual PVST+ regions cooperate together to form a single spanning tree for each corresponding VLAN inside all PVST+ regions, with CST regions merely serving the purpose of loop-free shared segments connecting the PVST+ regions together.

VLAN 1 on PVST+ trunks is actually handled specially: Both standard STP BPDUs and PVST+ BPDUs are sent for VLAN 1. However, only the STP BPDU is used both by CST and PVST+ switches in VLAN 1 to compute the spanning tree. PVST+ BPDU for VLAN 1 is used to detect native VLAN mismatches and is otherwise ignored upon arrival.

**Key Topic**

To summarize the sending and processing of PVST+ and ordinary IEEE BPDUs on ports, when *sending* BPDUs, access ports send only IEEE BPDUs relevant to their access VLAN. Trunk ports always send a set of BPDUs:

■   IEEE-formatted BPDUs for VLAN1, always untagged.

■   PVST+ BPDUs (also called SSTP BPDUs in Cisco documents) for all existing and allowed VLANs including VLAN1, tagged accordingly to the native VLAN of the trunk; that is, BPDUs for the native VLAN won't be tagged and all others will. Each of these PVST+ BPDUs carries the PVID TLV.

When processing *received* BPDUs, an access port must receive only IEEE BPDUs; otherwise a Type Inconsistent state is declared. These IEEE BPDUs will be processed by the STP instance for the access VLAN of the port. On trunk ports, the processing is a little more complex:

■   IEEE-formatted BPDUs will be immediately processed by the VLAN1 STP instance.

■   PVST+ BPDUs are processed according to this sequence of steps:

   **1.**   Assign the BPDU to the appropriate VLAN by looking at its 802.1Q tag. If the tag is present, the BPDU is assigned to the VLAN indicated by the tag. If the tag is not present, the BPDU is assigned to the native VLAN.

   **2.**   Check the PVID TLV in the BPDU. If the VLAN stored in the PVID TLV does not match the VLAN to which the BPDU was assigned, drop the BPDU and declare the PVID_Inconsistent state for the offending pair of VLANs. This is the native VLAN mismatch check.

3. BPDUs whose PVID TLV VLAN matches the assigned VLAN will be processed by STP in their appropriate VLANs except BPDUs for VLAN1. Because the information for VLAN1 is duplicated in the IEEE BPDUs and PVST+ BPDUs and the IEEE BPDUs always have to be processed, the PVST+ BPDU for VLAN1 served only the purpose of protection against native VLAN mismatch in VLAN1, and can be dropped afterward.

Figure 3-7 shows a network in which three CST regions of non-Cisco switches connect to two regions of Cisco PVST+ supporting switches.

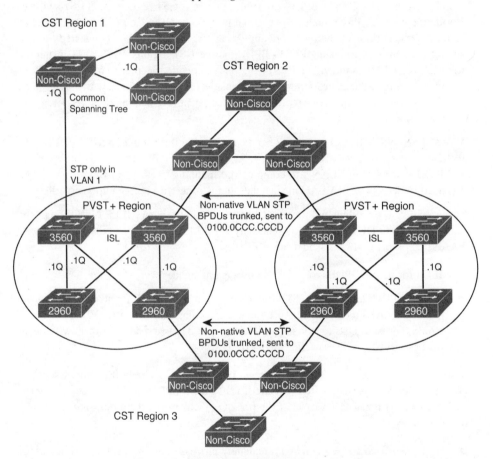

**Figure 3-7**   *Combining Standard IEEE 802.1Q and CST with PVST+*

The topology in Figure 3-7 consists of three CST and two PVST+ regions. CST regions use ordinary STP with no per-VLAN semantics. PVST+ regions run STP independently in each VLAN, and on PVST+ boundaries, they use the VLAN 1 STP instance to interact and interoperate with CST regions.

As CST and PVST+ VLAN 1 STP instances will interact and cooperate with each other, the result of this interaction is a tree that spans through the entire network. In CST regions, the loop-free topology will be shared by all VLANs; in PVST+ regions, the loop-free topology will be applied to VLAN 1 only. Assuming that the topmost switch in CST Region 2 is the root switch and all links have the same STP cost, the resulting loop-free topology in CST regions and in VLAN 1 in PVST+ regions is shown in Figure 3-8.

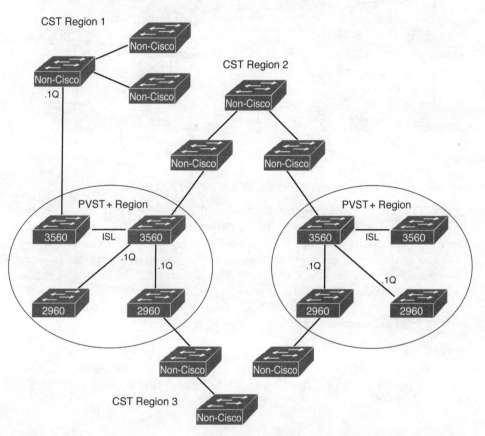

**Figure 3-8**  *Resulting Spanning Tree in CST Regions and in VLAN 1 in PVST+ Regions*

In simple terms, the result of CST and VLAN 1 STP interaction can be easily visualized simply by considering all switches to run a single STP instance and computing the spanning tree, ignoring all VLANs for the moment, then taking into consideration that in CST regions, this spanning tree will be shared by all VLANs, while in PVST+ regions, only VLAN 1 will be affected. Also, any CST region that interconnects two or more PVST+ regions is internally loop free and either continuous (as in CST Region 2; this region provides a transit connectivity between PVST+ regions) or partitioned (as in CST Region 3; this region does not provide transit connectivity to PVST+ regions).

This observation about CST regions being internally loop free is important to understand the operation of remaining non-VLAN 1 STP instances in PVST+ regions. After loops have been eliminated from CST regions, the resulting network as seen by PVST+ STP instances can be seen in Figure 3-9.

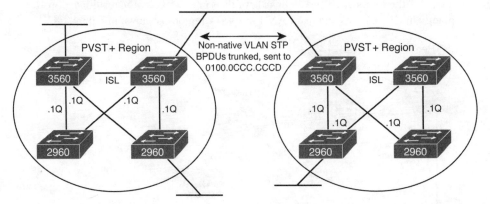

**Figure 3-9**   *Network as Perceived by Non-VLAN 1 PVST+ STP Instances*

As PVST+ BPDUs are effectively tunneled across CST regions, the CST regions simply appear as shared segments to non-VLAN 1 PVST+ STP instances. These shared segments are internally loop free and either interconnect PVST+ regions, in which case PVST+ will take care of eliminating any remaining possible loops between PVST+ regions, or do not even provide transit connectivity. PVST+ BPDUs will be flooded across the CST region without being processed. When forwarded PVST+ BPDUs reach the first Cisco PVST+ switch in the other PVST+ region, the switch, listening for multicasts to 0100.0CCC. CCCD, reads and interprets the BPDU.

**Note**   Along with 802.1s Multiple Spanning Tree Protocol (MSTP), 802.1Q allows 802.1Q trunks for supporting multiple STP instances. MST is covered later in this chapter.

## STP Configuration and Analysis

Example 3-1, based on Figure 3-10, shows some of the basic STP configuration and **show** commands. Take care to note that many of the upcoming commands allow the parameters to be set for all VLANs by omitting the VLAN parameter, or set per VLAN by including a VLAN parameter. Example 3-1 begins with SW1 coincidentally becoming the root switch. After that, SW2 is configured to become root, and SW3 changes its Root Port as a result of a configured port cost in VLAN 1.

Core Design

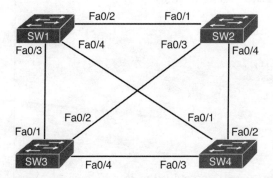

**Figure 3-10** *Network Used with Example 3-1*

**Example 3-1** *STP Basic Configuration and* show *Commands*

```
! First, note the Root ID column lists the root's bridge ID as two parts,
! first the priority, followed by the MAC address of the root. The root cost of
! 0 implies that SW1 (where the command is executed) is the root.


SW1# sh spanning-tree root

                                           Root    Hello Max Fwd
Vlan                   Root ID        Cost  Time  Age Dly Root Port
---------------- -------------------- ----- ----- --- --- ------------
VLAN0001          32769 000a.b7dc.b780    0    2   20  15
VLAN0011          32779 000a.b7dc.b780    0    2   20  15
VLAN0012          32780 000a.b7dc.b780    0    2   20  15
VLAN0021          32789 000a.b7dc.b780    0    2   20  15
VLAN0022          32790 000a.b7dc.b780    0    2   20  15


! The next command confirms that SW1 believes that it is the root of VLAN 1.


SW1# sh spanning-tree vlan 1 root detail
  Root ID    Priority    32769
             Address     000a.b7dc.b780
             This bridge is the root
             Hello Time   2 sec  Max Age 20 sec  Forward Delay 15 sec


! Next, SW2 is configured with a lower (better) priority than SW1,
! so it becomes the root. Note that because SW2 is defaulting to use
! the System ID Extension, the actual priority must be configured as a
! multiple of 4096.
```

```
SW2# conf t
Enter configuration commands, one per line.  End with CNTL/Z.
SW2(config)# spanning-tree vlan 1 priority ?
  <0-61440>  bridge priority in increments of 4096

SW2(config)# spanning-tree vlan 1 priority 28672
SW2(config)# ^Z
SW2# sh spanning-tree vlan 1 root detail
VLAN0001
   Root ID    Priority    28673
              Address     0011.92b0.f500
              This bridge is the root
              Hello Time   2 sec  Max Age 20 sec  Forward Delay 15 sec

! The System ID Extension field of the bridge ID is implied next. The output
! does not separate the 4-bit Priority field from the System ID field. The output
! actually shows the first 2 bytes of the bridge ID, in decimal. For VLAN1,
! the priority is 28,673, which is the configured 28,672 plus the VLAN ID,
! because the VLAN ID value is used in the System ID field in order to implement
! the MAC address reduction feature. The other VLANs have a base priority
! of 32768, plus the VLAN ID - for example, VLAN11 has priority 32779,
! (priority 32,768 plus VLAN 11), VLAN12 has 32780, and so on.

SW2# sh spanning-tree root priority
VLAN0001        28673
VLAN0011        32779
VLAN0012        32780
VLAN0021        32789
VLAN0022        32790

! Below, SW3 shows a Root Port of Fa0/2, with cost 19. SW3 gets Hellos
! directly from the root (SW2) with cost 0, and adds its default cost (19).
! This next command also details the breakdown of the priority and system ID.

SW3# sh spanning-tree vlan 1
VLAN0001
   Spanning tree enabled protocol ieee
   Root ID    Priority    28673
              Address     0011.92b0.f500
              Cost        19
              Port        2 (FastEthernet0/2)
              Hello Time   2 sec  Max Age 20 sec  Forward Delay 15 sec
```

```
  Bridge ID  Priority    32769  (priority 32768 sys-id-ext 1)
             Address     000e.837b.3100
             Hello Time   2 sec  Max Age 20 sec  Forward Delay 15 sec
             Aging Time 300


Interface         Role Sts Cost      Prio.Nbr Type
----------------  ---- --- --------- -------- --------------------------------
Fa0/1             Altn BLK 19        128.1    P2p
Fa0/2             Root FWD 19        128.2    P2p
Fa0/4             Desg FWD 19        128.4    P2p
Fa0/13            Desg FWD 100       128.13   Shr


! Above, the port state of BLK and FWD for each port is shown, as well as the
! Root Port and the Designated Ports.
! Below, Switch3's VLAN 1 port cost is changed on its Root Port (Fa0/2),
! causing SW3 to reconverge, and pick a new RP.


SW3# conf t
Enter configuration commands, one per line.  End with CNTL/Z.
SW3(config)# int fa 0/2
SW3(config-if)# spanning-tree vlan 1 cost 100
SW3(config-if)# ^Z


! The next command was done immediately after changing the port cost on
! SW3. Note the state listed as "LIS," meaning Listening. STP has already
! chosen Fa0/1 as the new RP, but it must now transition through Listening
! and Learning states.


SW3# sh spanning-tree vlan 1
VLAN0001
  Spanning tree enabled protocol ieee
  Root ID    Priority    28673
             Address     0011.92b0.f500
             Cost        38
             Port        1 (FastEthernet0/1)
             Hello Time   2 sec  Max Age 20 sec  Forward Delay 15 sec


  Bridge ID  Priority    32769  (priority 32768 sys-id-ext 1)
             Address     000e.837b.3100
             Hello Time   2 sec  Max Age 20 sec  Forward Delay 15 sec
             Aging Time 15
```

```
Interface        Role Sts Cost        Prio.Nbr Type
---------------- ---- --- --------    -------- ---------------------------------
Fa0/1            Root LIS 19          128.1    P2p
Fa0/2            Altn BLK 100         128.2    P2p
Fa0/4            Desg FWD 19          128.4    P2p
Fa0/13           Desg FWD 100         128.13   Shr
```

The preceding example shows one way to configure the priority to a lower value to become the root. Optionally, the **spanning-tree vlan** *vlan-id* **root** {**primary** | **secondary**} [**diameter** *diameter*] command could be used. This command causes the switch to set the priority lower. The optional **diameter** parameter causes this command to lower the Hello, ForwardDelay, and MaxAge timers. (This command does not get placed into the configuration, but rather it acts as a macro, being expanded into the commands to set priority and the timers.)

**Note** When using the **primary** option, the **spanning-tree vlan** command sets the priority to 24,576 if the current root has a priority larger than 24,576 or its priority is 24,576 and its MAC address is higher than the current switch's MAC (that is, if setting the priority of 24,576 allows the current switch to become the root). Otherwise, this command sets this switch's priority to 4096 less than the current root. With the **secondary** keyword, this switch's priority is always set to 28,672. Also note that this logic applies to when the configuration command is executed; it does not dynamically change the priority if another switch later advertises a better priority.

# Rapid Spanning Tree Protocol

IEEE 802.1w *Rapid Spanning Tree Protocol (RSTP)* enhances the 802.1D standard with one goal in mind: improving STP convergence. Updates to the entire protocol operation are multifold and result in a dramatic increase of its convergence speed—well below 1 second in properly designed networks.

## New Port Roles, States and Types, and New Link Types

RSTP has significantly reworked the classification of port and link properties to streamline and optimize its operation. Properties of ports include port *states*, port *roles*, and port *types*. In addition, links interconnecting RSTP switches also have their *types*.

The number of port *states* has been reduced from five to three: While 802.1D STP defines Disabled, Blocking, Listening, Learning, and Forwarding states, 802.1w RSTP defines only Discarding, Learning, and Forwarding states. Discarding and Forwarding states are stable states; Learning is a transitory state. This cleanup relates to the fact that a port can either be in stable state, that is, Forwarding or Discarding, for an unlimited time in the absence of any topological changes, or can be in a transitory Learning state, going from Discarding to Forwarding over a limited time period. Table 3-5 compares the port states defined by each protocol.

**Table 3-5**    *RSTP and STP Port States*

| Administrative State | STP State (802.1D) | RSTP State (802.1w) |
| --- | --- | --- |
| Disabled | Disabled | Discarding |
| Enabled | Blocking | Discarding |
| Enabled | Listening | Discarding |
| Enabled | Learning | Learning |
| Enabled | Forwarding | Forwarding |

In RSTP, a Discarding state means that the port does not forward data frames, receive data frames, or learn source MAC addresses, regardless of whether the port was shut down, failed, or simply does not have a reason to forward frames. Note that even a Discarding port, similarly to the Blocking state in legacy STP, continues to process received BPDUs; send BPDUs (depending on its role); and send and receive frames of inter-switch signaling protocols such as DTP, VTP, CDP, LLDP, PAgP, LACP, or LOOP. The Discarding is also the default state of a port that has newly come alive (with the exception of an Edge port whose default state is Forwarding).

RSTP decouples the state of the port from its purpose, or a *role*, in a topology, and defines four separate port roles:

- Root Port (maintains its usual meaning)

- Designated Port (maintains its usual meaning)

- Alternate Port (a prospective replacement for the switch's own Root Port)

- Backup Port (a prospective replacement for the switch's own Designated Port into a shared segment)

This decoupling allows for better definition of what function a port fulfills in a topology without inferring its role purely from its state. Also, this split underlines the fact that during transitory periods, Root and Designated Ports can be put into Discarding or Learning states, or—as is in the case of the Proposal/Agreement process—these can be skipped. Table 3-6 lists individual RSTP port roles, how they are determined, and their purpose.

**Table 3-6**  *RSTP Port Roles*

| RSTP Role | Definition |
| --- | --- |
| Root Port | Same as 802.1D Root Port. |
| Designated Port | Same as 802.1D Designated Port. |
| Alternate Port | A replacement Root Port. Alternate Ports are ports receiving BPDUs from other switches but not meeting requirements to become Root or Designated. Such a port is attached to a neighboring switch and provides a possible alternate path toward the root. Upon the loss of the current Root Port, the Alternate Port receiving the best resulting BPDUs will be rapidly promoted to the role of Root Port and moved to the Forwarding state. |
| Backup Port | A replacement Designated Port. Backup Ports are ports receiving BPDUs from the same switch but not meeting requirements to become Designated. Such a port is attached to the same link as another port on the same switch, but the other port is Designated for that segment. The Backup Port is ready to take over if the DP fails; however, this takeover is not rapid. Rather, it is driven by timers. |

The Alternate Port concept offers protection against the loss of a switch's Root Port, also called a *direct link failure*, by keeping track of the Alternate Ports with a path to the root. If the current Root Port fails, RSTP will simply compare the resulting BPDUs (BPDUs stored on ports after incrementing the Root Path Cost by the receiving port's cost) on Alternate Ports and choose the port with the superior resulting BPDU as the new Root Port. This port will be immediately declared Root Forwarding. Figure 3-11 illustrates this process.

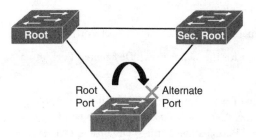

**Figure 3-11**  *Use of Alternate Port to Replace Lost Root Port (Direct Link Failure)*

The Backup Port role provides protection against losing the Designated Port attached to a shared link when the switch has another physical port attached to the same shared LAN. As this is a shared link, there is no rapid convergence. After the Designated Port fails, all Backup Ports for the same link become Designated Discarding after missing three BPDUs in a row from the former Designated Port (expiry of Rapid Spanning Tree [RST] BPDUs will be described in the next section). Out of them, only a single port will remain Designated Discarding; the others will again revert to Backup Discarding after receiving the BPDU from the newly elected Designated Port. This new Designated Port will gradually move from Discarding through Learning to Forwarding. As Proposals are not sent on ports connected to shared links, there is no way of safely moving a Backup Port to Designated rapidly.

The default role for a port that has newly come alive is Designated.

Finally, in RSTP, ports have *types*: A port can be either an Edge or a Non-Edge port. This property is already well known thanks to the Cisco PortFast feature. An Edge Port immediately becomes Designated Forwarding after coming up. It still sends BPDUs but it expects not to receive any. Should a BPDU be received by an Edge port, this port will revert to the Non-Edge type and start operating as a common RSTP port. No commands will be removed from the configuration; only the runtime operational type of the port will change. The port will again become an Edge port after it goes down and comes up again, either through disconnect/reconnect or through shutting it down and reactivating. There is no reliable way of automatically detecting whether a port is an Edge or a Non-Edge port. The default port type on Cisco Catalyst switches is Non-Edge.

Regarding links, RSTP recognizes two *link types*:

■ **Point-to-point link:** A link that connects an RSTP switch to at most one neighboring RSTP switch.

■ **Shared link:** A link that connects an RSTP switch to two or more neighboring switches.

In most modern LAN designs with no hubs or non-STP switches that create a shared communication environment from RSTP's viewpoint, all links would be of the point-to-point type. Most of RSTP's improvements in its reaction speed are usable only on point-to-point links. On shared links, RSTP reverts to slow operation driven by timers similar to STP. There is no reliable way of detecting whether a link is point-to-point or shared. However, Catalyst switches try to be somewhat smart in this aspect: If a port negotiates half-duplex operation with its connected neighbor, the switch assumes that the neighbor is a hub (as hubs are incapable of supporting full-duplex), and it will consider the link type to be shared. If a port negotiates full-duplex operation, the switch will assume that the neighbor is a switch running RSTP, and will treat the link as point-to-point. Obviously, this decision process is just a guess and there are easily presentable situations where this logic fails (for example, running half-duplex on a point-to-point link between two switches because of some technical difficulties or peculiarities of the link, or having three or more RSTP switches interconnected by an unmanaged switch together that do not run STP). There is no one-to-one correspondence between the duplex mode and the link type. In cases this heuristic fails, the link type can be configured on a per-port basis using the **spanning-tree link-type** { **point-to-point** | **shared** } command.

> **Note**    The default *port role* and *port state* are Designated Discarding—this is the combination of roles and states applied to a port at the moment it becomes live. The default *port type* is Non-Edge. The default *link type* depends on the duplex mode of the port—for full-duplex, it is point-to-point; for half-duplex, it is shared.

## Changes to BPDU Format and Handling

In RSTP, there is only a single type of BPDU used both for building a loop-free topology and for topology change notification purposes. TCN BPDUs are not used by RSTP. For RSTP, the Protocol Version field is set to 2 (legacy STP uses Version 0; Version 1 was an STP variant for Remote MAC Bridging according to the 802.1G standard but was never widely deployed).

The Flags field has been updated. In 802.1D STP BPDUs, only 2 bits out of 8 are used: TC (Topology Change) and TCA (Topology Change Acknowledgment). RSTP uses the 6 remaining bits as well to encode additional information: Proposal bit, Port Role bits, Learning bit, Forwarding bit, and Agreement bit. The TCA bit is not used by RSTP. This change allows implementing the Proposal/Agreement mechanism and also allows a BPDU to carry information about the originating port's role and state, forming the basis of RSTP's Dispute mechanism, protecting against issues caused by unidirectional links.

In STP, Configuration BPDUs are originated by the root switch only. A nonroot switch does not originate its own Configuration BPDUs; rather, it waits for a BPDU to arrive on its Root Port to relay it farther out its own Designated Ports after updating its contents. This delays an appropriate reaction to a sudden loss of received BPDUs on a port—their lack only indicates a problem somewhere between the root switch and the current switch. The switch needs to wait for MaxAge-MessageAge seconds for the BPDU stored on the Root Port to expire. In RSTP, each switch originates BPDUs on its own, with their contents nevertheless based on the information from the BPDU stored on the switch's Root Port. RSTP BPDUs therefore become more similar to a Hello mechanism known from routing protocols. If a switch ceases to receive RSTP BPDUs on its port, it is certain that the problem is contained on the link between this switch and its neighbor. This allows RSTP switches to age out BPDUs much sooner—in a *3x Hello* interval. Three missing Hellos in a row cause a port to age out the stored BPDU. The MessageAge field value no longer has an influence on BPDU's expiry. Instead, it serves the role of a hop count. Any BPDU whose MessageAge is equal to or higher than its MaxAge will be discarded upon arrival.

RSTP improves handling of inferior BPDUs sent by the designated switch on a segment. In STP, if a designated switch (that is, a switch having a Designated Port on a segment) suddenly started sending BPDUs that are inferior to the BPDUs sent earlier, remaining switches on the segment would ignore them until the superior BPDU expired from their ports, which is after MessageAge-MaxAge seconds (values taken from the superior BPDU). In RSTP, an inferior BPDU originated by a designated switch on a segment is accepted right away, immediately replacing previously stored BPDUs on receiving ports of attached switches. In other words, if a designated switch on a segment suddenly sends an inferior BPDU, other switches on the segment will immediately accept it as if the superior stored BPDU expired just when the inferior BPDU arrived, and reevaluate their own port roles and states on the segment according to usual rules. This behavior allows a switch to rapidly react to a situation where the neighboring switch experiences a disruptive change in its own connectivity toward the root switch (this is called an *indirect link failure*). Consider the situation in Figure 3-12.

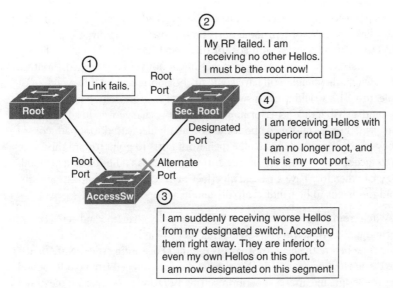

**Figure 3-12**  *Accepting Inferior BPDUs from Designated Switch (Indirect Link Failure)*

To better understand the need for this improvement, it is important to realize that if an inferior BPDU arrives from the designated switch, the designated switch or its own upstream switches must have encountered a change for the worse to their connectivity toward the root switch—the root path cost might have increased, or the Root Bridge ID itself might have changed to a higher value. If the root path cost has increased, the neighboring switch might no longer be using the shortest available path toward the root switch, and possibly, the next shortest path to the root switch might be through the current switch. If the Root Bridge ID has increased, the neighboring switch believes that the root switch has changed, but the true root switch might be different. In both cases, this inferior information has to be processed immediately to find out whether the neighboring switch has to be updated about the root switch's identity or about a better path toward it. This is accomplished by accepting and processing the inferior BPDU, and running the usual sequence of steps: reevaluating the role of the switch (whether it should become the root switch itself), reevaluating the choice of a Root Port, and reevaluating roles of remaining ports. If the port toward the neighbor becomes Designated (before the change, it could only have been Root or Alternate), it will start sending BPDUs, thereby updating the neighbor about the root switch and the available root path cost.

## Proposal/Agreement Process in RSTP

Improvements described so far allow a switch or its neighbors to rapidly recover from a *lost connectivity* to the root switch. However, a connectivity disruption can also be caused by *adding a new link* into the topology that causes one of the switches to reelect its Root Port and place it on the added link (that is, the added link provides a better path to the root switch). RSTP uses the Proposal/Agreement process on a point-to-point link to rapidly put such a link into operation without causing a temporary switching loop or significant interruptions in the communication.

If a newly added point-to-point link causes one of the attached switches to place its Root Port on this new link, the roles of remaining ports on this switch can move from Root or Alternate to Designated (the root path cost of this switch can decrease below the costs of its neighbors). As the neighboring switches might not yet be informed about the changes on this switch, they might still have some of their ports toward this switch in the Designated role, too. This would cause a switching loop. Therefore, a loop has to be prevented locally on the switch that is performing its Root Port changeover. In addition, after the neighboring switches are informed about the potentially decreased root path cost of this switch, they might also decide to change their Root Ports to point toward this switch, causing them to face the very same task as the current switch. An addition of a new link to the topology can therefore have a cascading effect of several switches updating their Root Ports, and this needs to be handled rapidly and in a loop-free manner.

Preventing a switch from creating a switching loop by rapidly changing and activating its Root Port can be done by having this switch put all its Non-Edge Designated ports into Discarding state before the new Root Port is put into Forwarding state. Note that the Non-Edge Designated ports include those ports that have moved from old Root and Alternate roles to Designated after a superior resulting BPDU was received on the new Root Port and the switch reevaluated the roles of all ports.

This procedure alone would allow a switch to rapidly change its Root Port while maintaining a loop-free topology, but at the same time, it would cause a major disruption in the communication because the switch is effectively isolated from the network: While its new Root Port might be made Forwarding, the upstream neighbor's Designated Port on the added link is still in the Discarding or Learning state. In addition, all Non-Edge Designated ports on this switch have been put into the Discarding state as well to prevent a possible loop. To avoid waiting twice for the ForwardDelay timer, an explicit signaling scheme between the switches needs to be used, allowing them to confirm that it is safe to put a Designated Port into the Forwarding state.

This signaling scheme is called *Proposal/Agreement*. The *Proposal* signifies the willingness of a port to become Designated Forwarding, while the *Agreement* stands for permission to do so immediately. After a new link point-to-point link is added between two switches, ports on both ends will come up as Designated Discarding, the default role and state for a Non-Edge port. Any Designated Port in a Discarding or Learning state sends BPDUs with the Proposal bit set. Both switches will therefore attempt to exchange BPDUs with the Proposal bit set (or simply a Proposal), assuming that they have the right to be Designated. However, if one of the ports receiving a Proposal discovers that the Proposal constitutes the best received resulting BPDU, its role will change from Designated to Root (the state will remain Discarding yet). Other port roles on that switch will also be updated accordingly. Furthermore, a switch receiving a Proposal on its Root Port will immediately put all its Non-Edge Designated ports into a Discarding state. This operation is called *Sync*. A switch in Sync state is now isolated from the network, preventing any switching loop from passing through it: Its Root Port is still in the Discarding state (and even if it was Forwarding, the neighboring Designated Port is still Discarding or Learning), and its own Designated Ports are intentionally moved to the Discarding state. Now it is safe to move the new Root Port to the Forwarding state and inform the upstream switch that it is now allowed to move its Designated Discarding or Learning port to the Forwarding state. This is accomplished by a switch sending a BPDU with the Agreement bit set (or simply an Agreement) through its Root Port after performing the Sync. Upon receiving an Agreement on its Designated Discarding or Learning port, the upstream switch will immediately move that port into the Forwarding state, completing the Proposal/Agreement exchange between two switches.

As a result of the Proposal/Agreement and Sync operation, all Non-Edge Designated ports on the switch with the new Root Port have been moved to the Discarding state. Because all Designated Discarding and Designated Learning ports send Proposals, the Proposal/Agreement exchange has effectively moved from "above" the switch to "beneath" it (with respect to the root switch being at the "top" of the spanning tree), constituting the cascading effect of switches pairwise reevaluating their choice of Root Ports, expressing their willingness to have their Designated Ports made Forwarding rapidly (Proposals), and eventually receiving approvals to do so (Agreements). This process is illustrated in Figure 3-13, showing a wave-like sending of Proposals, performing Sync and generating Agreements in turn while pushing the Proposal/Agreement exchange downstream.

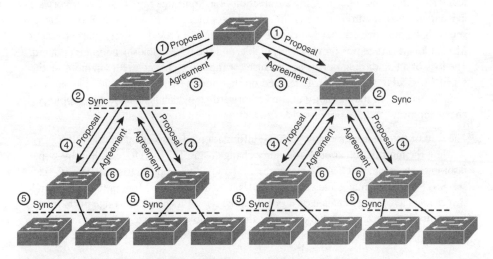

**Figure 3-13**   *Proposal/Agreement Mechanism in RSTP*

**Note**   Outages in a switched network can be caused by direct link failures (a switch losing its Root Port), indirect link failures (a neighbor losing its Root Port), adding a new root link, or a root switch changeover. RSTP has reaction mechanisms for each of these events: Direct link failures are handled by the best Alternate Port becoming a new Root Port, indirect link failures are handled by the concept of accepting inferior BPDUs from designated switches, adding a new root link is handled by the Proposal/Agreement mechanism, and the changeover of a root switch is handled by the combination of the mechanisms above.

**Note**   During the Proposal/Agreement exchange, all Non-Edge Designated ports will be moved to Discarding state (the Sync operation). If ports toward end hosts are not explicitly configured as Edge ports using the **spanning-tree portfast** port level command or the **spanning-tree portfast default** global level command (both have an effect on access ports only), they will become Discarding during Sync. Because end hosts are incapable of sending RSTP Agreements, these ports will require twice the ForwardDelay interval to become Forwarding again, and the end hosts will experience major connectivity outages. In RSTP, it is of crucial importance to configure ports toward end hosts as Edge ports; otherwise the performance of the network might be perceived as being even worse than with 802.1D STP.

## Topology Change Handling in RSTP

As opposed to STP, which recognizes four distinct events as topology change events, RSTP simplifies this concept: Only a transition of a Non-Edge port from a non-Forwarding state to the Forwarding state is considered a topology change event in RSTP. The reason is that a port that has newly become Forwarding can provide a better path to a set of MAC addresses than was previously available, and the CAM tables need to be updated. The loss of a Forwarding port is not a cause for topology change event anymore, as the set of MAC addresses previously learned on that port is definitely inaccessible unless some other port in the topology becomes Forwarding (which is handled as a topology change anyway) and possibly provides an alternate path toward them.

The way of propagating topology change information has also changed. Instead of forwarding the information about a topology change using TCN BPDUs in a hop-by-hop fashion to the root switch and causing the root switch to send BPDUs with the TC flag set, RSTP switches immediately flood BPDUs with TC flag set. More precisely, a switch that *detects* a topology change on a port (that is, one of its own Non-Edge ports transitions into the Forwarding state) or *learns* about a topology change on a port (a BPDU with the TC flag set is received on its Root or Designated Port) will do the following:

- Set a so-called tcWhile timer to the value of the Hello time plus one second (older revisions of RSTP set this value to twice the Hello time) on all remaining Non-Edge Designated ports and Root Port if any, except the port on which the topology change was detected or learned.

- Immediately flush all MAC addresses learned on these ports.

- Send BPDUs with the TC flag set on these ports every Hello seconds until the tcWhile timer expires.

This way, information about a topology change is rapidly flooded along the spanning tree in the form of BPDUs with the TC flag set, and causes switches to immediately flush their CAM tables for all ports except those ports on which the topology change was detected or learned, as they point in the direction of the topology change where a set of MAC addresses might have become reachable through a new or improved path.

Edge ports never cause a topology change event, and MAC addresses learned on them are not flushed during topology change event handling.

### Rapid Per-VLAN Spanning Tree Plus (RPVST+)

RPVST+ is a form of running RSTP on a per-VLAN basis, analogous to PVST+. This provides the subsecond convergence of RSTP with the advantages of PVST+ described in the previous section. Thus, RPVST+ and RSTP share the same characteristics such as convergence time, Hello behavior, the election process, port states, and so on. RPVST+ is backwardly compatible with PVST+. Also the rules of interoperation of RPVST+ with CST regions running RSTP are the same.

Configuring RPVST+ is straightforward. In global configuration mode, issue the **spanning-tree mode rapid-pvst** command. Also, it is very important to configure ports toward end hosts as Edge ports—either on a per-port basis using the **spanning-tree portfast** command or globally using the **spanning-tree portfast default** command. Both these commands have an effect only on ports operating in access mode. Additionally, as explained earlier, most RSTP improvements are applicable only on point-to-point links. If the physical connections between switches are of the point-to-point nature but operate in half-duplex (abnormal for a correct point-to-point interconnection!), Cisco switches will treat these links as shared, as also evidenced by the acronym Shr in the **show spanning-tree** output. In these rare cases, if the link is truly point-to-point, the link type can be overridden using the **spanning-tree link-type point-to-point** interface level command. Apart from these specific configurations, all other configuration commands are of the same meaning as in PVST+. See the "Further Reading" section, later in this chapter, for a source of more information on RPVST+.

**Note**   For RSTP and consequently RPVST+ to provide rapid reaction to changes in the network topology, all switches must run RSTP or RPVST+, all inter-switch links must be properly installed and recognized as point-to-point links, and all ports toward end stations must be properly identified as edge ports. Failure to meet these three requirements will degrade the RSTP and RPVST+ performance, voiding its advantages. Ports toward legacy switches will revert to legacy 802.1D STP or PVST+ operation. On shared links, RSTP and RPVST+ revert to timers. On non-edge ports, RSTP and RPVST+ rely on the Proposal/Agreement procedure to provide rapid reaction, and if the neighboring device does not speak RSTP or RPVST+, it will not be able to send an Agreement in response to a Proposal.

## Multiple Spanning Trees: IEEE 802.1s

IEEE 802.1s *Multiple Spanning Trees (MST)*, sometimes referred to as *Multiple STP (MSTP)*, defines a standards-based way to use multiple instances of STP in a network that uses 802.1Q VLANs. The following are some of the main benefits of 802.1s:

■   Like PVST+, it allows the tuning of STP parameters on a per-instance basis so that while some port blocks for one set of VLANs, the same port can forward in another set of VLANs.

- As opposed to PVST+, it does not run a separate STP instance for each and every VLAN because that is largely unnecessary: Usually only a handful of different spanning trees is required and configured in a network. Running a separate STP instance for each VLAN in PVST+ merely results in multiple instances creating exactly the same spanning tree while consuming multifold system resources. Instead, MST runs in instances whose existence is not directly related to any particular VLAN. Instances are created by configuration, and VLANs are subsequently mapped onto them. Spanning tree created by an MST instance is shared by all VLANs mapped onto that instance.

- Use 802.1w RSTP for rapid convergence in each instance, inheriting all its rapid convergence properties. The following advantages have been retained: general RSTP rules about BPDU expiry in a 3x Hello interval, acceptances of inferior BPDUs from designated switches, port roles/states/types, link types, Proposal/Agreement, and so on.

- At press time, various Catalyst platforms have a limit on the maximum number of concurrent STP instances. The 2960, 3560, and 3750 platforms, for example, support at most 128 STP instances. If more than 128 VLANs are created and active on ports, some VLANs will not have any STP instance running and will not be protected against switching loops. If decreasing the number of active VLANs is not an option, neither PVST+ nor RPVST+ can be used, and MST is the only choice.

- MST is the only standards-based and interoperable version of STP supporting VLANs and suitable in multivendor switched environments.

## MST Principles of Operation

**Key Topic**

MST organizes the network into one or more *regions*. An MST region is a group of switches that together use MST in a consistent way—they run the same number of MST instances and map the same sets of VLANs onto these instances, among other things. For example, in Figure 3-14, an MST region has been defined, along with connections to non-MST switches. Focusing on the left side of the figure, inside the MST region, you really need only two instances of STP—one each for roughly half of the VLANs. With two instances, the access layer switches will forward on their links to SW1 for one set of VLANs using one MST instance, and forward on their links to SW2 for the other set of VLANs using the second MST instance.

One of the key benefits of MST over PVST+ is that it requires only one MST instance for a group of VLANs. If this MST region had hundreds of VLANs, and used PVST+, hundreds of sets of STP messages would be used. With MST, only one set of STP messages is needed for each MST instance.

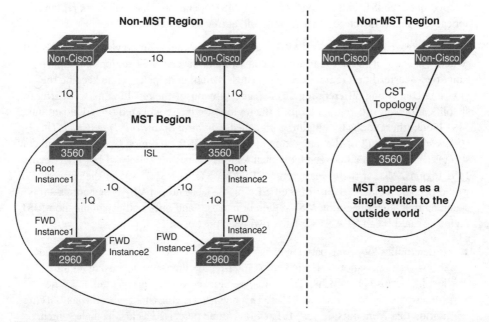

**Figure 3-14** *MST Operations*

MST reuses the concept of System ID Extension from IEEE 802.1t to embed the instance number into the Bridge ID. As the System ID Extension field contains 12 bits, the range of MST instance numbers is in the range of 0–4095, though at the time of this writing, different Catalyst platforms supported different ranges: 0–15 on Catalyst 2950, and 0–4094 on Catalyst 2960 and 3560. Furthermore, the MST standard allows for at most 65 active MST instances (instance 0 plus at most 64 user-definable instances). Apart from being higher than any reasonable network would require, this limit is also motivated by the fact that MST uses a *single* BPDU to carry information about all instances, and it must fit into a single Ethernet frame. While a typical Ethernet MTU of 1500B would allow for approximately 88 MST instances in total, the limit of 64 user-definable instances is sufficient for any practical needs and fits well into an ordinary Ethernet frame. In MST, a port sends BPDUs if it is Designated for at least one MST instance. As MST uses a single BPDU for all instances, it is possible to see both switches on a point-to-point link to send BPDUs to each other if each of these switches is Designated in a different MST instance.

Out of all MST instances, the instance 0 has a special meaning. This instance is also called the *Internal Spanning Tree*, or IST, and serves several purposes. First, this instance always exists even if no other MST instances are created, providing a loop-free environment to VLANs mapped onto it within a region. Without any additional configuration, all VLANs are mapped onto the IST. Second, the IST is the only instance that interacts with STP run on switches outside the MST region. Whatever port role and state are determined by the interaction of IST on a region boundary with a neighboring switch, this role and state will be inherited by all existing VLANs on that port, not just by VLANs mapped onto the IST. This is a part of overall MST operations that makes the region appear as a single switch to other regions and non-MST switches.

If the network consists of several MST regions, each of them can be visualized as a single switch. The view of the entire topology consisting of several MST regions can thus be simplified—instead of a region, imagine a single switch in its place while keeping the links interconnecting different regions in place. Obviously, the resulting network after this simplification can still contain loops if the regions are interconnected by redundant links. MST blocks these loops by building a so-called *Common Spanning Tree (CST)*. This CST is simply a result of the interaction of individual ISTs on region boundaries, and constitutes a spanning tree between individual regions, consisting purely of links between MST regions. Also, if there was a non-MST (either STP or RSTP) part of the network, it would become an integral part of the CST. This CST has no per-VLAN semantics—it is a spanning tree interconnecting MST region boundaries and optionally spanning non-MST regions, shared by all VLANs. CST has two main purposes:

■ It determines loop-free paths between regions. An important consequence is that loops between regions are blocked on inter-region links and not inside regions, just like loops between switches would be blocked on the inter-switch links, not somewhere "inside" those switches. This behavior is consistent with the simplifying notion that from outside, an MST region can be perceived as just a single switch.

■ CST is the only spanning tree that can be understood and participated in by non-MST (that is, STP and RSTP) switches, facilitating the interoperation between MST and its predecessors. In mixed environments with MST and STP/RSTP, STP/RSTP switches unknowingly participate in CST. Costs in CST reflect only the costs of links between regions and in non-MST parts of the network. These costs are called *external costs* by MST.

**Key Topic**

In each MST region, the CST on the region's boundary merges with the IST inside the region. The resulting tree consists of a loop-free interconnection between MST regions "glued together" with loop-free interconnection inside each MST region, and is called the *Common and Internal Spanning Tree*, or CIST. This tree is the union of CST between regions and ISTs inside individual regions, and is a single spanning tree that spans the entire switched topology. As each MST region has its own IST root, CIST—consisting of ISTs inside regions and CST between regions—can have multiple root switches as a result. These switches are recognized as the CIST Root Switch (exactly one for the entire CIST) and CIST Regional Root Switches (exactly one for the IST inside each region). CIST Regional Root Switch is simply a different name for an IST root switch inside a particular region.

The CIST Root Switch is elected by the lowest Bridge ID from all switches that participate in CIST, that is, from all MST switches across all regions according to their IST Bridge IDs (composed of IST priority, instance number 0, and their base MAC address), and from all STP/RSTP switches, if present, according to the only Bridge IDs they have. If running a pure MST-based network, the CIST Root Switch will be the switch whose IST priority is the lowest (numerically), and in the case of a tie, the switch with the lowest base MAC address. This switch will also become the root of IST inside its own MST region; that is, it will also be the CIST Regional Root Switch. As the CIST Root Switch has the lowest known Bridge ID in the CST, it is automatically the CST Root as well, although this observation would be important only in cases of mixed MST and non-MST environments.

In other MST regions that do not contain the CIST Root Switch, only MST switches at the region boundary (that is, having links to other regions) are allowed to join the IST root switch elections. The remaining internal switches in the region will not participate in these elections. Summing up the options, a switch is allowed to attempt to become the IST root switch only in the following two cases: Either it is the CIST Root Switch, in which case it becomes the IST root automatically, or it is a boundary switch receiving BPDUs from a different MST or a non-MST region. From boundary switches, IST root switches are elected first by their lowest *external root path cost* to the CIST Root Switch. The external root path cost is the sum of costs of inter-region links to reach the region with the CIST Root Switch, or in other words, the CST cost of reaching the region with the CIST Root Switch; costs of links inside regions are not taken into account. In case of a tie, the lowest IST Bridge ID of boundary switches is used. Note that these rules significantly depart from the usual concept of the root switch having the lowest Bridge ID. In MST regions that do not contain the CIST Root Switch, the regional IST root switches might not necessarily be the ones with the lowest Bridge IDs.

A CIST Regional Root Switch has a particular importance for a region: Its own CIST Root Port, that is, the Root Port to reach the CIST Root Switch outside the region, is called the Master port (this is an added port role in MST), and provides connectivity from the region toward the CIST Root for all MST instances inside the region.

## Interoperability Between MST and Other STP Versions

To understand the interoperation between MST and other STP versions, we first need to have a look at the way MST interoperates with non-MST switches running pure IEEE 802.1D STP or 802.1w RSTP without any per-VLAN semantics (let us call them simply non-MST switches). These non-MST switches run a single STP instance for all VLANs and so all VLANs share the same single spanning tree in the non-MST part of the network. Whatever role and state a non-MST switch puts a port into, this role and state are shared by all VLANs on that port. If a non-MST switch is to interoperate with one or more neighboring MST switches, these MST switches must give the impression of running a single STP or RSTP to non-MST switches. Also, because STP and RSTP do not understand nor see into the workings of MST in individual instances inside an MST region, the entire MST region is a single "black box" to STP and RSTP. It is quite logical, then, to treat this single "black box" as a single huge switch. This single switch must speak a single instance of STP or RSTP on its boundary ports toward its non-MST neighbors, and whatever decisions are made about port roles and states on this boundary, they must apply to all VLANs. The non-MST switches accomplish this trivially by the very way they run IEEE STP/RSTP; the MST switches do this by speaking exclusively the MST instance 0, also called the IST, on boundary ports, formatted into ordinary STP or RSTP BPDUs, and applying the negotiated port roles and states on boundary ports to all

VLANs on those ports. The MST instance 0 has a key role here—it speaks to non-MST neighbors and it processes BPDUs received from them.

The interoperation between an MST region and an older IEEE STP variant is relatively straightforward. The non-MST region speaks a single STP/RSTP instance. The MST region uses the IST to speak on behalf of the entire region to non-MST neighbors on boundary ports. The resulting boundary port roles and states derived from the interaction of IEEE STP/RSTP and IST are binding for all VLANs.

Interaction between MSTP and Cisco's PVST+ is significantly more complex to understand. PVST+ regions by definition run one STP or RSTP instance for each active VLAN. It might be tempting at first to have each received PVST+ BPDU processed by the particular MST instance to which the respective VLAN is mapped. This idea is futile, however. There can be two or more VLANs mapped to the same MST instance that have completely different root bridges, root path costs, and so on in the PVST+ region. Which root bridge IDs, root path costs, and other STP attributes shall be taken into account by this MST instance, then? Clearly, the idea of doing any "smart" mapping between PVST+ and MST instances is not the way to go.

Instead, the idea of interoperation between MST and PVST+ stems from the basic idea of interoperation between MST and IEEE STP/RSTP. For both MST and PVST+ regions, a *single* representative is chosen to speak on behalf of the entire region, and the interaction between these two representatives determines the boundary port roles and states for all VLANs. Doing this is trickier than it seems, though. While the role and state of an MST boundary will be unconditionally imposed on all VLANs active on that port (that is how MST boundary ports work), PVST+ ports have independent roles and states for each VLAN. If a single representative MST instance is chosen to speak on behalf of an MST region, its information must be delivered to PVST+ switches in such a way that every PVST+ instance receives the same information to make an identical, *consistent* choice. The word *consistent* becomes very important—it describes a process where both MST and PVST+ in all their instances arrive at the same port role and state determination even though only a single MST instance and a single PVST+ instance directly interact with each other. The purpose of the *PVST Simulation* mechanism is to allow for a consistent interoperation between MST and PVST+ regions.

In the MST-to-PVST+ direction, the MST region again chooses the IST as the representative, with the goal of speaking IST information to all PVST+ instances using PVST+ BPDUs. To allow the PVST+ region to make an identical, *consistent* decision based on IST's attributes for all known VLANs, all PVST+ instances must receive the same IST information formatted in PVST+ BPDUs. Therefore, MST boundary ports replicate the IST's BPDUs into PVST+ BPDUs for all active VLANs. This way, the MST supplies PVST+ neighbors with *consistent* information in all VLANs. A PVST+ neighbor receiving these BPDUs on any single port will therefore make an identical, *consistent* choice of that port's role and state for all VLANs.

In the opposite direction, MST takes the VLAN 1 as the representative of the entire PVST+ region, and processes the information received in VLAN 1's BPDUs in IST. The boundary port's role and state will be binding for all VLANs active on that port. However, MST must make sure that the boundary's port role and state as determined by interaction with VLAN 1's STP instance truly represent the choice that all other PVST+ instances would also make; that is, it must ascertain whether the result of IST's interaction with VLAN 1's STP instance is *consistent* with the state of STP instances run in other VLANs.

Let us analyze this in closer detail. The interaction of IST run on an MST boundary port and VLAN 1 PVST+ can basically result in three possible roles of the port: Designated, Root, or Non-Designated (whether that is Alternate or Backup is not relevant at this point).

An MST boundary port will become a Designated Port if the BPDUs it sends out (carrying IST data) are superior to incoming VLAN 1 PVST+ BPDUs. A Designated boundary port will unconditionally become Forwarding for all VLANs, not just for VLAN 1. Therefore, to make sure that the other PVST+ instances make a *consistent* decision, the boundary port must verify whether other PVST+ instances would also consider it to be a Designated Port. This is trivially accomplished by listening to all incoming PVST+ BPDUs and making sure that each of them is inferior to the boundary port's own BPDUs. This forms our first PVST Simulation consistency criterion:

> *PVST+ BPDUs for all VLANs arriving at a Designated boundary port must be inferior to its own BPDUs derived from IST.*

Conversely, an MST boundary port will become a Root Port toward the CIST root bridge if the incoming VLAN 1 PVST+ BPDUs are so superior that they not only beat the boundary port's own BPDUs but also are the best VLAN 1 PVST+ BPDUs received on any of the boundary ports. Obviously, this situation implies that the CIST Root is located in the PVST+ region and it is the root switch for VLAN 1. A root boundary port will unconditionally become forwarding for all VLANs. Therefore, to make sure that the other PVST+ instances make a consistent decision, the boundary port must also act like a Root Port toward root bridges in all remaining VLANs. This in turn implies that the root bridges for these VLANs must also be located in the PVST+ region and the Root Port toward them is exactly this particular boundary port. A simple, yet sufficient condition to make this happen is to verify whether incoming PVST+ BPDUs for VLANs other than 1 are identical or even superior to incoming PVST+ BPDUs for VLAN 1. This forms our second consistency PVST Simulation criterion:

> *PVST+ BPDUs for VLANs other than VLAN 1 arriving at a root boundary port must be identical or superior to PVST+ BPDUs for VLAN 1.*

Note that if System ID Extension is used, PVST+ BPDUs for different VLANs cannot be identical, and in fact, with the same priority on a PVST+ root switch for multiple VLANs, PVST+ BPDU for VLAN $x$ is inferior to BPDU for VLAN $y$ if $x>y$. Therefore, to meet the second consistency criterion, priorities for PVST+ root switches in VLANs other than VLAN 1 must be lower by at least 4096 from the priority of the PVST+ VLAN 1 root switch.

In both these cases, if the criterion for a particular port role is not met, the PVST Simulation process will declare a PVST Simulation inconsistency and will keep the port in the blocked state until the consistency criterion for the port's role is met again. Older switches report the offending port as Root Inconsistent; recent switches use the PVST Simulation Inconsistent designation instead.

Finally, an MST boundary port will become a Non-Designated port if the incoming VLAN 1 PVST+ BPDUs are superior to its own BPDUs but not that superior to make this port a Root Port. A Non-Designated boundary port will unconditionally become Blocking for all VLANs. Therefore, to make sure that the other PVST+ instances make a consistent decision, the boundary port should verify whether also other PVST+ instances would consider it to be a Non-Designated port. This could be trivially accomplished by listening to all incoming PVST+ BPDUs and making sure that each of them is superior to the boundary port's own BPDU; however, Cisco appears to have implemented a slight optimization here. If indeed this criterion was met, all PVST+ instances would consistently consider this port to be a Non-Designated port and the port would be blocked according to its Non-Designated role. If, however, this criterion was not met, that is, at least one non-VLAN1 PVST+ BPDU was inferior to this port's BPDU, the PVST Simulation inconsistency would be declared, and the port would be kept blocked. So in any case, the port will be blocked. Hence, for Non-Designated ports, there are no consistency checks performed because the port is blocked regardless.

If it is necessary to operate a mixed MST and PVST+ network, it is recommended to make sure that the MST region appears as a root switch to all PVST+ instances by lowering its IST root's priority below the priorities of all PVST+ switches in all VLANs.

It is noteworthy to mention that if a Cisco MST switch faces a pure 802.1D STP or 802.1w RSTP switch, it will revert to the appropriate STP version on the interconnecting port, that is, STP or RSTP, according to the neighbor type. However, if a Cisco MST switch is connected to a PVST+ or RPVST+ switch, it will *always* revert to PVST+. In other words, Cisco MST interoperates with RPVST+ regions using only PVST+, reverting to PVST+ operation on a region boundary. This is an implementor's decision made to simplify the interworking between MST and RPVST+ regions—it requires less state to be stored and processed, particularly with respect to the Proposal/Agreement mechanism.

**Note**   PVST Simulation consistency criteria require that for an MST Boundary port toward a PVST+ region to be Forwarding, one of the following conditions must be met:

■ Either the boundary port's own IST BPDUs are superior to all received PVST+ BPDUs regardless of their VLAN (in this case, the port becomes Designated; "if be Designated Port for VLAN 1, then be Designated Port for all VLANs")

■ Or the boundary port's own IST BPDUs are inferior to received PVST+ BPDUs for VLAN 1, and *they* are in turn identical or inferior to received PVST+ BPDUs for other VLANs (in this case, the port becomes Root Port; "if be Root Port for VLAN 1, then be Root Port for all VLANs")

## MST Configuration

Configuring MST requires a certain degree of prior planning. First, it is necessary to decide whether multiple regions shall be used and where their boundaries shall be placed. Multiple regions allow having independent numbers of MST instances, VLAN-to-instance mappings, and individual instance roots in each region. The overall network operation can become more complex to understand and maintain, though. Each region must be subsequently assigned its name, configuration revision number, and VLAN-to-instance mapping table. The name, revision number, and VLAN-to-instance mappings are three mandatory elements of MST configuration and must match on all switches of a single region. The name and configuration revision number are carried in MST BPDUs in their plain form. Instead of transmitting the entire VLAN-to-instance mapping table, an MD5 hash is performed over it and its value is carried in MST BPDUs. The region name, revision number, and the MD5 hash of the VLAN-to-instance mapping table are compared upon BPDU arrival and must match for two switches to consider themselves being in the same region. The hash value can be displayed using the **show spanning-tree mst configuration digest** EXEC command. On older switches, the **digest** keyword might be hidden but nevertheless accepted if typed in its entirety.

A modification to the MST region configuration (name, revision, mapping of VLANs onto instances) on a single switch causes the switch to create its own region and trigger a topology change, possibly causing a transient network outage. Upgrading an MST region to a new configuration will therefore require a maintenance window. As changes to VLAN-to-instance mappings are most common, it is recommended to premap VLANs into instances even before the VLANs are created. Creating (or deleting) a VLAN after it is mapped to an instance will not cause any topology change event with respect to MST.

If it is necessary to operate a mixed MST and PVST+ network, it is recommended to make sure that the MST region becomes the region containing the CIST Root Switch. This can be accomplished by lowering the IST root switch's priority (that is, the priority of the existing root of instance 0 in the MST region) below the priorities of all PVST+ switches in all VLANs.

Finally, older Cisco switches have implemented a prestandard version of MST that differs in the BPDU format and some other details. A quick test to verify whether the switch supports the standard or prestandard MST version is to issue the **show spanning-tree mst configuration digest** command. If there is only a single MD5 digest displayed in the output, the switch supports prestandard MST only. If there are two MD5 digests displayed, the switch supports standard MST and also the prestandard MST for backward compatibility. If a switch implementing standard MST is to be connected to a switch running prestandard MST, the port toward the prestandard switch must be configured with the **spanning-tree mst pre-standard** command; otherwise, permanent switching loops can ensue or the switch will keep the port blocking until configured with this command.

Configuration of MST can be accomplished by following these steps:

**Step 1.**   Enter MST configuration mode by using the **spanning-tree mst configuration** command.

**Step 2.**   From MST configuration mode, create an MST region name (up to 32 characters) by using the **name** subcommand.

**Step 3.**   From MST configuration mode, define an MST revision number by using the **revision** command.

**Step 4.**   From MST configuration mode, map VLANs to an MST STP instance by using the **instance** command.

**Step 5.**   From MST configuration mode, after reviewing the MST configuration before performing the changes using the **show current** command and after the changes using the **show pending** command, you can either apply the changes using the **exit** command or cancel the changes using the **abort** command. Both commands will exit from the MST configuration mode.

**Step 6.**   Globally enable MST using the **spanning-tree mode mst** command.

Example 3-2 demonstrates configuring a switch with an MST region.

**Example 3-2**   *MST Configuration and* **show** *Commands*

```
! First, the MST region configuration is entered, defining the name of the region
! to be CCIE, the configuration revision to 1, and creating four instances
! with different VLANs mapped onto them. Note that the VLANs do not need to be
! created at all; they can be pre-mapped into MST instances and created later.
! The show current shows the current (empty at the moment) MST configuration,
! the show pending shows the modified but still unapplied configuration.

SW1(config)# spanning-tree mst configuration
SW1(config-mst)# name CCIE
SW1(config-mst)# revision 1
SW1(config-mst)# instance 1 vlan 1-500
SW1(config-mst)# instance 2 vlan 501-1000
SW1(config-mst)# instance 3 vlan 1001-2047
SW1(config-mst)# instance 4 vlan 2048-4094
SW1(config-mst)# show current
Current MST configuration
Name       []
Revision   0     Instances configured 1


Instance  Vlans mapped
--------  -----------------------------------------------------------------------
0         1-4094
          -----------------------------------------------------------------------


SW1(config-mst)# show pending
Pending MST configuration
Name       [CCIE]
Revision   1     Instances configured 5


Instance  Vlans mapped
--------  -----------------------------------------------------------------------
0         none
1         1-500
```

```
2          501-1000
3          1001-2047
4          2048-4094
----------------------------------------------------------------------------
SW1(config-mst)# exit
SW1(config)# spanning-tree mode mst

! To modify the switch's priority, spanning-tree mst instance priority command
! must be used instead of spanning-tree vlan vlan-id priority. Also, modifying
! a port's cost or priority is accomplished using spanning-tree cost mst and
! spanning-tree port-priority mst commands instead of their counterparts utilizing
! the vlan keyword. They have no effect in MST mode.

SW1(config)# spanning-tree mst 0 priority 0
SW1(config)# spanning-tree mst 1 priority 4096
SW1(config)# spanning-tree mst 2 priority 8192

! If switches in the region support VTPv3 then VTPv3 can be used to synchronize
! the MST region configuration across all switches in the VTP domain. As all
! switches in the VTP domain will share the same MST region configuration, they
! will all become members of the same MST region. Hence, there is a 1:1 relation
! between a VTPv3 domain and the MST region.

SW1(config)# vtp domain CCIE
Changing VTP domain name from NULL to CCIE
*Mar 12 16:12:14.697: %SW_VLAN-6-VTP_DOMAIN_NAME_CHG: VTP domain name changed to
  CCIE.
SW1(config)# vtp version 3
SW1(config)#
*Mar 12 16:12:18.606: %SW_VLAN-6-OLD_CONFIG_FILE_READ: Old version 2 VLAN
  configuration file detected and read OK.  Version 3
    files will be written in the future.
SW1(config)# vtp mode server mst
Setting device to VTP Server mode for MST.
SW1(config)# do vtp primary mst
This system is becoming primary server for feature  mst
No conflicting VTP3 devices found.
Do you want to continue? [confirm]
*Mar 12 16:12:46.422: %SW_VLAN-4-VTP_PRIMARY_SERVER_CHG: 0023.ea41.ca00 has become
  the primary server for the MST VTP feature
SW1(config)#

! From this moment on, the entire spanning-tree mst configuration section will be
! synchronized across the entire VTPv3 domain, and changes to its contents on SW1
```

```
! as the primary server switch will be propagated to all switches in the domain.
! Note that MST region configuration revision is independent of VTPv3 revision
! number and will not be incremented by VTP automatically. VTP uses its own
! revision number which will be incremented.
```

# Protecting and Optimizing STP

This section covers several switch configuration tools that protect STP from different types of problems or attacks, depending on whether a port is a trunk or an access port.

The previous edition of this book covered Cisco-proprietary extensions to legacy STP—the UplinkFast and BackboneFast features. These additions have been dropped from the current exam blueprint, and in addition, their core ideas (tracking Alternate Ports, accepting inferior BPDUs from designated switches) have been leveraged in RSTP and MST, becoming an integral part of their design.

## PortFast Ports

**Key Topic**

The PortFast is a well-known improvement in legacy STP and PVST+, and is a standardized enhancement in RSTP and MST. Essentially, it defines an Edge port. We will use both *Edge port* and *PortFast port* terms interchangeably. An Edge port becomes forwarding immediately after coming up, does not generate topology change events, does not flush MAC addresses from the CAM table as a result of topology change handling, and is not influenced by the Sync step in the Proposal/Agreement procedure. An Edge port sends BPDUs but it expects not to receive any BPDUs back. If a BPDU does arrive at a PortFast port, the operational PortFast status will be disabled on the port until it goes down and back up.

The use of PortFast on ports toward end hosts is important for several reasons. First and foremost, it accelerates the port's transition into the Forwarding state. Apart from saving twice the ForwardDelay time, it also remediates problems with overly sensitive DHCP clients on end hosts that report an error if no response from a DHCP server is received within a couple of seconds. Second, a somewhat less obvious but far more grave reason to use PortFast is that in RSTP and MST, it prevents a port from being put into the Discarding state during Proposal/Agreement handling. Not taking care to configure Edge ports in a network running RSTP or MST will result in intermittent connectivity during topology changes, and while the network itself will reconverge in seconds at most (and usually much sooner), end hosts will suffer an outage for twice the ForwardDelay time.

PortFast ports can be configured either directly on ports using the **spanning-tree portfast** command or on a global level using the **spanning-tree portfast default** command. Both of these commands apply only to ports operating in access mode (that is, static access or dynamic mode that negotiated an access link). This behavior simply follows the logic that end hosts are usually connected to access ports while links to other switches operate as trunks. If PortFast is enabled globally, but some access port is nevertheless connected to another switch, PortFast can be explicitly disabled on that port using the **spanning-tree portfast disable** command.

If a trunk port is connected to an end device, such as a router or a server, it can be forced into PortFast mode using the **spanning-tree portfast trunk** interface level command. Be sure, however, to never activate PortFast on ports toward other switches. RSTP and MST will take care of their rapid handling if the other switch also speaks RSTP or MST.

## Root Guard, BPDU Guard, and BPDU Filter: Protecting Access Ports

Network designers probably do not intend for end users to connect a switch to an access port that is intended for attaching end-user devices. However, it happens—for example, someone just might need a few more ports in the meeting room down the hall, so he figures that he could just plug a small, cheap switch into the wall socket.

The STP topology can be changed based on one of these unexpected and undesired switches being added to the network. For example, this newly added and unexpected switch might have the lowest Bridge ID and become the root. To prevent such problems, BPDU Guard and Root Guard can be enabled on these access ports to monitor for incoming BPDUs—BPDUs that should not enter those ports, because they are intended for single end-user devices. Both features can be used together. Their base operations are as follows:

- **BPDU Guard:** Enabled per port or globally per PortFast-enabled ports; error disables the port immediately upon receipt of any BPDU.

- **Root Guard:** Enabled per port; ignores any received superior BPDUs to prevent this port from becoming the Root Port. Upon receipt of superior BPDUs, this switch puts the port in a root-inconsistent blocking state, ceasing forwarding and receiving data frames until the superior BPDUs cease.

Key Topic

The BPDU Guard can either be activated unconditionally on a per-port basis using the **spanning-tree bpduguard enable** interface command or globally using the **spanning-tree portfast bpduguard default** command. The global command, however, activates the BPDU Guard only on ports that operate as PortFast ports (it does not matter how the port was configured for PortFast operation). Again, in the case where BPDU Guard is enabled globally but it needs to be deactivated on a particular PortFast port, the **spanning-tree bpduguard disable** interface command can be used.

There is often confusion regarding the relation of PortFast and BPDU Guard to each other. In reality, the *only* dependence between these mechanisms is concerned with configuring the BPDU Guard on a global level. In this case, it will be automatically activated on those ports on which PortFast is also active; in other words, the global activation of BPDU Guard will activate it on all Edge ports. Besides this particular *configurational* dependency, PortFast and BPDU Guard are completely independent. On a port, BPDU Guard can be configured regardless of PortFast. PortFast, either per-port or globally, can be configured regardless of BPDU Guard.

Regardless of how the BPDU Guard is activated on an interface, when a BPDU is received on such a port, it will be immediately err-disabled.

Root Guard can be activated only on a per-port basis using the **spanning-tree guard root** interface command.

With BPDU Guard, the port does not recover from the *err-disabled* state unless additional configuration is added. You can tell the switch to change from the err-disabled state back to an up state after a certain amount of time. With Root Guard, the port recovers automatically when the undesired superior BPDUs are no longer received for the usual MaxAge-Message age in STP, or 3x Hello in RSTP (effectively, when they expire).

The BPDU Filter feature is concerned with stopping the transmission, and optionally the reception as well, of BPDUs on a port. Its behavior differs depending on how it is activated:

- If configured globally using **spanning-tree portfast bpdufilter default**, it applies only to Edge ports (that is, to ports on which PortFast is active). After these ports are connected to, they will start sending BPDUs each Hello interval; however, if during the next ten Hello intervals, no BPDU is received from the connected device, the port will stop sending BPDUs itself. As a result, the port will send only 11 BPDUs (one immediately after the port comes up, and then ten more during the ten Hello intervals) and then cease sending BPDUs. The port is still prepared to process any incoming BPDUs. If a BPDU arrives at any time, during the first ten Hello intervals or anytime after, BPDU Filter will be operationally deactivated on that port, and the port will start sending and receiving BPDUs according to usual STP rules. BPDU Filter operation on this port will be reinstated after the port is disconnected and reconnected. As usual, if the global configuration of BPDU Filter applies to an Edge port on which you do not want BPDU Filter to be activated, you can exempt the port using the **spanning-tree bpdufilter disable** command.

- If configured locally on a port using the **spanning-tree bpdufilter enable** command, BPDU Filter will cause the port to unconditionally stop sending and receiving BPDUs altogether.

The use of BPDU Filter depends on how it is configured. The global BPDU Filter configuration causes Edge ports to stop sending BPDUs after a certain time, assuming that it is not useful to send BPDUs to end devices as they do not speak STP. If it is discovered that such a port is actually connected to a switch by receiving a BPDU, the BPDU Filter will be deactivated on the port until the port goes down and comes back up (through disconnect/reconnect, or through shutting it down and activating it again). This can be considered an optimization in networks with many access ports toward end devices.

BPDU Filter configured directly on a port causes the port to stop sending and processing received BPDUs. No BPDUs will be sent; received BPDUs will be silently dropped. This configuration prevents STP from participating with any other switch on the port. Usually, this feature is used to split a network into separate independent STP domains. Because in this case, STP does not operate over these ports, it is unable to prevent a switching loop if the STP domains are redundantly interconnected. It is the responsibility of the administrator, then, to make sure that there are no physical loops between the STP domains.

Again, there is often confusion regarding the dependence of PortFast and BPDU Filter. Their true dependence is practically identical to that of BPDU Guard and PortFast. The *only* situation where BPDU Filter and PortFast are *configurationally* dependent is when BPDU Filter is configured on a global level, because in that case it automatically applies to all Edge ports (that is, ports with active PortFast). If a port on which BPDU Filter is active because global configuration (meaning that it must have been an Edge port) receives a BPDU, it will lose its Edge status, and because the global BPDU Filter configuration applies to Edge ports, BPDU Filter on this port will be deactivated as well. Apart from this, no other dependency between BPDU Filter and PortFast exists.

It is possible to combine globally configured BPDU Filter with BPDU Guard (the BPDU Guard can be also configured globally or per-port in this case). Should a port protected both with global BPDU Filter and BPDU Guard receive a BPDU, it will be automatically err-disabled.

On the other hand, it does not make sense to combine port-level BPDU Filter with BPDU Guard. As the port drops all received BPDUs, the BPDU Guard will never see them, meaning that it will never be able to put the port into an err-disabled state.

## Protecting Against Unidirectional Link Issues

Unidirectional links are links for which one of the two transmission paths on the link has failed, but not both. This can happen as a result of miscabling, cutting one fiber cable, unplugging one fiber, GBIC problems, or other reasons. Because STP monitors incoming BPDUs to know when to reconverge the network, adjacent switches on a unidirectional link could both become Forwarding, causing a loop, as shown in Figure 3-15.

Figure 3-15 shows the fiber link between SW1 and SW2 with both cables. SW2 starts in a Blocking state, but as a result of the failure on SW1's transmit path, SW2 ceases to hear Hellos from SW1. SW2 then transitions to the Forwarding state, and now all trunks on all switches are Forwarding. Even with the failure of SW1's transmit fiber, frames will now loop counterclockwise in the network.

On Catalyst switches, there are several mechanisms available to detect and avoid issues caused by unidirectional links. These mechanisms include UDLD, STP Loop Guard, Bridge Assurance, and the RSTP/MST Dispute mechanism.

Unidirectional Link Detection (UDLD), a Cisco-proprietary Layer 2 messaging protocol, serves as an echo mechanism between a pair of devices. Using UDLD messages, each switch advertises its identity and port identifier pair as the message originator, and a list of all neighboring switch/port pairs heard on the same segment. Using this information, a unidirectional link can be detected by looking for one of the following symptoms:

Key
Topic

■ UDLD messages arriving from a neighbor do not contain the exact switch/port pair matching the receiving switch and its port in the list of detected neighbors. This suggests that the neighbor either does not hear this switch at all (for example, a cut fiber) or the neighbor's port sending these UDLD messages is different from that neighbor's port receiving this switch's own UDLD messages (for example, a Tx fiber plugged into a different port than the Rx fiber).

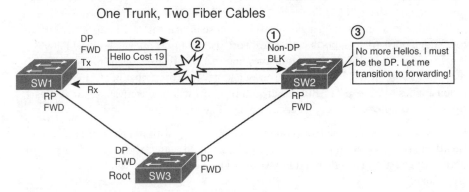

**Figure 3-15**  *STP Problems with Unidirectional Links*

■ UDLD messages arriving from a neighbor contain the same switch/port originator pair as used by the receiving switch. This suggests a self-looped port.

■ A switch has detected only a single neighbor but that neighbor's UDLD messages contain more than one switch/port pair in the list of detected neighbors. This suggests a shared media interconnection with an issue in its capability to provide full visibility between all connected devices.

If any of these symptoms are detected, UDLD will declare the link as unidirectional and will *err-disable* the port.

In addition, a unidirectional link can under circumstances also manifest itself by sudden loss of all incoming UDLD messages without the port going down. This symptom is not always a reliable indication of a unidirectional link, though. Assume, for example, two switches interconnected by a link utilizing a pair of metallic/optical media converters. If one switch is turned off, the other switch will not experience a link down event; just the UDLD messages stop arriving. Assuming that the link has become unidirectional would be presumptuous in this case.

Key
Topic

UDLD therefore has two modes of operation with the particular respect to the sudden loss of arriving UDLD messages. In the *normal* mode, if UDLD messages cease being received, a switch will try to reconnect with its neighbors (eight times), but if this attempt fails, UDLD takes absolutely no action. In particular, the port that stopped receiving UDLD messages will remain up. In the *aggressive* mode, after UDLD messages stop arriving, a switch will try eight times to reconnect with its neighbors, and if this attempt fails, UDLD will err-disable the port. The difference between the normal and aggressive mode therefore lies in the reaction to the sudden loss of incoming UDLD messages, that is, to an *implicit* indication of a possible unidirectional link condition. Note that both normal and aggressive modes will err-disable the port if the unidirectional link is *explicitly* detected by the three symptoms described earlier.

UDLD can be activated either on a global level or on a per-port basis, and needs to be activated on both interconnected devices. Global UDLD configuration applies only to fiber ports; per-port UDLD configuration activates it regardless of the underlying media type. On the global level, UDLD is activated with the **udld { enable | aggressive }** command, the **enable** keyword referring to the normal mode and **aggressive** referring to the aggressive mode. On a port, UDLD is activated using the **udld port [ aggressive ]** command. If the **aggressive** keyword is omitted, normal mode is used. Operational status of UDLD including port information and detected neighbors and their states can be displayed using **show udld** and **show udld neighbors** commands. If UDLD err-disables a port after detecting a unidirectional link condition, apart from shutting it down and bringing it back up to reactivate it, a port can also be reset from the privileged EXEC mode using the **udld reset** command.

STP Loop Guard is an added logic related to receiving BPDUs on Root and Alternate Ports on point-to-point links. In the case of a unidirectional link, these ports could move from Root or Alternate to Designated, thereby creating a switching loop. STP Loop Guard assumes that after BPDUs were being received on Root and Alternate Ports, it is not possible in a correctly working network for these ports to suddenly stop receiving BPDUs without them actually going down. A sudden loss of incoming BPDUs on Root and Alternate Ports therefore suggests that a unidirectional link condition might have occurred.

Following this logic, STP Loop Guard prevents Root and Alternate Ports from becoming Designated as a result of total loss of incoming BPDUs. If BPDUs cease being received on these ports and their stored BPDUs expire, Loop Guard will put them into a *loop-inconsistent* blocking state. They will be brought out of this state automatically after they start receiving BPDUs again.

Loop Guard can be activated either globally or on a per-port basis, and is a local protection mechanism (that is, it does not require other switches to be also configured with Loop Guard to work properly). If activated globally using the **spanning-tree loopguard default** command, it automatically protects all Root and Alternate Ports on STP point-to-point link types on the switch. Global Loop Guard does not protect ports on shared type links. It can also be configured on a per-port basis using the **spanning-tree guard loop** command, in which case it applies even to ports on shared links.

The Bridge Assurance, applicable only with RPVST+ and MST and only on point-to-point links, is a further extension of the idea used by Loop Guard. Bridge Assurance modifies the rules for sending BPDUs. With Bridge Assurance activated on a port, this port *always* sends BPDUs each Hello interval, whether it is Root, Designated, Alternate, or Backup. BPDUs thus essentially become a Hello mechanism between pairs of interconnected switches. A Bridge Assurance–protected port is absolutely required to receive BPDUs. If no BPDUs are received, the port will be put into a *BA-inconsistent* blocking state until it starts receiving BPDUs again. Apart from unidirectional links, Bridge Assurance also protects against loops caused by malfunctioning switches that completely stop participating in RPVST+/MST (entirely ceasing to process and send BPDUs) while opening all their ports. At the time of this writing, Bridge Assurance was supported on selected Catalyst 6500 and Nexus 7000 platforms. Configuring it on Catalyst 6500 Series requires activating it both globally using **spanning-tree bridge assurance** and on ports on STP point-to-point link types toward other switches using the **spanning-tree portfast network** interface command. The neighboring device must also be configured for Bridge Assurance.

The Dispute mechanism is yet another and standardized means to detect a unidirectional link. Its functionality is based on the information encoded in the Flags field of RST and MST BPDUs, namely, the role and state of the port forwarding the BPDU. The principle of operation is very simple: If a port receives an inferior BPDU from a port that claims to be Designated Learning or Forwarding, it will itself move to the Discarding state. Cisco has also implemented the Dispute mechanism into its RPVST+. The Dispute mechanism is not available with legacy STP/PVST+, as these STP versions do not encode the port role and state into BPDUs. The Dispute mechanism is an integral part of RSTP/MST and requires no configuration.

# Configuring and Troubleshooting EtherChannels

EtherChannel, also known as Link Aggregation, is a widely supported and deployed technology used to bundle several physical Ethernet links interconnecting a pair of devices into a single logical communication channel with increased total throughput. After an EtherChannel is established, it is represented to the devices as a single logical interface (called *Port-channel* in Cisco parlance), utilizing the bandwidth of all its member links. This allows for traffic load sharing between the member links, taking advantage of their combined bandwidth. Also, should a link in an EtherChannel bundle fail, the traffic will be spread over remaining working links without further influencing the state of the logical interface. Control plane protocols that see only the logical Port-channel interface and not its underlying physical members, such as STP, will only notice a change in the interface's bandwidth parameter (if not configured statically using the **bandwidth** command). The reaction to a failure or addition of a member link is therefore significantly more graceful than a reaction to a loss or reestablishment of a standalone link.

## Load Balancing Across Port-Channels

EtherChannel increases the available bandwidth by carrying multiple frames over multiple links. A single Ethernet frame is always transmitted over a single link in an EtherChannel bundle. A hashing function performed over selected frames' address fields produces a number identifying the physical link in the bundle over which the frame will be forwarded. The sequence of frames having an identical value in a particular address field (or a set of fields) fed into the hashing function is called a *conversation* or simply a *flow*. This hashing function is deterministic, meaning that all frames in a single flow produce the same hash value, and are therefore forwarded over the same physical link. Hence, the increase in the available bandwidth is never experienced by a single flow; rather, multiple flows have a chance of being distributed over multiple links, achieving higher aggregated throughput. The fact that a single flow is carried by a single link and thus does not benefit from a bandwidth increase can be considered a disadvantage; however, this approach also prevents frames from being reordered. This property is crucial, as EtherChannel—being a transparent technology—must not introduce impairments that would not be seen on plain Ethernet.

Load-balancing methods differ depending on the model of switch and software revision. Generally, load balancing is based on the contents of the Layer 2, 3, and/or 4 headers. If load balancing is based on only one header field in the frame, that single field is fed into the hashing function. If more than one header field is used, first, an XOR operation between the selected fields is used and only the result of this XOR is fed into the hashing function. The details of hashing functions in use are not public and can vary between different switch platforms.

For the best balancing effect, the header fields on which balancing is based need to vary among the mix of frames sent over the Port-channel. For example, for a Layer 2 Port-channel connected to an access layer switch, most of the traffic going from the access layer switch to the distribution layer switch is probably going from clients to the default router. So most of the frames have different source MAC addresses but the same destination MAC address. For packets coming back from a distribution switch toward the access layer switch, many of the frames might have a source address of that same router, with differing destination MAC addresses. So, you could balance based on source MAC at the access layer switch and based on destination MAC at the distribution layer switch—or balance based on both fields on both switches. The goal is simply to use a balancing method for which the fields in the frames vary.

The **port-channel load-balance** *type* global level command sets the type of load balancing. The *type* options include using source and destination MAC, IP addresses, and TCP and UDP ports—either a single field or both the source and destination. Because this command is global, it influences the operation of all EtherChannel bundles on a switch. Devices on opposite ends of an EtherChannel bundle can, and often do, use different load-balancing algorithms.

The maximum number of active member links in an EtherChannel bundle is eight. This limit is reasonable, considering that Ethernet variants differ in speed by orders of tens (10 Mbps, 100 Mbps, 1 Gbps, 10 Gbps, 100 Gbps). More than eight links in an EtherChannel bundle is simply closing in on the next faster Ethernet variant, so it is reasonable to consider using a faster Ethernet variant in such cases instead. On many Catalyst switch platforms, the hashing function therefore produces a 3-bit result in the range of 0–7 whose values are assigned to the individual member links. With eight physical links in a bundle, each link is assigned exactly one value from this range. If there are fewer physical links, some of the links will be assigned multiple values from this range, and as a result, some of the links will carry more traffic than the others. Table 3-7 describes the traffic amount ratios (P*n* denotes the *n*th port in a bundle).

**Table 3-7**   *Load Spread Ratios with Different Port Numbers in EtherChannel*

| Number of Ports in the EtherChannel | Load-Balancing Ratios |
|---|---|
| 8 | P1:P2:P3:P4:P5:P6:P7:P8 → 1:1:1:1:1:1:1:1 |
| 7 | P1:P2:P3:P4:P5:P6:P7:P1 → 2:1:1:1:1:1:1 |
| 6 | P1:P2:P3:P4:P5:P6:P1:P2 → 2:2:1:1:1:1 |
| 5 | P1:P2:P3:P4:P5:P1:P2:P3 → 2:2:2:1:1 |
| 4 | P1:P2:P3:P4:P1:P2:P3:P4 → 2:2:2:2 |
| 3 | P1:P2:P3:P1:P2:P3:P1:P2 → 3:3:2 |
| 2 | P1:P2:P1:P2:P1:P2:P1:P2 → 4:4 |

Under ideal conditions, the traffic distribution across member links will be equal only if the number of links is eight, four, or two. With the eight resulting values from a 3-bit hash function, each value represents 1/8=12.5% of the traffic. The spread of the traffic by multiples of 12.5% is quite coarse. The indicated ratios can also be computed by using DIV and MOD operations: For example, with three links in a bundle, each link will be assigned 8 DIV 3 = 2 resulting hash values, plus 8 MOD 3 = 2 links will be handling an additional hash result value, yielding a ratio of (2+1):(2+1):2 = 3:3:2, or 37.5% : 37.5% : 25%.

On other Cisco switch platforms, an 8-bit hash result is used although the EtherChannel is still limited to a maximum of eight links. Because the hash value allows for 256 possible results, each value represents a mere 1/256 = 0.390625% of the traffic. The spread of the traffic across links in a bundle is thus much more fine-grained. With three links, each of them would be assigned 256 DIV 3 = 85 resulting hash values, plus a 256 MOD 3 = 1 link would be handling an additional hash result value. So the traffic split ratio would be 86:85:85, or approximately 33.6% : 33.2% : 33.2%, much more balanced than 3:2:2.

It is sometimes incorrectly stated that a Port-channel can only operate with two, four, or eight links. That is incorrect—a Port-channel can operate with any number of links between one and eight, inclusive. The spreading of total traffic across links can be uneven, however, if the number of links is not a power of 2, as previously explained.

## Port-Channel Discovery and Configuration

When you are adding multiple ports to a particular Port-channel *on a single switch*, several configuration items must be identical, as follows:

- Same speed and duplex settings.

- Same operating mode (trunk, access, dynamic).

- If not trunking, same access VLAN.

- If trunking, same trunk type, allowed VLANs, and native VLAN.

- No ports can have SPAN configured.

Some of these limitations can change over time—it is recommended to consult the Configuration Guide for your particular switch platform and IOS version to stay up to date.

When a new Port-channel is created, an **interface Port-channel** is automatically added to the configuration. This interface inherits the configuration of the first physical interface added to the Port-channel, and the configuration of all other physical interfaces added to the same Port-channel will be compared to the **interface Port-channel** configuration. If they differ, the physical interface will be considered as *suspended* from the Port-channel, and it will not become a working member until its configuration is made identical to that of the Port-channel interface. Configuration changes performed on the **interface Port-channel** apply only to nonsuspended member ports; that is, commands applied to the Port-channel interface are pushed down only to those physical member ports whose configuration matched the **interface Port-channel** configuration before making the change. Therefore, reentering the configuration on the Port-channel interface in hopes of unifying the configuration of all member ports will not have an effect on those ports whose current configuration differs from that of the Port-channel interface. It is therefore recommended to adhere to the following guidelines when configuring Port-channels:

- Do not create the interface Port-channel manually before bundling the physical ports under it. Let the switch create it and populate its configuration automatically.

- On the other hand, when removing a Port-channel, make sure to manually remove the **interface Port-channel** from the running config so that its configuration does not cause issues when a Port-channel with the same number is re-created later.

- Be sure to make the configuration of physical ports identical before adding them to the same Port-channel.

- If a physical port's configuration differs from the **interface Port-channel** configuration, correct the physical port's configuration first. Only then proceed to perform changes to the Port-channel interface configuration.

■ A Port-channel interface can either be Layer 2 (switched) or Layer 3 (routed), depending on whether the physical bundled ports are configured as Layer 2 (**switchport**) or Layer 3 (**no switchport**). After a Port-channel has been created with a particular operating level, it is not possible to change it to the other mode without re-creating it. If it is necessary to change between Layer 2 and Layer 3 levels of operation, the Port-channel must be removed from configuration and re-created after the physical ports are reconfigured for the required level of operation. It is possible, though, to combine the Layer 2 Port-channel on one switch with the Layer 3 Port-channel on another, although not necessarily a best practice.

■ Whenever resolving an issue with err-disabled ports under a Port-channel interface, be sure to shut down both the physical interfaces and the **interface Port-channel** itself. Only then try to reactivate them. If the problem persists, it is recommended to remove the Port-channel altogether from the configuration, unbundling the ports as a result, and re-create the Port-channel.

You can statically configure interfaces to be in a Port-channel by using the **channel-group** *number* **mode on** interface subcommand. You would simply put the same command under each of the physical interfaces inside the Port-channel, using the same Port-channel number. This configuration forces the ports to become members of the same Port-channel without negotiating with the neighboring switch. This way of creating a Port-channel is strongly discouraged, though. If one switch considers multiple physical ports to be bundled under a single Port-channel while the neighboring switch still treats them as individual or assigns them into several bundles, permanent switching loops can occur. Also, this static Port-channel configuration is not capable of detecting whether the bundled ports are all connected to the same neighboring device. Having individual ports in a single Port-channel connect to different neighboring switches can again lead to permanent switching loops. To understand how the switch loop ensues, consider the topology shown in Figure 3-16.

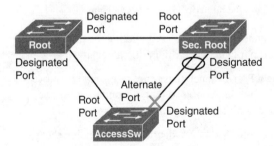

**Figure 3-16**  *Permanent Switching Loop in a Misconfigured EtherChannel*

In this topology, the ports on the Secondary Root switch toward AccessSw have already been bundled in a Port-channel using **mode on**, and the switch uses them as a single EtherChannel right away, without negotiating with AccessSw. However, AccessSw is not yet configured for Port-channel on these ports, and treats them as individual links.

**Key Topic**

Because Port-channel interfaces are treated as single ports by STP, only a single BPDU is sent for the entire Port-channel interface, regardless of how many physical links are bundled. This BPDU is also subject to the hashing function and forwarded over a single link in the entire Port-channel bundle. Assuming that the Secondary Root has the second-lowest priority in this network and that the BPDUs are forwarded over the left link toward AccessSw, the corresponding port on AccessSw is Alternate Discarding. However, the AccessSw port on the right link is not receiving any BPDUs and becomes Designated Forwarding as a result. Even though such a port sends BPDUs, they will be ignored by the Secondary Root switch because they are inferior to its own BPDUs. Hence, a permanent switching loop is created. This is also the reason why a switch shuts down all physical ports when **no interface Port-channel** is issued—to prevent switching loops when Port-channel configuration is being removed.

Note that if using RSTP/MST, the Dispute mechanism would detect this problem and put the Port-channel on the Secondary Root switch to the Discarding state, preventing this loop. In addition, Cisco has implemented yet another prevention mechanism called STP *EtherChannel Misconfig Guard* on its switches. This mechanism makes an assumption that if multiple ports are correctly bundled into a Port-channel at the neighbor side, all BPDUs received over links in this Port-channel must have the same source MAC address in their Ethernet header, as the Port-channel interface inherits the MAC address of one of its physical member ports. If BPDUs sourced from different MAC addresses are received on a Port-channel interface, it is an indication that the neighbor is still treating the links as individual, and the entire Port-channel will be err-disabled. Note that the detection abilities of the EtherChannel Misconfig Guard are limited. In the topology in Figure 3-16, this mechanism will not help because the Secondary Switch receives just a single BPDU from AccessSw over the right link, and has no other BPDU to compare the source MAC address to. The mechanism would be able to detect a problem if, for example, there were three or more links between Secondary Root and AccessSw, or if the two existing links were bundled at the AccessSw instead of Secondary Root. The EtherChannel Misconfig Guard is active by default and can be deactivated using the **no spanning-tree etherchannel guard misconfig** global configuration command.

It is therefore strongly recommended to use a dynamic negotiation protocol to allow switches to negotiate the creation of a Port-channel and verify whether the links are eligible for bundling. Those protocols are the Cisco-proprietary *Port Aggregation Protocol (PAgP)* and the open IEEE 802.1AX (formerly 802.3ad) *Link Aggregation Control Protocol (LACP)*. Both protocols offer relatively similar features though they are mutually incompatible. On a common Port-channel, both switches must use the same negotiation protocol; different Port-channel interfaces can use different negotiation protocols. Using LACP is generally preferred because of its open nature and widespread support.

PAgP allows a maximum of eight links in a Port-channel. A switch will refuse to add more than eight links to a PAgP Port-channel. On current Catalyst switches, PAgP has no user-configurable parameters apart from the frequency of sending PAgP messages. This frequency is configurable on a per-port basis using the **pagp timer** { **normal | fast** } command; **normal** frequency is 30 seconds after the Port-channel is established, and **fast** is a

1-second frequency. Other available commands related to PAgP have no effect on the forwarding behavior of the switch, and are kept only for backward compatibility with very old switches.

With LACP, a maximum of 16 links can be placed into a Port-channel. Out of these links, at most eight links will be active members of the Port-channel. Remaining links will be put into a so-called Standby (sometimes also called Hot-Standby) mode. If an active link fails, one of the Standby links will be used to replace it. A single switch is in charge of selecting which Standby link will be promoted to the active state—it is the switch with the lower LACP System ID that consists of a configurable priority and the switch MAC address (the same concept as in STP). If there are multiple Standby links, the switch in control will choose the link with the lowest Port ID that again consists of a configurable priority and the port number. LACP priority of a switch can be globally configured using the **lacp system-priority** command, and the priority of a port can be set up using the **lacp port-priority** command. Both priorities can be configured in the range of 0–65535.

To dynamically form a Port-channel using PAgP, you still use the **channel-group** command, with a mode of **auto** or **desirable**. To use LACP to dynamically create a Port-channel, use a mode of **active** or **passive**. Table 3-8 lists and describes the modes and their meanings.

**Key Topic**

**Table 3-8**  *PAgP and LACP Configuration Settings and Recommendations*

| PAgP Setting | LACP 802.1AX Setting | Action |
| --- | --- | --- |
| auto | passive | Uses PAgP or LACP, but waits on the other side to send the first PAgP or LACP message |
| desirable | active | Uses PAgP or LACP and initiates the negotiation |

**Note**  Using **auto** (PAgP) or **passive** (LACP) on both switches prevents a Port-channel from forming dynamically. Cisco recommends the use of **desirable** mode (PAgP) or **active** mode (LACP) on ports that you intend to be part of a Port-channel on both devices.

As remembering the mode keywords and the protocol they refer to (**desirable/auto** for PAgP; **active/passive** for LACP) can be awkward, Cisco implemented the helper command **channel-protocol** { **pagp | lacp** } that can be used on physical interfaces to limit the accepted mode keywords to the stated negotiation protocol. In other words, entering **channel-protocol pagp** will allow the subsequent use of **desirable** or **auto** modes only; the **active**, **passive**, and **on** modes will be rejected. Similarly, using **channel-protocol lacp** will only permit the subsequent use of **active** or **passive** modes; the **desirable**, **auto**, and **on** modes will be rejected.

**Note**    A common misunderstanding is that the **channel-protocol** command can be used in combination with the **on** mode to start a particular negotiation protocol. This is incorrect. The **channel-protocol** command only causes the CLI to refuse any mode keywords that do not imply running the chosen negotiation protocol.

When PAgP or LACP negotiate to form a Port-channel, the messages include the exchange of key information that allows detecting whether all links to be bundled under a single Port-channel are connected to the same neighbor and whether the neighbor is also willing to bundle them under a single Port-channel. These values include system IDs of both interconnected devices, identifiers of physical ports, and aggregation groups these ports fall under. It is sometimes believed that PAgP and LACP carry detailed information about individual port settings; that is incorrect. While PAgP and LACP make sure that the links to be bundled are all connected to the same neighboring switch and that both switches are willing to bundle them into a common Port-channel, they are neither capable nor supposed to verify whether ports on opposite sides of bundled links are otherwise identically configured.

**Note**    PAgP and LACP verify only whether the links to be bundled are consistently connected to the same neighboring device and are to be bundled into the same link aggregation group. However, neither of these protocols performs checks on whether the ports on this switch and its neighbor are configured identically with respect to their operating mode, allowed VLANs, native VLAN, encapsulation, and so on.

When PAgP or LACP completes the process, a new Port-channel interface exists and is used as if it were a single port for STP purposes, with balancing taking place based on the global load-balancing method configured on each switch.

## Troubleshooting Complex Layer 2 Issues

Troubleshooting is one of the most challenging aspects of CCIE study. The truth is, we can't teach you to troubleshoot in the pages of a book; only time and experience bring strong troubleshooting skills. We can, however, provide you with two things that are indispensable in learning to troubleshoot effectively and efficiently: process and tools. The focus of this section is to provide you with a set of Cisco IOS–based tools, beyond the more common ones that you already know, as well as some guidance on the troubleshooting process for Layer 2 issues that you might encounter.

In the CCIE Routing and Switching lab exam, you will encounter an array of troubleshooting situations that require you to have mastered fast, efficient, and thorough troubleshooting skills. In the written exam, you'll need a different set of skills—mainly, the knowledge of troubleshooting techniques that are specific to Cisco routers and switches, and the ability to interpret the output of various **show** commands and possibly debug output. You can also expect to be given an example along with a problem statement. You will need to quickly narrow the question down to possible solutions and then pinpoint the final solution. This requires a different set of skills than what the lab exam requires, but spending time on fundamentals as you prepare for the qualification exam will provide a good foundation for the lab exam environment.

As in all CCIE exams, you should expect that the easiest or most direct ways to a solution might be unavailable to you. In troubleshooting, perhaps the easiest way to the source of most problems is through the **show run** command or variations on it. Therefore, we'll institute a simple "no **show run**" rule in this section that will force you to use your knowledge of more in-depth troubleshooting commands in the Cisco IOS portion of this section.

In addition, you can expect that the issues you'll face in this part of the written exam will need more than one command or step to isolate and resolve.

## Layer 2 Troubleshooting Process

From the standpoint of troubleshooting techniques, two basic stack-based approaches come into play depending on what type of issue you're facing. The first of these is the climb-the-stack (or bottom-up) approach, where you begin at Layer 1 and work your way up until you find the problem. Alternatively, you can start at Layer 7 and work your way down in a top-down approach; however, in the context of the CCIE Routing and Switching exams, the climb-the-stack approach generally makes more sense.

Another approach is often referred to as the divide-and-conquer method. With this technique, you start in the middle of the stack (usually where you see the problem) and work your way down or up the stack from there until you find the problem. In the interest of time, which is paramount in an exam environment, the divide-and-conquer approach usually provides the best results. Because this section deals with Layer 2 issues, it starts at the bottom and works up.

Some lower-level issues that might affect Layer 2 connectivity include the following:

- **Cabling:** Check the physical soundness of the cable as well as the use of a correctly pinned cable. If the switch does not support Automatic Medium-Dependent Interface Crossover (Auto-MDIX), the correct choice of either crossover or straight-through cable must be made. On many Catalyst platforms (not all, though), configuring both speed and duplex statically on a port results in autonegotiation including Auto-MDIX to be deactivated on that port. That can lead both to duplex mismatches and to a link going down if the cable required the port to perform automatic crossover.

- **Speed or duplex mismatch:** Most Cisco devices will correctly sense speed and duplex when both sides of the link are set to Auto, but a mismatch can cause the line protocol on the link to stay down.

- **Device physical interface:** It is possible for a physical port to break.

## Layer 2 Protocol Troubleshooting and Commands

In addition to the protocol-specific troubleshooting commands that you have learned so far, this section addresses commands that can help you isolate problems through a solid understanding of the information they present. We will use a variety of examples of command output to illustrate the key parameters you should understand.

### Troubleshooting Using Cisco Discovery Protocol

Cisco Discovery Protocol (CDP) is a proprietary protocol that is used to help administrators collect information about neighboring Cisco devices. CDP makes it possible to gather hardware and protocol information about neighbor devices, which is useful information for troubleshooting or network discovery.

CDP messages are generated every 60 seconds as Layer 2 multicast messages on each of a device's active interfaces. The information shared in a CDP packet about a device includes, but is not limited to, the following:

- Name of the device configured with the **hostname** command

- IOS software version

- Hardware capabilities, such as routing, switching, and/or bridging

- Hardware platform, such as 2800, 2960, or 1900

- The Layer 3 address(es) of the device

- The interface that the CDP update was generated on

- Duplex setting of the interface that CDP was generated on

- VTP domain of the device if relevant

- Native VLAN of the sending port if relevant

CDP enables devices to share basic configuration information without even configuring any protocol-specific information and is enabled by default on all common interfaces (CDP might be deactivated on less typical interfaces such as Virtual-Template or multipoint Frame Relay). CDP is a Data Link Layer utility found in IOS that resides at Layer 2 of the OSI model; as such, CDP is not routable and can only operate over directly connected interfaces. As a general rule, CDP is active by default on devices.

CDP updates are generated every 60 seconds with a hold-down period of 180 seconds for a missing neighbor. The **no cdp run** command globally disables CDP, while the **no cdp enable** command disables CDP on an interface. Disabling CDP globally and enabling it on individual interfaces is not possible. We can use the **show cdp neighbors** command to list any directly connected Cisco neighboring devices. Additionally, we can use the **detail** keyword to display detailed information about the neighbor, including its Layer 3 addressing.

Example 3-3 shows the CDP timer, which is how often CDP packets are sent, and the CDP holdtime, which is the amount of time that the device will hold packets from neighbor devices.

**Example 3-3**  *CDP Timers*

```
Router_2# show cdp
Global CDP information:
        Sending CDP packets every 60 seconds
        Sending a holdtime value of 180 seconds
```

Example 3-4 shows how we can use the following commands to set CDP timer and holdtime values to something other than the defaults.

**Example 3-4**  *Adjusting CDP Timers*

```
Router_2# conf t
Enter configuration commands, one per line.  End with CNTL/Z.
Router_2(config)# cdp timer 90
Router_2(config)# cdp holdtime 360
```

CDP can be disabled with the **no cdp run** command in global configuration mode.

Because a device stores the CDP information in its runtime memory, you can view it with a **show** command. It will only show information about directly connected devices because CDP packets are not passed through Cisco devices. Example 3-5 shows such output.

**Example 3-5**  *CDP Verification Commands*

```
Router_2# show cdp neighbors
Capability Codes: R - Router, T - Trans Bridge, B - Source Route Bridge
                  S - Switch, H - Host, I - IGMP, r - Repeater


Device ID          Local Intrfce     Holdtme    Capability  Platform  Port ID
Router3            Ser 1             120          R          2500      Ser 0
Router1            Eth 1             180          R          2500      Eth 0
Switch1            Eth 0             240          S          1900      2


! CDP Neighbor Information includes
! Neighbor's device ID
! Local port type and number
! Holdtime value (in seconds)
! Neighbor's network device capability
! Neighbor's hardware platform
! Neighbor's remote port type and number


! In addition to this we can employ the show cdp entry device-id
! command to show  more information about a specified neighbor.
```

```
Router_2# show cdp entry Router1
------------------------

Device ID: Router1
Entry address(es):
 IP address: 192.168.1.2
Platform: cisco 2500, Capabilities: Router
Interface: Ethernet1,  Port ID (outgoing port): Ethernet0
Holdtime : 180 sec

Version:
Cisco Internetwork Operating System Software
IOS (tm) 2500 Software (2500-JS-L), Version 11.2(15)
RELEASED SOFTWARE (fc1)
Copyright (c) 1986-1998 by Cisco Systems, Inc.
Compiled Mon 06-Jul-98 22:22 by tmullins

! The following is a sample output for one neighbor from the show cdp neighbors
! detail command. Additional detail is shown about neighbors, including network
! address, enabled protocols, and software version.

Router_2# show cdp neighbors detail

Device ID: 008024 1EEB00 (milan-sw-1-cat9k)
Entry address(es):
   IP address: 1.15.28.10
Platform: CAT5000, Capabilities: Switch
Interface: Ethernet1/0, Port ID (outgoing port): 2/7
Holdtime : 162 sec

Version :
Cisco Catalyst 5000
Duplex Mode: full
Native VLAN: 42
VTP Management Domain: 'Accounting Group'
```

## Troubleshooting Using Link Layer Discovery Protocol

Where Cisco Discovery Protocol (CDP) is a device discovery protocol that runs over
Layer 2 on all Cisco-manufactured devices (routers, bridges, access servers, and switches)
that allows network management applications to automatically discover and learn about
other Cisco devices connected to the network, we have to ask the question, "What happens if we have to work with non-Cisco equipment?"

To support non-Cisco devices and to allow for interoperability between other devices, IOS also supports the IEEE 802.1AB Link Layer Discovery Protocol (LLDP). LLDP is a neighbor discovery protocol similar to CDP that is used for network devices to advertise information about themselves to other devices on the network. This protocol runs over the Data Link Layer, which allows two systems running different network layer protocols to learn about each other.

LLDP supports a set of attributes that it uses to discover neighbor devices. These attributes contain type, length, and value descriptions and are referred to as TLVs. LLDP-supported devices can use TLVs to receive and send information to their neighbors. This protocol can advertise details such as configuration information, device capabilities, and device identity.

The switch supports these basic management TLVs. These are mandatory LLDP TLVs:

- Port description TLV

- System name TLV

- System description TLV

- System capabilities TLV

- Management address TLV

Similar to CDP, configuration on a Cisco device can be made in the global or interface mode.

Example 3-6 shows how to globally enable LLDP and to manipulate its configuration.

**Example 3-6**  *LLDP Configuration and Verification*

```
! This example shows how to enable LLDP. First, LLDP must be
! activated globally. Then, instead of having a single
! enable keyword similar to cdp enable, LLDP has lldp transmit and lldp receive
! commands. By default, they are both set, so a port automatically sends and
! receives LLDP messages. The following example shows the use of the commands.

Switch# configure terminal
Switch(config)# lldp run
Switch(config)# interface fa0/1
Switch(config-if)# lldp transmit
Switch(config-if)# lldp receive
Switch(config-if)# end


! You can configure the frequency of LLDP updates, the amount of time to hold the
! information before discarding it, and the initialization delay time.
```

```
Switch# configure terminal
Switch(config)# lldp holdtime 120
Switch(config)# lldp reinit 2
Switch(config)# lldp timer 30
Switch(config)# end
```

## Troubleshooting Using Basic Interface Statistics

The **show interfaces** command is a good place to start troubleshooting interface issues. It will tell you whether the interface has a physical connection and whether it was able to form a logical connection. The link duplex and bandwidth are shown, along with errors and collisions. Example 3-7 shows output from this command, with important statistics highlighted.

**Example 3-7**   *Troubleshooting with the* **show interface** *Command*

```
! Shows a physical and logical connection

SW4# show int fa0/21
FastEthernet0/21 is up, line protocol is up (connected)
   Hardware is Fast Ethernet, address is 001b.d4b3.8717 (bia 001b.d4b3.8717)
   MTU 1500 bytes, BW 100000 Kbit, DLY 100 usec,
      reliability 255/255, txload 1/255, rxload 1/255
   Encapsulation ARPA, loopback not set
   Keep alive set (10 sec)

! Negotiated or configured speed and duplex

   Full-duplex, 100Mb/s, media type is 10/100BaseTX
   input flow-control is off, output flow-control is unsupported
   ARP type: ARPA, ARP Timeout 04:00:00
   Last input 00:00:01, output 00:00:08, output hang never
   Last clearing of "show interface" counters never
   Input queue: 0/75/0/0 (size/max/drops/flushes); Total output drops: 0
   Queueing strategy: fifo
   Output queue: 0/40 (size/max)
   5 minute input rate 0 bits/sec, 0 packets/sec
   5 minute output rate 0 bits/sec, 0 packets/sec
      16206564 packets input, 1124307496 bytes, 0 no buffer
      Received 14953512 broadcasts (7428112 multicasts)

   ! CRC errors, runts, frames, collisions or late collisions
   ! may indicate a duplex mismatch

      0 runts, 0 giants, 0 throttles
```

```
0 input errors, 0 CRC, 0 frame, 0 overrun, 0 ignored
0 watchdog, 7428112 multicast, 0 pause input
0 input packets with dribble condition detected
2296477 packets output, 228824856 bytes, 0 underruns
0 output errors, 0 collisions, 1 interface resets
0 babbles, 0 late collision, 0 deferred
0 lost carrier, 0 no carrier, 0 PAUSE output
0 output buffer failures, 0 output buffers swapped out
```

If an interface shows as up/up, you know that a physical and logical connection has been made, and you can move on up the stack in troubleshooting. If it shows as up/down, you have some Layer 2 troubleshooting to do. An interface status of err-disable could be caused by many different problems, some of which are discussed in this chapter. Common causes include a security violation or detection of a unidirectional link. Occasionally, a duplex mismatch will cause this state.

Chapter 1, "Ethernet Basics," showed examples of a duplex mismatch, but the topic is important enough to include here. Duplex mismatch might be caused by hard-coding one side of the link to full duplex but leaving the other side to autonegotiate duplex. A 10/100 interface will default to half duplex if the other side is 10/100 and does not negotiate. It could also be caused by an incorrect manual configuration on both sides of the link. A duplex mismatch usually does not bring the link down; it just creates suboptimal performance by causing collisions.

You would suspect a duplex mismatch if you saw collisions on a link that should be capable of full duplex, because a full-duplex link should by definition never have collisions. A link that is half duplex on both sides will show some interface errors. But more than about 1 percent to 2 percent of the total traffic is cause for a second look. Watch for the following types of errors:

- **Runts:** Runts are frames smaller than 64 bytes.

- **CRC errors:** The frame's cyclic redundancy checksum value does not match the one calculated by the switch or router.

- **Frames:** Frame errors have a CRC error and contain a noninteger number of octets.

- **Alignment:** Alignment errors have a CRC error and an odd number of octets.

- **Collisions:** Look for collisions on a full-duplex interface (meaning that the interface operated in half-duplex mode at some point in the past), or excessive collisions on a half-duplex interface.

- **Late collisions on a half-duplex interface:** A late collision occurs after the first 64 bytes of a frame.

Another command to display helpful interface statistics is **show controllers**, shown in Example 3-8. The very long output from this command is another place to find the number of frames with bad frame checks, CRC errors, collisions, and late collisions. In addition, it tells you the size breakdown of frames received and transmitted. A preponderance of one-size frames on an interface that is performing poorly can be a clue to the application sending the frames. Another useful source of information is the interface autonegotiation status and the speed/duplex capabilities of it and its neighbor, shown at the bottom of Example3-8.

**Example 3-8**   *Troubleshooting with the* **show controllers** *Command*

```
R1# show controllers fastEthernet 0/0
Interface FastEthernet0/0
Hardware is MV96340
HWIDB: 46F92948, INSTANCE: 46F939F0, FASTSEND: 4374CB14, MCI_INDEX: 0
Aggregate MIB Counters
----------------------
  Rx Good Bytes: 27658728              Rx Good Frames: 398637
  Rx Bad Bytes: 0                      Rx Bad Frames: 0
  Rx Broadcast Frames: 185810          Rx Multicast Frames: 181353
  Tx Good Bytes: 3869662               Tx Good Frames: 36667
  Tx Broadcast Frames: 0               Tx Multicast Frames: 5684
  Rx+Tx Min-64B Frames: 412313         Rx+Tx 65-127B Frames: 12658
  Rx+Tx 128-255B Frames: 0             Rx+Tx 256-511B Frames: 10333
  Rx+Tx 512-1023B Frames: 0            Rx+Tx 1024-MaxB Frames: 0
  Rx Unrecog MAC Ctrl Frames: 0
  Rx Good FC Frames: 0                 Rx Bad FC Frames: 0
  Rx Undersize Frames: 0               Rx Fragment Frames: 0
  Rx Oversize Frames: 0                Rx Jabber Frames: 0
  Rx MAC Errors: 0                     Rx Bad CRCs: 0
  Tx Collisions: 0                     Tx Late Collisions: 0


! [output omitted]


AUTONEG_EN
PHY Status (0x01):
AUTONEG_DONE LINK_UP
Auto-Negotiation Advertisement (0x04):
100FD 100HD 10FD 10HD
Link Partner Ability (0x05):
100FD 100HD 10FD 10HD


! output omitted
```

## Troubleshooting Spanning Tree Protocol

Spanning-tree issues are possible in a network that has not been properly configured. Previous sections of this chapter discussed ways to secure STP. One common STP problem is a change in the root bridge. If the root bridge is not deterministically configured, a change in the root can affect network connectivity. To lessen the chance of this, use Rapid STP and all the tools necessary to secure the root and user ports. Example 3-1 showed commands to check the root bridge and other STP parameters, including the following:

```
show spanning-tree [ vlan number ] root [ detail | priority [
    system-id ] ]
```

Keep in mind that when BPDU Guard is enabled, a port is error-disabled if it receives a BPDU. You can check this with the **show interfaces status err-disabled** command. In addition, switching loops can result if the **spanning-tree portfast trunk** command is enabled on a trunk port toward another switch, or an interface has a duplex mismatch. One symptom of a loop is flapping MAC addresses. A port protected by Root Guard is put in a root-inconsistent state if it tries to become a Root Port: a Root and Alternate Port with Loop Guard configured is put in a loop-inconsistent state if it stops receiving BPDUs. You can check this with the **show spanning-tree inconsistent ports** command. Whether an interface is error-disabled or put into an inconsistent state, the port is effectively shut down to user traffic.

Cisco STP implementation recognizes many kinds of port inconsistencies. Table 3-9 summarizes them and the reasons causing them.

**Table 3-9**  *Types of STP Inconsistencies and Their Causes*

| Inconsistency Type | Description and Probable Cause of Inconsistency |
|---|---|
| Type (*TYPE_Inc) | PVST+ BPDUs are received on a non-802.1Q port. Usually caused by interconnecting access and trunk ports. |
| Port VLAN ID (*PVID_Inc) | PVST+ BPDUs are received in a different VLAN than they were originated in. Usually caused by native VLAN mismatch on a trunk. |
| PVST Simulation (*PVST_Inc) | PVST+ BPDUs received on an MST boundary port do not meet the PVST Simulation consistency criteria. |
| Loop (*LOOP_Inc) | A Root or Alternate Port tried to become Designated after BPDUs stopped arriving. Seen only on Loop Guard–protected ports. |
| Root (*ROOT_Inc) | A port tried to become a Root Port after receiving superior BPDUs. Seen only on Root Guard-protected ports. Also, on older switches, this state was displayed in place of the PVST_Inc state if PVST Simulation Inconsistency was encountered on a port. |
| Bridge Assurance (*BA_Inc) | A port stopped receiving BPDUs. Seen only on Bridge Assurance–protected ports. |

## Troubleshooting Trunking

Trunks that fail to form can result from several causes. With an 802.1Q trunk, a native VLAN mismatch is usually the first thing troubleshooters look at. You should additionally check the Dynamic Trunking Protocol (DTP) negotiation mode of each side of the trunk. Table 2-9 in Chapter 2, "Virtual LANs and VLAN Trunking," lists the combinations of DTP configurations that will lead to successful trunking.

A VLAN Trunking Protocol (VTP) domain mismatch has been known to prevent trunk formation, even in switches that are in VTP Transparent mode, because the VTP domain name is carried in DTP messages. The switch's logging output will help you greatly. This is shown in Example 3-9, along with some commands that will help you troubleshoot trunking problems. In Example 3-9, two switches are configured with 802.1Q native VLANs 10 and 99, and DTP mode desirable. Both are VTP transparent and have different VTP domain names. Some output irrelevant to the example is omitted.

**Example 3-9**   *Troubleshooting Trunking*

```
! These errors messages were logged by the switch

%CDP-4-NATIVE_VLAN_MISMATCH: Native VLAN mismatch discovered on FastEthernet1/0/21
  (10), with sw4 FastEthernet0/21 (99)
%SPANTREE-2-RECV_PVID_ERR: Received BPDU with inconsistent peer vlan id 99 on
  FastEthernet1/0/21 VLAN10
%DTP-5-DOMAINMISMATCH: Unable to perform trunk negotiation on port Fa1/0/21 because
  of VTP domain mismatch.


! This command shows that the port is configured to trunk
! (Administrative Mode) but is not performing as a trunk
! (Operational Mode)

SW2# show int fa 1/0/1 switchport
Name: Fa1/0/1
Switchport: Enabled
Administrative Mode: dynamic desirable
Operational Mode: static access
Administrative Trunking Encapsulation: negotiate
Operational Trunking Encapsulation: native
Negotiation of Trunking: On
Access Mode VLAN: 1 (default)
Trunking Native Mode VLAN: 10 (NATIVE_10)
Administrative Native VLAN tagging: enabled
! output omitted


! Trunking VLANs Enabled: 3,99


! The port is shown as inconsistent due to native VLAN mismatch
```

```
SW4# show spanning-tree inconsistentports
Name            Interface                   Inconsistency
------------    -------------------------   ------------------
VLAN0099        FastEthernet0/21            Port VLAN ID Mismatch
Number of inconsistent ports (segments) in the system : 1


! Once the errors are corrected, the interface shows as a trunk


SW4# show interfaces trunk
Port         Mode         Encapsulation  Status       Native vlan
Fa0/21       desirable    802.1q         trunking     99
! Output omitted
```

If your trunks are connected and operating, but user connectivity is not working, check the VLANs allowed on each trunk. Make sure that the allowed VLANs match on each side of the trunk, and that the users' VLAN is on the allowed list (assuming that it should be). Either look at the interface configuration or use the **show interfaces trunk** and **show interfaces switchport** commands shown in Example 3-9 to find that information.

## Troubleshooting VTP

If you choose to use anything other than VTP Transparent mode in your network, you should be aware of the ways to break it. VTP will fail to negotiate a neighbor status if the following items do not match:

- VTP version
- VTP domain
- VTP password

In addition, recall that VTP runs over trunk links only, so you must have an operational trunk before expecting VTP to act. To prevent your VLAN database from being altered when adding a VTPv1 or VTPv2 switch to the VTP domain, follow these steps:

**Step 1.** Change the VTP mode to Transparent, which will reset the configuration revision number to 0.

**Step 2.** Configure the remaining appropriate VTP parameters.

**Step 3.** Configure trunking.

**Step 4.** Connect the switch to the network.

VTPv3 prevents a switch, even with a higher revision number, from asserting its database over other switches if its idea of who is the primary server differs from that of its neighbors.

The first part of Example 3-10 shows a VTP client with a password that doesn't match its neighbor (note the error message). The switch does not show an IP address in the last line because it has not been able to negotiate a VTP relationship with its neighbor. In the second part of the example, the configuration has been corrected. Now the neighbor's IP address is listed as the VTP updater.

**Example 3-10**  *Troubleshooting VTP*

```
! Wrong password is configured


SW4# show vtp status
VTP Version                     : running VTP1 (VTP2 capable)
Configuration Revision          : 0
Maximum VLANs supported locally : 1005
Number of existing VLANs        : 5
VTP Operating Mode              : Client
VTP Domain Name                 : CCIE
VTP Pruning Mode                : Disabled
VTP V2 Mode                     : Disabled
VTP Traps Generation            : Disabled
MD5 digest                      : 0xA1 0x7C 0xE8 0x7E 0x4C 0xF5 0xE3 0xC8
*** MD5 digest checksum mismatch on trunk: Fa0/23 ***
*** MD5 digest checksum mismatch on trunk: Fa0/24 ***
Configuration last modified by 0.0.0.0 at 7-24-09 03:12:27


! On some IOS versions, a message about MD5 digest failing is not displayed.
! In these cases, using debug sw-vlan vtp events may be helpful - look for output
! similar to this:


*Jul 24 11:01:42.558: VTP LOG RUNTIME: MD5 digest failing
calculated = D7 17 28 01 4E 1D E6 65 67 0A 9D 73 71 EA 5A 5C
transmitted = C2 93 A7 15 E5 0C 0B 9D DD 24 BB ED 18 4C 97 45


! Command output after the misconfiguration was corrected


SW4# show vtp status
VTP Version                     : running VTP2
Configuration Revision          : 5
Maximum VLANs supported locally : 1005
Number of existing VLANs        : 9
VTP Operating Mode              : Client
VTP Domain Name                 : CCIE
VTP Pruning Mode                : Disabled
VTP V2 Mode                     : Enabled
VTP Traps Generation            : Disabled
MD5 digest                      : 0xDD 0x6C 0x64 0xF5 0xD2 0xFE 0x9B 0x62
Configuration last modified by 192.168.250.254 at 7-24-09 11:02:43
```

## Troubleshooting EtherChannels

Table 3-8 listed the LACP and PAgP settings. If your EtherChannel is not coming up, check these settings. If you are using LACP, at least one side of each link must be set to **active**. If you are using PAgP, at least one side of the link must be set to **desirable**. If you are not using a channel negotiation protocol, make sure that both sides of the links are set to **on**.

Remember that the following rules apply to all ports within an EtherChannel:

- Speed and duplex must match.

- Interface type—access, trunk, or routed—must match.

- Trunk configuration—encapsulation, allowed VLANs, native VLAN, and DTP mode—must match.

- If a Layer 2 EtherChannel is not a trunk, all ports must be assigned to the same VLAN.

- No port in the EtherChannel can be a Switched Port Analyzer (SPAN) port.

- On a Layer 3 EtherChannel, the IP address must be on the Port-channel interface, not a physical interface.

To troubleshoot an EtherChannel problem, check all the parameters in the preceding list. Example 3-11 shows some commands to verify the logical and physical port configuration for an EtherChannel. QoS configuration must match and must be configured on the physical ports, not the logical one.

**Example 3-11**    *Troubleshooting EtherChannels*

```
! The show etherchannel summary command gives an overview of the
! channels configured, whether they are Layer 2 or Layer 3, the
! interfaces assigned to each, and the protocol used if any


L3SW4# show etherchannel summary
Flags:  D - down         P - bundled in port-channel
        I - stand-alone s - suspended
        H - Hot-standby (LACP only)
        R - Layer3       S - Layer2
        U - in use       f - failed to allocate aggregator
        M - not in use, minimum links not met
        u - unsuitable for bundling
        w - waiting to be aggregated
        d - default port
Number of channel-groups in use: 3
```

```
Number of aggregators:          3
Group  Port-channel  Protocol  Ports
------+-------------+---------+-------------------------------------------
14     Po14(SU)      LACP      Fa0/3(P)
24     Po24(RU)      -         Fa0/7(P)  Fa0/8(P)  Fa0/9(P)  Fa0/10(P)
34     Po34(RU)      PAgP      Fa0/1(P)  Fa0/2(P)

! The show interface etherchannel command lets you verify that the
! interface is configured with the right channel group and
! protocol settings

L3SW3# show int fa0/1 etherchannel
Port state    = Up  Mstr In-Bndl
Channel group = 34       Mode = On     Gcchange = -
Port-channel  = Po34     GC   = -      Pseudo port-channel = Po34
Port index    = 0        Load = 0x00   Protocol  = PAgP
Age of the port in the current state: 1d:07h:28m:19s

! The show interface portchannel command produces output similar
! to a physical interface. It allows you to verify the ports
! assigned to the channel and the type of QoS used

L3SW3# show int port-channel 23
Port-channel23 is up, line protocol is up (connected)
Hardware is EtherChannel, address is 001f.2721.8643 (bia 001f.2721.8643)
Internet address is 10.1.253.13/30
MTU 1500 bytes, BW 200000 Kbit, DLY 100 usec,
reliability 255/255, txload 1/255, rxload 1/255
Encapsulation ARPA, loopback not set
Keepalive set (10 sec)
Full-duplex, 100Mb/s, link type is auto, media type is unknown
input flow-control is off, output flow-control is unsupported
Members in this channel: Fa0/3 Fa0/4
ARP type: ARPA, ARP Timeout 04:00:00
Last input 00:00:02, output 00:00:00, output hang never
Last clearing of "show interface" counters never
Input queue: 0/75/0/0 (size/max/drops/flushes); Total output drops: 0
Queueing strategy: fifo
```

## Approaches to Resolving Layer 2 Issues

Table 3-10 presents some generalized types of Layer 2 issues and ways of approaching them, including the relevant Cisco IOS commands.

**Table 3-10**   *Layer 2 Troubleshooting Approach and Commands*

| Problem | Approach | Helpful IOS Commands |
|---|---|---|
| Lack of reachability to devices in the same VLAN | Eliminate Layer 1 issues with **show interface** commands.<br><br>Verify that the VLAN exists on the switch.<br><br>Verify that the interface is assigned to the correct VLAN.<br><br>Verify that the VLAN is allowed on the trunk. | **show interface**<br><br>**show vlan**<br><br>**show interface switchport**<br><br>**traceroute mac** *source-mac destination-mac*<br><br>**show interface trunk** |
| Intermittent reachability to devices in the same VLAN | Check for excessive interface traffic.<br><br>Check for unidirectional links.<br><br>Check for spanning-tree problems such as BPDU floods or flapping MAC addresses. | **show interface**<br><br>**show spanning-tree**<br><br>**show spanning-tree root**<br><br>**show mac address-table** |
| No connectivity between switches | Check for interfaces that are shut down.<br><br>Verify that trunk links and EtherChannels are active.<br><br>Verify that BPDU Guard is not enabled on a trunk interface. | **show interfaces status err-disabled**<br><br>**show interfaces trunk**<br><br>**show etherchannel summary**<br><br>**show spanning-tree detail** |
| Poor performance across a link | Check for a duplex mismatch. | **show interface** |

In summary, when troubleshooting Layer 2 issues, check for interface physical problems or configuration mismatches. Verify that STP is working as expected. If you are using VTP, make sure that it is configured properly on each switch. For trunking problems, check native VLAN and DTP configuration. When troubleshooting port channels, verify that the interface parameters are the same on both sides.

# Foundation Summary

This section lists additional details and facts to round out the coverage of the topics in this chapter. Unlike most of the Cisco Press Exam Certification Guides, this "Foundation Summary" does not repeat information presented in the "Foundation Topics" section of the chapter. Please take the time to read and study the details in the "Foundation Topics" section of the chapter, as well as review items noted with a Key Topic icon.

Table 3-11 lists the protocols mentioned in this chapter and their respective standards documents.

**Table 3-11** *Protocols and Standards for Chapter 3*

| Name | Standards Body |
|------|---------------|
| RSTP | IEEE 802.1D (formerly 802.1w) |
| MST | IEEE 802.1Q (formerly 802.1s) |
| STP | Formerly IEEE 802.1D |
| LACP | IEEE 802.1AX (formerly 802.3AD) |
| Dot1Q trunking | IEEE 802.1Q |
| PVST+ | Cisco |
| RPVST+ | Cisco |
| PAgP | Cisco |

Table 3-12 lists the three key timers that impact STP convergence.

**Table 3-12** *IEEE 802.1D STP Timers*

| Timer | Default | Purpose |
|-------|---------|---------|
| Hello | 2 sec | Interval at which the root sends Configuration BPDUs |
| Forward Delay | 15 sec | Time that switch leaves a port in the Listening state and the Learning state; also used as the short CAM timeout timer |
| MaxAge | 20 sec | Time without hearing a Hello before expiring the stored BPDU |

Table 3-13 lists some of the key IOS commands related to the topics in this chapter. The command syntax for switch commands was taken from the *Catalyst 3560 Switch Command Reference, 15.0(2)SE.*

**Table 3-13**   *Command Reference for Chapter 3*

| Command | Description |
|---|---|
| **spanning-tree mode {mst | pvst | rapid-pvst}** | Global config command that sets the STP mode. |
| **[no] spanning-tree vlan** *vlan-id* | Enables or disables STP inside a particular VLAN when using PVST+ or RPVST+. |
| **spanning-tree vlan** *vlan-id* **{forward-time** *seconds* | **hello-time** *seconds* | **max-age** *seconds* | **priority** *priority* | **{root {primary | secondary} [diameter** *net-diameter* **[hello-time** *seconds*]]}}** | Global config command to set a variety of STP parameters when using PVST+ or RPVST+. |
| **spanning-tree [ vlan** *x* | **mst** *x* **] cost** *y* | Interface subcommand used to set interface costs, per VLAN. If the **vlan** or **mst** keyword is omitted, applies to all unspecified VLANs or MST instances. |
| **spanning-tree [ vlan** *x* | **mst** *x* **] port-priority** *y* | Interface subcommand used to set port priority, per VLAN. If the **vlan** or **mst** keyword is omitted, applies to all unspecified VLANs or MST instances. |
| **channel-group** *channel-group-number* **mode {auto [non-silent] | desirable [non-silent] | on | active | passive}** | Interface subcommand that places the interface into a Port-channel, and sets the negotiation parameters. |
| **channel-protocol {lacp | pagp}** | Interface subcommand to define which protocol to allow to configure for EtherChannel negotiation. |
| **interface port-channel** *port-channel-number* | Global command that allows entering the logical interface representing the Port-channel bundle. |
| **spanning-tree portfast [ trunk ]** | Interface subcommand that enables PortFast on the interface. |
| **spanning-tree bpduguard {enable | disable}** | Interface command that enables or disables BPDU Guard on the interface. |
| **spanning-tree mst** *instance-id* **priority** *priority* | Global command used to set the priority of an MST instance. |
| **spanning-tree mst configuration** | Global command that puts the user in MST configuration mode. |
| **show spanning-tree bridge | root | brief | summary** | EXEC command to show various details about STP operation. |
| **show interfaces** | Displays Layer 1 and 2 information about an interface. |
| **show interfaces trunk** | Displays the interface trunk configuration. |
| **show etherchannel [summary]** | Lists EtherChannels configured and their status. |

| Command | Description |
|---|---|
| show interfaces switchport | Displays the interface trunking and VLAN configuration. |
| show vtp status | Displays the VTP configuration. |
| show controllers | Displays physical interface characteristics as well as traffic and error types. |

# Memory Builders

The CCIE Routing and Switching written exam, like all Cisco CCIE written exams, covers a fairly broad set of topics. This section provides some basic tools to help you exercise your memory about some of the broader topics covered in this chapter.

## Fill in Key Tables from Memory

Appendix E, "Key Tables for CCIE Study," on the CD in the back of this book, contains empty sets of some of the key summary tables in each chapter. Print Appendix E, refer to this chapter's tables in it, and fill in the tables from memory. Refer to Appendix F, "Solutions for Key Tables for CCIE Study," on the CD to check your answers.

## Definitions

Next, take a few moments to write down the definitions for the following terms:

CST, CIST, STP, MST, RSTP, Hello timer, MaxAge timer, ForwardDelay timer, Blocking state, Forwarding state, Listening state, Learning state, Disabled state, Alternate role, Discarding state, Backup role, Root Port, Designated Port, superior BPDU, inferior BPDU, PVST+, RPVST+, PortFast, Root Guard, BPDU Guard, UDLD, Loop Guard, LACP, PAgP

Refer to the glossary to check your answers.

## Further Reading

The topics in this chapter tend to be covered in slightly more detail in CCNP Switching exam preparation books. For more details on these topics, refer to the Cisco Press CCNP preparation books found at www.ciscopress.com/ccnp.

*Cisco LAN Switching*, by Kennedy Clark and Kevin Hamilton, covers STP logic and operations in detail.

More details about UDLD can be found in RFC 5171 and in U.S. Patent No. 7,480,251.

Cisco.com has an unusually extensive set of high-quality documents covering selected topics from this chapter. Instead of posting the URLs that can change over time, following is Table 3-14 of selected documents' names and Document ID numbers you can use in the Search function to locate the appropriate document. So, for example, when looking for "Understanding Spanning Tree Protocol Topology Changes," type the string "Document ID 12013" in the Search box on the Cisco website. If "PDF" is indicated instead of a numerical Document ID, the document has no Document ID and must be searched for only using its name. Some of the documents cover topics that are outdated and/or have been dropped from the current exam blueprint but which are nevertheless worth reading to reinforce your understanding. Most of the indicated documents are a must-read, though.

**Table 3-14** *Recommended Further Reading at Cisco.com*

| Document Name | Document ID |
| --- | --- |
| Understanding Spanning-Tree Protocol Topology Changes | 12013 |
| VLAN Load Balancing Between Trunks Using the Spanning-Tree Protocol Port Priority | 10555 |
| Understanding and Tuning Spanning Tree Protocol Timers | 19120 |
| Understanding and Configuring the Cisco UplinkFast Feature | 10575 |
| Understanding and Configuring Backbone Fast on Catalyst Switches | 12014 |
| Understanding Rapid Spanning Tree Protocol (802.1w) | 24062 |
| Understanding Multiple Spanning Tree Protocol (802.1s) | 24248 |
| PVST Simulation on MST Switches | 116464 |
| Using PortFast and Other Commands to Fix Workstation Startup Connectivity Delays | 10553 |
| Spanning Tree PortFast BPDU Guard Enhancement | 10586 |
| Spanning Tree Protocol Root Guard Enhancement | 10588 |
| Spanning-Tree Protocol Enhancements using Loop Guard and BPDU Skew Detection Features | 10596 |
| Understanding and Configuring the Unidirectional Link Detection Protocol Feature | 10591 |
| Spanning Tree from PVST+ to Rapid-PVST Migration Configuration Example | 72836 |
| Configuration Example to Migrate Spanning Tree from PVST+ to MST | 72844 |
| Cisco AVVID Network Infrastructure: Implementing 802.1w and 802.1s in Campus Networks | PDF |

| Document Name | Document ID |
|---|---|
| Best Practices for Catalyst 6500/6000 Series and Catalyst 4500/4000 Series Switches Running Cisco IOS Software | 24330 |
| Troubleshooting Transparent Bridging Environments | 10543 |
| Troubleshooting LAN Switching Environments | 12006 |
| Spanning Tree Protocol Problems and Related Design Considerations | 10556 |
| Troubleshooting STP on Catalyst Switches Running Cisco IOS System Software | 28943 |
| Troubleshooting Spanning Tree PVID- and Type-Inconsistencies | 24063 |
| Understanding EtherChannel Load Balancing and Redundancy on Catalyst Switches | 12023 |
| Understanding EtherChannel Inconsistency Detection | 20625 |
| Catalyst 6500, 4500, and 3750 Series Switches EtherChannel Load-Balancing | 116385 |
| Errdisable Port State Recovery on the Cisco IOS Platforms | 69980 |

**Blueprint topics covered in this chapter:**

This chapter covers the following subtopics from the Cisco CCIE Routing and Switching written exam blueprint. Refer to the full blueprint in Table I-1 in the Introduction for more details on the topics covered in each chapter and their context within the blueprint.

- IP Operation

- TCP Operation

- UDP Operation

- IPv4 Addressing

- IPv4 Subnetting

- IPv4 VLSM

- Route Summarization

- NAT

- IPv6 Addressing

- IPv6 Subnetting

- Migrating from IPv4 to IPv6

## CHAPTER 4

# IP Addressing

Complete mastery of IP addressing and subnetting is required for any candidate to have a reasonable chance at passing both the CCIE written and lab exam. In fact, even the CCNA exam has fairly rigorous coverage of IP addressing and the related protocols. For the CCIE exam, understanding these topics is required to answer much deeper questions. For example, a question might ask for the interpretation of the output of a **show ip bgp** command and a configuration snippet to decide what routes would be summarized into a new prefix. To answer such questions, you must be familiar with the basic concepts and math behind subnetting.

## "Do I Know This Already?" Quiz

Table 4-1 outlines the major headings in this chapter and the corresponding "Do I Know This Already?" quiz questions.

**Table 4-1** *"Do I Know This Already?" Foundation Topics Section-to-Question Mapping*

| Foundation Topics Section | Questions Covered in This Section | Score |
|---|---|---|
| IP Addressing and Subnetting | 1–4 | |
| CIDR, Private Addresses, and NAT | 5–8 | |
| IPv6 Addressing and Tunneling | 9–11 | |
| **Total Score** | | |

To best use this pre-chapter assessment, remember to score yourself strictly. You can find the answers in Appendix A, "Answers to the 'Do I Know This Already?' Quizzes."

1. In what subnet does address 192.168.23.197/27 reside?

   a. 192.168.23.0

   b. 192.168.23.128

   c. 192.168.23.160

   d. 192.168.23.192

   e. 192.168.23.196

2.  Router1 has four LAN interfaces, with IP addresses 10.1.1.1/24, 10.1.2.1/24, 10.1.3.1/24, and 10.1.4.1/24. What is the smallest summary route that could be advertised out a WAN link connecting Router1 to the rest of the network, if subnets not listed here were allowed to be included in the summary?

    a.  10.1.2.0/22

    b.  10.1.0.0/22

    c.  10.1.0.0/21

    d.  10.1.0.0/16

3.  Router1 has four LAN interfaces, with IP addresses 10.22.14.1/23, 10.22.18.1/23, 10.22.12.1/23, and 10.22.16.1/23. Which one of the answers lists the smallest summary route(s) that could be advertised by Router1 without also including subnets not listed in this question?

    a.  10.22.12.0/21

    b.  10.22.8.0/21

    c.  10.22.8.0/21 and 10.22.16.0/21

    d.  10.22.12.0/22 and 10.22.16.0/22

4.  Which two of the following VLSM subnets, when taken as a pair, overlap?

    a.  10.22.21.128/26

    b.  10.22.22.128/26

    c.  10.22.22.0/27

    d.  10.22.20.0/23

    e.  10.22.16.0/22

5.  Which of the following protocols or tools includes a feature like route summarization, plus administrative rules for global address assignment, with a goal of reducing the size of Internet routing tables?

    a.  Classless interdomain routing

    b.  Route summarization

    c.  Supernetting

    d.  Private IP addressing

6. Which of the following terms refer to a NAT feature that allows for significantly fewer IP addresses in the enterprise network as compared with the required public registered IP addresses?

   a. Static NAT

   b. Dynamic NAT

   c. Dynamic NAT with overloading

   d. PAT

   e. VAT

7. Consider an enterprise network using private class A network 10.0.0.0, and using NAT to translate to IP addresses in registered class C network 205.1.1.0. Host 10.1.1.1 has an open www session to Internet web server 198.133.219.25. Which of the following terms refers to the destination address of a packet, sent by the web server back to the client, when the packet has not yet made it back to the enterprise's NAT router?

   a. Inside Local

   b. Inside Global

   c. Outside Local

   d. Outside Global

8. Router1 has its fa0/0 interface, address 10.1.2.3/24, connected to an enterprise network. Router1's S0/1 interface connects to an ISP, with the interface using a publicly registered IP address of 171.1.1.1/30. Which of the following commands could be part of a valid NAT overload configuration, with 171.1.1.1 used as the public IP address?

   a. ip nat inside source list 1 int s0/1 overload

   b. ip nat inside source list 1 pool fred overload

   c. ip nat inside source list 1 171.1.1.1 overload

   d. None of the answers are correct.

9. What feature is built into the IPv6 protocol to facilitate intranet-wide address management that enables a large number of IP hosts to easily discover the network and get new and globally unique IPv6 addresses associated with their location?

   a. ISATAP

   b. Address autoconfiguration

   c. Interface Overload

   d. None of the answers are correct.

**10.** What IPv6 transition strategy involves configuring devices to be able to run IPv4 and IPv6 simultaneously?

  **a.** ISATAP

  **b.** IPv4-in-IPv6 Tunnels

  **c.** Dual Stack

  **d.** 6to4 Tunnels

**11.** If you use static configuration, all autoconfiguration features provided by IPv6 will be disabled.

  **a.** True

  **b.** False

## Foundation Topics

## IP Operation

IP is a protocol, and a protocol is best described as a series of rules governing how things work in a certain technologies, the ultimate goal being an operational standardization. When put into a network communication context, a protocol is the set of rules governing how packets are transmitted over a network. When you have a protocol, you are sure that all machines on a network (or in the world, when it comes to the Internet) speak the "same language" and can integrate into a holistic framework. IP is probably the most common protocol over the Internet. It is the set of rules governing how packets are transmitted over the Internet.

The IP protocol standardizes the way that machines over the Internet or any IP network forward or route their packets based on their IP addresses. The most fundamental and basic operation we observe in IP is the ability to perform routing. The routing of IP packets and its unique addressing scheme is one of the main functions of the IP protocol. Routing consists of forwarding IP packets from source to destination machines over a network, based on their IP addresses. IP is probably the most common and widely used protocol in existence as a result of its ease and use, but IP on its own is not sufficient to every task that we might have in networking. It must be noted that the operation of IP is also governed by the manner in which we deliver what to packets. Yes, the routing protocol allows the delivery, but without certain additional components, IP will not, for example, provide reliable packet delivery. To meet this goal of adding features like reliable transport and acknowledgment, we need to rely on another feature known as Transport Control Protocol (TCP).

## TCP Operation

When TCP couples with IP, you get a traffic controller that manages reliable exchange. TCP and IP work together to transmit data over the Internet, but at different levels. As we mentioned previously, IP does not guarantee reliable packet delivery over a network, and it is TCP that takes charge of making packet exchange reliable.

TCP is the protocol that ensures reliability in a transmission with minimal loss of packets. Additional duties in the operation of TCP include assuring that packets maintain the right order, and that any delay is kept to an acceptable level. Also, it is TCP that prevents the possibility of packet duplication. All this is to ensure that the data received is consistent, in order, complete, and smooth.

TCP operates in the protocol stack at the transport layer of the Open Systems Interconnection (OSI) model, which means that during data transmission, TCP works just before IP. TCP bundles data into TCP packets before sending these to IP, which in turn encapsulates these into IP packets.

An IP packet is a packet of data that carries a data payload and an IP header. Any piece of data is broken into bits and placed into these packets and transmitted over the network. When the packets reach their destination, they are reassembled into the original data.

## UDP Operation

The previous section discussed the nature of reliable transport that is provided by TCP, but there are instances in many networks where you either do not need reliable packet delivery or where you cannot afford to pay the associated costs of reliable delivery. Reliable packet delivery is slow, and many applications that can be deployed on a modern network find TCP too slow. A perfect example is voice and video traffic. But a more general explanation would be that TCP traffic is considered to be connection-oriented, whereas User Datagram Protocol (UDP) traffic is connectionless. This means that UDP packets do not contain anywhere near the amount of information as a TCP packet and thus they are smaller. This small size, coupled with their speed, makes them ideal for applications that are sensitive to the packet loss or delay such as IP voice or video solutions.

But no matter the transport method, TCP or UDP, your IP packets are delivered and managed in the context of IOS through their unique logical addressing and the ability to partition sections of addresses into usable networks.

## IP Addressing and Subnetting

You need a postal address to receive letters; similarly, computers must use an IP address to be able to send and receive data using the TCP/IP protocols. Just as the postal service dictates the format and meaning of a postal address to aid the efficient delivery of mail, the TCP/IP protocol suite imposes some rules about IP address assignment so that routers can efficiently forward packets between IP hosts. This chapter begins with coverage of the format and meaning of IP addresses, with required consideration for how they are grouped to aid the routing process.

### IP Addressing and Subnetting Review

First, here's a quick review of some of the core facts about IPv4 addresses that should be fairly familiar to you:

- A 32-bit binary number.

- Written in "dotted decimal" notation (for example, 1.2.3.4), with each decimal octet representing 8 bits.

- Addresses are assigned to network interfaces, so computers or routers with multiple interfaces have multiple IP addresses.

- A computer with an IP address assigned to an interface is an *IP host*.

- A group of IP hosts that are not separated from each other by an IP router are in the same grouping.

- These groupings are called *networks*, *subnets*, or *prefixes*, depending on the context.

- IP hosts separated from another set of IP hosts by a router must be in separate groupings (network/subnet/prefix).

IP addresses can be analyzed using *classful* or *classless* logic, depending on the situation. Classful logic simply means that the main class A, B, and C rules from RFC 791 are considered. The next several pages present a classful view of IP addresses, as reviewed in Table 4-2.

With classful addressing, class A, B, and C networks can be identified as such by their first several bits (shown in the last column of Table 4-2) or by the range of decimal values for their first octets. Also, each class A, B, or C address has two parts (when not subnetted): a *network part* and a *host part*. The size of each is implied by the class, and can be stated explicitly using the default mask for that class of network. For example, mask 255.0.0.0, the default mask for class A networks, has 8 binary 1s and 24 binary 0s, representing the size of the network and host parts, respectively.

Key Topic

**Table 4-2**  *Classful Network Review*

| Class of Address | Size of Network and Host Parts of the Addresses | Range of First Octet Values | Default Mask for Each Class of Network | Identifying Bits at Beginning of Address |
|---|---|---|---|---|
| A | 8/24 | 1–126 | 255.0.0.0 | 0 |
| B | 16/16 | 128–191 | 255.255.0.0 | 10 |
| C | 24/8 | 192–223 | 255.255.255.0 | 110 |
| D | — | 224–239 | — | 1110 |
| E | — | 240–255 | — | 1111 |

## Subnetting a Classful Network Number

With classful addressing, and no subnetting, an entire class A, B, or C network is needed on each individual instance of a data link. For example, Figure 4-1 shows a sample internetwork, with dashed-line circles representing the set of hosts that must be in the same IP network—in this case requiring three networks. Figure 4-1 shows two options for how IP addresses can be assigned and grouped together for this internetwork topology.

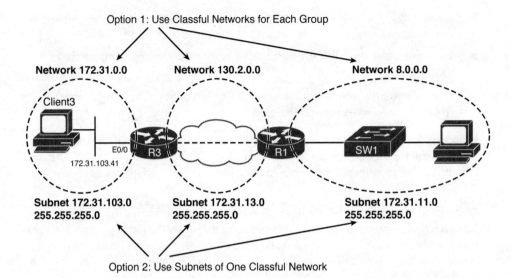

**Figure 4-1** *Sample Internetwork with Two Alternatives for Address Assignment—Without and With Subnetting*

Option 1 uses three classful networks; however, it wastes a lot of IP addresses. For example, all hosts in class A network 8.0.0.0 must reside on the LAN on the right side of the figure.

Of course, the much more reasonable alternative is to reserve one classful IP network number and use *subnetting* to subdivide that network into at least three subdivisions, called *subnets*. Option 2 (bottom of Figure 4-1) shows how to subdivide a class A, B, or C network into subnets.

To create subnets, the IP addresses must have three fields instead of just two—the network, *subnet*, and host. When using classful logic to interpret IP addresses, the size of the network part is still defined by classful rules—either 8, 16, or 24 bits based on class. To create the subnet field, the host field is shortened, as shown in Figure 4-2.

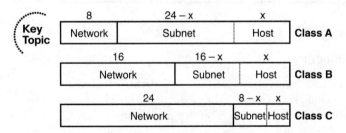

**Figure 4-2** *Formats of IP Addresses when Subnetting*

**Note**  The term *internetwork* refers to a collection of computers and networking hardware; because TCP/IP discussions frequently use the term *network* to refer to a classful class A, B, or C IP network, this book uses the term *internetwork* to refer to an entire network topology, as shown in Figure 4-1.

To determine the size of each field in a subnetted IP address, you can follow the three easy steps shown in Table 4-3. Note that Figure 4-1 also showed alternative addressing for using subnets, with the last column in Table 4-3 showing the size of each field for that particular example, which used class B network 172.31.0.0, mask 255.255.255.0.

**Table 4-3**  *Finding the Size of the Network, Subnet, and Host Fields in an IP Address*

| Name of Part of the Address | Process to Find Its Size | Size per Figure 4-1 Example |
|---|---|---|
| Network | 8, 16, or 24 bits based on class rules | 16 |
| Subnet | 32 minus network and host bits | 8 |
| Host | Equal to the number of binary 0s in the mask | 8 |

## Comments on Classless Addressing

The terms *classless* and *classful* can be applied to three popular topics that are all related to IP. This chapter explains classful and classless IP addressing, which are relatively simple concepts. Two other chapters explain the other uses of the terms classless and classful: Chapter 6, "IP Forwarding (Routing)," describes classless/classful routing, and Chapter 7, "RIPv2 and RIPng," covers classless/classful routing protocols.

Classless IP addressing, simply put, means that class A, B, and C rules are ignored. Each address is viewed as a two-part address, formally called the *prefix* and the *host* parts of the address. The prefix simply states how many of the beginning bits of an IP address identify or define the group. It is the same idea as using the combined network and subnet parts of an address to identify a subnet. All the hosts with identical prefixes are in effect in the same group, which can be called a *subnet* or a *prefix*.

Just as a classful subnet must be listed with the subnet mask to know exactly which addresses are in the subnet, a prefix must be listed with its *prefix length*. The prefix itself is a dotted-decimal number. It is typically followed by a / symbol, after which the prefix length is listed. The prefix length is a decimal number that denotes the length (in bits) of the prefix. For example, 172.31.13.0/24 means a prefix of 172.31.13.0 and a prefix length of 24 bits. Also, the prefix can be implied by a subnet mask, with the number of 1s in the binary version of the mask implying the prefix length.

Classless and classful addressing are mainly just two ways to think about IP address formats. For the exam, make sure to understand both perspectives and the terminology used by each.

## Subnetting Math

Knowing how to interpret the meaning of addresses and masks, routes and masks in the routing table, and addresses and masks in access control lists (ACL) and how to configure route filtering are all very important topics for the CCIE Routing and Switching written and lab exams. This section covers the binary math briefly, with coverage of some tricks to do the math quickly without binary math. Several subsequent chapters cover the configuration details of features that require this math.

### Dissecting the Component Parts of an IP Address

First, deducing the size of the three parts (classful view) or two parts (classless view) of an IP address is important, because it allows you to analyze information about that subnet and other subnets. Every internetwork requires some number of subnets, and some number of hosts per subnet. Analyzing the format of an existing address, based on the mask or prefix length, enables you to determine whether enough hosts per subnet exist, or whether enough subnets exist to support the number of hosts. The following list summarizes some of the common math facts about subnetting related to the format of IP addresses:

- If a subnet has been defined with $y$ host bits, there are $2^y - 2$ valid usable IP addresses in the subnet, because two numeric values are reserved.

- One reserved IP address in each subnet is the subnet number itself. This number, by definition, has binary 0s for all host bits. This number represents the subnet, and is typically seen in routing tables.

- The other reserved IP address in the subnet is the subnet broadcast address, which by definition has binary 1s for all host bits. This number can be used as a destination IP address to send a packet to all hosts in the subnet.

- When you are thinking classfully, if the mask implies $x$ subnet bits, then $2x$ possible subnets exist for that classful network, assuming that the same mask is used throughout the network.

- Although there are no truly reserved values for the subnet numbers, two (lowest and highest values) can be discouraged from use in some cases:

  - **Zero subnet:** The subnet field is all binary 0s; in decimal, each zero subnet is the exact same dotted-decimal number as the classful network number, potentially causing confusion.

  - **Broadcast subnet:** The subnet field is all binary 1s; in decimal, this subnet's broadcast address is the same as the network-wide broadcast address, potentially causing confusion.

In Cisco routers, by default, zero subnets and broadcast subnets work fine. You can disable the use of the zero subnet with the **no ip subnet-zero** global command. The only time that using the zero subnet typically causes problems is when classful routing protocols are used.

## Finding Subnet Numbers and Valid Range of IP Addresses—Binary

When examining an IP address and mask, the process of finding the subnet number, the broadcast address, and the range of valid IP addresses is as fundamental to networking as is addition and subtraction for advanced math. Possibly more so for the CCIE Routing and Switching lab exam, mastery of the math behind subnetting, which is the same basic math behind route summarization and filtering, will improve your speed in completing complex configurations on the exam.

The range of valid IP addresses in a subnet begins with the number that is 1 larger than the subnet number, and ends with the address that is 1 smaller than the broadcast address for the subnet. So, to determine the range of valid addresses, just calculate the subnet number and broadcast address, which can be done as follows:

- **To derive the subnet number:** Perform a bitwise Boolean AND between the IP address and mask.

- **To derive the broadcast address:** Change all host bits in the subnet number from 0s to 1s.

A bitwise Boolean AND means that you place two long binary numbers on top of each other, and then AND the two bits that line up vertically. (A Boolean AND results in a binary 1 only if both bits are 1; otherwise, the result is 0.) Table 4-4 shows an easy example based on subnet 172.31.103.0/24 from Figure 4-1.

**Table 4-4**  *Binary Math to Calculate the Subnet Number and Broadcast Address*

| Address | 172.31.103.41 | 1010 1100 0001 1111 0110 0111 **0010 1001** |
|---|---|---|
| Mask | 255.255.255.0 | 1111 1111 1111 1111 1111 1111 **0000 0000** |
| Subnet Number (Result of AND) | 172.31.103.0 | 1010 1100 0001 1111 0110 0111 **0000 0000** |
| Broadcast | 172.31.103.255 | 1010 1100 0001 1111 0110 0111 **1111 1111** |

Probably almost everyone reading this already knew that the decimal subnet number and broadcast addresses shown in Table 4-4 were correct, even without looking at the binary math. The important part is to recall the binary process, and practice until you can confidently and consistently find the answer without using any binary math. The only parts of the math that typically trip people up are the binary-to-decimal and decimal-to-binary conversions. When working in binary, keep in mind that you will not have a calculator for the written exam, and that when converting to decimal, you always convert 8 bits at a time—even if an octet contains some prefix bits and some host bits. (Appendix C, "Decimal-to-Binary Conversion Table," contains a conversion table for your reference.)

## Decimal Shortcuts to Find the Subnet Number and Valid Range of IP Addresses

Many of the IP addressing and routing related problems on the exam come back to the ability to solve a couple of classic basic problems. One of those problems runs as follows:

> Given an IP address and mask (or prefix length), determine the subnet number/prefix, broadcast address, and range of valid IP addresses.

If you can already solve such problems with only a few seconds' thought, even with tricky masks, you can skip this section of the chapter. If you cannot solve such questions easily and quickly, this section can help you learn some math shortcuts that allow you to find the answers without needing to use any Boolean math.

**Note** The next several pages of this chapter describe some algorithms that you can use to find many important details related to IP addressing, without needing to convert to and from binary. In my experience, some people simply work better performing the math in binary until the answers simply start popping into their heads. Others find that the decimal shortcuts are more effective.

If you use the decimal shortcuts, it is best to practice them until you no longer really use the exact steps listed in this book; rather, the processes should become second nature. To that end, CD-only Appendix D, "IP Addressing Practice," lists several practice problems for each of the algorithms presented in this chapter.

To solve the "find the subnet/broadcast/range of addresses" type of problem, at least three of the four octets should have pretty simple math. For example, with a nice, easy mask like 255.255.255.0, the logic used to find the subnet number and broadcast address is intuitive to most people. The more challenging cases occur when the mask or prefix does not divide the host field at a byte boundary. For example, the same IP address 172.31.103.41, with mask 255.255.252.0 (prefix /22), is actually in subnet 172.31.100.0. Working with the third octet in this example is the hard part, because the mask value for that octet is not 0 or 255; for the upcoming process, this octet is called the *interesting octet*. The following process finds the subnet number, using decimal math, even with a challenging mask:

**Step 1.**  Find the mask octets of value 255; copy the same octets from the IP address.

**Step 2.**  Find the mask octets of value 0; write down 0s for the same octets.

**Step 3.**  If one octet has not yet been filled in, that octet is the interesting octet. Find the subnet mask's value in the interesting octet and subtract it from 256. Call this number the "magic number."

**Step 4.**  Find the integer multiple of the magic number that is closest to, but not larger than, the interesting octet's value.

An example certainly helps, as shown in Table 4-5, with 172.31.103.41, mask 255.255.252.0. The table separates the address into its four component octets. In this example, the first, second, and fourth octets of the subnet number are easily found from Steps 1 and 2 in the process. Because the interesting octet is the third octet, the magic number is 256 – 252, or 4. The integer multiple of 4, closest to 103 but not exceeding 103, is 100—making 100 the subnet number's value in the third octet. (Note that you can use this same process even with an easy mask, and Steps 1 and 2 will give you the complete subnet number.)

**Table 4-5**   *Quick Math to Find the Subnet Number—172.31.103.41, 255.255.252.0*

|  | Octet | | | | Comments |
| --- | --- | --- | --- | --- | --- |
|  | **1** | **2** | **3** | **4** |  |
| Address | 172 | 31 | 103 | 41 |  |
| Mask | 255 | 255 | 252 | 0 | Equivalent to /22. |
| Subnet number results after Steps 1 and 2 | 172 | 31 |  | 0 | Magic number will be 256 – 252 = 4. |
| Subnet number after completing the interesting octet | 172 | 31 | 100 | 0 | 100 is the multiple of 4 closest to, but not exceeding, 103. |

A similar process can be used to determine the subnet broadcast address. This process assumes that the mask is tricky. The detailed steps are as follows:

**Step 1.** Start with the subnet number.

**Step 2.** Decide which octet is interesting, based on which octet of the mask does not have a 0 or 255.

**Step 3.** For octets to the left of the interesting octet, copy the subnet number's values into the place where you are writing down the broadcast address.

**Step 4.** For any octets to the right of the interesting octet, write 255 for the broadcast address.

**Step 5.** Calculate the magic number: Find the subnet mask's value in the interesting octet and subtract it from 256.

**Step 6.** Take the subnet number's interesting octet value, add the magic number to it, and subtract 1. Fill in the broadcast address's interesting octet with this number.

Table 4-6 shows the 172.31.103.41/22 example again, using this process to find the subnet broadcast address.

**Table 4-6**    *Quick Math to Find the Broadcast Address—172.31.103.41, 255.255.252.0*

| | Octet | | | | Comments |
|---|---|---|---|---|---|
| | **1** | **2** | **3** | **4** | |
| Subnet number (per Step 1) | 172 | 31 | 100 | 0 | |
| Mask (for reference) | 255 | 255 | 252 | 0 | Equivalent to /22 |
| Results after Steps 1 to 4 | 172 | 31 | | 255 | Magic number will be 256 − 252 = 4 |
| Subnet number after completing the empty octet | 172 | 31 | 103 | 255 | Subnet's third octet (100), plus magic number (4), minus 1 is 103 |

**Note**    If you have read the last few pages to improve your speed at dissecting a subnet without requiring binary math, it is probably a good time to pull out the CD in the back of the book. CD-only Appendix D, "IP Addressing Practice," contains several practice problems for finding the subnet and broadcast address, as well as for many other math issues related to IP addressing.

### Determining All Subnets of a Network—Binary

Another common question, typically simply a portion of a more challenging question on the CCIE written exam, relates to finding all subnets of a network. The base underlying question might be as follows:

> Given a particular class A, B, or C network, and a mask/prefix length used on all subnets of that network, what are the actual subnet numbers?

The answers can be found using binary or using a simple decimal algorithm. This section first shows how to answer the question using binary, using the following steps. Note that the steps include details that are not really necessary for the math part of the problem; these steps are mainly helpful for practicing the process.

Key Topic

**Step 1.**    Write the binary version of the classful network number; that value is actually the zero subnet as well.

**Step 2.**    Draw two vertical lines through the number, one separating the network and subnet parts of the number, the other separating the subnet and host part.

**Step 3.**    Calculate the number of subnets, including the zero and broadcast subnet, based on $2^y$, where $y$ is the number of subnet bits.

**Step 4.**    Write $y-1$ copies of the binary network number below the first one, but leave the subnet field blank.

**Step 5.**    Using the subnet field as a binary counter, write the values, top to bottom, in which the next value is 1 greater than the previous.

**Step 6.**    Convert the binary numbers, 8 bits at a time, back to decimal.

This process takes advantage of a couple of facts about the binary form of IP subnet numbers:

■ All subnets of a classful network have the same value in the network portion of the subnet number.

■ All subnets of any classful network have binary 0s in the host portion of the subnet number.

Step 4 in the process simply makes you write the network and host parts of each subnet number, because those values are easily predicted. To find the different subnet numbers, you then just need to discover all possible different combinations of binary digits in the subnet field, because that is the only part of the subnet numbers that differs from subnet to subnet.

For example, consider the same class B network 172.31.0.0, with static length subnet masking (SLSM) assumed, and a mask of 255.255.224.0. Note that this example uses 3 subnet bits, so there will be $2^3=8$ subnets. Table 4-7 lists the example.

**Table 4-7**  *Binary Method to Find All Subnets—Steps 1 Through 4*

| | Octet | | | |
|---|---|---|---|---|
| **Subnet** | **1** | **2** | **3** | **4** |
| Network number/zero subnet | 10101100 | 000 11111 | 000 00000 | 00000000 |
| 2nd subnet | 10101100 | 000 11111 | 00000 | 00000000 |
| 3rd subnet | 10101100 | 000 11111 | 00000 | 00000000 |
| 4th subnet | 10101100 | 000 11111 | 00000 | 00000000 |
| 5th subnet | 10101100 | 000 11111 | 00000 | 00000000 |
| 6th subnet | 10101100 | 000 11111 | 00000 | 00000000 |
| 7th subnet | 10101100 | 000 11111 | 00000 | 00000000 |
| 8th subnet ($2^y = 8$); broadcast subnet | 10101100 | 000 11111 | 00000 | 00000000 |

At this point, you have the zero subnet recorded at the top, and you are ready to use the subnet field (the missing bits in the table) as a counter to find all possible values. Table 4-8 completes the process.

**Table 4-8**  *Binary Method to Find All Subnets—Step 5*

| | Octet | | | |
|---|---|---|---|---|
| **Subnet** | **1** | **2** | **3** | **4** |
| Network number/zero subnet | 10101100 | 00011111 | 000 00000 | 00000000 |
| 2nd subnet | 10101100 | 00011111 | 001 00000 | 00000000 |
| 3rd subnet | 10101100 | 00011111 | 010 00000 | 00000000 |
| 4th subnet | 10101100 | 00011111 | 011 00000 | 00000000 |
| 5th subnet | 10101100 | 00011111 | 100 00000 | 00000000 |
| 6th subnet | 10101100 | 00011111 | 101 00000 | 00000000 |
| 7th subnet | 10101100 | 00011111 | 110 00000 | 00000000 |
| 8th subnet ($2^y = 8$); broadcast subnet | 10101100 | 00011111 | 111 00000 | 00000000 |

The final step to determine all subnets is simply to convert the values back to decimal. Take care to always convert 8 bits at a time. In this case, you end up with the following subnets: 172.31.0.0, 172.31.32.0, 172.31.64.0, 172.31.96.0, 172.31.128.0, 172.31.160.0, 172.31.192.0, and 172.31.224.0.

## Determining All Subnets of a Network—Decimal

You might have noticed the trend in the third octet values in the subnets listed in the previous paragraph. When assuming SLSM, the subnet numbers in decimal do have a regular increment value, which turns out to be the value of the magic number. For example, instead of the binary math in the previous section, you could have thought the following:

■   The interesting octet is the third octet.

■   The magic number is 256 − 224 = 32.

■   172.31.0.0 is the zero subnet, because it is the same number as the network number.

■   The other subnet numbers are increments of the magic number inside the interesting octet.

If that logic already clicks in your head, you can skip to the next section in this chapter. If not, the rest of this section outlines a decimal algorithm that takes a little longer pass at the same general logic. First, the question and the algorithm assume that the same subnet mask is used on all subnets of this one classful network—a feature sometimes called *static length subnet masking (SLSM)*. In contrast, *variable length subnet masking (VLSM)* means that different masks are used in the same classful network. The algorithm assumes a subnet field of 8 bits or less just to keep the steps uncluttered; for longer subnet fields, the algorithm can be easily extrapolated.

**Key Topic**

**Step 1.**   Write the classful network number in decimal.

**Step 2.**   For the first (lowest numeric) subnet number, copy the entire network number. That is the first subnet number, and is also the zero subnet.

**Step 3.**   Decide which octet contains the entire subnet field; call this octet the interesting octet. (Remember, this algorithm assumes 8 subnet bits or less, so the entire subnet field will be in a single interesting octet.)

**Step 4.**   Calculate the magic number by subtracting the mask's interesting octet value from 256.

**Step 5.**   Copy the previous subnet number's noninteresting octets onto the next line as the next subnet number; only one octet is missing at this point.

**Step 6.**   Add the magic number to the previous subnet's interesting octet, and write that as the next subnet number's interesting octet, completing the next subnet number.

**Step 7.**   Repeat Steps 5 and 6 until the new interesting octet is 256. That subnet is not valid. The previously calculated subnet is the last valid subnet, and also the broadcast subnet.

For example, consider the same class B network 172.31.0.0, with SLSM assumed, and a mask of 255.255.224.0. Table 4-9 lists the example.

**Table 4-9**   *Subnet List Chart—172.31.0.0/255.255.224.0*

|  | Octet | | | | Comments |
|---|---|---|---|---|---|
|  | **1** | **2** | **3** | **4** |  |
| Network number | 172 | 31 | 0 | 0 | Step 1 from the process. |
| Mask | 255 | 255 | 224 | 0 | Magic number is 256 − 224 = 32. |
| Subnet zero | 172 | 31 | 0 | 0 | Step 2 from the process. |
| First subnet | 172 | 31 | 32 | 0 | Steps 5 and 6; previous interesting octet 0, plus magic number (32). |
| Next subnet | 172 | 31 | 64 | 0 | 32 plus magic number is 64. |
| Next subnet | 172 | 31 | 96 | 0 | 64 plus magic number is 96. |
| Next subnet | 172 | 31 | 128 | 0 | 96 plus magic number is 128. |
| Next subnet | 172 | 31 | 160 | 0 | 128 plus magic number is 160. |
| Next subnet | 172 | 31 | 192 | 0 | 160 plus magic number is 192. |
| Last subnet (broadcast) | 172 | 31 | 224 | 0 | The broadcast subnet in this case. |
| Invalid; easy-to-recognize stopping point | 172 | 31 | 256 | 0 | 256 is out of range; when writing this one, note that it is invalid, and that the previous one is the last valid subnet. |

You can use this process repeatedly as needed until the answers start jumping out at you without the table and step-wise algorithm. For more practice, refer to CD-only Appendix D.

## VLSM Subnet Allocation

So far in this chapter, most of the discussion has been about examining existing addresses and subnets. Before deploying new networks, or new parts of a network, you must give some thought to the ranges of IP addresses to be allocated. Also, when assigning subnets for different locations, you should assign the subnets with thought for how routes could then be summarized. This section covers some of the key concepts related to subnet allocation and summarization. (This section focuses on the concepts behind summarization; the configuration of route summarization is routing protocol–specific and thus is covered in the individual chapters covering routing protocols.)

Many organizations purposefully use SLSM to simplify operations. Additionally, many internetworks also use private IP network 10.0.0.0, with an SLSM prefix length of /24, and use NAT for connecting to the Internet. Operations and troubleshooting can be a lot easier when you use SLSM, particularly with a nice, easy prefix like /24.

In some cases, VLSM is required or preferred when allocating addresses. VLSM is typically chosen when the address space is constrained to some degree. The VLSM subnet assignment strategy covered here complies with the strategy you might remember from the Cisco BSCI course or from reading the Cisco Press CCNP Routing certification books.

Similar to when assigning subnets with SLSM, you should use an easily summarized block of addresses for a new part of the network. Because VLSM network addresses are likely constrained to some degree, you should choose the specific subnets wisely. The general rules for choosing wisely are as follows:

Key Topic

**Step 1.**   Determine the shortest prefix length (in other words, the largest block) required.

**Step 2.**   Divide the available address block into equal-sized prefixes based on the shortest prefix from Step 1.

**Step 3.**   Allocate the largest required subnets/prefixes from the beginning of the IP address block, leaving some equal-sized unallocated address blocks at the end of the original large address block.

**Step 4.**   Choose an unallocated block that you will further subdivide by repeating the first three steps, using the shortest required prefix length (largest address block) for the remaining subnets.

**Step 5.**   When allocating very small address blocks for use on links between routers, consider using subnets at the end of the address range. This leaves the largest consecutive blocks available in case future requirements change.

For example, imagine that a network engineer plans a new site installation. He allocates the 172.31.28.0/23 address block for the new site, expecting to use the block as a single summarized route. When planning, the engineer then subdivides 172.31.28.0/23 per the subnet requirements for the new installation, as shown in Figure 4-3. The figure shows three iterations through the VLSM subnet assignment process, because the requirements call for three different subnet sizes. Each iteration divides a remaining block into equal sizes, based on the prefix requirements of the subnets allocated at that step. Note that the small /30 prefixes were allocated from the end of the address range, leaving the largest possible consecutive address range for future growth.

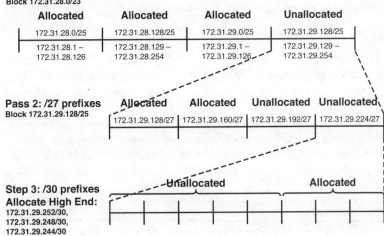

**Figure 4-3** *Example of VLSM Subnet Allocation Process*

## Route Summarization Concepts

The ability to recognize and define how to most efficiently summarize existing address ranges is an important skill on both the written and lab exams. For the written exam, the question might not be as straightforward as, "What is the most efficient summarization of the following subnets?" Rather, the math required for such a question might simply be part of a larger question. Certainly, such math is required for the lab exam. This section looks at the math behind finding the best summarization; other chapters cover specific configuration commands.

Good IP address assignment practices should always consider the capabilities for route summarization. For example, if a division of a company needs 15 subnets, an engineer needs to allocate those 15 subnets from the unused portions of the address block available to that internetwork. However, assigning subnets 10.1.101.0/24 through 10.1.115.0/24 would be a poor choice, because those do not easily summarize. Rather, allocate a range of addresses that can be easily summarized into a single route. For example, subnets

10.1.96.0/24 through 10.1.111.0/24 can be summarized as a single 10.1.96.0/20 route, making those routes a better choice.

There are two main ways to think of the word *best* when you are looking for the "best summarization":

- **Inclusive summary routes:** A single summarized route that is as small a range of addresses as possible, while including all routes/subnets shown, and *possibly including subnets that do not currently exist.*

- **Exclusive summary routes:** As few as possible summarized routes that include all to-be-summarized address ranges, but *excluding all other routes/subnets.*

**Note** The terms *inclusive summary*, *exclusive summary*, and *candidate summary* are simply terms I invented for this book and will continue to use later in the chapter.

For example, with the VLSM example in Figure 4-3, the network engineer purposefully planned so that an inclusive summary of 172.31.28.0/23 could be used. Even though not all subnets are yet allocated from that address range, the engineer is likely saving the rest of that address range for future subnets at that site, so summarizing using an inclusive summary is reasonable. In other cases, typically when trying to summarize routes in an internetwork for which summarization was not planned, the summarization must exclude routes that are not explicitly listed, because those address ranges can actually be used in another part of the internetwork.

## Finding Inclusive Summary Routes—Binary

Finding the best inclusive summary lends itself to a formal binary process, as well as to a formal decimal process. The binary process runs as follows:

**Step 1.** Write the binary version of each component subnet, one on top of the other.

**Step 2.** Inspect the binary values to find how many consecutive bits have the exact same value in all component subnets. That number of bits is the prefix length.

**Step 3.** Write a new 32-bit number at the bottom of the list by copying $y$ bits from the prior number, $y$ being the prefix length. Write binary 0s for the remaining bits. This is the inclusive summary.

**Step 4.** Convert the new number to decimal, 8 bits at a time.

Table 4-10 shows an example of this process, using four routes, 172.31.20.0, .21.0, .22.0, and .23.0, all with prefix /24.

**Table 4-10**   *Example of Finding the Best Inclusive Summary—Binary*

|                    | Octet 1   | Octet 2   | Octet 3    | Octet 4   |
|--------------------|-----------|-----------|------------|-----------|
| 172.31.20.0/24     | 10101100  | 00011111  | 000101 00  | 00000000  |
| 172.31.21.0/24     | 10101100  | 00011111  | 000101 01  | 00000000  |
| 172.31.22.0/24     | 10101100  | 00011111  | 000101 10  | 00000000  |
| 172.31.23.0/24     | 10101100  | 00011111  | 000101 11  | 00000000  |
| Prefix length: 22  |           |           |            |           |
| Inclusive summary  | 10101100  | 00011111  | 000101 00  | 00000000  |

The trickiest part is Step 2, in which you have to simply look at the binary values and find the point at which the bits are no longer equal. You can shorten the process by, in this case, noticing that all component subnets begin with 172.31, meaning that the first 16 bits will certainly have the same values.

## Finding Inclusive Summary Routes—Decimal

To find the same inclusive summary using only decimal math, use the following process. The process works just fine with variable prefix lengths and nonconsecutive subnets.

**Step 1.**   Count the number of subnets; then, find the smallest value of $y$, such that $2^y$ => that number of subnets.

**Step 2.**   For the next step, use a prefix length based on the longest prefix length of the component subnets, minus $y$.

**Step 3.**   Pretend that the lowest numeric subnet number in the list of component subnets is an IP address. Using the new, smaller prefix from Step 2, calculate the subnet number in which this pretend address resides.

**Step 4.**   Repeat Step 3 for the largest numeric component subnet number and the same prefix. If it is the same subnet derived as in Step 3, the resulting subnet is the best summarized route, using the new prefix.

**Step 5.**   If Steps 3 and 4 do not yield the same resulting subnet, repeat Steps 3 and 4 with another new prefix length of 1 less than the last prefix length.

Table 4-11 shows two examples of the process. The first example has four routes, 172.31.20.0, .21.0, .22.0, and .23.0, all with prefix /24. The second example adds 172.31.24.0 to that same list.

**Table 4-11**   *Example of Finding the Best Summarizations*

| Step | Range of .20.0, .21.0, .22.0, and .23.0, /24 | Same Range, Plus 172.31.24.0 |
|---|---|---|
| Step 1 | $2^2 = 4$, $y = 2$ | $2^3 = 8$, $y = 3$ |
| Step 2 | $24 - 2 = 22$ | $24 - 3 = 21$ |
| Step 3 | Smallest subnet 172.31.20.0, with /22, yields **172.31.20.0/22** | Smallest subnet 172.31.20.0, with /21, yields **172.31.16.0/21** |
| Step 4 | Largest subnet 172.31.23.0, with /22, yields **172.31.20.0/22** | Largest subnet 172.31.24.0, with /21, yields **172.31.24.0/21** |
| Step 5 | — | $21 - 1 = 20$; new prefix |
| Step 3, 2nd time | — | 172.31.16.0/20 |
| Step 4, 2nd time | — | 172.31.16.0/20; the same as prior step, so that is the answer |

With the first example, Steps 3 and 4 yielded the same answer, which means that the best inclusive summary had been found. With the second example, a second pass through the process was required. CD-only Appendix D contains several practice problems to help you develop speed and make this process second nature.

## Finding Exclusive Summary Routes—Binary

A similar process, listed next, can be used to find the exclusive summary. Keep in mind that the best exclusive summary can be composed of multiple summary routes. Once again, to keep it simple, the process assumes SLSM.

**Step 1.**   Find the best *exclusive* summary route; call it a *candidate exclusive* summary route.

**Step 2.**   Determine whether the candidate summary includes any address ranges it should not. To do so, compare the summary's implied address range with the implied address ranges of the component subnets.

**Step 3.**   If the candidate summary only includes addresses in the ranges implied by the component subnets, the candidate summary is part of the best exclusive summarization of the original component subnets.

**Step 4.**   If instead the candidate summary includes some addresses that match the candidate summary routes and some addresses that do not, split the current candidate summary in half, into two new candidate summary routes, each with a prefix 1 *longer* than before.

**Step 5.**   If the candidate summary only includes addresses outside the ranges implied by the component subnets, the candidate summary is not part of the best exclusive summarization, and it should not be split further.

**Step 6.**    Repeat Steps 2 through 4 for each of the two possible candidate summary routes created at Step 4.

For example, take the same five subnets used with the inclusive example—172.31.20.0/24, .21.0, .22.0, .23.0, and .24.0. The best inclusive summary is 172.31.16.0/20, which implies an address range of 172.31.16.0 to 172.31.31.255—clearly, it includes more addresses than the original five subnets. So, repeat the process of splitting the summary in half, and repeating, until summaries are found that do not include any unnecessary address ranges. Figure 4-4 shows the idea behind the logic.

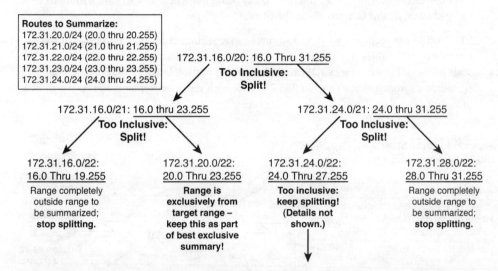

**Figure 4-4**   *Example of Process to Find Exclusive Summary Routes*

The process starts with one candidate summary. If it includes some addresses that need to be summarized and some addresses it should not summarize, split it in half and try again with each half. Eventually, the best exclusive summary routes are found, or the splitting keeps happening until you get back to the original routes. In fact, in this case, after a few more splits (not shown), the process ends up splitting to 172.31.24.0/24, which is one of the original routes—meaning that 172.31.24.0/24 cannot be summarized any further in this example.

# CIDR, Private Addresses, and NAT

The sky was falling in the early 1990s in that the commercialization of the Internet was rapidly depleting the IP version 4 address space. Also, Internet routers' routing tables were doubling annually (at least). Without some changes, the incredible growth of the Internet in the 1990s would have been stifled.

To solve the problems associated with this rapid growth, several short-term solutions were created, as well as an ultimate long-term solution. The short-term solutions included classless interdomain routing (CIDR), which helps reduce the size of routing tables by aggregating routes, and Network Address Translation (NAT), which reduces the number of required public IP addresses used by each organization or company. This section covers the details of CIDR and NAT, plus a few related features.

## Classless Interdomain Routing

CIDR is a convention defined in RFCs 1517 through 1520 that calls for aggregating routes for multiple classful network numbers into a single routing table entry. The primary goal of CIDR is to improve the scalability of Internet routers' routing tables. Imagine the implications of an Internet router being burdened by carrying a route to every class A, B, and C network on the planet!

CIDR uses both technical tools and administrative strategies to reduce the size of the Internet routing tables. Technically, CIDR uses route summarization, but with Internet scale in mind. For example, CIDR might be used to allow a large ISP to control a range of IP addresses from 198.0.0.0 to 198.255.255.255, with the improvements to routing shown in Figure 4-5.

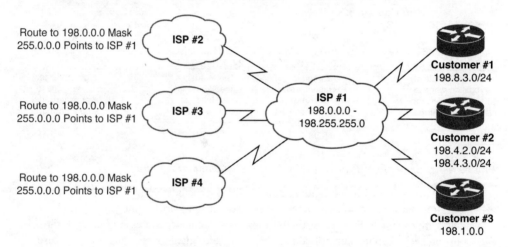

**Figure 4-5**  *Typical Use of CIDR*

ISPs 2, 3, and 4 need only one route (198.0.0.0/8) in their routing tables to be able to forward packets to all destinations that begin with 198. Note that this summary actually summarizes multiple class C networks—a typical feature of CIDR. ISP 1's routers contain more detailed routing entries for addresses beginning with 198, based on where they allocate IP addresses for their customers. ISP 1 would reduce its routing tables similarly with large ranges used by the other ISPs.

CIDR attacks the problem of large routing tables through administrative means as well. As shown in Figure 4-5, ISPs are assigned contiguous blocks of addresses to use when assigning addresses for their customers. Likewise, regional authorities are assigned large address blocks, so when individual companies ask for registered public IP addresses, they ask their regional registry to assign them an address block. As a result, addresses assigned by the regional agency will at least be aggregatable into one large geographic region of the world. For example, the Latin American and Caribbean Internet Addresses Registry

(LACNIC, www.lacnic.net) administers the IP address space of the Latin American and Caribbean region (LAC) on behalf of the Internet community.

In some cases, the term *CIDR* is used a little more generally than the original intent of the RFCs. Some texts use the term CIDR synonymously with the term *route summarization*. Others use the term CIDR to refer to the process of summarizing multiple classful networks together. In other cases, when an ISP assigns subsets of a classful network to a customer who does not need an entire class C network, the ISP is essentially performing subnetting; once again, this idea sometimes gets categorized as CIDR. But CIDR itself refers to the administrative assignment of large address blocks, and the related summarized routes, for the purpose of reducing the size of the Internet routing tables.

> **Note**   Because CIDR defines how to combine routes for multiple classful networks into a single route, some people think of this process as being the opposite of subnetting. As a result, many people refer to CIDR's summarization results as *supernetting*.

## Private Addressing

One of the issues with Internet growth was the assignment of all possible network numbers to a small number of companies or organizations. Private IP addressing helps to mitigate this problem by allowing computers that will never be directly connected to the Internet to not use public, Internet-routable addresses. For IP hosts that will purposefully have no direct Internet connectivity, you can use several reserved network numbers, as defined in RFC 1918 and listed in Table 4-12.

**Table 4-12**   *RFC 1918 Private Address Space*

| Range of IP Addresses | Class of Networks | Number of Networks |
|---|---|---|
| 10.0.0.0 to 10.255.255.255 | A | 1 |
| 172.16.0.0 to 172.31.255.255 | B | 16 |
| 192.168.0.0 to 192.168.255.255 | C | 256 |

In other words, any organization can use these network numbers. However, no organization is allowed to advertise these networks using a routing protocol on the Internet. Furthermore, all Internet routers should be configured to reject these routes.

## Network Address Translation

NAT, defined in RFC 1631, enables a host that does not have a valid registered IP address to communicate with other hosts on the Internet. NAT has gained such widespread acceptance that the majority of enterprise IP networks today use private IP addresses for most hosts on the network and use a small block of public IP addresses, with NAT translating between the two.

NAT translates, or changes, one or both IP addresses inside a packet as it passes through a router. (Many firewalls also perform NAT; for the CCIE Routing and Switching exam, you do not need to know NAT implementation details on firewalls.) In most cases, NAT changes the (typically private range) addresses used inside an enterprise network into addresses from the public IP address space. For example, Figure 4-6 shows static NAT in operation; the enterprise has registered class C network 200.1.1.0/24, and uses private class A network 10.0.0.0/8 for the hosts inside its network.

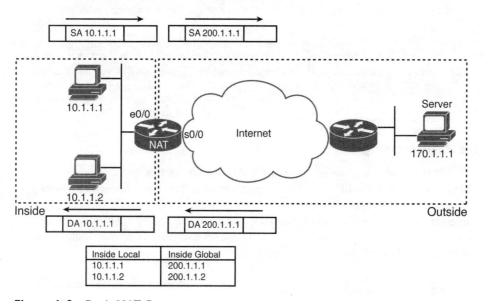

**Figure 4-6**  *Basic NAT Concept*

Beginning with the packets sent from a PC on the left to the server on the right, the private IP source address 10.1.1.1 is translated to a public IP address of 200.1.1.1. The client sends a packet with source address 10.1.1.1, but the NAT router changes the source to 200.1.1.1—a registered public IP address. When the server receives a packet with source IP address 200.1.1.1, the server thinks it is talking to host 200.1.1.1, so it replies with a packet sent to destination 200.1.1.1. The NAT router then translates the destination address (200.1.1.1) back to 10.1.1.1.

Figure 4-6 provides a good backdrop for the introduction of a couple of key terms, *Inside Local* and *Inside Global*. Both terms take the perspective of the owner of the enterprise network. In Figure 4-6, address 10.1.1.1 is the Inside Local address, and 200.1.1.1 is the Inside Global address. Both addresses represent the client PC on the left, which is *inside the enterprise network*. Address 10.1.1.1 is from the enterprise's IP address space, which is only *locally* routable inside the enterprise—hence the term Inside Local. Address 200.1.1.1 represents the local host, but the address is from the globally routable public IP address space—hence the name Inside Global. Table 4-13 lists and describes the four main NAT address terms.

**Table 4-13**  *NAT Terminology*

| Name | Location of Host Represented by Address | IP Address Space in Which Address Exists |
|---|---|---|
| Inside Local address | Inside the enterprise network | Part of the enterprise IP address space; typically a private IP address |
| Inside Global address | Inside the enterprise network | Part of the public IP address space |
| Outside Local address | In the public Internet; or, outside the enterprise network | Part of the enterprise IP address space; typically a private IP address |
| Outside Global address | In the public Internet; or, outside the enterprise network | Part of the public IP address space |

### Static NAT

Static NAT works just like the example in Figure 4-6, but with the IP addresses statically mapped to each other through configuration commands. With static NAT

- A particular Inside Local address always maps to the same Inside Global (public) IP address.

- If used, each Outside Local address always maps to the same Outside Global (public) IP address.

- Static NAT does not conserve public IP addresses.

Although static NAT does not help with IP address conservation, static NAT does allow an engineer to make an inside server host available to clients on the Internet, because the inside server will always use the same public IP address.

Example 4-1 shows a basic static NAT configuration based on Figure 4-6. Conceptually, the NAT router has to identify which interfaces are inside (attach to the enterprise's IP address space) or outside (attach to the public IP address space). Also, the mapping between each Inside Local and Inside Global IP address must be made. (Although not needed for this example, outside addresses can also be statically mapped.)

**Example 4-1**  *Static NAT Configuration*

```
!!!!!!!!!!!!!!!!!!!!!!!!!!!!!!!!!!!!!!!!!!!!!!!!!!!!!!!!!!!!!!!!!!!!!!!!!!!!!!!!!!!!
! E0/0 attaches to the internal Private IP space, so it is configured as an inside
! interface.
interface Ethernet0/0
 ip address 10.1.1.3 255.255.255.0
```

```
 ip nat inside
! S0/0 is attached to the public Internet, so it is defined as an outside
! interface.
interface Serial0/0
 ip address 200.1.1.251 255.255.255.0
 ip nat outside
! Next, two inside addresses are mapped, with the first address stating the
! Inside Local address, and the next stating the Inside Global address.
ip nat inside source static 10.1.1.2 200.1.1.2
ip nat inside source static 10.1.1.1 200.1.1.1
! Below, the NAT table lists the permanent static entries from the configuration.
NAT# show ip nat translations
Pro Inside global     Inside local      Outside local     Outside global
--- 200.1.1.1         10.1.1.1          ---               --
--- 200.1.1.2         10.1.1.2          ---               ---
```

The router is performing NAT only for inside addresses. As a result, the router processes packets entering E0/0—packets that could be sent by inside hosts—by examining the source IP address. Any packets with a source IP address listed in the Inside Local column of the **show ip nat translations** command output (10.1.1.1 or 10.1.1.2) will be translated to source address 200.1.1.1 or 200.1.1.2, respectively, per the NAT table. Likewise, the router examines the destination IP address of packets entering S0/0, because those packets would be destined for inside hosts. Any such packets with a destination of 200.1.1.1 or .2 will be translated to 10.1.1.1 or .2, respectively.

In cases with static outside addresses being configured, the router also looks at the destination IP address of packets sent from the inside to the outside interfaces, and the source IP address of packets sent from outside interfaces to inside interfaces.

## Dynamic NAT Without PAT

Dynamic NAT (without PAT), like static NAT, creates a one-to-one mapping between an Inside Local and Inside Global address. However, unlike static NAT, it does so by defining a set or pool of Inside Local and Inside Global addresses, and dynamically mapping pairs of addresses as needed. For example, Figure 4-7 shows a pool of five Inside Global IP addresses—200.1.1.1 through 200.1.1.5. NAT has also been configured to translate any Inside Local addresses whose address starts with 10.1.1.

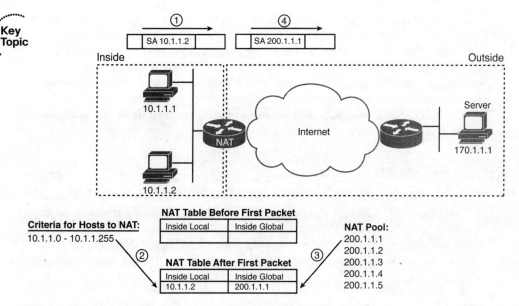

**Figure 4-7** *Dynamic NAT*

The numbers 1, 2, and 3 in Figure 4-7 refer to the following sequence of events:

1. Host 10.1.1.2 starts by sending its first packet to the server at 170.1.1.1.

2. As the packet enters the NAT router, the router applies some matching logic to decide whether the packet should have NAT applied. Because the logic has been configured to mean "translate Inside Local addresses that start with 10.1.1," the router dynamically adds an entry in the NAT table for 10.1.1.2 as an Inside Local address.

3. The NAT router needs to allocate a corresponding IP address from the pool of valid Inside Global addresses. It picks the first one available (200.1.1.1 in this case) and adds it to the NAT table to complete the entry.

With the completion of Step 3, the NAT router can actually translate the source IP address and forward the packet. Note that as long as the dynamic NAT entry exists in the NAT table, only host 10.1.1.2 can use Inside Global IP address 200.1.1.1.

## Overloading NAT with Port Address Translation

As mentioned earlier, NAT is one of the key features that helped to reduce the speed at which the IPv4 address space was being depleted. *NAT overloading*, also known as *Port Address Translation (PAT)*, is the NAT feature that actually provides the significant savings of IP addresses. The key to understanding how PAT works is to consider the following: From a server's perspective, there is no significant difference between 100 different TCP connections, each from a different host, and 100 different TCP connections all from the same host.

PAT works by making large numbers of TCP or UDP flows from many Inside Local hosts appear to be the same number of large flows from one (or a few) host's Inside Global addresses. With PAT, instead of just translating the IP address, NAT also translates the port numbers as necessary. And because the port number fields are 16 bits in length, each Inside Global IP address can support over 65,000 concurrent TCP and UDP flows. For example, in a network with 1000 hosts, a single public IP address used as the only Inside Global address could handle an average of sixty concurrent flows from each host to and from the hosts on the Internet.

## Dynamic NAT and PAT Configuration

Like static NAT, dynamic NAT configuration begins with identifying the inside and outside interfaces. Additionally, the set of Inside Local addresses is configured with the **ip nat inside** global command. If you are using a pool of public Inside Global addresses, the set of addresses is defined by the **ip nat pool** command. Example 4-2 shows a dynamic NAT configuration based on the internetwork shown in Figure 4-7. The example defines 256 Inside Local addresses and two Inside Global addresses.

**Example 4-2**  *Dynamic NAT Configuration*

```
! First, the ip nat pool fred command lists a range of IP addresses. The ip nat
! inside source list 1 pool fred command points to ACL 1 as the list of Inside
! Local addresses, with a cross-reference to the pool name.
interface Ethernet0/0
 ip address 10.1.1.3 255.255.255.0
 ip nat inside
!
interface Serial0/0
 ip address 200.1.1.251 255.255.255.0
 ip nat outside
!
ip nat pool fred 200.1.1.1 200.1.1.2 netmask 255.255.255.252
ip nat inside source list 1 pool fred
!
access-list 1 permit 10.1.1.0 0.0.0.255
! Next, the NAT table begins as an empty table, because no dynamic entries had
! been created at that point.
NAT# show ip nat translations

! The NAT statistics show that no hits or misses have occurred. Hits occur when
! NAT looks for a mapping, and finds one. Misses occur when NAT looks for a NAT
! table entry, does not find one, and then needs to dynamically add one.
NAT# show ip nat statistics
Total active translations: 0 (0 static, 0 dynamic; 0 extended)
```

```
Outside interfaces:
  Serial0/0
Inside interfaces:
  Ethernet0/0
Hits: 0  Misses: 0
Expired translations: 0
Dynamic mappings:
-- Inside Source
access-list 1 pool fred refcount 0
 pool fred: netmask 255.255.255.252
    start 200.1.1.1 end 200.1.1.2
    type generic, total addresses 2, allocated 0 (0%), misses 0
! At this point, a Telnet session from 10.1.1.1 to 170.1.1.1 started.
! Below, the 1 "miss" means that the first packet from 10.1.1.2 did not have a
! matching entry in the table, but that packet triggered NAT to add an entry to the
! NAT table. Host 10.1.1.2 has then sent 69 more packets, noted as "hits" because
! there was an entry in the table.
NAT# show ip nat statistics
Total active translations: 1 (0 static, 1 dynamic; 0 extended)
Outside interfaces:
  Serial0/0
Inside interfaces:
  Ethernet0/0
Hits: 69  Misses: 1
Expired translations: 0
Dynamic mappings:
-- Inside Source
access-list 1 pool fred refcount 1
 pool fred: netmask 255.255.255.252
    start 200.1.1.1 end 200.1.1.2
    type generic, total addresses 2, allocated 1 (50%), misses 0
! The dynamic NAT entry is now displayed in the table.
NAT# show ip nat translations
Pro Inside global      Inside local      Outside local      Outside global
--- 200.1.1.1          10.1.1.2          ---                ---
! Below, the configuration uses PAT via the overload parameter. Could have used the
! ip nat inside source list 1 int s0/0 overload command instead, using a single
! IP Inside Global IP address.
NAT(config)# no ip nat inside source list 1 pool fred
NAT(config)# ip nat inside source list 1 pool fred overload
! To test, the dynamic NAT entries were cleared after changing the NAT
! configuration. Before the next command was issued, host 10.1.1.1 had created two
! Telnet connections, and host 10.1.1.2 created 1 more TCP connection.
```

```
NAT# clear ip nat translations *
NAT# show ip nat translations
Pro Inside global        Inside local        Outside local        Outside global
tcp 200.1.1.1:3212       10.1.1.1:3212       170.1.1.1:23         170.1.1.1:23
tcp 200.1.1.1:3213       10.1.1.1:3213       170.1.1.1:23         170.1.1.1:23
tcp 200.1.1.1:38913      10.1.1.2:38913      170.1.1.1:23         170.1.1.1:23
```

# IPv6

In the TCP/IP stack, IP is where packet sorting and delivery take place. At this layer, each incoming or outgoing packet is referred to as a *datagram*. Each IP datagram bears the source IP address of the sender and the destination IP address of the intended recipient. Unlike MAC addresses, IP addresses in a datagram remain the same throughout a packet's journey across an internetwork.

As we have discussed before, the operation of IP is central to the TCP/IP stack—all other TCP/IP protocols use IP—and all data passes through it. IP is a connectionless protocol and has some limitations. If IP attempts packet delivery and in the process a packet is lost, delivered out of sequence, duplicated, or delayed, neither sender nor receiver is informed. Packet acknowledgment is handled by a higher-layer transport protocol, such as TCP, which we have discussed previously.

IP is responsible for addressing and routing packets between hosts, and determines whether fragmentation is necessary. Fragmentation involves breaking a datagram into smaller pieces for optimized routing. The IP protocol will fragment packets prior to sending them and will also reassemble them when they reach their destination.

The issue with IP in the modern internetwork has more to do with capacity constraints rather than operational issues. In short, we can best describe the Achilles heel of IP by pointing out the fact that the Internet has grown so significantly over the decades that there are not enough IP addresses to go around. We obviously are talking about IPv4 addresses. The version 4 address space, as discussed previously, is composed of addresses defined by a series of 32 bits broken up into four separate octets through the use of "dotted decimal" notation. This means that we have a very finite number of addresses available to use at the onset, and this limitation is further compounded by the fact that many addresses in this total range have either been "reserved" for special operations or "wasted" with regard to being inefficiently issued to users.

In short, we need another solution. That solution is the next generation IP that is being widely adopted across the globe as we speak: IPv6. IP version 6 is considered to be the best fit for the modern network because of the fact that it supports a substantially larger address space to begin with. Whereas IPv4 addresses were 32 bits long, an IPv6 address is 128 bits long. This means that the older IPv4 only supports a maximum of $2^{32}$ IP addresses, which translates to roughly 4.29 billion total addresses. IPv6, because it utilizes 128 bits, supports a maximum of $2^{128}$ available addresses:

340,282,366,920,938,463,463,374,607,431,768,211,456

For those who care to know, that number would be read as 340 undecillion, 282 decillion, 366 nonillion, 920 octillion, 938 septillion, 463 sextillion, 463 quintillion, 374 quadrillion, 607 trillion, 431 billion, 768 million, 211 thousand, and 456. For the rest of us, we can just say it's a very big number.

IPv6 introduces some new concepts with regard to how we annotate addresses and how we implement and categorize address assignment.

## IPv6 Address Format

IPv6 uses 16-byte hexadecimal number fields separated by colons (:) to represent the 128-bit addressing format that makes the address representation less cumbersome and error-prone. Here is an example of a valid IPv6 address:

    2001:db8:130F:0000:0000:09C0:876A:130B

Additionally, to shorten the IPv6 address and make the address easier to represent, IPv6 uses the following conventions:

- Leading 0s in the address field are optional and can be compressed.

    For example: The following hexadecimal numbers can be represented as shown in a compressed format:

    - Example 1: 0000 = 0 (compressed form)
    - Example 2: 2001:db8:130F:0000:0000:09C0:876A:130B = 2001:db8:130F:0:0:9C0:876A:130B (compressed form)

- A pair of colons (::) represents successive fields of 0. However, the pair of colons is allowed just once in a valid IPv6 address.

    - Example 1: 2001:db8:130F:0:0:9C0:876A:130B = 2001:db8:130F::9C0:876A:130B (compressed form)
    - Example 2: FF01:0:0:0:0:0:1 = FF01::1 (compressed form)

An address parser can easily identify the number of missing 0s in an IPv6 address by separating the two parts of the address and filling in the 0s until the 128-bit address is complete. However, if two pairs of colons are placed in the same address, there is no way to identify the size of each block of 0s. The use of the :: makes many IPv6 addresses very small.

## Network Prefix

In IPv6, there are references to prefixes that, in IPv4 terms, loosely equate to subnets. The IPv6 prefix is made up of the leftmost bits and acts as the network identifier. The IPv6 prefix is represented using the IPv6-prefix or prefix-length format just like an IPv4 address is represented in the classless interdomain routing (CIDR) notation.

The / prefix-length variable is a decimal value that indicates the number of high-order contiguous bits of the address that form the prefix, which is the network portion of the address. For example, 2001:db8:8086:6502::/64 is an acceptable IPv6 prefix. If the address ends in a double colon, the trailing double colon can be omitted. So the same address can be written as 2001:db8:8086:6502/64. In either case, the prefix length is written as a decimal number 64 and represents the leftmost bits of the IPv6 address. A similar address in IPv4 would be xxx.xxx.xxx.xxx/16.

## IPv6 Address Types

There is a major difference in the IP address requirements between an IPv4 host and an IPv6 host. An IPv4 host typically uses one IP address, but an IPv6 host can have more than one IP address.

There are three major types of IPv6 addresses:

■ **Unicast:** An address for a single interface. A packet that is sent to a unicast address is delivered to the interface identified by that address.

■ **Anycast:** An address for a set of interfaces that typically belong to different nodes. A packet sent to an anycast address is delivered to the closest interface, as defined by the routing protocols in use and identified by the anycast address.

■ **Multicast:** An address for a set of interfaces (in a given scope) that typically belong to different nodes. A packet sent to a multicast address is delivered to all interfaces identified by the multicast address (in a given scope).

Note that in the context of IPv6, there is no concept of Broadcast.

## Address Management and Assignment

There are four ways to configure a host address in IPv6:

■ **Static Configuration:** Similar to IPv4, the host address, mask, and gateway address are manually defined.

■ **Stateless Address Autoconfiguration (SLAAC):** In this case, the host autonomously configures its own address. Router solicitation messages are sent by booting nodes to request Router Advertisements (RA) for configuring the interfaces (RFC 2462).

■ **Stateful DHCPv6:** The host uses Dynamic Host Configuration Protocol (DHCP) to get its IPv6 address. This addressing management is similar to IPv4 behavior (RFC 3315).

■ **Stateless DHCP:** The host uses SLAAC and also DHCP to get additional parameters such as TFTP Server, WINS, and so on.

The configuration choice relies on Router Advertisement (RA) flags sent by the router on the LAN. The sections that follow take a cursory look at each of these methods.

## Static Configuration

As in IPv4, the host address can be statically defined. In this case, the IPv6 address, mask, and gateway address are all manually defined on the host.

Static address configuration is typically used for router interface configuration but is not likely to be used for hosts in IPv6. Keep in mind that using static configuration means that all autoconfiguration features provided by IPv6 will be disabled.

## Stateless Address Autoconfiguration

Nodes can use IPv6 Stateless Address Autoconfiguration to generate addresses without the necessity of a DHCP server. IPv6 addresses are formed by combining network prefixes with an interface identifier. On interfaces with embedded Institute of Electrical and Electronics Engineers (IEEE) identifiers, the interface identifier is typically derived from the IEEE identifier.

The address autoconfiguration feature is built into the IPv6 protocol to facilitate intranet-wide address management that enables a large number of IP hosts to easily discover the network and get new and globally unique IPv6 addresses associated with their location. The autoconfiguration feature enables plug-and-play Internet deployment of new consumer devices, such as cell phones, wireless devices, home appliances, and so on. As a result, network devices can connect to the network without manual configuration and without any servers, such as DHCP servers. We need to take a slightly closer look at the principles behind this feature.

A router on a local link sends network-type information through RA messages, such as the prefix of the local link and the default route in its router advertisements. The router provides this information to all the nodes on the local link.

A host can then build its address by appending a host identifier to the /64 prefix received from the router. As a result, Ethernet hosts can autoconfigure themselves by appending their 48-bit link-layer address (MAC address) in an extended universal identifier EUI-64-bit format to the 64 bits of the local link prefix advertised by the router.

Another hugely beneficial aspect to this approach is the ease with which address renumbering can be implemented. In IPv6 networks, the autoconfiguration feature makes renumbering an existing network simple and relatively easy compared to IPv4. The router sends the new prefix from the new upstream provider in its router announcements. The hosts in the network automatically pick the new prefix from the router advertisements and then use it to create their new addresses. As a result, the transition from provider A to B becomes manageable for network operators.

## Stateful DHCPv6

Many enterprises currently use DHCP to distribute addresses to their hosts. IPv6 can be deployed with the same DHCP mechanism.

The process for acquiring configuration data for a client in IPv6 is similar to that in IPv4. However, DHCPv6 uses multicast for many of its messages. Initially, the client must first detect the presence of routers on the link using neighbor discovery messages. If a router is found, the client examines the router advertisements to determine whether DHCP should be used. If the router advertisements enable the use of DHCP on that link (disabling the Autoconfiguration flag and enabling the Managed flag in RA messages allows a host to use DHCPv6 to obtain an IPv6 address), the client starts a DHCP solicitation phase to find a DHCP server.

Using DHCPv6 provides the following benefits:

- More control than serverless/stateless autoconfiguration.

- It can be used concurrently with stateless autoconfiguration.

- It can be used for renumbering.

- It can be used for automatic domain name registration of hosts using dynamic DNS.

- It can be used to delegate the IPv6 prefix to leaf customer premises equipment (CPE) routers.

### Stateless DHCP

Stateless DHCPv6 normally combines stateless autoconfiguration for address assignment with DHCPv6 exchange for all other configuration settings. In this case, DHCPv6 is only used for the host to acquire additional parameters, such as a TFTP server, a DNS server, and so on.

A host builds its address by appending a host identifier to the /64 prefix received from the router and then issues a DHCP solicit message to the DHCP server.

## IPv6 Transition Technologies

The success of IPv6 originally was thought to depend on the new applications that run over it. However, it is becoming very clear that the exhaustion of IPv4 will ultimately end up being the driver for IPv6 adoption. A key part of any good IPv6 design is its ability to integrate into and coexist with existing IPv4 networks. IPv4 and IPv6 hosts need to coexist for a substantial length of time during the steady migration from IPv4 to IPv6, and the development of transition strategies, tools, and mechanisms has been part of the basic IPv6 design from the start.

There are three IPv6 transition technologies: dual stack, tunneling, and translation.

### Dual Stack

Dual stack is the basic strategy to use for large agencies that are adopting IPv6. It involves configuring devices to be able to run IPv4 and IPv6 simultaneously. IPv4 communication uses the IPv4 protocol stack, and IPv6 communication uses the IPv6 protocol stack.

Applications choose between using IPv4 or IPv6 based on the response to DNS requests. The application selects the correct address based on the type of IP traffic. Because dual stack allows hosts to simultaneously reach existing IPv4 content and IPv6 content as it becomes available, dual stack offers a very flexible adoption strategy. However, because IPv4 addresses are still required, dual stack is not a long-term solution to address exhaustion.

Dual stack also avoids the need to translate between protocol stacks. Translation is a valid adoption mechanism, but it introduces operational complexity and lower performance. Because a host automatically selects the right transport to use to reach a destination based on DNS information, there should not be a need to translate between an IPv6 host and an IPv4 server.

## Tunneling

Tunnels encapsulate IPv6 traffic within IPv4 packets, and are primarily used for communication between IPv6 (or dual stack) sites or for connection to remote IPv6 networks or hosts over an IPv4 backbone. There are many different tunneling techniques, including 6to4, ISATAP, Teredo, 6PE, 6VPE, and mGRE v6 over v4. Tunnels can be manually configured or automatically configured. Most modern operating systems include support for tunneling in addition to dual stack.

Example 4-3 presents a simple 6to4 tunnel configuration.

**Example 4-3**  *Dynamic 6to4 Tunnel Configuration*

```
On R2


R2(config)# int tunnel 23
R2(config-if)# ipv6 addr 23::2/64
R2(config-if)# tunnel source lo0
R2(config-if)# tunnel destination 3.3.3.3
R2(config-if)# tunnel mode ipv6ip


You should see the following console message stating that the tunnel interface is
  UP:


%LINEPROTO-5-UPDOWN: Line protocol on Interface Tunnel23, changed state
to up
On R3


R3(config)# int tunnel 32
R3(config-if)# ipv6 addr 23::3/64
R3(config-if)# tunnel source lo0
R3(config-if)# tunnel destination 2.2.2.2
R3(config-if)# tunnel mode ipv6ip
```

```
You should see the following console message stating that the tunnel interface is
  UP:

%LINEPROTO-5-UPDOWN: Line protocol on Interface Tunnel32, changed state
to up
On R2


R2# Ping 23::3

Type escape sequence to abort.
Sending 5, 100-byte ICMP Echos to 23::3, timeout is 2 seconds:
!!!!!
Success rate is 100 percent (5/5), round-trip min/avg/max = 56/58/60 ms
```

## Translation

Address Family Translation (AFT) is the process of translating addresses from one
address family to another. During the adoption phase, AFT is primarily used to translate
between IPv6 hosts and IPv4 content. AFT can be stateless, where reserved portions
of the IPv6 address space are automatically mapped to IPv4, or it can be stateful, with
addresses from a configured range used to map packets between address families.

Nearly all enterprise deployments of IPv6 use dual stack internally. Dual stack offers a
nondisruptive way to learn about and gain operational experience with a new address
family, which is an important part of successfully managing the transition.

Pilots and trials depend on specific requirements.

# Foundation Summary

This section lists additional details and facts to round out the coverage of the topics in this chapter. Unlike most of the Cisco Press Exam Certification Guides, this "Foundation Summary" does not repeat information presented in the "Foundation Topics" section of the chapter. Please take the time to read and study the details in the "Foundation Topics" section of the chapter, as well as review items noted with a Key Topic icon.

Table 4-14 lists and briefly explains several variations on NAT.

**Table 4-14**  *Variations on NAT*

| Name | Function |
| --- | --- |
| Static NAT | Statically correlates the same public IP address for use by the same local host every time. Does not conserve IP addresses. |
| Dynamic NAT | Pools the available public IP addresses, shared among a group of local hosts, but with only one local host at a time using a public IP address. Does not conserve IP addresses. |
| Dynamic NAT with overload (PAT) | Like dynamic NAT, but multiple local hosts share a single public IP address by multiplexing using TCP and UDP port numbers. Conserves IP addresses. |
| NAT for overlapping address | Can be done with any of the first three types. Translates both source and destination addresses, instead of just the source (for packets going from enterprise to the Internet). |

Table 4-15 lists the protocols mentioned in this chapter and their respective standards documents.

**Table 4-15**  *Protocols and Standards for Chapter 4*

| Name | Standardized In |
| --- | --- |
| IP | RFC 791 |
| Subnetting | RFC 950 |
| NAT | RFC 1631 |
| Private addressing | RFC 1918 |
| CIDR | RFCs 1517–1520 |
| DHCPv6 | RFC 3315 |
| Internet Protocol version 6 (IPv6) Addressing Architecture | RFC 3513 |
| IPv6 Global Unicast Address Format | RFC 3587 |

Table 4-16 lists and describes some of the most commonly used IOS commands related to the topics in this chapter.

**Table 4-16**   *Command Reference for Chapter 4*

| Command | Description |
|---|---|
| **ip address** *ip-address mask* [**secondary**] | Interface subcommand to assign an IPv4 address |
| **ip nat** {**inside** \| **outside**} | Interface subcommand; identifies inside or outside part of network |
| **ip nat inside source** {**list** {*access-list-number* \| *access-list-name*} \| **route-map** *name*} {**interface** *type number* \| **pool** *pool-name*} [**overload**] | Global command that defines the set of inside addresses for which NAT will be performed, and corresponding outside addresses |
| **ip nat inside destination list** {*access-list-number* \| *name*} **pool** *name* | Global command used with destination NAT |
| **ip nat outside source** {**list** {*access-list-number* \| *access-list-name*} \| **route-map** *name*} **pool** *pool-name* [**add-route**] | Global command used with both destination and dynamic NAT |
| **ip nat pool** *name start-ip end-ip* {**netmask** *netmask* \| **prefix-length** *prefix-length*} [**type rotary**] | Global command to create a pool of addresses for dynamic NAT |
| **show ip nat statistics** | Lists counters for packets and for NAT table entries, as well as basic configuration information |
| **show ip nat translations** [**verbose**] | Displays the NAT table |
| **clear ip nat translation** {* \| [**inside** *global-ip local-ip*] [**outside** *local-ip global-ip*]} | Clears all or some of the dynamic entries in the NAT table, depending on which parameters are used |
| **debug ip nat** | Issues log messages describing each packet whose IP address is translated with NAT |
| **show ip interface** [*type number*] [**brief**] | Lists information about IPv4 on interfaces |

Figure 4-8 shows the IP header format.

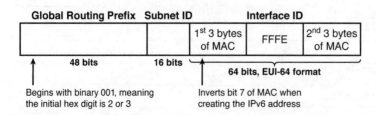

**Figure 4-8**   *IP Header*

Table 4-17 lists the terms and meanings of the fields inside the IP header.

**Key Topic**

**Table 4-17**    *IP Header Fields*

| Field | Meaning |
|---|---|
| Version | Version of the IP protocol. Most networks use IPv4 today, with IPv6 becoming more popular. The header format reflects IPv4. |
| Header Length | Defines the length of the IP header, including optional fields. Because the length of the IP header must always be a multiple of 4, the IP header length (IHL) is multiplied by 4 to give the actual number of bytes. |
| DS Field | Differentiated Services Field. This byte was originally called the Type of Service (ToS) byte, but was redefined by RFC 2474 as the DS Field. It is used for marking packets for the purpose of applying different quality of service (QoS) levels to different packets. |
| Packet Length | Identifies the entire length of the IP packet, including the data. |
| Identification | Used by the IP packet fragmentation process. If a single packet is fragmented into multiple packets, all fragments of the original packet contain the same identifier so that the original packet can be reassembled. |
| Flags | 3 bits used by the IP packet fragmentation process. |
| Fragment Offset | A number set in a fragment of a larger packet that identifies the fragment's location in the larger original packet. |
| Time to Live (TTL) | A value used to prevent routing loops. Routers decrement this field by 1 each time the packet is forwarded; when it decrements to 0, the packet is discarded. |
| Protocol | A field that identifies the contents of the data portion of the IP packet. For example, protocol 6 implies that a TCP header is the first thing in the IP packet data field. |
| Header Checksum | A value used to store a frame check sequence (FCS) value, whose purpose is to determine whether any bit errors occurred in the IP header (not the data) during transmission. |
| Source IP Address | The 32-bit IP address of the sender of the packet. |
| Destination IP Address | The 32-bit IP address of the intended recipient of the packet. |
| Optional Header Fields and Padding | IP supports additional header fields for future expansion through optional headers. Also, if these optional headers do not use a multiple of 4 bytes, padding bytes are added, composed of all binary 0s, so that the header is a multiple of 4 bytes in length. |

Table 4-18 lists some of the more common IP protocol field values.

**Table 4-18**   *IP Protocol Field Values*

| Protocol Name | Protocol Number |
|---------------|-----------------|
| ICMP | 1 |
| TCP | 6 |
| UDP | 17 |
| EIGRP | 88 |
| OSPF | 89 |
| PIM | 103 |

Figure 4-9 Illustrates an IPv6 header.

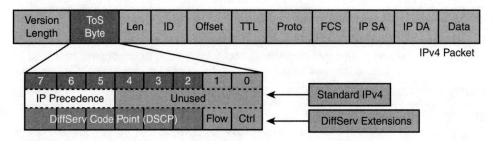

**Figure 4-9**   *IPv4 Header*

Table 4-19 lists the terms and meanings for the fields in the header illustration.

**Table 4-19**   *IPv6 Header Fields*

| Field | Meaning |
|-------|---------|
| Version | 4 bits. IPv6 version number. |
| Traffic Class | 8 bits. Internet traffic priority delivery value. |
| Flow Label | 20 bits. Used for specifying special router handling from the source to the destination(s) for a sequence of packets. |
| Payload Length | 16 bits. Specifies the length of the data in the packet. When cleared to 0, the option is a hop-by-hop Jumbo payload. |
| Next Header | 8 bits. Specifies the next encapsulated protocol. The values are compatible with those specified for the IPv4 protocol field. |
| Hop Limit | 8 bits. For each router that forwards the packet, the hop limit is decremented by 1. When the hop limit field reaches 0, the packet is discarded. This replaces the TTL field in the IPv4 header that was originally intended to be used as a time-based hop limit. |
| Source Address | 16 bytes. The IPv6 address of the sending node. |
| Destination Address | 16 bytes. The IPv6 address of the destination node. |

# Memory Builders

The CCIE Routing and Switching written exam, like all Cisco CCIE written exams, covers a fairly broad set of topics. This section provides some basic tools to help you exercise your memory about some of the broader topics covered in this chapter.

## Fill in Key Tables from Memory

Appendix E, "Key Tables for CCIE Study," on the CD in the back of this book, contains empty sets of some of the key summary tables in each chapter. Print Appendix E, refer to this chapter's tables in it, and fill in the tables from memory. Refer to Appendix F, "Solutions for Key Tables for CCIE Study," on the CD to check your answers.

## Definitions

Next, take a few moments to write the definitions for the following terms:

subnet, prefix, classless IP addressing, classful IP addressing, CIDR, NAT, IPv4, subnet broadcast address, subnet number, subnet zero, broadcast subnet, subnet mask, private addresses, SLSM, VLSM, Inside Local address, Inside Global address, Outside Local address, Outside Global address, PAT, overloading, quartet, IPv6, 6to4 Tunnel, ISATAP, DHCPv6, AFT

Refer to the glossary to check your answers.

## Further Reading

All topics in this chapter are covered in varying depth for the CCNP Routing exam. For more details on these topics, look for the CCNP routing study guides at www.ciscopress.com/ccnp.

**Blueprint topics covered in this chapter:**

This chapter covers the following subtopics from the Cisco CCIE Routing and Switching written exam blueprint. Refer to the full blueprint in Table I-1 in the Introduction for more details on the topics covered in each chapter and their context within the blueprint.

- Hot Standby Router Protocol (HSRP)
- Gateway Load Balancing Protocol (GLBP)
- Virtual Router Redundancy Protocol (VRRP)
- Dynamic Host Configuration Protocol (DHCP)
- Network Time Protocol (NTP)
- Web Cache Communication Protocol (WCCP)
- Network Management
- Logging and Syslog
- Troubleshoot Network Services
- Implement IP Service Level Agreement (IP SLA)
- Object Tracking
- Implement NetFlow
- Implement Router IP Traffic Export (RITE)
- Implement SNMP
- Implement Cisco IOS Embedded Event Manager (EEM)
- Implement Remote Monitoring (RMON)
- Implement FTP
- Implement TFTP
- Implement TFTP Server on Router
- Implement Secure Copy Protocol (SCP)
- Implement HTTP and HTTPS
- Implement Telnet
- Implement SSH

## CHAPTER 5

# IP Services

IP relies on several protocols to perform a variety of tasks related to the process of routing packets. This chapter provides a reference for the most popular of these protocols. In addition, this chapter covers a number of management-related protocols and other blueprint topics related to IP services.

## "Do I Know This Already?" Quiz

Table 5-1 outlines the major headings in this chapter and the corresponding "Do I Know This Already?" quiz questions.

**Table 5-1** *"Do I Know This Already?" Foundation Topics Section-to-Question Mapping*

| Foundation Topics Section | Questions Covered in This Section | Score |
|---|---|---|
| ARP, Proxy ARP, Reverse ARP, BOOTP, and DHCP | 1–3 | |
| HSRP, VRRP, and GLBP | 4–6 | |
| Network Time Protocol | 7 | |
| SNMP | 8–9 | |
| Web Cache Communication Protocol | 10–11 | |
| Implement SSH | 12 | |
| Implement SSH, HTTPS, FTP, SCP, TFTP | 13 | |
| Implement RMON | 14 | |
| Implement IP SLA, NetFlow, RITE, EEM | 15 | |
| Total Score | | |

To best use this pre-chapter assessment, remember to score yourself strictly. You can find the answers in Appendix A, "Answers to the 'Do I Know This Already?' Quizzes."

1. Two hosts, named PC1 and PC2, sit on subnet 172.16.1.0/24, along with Router R1. A web server sits on subnet 172.16.2.0/24, which is connected to another interface of R1. At some point, both PC1 and PC2 send an ARP request before they successfully send packets to the web server. With PC1, R1 makes a normal ARP reply, but for PC2, R1 uses a proxy ARP reply. Which two of the following answers could be true given the stated behavior in this network?

   a. PC2 set the proxy flag in the ARP request.

   b. PC2 encapsulated the ARP request inside an IP packet.

   c. PC2's ARP broadcast implied that PC2 was looking for the web server's MAC address.

   d. PC2 has a subnet mask of 255.255.0.0.

   e. R1's proxy ARP reply contains the web server's MAC address.

2. Host PC3 is using DHCP to discover its IP address. Only one router attaches to PC3's subnet, using its fa0/0 interface, with an **ip helper-address 10.5.5.5** command on that same interface. That same router interface has an **ip address 10.4.5.6 255.255.252.0** command configured as well. Which of the following are true about PC3's DHCP request?

   a. The destination IP address of the DHCP request packet is set to 10.5.5.5 by the router.

   b. The DHCP request packet's source IP address is unchanged by the router.

   c. The DHCP request is encapsulated inside a new IP packet, with source IP address 10.4.5.6 and destination 10.5.5.5.

   d. The DHCP request's source IP address is changed to 10.4.5.255.

   e. The DHCP request's source IP address is changed to 10.4.7.255.

3. Which of the following statements are true about BOOTP, but not true about RARP?

   a. The client can be assigned a different IP address on different occasions, because the server can allocate a pool of IP addresses for allocation to a set of clients.

   b. The server can be on a different subnet from the client.

   c. The client's MAC address must be configured on the server, with a one-to-one mapping to the IP address to be assigned to the client with that MAC address.

   d. The client can discover its IP address, subnet mask, and default gateway IP address.

**4.** R1 is HSRP active for virtual IP address 172.16.1.1, with HSRP priority set to 115. R1 is tracking three separate interfaces. An engineer configures the same HSRP group on R2, also connected to the same subnet, only using the **standby 1 ip 172.16.1.1** command, and no other HSRP-related commands. Which of the following would cause R2 to take over as HSRP active?

    **a.** R1 experiences failures on tracked interfaces, totaling 16 or more lost points.

    **b.** R1 experiences failures on tracked interfaces, totaling 15 or more lost points.

    **c.** R2 could configure a priority of 116 or greater.

    **d.** R1's fa0/0 interface fails.

    **e.** R2 would take over immediately.

**5.** Which Cisco IOS feature does HSRP, GLBP, and VRRP use to determine when an interface fails for active switching purposes?

    **a.** Each protocol has a built-in method of tracking interfaces.

    **b.** When a physical interface goes down, the redundancy protocol uses this automatically as a basis for switching.

    **c.** Each protocol uses its own hello mechanism for determining which interfaces are up or down.

    **d.** The Cisco IOS object tracking feature.

**6.** Which is the correct term for using more than one HSRP group to provide load balancing for HSRP?

    **a.** LBHSRP

    **b.** LSHSRP

    **c.** RHSRP

    **d.** MHSRP

    **e.** None of these is correct. HSRP does not support load balancing.

**7.** Which of the following NTP modes in a Cisco router requires a predefinition of the IP address of an NTP time source??

    **a.** Server mode

    **b.** Static client mode

    **c.** Broadcast client mode

    **d.** Symmetric active mode

**8.** Which of the following are true about SNMP security?

    **a.** SNMP Version 1 calls for the use of community strings that are passed as clear text.

    **b.** SNMP Version 2c calls for the use of community strings that are passed as MD5 message digests generated with private keys.

    **c.** SNMP Version 3 allows for authentication using MD5 message digests generated with private keys.

    **d.** SNMP Version 3 authentication also requires concurrent use of encryption, typically done with DES.

**9.** Which of the following statements are true regarding features of SNMP based on the SNMP version?

    **a.** SNMP Version 2 added the GetNext protocol message to SNMP.

    **b.** SNMP Version 3 added the Inform protocol message to SNMP.

    **c.** SNMP Version 2 added the Inform protocol message to SNMP.

    **d.** SNMP Version 3 expanded the SNMP Response protocol message so that it must be used by managers in response to Traps sent by agents.

    **e.** SNMP Version 3 enhanced SNMP Version 2 security features but not other features.

**10.** WCCP uses what protocol and port for communication between content engines and WCCP routers?

    **a.** UDP 2048

    **b.** TCP 2048

    **c.** UDP 4082

    **d.** TCP 4082

**11.** In a WCCP cluster, which content engine becomes the lead engine after the cluster stabilizes?

    **a.** The content engine with the lowest IP address.

    **b.** The content engine with the highest IP address.

    **c.** There is no such thing as a lead content engine; the correct term is designated content engine.

    **d.** All content engines have equal precedence for redundancy and the fastest possible load sharing.

**12.** Which configuration commands are required to enable SSH on a router?

 a. hostname

 b. ip domain-name

 c. ip ssh

 d. crypto key generate rsa

 e. http secure-server

**13.** Which protocol is the most secure choice, natively, for transferring files from a router?

 a. SSH

 b. HTTPS

 c. FTP

 d. TFTP

 e. SCP

**14.** In RMON, which type of configured option includes rising and falling thresholds, either relative or absolute, and is monitored by another type of RMON option?

 a. Event

 b. Alert

 c. Notification

 d. Port

 e. Probe

**15.** Which Cisco IOS feature permits end-to-end network performance monitoring with configuration on devices at each end of the network?

 a. Flexible NetFlow

 b. IP SLA

 c. EEM

 d. RITE

## Foundation Topics

# ARP, Proxy ARP, Reverse ARP, BOOTP, and DHCP

The heading for this section might seem like a laundry list of a lot of different protocols. However, these five protocols do have one central theme, namely, that they help a host learn information so that it can successfully send and receive IP packets. Specifically, Address Resolution Protocol (ARP) and proxy ARP define methods for a host to learn another host's MAC address, whereas the core functions of Reverse ARP (RARP), Bootstrap Protocol (BOOTP), and DHCP define how a host can discover its own IP address, plus additional related information.

## ARP and Proxy ARP

You would imagine that anyone getting this far in his CCIE study would already have a solid understanding of the Address Resolution Protocol (ARP, RFC 826). However, proxy ARP (RFC 1027) is often ignored, in part because of its lack of use today. To see how they both work, Figure 5-1 shows an example of each, with Fred and Barney both trying to reach the web server at IP address 10.1.2.200.

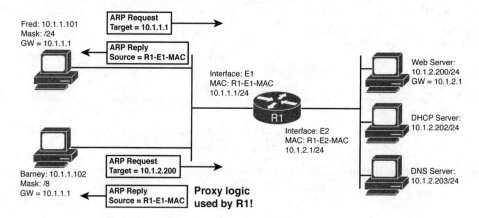

**Figure 5-1**  *Comparing ARP and Proxy ARP*

Fred follows a normal ARP process, broadcasting an ARP request, with R1's E1 IP address as the target. The ARP message has a *Target* field of all 0s for the MAC address that needs to be learned, and a target IP address of the IP address whose MAC address it is searching, namely, 10.1.1.1 in this case. The ARP reply lists the MAC address associated with the IP address, in this case, the MAC address of R1's E1 interface.

**Note**  The ARP message itself does not include an IP header, although it does have destination and source IP addresses in the same relative position as an IP header. The ARP request lists an IP destination of 255.255.255.255. The ARP Ethernet protocol type is 0x0806, whereas IP packets have an Ethernet protocol type of 0x0800.

Proxy ARP uses the exact same ARP message as ARP, but the ARP request is actually requesting a MAC address that is not on the local subnet. Because the ARP request is broadcast on the local subnet, it will not be heard by the target host—so if a router can route packets to that target host, the router issues a proxy ARP reply on behalf of that target.

For example, Barney places the web server's IP address (10.1.2.200) in the Target field, because Barney thinks that he is on the same subnet as the web server because of Barney's mask of 255.0.0.0. The ARP request is a LAN broadcast, so R1, being a well-behaved router, does not forward the ARP broadcast. However, knowing that the ARP request will never get to the subnet where 10.1.2.200 resides, R1 saves the day by replying to the ARP on behalf of the web server. R1 takes the web server's place in the ARP process, hence the name *proxy* ARP. Also, note that R1's ARP reply contains R1's E1 MAC address, so that Barney will forward frames to R1 when Barney wants to send a packet to the web server.

Before the advent of DHCP, many networks relied on proxy ARP, configuring hosts to use the default masks in their respective networks. Regardless of whether the proxy version is used, the end result is that the host learns a router's MAC address to forward packets to another subnet.

## RARP, BOOTP, and DHCP

The ARP and proxy ARP processes both occur after a host knows its IP address and subnet mask. RARP, BOOTP, and DHCP represent the evolution of protocols defined to help a host dynamically learn its IP address. All three protocols require the client host to send a broadcast to begin discovery, and all three rely on a server to hear the request and supply an IP address to the client. Figure 5-2 shows the basic processes with RARP and BOOTP.

A RARP request is a host's attempt to find its own IP address. So RARP uses the same old ARP message, but the ARP request lists a MAC address target of its own MAC address and a target IP address of 0.0.0.0. A preconfigured RARP server, which must be on the same subnet as the client, receives the request and performs a table lookup in its configuration. If that target MAC address listed in the ARP request is configured on the RARP server, the RARP server sends an ARP reply, after entering the configured IP address in the Source IP address field.

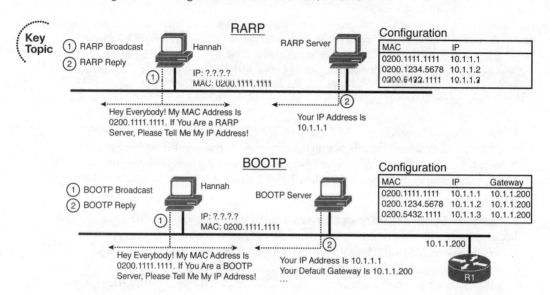

**Figure 5-2** *RARP and BOOTP—Basic Processes*

BOOTP was defined in part to improve IP address assignment features of RARP. BOOTP uses a completely different set of messages, defined by RFC 951, with the commands encapsulated inside an IP and UDP header. With the correct router configuration, a router can forward the BOOTP packets to other subnets—allowing the deployment of a centrally located BOOTP server. Also, BOOTP supports the assignment of many other tidbits of information, including the subnet mask, default gateway, DNS addresses, and its namesake, the IP address of a boot (or image) server. However, BOOTP does not solve the configuration burden of RARP, still requiring that the server be preconfigured with the MAC addresses and IP addresses of each client.

## DHCP

DHCP represents the next step in the evolution of dynamic IP address assignment. Building on the format of BOOTP protocols, DHCP focuses on dynamically assigning a variety of information and provides flexible messaging to allow for future changes, without requiring predefinition of MAC addresses for each client. DHCP also includes temporary leasing of IP addresses, enabling address reclamation, pooling of IP addresses, and, recently, dynamic registration of client Domain Name System (DNS) fully qualified domain names (FQDN). (See www.ietf.org for more information on FQDN registration.)

DHCP servers typically reside in a centralized location, with remote routers forwarding the LAN-broadcast DHCP requests to the DHCP server by changing the request's destination address to match the DHCP server. This feature is called DHCP relay agent. For example, in Figure 5-1, if Fred and Barney were to use DHCP, with the DHCP server at 10.1.2.202, R1 would change Fred's DHCP request from a destination of 255.255.255.255 to a destination of 10.1.2.202. R1 would also list its own IP address in the message, in the gateway IP address (giaddr) field, notifying the DHCP server of the IP address to which the response should be sent. The source address is also changed to the LAN broadcast, so that reply packets from the DHCP server are forwarded to the client's LAN. The only configuration requirement on the router is an **ip helper-address 10.1.2.202** interface subcommand on its E1 interface.

Alternatively, R1 could be configured as a DHCP server—a feature that is not often configured on routers in production networks but is certainly fair game for the CCIE written and lab exams. Configuring DHCP on a router consists of several required steps:

**Step 1.**    Configure a DHCP pool.

**Step 2.**    Configure the router to exclude its own IP address from the DHCP pool.

**Step 3.**    Disable DHCP conflict logging or configure a DHCP database agent.

The DHCP pool includes key items such as the subnet (using the **network** command within DHCP pool configuration), default gateway (*default-router*), and the length of time for which the DHCP lease is valid (*lease*). Other items, including the DNS domain name and any DHCP options, are also defined within the DHCP pool.

Although not strictly necessary in DHCP configuration, it is certainly a best practice to configure the router to make its own IP address in the DHCP pool subnet unavailable for allocation through DHCP. The same is true for any other static IP addresses within the DHCP pool range, such as those of servers and other routers. Exclude host IP addresses from the DHCP process using the **ip dhcp excluded-address** command.

**Note**    The **ip dhcp excluded-address** command is one of the relatively few Cisco IOS **ip** commands that is a global configuration command rather than an interface command.

The Cisco IOS DHCP server also provides a mechanism for logging DHCP address conflicts to a central server called a DHCP database agent. IOS requires that you either disable conflict logging by using the **no ip dhcp conflict-logging** command or configure a DHCP database agent on a server by using the **ip dhcp database** command. Example 5-1 shows R1's configuration for a DHCP relay agent, as well as an alternative for R1 to provide DNS services for subnet 10.1.1.0/24.

**Example 5-1**    *DHCP Configuration Options—R1, Figure 5-1*

```
! UDP broadcasts coming in E0 will be forwarded as unicasts to 10.1.2.202.
! The source IP will be changed to 10.1.1.1, so that the reply packets will be
! processed by the relay agent and subsequently broadcasted back out E1.
interface Ethernet1
 ip address 10.1.1.1 255.255.255.0
 ip helper-address 10.1.2.202
! Below, an alternative configuration, with R1 as the DHCP server. R1 assigns IP
! addresses other than the excluded first 20 IP addresses in the subnet, and
! informs the clients of their IP addresses, mask, DNS, and default router. Leases
```

```
! are for 0 days, 0 hours, and 20 minutes.
ip dhcp excluded-address 10.1.1.0 10.1.1.20
!
ip dhcp pool subnet1
   network 10.1.1.0 255.255.255.0
   dns-server 10.1.2.203
   default-router 10.1.1.1
   lease 0 0 20
```

Table 5-2 summarizes some of the key comparison points with RARP, BOOTP, and DHCP.

**Table 5-2**   *Comparing RARP, BOOTP, and DHCP*

| Feature | RARP | BOOTP | DHCP |
|---|---|---|---|
| Relies on server to allocate IP addresses | Yes | Yes | Yes |
| Encapsulates messages inside IP and UDP so that they can be forwarded to a remote server | No | Yes | Yes |
| Client can discover its own mask, gateway, DNS, and download server | No | Yes | Yes |
| Dynamic address assignment from a pool of IP addresses, without requiring knowledge of client MACs | No | No | Yes |
| Allows temporary lease of IP address | No | No | Yes |
| Includes extensions for registering client's FQDN with a DNS | No | No | Yes |

# HSRP, VRRP, and GLBP

IP hosts can use several methods of deciding which default router or default gateway to use—DHCP, BOOTP, ICMP Router Discovery Protocol (IRDP), manual configuration, or even by running a routing protocol (although having hosts run a routing protocol is not common today). The most typical methods—using DHCP or manual configuration—result in the host knowing a single IP address of its default gateway. Hot Standby Router Protocol (HSRP), Virtual Router Redundancy Protocol (VRRP), and Gateway Load Balancing Protocol (GLBP) represent a chronological list of some of the best tools for overcoming the issues related to a host knowing a single IP address as its path to get outside the subnet.

**Key Topic**

HSRP allows multiple routers to share a virtual IP and MAC address so that the end-user hosts do not realize when a failure occurs. Some of the key HSRP features are as follows:

■  Virtual IP address and virtual MAC are active on the HSRP Active router.

■  Standby routers listen for Hellos from the Active router, defaulting to a 3-second hello interval and 10-second dead interval.

■  Highest priority (IOS default 100, range 1–255) determines the Active router, with preemption disabled by default.

■  Supports tracking, whereby a router's priority is decreased when a tracked object (interface or route) fails.

■  Up to 255 HSRP groups per interface, enabling an administrative form of load balancing.

■  Virtual MAC of 0000.0C07.ACxx, where xx is the hex HSRP group.

■  Virtual IP address must be in the same subnet as the routers' interfaces on the same LAN.

■  Virtual IP address must be different from any of the routers' individual interface IP addresses.

■  Supports clear-text and MD5 authentication (through a key chain).

Example 5-2 shows a typical HSRP configuration, with two groups configured. Routers R1 and R2 are attached to the same subnet, 10.1.1.0/24, both with WAN links (S0/0.1) connecting them to the rest of an enterprise network. Cisco IOS provides the tracking mechanism shown in Example 5-2 to permit many processes, including HSRP, VRRP, and GLBP, to track interface states. A tracking object can track based on the line protocol (shown here) or the IP routing table. The example contains the details and explanation of the configuration.

**Key Topic**

**Example 5-2**  *HSRP Configuration*

```
! First, on Router R1, a tracking object must be configured so that
! HSRP can track the interface state.
track 13 interface Serial0/0.1 line-protocol
! Next, on Router R1, two HSRP groups are configured. R1 has a higher priority
! in group 21, with R2 having a higher priority in group 22. R1 is set to preempt
! in group 21, as well as to track interface s0/0.1 for both groups.
interface FastEthernet0/0
 ip address 10.1.1.1 255.255.255.0
 standby 21 ip 10.1.1.21
continues
 standby 21 priority 105
 standby 21 preempt
 standby 21 track 13
 standby 22 ip 10.1.1.22
```

```
 standby 22 track 13
```

```
! Next, R2 is configured with a higher priority for HSRP group 22, and with
! HSRP tracking enabled in both groups. The tracking "decrement" used by R2,
! when S0/0.1 fails, is set to 9 (instead of the default of 10).
! A tracking object must be configured first, as on R1.
track 23 interface Serial0/0.1 line-protocol
interface FastEthernet0/0
 ip address 10.1.1.2 255.255.255.0
 standby 21 ip 10.1.1.21
 standby 21 track 23
 standby 22 ip 10.1.1.22
 standby 22 priority 105
 standby 22 track 23 decrement 9
```

```
!!!!!!!!!!!!!!!!!!!!!!!!!!!!!!!!!!!!!!!!!!!!!!!!!!!!!!!!!!!!!!!!!!!!!!!!!!!!!!!!!!!!!!!!!!
! On R1 below, for group 21, the output shows that R1 is active, with R2
! (10.1.1.2) as standby.
! R1 is tracking s0/0.1, with a default "decrement" of 10, meaning that the
! configured priority of 105 will be decremented by 10 if s0/0.1 fails.
Router1# sh standby fa0/0
FastEthernet0/0 - Group 21
  State is Active
    2 state changes, last state change 00:00:45
  Virtual IP address is 10.1.1.21
  Active virtual MAC address is 0000.0c07.ac15
    Local virtual MAC address is 0000.0c07.ac15 (v1 default)
  Hello time 3 sec, hold time 10 sec
    Next hello sent in 2.900 secs
  Preemption enabled
  Active router is local
  Standby router is 10.1.1.2, priority 100 (expires in 7.897 sec)
  Priority 105 (configured 105)
    Track object 13 state Up decrement 10
  IP redundancy name is "hsrp-Fa0/0-21" (default)
! output omitted
! NOT SHOWN—R1 shuts down S0.0.1, lowering its priority in group 21 by 10.
! The debug below shows the reduced priority value. However, R2 does not become
! active, because R2's configuration did not include a standby 21 preempt command.
Router1# debug standby
*Mar  1 00:24:04.122: HSRP: Fa0/0 Grp 21 Hello  out 10.1.1.1 Active  pri 95 vIP
   10.1.1.21
```

Because HSRP uses only one Active router at a time, any other HSRP routers are idle. To provide load sharing in an HSRP configuration, the concept of Multiple HSRP, or MHSRP, was developed. In MHSRP, two or more HSRP groups are configured on each HSRP LAN interface, where the configured priority determines which router will be active for each HSRP group.

MHSRP requires that each DHCP client and statically configured host are issued a default gateway corresponding to one of the HSRP groups and requires that they're distributed appropriately. Thus, in an MHSRP configuration with two routers and two groups, all other things being equal, half of the hosts should have one HSRP group address as its default gateway, and the other half of the hosts should use the other HSRP group address. If you now revisit Example 5-2, you will see that it is an MHSRP configuration.

HSRP is Cisco proprietary, has been out a long time, and is widely popular. VRRP (RFC 3768) provides a standardized protocol to perform almost the exact same function. The Cisco VRRP implementation has the same goals in mind as HSRP but with these differences:

- VRRP uses a multicast virtual MAC address (0000.5E00.01$xx$, where $xx$ is the hex VRRP group number).

- VRRP uses the IOS object tracking feature, rather than its own internal tracking mechanism, to track interface states for failover purposes.

- VRRP defaults to use preemption, but HSRP defaults to not use preemption. Both can be configured to either use preemption or not.

- The VRRP term *Master* means the same thing as the HSRP term *Active*.

- In VRRP, the VRRP group IP address is the interface IP address of one of the VRRP routers.

GLBP is a newer Cisco-proprietary tool that adds load-balancing features in addition to gateway-redundancy features. Hosts still point to a default gateway IP address, but GLBP causes different hosts to send their traffic to one of up to four routers in a GLBP group. To do so, the GLBP Active Virtual Gateway (AVG) assigns each router in the group a unique virtual MAC address, following the format 0007.B40X.$xxyy$, where X$xx$ is the 10-bit wide GLBP group number (hence only the lowmost 2 bits from X are used for the group number), and $yy$ is a different number for each router (01, 02, 03, or 04). When a client ARPs for the (virtual) IP address of its default gateway, the GLBP AVG replies with one of the four possible virtual MACs. By replying to ARP requests with different virtual MACs, the hosts in that subnet will in effect balance the traffic across the routers, rather than send all traffic to the one active router.

Cisco IOS devices with GLBP support permit configuring up to 1024 GLBP groups per physical interface and up to four hosts per GLBP group.

# Network Time Protocol

NTP Version 3 (RFC 1305) allows IP hosts to synchronize their time-of-day clocks with a common source clock. For example, routers and switches can synchronize their clocks to make event correlation from an SNMP management station more meaningful, by ensuring that any events and traps have accurate time stamps.

By design, most routers and switches use NTP *client mode*, adjusting their clocks based on the time as known by an NTP server. NTP defines the messages that flow between client and server, and the algorithms a client uses to adjust its clock. Routers and switches can also be configured as NTP servers, as well as using NTP *symmetric active mode*—a mode in which the router or switch mutually synchronizes with another NTP host.

NTP servers can reference other NTP servers to obtain a more accurate clock source as defined by the *stratum level* of the ultimate source clock. For example, atomic clocks and Global Positioning System (GPS) satellite transmissions provide a source of stratum 1 (lowest/best possible stratum level). For an enterprise network, the routers and switches can refer to a low-stratum NTP source on the Internet, or purpose-built rack-mounted NTP servers, with built-in GPS capabilities, can be deployed.

Example 5-3 shows a sample NTP configuration on four routers, all sharing the same 10.1.1.0/24 Ethernet subnet. Router R1 will be configured as an NTP server. R2 acts as an *NTP static client* by virtue of the static configuration referencing R1's IP address. R3 acts as an *NTP broadcast client* by listening for R1's NTP broadcasts on the Ethernet. Finally, R4 acts in NTP symmetric active mode, configured with the **ntp peer** command.

**Example 5-3**  *NTP Configuration*

```
!!!!!!!!!!!!!!!!!!!!!!!!!!!!!!!!!!!!!!!!!!!!!!!!!!!!!!!!!!!!!!!!!!!!!!!!!!!!!!!!!!!!!!!
! First, R1's configuration, the ntp broadcast command under interface fa0/0
! causes NTP to broadcast NTP updates on that interface. The first three of the
! four global NTP commands configure authentication; these commands are identical
! on all the routers.
R1# show running-config
interface FastEthernet0/0
 ntp broadcast
!
ntp authentication-key 1 md5 1514190900 7
ntp authenticate
ntp trusted-key 1
ntp master 7
! Below, the "127.127.7.1" notation implies that this router is the NTP clock
! source. The clock is synchronized, with stratum level 7, as configured on the
! ntp master 7 command above.
R1# show ntp associations
```

```
         address          ref clock      st  when  poll reach  delay  offset    disp
*~127.127.7.1        127.127.7.1      6    22    64  377    0.0    0.00     0.0
 * master (synced), # master (unsynced), + selected, - candidate, ~ configured
R1# show ntp status
Clock is synchronized, stratum 7, reference is 127.127.7.1
nominal freq is 249.5901 Hz, actual freq is 249.5901 Hz, precision is 2**16
reference time is C54483CC.E26EE853 (13:49:00.884 UTC Tue Nov 16 2004)
clock offset is 0.0000 msec, root delay is 0.00 msec
root dispersion is 0.02 msec, peer dispersion is 0.02 msec
! R2 is configured below as an NTP static client. Note that the ntp clock-period
! command is automatically generated as part of the synchronization process, and
! should not be added to the configuration manually.
R2# show run | begin ntp
ntp authentication-key 1 md5 1514190900 7
ntp authenticate
ntp trusted-key 1
ntp clock-period 17208144
ntp server 10.1.1.1
end
! Next, R3 has been configured as an NTP broadcast client. The ntp broadcast client
! command on R3 tells it to listen for the broadcasts from R1. This configuration
! relies on the ntp broadcast subcommand on R1's Fa0/0 interface, as shown at the
! beginning of this example.
R3# show run
interface Ethernet0/0
 ntp broadcast client
! R4's configuration is listed, with the ntp peer
! command implying the use of symmetric active mode.
R4# show run | beg ntp
ntp authentication-key 1 md5 0002010300 7
ntp authenticate
ntp trusted-key 1
ntp clock-period 17208233
ntp peer 10.1.1.1
```

# SNMP

This section of the chapter summarizes some of the core Simple Network Management Protocol (SNMP) concepts and details, particularly with regard to features of different SNMP versions. SNMP or, more formally, the *Internet Standard Management Framework*, uses a structure in which the device being managed (the SNMP agent) has information that the management software (the SNMP manager) wants to display to someone operating the network. Each SNMP agent keeps a database, called a *Management Information Base (MIB)*, that holds a large variety of data about the operation of the device on which the agent resides. The manager collects the data by using SNMP.

SNMP has been defined with four major functional areas to support the core function of allowing managers to manage agents:

- **Data Definition:** The syntax conventions for how to define the data to an agent or manager. These specifications are called the *Structure of Management Information (SMI)*.

- **MIBs:** More than 100 Internet standards define different MIBs, each for a different technology area, with countless vendor-proprietary MIBs as well. The MIB definitions conform to the appropriate SMI version.

- **Protocols:** The messages used by agents and managers to exchange management data.

- **Security and Administration:** Definitions for how to secure the exchange of data between agents and managers.

Interestingly, by separating SNMP into these major functional areas, each part has been improved and expanded independently over the years. However, it is important to know a few of the main features added for each official SNMP version, as well as for a pseudo-version called SNMPv2c, as summarized in Table 5-3.

Key Topic

**Table 5-3**   *SNMP Version Summaries*

| SNMP Version | Description |
|---|---|
| 1 | Uses SMIv1, simple authentication with communities, but used MIB-I originally. |
| 2 | Uses SMIv2, removed requirement for communities, added GetBulk and Inform messages, but began with MIB-II originally. |
| 2c | Pseudo-release (RFC 1905) that allowed SNMPv1-style communities with SNMPv2; otherwise, equivalent to SNMPv2. |
| 3 | Mostly identical to SNMPv2, but adds significantly better security, although it supports communities for backward compatibility. Uses MIB-II. |

Table 5-3 hits the highlights of the comparison points between the various SNMP versions. As you might expect, each release builds on the previous one. For example, SNMPv1 defined *community strings* for use as simple clear-text passwords. SNMPv2 removed the requirement for community strings—however, backward compatibility for SNMP communities was defined through an optional RFC (1901). Even SNMPv3, with much better security, supports communities to allow backward compatibility.

> **Note**   The use of SNMPv1 communities with SNMPv2, based on RFC 1901, has popularly been called *SNMP Version 2c*, with *c* referring to "communities," although it is arguably not a legitimate full version of SNMP.

The next few sections provide a bit more depth about the SNMP protocol, with additional details about some of the version differences.

## SNMP Protocol Messages

The SNMPv1 and SNMPv2 protocol messages (RFC 3416) define how a manager and agent, or even two managers, can communicate information. For example, a manager can use three different messages to get MIB variable data from agents, with an SNMP *Response* message returned by the agent to the manager supplying the MIB data. SNMP uses UDP exclusively for transport, using the SNMP Response message to both acknowledge receipt of other protocol messages and supply SNMP information.

Table 5-4 summarizes the key information about each of the SNMP protocol messages, including the SNMP version in which the message first appeared.

Key Topic

**Table 5-4**   *SNMP Protocol Messages (RFCs 1157 and 1905)*

| Message | Initial Version | Response Message | Typically Sent By | Main Purpose |
|---------|-----------------|------------------|-------------------|--------------|
| Get | 1 | Response | Manager | A request for a single variable's value. |
| GetNext | 1 | Response | Manager | A request for the next single MIB leaf variable in the MIB tree. |
| GetBulk | 2 | Response | Manager | A request for multiple consecutive MIB variables with one request. Useful for getting complex structures, for example, an IP routing table. |
| Response | 1 | None | Agent | Used to respond with the information in Get and Set requests. |
| Set | 1 | Response | Manager | Sent by a manager to an agent to tell the agent to set a variable to a particular value. The agent replies with a Response message. |
| Trap | 1 | None | Agent | Allows agents to send unsolicited information to an SNMP manager. The manager does not reply with any SNMP message. |
| Inform | 2 | Response | Manager | A message used between SNMP managers to allow MIB data to be exchanged. |

The three variations of the SNMP Get message, and the SNMP Response message, are typically used when someone is actively using an SNMP manager. When a user of the SNMP manager asks for information, the manager sends one of the three types of Get commands to the agent. The agent replies with an SNMP Response message. The different variations of the Get command are useful, particularly when the manager wants to view large portions of the MIB. An agent's entire MIB—whose structure can vary from agent to agent—can be discovered with successive GetNext requests, or with GetBulk requests, using a process called a *MIB walk*.

The SNMP Set command allows the manager to change something on the agent. For example, the user of the management software can specify that a router interface should be shut down; the management station can then issue a Set command for a MIB variable on the agent. The agent sets the variable, which tells Cisco IOS Software to shut down the interface.

SNMP Traps are unsolicited messages sent by the agent to the management station. For example, when an interface fails, a router's SNMP agent could send a Trap to the SNMP manager. The management software could then highlight the failure information on a screen, email first-level support personnel, page support, and so on. Also of note, there is no specific message in response to the receipt of a Trap; technically, of the messages in Table 5-4, only the Trap and Response messages do not expect to receive any kind of acknowledging message.

Finally, the Inform message allows two SNMP managers to exchange MIB information about agents that they both manage.

## SNMP MIBs

SNMP Versions 1 and 2 included a standard generic MIB, with initial MIB-I (version 1, RFC 1156) and MIB-II (version 2, RFC 1213). MIB-II was actually created in between the release of SNMPv1 and v2, with SNMPv1 supporting MIB-II as well. After the creation of the MIB-II specification, the IETF SNMP working group changed the strategy for MIB definition. Instead of the SNMP working group creating standard MIBs, other working groups, in many different technology areas, were tasked with creating MIB definitions for their respective technologies. As a result, hundreds of standardized MIBs are defined. Additionally, vendors create their own vendor-proprietary MIBs.

The Remote Monitoring MIB (RMON, RFC 2819) is a particularly important standardized MIB outside MIB-II. An SNMP agent that supports the RMON MIB can be programmed, through SNMP Set commands, to capture packets, calculate statistics, monitor thresholds for specific MIB variables, report back to the management station when thresholds are reached, and perform other tasks. With RMON, a network can be populated with a number of monitoring probes, with SNMP messaging used to gather the information as needed.

## SNMP Security

SNMPv3 added solid security to the existing SNMPv2 and SNMPv2c specifications.
SNMPv3 adds two main branches of security to SNMPv2: authentication and encryption. SNMPv3 specifies the use of message digest algorithm 5 (MD5) and secure hash
algorithm (SHA) to create a message digest for each SNMPv3 protocol message. Doing
so enables authentication of endpoints and prevents data modification and masquerade
types of attacks. Additionally, SNMPv3 managers and agents can use Digital Encryption
Standard (DES) to encrypt the messages, providing better privacy. (SNMPv3 suggests
future support of Advanced Encryption Standard [AES] as well, but that is not a part of
the original SNMPv3 specifications.) The encryption feature remains separate because of
the U.S. government export restrictions on DES technology.

Example 5-4 shows a typical SNMP configuration with the following goals:

■ Enable SNMP and send traps to 192.168.1.100.

■ Send traps for a variety of events to the SNMP manager.

■ Set optional information to identify the router chassis, contact information, and
location.

■ Set read-write access to the router from the 192.168.1.0/24 subnet (filtered by access
list 33).

**Example 5-4**  *Configuring SNMP*

```
access-list 33 permit 192.168.1.0 0.0.0.255
snmp-server community public RW 33
snmp-server location B1
snmp-server contact routerhelpdesk@mail.local
snmp-server chassis-id 2511_AccessServer_Canadice
snmp-server enable traps snmp
snmp-server enable traps hsrp
snmp-server enable traps config
snmp-server enable traps entity
snmp-server enable traps bgp
snmp-server enable traps rsvp
snmp-server enable traps frame-relay
snmp-server enable traps rtr
snmp-server host 192.168.1.100 public
```

# Syslog

Event logging is nothing new to most CCIE candidates. Routers and switches, among
other devices, maintain event logs that reveal a great deal about the operating conditions
of that device, along with valuable time-stamp information to help troubleshoot problems
or chains of events that take place.

By default, Cisco routers and switches do not log events to nonvolatile memory. They can be configured to do so using the **logging buffered** command, with an additional argument to specify the size of the log buffer. Configuring a router, for example, for SNMP management provides a means of passing critical events from the event log, as they occur, to a network management station in the form of traps. SNMP is, however, fairly involved to configure. Furthermore, if it's not secured properly, SNMP also opens attack vectors to the device. However, disabling SNMP and watching event logs manually is at best tedious, and this approach simply does not scale.

Syslog, described in RFC 5424, is a lightweight event-notification protocol that provides a middle ground between manually monitoring event logs and a full-blown SNMP implementation. It provides real-time event notification by sending messages that enter the event log to a Syslog server that you specify. Syslog uses UDP port 514 by default.

Cisco IOS devices configured for Syslog, by default, send all events that enter the event log to the Syslog server. You can also configure Syslog to send only specific classes of events to the server.

Syslog is a clear-text protocol that provides event notifications without requiring difficult, time-intensive configuration or opening attack vectors. In fact, it's quite simple to configure basic Syslog operation:

**Step 1.**   Install a Syslog server on a workstation with a fixed IP address.

**Step 2.**   Configure the logging process to send events to the Syslog server's IP address using the **logging host** command.

**Step 3.**   Configure any options, such as which severity levels (0–7) you want to send to the Syslog server using the **logging trap** command.

# Web Cache Communication Protocol

To ease pressure on congested WAN links in networks with many hosts, Cisco developed WCCP to coordinate the work of edge routers and content engines (also known as cache engines). Content engines collect frequently accessed data, usually HTTP traffic, locally, so that when hosts access the same pages, the content can be delivered from the cache engine rather than crossing the WAN. WCCP differs from web proxy operation in that the hosts accessing the content have no knowledge that the content engine is involved in a given transaction.

WCCP works by allowing edge routers to communicate with content engines to make each aware of the other's presence and to permit the router to redirect traffic to the content engine as appropriate. Figure 5-3 shows how WCCP functions between a router and a content engine when a user requests a web object using HTTP.

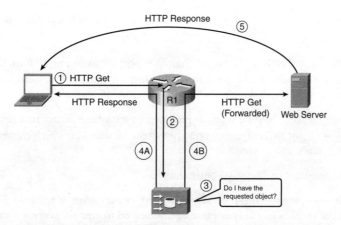

**Figure 5-3** *WCCP Operations Between a Router and a Content Engine*

The figure shows the following steps, with the main decision point on the content engine coming at Step 4:

**Step 1.** The client sends an HTTP Get request with a destination address of the web server, as normal.

**Step 2.** The router's WCCP function notices the HTTP Get request and redirects the packet to the content engine.

**Step 3.** The content engine looks at its disk storage cache to discover whether the requested object is cached.

**Step 4A.** If the object is cached, the content engine sends an HTTP response, which includes the object, back to the client.

**Step. 4B** If the object is not cached, the content engine sends the original HTTP Get request on to the original server.

**Step 5.** If Step 4B was taken, the server replies to the client, with no knowledge that the packet was ever redirected to a content engine.

Using WCCP, which uses UDP port 2048, a router and a content engine, or a pool of content engines (known as a cluster), become aware of each other. In a cluster of content engines, the content engines also communicate with each other using WCCP. Up to 32 content engines can communicate with a single router using WCCPv1. If more than one content engine is present, the one with the lowest IP address is elected as the lead engine.

WCCP also provides a means for content engines within a cluster to become aware of each other. Content engines request information on the cluster members from the WCCP router, which replies with a list. This permits the lead content engine to determine how traffic should be distributed to the cluster.

In WCCPv1, only one router can redirect traffic to a content engine or a cluster of content engines. In WCCPv2, multiple routers and multiple content engines can be configured as a WCCP service group. This expansion permits much better scalability in content caching. Furthermore, WCCPv1 supports only HTTP traffic (TCP port 80, specifically).

WCCPv2 supports several other traffic types and has other benefits compared to WCCPv1:

- Supports TCP and UDP traffic other than TCP port 80, including FTP caching, FTP proxy handling, web caching for ports other than 80, Real Audio, video, and telephony.

- Permits segmenting caching services provided by a caching cluster to a particular protocol or protocols, and uses a priority system for deciding which cluster to use for a particular cached protocol.

- Supports multicast to simplify configuration.

- Supports multiple routers (up to 32 per cluster) for redundancy and load distribution. (All content engines in a cluster must be configured to communicate with all routers in that cluster.)

- Provides for MD5 security in WCCP communication using the global configuration command **ip wccp password** *password*.

- Provides load distribution.

- Supports transparent error handling.

When you enable WCCP globally on a router, the default version used is WCCPv2. Because the WCCP version is configured globally for a router, the version number affects all interfaces. However, multiple services can run on a router at the same time. Routers and content engines can also simultaneously participate in more than one service group. These WCCP settings are configured on a per-interface basis.

Configuring WCCP on a router is not difficult because a lot of the configuration in a caching scenario takes place on the content engines; the routers need only minimal configuration. Example 5-5 shows a WCCPv2 configuration using MD5 authentication and multicast for WCCP communication.

**Example 5-5**  *WCCP Configuration Example*

```
! First we enable WCCP globally on the router,
! specifying a service (web caching), a multicast address for
! the WCCP communication, and an MD5 password:
ip wccp web-cache group-address 239.128.1.100 password cisco
! Next we configure an interface to redirect WCCP web-cache
! traffic outbound to a content engine:
int fa0/0
 ip wccp web-cache redirect out
! Finally, inbound traffic on interface fa0/1 is excluded from redirection:
int fa0/1
 ip wccp redirect exclude in
```

Finally, WCCP can make use of access lists to filter traffic only for certain clients (or to exclude WCCP use for certain clients) using the **ip wccp web-cache redirect-list** *access-list* global command. WCCP can also use ACLs to determine which types of redirected traffic the router should accept from content engines, using the global command **ip wccp web-cache group-list** *access-list*.

## Implementing the Cisco IOS IP Service Level Agreement (IP SLA) Feature

The Cisco IOS IP SLA feature, formerly known as the Service Assurance Agent (SAA), and prior to that simply the Response Time Reporter (RTR) feature, is designed to provide a means of actively probing a network to gather performance information from it. Whereas most of the tools described in the following sections are designed to monitor and collect information, IP SLA is based on the concept of generating traffic at a specified interval, with specifically configured options, and measuring the results. It is built around a source-responder model, where one device (the source) generates traffic and either waits for a response from another device (the responder) or another device configured as a responder captures the sender's traffic and does something with it. This model provides the ability to analyze actual network performance over time, under very specific conditions, to measure performance, avert outages, evaluate quality of service (QoS) performance, identify problems, verify SLAs, and reduce network outages. The IP SLA feature is extensively documented at www.cisco.com/go/ipsla.

The IP SLA feature allows measuring the following parameters in network performance:

- Delay (one-way and round-trip)

- Jitter (directional)

- Packet loss (directional)

- Packet sequencing

- Path (per hop)

- Connectivity (through the UDP Echo, ICMP Echo, ICMP Path Echo, and TCP Connect functions)

- Server or website download time

- Voice-quality metrics (MOS)

Implementing the IP SLA feature requires these steps:

**Step 1.**  Configure the SLA operation type, including any required options.

**Step 2.**  Configure any desired threshold conditions.

**Step 3.**  Configure the responder(s), if appropriate.

**Step 4.**   Schedule or start the operation and monitor the results for a sufficient period of time to meet your requirements.

**Step 5.**   Review and interpret the results. You can use the Cisco IOS CLI or an SNMP manager to do this.

After IP SLA monitors have been configured, they cannot be edited or modified. You must delete an existing IP SLA monitor to reconfigure any of its options. Also, when you delete an IP SLA monitor to reconfigure it, the associated schedule for that IP SLA monitor is deleted, too.

IP SLAs can use MD5 authentication. These are configured using the **ip sla key-chain** command.

Example 5-6 shows a basic IP SLA configuration with the UDP Echo function. On the responding router, the only required command is global config **ip sla monitor responder**. On the originating router, the configuration shown in the example sets the source router to send UDP echo packets every 5 seconds for one day to 200.1.200.9 on port 1330.

**Example 5-6**   *IP SLA Basic Configuration*

```
SLAdemo# config term
SLAdemo(config)# ip sla monitor 1
SLAdemo(config-sla-monitor)# type udpEcho dest-ipaddr 200.1.200.9 dest-port 1330
SLAdemo(config-sla-monitor)# frequency 5
SLAdemo(config-sla-monitor)# exit
SLAdemo(config)# ip sla monitor schedule 1 life 86400 start-time now
```

A number of **show** commands come in handy in verifying IP SLA performance. On the source router, the most useful commands are **show ip sla monitor statistics** and **show ip sla monitor configuration**. Here's a sample of the **show ip sla monitor statistics** command for the sending router in the configuration in Example 5-6:

```
SLAdemo# show ip sla monitor statistics
Round trip time (RTT)   Index 1
       Latest RTT: 26 ms
Latest operation start time: 19:42:44.799 EDT Tue Jun 9 2009
Latest operation return code: OK
Number of successes: 228
Number of failures: 0
Operation time to live: 78863 sec
```

## Implementing NetFlow

NetFlow is a software feature set in Cisco IOS that is designed to provide network administrators information about what is happening in the network, so that those responsible for the network can make appropriate design and configuration changes and monitor for network attacks. NetFlow has been included in Cisco IOS for a long time, and has evolved through several versions (currently version 9). Cisco has renamed the feature Cisco Flexible NetFlow. It is more than just a renaming, however. The original NetFlow implementation included a fixed seven tuples that identified a flow. Flexible NetFlow allows a user to configure the number of tuples to more specifically target a particular flow to monitor.

The components of NetFlow are

- **Records:** A set of predefined and user-defined key fields (such as source IP address, destination IP address, source port, and so on) for network monitoring.

- **Flow monitors:** Applied to an interface, flow monitors include records, a cache, and optionally a flow exporter. The flow monitor cache collects information about flows.

- **Flow exporters:** These export the cached flow information to outside systems (typically a server running a NetFlow collector).

- **Flow samplers:** Designed to reduce the load on NetFlow-enabled devices, flow samplers allow specifying the sample size of traffic, NetFlow analyzes to a ratio of 1:2 through 1:32768 packets. That is, the number of packets analyzed is configurable from 1/2 to 1/32768 of the packets flowing across the interface.

Configuring NetFlow in its most basic form uses predefined flow records, configured for collection by a flow monitor, and at least one flow exporter. Example 5-7 shows a basic NetFlow configuration for collecting information and statistics on IPv4 traffic using the predefined IPv4 record, and for configuring some timer settings to show their structure. An exporter is configured to send the collected information to a server at 192.168.1.110 on UDP port 1333, and with a Differentiated Services Code Point (DSCP) of 8 on the exported packets. The process consists of three steps: configuring the NetFlow monitor, applying it to an interface, and configuring an exporter.

**Example 5-7**   *Basic NetFlow Monitor and Exporter Configuration*

```
EastEdge# show run | begin flow
flow exporter ipv4flowexport
 destination 192.168.1.110
 dscp 8
 transport udp 1333
!
flow monitor ipv4flow
 description Monitors all IPv4 traffic
 record netflow ipv4 original-input
 cache timeout inactive 600
 cache timeout active 180
 cache entries 5000
 statistics packet protocol
!
```

```
interface FastEthernet0/0
 ip address 192.168.39.9 255.255.255.0
 ip flow monitor ipv4flow input
! output omitted
```

You can verify NetFlow configuration using these commands:

- show flow record
- show flow monitor
- show flow exporter
- show flow interface

## Implementing Router IP Traffic Export

IP Traffic Export, or Router IP Traffic Export (RITE), exports IP packets to a VLAN or LAN interface for analysis. RITE does this only for traffic received on multiple WAN or LAN interfaces simultaneously as would typically take place only if the device were being targeted in a denial of service attack. The primary application for RITE is in intrusion detection system (IDS) implementations, where duplicated traffic can indicate an attack on the network or device. In case of actual attacks where identical traffic is received simultaneously on multiple ports of a router, it's useful to have the router send that traffic to an IDS for alerting and analysis—that's what RITE does.

When configuring RITE, you enable it and configure it to direct copied packets to the MAC address of the IDS host or protocol analyzer. You can configure forwarding of inbound traffic (the default), outbound traffic, or both, and filtering on the number of packets forwarded. Filtering can be performed with access lists and based on one-in-$n$ packets.

In Example 5-8, a router is configured with a RITE profile that's applied to the fa0/0 interface and exports traffic to a host with the MAC address 0018.0fad.df30. The router is configured for bidirectional RITE, and to send one in every 20 inbound packets and one in every 100 outbound packets to this MAC address. The egress interface (toward the IDS host) is fa0/1. For simplicity, Example 5-8 shows only one ingress interface. Configuration for other ingress interfaces uses the same steps shown here for the fa0/0 interface.

**Example 5-8**  *Router IP Traffic Export Example*

```
Edge# config term
Edge(config)# ip traffic-export profile export-this
Edge(config-rite)# interface fa0/0
Edge(config-rite)# bidirectional
Edge(config-rite)# mac-address 0018.0fad.df30
Edge(config-rite)# incoming sample one-in-every 20
Edge(config-rite)# outgoing sample one-in-every 100
```

```
Edge(config-rite)# exit
Edge(config)# interface fa0/1
Edge(config-if)# ip traffic-export apply export-this
Edge(config-if)# end
Edge#
%RITE-5-ACTIVATE: Activated IP traffic export on interface FastEthernet 0/1.
```

## Implementing Cisco IOS Embedded Event Manager

The Embedded Event Manager is a software component of Cisco IOS that is designed to make life easier for administrators by tracking and classifying events that take place on a router and providing notification options for those events. The Cisco motivation for including EEM was to reduce downtime, thus improving availability, by reducing the mean time to recover from various system events that previously required a manual troubleshooting and remediation process.

In some ways, EEM overlaps with RMON functionality, but EEM is considerably more powerful and flexible. EEM uses *event detectors* and *actions* to provide notifications of those events. Event detectors that EEM supports include the following:

- Monitoring SNMP objects

- Screening Syslog messages for a pattern match (using regular expressions)

- Monitoring counters

- Timers (absolute time-of-day, countdown, watchdog, and CRON)

- Screening CLI input for a regular expression match

- Hardware insertion and removal

- Routing table changes

- IP SLA and NetFlow events

- Generic On-Line Diagnostics (GOLD) events

- Many others, including redundant switchover events, inbound SNMP messages, and others

Event actions that EEM provides include the following:

- Generating prioritized Syslog messages

- Reloading the router

- Switching to a secondary processor in a redundant platform

- Generating SNMP traps

- Setting or modifying a counter

- Executing a Cisco IOS command

- Sending a brief email message

- Requesting system information when an event occurs

- Reading or setting the state of a tracked object

EEM policies can be written using either the Cisco IOS CLI or using the Tcl command interpreter language. For the purposes of the CCIE Routing and Switching qualification exam, you're more likely to encounter CLI-related configuration than Tcl, but both are very well documented at www.cisco.com/go/eem. Example 5-9 is a brief example configuration that shows the CLI configuration of an EEM event that detects and then sends a notification that a console user has issued the **wr** command, as well as the associated console output when the command is issued.

**Example 5-9** *EEM Configuration Example*

```
R9(config)# event manager applet CLI-cp-run-st
R9(config-applet)# event cli pattern "wr" sync yes
R9(config-applet)# action 1.0 syslog msg "$_cli_msg Command Executed"
R9(config-applet)# set 2.0 _exit_status 1
R9(config-applet)# end
R9# wr
Jun  9 19:23:21.989: %HA_EM-6-LOG: CLI-cp-run-st: write Command Executed
```

The Cisco IOS EEM has such vast capability that an entire book on the subject is easily conceivable, but considering the scope of the CCIE Routing and Switching qualifying exam, these fundamental concepts should provide you with enough working knowledge to interpret questions you might encounter.

## Implementing Remote Monitoring

Remote Monitoring, or RMON, is an event-notification extension of the SNMP capability on a Cisco router or switch. RMON enables you to configure thresholds for alerting based on SNMP objects, so that you can monitor device performance and take appropriate action to any deviations from the normal range of performance indications.

RMON is divided into two classes: alarms and events. An event is a numbered, user-configured threshold for a particular SNMP object. You configure events to track, for example, CPU utilization or errors on a particular interface, or anything else you can do with an SNMP object. You set the rising and falling thresholds for these events, and then tell RMON which RMON alarm to trigger when those rising or falling thresholds are crossed. For example, you might want to have the router watch CPU utilization and trigger an SNMP trap or log an event when the CPU utilization rises faster than, say, 20 percent per minute. Or you might configure it to trigger an alarm when the CPU utilization rises to some absolute level, such as 80 percent. Both types of thresholds (relative, or "delta," and absolute) are supported. Then, you can configure a different alarm notification as the CPU utilization falls, again at some delta or to an absolute level you specify.

The alarm that corresponds to each event is also configurable in terms of what it does (logs the event or sends a trap). If you configure an RMON alarm to send a trap, you also need to supply the SNMP community string for the SNMP server.

Event and alarm numbering are locally significant. Alarm numbering provides a pointer to the corresponding event. That is, the configured events each point to specific alarm numbers, which you must also define.

Example 5-10 shows the configuration required to identify two pairs of events, and the four corresponding alarm notifications. The events being monitored are the interface error counter on the FastEthernet 0/0 interface (SNMP object ifInErrors.1) and the Serial 0/0 interface (SNMP object ifInErrors.2). In the first case, the RMON event looks for a delta (relative) rise in interface errors in a 60-second period, and a falling threshold of five errors per 60 seconds. In the second case, the numbers are different and the thresholds are absolute, but the idea is the same. In each case, the RMON events drive RMON alarms 1, 2, 3, or 4, depending on which threshold is crossed.

**Example 5-10**   *RMON Configuration Example*

```
rmon event 1 log trap public description Fa0.0RisingErrors owner config
rmon event 2 log trap public description Fa0.0FallingErrors owner config
rmon event 3 log trap public description Se0.0RisingErrors owner config
rmon event 4 log trap public description Se0.0FallingErrors owner config
rmon alarm 11 ifInErrors.1 60 delta rising-threshold 10 1 falling-threshold 5 2
  owner config
rmon alarm 20 ifInErrors.2 60 absolute rising-threshold 20 3 falling-threshold 10 4
  owner   config
```

To monitor RMON activity and to see the configured alarms and events, use the **show rmon alarm** and **show rmon event** commands. Here's an example of the console events that take place when the previously configured events trigger the corresponding alarms:

```
Jun  9 12:54:14.787: %RMON-5-FALLINGTRAP: Falling trap is generated
  because the value  of ifInErrors.1 has fallen below the falling-
  threshold value 5
Jun  9 12:55:40.732: %RMON-5-FALLINGTRAP: Falling trap is generated
  because the value  of ifInErrors.2 has fallen below the falling-
  threshold value 10
```

## Implementing and Using FTP on a Router

You can use the Cisco IOS FTP client to send or receive files from the CLI. Cisco IOS does not support configuration as an FTP server, but you can configure a TFTP server (see the next section of this chapter for details).

To transfer files using FTP from the CLI, use the **ip ftp** command with the appropriate options. You can specify the username and password to use for an FTP transfer using the **ip ftp username** and **ip ftp password** commands. You can also specify the source interface used for FTP transfers using the **ip ftp** *source-interface* command.

To initiate an FTP transfer, use the **copy** command with the **ftp** keyword in either the source or destination argument. For example, to send the startup configuration file on a router to an FTP server at 10.10.200.1, where it will be stored as r8-startup-config, the transaction is shown in Example 5-11.

**Example 5-11**  *Using FTP to Copy a Configuration File*

```
R8# copy startup-config ftp:
Address or name of remote host []? 10.10.200.1
Destination filename [r8-confg]? r8-startup-config
Writing r8-startup-config  !
3525 bytes copied in 0.732 secs
```

FTP can also be used to send an exception dump to an FTP server in the event of a crash. Example 5-12 shows a router configured to send an exception dump of 65,536 bytes to 172.30.19.63 using the username JoeAdmin and password c1sco.

**Example 5-12**  *Using FTP to Send an Exception Dump*

```
ip ftp username JoeAdmin
ip ftp password c1sco
!
exception protocol ftp
exception region-size 65536
exception dump 172.30.19.63
```

Finally, you can set the router for passive-mode FTP connections by configuring the **ip ftp passive** command.

## Implementing a TFTP Server on a Router

TFTP is commonly used for IOS and configuration file transfers on routers and switches. Cisco IOS supports configuring a TFTP server on a router, and the process is straightforward. It should be noted that TFTP is a tool that allows files to be "pulled" from one device to another.

To enable TFTP, issue the **tftp-server** command, which has several arguments. You can specify the memory region where the file resides (typically flash, but other regions are supported), the filename, and an access list for controlling which hosts can access the file. Here's an example that shows the commands to permit TFTP access to flash:c1700-advipservicesk9-mz.124-23.bin to hosts that are identified by access list 11. This example also shows how the alias command-line option can be used to make the file available with a name other than the one that it has natively in flash, specifically supersecretfile.bin:

```
tftp-server flash:c1700-advipservicesk9-mz.124-23.bin alias
  supersecretfile.bin 11
```

## Implementing Secure Copy Protocol

Secure Copy Protocol (SCP) is a service you can enable on a Cisco IOS router or switch to provide file copy services. SCP uses Secure Shell (SSH) (TCP port 22) for its transport protocol. It enables file transfer using the IOS **copy** command.

SCP requires authentication, authorization, and accounting (AAA) for user authentication and authorization. Therefore, you must enable AAA before turning on SCP. In particular, because **copy** is an exec command, you must configure the **aaa authorization** command with the **exec** option. After you've enabled AAA, use the **ip scp server enable** command to turn on the SCP server.

## Implementing HTTP and HTTPS Access

Cisco IOS routers and switches support web access for administration, through both HTTP and HTTPS. Enabling HTTP access requires the **ip http server** global configuration command. HTTP access defaults to TCP port 80. You can change the port used for HTTP by configuring the **ip http port** command. You can restrict HTTP access to a router using the **ip http access-class** command, which applies an extended access list to connection requests. You can also specify a unique username and password for HTTP access using the **ip http client username** and **ip http client password** commands. If you choose, you can also configure HTTP access to use a variety of other access-control methods, including AAA, using **ip http authentication [aaa | local | enable | tacacs]**.

You can also configure a Cisco IOS router or switch for Secure Sockets Layer (SSL) access. By default, HTTPS uses TCP port 443, and the port is configurable in much the same way as it is with HTTP access. Enabling HTTPS access requires the **ip http secure-server** command. When you configure HTTPS access in most IOS Release 12.4 versions, the router or switch automatically disables HTTP access, if it has been configured. However, you should disable it manually if the router does not do it for you.

HTTPS router access also gives you the option of specifying the cipher suite of your choice. This is the combination of encryption methods that the router will enable for HTTPS access. By default, all methods are enabled, as shown in the sample **show** *command* output of Example 5-13.

**Example 5-13**  *HTTPS Configuration Output on a Router*

```
R8# sh ip http server secure status
HTTP secure server status: Enabled
HTTP secure server port: 443
HTTP secure server ciphersuite: 3des-ede-cbc-sha des-cbc-sha rc4-128-md5
  rc4-128-sha
HTTP secure server client authentication: Disabled
HTTP secure server trustpoint:
HTTP secure server active session modules: ALL
R8#
```

## Implementing Telnet Access

Telnet is such a ubiquitous method of access on Cisco IOS routers and switches that it needs little coverage here. Still, a few basic points are in order.

Telnet requires a few configuration specifics to work. On the vty lines, the **login** command (or a variation of it such as **login local**) must be configured. If a **login** command is not configured, the router or switch will refuse all Telnet connection attempts.

By default, Telnet uses TCP port 23. However, you can configure the vty lines to use rotary groups, also known as rotaries, to open access on other ports. If you configure this option, you should use an extended access list to enforce connection on the desired ports. By default, rotaries support connections on a number of ports. For example, if you configure **rotary 33** on the vty lines, the router will accept Telnet connections on ports 3033, 5033, and 7033. Therefore, filtering undesired ports is prudent. Remember that applying access lists to vty lines requires the **access-class** *list* **in** command.

## Implementing SSH Access

Secure Shell (SSH) is much more secure than Telnet because it uses SSL rather than clear text. Therefore, today, nearly all Cisco router and switch deployments use SSH rather than Telnet for secure access. Enabling SSH on a Cisco router is a four-step process. This is because SSH requires a couple of items to be configured before you can enable SSH itself, and those prerequisites are not intuitive. The steps in configuring SSH are as follows:

**Step 1.**   Configure a host name using the **hostname** command.

**Step 2.**   Configure a domain name using the **ip domain-name** command.

**Step 3.**   Configure RSA keys using the **crypto key generate rsa** command.

**Step 4.**   Configure the terminal lines to permit SSH access using the **transport input ssh** command.

SSH supports rotaries on vty lines just as Telnet does, so you can use rotaries to specify the port or ports on which SSH access is permitted on vty lines.

# Foundation Summary

This section lists additional details and facts to round out the coverage of the topics in this chapter. Unlike most of the Cisco Press Exam Certification Guides, this "Foundation Summary" does not repeat information presented in the "Foundation Topics" section of the chapter. Please take the time to read and study the details in the "Foundation Topics" section of the chapter, as well as review items noted with a Key Topic icon.

Table 5-5 lists the protocols mentioned in this chapter and their respective standards documents.

**Table 5-5**   *Protocols and Standards for Chapter 5*

| Name | Standardized In |
|---|---|
| ARP | RFC 826 |
| Proxy ARP | RFC 1027 |
| RARP | RFC 903 |
| BOOTP | RFC 951 |
| DHCP | RFC 2131 |
| DHCP FQDN option | Internet-Draft |
| HSRP | Cisco proprietary |
| VRRP | RFC 3768 |
| GLBP | Cisco proprietary |
| CDP | Cisco proprietary |
| NTP | RFC 1305 |
| Syslog | RFC 5424 |
| SNMP Version 1 | RFCs 1155, 1156, 1157, 1212, 1213, 1215 |
| SNMP Version 2 | RFCs 1902–1907, 3416 |
| SNMP Version 2c | RFC 1901 |
| SNMP Version 3 | RFCs 2578–2580, 3410–3415 |
| Good Starting Point: | RFC 3410 |

Table 5-6 lists some of the most popular Cisco IOS commands related to the topics in this chapter.

**Table 5-6**   *Command Reference for Chapter 5*

| Command | Description |
| --- | --- |
| **ip dhcp pool** *name* | Creates DHCP pool. |
| **default-router** *address* [*address2...address8*] | DHCP pool subcommand to list the gateways. |
| **dns-server** *address* [*address2...address8*] | DHCP pool subcommand to list DNS servers. |
| **lease** {*days* [*hours*][*minutes*] \| **infinite**} | DHCP pool subcommand to define the lease length. |
| **network** *network-number* [*mask* \| *prefix-length*] | DHCP pool subcommand to define IP addresses that can be assigned. |
| **ip dhcp excluded-address** [*low-address high-address*] | Global command to disallow these addresses from being assigned. |
| **host** *address* [*mask* \| *prefix-length*] | DHCP pool subcommand, used with *hardware-address* or *client-identifier*, to predefine a single host's IP address. |
| **hardware-address** *hardware-address type* | DHCP pool subcommand to define MAC address; works with the **host** command. |
| **show ip dhcp binding** [*ip-address*] | Lists addresses allocated by DHCP. |
| **show ip dhcp server statistics** | Lists stats for DHCP server operations. |
| **standby** [*group-number*] **ip** [*ip-address* [**secondary**]] | Interface subcommand to enable an HSRP group and define the virtual IP address. |
| **track** *object-number* **interface** *type-number* {*line-protocol* \| *ip routing*} | Configures a tracking object that can be used by HSRP, VRRP, or GLBP to track the status of an interface. |
| **standby** [*group-number*] **preempt** [**delay** {**minimum** *delay* \| **reload** *delay* \| **sync** *delay*}] | Interface subcommand to enable preemption and set delay timers. |
| **show track** [*object-number* [**brief**] \| **interface** [**brief**] \| **ip route** [**brief**] \| **resolution** \| **timers**] | Displays status of tracked objects. |
| **standby** [*group-number*] **priority** *priority* | Interface subcommand to set the HSRP group priority for this router. |
| **standby** [*group-number*] **timers** [**msec**] *hellotime* [**msec**] *holdtime* | Interface subcommand to set HSRP group timers. |
| **standby** [*group-number*] **track** *object-number* | Interface subcommand to enable HSRP to track defined objects, usually for the purpose of switching active routers on an event related to that object. |

| Command | Description |
|---------|-------------|
| show standby [*type number* [*group*]] [brief \| all] | Lists HSRP statistics. |
| ntp peer *ip-address* [version *number*] [key *keyid*] [source *interface*] [prefer] | Global command to enable symmetric active mode NTP. |
| ntp server *ip-address* [version *number*] [key *keyid*] [source *interface*] [prefer] | Global command to enable static client mode NTP. |
| ntp broadcast [version *number*] | Interface subcommand on an NTP server to cause NTP broadcasts on the interface. |
| ntp broadcast client | Interface subcommand on an NTP client to cause it to listen for NTP broadcasts. |
| ntp master [*stratum*] | Global command to enable NTP server. |
| show ntp associations | Lists associations with other NTP servers and clients. |
| show ntp status | Displays synchronization status, stratum level, and other basic information. |
| logging trap level | Sets the severity level for syslog messages; arguments are 0–7, where 0=emergencies, 1=alerts, 2=critical, 3=errors, 4=warnings, 5=notifications, 6=informational, 7=debugging (default). |
| logging host {{*ip-address* \| *hostname*} \| {ipv6 *ipv6-address* \| *hostname*}} [transport {udp [port *port-number*] \| tcp [port *port-number*]}] [alarm [*severity*]] | Configures the IP or IPv6 address or host name to which to send syslog messages and permits setting the transport protocol and port number. |
| ip wccp {web-cache \| *service-number*} [service-list *service-access-list*] [mode {open \| closed}] [group-address *multicast-address*] [redirect-list *access-list*] [group-list *access-list*] [password [0-7] *password*] | Enables WCCP and configures filtering and service parameters. |
| ip wccp {web-cache \| *service-number*} redirect {in \| out} | Interface configuration command to enable WCCP and configure it for outbound or inbound service. |
| show ip wccp | Displays WCCP configuration settings and statistics. |
| snmp-server enable traps | Enables sending of all types of traps available on the router or switch. |

| Command | Description |
|---------|-------------|
| **snmp-server host** {*hostname* \| *ip-address*} [**vrf** *vrf-name*] [**traps** \| **informs**] [**version** {**1** \| **2c** \| **3** [**auth** \| **noauth** \| **priv**]}] **community-string** [**udp-port** *port*] [*notification-type*] | Configures the SNMP server to send traps or informs to a particular host, along with options for setting the SNMP version for traps and the UDP port (default is 162). The notification-type field specifies the types of traps to send; if no types are specified, all available categories of traps will be sent. |
| **snmp-server community** *string* [**view** *view-name*] [**ro** \| **rw**] [*access-list-number*] | Sets the read-only or read-write community string and access list for host filtering for access to SNMP reads and writes on the router or switch. |
| **show snmp mib ifmib ifindex** *interface-id* | Shows the router's interface ID for a particular interface. Particularly useful for RMON configuration. |
| **ip sla monitor** *operation-index* | Enters IP SLA monitor configuration mode for an individual monitor function. |
| **type** [**jitter** \| **udp-echo** \| **echo protocol icmpecho** \| **dns** \| **ftp operation** \| **http operation** \| **mpls ping ipv4** \| **pathecho** \| **pathjitter** \| **tcpconnect** \| **voip delay post-dial** \| **udp-jitter** \| **udp-jitter** *codec*] | Configures the IP SLA monitor type with options (not shown) including source and destination IP address and source and destination port number, plus other relevant options to the particular type. |
| **ip sla key-chain** *key-chain-name* | Configures a key chain for MD5 authentication of IP SLA operations. |
| **ip sla monitor schedule** *operation-number* [**life** {**forever** \| *seconds*}] [**start-time** {*hh:mm*[*:ss*] [*month day* \| *day month*] \| **pending** \| **now** \| **after** *hh:mm:ss*}] [**ageout** *seconds*] [**recurring**] | Configures the schedule for a particular IP SLA monitor. If the IP SLA monitor is deleted from the configuration, the schedule is also deleted. |
| **ip sla monitor responder** | Enables the IP SLA responder function globally. More specific options for this command can be configured for specific responder types, ports, and so on. |
| **show ip sla monitor statistics** [*operation*] **detail** | Shows the statistics for a specified IP SLA operation or all configured IP SLA operations. |
| **show ip sla responder** | Shows currently configured IP SLA responders and recent activity (source IP address, and so on). |
| **ip ssh** [**timeout** *seconds* \| **authentication-retries** *integer*] | Sets SSH access crypto key. |
| **crypto key generate rsa** | Generates RSA keys. Required for SSH configuration. |

| Command | Description |
|---|---|
| transport input ssh | In vty configuration mode, permits SSH connections. |
| ip http server | Enables HTTP server. |
| ip http secure-server | Enables HTTPS server. |
| ip traffic-export profile *profile-name* | Enables and enters configuration mode for a RITE profile. |
| ip traffic-export apply *profile-name* | Applies a RITE profile to an interface. |
| event manager applet *applet-name* [class *class-options*] [trap] | Enters EEM applet configuration mode. |
| event cli pattern *regular-expression* {[default] [enter] [questionmark] [tab]} [sync {yes | no}] skip {yes | no}] [mode *variable*] [occurs *num-occurrences*] [period *period-value*] [maxrun *maxruntime-number*] | Configures EEM to match a CLI command string. |
| ip flow-top-talkers | NetFlow aggregator. Aggregates traffic for unclassified top talkers. |
| flow monitor *flow-name* | Enters configuration mode for a NetFlow monitor. |
| flow exporter *exporter-name* | Configures a NetFlow exporter and the destination server to which to send NetFlow information for a particular flow monitor. |
| rmon event | Configures an event action for an RMON alarm's rising or falling threshold. |
| rmon alarm | Configures an RMON alarm to monitor a particular SNMP object, along with rising and falling thresholds |
| Copy | With FTP option in the source or destination field, copies a file to or from an FTP server. |
| tftp-server flash [*partition-number:*] *filename1* [alias *filename2*] [*access-list-number*] | Configures a TFTP server on the router to serve a file, optionally with an alias, and optionally through an ACL. |
| aaa new-model | Enables AAA on the router. |
| aaa authentication | Configures AAA authentication methods. |
| aaa authorization | Configures AAA authorization methods. |
| ip scp server enable | Enables the SCP server on the router. Requires AAA authentication and AAA authorization to be configured. |

## Memory Builders

The CCIE Routing and Switching written exam, like all Cisco CCIE written exams, covers a fairly broad set of topics. This section provides some basic tools to help you exercise your memory about some of the broader topics covered in this chapter.

### Fill In Key Tables from Memory

Appendix E, "Key Tables for CCIE Study," on the CD in the back of this book, contains empty sets of some of the key summary tables in each chapter. Print Appendix E, refer to this chapter's tables in it, and fill in the tables from memory. Refer to Appendix F, "Solutions for Key Tables for CCIE Study," on the CD to check your answers.

### Definitions

Next, take a few moments to write down the definitions for the following terms:

HSRP, VRRP, GLBP, ARP, RARP, proxy ARP, BOOTP, DHCP, NTP symmetric active mode, NTP server mode, NTP client mode, NTP, virtual IP address, VRRP Master router, SNMP agent, SNMP manager, Get, GetNext, GetBulk, MIB-I, MIB-II, Response, Trap, Set, Inform, SMI, MIB, MIB walk, lead content engine

Refer to the glossary to check your answers.

### Further Reading

More information about several of the topics in this chapter can be easily found in a large number of books and online documentation. The RFCs listed in Table 5-5 of the "Foundation Summary" section also provide a great deal of background information for this chapter. Here are a few references for more information about some of the less popular topics covered in this chapter:

■   **Proxy ARP:** www.cisco.com/en/US/tech/tk648/tk361/technologies_tech_note-09186a0080094adb.shtml.

■   **GLBP:** www.cisco.com/en/US/docs/ios/12_2t/12_2t15/feature/guide/ft_glbp.html.

■   **VRRP:** www.cisco.com/en/US/docs/ios/12_0st/12_0st18/feature/guide/st_vrrpx.html.

■   **SNMP:** Any further reading of SNMP-related RFCs should begin with RFC 3410, which provides a great overview of the releases and points to the more important of the vast number of SNMP-related RFCs.

**Blueprint topics covered in this chapter:**

This chapter covers the following subtopics from the Cisco CCIE Routing and Switching written exam blueprint. Refer to the full blueprint in Table I-1 in the Introduction for more details on the topics covered in each chapter and their context within the blueprint.

- Cisco Express Forwarding Concepts
- Routing Protocol Migration
- Policy-Based Routing

## CHAPTER 6

# IP Forwarding (Routing)

This chapter begins with coverage of the details of the forwarding plane—the actual forwarding of IP packets. This process of forwarding IP packets is often called *IP routing*, or simply *routing*. Also, many people also refer to IP routing as the *data plane*, meaning the plane (topic) related to the end-user data.

Chapters 7 through 11 cover the details of the IP *control plane*. In contrast to the term *data plane*, the control plane relates to the communication of control information—in short, routing protocols like OSPF and BGP. These chapters cover the routing protocols on the exam, plus an additional chapter on redistribution and route summarization.

## "Do I Know This Already?" Quiz

Table 6-1 outlines the major headings in this chapter and the corresponding "Do I Know This Already?" quiz questions.

**Table 6-1** *"Do I Know This Already?" Foundation Topics Section-to-Question Mapping*

| Foundation Topics Section | Questions Covered in This Section | Score |
| --- | --- | --- |
| IP Forwarding | 1–6 | |
| Multilayer Switching | 7–9 | |
| Policy Routing | 10–11 | |
| Total Score | | |

To best use this pre-chapter assessment, remember to score yourself strictly. You can find the answers in Appendix A, "Answers to the 'Do I Know This Already?' Quizzes."

**1.** What command is used to enable CEF globally for IPv4 packets?

  **a.** enable cef

  **b.** ip enable cef

  **c.** ip cef

  **d.** cef enable

  **e.** cef enable ip

  **f.** cef ip

**2.** What command is used to enable CEF globally for IPv6 packets?

   **a.** enable cef6

   **b.** ipv6 enable cef

   **c.** ipv6 cef

   **d.** ip cef (the command automatically enables CEF for IPv4 and IPv6)

**3.** Can CEF for IPv6 be enabled independently of CEF for IPv4?

   **a.** Yes

   **b.** No

**4.** Which of the following triggers an update to a CEF FIB?

   **a.** Receipt of an ICMPv6 Neighbor Advertisement message with previously unknown information

   **b.** Receipt of a LAN ARP reply message with previously unknown information

   **c.** Addition of a new route to the IP routing table by EIGRP

   **d.** Addition of a new route to the IP routing table by adding an **ip route** command

   **e.** The removal of a route from the IP routing table by EIGRP

**5.** Which of the following triggers an update to a CEF adjacency table?

   **a.** Receipt of a CDP multicast on the PVC connected to Router1

   **b.** Receipt of an ARP response with previously unknown information

   **c.** Receipt of a packet that needs to be routed to another router over a point-to-point interface

   **d.** Receipt of an ICMPv6 Neighbor Advertisement with previously unknown information

**6.** Which of the following packet-switching paths is considered to be the slowest?

   **a.** Process Switching

   **b.** Fast Switching

   **c.** Route Cache

   **d.** Cisco Express Forwarding

**7.** Which of the following commands is used on a Cisco IOS Layer 3 switch to use the interface as a *routed interface* instead of a *switched interface*?

   **a.** **ip routing** or **ipv6 unicast-routing** global command

   **b.** **ip routing** or **ipv6 unicast-routing** interface subcommand

   **c.** **ip address** interface subcommand

   **d.** **switchport mode routed** interface subcommand

   **e.** **no switchport** interface subcommand

**8.** On a Cisco Catalyst 3560 switch, the first line of the output of a **show interface vlan 55** command lists the state as "Vlan 55 is down, line protocol is down." Which of the following might be causing that state to occur?

   **a.** VLAN interface has not been **no shut** yet.

   **b.** The **ip routing** global command is missing from the configuration.

   **c.** On at least one interface in the VLAN, a cable that was previously plugged in has been unplugged.

   **d.** VTP mode is set to transparent.

   **e.** The VLAN has not yet been created on this switch, or is not in the active state.

**9.** On a Cisco Catalyst 3560 switch, the first line of the output of a **show interface vlan 55** command lists the state as "Vlan 55 is up, line protocol is down." Which of the following might be causing that state to occur?

   **a.** VLAN interface has not been **no shut** yet.

   **b.** The **ip routing** global command is missing from the configuration.

   **c.** There is no switch port on the switch with this VLAN allowed and in the STP forwarding state.

   **d.** STP has been administratively deactivated for this VLAN.

   **e.** The VLAN has not yet been created on this switch, or is not in the active state.

**10.** Imagine a route map used for policy routing, in which the route map has a **set default interface serial0/0** command. Serial0/0 is a point-to-point link to another router. A packet arrives at this router, and the packet matches the policy routing **route-map** clause whose only **set** command is the one just mentioned. Which of the following general characterizations is true?

   **a.** The packet will be routed out interface s0/0; if s0/0 is down, it will be routed using the default route from the routing table.

   **b.** The packet will be routed using the default route in the routing table; if there is no default, the packet will be routed out s0/0.

   **c.** The packet will be routed using the best match of the destination address with the routing table; if no match is found, the packet will be routed out s0/0.

   **d.** The packet will be routed out interface s0/0; if s0/0 is down, the packet will be discarded.

**11.** Router1 has an fa0/0 interface and two point-to-point WAN links back to the core of the network (s0/0 and s0/1, respectively). Router1 accepts routing information only over s0/0, which Router1 uses as its primary link. When s0/0 fails, Router1 uses policy routing to forward the traffic out the relatively slower s0/1 link. Which of the following **set** commands in Router1's policy routing route map could have been used to achieve this function?

    **a.**  set ip default next-hop

    **b.**  set ip next-hop

    **c.**  set default interface

    **d.**  set interface

# Foundation Topics

## IP Forwarding

*IP forwarding*, or *IP routing*, is the process of receiving an IP packet, making a decision of where to send the packet next, and then forwarding the packet. The forwarding process needs to be relatively simple, or at least streamlined, for a router to forward large volumes of packets. Ignoring the details of several Cisco optimizations to the forwarding process for a moment, the internal forwarding logic in a router works basically as shown in Figure 6-1.

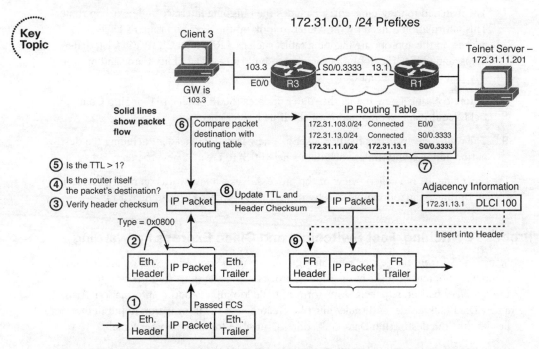

**Figure 6-1** *Forwarding Process at Router3, Destination Telnet Server*

The following list summarizes the key steps shown in Figure 6-1:

1. A router receives the frame and checks the received frame check sequence (FCS); if errors occurred, the frame is discarded. The router makes no attempt to recover the lost packet.

2. If no errors occurred, the router checks the Ethernet Type field for the packet type and extracts the packet. The Data Link header and trailer can now be discarded.

3. Assuming an IPv4 packet, its header checksum is first verified. In case of mismatch, the packet is discarded. With IPv6 packets, this check is skipped, as IPv6 headers do not contain a checksum.

4.  If the header checksum passed, the router checks whether the destination IP address is one of the addresses configured on the router itself. If it does, the packet has just arrived at its destination. The router analyzes the Protocol field in the IP header, identifying the upper-layer protocol, and hands the packet's payload over to the appropriate upper-protocol driver.

5.  If the destination IP address does not match any of the router's configured addresses, the packet must be routed. The router first verifies whether the TTL of the packet is greater than 1. If not, the packet is dropped and an ICMP Time Exceeded message is sent to the packet's sender.

6.  The router checks its IP routing table for the most specific prefix match of the packet's destination IP address.

7.  The matched routing table entry includes the outgoing interface and next-hop router. This information is used by the router to look up the next-hop router's Layer 2 address in the appropriate mapping table, such as ARP, IP/DLCI, IP/VPI-VCI, dialer maps, and so on. This lookup is needed to build a new Data Link frame and optionally dial the proper number.

8.  Before creating a new frame, the router updates the IP header TTL or Hop Count field, requiring a recomputation of the IPv4 header checksum.

9.  The router encapsulates the IP packet in a new Data Link header (including the destination address) and trailer (including a new FCS) to create a new frame.

The preceding list is a generic view of the process. Next, a few words on how Cisco routers can optimize the routing process by using Cisco Express Forwarding (CEF).

## Process Switching, Fast Switching, and Cisco Express Forwarding

Steps 6 and 7 from the generic routing logic shown in the preceding section are the most computation-intensive tasks in the routing process. A router must find the best route to use for every packet, requiring some form of table lookup of routing information. Also, a new Data Link header and trailer must be created, and the information to put in the header (like the destination Data Link address) must be found in another table.

Cisco has created several different methods to optimize the forwarding processing inside routers, termed *switching paths*. This section examines the two most likely methods to exist in Cisco router networks today: fast switching and CEF.

With fast switching, the first packet to a specific destination IP address is *process switched*, meaning that it follows the same general algorithm as shown in Figure 6-1. With the first packet, the router adds the results of this daunting lookup to the *fast-switching cache*, sometimes called the *route cache*, organized for fast lookups. The cache contains the destination IP address, the next-hop information, and the data-link header information that needs to be added to the packet before forwarding (as in Step 6 in Figure 6-1). Future packets to the same destination address match the cache entry, so it takes the router less time to process and forward the packet, as all results are already stored in the cache. This approach is also sometimes termed *route once, forward many times*.

Although it is much better than process switching, fast switching has significant draw-backs. The first packet must be process switched, because an entry can be added to the cache only when a packet is routed and the results of its routing (next hop, egress inter-face, Layer 2 rewrite information) are computed. A huge inflow of packets to destinations that are not yet recorded in the route cache can have a detrimental effect on the CPU and the router's performance, as they all need to be process switched. The cache entries are timed out relatively quickly, because otherwise the cache could get overly large as it has an entry per each destination address, not per destination subnet/prefix. If the rout-ing table or Layer 3–to–Layer 2 tables change, parts of the route cache must be invali-dated rather than updated, causing packets for affected destinations to become process switched again. Also, load balancing can only occur per destination with fast switching. Overall, fast switching was a great improvement at the time it was invented, but since that time, better switching mechanisms have been developed. One of them, Cisco Express Forwarding (CEF), has become the major packet-forwarding mechanism in all current Cisco IP routing implementations, with fast switching becoming practically unused. The support for unicast fast switching has therefore been discontinued and removed from IOS Releases 12.2(25)S and 12.4(20)T onward.

**Key Topic**

To learn the basic idea behind CEF as an efficient mechanism to perform routing deci-sions, it is important to understand that the crucial part of routing a packet through a router is finding out how to construct the Layer 2 frame header to allow the packet to be properly encapsulated toward its next hop, and forward the packet out the correct interface. Often, this operation is called a Layer 2 frame rewrite because that is what it resembles: A packet arrives at a router, and the router rewrites the Layer 2 frame, encap-sulating the packet appropriately, and sends the packet toward the next hop. The packet's header does not change significantly—in IPv4, only the TTL and checksum are modi-fied; with IPv6, only the Hop Count is decremented. An efficient routing mechanism should therefore focus on speeding up the construction of Layer 2 rewrite information and egress interface lookup. The process switching is highly inefficient in this aspect: The routing table lookup is relatively slow and might need recursive iterations until the direct-ly attached next hop and egress interface are identified. The next-hop information must then be translated in ARP or other Layer 3–to–Layer 2 mapping tables to the appropriate Layer 2 address and the frame header must be constructed, and only then the packet can be encapsulated and forwarded. With each subsequent packet, this process repeats from the beginning.

**Key Topic**

One important observation is that while the routing table can hold tens of thousands of destination networks (prefixes), a router typically has only a handful of neighbors—the next hops toward all the known destinations. All destinations reachable through a par-ticular next hop are using the same Layer 2 rewrite information. To reach any of the networks behind a particular *adjacent* next hop, the packets will be encapsulated into frames having the same Layer 2 header addresses and sent out the same egress interface. It makes sense, then, to trade memory for speed: Preconstruct the Layer 2 frame headers and egress interface information for each neighbor, and keep them ready in an *adjacency table* stored in the router's memory. This adjacency table can be constructed immediately as the routing table is populated, using IP addresses of next hops in the routing table and utilizing ARP or other Layer 3–to–Layer 2 mapping tables to translate next-hop

IP addresses into their corresponding Layer 2 addresses. A packet that is to be routed through a particular next hop will then simply use the preconstructed Layer 2 frame header for that next hop, without needing to visit the ARP or similar tables over and over again. The process of routing a packet will then transform itself to the process of deciding which entry from the adjacency table should be used to encapsulate and forward the packet. After the proper entry is selected, encapsulating the packet and forwarding it out the egress interface can be done in an extremely rapid way, as all necessary data is readily available.

**Key Topic**

Another important observation is that the routing table itself is not truly optimized for rapid lookups. It contains lots of information crucial to its construction but not that important for routing lookups, such as origin and administrative distances of routes, their metrics, age, and so on. Entries in the routing table can require recursive lookups: After matching a destination network entry, the next-hop information might contain only the IP address of the next hop but not the egress interface, so the next hop's IP address has to be looked up in the routing table in the next iteration—and the depth of this recursion is theoretically unlimited. Even after matching the ultimate entry in the routing table that finally identifies the egress interface, it does not really say anything about the Layer 2 rewrite that is necessary to forward the packet. The last found next-hop IP address during this lookup process has to be further matched in the ARP or similar mapping tables for the egress interface to find out how to construct the Layer 2 frame header. All these shortcomings can be improved, though: The destination prefixes alone from the routing table can be stored in a separate data structure called the *Forwarding Information Base*, or FIB, optimized for rapid lookups (usually, tree-based data structures meet this requirement). Instead of carrying the plain next hop's IP address from the routing table over into the FIB, each entry in the FIB that represents a destination prefix can instead contain a pointer toward the particular entry in the adjacency table that stores the appropriate rewrite information: Layer 2 frame header and egress interface indication. Any necessary recursion in the routing table is resolved while creating the FIB entries and setting up the pointers toward appropriate adjacency table entries. No other information needs to be carried over from the routing table into the FIB. In effect, the FIB stores only destination prefixes alone. The forwarding information itself is stored as Layer 2 rewrite information in the adjacency table, and entries in the FIB point toward appropriate entries in the adjacency table. All FIB entries that describe networks reachable through a particular next hop point to the same adjacency table entry that contains prepared Layer 2 header and egress information toward that next hop.

**Key Topic**

After the FIB and adjacency table are created, the routing table is not used anymore to route packets for which all forwarding information is found in the FIB/adjacency table. With FIB-based routers, the routing table can be used for packets that require more complex processing not available through straightforward Layer 2 rewrite; however, for plain packet routing, only the FIB and the adjacency table are used. The routing table therefore becomes more of a source of routing data to build the FIB and adjacency table contents but is not necessarily used to route packets anymore. Therefore, such a routing table is called the *Routing Information Base (RIB)*—it is the master copy of routing information from which the FIB and other structures are populated, but it is not necessarily used to route packets itself. Note that many routing protocols including Open Shortest Path First (OSPF) and Border Gateway Protocol (BGP) construct their own internal routing tables that are also called RIBs. These per-protocol RIBs are usually separate from the router's routing table and shall not be confused with the RIB discussed in this chapter.

Advantages of this approach should be immediately obvious. The FIB contains only the essential information to match a packet's destination address to a known prefix. A single lookup in the FIB immediately produces a pointer toward complete Layer 2 rewrite information for the packet to be forwarded. If the next hop for a destination changes, only the pointer in the respective FIB entry needs to be updated to point toward the new adjacency table entry; the FIB entry itself that represents the destination prefix is unchanged. Both FIB and adjacency tables can be readily constructed from the routing table and the available Layer 3–to–Layer 2 mapping tables, without requiring any packet flows as was the case in fast switching. To those readers familiar with database systems, the FIB can be seen as an index over the adjacency table, with IP prefixes being the lookup keys and the indexed data being the Layer 2 rewrite entries in the adjacency table.

These ideas are at the core of Cisco Express Forwarding, or CEF. Conceptually, CEF consists of two parts—the *Forwarding Information Base* and the *adjacency table*. The FIB contains all known destination prefixes from the routing table, plus additional specific entries, organized as a so-called *mtrie* or a *multiway prefix tree*. The adjacency table contains a Layer 2 frame header prepared for each known next hop or directly attached destination.

The CEF as just described can be implemented in a relatively straightforward way in software, and this is exactly what all software-based Cisco routers do: They implement CEF purely in software, as part of the operating system they run. Both FIB and adjacency tables are maintained in router's memory, and lookups in these structures are done by the CPU as part of interrupt handler executed when a packet is received. Figure 6-2, reused from the Cisco document "How to Choose the Best Router Switching Path for Your Network," Document ID 13706 available on the Cisco website, illustrates the concept.

Multilayer switches and high-end Cisco router platforms go even further, and instead of software-based FIB, they use specialized circuits (specifically, Ternary Content Addressable Memory [TCAM]) to store the FIB contents and perform even faster lookups. Using a TCAM, an address lookup is performed in an extremely short time that does not depend on the number of FIB entries, as the TCAM performs the matching on its entire contents in parallel. On these platforms, the CEF structures are distributed to individual linecards if present, and stored in TCAMs and forwarding ASICs.

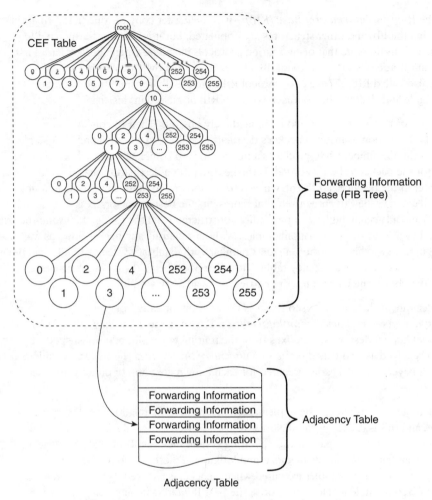

**Figure 6-2**  *Cisco Express Forwarding Basic Architecture*

To illustrate the CEF in action, consider the network in Figure 6-3 and related Example 6-1.

In this network, Router R1 is connected to two other routers and one multilayer switch. The Data Link Layer technologies interconnecting the devices are diverse: Between R1 and R2, HDLC is used; R1 and R3 are connected over a PPP link; R1 and MLS4 are using Ethernet interconnection in two VLANs—native VLAN and VLAN 2. OSPF is the routing protocol in use. R2 advertises networks 10.2.0.0/24 through 10.2.3.0/24 and FD00:2::/64 through FD00:2:3::/64. In a similar fashion, R3 advertises networks 10.3.4.0/24 through 10.3.7.0/24 and FD00:3:4::/64 through FD00:3:7::/64. MLS4 advertises networks 10.4.8.0/24 and 10.4.9.0/24, and FD00:4:8::/64 and FD00:4:9::/64, over both VLANs. Multiple interface encapsulations and multiple networks reachable over a single next hop are used in this example to show how potentially numerous destination prefixes map to a single adjacent next hop and how the Layer 2 rewrite information is built depending on the Data Link Layer technology. CEF is activated for both IPv4 and IPv6 using the **ip cef** and **ipv6 cef** global configuration commands on R1.

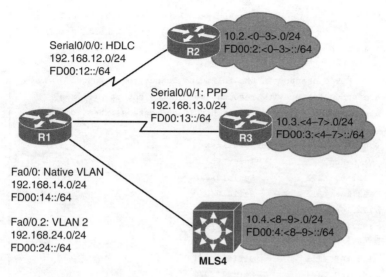

**Figure 6-3** *Example Network Showcasing CEF Operation*

**Example 6-1** *CEF FIB and Adjacency Table*

```
! On R1, show ip route ospf shows a portion of the RIB


R1# show ip route ospf
     10.0.0.0/8 is variably subnetted, 12 subnets, 2 masks
O       10.2.0.0/24 [110/782] via 192.168.12.2, 00:07:06, Serial0/0/0
O       10.2.1.0/24 [110/782] via 192.168.12.2, 00:07:06, Serial0/0/0
O       10.2.2.0/24 [110/782] via 192.168.12.2, 00:07:06, Serial0/0/0
O       10.2.3.0/24 [110/782] via 192.168.12.2, 00:07:06, Serial0/0/0
O       10.3.4.1/32 [110/782] via 192.168.13.3, 00:07:06, Serial0/0/1
O       10.3.5.0/24 [110/782] via 192.168.13.3, 00:07:06, Serial0/0/1
O       10.3.6.0/24 [110/782] via 192.168.13.3, 00:07:06, Serial0/0/1
O       10.3.7.0/24 [110/782] via 192.168.13.3, 00:07:06, Serial0/0/1
O       10.4.8.0/24 [110/2] via 192.168.24.4, 00:07:06, FastEthernet0/0.2
                    [110/2] via 192.168.14.4, 00:07:06, FastEthernet0/0
O       10.4.9.0/24 [110/2] via 192.168.24.4, 00:07:06, FastEthernet0/0.2
                    [110/2] via 192.168.14.4, 00:07:06, FastEthernet0/0


! Another crucial part of information is the ARP table that resolves
! next hop IP addresses of hosts connected via Ethernet to MAC addresses
! Serial interface technologies in this example are point-to-point and
! hence require no Layer 3-to-Layer 2 mapping tables. This information will
! be used in construction of adjacency table entries


R1# show ip arp
Protocol  Address          Age (min)  Hardware Addr   Type    Interface
Internet  192.168.14.4           41   0017.9446.b340  ARPA    FastEthernet0/0
```

```
Internet  192.168.14.1       -    0019.e87f.38e4  ARPA   FastEthernet0/0
Internet  192.168.24.1       -    0019.e87f.38e4  ARPA   FastEthernet0/0.2
Internet  192.168.24.4       41   0017.9446.b341  ARPA   FastEthernet0/0.2


! show ip cef shows the FIB contents. In the following output, only routes
! learned via OSPF are shown for brevity reasons. Note how a set of prefixes
! resolves through a particular adjacency (next hop IP and egress interface).


R1# show ip cef 10.0.0.0 255.0.0.0 longer-prefixes
Prefix              Next Hop            Interface
10.2.0.0/24         192.168.12.2        Serial0/0/0
10.2.1.0/24         192.168.12.2        Serial0/0/0
10.2.2.0/24         192.168.12.2        Serial0/0/0
10.2.3.0/24         192.168.12.2        Serial0/0/0
10.3.4.1/32         192.168.13.3        Serial0/0/1
10.3.5.0/24         192.168.13.3        Serial0/0/1
10.3.6.0/24         192.168.13.3        Serial0/0/1
10.3.7.0/24         192.168.13.3        Serial0/0/1
10.4.8.0/24         192.168.24.4        FastEthernet0/0.2
                    192.168.14.4        FastEthernet0/0
10.4.9.0/24         192.168.24.4        FastEthernet0/0.2
                    192.168.14.4        FastEthernet0/0


! Similarly, for IPv6, the relevant outputs are:


R1# show ipv6 route ospf
! Output shortened and reformatted for brevity
O    FD00:2::/64 [110/782]   via FE80::2, Serial0/0/0
O    FD00:2:1::/64 [110/782] via FE80::2, Serial0/0/0
O    FD00:2:2::/64 [110/782] via FE80::2, Serial0/0/0
O    FD00:2:3::/64 [110/782] via FE80::2, Serial0/0/0
O    FD00:3:4::/64 [110/782] via FE80::3, Serial0/0/1
O    FD00:3:5::/64 [110/782] via FE80::3, Serial0/0/1
O    FD00:3:6::/64 [110/782] via FE80::3, Serial0/0/1
O    FD00:3:7::/64 [110/782] via FE80::3, Serial0/0/1
O    FD00:4:8::/64 [110/2]   via FE80:24::4, FastEthernet0/0.2
                             via FE80:14::4, FastEthernet0/0
O    FD00:4:9::/64 [110/2]   via FE80:24::4, FastEthernet0/0.2
                             via FE80:14::4, FastEthernet0/0


R1# show ipv6 neighbors
IPv6 Address                      Age Link-layer Addr State Interface
FD00:14::4                          1 0017.9446.b340  STALE Fa0/0
FD00:24::4                          1 0017.9446.b341  STALE Fa0/0.2
FE80::3                             - -               REACH Se0/0/1
FE80:14::4                          2 0017.9446.b340  STALE Fa0/0
```

```
FE80:24::4                              1 0017.9446.b341   STALE Fa0/0.2


R1# show ipv6 cef
! Output shortened and reformatted for brevity
FD00:2::/64    nexthop FE80::2 Serial0/0/0
FD00:2:1::/64 nexthop FE80::2 Serial0/0/0
FD00:2:2::/64 nexthop FE80::2 Serial0/0/0
FD00:2:3::/64 nexthop FE80::2 Serial0/0/0
FD00:3:4::/64 nexthop FE80::3 Serial0/0/1
FD00:3:5::/64 nexthop FE80::3 Serial0/0/1
FD00:3:6::/64 nexthop FE80::3 Serial0/0/1
FD00:3:7::/64 nexthop FE80::3 Serial0/0/1
FD00:4:8::/64 nexthop FE80:24::4 FastEthernet0/0.2
              nexthop FE80:14::4 FastEthernet0/0
FD00:4:9::/64 nexthop FE80:24::4 FastEthernet0/0.2
              nexthop FE80:14::4 FastEthernet0/0


! The show adjacency shows an abbreviated list of adjacency table entries
! Note that separate entries are created for IPv4 and IPv6 adjacencies,
! as the Protocol or EtherType field value in pre-constructed frame headers
! is different for IPv4 and IPv6


R1# show adjacency
Protocol Interface             Address
IPV6     Serial0/0/0           point2point(12)
IP       Serial0/0/0           point2point(13)
IPV6     Serial0/0/1           point2point(10)
IP       Serial0/0/1           point2point(15)
IPV6     FastEthernet0/0.2     FE80:24::4(12)
IP       FastEthernet0/0       192.168.14.4(23)
IPV6     FastEthernet0/0       FE80:14::4(12)
IP       FastEthernet0/0.2     192.168.24.4(23)
IPV6     Serial0/0/1           point2point(4)
IPV6     FastEthernet0/0.2     FD00:24::4(5)
IPV6     FastEthernet0/0       FD00:14::4(7)


! Now focus on the adjacency table details. There are adjacencies via multiple
! interfaces. Serial0/0/0 is running HDLC. Note in the show adjacency detail
! command output the prepared HDLC header for all IPv6 prefixes (0F0086DD)
! and IP prefixes (0F000800) resolving through this adjacency.


R1# show adjacency s0/0/0 detail
Protocol Interface             Address
IPV6     Serial0/0/0           point2point(12)
                               0 packets, 0 bytes
                               0F0086DD
```

```
                                    IPv6 CEF    never
                                    Epoch: 2
IP         Serial0/0/0              point2point(13)
                                    0 packets, 0 bytes
                                    0F000800
                                    CEF    expires: 00:02:43
                                           refresh: 00:00:43
                                    Epoch: 2
```

! Similar output can be achieved for Serial0/0/1 that runs PPP. In the following
! output, note the prepared PPP headers for IPv6 (FF030057) and IPv4 (FF030021)
! prefixes resolving through these adjacencies. There are two IPv6 adjacencies
! present as IPV6CP specifically installs an adjacency towards the neighbor's link
! local address.

```
R1# show adjacency s0/0/1 detail
Protocol Interface               Address
IPV6     Serial0/0/1             point2point(10)
                                 0 packets, 0 bytes
                                 FF030057
                                 IPv6 CEF    never
                                 Epoch: 2
IP       Serial0/0/1             point2point(15)
                                 0 packets, 0 bytes
                                 FF030021
                                 CEF    expires: 00:02:30
                                        refresh: 00:00:30
                                 Epoch: 2
IPV6     Serial0/0/1             point2point(4)
                                 0 packets, 0 bytes
                                 FF030057
                                 IPv6 ND     never
                                 IPv6 ND     never
                                 Epoch: 2
```

! Adjacencies on Fa0/0 show preconstructed Ethernet headers for the neighbors
! 192.168.14.4, FE80:14::4 and FD00:14::4 - destination MAC, source MAC, EtherType.
! Compare the MAC addresses with contents of ARP and IPv6 ND tables above.

```
R1# show adjacency fa0/0 detail
Protocol Interface               Address
IP       FastEthernet0/0         192.168.14.4(23)
                                 0 packets, 0 bytes
                                 00179446B3400019E87F38E40800
                                 ARP         02:29:07
                                 Epoch: 2
```

```
IPV6       FastEthernet0/0            FE80:14::4(12)
                                      0 packets, 0 bytes
                                      00179446B3400019E87F38E486DD
                                      IPv6 ND    never
                                      Epoch: 2
IPV6       FastEthernet0/0            FD00:14::4(7)
                                      0 packets, 0 bytes
                                      00179446B3400019E87F38E486DD
                                      IPv6 ND    never
                                      Epoch: 2

! Finally, adjacencies on Fa0/0.2 show preconstructed Ethernet headers for
! neighbors 192.168.24.4, FE80:24::4 and FD00:24::4 - destination MAC, source MAC,
! 802.1Q VLAN tag, EtherType. Compare the MAC addresses with contents of ARP and
! IPv6 ND tables.


R1# show adjacency fa0/0.2 detail
Protocol Interface                    Address
IPV6       FastEthernet0/0.2          FE80:24::4(12)
                                      0 packets, 0 bytes
                                      00179446B3410019E87F38E481000002
                                      86DD
                                      IPv6 ND    never
                                      Epoch: 2
IP         FastEthernet0/0.2          192.168.24.4(23)
                                      0 packets, 0 bytes
                                      00179446B3410019E87F38E481000002
                                      0800
                                      ARP        02:26:57
                                      Epoch: 2
IPV6       FastEthernet0/0.2          FD00:24::4(5)
                                      0 packets, 0 bytes
                                      00179446B3410019E87F38E481000002
                                      86DD
                                      IPv6 ND    never
                                      Epoch: 2
```

Table 6-2 summarizes a few key points about the three main options for router switching paths.

**Table 6-2**  *Matching Logic and Load-Balancing Options for Each Switching Path*

| Switching Path | Structures That Hold the Forwarding Information | Load-Balancing Method |
|---|---|---|
| Process switching | Routing table | Per packet |
| Fast switching | Fast-switching cache (per flow route cache) | Per destination IP address |
| CEF | FIB tree and adjacency table | Per a hash of the packet source and destination, or per packet |

The **ip cef** global configuration command enables CEF for all interfaces on a Cisco router. For IPv6, the **ipv6 cef** command is used to activate CEF support. Note that it is possible to run IPv4 CEF without IPv6 CEF, but the converse is not true: To run IPv6 CEF, IPv4 CEF must be active. The **no ip route-cache cef** interface subcommand can then be used to selectively disable CEF on an interface.

## Load Sharing with CEF and Related Issues

One of major advantages of CEF is its native support for different load-sharing mechanisms, allowing the use of multiple paths toward a destination network if present in the FIB. CEF supports two modes of load sharing: per-packet and per-destination. With per-packet load sharing, packets destined to a destination network are distributed across multiple paths in a packet-by-packet fashion. With the per-destination mode, the CEF actually takes the source and destination IP address and optionally other data to produce a hash value that identifies the particular path to carry the packet. In effect, for a particular source and destination pair, all packets flow through a single path. Other particular source/destination address combinations toward the same destination network can produce a different hash and thus be forwarded over a different path. In fact, the per-destination load-sharing mode in CEF would be better called per-flow load sharing. The per-destination load-sharing mode is the default (hardware-based CEF implementations might not support the per-packet load sharing mode), and in general, it is preferred because it avoids packet reordering within a single conversation.

Per-destination load sharing in CEF is technically achieved by placing a so-called load-share table between the FIB and the adjacency table. This loadshare table contains up to 16 pointers to entries in the adjacency table, and the individual loadshare entries are populated so that the counts of loadshare pointers to particular adjacency entries are proportional to the costs of parallel routes toward the same destination. (That is, if there are two equal-cost paths to the same destination, eight loadshare entries will point to one next-hop adjacency entry while another eight loadshare entries will point to another next-hop adjacency entry. If there are three equal cost paths, only 15 loadshare entries will be populated, with each five loadshare entries pointing to one of the three next-hop adjacency entries.) When a packet arrives, the router performs a hashing operation over the packet's source and destination address fields, and uses the hash result value as an index into the loadshare table to select one of the possible paths toward the destination. This concept is illustrated in Figure 6-4, also taken from the Cisco document "How to Choose the Best Router Switching Path for Your Network," Document ID 13706.

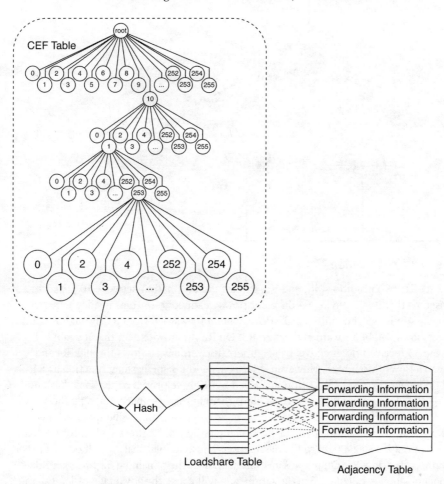

**Figure 6-4**   *CEF Load Balancing*

The particular method of per-packet or per-destination load sharing can be activated on *egress* interfaces of a router using the **ip load-share** { **per-destination** | **per-packet** } interface-level command. The availability of this command might be limited depending on the hardware capabilities of the device. Often, multilayer switches performing hardware-accelerated switching do not support this command while software-based ISR routers do.

With the hashing performed over fixed packet and/or segment address fields, a single hash function produces the same result for all packets in a flow. While this is desirable on a single router to always select a single path for a flow, it leads to unpleasant consequences in a network where multiple routers down a path to a destination have multiple routes toward it.

Consider the network shown in the Figure 6-5.

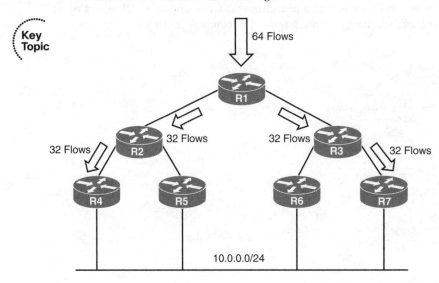

**Figure 6-5**  *CEF Polarization*

Router R1 has two neighbors, R2 and R3, toward the destination network 10.0.0.0/24. Let's assume that it is receiving 64 different flows destined to stations inside the network 10.0.0.0/24. Under ideal conditions, 32 flows will be forwarded from R1 through R2 and 32 other flows will be forwarded through R3. On R2, we now expect that it again balances the 32 received flows across its neighbors, forwarding 16 flows through R4 and another 16 flows through R5. However, if R2 is using the same hashing function as R1, this is no longer the case. All 32 flows received by R2 have produced the same hashing value on R1—that is why R2 is receiving all of them in the first place. Running the same hashing function over these 32 flows will again produce the same value for all of them, and as a result, R2 will no longer load-share them; rather, all 32 flows will be forwarded from R2 through a single path to the destination. Thus, no load sharing will occur farther down the path below R1. Quite the same fate will meet the remaining 32 flows on R3. This phenomenon is called CEF polarization, and will cause the advantage of load sharing to be lost quickly.

To avoid this, the basic CEF load-sharing mechanism has been enhanced. Each router chooses a random 4B-long number called a Universal ID (details of its selection are not public). This Universal ID is used as a seed in the hashing function used by CEF. Because with high probability, different routers will have unique Universal IDs, they will also produce different hashing results for a particular packet flow. As a result, a set of flows producing a single hashing value on one router might produce a set of different hashing values on another router, enabling the set of flows to be load-balanced again across multiple paths.

In recent IOSs, there are multiple variations of the CEF load-sharing algorithm:

- **Original algorithm:** As the name suggests, this is the original unseeded implementation prone to CEF polarization.

- **Universal algorithm:** An improved algorithm using the Universal ID to avoid the CEF polarization.

- **Tunnel algorithm:** A further improvement on the Universal algorithm especially suitable to environments where tunnels are extensively deployed, possibly resulting in a relatively small number of outer source/destination pairs. Avoids the CEF polarization. Might not be available for IPv6 CEF.

- **L4 port algorithm:** Based on the Universal algorithm while also taking the L4 source and/or destination ports into account. Avoids the CEF polarization.

Except from the Original algorithm, all other algorithms listed here avoid the CEF polarization issue by seeding the hash function using the Universal ID. This ID can be specified for these algorithms in the **ip cef load-sharing algorithm** and **ipv6 cef load-sharing algorithm** global configuration commands manually if necessary. This command is also used to select the particular load-sharing algorithm as described in the preceding list. To verify the current load-sharing mechanism and Universal ID value, the output of **show cef state**, **show ip cef summary**, or **show ip cef detail**, especially the heading, shall be examined (the output of these commands differs on different platforms).

The Catalyst 6500 platform (and some others that are directly derived from it, such as selected 7600 Series supervisors and linecards), enjoying a long history of existence during the time the details of CEF were fleshed out and perfected in software-based IOSs, has its own set of workarounds about the CEF polarization problem. On this platform, instead of the **ip cef load-sharing algorithm** command, the **mls ip cef load-sharing** command is used to select the load-sharing algorithm. The individual options are as follows:

- Default (**default mls ip cef load-sharing**): Uses source and destination IP, plus the Universal ID if supported by the hardware. Avoids CEF polarization.

- Full (**mls ip cef load-sharing full**): Uses source IP, destination IP, source L4 port, and destination L4 port. Does not use Universal ID. Prone to CEF polarization. However, to alleviate its impact, this load-balancing algorithm causes the traffic to split equally among multiple paths only if the number of paths is odd. With an even number of parallel paths, the ratio of traffic split will not be uniform.

- Simple (**mls ip cef load-sharing simple**): Uses source and destination IP only. Does not use Universal ID. Prone to CEF polarization.

- Full Simple (**mls ip cef load-sharing full simple**): Uses source IP, destination IP, source L4 port, and destination L4 port. Does not use Universal ID. Prone to CEF polarization. The difference from Full mode is that all parallel paths receive an equal weight, and fewer adjacency entries in hardware are used. This mode avoids unequal traffic split seen with Full mode.

# Multilayer Switching

*Multilayer Switching (MLS)* refers to the process by which a LAN switch, which operates at least at Layer 2, also uses logic and protocols from layers other than Layer 2 to forward data. The term *Layer 3 switching* refers specifically to the use of the Layer 3 destination address, compared to the routing table (or equivalent), to make the forwarding decision. (The latest switch hardware and software from Cisco uses CEF switching to optimize the forwarding of packets at Layer 3.)

## MLS Logic

Layer 3 switching configuration works similarly to router configuration—IP addresses are assigned to interfaces, and routing protocols are defined. The routing protocol configuration works just like a router. However, the interface configuration on MLS switches differs slightly from routers, using VLAN interfaces, routed interfaces, and Port-channel Layer 3 interfaces.

*VLAN interfaces* give a Layer 3 switch a Layer 3 interface attached to a VLAN. Cisco often refers to these interfaces as *switched virtual interfaces (SVI)*. To route between VLANs, a switch simply needs a virtual interface attached to each VLAN, and each VLAN interface needs an IP address in the respective subnets used on those VLANs.

**Note**   Although it is not a requirement, the devices in a VLAN are typically configured in the same single IP subnet. However, you can use secondary IP addresses on VLAN interfaces to configure multiple subnets in one VLAN, just like on other router interfaces.

The operational state of SVI interfaces deserves a word on its own. For an MLS, an SVI is *the* Layer 3 interface that interconnects the internal "router" inside the MLS with the particular VLAN, much like an interface on a real router connects it to a particular network. An MLS can directly send packets to or through a particular VLAN by forwarding them over the corresponding SVI. These SVIs will be present in an MLS's routing table as egress interfaces for packets delivered into or through particular VLANs. The operational state of an SVI should therefore reflect the true ability of the MLS to directly forward packets into the corresponding VLAN. The SVI—despite being a virtual interface—must not be in the "up, line protocol up" state if the MLS is not truly capable of forwarding packets into the corresponding VLAN. In other words, the state of SVIs must mimic the behavior of ordinary routers. If an interface is not in the "up, line protocol up" state, the configured directly connected network on that interface and all routes formerly reachable over it must be removed from the routing table, and can be put back only if the interface becomes fully operational again.

There are two primary reasons why an MLS might be unable to forward packets into a particular VLAN: Either that VLAN is not created and active on the MLS, or the VLAN exists and is active but there is no physical Layer 2 interface on the switch allowing it to forward frames into that VLAN. Consequently, the state of an SVI can be one of the following:

- **Administratively down, line protocol down:** The SVI interface is shut down.

- **Down, line protocol down:** The corresponding VLAN does not exist, or is not in an active state (the **state suspend** or **shutdown** commands were issued in the VLAN's configuration).

- **Up, line protocol down:** The corresponding VLAN exists, but it is not allowed and in an STP forwarding state on any Layer 2 switch port (access or trunk).

- **Up, line protocol up:** The VLAN is created and the MLS is capable of forwarding frames (and hence packets) into that VLAN.

To avoid the "up, line protocol down," at least one of the following conditions must be true:

- At least one physical trunk that is itself in the "up, line protocol up" state must have this VLAN allowed, not VTP pruned, and in the STP forwarding state. This can be verified, for example, using the **show interfaces trunk** command (check the bottom-most section labeled with "Vlans in spanning tree forwarding state and not pruned").

- At least one physical switch port that is itself in the "up, line protocol up" state must have this VLAN configured as an access or voice VLAN and in the STP forwarding state. This can be verified, for example, using **show vlan** and **show spanning-tree** commands.

When using VLAN interfaces, the switch must take one noticeable but simple additional step when routing a packet. Like typical routers, MLS makes a routing decision to forward a packet. As with routers, the routes in an MLS routing table entry list an outgoing interface (a VLAN interface in this case), as well as a next-hop Layer 3 address. The adjacency information (for example, the IP ARP table or the CEF adjacency table) lists the VLAN number and the next-hop device's MAC address to which the packet should be forwarded—again, typical of normal router operation.

At this point, a true router would know everything it needs to know to forward the packet. An MLS switch, however, then also needs to use Layer 2 logic to decide which physical interface to physically forward the packet already encapsulated in a Layer 2 frame. The switch will simply find the next-hop device's MAC address in the CAM and forward the frame to that address based on the CAM.

## Using Routed Ports and Port-channels with MLS

In some point-to-point topologies, VLAN interfaces are not required. For example, when an MLS switch connects to a router using a cable from a switch interface to a router's LAN interface, and the only two devices in that subnet are the router and that one physical interface on the MLS switch, the MLS switch can be configured to treat that one interface as a *routed port*. (Another typical topology for using routed ports is when two MLS switches connect for the purpose of routing between the switches, again creating a case with only two devices in the VLAN/subnet.)

A routed port on an MLS switch has the following characteristics:

■ The interface is not placed into any user-defined VLAN (internally in an MLS switch, an *internal usage VLAN* is created for each individual routed port).

■ On most Catalyst platforms, a routed port cannot be configured with subinterfaces.

■ The switch does not keep any Layer 2 switching table information for the interface.

■ Layer 3 settings, such as the IP address, are configured under the physical interface, just like a router.

■ The adjacency table lists the outgoing physical interface or Port-channel, which means that Layer 2 switching logic is not required in these cases.

The *internal usage VLAN* created on behalf of a routed port deserves a special mention. For a VLAN-aware MLS, all operations are performed within the context of a VLAN in which the frame or packet is processed. The most natural way for these switches to implement a routed port is in fact to create a hidden, standalone, and dedicated VLAN for each separate routed port, and deactivate the typical Layer 2 control plane protocols on it. These dedicated VLANs are called *internal usage VLANs*. On Catalyst switches supporting an extended VLAN range, these internal usage VLANs are allocated from the extended range, depending on the setting of the **vlan internal allocation policy { ascending | descending }** global configuration command. If the **ascending** option is used, internal usage VLANs are allocated from VLAN ID 1006 upward. Conversely, if the **descending** option is used, internal usage VLANs are allocated from VLAN ID 4094 downward. On lower-end Catalyst platforms, this command is present in the configuration with the **ascending** option but cannot be modified.

The current allocation of internal usage VLANs can be displayed only using the **show vlan internal usage** command; they do not appear in common **show vlan** output. As an example, observe the output in the Example 6-2.

**Example 6-2**  *Internal Usage VLANs Created for Routed Ports*

```
! On this 3560G switch, ports GigabitEthernet0/12 and GigabitEthernet0/13 will
! be configured as routed ports, and the internal usage VLANs will be observed.
! The switch is configured with vlan internal allocation policy ascending

Switch(config)# do show vlan internal usage


VLAN Usage
---- --------------------


Switch(config)# interface gi0/12
Switch(config-if)# no switchport
Switch (config-if)# do show vlan internal usage
```

```
VLAN Usage
---- --------------------
1006 GigabitEthernet0/12


Switch(config-if)# exit
Switch(config)# interface gi0/13
Switch(config-if)# no switchport
Switch(config-if)# do show vlan internal usage


VLAN Usage
---- --------------------
1006 GigabitEthernet0/12
1007 GigabitEthernet0/13
```

Internal usage VLANs are internal to the switch, and regardless of the VTP mode, they are not stored in the VLAN database and are not advertised to any other switch in the VTP domain. The assignment of internal usage VLANs to routed ports is therefore only done at runtime and can differ between restarts of a switch, depending on the order that the routed ports are configured and on the unused extended VLAN IDs.

Because of the relatively discreet nature of internal usage VLANs (they are not visible in ordinary **show vlan** output), conflicts can ensue if an administrator tries to create an extended VLAN whose ID is—unknowingly to the administrator—already used by an internal usage VLAN, as shown in the Example 6-3.

**Example 6-3**   *Possible Internal Usage VLAN Conflict While Creating Extended VLANs*

```
! Building on the previous example, internal usage VLANs 1006 and 1007 exist
! on this switch. An administrator is not aware about their existence, though,
! and tries to create VLAN 1006 for its own use. Notice how the switch refuses
! to add the VLAN only after exiting the VLAN configuration.


Switch(config)# do show vlan internal usage


VLAN Usage
---- --------------------
1006 GigabitEthernet0/12
1007 GigabitEthernet0/13


Switch(config)# vlan 1006
Switch(config-vlan)# name SomeExtendedVLAN
Switch(config-vlan)# exit
% Failed to create VLANs 1006
VLAN(s) not available in Port Manager.
%Failed to commit extended VLAN(s) changes.
```

This problem can become especially unpleasant if VTPv3 is used that is capable of handling extended VLAN IDs. If the administrator creates an extended range VLAN on a VTP Primary Server switch, and the particular VLAN ID is already used by an internal usage VLAN on some other switch in the domain, VTP will fail to create this VLAN on that switch, resulting in connectivity issues. The conflict will be logged only on the switch experiencing the VLAN ID collision and so can elude the administrator's attention.

It is therefore generally recommended that if extended VLANs are used, they should be allocated from the end of the extended VLAN range that is opposite to the current internal VLAN allocation policy, to minimize the risk of creating VLAN ID collisions.

Keeping all these facts in mind, a routed port is practically equivalent to a switch port placed into a dedicated VLAN, with the Layer 2 control plane protocols deactivated on that port. From this viewpoint, a routed port is a syntactical device in the configuration to make the configuration quick and convenient, while the switch continues to handle the port internally as a switch port with a slightly modified operation.

The following two configuration snippets in Example 6-4 are practically equivalent; just the routed port is simpler to configure.

**Example 6-4**  *Routed Port and Its Internal Treatment by a Multilayer Switch*

```
! Following the previous example, assume the Gi0/12 is configured as follows:

Switch(config)# int gi0/12
Switch(config-if)# no switchport
Switch(config-if)# ip address 192.168.12.1 255.255.255.0
Switch(config-if)# do show vlan internal usage


VLAN Usage
---- -------------------
1006 GigabitEthernet0/12
```

```
! The above configuration is effectively equivalent to the following configuration:

Switch(config)# vlan 1006
Switch(config-vlan)# exit
Switch(config)# no spanning-tree vlan 1006
Switch(config)# no mac address-table learning vlan 1006
Switch(config)# interface GigabitEthernet0/12
Switch(config-if)# switchport mode access
Switch(config-if)# switchport access vlan 1006
Switch(config-if)# switchport nonegotiate
Switch(config-if)# no vtp
Switch(config-if)# exit
Switch(config)# interface Vlan1006
Switch(config-if)# ip address 192.168.12.1 255.255.255.0
```

Ethernet Port-channels can be used as routed interfaces as well. To do so, physical interfaces must be configured with the **no switchport** command *before* adding them to a channel group. The automatically created Port-channel interface inherits the configuration of the first physical interface added to the channel group; if that interface is configured as a routed interface, the entire Port-channel will be working as a routed port. An existing Layer 2 Port-channel cannot be changed from Layer 2 to Layer 3 operation and vice versa. If such a modification is necessary, it is first required to completely delete the entire Port-channel, unbundle the physical ports, reconfigure them into the desired mode of operation, and then add them into a channel group again, re-creating the Port-channel interface in the process. Also, when using a Port-channel as a routed interface, Port-channel load balancing should be based on Layer 3 addresses because the Layer 2 addresses will mostly be the MAC addresses of the two MLS switches on either end of the Port-channel. Port-channels can also be used as Layer 2 interfaces when doing MLS. In that case, VLAN interfaces would be configured with an IP address, and the Port-channel would simply act as any other Layer 2 interface.

Table 6-3 lists some of the specifics about each type of Layer 3 interface.

**Table 6-3**   *MLS Layer 3 Interfaces*

| Interface | Forwarding to Adjacent Device | Configuration Requirements |
|---|---|---|
| VLAN interface | Uses Layer 2 logic and Layer 2 MAC address table | Create VLAN interface; VLAN must also exist |
| Physical (routed) interface | Forwards out physical interface | Use the **no switchport** command to create a routed interface |
| Port-channel (switched) interface | Not applicable; just used as another Layer 2 forwarding path | No special configuration; useful with VLAN interfaces |
| Port-channel (routed) interface | Balances across links in Port-channel | Needs the **no switchport** command to be used as a routed interface; optionally change load-balancing method |

## MLS Configuration

The upcoming MLS configuration example is designed to show all the configuration options. The network design is shown in Figures 6-6 and 6-7. In Figure 6-6, the physical topology is shown, with routed ports, VLAN trunks, a routed Port-channel, and access links. Figure 6-7 shows the same network, with a Layer 3 view of the subnets used in the network.

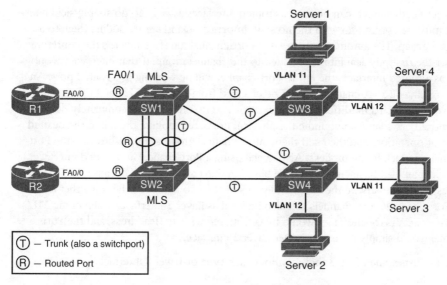

**Figure 6-6**   *Physical Topology: Example Using MLS*

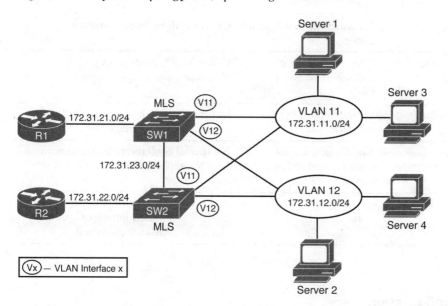

**Figure 6-7**   *Layer 3 Topology View: Example Using MLS*

A few design points bear discussion before jumping into the configuration. First, SW1 and SW2 need Layer 2 connectivity to support traffic in VLANs 11 and 12. In this particular example, a trunk is used between SW1 and SW2 as well as between SW1/ SW2 and SW3/SW4. Focusing on the Layer 2 portions of the network, SW1 and SW2, both distribution MLS switches, connect to SW3 and SW4, which are access layer switches. SW1 and SW2 are responsible for providing full connectivity in VLANs 11 and 12. Having full Layer 2 connectivity between switches in a topology is the traditional approach. In newer deployments, a new approach is favored in which SW1 and SW2 are interconnected through a routed port (Layer 3 link) only, and the connections toward access layer switches are Layer 2 or even Layer 3. This allows for shrinking the size of Layer 2 domain and the resulting scope of STP operation. If only a routed link was left between SW1 and SW2, the Layer 2 topology between SW1/SW2 and SW3/SW4 would be physically loop-free and there would be no ports blocked by STP, requiring little or no reaction of STP if a link is added or removed.

Additionally, this design uses SW1 and SW2 as Layer 3 switches, so the hosts in VLANs 11 and 12 will use SW1 or SW2 as their default gateway. For better availability, the two switches should use HSRP, VRRP, or GLBP. Regardless of which protocol is used, both SW1 and SW2 need to be in VLANs 11 and 12, with connectivity in those VLANs, to be effective as default gateways.

In addition to a Layer 2 trunk between SW1 and SW2, to provide effective routing, it makes sense for SW1 and SW2 to have a routed path between each other as well. Certainly, SW1 needs to be able to route packets to Router R1, and SW2 needs to be able to route packets to Router R2. However, routing between SW1 and SW2 allows for easy convergence if R1 or R2 fails.

Figure 6-6 shows two alternatives for routed connectivity between SW1 and SW2, and one option for Layer 2 connectivity. For Layer 2 connectivity, a VLAN trunk needs to be used between the two switches. Figure 6-6 shows a pair of trunks between SW1 and SW2 (labeled with a circled T) as a Layer 2 Port-channel. The Port-channel would support the VLAN 11 and 12 traffic.

To support routed traffic, the figure shows two alternatives: Simply route over the Layer 2 Port-channel using VLAN interfaces or use a separate routed Port-channel. First, to use the Layer 2 Port-channel, SW1 and SW2 could simply configure VLAN interfaces in VLANs 11 and 12. The alternative configuration uses a second Port-channel that will be used as a routed Port-channel. However, the routed Port-channel does not function as a Layer 2 path between the switches, so the original Layer 2 Port-channel must still be used for Layer 2 connectivity. Upcoming Example 6-5 shows both configurations.

Finally, a quick comment about Port-channels is needed. This design uses Port-channels between the switches, but they are not required. Most links between switches today use at least two links in a Port-channel, for the typical reasons—better availability, better convergence, and less STP overhead. This design includes the Port-channel to point out a small difference between the routed interface configuration and the routed Port-channel configuration.

Example 6-5 shows the configuration for SW1, with some details on SW2.

**Example 6-5**  *MLS-Related Configuration on Switch1*

```
! Below, note that the switch is in VTP transparent mode, and VLANs 11 and 12 are
! configured, as required. Also note the ip routing global command, without which
! the switch will not perform Layer 3 switching of IP packets.

vlan 11
!
vlan 12

! The ip routing global command is required before the MLS will perform
! Layer 3 forwarding. Similarly, ipv6 unicast-routing is required for
! IPv6 routing to be enabled. On selected Catalyst platforms, the use of
! distributed keyword is required, as the CEF operates in distributed mode
! on these switches - over multiple ASICs or line cards.

ip routing
ipv6 unicast-routing distributed
!
vtp domain CCIE-domain
vtp mode transparent

! Next, the configuration shows basic Port-channel creation commands, with the
! no switchport command being required before bundling physical ports into
! a Port-channel. Note the Port-channel interface will be created automatically.

interface GigabitEthernet0/1
 no switchport
 no ip address
 channel-group 1 mode desirable
!
interface GigabitEthernet0/2
 no switchport
 no ip address
 channel-group 1 mode desirable


! Next, the Port-channel interface is assigned an IP address.

interface Port-channel1
 ip address 172.31.23.201 255.255.255.0

! Below, similar configuration on the interface connected to Router1.
```

```
interface FastEthernet0/1
 no switchport
 ip address 172.31.21.201 255.255.255.0

! Next, interface Vlan 11 gives Switch1 an IP presence in VLAN11. Devices in VLAN
! 11 can use 172.31.11.201 as their default gateway. However, using HSRP is
! better, so Switch1 has been configured to be HSRP primary in VLAN11, and Switch2
! to be primary in VLAN12, with tracking so that if Switch1 loses its connection
! to Router1, HSRP will fail over to Switch2.

interface Vlan11
 ip address 172.31.11.201 255.255.255.0
 standby 11 ip 172.31.11.254
 standby 11 priority 90
 standby 11 preempt
 standby 11 track FastEthernet0/1

! Below, VLAN12 has similar configuration settings, but with a higher (better)
! HSRP priority than Switch2's VLAN 12 interface.

interface Vlan12
 ip address 172.31.12.201 255.255.255.0
 standby 12 ip 172.31.12.254
 standby 12 priority 110
 standby 12 preempt
 standby 12 track FastEthernet0/1
```

**Note**  For MLS switches to route using VLAN interfaces, the **ip routing** global command must be configured. MLS switches will not perform Layer 3 routing without the **ip routing** command, which is not enabled by default. Similar comments apply to IPv6 routing that needs to be enabled by **ipv6 unicast-routing**.

As stated earlier, the routed Port-channel is not required in this topology. It was included to show an example of the configuration, and to provide a backdrop from which to discuss the differences. However, as configured, SW1 and SW2 are Layer 3 adjacent over the routed Port-channel as well as through their VLAN 11 and 12 interfaces. So, they could exchange interior gateway protocol (IGP) routing updates over three separate subnets. In such a design, the routed Port-channel was probably added so that it would be the normal Layer 3 path between SW1 and SW2. Care should be taken to tune the IGP implementation so that this route is chosen instead of the routes over the VLAN interfaces.

# Policy Routing

All the options for IP forwarding (routing) in this chapter had one thing in common: The destination IP address in the packet header was the only thing in the packet that was used to determine how the packet was forwarded. Policy routing (or Policy-Based Routing [PBR]) allows a router to make routing decisions based on information besides the destination IP address.

Policy routing's logic begins, depending on IPv4 or IPv6 in use, with the **ip policy** or **ipv6 policy** command on an interface. This command tells the IOS to process *incoming* packets on that interface with different logic before the normal forwarding logic takes place. (To be specific, policy routing intercepts the packet after Step 4, but before Step 5, in the routing process shown in Figure 6-1.) The IOS compares the received packets using the **route-map** referenced in the **ip policy** or **ipv6 policy** command. Figure 6-8 shows the basic logic.

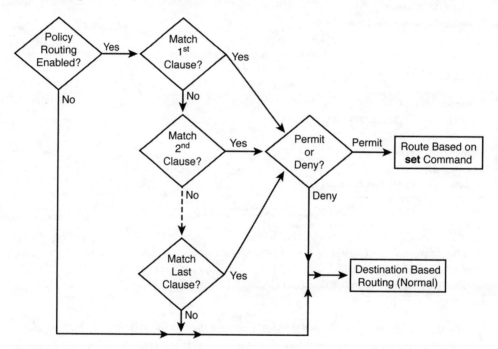

**Figure 6-8**   *Basic Policy Routing Logic*

Specifying the matching criteria for policy routing is relatively simple compared to defining the routing instructions using the **set** command. The route maps used by policy routing must match either based on referring to an ACL (numbered or named IPv4/IPv6 ACL, using the **match ip address** or **match ipv6** address command) or based on packet length (using the **match length** command). To specify the routing instructions—in other words, where to forward the packet next—use the **set** command. Table 6-4 lists the **set** commands and provides some insight into their differences.

**Table 6-4**  *Policy Routing Instructions (set Commands)*

| Command | Comments |
|---|---|
| **set ip next-hop** *ip-address* [.... *ip-address*] | Next-hop addresses must be in a connected subnet; forwards to the first address in the list for which the associated interface is up. Supported for both IPv4 and IPv6. |
| **set ipv6 next-hop** *ipv6-address* [ ... *ipv6-address* ] | |
| **set ip default next-hop** *ip-address*[.... *ip-address*] | Same logic as previous command, except policy routing first attempts to route based on the routing table, and only if no match is found in the routing table, the packet will be handled by PBR. Default route in the routing table is ignored; that is, if the packet's destination is matched only by the default route, the packet will be handled by PBR. Supported for both IPv4 and IPv6. |
| **set ipv6 default next-hop** *ipv6-address* [... *ipv6-address* ] | |
| **set interface** *interface-type interface-number* [.... *interface-type interface-number*] | Forwards packets using the first interface in the list that is up. Recommended only for point-to-point interfaces; strongly discouraged for multiaccess interfaces. Supported for both IPv4 and IPv6. |
| **set default interface** *interface-type interface-number* [... *interface-type interface-number*] | Same logic as previous command, except policy routing first attempts to route based on the routing table, and only if no match is found in the routing table, the packet will be handled by PBR. Default route in the routing table is ignored, that is, if the packet's destination is matched only by the default route, the packet will be handled by PBR. Recommended only for point-to-point interfaces; strongly discouraged for multiaccess interfaces. Supported for both IPv4 and IPv6. |
| **set ip df** *number* | Sets the IP DF bit; can be either 0 or 1. Supported only for IPv4. |
| **set ip precedence** *number* | *name* | Sets IP precedence bits; can be a decimal value in the range 0–7 or a textual name (IPv4 only). Supported for both IPv4 and IPv6. |
| **set ipv6 precedence** *number* | |
| **set ip tos** *number* | *name* | Sets the ToS bits (delay, throughput, reliability, monetary cost); can be decimal value or ASCII name. Supported for IPv4 only. |

The first four **set** commands in Table 6-4 are the most important ones to consider. Essentially, you set either the next-hop IP address or the outgoing interface. Use the outgoing interface option *only* when it is of point-to-point technology type—for example, do not refer to a LAN interface or multipoint Frame Relay subinterface. This will almost certainly cause the policy-based routing to fail or act unexpectedly; details will be discussed later. Most importantly, note the behavior of the **default** keyword in the **set** commands. Use of the **default** keyword essentially means that policy routing tries the default (destination-based) routing first, and resorts to using the **set** command details only when the router finds no matching route in the routing table. Note that a default route is not considered a matching route by the **default** keyword. If a packet's destination is matched only by the default route, PBR treats this as if no match occurred, and the packet is eligible to be forwarded according to the **set** commands using the **default** keyword.

The remaining **set** commands set the bits inside the ToS byte of the packet; refer to Chapter 5, "Classification and Marking," in Volume II for more information about the ToS byte and QoS settings. Note that you can have multiple **set** commands in the same **route-map** clause. For example, you might want to define the next-hop IP address and mark the packet's ToS at the same time. A single route map entry can even contain multiple set statements specifying where the packet shall be forwarded. In such cases, the **set** statements are evaluated in the following order:

**Key Topic**

1.  **set ip next-hop / set ipv6 next-hop**

2.  **set interface**

3.  **set ip default next-hop / set ipv6 default next-hop**

4.  **set default interface**

The use of **set interface** and **set default interface** is strongly recommended only with point-to-point interfaces. Using multiaccess interfaces in these commands will lead to PBR failing in most cases. IPv6 PBR using **set [ default ] interface** with a multiaccess interface fails outright; differences in very selected cases have been observed under different IOS versions. IPv4 PBR under the same circumstances might appear to work but the background processes are unintuitive: The router first performs a normal routing table lookup for the packet's destination IP address to look for the connected next-hop address, and then tries to translate this next-hop address into the appropriate Layer 2 address on the multiaccess interface specified in the **set [ default ] interface** command. This can fail for obvious reasons: The routing table might provide no match for the packet's destination and thus the **set [ default ] interface** is skipped, or the next hop itself might be connected to a different interface. Even Proxy ARP, if applicable, is not going to help much—Cisco routers perform a validity check on received ARP responses similar to a unicast reverse path forwarding check. A router verifies using its routing table whether the sender IPv4 address in the ARP response's body (the address whose MAC address is being asked for) is reachable through the interface the ARP response came in. If this check fails, the router will drop the ARP response, claiming that it arrived over the "wrong cable" in the **debug arp** output. Once again, the use of **set [ default ] interface** is appropriate only with point-to-point interfaces. IOS Releases 15.x display an explicit warning if the command is used with multiaccess interface types.

The IPv6 PBR with **set interface** in particular has one more peculiarity: In some IOS versions, the router checks whether there is a matching route (ignoring the default route) for the packet's destination even if the packet is to be handled by PBR. If there is no matching route in the routing table, the **set interface** command is ignored. It is also noteworthy to mention that on some platforms, this behavior also depends on the state IPv6 CEF. The particular behavior of the IOS in question should therefore be verified using **debug ipv6 policy.**

**Key Topic**

If PBR is required on a multilayer switch, many lower-end switches, such as Catalyst 3550, 3560, or 3750, require that the TCAM in the switch is repartitioned in a different way, providing TCAM space for PBR entries while taking away space from entries of other types. On these platforms, the size of TCAM regions for individual applications cannot be configured individually; instead, a set of templates is prepared for typical switch deployments. A switch should be configured with an appropriate TCAM partitioning template that allocates the most space to the types of entries most required in the particular switch's mode of deployment. A template that provides space for PBR entries must be active before the PBR can be configured. These templates are called Switch Database Management templates, or SDM templates for short. Current SDM templates can be shown using the **show sdm prefer** command, also displaying an approximate space for different TCAM entry types. This command can be also used to view the TCAM allocation policy for different templates if the **show sdm prefer** *template-name* form is used. To allow for PBR usage on the switch models mentioned previously, either the **routing**, **access**, or **dual-ipv4-and-ipv6 routing** (if supported) SDM template needs to be used. On Catalyst 3650 and 3850 Series, the **advanced** SDM template is required. To activate a particular template, the **sdm prefer** *template-name* global configuration level command is used. After you issue this command, the switch must be reloaded. It is strongly recommended to consult the appropriate switch model documentation for the list of supported SDM templates and the individual features they activate.

Apart from PBR, changing the SDM template on an MLS might also be required if routing or IPv6 support are to be activated. One of indications that an inappropriate SDM template is currently active is very visible: The IOS CLI appears to lack the commands necessary to configure routing, PBR, or IPv6, even though the IOS should support these features and the appropriate licenses are in place.

## Routing Protocol Changes and Migration

The proper selection of a routing protocol for a network is always a sensitive (and understandably difficult) task. Many factors need to be taken into consideration, ranging from the protocol's scalability and speed of convergence through advanced features, ending with compatibility issues especially in multivendor environments; all of these are related to the network's design and requirements. As the network evolves, it might become necessary to reevaluate the choice of a particular routing protocol, and if it is found to be inappropriate, it might need to be replaced.

Migrating from one routing protocol to another is always a disruptive change to the network. It requires careful planning to minimize the outages, and even then, they are inevitable, although their duration can be kept very low. Therefore, a routing protocol migration always requires a maintenance window.

Routing protocol migration is usually accomplished with the following steps:

**Step 1.**   Plan the migration strategy.

**Step 2.**   Activate the new routing protocol on all routers in the topology, raising its administrative distance (AD) above the ADs of the current IGP. If the new IGP is Routing Information Protocol (RIP) or Enhanced Interior Gateway Routing Protocol (EIGRP), redistribution from the current into the new IGP has to be configured on each router as well. The current IGP is left intact.

**Step 3.**   Verify the new IGP's adjacencies and optionally the working database contents.

**Step 4.**   Deactivate the current IGP in a gradual fashion.

**Step 5.**   Remove the temporary settings from the new IGP.

We describe each of these steps in closer detail.

## Planning the Migration Strategy

The deployment of a new routing protocol should be preplanned for the entire network, including the division of network into separate areas if and when a link-state IGP is to be used. Additionally, protocol features such as prefix summarization/filtration, stub features, and external information redistribution can further isolate areas of the network from one another. This planning should also involve the order in which routers will be migrated over from the current IGP to the new one. Ideally, routers should be migrated so that they form a contiguous, ever-growing part of the network running the new IGP, gradually shrinking the contiguous remainder of the network in which both the current and new IGP are run. If the current IGP is a link-state protocol, it is advisable to perform the migration in a per-area fashion. The backbone routers should be the last ones to migrate.

## Activating New IGP While Keeping the Current IGP Intact

According to the planning in the previous step, the new IGP should be activated on the routers in the network, first setting its administrative distance (AD) to a higher value than the current IGP's AD, and only then adding interfaces and networks to the new IGP and activating selected features. The current IGP is left running and its configuration is unchanged throughout this entire step. If the current IGP uses various ADs for different network types (for example, EIGRP uses 90 and 170 for internal and external routes, respectively), the new IGP's AD should be reconfigured to be higher than the highest AD used by the existing IGP. As an example, if the current IGP is OSPF and the new IGP should be EIGRP, the ADs of EIGRP should, for the duration of the migration, be reconfigured to, say, 210 and 220 for internal and external EIGRP routes, respectively. This way, the new IGP can be deployed across the network, creating adjacencies between routers as usual but not influencing the routing tables and routing just yet. If the current IGP configuration includes redistribution from other sources (static routes, directly connected networks, and so on), the new IGP shall be configured similarly.

If the new IGP is a distance-vector routing protocol (RIP or EIGRP), each router must also be configured with redistribution from the current IGP into the new IGP. Reasons for this are explained later in the chapter.

## Verifying New IGP Adjacencies and Working Database Contents

After the new IGP has been configured across the entire network, it should have created adjacencies in the usual fashion though the routing tables are not populated by its routes yet. These adjacencies should be verified to make sure that they are complete. After the current IGP is deactivated, these adjacencies are the only routing protocol adjacencies left between migrated routers, and so must be working as expected before the current IGP starts being removed.

It is often recommended to verify the contents of the working databases in the new IGP to check whether all expected networks are present, even though not placed into routing tables because of higher ADs. This step might be difficult to accomplish, though, because of two reasons. First, the amount and format of the data can be overwhelming to a human, requiring some kind of automated processing. The second reason is relevant only if the new IGP is a distance-vector protocol, that is, either RIP or EIGRP. These protocols advertise a learned route only if it is also installed in the routing table by the same protocol. This additional advertisement logic in distance-vector routing protocols is based on the fact that a router should not advertise a route it is not using itself. Because the AD of the new IGP has been configured to be higher than the current IGP's AD, routes learned by the new IGP will not be placed into the router's routing table as long as the current IGP is still running on the router, and hence will not be advertised further. As a result, if the new IGP is RIP or EIGRP, its working databases will contain only partial contents until the migration starts, making the verification before migration impossible. This behavior of distance-vector IGPs will be discussed in closer detail later in the chapter. Note that this additional advertisement logic does not apply to link-state IGPs such as OSPF and IS-IS, as the nature of routing information they generate and the flooding mechanism are strongly different from distance-vector IGPs and do not allow for such additional checks.

## Deactivating Current IGP

The next step in the routing protocol migration involves the actual removal of the current IGP from a contiguous set of routers, one router at a time, allowing the new routing protocol to populate the routing table instead, and then proceeding to the next router. Alternatively, instead of plainly deleting the current IGP configuration from the router, it can be configured using the **passive-interface default** command that will effectively shut it down. In recent IOS versions, selected routing protocols even support the **protocol shutdown** or **shutdown** command. The obvious advantage of this approach is that the configuration of the current IGP is preserved, should it ever be necessary to activate it again quickly.

The removal or deactivation of the current IGP should be done in such a way that the network always consists of at most two regions. In one, both routing protocols are run (the unmigrated part of network), and in the other, only the new protocol is running (the migrated part of the network) and both regions are contiguous.

**Key Topic**

During a properly executed migration, the network consists of a contiguous region that runs both IGPs and of a contiguous region that runs the new IGP only. Traffic crossing the network enters either an unmigrated or a migrated router, and is destined to a network that is directly connected to a router that is again either migrated or unmigrated yet. These options have an impact on which IGPs carry the information about the destination and thus what source of routing information is used by routers along the way.

If traffic enters an *unmigrated* router and is destined to a network connected to an *unmigrated* router, the destination network is advertised in both IGPs but the new IGP has been configured with a higher AD, so it has no impact on the routing table contents. Consequently, the traffic completely follows the path provided by the current IGP, as if no migration was taking place.

If traffic enters a *migrated* router and is destined to a network connected to a *migrated* router, the destination network is advertised only in the new IGP, as the current IGP has been removed from the destination router. The current IGP does not advertise this network anymore and does not compete about this particular network with the new IGP (recall that it would otherwise be resolved in favor of the current IGP thanks to its lower AD). Consequently, all routers, both migrated and unmigrated, know about this destination only through the new IGP, and follow the path provided by the new IGP.

If traffic enters an *unmigrated* router and is destined to a network connected to a *migrated* router, the situation is very similar. As the current IGP has been removed from the destination router, the destination network is advertised only in the new IGP. All routers therefore know about this network through the new IGP only and follow the path provided by the new IGP.

Finally, if traffic enters a *migrated* router and is destined to a network connected to an *unmigrated* router, the situation is slightly more complex. The destination router advertises the network through both IGPs. Other unmigrated routers know the destination network through both IGPs and prefer the current IGP, while migrated routers, including the ingress router, know the network through the new IGP only. In the migrated path of the network, the traffic will be routed according to the new IGP until it is forwarded to the first unmigrated router. Starting with this router, all other routers on the path toward the destination still prefer the path provided by the current IGP. Therefore, beginning with this router, the traffic will be routed according to the current IGP.

This analysis shows that during a properly executed migration, the network remains fully connected and destinations should remain fully reachable. Transient outages can occur at the moment when the current IGP is removed from a router, as the routes provided by the current IGP will need to be flushed from the routing table and replaced by routes learned through the new IGP.

## Removing New IGP's Temporary Settings

After the network has been completely migrated to the new IGP and the previous IGP has been completely removed from all routers, the new IGP still contains temporary settings that were necessary for a seamless migration, especially the modified AD values, leftovers from redistribution of the previous IGP into the new IGP, and so on. These settings should be removed as the last step of the migration procedure. In link-state routing protocols, removing the temporary settings should not cause any additional interruptions in network service. However, in EIGRP, modifying the AD values causes the router to drop and reestablish its EIGRP adjacencies with neighboring routers, causing a transient disruption in network connectivity. These changes must therefore be also performed during a maintenance window.

## Specifics of Distance-Vector Protocols in IGP Migration

Ideally, migrating to a different routing protocol should not involve any route redistribution between the current and the new IGP, as the redistribution involves additional complexity to the migration process. However, if the new IGP is a distance-vector protocol (such as RIP or EIGRP), a temporary redistribution is inevitable. The reason lies in the advertisement logic of these routing protocols: A learned route will be advertised further *only* if the router has placed that very learned route into the routing table as well. In other words, a learned route is advertised through the same routing protocol only if the router is using that route itself. As the migration process involves temporarily configuring the new IGP's administrative distance (AD) to be higher than the AD of the current IGP, none of the learned routes through the new IGP are going to be placed into the routing table if the current IGP is still running. If the new IGP happens to be RIP or EIGRP, any route learned through that protocol won't make it into the router's routing table and will not be advertised further as a result. To illustrate this concept, consider the network in Figure 6-9 (split horizon rules in EIGRP have been omitted for simplicity).

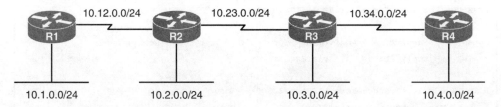

| EIGRP | R1 | R2 | R3 | R4 |
|---|---|---|---|---|
| Advertises | 10.1.0.0/24<br>10.12.0.0/23 | 10.12.0.0/24<br>10.2.0.0/24<br>10.23.0.0/24 | 10.23.0.0/24<br>10.3.0.0/24<br>10.34.0.0/24 | 10.34.0.0/24<br>10.4.0.0/24 |
| Learns | 10.2.0.0/24<br>10.23.0.0/24 | 10.1.0.0/24<br>10.3.0.0/24<br>10.34.0.0/24 | 10.12.0.0/24<br>10.2.0.0/24<br>10.4.0.0/24 | 10.23.0.0/24<br>10.3.0.0/24 |

**Figure 6-9**  *Example Network Topology for Routing Protocol Migration*

OSPF is the current routing protocol in this network, and the network is planned to be migrated to EIGRP. All four routers are therefore configured with EIGRP as well, the EIGRP AD is set to 210 for internal and 220 for external routes, and all interfaces are added to EIGRP on all routers. OSPF's operation is not influenced in any way, and because its AD remains at 110, routers still keep OSPP-learned routes in their routing table. If we focus on R1's operation and on the 10.1.0.0/24 network in particular, R1 advertises its directly connected networks, including 10.1.0.0/24 to R2 through EIGRP. R2 will have this route in its EIGRP topology table but will be unable to install it into the routing table because of EIGRP's modified AD of 210. As a result, R2 will not propagate the EIGRP-learned route 10.1.0.0/24 through EIGRP to R3, so neither R3 nor R4 will learn about this network through EIGRP. This limited propagation of networks in EIGRP will take place on each router in this topology: Each router will advertise its directly connected networks in EIGRP to its immediate neighbors, but these neighbors are prevented from advertising them further, as shown in Figure 6-9. Looking into EIGRP topology tables of all routers confirms this, as shown in Example 6-6.

**Example 6-6**  *Contents of EIGRP Topology Tables in Figure 6-9 Topology*

```
! On all routers in the topology from Figure 6-9, EIGRP is configured identically:

router eigrp 1
 network 10.0.0.0
 distance eigrp 210 220
 no auto-summary

! It is assumed that OSPF is also running on all four routers.

! show ip eigrp topology on R1:

R1# show ip eigrp topology
IP-EIGRP Topology Table for AS(1)/ID(10.12.0.1)

Codes: P - Passive, A - Active, U - Update, Q - Query, R - Reply,
       r - reply Status, s - sia Status

P 10.12.0.0/24, 1 successors, FD is 832000
        via Connected, Serial0/0/0
P 10.2.0.0/24, 0 successors, FD is Inaccessible
        via 10.12.0.2 (857600/281600), Serial0/0/0
P 10.1.0.0/24, 1 successors, FD is 281600
        via Connected, FastEthernet0/0
P 10.23.0.0/24, 0 successors, FD is Inaccessible
        via 10.12.0.2 (1344000/832000), Serial0/0/0

! show ip eigrp topology on R2:

R2# show ip eigrp topology
```

```
IP-EIGRP Topology Table for AS(1)/ID(10.23.0.2)


Codes: P - Passive, A - Active, U - Update, Q - Query, R - Reply,
       r - reply Status, s - sia Status


P 10.12.0.0/24, 1 successors, FD is 832000
        via Connected, Serial0/0/1
P 10.2.0.0/24, 1 successors, FD is 281600
        via Connected, FastEthernet0/0
P 10.3.0.0/24, 0 successors, FD is Inaccessible
        via 10.23.0.3 (857600/281600), Serial0/0/0
P 10.1.0.0/24, 0 successors, FD is Inaccessible
        via 10.12.0.1 (857600/281600), Serial0/0/1
P 10.23.0.0/24, 1 successors, FD is 832000
        via Connected, Serial0/0/0
P 10.34.0.0/24, 0 successors, FD is Inaccessible
        via 10.23.0.3 (1344000/832000), Serial0/0/0

! show ip eigrp topology on R3:

R3# show ip eigrp topology
IP-EIGRP Topology Table for AS(1)/ID(10.34.0.3)


Codes: P - Passive, A - Active, U - Update, Q - Query, R - Reply,
       r - reply Status, s - sia Status


P 10.12.0.0/24, 0 successors, FD is Inaccessible
        via 10.23.0.2 (1344000/832000), Serial0/0/1
P 10.2.0.0/24, 0 successors, FD is Inaccessible
        via 10.23.0.2 (857600/281600), Serial0/0/1
P 10.3.0.0/24, 1 successors, FD is 281600
        via Connected, FastEthernet0/0
P 10.4.0.0/24, 0 successors, FD is Inaccessible
        via 10.34.0.4 (857600/281600), Serial0/0/0
P 10.23.0.0/24, 1 successors, FD is 832000
        via Connected, Serial0/0/1
P 10.34.0.0/24, 1 successors, FD is 832000
        via Connected, Serial0/0/0

! show ip eigrp topology on R4:

R4# show ip eigrp topology
IP-EIGRP Topology Table for AS(1)/ID(10.34.0.4)


Codes: P - Passive, A - Active, U - Update, Q - Query, R - Reply,
       r - reply Status, s - sia Status
```

```
P 10.3.0.0/24, 0 successors, FD is Inaccessible
        via 10.34.0.3 (857600/281600), Serial0/0/1
P 10.4.0.0/24, 1 successors, FD is 281600
        via Connected, FastEthernet0/0
P 10.23.0.0/24, 0 successors, FD is Inaccessible
        via 10.34.0.3 (1344000/832000), Serial0/0/1
P 10.34.0.0/24, 1 successors, FD is 832000
        via Connected, Serial0/0/1
```

Note that on each router, only directly connected networks of its immediate neighbors are learned through EIGRP, and all these networks are marked with a "0 successors, FD is Inaccessible" indication in their heading, preventing them from being advertised further.

After OSPF is removed from R4's configuration as a step in the migration procedure, the OSPF-learned 10.1.0.0/24 will be removed from R4's routing table without being replaced by an EIGRP-learned route, as R2 is still running OSPF and does not advertise this route through EIGRP. This will cause connectivity outages: R4 will learn only about directly connected networks from R3 through EIGRP, missing all other networks, and R3—still running OSPF—will be unable to forward EIGRP-learned routes from R4 back to R2. Clearly, full connectivity in this network will be restored only after OSPF is completely removed.

The solution to this problem is to configure route redistribution from the current IGP into the new IGP on each router in the topology. In the example network, the situation will be significantly different, then: Because each router knows about all networks through OSPF, redistributing them from OSPF into EIGRP allows each router to advertise them all to each directly connected neighbor. While the neighbor will not be allowed to advertise them further if still running OSPF, its EIGRP topology database will nonetheless be populated with the full set of networks from its own neighbors. When OSPF is deactivated on a router, EIGRP-learned routes will take over—they will get installed into the routing table, and the router will be able to forward them further.

If the new IGP is a link-state protocol, this redistribution is unnecessary and shall not be configured. Flooding of topological information in link-state protocols is not constrained by routing table contents. Routers will always flood the routing information in a link-state protocol, regardless of whether routes derived from that information are installed into routing tables or not.

To analyze how this approach works, assume that the migration of the network in Figure 6-9 continues by gradual deactivation of OSPF, starting on R4 and proceeding router by router toward R1. Table 6-5 summarizes how the individual networks are visible in the routing tables of individual routers. Only the first two octets of each prefix are listed for brevity. Prefixes in the O row are learned by OSPF; prefixes in the D row are learned by EIGRP. Directly connected networks are not listed, as they are not influenced by changes in routing protocols.

**Table 6-5**   *Contents of Routing Tables in Different Migration Stages*

| OSPF Run On | | R1 | R2 | R3 | R4 |
|---|---|---|---|---|---|
| R1 to R4 | O | 10.2/24 | 10.1/24 | 10.1/24 | 10.1/24 |
| | | 10.23/24 | 10.3/24 | 10.12/24 | 10.12/24 |
| | | 10.3/24 | 10.34/24 | 10.2/24 | 10.2/24 |
| | | 10.34/24 | 10.4/24 | 10.4/24 | 10.23/24 |
| | | 10.4/24 | | | 10.3/24 |
| | D | None | None | None | None |
| R1 to R3 | O | 10.2/24 | 10.1/24 | 10.1/24 | None |
| | | 10.23/24 | 10.3/24 | 10.12/24 | |
| | | 10.3/24 | 10.34/24 | 10.2/24 | |
| | | 10.34/24 | | | |
| | D | 10.4/24 | 10.4/24 | 10.4/24 | 10.1/24 (EX) |
| | | | | | 10.12/24 (EX) |
| | | | | | 10.2/24 (EX) |
| | | | | | 10.23/24 |
| | | | | | 10.3/24 |
| R1 to R2 | O | 10.2/24 | 10.1/24 | None | None |
| | | 10.23/24 | | | |
| | D | 10.3/24 | 10.3/24 | 10.1/24 (EX) | 10.1/24 (EX) |
| | | 10.34/24 | 10.34/24 | 10.12/24 | 10.12/24 |
| | | 10.4/24 | 10.4/24 | 10.2/24 | 10.2/24 |
| | | | | 10.4/24 | 10.23/24 |
| | | | | | 10.3/24 |
| R1 only | O | None | None | None | None |
| | D | 10.2/24 | 10.1/24 | 10.1/24 | 10.1/24 |
| | | 10.23/24 | 10.3/24 | 10.12/24 | 10.12/24 |
| | | 10.3/24 | 10.34/24 | 10.2/24 | 10.2/24 |
| | | 10.34/24 | 10.4/24 | 10.4/24 | 10.23/24 |
| | | 10.4/24 | | | 10.3/24 |

Key observations about this table are as follows:

- Prefixes advertised from routers running both the original and new routing protocol are learned by the original routing protocol on all routers still running it.

- Prefixes advertised from routers running only the new routing protocol are learned by the new routing protocol across the entire network.

- At all times, all routers know about all prefixes.

- Traffic entering a router running both routing protocols and destined to a network on a router running both protocols is routed completely according to the original routing protocol without changes. This is because the network is advertised in both protocols and the new routing protocol's AD has been intentionally raised above the original protocol's AD.

- Traffic entering a router running the new routing protocol and destined to a network on a router running the new protocol is routed completely according to the new routing protocol. This is because the network in question is not injected into the original routing protocol anymore, so the only source of the information is the new protocol.

- Traffic entering a router running both routing protocols and destined to a network on a router running the new routing protocol is routed completely according to the new routing protocol. The reason is the same as in the previous item.

- Traffic entering a router running the new routing protocol and destined to a network on a router running both routing protocols will be routed according to the new routing protocol until it hits the first router that still runs both routing protocols. Afterward, it will be routed according to the original routing protocol. This is because in the migrated part of the network, routers run only the new routing protocol, while in the remaining part of network running both protocols, the original routing protocol is preferred.

The last four items are valid if the migration is performed in such a way that the network always consists of at most two contiguous regions. In one, both routing protocols are run (the unmigrated part of network), and in the other, only the new protocol is running (the migrated part of the network). Also, if this rule is maintained throughout the migration process, the boundary between the new and original routing protocol as described in the last item is crossed only once.

# Foundation Summary

This section lists additional details and facts to round out the coverage of the topics in this chapter. Unlike most of the Cisco Press Exam Certification Guides, this "Foundation Summary" does not repeat information presented in the "Foundation Topics" section of the chapter. Please take the time to read and study the details in the "Foundation Topics" section of the chapter, as well as review items noted with a Key Topic icon.

Table 6-6 lists the protocols mentioned in or pertinent to this chapter and their respective standards documents.

**Table 6-6**  *Protocols and Standards for Chapter 6*

| Name | Standardized In |
| --- | --- |
| Address Resolution Protocol (ARP) | RFC 826 |
| IPv6 Neighbor Discovery | RFC 4861, RFC 5942 |
| Differentiated Services Code Point (DSCP) | RFC 2474 |

Table 6-7 lists some of the key IOS commands related to the topics in this chapter. (The command syntax for switch commands was taken from the *Catalyst 3560 Multilayer Switch Command Reference, 15.0(2)SE*. Router-specific commands were taken from the IOS Release 15 mainline Command Reference.)

**Table 6-7**  *Command Reference for Chapter 6*

| Command | Description |
| --- | --- |
| **show ip arp** | EXEC command that displays the contents of the IP ARP cache. |
| **show ipv6 neighbors** | EXEC command that displays the contents of the IPv6 neighbor cache. |
| [no] **switchport** | Switch interface subcommand that toggles an interface between a Layer 2 switched function (**switchport**) and a routed port (**no switchport**). |
| [no] **ip route-cache cef** | Interface subcommand that enables or disables CEF switching on an interface. |
| [no] **ip cef** | Global configuration command to enable (or disable) CEF on all interfaces. |
| [no] **ipv6 cef** | Global configuration command to enable (or disable) CEF for IPv6 on all interfaces. For IPv6 CEF to be activated, **ip cef** must also be present. |

| Command | Description |
|---|---|
| [no] ip routing | Enables IP routing; defaults to **no ip routing** and **no ipv6** |
| [no] ipv6 unicast-routing | **unicast-routing** on a multilayer switch. |
| ip policy route-map *map-tag* | Router interface subcommand that enables policy routing |
| ipv6 policy route-map *map-tag* | for the packets entering the interface. |

Refer to Table 6-4 for the list of **set** commands related to policy routing.

# Memory Builders

The CCIE Routing and Switching written exam, like all Cisco CCIE written exams, covers a fairly broad set of topics. This section provides some basic tools to help you exercise your memory about some of the broader topics covered in this chapter.

## Fill In Key Tables from Memory

Appendix E, "Key Tables for CCIE Study," on the CD in the back of this book, contains empty sets of some of the key summary tables in each chapter. Print Appendix E, refer to this chapter's tables in it, and fill in the tables from memory. Refer to Appendix F, "Solutions for Key Tables for CCIE Study," on the CD to check your answers.

## Definitions

Next, take a few moments to write down the definitions for the following terms:

> policy routing, process switching, CEF, polarization, MLS, ARP, Proxy ARP, routed interface, fast switching, TTL, RIB, FIB, adjacency table, control plane, switched interface, data plane, IP routing, IP forwarding

Refer to the glossary to check your answers.

## Further Reading

For a great overview of router switching paths, refer to www.cisco.com/en/US/tech/tk827/tk831/technologies_white_paper09186a00800a62d9.shtml.

For a good reference on load balancing with CEF, refer to http://cisco.com/en/US/tech/tk827/tk831/technologies_tech_note09186a0080094806.shtml.

Details on implementing and troubleshooting static routing can be found in numerous documents on the Cisco website. Recommended documents include "Specifying a Next Hop IP Address for Static Routes" (Document ID 27082), "Route Selection in Cisco Routers" (Document ID 8651), and "IOS Configuration Guide," in particular, the "IP Routing: Protocol-Independent Configuration Guide" section.

**Blueprint topics covered in this chapter:**

This chapter covers the following subtopics from the Cisco CCIE Routing and Switching written exam blueprint. Refer to the full blueprint in Table I-1 in the Introduction for more details on the topics covered in each chapter and their context within the blueprint.

■  Introduction to dynamic routing protocols

■  Routing Information Protocol v.2

■  Routing Information Protocol for IPv6

## CHAPTER 7

# RIPv2 and RIPng

This chapter covers Routing Information Protocol version 2 (RIPv2) and Routing Information Protocol next generation (RIPng) for IPv6, including most of the features, concepts, and commands. Chapter 11, "IGP Route Redistribution, Route Summarization, Default Routing, and Troubleshooting," covers some RIP details, in particular, route redistribution between RIP and other routing protocols, and route summarization.

## "Do I Know This Already?" Quiz

Table 7-1 outlines the major headings in this chapter and the corresponding "Do I Know This Already?" quiz questions.

**Table 7-1** *"Do I Know This Already?" Foundation Topics Section-to-Question Mapping*

| Foundation Topics Section | Questions Covered in This Section | Score |
|---|---|---|
| RIPv2 Basics | 1–2 | |
| RIPv2 Convergence and Loop Prevention | 3–5 | |
| RIPv2 Configuration | 6–7 | |
| Total Score | | |

To best use this pre-chapter assessment, remember to score yourself strictly. You can find the answers in Appendix A, "Answers to the 'Do I Know This Already?' Quizzes."

1. Which of the following items are true of RIP version 2?

    a. Supports VLSM

    b. Sends Hellos to 224.0.0.9

    c. Allows for route tagging

    d. Defines infinity as 255 hops

    e. Authentication allows the use of 3DES

**2.** In an internetwork that solely uses RIPv2, after the network is stable and converged, which of the following is true?

   **a.** Routers send updates every 30 seconds.

   **b.** Routers send updates every 90 seconds.

   **c.** Routers send Hellos every 10 seconds, and send updates only when routes change.

   **d.** A routing update sent out a router's Fa0/0 interface includes all RIPv2 routes in the IP routing table.

   **e.** A RIPv2 update's routes list the same metric as is shown in that router's IP routing table.

**3.** R1 previously had heard about only one route to 10.1.1.0/24, metric 3, through an update received on its S0/0 interface, so it put that route in its routing table. R1 gets an update from that same neighboring router, but the same route now has metric 16. R1 immediately sends a RIP update out all its interfaces that advertises a metric 16 route for that same subnet. Which of the following are true for this scenario?

   **a.** Split Horizon must have been disabled on R1's S0/0 interface.

   **b.** R1's update is a triggered update.

   **c.** R1's metric 16 route advertisement is an example of a route poisoning.

   **d.** The incoming metric 16 route was the result of a counting-to-infinity problem.

**4.** R1 is in a network that uses RIPv2 exclusively, and RIP has learned dozens of subnets through several neighbors. Which of the following commands displays the current value of at least one route's age?

   **a.** show ip route

   **b.** show ip rip database

   **c.** debug ip rip

   **d.** debug ip rip event

**5.** R1 is in a network that uses RIPv2 exclusively, and RIP has learned dozens of subnets through several neighbors. From privileged EXEC mode, the network engineer types in the command **clear ip route *.** What happens?

   **a.** R1 removes all routes from its IP routing table and tries to repopulate it.

   **b.** R1 removes only RIP routes from its IP routing table.

   **c.** After the command, R1 will relearn its routes when the neighboring router's Update timers cause them to send their next updates.

   **d.** R1 immediately sends updates on all interfaces, poisoning all routes, so that all neighbors immediately send triggered updates—which allow R1 to immediately relearn its routes.

   **e.** R1 will relearn its routes immediately by sending RIP requests out all its RIP-enabled nonpassive interfaces.

   **f.** None of the other answers is correct.

**6.** R1 has been configured for RIPv2 using only **version 2**, **network** statements and **no auto-summary.** The configuration includes a **network 10.0.0.0** command. Which of the following statements are true about R1's RIP behavior?

   **a.** R1 will send advertisements out any of its nonpassive interfaces in network 10.0.0.0.

   **b.** R1 will process received advertisements in any of its interfaces in network 10.0.0.0, including passive interfaces.

   **c.** R1 will send updates only after receiving a RIP Hello message from a neighboring router.

   **d.** R1 can disable the sending of routing updates on an interface using the **passive-interface** *interface* subcommand.

   **e.** R1 will advertise the subnets of any of its interfaces connected to subnets of network 10.0.0.0.

**7.** Which of the following represents a default setting for the Cisco IOS implementation of RIPv2?

   **a.** Split Horizon is enabled on all types of interfaces.

   **b.** Split Horizon is disabled on Frame Relay physical interfaces and multipoint subinterfaces.

   **c.** The default authentication mode, normally set with the **ip rip authentication mode** interface subcommand, is MD5 authentication.

   **d.** RIP will send triggered updates when a route changes.

## Foundation Topics

## Introduction to Dynamic Routing

Chapter 6, "IP Forwarding (Routing)," focused on the processes concerned with using a router's routing table contents after it has been populated. Creating the contents of a routing table and sharing it among routers, however, is one of the largest—and arguably the most interesting—aspects of router operation. Apart from static routing, which is the elementary approach to populating a routing table, dynamic routing protocols are used in the majority of cases to fill routing tables on routers with correct information about reachable networks and appropriate routes to them. Dynamic routing protocols constitute messages exchanged between routers to detect their mutual presence and convey information about the existing networks in the topology, and algorithms necessary to process this information and advertise it throughout the network.

Each dynamic routing protocol covered on the CCIE Routing and Switching exam will be devoted a separate chapter in this book. The general characteristics of all routing protocols given in this particular section should therefore be taken as an introduction into the subject matter, establishing the basic terminology and concepts. Although the chapter focuses on an archetypal distance-vector routing protocol, RIP, this section also introduces path-vector and link-state paradigms and compares them to the distance-vector approach, so that the similarities and differences between the individual routing protocol principles can be highlighted in one place.

Cisco routers and multilayer switches support a number of routing protocols, including RIPv2, EIGRP, OSPF, IS-IS, and BGP. Each of these can be categorized by different criteria. However, one of the most common—and most discerning—is the underlying principle and nature of information the routing protocol uses to construct the routing table contents: distance-vector and link-state.

Distance-vector-type routing protocols are principally founded on the exchange of *distance vectors*; that is, *arrays of distances* to known networks. The term *vector* here refers to a unidimensional array; in computer science, terms *vector* and *unidimensional array* are synonyms. The term *distance* refers to the measure of feasibility, or a metric, of reaching a particular network. Indeed, in distance-vector routing protocols, key messages exchanged between routers contain arrays, with each element containing information about one particular network known to the router originating the message, and that router's distance to this network. A router learns about the existence of a network by receiving a message from its neighboring router that advertises the network. This neighbor then becomes the next hop toward this network. If there are multiple neighbors that advertise the same network, the router will choose that neighbor which provides the least total metric to the network. If there are multiple such routers available, all of them can be used as next hops (equal-cost multipath). After a router learns about a network from one or more of its neighbors, chooses a next hop, and installs the route into its routing table, it advertises the route itself, announcing its own distance from the destination. As a consequence, each router advertises its own directly connected networks added to the routing protocol, plus all routes learned by that protocol that have been placed into the routing table. (This is a sanity check performed by all distance-vector routing protocols on Cisco routers: A route learned by a routing protocol will be further advertised only if it is also placed into the router's routing table; a router advertises only those routes used by itself.)

In distance-vector routing protocols, routers by definition exchange only lists of known networks and their distances. They do not exchange information about the network's topology. Information present in any router's working database does not allow reconstructing the topology of the network. Processing the exchanged information is, from the viewpoint of memory and algorithmic complexity, relatively simple. However, the simplicity and limited nature of the information also makes these protocols generally prone to the creation of routing loops. Various methods have been implemented to avoid the creation of routing loops; however, only Enhanced Interior Gateway Routing Protocol (EIGRP), using its advanced properties, is guaranteed to provide loop-free routing at every instant. Both RIPv2 and EIGRP are distance-vector routing protocols.

An extension of the distance-vector principle is the path-vector routing protocol. The path-vector paradigm is fundamentally the same as with distance-vector routing protocols. Routers exchange messages about known networks and their distances, but in addition, each network is also accompanied by a list of *path elements* describing the path toward the network. These path elements can be theoretically anything—router IDs of individual routers, area numbers, and so on. In Border Gateway Protocol (BGP), the most widely used path-vector routing protocol, these path elements are autonomous system numbers: the list of autonomous systems the packet must traverse to reach its destination. This path description can be used as a part of a best-path selection algorithm, but its primary purpose is different: to allow routing loop avoidance. A router will not accept an advertisement about a network whose path description already includes the identifier the router would put into that advertisement itself. This prevents routing loops from occurring. BGP is the only common routing protocol of the path-vector type. Some sources even consider BGP simply as a distance-vector protocol.

In contrast to the distance-vector and path-vector paradigm, a *link-state* routing protocol exchanges information about individual objects in the topology and their mutual interconnection. These objects include routers, multiaccess networks, routers on borders of areas or entire autonomous systems, and networks from other areas or from outside the autonomous system. In fact, the primary objects of interest in the link-state routing protocol are the routers themselves, and their links—interfaces connecting them together. IP prefixes are often treated only as attributes, or properties, of these objects. After a router has generated a message in which it describes itself and its links to immediately neighboring objects, this message is flooded without any modification to every other router in an area. As a result, every router has exact information about the entire area's topology: It knows every router, every network, and every link. This detailed information about each object in an area then allows the router to construct a so-called directed graph of the topology (in essence a map of the topology) and use one of possibly many algorithms that computes a tree of shortest paths (also called a shortest path tree) on this graph to find all reachable destinations and least-cost paths toward them. Usually, the Shortest Path First (SPF) algorithm invented by Edsger W. Dijkstra is used.

Link-state routing protocols operate over a very detailed representation of the network. Dijkstra's algorithm by its very nature does not construct routes containing loops. Therefore, link-state routing protocols are significantly less prone to, though not guaranteed to avoid, routing loop creation. Temporary routing loops, or microloops, can still occur when routers do not compute shortest paths using the same information—usually during network convergence. A single router's detailed knowledge about the network topology allows running network applications not possible with distance-vector approaches, such as MPLS Traffic Engineering and MPLS Fast Re-Route (note that these particular technologies are indicated as examples; they are not part of the CCIE Routing & Switching blueprint).

It is often perceived that the downside to the link-state approach is the amount and complexity of data that needs to be maintained in a router's working database, as each router has complete knowledge of the network topology. It is true that link-state routing protocols require a router to hold more information, and processing the information into a shortest-path tree is more CPU intensive in comparison to the distance-vector approach. However, with the amounts of RAM and CPU power in modern routers, this argument has become moot, and so have the rules of thumb that recommend no more than 50 routers in a single area.

What is, however, a fundamental property of link-state routing protocols—one that can indeed be considered a downside—is their inability to perform route summarization, filtering, or applying offset-lists in arbitrary places in network. This is because the topological information can only be modified by its originating router, and must not be otherwise altered or filtered by any other router. Route summarization, filtering, and applying offset-lists, on the other hand, constitute just that: modifying information that was possibly originated by a different router. Within an area, therefore, none of these operations is available. If route summarization or filtering is required, it can be accomplished only on area border routers, as these routers are in charge of carrying (that is, re-originating) information in a distance-vector fashion from one area to another. Multiarea design with link-state protocols in modern network deployments is therefore driven more by the requirement to perform route summarization, filtering, and failure domain containment rather than saving memory or CPU cycles.

As with all other mechanisms, there is no perfect routing protocol that suits each and every purpose. The choice of a routing protocol is always an iterative task taking multiple variables into account, and any particular choice might possibly require revisiting as the network evolves and requirements change.

## RIPv2 Basics

CCIE candidates might already know many of the features and configuration options of RIPv2. Although RIPv2 is among the simplest routing protocols, it is clearly helpful to review its operations to strengthen your grasp on interior gateway protocols (IGP) in general and the differences between distance-vector and link-state protocols. This chapter summarizes RIPv2's protocol features and concepts. Table 7-2 provides a high-level overview of RIPv2's operation. We completely omit the details about RIPv1, though; the classful nature of this protocol makes it unsuitable for today's networks.

**Table 7-2** *RIPv2 Feature Summary*

| Function | Description |
|---|---|
| General characteristic | Classless, distance-vector, timer-driven routing protocol |
| Transport protocol | User Datagram Protocol (UDP), port 520 |
| Metric | Hop count, with 15 as the maximum usable metric, and 16 considered to be infinite |
| Hello interval | None; RIPv2 relies on the regular full routing updates instead |
| Update destination | 224.0.0.9 multicast for RIPv2 |
| Update interval | 30 seconds |
| Full or partial updates | Full updates each interval. For on-demand circuits, allows RIPv2 to send full updates once, and then remain silent until changes occur, per RFC 2091 |
| Triggered updates | Yes, when routes change |
| Authentication | Allows both plain-text and MD5 authentication |
| Route tags | Allows RIPv2 to tag routes as they are redistributed into RIPv2 |
| Next Hop field | Supports the assignment of a next-hop IP address for a route, allowing a router to advertise a next-hop router that is different from itself |

RIPv2 exchanges routes by sending RIPv2 updates on each RIPv2-enabled interface based on the Update timer (update interval). A RIPv2 router advertises its connected routes, as well as other RIPv2-learned routes that are in the router's IP routing table. RIPv2 routers do not form neighbor relationships, nor do they use a Hello protocol. Each router simply sends updates, with destination address 224.0.0.9. RIPv2 routers can also be configured to use the 255.255.255.255 broadcast IP address using the **ip rip v2-broadcast** per-interface command, although this is not commonly done.

RIPv2 actually uses two types of messages: Requests and Responses. The message format for both message types is identical and is shown in Figure 7-1.

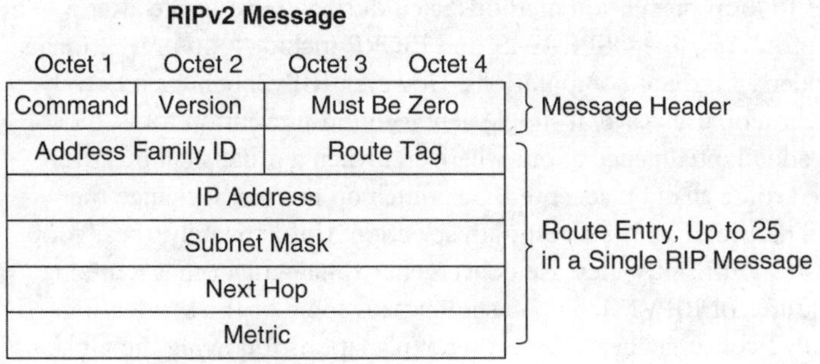

**Figure 7-1** *RIPv2 Message Format*

A RIP message consists of a 4B-long header containing the command field (set to 1 for Request, 2 for Response) and the version field (2 for RIPv2). The remaining two octets are unused. The remainder of the message consists of routing entries, with each routing entry occupying 20 octets in total. At most 25 routing entries can be placed into a single RIP message. Each routing entry contains the address family identifier identifying the format of the address information carried in the routing entry (only the value 2, IPv4— also known as AF_INET—is commonly supported), route tag, and the route itself—its address, netmask, recommended next hop, and metric.

A Request message is used to ask a neighbor to send a partial or a full RIP update immediately, rather than waiting for the Update timer to expire, speeding the convergence. A full RIP update is requested by a Request message containing exactly one routing entry with the address family ID set to 0 and metric set to 16. Otherwise, if a Request message lists one or more particular networks, only the update on these networks is requested. On Cisco routers, Request messages for full updates are sent when the RIP process is being started, a RIP-enabled interface comes up, or when the **clear ip route** * command is used to clear the routing table. Partial requests do not appear to be used.

RIPv2 uses the hop-count metric, counting the number of routers that need to be traversed till the destination network is reached, with 15 being the largest valid metric, and 16 considered to be infinity. Interestingly, a RIPv2 router does not put its own metric in the route of a sent routing update; rather, it first adds 1 to each metric when building the update. For example, if a router has a route with metric 2, it advertises that route with metric 3. In essence, RIPv2 increments the metric when sending updates; RIPng and EIGRP increment metrics when receiving updates.

When Cisco RIPv2 routers learn multiple routes to the same subnet, the lowest-metric route is chosen, of course. If multiple equal-hop routes exist, the router (by default) installs up to 4 such routes in its routing table by default, or between 1 and 16 or even 32 of such routes, based on the **maximum-paths** setting under the **router rip** section. The actual upper limit depends on the IOS version and router platform, and is not in fact related to RIPv2 or any other protocol.

## RIPv2 Convergence and Loop Prevention

The most interesting and complicated part of RIPv2—if there is anything truly complicated in RIPv2—relates to loop-prevention methods used during convergence after a route has failed. Some protocols, like OSPF, IS-IS, and EIGRP, include loop prevention as a side effect of their underlying route computations. However, RIPv2, being a relatively naïve distance vector protocol, uses several supplementary loop-prevention tools, most of which constitute an added intelligence about where and when a route shall be advertised and when a learned route shall be accepted, but which do not really change the underlying fundamental nature of RIPv2's best-path selection. Unfortunately, these loop-prevention tools can also significantly increase convergence time—a fact that is among the biggest negative features of RIPv2. Table 7-3 summarizes some of the key features and terms related to RIPv2 convergence, with further explanations following the table.

**Table 7-3**  *RIPv2 Features Related to Convergence and Loop Prevention*

| Function | Description |
|---|---|
| Counting to Infinity | If the next hop to a particular destination network advertises that network with a suddenly increased metric, accept the advertisement immediately and update our metric accordingly. If the updated metric reaches infinity, stop using that next hop. |
| Split Horizon | Instead of advertising all routes out a particular interface, RIPv2 omits the routes whose outgoing interface field matches the interface out which the update would be sent. |
| Split Horizon with Poisoned Reverse | A stronger variant of Split Horizon: All routes whose outgoing interface matches the interface out which the update would be sent are advertised with an infinite metric. |
| Route poisoning | The process of sending an infinite-metric route in routing updates when that route fails, prompting its rapid removal from routing tables. |
| Triggered update | The immediate sending of a new update when routing information changes, instead of waiting for the Update timer to expire. Only the changed network is sent in the triggered update. Complete updates continue to be sent in regular intervals. |
| *Update* timer | The timer that specifies the time interval over which updates are sent, defaulting to 30 seconds. |
| *Invalid after* timer | A per-route timer (default 180 seconds) that is reset and begins after an update about a route has been received from its next hop. If the updates about the route from its next hop cease to be received and the *Invalid after* timer reaches its limit, the route is declared invalid and the *Holddown* timer starts for this route. |
| *Holddown* timer | A per-route timer (default 180 seconds) that begins after a route has been declared invalid (that is, after the *Invalid after* timer expires). The router starts advertising that route as unreachable, does not accept any updated information, and does not modify the routing table entry for that route until the *Holddown* timer for that route expires. |
| *Flushed after* timer | A per-route timer (default 240 seconds) that is reset and begins after an update about a route has been received from its next hop. If the updates about the route from its next hop cease to be received and the *Flushed after* timer reaches its limit, the router removes the route from the routing table entirely. |

Several of these mechanisms are surprisingly misunderstood and even poorly documented. A few words about each of them are therefore in order.

The basic working principle of distance-vector routing protocols states that routers exchange lists (that is, vectors) of known networks and their distances. For each network, a router chooses the neighbor providing the least total metric as the next hop toward that network, and installs the network through that particular neighbor into its routing table. All other routers advertising the same network with a higher total distance are ignored. There is only one crucial exception to this rule: If the next-hop router for a destination network suddenly advertises a higher distance than the last time, this advertisement is not ignored but rather accepted immediately. The receiving router will update the total distance to the network in its routing table, and it will advertise the increased total distance itself but it will otherwise keep the network and its current next hop in the routing table. Only a subsequent arrival of an update from a different neighbor providing a lower total metric would cause the router to change the next hop. While perhaps slightly surprising, the logic here is straightforward: If a next hop has become more distant from the destination than it was before, so have become all routers that still traverse through this next hop.

This logic immediately leads to the existence of the mechanism known as Counting to Infinity. If, for some reason (usually caused by deactivated Split Horizon and race conditions in timing), two neighboring routers start mutually considering themselves as next hops toward the same destination network, each of them will derive its own metric from the metric of its neighbor. Assume two neighbors, routers X and Y, pointing to each other in a tight routing loop for a destination network N. If X advertises the network N with a metric of 1, Y will advertise this network with a metric of 2. Because Y is X's next hop, X will accept this update right away and increase its own metric to 3. After advertising it, Y will also accept this update immediately, as X is Y's next hop, and increase its own metric to 4. After Y sends another advertisement to X, the metric on X will increase to 5, after which X will advertise this network to Y, causing it to raise its distance to 7, and so on. This process will—theoretically—continue ad infinitum, hence the name Counting to Infinity. Because distance-vector routing protocols have a concept of an infinite metric— a metric whose value represents an unreachable network—after one of routers X or Y reaches this metric, it will drop the route from its routing table, finally breaking the loop. This is how the Counting to Infinity mechanism leads to gradual, albeit slow, elimination of routing loops after they have occurred. It is noteworthy to mention that Counting to Infinity is not an additional enhancement to the distance-vector principle but simply a consequence of it.

The Split Horizon is a well-known principle, stating that *a network should never be advertised back over the interface that is used to reach that network*, because that interface leads back to the next hop toward that route and we do not want to risk a situation where the next hop suddenly loses the route while we inadvertently trick it into believing we are providing a backup path. In the Cisco RIPv2 implementation, Split Horizon is by default activated on most interfaces, notable exceptions being physical Frame Relay and ATM interfaces. The state of RIPv2 Split Horizon can be verified in the **show ip interface** command output.

An augmented version of Split Horizon is the addition of the *Poisoned Reverse* mechanism, resulting in Split Horizon with Poisoned Reverse. This principle states that *a network should always be explicitly advertised as unreachable over the interface that is used to reach that network*. This version of Split Horizon is stronger than its basic version: Instead of simply not advertising the route back toward its next hop, silently hoping the next hop has never considered us a possible backup for this path, we explicitly force the next-hop router to avoid and ignore us when choosing the best path to the network. While more effective, it is not implemented in the Cisco RIPv2.

Route Poisoning is a mechanism used to rapidly flush a route that has become unreachable. Doing this is accomplished by advertising this route with the metric set to infinity. A router that receives an update about a network *from its next hop* with an infinite metric will immediately remove the route to the network through that particular next hop from its routing table. If this was the only route to the network, the router will itself advertise that network as being unreachable to its neighbors. As a result, the information about the unreachability will propagate toward and through all routers whose old path to the (now unreachable) network traversed through the failure point. Routers that receive an update about an unreachable network from different neighbors than their respective next hops are not influenced (the message is indistinguishable from a Split Horizon with Poisoned Reverse advertisement—they process it accordingly but it has no effect on their routing tables). Hence, routers on the affected route expire the old route rapidly, allowing it to converge on a backup path significantly faster.

Even though a route is removed from the routing table during a Route Poisoning procedure, RIP will still keep the route in its internal database (see the **show ip rip database** command), marked as *possibly down*. This is done to allow the route to be repeatedly advertised as unreachable, as a single advertisement can get lost (keep in mind that RIP is UDP-based and has no acknowledgments). The unreachable route will be flushed from the RIP internal database after *Flushed after – Invalid after* seconds. These timers will be discussed in more detail further in the chapter.

It is important to distinguish between the relatively similar terms *Poisoned Reverse* and *Route Poisoning*. They both refer to an action of advertising a network with an infinite metric. What makes the two terms different is the purpose of advertising a network as unreachable: *Poisoned Reverse* is an extension to the Split Horizon principle that advertises a route as unreachable back to its next hop to prevent it from creating a routing loop, while *Route Poisoning* advertises a truly unreachable route to quickly flush it from routing tables and to allow a backup path to take over.

Triggered updates are updates in RIPv2 that are sent in the moment of detecting a change in reachability of a network, rather than waiting for the full Update interval to expire. Connecting or learning about a new network, disconnecting it or learning about its unreachability, or a change to its metric will cause a router to immediately send an advertisement with the updated information. This update commonly carries only the changed network, without listing all other known networks. They continue to be advertised, along with the changed information, in regular intervals driven by the Update timer. In debugs and Cisco documents, these triggered updates are also called *flash updates*. Triggered updates in RIPv2 shall not be confused with Triggered Extensions to RIPv2 covered in

RFC 2091, which are a different mechanism (adaptation of RIPv2 for on-demand circuits so that the updates are sent only in moments of topology change to avoid keeping the on-demand circuit permanently up).

The Holddown mechanism is frequently misunderstood. Its main purpose is to *delay processing updates about a network whose reachability has become questionable, as the received updates might not yet contain up-to-date information*. To understand this mechanism better, assume that a router suddenly stopped receiving updates about a particular network from its only next hop toward that network. This network has not been declared unreachable by the next hop. Rather, updates (if any) received from that next hop simply do not list that network anymore. This can happen for various reasons, including the following:

■ Update might have been lost in transit or dropped (ACLs, rate limit, and so on).

■ Next-hop router might have been turned off or crashed without the link going down.

■ Next-hop router might have started considering us as its own next hop and uses plain Split Horizon.

■ RIPv2 process on the next-hop router might have been removed.

■ Summarization, route filtering, or passive interface might have been activated.

■ Next-hop router might be running a RIPv2 implementation that does not support Route Poisoning, so when a network truly goes down, it simply stops being advertised.

In any case, the ongoing lack of any information about a network from its next hop is tolerable for a limited time period (to account for UDP's lack of reliability), but if its absence exceeds a reasonable time, it is clear that "something happened." Unfortunately, it is not clear what exactly has occurred, and it is even less clear whether the non-next-hop neighbors that claim reachability to this network already know about this possible outage and use a different route. Therefore, the router that has detected a sudden loss of reachability information for a network must not immediately accept the updates from its neighbors; rather, it must give them certain time to learn about the outage and converge to a different path. Only after this time, updates from other routers regarding the missing network can be accepted as trustworthy again.

To accomplish this, Cisco routers implement two independent RIPv2 timers: the *Invalid after* timer and the *Holddown* timer. The *Invalid after* timer is reset every time an update about a network from its next hop arrives, and is incremented each second. A route is considered perfectly usable if an update about it has been received within the last 180 seconds, which is the default upper limit for the *Invalid after* timer. If, however, the *Invalid after* timer has reached the upper limit and an update about this network has not been received, the network is considered invalid. In such case, the following happens:

■ Router declares the network invalid—to be of questionable reachability. This is visible in the **show ip route** output by a comment of "is possibly down." The *Invalid after* timer is stopped for this network.

- Router starts the *Holddown* timer for this network. While the timer runs (180 seconds by default), the router itself advertises the network with infinite metric (Route Poisoning) to force its neighbors to find an alternative route if possible. Additionally, the router locks the routing entry in its routing table, still pointing toward the former next hop. Absolutely no updates whatsoever are accepted until the *Holddown* timer expires, regardless of who sends them and what metric they claim.

- After the *Holddown* timer expires, the router unlocks the routing entry in its routing table and converges through a neighbor that offers the lowest metric route to the network.

There are a number of noteworthy facts about this entire procedure. First, the procedure is *not* triggered by the arrival of an update that advertises an unreachable network. Such an update would be nothing else than Route Poisoning that would cause the route to be dropped from the routing table immediately (even though it would be kept in the RIP internal database for *Flushed after – Invalid after* seconds as described earlier, to allow the route to be advertised as unreachable for a period of time). Rather, this procedure is invoked after the reachability of a network can be neither confirmed nor refuted for a period of time.

Second, after a router puts a route into the invalid state, it advertises that route as unreachable itself. This action is very natural—it is like saying: "I know there is some problem in reaching this network, although I do not know what exactly happened. Whoever uses me as a next hop, stop doing that, and try to find another route that bypasses me." As a result, after a router has put a route into the invalid state, it forces its neighbors to find a detour if any exists. If a neighbor still advertises the network some time after it has been told it is not reachable through us anymore, it must know a different path to it.

Third, a router never updates an invalid route while the *Holddown* timer runs. Before it was declared invalid, it pointed toward a next hop. After the next hop stopped advertising that network altogether and the *Invalid after* timer expired, the route was declared invalid and started being advertised as unreachable, but the router still keeps it locked in the routing table, pointing toward the former next hop, until the *Holddown* timer expires. The general idea here is that it is better to blackhole the traffic rather than create a routing loop by prematurely trusting a different neighbor that claims to have a route toward the failed network.

Fourth, the last bullet in the previous holddown procedure assumes that there is an alternative route to the destination. If there truly is a detour path, the router will learn about it after the *Holddown* timer expires and the routing entry is unlocked. However, the failed route might have been the only path to the destination, and there might be no alternative path available, so no neighbor will advertise it. That would cause the routing entry to linger in the routing table indefinitely, still pointing toward the previous next hop.

Therefore, to prevent a route that has stopped being advertised from lingering in routing tables indefinitely, yet another timer is present: the *Flushed after* timer. Similarly to *Invalid after*, the *Flushed after* timer is reset every time an update about a network from its next hop arrives, and is incremented each second. If the *Flushed after* timer reaches its upper limit, the route is immediately flushed from the routing table. If this was the last instance of the route toward a particular network, the network will be also advertised as unreachable along with its removal. That will conclude its existence in routing tables.

The default setting of RIPv2 timers on Cisco routers is 30 seconds for *Update*, 180 seconds for *Invalid after* and *Holddown*, and 240 seconds for *Flushed after*. The default timer setting actually does not allow the *Holddown* timer to completely expire. If a network stops being advertised by its next hop, it will be put into an invalid state 180 seconds after the last update about it arrived from the next hop. The *Holddown* timer then starts, but after 60 seconds, the *Flushed after* timer that starts in tandem with the *Invalid after* timer will expire, and the router will remove the route entirely along with all associated timers. As a result, the effective *Holddown* period is only 60 seconds.

It turns out that in Cisco implementation, the *Flushed after* timer's value is verified only after the route has been moved to invalid state (that is, after the *Invalid after* timer expires). As an example, if the *Invalid after* was set to 180 seconds but the *Flushed after* was set just to 120 seconds, both timers would be reset and increasing simultaneously after the last update, but if the updates ceased, the route would be kept in the routing table until the *Invalid after* timer fired, that is, the next 180 seconds. At that moment, the router would also check the *Flushed after* timer and find out the route should have been removed 60 seconds ago, so it would remove it within a few seconds. In other words, the *Flushed after* timer has no effect on a route that is still considered valid (that is, its age is less than the upper limit of *Invalid after*). If you perform an experiment to verify this behavior in a lab, you might find that the reaction to the *Flushed after* timer is delayed by roughly 10 seconds, probably caused by the timing granularity used by IOS.

The rest of this section shows examples of the convergence features, using RIP **show** and **debug** command output to show examples of their use. Figure 7-2 shows the sample internetwork that is used in these examples of the various loop-prevention tools.

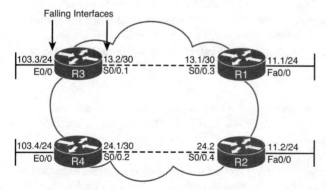

**Figure 7-2**   *Sample Internetwork Used for Loop-Prevention Examples*

## Converged Steady-State Operation

Example 7-1 shows a few details of R1's operation while all interfaces in Figure 7-2 are up and working. The example lists the basic (and identical) RIPv2 configuration on all four routers; configuration will be covered in more detail later in the chapter. As configured, all four routers are using only RIPv2, on all interfaces shown in Figure 7-2. Read the comments in Example 7-1 for explanations of the output. In a stable network, no triggered updates need to be sent, and all routers send their updates each Update interval seconds, which is 30 by default.

**Example 7-1** *Steady-State RIPv2 Operation in Figure 7-2*

```
! All routers use the same three lines of RIPv2 configuration.

router rip
 network 172.31.0.0
 version 2

! Below, the show ip protocols command lists many of RIPv2's operational settings,
! including RIPv2 timers, version used, and neighbors from which RIPv2 updates have
! been received (listed as "Routing Information Sources").

R1# show ip protocols
Routing Protocol is "rip"
 Sending updates every 30 seconds, next due in 24 seconds
 Invalid after 180 seconds, hold down 180, flushed after 240
 Outgoing update filter list for all interfaces is not set
 Incoming update filter list for all interfaces is not set
 Redistributing: RIPv2
 Default version control: send version 2, receive version 2
   Interface            Send  Recv  Triggered RIP  Key-chain
   FastEthernet0/0        2     2
   Serial0/0.3            2     2
 Automatic network summarization is in effect
 Maximum path: 4
 Routing for Networks:
   172.31.0.0
 Routing Information Sources:
   Gateway         Distance      Last Update
   172.31.11.2     120           00:00:15
   172.31.13.2     120           00:00:08
 Distance: (default is 120)

! Below, the current age is listed by each RIP route. Note that it took
! about 3 seconds between the above show ip protocols command and the upcoming
! show ip route command, so the last update from 172.31.13.2 (above)
! was 8 seconds; 3 seconds later, the age for a route learned from
```

```
! 172.31.13.2 is now 11 seconds.

R1# show ip route
Codes: C - connected, S - static, R - RIP, M - mobile, B - BGP
   D - EIGRP, EX - EIGRP external, O - OSPF, IA - OSPF inter area
   N1 - OSPF NSSA external type 1, N2 - OSPF NSSA external type 2
   E1 - OSPF external type 1, E2 - OSPF external type 2
   i - IS-IS, su - IS-IS summary, L1 - IS-IS level-1, L2 - IS-IS level-2
   ia - IS-IS inter area, * - candidate default, U - per-user static route
   o - ODR, P - periodic downloaded static route

Gateway of last resort is not set
     172.31.0.0/16 is variably subnetted, 4 subnets, 2 masks
R       172.31.24.0/30 [120/1] via 172.31.11.2, 00:00:18, FastEthernet0/0
C       172.31.11.0/24 is directly connected, FastEthernet0/0
C       172.31.13.0/30 is directly connected, Serial0/0.3
R       172.31.103.0/24 [120/1] via 172.31.13.2, 00:00:11, Serial0/0.3

! Below, the show ip rip database command lists information for each route
! considered by RIP.

R1# show ip rip database
172.31.0.0/16 auto-summary
172.31.11.0/24 directly connected, FastEthernet0/0
172.31.13.0/30 directly connected, Serial0/0.3
172.31.24.0/30
 [1] via 172.31.11.2, 00:00:01, FastEthernet0/0
172.31.103.0/24
 [1] via 172.31.13.2, 00:00:23, Serial0/0.3
```

**Note**   The **show ip rip database** command lists all RIP learned routes and all connected routes that RIP is advertising.

## Triggered (Flash) Updates and Poisoned Routes

When RIPv2 knows for sure that a route to a subnet has failed, RIPv2 can converge to an alternate route relatively quickly. Example 7-2 details the steps behind one such example, using Figure 7-2, with the steps outlined in the following list (the comments in Example 7-2 refer to these steps by number):

1.   RIPv2 **debug** messages show R1's RIPv2 updates, including R1's use of split horizon.

2.   R3's E0/0 interface is shut down, simulating a failure.

3. R3 immediately sends a triggered update (also called a flash update), because R3 knows for sure that the route has failed. R3's behavior combines a triggered update with route poisoning, as R3's advertised route is a poisoned route to now unreachable network 172.31.103.0/24.

4. R1 immediately (because of triggered updates) sends a triggered update out all its interfaces, advertising a poisoned route for 172.31.103.0/24.

5. R1 removes its route to 172.31.103.0/24 from its routing table.

6. R1 waits for R2's next update, sent based on R2's Update timer on its Fa0/0 interface. That update includes a route to 172.31.103.0/24. R1 adds that route to its routing table.

**Example 7-2**    *R1's Convergence for 172.31.103.0/24 Upon R3's E0/0 Interface Failure*

```
! First, the debug ip RIPv2 command enables RIPv2 debugging. This command will show
! messages that show every route in the sent and received updates.


R1# debug ip RIPv2
RIPv2 protocol debugging is on


! (Step 1) Below, the output exhibits split horizon - for example, 172.31.103.0/24
! is not advertised out s0/0.3, but it is advertised out Fa0/0.


*Mar 3 22:44:08.176: RIPv2: sending v2 update to 224.0.0.9 via S0/0.3 (172.31.13.1)
*Mar 3 22:44:08.176: RIPv2: build update entries
*Mar 3 22:44:08.176:    172.31.11.0/24 via 0.0.0.0, metric 1, tag 0
*Mar 3 22:44:08.176:    172.31.24.0/30 via 0.0.0.0, metric 2, tag 0
*Mar 3 22:44:12.575: RIPv2: sending v2 update to 224.0.0.9 via Fa0/0 (172.31.11.1)
*Mar 3 22:44:12.575: RIPv2: build update entries
*Mar 3 22:44:12.575:    172.31.13.0/30 via 0.0.0.0, metric 1, tag 0
*Mar 3 22:44:12.575:    172.31.103.0/24 via 0.0.0.0, metric 2, tag 0


! Next, R1 receives a RIPv2 update from R3. The metric 1 route in the update below
! is R1's best route, and is placed into R1's routing table. Note that the metric
! in the received update is R1's actual metric to reach the route.


*Mar 3 22:44:21.265: RIPv2: received v2 update from 172.31.13.2 on S0/0.3
*Mar 3 22:44:21.269:        172.31.24.0/30 via 0.0.0.0 in 2 hops
*Mar 3 22:44:21.269:        172.31.103.0/24 via 0.0.0.0 in 1 hops


! (Step 2) R3's E0/0 interface is shut down at this point. (Not shown).
! (Step 3) Below, R1 receives a triggered update, with two poisoned routes from
! R3 - the same two routes that R3 advertised in the previous routing update above.
! Note that the triggered update only includes changed routes, with full updates
! continuing on the same update interval.
```

```
*Mar 3 22:44:46.338: RIPv2: received v2 update from 172.31.13.2 on S0/0.3
*Mar 3 22:44:46.338:     172.31.24.0/30 via 0.0.0.0 in 16 hops (inaccessible)
*Mar 3 22:44:46.338:     172.31.103.0/24 via 0.0.0.0 in 16 hops (inaccessible)

! (Step 4) Above, R1 reacts to its receipt of poisoned routes, sending a triggered
! update out its Fa0/0 interface. Note that the debug refers to the triggered
! update as a flash update.

*Mar 3 22:44:48.341: RIPv2: sending v2 flash update to 224.0.0.9 via Fa0/0
   (172.31.11.1)
*Mar 3 22:44:48.341: RIPv2: build flash update entries
*Mar 3 22:44:48.341:     172.31.103.0/24 via 0.0.0.0, metric 16, tag 0

! (Step 4) R1 also sends a triggered update out S0/0.3 to R3, which includes
! a poison reverse route to 172.31.103.0/24, back to R3. R1 does not send back a
! poison route to 172.31.24.0, because R1's route to 172.31.24.0 was
! pointing towards R2, not R3 - so R1's route to 172.31.24.0/24 did not fail.

*Mar 3 22:44:48.345: RIPv2: sending v2 flash update to 224.0.0.9 via S0/0.3
   (172.31.13.1)
*Mar 3 22:44:48.345: RIPv2: build flash update entries
*Mar 3 22:44:48.345:     172.31.103.0/24 via 0.0.0.0, metric 16, tag 0

! (Step 5) Below, note the absence of a route to 103.0/24 in R1's routing table.

R1# show ip route 172.31.103.0 255.255.255.0
% Subnet not in table

! (Step 6) Below, 23 seconds since the previous message, R2's next routing
! update arrives at R1, advertising 172.31.103.0/24. Following that, R1 now has
! a 2-hop route, through R2, to 172.31.103.0/24.

*Mar 3 22:45:11.271: RIPv2: received v2 update from 172.31.11.2 on Fa0/0
*Mar 3 22:45:11.271:     172.31.24.0/30 via 0.0.0.0 in 1 hops
*Mar 3 22:45:11.271:     172.31.103.0/24 via 0.0.0.0 in 2 hops

R1# show ip route 172.31.103.0 255.255.255.0
Routing entry for 172.31.103.0/24
 Known via "RIPv2", distance 120, metric 2
 Redistributing via RIPv2
 Last update from 172.31.11.2 on FastEthernet0/0, 00:00:01 ago
 Routing Descriptor Blocks:
 * 172.31.11.2, from 172.31.11.2, 00:00:01 ago, via FastEthernet0/0
      Route metric is 2, traffic share count is 1
```

If you examine the debug message time stamps in Example 7-2, you will see that between 25 and 45 seconds passed from when R1 heard the poisoned routes until R1 heard R2's new routing update with a now-best route to 172.31.103.0/24. While not on par with EIGRP or OSPF, this convergence is reasonably fast for RIPv2.

> **Note**  Do not confuse the term *triggered update* with the term *triggered extensions to RIPv2*. RFC 2091 defines how RIPv2 can choose to send full updates only once, and then be silent, to support demand circuits. The feature is enabled per interface by the **ip rip triggered** interface subcommand.

## RIPv2 Convergence When Routing Updates Cease

When a router ceases to receive routing updates, RIPv2 must wait for some timers to expire before it decides that routes previously learned from the now-silent router can be considered to be failed routes. To deal with such cases, RIPv2 uses its *Invalid after*, *Flushed after*, and *Holddown* timers to prevent loops. Coincidentally, RIPv2's convergence time increases to several minutes as a result.

Example 7-3 details just such a case, where R1 simply ceases to hear RIPv2 updates from R3. (To create the failure, R3's s0/0.1 subinterface was configured as passive, emulating a silent passing away of the router without the interface actually going down.) The example uses the internetwork illustrated in Figure 7-2 again, and begins with all interfaces up, and all four routes known in each of the four routers. The example follows this sequence (the comments in Example 7-3 refer to these steps by number):

1. R3's s0/0.1 subinterface fails, but R1's subinterface stays up, so R1 must use its timers to detect route failures.

2. R1's *Invalid after* and *Flushed after* timers for route 172.31.103.0/24 grow because R1 does not hear any further updates from R3.

3. After the *Invalid after* timer expires (180 seconds) for R1's route to 172.31.103.0/24, R1 starts a *Holddown* timer for the route. *Holddown* starts at (default) 180 seconds and counts down.

4. The *Flushed after* timer expires after a total of 240 seconds, or 60 seconds past the *Invalid after* timer. As a result, R1 flushes the route to 172.31.103.0/24 from its routing table, which also removes the *Holddown* timer for the route.

**Example 7-3**  *R1 Ceases to Hear R3's Updates: Invalid After, Flushed After, Holddown Timers*

```
! First, the debug ip ripv2 event command is used which displays messages when
! updates are sent and received, but does not display the contents of the updates.


R1# debug ip ripv2 event
RIPv2 event debugging is on
```

```
! (Step 1) Not Shown: R3's S0/0.1 subinterface is made passive.
! (Step 2) Below, the age for 172.31.103.0/24 has reached 35 seconds, meaning
! that 35 seconds have passed since the last received update from which this route
! was learned. An age of a RIPv2-learned route over 30 seconds means that at least
! one RIPv2 update was not received.

R1# show ip route
Codes: C - connected, S - static, R - RIP, M - mobile, B - BGP
       D - EIGRP, EX - EIGRP external, O - OSPF, IA - OSPF inter area
       N1 - OSPF NSSA external type 1, N2 - OSPF NSSA external type 2
       E1 - OSPF external type 1, E2 - OSPF external type 2
       i - IS-IS, su - IS-IS summary, L1 - IS-IS level-1, L2 - IS-IS level-2
       ia - IS-IS inter area, * - candidate default, U - per-user static route
       o - ODR, P - periodic downloaded static route

Gateway of last resort is not set

     172.31.0.0/16 is variably subnetted, 4 subnets, 2 masks
R       172.31.24.0/30 [120/1] via 172.31.11.2, 00:00:09, FastEthernet0/0
C       172.31.11.0/24 is directly connected, FastEthernet0/0
C       172.31.13.0/30 is directly connected, Serial0/0.3
R       172.31.103.0/24 [120/1] via 172.31.13.2, 00:00:35, Serial0/0.3

! Below, one example set of debug messages are shown. (Many more debug messages
! occurred while waiting for convergence, but those were omitted.) The messages
! about R1's received updates from R2 occur every 30 seconds or so. The contents
! include a 2-hop route to 172.31.103.0/24, which R1 ignores until the Flushed
! after timer expires.

*Mar 3 21:59:58.921: RIPv2: received v2 update from 172.31.11.2 on FastEthernet0/0
*Mar 3 21:59:58.921: RIPv2: Update contains 2 routes

! (Step 3) Below, the Invalid after timer expires, roughly 3 minutes after the
! failure. Note that the route is listed as "possibly down," which occurs when the
! Invalid after timer has expired but the Flushed after timer has not.

R1# show ip route 172.31.103.0 255.255.255.0
Codes: C - connected, S - static, R - RIP, M - mobile, B - BGP
       D - EIGRP, EX - EIGRP external, O - OSPF, IA - OSPF inter area
       N1 - OSPF NSSA external type 1, N2 - OSPF NSSA external type 2
       E1 - OSPF external type 1, E2 - OSPF external type 2
       i - IS-IS, su - IS-IS summary, L1 - IS-IS level-1, L2 - IS-IS level-2
       ia - IS-IS inter area, * - candidate default, U - per-user static route
       o - ODR, P - periodic downloaded static route
```

```
Gateway of last resort is not set


      172.31.0.0/16 is variably subnetted, 4 subnets, 2 masks
R        172.31.24.0/30 [120/1] via 172.31.11.2, 00:00:20, FastEthernet0/0
C        172.31.11.0/24 is directly connected, FastEthernet0/0
C        172.31.13.0/30 is directly connected, Serial0/0.3
R        172.31.103.0/24 is possibly down,
             routing via 172.31.13.2, Serial0/0.3


! (Step 3) Next, the command shows the metric as inaccessible, meaning an
! infinite metric, as well as the current age timer (3:23), which counts up.
! While not shown in this example, R1 itself advertises the route with infinite
! metric as the Invalid after timer expired and the route has been declared
! invalid. Also, the Holddown timer for this route has started (at 180 seconds),
! with 159 seconds in its countdown. The Holddown timer prevents R1 from using
! the route heard from R2.

R1# show ip route 172.31.103.0 255.255.255.0
Routing entry for 172.31.103.0/24
  Known via "RIPv2", distance 120, metric 4294967295 (inaccessible)
  Redistributing via RIPv2
  Last update from 172.31.13.2 on Serial0/0.3, 00:03:23 ago
  Hold down timer expires in 159 secs

! (Step 4) Below, just after 4 minutes has passed, the Flushed after timer has
! expired, and the route to 172.31.103.0/24 has been flushed from the routing
! table.

R1# show ip route 172.31.103.0 255.255.255.0
% Subnet not in table
```

At the end of the example, the only remaining step for convergence is for R1 to receive R2's next regular full routing update, which includes a two-hop route to 172.31.103.0/24. R2 will send that update based on R2's regular Update interval. R1 would place that route in its routing table, completing convergence.

Note that either the *Flushed after* timer or the *Holddown* timer must expire before new routing information would be used in this case. Here, the *Flushed after* timer for route 172.31.103.0/24 expired first, resulting in the route being removed from R1's routing table. When the route is flushed (removed), any associated timers are also removed, including the *Holddown* timer. Had the *Holddown* timer been smaller, and had it expired before the *Flushed after* timer, R1 would have been able to use the route advertised by R2 at that point in time.

### Convergence Extras

Convergence in Example 7-3 took a little over 4 minutes, but it could be improved in some cases. The RIPv2 timers can be tuned with the **timers basic** *update invalid hold-down flush* subcommand under **router rip**, although care should be taken when changing these timers. The timers should be consistent across routers, and smaller values increase the chance of transient routing loops being formed during convergence.

The **clear ip route** * command also speeds convergence by removing all routes (not just RIP-learned) from the routing table, along with any per-route timers. In Example 7-3, the **clear ip route 172.31.103.0** command would have worked as well, just deleting that one route. Because the **clear** command bypasses loop-prevention features by deleting the route and timers, it can be risky, but it certainly speeds convergence. Also, after the **clear ip route** * command, R1 would immediately issue RIPv2 request packets, which cause the neighboring routers to send full routing updates to R1, instead of waiting on their next update time.

## RIPv2 Configuration

This chapter does not go into detail on configuring RIPv2. However, make sure to review the list of RIPv2 configuration commands, and command syntax, listed in Table 7-6 of the "Foundation Summary" section for this chapter.

Figure 7-3 shows the internetwork that will be used to illustrate RIPv2 configuration concepts in Example 7-4. Note that most of the subnets are part of network 172.31.0.0, except where noted.

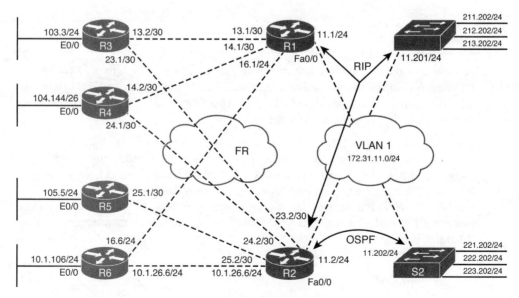

**Figure 7-3**   *Sample Internetwork Used for RIPv2 Configuration Examples*

## Enabling RIPv2 and the Effects of Autosummarization

Example 7-4 covers basic RIPv2 configuration, the meaning and implication of the RIPv2 **network** command, and the effects of the default setting for autosummarization. To examine just those functions, Example 7-4 shows the related RIPv2 configuration on R1, R2, and R6, along with some command output.

**Example 7-4** *Basic RIPv2 Configuration on R1, R2, R4, and S1*

```
! First, the three lines of configuration are the same on R1 and S1
! (Point 1): the version 2 command tells R1 to send and receive only RIPv2
! updates, and to ignore RIPv1 updates. The network command always recomputes
! its argument (the network address) into a classful representation.

router rip
 version 2
 network 172.31.0.0

! Next, the configuration for R2 and R6 is shown, which includes a network 10.0.0.0
! command, enabling RIPv2 on their interfaces in network 10.0.0.0/8.

router rip
 version 2
 network 10.0.0.0
 network 172.31.0.0

! Below, R1 shows that only v2 updates are being sent and received, and that
! autosummarization is in effect.

R1# show ip protocols
Routing Protocol is "RIPv2"
  Sending updates every 30 seconds, next due in 26 seconds
  Invalid after 180 seconds, hold down 180, flushed after 240
  Outgoing update filter list for all interfaces is not set
  Incoming update filter list for all interfaces is not set
  Redistributing: RIPv2
  Default version control: send version 2, receive version 2
    Interface          Send  Recv  Triggered RIPv2  Key-chain
    FastEthernet0/0     2     2             carkeys
    Serial0/0.3         2     2
    Serial0/0.4         2     2             anothersetofkeys
    Serial0/0.6         2     2
Automatic network summarization is in effect

! Lines omitted for brevity
! Below, the show ip route 10.0.0.0 command lists all of R1's known routes to
! network 10.0.0.0; the only route is for 10.0.0.0/8, because R2 and R6
```

```
! automatically summarize (by default) at the classful network boundary.


R1# show ip route 10.0.0.0
Routing entry for 10.0.0.0/8
  Known via "RIPv2", distance 120, metric 1
  Redistributing via RIPv2
  Last update from 172.31.11.2 on FastEthernet0/0, 00:00:01 ago
  Routing Descriptor Blocks:
    172.31.16.6, from 172.31.16.6, 00:00:08 ago, via Serial0/0.6
      Route metric is 1, traffic share count is 1
  * 172.31.11.2, from 172.31.11.2, 00:00:01 ago, via FastEthernet0/0
      Route metric is 1, traffic share count is 1
```

A couple of points from this example need a little more explanation. The RIPv2 **network** command only allows for a classful network as a parameter, which in turn enables RIPv2 on all of that router's interfaces that are part of that network. Even if a subnetwork address is entered as the **network** command's parameter, the router will automatically compute the corresponding classful network's address and store it in the configuration. Enabling RIPv2 on an interface makes the router begin sending RIPv2 updates, listening for RIPv2 updates (UDP port 520), and advertising that interface's connected subnet.

Because the RIPv2 **network** command has no way to simply match one interface at a time, a RIPv2 configuration might enable these three functions on an interface for which some or all of these functions are not required. The three RIPv2 functions can be individually disabled on an interface with some effort. Table 7-4 lists these three functions, along with how to disable each feature.

**Key Topic**

**Table 7-4**    *RIPv2 Per-Interface Actions, and How to Disable Them When Enabled*

| RIPv2 Function | How to Disable |
|---|---|
| Sending RIPv2 updates | Make the interface passive: configure **router rip**, followed by **passive-interface** *type number* |
| Listening for RIPv2 updates | Filter all incoming routes using a distribute list, or filter incoming RIPv2 packets using a per-interface ACL |
| Advertising the connected subnet | Filter outbound advertisements on other interfaces using distribute lists, filtering an interface's connected subnet |

Another way that you can limit advertisements on multiaccess networks is to use the **neighbor** *ip-address* RIP subcommand. This command tells RIP to send unicast RIP updates to that neighbor. For example, when using a multipoint Frame Relay subinterface, there might be four routers reachable using that subinterface. If you want to send RIP updates to only one of them, make the interface passive, and then use the **neighbor** command to cause RIP to send updates, but only to that particular neighbor.

RIPv2 uses autosummarization at classful network boundaries by default. To reiterate, automatic summarization applies whenever a router intends to advertise a subnetwork of a particular classful network X (also called *major network*) out an interface that is itself in a different classful network Y. In that case, the router will advertise only the classful network X instead of the individual subnet. In Example 7-4, R2 and R6 connect to parts of classful networks 10.0.0.0/8 and network 172.31.0.0/16. Advertisements sent out interfaces in network 172.31.0.0/16 advertise a summarized route of the complete class A network 10.0.0.0/8. In the example, R2 and R6 both advertise a summarized network 10.0.0.0/8 to R1. As a result, as seen with the **show ip route 10.0.0.0** command on R1, R1 knows two equal-cost routes to classful network 10.0.0.0. In this case, R1 would send some packets meant for subnet 10.1.106.0/24 through R2 first, a seemingly poor choice. To advertise the subnets of network 10.0.0.0, R2 and R6 could be configured with the **no auto-summary** command under **router rip**. Disabling the automatic summarization should be considered a mandatory part of any RIPv2 configuration.

Note that RIPv2 allows for discontiguous networks, but autosummarization must be disabled for a design using discontiguous networks to work.

## RIPv2 Authentication

RIPv2 authentication, much like EIGRP and OSPF authentication, requires the creation of keys and requires authentication to be enabled on an interface. The keys are used either as clear-text passwords or as the secret (private) key used in an MD5 calculation.

Multiple keys are allowed, and are grouped together using a construct called a *key chain*. A key chain is simply a set of related keys, each of which has a different number and might be restricted to a time period. By allowing multiple related keys in a key chain, with each key valid during specified time periods, the engineer can easily plan for migration to new keys in the future. (NTP is recommended when keys are restricted by time ranges. Beware of a chicken-and-egg problem, though, when keys are not considered usable until correct time is set on a router, and a correct time cannot be obtained from a remote NTP server because the routing requires the use of correct keys.)

**Key Topic**

Cisco IOS enables the RIPv2 (and EIGRP) authentication process on a per-interface basis, referring to the key chain that holds the keys with the **ip rip authentication key-chain name** interface subcommand. The router looks in the key chain and selects the key(s) valid at that particular time. If multiple keys are valid for signing outgoing RIPv2 packets, the key with the lowest sequence number will be used. With RIPv2, the type of authentication (clear-text password or MD5 digest) is chosen per interface as well, using the **ip rip authentication mode {text | md5}** interface subcommand. If this command is omitted, the authentication type defaults to **text**, meaning that the key is used as a clear-text password.

When authentication is enabled, the maximum number of prefixes that can be advertised in a RIPv2 message is reduced by 1 to a value of 24. The first route entry in each RIPv2 message would be carrying 20 bytes of authentication data. If cryptographic authentication methods are used, further authentication data is placed after the entire RIPv2 message. As a single RIPv2 message can carry at most 25 route entries, the first one would be occupied by authentication data, the remaining 24 entries would carry routing information, and the remaining authentication data would be placed after the 25th entry.

### RIPv2 Next-Hop Feature and Split Horizon

This section covers the split horizon and next-hop features of RIPv2. These two features do not typically need to be considered at the same time, but in some cases they do.

First, Cisco IOS controls the split horizon setting per interface, using the [**no**] **ip split-horizon** interface subcommand. Split Horizon is on by default, except for cases in which Frame Relay or ATM is configured with the IP address on the physical interface.

The RIPv2 next-hop feature allows a RIPv2 router to advertise a different next-hop router than the advertising router. Although this is not a common requirement, this little-known feature permits a RIPv2 router to point to a different next hop on the same segment than itself, potentially eliminating an extra hop. The original motivation for the next-hop feature is described in RFC 2453 Appendix A. On Cisco routers, this feature is not configurable, though, and is almost unused. In fact, the only instance in which the next-hop field was seen to be set to a nonzero address is when RIPv2 is run over Non Broadcast Multiple Access (NBMA) interfaces, facilitating direct spoke-to-spoke routing (and possibly causing issues if direct spoke-to-spoke communication is not available).

### RIPv2 Offset Lists

RIPv2 offset lists allow RIPv2 to add to a route's metric, either before sending an update, or for routes received in an update. The offset list refers to an ACL (standard, extended, or named) to match the routes; the router then adds the specified offset, or extra metric, to any matching routes. Any routes not matched by the offset list are unchanged. The offset list also specifies which routing updates to examine by referring to a direction (**in** or **out**) and, optionally, an interface. If the interface is omitted from the command, all updates for the defined direction are examined.

### Route Filtering with Distribute Lists and Prefix Lists

Outbound and inbound RIPv2 updates can be filtered at any interface, or for the entire RIPv2 process. To filter the routes, the **distribute-list** command is used under **router rip**, referencing an IP ACL or an IP prefix list. Any subnets matched with a **permit** clause in the ACL make it through; any that match with a **deny** action are filtered. The distribution list filtering can be performed for either direction of flow (**in** or **out**) and, optionally, for a particular interface. If the interface option is omitted, all updates coming into or out of the RIPv2 process are filtered. (Routes can also be filtered at redistribution points, a topic covered in Chapter 11.)

The generic command, when creating a RIPv2 distribution list that uses an ACL, is

```
distribute-list { access-list-number | name } { in | out }
    [interface-type interface-number]
```

A RIPv2 distribute list might refer to a prefix list instead of an ACL to match routes. Prefix lists are designed to match a range of subnets, as well as a range of subnet masks associated with the subnets. The distribute list must still define the direction of the updates to be examined (**in** or **out**), and optionally an interface.

Chapter 11 includes a more complete discussion of the syntax and formatting of prefix lists; this chapter focuses on how to call and use a prefix list for RIPv2. Use of prefix lists is generally recommended. To reference a prefix list, use the following **router rip** subcommand:

```
distribute-list prefix prefix-list-name { in | out } [interface-type
   interface-number]
```

# RIPng for IPv6

While RIP is in many aspects an inferior protocol to EIGRP, OSPF, or IS-IS, its simplicity nonetheless makes it suitable for small office/home office (SOHO) routers and simple networks. Its wide adoption and support over a wide range of routers from multiple vendors prompted the creation of the IPv6 version of RIP named *RIP next generation (RIPng)*.

Although the name RIPng suggests major reworking, RIPng is in fact just a straightforward adaptation of RIPv2 for IPv6 operation with practically no changes to underlying protocol mechanisms. RIPng remains a plain distance-vector protocol utilizing User Datagram Protocol (UDP) as its transport protocol, using port 521 instead of 520 to avoid clashes with existing RIPv1/RIPv2 implementations. The destination IPv6 address for multicasted RIPng messages is FF02::9. Metric is again based on hop count, with 15 being the maximum usable metric and 16 representing infinity. RIPng differs, though, in its metric handling: The metric is incremented by the receiver of a RIPng advertisement, not by the advertisement sender anymore. All loop avoidance techniques described in previous sections are used by RIPng in precisely the same way.

Figure 7-4 shows the RIPng message format—similar to RIPv2 messages.

**RIPng Message**

| Octet 1 | Octet 2 | Octet 3 | Octet 4 | |
|---------|---------|---------|---------| |
| Command | Version | Must Be Zero | | } Message Header |
| IPv6 Prefix | | | | } Route Entry, as Many Entries as Permitted by Link MTU |
| Route Tag | | Prefix Len | Metric | |

**Figure 7-4** *RIPng Message Format*

Similar to RIPv2, the RIPng message starts with a header containing a Command field (value 1 for Request, 2 for Response) and a Version field (currently set to 1). After the header, a variable number of route entries follows. The number of route entries in a RIPng message is limited only by the IPv6 MTU on the link, and the protocol itself poses no limitations on their count. Route entry fields are self-explanatory. Two facts are worth mentioning:

■ As RIPng does not assume any multiprotocol capability, the address family ID field has been omitted.

■ Because the next-hop field was relatively unused in RIPv2, keeping a per-prefix next-hop field in a route entry would uselessly occupy quite a significant space (128 bits). Therefore, the next hop field—if necessary—is specified by a separate route entry containing the IPv6 next-hop address (a link-local address) in the IPv6 prefix field, the metric value set to 255, and route tag and prefix length fields set to 0. All subsequent route entries are to be processed with this particular next hop until another next-hop route entry is encountered in the RIPng message. A route entry with the IPv6 next-hop address set to :: (all-zero) will revert to the sender of the message being the next hop.

Authentication is not handled by RIPng anymore; rather, similar to OSPFv3, these functions are offloaded to IPsec. RIPng implementation in current Cisco IOS is relatively simple and lacks several features supported by RIPv2:

■ Authentication or encryption by IPsec is not supported.

■ Split Horizon can be activated or deactivated only on a per-process basis, not on individual interfaces.

■ Passive interfaces are not supported.

■ Static (manual) neighbors cannot be configured (no **neighbor** command).

■ Per-process offset lists are not supported.

Still, there are management improvements over RIPv2 implemented in the Cisco RIPng:

■ Multiple RIPng processes can be run on a router; however, at the time of writing, at most four simultaneously running RIPng processes were supported on IOS-based routers. Individual processes are distinguished by an alphanumeric name that is local to the router and does not need to match between different routers.

■ Route Poisoning, as an enhancement of the Split Horizon mechanism, can be activated on a per-process basis.

■ Interfaces can be configured with a *metric-offset* value that is added to the metric in all received advertisements over that interface, effectively allowing RIPng to operate with link costs rather than hop counts.

■ The default route can be originated on a per-interface basis, including an option of suppressing all other updates over that interface.

Example 7-5 shows a simple configuration of RIPng on a router with two interfaces.

**Example 7-5**  *Basic RIPng Configuration on a Router*

```
! First, IPv6 unicast routing support must be activated, and IPv6 CEF is activated
! as well

ipv6 unicast-routing
ipv6 cef
```

```
! Fa0/0 interface is connected to a stub router. Only default route needs to be
! sent.

R1(config)# interface FastEthernet0/0
R1(config-if)# ipv6 address 2001:DB8:1::1/64
R1(config-if)# ipv6 rip 1 enable
R1(config-if)# ipv6 rip 1 default-information only


! S0/0/0 interface simply connects to another router. However, the metric of this
! interface is increased to 3 from 1

R1(config)# interface Serial0/0/0
R1(config-if)# ipv6 address 2001:DB8:2::1/64
R1(config-if)# ipv6 rip 1 enable
R1(config-if)# ipv6 rip 1 metric-offset 3


! In global IPv6 RIPng process 1, Poison Reverse is activated and settings are
! verified afterwards using show ipv6 rip command

R1(config)# ipv6 router rip 1
R1(config-rtr)# poison-reverse
R1(config-rtr)# do show ipv6 rip
RIP process "1", port 521, multicast-group FF02::9, pid 246
     Administrative distance is 120. Maximum paths is 16
     Updates every 30 seconds, expire after 180
     Holddown lasts 0 seconds, garbage collect after 120
     Split horizon is on; poison reverse is on
     Default routes are generated
     Periodic updates 18, trigger updates 2
     Full Advertisement 2, Delayed Events 0
   Interfaces:
     Serial0/0/0
     FastEthernet0/0
   Redistribution:
     None
```

# Foundation Summary

This section lists additional details and facts to round out the coverage of the topics in this chapter. Unlike most of the Cisco Press Exam Certification Guides, this "Foundation Summary" does not repeat information presented in the "Foundation Topics" section of the chapter. Please take the time to read and study the details in the "Foundation Topics" section of the chapter, as well as review items noted with a Key Topic icon.

Table 7-5 lists the protocols mentioned in this chapter and their respective standards documents.

**Table 7-5**  *Protocols and Standards for Chapter 7*

| Protocol or Feature | Standard |
| --- | --- |
| RIPv2 (RIP version 2) | RFC 2453 |
| RIPv2 Cryptographic Authentication | RFC 4822 |
| RIPv2 Triggered Extensions for On-Demand Circuits | RFC 2091 |
| RIPng for IPv6 | RFC 2080 |

Table 7-6 lists some of the most significant Cisco IOS commands related to the topics in this chapter.

**Table 7-6**  *Command Reference for Chapter 7*

| Command | Command Mode and Description |
| --- | --- |
| **router rip** | Global config; puts user in RIP configuration mode. |
| **network** *ip-address* | RIP config mode; defines classful network, with all interfaces in that network sending and able to receive RIP advertisements. |
| **[ no ] auto-summary** | RIP config mode; activates or deactivates automatic network summarization on classful boundaries whenever a prefix from one major network is advertised out an interface in a different major network. |
| **distribute-list** [*access-list-number* \| *name* \| **prefix** *name*] \| {**in** \| **out**} [*interface-type interface-number*] | RIP config mode; defines ACL or prefix list to filter RIP updates. |
| **[ no ] ip split-horizon** | Interface mode; enables or disables split horizon. |
| **ip summary-address rip** *address netmask* | Interface mode; defines manual network summarization. |

| Command | Command Mode and Description |
|---------|------------------------------|
| **passive-interface** [**default**] {*interface-type interface-number*} | RIP config mode; causes RIP to stop sending updates on the specified interface. |
| **timers basic** *update invalid holddown flush* | RIP config mode; sets the values for RIP timers. |
| **version** {**1** \| **2**} | RIP config mode; sets the RIP version to version 1 or version 2. |
| **offset-list** {*access-list-number* \| *access-list-name*} {**in** \| **out**} *offset* [*interface-type interface-number*] | RIP config mode; defines rules for RIP to add to the metrics of particular routes. |
| **neighbor** *ip-address* | RIP config mode; identifies a neighbor to which unicast RIP updates will be sent. |
| **show ip route rip** | User mode; displays all routes in the IP routing table learned by RIP. |
| **show ip rip database** | User mode; lists all routes learned by RIP even if a route is not in the routing table because of a route with lower administrative distance. |
| **debug ip rip** | Enable mode; displays details of RIP processing |
| **show ip protocols** | User mode; lists RIP timer settings, current protocol status, autosummarization actions, and update sources. |
| **clear ip route** {*network* [*mask*] \| *\**} | Enable mode; clears the routing table entry, and with RIP, sends RIP requests, quickly rebuilding the routing table. |
| **show ip interface** [*type number*] [**brief**] | User mode; lists many interface settings, including split horizon. |
| **key chain** *name-of-chain* | Global config; defines name of key chain for routing protocol authentication. |
| **key** *key-id* | Key config mode; identifies a key by number. |
| **key-string** *string* | Key config mode; defines the text of the key. |
| **send-lifetime** [*start-time* {**infinite** \| *end-time* \| **duration** *seconds*}] | Key config mode; defines when the key is valid to be used for sent updates. |
| **accept-lifetime** [*start-time* {**infinite** \| *end-time* \| **duration** *seconds*}] | Key config mode; defines when the key is valid for received updates. |
| **ip rip authentication key-chain** *name-of-chain* | Interface mode; enables RIPv2 authentication on the interface. |
| **ip rip authentication mode** {**text** \| **md5**} | Interface mode; defines RIPv2 authentication as clear text (default) or MD5. |

| Command | Command Mode and Description |
|---|---|
| ipv6 router rip *word* | Global config; puts user in RIPng configuration mode. The word is the name of the RIPng instance. |
| distribute-list prefix *name* { in | out} [*interface-type interface-number*] | RIPng config mode; defines an IPv6 prefix list to filter RIPng updates. |
| split-horizon | RIPng config mode; activates simple Split Horizon. |
| poison-reverse | RIPng config mode; activates Split Horizon with Poisoned Reverse. If both split-horizon and poison-reverse are configured, poison-reverse takes precedence. |
| port *port* multicast-group *group* | RIPng config mode; defines the UDP port and multicast address to send and listen for RIPng packets. Used if multiple processes are to communicate over a single interface, as multiple processes cannot listen on the same UDP port. |
| timers *update timeout holddown garbage-collection* | RIPng config mode; defines the RIPng timers. *Update* is the time between RIPng update messages, *Timeout* is equivalent to the *Invalid after* timer, *Holddown* is the hold down timer, and the *Garbage Collection* timer is similar to *Flushed after* with a notable difference: The *Garbage Collection* timer starts only after the *Timeout* timer expired. The default values of these timers are 30, 180, 0, 120, respectively. |
| ipv6 rip *word* enable | Interface mode; activates a RIPng instance identified by the *word* on the interface. All unicast prefixes of this interface except the link-local address will be advertised by RIPng. |
| ipv6 rip *word* default-information { only | originate } [ metric *metric* ] | Interface mode; advertises the default route out the interface. If the only keyword is used, all other prefixes are suppressed. |
| ipv6 rip *word* metric-offset *offset* | Interface mode; defines the offset by which the metric in received RIPng updates is incremented. By default, the *offset* value is 1. |
| ipv6 rip *word* summary-address *ipv6-prefix/prefix-length* | Interface mode; defines manual prefix summarization. |

# Memory Builders

The CCIE Routing and Switching written exam, like all Cisco CCIE written exams, covers a fairly broad set of topics. This section provides some basic tools to help you exercise your memory about some of the broader topics covered in this chapter.

Appendix E, "Key Tables for CCIE Study," on the CD in the back of this book, contains empty sets of some of the key summary tables in each chapter. Print Appendix E, refer to this chapter's tables in it, and fill in the tables from memory. Refer to Appendix F, "Solutions for Key Tables for CCIE Study," on the CD to check your answers.

## Definitions

Next, take a few moments to write down the definitions for the following terms:

> Holddown timer, Invalid after timer, Flushed after timer, authentication, Update timer, triggered updates, flash updates, split horizon, route poisoning, poison reverse, counting to infinity, hello interval, full update, partial update, Route Tag field, Next Hop field, Triggered Extensions to RIPv2 for On-Demand Circuits, MD5, offset list, prefix list, distribution list, distance vector, metric

Refer to the glossary to check your answers.

## Further Reading

This chapter focuses on TCP/IP protocols; much more information can be found in the RFCs mentioned throughout the chapter.

The RIP RFCs listed in Table 7-5 provide good references for RIPv2 concepts.

Jeff Doyle's *Routing TCP/IP, Volume I*, Second Edition (Cisco Press), has several excellent configuration examples and provides a complete explanation of RIPv2 concepts.

**Blueprint topics covered in this chapter:**

This chapter covers the following subtopics from the Cisco CCIE Routing and Switching written exam blueprint. Refer to the full blueprint in Table I-1 in the Introduction for more details on the topics covered in each chapter and their context within the blueprint.

- Describe Packet Types

- Implement and Troubleshoot Neighbor Relationship

- Implement and Troubleshoot Loop-Free Path Selection

- Implement and Troubleshoot Operations

- Implement and Troubleshoot EIGRP Stub

- Implement and Troubleshoot Load Balancing

- Implement EIGRP Named Mode

- Implement, Troubleshoot, and Optimize EIGRP Convergence and Scalability

## CHAPTER 8

# EIGRP

This chapter covers most of the features, concepts, and commands related to Enhanced Interior Gateway Routing Protocol (EIGRP). Chapter 11, "IGP Route Redistribution, Route Summarization, Default Routing, and Troubleshooting," covers a few other details of EIGRP—in particular, route redistribution, route filtering when redistributing, and route summarization.

## "Do I Know This Already?" Quiz

Table 8-1 outlines the major headings in this chapter and the corresponding "Do I Know This Already?" quiz questions.

**Table 8-1** *"Do I Know This Already?" Foundation Topics Section-to-Question Mapping*

| Foundation Topics Section | Questions Covered in This Section | Score |
|---|---|---|
| EIGRP Metrics, Packets, and Adjacencies | 1–11 | |
| Diffusing Update Algorithm | 12–25 | |
| EIGRP Named Mode | 26 | |
| Additional and Advanced EIGRP Features | 27–31 | |
| Total Score | | |

To best use this pre-chapter assessment, remember to score yourself strictly. You can find the answers in Appendix A, "Answers to the 'Do I Know This Already?' Quizzes."

**1.** Which of the following items are true of EIGRP?

    **a.** Authentication can be done using MD5 or clear text.

    **b.** Uses UDP port 88.

    **c.** Sends full or partial updates as needed.

    **d.** Multicasts updates to 224.0.0.10 or FF02::A.

**2.** What classic metric components can be used by EIGRP for metric computation and best path selection?

    **a.** Bandwidth

    **b.** Cost

    **c.** Delay

    **d.** Hop count

    **e.** Load

    **f.** Expense

    **g.** MTU

    **h.** Reliability

**3.** Which of the following accurately describe the manipulation with the component metrics?

    **a.** Reliability is maximized.

    **b.** Delay is summed.

    **c.** Load is minimized.

    **d.** Reliability is minimized.

    **e.** Bandwidth is summed.

    **f.** Load is maximized.

    **g.** Bandwidth is minimized.

**4.** Which statement is true regarding EIGRP's use of Reliability and Load metric components on regular interfaces such as Ethernet or PPP?

    **a.** EIGRP sends updates and recalculates the composite metric immediately whenever the Reliability and Load values on an interface change, regardless of K-value settings.

    **b.** EIGRP sends updates and recalculates the composite metric immediately whenever the Reliability and Load values on an interface change but only when K-values are configured to take these components into account.

    **c.** EIGRP samples the Reliability and Load in regular intervals and sends updates along with recalculating the composite metric when the sampled Reliability and Load values change.

    **d.** EIGRP takes a snapshot of the interface Reliability and Load values in the moment of advertising a network, but changes to their values do not trigger sending further updates.

5. What are the shortcomings solved by Wide Metrics?

   a. Gradual loss of resolution caused by repetitive descaling and scaling of Bandwidth and Delay components in integer arithmetics

   b. Inability to use Reliability and Load without incurring routing table instabilities

   c. Loss of resolution for interfaces with speeds over 1 Gbps

   d. Inability to extend the metrics with additional future factors

6. What are the component metrics used in Wide Metrics that can be used for best path selection?

   a. Throughput

   b. Latency

   c. Reliability

   d. Load

   e. MTU

   f. Hop Count

   g. Extended Metrics

7. Which of the following EIGRP packets are considered reliable packets?

   a. Hello

   b. Ack

   c. Update

   d. Query

   e. Reply

   f. SIA-Query

   g. SIA-Reply

8. Which of the following EIGRP packets can be sent as multicasts?

   a. Hello

   b. Ack

   c. Update

   d. Query

   e. Reply

   f. SIA-Query

   g. SIA-Reply

**9.** Which statements are true about Hello packets?

   **a.** Hello packets must be confirmed.

   **b.** Hello packets sent by a router contain a list of all detected neighbors on the interface.

   **c.** Hello packets are usually sent as multicasts.

   **d.** Default interval between Hello packets is 5 seconds on all interfaces.

   **e.** Hello packets do not contain routing information.

**10.** Which EIGRP packet types are acknowledged?

   **a.** Hello

   **b.** Ack

   **c.** Update

   **d.** Query

   **e.** Reply

   **f.** SIA-Query

   **g.** SIA-Reply

**11.** Which EIGRP packet types can themselves act as acknowledgments?

   **a.** Hello

   **b.** Ack

   **c.** Update

   **d.** Query

   **e.** Reply

   **f.** SIA-Query

   **g.** SIA-Reply

**12.** What is the Computed Distance for a destination?

   **a.** The current total distance to the destination computed over a particular neighbor router

   **b.** The lowest known distance to the destination since the last time the destination transitioned from Active to Passive state

   **c.** The current distance of a particular neighbor to the destination

   **d.** The lowest known distance of a particular neighbor to the destination since the last time the destination transitioned from Active to Passive state

**13.** How many Computed Distances for a destination exist?

    **a.** Only one, not bound to any particular neighbor

    **b.** One per each neighbor that advertises the destination

    **c.** One per each Successor

    **d.** One per each Feasible Successor

**14.** What is the Reported Distance for a destination?

    **a.** The current total distance to the destination computed over a particular neighbor router

    **b.** The lowest known distance to the destination since the last time the destination transitioned from Active to Passive state

    **c.** The current distance of a particular neighbor to the destination

    **d.** The lowest known distance of a particular neighbor to the destination since the last time the destination transitioned from Active to Passive state

**15.** How many Reported Distances for a destination exist?

    **a.** Only one, not bound to any particular neighbor

    **b.** One per each neighbor that advertises the destination

    **c.** One per each Successor

    **d.** One per each Feasible Successor

**16.** What is the Feasible Distance for a destination?

    **a.** The current total distance to the destination computed over a particular neighbor router

    **b.** The lowest known distance to the destination since the last time the destination transitioned from Active to Passive state

    **c.** The current distance of a particular neighbor to the destination

    **d.** The lowest known distance of a particular neighbor to the destination since the last time the destination transitioned from Active to Passive state

**17.** How many Feasible Distances for a destination exist?

    **a.** Only one, not bound to any particular neighbor

    **b.** One per each neighbor that advertises the destination

    **c.** One per each Successor

    **d.** One per each Feasible Successor

**18.** Which statement correctly constitutes the Feasibility Condition in EIGRP?

   **a.** The neighbor must be closer to the destination than I have ever been since the last time the destination became Passive.

   **b.** The neighbor must be closer to the destination than I am.

   **c.** The neighbor must be farther from the destination than I am.

   **d.** The neighbor must be farther from the destination than I have ever been.

**19.** What statements correctly apply to a Successor?

   **a.** It is a route over a particular neighbor.

   **b.** It is a particular neighbor.

   **c.** It must provide a loop-free path.

   **d.** The Computed Distance over the Successor must be the lowest available.

   **e.** The Computed Distance over the Successor does not need to be the lowest available.

   **f.** In a connected network, there is always at least one Successor to a destination.

**20.** What statements correctly apply to a Feasible Successor?

   **a.** It is a route over a particular neighbor.

   **b.** It is a particular neighbor.

   **c.** It must provide a loop-free path.

   **d.** The Computed Distance over the Feasible Successor must be the lowest available.

   **e.** The Computed Distance over the Feasible Successor does not need to be the lowest available.

   **f.** There is always at least one Feasible Successor to a destination.

**21.** What is a local computation?

   **a.** The process of local processing of all received Updates and Replies

   **b.** The process of reevaluating and possibly changing a next hop to a destination locally that does not require the router to send Queries and wait for Replies before making its own decision

   **c.** The process of computing the composite metric from individual components

   **d.** The process of coordinating a change in the next hop to a destination by sending out Queries and waiting for Replies before making its own next-hop selection

**22.** What is a diffusing computation?

    **a.** The process of local processing of all received Updates and Replies

    **b.** The process of reevaluating and possibly changing a next hop to a destination locally that does not require the router to send Queries and wait for Replies before making its own decision

    **c.** The process of computing the composite metric from individual components

    **d.** The process of coordinating a change in the next hop to a destination by sending out Queries and waiting for Replies before making its own next-hop selection

**23.** Is the following statement true? "If a router has a Feasible Successor for a destination identified in its topology table, it will always be used in place of the current Successor if the Successor fails."

    **a.** Yes

    **b.** No

**24.** How long at most will a diffusing computation run by default on a router before being terminated forcibly?

    **a.** Indefinitely

    **b.** 3 minutes

    **c.** 3 minutes if the SIA-Query and SIA-Reply messages are not supported; 6 minutes if the SIA-Query and SIA-Reply are supported

    **d.** 15 seconds

**25.** What are some of the factors contributing to the occurrence of SIA states?

    **a.** The use of route filtering and summarization

    **b.** Excessive redundancy in the network

    **c.** The use of the EIGRP Stub feature

    **d.** Excessive network diameter

    **e.** Large amount of routing information

    **f.** The use of the EIGRP Add-Path feature

**26.** What statements are true about running EIGRP Named Mode?

  **a.** Verbal names of EIGRP processes on neighboring routers must match for the routers to establish adjacencies.

  **b.** Multiple autonomous system instances for a single address family can be run in a single EIGRP named process.

  **c.** Multiple autonomous system instances for different address families can be run in a single EIGRP named process.

  **d.** Both classic and named mode can be used on a router as long as they do not conflict on the address family and the autonomous system number.

  **e.** The use of named mode still permits that per-interface commands can be applied to interfaces to maintain backward compatibility.

  **f.** The named mode contains a superset of all commands from the classic mode.

**27.** What statements are true about EIGRP RID?

  **a.** EIGRP has no concept of a RID.

  **b.** The RID is equal to the autonomous system number.

  **c.** The RID is advertised with all external and, in recent IOS releases, also with all internal routes.

  **d.** The RID indicates the immediate neighbor advertising a route.

  **e.** The RID indicates the originator of the routing information.

**28.** What statements are true about unequal cost load balancing in EIGRP?

  **a.** Feasible Successors are required for this feature.

  **b.** Multiple unequal cost paths can be advertised by a router to its neighbors.

  **c.** Each unequal-cost path will be assigned a share of traffic in inverse proportion to how many times worse it is than the current best path.

  **d.** EIGRP allows using any worse-cost path as long as the neighbor advertising this path is closer to the destination than this router.

**29.** What statements are true about the EIGRP Stub Router feature?

  **a.** No Queries are sent by a stub router.

  **b.** No Queries are usually sent to a stub router.

  **c.** All Queries sent to a stub router are responded to by Replies indicating unreachability.

  **d.** Depending on what routes the stub router is allowed to advertise, some Queries can be responded to normally while others will elicit a Reply indicating unreachability.

  **e.** Neighbors of a stub router must be configured to treat that router as a stub.

  **f.** A router is capable of advertising itself as a stub.

**30.** What statements are true about EIGRP authentication?

    **a.** In recent IOS versions, SHA-2 with 256-bit digests is supported.

    **b.** MD5 digest is always supported.

    **c.** Key chains or passwords can be used for SHA-2 authentication.

    **d.** Key chains or passwords can be used for MD5 authentication.

    **e.** IPv6 EIGRP uses IPsec for authentication purposes.

**31.** What of the following are true regarding the default route injection into EIGRP?

    **a.** The **network 0.0.0.0** command is the preferred way of injecting the default route into EIGRP.

    **b.** A default route can be injected into EIGRP by redistribution.

    **c.** A default route can be injected into EIGRP by summarization.

    **d.** Neighbors of stub routers send a default route to stub routers automatically.

# Foundation Topics

## EIGRP Basics and Evolution

Many CCIE candidates have already learned the majority of the details of EIGRP operation and configuration. Because of its former proprietary nature, however, there are many misconceptions and misunderstandings about various fundamental details of EIGRP operation. With that in mind, this chapter strives to review the key terms and concepts in depth, and then get to specific examples that detail EIGRP operation on a Cisco router.

It is noteworthy to mention that in 2013, Cisco decided to open up the EIGRP specification and publish it as an IETF Internet Draft, a precursor to an RFC; the document name is *draft-savage-eigrp*. Basic EIGRP is thus no longer a closed, proprietary protocol. An open source EIGRP implementation based on the Quagga routing platform already exists and is being actively developed.

Table 8-2 lists the selected key features related to EIGRP.

**Table 8-2**   *EIGRP Feature Summary*

| Feature | Description |
| --- | --- |
| Transport | IP, protocol type 88 (does not use UDP or TCP). Implements its own Reliable Transport Protocol, providing reliable unicast and multicast packet delivery. |
| Metric | Based on constrained bandwidth and cumulative delay by default, and optionally load reliability, and extended metrics. |
| Hello interval | Interval at which a router sends EIGRP Hello messages on an interface. |
| Hold timer | Timer used to determine when a neighboring router has failed, based on a router not receiving any EIGRP messages, including Hellos, in this timer period. |
| Update destination address | Normally sent to 224.0.0.10 or FF02::A, with retransmissions being sent to each neighbor's unicast IP address. |
| Full or partial updates | Full updates are used when new neighbors are discovered; otherwise, partial updates are used. |
| Authentication | Supports MD5 and SHA-based authentication. |
| VLSM/classless | EIGRP includes the mask with each route, also allowing it to support discontiguous networks and VLSM. |
| Route Tags | Enables EIGRP to tag and filter internal and external routes using distribute-lists and route-maps. |
| Next-hop field | Supports the advertisement of routes with a different next-hop router than the advertising router. |

| Feature | Description |
|---------|-------------|
| Manual route summarization | Allows route summarization at any point in the EIGRP network. |
| Multiprotocol | Supports the advertisement of IPv4 and IPv6. Former implementations also supported IPX and AppleTalk routes. |

## EIGRP Roots: Interior Gateway Routing Protocol

To understand EIGRP roots better, we start our discussion with a brief look into the past, focusing on a dead protocol that was an immediate predecessor to EIGRP.

In the mid-1980s, Cisco developed the Interior Gateway Routing Protocol (IGRP), an alternative protocol to Routing Information Protocol version 1 (RIPv1). The most significant goal was to eliminate RIP's working but naïve hop count metric and the hop network diameter limitation of 15 hops. IGRP relied on a composite metric made up of a variety of route variables and even went so far as to provide a way for the weighting of specific variables over others so that the protocol could reflect the specific characteristics and needs of a diverse array of networks.

Benefits that IGRP offered over RIP included

■ Wider network diameter, up to 255 hops

■ Complex multivariate metric

■ Unequal-cost load sharing

■ An update period of 90 seconds, three times longer than RIP's

■ A more efficient update packet format

IGRP was designed to interoperate with multiple routed protocols including IPv4, ISO Connectionless Network Protocol (CLNP), Novell IPX, or AppleTalk. Like RIP, IGRP broadcasted a Request packet out all IGRP-enabled interfaces at startup and performed a sanity check on received Update packets to verify that the source address of the packet belonged to the same subnet on which the Update was received. Update packets themselves were sent periodically each 90 seconds.

IGRP was also like RIPv1 in that it was a classful distance-vector protocol that periodically broadcasted its entire gathered knowledge. The protocol also relied on Split Horizon, triggered updates, Invalid after, and Holddown and Flushed after timers for functional stability; IGRP summarized advertised addresses at network boundaries.

Overall, IGRP was better than RIP for larger networks but it still had many of the fundamental limitations found in RIP that had an adverse impact on its scalability and speed of convergence.

## Moving from IGRP to Enhanced IGRP

Most significant IGRP weaknesses and detractors include

- Sending full routing updates periodically

- The lack of variable-length subnet mask (VLSM) support

- Slow convergence

- The lack of adequate loop-prevention mechanisms

Making changes to the metric calculation did not remove the fundamental shortcomings of the basic distance-vector routing protocol paradigm; a new approach was necessary.

To address these specific issues, Cisco created an "Enhanced" version of IGRP. Enhanced Interior Gateway Routing Protocol (EIGRP) is a protocol that is significantly more capable than its predecessor, containing numerous improvements over IGRP. In fact, EIGRP is so much different that simply calling it an "Enhanced IGRP" is somewhat of an understatement. There is in fact very little left of the original IGRP in EIGRP—even though EIGRP still is a distance-vector routing protocol, albeit an advanced one.

IGRP was based on timers, and similarly to RIP, it advertised its entire database of known networks on each Update interval expiry. In both RIP and IGRP, the periodic origination of Update packets served multiple purposes: detecting neighbors, verifying their continuous presence, learning new routes, and refreshing or withdrawing existing learned routes. In fact, these periodic Updates provide two separate and unrelated functions—first, detecting neighbors and their liveliness, and second, carrying routing information. To allow EIGRP to become an incremental, event-based protocol, it was first necessary to decouple building and maintaining adjacencies from exchanging routing information. The first task is accomplished in EIGRP by using a *Hello protocol*. Thanks to the Hello protocol, it is no longer necessary to periodically send Update packets to announce a router's continuous presence on a network; instead, the Hello protocol takes over this responsibility. EIGRP routers use the Hello protocol to build and maintain neighbor adjacencies in a way that's similar to Open Shortest Path First (OSPF) and other protocols. The Hello protocol keeps the periodic nature of former Update packets without carrying the routing information.

To advertise routing information whenever there is a change, without requiring routers to advertise it periodically, EIGRP implements the *Reliable Transport Protocol* (RTP; do not confuse it with the Real-time Transport Protocol, which is a different and unrelated protocol used in media-streaming applications), a Layer 3–independent transport protocol capable of reliable unicast and multicast delivery. The use of RTP allows routers to initially exchange the complete routing information when synchronizing for the first time, and afterward, advertise changed routes only. RTP makes sure that all updates—if any—are delivered reliably. The lack of updates therefore does not indicate a connectivity issue but rather simply a stable network state in which the routing information does not change. The use of Hellos to establish and maintain router adjacencies and RTP to carry all updates reliably allows EIGRP to completely abandon the periodic updating process and operate in an event-driven, incremental fashion.

IGRP as a distance-vector routing protocol was prone to the creation of temporary routing loops during network convergence. To maintain a loop-free operation at every instant, EIGRP uses a so-called *Feasibility Condition* criterion to identify neighbors, providing guaranteed loop-free paths to a given destination. This criterion allows an EIGRP router to avoid forwarding packets to a neighbor that could, even possibly, form a routing loop. Considering the fact that EIGRP is still a distance-vector protocol and carries the same detail of information about the network as IGRP in its messages, the importance of the Feasibility Condition is paramount.

Another important addition working in tandem with the Feasibility Condition is the use of the so-called *diffusing computations.* Under circumstances, a router detecting a topology change can be adversely affected by this change, meaning that the Feasibility Condition can cause its neighbor providing the current least-cost path to be considered ineligible. In this case, an EIGRP router can actively query all its neighbors to update their own best-path selection with respect to the topology change that triggered this event, and reply with their updated distances. Neighbors that are not adversely affected will simply respond right away with a (possibly updated) distance; neighbors that are adversely affected will propagate the query further and can respond only after receiving all replies and making a choice themselves. In a sense, the task of searching for a replacement path to a destination *diffuses* into the affected part of the network, hence the name *diffusing computations.* This way, EIGRP actively involves the affected part of the network into updating the best-path selection in a highly coordinated manner. The use of diffusing computations is at the core of EIGRP's rapid convergence.

To handle multiple topology changes during a single diffusing computation, EIGRP implements a finite state machine called *Diffusing Update Algorithm (DUAL)* that controls the run of a diffusing computation, processing the replies and eventually inserting the gathered information into the routing table or commencing an additional diffusing computation. The DUAL is not the diffusing computation algorithm itself; it is a control mechanism on top of diffusing computations that decides when it is necessary to start a diffusing computation and how the results should be processed.

EIGRP was designed as a successive version of IGRP to allow for an easy migration path. While the mechanisms used in IGRP and EIGRP strongly differ, many of the ideas that worked very well for IGRP were applied to EIGRP. As an example, EIGRP has a default hop-count limitation of 100; however, this value can be manually adjusted using the command illustrated in Example 8-1.

**Example 8-1**  *Adjusting Hop-Count Limitation*

```
Router(config-router)# metric maximum-hops ?
  <1-255>  Hop count
```

Another area of similarity is the choice of metric components. EIGRP basically reuses the metric computation first used by IGRP, including the component metrics of bandwidth, delay, and optionally reliability and load. This similarity will be discussed in further detail in the upcoming sections.

EIGRP makes a distinction between internal and external routes. Internal routes are those injected into EIGRP by the **network** command. External routes are redistributed into EIGRP from a different routing source. EIGRP internal and external routes can be distinguished within the routing table by their default administrative distance (AD). Internal prefixes will have an AD of 90, and external will be 170 by default. Example 8-2 demonstrates how these default values can be changed under the routing protocol.

**Example 8-2**   *Adjusting Administrative Distance Based on Route Type*

```
Router(config-router)# distance eigrp ?
  <1-255>  Distance for internal routes
Router(config-router)# distance eigrp 90 ?
  <1-255>  Distance for external routes
Router(config-router)# distance eigrp 90 100
```

After this fleeting overview of what enhancements EIGRP has over other distance-vector routing protocols, it is time to take an even closer look at the protocol's operation and features.

# EIGRP Metrics, Packets, and Adjacencies

Many people are tempted to overlook or browse past this type of content. Reading through a topic that appears to be all too familiar can be tiring at first, but we nonetheless encourage you to read the following sections very carefully. There are lots of hidden details about EIGRP that we have strived to uncover. Also, it will make concepts like filtration, summarization, and stub routing (to name a few) easier for you to understand.

## EIGRP Classic Metrics

EIGRP uses several types of metrics, also called *component metrics* or *metric components*, to describe selected technical properties of a route. These component metrics are bandwidth, delay, reliability, load, MTU, and hop count. Out of these six components, the first four are combined together using a well-known formula to produce a single number that we will call the *composite metric* or, where there is no risk of confusion, simply as *metric, distance,* or *cost*. This single composite metric is then used by EIGRP to choose the best path toward a destination. Originally, the idea of combining several technical measures of a route into a single number came in IGRP that strived to be "smarter" than RIP and cover more properties of a route in a single metric value. When EIGRP was developed, to serve as a drop-in replacement for IGRP, it retook its system of metric calculation.

The component metrics as described in this section are also called Classic Metrics and are the standard set of metrics supported by all current EIGRP implementations. EIGRP shipped with recent IOS versions also supports so-called Wide Metrics, which expand the allowable range of existing Classic Metrics. These Wide Metrics will be described in the next section.

Let us now have a closer look at the individual Classic Metric components and how EIGRP uses them.

## Bandwidth Metric Component

The bandwidth is a static metric assigned to each router interface using the **bandwidth** interface level command. The meaning of this metric component is obvious: It describes the transmission speed of an interface. The **bandwidth** command expresses the interface bandwidth in terms of kilobits per second. If no **bandwidth** command is configured explicitly, IOS assigns an implicit bandwidth value to each interface, depending on its hardware type and operational characteristics. With selected interface types, as with Ethernet interfaces, the implicit bandwidth value reflects the true speed negotiated by the interface with its link partner. On other interface types, the value has no realistic relation to the interface capabilities (common with Serial or Tunnel interfaces, for example).

When calculating the composite metric to a destination, EIGRP takes the *minimal bandwidth* along the route into account. This is done by comparing the bandwidth as advertised by a neighboring router to the bandwidth of the interface toward the advertising neighbor, and taking the lower value of these two.

With Classic Metrics, EIGRP is capable of describing the bandwidth in the range of 1 kbps up to 10 Gbps.

## Delay Metric Component

The delay is a static metric assigned to each interface using the **delay** interface command. This metric component estimates the serialization delay incurred by the interface. Of course, in real life, the serialization delay would depend both on the interface transmission speed as well as the serialized packet's size. Being a static value not related to any true characteristic of an interface, the delay metric component of an interface can be seen more like an average delay incurred by the interface for typical traffic.

The **delay** command expresses the delay in somewhat inconvenient units—tens of microseconds. Configuring a **delay** of 123 on an interface defines its delay to be 1230 microseconds. The **show interface** command output already reports interface delay directly in microseconds. This difference between the units used in **show interface** output and in the **delay** command is subtle but significant. The **show interface** output will always display a value ten times higher than the configured value. If the **delay** is not configured explicitly, IOS assigns an implicit delay value to each interface, depending on the interface hardware type.

When calculating the composite metric to a destination, EIGRP takes the *total delay* into account. This is done by taking the delay as advertised by a neighboring router and summing it with the delay of the interface toward the advertising neighbor.

With Classic Metrics, EIGRP is capable of describing the delay in the range of 10 to 167,772,140 microseconds (1 to 16,777,214 tens of microseconds). A delay of 16,777,215 tens of microseconds is used to indicate an infinite distance and is the key to the ability of advertising an unreachable network. Split Horizon with Poisoned Reverse, Route

Poisoning, withdrawing a route—all these techniques in EIGRP use the maximum delay as an indication of an unreachable route.

## Reliability Metric Component

The reliability is a dynamically estimated metric of an interface that evaluates its reliability, or the ratio between the count of successfully received and the count of all received frames. This ratio is expressed as a fraction of 255. To illustrate, a reliability of 255 expresses a 100 percent reliability, a reliability of 230 expresses a 90 percent reliability, and a reliability of 26 expresses a 10 percent reliability. The reliability metric is dynamically updated by IOS.

When calculating the composite metric to a destination, EIGRP takes the *minimal reliability* into account. This is done by comparing the reliability as advertised by a neighboring router to the reliability of the interface toward the advertising neighbor, and taking the lower value of these two.

There is an important fact regarding the EIGRP's handling of reliability metric. While EIGRP does advertise the information about the path reliability and optionally factors it into the composite metric (this depends on K-value settings described later in this section), EIGRP *does not* send updates when an interface's reliability changes. In other words, a change in interface reliability value does not trigger sending EIGRP updates. The reliability metric of a route is just a snapshot of its then-current reliability when it was last advertised.

To understand this, recall that EIGRP metrics are retaken from IGRP, which was a timer-driven protocol. EIGRP, on the other hand, is an event-driven protocol. If the reliability metric change was a trigger event for EIGRP, it could potentially induce a routing table oscillation into the network, bringing the traffic on and off the unreliable link and aggravating the swings in the reliability metric more and more, creating a feedback loop. In fact, the reliability metric component was retaken into EIGRP primarily to facilitate the smooth transition from IGRP. As a result, in EIGRP, the reliability metric component is currently just a relic carried over from its predecessor, with no particular usability.

## Load Metric Component

The load is a dynamically estimated metric of an interface that measures the amount of traffic flowing through the interface in relation to its maximum capacity. Similar to reliability, the load is also expressed as a fraction of 255, with the load of 1 representing an empty interface and the load of 255 representing a fully utilized interface. To account for large differences in the momentary load caused by bursty traffic, IOS actually computes an exponentially weighted average over the momentary load that smooths out short-lived load swings. Because an interface can be differently utilized in the ingress and egress data flow direction, IOS maintains two independent load metric counters, the Txload for outgoing traffic and Rxload for incoming traffic.

When calculating the composite metric to a destination, EIGRP takes the *maximal Txload* into account. This is done by comparing the load as advertised by a neighboring router to the Txload of the interface toward the advertising neighbor, and taking the higher value of these two.

EIGRP's handling of the load metric component is the same as with reliability: While advertised and optionally factored into the composite metric, the changes in the Txload values on interfaces do not trigger EIGRP updates. The load metric of a route is just a snapshot of its then-current load when it was last advertised. The load, along with the reliability, is a relic from IGRP with no particular usability in EIGRP.

## MTU Metric Component

There is widespread confusion regarding the maximum transmission unit (MTU) metric component in EIGRP and its use. Similar to bandwidth and reliability, EIGRP advertises the minimum MTU along the route to the destination. However, even though carried in EIGRP messages, the MTU is completely unused in the best-path selection process. It is not factored into the composite metric, nor is it used as any kind of a tiebreaker. Simply put, the use of the MTU in EIGRP's best-path selection algorithm has never been implemented.

## Hop Count Metric Component

The hop count metric component is simply a counter of routers (hops) in the path toward the destination. It is just a fallback security measure: EIGRP routers can be configured to advertise each route having its hop count over a predefined threshold as unreachable, thereby breaking any potential routing loops. By default, this limit is 100, and can be configured in the range of 1 to 255. The hop count is not factored into the composite metric calculation and does not impact the best-path selection in any way.

## Calculating the Composite Metric

Because EIGRP treats each metric component differently (delay is summed, bandwidth and reliability are minimized, load is maximized), EIGRP routers exchange these component metrics as separate values. To arrive at a single composite metric value, each router must independently compute the resulting composite metric on its own. This composite metric is used locally on a router, and is never advertised as a single number in EIGRP messages. The only exception to this rule is when a route is redistributed from one EIGRP process to another. Even in this case, however, the composite metric of the redistributed route is retaken only for diagnostic purposes and carried separately from the seed component metrics specified in the **redistribute** command that activates the redistribution and defines the starting component metrics for redistributed routes.

Using the bandwidth, delay, reliability, and load, each EIGRP router computes a composite metric value using the formula shown in Figure 8-1.

$$ CM = \left( K_1 \cdot BW_S + K_2 \cdot \frac{BW_S}{256 - Lo_{Max}} + K_3 \cdot D_S \right) \cdot \left( \frac{K_5}{K_4 + R_{Min}} \right) $$

$$ BW_S = \frac{256 \cdot 10^7}{Bandwidth_{Min}} $$

$$ D_S = 256 \cdot Delay_{Summed} $$

**Figure 8-1**   *Classic Composite Metric Computation Formula*

The constants $K_1$ through $K_5$, commonly called K-values, are weight constants in the range 0–255 that can be tweaked to influence the impact of individual metric components on the overall composite metric. It is crucial that all EIGRP routers in an autonomous system compute the composite metric in the same way. Therefore, K-values on all routers must match. If K-values on two neighboring routers differ, the routers will be unable to establish an adjacency. By default, $K_1$ and $K_3$ are set to 1, and all other K-values are set to 0, causing EIGRP to take only bandwidth and delay into account. If $K_5$ is 0 (which it is by default), the entire term in the right parentheses, that is, $K_5/(K_4 + R_{Min})$, is not used in the metric computation.

The $BW_{Scaled}$ term is in effect telling how many times the minimal bandwidth along the path is smaller than a $10^7$-Kbps = 10-Gbps link, multiplied by 256. The $D_{Scaled}$ term is a sum of all interface delays along the path to the destination in tens of microseconds, multiplied by 256. The multiplication by 256 in both terms is the result of expanding the former IGRP 24-bit metric into a 32-bit metric used by EIGRP. The remaining terms—$Lo_{Max}$ standing for maximum load and $R_{Min}$ standing for minimum reliability—are taken without further modification.

Note once again that neither MTU nor hop count is a part of the composite metric formula. The hop count only causes a route reaching the predefined hop count limit to be advertised as unreachable; the MTU is unused. Neither of these metric components influences the choice of best path.

## EIGRP Wide Metrics

With the speeds of interfaces ever increasing, the EIGRP Classic Metrics faced issues with interfaces faster than 1 Gbps. The Bandwidth component itself is unable to differentiate between a 10-Gbps and faster interfaces. In addition, the default Delay component metric is already set to the lowest value of 1 (10 microseconds) on 1-Gbps interfaces and cannot be made smaller on faster interfaces. Also, the bandwidth and delay metric components are carried in EIGRP packets in their scaled form. This requires each router to descale them first to obtain the $Bandwidth_{Min}$ and $Delay_{Summed}$ values to perform the necessary minimization of bandwidth and summing the delay, and then scale them again when computing the composite metric and advertising the route to its neighbors. Because Cisco routers perform integer arithmetic, the round-off errors during this repetitive scaling and descaling can introduce a gradual loss of resolution.

These reasons prompted EIGRP developers to design an improved set of metrics that allow for a greater range of key parameters and that are carried in EIGRP packets in their raw form, avoiding the loss of precision. These metrics are amply named Wide Metrics. To see whether your router supports Wide Metrics, check out the output of selected **show eigrp** commands, as shown in Example 8-3.

**Example 8-3**    *Confirming the Presence of EIGRP Wide Metrics Support*

```
! In the show eigrp plugins command output, check whether the version
! of eigrp-release plugin is at least 8.00.00. In this output,
! the eigrp-release plugin is of version 12.00.00.

Router# show eigrp plugins
EIGRP feature plugins::::
    eigrp-release    :  12.00.00 : Portable EIGRP Release
                     :   2.00.09 : Source Component Release(rel12)
    parser           :   2.02.00 : EIGRP Parser Support
    igrp2            :   2.00.00 : Reliable Transport/Dual Database
[ ... output omitted ... ]

! Alternatively, check out the output of show eigrp tech-support command
! and look for Wide Metrics support claimed explicitly

Router# show eigrp tech-support
EIGRP feature plugins::::
    eigrp-release    :  12.00.00 : Portable EIGRP Release
                     :   2.00.09 : Source Component Release(rel12)
                                   + HMAC-SHA-256 Authentication
    parser           :   2.02.00 : EIGRP Parser Support
    igrp2            :   2.00.00 : Reliable Transport/Dual Database
                                   + Wide Metrics
[ ... output omitted ... ]

! Yet another easy way of detecting the support of Wide Metrics is the
! show ip protocols output. Note the presence of the K₆ constant,
! the rib-scale of 128 and 64-bit metric version - all these indicate
! that Wide Metrics are supported.

Router# show ip protocols
Routing Protocol is "eigrp 1"
  Outgoing update filter list for all interfaces is not set
  Incoming update filter list for all interfaces is not set
  Default networks flagged in outgoing updates
  Default networks accepted from incoming updates
  EIGRP-IPv4 VR(Test) Address-Family Protocol for AS(1)
    Metric weight K1=0, K2=0, K3=1, K4=0, K5=0 K6=0
    Metric rib-scale 128
    Metric version 64bit
[ ... output omitted ... ]
```

With Wide Metrics, the general philosophy of EIGRP metrics is maintained; however, the metric components whose range has been extended carry a new name to distinguish them from their classic counterparts.

EIGRP Wide Metrics consist of following components:

- **Throughput:** This metric is analogous to the classic Bandwidth component. The throughput metric of an interface is calculated as $65536 \times 10^7$/Interface Bandwidth, with the interface bandwidth expressed in kbps. The throughput component effectively tells how many times slower the interface is than a 655.36-Tbps link.

- **Latency:** This metric is analogous to the classic Delay component. The latency metric of an interface is calculated as $65536 \times$ Interface Delay/$10^6$, with the interface delay expressed in picoseconds. Because the delay metrics have sensible defaults only on interfaces with physical bandwidths up to 1 Gbps, the computation of per-interface delay metric differs based on its physical capability and configuration, making it somewhat counterintuitive.

  - On interfaces physically operating on speeds of 1 Gbps and lower without **bandwidth** and **delay** commands, the interface delay is simply its IOS-based *default delay* converted to picoseconds.

  - On interfaces physically operating on speeds over 1 Gbps without **bandwidth** and **delay** commands, the interface delay is computed as $10^{13}$ / interface *default bandwidth*.

  - On interfaces configured with the explicit **bandwidth** command and without the **delay** command, regardless of their physical operating speed, the interface delay is the IOS-based *default delay* converted to picoseconds.

  - On interfaces configured with explicit **delay** command, regardless of their physical operating speed and the **bandwidth** setting, the interface delay is computed as its specified delay value converted to picoseconds, that is, $10^7 \times$ value of the **delay** command (recall that the **delay** command defines the delay in tens of microseconds).

- **Reliability:** This metric is identical to the classic Reliability component and has not changed in Wide Metrics.

- **Load:** This metric is identical to the classic Load metric component and has not changed in Wide Metrics.

- **MTU:** This metric is identical to the classic MTU metric component, and just like in Classic Metrics, it is advertised but unused.

- **Hop Count:** This metric is identical to the classic Hop Count metric component, and just like in Classic Metrics, it is advertised but unused in path selection; it only prevents potential routing loops.

- **Extended Metrics:** These metric components are considered as placeholders for future extensions to the composite metric computation. As of this writing, three extended metrics were defined: Jitter, Energy, and Quiescent Energy. To incorporate these components into the composite metric, the $K_6$ constant was introduced. These metric components are not usually used or supported.

Using the throughput, latency, reliability, load, and extended metrics, each EIGRP router computes a wide composite metric value using the formula shown in Figure 8-2.

$$WM = \left( K_1 \cdot T_{Min} \;+\; K_2 \cdot \frac{T_{Min}}{256 - Lo_{Max}} \;+\; K_3 \cdot La_{Summed} \right.$$
$$\left. +\; K_6 \cdot ExtM \right) \cdot \left( \frac{K_5}{K_4 + R_{Min}} \right)$$

$$T_{Min} = \frac{65536 \cdot 10^7}{Bandwidth_{Min}}$$

$$La_{Summed} = \sum \frac{65536 \cdot Delay_{Interface}}{10^6}$$

$$Delay_{Interface} = \begin{cases} DefaultDelay_{Interface} \; [\text{picosec}] & \text{for interfaces} \le 1 \text{ Gbps} \\ & \text{or where } \textbf{bandwidth} \text{ is configured,} \\[2ex] \dfrac{10^{13}}{DefaultBandwidth_{Interface}} & \text{for interfaces} > 1 \text{ Gbps,} \\[2ex] 10^7 \cdot ConfiguredDelay_{Interface} & \text{where } \textbf{delay} \text{ is configured} \end{cases}$$

**Figure 8-2**  *Wide Composite Metric Computation Formula*

In this formula, $T_{Min}$ is the throughput computed using the least bandwidth along the path to the destination, $La_{Summed}$ is the sum of latencies for each interface along the path to the destination, $Lo_{Max}$ is the maximum load on the path, $R_{Min}$ is the minimum reliability on the path, and ExtM are the extended metrics.

The Wide Metric support is available when EIGRP is configured in named mode as described later in the chapter, and is automatically activated—there is no command to control the activation of Wide Metrics. EIGRP routers supporting Wide Metrics automatically detect whether their neighbors also support Wide Metrics, and use the appropriate metric type when talking to them. Wide Metrics are preferred; if all neighbors on an interface support Wide Metrics, they will be used automatically instead of Classic Metrics. In the case of mixed neighbors on a common interface, EIGRP routers supporting Wide Metrics will use both metric formats in their messages, allowing each neighbor to process the metric format it supports.

Because the Wide Metrics composite value can well result in a number wider than 32 bits while the routing table (Routing Information Base, RIB) is capable of handling only 32-bit metrics, the Wide Metrics composite value has to be downscaled before the route can be passed down to the RIB in IOS. This is done by dividing the Wide Metrics composite value by a factor configured in the **metric rib-scale** EIGRP command. The default value is 128 and can be configured in the range 1–255. Note that this downscaled value is not used by EIGRP in any way. EIGRP makes all its path selections based on the Wide Metrics composite value; only after a best path toward a destination is selected, its composite metric value is downscaled as the route is installed to the RIB.

## Tweaking Interface Metrics to Influence Path Selection

As should be obvious from the discussion about EIGRP metric components so far, the only EIGRP metric components that can be manually influenced are the Bandwidth and Delay. It might be tempting to use the **bandwidth** command to force EIGRP to use or not to use a particular path. The answer to this idea, however, is a resolute and resounding *no*. Following is an adapted quotation from the public EIGRP Internet Draft document *draft-savage-eigrp* that considers this issue to be grave enough to warrant a special mention:

*When trying to manually influence EIGRP path selection through interface bandwidth/delay configuration, the modification of bandwidth is discouraged for following reasons:*

■ *The change will only affect the path selection if the configured value is the lowest bandwidth over the entire path. Changing the bandwidth can have impact beyond affecting the EIGRP metrics. For example, quality of service (QoS) also looks at the bandwidth on an interface.*

■ *EIGRP by default throttles to use 50 percent of the configured bandwidth. Lowering the bandwidth can cause problems like starving EIGRP neighbors from getting packets because of the throttling back. Configuring an excessively high bandwidth can lead EIGRP to consume more bandwidth than physically available, leading to packet drops.*

■ *Changing the delay does not impact other protocols nor does it cause EIGRP to throttle back, and because, as it's the sum of all delays, has a direct effect on path selection.*

In other words, the **bandwidth** parameter of an interface should always be configured to the true bandwidth of the interface and should *never* be used to influence EIGRP's path selection. Instead, the **delay** is a parameter that has absolutely no impact on any other IOS subsystem and even to EIGRP; it constitutes only a constant to be summed together with the existing path delay to compute the total path delay. Being the only cumulative parameter in EIGRP's metric computation, the **delay** is the right metric that can be manually modified to affect the best-path selection.

## EIGRP Packet Format

EIGRP packets are carried directly in IP packets, using protocol number 88. The maximum length of an EIGRP packet is derived from the maximum IP MTU on the particular interface—typically 1500 bytes for the entire IP packet, leaving 1480 bytes for the EIGRP packet itself.

Figure 8-3 and Table 8-3 explain the generic format of an EIGRP packet. Each EIGRP packet carries a 20-byte header, followed by a variably sized body indicated in Figure 8-3 as *TLVs*, standing for Type-Length-Value triplets. These TLVs carry diverse information including EIGRP and TLV versions, K-values, Hold timers, control information to facilitate reliable multicasting, and most importantly, route reachability information. With respect to RTP, there is no clearly delineated RTP header. Instead, the Flags, Sequence number, and Acknowledgment number fields are the ones that provide most of the RTP functionality in EIGRP; some others are implemented using specific TLVs. With a certain degree of simplification, the entire EIGRP packet header can also be considered an RTP header.

```
|<------------------------------ 32 Bit ------------------------------>|

|  VERSION=2  |   OPCODE   |             CHECKSUM              |
|                          FLAGS                              |
|                    SEQUENCE NUMBER                          |
|                 ACKNOWLEDGMENT NUMBER                       |
|   VIRTUAL ROUTER ID    |   AUTONOMOUS SYSTEM NUMBER         |
|                          TLVs                               |
|                          ...                                |
|                          ...                                |
|                          ...                                |
```

**Figure 8-3**  *Basic EIGRP Packet Format*

**Table 8-3**  *EIGRP Packet Format Details*

| Field | Description |
|---|---|
| Version Field | 4-bit field used to indicate the protocol version of the originating EIGRP process. The version of the EIGRP protocol itself has not changed since its release and is set to 2. |
| Opcode | 4-bit field that specifies the EIGRP packet type. Relevant types are 1 = Update, 3 = Query, 4 = Reply, 5 = Hello/Ack, 10 = SIA Query, 11 = SIA Reply. Other types have been allocated for different, mostly unimplemented purposes, or are obsolete; only the indicated packet types are used. |
| Checksum | 24-bit field that is used to run a sanity check on the EIGRP packet. This field is based on the entire EIGRP packet excluding the IP header. |
| Flags | 32-bit field indicating specific flags: 0x1 = Init (used during initial adjacency buildup), 0x2 = Conditional Receive (used by RTP to allow this message to be received only by a subset of receivers), 0x4 = Restart (indicates that a router has restarted), 0x8 = End-of-Table (indicates that the transmission of the entire EIGRP database is complete). |

| Field | Description |
|---|---|
| Sequence | 32-bit field that contains a sequence number used by RTP. This facilitates orderly delivery of reliable packets. |
| Acknowledgment | 32-bit field used by RTP that contains the sequence number of the last packet heard from the neighbor to which this packet is being sent. A Hello packet with a nonzero ACK field will be treated as an ACK packet rather than as a Hello. Note that an ACK field will only be nonzero if the packet itself is unicast because acknowledgments are never multicasted. |
| Virtual Router ID | 16-bit field identifying the virtual router this packet is associated with. Currently used values are 0x1 = Unicast Address Family, 0x2 = Multicast Address Family, 0x8000 = Unicast Service Address Family (in Service Advertisement Framework). |
| Autonomous System Number | 16-bit field that identifies the number of the EIGRP domain. |
| Type-Length-Value | Field used to carry route entries as well as provide EIGRP DUAL information. EIGRP supports several different types of TLVs: |
| | 0x0001 EIGRP Parameters (*General TLV Types*) |
| | 0x0002 Authentication Type (*General TLV Types*) |
| | 0x0003 Sequence (*General TLV Types*) |
| | 0x0004 Software Version (*General TLV Types*) |
| | 0x0005 Next Multicast Sequence (*General TLV Types*) |
| | 0x0102 IPv4 Internal Routes (*IP-Specific TLV Types*) |
| | 0x0103 IPv4 External Routes (*IP-Specific TLV Types*) |
| | 0x0402 IPv6 Internal Routes (*IP-Specific TLV Types*) |
| | 0x0403 IPv6 External Routes (*IP-Specific TLV Types*) |
| | 0x0602 Multi Protocol Internal Routes (*AFI-Specific TLV Types*) |
| | 0x0603 Multi Protocol External Routes (*AFI-Specific TLV Types*) |

TLVs (Type-Length-Values) are a particular format of storing and transmitting different types of information in a single datagram; each TLV contains a particular piece of information that the sender wants to advertise. TLVs are not only found within EIGRP packets; they are also common in other protocols like IS-IS, CDP, and LLDP as well.

As the name suggests, TLVs are formatted as triplets containing Type, Length, and Value fields. The Type and Length fields are fixed in size (typically 1–4 bytes), and the Value field is of variable size.

■ **Type:** A numeric code that indicates the kind of information stored in the Value field.

- **Length:** The total size of Type, Length, and Value fields. Note that some other protocols (not EIGRP) store only the length of the Value field in the Length.

- **Value:** Variable-sized series of bytes that contain the actual information.

Each Internal and External Route TLV contains a single route entry. The Update, Query, Reply, SIA-Query, and SIA-Reply packets contain at least one such TLV to advertise a particular network or to query for it. The list, or the array (the vector), of Internal and External Route TLVs in these packets is what constitutes the distance-vector nature of EIGRP. Each TLV advertises a particular network and a distance toward it, with multiple TLVs constituting a vector of such distances.

Details about the format and use of individual TLVs in EIGRP can be found in the EIGRP Internet Draft published on the Internet Engineering Task Force (IETF) web page, at the time of this writing named *draft-savage-eigrp*.

## EIGRP Packets

EIGRP uses seven different packet types when communicating with its neighboring routers:

- Hello packets
- Acknowledgment packets
- Update packets
- Query packets
- Reply packets
- SIA-Query packets
- SIA-Reply packets

The Update, Query, Reply, SIA-Query, and SIA-Reply packets are also called *reliable packets* because EIGRP makes sure that they are all delivered and in proper order.

### EIGRP Packets in Action

Statistics about all sent and received EIGRP packets can be obtained using the **show ip eigrp traffic** command, as illustrated in Example 8-4.

**Example 8-4**  *EIGRP Traffic Counters*

```
R1# show ip eigrp traffic
EIGRP-IPv4 VR(CCIE) Address-Family Traffic Statistics for AS(1)
  Hellos sent/received: 1132/6090
  Updates sent/received: 169/428
  Queries sent/received: 0/0
  Replies sent/received: 0/0
  Acks sent/received: 74/191
```

```
SIA-Queries sent/received: 0/0
SIA-Replies sent/received: 0/0
Hello Process ID: 246
PDM Process ID: 244
Socket Queue: 0/10000/7/0 (current/max/highest/drops)
Input Queue: 0/2000/7/0 (current/max/highest/drops)
```

The sections that follow describe all these packets in more detail.

## Hello Packets

EIGRP sends periodic Hello packets once it has been enabled on a router for a particular interface. These Hello messages are used to identify neighbors, verify whether these neighbors are compatibly configured (residing on a common IP subnet, using the same AS number, K-values, and authentication if configured), and serve as a keepalive mechanism between neighbors. EIGRP Hello packets are sent to the link-local multicast group address 224.0.0.10 in IPv4, and FF02::A in IPv6. If static neighbors are configured, Hello packets are sent as unicasts to the neighbor's explicitly configured address. The default Hello interval is 5 seconds; on NBMA interfaces with the bandwidth setting of 1544 kbps and less, the default Hello interval is 60 seconds. EIGRP Hello packets have an Opcode of 5 and are not acknowledged.

## Acknowledgment Packets

An EIGRP Acknowledgment (ACK) packet is used to acknowledge selected received EIGRP packets to facilitate their reliable delivery. ACKs are sent in response to Update, Query, Reply, SIA-Query, and SIA-Reply packets, and are always unicasted to the sender of the acknowledged packet. With respect to the packet format, EIGRP ACK is essentially a Hello packet with an empty body (that is, no TLVs), carrying only the common EIGRP packet header as shown in Figure 8-3, and having a non-zero Acknowledgment number field whose value is set to the Sequence number of the reliable packet being acknowledged. The ACK uses the same Opcode as the Hello packet, that is, 5.

Note in Figure 8-3 that the header of each EIGRP packet carries an Acknowledgment number field. In EIGRP, it is allowed to use any unicast reliable packet to also carry an acknowledgment number. If a router has both a unicast reliable packet to send to a neighbor and also needs to acknowledge a previously received reliable packet from that neighbor, the sequence number of the received reliable packet can be sent along with the outbound reliable packet in its Acknowledgment number field. It is not necessary to send a standalone ACK in this case; the unicast reliable packet carrying a nonzero Acknowledgment number field will be processed by its recipient both by its true type and as an ACK.

EIGRP's use of the Acknowledgment number field is very similar to that of TCP: After a TCP session is established, each TCP segment can both contain data in its payload and carry an acknowledgment in its Acknowledgment number header field. If a sender of a

TCP segment has any data to send to its peer, it will send it along with the acknowledgment of the last received octet (plus 1). If there is no data to be sent to the peer, only a TCP segment header with an empty body is sent, carrying the proper acknowledgment. In EIGRP, it is quite the same: If both an ACK and a reliable packet are waiting to be sent to the same neighbor, EIGRP can put the acknowledgment number into the reliable packet's Acknowledgment number field, saving the need to send a standalone ACK. If there is no reliable packet waiting to be sent to a neighbor, just an acknowledgment is outstanding, EIGRP chooses the packet type for which it makes most sense to have an empty body, which is obviously a Hello packet, to carry the acknowledgment number, hence the standalone ACK—in reality a Hello with no TLVs and just its Acknowledgment number field set. Noting that the ACK essentially consists of just the EIGRP packet header, the similarity to TCP's use of segment headers with empty payloads to carry acknowledgments is striking.

Keep in mind that out of reliable packets, only those that are unicasted can be also used to carry acknowledgment numbers. It would not make sense to put acknowledgment numbers into multicast reliable packets as they are received by multiple routers while the acknowledgment is itself always relevant only to a single packet from a single neighbor.

## Update Packets

EIGRP Update packets contain routing information updates and are used to convey the reachability of destinations. Update packets can be both unicasted and multicasted. Regarding the use of multicast or unicast to send Update packets, the rules can be summarized as follows:

- During a new adjacency buildup, Update packets are unicasted between the newly discovered neighbors. In specific cases, when multiple new neighbors are detected on a single multiaccess interface in a short time span, EIGRP might choose to synchronize to them using multicasts for efficiency reasons (for example, when a hub router in a Dynamic Multipoint VPN [DMVPN] network starts and detects tens or hundreds of spoke routers). Details on the choice process of unicast or multicast Update packets during adjacency buildup are proprietary. The particular choice only impacts the efficiency of the initial synchronization process, and has no influence on the actual contents of exchanged information.

- After routers have fully synchronized, further Updates are sent as multicasts.

- If a neighbor does not acknowledge the arrival of an Update packet, EIGRP will retransmit the Update as unicast to the unresponsive neighbor.

- On point-to-point interfaces and for statically configured neighbors, EIGRP always uses unicast to send Updates.

Update packets are delivered reliably, meaning that they are always acknowledged and retransmitted if no acknowledgment is heard in a certain time. Update packets are assigned an Opcode of 1.

## Query Packet

EIGRP Query packets are used to involve neighbors in the task of searching for the best route toward a destination. Similarly to Updates, Queries are also delivered reliably. Queries can be both unicasted and multicasted; by default, on multiaccess interfaces with only dynamic neighbors, Queries are sent as multicasts. If not acknowledged in proper time by a neighbor, a Query is retransmitted to the unresponsive neighbor as unicast. On point-to-point interfaces and toward statically configured neighbors, Queries are always sent as unicasts. Note that while each received Query must be acknowledged by sending an ACK, this ACK does not constitute a response to the Query message, only an acknowledgment that the Query has been received. The following packet type, the Reply, is used for that purpose. EIGRP Query packets are assigned an Opcode of 3.

## Reply Packets

EIGRP Reply packets are sent in response to Query packets and carry their sender's current distance to the destination after taking into account the topology change that prompted the Query. Reply packets are always unicasted to the originator of the Query and delivered reliably. The EIGRP Reply packets are assigned an Opcode of 4.

## SIA-Query and SIA-Reply Packets

These two packet types are used during a prolonged diffusing computation to verify whether a neighbor that has not yet sent a Reply to a Query is truly reachable and still engaged in the corresponding diffusing computation. The SIA-Query packet is used to ask a particular neighbor to confirm that it is still working on the original Query. If the neighbor is reachable and is still engaged in the diffusing computation for the destination specified in the SIA-Query, it will immediately respond with an SIA-Reply packet. As a result, the timer that governs the maximum time a diffusing computation is allowed to run is reset, giving the computation extra time to finish. Both SIA-Query and SIA-Reply packets are unicast and reliably delivered. SIA-Query uses an Opcode of 10, and SIA-Reply uses an Opcode of 11.

## Reliable Transport Protocol

The Reliable Transport Protocol (RTP) manages the delivery and reception of EIGRP packets. Reliable delivery means that delivery is guaranteed and that packets will be delivered in order. This is accomplished by means of a Cisco-invented algorithm known as reliable multicast. Packet types that are to be delivered reliably are Update, Query, Reply, SIA-Query, and SIA-Reply, regardless of whether they are unicasted or multicasted (SIA-Query, Reply, and SIA-Reply are only unicasted, of course). Each of these packets carries a nonzero Sequence number in its header. The Sequence number is a global value maintained per each EIGRP process instance on a router and is incremented whenever one of these packets is originated by the instance, regardless of which EIGRP-enabled interface the packet is going to be sent from. Each neighbor receiving an Update, Query, Reply, SIA-Query, or SIA-Reply is required to send back an ACK packet with the

Acknowledgment number set to the Sequence number of the packet to be acknowledged. A neighbor can also acknowledge a reliable packet by "piggybacking" the acknowledgment onto its own reliable packet (if it has any to send to this router) by appropriately setting the Acknowledgment number field in the packet's header, as explained earlier in the "Acknowledgment Packets" section. If an acknowledgment is not received within a certain time period, the packet is retransmitted as unicast to the unresponsive neighbor.

Packets that are not to be delivered reliably (Hello and ACK packets) set their Sequence number to zero and do not cause the global Sequence number to increase.

With a naïve reliable multicast, each recipient of a multicasted message must acknowledge its arrival before the sender can move on to transmit another message. If some recipient does not acknowledge the message, the sender has to postpone further sending of multicast packets and retransmit the missing message to the intended recipient as unicast until the recipient successfully acknowledges its arrival. Obviously, a single misbehaving, overloaded, or poorly connected recipient can negatively impact the performance of the entire reliable multicast streaming. A natural solution would be to continue sending the multicast packets while, in parallel, retransmitting the unacknowledged and subsequent delayed packets in their proper order to the "lagging" recipient as unicasts to allow it to eventually catch up. This poses a problem, however: The lagging neighbor is still a member of the multicast group, and if it by chance received the next multicast packet without first receiving the packet it has missed before, it would be processing the streamed messages out of correct order.

To cope with this situation, RTP has an additional distinctive feature called Conditional Receive. This feature allows EIGRP to partition all its neighbors on a multiaccess interface into two groups: a group of well-behaved neighbors that have been able to acknowledge all multicast messages sent so far and a group of "lagging" routers that have failed to acknowledge at least one transmitted reliable EIGRP packet and that must be handled individually. If EIGRP wants to continue sending the multicast packets in parallel with retransmitting the unacknowledged packets to the lagging routers as unicasts, it has to send the in-order multicast packets with a special flag saying "this packet is only for those routers that have received all multicast packets so far."

This is accomplished by the sender first transmitting a Hello packet with two specific TLVs called the Sequence TLV and the Next Multicast Sequence TLV, often called a Sequenced Hello. The Next Multicast Sequence TLV contains the upcoming sequence number of the next reliable multicasted message. The Sequence TLV contains a list of all lagging neighbors by their IP address, in effect saying "whoever finds himself in this list, *ignore* the next multicast message with the indicated sequence number." A neighbor receiving this Sequenced Hello packet and *not finding* itself in the Sequence TLV will know that it is expected to receive the upcoming multicast packet, and will put itself into a so-called Conditional Receive mode (CR-mode). A neighbor receiving this Sequenced Hello packet and finding itself in the Sequence TLV, or a neighbor not receiving this Hello packet at all for whatever reason will not put itself into the CR-mode. Afterward, the sending router will send the next multicast packet with the CR flag set in its Flags field. Routers in CR-mode will process this packet as usual and then exit the CR-mode; routers not in CR-mode will ignore it. As a result, the router is able to continue using multicast with those routers that have no issues receiving and acknowledging it, while making sure that the lagging neighbors won't process the multicasts until they are able to catch up. Each lagging neighbor that has not acknowledged one or more multicast packets will be sent these packets as unicasts in their proper sequence.

The time to wait for an ACK before declaring a neighbor as lagging and switching from multicast to unicast is specified by the *multicast flow timer*. The time between the subsequent unicasts is specified by the *retransmission timeout (RTO)*. Both the multicast flow timer and the RTO are calculated for each neighbor from the *smooth round-trip time (SRTT)*. The SRTT is the average elapsed time, measured in milliseconds, between the transmission of a reliable packet to the neighbor and the receipt of an acknowledgment. The formulas for calculating the exact values of the SRTT, the RTO, and the multicast flow timer are beyond the scope of this book.

## Router Adjacencies

EIGRP routers establish and maintain neighbor adjacencies. EIGRP by default discovers neighboring routers dynamically, or it can discover neighbors through manual administrator configuration (static).

*Dynamic* neighbor discovery is performed by sending EIGRP Hello packets to the destination multicast group address 224.0.0.10 or FF02::A. This is performed as soon as EIGRP is activated on an interface. *Static* EIGRP neighbor relationships require manual neighbor configuration on the router. When static EIGRP neighbors are configured, the local router uses the unicast neighbor address to send packets to these routers. You would typically use static neighbor configuration when being deployed across media that does not natively support broadcast or multicast packets, such as Frame Relay.

After a static neighbor is defined, all EIGRP multicasts on the interface through which the neighbor is reachable will be disabled. As a result, EIGRP-enabled routers will not establish an adjacency if one router is configured to use unicast (static) while another uses multicast (dynamic) on the same link. Here's another way of putting this rule: Either all neighbors on a common network segment are statically configured for each other, or none of them are.

It is important to understand that simply enabling EIGRP between two or more routers does not guarantee that a neighbor relationship will be established. An EIGRP neighbor relationship requires that neighbors agree on all the following parameters:

- EIGRP Authentication Parameters (if configured)

- EIGRP K-Values

- EIGRP Autonomous System (AS) Number

- Use of primary addresses for EIGRP neighbor relationships

- Use of the common IP network address on a single subnet

If two routers differ in any of these parameters, they will not become EIGRP neighbors.

Note that the timers (that is, Hello and Hold) do not need to match between neighbors. The default *Hello* interval (60 seconds on nonbroadcast multiaccess [NBMA] interfaces with the configured bandwidth equal to T1 or slower, and 5 seconds on all other interfaces) can be changed with the interface command illustrated in Example 8-5.

**Example 8-5**  *Adjusting EIGRP Hello Intervals*

```
Router(config-if)# ip hello-interval eigrp 100 ?
  <1-65535>  Seconds between hello transmissions
```

The *Hold* time tells the router the maximum time it should wait to receive subsequent valid EIGRP packets from a neighbor. If the Hold timer expires before any acceptable EIGRP packet is received, the neighbor is declared unreachable and DUAL is informed of the loss of a neighbor. By default, the Hold time is three times the Hello, equaling either 15 or 180 seconds, depending on the interface type. Be aware, however, that changing the Hello interval does not result in automatic recalculation of the Hold time. This can, under certain circumstances, result in problems with flapping adjacencies if the Hello interval is manually configured to be close or even higher than the default Hold time, without changing the Hold timer itself.

As detailed in Example 8-6, these defaults can be changed at the interface level.

**Example 8-6**  *Adjusting EIGRP Hold Time*

```
Router(config-if)# ip hold-time eigrp 100 ?
  <1-65535>  Seconds before neighbor is considered down
```

The process of establishing adjacency in EIGRP is illustrated in Figure 8-4.

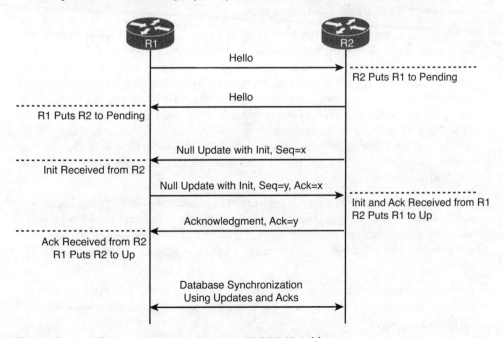

**Figure 8-4**  *Adjacency Creation Between EIGRP Neighbors*

The process starts by a router discovering its new neighbor by receiving a Hello packet from it. In Figure 8-4, R2 receives a Hello packet from R1. R2 will expedite sending its own Hello packet onto the interface, allowing R1 to quickly discover it as well. As soon as a new neighbor is discovered through a Hello packet, it is put into a so-called Pending state. The purpose of this Pending state is to defer sending and accepting any EIGRP messages containing routing information between these neighbors until their bidirectional connectivity has been confirmed.

Continuing the process, R2 sends R1 an empty Update packet, also called a null Update, with the Init flag set. This null Update carries a nonzero sequence number but contains no routing information. The Init flag is an indication to the neighbor that this adjacency is starting over from scratch and the neighbor is requested to send its full database after the bidirectional visibility is confirmed. R1 is required to acknowledge the arrival of this null Update, thereby confirming the bidirectional connectivity, and it must also send R2 its own null Update packet with the Init flag set, acknowledging that the neighbor also considers this adjacency to be starting over from scratch. R2 finally acknowledges R1's null Update, completing the initial exchange. The acknowledgments in this procedure can either be sent as standalone ACK packets, or they can be carried in the null Update packets by setting the Acknowledgment Number field in their header to the sequence number of the other router's null Update packet—either of these options is valid.

While in Pending state, the only packets that can be exchanged in both directions with the neighbor are the unreliable packets (Hello, Ack) and reliable packets with the Init flag set that indicate the startup of an adjacency. In addition, because the bidirectional connectivity with a neighbor in the Pending state has not yet been confirmed, it makes no sense to send or process reliable packets containing meaningful routing information. As a result, the only sensible reliable packet that can be exchanged with a neighbor in the Pending state is exactly the null Update packet.

A neighbor is moved from the Pending to the Up state if and only if it acknowledges the null Update received from the router and sends its own null Update with the Init flag set to this router (in any order). In other words, the router must receive an acknowledgment for its own null Update to the neighbor and must receive an Init-flagged packet from the neighbor to move the neighbor from the Pending to the Up state. In a sense, this procedure can be likened to the process of opening a TCP session. The Init flag is similar to the SYN flag in TCP. The first null Update+Init from R2 toward R1 is similar to a TCP SYN segment, R1's null Update+Init with the piggybacked acknowledgment is similar to a TCP SYN/ACK segment, and R2's Ack packet confirming the R1's null Update+Init is similar to a TCP ACK segment.

After this initial three-way handshake, the routers will exchange complete routing information using Update packets. After the synchronization is completed, EIGRP neighbors will send only incremental updates to advise neighbors of status or routing changes and will not send their full databases again unless restarted or resynchronization is manually invoked.

Information about each neighbor is recorded in a *neighbor table*. To see the contents of the neighbor table, use the **show ip eigrp neighbors** command in accordance with Example 8-7.

**Example 8-7**    *EIGRP Neighbor Table*

```
R1# show ip eigrp neighbors
IP-EIGRP neighbors for process 1
H    Address               Interface        Hold Uptime    SRTT   RTO   Q    Seq
                                            (sec)          (ms)         Cnt  Num
1    10.10.10.3            Fa0/0             11 00:00:08     87   522   0    6
0    10.10.10.2            Fa0/0             14 00:01:54   1300  5000   0    3
```

The *neighbor table* records information about each detected neighbor with whom this router has established an adjacency. The *H (Handle)* column shows the internal number that EIGRP assigns to each neighbor. The handle number is used in EIGRP to internally identify neighbors in an address-family independent way. The *Address* and *Interface* columns hold the neighbor's IP address and this router's interface toward the neighbor. The *Hold* time is derived from the value advertised by the neighbor and decremented each second; it is reset every time any acceptable EIGRP packet from the neighbor is received. The *Uptime* shows the time the neighbor has been up for the last time.

The *SRTT*, the Smooth Round Trip Time, estimates the turnover time between sending a reliable packet to the neighbor and receiving an appropriate acknowledgment. The *RTO,* or Retransmit Time Out, is the time that the router will wait for an acknowledgment of a retransmitted unicast packet after its previous delivery was not acknowledged. If the *RTO* expires before an ACK is received, another copy of the queued packet is sent. Both these timers are shown in milliseconds.

The *Q Cnt* indicates the number of enqueued reliable packets, that is, packets that have been prepared for sending and even possibly sent but for which no ACK has been received yet from the neighbor. In a stable network, the *Q Cnt* value must be zero; non-zero values are normal during initial router database synchronization or during network convergence. If the Q Cnt value remains nonzero for prolonged periods of time, however, it indicates a communication problem with the neighbor.

Finally, the *Sequence number* shows the sequence number of the last reliable packet (Update, Query, Reply, SIA-Query, or SIA-Reply) received from the neighbor. RTP tracks these sequence numbers to ensure that reliable packets from the neighbor are processed in ascending order. Note that the Sequence number in EIGRP is a per-process variable incremented each time a new reliable packet is originated and transmitted. If a neighbor is involved in a reliable communication on one of its interfaces and then needs to send another reliable packet to this router, the sequence number in this column might increment by more than 1. It is thus normal to see sequence numbers increasing by different increments as long as they form an ascending series.

Table 8-4 summarizes the fields you see in the neighbor table.

**Table 8-4**   *EIGRP Neighbor Table Columns*

| Field | Description |
|---|---|
| H | Internal reference to a neighbor, also called a neighbor handle, starting at 0. |
| Address | The IP address of the neighbor. |
| Interface | The interface toward the neighbor. |
| Hold | The Hold timer for the neighbor. If it decreases to 0, the neighbor is considered down. |
| Uptime | Timer for how long the neighbor relationship has been up. |
| SRTT | This is the Smooth Round Trip Time, which is the time it takes to send a reliable EIGRP packet and receive an acknowledgment. |
| RTO | This is the Retransmission Time Out, which is the amount of time the router will wait between retransmitting an EIGRP reliable packet if an Ack is not received. |
| Q Cnt | This is the number of EIGRP reliable packets sent and waiting to be sent to the neighbor but not acknowledged yet. |
| Seq Num | This is the sequence number of the last EIGRP reliable packet received from the neighbor. This is to ensure that packets from the neighbor are processed in the correct order. |

# Diffusing Update Algorithm

The Diffusing Update Algorithm (DUAL) is a convergence algorithm that replaces the Bellman-Ford algorithm used by other distance-vector protocols. Routing loops, even those that might come into existence temporarily as our protocols fully converge, are detrimental to the performance of a network. To prevent the possibility of loop formation, DUAL uses a concept of diffusing computations to perform distributed shortest-path computation while maintaining freedom from loops during those calculations. DUAL is at the center of the EIGRP routing protocol.

## Topology Table

The central data store of an EIGRP process is the *topology table*. The choice of this name is perhaps not particularly fortunate, as EIGRP, being a distance-vector routing protocol, has no information about the network's topology per se. Nonetheless, the topology table is the place where EIGRP stores its entire routing information including

■  The prefix of each known destination network (address/netmask)

■  Feasible Distance of the destination network

■  Address of each neighboring router that advertised the destination network, including the egress interface toward the neighbor

■ Metrics of the destination network as advertised by each neighbor, and the resulting metrics of the path to the destination network through that neighbor

■ State of the destination network

■ Additional information about the network (various internal flags, network type and origin, and others)

The topology table is populated and updated by locally injected networks (directly connected interfaces added to EIGRP, routes redistributed locally) and by contents of received EIGRP Update, Query, Reply, SIA-Query, and SIA-Reply messages. For each remote network learned through EIGRP and stored in the topology table, EIGRP will look up the neighbor that provides the least total cost path to the destination and verify that the neighbor provides a loop-free path, and if so, install the network through that neighbor into the routing table. An important fact to remember is that a remote network must first be present in the topology table before being installed in the routing table.

Each network recorded in the topology table has a state associated with it. This state can be either *Passive*, meaning that the shortest path to the network has already been found and EIGRP is satisfied with it, or it can be *Active*, meaning that EIGRP is currently actively involved in a search for a new shortest path. In a stable topology, all routes shall be in the Passive state. The Active state is always related to the router sending Query packets, asking its neighbors for cooperation in the search for a new path. While in an Active state, the router is prohibited from modifying the routing table entry for this network, meaning that the route must not be removed or its next hop changed. The Active state can be successfully terminated only by this router receiving a Reply from all its neighbors. Only then can the route enter the Passive state again and the router can make a new shortest-path selection, finally updating the routing table. As already stated, EIGRP is designed to avoid routing loops at every instant. Keeping the formerly usable (and loop-free) route unchanged in the routing table during the Active state makes sure that the router stays with the former route—it might be suboptimal or cause traffic blackholing but is still loop-free. After the computation terminates, the router can choose a new loop-free best path and start using it. EIGRP essentially behaves in a transactional way, always moving from a loop-free path to another loop-free path, with no intermediary states of transient routing loops ever possible. The exact rules of entering the Active state will be explained later in the "Local and Diffusing Computations in EIGRP" section; at this point, they can be summarized as follows:

■ Whenever a router needs to select a new shortest path and the neighbor providing that path can be proven not to create a routing loop, the route stays in the Passive state because the router already has all the information to make a correct choice.

■ If the neighbor providing the least-cost path cannot be guaranteed to avoid a routing loop, or if no such neighbor exists, the route will need to enter the Active state.

Example 8-8 shows the contents of an EIGRP topology table of a router. Outputs in this example were taken from Router R1 shown in Figure 8-5 in the following section. This network runs IPv6 EIGRP, with the serial links between R1 and all other routers configured using only IPv6 link-local addresses in the form of FE80::<*RouterNumber*>. The

LAN at the right side of Figure 8-5 is configured as a passive network (R2, R3, and R4 have their interfaces into the LAN configured as passive; hence, no EIGRP adjacencies are established over it), and it is assigned a global IPv6 prefix of 2001:DB8:CC1E::/64. R4 also redistributes a static route toward 2001:DB8:FFFF::/48 into EIGRP. To simplify metric calculations, EIGRP in this network is configured to take only the delay metric component into account ($K_3 = 1$, all other K-values are set to 0). Delays on individual interfaces are configured to the values shown in the figure. IPv6 is chosen for this example because it allows operating this network with most interconnections configured with link-local addresses only. This makes the outputs of various **show** and **debug** commands much more readable. Also, for simplicity, this example was created on routers using the Classic Metrics. Keep in mind that EIGRP multiplies the calculated classic metric by 256. Take care to read the comments in the example carefully.

**Example 8-8** *EIGRP Topology Table Contents*

```
! The show ipv6 eigrp topology output shows the AS number of the EIGRP process,
! its Router ID, and the collected knowledge of all networks locally injected
! into EIGRP or learned from other EIGRP neighbors. Towards 2001:DB8:CC1E::/64,
! only next hops FE80::2 (R2) and FE80::3 (R3) are displayed, as R4 currently
! does not meet the Feasibility Condition to be considered a prospective next hop.
! The show ipv6 eigrp topology is one of very few commands in EIGRP that actually
! shows the Router ID of the EIGRP process.

R1# show ipv6 eigrp topology
IPv6-EIGRP Topology Table for AS(1)/ID(10.255.255.1)

Codes: P - Passive, A - Active, U - Update, Q - Query, R - Reply,
       r - reply Status, s - sia Status

P 2001:DB8:FFFF::/48, 1 successors, FD is 1024
        via FE80::4 (1024/1), Serial1/2
P 2001:DB8:CC1E::/64, 1 successors, FD is 2560
        via FE80::2 (2560/256), Serial1/0
        via FE80::3 (5120/1280), Serial1/1


! Using the all-links keyword, all neighbors advertising a network, including
! those who fail to meet the Feasibility Condition check, are displayed.
! The reason there is just a single neighbor for the 2001:DB8:FFFF::/48
! displayed even with all-links is the Split Horizon with Poisoned Reverse
! used by EIGRP. As routers R2 and R3 are using R1 as their next hop towards
! 2001:DB8:FFFF::/48, they advertise it back to R1 with an infinite metric.


R1# show ipv6 eigrp topology all-links
IPv6-EIGRP Topology Table for AS(1)/ID(10.255.255.1)
```

```
Codes: P - Passive, A - Active, U - Update, Q - Query, R - Reply,
       r - reply Status, s - sia Status


P 2001:DB8:FFFF::/48, 1 successors, FD is 1024, serno 3
        via FE80::4 (1024/1), Serial1/2
P 2001:DB8:CC1E::/64, 1 successors, FD is 2560, serno 2
        via FE80::2 (2560/256), Serial1/0
        via FE80::4 (4096/3072), Serial1/2
        via FE80::3 (5120/1280), Serial1/1


! By referencing a particular network, detailed information about it can be
! displayed. Notice the individual information stored about the network:
! State, Number of Successors, Feasible Distance, per-neighbor information
! covering the route type, individual metric components of the path over
! the neighbor, and resulting composite calculated metrics.


R1# show ipv6 eigrp topology 2001:DB8:CC1E::/64
IPv6-EIGRP (AS 1): Topology entry for 2001:DB8:CC1E::/64
  State is Passive, Query origin flag is 1, 1 Successor(s), FD is 2560
  Routing Descriptor Blocks:
  FE80::2 (Serial1/0), from FE80::2, Send flag is 0x0
      Composite metric is (2560/256), Route is Internal
      Vector metric:
        Minimum bandwidth is 1544 Kbit
        Total delay is 100 microseconds
        Reliability is 255/255
        Load is 1/255
        Minimum MTU is 1500
        Hop count is 1
  FE80::4 (Serial1/2), from FE80::4, Send flag is 0x0
      Composite metric is (4096/3072), Route is Internal
      Vector metric:
        Minimum bandwidth is 1544 Kbit
        Total delay is 160 microseconds
        Reliability is 255/255
        Load is 1/255
        Minimum MTU is 1500
        Hop count is 1
  FE80::3 (Serial1/1), from FE80::3, Send flag is 0x0
      Composite metric is (5120/1280), Route is Internal
      Vector metric:
        Minimum bandwidth is 1544 Kbit
        Total delay is 200 microseconds
        Reliability is 255/255
        Load is 1/255
        Minimum MTU is 1500
        Hop count is 1
```

```
! If detailed information about an external (redistributed) network is
! pulled from the topology table, apart from the obvious information,
! external networks also carry information about the router that performs
! the redistribution, and about the origins of the redistributed route
! such as what is its original type, AS number, or metric.


R1# show ipv6 eigrp topology 2001:DB8:FFFF::/48
IPv6-EIGRP (AS 1): Topology entry for 2001:DB8:FFFF::/48
  State is Passive, Query origin flag is 1, 1 Successor(s), FD is 1024
  Routing Descriptor Blocks:
  FE80::4 (Serial1/2), from FE80::4, Send flag is 0x0
      Composite metric is (1024/1), Route is External
      Vector metric:
        Minimum bandwidth is 1544 Kbit
        Total delay is 40 microseconds
        Reliability is 0/255
        Load is 1/255
        Minimum MTU is 1500
        Hop count is 1
      External data:
        Originating router is 10.255.255.4
        AS number of route is 0
        External protocol is Static, external metric is 0
        Administrator tag is 0 (0x00000000)
```

## Computed, Reported, and Feasible Distances, and Feasibility Condition

Toward a particular destination network, EIGRP keeps track of various distances as a part of its operation. Unfortunately, the details about these distances, and their purpose and operation, are often poorly explained and understood. A correct in-depth understanding of EIGRP therefore requires that we revisit these concepts in detail. EIGRP uses a composite metric; however, for simplicity, the remainder of this section assumes that the EIGRP metric is a single dimensionless number, as it makes no difference to the operation of underlying mechanisms. As explained in the "EIGRP Classic Metrics" and "EIGRP Wide Metrics" sections, earlier in the chapter, the metric components are combined into a single number; the words *distance* and *cost* used interchangeably in this section refer to this combined value. Also, for simplicity, throughout this section, EIGRP routers are assumed to operate without Split Horizon.

Consider the topology shown in Figure 8-5.

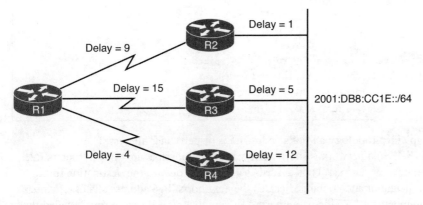

**Figure 8-5**  *Sample Network Operating EIGRP in IPv6 Mode*

Assuming that the network has been properly configured and EIGRP has converged, Example 8-9 shows the output of selected **show** commands issued on R1 that we will analyze in greater detail. Throughout this discussion, we focus on R1's behavior toward destination network 2001:DB8:CC1E::/64. The redistribution on R4 has been removed.

**Example 8-9**  *EIGRP Topology Table on R1*

```
R1# show ipv6 route eigrp
IPv6 Routing Table - 2 entries
Codes: C - Connected, L - Local, S - Static, R - RIP, B - BGP
       U - Per-user Static route, M - MIPv6
       I1 - ISIS L1, I2 - ISIS L2, IA - ISIS interarea, IS - ISIS summary
       O - OSPF intra, OI - OSPF inter, OE1 - OSPF ext 1, OE2 - OSPF ext 2
       ON1 - OSPF NSSA ext 1, ON2 - OSPF NSSA ext 2
       D - EIGRP, EX - EIGRP external
D    2001:DB8:CC1E::/64 [90/2560]
     via FE80::2, Serial1/0

R1# show ipv6 eigrp topology
IPv6-EIGRP Topology Table for AS(1)/ID(10.255.255.1)

Codes: P - Passive, A - Active, U - Update, Q - Query, R - Reply,
       r - reply Status, s - sia Status

P 2001:DB8:CC1E::/64, 1 successors, FD is 2560
        via FE80::2 (2560/256), Serial1/0
        via FE80::3 (5120/1280), Serial1/1

R1# show ipv6 eigrp topology all-links
IPv6-EIGRP Topology Table for AS(1)/ID(10.255.255.1)
```

```
Codes: P - Passive, A - Active, U - Update, Q - Query, R - Reply,
       r - reply Status, s - sia Status


P 2001:DB8:CC1E::/64, 1 successors, FD is 2560, serno 4
        via FE80::2 (2560/256), Serial1/0
        via FE80::3 (5120/1280), Serial1/1
        via FE80::4 (4096/3072), Serial1/2
```

The **show ip eigrp topology all-links** command is of particular interest. The 2001:DB8:CC1E::/64 network is shown here with three possible next hops: Routers R2, R3, and R4. Each of the "via" lines describes a possible route to the destination through a particular neighbor and contains, besides the next hop's IPv6 address and egress interface, two numbers enclosed in parentheses. The number after the slash sign is called the *Reported Distance (RD)* and corresponds to the current best distance of the particular neighbor to the destination. In other words, the RD is the neighbor's distance to the destination as *reported* in an EIGRP packet received from that neighbor. R1 learns about these distances by receiving an EIGRP message from these neighbors that carries routing information—an Update, Query, Reply, SIA-Query, or SIA-Reply. In some sources, RD is also called an *Advertised Distance*, but because this term (and its acronym AD) is easily confused with Administrative Distance, we will avoid using it. The RD values for routers R2, R3, and R4 shown in Example 8-9 correspond to their delay values indicated in Figure 8-5 multiplied by 256 (256 = 1 × 256, 1280 = 5 × 256, 3072 = 12 × 256).

The number in parentheses before the slash sign is called the *Computed Distance (CD)* and shows the total metric of reaching the destination over the particular neighbor. The CD is computed as the RD of the neighbor plus the cost of the link between R1 and the neighbor. Current values in Example 8-9 correspond to the total sum of delays from R1 through each particular neighbor multiplied by 256 (2560 = 10 × 256, 5120 = 20 × 256, 4096 = 16 × 256).

For each destination network, there is exactly one CD and one RD per each neighbor. These distances are displayed in the "via" lines of the **show ip eigrp topology** output in the form of (CD/RD).

Just as with any other routing protocol, EIGRP's goal is to identify paths with the least metric to the destination. To accomplish this, EIGRP chooses the path with the lowest CD and installs it, after verifying that the path is not looped, into the routing table. Example 8-9 shows that currently, the smallest distance to the destination network is through R2 with the CD of 2560. This route is also installed into R1's routing table, using this CD as the route metric.

Both CD and RD correspond to the *current* distance, that is, the momentary total distance of this router to the destination through a particular neighbor (CD), and the neighbor's own distance to that destination as known by this router (RD). EIGRP also maintains a record of yet another distance for each destination: the *Feasible Distance (FD)*. The FD is one of the most misunderstood and poorly explained concepts in EIGRP. For each destination, *FD is a record of the lowest known distance since the last transition*

*from the Active to Passive state*. In other words, FD is a *historical* record, or a *historical* copy, of the smallest known CD toward a particular destination, with the *history* starting anew with the last Active-to-Passive transition. Being a record of the smallest known CD since the route entered the Passive state for the last time, FD is *not necessarily equal* to the current best CD to a destination. By its definition, in the Passive state, after the FD has been initialized, it can only decrease (if the current best CD happens to fall below the current value of FD) or remain at its current value (if the current best CD rises but the route remains Passive). There is exactly one FD per each destination, regardless of the number of neighbors. It is important to note that the FD is an internal variable maintained for each network known to EIGRP whose value is never advertised to another router.

To better illustrate the behavior of FD, consider Example 8-10, with comments inserted directly into the output. Keep in mind that all metric modifications in this example are carefully chosen to avoid violating the Feasibility Condition and causing the route toward 2001:DB8:CC1E::/64 entering the Active state. This example shows the behavior of the FD while the route is kept in the Passive state.

**Example 8-10**  *Feasible Distance Behavior in EIGRP*

**Key Topic**

```
! Before performing any changes to the network, it is in the state shown
! in Figure 8-5 and Example 8-9. Now assume that the delay of link between
! R1 and R2 has increased from 9 to 11. Note in the following output that
! while the CD via R2 has changed from 2560 to 3072 and so has the metric
! in the routing table, FD indicated in the network heading remained at its
! current value of 2560. At this moment, the value of FD says that "at some
! point in the past, R1 was as close as 2560 units to the destination", even
! though the current best CD is different. R2's RD did not change, either,
! because R2's best path to the destination has not been influenced in any way.

R1# show ipv6 eigrp topology all-links
! Legend removed for brevity
P 2001:DB8:CC1E::/64, 1 successors, FD is 2560, serno 5
        via FE80::2 (3072/256), Serial1/0
        via FE80::3 (5120/1280), Serial1/1
        via FE80::4 (4096/3072), Serial1/2


R1# show ipv6 route eigrp
! Legend removed for brevity
D   2001:DB8:CC1E::/64 [90/3072]
     via FE80::2, Serial1/0


! Further assume that subsequently, R2's LAN interface's delay increases
! from 1 to 3. Now, both R2's RD and CD through R2 change: R2's RD increases
! to 768 and CD via R2 increases to 3584 but again, the FD remains at its
! former value of 2560, as at some point in the past, our best CD was 2560.
```

```
R1# show ipv6 eigrp topology all-links
! Legend removed for brevity
P 2001:DB8:CC1E::/64, 1 successors, FD is 2560, serno 6
        via FE80::2 (3584/768), Serial1/0
        via FE80::3 (5120/1280), Serial1/1
        via FE80::4 (4096/3072), Serial1/2


R1# show ipv6 route eigrp
! Legend removed for brevity
D    2001:DB8:CC1E::/64 [90/3584]
     via FE80::2, Serial1/0


! Now, assume that R2's LAN interface's delay returns back to 1, and moreover,
! the delay of R1-R2 link decreases to 7. Because the total delay of 8 is now
! better than any experienced so far, not only the R2's RD and CD via R2 change,
! but also the FD as the record of the smallest known CD changes from 2560 to 2048.


R1# show ipv6 eigrp topology all-links
! Legend removed for brevity
P 2001:DB8:CC1E::/64, 1 successors, FD is 2048, serno 8
        via FE80::2 (2048/256), Serial1/0
        via FE80::3 (5120/1280), Serial1/1
        via FE80::4 (4096/3072), Serial1/2


R1# show ipv6 route eigrp
! Legend removed for brevity
D    2001:DB8:CC1E::/64 [90/2048]
     via FE80::2, Serial1/0


! Now when the delay of the R1-R2 link increases back to 9, the CD via R2
! increases and the best distance returns to the former value of 2560. However,
! FD will now keep its value of 2048 as this distance has become the new
! historical minimum of the distance towards 2001:DB8:CC1E::/64. At the end
! of this example, the delays on network interfaces have completely returned
! back to the original state from Figure 8-5; yet, because of its properties,
! the FD has changed from 2560 to 2048 although the CD of the current best
! route via FE80::2 is back to the original value of 2560.


R1# show ipv6 eigrp topology all-links
! Legend removed for brevity
P 2001:DB8:CC1E::/64, 1 successors, FD is 2048, serno 9
        via FE80::2 (2560/256), Serial1/0
        via FE80::3 (5120/1280), Serial1/1
        via FE80::4 (4096/3072), Serial1/2
```

```
R1# show ipv6 route eigrp
! Legend removed for brevity
D    2001:DB8:CC1E::/64 [90/2560]
      via FE80::2, Serial1/0
```

Note how, in several cases in Example 8-10, FD was different from the actual lowest CD that was also visible in the **show ipv6 route** output. When advertising its distance to the 2001:DB8:CC1E::/64, R1 would advertise its actual distance instead of FD. Once again, FD is an internal value that is used by EIGRP to select loop-free paths, but its value is never advertised in any EIGRP packets.

To explain the motivation behind the FD as previously described, consider the scenario in Figure 8-6. This topology is similar to Figure 8-5, with a change: R4 is only connected to R1 and is not connected to the LAN. The delay on the R1–R4 link is configured to 2. As a result, R4 points to R1 to reach 2001:DB8:CC1E::/64, and R4's total metric to this network will be $(2+9+1) \times 256 = 12 \times 256 = 3072$, identical to the original situation in Figure 8-5.

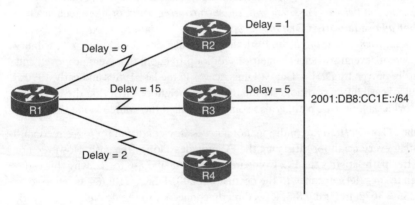

**Figure 8-6**  *Modified Sample Network Operating EIGRP in IPv6 Mode*

Assume now that the R1–R2 link suddenly fails. At the exact moment of the failure, R1 and R2 are the only routers that are aware of the topology change. Neither R3 nor R4 knows about the change yet. If R1 immediately proceeded to choose a replacement next hop toward the destination, it would choose R4 because with R2 unreachable, R4 apparently provides the next least-cost path with the metric of $(2+12) \times 256 = 3584$. However, this would cause a routing loop because at the moment the R1–R2 link failed and R1 tried to find another next hop, R4 was not yet updated about the topology change, and therefore its RD of $12 \times 256 = 3072$ was outdated. Trusting it blindly would be a mistake.

Key Topic

This is where FD comes in. With the FD set to 2560, R1 knows that at some point in the past, it had a workable, loop-free path to the destination with the distance as low as 2560. Naturally, by virtue of all links in the topology having positive (that is, non-negative and nonzero) costs, neighbors that provided this path must have been even closer, meaning that their RDs must have been strictly less than 2560. At that point in the past, any neighbor whose distance was less than 2560 was safe to be used by R1, as that neighbor would never forward packets back to R1, neither directly nor over any chain of multiple routers looping back to R1: If the neighbor's own distance was less than R1's, why would it forward packets over a path whose distance was higher than its own?

Now if R1's actual distance increases over time, it is one more reason for these neighbors with their distances less than 2560 to avoid using R1 to reach the network because, just as before, why should they forward packets through R1 whose distance was higher than their own and even grew further? Note that in this logic, the neighbors do not even need to know that R1's distance has increased from 2560 to a higher value, so to make this *feasibility check*, it is not even important they have up-to-date information from R1—which is exactly what we need!

**Key Topic**

This idea forms the basis of Feasible Distance and the related Feasibility Condition check. FD, being the record of the smallest known distance to a destination since the last time the route went Passive, is a value that describes the metric of the best path to the destination this router has known. Any neighbor whose current distance is lower would never pass packets back to this router, and it would even less consider passing packets back if it knew that this router's distance has increased for whatever reasons. Therefore, *any neighbor that is closer to the destination than this router has been since the last time the destination became Passive cannot form a routing loop*, or more technically, *any neighbor whose Reported Distance is strictly smaller than this router's Feasible Distance cannot form a routing loop*. Both these formulations constitute the Feasibility Condition, one of several sufficient conditions for loop freedom that were proposed and mathematically proven by Dr. J. J. Garcia-Luna-Aceves in the late 1980s and early 1990s. This particular Feasibility Condition, stating that every neighbor satisfying the inequality RD < FD provides a loop-free path, is also sometimes called the Source Node Condition.

Note that the FC is a *sufficient* condition, not a *necessary* condition for loop freedom; this means that every neighbor satisfying the FC provides a loop-free path. However, not every loop-free path satisfies the FC. Compare Figures 8-5 and 8-6 to see why this is the case. In both figures, R4's distance to the destination 2001:DB8:CC1E::/64 as reported to R1 is 12 × 256 = 3072. In Figure 8-5, R4 is directly connected to the destination network and forwards packets to this network directly. If R4 received packets from R1 toward the LAN, it would forward them onto the LAN without causing any routing loop. In Figure 8-6, however, R4 uses R1 as its next hop toward the LAN network, and if R1 tried to route packets to the LAN through R4, it would receive them back in a routing loop. In other words, if a neighbor's RD is equal to or higher than R1's FD, it might (Figure 8-6) or might not (Figure 8-5) cause a routing loop; in the distance-vector approach, R1 has no further information to verify that. However, it is certain and guaranteed that if a neighbor's RD is lower than R1's FD (that is, if the neighbor is closer to the destination than R1 has ever been since the last time the destination became Passive), it will not cause a routing loop. The FC basically splits all neighbors of a router into two groups: neighbors that are guaranteed to provide a loop-free path and all other neighbors about which the router cannot be sure.

For a destination, all neighbors that pass the FC and thus are safe to use as next hops are called *Feasible Successors*. In other words, a Feasible Successor is a neighbor that is guaranteed to provide a loop-free path toward a destination; Feasible Successors are identified by passing the FC check. Among these Feasible Successors, one or more provide the least CD to the destination; these are called *Successors*. Both Feasible Successors and Successors must meet the FC and thus are guaranteed to provide a loop-free path; Successors must in addition provide the shortest path available. Technically, each Successor is also a Feasible Successor because it meets the FC. However, in common language, the term *Feasible Successor* is used to denote only the neighbor that provides a loop-free, yet not the shortest, path available. All Successors and Feasible Successors to a destination can be seen in the **show ip eigrp topology** output. Neighbors that do not meet the FC are not displayed in this output; to display them as well, the **show ip eigrp topology all-links** command must be used.

In Figure 8-6, using the FC will prevent R1 from creating a routing loop through R4 when the R1–R2 link fails. Because R4's RD is 3584 while R1's FD is 2560, R1 assumes that R4 *might be using it* as its own next hop to the LAN. Therefore, R4 does not pass the FC check and is not considered a Feasible Successor. In the precise moment of R1–R2 link failure, when only R1 and R2 are aware of the failure, R1 now knows that even though R4 appears to provide the next least-cost path, it cannot be trusted. This prevents R1 from pointing toward R4, creating a temporary routing loop.

An EIGRP router is always allowed to use any Successor and Feasible Successor to reach the destination, without any further coordination with them. Using a Successor will make the packets flow to the destination through the shortest loop-free path; using a Feasible Successor will cause the packets to go over a longer but still loop-free path. While the route is in the Passive state, there is usually no reason to route packets through Feasible Successors because that would make them flow over suboptimal paths, yet this is exactly the idea of unequal-cost load balancing that EIGRP is capable of.

## Local and Diffusing Computations in EIGRP

After having explained the concepts of Reported Distance, Computed Distance, Feasible Distance, and Feasibility Condition, describing the handling of topology changes in EIGRP is relatively straightforward. A topology change occurs whenever the distance to a network changes or a new neighbor comes online that advertises the network. The distance change can be detected either through receiving an Update, Query, Reply, SIA-Query, or SIA-Reply packet from a neighbor that carries updated metric information about the network, or because a local interface metric has changed. Also, the event of a neighbor going down is processed by setting the CD/RD of all networks reachable through that neighbor to infinity. Whatever the reason for the topology change is, the router can immediately verify in its topology table whether the new shortest path is provided by a router passing the FC check, that is, a Feasible Successor. If it is, the router performs the following steps:

**Key Topic**

1. The Feasible Successor providing the least CD is made the new Successor.

2. If the CD over the new Successor is less than the current FD, the FD will be updated to the new CD; otherwise it stays at its current value.

3. The routing table is updated to point toward the new Successor.

4. If the current distance to the destination has changed as a result of switching to a new Successor, an Update packet is sent to all neighbors, advertising the router's updated distance to the destination.

This action is called a *local computation* in EIGRP, performed solely by using information already stored in the router's topology table, without needing to coordinate with the neighboring routers. Throughout this procedure, the route has remained in the Passive state.

If, however, after detecting a topology change, the router finds out that the new shortest path is provided by a neighbor that is not a Feasible Successor, the router cannot use such a neighbor right away because it could cause a routing loop. Therefore, the router commences a *diffusing computation* by performing the following steps:

**Key Topic**

1. The entry in the routing table, still pointing to the current unchanged Successor, is locked: It must not be removed nor its next hop changed until the diffusing computation is finished and the route has been moved to the Passive state again.

2. The FD is set to the current (possibly increased) CD through the current unchanged Successor. Also, if this router ever needs to advertise its distance to the network while in the Active state, it will also use the value of the current CD through the Successor.

3. The network is put into the Active state and the router sends out a Query packet to all its neighbors. This Query packet contains the Active network's prefix and the router's current CD toward it.

Each neighbor receiving a Query packet will process it by updating its own topology table using the distance information advertised in the Query and reevaluating its own choice of Successors and Feasible Successors. Two possibilities now exist: Either the neighbor still has its own Feasible Successor or a Successor that provides it with the least-cost loop-free path, or the information contained in the Query causes the neighbor to stop considering the path through its current Successor the shortest available and none of its own neighbors that offer the shortest path are a Feasible Successor.

In the first case, when the neighbor still has a Successor, it will simply send back a Reply packet, indicating the neighbor's current distance to the destination (performing its own local computation if necessary). The neighbor did not become engaged in the diffusing computation as it did not need to put the network into the Active state itself. Thanks to this, the diffusing computation was bounded by this neighbor and did not propagate further.

In the second case, the neighbor will itself join the diffusing computation, send out its own Query packet, and advertise its own current distance through its current Successor. As a result, the wave of Query messages propagates through the part of the network that is affected by the change. Other parts of the network that are not affected will not engage in the diffusing computation. This fact explains the somewhat more marketing than technical claims about EIGRP using "partial, bounded updates": any EIGRP signaling that by its nature covers only the changed information (partial) and is propagated only into the affected part of the network (bounded).

After a router becomes Active for a destination and sends out Query packets to its neighbors, it must wait for a Reply packet from each of its neighbors to come back. Until then, the route remains in the Active state, and its routing table is unchanged. Only after all Reply packets are received, the router can put the route back to the Passive state, simply choose the neighbor offering the shortest path available while skipping the FC check, and reinitialize the FD to the CD offered by the selected neighbor. Now the routing table entry can finally be updated. If this router itself became Active by receiving a Query, it now starts sending its own Reply and possibly Update packets, as only now its own distance to the destination has been determined; otherwise, the router sends out Update packets only.

It is noteworthy to mention that the crucial information carried in Update, Query, Reply, SIA-Query, and SIA-Reply packets is always simply the sender's current distance to a particular destination, informing its receiver about the packet originator's distance to the destination and optionally requesting a response (in the case of Query and SIA-Query packets). Whether any of these packets causes its receiver to go Active for a destination depends exclusively on how the information in the message impacts the receiver's choice of the shortest path and FC check performed over its neighbor offering the shortest path.

It is a widespread belief about EIGRP that if the current Successor fails, a Feasible Successor (if one exists) will always be promoted to the Successor role. This statement is not entirely correct, however. Consider again the topology in Figure 8-5 in the state we have left it at the end of Example 8-10. On R1, the FD of the LAN remained at 2048, and the best path currently goes through R2, the Successor, its CD being 2560. R3 is identified as the Feasible Successor as its RD is 1280, less than the FD (2048), and the CD through R3 is 5120. Note that R4 actually provides a better path than R3 with the CD of 4096, but because of R4's RD of 3072, R4 does not pass the FC and R1 does not consider it to be a Feasible Successor.

If the link between R1 and R2 fails, the common belief is that R1 would first check whether it has a Feasible Successor available—and it does indeed; it is R3—so it would be promoted to the Successor role and R1 would install a route to the LAN through R3. This would not be correct, however. If R1 was simply satisfied with R3, it would be using a workable but not necessarily the shortest available path, and would never explore the possibility of using a shorter path. What really happens in EIGRP is the following:

**Key Topic**

- Whenever EIGRP detects a topology change, it first records the change into the topology table and updates the RD and CD of the neighbor that advertised the change (in case of a received EIGRP message) or was influenced by it (in case of a link metric change).

- From among all neighbors that advertise the network, EIGRP identifies the one that provides the least CD, taking into account the updated CDs. Note that the FC is not invoked at this step.

- Only after identifying the neighbor offering the least CD, EIGRP verifies whether this neighbor meets the FC and is therefore a Feasible Successor. If it is, EIGRP will promote it to the Successor and start using it right away. If, however, that neighbor does not meet the FC, EIGRP will put the route into the Active state and send out Queries, asking its neighbors to assist in locating the best route.

In other words, EIGRP—just like any other routing protocol—always tries to choose the shortest path toward a destination, but before using it, EIGRP verifies whether it meets the FC to be loop-free. If it does, EIGRP will use it. If it does not, EIGRP puts the destination into the Active state.

Consider Example 8-11, which explains how the network in Figure 8-5 would react if the R1–R2 link was shut down. Read the comments in the example carefully.

**Example 8-11**  *Use of a Neighbor Failing the FC and Providing the Next Least Distance*

```
! The IPv6 routing table shows the LAN network routed via R2


R1# show ipv6 route eigrp
! Legend removed for brevity
D   2001:DB8:CC1E::/64 [90/2560]
     via FE80::2, Serial1/0


! In the EIGRP topology table, R2 is identified as the Successor, and R3
! is identified as the Feasible Successor. R4 is not displayed here, as
! it does not meet the FC. Note the FD remained at 2048 after the changes
! performed in the Example 8-10; the delays on links have nonetheless been
! configured back to the values shown in Figure 8-5.


R1# show ipv6 eigrp topology
! Legend removed for brevity
P 2001:DB8:CC1E::/64, 1 successors, FD is 2048
        via FE80::2 (2560/256), Serial1/0
        via FE80::3 (5120/1280), Serial1/1


! Using the all-links keyword, R4 can be displayed as well but it is clear
! from the (CD/RD) values that R4's RD of 3072 is not strictly less than
! the FD of 2048. R2 and R3 pass this check, however.


R1# show ipv6 eigrp topology all-links
! Legend removed for brevity
P 2001:DB8:CC1E::/64, 1 successors, FD is 2048, serno 9
        via FE80::2 (2560/256), Serial1/0
        via FE80::3 (5120/1280), Serial1/1
        via FE80::4 (4096/3072), Serial1/2
```

```
! The debug eigrp fsm is used to display EIGRP's DUAL FSM actions.


R1# debug eigrp fsm
EIGRP FSM Events/Actions debugging is on



R1# conf t
Enter configuration commands, one per line.  End with CNTL/Z.
R1(config)# int s1/0
R1(config-if)# shutdown
*Mar  1 12:20:35.380: %DUAL-5-NBRCHANGE: IPv6-EIGRP(0) 1: Neighbor FE80::2
(Serial1/0) is down: interface down
*Mar  1 12:20:35.384: DUAL: linkdown: start - FE80::2 via Serial1/0


! After the Serial1/0 interface is shut down, note that the loss of R2
! is represented in the topology table as if R2 advertised an infinite metric.
! R1 evaluates all neighbor entries for the destination in the topology table
! and determines that while the minimum available distance (Dmin) is 4096,
! obviously via R4, this router does not meet the FC - that is the reason
! of the "not found" comment in the debug output; the "not found" does not
! really relate to the FE80::4 line on which it is printed out (the debug
! output is just wrapped confusingly).


*Mar  1 12:20:35.384: DUAL: Destination 2001:DB8:CC1E::/64
*Mar  1 12:20:35.384: DUAL: Find FS for dest 2001:DB8:CC1E::/64. FD is 2048, RD is
  2560
*Mar  1 12:20:35.384: DUAL:      FE80::2 metric 4294967295/4294967295
*Mar  1 12:20:35.384: DUAL:      FE80::3 metric 5120/1280
*Mar  1 12:20:35.384: DUAL:      FE80::4 metric 4096/3072 not found Dmin is 4096
*Mar  1 12:20:35.384: DUAL: Peer total 2 stub 0 template 2


! Because the neighbor providing the least cost path does not meet the FC,
! R1 enters the Active state, sends out Queries, and expects Replies.


*Mar  1 12:20:35.384: DUAL: Dest 2001:DB8:CC1E::/64 entering active state.
*Mar  1 12:20:35.384: DUAL: Set reply-status table. Count is 2.
*Mar  1 12:20:35.384: DUAL: Not doing split horizon
*Mar  1 12:20:35.384: DUAL: linkdown: finish


! R3 responds; it is not influenced by the failure of the R1/R2 link, so
! the CD/RD are the same as already stored.


*Mar  1 12:20:35.440: DUAL: rcvreply: 2001:DB8:CC1E::/64 via FE80::3 metric
  5120/1280
*Mar  1 12:20:35.440: DUAL: reply count is 2
*Mar  1 12:20:35.440: DUAL: Clearing handle 2, count now 1
```

```
! R4 responds; it is not influenced by the failure of the R1/R2 link, so
! the CD/RD are the same as already stored.


*Mar  1 12:20:35.440: DUAL: rcvreply: 2001:DB8:CC1E::/64 via FE80::4 metric
  4096/3072
*Mar  1 12:20:35.440: DUAL: reply count is 1
*Mar  1 12:20:35.440: DUAL: Clearing handle 1, count now 0
*Mar  1 12:20:35.440: DUAL: Freeing reply status table


! Now that all replies have been received, R1 is free to reset the FD
! and choose any neighbor that provides the least CD. Obviously, it is R4.
! The "RT installed" shows the route and the next hop that are installed
! into the routing table.


*Mar  1 12:20:35.444: DUAL: Find FS for dest 2001:DB8:CC1E::/64. FD is 4294967295,
  RD is 4294967295 found
*Mar  1 12:20:35.444: DUAL: Removing dest 2001:DB8:CC1E::/64, nexthop FE80::2,
  infosource FE80::2
*Mar  1 12:20:35.448: DUAL: RT installed 2001:DB8:CC1E::/64 via FE80::4
*Mar  1 12:20:35.448: DUAL: Send update about 2001:DB8:CC1E::/64.  Reason: metric
  chg
*Mar  1 12:20:35.448: DUAL: Send update about 2001:DB8:CC1E::/64.  Reason: new if
*Mar  1 12:20:37.308: %LINK-5-CHANGED: Interface Serial1/0, changed state to
  administratively down
*Mar  1 12:20:38.308: %LINEPROTO-5-UPDOWN: Line protocol on Interface Serial1/0,
  changed state to down


! The outputs below now show that the FD has been reset and updated to the new
! least CD available - 4096 via R4. The route via R4 is also installed into
! the IPv6 routing table. Note that R3 was, and has remained, a Feasible Successor
! without being ever promoted to the Successor role.


R1(config-if)# do show ipv6 eigrp topology
! Legend removed for brevity
P 2001:DB8:CC1E::/64, 1 successors, FD is 4096
        via FE80::4 (4096/3072), Serial1/2
        via FE80::3 (5120/1280), Serial1/1


R1(config-if)# do show ipv6 route eigrp
! Legend removed for brevity
D   2001:DB8:CC1E::/64 [90/4096]
     via FE80::4, Serial1/2
```

## DUAL FSM

The mechanisms described so far—the concept of Feasible Distance, Successors and Feasible Successors, local computations, and diffusing computations that grow by sending Queries and shrink by receiving Replies—allow a router to efficiently compute a new path to a destination, assuming that over the entire duration of the diffusing computation, no other topological changes take place. However, this is a very strong assumption. Therefore, on top of all these mechanisms, EIGRP uses a control mechanism called the Diffusing Update Algorithm, or DUAL, that takes care of handling multiple topology changes occurring during a single diffusing computation. Figure 8-7 shows the DUAL Finite State Machine (FSM).

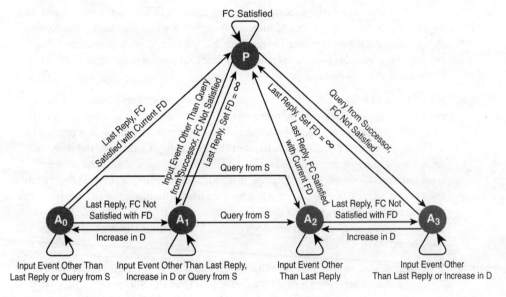

**Figure 8-7**   *Diffusing Update Algorithm Finite State Machine*

In Figure 8-7, the acronyms D, S, FC, and FD stand for Distance, Successor, Feasible Condition, and Feasible Distance, respectively. The DUAL FSM has one passive and four active states denoted as P and $A_0$ through $A_3$. These Active states also have names by which we will refer to them later in the section, and the names refer to the origin of the diffusing computation—which router appears to have started it:

- $A_0$: Local Origin with Distance Increase
- $A_1$: Local Origin
- $A_2$: Multiple Origins
- $A_3$: Successor Origin

Comments by the arrows explain events that the DUAL FSM reacts to, and the arrows describe the state transitions caused by these events. Explaining the DUAL FSM in depth is beyond the scope of this book; however, its basic behavior can be summarized in these rules (all rules always focusing on a single particular destination at a time):

■ Unless a change in distance occurs such that the neighbor providing the least Computed Distance fails to meet the Feasibility Condition, the route remains passive.

■ If a Query is received from the current Successor and, after processing the distance indicated in this Query, the neighbor that provides the least Computed Distance fails to meet the Feasibility Condition, the route will enter the $A_3$ active state, also called the *Successor Origin* Active State. The router will send out Queries and wait for Replies. If no further distance increase is detected while waiting for the Replies, the last Reply allows the router to transition back to the Passive state, reinitialize the Feasible Distance, and choose any neighbor that provides the least Computed Distance as the new Successor.

■ If a distance change caused by other means than a Query from a Successor is detected (this can be caused by receiving an Update, changing an interface metric, or losing a neighbor) and after processing the change, the neighbor that provides the least Computed Distance fails to meet the Feasibility Condition, the route will enter the $A_1$ active state, also called the *Local Origin* Active State. The router will send out Queries and wait for Replies. If no further distance increase or Query from the current Successor is received while waiting for the Replies, the last Reply allows the router to transition back to the Passive state, reinitialize the Feasible Distance, and choose any neighbor that provides the least Computed Distance as the new Successor.

■ If during the stay in the $A_3$ (Successor Origin) or $A_1$ (Local Origin) active states, another distance increase caused by other means than the Successor's Query is detected, another topology change during the diffusing computation has occurred. Because the router cannot advertise this updated distance while it is in the Active state, other routers might not be informed about it and their Replies might not take this new increased distance into account. Therefore, extra scrutiny is applied to the received Replies instead of simply choosing the neighbor that provides the least Computed Distance. This is accomplished first by changing the state from $A_3$ (Successor Origin) to $A_2$ (called *Multiple Origins*), or from $A_1$ (Local Origin) to $A_0$ (no official name; we will call it *Local Origin with Distance Increase*) states. In $A_2$ or $A_0$ states, the router waits to receive all remaining Replies. When the last Reply arrives, the router will first check whether the neighbor providing the least Computed Distance passes the Feasible Condition check using the Feasibility Distance value set when the route entered the Active state (recall that it was set to the increased distance through the current Successor at the moment of transitioning to the Active state). This extra check essentially mimics a situation in which the router is actually using the path through the current Successor and has just detected the distance increase, so it uses the current value of Feasibility Distance to verify whether the neighbor providing the least Computed Distance passes the Feasibility

Condition. If it does, the route becomes Passive again, and the neighbor is chosen as the Successor. If it does not, however, the route will return from $A_0$ (Local Origin with Distance Increase) to $A_1$ (Local Origin) or from $A_2$ (Multiple Origins) to $A_3$ (Successor Origin) and the router will commence another diffusing computation by again sending a Query.

■ If during the stay in $A_1$ (Local Origin) or $A_0$ (Local Origin with Distance Increase) active states a Query from the Successor is received, another topology change during the diffusing computation has occurred. Because the router cannot advertise this updated distance while it is in the Active state, other routers might not be informed about it and their Replies might not take this new increased distance into account. Therefore, extra scrutiny is applied to the received Replies. This is accomplished by changing the state to $A_2$ (Multiple Origins) and then proceeding from that state just like in the previous case.

The number of the Active state, that is, 0 to 3, is stored in a so-called query origin flag that is visible in the EIGRP topology table during the Active state. Consult Example 8-12 for more information. Routers in this example are running IPv4 EIGRP and have again been configured to take only the Delay metric component into account. The routers in this topology have been daisy-chained (RouterX is connected to RouterY; RouterY is connected to RouterZ and not shown in the example). To elicit long-lasting Active states, the Hold timers on interfaces have been configured to 10000 seconds and the **timers active-time disabled** command was used on all routers to allow the diffusing computation to run indefinitely. In addition, an access list dropping all inbound packets was placed on the RouterY interface toward RouterX before causing a topology change; this ACL prevented Queries and Replies from being exchanged between RouterX and RouterY, causing the diffusing computation to stall. Topology changes were caused by shutting down loopback interfaces whose networks were advertised in EIGRP, and optionally increasing the Delay metrics on interfaces during the diffusing computation.

**Example 8-12**  *Active States of an EIGRP Route*

```
! In this example, a local loopback interface has been shut down, prompting
! the router to start a diffusing computation. The following outputs show
! that the origin of the query is the local router. In the output of
! show ip eigrp topology active command, the query-origin is shown as
! "Local origin", and the detailed output on the 10.255.255.1/32 entry
! claims the Query origin flag to be 1, hinting at the A1 state.

RouterX(config-if)# do show ip eigrp topology active
IP-EIGRP Topology Table for AS(1)/ID(10.255.255.1)

Codes: P - Passive, A - Active, U - Update, Q - Query, R - Reply,
       r - reply Status, s - sia Status

A 10.255.255.1/32, 1 successors, FD is Inaccessible, Q
    1 replies, active never, query-origin: Local origin
       via Connected (Infinity/Infinity), Loopback0
```

```
         Remaining replies:
             via 10.0.12.2, r, Serial1/0


RouterX(config-if)# do show ip eigrp topology 10.255.255.1/32
IP-EIGRP (AS 1): Topology entry for 10.255.255.1/32
   State is Active, Query origin flag is 1, 1 Successor(s), FD is 4294967295
Waiting for 1 replies
   Routing Descriptor Blocks:
   0.0.0.0 (Loopback0), from Connected, Send flag is 0x0
         Composite metric is (4294967295/4294967295), Route is Internal
         Vector metric:
            Minimum bandwidth is 0 Kbit
            Total delay is 167772159 microseconds
            Reliability is 0/255
            Load is 0/255
            Minimum MTU is 1514
            Hop count is 0


! In the next output, an entry is shown for which the router received a Query
! from its Successor. The query-origin is indicated as "Successor Origin",
! and the Query origin flag having the value of 3, hinting at the A₃ state.

RouterY(config-if)# do show ip eigrp topology active
IP-EIGRP Topology Table for AS(1)/ID(10.255.255.2)

Codes: P - Passive, A - Active, U - Update, Q - Query, R - Reply,
       r - reply Status, s - sia Status


A 10.255.255.3/32, 1 successors, FD is Inaccessible, Q
     1 replies, active never, query-origin: Successor Origin
         via 10.0.23.3 (Infinity/Infinity), Serial1/0
      Remaining replies:
          via 10.0.12.1, r, Serial1/1


RouterY(config-if)# do show ip eigrp topology 10.255.255.3/32
IP-EIGRP (AS 1): Topology entry for 10.255.255.3/32
   State is Active, Query origin flag is 3, 1 Successor(s), FD is 4294967295
Waiting for 1 replies
   Routing Descriptor Blocks:
   10.0.23.3 (Serial1/0), from 10.0.23.3, Send flag is 0x0
         Composite metric is (4294967295/4294967295), Route is Internal
         Vector metric:
            Minimum bandwidth is 0 Kbit
            Total delay is 167772159 microseconds
            Reliability is 0/255
            Load is 0/255
```

```
        Minimum MTU is 1514
        Hop count is 0


! The following output shows a router that received an Update from its Successor
! that forced it to enter the A₁ state, and detecting another distance increase
! during the diffusing computation, moving it to the A₀ state. Note that the
! verbose name of the query-origin is displayed as "Clear", having no meaning.
! The numerical value of the Query origin flag is 0, hinting at the A₀ state.

RouterY(config-if)# do show ip eigrp topology active
IP-EIGRP Topology Table for AS(1)/ID(10.255.255.2)


Codes: P - Passive, A - Active, U - Update, Q - Query, R - Reply,
       r - reply Status, s - sia Status


A 10.255.255.4/32, 1 successors, FD is 256256, Q
    1 replies, active never, query-origin: Clear
        via 10.0.23.3 (512000/256000), Serial1/0
      Remaining replies:
         via 10.0.12.1, r, Serial1/1


RouterY(config-if)# do show ip eigrp topo 10.255.255.4/32
IP-EIGRP (AS 1): Topology entry for 10.255.255.4/32
  State is Active, Query origin flag is 0, 1 Successor(s), FD is 256256
Waiting for 1 replies
  Routing Descriptor Blocks:
  10.0.23.3 (Serial1/0), from 10.0.23.3, Send flag is 0x0
      Composite metric is (512000/256000), Route is Internal
      Vector metric:
        Minimum bandwidth is 1000 Kbit
        Total delay is 20000 microseconds
        Reliability is 255/255
        Load is 1/255
        Minimum MTU is 1500
        Hop count is 1


! Finally, the next output shows a router that, during the diffusing computation,
! detected a distance increase and received a Query from its Successor. Note
! the Query origin being displayed as "Multiple Origins" and the value of the
! Query origin flag is 2, hinting at the A₂ state.


RouterY(config-if)# do show ip eigrp topology active
IP-EIGRP Topology Table for AS(1)/ID(10.255.255.2)


Codes: P - Passive, A - Active, U - Update, Q - Query, R - Reply,
       r - reply Status, s - sia Status
```

```
A 10.255.255.5/32, 1 successors, FD is 256256, Q
    1 replies, active never, query-origin: Multiple Origins
        via 10.0.23.3 (Infinity/Infinity), Serial1/0
      Remaining replies:
        via 10.0.12.1, r, Serial1/1


RouterY(config-if)# do show ip eigrp topology 10.255.255.5/32
IP-EIGRP (AS 1): Topology entry for 10.255.255.5/32
  State is Active, Query origin flag is 2, 1 Successor(s), FD is 256256
Waiting for 1 replies
  Routing Descriptor Blocks:
  10.0.23.3 (Serial1/0), from 10.0.23.3, Send flag is 0x0
      Composite metric is (4294967295/4294967295), Route is Internal
      Vector metric:
        Minimum bandwidth is 0 Kbit
        Total delay is 167772159 microseconds
        Reliability is 0/255
        Load is 0/255
        Minimum MTU is 1514
        Hop count is 0
```

## Stuck-In-Active State

If a router joins the diffusing computation for a particular destination by putting it into the Active state and sending out Queries, it must first wait for all its neighbors to send back a Reply before it can conclude the diffusing computation itself, make a new best-path selection, and start sending its own Replies. Consequently, if a router sends a Query and that Query causes at least one of its directly connected neighbors to also become Active, the router will now become dependent not only on its Active neighbor but also on that neighbor's own neighbors. If they fail to respond, the router's neighbor cannot conclude the diffusing computation and send a final Reply back to the router, meaning that the router cannot conclude the diffusing computation either. By simple extension, a router in the Active state is dependent on the entire chained sequence of routers that have become Active as a result of this router's Query. Any single misbehaving router up this chain that is unable to send a Reply for whatever reason will cause all the routers depending on it to stall, possibly never being allowed to conclude the diffusing computation and converge.

There are several reasons why the EIGRP neighbor router(s) might not respond to the Query. Common reasons for this include the following:

**Key Topic**

- The neighbor router's CPU is overloaded and the router either cannot respond in time or is even unable to process all incoming packets including the EIGRP packets.

- Quality issues on the link are causing packets to be lost.

- Low-bandwidth links are congested and packets are being delayed or dropped.

■ The network topology is excessively large or complex, either requiring the Query to propagate to a significant depth or causing an inordinate number of prefixes to be impacted by a single link or node failure.

This chained dependency of routers in the Active state is somewhat of EIGRP's Achilles heel. Therefore, EIGRP implements multiple mechanisms to cope with this situation.

When a Query is first sent out by a router, a timer called the Active timer for the route is started. The default value of the Active timers is 3 minutes and it can be set to any value between 1 and 65535 minutes or set to infinity using the **timers active-time** command in the **router eigrp** context. If all expected Replies are not received before the Active timer expires, the route in question will be designated as Stuck-In-Active (SIA). The neighbor or neighbors that did not reply will be removed from the neighbor table and their adjacencies torn down, and the diffusing computation will consider these neighbors to have responded with an infinite metric.

SIA states in EIGRP are extremely unpleasant and generally difficult to diagnose. In the worst case, an unresponsive router can prevent a significant portion of the network from ever converging in the time allotted by the Active timer. In addition, dropping an adjacency to a neighbor as a consequence of the SIA state can introduce further instability to the network, as all networks learned from that neighbor will be flushed and possibly learned again after the neighbor comes back up within the Hello interval time.

The difficulty in solving the SIA states in first EIGRP implementations was aggravated by the fact that if a neighbor did not send a Reply until the Active timer expired, the router would drop the adjacency toward that neighbor even though the neighbor itself was not the root cause of the SIA. Clearly, doing so unlocked the SIA state, but at the same time, it penalized a router that might have been innocent and provided no hint as to where the real cause of the problem was located. To at least partially contain and localize the true place where a difficulty in the Query/Reply message exchange causes the diffusing computation to stall, more recent EIGRP implementations use the SIA-Query and SIA-Reply messages.

Key
Topic

If a neighbor does not respond to a Query message with its Reply within half of the Active timer time, the router will send the neighbor a SIA-Query message. The SIA-Query stands for a message saying "Are you still working on my Query?" If the neighbor is able to receive and process this SIA-Query, it will immediately respond with the SIA-Reply message. The contents of the SIA-Reply can either say "Yes, I still expect my own neighbors to send me the Replies I've asked them for" or "No, the computation is finished; this is my current metric to the destination." In any case, the SIA-Reply is sent immediately as a response to the SIA-Query message; there is nothing to wait for. Receiving an SIA-Reply allows the Active timer to be reset, giving the diffusing computation an additional time to complete. At most three SIA-Queries can be sent, each after half of the Active timer. If the diffusing computation is not finished by the time the third SIA-Query was replied to by an SIA-Reply and the half of the Active timer expired again, the adjacency to the neighbor will be dropped. The same will happen if an SIA-Query is not responded to by an SIA-Reply within the next half of the Active timer. With the default setting of the Active timer to 180 seconds, three consecutive SIA-Query packets allow extending the diffusing computation to a maximum of 4 × 90 = 360 seconds (90 seconds to the first SIA-Query, plus each SIA-Query buying another 90 seconds).

As a result, if two neighbors can communicate without issues, an SIA-Query will be responded to by an SIA-Reply almost instantly. If, however, two routers have issues talking to each other, it is also probably the place where the normal Query and Reply messages are lost, and there is a good chance of the SIA-Query also going unanswered. Hence, the adjacency will be dropped between the routers that are likely to be the cause of the SIA state.

Example 8-13 shows an SIA situation. Similar to Example 8-12, three routers in a row, RouterX, RouterY, and RouterZ (not shown in the topology) are connected, running IPv4 EIGRP. The Active timer is at its default setting of 3 minutes. The Hold interval is increased to 10000 seconds on each interface in the topology, and an ACL dropping all packets is placed in the inbound direction on the RouterY interface toward RouterZ. On RouterX, the local loopback is shut down. RouterX sends a Query to RouterY, which in turn sends a Query to RouterZ. However, because of the ACL, the Reply from RouterZ is not received by RouterY, leading to an SIA state. The following example documents the EIGRP's handling of the issue. Read the comments in the example carefully.

**Example 8-13**    *Handling of Stuck-In-Active State*

```
! Right after the loopback is shut down on RouterX, it sends out a Query to
! its neighbor RouterY. Note the origin of the Query is Local.
! The lowercase 'r' flag shown in the "Remaining replies" section indicates
! a Reply packet is expected from 10.0.12.2 (RouterY) but has not arrived yet.
! Until a SIA-Query has been sent, the output of show ip eigrp topology and
! show ip eigrp topology active is entirely identical, with the active keyword
! automatically limiting output just to active entries.

RouterX(config-if)# do show ip eigrp topology
IP-EIGRP Topology Table for AS(1)/ID(10.255.255.1)

Codes: P - Passive, A - Active, U - Update, Q - Query, R - Reply,
       r - reply Status, s - sia Status

! Lines omitted for brevity

A 10.255.255.1/32, 1 successors, FD is Inaccessible
    1 replies, active 00:00:10, query-origin: Local origin
      Remaining replies:
          via 10.0.12.2, r, Serial1/0

RouterX(config-if)# do show ip eigrp topology active
IP-EIGRP Topology Table for AS(1)/ID(10.255.255.1)

Codes: P - Passive, A - Active, U - Update, Q - Query, R - Reply,
       r - reply Status, s - sia Status
```

```
A 10.255.255.1/32, 1 successors, FD is Inaccessible
    1 replies, active 00:00:10, query-origin: Local origin
         via Connected (Infinity/Infinity), Loopback0
       Remaining replies:
          via 10.0.12.2, r, Serial1/0


R1(config-if)# do show ip eigrp topology 10.255.255.1/32
IP-EIGRP (AS 1): Topology entry for 10.255.255.1/32
  State is Active, Query origin flag is 1, 1 Successor(s), FD is 4294967295
Waiting for 1 replies
  Routing Descriptor Blocks:
  0.0.0.0 (Loopback0), from Connected, Send flag is 0x0
      Composite metric is (4294967295/4294967295), Route is Internal
      Vector metric:
        Minimum bandwidth is 0 Kbit
        Total delay is 167772159 microseconds
        Reliability is 0/255
        Load is 0/255
        Minimum MTU is 1514
        Hop count is 0


! On RouterY, the route is reported with the Query origin of Successor Origin.
! Also here notice the 'r' flag in the "Remaining replies" section, indicating
! a Reply packet is expected from 10.0.23.3 (RouterZ) but has not arrived yet.
! This Reply will never arrive due to the ACL between RouterY and RouterZ.
! The 'Q' flag in the entry heading indicates that a Query has been sent for
! this route but it has not been acknowledged yet (also due to the ACL).


RouterY(config-if)# do show ip eigrp topology
IP-EIGRP Topology Table for AS(1)/ID(10.255.255.2)


Codes: P - Passive, A - Active, U - Update, Q - Query, R - Reply,
       r - reply Status, s - sia Status


! Lines omitted for brevity


A 10.255.255.1/32, 1 successors, FD is Inaccessible, Q
    1 replies, active 00:00:16, query-origin: Successor Origin
      Remaining replies:
          via 10.0.23.3, r, Serial1/0


RouterY(config-if)# do show ip eigrp topology active
IP-EIGRP Topology Table for AS(1)/ID(10.255.255.2)


Codes: P - Passive, A - Active, U - Update, Q - Query, R - Reply,
       r - reply Status, s - sia Status
```

```
A 10.255.255.1/32, 1 successors, FD is Inaccessible, Q
    1 replies, active 00:00:16, query-origin: Successor Origin
        via 10.0.12.1 (Infinity/Infinity), Serial1/1
      Remaining replies:
        via 10.0.23.3, r, Serial1/0


RouterY(config-if)# do show ip eigrp topology 10.255.255.1/32
IP-EIGRP (AS 1): Topology entry for 10.255.255.1/32
  State is Active, Query origin flag is 3, 1 Successor(s), FD is 4294967295
Waiting for 1 replies
  Routing Descriptor Blocks:
  10.0.12.1 (Serial1/1), from 10.0.12.1, Send flag is 0x0
      Composite metric is (4294967295/4294967295), Route is Internal
      Vector metric:
        Minimum bandwidth is 0 Kbit
        Total delay is 167772159 microseconds
        Reliability is 0/255
        Load is 0/255
        Minimum MTU is 1514
        Hop count is 0


! After the half of the Active timer elapses, both RouterX and RouterY will
! try to find out whether their neighbors that have not responded yet are
! still working on the Query. To accomplish this, both RouterX and RouterY
! will send a SIA-Query to their unresponsive neighbors.

! The "retries(1)" on RouterX shows that it has sent one SIA-Query to
! RouterY and has received a SIA-Reply response. This is visible in a number
! of places: a topology table entry of Infinity/Infinity via 10.0.12.2
! has been added in the show ip eigrp active output as a result of receiving
! the SIA-Reply, and this entry has an 'r' flag indicating that a regular
! Reply is still being expected but has no 's' flag that would indicate
! that no SIA-Reply was received. Compare this output later to the output of
! RouterY below.

RouterX(config-if)# do show ip eigrp topology
IP-EIGRP Topology Table for AS(1)/ID(10.255.255.1)

Codes: P - Passive, A - Active, U - Update, Q - Query, R - Reply,
       r - reply Status, s - sia Status

! Lines omitted for brevity

A 10.255.255.1/32, 1 successors, FD is Inaccessible
    1 replies, active 00:01:41, query-origin: Local origin, retries(1)
```

```
        Remaining replies:
            via 10.0.12.2, r, Serial1/0


RouterX(config-if)# do show ip eigrp topology active
IP-EIGRP Topology Table for AS(1)/ID(10.255.255.1)


Codes: P - Passive, A - Active, U - Update, Q - Query, R - Reply,
       r - reply Status, s - sia Status


A 10.255.255.1/32, 1 successors, FD is Inaccessible
    1 replies, active 00:01:41, query-origin: Local origin, retries(1)
        via Connected (Infinity/Infinity), Loopback0
        via 10.0.12.2 (Infinity/Infinity), r, Serial1/0, serno 20


RouterX(config-if)# do show ip eigrp topology 10.255.255.1/32
IP-EIGRP (AS 1): Topology entry for 10.255.255.1/32
  State is Active, Query origin flag is 1, 1 Successor(s), FD is 4294967295
Waiting for 1 replies
  Routing Descriptor Blocks:
  0.0.0.0 (Loopback0), from Connected, Send flag is 0x0
      Composite metric is (4294967295/4294967295), Route is Internal
      Vector metric:
        Minimum bandwidth is 0 Kbit
        Total delay is 167772159 microseconds
        Reliability is 0/255
        Load is 0/255
        Minimum MTU is 1514
        Hop count is 0
  10.0.12.2 (Serial1/0), from 10.0.12.2, Send flag is 0x0, outstanding reply
      Composite metric is (4294967295/4294967295), Route is Internal
      Vector metric:
        Minimum bandwidth is 1000 Kbit
        Total delay is 167772159 microseconds
        Reliability is 255/255
        Load is 1/255
        Minimum MTU is 1500
        Hop count is 0


! On RouterY, it is also visible that a SIA-Query has been sent to RouterZ.
! However, this SIA-Query has not been responded to. In the basic
! show ip eigrp topology command output, the RouterZ (10.0.23.3) is marked
! as SIA-Stuck. In the show ip eigrp topology active output, the topology
! table entry for RouterZ (10.0.23.3) shows that not only a Reply is still
! expected (the 'r' flag) but also that a SIA-Reply is expected (the 's' flag)
! but has not arrived yet. The 'q' flag indicates that a SIA-Query was sent
! to the neighbor but no ACK was received yet (because of the ACL).
```

```
!
! Eventually, after next half Active timer interval with no SIA-Reply arriving,
! RouterY decides to drop the adjacency to RouterZ.

RouterY(config-if)# do show ip eigrp topology
IP-EIGRP Topology Table for AS(1)/ID(10.255.255.2)


Codes: P - Passive, A - Active, U - Update, Q - Query, R - Reply,
       r - reply Status, s - sia Status


! Lines omitted for brevity

A 10.255.255.1/32, 1 successors, FD is Inaccessible, Qqr
    1 replies, active 00:01:46, query-origin: Successor Origin, retries(1)
      Remaining replies:
          via 10.0.23.3, r, Serial1/0
    SIA-Stuck: 1 peers
      Peers:
          via 10.0.23.3, s, Serial1/0


RouterY(config-if)# do show ip eigrp topology active
IP-EIGRP Topology Table for AS(1)/ID(10.255.255.2)


Codes: P - Passive, A - Active, U - Update, Q - Query, R - Reply,
       r - reply Status, s - sia Status


A 10.255.255.1/32, 1 successors, FD is Inaccessible, Qqr
    1 replies, active 00:01:47, query-origin: Successor Origin, retries(1)
          via 10.0.12.1 (Infinity/Infinity), Serial1/1, serno 24
          via 10.0.23.3 (Infinity/Infinity), rs, q, Serial1/0, serno 23, anchored

RouterY(config-if)# do show ip eigrp topology 10.255.255.1/32
IP-EIGRP (AS 1): Topology entry for 10.255.255.1/32
  State is Active, Query origin flag is 3, 1 Successor(s), FD is 4294967295
Waiting for 1 replies
  Routing Descriptor Blocks:
  10.0.12.1 (Serial1/1), from 10.0.12.1, Send flag is 0x0
      Composite metric is (4294967295/4294967295), Route is Internal
      Vector metric:
        Minimum bandwidth is 0 Kbit
        Total delay is 167772159 microseconds
        Reliability is 0/255
        Load is 0/255
        Minimum MTU is 1514
        Hop count is 0
  10.0.23.3 (Serial1/0), from 10.0.23.3, Send flag is 0x40, outstanding reply
```

```
        Composite metric is (4294967295/4294967295), Route is Internal
        Vector metric:
          Minimum bandwidth is 1000 Kbit
          Total delay is 167772159 microseconds
          Reliability is 255/255
          Load is 1/255
          Minimum MTU is 1500
          Hop count is 0
R2(config-if)#

*Mar  1 00:14:35.919: %DUAL-3-SIA: Route 10.255.255.1/32 stuck-in-active state in
  IP-EIGRP(0) 1.  Cleaning up
*Mar  1 00:14:35.927: %DUAL-5-NBRCHANGE: IP-EIGRP(0) 1: Neighbor 10.0.23.3
  (Serial1/0) is down: stuck in active
```

Note that it is possible for a router to receive a Query for a destination while it is Active for that destination. Assume the topology shown in Figure 8-8.

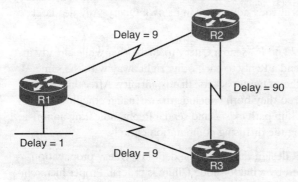

**Figure 8-8**   *Active State in a Network with Physical Loops*

The situation would be as follows:

■ R1 has a LAN network directly connected.

■ Both R2 and R3 will choose R1 as their next hop toward the LAN, with the Computed Distance of 10.

■ Neither R2 nor R3 considers itself to be a Feasible Successor for the route toward the R1 LAN.

■ After the LAN interface on R1 is shut down, R1 will send out a Query for this network to all its neighbors, indicating an infinite distance. Assume, however, that there are significant delays in the delivery of the Query packet to R1's neighbors, and R2 is the first router to receive this Query.

■ Because the Query causes R2 to stop considering R1 as the Successor (it no longer passes the FC check on R2) and R2 has no Feasible Successors, it will go Active and send its own Query to R3.

■ Meanwhile, assume that R1's Query arrived at R3. For R3, the situation is identical. R3 will also become Active and send a Query to R2, while R2's Query is already being transmitted down the R2/R3 link.

■ As a result, R2 and R3 have sent a Query to each other, causing each of them to receive a Query for a destination while already being in the Active state for that destination.

Some sources state that precisely this situation causes the SIA states, as they assume that this causes a deadlock. A router in an Active state for a destination has not concluded its computation yet and cannot send Replies, causing the two or more routers to mutually wait for themselves and never receive the expected Reply to each other. In reality, this is a gross misunderstanding. Such situations never cause SIA states to occur. Recall that when a router enters the Active state for a destination, it sends out a Query indicating its current distance to the destination after the topology change that triggered the transition to the Active state. If, during the Active state, the router receives another Query for this destination, it simply sends back a Reply packet immediately, claiming exactly the same distance as originally advertised in its own Query packet. In other words, the router simply restates the same distance it has already advertised in its own Query. Any deadlock scenario is thereby averted.

With respect to Figure 8-8, after R2 and R3 send a Query to each other while already in the Active state, they will simply send a Reply to each other right away with the same distance they already indicated in their Query packets, that is, infinity. After this, R2 and R3 receive all Replies they wait for, so they both conclude the diffusing computation, arrive at the conclusion that no backup path exists, and send a Reply indicating an infinite distance back to R1, terminating the diffusing computation entirely.

To avoid SIA states, proper network design that limits the depth of Query propagation and the number of prefixes impacted by a link or node failure is crucial. Proper hierarchical network design coupled with judicious use of passive interfaces, appropriate route filtering and/or summarization, and the EIGRP Stub feature are the key tools that help limit the probability of an SIA state occurrence to an absolute minimum.

# EIGRP Named Mode

Starting with IOS Release 15.0(1)M, an EIGRP process on a router can be configured using a so-called *named mode*. The common way of configuring EIGRP processes directly by their autonomous system numbers separately for IPv4 and IPv6 was retroactively named the *classic mode*, sometimes also called the *autonomous system mode*. The named mode is the preferred mode of configuring EIGRP after the IOS supports it, and all commands for new features in EIGRP will be made available in the named mode only. The classic mode remains to provide backward compatibility with older configurations but it will not be enhanced with new commands. On a single router, you can run multiple EIGRP processes, some configured using the classic mode and others configured in named mode.

Reasons for EIGRP developers to move to named mode were motivated primarily by the fact that many new features were added both to IPv4 and IPv6 EIGRP. It was becoming clear that this called for a better unified, more consistent configuration interface, ultimately provided by the named configuration mode. Readers knowledgeable with Border Gateway Protocol (BGP) configuration will find the EIGRP named mode actually familiar: a single EIGRP process configuration that consists of one or more address family sections, each of them specifying details of EIGRP operation for the particular address family. The unification in the named mode configuration even went as far as providing commands to configure *every* aspect of EIGRP operation including former per-interface commands (timers, authentication, next hop handling, Split Horizon, summarization, and others) within the context of the named mode. With named mode, the entire EIGRP configuration is located in a single place. If an EIGRP instance is configured in named mode, all EIGRP-related commands outside the named mode (such as per-interface commands) will be ignored if configured.

It is very important to stress that the classic and named mode are just two different ways of how EIGRP is configured. They *do not* constitute two different versions of EIGRP. There is no difference to EIGRP packet format or operation, except (of course) the new configurable features for which the commands are available only in the named mode.

As the named mode is best explained in a real configuration, Example 8-14 contains a fairly typical named mode configuration for an IPv4/IPv6 EIGRP on a router. Three building blocks of a named EIGRP configuration can be discerned:

■ **Address Family (AF) section:** Created using the **address-family** command, this is a mandatory section directly inside **router eigrp** *name* configuration that specifies the particular address family for which an EIGRP instance shall be started. The autonomous system number is a part of the AF section definition.

■ **Per-AF-interface section:** This optional section configured by the **af-interface** command and located inside a particular AF holds EIGRP settings pertaining to the specified interface and AF. One per-AF-interface section can be created for each routed interface or subinterface. In addition, a per-AF-interface section is configured using **af-interface default** holds settings that will be applied to all interfaces enabled for EIGRP. In the case both **af-interface default** and an interface-specific **af-interface** section define the same setting, the interface-specific section is preferred.

■ **Per-AF-topology section:** This is a section present inside a particular AF, related to the support of Multi Topology Routing (MTR) in EIGRP. The **topology base** per-AF-topology section will always be present in the configuration, even if the IOS has no support for multiple routing topologies.

Read the comments in the example carefully.

**Example 8-14**  *EIGRP Named Mode Configuration*

```
! Named mode is entered for both IPv4 and IPv6 EIGRP using the router eigrp
! command and referring to an arbitrary name.

router eigrp CCIE

! Here, IPv4 EIGRP address family for AS number 1 is enabled.

address-family ipv4 unicast autonomous-system 1

! Within the AF section, a number of per-AF-interface sections is created.
! The af-interface default section contains timer settings that apply to
! all EIGRP-enabled interfaces. The af-interface Loopback0 section defines
! the Lo0 interface to be passive.

  af-interface default
   hello-interval 1
   hold-time 3
  exit-af-interface
  !
  af-interface Loopback0
   passive-interface
  exit-af-interface

! The topology base section defines EIGRP behavior related to the base routing
! topology. On routers without Multi Topology Routing support, this will be
! the only per-AF-topology section present. Here, the variance is configured
! and the number of parallel paths to the same destination is increased.

  topology base
   maximum-paths 6
   variance 4
  exit-af-topology

! The network commands to enable EIGRP on selected interfaces are placed
! in the AF section itself.

  network 10.0.0.1 0.0.0.0
  network 10.255.255.1 0.0.0.0
 exit-address-family

! In the same EIGRP process, an IPv6 address family for AS number 1 is enabled.

  address-family ipv6 unicast autonomous-system 1
```

```
! Somewhat surprisingly, each interface on which IPv6 is enabled is automatically
! added to IPv6 EIGRP. In other words, as soon as the IPv6 EIGRP address family
! is configured, it immediately runs on all IPv6-enabled interfaces.
! The following af-interface default section therefore stops this EIGRP instance
! from automatically running on all IPv6-enabled interfaces. Selected interfaces
! are then added to this instance in their specific af-interface sections.

 af-interface default
  shutdown
 exit-af-interface
 !
 af-interface Loopback0
  no shutdown
 exit-af-interface
 !
 af-interface FastEthernet0/0
  no shutdown
 exit-af-interface

! Here, the Active timer defining the maximum time for a diffusing computation
! is shortened to one minute.

 topology base
  timers active-time 1
 exit-af-topology
exit-address-family
```

After briefly getting used to the new location of familiar commands, the named mode configuration comes off as a very natural way of configuring EIGRP and all related settings in a single place.

A few notes about the named mode are in order. The named mode is entered using the **router eigrp** *name* global configuration command, where *name* is an arbitrary text name, also called a virtual instance name, of the EIGRP process. Multiple-name EIGRP processes can be started on a single router as long as their names are unique. The process name is not sent in EIGRP messages; it is a locally significant value and is never compared to process names on other routers.

Each named EIGRP process can hold only a single instance for an address family. In other words, it is not allowed to run two or more instances for the same address family inside a single named EIGRP process. If it is necessary to run, say, two IPv4 EIGRP instances, one for AS number 1 and the other for AS number 64512, each of them must be placed into a separate EIGRP process with a unique name. Also, two or more distinct named EIGRP processes cannot run the same address family instance with the same AS number. Simply put, there is a one-to-one correspondence between an EIGRP named process and an address family instance with a particular AS number.

On the other hand, running several different address families under a single named EIGRP process is perfectly allowed, as shown in Example 8-14. In this case, the AS numbers of EIGRP instances for individual address families in the same EIGRP process do not even need to match (meaning that you can run an IPv4 instance for AS number 1 and an IPv6 instance in the same process for AS number 2), but such a configuration is confusing at best, so it is not recommended.

Readers familiar with the classic mode configuration of IPv6 EIGRP surely remember the fact that an IPv6 EIGRP process was shut down by default after configuring it, and a **no shutdown** command was necessary to actually start it. In the named configuration mode, this is no longer true. In fact, there is an opposite extreme already described in Example 8-14: As soon as you configure an IPv6 address family, it automatically adopts all interfaces on which IPv6 has been enabled (even a link-local address is sufficient) and starts running on them. As this is usually not the desired behavior for production networks, Example 8-14 shows how to use the **af-interface default** section to first keep the IPv6 address family instance off all interfaces, and only activate it on selected interfaces later. Note the difference between deactivating an EIGRP address family instance on an interface using the **shutdown** command and declaring an interface as passive using the **passive-interface** command (both used in an **af-interface** section): No EIGRP adjacencies will be formed over a passive interface, but its global prefixes will still be advertised over other interfaces. Deactivating an EIGRP address family instance makes the EIGRP completely ignore the interface, not forming any adjacencies over it and also not advertising any of its prefixes.

Let us now have a closer look at the commands available in each of the three AF-related sections of named EIGRP configuration.

## Address Family Section

This section is where any configurations specific to the EIGRP process itself are applied. Commonly used commands include **network** and **neighbor** statements, or a manual EIGRP Router ID specification. It is also the section that holds the per-AF-interface and per-AF-topology sections. Example 8-15 shows the first-order commands available in the IPv4 Address Family section.

**Example 8-15**   *EIGRP Address Family Configuration Mode*

```
R1(config-router-af)# ?
Address Family configuration commands:
  af-interface        Enter Address Family interface configuration
  default             Set a command to its defaults
  eigrp               EIGRP Address Family specific commands
  exit-address-family Exit Address Family configuration mode
  help                Description of the interactive help system
  maximum-prefix      Maximum number of prefixes acceptable in aggregate
  metric              Modify metrics and parameters for advertisement
  neighbor            Specify an IPv4 neighbor router
  network             Enable routing on an IP network
```

```
no                      Negate a command or set its defaults
shutdown                Shutdown address family
timers                  Adjust peering based timers
topology                Topology configuration mode
```

## Per-AF-Interface Configuration Section

This configuration section is where all EIGRP interface-specific commands are applied. Except non-EIGRP-specific commands such as **bandwidth** and **delay** (although arguably, the **delay** is used only by EIGRP), every other EIGRP-related command can now be configured in this section. This includes, but is not limited to, features such as EIGRP authentication, Split Horizon, and manual summarization. Example 8-16 shows the list of all first-order commands available in a per-AF-interface section for a selected interface. Note that the list of commands for the **af-interface default** section would omit the **summary-address** command; otherwise the list of supported commands would be identical.

**Example 8-16**  *EIGRP Address-Family Interface Configuration Mode*

```
R1(config-router-af-interface)# ?
Address Family Interfaces configuration commands:
  add-paths             Advertise add paths
  authentication        authentication subcommands
  bandwidth-percent     Set percentage of bandwidth percentage limit
  bfd                   Enable Bidirectional Forwarding Detection
  dampening-change      Percent interface metric must change to cause update
  dampening-interval    Time in seconds to check interface metrics
  default               Set a command to its defaults
  exit-af-interface     Exit from Address Family Interface configuration mode
  hello-interval        Configures hello interval
  hold-time             Configures hold time
  next-hop-self         Configures EIGRP next-hop-self
  no                    Negate a command or set its defaults
  passive-interface     Suppress address updates on an interface
  shutdown              Disable Address-Family on interface
  split-horizon         Perform split horizon
  summary-address       Perform address summarization
```

One of the neat consequences of having all EIGRP-related interface commands centralized in the **af-interface** section is that there is no longer a requirement for the **eigrp** keyword in any of these commands. This globalizes the EIGRP commands against the format used through any of the other routing protocols, and simultaneously provides a place for all configurations that affect the operation, implementation, and regulation of EIGRP as a whole.

## Per-AF-Topology Configuration Section

This configuration mode relates to the support of multiple routing topologies in EIGRP. While multiple routing topologies are outside the scope of CCIE Routing and Switching certification, a few words are certainly useful as the named EIGRP mode always presents us with the **topology base** configuration section.

Within the context of Multi Topology Routing, a *topology* is defined as a subset of routers and links in a network for which a separate set of routes is calculated. The entire network itself, for which the usual set of routes is calculated, is known as the *base topology*. The base topology is the default routing environment that exists prior to enabling MTR. Any additional topologies are known as class-specific topologies and are a subset of the base topology. Each class-specific topology carries a class of traffic and is characterized by an independent set of Network Layer Reachability Information (NLRI) that is used to maintain separate routing tables and FIB databases. This design allows the router to perform independent route calculation and forwarding for each topology. Multiple topologies can be used to segregate different classes of traffic, such as data, voice, and video, and carry them over different links in the same physical network, or to keep separate and independent topologies for IPv4 and IPv6 routing. Multiple topologies are not equivalent to Virtual Routing and Forwarding (VRF) tables because they share the common address space, and they are not intended to provide address conservation or reuse.

EIGRP is capable of keeping separate routing information for different topologies, and its behavior per specific topology within an address family can be configured in the per-AF-topology section. On routers without MTR support, only the **topology base** command will be available; on routers supporting MTR, the **topology** command will allow referencing a particular separate topology table definition by its name.

Example 8-17 shows the first-order commands available in the **topology base** section. Note that these commands comprise the most commands related to route and metric handling.

**Example 8-17**  *EIGRP Address-Family Topology Configuration Mode*

```
R1(config-router-af-topology)# ?
Address Family Topology configuration commands:
  auto-summary         Enable automatic network number summarization
  default              Set a command to its defaults
  default-information  Control distribution of default information
  default-metric       Set metric of redistributed routes
  distance             Define an administrative distance
  distribute-list      Filter entries in eigrp updates
  eigrp                EIGRP specific commands
  exit-af-topology     Exit from Address Family Topology configuration mode
  maximum-paths        Forward packets over multiple paths
  metric               Modify metrics and parameters for advertisement
  no                   Negate a command or set its defaults
  offset-list          Add or subtract offset from EIGRP metrics
  redistribute         Redistribute IPv4 routes from another routing protocol
```

| | |
|---|---|
| snmp | Modify snmp parameters |
| summary-metric | Specify summary to apply metric/filtering |
| timers | Adjust topology specific timers |
| traffic-share | How to compute traffic share over alternate paths |
| variance | Control load balancing variance |

To sum up the EIGRP named mode configuration, as you might have learned by now, everything you know about EIGRP classic mode configuration still applies in the EIGRP named mode. The only slight inconvenience is related to relearning the placement of the well-known commands into individual per-AF sections.

Together with the named mode, related **show** commands have also been updated. Instead of **show ip eigrp ...** the new **show eigrp address-family ipv4 ...** syntax is used. Similarly, instead of **show ipv6 eigrp ...** the new **show eigrp address-family ipv6 ...** syntax is used. The older **show** commands will still be accepted, though, even if EIGRP is configured in the named mode. Be aware, though, that for new EIGRP features, relevant **show** commands might be only available in the new command syntax.

# Additional and Advanced EIGRP Features

This section covers selected advanced EIGRP features.

## Router ID

As with many protocols, EIGRP also uses a concept of a Router ID (RID), a single 4-byte number representing a particular router instance. Each address family instance has its own independent RID. It is however allowed for multiple EIGRP processes and address family instances on the same router to use the same RID.

Originally, the primary use of the EIGRP RID has been to prevent routing loops in EIGRP environments using redistribution. The RID identifies the originating router for external routes injected into the EIGRP domain. Each external route was attached the RID of the router that redistributed it into EIGRP. If an external route is received with the same RID as the local router, the route is discarded. This feature is designed to reduce the possibility of routing loops in networks where route redistribution is being performed on more than one router. EIGRP RID was not originally advertised with internal routes.

With recent IOS releases, however, the EIGRP RID is also advertised with internal routes. As a result, each route advertised in EIGRP, internal or external, carries the RID of the router that injected it into EIGRP. The logic of using the RID remains the same—a router will discard every received route carrying the router's own RID. Example 8-18 shows the EIGRP RID carried along with advertised routes.

**Example 8-18**  *EIGRP Router ID*

```
! The 10.0.2.0/24 is reported as internal, yet the route carries the RID
! of the advertising router - it is 10.255.255.2.

R1# show eigrp address-family ipv4 topology 10.0.2.0/24
EIGRP-IPv4 VR(CCIE) Topology Entry for AS(1)/ID(10.255.255.1) for 10.0.2.0/24
  State is Passive, Query origin flag is 1, 1 Successor(s), FD is 13189120, RIB is
    103040
  Descriptor Blocks:
  10.0.0.2 (FastEthernet0/0), from 10.0.0.2, Send flag is 0x0
      Composite metric is (13189120/163840), route is Internal
      Vector metric:
        Minimum bandwidth is 100000 Kbit
        Total delay is 101250000 picoseconds
        Reliability is 255/255
        Load is 1/255
        Minimum MTU is 1500
        Hop count is 1
        Originating router is 10.255.255.2


! The next output shows a redistributed route 192.0.2.0/24 also carrying
! the originating router's ID. It is 10.255.255.2, also originated by the same
! router as before.


R1# show eigrp address-family ipv4 topology 192.0.2.0/24
EIGRP-IPv4 VR(CCIE) Topology Entry for AS(1)/ID(10.255.255.1) for 192.0.2.0/24
  State is Passive, Query origin flag is 1, 1 Successor(s), FD is 13172736, RIB is
102912
  Descriptor Blocks:
  10.0.0.2 (FastEthernet0/0), from 10.0.0.2, Send flag is 0x0
      Composite metric is (13762560/7208960), route is External
      Vector metric:
        Minimum bandwidth is 100000 Kbit
        Total delay is 110000000 picoseconds
        Reliability is 255/255
        Load is 1/255
        Minimum MTU is 1500
        Hop count is 1
        Originating router is 10.255.255.2
      External data:
        AS number of route is 0
        External protocol is Static, external metric is 0
        Administrator tag is 0 (0x00000000)
```

The rules of RID value selection are the same as with OSPF. First, the **eigrp router-id** command in EIGRP configuration is preferred. If not configured, the highest IP address among nonshutdown loopback interfaces is chosen as the RID. If no loopback interfaces are configured or active, the highest IP address among all other nonshutdown interfaces is used as the RID. After it is chosen, the RID will not be reinitialized until the EIGRP process is removed, the RID is manually configured, or a manually configured RID is removed. If you are configuring RID manually using the **eigrp router-id** command, the values 0.0.0.0 and 255.255.255.255 are disallowed. Any other RID value is valid and usable. If a router's RID changes, it drops and reestablishes its adjacencies; a brief connectivity outage might therefore ensue.

When you are changing interface addresses of a running router without restarting it, the EIGRP RID will remain unchanged. This can cause unpleasant issues when a new router is introduced into the network, retaking other routers' addresses and tasks, while the old router is renumbered without restarting it. As a result, it is possible that these two routers have the same EIGRP RID and they will not learn routes injected into EIGRP by each other. There is no logging message to point to this phenomenon, apart from a relatively obscure logging message in the EIGRP event log, as shown in Example 8-19.

**Example 8-19**   *Message in EIGRP Event Log If Route Is Denied Because of Duplicate RID*

```
! The 172.16.1.0/24 route is ignored in a received update because the RID
! of the router that injected the route into EIGRP matches this router's RID.


R7# show eigrp address-family ipv4 events
Event information for AS 1:
1    19:15:07.806 Ignored route, metric: 172.16.1.0/24 metric(3283435520)
2    19:15:07.802 Ignored route, dup routerid int: 10.255.255.1
! Output omitted
```

Finding out the current RID value was originally somewhat cumbersome. In older IOS revisions, the only place that displayed the router's RID was the heading of the **show ip eigrp topology** and **show ipv6 eigrp topology** command output, as shown in Example 8-18. Starting with IOS Release 15.0(1)M, there is a new **show eigrp protocols** command that also contains information about the EIGRP RID. In newer IOS revisions, the EIGRP RID is displayed in the **show ip protocols** command output as well.

Example 8-20 demonstrates the ways of displaying the RID. The router on which this output was captured is the R1 router configured according to Example 8-14. Its RID is initialized from a loopback interface 10.255.255.1/32.

**Example 8-20**   *EIGRP Router ID*

```
! The following two commands all display the same output, as for both IPv4
! and IPv6, this router uses the same RID. In place of these commands,
! the new show eigrp address-family ipv4 topology
! and show eigrp address-family ipv6 topology commands can be used.
```

```
R1# show ip eigrp topology | i Topology
EIGRP-IPv4 VR(CCIE) Topology Table for AS(1)/ID(10.255.255.1)
R1# show ipv6 eigrp topology | i Topology
EIGRP-IPv6 VR(CCIE) Topology Table for AS(1)/ID(10.255.255.1)

! The show eigrp protocols command covers all configured processes and address
! family instances in a single output. RID is displayed in the Router-ID line.

R1# show eigrp protocols
EIGRP-IPv4 VR(CCIE) Address-Family Protocol for AS(1)
  Metric weight K1=1, K2=0, K3=1, K4=0, K5=0 K6=0
  Metric rib-scale 128
  Metric version 64bit
  NSF-aware route hold timer is 240
  Router-ID: 10.255.255.1
  Topology : 0 (base)
! Lines omitted for brevity

EIGRP-IPv6 VR(CCIE) Address-Family Protocol for AS(1)
  Metric weight K1=1, K2=0, K3=1, K4=0, K5=0 K6=0
  Metric rib-scale 128
  Metric version 64bit
  NSF-aware route hold timer is 240
  Router-ID: 10.255.255.1
  Topology : 0 (base)
! Lines omitted for brevity
```

## Unequal-Cost Load Balancing

Unlike most internal routing protocols, EIGRP has a feature that allows you to distribute the load of your traffic across multiple unequal-cost paths and not just over paths providing the least distance to a destination. This feature is amply named *unequal-cost load balancing*.

The key to unequal-cost load balancing is the presence of Feasible Successors. These routers provide a guaranteed loop-free path to the destination, although not necessarily the shortest one. Precisely this fact can be leveraged by EIGRP: Paths through Feasible Successors can be installed to the routing table and used along with the best available path even when the route is in the Passive state.

Unequal-cost load balancing is enabled through the **variance** *multiplier* command. In named mode, the **variance** is configured in the **topology base** section. The *multiplier* value essentially defines how many times worse than the best path a route through a Feasible Successor can be to be still used by EIGRP for unequal-cost load balancing. More precisely, if the **variance** is set to the value V, for each destination individually, the router checks whether any path over a Feasible Successor meets the following condition (CD stands for Computed Distance):

CD via Successor < CD via Feasible Successor in question < V × CD via Successor

If it does, it will be installed into the routing table through the corresponding Feasible Successor.

A multiplier of 1, which is the default, implies that no unequal-cost load balancing is being performed. The current value of the variance multiplier can always be verified in the **show ip protocols** command output.

If multiple unequal-cost paths to a destination are installed into the routing table, the router will forward proportionally less traffic over the worse paths, and vice versa. The amount of traffic flowing over a particular path can be computed as this ratio:

Highest Installed Path Metric / Path Metric

As an example, if there are four paths over Successors and Feasible Successors to a destination with metrics 1100, 1100, 2000, and 4000, the amounts of traffic over these paths would be 4000/1100 = 3, 4000/1100 = 3, 4000/2000 = 2, and 4000/4000 = 1, so the true traffic share ratio would be 3:3:2:1 (recall that IOS routers perform integer division).

It is once again important to realize that the key to performing unequal-cost load balancing is first to have Feasible Successors toward a destination identified in the topology table. Routers that do not meet the Feasibility Condition and thus are not considered Feasible Successors are not considered in the unequal-cost load balancing, either. To utilize several neighbors as Feasible Successors, you might need to perform judicious metric tweaking so that the neighbors pass the Feasibility Condition check.

Keep in mind that the unequal-cost paths installed into the routing table also count toward the maximum number of parallel paths to a destination configured using the **maximum-paths** command. Depending on your network topology and requirements, it might be necessary to modify this setting.

## Add-Path Support

In certain scenarios, such as Dynamic Multipoint VPN (DMVPN) deployments in which multiple branch offices are dual homed, hub routers usually have information about both routes to a particular dual-homed branch office, and can perform equal-cost load balancing on their end. However, without an additional mechanism, a hub is unable to advertise these equal-cost routes to other spoke routers. As a result, the other spokes only see a single route to the dual-homed branch office without an ability to perform load balancing over multiple paths, and if the single route they know about fails, they need to go over the usual reconvergence process in EIGRP to learn about the other route.

To support these scenarios, starting with IOS Release 15.3(2)T, EIGRP was extended with a so-called Add-Path support, allowing a hub to advertise multiple equal-cost routes to the same destination. The prerequisite for a hub router to be able to advertise multiple equal-cost routes is to first have them installed in its routing table. This might require tuning the metrics and the **maximum-paths** command value first. Also, the hub router must have the Split Horizon deactivated on the multipoint tunnel interface toward individual spokes.

The Add-Path feature can be configured only in the named mode, and is controlled on a per-interface basis using the **add-paths** *path-count* command in the **af-interface** section. The **add-paths** command allows advertising additional *path-count* equal-cost routes in addition to the route that would be advertised nonetheless. The *path-count* is a mandatory argument in the range of 1 to 4. Using the Add-Path feature, therefore, at most four additional equal-cost paths to any destination can be advertised from a hub router, in total allowing the spokes to learn about five different equal paths to a particular destination.

Spoke routers do not need to be specifically configured for the Add-Path feature, apart from possible tuning of the **maximum-paths** command to be allowed to insert multiple equal-cost paths into their routing tables.

The Variance (Unequal Cost Load Balancing) and Add-Path features are not compatible with each other. When using the Add-Path, always be sure to set the **variance** to 1.

Example 8-21 shows the use of the Add-Path feature.

**Example 8-21**   *Configuring the EIGRP Add-Path Feature*

```
! First, the variance is deactivated, and the maximum-paths is set to 6.
! Then, on the Tunnel0 interface, split horizon is deactivated (a mandatory
! step; otherwise, multiple equal cost paths cannot be advertised to spokes).
! In addition, the next-hop-self setting must be deactivated, allowing the R1-Hub
! to retain the original next hop value instead of asserting itself as the
! next hop. Finally, the add-paths 4 allows advertising additional 4 equal-cost
! routes to a destination if the hub knows about them via the same EIGRP process
! instance and has them installed in its own routing table.

R1-Hub(config)# router eigrp CCIE
R1-Hub(config-router)# address-family ipv4 unicast autonomous-system 1
R1-Hub(config-router-af)# topology base
R1-Hub(config-router-af-topology)# variance 1
R1-Hub(config-router-af-topology)# maximum-paths 6
R1-Hub(config-router-af-topology)# exit
R1-Hub(config-router-af)# af-interface Tunnel0
R1-Hub(config-router-af-interface)# no split-horizon
R1-Hub(config-router-af-interface)# no next-hop-self
R1-Hub(config-router-af-interface)# add-paths 4
```

The **no next-hop-self** command has an additional **no-ecmp-mode** keyword not included in Example 8-21. To understand what this keyword does, first assume a topology in which a DMVPN hub is dual homed itself, using two ISPs and two different multipoint tunnel interfaces to reach the spoke routers. It is now possible for the hub to learn about equal-cost paths to a spoke site over each tunnel interface, for example, two equal-cost paths over Tunnel1 and next hops $N_{11}$ and $N_{12}$, and two more equal-cost paths over

Tunnel2 and next hops $N_{21}$ and $N_{22}$. When using the **next-hop-self** command on these tunnel interfaces, EIGRP internally optimizes its work: It takes only the first entry in the topology table (obviously pointing to a Successor) and verifies whether the Successor is reachable over the tunnel interface through which the route is going to be readvertised (thanks to deactivated Split Horizon), and if it is, the hub will keep the Successor address in the advertisement, not asserting itself as the next hop. Additional entries in the topology table are not subject to this test. This can lead to the **no next-hop-self** setting on an interface being ignored for an advertised route, causing the hub router to impose itself as the next hop even though it is not supposed to. For example, if the first entry in the topology table is learned over Tunnel1 and next hop $N_{11}$, this route will be advertised over the Tunnel2 interface with the hub imposing itself as the next hop. The fact that the same route with the same cost is also learned over Tunnel2 and next hops $N_{21}$ and $N_{22}$ reachable on this interface, and should in fact be subject to **no next-hop-self**, will be ignored.

The **no-ecmp-mode** command deactivates this internal optimization and forces EIGRP to always walk over all equal-cost paths to a destination recorded in the topology table, making sure that if any of these routes' Successors can be reached over the interface on which the route is going to be readvertised, the **no next-hop-self** command will be honored and the Successor's address will be retained in the advertisement. The use of **no-ecmp-mode** is recommended with the Add-Path feature if the hub uses multiple tunnel interfaces to reach the spoke sites.

## Stub Routing

Stub routing is an EIGRP feature primarily designed to improve network scalability and stability. The stub routing feature is most commonly used in hub-and-spoke networks. This feature is configured only on spoke routers. When configured on a spoke router, the router announces its stub router status using an additional TLV in its EIGRP Hello messages. The results of configuring a router as a stub are multifold:

- A stub router does not propagate routes learned through EIGRP to its neighbors, with the exception of EIGRP-learned routes that are explicitly selected using a so-called **leak-map** construct. This prevents a stub router from ever being considered a Feasible Successor for remote networks by its neighbors and possibly becoming a transit router at some point in the future.

- A stub router advertises only a subset of its own EIGRP-enabled networks to its neighbors. This subset can be defined in the **eigrp stub** command using the **summary**, **connected**, **static**, **redistributed**, and **receive-only** keywords.

- Neighbors of a stub router aware of its stub status (thanks to the specific TLV in the stub router's Hello packets) will never send a Query packet to a stub router. This prevents the neighbors from converging through a stub router to reach networks that are remote to the stub router.

There is a slight misunderstanding related to how a stub router itself handles Queries. Several sources, including documents on the Cisco website, insist that a stub router summarily responds to every received Query immediately with a Reply indicating infinite distance. This is not entirely true. The following rules summarize the stub router behavior with respect to handling Query packets:

**Key Topic**

■ *Originating Query packets* is not modified in any way. Rules for entering the Active state and sending Queries are precisely the same.

■ *Processing received Query packets* depends on what network was queried for. If the network in the received Query is a network the stub router is allowed to advertise, meaning that it falls under the configured category of **summary**, **connected**, **static**, or **redistributed**, the router will process the Query normally (even possibly causing the stub router to become Active itself) and send back an appropriate Reply. The same is valid for an EIGRP-learned network that is allowed to be further advertised using a **leak-map**—a Query for such a network would be processed and responded to in the usual way. If the Query contains a network that the stub router knows about but is not allowed to advertise (the network does not fall under the configured category, or is learned through EIGRP but not allowed for further advertisement by a **leak-map**), it will be processed in the usual way as described earlier, but the Reply will always indicate infinite distance, regardless of what the stub router truly knows about the network. Receiving a Query for an unknown network will immediately cause the router to respond with a Reply and an infinite distance; however, this is regular EIGRP behavior not related to the stub feature.

At this point, you might ask why a stub router would receive a Query, as its stub status should instruct its neighbors to avoid sending Queries to it. There are two primary reasons why even a stub router might receive a Query. First, a stub router's neighbor might be running an old IOS that does not recognize the stub TLV yet. Such a neighbor will create an adjacency to a stub router just fine, but it will also happily send Queries to it, not knowing that the router is a stub router. Second, if there are multiple routers on a common segment and all of them are configured as stub routers, if any of these stub routers need to send a Query, it will also send it to all its stub neighbors. This is done to support multihomed branch offices that usually have two branch routers configured as stubs. Each of these branch routers is connected to the headquarters through its own uplink, and they are also connected together by a common intra-site link. If the uplink on one of the branch routers fails, the affected router needs to converge through its neighbor branch router, and this might require a permission to send Queries to its fellow stub neighbor. Therefore, on a common segment with all routers configured as stubs, Queries are sent as usual.

In case of multiaccess segments with mixed neighbors (stub and nonstub), EIGRP solves the problem of sending Queries only to nonstub neighbors in two ways: Either it sends the Queries as unicasts to the nonstub neighbors or it uses the Conditional Receive mode in RTP to send multicast Queries in such a way that only nonstub routers will process them. The choice of a particular mechanism depends on the number of nonstub neighbors. While mixing stub and nonstub routers on a common segment is not a recommended practice, it is inevitable, for example, in cases where the hubs and spokes are interconnected by a DMVPN or a VPLS service.

The EIGRP stub routing feature provides important advantages when implemented in hub-and-spoke networks:

■ It prevents suboptimal routing from occurring within hub-and-spoke networks.

■ It prevents stub routers with low-speed links from being used as transit routers.

■ It significantly limits the number of Query packets and the depth of their propagation, allowing the EIGRP network to convergence faster and avoid the SIA states.

The advantage of limiting the propagation of a Query packet should be immediately obvious. Assume a network with 100 branch office routers, each of these branch office routers being connected through a pair of point-to-point links to hub routers at the headquarters (dual-hub design). Any Query originating at the headquarters can possibly propagate to any branch office router through both links, and if a branch router is unable to respond, it might need to originate a Query itself. The number of Queries and Replies expected grows easily to orders of hundreds. A single misbehaving router, or an overloaded or faulty link, can cause major trouble and the diffusing computation will have difficulties terminating, again risking the SIA state. With the stub feature, these issues are eliminated easily.

Stub routing is enabled with the router process command demonstrated in Example 8-22. In named mode, the **eigrp stub** command is used in the particular address family section.

**Example 8-22**   *EIGRP Stub Router Configuration*

```
Router(config-router)# eigrp stub ?
  connected      Do advertise connected routes
  leak-map       Allow dynamic prefixes based on the leak-map
  receive-only   Set IP-EIGRP as receive only neighbor
  redistributed  Do advertise redistributed routes
  static         Do advertise static routes
  summary        Do advertise summary routes
  <cr>
```

The **receive-only** keyword configures the router as a receive-only router. In other words, when this keyword is used, the stub router does not advertise any prefixes. It only receives prefixes advertised to it by its neighbors. Obviously, either static routing on its neighbors or NAT/PAT on the stub router is required in this case to allow the networks behind the stub router to communicate with the outside world. This keyword cannot be used with any other keywords when configuring stub routing.

The **leak-map** *name* keyword configures the stub router to advertise selected EIGRP-learned routes that would not be ordinarily advertised. The *name* references a route-map that matches one or more ACLs or prefix lists that permit the matched subnets or addresses to be leaked. This leaking is crucial in scenarios where a branch office uses a pair of interconnected routers configured as stub routers. If these routers are to provide backup connectivity to each other, they must be allowed to readvertise EIGRP-learned routes to each other, even in stub mode. Route leaking accomplishes that.

The **connected** keyword configures the stub router to advertise connected subnets. These are subnets on any interface directly connected to the router. Note that the directly connected interfaces will not be advertised automatically; it is still necessary to add them to EIGRP using the usual **network** command.

The **static** keyword configures the stub router to advertise static routes. The static routes need to be redistributed into EIGRP to be advertised.

The **summary** keyword configures the stub router to advertise summary routes if configured on interfaces.

The **redistributed** keyword configures the stub router to advertise routes that have been redistributed into EIGRP from other route sources.

By default, when this command is enabled without additional keywords, both **connected** and **summary** are assumed.

To check the current stub settings, inspect the **show ip protocols** output, as shown in Example 8-23. The current stub mode, if any, will be indicated in the output. Also, if it is necessary to verify whether any neighbor is configured as a stub, use the **show ip eigrp neighbors detail** command. If a neighbor is configured as a stub router, this command will reveal it along with the information about which route categories it is advertising. Keep in mind that activating, deactivating, or modifying the stub feature settings on a router will cause it to drop and reestablish adjacencies with its neighbors.

**Example 8-23**  *EIGRP Stub Status as Advertised in* **show** *Commands*

```
! On R2, EIGRP Stub is configured. The show ip protocols shows that both
! connected and summary networks will be advertised.

R2# show ip protocols
Routing Protocol is "eigrp 1"
  Outgoing update filter list for all interfaces is not set
  Incoming update filter list for all interfaces is not set
  Default networks flagged in outgoing updates
  Default networks accepted from incoming updates
  EIGRP metric weight K1=1, K2=0, K3=1, K4=0, K5=0
  EIGRP maximum hopcount 100
  EIGRP maximum metric variance 1
  EIGRP stub, connected, summary
  Redistributing: eigrp 1
  EIGRP NSF-aware route hold timer is 240s
  Automatic network summarization is not in effect
  Maximum path: 4
  Routing for Networks:
    10.0.0.0
  Routing Information Sources:
    Gateway         Distance      Last Update
```

```
     10.0.12.1              90        00:00:07
   Distance: internal 90 external 170


! On R1 which is R2's direct neighbor, the show ip eigrp neighbors detail reveals
! that R2 is a stub connected+summary router, and R1 will not send Queries to R2.

R1# show ip eigrp neighbors detail
IP-EIGRP neighbors for process 1
H   Address              Interface       Hold Uptime   SRTT   RTO  Q   Seq
                                         (sec)         (ms)        Cnt Num
0   10.0.12.2            Se1/0             10 00:03:50  26    300  0   3
    Version 12.4/1.2, Retrans: 1, Retries: 0, Prefixes: 1
    Stub Peer Advertising ( CONNECTED SUMMARY ) Routes
    Suppressing queries
```

Note that the stub router feature has no impact on what routes the hub router will advertise to its stub spokes. Without an additional configuration on the hub router, the spokes
will be populated with full routing tables. Considering the fact that in a hub-and-spoke
network, any other network beyond the branch networks is reachable through the hub,
having full routing tables on spoke routers with most of their entries pointing toward the
hub router is not particularly useful. Therefore, in these networks, the stub feature on
spokes is usually combined with route filtering and summarization on the hub router. The
hub router can be configured to advertise only the default route to the spoke router(s),
filtering out all other more specific route entries, effectively reducing the routing table on
the spoke to a single EIGRP-learned default route entry.

## Route Summarization

Already a well-known concept to all CCIE Routing and Switching candidates, route
summarization reduces the amount of routing information that routers must exchange,
process, and maintain, which allows for faster convergence and less router load within
the network. Summarization also restricts the size of an area that is affected by network
changes by hiding the changes in the individual networks behind a single advertised summary route.

With particular respect to EIGRP, summarization is also a powerful tool to create a
boundary for Query propagation: If a router receives a Query for a network it does not
have in its topology table, it will immediately send back a Reply indicating an unreachable
destination, without itself going active and propagating the Query further. With summarization, this is a natural scenario. Neighbors of a router performing route summarization
do not know the individual component routes. Queries originated inside the summarized
part of network, including those for component routes, will be propagated according
to the usual rules; a router performing route summarization does not modify the Query
contents nor influence its flooding scope. However, when a Query asking for a particular
component route is forwarded to the summarizing router's neighbor, this neighbor has no
knowledge of the component, so it immediately responds with a Reply containing infinite

distance. As a result, summarization causes the propagation of Queries to be bounded by directly connected neighbors of routers that perform route summarization.

Historically, EIGRP supports two types of route summarization: automatic summarization and manual summarization. Automatic summarization is a concept originally utilized in classful routing protocols, whereby a subnet of a particular major network is advertised as the major network itself if the subnet is to be advertised out an interface that lies in a different major network. In EIGRP, automatic summarization does not apply to external routes unless there is also an internal network that belongs to the same major network as the external routes. EIGRP is a classless protocol, though, and the automatic summarization was implemented in it mostly to provide a smooth transition from classful protocols to EIGRP. However, the concept of automatic summarization is practically unusable in today's networks, and in fact, starting with IOS Release 15.0(1)M, it is deactivated by default; for older IOS releases, the **no auto-summary** command should be used in the EIGRP configuration to deactivate it.

Manual summarization allows summarizing routes at any chosen router and its interface in the network. As opposed to RIP implementation in IOS that does not allow supernetting in summarization (using a shorter-than-classful netmask), EIGRP poses no limitations on the particular manual summary address/netmask combination. If it suits you, you can summarize even into a default route. Furthermore, configuring multiple overlapping summary addresses on an interface is also supported—in that case, EIGRP will advertise each configured summary address for which at least one component route exists. This allows for a sort of traffic engineering in which a part of a network with multiple border routers advertises the same summary route covering the entire contained address range from each border router (for example, 172.20.32.0/19), plus each of the border routers also advertising a different, more specific summary route covering only a portion of the contained address range (for example, one border router advertising 172.20.32.0/20 and the other advertising 172.20.48.0/20). Routers in other parts of the network will learn both the less specific summary route from all border routers, thereby knowing that each border router can be used to reach this prefix, and the more specific summaries, each advertised from a different border router. Thanks to the longest prefix match paradigm in IP routing, traffic to different destinations in the summarized part of the network will first follow the path through the border router that advertised the more specific summary route matching the destination. Only if that border router is unavailable or does not advertise the more specific summary, traffic will follow the shortest route toward the less specific summary through the nearest border router.

In EIGRP, manual summarization is configured on a per-interface basis. If you are using the classic configuration mode, summarization is configured directly on an interface using the **ip summary-address eigrp** *autonomous-system address netmask* [ *distance* ] [ **leak-map** *name* ] command. In named mode, summarization is configured in the corresponding **af-interface** section using the **summary-address** *address netmask* [ **leak-map** *name* ] command. The optional **leak-map** argument allows referring to a route-map to allow more specific components of the summary route to be selectively advertised as unsummarized along with the summary route. This is used in certain scenarios where leaking a particular component route helps to avoid suboptimal routing toward it.

Whenever a summary route is advertised, the router performing the summarization auto-matically installs a so-called *discard route* for this summary route into its routing table. The network and netmask in this discard route are identical to the network and netmask of the advertised summary, and the outgoing interface is set to Null0. The discard route prevents suboptimal routing or routing loops in situations when a router advertises a summary route but has no knowledge of a more specific matching subnet for incoming traffic. By virtue of the longest prefix match rule, any known component routes of a summary route would be matched in the routing table before hitting the corresponding discard route, and hence routed normally. For any presently unknown destinations within an advertised summary, the discard route makes sure that the traffic is dropped rather than routed over a possibly unrelated route, such as a default route.

A discard route's administrative distance is 5 by default. In most scenarios, it is not nec-essary to modify it. However, there are situations in which the summarizing router is configured to advertise a manual summary route exactly matching a route that is already learned by the router from another source. In that case, adding the corresponding discard route can possibly replace the learned route in the routing table, rendering it unreachable. For example, when summarizing into the default route, the router will attempt to install a discard route to 0.0.0.0/0 into its routing table. If there already is a default route in the routing table with its administrative distance higher than 5, the discard route will replace it, causing the router to lose connectivity provided by the former default route. In such cases, it is necessary to raise the discard route's administrative distance above that of the learned route. This can be accomplished using either the *admin-distance* optional argu-ment in the **ip summary-address eigrp** per-interface command when using classic con-figuration mode, or in the named mode by entering the **topology base** section and using the **summary-metric** *address netmask* **distance** *admin-distance* command. In recent IOS releases that support the named EIGRP configuration mode, the *admin-distance* argument is removed from the **ip summary-address eigrp** command, and the **summary-metric** command in the **topology base** mode must be used to change the administrative distance.

Be careful about setting the discard route's administrative distance to 255. In earlier IOS releases, this prevented the discard route from being installed into the routing table, but the summary address was nonetheless advertised. In more recent IOS releases, setting the administrative distance of a discard route to 255 not only prevents the router from install-ing the discard route into its routing table, but it also causes it to stop advertising the summary route altogether. In other words, neither the summary route nor the component routes will be advertised to neighbors, and the discard route will not be installed into the routing table. This is similar to the OSPF **area range** *address mask* **not-advertise** com-mand, which essentially prevents all routes falling under the defined address and mask from being advertised, not even advertising the summarized route or installing a discard route.

By default, when an EIGRP router originates a summary route, it looks up the lowest met-ric from among all known component routes that are covered by this summary, and uses this metric as the metric of the summary route itself. This means, however, that whenever the lowest metric from among all known component routes changes, EIGRP has to select the new lowest metric and advertise the summary route again with an updated metric.

In scenarios when multiple hundreds or thousands of component routes are summarized into a single summary route, walking through this number of routes and identifying the new lowest metric each time a component route is updated (added, removed, its metric changed) can be CPU intensive, and at the same time, not worth the effort: The summary route itself does not change; only its metric is updated. Therefore, the **summary-metric** command in the **topology base** section can also be used to define a static metric for a particular summary route. The summary route will then always be advertised with the configured metric, relieving the router of the need to walk the topology table to identify the least metric of covered components.

Example 8-24 shows the use of summarization commands in named mode, and selected commands to verify whether the summarization has been configured properly.

**Example 8-24**   *Summarization Configuration and Verification in Named Mode*

```
! A prefix list and a route-map for route leaking are configured, allowing
! the 172.20.63.0/24 prefix to be leaked unsummarized

R2(config)# ip prefix-list LeakPrefixes permit 172.20.63.0/24
R2(config)# route-map EIGRPLeak permit 10
R2(config-route-map)# match ip address prefix-list LeakPrefixes

! In the EIGRP process, manual summarization is configured on the Fa0/0 interface
! to advertise a summary network of 172.20.32.0/19. Notice that the CIDR notation
! is also accepted in the command. A route-map is referenced in the leak-map
! optional keyword, allowing the prefixes permitted by the route-map to be
! advertised unsummarized along with the summary route.

R2(config-route-map)# router eigrp CCIE
R2(config-router)# address-family ipv4 unicast autonomous-system 1
R2(config-router-af)# af-interface FastEthernet0/0
R2(config-router-af-interface)# summary-address 172.20.32.0/19 leak-map EIGRPLeak
R2(config-router-af-interface)# exit-af-interface

! For this summary address, a static metric is configured in standard EIGRP
! component form, specifying the bandwidth of 1000000, delay of 1, reliability
! of 255, load of 1, and MTU of 1500. Setting the metric of the summary route
! statically allows the router to save CPU cycles by alleviating it from
! the need to traverse the topology table and search for the minimum metric
! among all covered component routes. Also, the administrative distance of the
! discard route is set to 10. For typographical reasons, the command keywords
! have been truncated; summary-m stands for summary-metric, dist stands for distance

R2(config-router-af)# topology base
R2(config-router-af-topology)# summary-m 172.20.32.0/19 1000000 1 255 1 1500 dist 10
R2(config-router-af-topology)# exit-af-topology
```

```
! There are several ways to verify the configured summarization. Following are
! selected ways of checking whether the summarization is configured and active.
! The show ip protocols command will list all configured summaries and interfaces
! they are placed on, including the advertised computed metric. In show ip route
! the corresponding discard route will be shown if the summary is being advertised,
! and the EIGRP topology table will contain the advertised summary route with
! the Null0 as the next hop interface.

R2(config-router-af)# do show ip protocols | section Summ
  Automatic Summarization: disabled
  Address Summarization:
    172.20.32.0/19 for Fa0/0
      Summarizing 32 components with metric 1310720


R2(config-router-af)# do show ip route eigrp | i Null
D        172.20.32.0/19 is a summary, 00:31:34, Null0

R2(config-router-af)# do show eigrp address-family ipv4 topology 172.20.32.0/19
EIGRP-IPv4 VR(CCIE) Topology Entry for AS(1)/ID(10.255.255.2) for 172.20.32.0/19
  State is Passive, Query origin flag is 1, 1 Successor(s), FD is 1310720, RIB is
    10240
  Descriptor Blocks:
  0.0.0.0 (Null0), from 0.0.0.0, Send flag is 0x0
      Composite metric is (1310720/0), route is Internal
      Vector metric:
        Minimum bandwidth is 1000000 Kbit
        Total delay is 10000000 picoseconds
        Reliability is 255/255
        Load is 1/255
        Minimum MTU is 1500
        Hop count is 0
        Originating router is 10.255.255.2
R2(config-router)#
```

## Passive Interfaces

When EIGRP is enabled for a network, the router begins to send out Hello packets and process incoming EIGRP packets on all interfaces that fall within the specified network range. This allows EIGRP to dynamically discover neighbors and establish network relationships, as we have previously discussed. This is desired on interfaces that are actually connected toward neighboring routers. However, this default behavior also results in an unnecessary waste of router resources on logical interfaces, such as loopback interfaces, that will never have any other device connected or have an EIGRP neighbor relationship form. Also, it is useless, even dangerous, to send and process EIGRP packets on interfaces connected to networks with end hosts where no further routers are intended to be.

To prevent this type of squandering of router resources, you can use the **passive-interface** command. A passive interface does not send or process received EIGRP packets, but the network configured on the interface is still advertised. In the classic configuration mode, the **passive-interface** command accepts an interface name or the **default** keyword, causing all interfaces to be considered passive; in that case, the **no passive-interface** command can subsequently be used to make selected interfaces active again. In the named configuration mode, the **passive-interface** command is used in the corresponding **af-interface** sections, as already shown in Example 8-24. To make all interfaces passive by default, use the **passive-interface** command in the **af-interface default** section, and **no passive-interface** in the specific **af-interface** sections for those interfaces that you want to keep active.

## Graceful Shutdown

Graceful Shutdown in EIGRP is a long-implemented feature that cannot in fact be controlled—it is only used, mostly not even knowing it is there. The Graceful Shutdown allows a router to advertise that it is being deactivated, either on an interface, for a particular address family, or as the entire process, thereby allowing its neighbors to react immediately, rather than wait for the Hold timer to expire. Technically, the Graceful Shutdown is accomplished by means of a Goodbye message, which is really a normal Hello packet having all K-values set to 255.

Classic EIGRP configuration mode allows you to gracefully shut down an EIGRP instance only for IPv6 EIGRP using the **shutdown** command. IPv4 EIGRP has no direct **shutdown** command. In the classic mode, the Goodbye message was usually sent when shutting down interfaces, configuring them as passive, removing the related **network** or **ipv6 eigrp** commands, or removing the entire EIGRP process or restarting the router.

In the named mode, the **shutdown** command can be used in various places:

- Directly in the **router eigrp** mode, causing all configured address family instances under that process name to be deactivated

- In the particular address family mode, causing the entire particular address family instance to be deactivated

- In the particular **af-interface** section in the address family mode, causing the EIGRP to cease all operations on that interface for the particular address family, effectively ignoring the interface altogether

## Securing EIGRP with Authentication

Since its inception, EIGRP supports Message Digest 5 (MD5) hashing to ensure the integrity of EIGRP messages and to prevent the injection of false routing information into the EIGRP domain. In addition, starting with IOS Releases 15.1(2)S and 15.2(1)T, EIGRP authentication support has been extended with the second-generation Secure Hash Algorithm, also known as SHA-2, in particular, with its 256-bit variant. MD5 authentication can be configured both in classic and named mode; SHA authentication can only be configured in the named mode.

The configuration of EIGRP authentication is fairly straightforward and consists of configuring at least one key chain to hold the used keys along with their numbers (also called key IDs), key strings, and optionally the validity time ranges, and activating the authentication on selected interfaces. As with all key chain–based authentication schemes, for the authentication between two neighbors to succeed, they must match on the key ID and key string used to authenticate exchanged packets. The key chain names themselves are used only locally in the configuration and do not need to match.

With SHA authentication, there is also an option of configuring passwords directly in the interface configuration, without creating key chains. This approach might be slightly simpler to configure; however, it will prevent you from performing a seamless rollover to a new key, as there can always be only a single per-interface key configured.

If using the classic mode, the per-interface commands to activate MD5 EIGRP authentication are the **ip authentication mode eigrp** and **ip authentication key-chain eigrp** commands. There is no way to configure EIGRP authentication for all interfaces at once; each EIGRP-enabled interface has to be configured individually. In named mode, per-interface configuration steps are accomplished in the **af-interface** section using the **authentication mode** and **authentication key-chain** commands. If used in the **af-interface default** section, the authentication settings will apply automatically to all EIGRP-enabled interfaces; these can be overridden later on selected interfaces using the appropriate **af-interface** section.

Example 8-25 shows a process of configuring various types of authentication in EIGRP named mode. Read the comments in the example carefully.

**Example 8-25**   *EIGRP Authentication*

```
! Key chain EIGRPKeys with a single key is configured

R1(config)# key chain EIGRPKeys
R1(config-keychain)# key 1
R1(config-keychain-key)# key-string EIGRPRocks


! MD5 authentication is configured on all EIGRP-enabled interfaces,
! using the EIGRPKeys key chain


R1(config)# router eigrp CCIE
R1(config-router)# address-family ipv4 autonomous-system 1
R1(config-router-af)# af-interface default
R1(config-router-af-interface)# authentication mode md5
R1(config-router-af-interface)# authentication key-chain EIGRPKeys
R1(config-router-af-interface)# exit


! On Fa0/0, the authentication type is overridden to SHA-256, using the key
! configured in the EIGRPKeys key chain. Note a particular peculiarity:
! At the time of writing, the authentication mode hmac-sha-256 command
! required that a password was specified even if a key chain was being used.
```

```
! In such case, both will be used for authentication. Also notice that the use of
! the EIGRPKeys key chain is already specified in the af-interface default
! section. Referring to the same key chain in the section for Fa0/0 is
! therefore not required, and the authentication key-chain EIGRPKeys command
! would in fact not appear in the af-interface Fa0/0 section. Nevertheless,
! always specifying it explicitly when SHA-256 authentication with a key chain
! is to be used can be considered a best practice.

R1(config-router-af)# af-interface FastEthernet0/0
R1(config-router-af-interface)# authentication mode hmac-sha-256 SomePhonyPass
R1(config-router-af-interface)# authentication key-chain EIGRPKeys
R1(config-router-af-interface)# exit

! On Fa0/1, the authentication type is overridden to SHA-256, using
! a per-interface configured password. Notice that to specifically stop
! using the EIGRPKeys key chain defined for all EIGRP-enabled interfaces
! in the af-interface default section, the no authentication key-chain command
! is used. Again, always stating it explicitly when a SHA-256 with a per-interface
! password authentication is to be used can be considered a best practice. If no
! default key chain is configured, the command will not appear in the config.

R1(config-router-af)# af-interface FastEthernet0/1
R1(config-router-af-interface)# authentication mode hmac-sha-256 BigP4ssw0rd
R1(config-router-af-interface)# no authentication key-chain
R1(config-router-af-interface)# exit

! Finally, the Serial1/0 interface is entirely exempted from authentication
! that would otherwise apply to it because of the af-interface default section.

R1(config-router-af)# af-interface Serial1/0
R1(config-router-af-interface)# no authentication mode
R1(config-router-af-interface)# exit

! Apart from verifying the configuration using show run | section router eigrp
! the authentication, if any, can be checked for a particular interface by
! the show eigrp address-family ... interfaces detail command.

R1(config-router-af)# do show eigrp address-family ipv4 int detail fa0/0
! Lines omitted for brevity
  Authentication mode is HMAC-SHA-256, key-chain is "EIGRPKeys"

R1(config-router-af)# do show eigrp address-family ipv4 int detail fa0/1
! Lines omitted for brevity
  Authentication mode is HMAC-SHA-256, key-chain is not set
```

```
R1(config-router-af)# do show eigrp address-family ipv4 int detail s1/1
! Lines omitted for brevity
  Authentication mode is md5,  key-chain is "EIGRPKeys"


R1(config-router-af)# do show eigrp address-family ipv4 int detail s1/0
! Lines omitted for brevity
  Authentication mode is not set
```

When using key chains, each key can be time limited in its usability to sign sent packets (by the **send-lifetime** per-key command) and to authenticate received packets (by the **accept-lifetime** per-key command). If multiple keys in the key chain are eligible to sign egress packets, the key with *the lowest* key ID will be used. To authenticate received packets, EIGRP will try to use the key indicated by its ID in the received packet if the key is still valid. This behavior allows for a seamless key rollover procedure:

- On all routers, add the new key with a higher key ID into the key chain. While the key chain will now hold both the old and the new key, the old key (assuming that it has a lower key ID than the new key) will continue to be used both to sign outgoing packets and authenticate incoming packets.

- After the new key has been added to all routers, configure the old key on all routers with a **send-lifetime** that is already in the past. This will cause each router to stop using the old key and migrate to using the new key. Note that regardless of which key (the old or the new) a router uses to sign outgoing packets, its neighbors will accept them because the particular key ID used to sign a packet is carried in the packet, and both old and new keys are still valid to authenticate received packets.

- After the **send-lifetime** has been set to a past time for the old key on all routers, the entire network now uses the new key both to sign sent and authenticate received packets. The old key can now be removed completely from key chains, completing the migration.

## Default Routing Using EIGRP

EIGRP has no dedicated command to inject a default route into an EIGRP domain. Instead, it uses other well-known techniques to advertise a default route:

- Redistributing the default route from other routing source into EIGRP, often the most straightforward method.

- Using manual summarization to summarize all advertised routes into a default route. Often used in hub-and-spoke scenarios, this requires a suitable topology.

EIGRP formerly also supported the use of the **ip default-network** command, originally retaken from IGRP, to flag a specific advertised route as a so-called candidate default network. This network, however, had to be a classful network and had to be advertised in EIGRP in addition to being flagged as a candidate default. The overall configuration required to advertise this classful network into EIGRP and flagging it as a candidate default network was of the same complexity, if not higher, as redistributing the default route directly. As a result, this approach was seldom feasible, and in recent IOS versions, EIGRP no longer appears to honor the candidate default flag. It is best to avoid using this command altogether.

Many sources claim that the **network 0.0.0.0** command causes EIGRP to generate and inject the default route into the routing domain. Such claims are based on a somewhat confusing behavior of EIGRP: If a static route is configured using only the egress interface and not the next-hop IP address, IOS treats this route also as being directly connected. As a result, the **network** command can be used to advertise such a *directly connected static route* in EIGRP much like any other directly connected network. If the default route happens to be configured as a static route out an interface, for example, **ip route 0.0.0.0 0.0.0.0 Dialer0**, using the **network 0.0.0.0** command in EIGRP seemingly does the right thing—it makes EIGRP advertise this default route. In reality, however, configuring **network 0.0.0.0** is almost *never* a good idea:

- It will cause all IPv4-enabled interfaces on the router to be enabled for EIGRP. In other words, EIGRP will start advertising all directly connected IPv4 networks on the router, and it will try to establish adjacencies over any IPv4 interface.

- If the default route on the router is not configured specifically as a directly connected static route, the **network 0.0.0.0** command has no effect on it and will not cause it to be advertised, defeating the entire purpose of configuring it in the first place.

## Split Horizon

Split Horizon is a generic distance-vector protocol feature that mandates that a route must not be advertised over an interface used to reach it. This prevents the "re-advertising" of routing information back to the next hop from which it is learned in the first place. EIGRP in particular uses the Split Horizon with Poisoned Reverse, advertising each learned network out the interface toward its Successor with an infinite metric.

While Split Horizon with Poisoned Reverse is a powerful loop-prevention mechanism, it is sometimes necessary to deactivate it. This is particularly important in hub-and-spoke networks, where multiple spoke routers are reachable over a single interface on a hub. Examples include neighbors reachable over Frame Relay or ATM multipoint interfaces, or spoke routers reachable through multipoint GRE tunnels in DMVPN deployments. With the Split Horizon with Poisoned Reverse in place, a hub learns about networks from each spoke but is forced to advertise each of these networks as unreachable out the same interface toward other spokes. As a result, neither spoke will learn about networks on other spokes.

If the topology and requirements permit it, the most scalable solution to this issue is to advertise a default route to all spokes, making the hub attract all spoke-to-spoke traffic for which the spokes have no more specific routes. The spoke-to-spoke traffic will then naturally flow through the hub. In cases where this approach is not usable, EIGRP can be configured to deactivate the Split Horizon with Poisoned Reverse on a per-interface basis.

In the classic mode, the **no { ip | ipv6 } split-horizon eigrp** interface command can be used to deactivate the Split Horizon. In the named mode, the corresponding **no split-horizon** command in an **af-interface** section can be used.

## EIGRP Over the ToP

A fairly recent addition to the EIGRP feature collection is the so-called Over the ToP, or OTP. This feature allows creating overlay multipoint VPNs between customer edge routers running EIGRP without any special cooperation with the service provider that operates the network interconnecting the edge routers, greatly simplifying many issues that usually arise with operating a possibly multihomed Layer 3 VPN over a service provider's network.

The key to the OTP functionality is the Locator/Identifier Separation Protocol, or LISP. While LISP is beyond the scope of the CCIE Routing and Switching exam, it is necessary to explain its basic principles very briefly to understand how EIGRP and OTP make use of it.

In traditional understanding, an IP address consists of two parts: the network prefix and the host suffix (the network ID and the host ID). In essence, the network prefix identifies the location of the particular host, while the host suffix identifies the host itself. When the host moves to a different network, its entire IP address changes (possibly both in network and host parts) even though the host is still the same; just its location has changed. Also, because the location and identity are tied together in a single address of a particular type (either IPv4 or IPv6), a single address also implies—and limits—communication with the particular host to the corresponding protocol only.

The Locator/Identifier Separation Protocol (LISP) aims at decoupling the location of a host from its identity, allowing the host to retain its identity regardless of its location in a network. The general idea in LISP is to separate the identity and location into two independent entities, each of them represented by a complete address, and provide a mapping service so that the address representing the identity of a host can be resolved into the address that represents its location. A tunneling mechanism is then used to encapsulate packets between end hosts addressed using end host identities into new packets that are destined to the addresses representing end host locations. This allows a host to change its location while retaining its identity and all open sessions without losing connectivity, and it also allows for interesting IPv4/IPv6 migration scenarios in which the location of a host (say, IPv6) is different from its location (reachable over an IPv4 network).

More precisely, in LISP, a host has an Endpoint ID, or EID, that identifies its identity that never needs to change. This EID can be an IPv4 address, an IPv6 address, or any other address format as needed, although at the time of this writing, IPv4 and IPv6 were the only supported formats. In Figure 8-9, all hosts at the LISP Site 1 have an EID in the space 10.0.1.0/24, while all hosts at the LISP Site 2 have an EID in the space 10.0.2.0/24. To reach any host at these sites from outside, packets must be tunneled to the router behind which this host is currently located. The outside address of this router effectively represents the location of the EID and is denoted as Routing Locator, or RLOC. Many EIDs can be located behind a single RLOC. In Figure 8-9, the RLOC for all EIDs in the space 10.0.1.0/24 is the R1 address 192.0.2.31. The RLOC for all EIDs in the space 10.0.2.0/24 is the R2 address 198.51.100.62. Traffic flowing from the source 10.0.1.11 at LISP Site 1 to the destination 10.0.2.12 at LISP Site 2 will be encapsulated by R1 into new packets and destined to the RLOC of 198.51.100.62, the R2's address. Responses flowing back to 10.0.1.11 will be encapsulated by R2 and sent to the RLOC of 192.0.2.31, the R1's address. These routers perform ingress and egress tunneling of traffic that flows between the LISP sites, and are also responsible for making all necessary EID-to-RLOC registration and resolution to allow the LISP sites to communicate successfully.

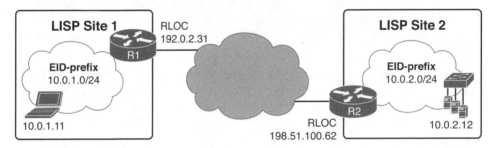

**Figure 8-9** *Location and Identifier Separation in LISP*

LISP hence has both a control and a data plane. The control plane in LISP comprises the registration protocol and procedures by which the tunnel routers R1 and R2 register the EIDs they are responsible for along with their RLOCs in a LISP-mapping service, and using these registrations they map EIDs into RLOCs. The data plane defines the actual tunnel encapsulation used between Routers R1 and R2 when two hosts from each LISP sites communicate.

**Key Topic**

In OTP, EIGRP serves as the replacement for LISP control plane protocols. Instead of doing dynamic EID-to-RLOC mappings in native LISP-mapping services, EIGRP routers running OTP over a service provider cloud create targeted sessions, use the IP addresses provided by the service provider as RLOCs, and exchange routes as EIDs. Consider Figure 8-9 again. If R1 and R2 ran OTP to each other, R1 would learn about the network 10.0.2.0/24 from R2 through EIGRP, treat the prefix 10.0.2.0/24 as an EID prefix, and take the advertising next hop 198.51.100.62 as the RLOC for this EID prefix. Similarly, R2 would learn from R1 about the network 10.0.1.0/24 through EIGRP, treat the prefix 10.0.1.0/24 as an EID prefix, and take the advertising next hop 192.0.2.31 as the RLOC for this EID prefix. On both routers, this information would be used to populate the LISP mapping tables. Whenever a packet from 10.0.1.0/24 to 10.0.2.0/24 would arrive at R1, it would use its LISP mapping tables just like in ordinary LISP to discover that the packet has to be LISP encapsulated and tunneled toward 198.51.100.62, and vice versa. The LISP data plane is reused in OTP and does not change; however, the native LISP mapping and resolving mechanisms are replaced by EIGRP.

OTP is based on creating targeted EIGRP sessions between customer edge routers, and using the routing information carried by EIGRP to populate both routing tables and LISP mapping tables. The edge routers do not exchange any routing information with the service provider routers. Thus, this solution is fully controlled by a customer and requires no cooperation with the service provider, apart from providing full IP connectivity between customer routers. In many ways, the resulting connectivity between customer sites closely resembles a Dynamic Multipoint VPN (DMVPN). The key differences are

- DMVPN uses multipoint GRE tunnels, encapsulating both data and control plane traffic. As a result, certain priming in DMVPN is necessary for it to start, such as creating tunnel interfaces on all member routers, assigning addresses to these tunnels, and manually mapping the tunnel address of the hub router to its real address on each spoke. OTP uses LISP UDP-based encapsulation for data plane traffic while running EIGRP natively, without additional encapsulation, between the customer edge routers. No tunnel interface configuration is required, and the only mandatory static configuration is specifying the remote static neighbor in EIGRP configuration. Optionally, the entire OTP traffic (both control and data plane) can be protected using Group Encrypted Transport Virtual Private Network (GETVPN).

- Apart from running a routing protocol such as EIGRP, DMVPN also depends on running the Next Hop Resolution Protocol (NHRP) to provide mappings between multipoint tunnel interfaces and real router addresses. In OTP, EIGRP itself serves as the mapping mechanism. No other control plane protocol is required.

Configuring two or more routers for direct EIGRP OTP peerings is as simple as configuring static EIGRP neighbors; see Example 8-26 and included comments.

**Example 8-26**  *EIGRP Over the ToP Configuration and Verification for a Pair of Routers*

```
! On R1, Gi0/0 is the interface toward the service provider. Basic IP
! configuration is performed, followed by LISP and EIGRP configuration.
! Configuring the LISP0 interface is not required; however, the default
! bandwidth setting on the LISP0 interface is 56 Kbps, causing EIGRP to
! compute very high metric values, therefore, the setting was updated.
! The OTP is started by the neighbor command referring to the remote neighbor
! 198.51.100.62 reachable over the Gi0/0 interface, specifying a hop count
! of 100 and the lisp-encap activating the LISP-based OTP functionality.
! At the time of writing, it was required to add the Gi0/0 interface
! to EIGRP, otherwise no static neighborships would form over it,
! hence the network 192.0.2.31 0.0.0.0 command. This was conformant to
! the usual EIGRP behavior that static neighborships form only over interfaces
! added to EIGRP. This limitation may be lifted in future. Also, a local
! network 10.0.1.0/24 is advertised in EIGRP.

interface LISP0
 bandwidth 1000000
!
interface GigabitEthernet0/0
 ip address 192.0.2.31 255.255.255.0
!
ip route 0.0.0.0 0.0.0.0 192.0.2.2
!
router eigrp CCIE
```

```
 !
  address-family ipv4 unicast autonomous-system 64512
   !
   topology base
   exit-af-topology
   neighbor 198.51.100.62 GigabitEthernet0/0 remote 100 lisp-encap
   network 10.0.1.0 0.0.0.255
   network 192.0.2.31 0.0.0.0

! On R2, the configuration is very similar:

interface LISP0
 bandwidth 1000000
!
interface GigabitEthernet0/1
 ip address 198.51.100.62 255.255.255.0
!
ip route 0.0.0.0 0.0.0.0 198.51.100.1
!
router eigrp CCIE
 !
 address-family ipv4 unicast autonomous-system 64512
  !
  topology base
  exit-af-topology
  neighbor 192.0.2.31 GigabitEthernet0/1 remote 100 lisp-encap
  network 10.0.2.0 0.0.0.255
  network 198.51.100.62 0.0.0.0

! On R1, show ip route and show eigrp address-family ipv4 neighbor commands
! produce a fairly common output, showing that the remote network 10.0.2.0/24
! is reachable over LISP0 interface while the remote neighbor itself can be
! reached through Gi0/0 interface (recall that control plane traffic in OTP is
! sent natively while data plane traffic is LISP-encapsulated). The show ip cef
! command shows that the traffic for 10.0.2.0/24 will be LISP-encapsulated
! and forwarded over the current default route next hop 192.0.2.2 to the other
! tunnel endpoint 198.51.100.62.

R1# show ip route eigrp
! Lines omitted for brevity
      10.0.0.0/8 is variably subnetted, 4 subnets, 2 masks
D        10.0.2.0/24 [90/2570880] via 198.51.100.62, 00:36:24, LISP0

R1# show eigrp addr ipv4 nei
EIGRP-IPv4 VR(CCIE) Address-Family Neighbors for AS(64512)
```

| H | Address | Interface | Hold Uptime | SRTT | RTO | Q | Seq |
|---|---------|-----------|-------------|------|-----|---|-----|
| | | | (sec) | (ms) | | Cnt | Num |
| 0 | 198.51.100.62 | Gi0/0 | 13 00:36:55 | 11 | 100 | 0 | 6 |

```
R1# show ip cef 10.0.2.0/24 internal
10.0.2.0/24, epoch 0, RIB[I], refcnt 5, per-destination sharing
  sources: RIB
  feature space:
   IPRM: 0x00028000
  ifnums:
   LISP0(17): 198.51.100.62
  path list 1381A4AC, 3 locks, per-destination, flags 0x49 [shble, rif, hwcn]
   path 12BED5A0, share 1/1, type attached nexthop, for IPv4
    nexthop 198.51.100.62 LISP0, IP midchain out of LISP0, addr 198.51.100.62
13C2AD00
  output chain:
   IP midchain out of LISP0, addr 198.51.100.62 13C2AD00
   IP adj out of GigabitEthernet0/0, addr 192.0.2.2 1289B118
```

Running OTP between remote routers does not even require that a route toward the remote neighbor (including a default route) is configured on the router. Because the **neighbor** command specifies the interface toward the remote neighbor, EIGRP in fact places its packets on the interface queue directly, bypassing the routing table and causing the IP driver to simply do its job after it has a packet enqueued: Do the encapsulation of the packet into a data link layer frame, using the packet's destination IP address to look up the particular destination Layer 2 address to put into the frame. If the interface is a point-to-point interface, the task of encapsulating the EIGRP packet into a frame is simple. If the interface is an Ethernet interface, however, this will cause the router to send ARP requests for the static remote neighbor's IP address out the interface to the service provider, effectively relying on the Proxy ARP feature activated on the service provider's edge router. Note that this is an unintuitive fact, and if the service provider disables Proxy ARP on its edge router, the OTP peering will not come up until static ARP mappings are configured on the OTP router.

**Key Topic**

With just a few OTP routers, configuring a full mesh of static neighbors is relatively easy. However, if the OTP network grows, this would not be a scalable approach. Therefore, OTP also introduces a special router role, a so-called *route reflector*. This router role borrows heavily from BGP, and in fact, it provides the same functionality to EIGRP: It allows collapsing the full mesh of OTP neighbors to a hub-and-spoke model of neighbor configuration, with the route reflector collecting learned networks from its clients and readvertising them back to individual clients, optionally maintaining the original next-hop value. With route reflectors, all clients of a route reflector are configured similarly to Router R2, as shown in Example 8-26, with the route reflector being their only statically defined OTP neighbor; there is otherwise no change to their configuration. The configuration of the route reflector router is shown in Example 8-27, now assuming that R1 is the route reflector.

**Example 8-27**   *EIGRP Over the ToP Route Reflector Configuration*

```
! The basic IP configuration is similar to the Example 8-26.

interface LISP0
 bandwidth 1000000
!
interface GigabitEthernet0/0
 ip address 192.0.2.31 255.255.255.0
!
ip route 0.0.0.0 0.0.0.0 192.0.2.2

! Instead of configuring neighbors on the route reflector statically,
! the remote-neighbors command is used, identifying the interface whose
! IP address is used by remote neighbors to reach this route reflector
! (meaning that this interface's IP address is used in the neighbor command
! on the remote neighbors) and that will be used by R1 to speak to remote
! neighbors. Usually, the physical interface toward the service provider
! network or a loopback will be used here. Just as before, this interface
! also must be added to EIGRP using the corresponding network command.
! In addition, the af-interface section for this interface specifies two
! commands: no split-horizon to allow learned routes to be reflected to other
! neighbors, accomplishing the very task of R1 as a route reflector,
! and no next-hop-self, facilitating direct spoke-to-spoke communication. If
! all traffic is intended to flow over the route reflector as in hub-and-spoke
! scenarios, the no next-hop-self can be omitted. The no split-horizon, however,
! must always be present.

router eigrp CCIE
 !
 address-family ipv4 unicast autonomous-system 64512
  !
  af-interface GigabitEthernet0/0
   no next-hop-self
   no split-horizon
  exit-af-interface
  !
  topology base
  exit-af-topology
  remote-neighbors source GigabitEthernet0/0 unicast-listen lisp-encap
  network 10.0.1.1 0.0.0.0
  network 192.0.2.31 0.0.0.0
```

The **remote-neighbors** command also allows you to refer to a named ACL using the optional **allow-list** *acl-name* keyword, narrowing the source addresses of permitted route reflector clients.

## EIGRP Logging and Reporting

EIGRP event logging configuration parameters are configured in router configuration mode, as demonstrated in Example 8-28. If named mode is used, these commands are located in the address family section.

**Example 8-28**   *EIGRP Logging and Reporting*

```
Router(config-router)# eigrp ?
  event-log-size         Set EIGRP maximum event log entries
  event-logging          Log IP-EIGRP routing events
  log-neighbor-changes   Enable/Disable IP-EIGRP neighbor logging
  log-neighbor-warnings  Enable/Disable IP-EIGRP neighbor warnings
```

The **eigrp event-logging** configuration command is the default. This EIGRP command enables the router to store a log of EIGRP events. The contents of the EIGRP log can be viewed by issuing the **show eigrp address-family** { **ipv4** | **ipv6** } **events** command. By default, the EIGRP event log stores up to 500 lines of events. This default behavior can be changed by running the command, under router processor, **event-log-size** *<0-443604>*. The **eigrp log-neighbor-changes** router configuration command allows the router to log EIGRP neighbor relationship changes. This command is enabled by default. The **eigrp log-neighbor-warnings** [*seconds*] router configuration command is also enabled by default. This command logs EIGRP neighbor warning messages at 10-second intervals.

## EIGRP Route Filtering

Outbound and inbound EIGRP updates can be filtered at any interface, or for the entire EIGRP address family instance, in either direction. To filter the routes, the **distribute-list** command is used. In classic mode, the command is applied directly in the EIGRP process configuration. In named mode, **distribute-list** is configured under **topology base** in the particular address family.

EIGRP allows ACLs, prefix lists, and route-maps to be used for route filtering in a **distribute-list** command. Depending on the filtering mechanism, there are multiple variants of this command available:

- ACLs: distribute-list *acl-number* | *acl-name* { **in** | **out** } [ *interface* ]
- Prefix lists: distribute-list prefix *prefix-list-name* { **in** | **out** } [ *interface* ]
- Route maps: distribute-list route-map *route-map-name* { **in** | **out** } [ *interface* ]

In general, the use of prefix lists is recommended, as they are specifically designed to match ranges of networks and netmasks.

Interestingly enough, distribute lists do not directly limit the propagation of Queries. Instead, what they do is more involved:

- For distribute lists in the **out** direction: All outgoing Updates, Queries, Replies, SIA-Queries, and SIA-Replies will indicate the correct metric for permitted prefixes and infinite metric for denied prefixes.

- For distribute lists in the **in** direction: In all incoming Updates, Replies, and SIA-Replies, permitted prefixes are processed normally while denied prefixes are ignored. Received Queries and SIA-Queries are not influenced by the distribute list and are processed without modification.

## EIGRP Offset Lists

EIGRP *offset lists* allow EIGRP to add to a route's metric, either before sending an update or for routes received in an update. The offset list refers to an ACL (standard, extended, or named) to match the routes; any matched routes have the specified *offset*, or extra metric, added to their Delay metric component. Any routes not matched by the offset list are unchanged. The offset list also specifies which routing updates to examine by specifying a direction (in or out) and, optionally, an interface. If the interface is omitted from the command, all updates for the defined direction will be examined.

Offset lists are much more applicable to RIP than EIGRP because RIP has such a limited metric range. With EIGRP, because of the metric's complexity, it is doubtful that you would manipulate EIGRP metrics this way. Because several other filtering methods and ways to influence EIGRP metrics are available, offset lists see limited use in EIGRP and are therefore not covered in more detail in this chapter.

## Clearing the IP Routing Table

The **clear ip route \*** command clears the IP routing table. However, because EIGRP keeps all possible routes in its topology table, a **clear ip route \*** command does not cause EIGRP to send any messages or learn any new topology information; the router simply refills the IP routing table with the best routes from the existing topology table.

The **clear eigrp address-family** { **ipv4** | **ipv6** } **neighbors** command can be used to clear all neighbor relationships and have the router reestablish them from scratch. An optional **soft** keyword allows for a graceful restart, in which the topology databases between the router and its neighbors are resynchronized but the adjacencies are not torn down.

# Foundation Summary

This section lists additional details and facts to round out the coverage of the topics in this chapter. Unlike most of the Cisco Press Exam Certification Guides, this "Foundation Summary" does not repeat information presented in the "Foundation Topics" section of the chapter. Please take the time to read and study the details in the "Foundation Topics" section of the chapter, as well as review items noted with a Key Topic icon.

Table 8-5 lists some of the most popular Cisco IOS commands related to the topics in this chapter.

**Table 8-5**   *Command Reference for Chapter 8*

| Command | Command Mode and Description |
|---|---|
| [ipv6] router eigrp *as-number*<br><br>router eigrp *name* | Global config; puts user in EIGRP classic configuration mode (first command) or in named configuration mode (second command). |
| eigrp upgrade-cli *name* | EIGRP classic mode. Automatically converts the classic configuration to the named configuration using the entered *name* as the process name. |
| address-family { ipv4 \| ipv6 } [ vrf *vrf-name* ] autonomous-system *as-number* | Named EIGRP mode, creates an instance for a particular address family and configures it with an autonomous system number. |
| af-interface { default \| *interface-type interface-number* } | Named EIGRP mode, address family instance. Holds per-interface EIGRP settings. |
| topology { base \| *topology-name* tid *number* } | Named EIGRP mode, address family instance. Holds EIGRP settings for a particular routing topology. |
| eigrp router-id | EIGRP classic config mode or address family named mode. Configures RID manually. |
| eigrp stub [receive-only] \| { [ leak-map *name* ] [connected] [static] [summary] [redistributed] } | EIGRP classic config mode or address family named mode. Designates the router as a stub router. |
| network *ip-address* [*wildcard-mask*] | EIGRP classic config mode or IPv4 address family named mode; defines matching parameters, compared to interface IP addresses, to pick interfaces on which to enable EIGRP. |
| ipv6 eigrp *as-number* | Interface subcommand; activates interface for IPv6 EIGRP. Used only in classic mode config. |

| Command | Command Mode and Description |
|---|---|
| [no] {ip | ipv6} split-horizon eigrp *autonomous-system*<br><br>[no] split-horizon | Interface subcommand; enables or disables Split Horizon. The first form is used in the classic mode configuration. The second form is used in the **af-interface** section in named mode. |
| [no] passive-interface [default] {*interface-type interface-number*}<br><br>[no] passive-interface | EIGRP config mode; causes EIGRP to stop sending and processing EIGRP packets on the specified interface, or enables them again. The first form is used in the classic mode configuration. The second form is used in the **af-interface** section in named mode. |
| [no] shutdown | EIGRP named mode, valid in the **router eigrp** section, particularly the address family section or **af-interface** section. Deactivates or activates the EIGRP operation within the defined scope. |
| {ip | ipv6} hello-interval eigrp *as-number seconds*<br><br>hello-interval *seconds* | Interface subcommand; sets the interval for periodic Hellos sent by this interface. The first form is used in the classic mode configuration. The second form is used in the **af-interface** section in named mode. |
| {ip | ipv6} hold-time eigrp *as-number seconds*<br><br>hold-time *seconds* | Interface subcommand; sets the countdown timer to be used by a router's neighbor when monitoring for incoming EIGRP messages from this interface. The first form is used in the classic mode configuration. The second form is used in the **af-interface** section in named mode. |
| [no] auto-summary | EIGRP classic config mode or per-AF-topology named mode; enables or disables automatic summarization at classful network boundaries. |
| {ip | ipv6} summary-address eigrp *as-number prefix* [*admin-distance*] [ leak-map *name* ]<br><br>summary-address *prefix* [ *admin-distance* [ leak-map *name* ] ] | Interface subcommand; configures the manual summarization and optional route leaking. The first form is used in the classic mode configuration. The second form is used in the **af-interface** section in named mode. |
| summary-metric *prefix* { *Bandwidth Delay Reliability Load MTU* [ distance *administrative-distance* ] | distance *administrative-distance* } | Named EIGRP mode, per-AF-topology section. Defines a constant advertised metric for an advertised summary route, optionally also modifying the corresponding discard route's administrative distance. |

| Command | Command Mode and Description |
|---|---|
| **metric weights** *0 $k_1$ $k_2$ $k_3$ $k_4$ $k_5$ [ $k_6$ ]* | EIGRP classic config mode or per-AF-topology named mode; defines the per-ToS K-values to be used in EIGRP metric calculations; however, only ToS 0 is supported. |
| **metric rib-scale** *scale-value* | EIGRP address family named mode. Defines a scaling value to downscale the computed wide metrics into a metric value offered to RIB. |
| {**ip** \| **ipv6**} **bandwidth-percent eigrp** *as-number percent*<br><br>**bandwidth-percent** *percent* | Interface subcommand; defines the maximum percentage of interface bandwidth to be used for EIGRP messages. The first form is used in the classic mode configuration. The second form is used in the **af-interface** section in named mode. |
| {**ip** \| **ipv6**} **authentication mode eigrp** *as-number* **md5**<br><br>**authentication mode** { **md5** \| **hmac-sha-256** *password* } | Enables authentication of EIGRP packets. The first form is used directly on an interface for classic configuration mode, and allows only for MD5 authentication. The second form is used in the **af-interface** section in named mode, and allows choosing the hashing algorithm. The *password* for SHA-256 is used only if no key chain is specified. |
| {**ip** \| **ipv6**} **authentication key-chain eigrp** *as-number key-chain-name*<br><br>**authentication key-chain** *key-chain-name* | Specifies the authentication key chain for EIGRP. The first form is used directly on an interface for classic configuration mode. The second form is used in **af-interface** section in named mode. |
| [**no**] {**ip** \| **ipv6**} **split-horizon eigrp** *as-number*<br><br>[**no**] **split-horizon** | Interface subcommand; allows activating or deactivating the Split Horizon mechanism. The first form is used in the classic mode configuration. The second form is used in the **af-interface** section in named mode. |
| [**no**] {**ip** \| **ipv6**} **next-hop-self eigrp** *as-number*<br><br>[**no**] **next-hop-self** | Interface subcommand; allows or prevents the router from asserting itself as the next hop in routes readvertised over the interface. The first form is used in the classic mode configuration. The second form is used in the **af-interface** section in named mode. |
| **add-paths** *path-count* | Named EIGRP mode, **af-interface** section. Allows the router to advertise up to four additional equal-cost paths. |

| Command | Command Mode and Description |
| --- | --- |
| variance *multiplier* | EIGRP classic config mode or per-AF-topology named mode. Allows the router to use worse paths over Feasible Successors whose metric is up to *multiplier* times worse than the current best-path metric. |
| neighbor { *ip-address* \| *ipv6-address* } *interface-type interface-number* [ **remote** *maximum-hops* [ **lisp-encap** [ *lisp-id* ] ] ] | EIGRP classic config mode or address family named mode. Specifies a static neighbor. OTP-related keywords are available only in named mode. |
| remote-neighbors source *interface-type interface-number* { **multicast-group** *group-address* \| **unicast-listen lisp-encap** [ *lisp-top-id* ] } [ **allow-list** *access-list-name* ] [ **max-neighbor** *max-remote-peers* ] | EIGRP address family named mode. Defines dynamic remote neighbor discovery, required for OTP route reflector functionality. |
| distribute-list {*access-list-number* \| *name*} { **in** \| **out** } [ *interface-type interface-number* ] | EIGRP classic config mode or per-AF-topology named mode. Specifies an access list for filtering routing updates to/from the EIGRP topology table. |
| distribute-list prefix *prefix-list-name* {**in** \| **out**} [ *interface-type interface-number* ] | EIGRP classic config mode or per-AF-topology named mode. Specifies a prefix list for filtering routing updates to/from the EIGRP topology table. |
| timers active-time [*time-limit* \| **disabled**] | EIGRP classic config mode or per-AF-topology named mode; sets the time limit for how long a route is in the active state before becoming stuck-in-active. |
| show {**ip** \| **ipv6**} eigrp topology [ **vrf** *vrf-name* \| *as-number* \| *network* [ *mask* ] \| *prefix* \| **active** \| **all-links** \| **detail-links** \| **frr** \| **name** \| **pending** \| **summary** \| **zero-successors** ]<br><br>show eigrp address-family { **ipv4** \| **ipv6** } [ **vrf** *vrf-name* ] [ *as-number* ] [**multicast**] **interfaces** [**detail**] [ *interface-type interface-number* ] | User mode; lists different parts of the EIGRP topology table, depending on the options used. |
| show ip eigrp [ **vrf** *vrf-name* ] [ *as-number* ] **interfaces** [ **detail** ] [ *type number* ]<br><br>show eigrp address-family { **ipv4** \| **ipv6** } [ **vrf** *vrf-name* ] [ *as-number* ] [**multicast**] **interfaces** [**detail**] [ *interface-type interface-number* ] | User mode; lists EIGRP protocol timers and statistics per interface. |

| Command | Command Mode and Description |
|---|---|
| show {ip \| ipv6} eigrp traffic [*as-number*] | User mode; displays EIGRP traffic statistics. |
| show eigrp address-family { ipv4 \| ipv6 } [ vrf *vrf-name* ] [ *as-number* ] [multicast] traffic | |
| show {ip \| ipv6} protocols | User mode; lists EIGRP timer settings, current protocol status, automatic summarization actions, and update sources. |
| show {ip \| ipv6} eigrp [*as-number*] neighbors | User mode; lists EIGRP neighbors. |
| show eigrp address-family { ipv4 \| ipv6 } [ vrf *vrf-name* ] [ *as-number* ] [multicast] neighbors [static] [detail] [ *interface-type interface-number* ] | |
| clear ip eigrp [ vrf *vrf-name* [*as-number*] \| *as-number* ] neighbors [ *ip-address* \| *interface-type interface-number* ] [soft] | Privileged mode; drops current neighbor adjacencies, removing topology table entries associated with each neighbor. The **soft** keyword causes the router to perform resynchronization with neighbors without dropping adjacencies. |
| show ip interface [*type number*] | User mode; lists many interface settings, including Split Horizon. |

Table 8-6 summarizes the types of EIGRP packets and their purposes.

**Table 8-6**  *EIGRP Message Summary*

| EIGRP Packet | Purpose |
|---|---|
| Hello | Identifies neighbors, exchanges parameters, and is sent periodically as a keepalive function |
| Ack | Acknowledges Update, Query, Reply, SIA-Query, and SIA-Reply packets |
| Update | Informs neighbors about updated routing information |
| Query | Asks neighboring routers to update their routing tables in a coordinated fashion and respond with their actual distance after having their routing tables updated |
| Reply | Sent by neighbors to reply to a Query, informing the router about the actual neighbor's distance to the destination after processing the information in the Query |
| SIA-Query | Asks a particular neighbor whose Reply to a Query packet is outstanding for a prolonged time to confirm whether it is still working on this router's Query |
| SIA-Reply | Sent by a neighbor as a response to an SIA-Query to ascertain its state |

## Memory Builders

The CCIE Routing and Switching written exam, like all Cisco CCIE written exams, covers a fairly broad set of topics. This section provides some basic tools to help you exercise your memory about some of the broader topics covered in this chapter.

### Fill In Key Tables from Memory

Appendix E, "Key Tables for CCIE Study," on the CD in the back of this book, contains empty sets of some of the key summary tables in each chapter. Print Appendix E, refer to this chapter's tables in it, and fill in the tables from memory. Refer to Appendix F, "Solutions for Key Tables for CCIE Study," on the CD, to check your answers.

### Definitions

Next, take a few moments to write down the definitions for the following terms:

hello interval, full update, partial update, MD5, DUAL, Hold timer, K-value, neighbor, adjacency, RTP, SRTT, RTO, Update, Ack, Query, Reply, Hello, Goodbye, RD, FD, feasibility condition, successor route, Feasible Successor, input event, local computation, active, passive, going active, stuck-in-active, query scope, EIGRP stub router, limiting query scope, variance, Named Mode

Refer to the glossary to check your answers.

### Further Reading

Jeff Doyle's *Routing TCP/IP*, Volume I, Second Edition (Cisco Press), has several excellent examples of configuration, as well as several examples of the DUAL algorithm and the Active Query process.

*EIGRP Network Design Solutions*, by Ivan Pepelnjak, contains wonderfully complete coverage of EIGRP. It also has great, detailed examples of the Query process.

*draft-savage-eigrp*, an Internet draft available through Internet Engineering Task Force web pages, documents the open parts of the protocol.

The CCIE Routing and Switching v5.0 exam blueprint also mentions the EIGRP IP Fast Reroute feature. More information about it can be found on the Cisco website in the *IP Routing EIGRP Configuration Guide* for Cisco IOS Release 15S, specifically in the "EIGRP Loop-Free Alternate Fast Reroute" section. Also, many Cisco Live! sessions cover this feature, including "IP LFA (Loop-Free-Alternative): Architecture and Troubleshooting" (BRKRST-3020) and "Routed Fast Convergence" (BRKRST-3363), available at www.ciscolive365.com. At the time of writing, this feature was supported only on service provider IOS, IOS-XE, and IOS-XR image builds and will not be present on the Lab exam. The Written exam might cover general properties of this feature.

**Blueprint topics covered in this chapter:**

This chapter covers the following subtopics from the Cisco CCIE Routing and Switching written exam blueprint. Refer to the full blueprint in Table I-1 in the Introduction for more details on the topics covered in each chapter and their context within the blueprint.

- Packet Types

- LSA Types

- Route Types

- Neighbor Relationship and Database Synchronization

- Network Types, Area Types, and Router Types

- Path Preference

- Metrics

- SPF Tuning

## CHAPTER 9

# OSPF

This chapter covers Open Shortest Path First (OSPF), one of the two link-state routing protocols covered by the CCIE Routing and Switching exam blueprint. As with the other routing protocol chapters, this chapter includes most of the features, concepts, and commands related to OSPF. Chapter 11, "IGP Route Redistribution, Route Summarization, Default Routing, and Troubleshooting," covers a few other details of OSPF, in particular, route redistribution, route filtering in redistribution, and route summarization.

## "Do I Know This Already?" Quiz

Table 9-1 outlines the major sections in this chapter and the corresponding "Do I Know This Already?" quiz questions.

**Table 9-1** *"Do I Know This Already?" Foundation Topics Section-to-Question Mapping*

| Foundation Topics Section | Questions Covered in This Section | Score |
|---|---|---|
| OSPF Database Exchange | 1–5 | |
| OSPF Design and LSAs | 6–9 | |
| OSPF Configuration | 10–12 | |
| OSPFv3 | 13–16 | |
| Total Score | | |

To best use this pre-chapter assessment, remember to score yourself strictly. You can find the answers in Appendix A, "Answers to the 'Do I Know This Already?' Quizzes."

1. R1 has received an OSPF LSU from R2. Which of the following methods can be used by R1 to acknowledge receipt of the LSU from R2?

    a. TCP on R1 acknowledges using the TCP Acknowledgment field.

    b. R1 sends back an identical copy of the LSU.

    c. R1 sends back an LSAck to R2.

    d. R1 sends back a DD packet with LSA headers whose sequence numbers match the sequence numbers in the LSU.

**2.** Fredsco has an enterprise network with one core Frame Relay connected router, with a hub-and-spoke network of PVCs connecting to ten remote offices. The network uses OSPF exclusively. The core router (R-core) has all ten PVCs defined under multipoint subinterface s0/0.1. Each remote router also uses a multipoint subinterface. Fred, the engineer, configures an **ip ospf network non-broadcast** command under the subinterface on R-core and on the subinterfaces of the ten remote routers. Fred also assigns an IP address to each router from subnet 10.3.4.0/24, with R-core using the .100 address, and the remote offices using .1 through .10. Assuming that all other related options are using defaults, which of the following would be true about this network?

   **a.** The OSPF hello interval would be 30 seconds.

   **b.** The OSPF dead interval would be 40 seconds.

   **c.** The remote routers could learn all routes to other remote routers' subnets, but only if R-core became the designated router.

   **d.** No designated router will be elected in subnet 10.3.4.0/24.

**3.** Which of the following interface subcommands, used on a multipoint Frame Relay subinterface, creates a requirement for a DR to be elected for the attached subnet?

   **a.** **ip ospf network point-to-multipoint**

   **b.** **ip ospf network point-to-multipoint non-broadcast**

   **c.** **ip ospf network non-broadcast**

   **d.** None of these answers is correct.

**4.** The following routers share the same LAN segment and have the stated OSPF settings: R1: RID 1.1.1.1, hello 10, priority 3; R2: RID 2.2.2.2, hello 9, priority 4; R3, RID 3.3.3.3, priority 3; and R4: RID 4.4.4.4, hello 10, priority 2. The LAN switch fails and recovers, and all routers attempt to elect an OSPF DR and form neighbor relationships at the same time. No other OSPF-related parameters were specifically set. Which of the following are true about negotiations and elections on this LAN?

   **a.** R1, R3, and R4 will expect Hellos from R2 every 9 seconds.

   **b.** R2 will become the DR but have no neighbors.

   **c.** R3 will become the BDR.

   **d.** R4's dead interval will be 40 seconds.

   **e.** All routers will use R2's hello interval of 9 after R2 becomes the designated router.

5.  Which of the following must be true for two OSPF routers that share the same LAN data link to be able to become OSPF neighbors?

    a.  Must be in the same area

    b.  Must have the same LSRefresh setting

    c.  Must have differing OSPF priorities

    d.  Must have the same Hello timer, but can have different dead intervals

6.  R1 is an OSPF ASBR that injects an E1 route for network 200.1.1.0/24 into the OSPF backbone area. R2 is an ABR connected to area 0 and to area 1. R2 also has an Ethernet interface in area 0, IP address 10.1.1.1/24, for which it is the designated router, and has established OSPF adjacencies over this interface with other routers. R3 is a router internal to area 1. Enough links are up and working for the OSPF design to be working properly. Which of the following are true regarding this topology? (Assume that no other routing protocols are running, and that area 1 is not a stub area.)

    a.  R1 creates a type 7 LSA and floods it throughout area 0.

    b.  R3 will not have a specific route to 200.1.1.0/24.

    c.  R2 forwards the LSA that R1 created for 200.1.1.0/24 into area 1.

    d.  R2 will create a type 2 LSA for subnet 10.1.1.0/24 and flood it throughout area 0.

7.  R1 is an OSPF ASBR that injects an E1 route for network 200.1.1.0/24 into the OSPF backbone area. R2 is an ABR connected to area 0 and to area 1. R2 also has an Ethernet interface in area 0, IP address 10.1.1.1/24, for which it is the designated router but there are no other OSPF routers on the segment. R3 is a router internal to area 1. Enough links are up and working for the OSPF design to be working properly. Which of the following are true regarding this topology? (Assume that no other routing protocols are running, and that area 1 is a totally NSSA.)

    a.  R3 could inject external routes into the OSPF domain.

    b.  R3 will not have a specific route to 200.1.1.0/24.

    c.  R2 forwards the LSA that R1 created for 200.1.1.0/24 into area 1.

    d.  R2 will create a type 2 LSA for subnet 10.1.1.0/24 and flood it throughout area 0.

   **8.** The routers in area 55 all have the **area 55 stub no-summary** command configured under the **router ospf** command. OSPF has converged, with all routers in area 55 holding an identical link-state database for area 55. All IP addresses inside the area come from the range 10.55.0.0/16; no other links outside area 55 use addresses in this range. R11 is the only ABR for the area. Which of the following is true about this design?

   **a.**  The area is a stubby area.

   **b.**  The area is a totally stubby area.

   **c.**  The area is an NSSA.

   **d.**  ABR R11 is not allowed to summarize the type 1 and 2 LSAs in area 55 into the 10.55.0.0/16 prefix because of the **no-summary** keyword.

   **e.**  Routers internal to area 55 can have routes to specific subnets inside area 0.

   **f.**  Routers internal to area 55 can have routes to E1, but not E2, OSPF routes.

   **9.** R1 is an OSPF ASBR that injects an E1 route for network 200.1.1.0/24 into the OSPF backbone area. R2 is an ABR connected to area 0 and to area 1. R2 also has an Ethernet interface in area 0, IP address 10.1.1.1/24, for which it is the designated router. R3 is a router internal to area 1. Enough links are up and working for the OSPF design to be working properly. Which of the following are true regarding this topology? (Assume that no other routing protocols are running, and that area 1 is not a stubby area.)

   **a.**  R3's cost for the route to 200.1.1.0 will be the cost of the route as it was injected into the OSPF domain by R1, without considering any internal cost.

   **b.**  R3's cost for the route to 200.1.1.0 will be the cost of reaching R1, plus the external cost listed in the LSA.

   **c.**  R3's cost for the route to 10.1.1.0/24 will be the same as its cost to reach ABR R2.

   **d.**  R3's cost for the route to 10.1.1.0/24 will be the sum of its cost to reach ABR R2 plus the cost listed in the type 3 LSA created for 10.1.1.0/24 by ABR R2.

   **e.**  It is impossible to characterize R3's cost to 10.1.1.0/24 because R3 uses a summary type 3 LSA, which hides some of the costs.

**10.** R1 and R2 each connect through Fast Ethernet interfaces to the same LAN, which should be in area 0. R1's IP address is 10.1.1.1/24, and R2's is 10.1.1.2/24. The only OSPF-related configuration is as follows:

```
hostname R1
router ospf 1
 network 0.0.0.0 255.255.255.255 area 0
 auto-cost reference-bandwidth 1000
!
hostname R2
router ospf 2
 network 10.0.0.0 0.0.0.255 area 0
```

Which of the following statements are true about the configuration?

   **a.** The **network** command on R2 does not match IP address 10.1.1.2, so R2 will not attempt to send Hellos or discover neighbors on the LAN.

   **b.** The different process IDs in the **router ospf** command will prevent the two routers from becoming neighbors on the LAN.

   **c.** R2 will become the DR as a result of having a cost of 1 associated with its Fast Ethernet interface.

   **d.** R1 and R2 could never become neighbors because of the difference in cost values.

   **e.** R1's OSPF cost for its Fast Ethernet interface would be 10.

**11.** Which of the following are true about setting timers with OSPF?

   **a.** The **ip ospf dead-interval minimal hello-multiplier 4** interface subcommand sets the hello interval to 4 ms.

   **b.** The **ip ospf dead-interval minimal hello-multiplier 4** interface subcommand sets the dead interval to 4 seconds.

   **c.** The **ip ospf dead-interval minimal hello-multiplier 4** interface subcommand sets the hello interval to 250 ms.

   **d.** On all interfaces, the **ip ospf hello-interval 30** interface subcommand changes the hello interval from 10 to 30.

   **e.** The **ip ospf hello-multiplier 5** interface subcommand sets the dead interval to five times the then-current hello interval.

   **f.** Cisco IOS defaults the hello and dead intervals to 30/120 on interfaces using the OSPF nonbroadcast network type.

**12.** R1 has been configured for OSPF authentication on its Fa0/0 interface as shown here. Which of the following is true about the configuration?

```
interface Fa0/0
 ip ospf authentication-key hannah
 ip ospf authentication
 ip ospf message-digest-key 2 md5 jessie
router ospf 2
 area 0 authentication message-digest
```

   **a.** R1 will attempt simple-text authentication on the LAN with key **hannah**.

   **b.** R1 will attempt MD5 authentication on the LAN with key **jessie**.

   **c.** R1 will attempt OSPF type 2 authentication on Fa0/0.

   **d.** R1 will attempt OSPF type 3 authentication on Fa0/0.

**13.** Which of the following statements about OSPFv3 are true?

   **a.** Type 1 and 2 LSAs do not carry addressing information.

   **b.** OSPFv3 messages are encapsulated directly into Layer 2 frames.

   **c.** OSPFv3 uses 128-bit Router IDs.

   **d.** There are three flooding scopes defined for OSPFv3 LSAs: link, area, and AS.

   **e.** Multiple OSPFv3 instances can run over a single link.

   **f.** OSPFv3 implements its own authentication mechanisms.

**14.** Which statements are true about Link LSA and Intra-Area-Prefix LSA in OSPFv3?

   **a.** Link LSAs have AS flooding scope.

   **b.** Intra-Area-Prefix LSAs have area flooding scope.

   **c.** Link LSAs carry information about link-local addresses.

   **d.** Intra-Area-Prefix LSAs carry information about global prefixes.

   **e.** When an updated Link or Intra-Area-Prefix LSA is flooded, a router is required to schedule a full SPF run.

   **f.** Link and Intra-Area-Prefix LSAs have entirely replaced the Router and Network LSAs.

**15.** How does OSPFv3 handle authentication?

   **a.** OSPFv3 implements its own authentication and encryption mechanisms.

   **b.** SSL/TLS is used by OSPFv3 to provide authentication and encryption.

   **c.** OSPFv3 relies on IPsec to authenticate and encrypt its packets.

   **d.** OSPFv3 makes use of ISAKMP/IKE protocols to negotiate authentication and encryption parameters between routers.

   **e.** The use of AH and ESP is mutually exclusive in OSPFv3.

**16.** Which statements are true about address family support in OSPFv3?

    **a.** When running multiple address families, a single link-state database on a router holds information from all address families.

    **b.** Each address family is run as a separate OSPFv3 instance, keeping all its data and state separate.

    **c.** Multiple address families are distinguished by separate OSPFv3 process IDs.

    **d.** Running IPv4 and IPv6 address families simultaneously under a single OSPFv3 process will result in a significantly smaller memory footprint than running a separate IPv4 OSPFv2 and IPv6 OSPFv3 process.

    **e.** Type 8 and 9 LSAs are reused to carry both IPv4 and IPv6 prefixes.

    **f.** Even if running OSPFv3 for IPv4 address family, interfaces must be configured for IPv6 connectivity.

# Foundation Topics

Link-state routing protocols define the content and structure of data that describes network topology, and define the processes by which routers exchange that detailed topology information. The name "link state" refers to the fact that the topology information includes information about each data *link*, along with each link's current operational *state*. All the topological data together comprises the *link-state database (LSDB)*. Each link-state router applies the Dijkstra algorithm to the database to calculate the current best routes to each subnet.

This chapter breaks down the OSPF coverage into three major sections. The first section details how the topology data is exchanged. The second section covers OSPF design and the contents of the LSDB, which comprises different types of *link-state advertisements (LSA)*. (The second section covers both design and the LSDB because the design choices directly impact which types of LSAs are forwarded into the differing parts of an OSPF network.) The third section covers the majority of the OSPF configuration details of OSPF for this chapter, although a few configuration topics are interspersed in the first two sections.

## OSPF Database Exchange

OSPF defines five different messages that routers can use to establish adjacencies and exchange routing information. The process by which LSAs are exchanged does not change whether a single area or multiple areas are used, so this section will use a single OSPF area (area 0).

### OSPF Router IDs

Before an OSPF router can send any OSPF messages, it must choose a unique 32-bit identifier called the OSPF *router identifier (RID)*. Cisco routers use the following sequence to choose their OSPF RID, only moving on to the next step in this list if the previous step did not supply the OSPF RID:

1. Use the router ID configured in the **router-id** *id* subcommand under **router ospf**.

2. Use the highest numeric IP address on any currently nonshutdown loopback interface that has not yet been allocated as a RID by any other OSPF process.

3. Use the highest numeric IP address on any currently nonshutdown, nonloopback interface that has not yet been allocated as a RID by any other OSPF process.

The sequence and logic are very simple, but some details are hidden in the sequence:

■   Multiple OSPF processes running on a single router try to choose unique RIDs. Each of the OSPF processes performs the same three steps to choose a RID, skipping IP addresses that have already been used as RIDs by other OSPF processes running on the router.

- The interface from which the RID is taken does not have to be matched by an OSPF **network** command.

- It is sufficient for the interface to be in the *down/down* state to be considered by OSPF as a prospective interface for RID selection.

- OSPF does not have to advertise a route to reach the RID's subnet.

- The RID does not have to be reachable per the IP routing table.

- Steps 2 and 3 look at the then-current interface state to choose the RID when the OSPF process is started.

- Routers consider changing the OSPF RID when the OSPF process is restarted, or when the RID is changed through configuration.

- If a router's RID changes, the rest of the routers in the same area will have to perform a new SPF calculation, even if the network topology has not changed. The reason is that a RID change is indistinguishable from a process of replacing one router with another.

- If the RID is configured with the **router-id** command, and the command remains unchanged, that router's RID will never change.

For these reasons, many people set their RIDs with the **router-id** command and use an obvious numbering scheme to make it easy to identify a router by its RID.

## Becoming Neighbors, Exchanging Databases, and Becoming Adjacent

OSPF directly encapsulates the five different types of OSPF messages inside IP packets, using IP protocol 89, as listed in Table 9-2.

**Table 9-2**   *OSPF Messages*

| Message | Description |
|---|---|
| Hello | Used to discover neighbors, bring a neighbor relationship to a 2-Way state, and monitor a neighbor's continuous liveliness |
| Database Description (DD or DBD) | Used to exchange LSA headers during the initial topology exchange, so that a router knows a list of that neighbor's LSAs including their versions |
| Link-State Request (LSR) | A packet that identifies one or more LSAs about which the sending router would like the neighbor to supply full details about the LSAs |
| Link-State Update (LSU) | A packet that contains fully detailed LSAs, sent in response to an LSR message or in the event of a topological change |
| Link-State Acknowledgment (LSAck) | Sent to confirm receipt of an LSU message |

These messages together allow routers to discover each other's presence (Hello), learn which LSAs are missing from their LSDBs (DD), request and reliably exchange the LSAs (LSR/LSU/LSAck), and monitor their neighbors for any changes in the topology (Hello). Note that the LSAs themselves are not OSPF messages. An LSA is a data structure, held inside a router's LSDB and exchanged inside LSU messages.

When a particular data link first comes up, OSPF routers first become neighbors using the Hello message. At that point, they exchange topology information using the other four OSPF messages. Figure 9-1 outlines the overall process between two routers.

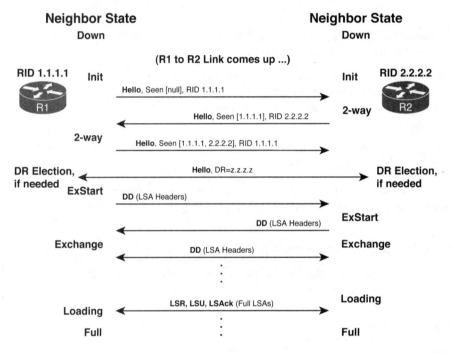

**Figure 9-1** *Overview of OSPF LSDB Exchange*

Figure 9-1 shows the overall message flow, along with the neighbor state on each router. An OSPF router keeps a state machine for each neighbor, listing the current neighbor state in the output of the **show ip ospf neighbor** command. These neighbor states change as the neighbors progress through their messaging; in this example, the neighbors settle into a *full state*, meaning *fully adjacent*, when the process is completed.

The "Foundation Summary" section at the end of this chapter includes a reference table (Table 9-14) listing the neighbor states and their meanings. The next few sections explain the details behind the process shown in Figure 9-1.

## OSPF Neighbor States

OSPF routers go through a series of adjacency states when establishing a relation. Some of these states are transitory, reflecting different stages of building an adjacency, while some of them are stable states in which routers can, in the absence of topological changes, remain for an unlimited period of time. The knowledge of these states is crucial for proper understanding of OSPF adjacency buildup and troubleshooting.

Before diving into the details, it is important to note that these states are in fact neighbor states—they indicate how a router treats its particular neighbor. Although sometimes popularly described as adjacency states, these states do not reflect the state of the entire adjacency but rather a state of a particular router's neighbor in this adjacency. Two routers building an adjacency can temporarily, though validly, consider each other to be in a different state (for example, one router might consider the other to be in the Loading state while the other might consider the first one to be already in the Full state). Ultimately, however, both routers must arrive at the same state.

■ **Down:** This is the initial state for a neighbor. This state is mostly seen when a working adjacency to a neighbor is torn down (for example, because no valid OSPF packets have been received during the Dead interval), or when a manually configured neighbor does not respond to our initial Hello packets. Note that having a neighbor in the Down state implies that the router already knows about this neighbor's IP address.

■ **Attempt:** This state is valid only on nonbroadcast multiaccess (NBMA) and point-to-multipoint nonbroadcast networks. On these networks, a neighbor is immediately placed into the Attempt state and contacted by Hello packets sent at usual intervals. If, however, the neighbor does not respond within the Dead interval, it will be placed back into the Down state, and contacted at a (possibly) reduced rate.

■ **Init:** A neighbor is placed into the Init state if a valid Hello packet has been received from it but the list of seen routers in this Hello packet does not contain the receiving router's RID. This means that this router can hear the other router but it is not certain whether the other router can hear this router.

■ **2-Way:** A neighbor is placed into the 2-Way state if a valid Hello packet has been received from it and the list of seen routers in this Hello packet includes the receiving router's RID. This state confirms a bidirectional visibility between the two routers. The 2-Way is a stable state between routers on multiaccess networks that do not intend to become fully adjacent.

■ **ExStart:** A neighbor is moved from Init or 2-Way into the ExStart state if the bidirectional visibility has been confirmed and it is decided that this router shall become fully adjacent to it. The purpose of the ExStart state is to establish the Master/Slave relationship. In the ExStart state, routers exchange empty Database Description packets to compare their Router IDs, determine the Master and Slave roles for each router, and agree on a common starting sequence number used to acknowledge subsequent Database Description packets used in the Exchange state.

■ **Exchange:** A neighbor is moved from ExStart to Exchange state after the Master/Slave relationship has been established. During the Exchange state, Database Description packets are exchanged between the routers carrying the list of link-state database elements (that is, LSAs) known by each router. During the Exchange state, each router builds a list of LSAs to be subsequently downloaded from the other router.

■ **Loading:** A neighbor is moved from the Exchange to Loading state after it has advertised the complete list of LSAs and this router needs to download some of the LSAs from the neighbor. The neighbor is kept in the Loading state during the LSA download.

■ **Full:** A neighbor is moved from the Exchange or Loading state to the Full state when all required LSAs have been downloaded from the neighbor, so all missing or outdated LSAs have been acquired. The Full state is a stable state between routers that have become fully adjacent.

### Becoming Neighbors: The Hello Process

Hello messages perform four major functions:

■ Discover other OSPF-speaking routers on common subnets

■ Check for agreement on selected configuration parameters

■ Verify bidirectional visibility between routers

■ Monitor health of the neighbors to react if the neighbor fails

To discover neighbors, Cisco OSPF routers listen for multicast Hello messages sent to 224.0.0.5—the *All OSPF Routers* multicast address—on any interfaces that have been enabled for OSPF. The Hellos are sourced from that router's primary IP address on the interface; in other words, Hellos are not sourced from secondary IP addresses. (OSPF routers will advertise secondary IP addresses, but they will not send Hellos from those IP addresses, and never form neighbor relationships using secondary addresses. This holds for EIGRP and RIP as well.) Furthermore, OSPF neighbors will become fully adjacent if one or both of the neighbors are using unnumbered interfaces for the connection between them.

After two routers discover each other by receiving Hellos from the other router, the routers perform the following parameter checks based on the receive Hellos:

■ Must pass the authentication process

■ Must be in the same primary subnet, including the same subnet mask

■ Must be in the same OSPF area

■ Must be of the same area type (regular, stub, not-so-stubby area [NSSA])

■ Must not have duplicate RIDs

■ OSPF Hello and Dead timers must be equal

If any of these items do not match, the two routers simply do not form a neighbor relationship. Also of note is one important item that does not have to match: the OSPF process ID (PID), as configured in the **router ospf** *process-id* command. Be aware of the fact that the maximum transmission unit (MTU) must be equal for the DD packets to be successfully processed between neighbors, but this parameter check is technically not part of the Hello process. The MTU mismatch would negatively affect the database synchronization process in the ExStart and Exchange phases, but it would not prevent routers from becoming successful neighbors up to and including the 2-Way state.

The third function of Hello packets is to verify bidirectional visibility between routers on the same segment. Each Hello packet contains a list of neighbors from whom the sending router received valid and acceptable Hellos. This list of variable size is located in the trailing part of each Hello and contains RIDs of routers whose Hellos were seen and accepted by the router originating this Hello. If a router finds its own RID in the list of seen routers in a Hello received from a neighbor, it can be sure that they can hear each other.

Finally, the fourth important function for a Hello is to maintain a heartbeat function between neighbors. The neighbors send Hellos every *hello interval*; failure to receive a Hello within the longer *dead interval* causes a router to believe that its neighbor has failed. The hello interval defaults to 10 seconds on interfaces with an OSPF broadcast or point-to-point network type, and 30 seconds on interfaces with an OSPF nonbroadcast or point-to-multipoint network type; the dead interval defaults to four times the hello interval.

Example 9-1 lists some basic OSPF command output related to the neighbor establishment with Hellos, and the hello and dead intervals.

**Example 9-1**  *Hello Mismatches and Basic Neighbor Parameters*

```
! Below, debug messages show that this router disagrees with the hello and dead
! intervals on router 10.1.111.4; The "C" and "R" mean "configured" and "received,"
! respectively, meaning that this router uses 30/120 for hello/dead, and the other
! router is trying to use 10/40.

R1# debug ip ospf hello
OSPF hello events debugging is on
Jan 12 06:41:20.940: OSPF: Mismatched hello parameters from 10.1.111.4
Jan 12 06:41:20.940: OSPF: Dead R 40 C 120, Hello R 10 C 30  Mask R 255.255.255.0 C
  255.255.255.0

! Below, R1's hello and dead intervals are listed for the same interface.

R1# show ip ospf int s 0/0.100
Serial0/0.100 is up, line protocol is up
  Internet Address 10.1.111.1/24, Area 0
  Process ID 1, Router ID 1.1.1.1, Network Type NON_BROADCAST, Cost: 64
  Transmit Delay is 1 sec, State DR, Priority 1
  Designated Router (ID) 1.1.1.1, Interface address 10.1.111.1
  No backup designated router on this network
```

```
   Timer intervals configured, Hello 30, Dead 120, Wait 120, Retransmit 5
! Lines omitted for brevity


! Below, R1 shows a neighbor on S0/0.100, in the full state, meaning the routers
! have completed LSDB exchange. Note the current Dead timer counts down, in this
! case from 2 minutes; the value of 1:58 means R1 last received a Hello from
! neighbor 10.1.111.6 two seconds ago.

R1# sh ip ospf neighbor 6.6.6.6
 Neighbor 6.6.6.6, interface address 10.1.111.6
    In the area 0 via interface Serial0/0.100
    Neighbor priority is 0, State is FULL, 8 state changes
    DR is 10.1.111.1 BDR is 0.0.0.0
    Poll interval 120
    Options is 0x42
    Dead timer due in 00:01:58
    Neighbor is up for 00:17:22
! Lines omitted for brevity
```

### Transmitting LSA Headers to Neighbors

When two routers hear Hellos, and the parameter check passes, they do not immediately send packets holding the LSAs. Instead, each router creates and sends *Database Description* (*DD*, or sometimes called *DBD*) packets, which contain the headers of each LSA. The headers include just enough information to uniquely identify each LSA and its revision without transmitting its body. Essentially, the routers exchange an index list of all the LSAs they each know about; the next step in the process is letting a router request a new copy of only those LSAs it does not have or which are less recent.

The DD messages use an OSPF-defined simple error-recovery process. Each DD packet, which can contain several LSA headers, has a sequence number assigned. The receiver acknowledges a received DD packet by sending a DD packet with the identical sequence number back to the sender. The sender uses a window size of one packet and then waits for the acknowledgment before sending the next DD packet.

### Database Description Exchange: Master/Slave Relationship

As a neighbor relationship forms between two routers (specifically, at the ExStart stage of the neighborship), the neighbors determine which router is to be the master and which is to be the slave during the database exchange between them. The roles of master and slave define the responsibilities of routers during the exchange of DD packets. Only the master is allowed to send DD packets on its own accord as well as to set and increase their sequence numbers. A slave is allowed to send a DD packet only as a response to a DD packet received from master router, and must use the same sequence number. In effect, a slave is *polled* by the master and only responds to it.

Among other fields, a DD packet header contains three flags:

- **Master (MS) flag:** Set in all DD packets sent by the master, and cleared in all packets sent by the slave

- **More (M) flag:** Set when a router intends to send an additional DD packet after this one

- **Init (I) flag:** Indicates that this is the initial DD packet that starts the exchange, and subsequent DD packets, either from master or slave, have the I flag cleared

The M flag requires further explanation. Before two routers synchronize their link-state databases, the count of LSAs in their databases can considerably differ. One router might hold hundreds or more LSAs in its database while the other might have just a handful of them. During the DD packet exchange, one router might need to send many DD packets while the other might be able to list all its known LSAs in a single DD packet. There are, however, two rules to sending DD packets that must be observed at all times:

1. Each DD packet sent from the master must be replied to by the slave (that is, the number of DD packets sent from master to slave must match the number of DD packets sent from slave to master).

2. A slave can send a DD packet *only as a response* to receiving a master's DD packet (that is, without receiving a DD packet from master, a slave is not allowed to send a DD packet on its own).

How shall these rules be obeyed if the routers have different counts of DD packets to send?

Satisfying the first rule is actually very simple: If a router has no more LSA headers to advertise but its peer requires it to send more DD packets, the router will simply send empty DD packets.

Satisfying the second rule is really concerned about the slave letting the master know whether it has more DD packets to send. If it does, the master must continue polling the slave, even if it has no more LSAs to advertise itself. This is accomplished by the slave setting the M flag in its DD packet sent in response to the master's DD packet. If the master receives a DD packet from the slave with the M flag set, it knows that the slave has at least one more DD packet to send, so it must poll it again. A master will stop send sending DD packets to a slave when it has no more LSA headers to advertise, *and* the slave's last received DD packet has the M flag cleared, indicating that the slave itself has advertised its entire LSA list.

Apart from the slave setting the M flag to ask the master to poll it again, both master and slave appropriately set the M flag in their DD packets to indicate when they have completed advertising their entire link-state database. This knowledge is necessary to move the neighbor to the appropriate state, either Loading or Full, when the complete list of LSAs in the neighbor's database is known.

In the beginning of the exchange, each router places the other into the ExStart state. Each of them considers itself to be the master, and sends an empty DD packet to the other router, containing a randomly chosen sequence number, and MS (Master), M (More), and I (Init) flags set to 1. After receiving the neighbor's DD packet, however, the router with the lower RID will change its role to slave, and it will respond with a DD packet with MS and I flags cleared and the sequence number set to the sequence number of master's DD packet. This accomplishes the master/slave selection, and both routers move to the Exchange state. The master will then send a DD packet with the sequence number incremented by 1, optionally containing one or more LSA headers, and the slave will respond with a DD packet reusing the same sequence number from the received packet, optionally advertising its own LSA headers. The exchange continues in the same fashion, with the master incrementing the sequence number of each subsequent DD packet, until both routers have advertised all known all LSA headers (the master will stop sending DD packets when it has advertised all LSA headers itself and the last DD response from the slave has the M flag cleared).

## Requesting, Getting, and Acknowledging LSAs

After all LSA headers have been exchanged using DD packets, each neighboring router has a list of LSAs known by the neighbor. Using that knowledge, a router needs to request a full copy of each LSA that is missing from its own LSDB.

To know whether a neighbor has a more recent copy of a particular LSA, a router looks at the sequence number of the LSA in its LSDB and compares it to the sequence number of that same LSA learned from the DD packet. Each LSA's sequence number is incremented every time the LSA changes or is reoriginated. So, if a router received (through a DD packet) an LSA header with a later sequence number for a particular LSA (as compared with the LSA in the LSDB), that router knows that the neighbor has a more recent LSA. For example, R1 sent R2 an LSA header for the type 1 LSA that describes R1 itself, with sequence number 0x80000004. If R2's database already held that LSA, but with a sequence number of 0x80000003, R2 would know that it needs to ask R1 to send the latest copy (sequence number 0x80000004) of that LSA.

**Note**   In OSPF, LSA sequence numbers form a space of linearly ordered *signed* 32-bit integers going from $-2^{31}+1$ to $2^{31}-1$, or from $-2,147,483,647$ to $2,147,483,647$. The value $2^{31}$ is reserved to detect when the LSA numbers wrap, and is not used as a sequence number. Because in most computer systems, negative integers are stored in two's complement, printing out the value of the two's complement of a negative number in hexadecimal form yields values 0x80000001 (corresponds to $-2^{31}+1$) through 0xFFFFFFFF (corresponds to $-1$). Hence, when printed out in hexadecimal, LSA sequence numbers start with 0x80000001 ($-2^{31}+1$); increase through 0xFFFFFFFF ($-1$), 0x00000000 (0), and 0x00000001 (1); and finish at 0x7FFFFFFF ($2^{31}-1$). If the sequence number of an LSA was to be increased to 0x80000000, this LSA would need to be flushed from the LSDB and then reoriginated with the sequence number starting again at 0x80000001. The sequence number 0x80000000 never appears on the wire.

Routers use *Link-State Request (LSR)* packets to request one or more LSAs from a neighbor. The neighboring router replies with *Link-State Update (LSU)* packets, which hold one or more full LSAs. As shown in Figure 9-1, both routers sit in a Loading state while the LSR/LSA process continues. After the process is complete, they settle into a *Full* state, which means that the two routers should have fully exchanged their databases, resulting in identical copies of the LSDB entries for that area on both routers.

The LSR/LSA process uses a reliable protocol that has two options for acknowledging packets. First, an LSU can be acknowledged by the receiver of the LSU simply repeating the exact same LSU back to the sender. Alternatively, a router can send back an *LSAck* packet to acknowledge the packet, which contains a list of acknowledged LSA headers.

At the end of the process outlined in Figure 9-1, two neighbors have exchanged their LSDBs. As a result, their LSDBs should be identical. At this point, they can each independently run the Dijkstra's Shortest Path First (SPF) algorithm to calculate the best routes from their own perspectives.

## Designated Routers on LANs

OSPF optimizes the LSA flooding process on multiaccess data links by using the concept of a *designated router (DR)*. Without the concept of a DR, each pair of routers that share a data link would become fully adjacent neighbors. Each pair of routers would directly exchange their LSDBs with each other, as shown in Figure 9-1. On a LAN with only six routers, without a DR, 15 different pairs of routers would exist, and 15 different instances of full database flooding would occur. OSPF uses a DR (and a *backup DR*, or *BDR*) on a LAN or other multiaccess network. The flooding occurs through the DR, reducing the unnecessary exchange of redundant LSAs.

**Note**  The true optimization of flooding provided by the DR depends on the situation that prompts the flooding. If a router on a common segment needs to advertise an update, the concept of a DR requires that the update is actually flooded twice: first from the router that advertises the update to the DR/BDR, and second, from the DR to all routers on the segment. This double flooding can hardly be considered an optimization. However, when a new multiaccess segment with multiple routers boots up, or if a new router is connected to such a segment, the presence of a DR/BDR allows the routers to synchronize only to a DR and BDR, alleviating the need of synchronizing to each other, possibly flooding the same set of LSAs multiple times. Hence, the optimization provided by the DR/BDR is most visible during the initial synchronization of router databases.

In reality, DRs have a different crucial and the only truly irreplaceable function: They create a type 2 LSA that represents the multiaccess network segment. LSA types are covered in the next major section, "OSPF Design and LSAs."

The next section goes through the basics of the DR/BDR process on LANs, which is followed by coverage of options of OSPF network types and how they impact OSPF flooding on Frame Relay links.

## Designated Router Optimization on LANs

The basic rule about exchanging LSDB contents states that only routers in the Full state are allowed to exchange LSAs. On a multiaccess segment, every router is in the Full state only with DR and BDR routers. The DR and BDR are in the Full state with all routers on the segment and with each other as well. If the DR or BDR needs to send an update, it simply does it directly by sending an LSU packet containing the updated LSA to the multicast IP address 224.0.0.5, the All OSPF Routers group. Every other OSPF router on the multiaccess segment will receive this LSU and acknowledge its arrival by sending a unicast LSAck packet to the router that sourced the LSU.

A router on a multiaccess segment that is neither DR nor BDR is in the Full state only with the DR and BDR. If it needs to send an update, it sends an LSU packet to the multicast IP address 224.0.0.6, the All OSPF DR Routers group that contains only the DR and BDR. Both the DR and BDR will store the updated LSA from the LSU in their LSDB. The DR then floods a new LSU packet containing the same updated LSA to all OSPF routers on the segment using the multicast IP address 224.0.0.5. Neither the DR nor BDR acknowledge the original LSU with an LSAck—while they could, and it would be a valid acknowledgment, it is not necessary. Instead, the LSU flooded by the DR serves as an implicit acknowledgment to the original router that sent the update. Other routers on the segment including the BDR, except the original router, will acknowledge the DR's LSU with a unicast LSAck sent to the DR.

**Note**    In topologies without a DR, the LSU packets are typically sent to the 224.0.0.5 All OSPF Routers multicast IP address.

Example 9-2 shows the output of a **show ip ospf neighbor** command issued on Router R1 connected to a common Fast Ethernet segment with three other routers. According to this output, the router with the OSPF RID of 8.8.8.8 is the DR, the router with the OSPF RID of 7.7.7.7 is the BDR, and both these neighbors have reached the Full state with respect to R1. Another router on the segment with the OSPF RID of 2.2.2.2 is neither the DR nor the BDR. Because R1 is obviously not a DR or BDR itself, Routers R1 and 2.2.2.2 remain in the 2-Way state.

**Example 9-2**    show ip ospf neighbor *Command*

```
R1# sh ip ospf neighbor fa 0/0
Neighbor ID     Pri    State         Dead Time    Address      Interface
2.2.2.2          1     2WAY/DROTHER  00:00:35     10.1.1.2     FastEthernet0/0
7.7.7.7          1     FULL/BDR      00:00:38     10.1.1.3     FastEthernet0/0
8.8.8.8          1     FULL/DR       00:00:34     10.1.1.4     FastEthernet0/0
```

When a DR is used on a link, routers end up as DR, BDR, or neither; a router that is neither a DR or a BDR is called a *DROther* router. The DR and BDR form full adjacencies with all other neighbors on the link, so they reach a Full state when the database exchange process is complete. However, two neighbors that are both DROthers do not become fully adjacent; they stop at the 2-Way state, as shown in Example 9-2. Stopping at the 2-Way state between two DROther routers is normal. It simply means that the Hello parameter match and bidirectional visibility check worked, but the neighbors do not need to proceed to the point of synchronizing their LSDBs directly, because they do not need to when a DR is present.

To describe the fact that some neighbors do not directly exchange DD and LSU packets, OSPF makes a distinction between the terms *neighbors* and *adjacent*, as follows:

- **Neighbors:** Two routers that share a common data link and that exchange Hello messages, and the Hellos must match for certain parameters.

- **Adjacent (fully adjacent):** Two neighbors that have completed the process of fully exchanging DD and LSU packets directly between each other.

Note that although DROther routers do not exchange DD and LSU packets directly with each other, like R1 and R2 in Figure 9-2, the DROther routers do end up with an identical copy of the LSDB entries by exchanging them with the DR.

## DR Election on LANs

As noted in Figure 9-1, if a DR is elected, the election occurs after the routers have become neighbors, but before they send DD packets and reach the ExStart neighbor state. When an OSPF router reaches the 2-Way state with the first neighbor on an interface, it has already received at least one Hello from that neighbor and has found its RID in the list of seen routers in the received Hello. If the Hello messages state a DR of 0.0.0.0— meaning that none have been elected—the router waits before attempting to elect a DR. This typically occurs after a failure on the LAN. OSPF routers wait with the goal of giving all the routers on that subnet a chance to finish initializing after a failure so that all the routers can participate in the DR election; otherwise, the first router to become active would always become the DR. (The time period is called the OSPF *wait time*, which is set to the same value as the Dead timer.)

However, if the received Hellos already list the DR's RID, the router does not have to wait before beginning the election process. This typically occurs when one router lost its connection to the LAN, but other routers remained and continued to work. In this case, the newly connected router does not attempt to elect a new DR, assuming that the DR listed in the received Hello is indeed the current DR.

The election process allows for the possibility of many different scenarios for which routers might and might not become the DR or BDR. Generally speaking, the following rules govern the DR/BDR election process:

- Any router with its OSPF priority set to 1–255 inclusive is eligible to become a DR or BDR. A router with its OSPF priority set to 0 is ignored in DR/BDR elections.

- Each router performs the elections locally based on the collected data from other neighbors on the segment; however, the algorithm makes sure that all routers ultimately arrive at the same conclusion.

■ During the wait interval, whose length is automatically set to the Dead interval on the interface, each router collects the priorities and RIDs of other neighbors on the segment by listening to received Hellos, adding its own RID and priority to the list as well. However, a router does not assert itself as the DR or BDR during the wait interval, and all Hellos it sends indicate that the DR and BDR are not yet elected (the IP addresses in the DR and BDR fields in Hellos are set to 0.0.0.0).

■ If, during the wait interval, a Hello packet arrives from a neighbor that claims itself to be the BDR (meaning both DR and BDR have already been elected and the BDR is alive), or if a neighbor that claims to be the DR and no BDR address is indicated in the Hello (meaning that the DR has already been elected and there is no BDR present on the network), the router immediately proceeds to the DR/BDR election process. Otherwise, the full wait interval period on the interface needs to expire.

■ The election is performed only for those roles that are not yet claimed in neighbor Hellos (either both DR and BDR, or just BDR). A router examines the list of priorities and RIDs it has collected over the wait interval, choosing the router with the highest priority as the DR (if the role is not taken already) and the router with the second-highest priority as the BDR (if the role is not taken already). If multiple routers advertise the same highest or second-highest priority, still competing for the role of DR or BDR, the higher RID is used to break the tie.

■ After the election has completed, if a new router arrives or an existing router improves its priority, it cannot preempt the existing DR and take over as DR (or as BDR).

■ When a DR is elected and the DR fails, the BDR becomes the DR, and a new election is held for a new BDR.

In certain scenarios, two or more routers might temporarily arrive at a different result of DR/BDR elections. This can happen if, for example, two or more routers are connected to a switched network that undergoes an STP topology change that requires 50 seconds to heal (for example, an indirect link failure). While the network is partitioned, routers arrive at different results of DR/BDR elections, as each network partition will elect its own DR and BDR. After the network becomes connected again, different routers will claim different DRs/BDRs in their Hellos. When this happens, the rule about DR/BDR elections being nonpreemptive is ignored (upholding it would prevent the routers from arriving at a single DR/BDR), and the contending routers enter the election phase again.

## Designated Routers on WANs and OSPF Network Types

Using a DR makes good sense on a LAN because it might improve LSA flooding efficiency. Likewise, not using a DR on a point-to-point WAN link also makes sense, because with only two routers on the subnet, there is no inefficiency upon which to improve. However, on nonbroadcast multiaccess (NBMA) networks, arguments can be made regarding whether a DR is helpful. So, OSPF includes several options that include a choice of whether to use a DR on WAN interfaces.

Cisco router interfaces can be configured to use, or not use, a DR, plus a couple of other key behaviors, based on the *OSPF network type* for each interface. The OSPF network type determines that router's behavior regarding the following:

■ Whether the router tries to elect a DR on that interface

■ Whether the router must statically configure a neighbor (with the **neighbor** command), or find neighbors using the typical multicast Hello packets

■ Whether more than two neighbors should be allowed on the same subnet

For example, LAN interfaces default to use an OSPF network type of *broadcast*. OSPF broadcast networks elect a DR, use Hellos to dynamically find neighbors, and allow more than two routers to be in the same subnet on that LAN. For High-Level Data Link Control (HDLC) and Point-to-Point Protocol (PPP) links, OSPF uses a network type of *point-to-point*, meaning that no DR is elected, only two IP addresses are in the subnet, and neighbors can be found through Hellos.

Table 9-3 summarizes the OSPF interface types and their meanings. Note that the interface type values can be set with the **ip ospf network** *type* interface subcommand; the first column in the table not only describes the interface type but also lists the exact keyword for the *type* argument. Also, for cases in which a DR is not elected, all routers that become neighbors also attempt to become adjacent by the direct exchange of DD, LSR, and LSU packets.

**Table 9-3**  *OSPF Network Types*

| Interface Type | Uses DR/ BDR? | Default Hello Interval | Requires a neighbor Command? | More Than Two Hosts Allowed in the Subnet? |
|---|---|---|---|---|
| Broadcast | Yes | 10 | No | Yes |
| Point-to-point[1] | No | 10 | No | No |
| Non-broadcast[2] (NBMA) | Yes | 30 | Yes | Yes |
| Point-to-multipoint | No | 30 | No | Yes |
| Point-to-multipoint nonbroadcast | No | 30 | Yes | Yes |
| Loopback[3] | No | – | – | No |

[1] Default on Frame Relay point-to-point subinterfaces.

[2] Default on Frame Relay physical and multipoint subinterfaces.

[3] Cannot be configured manually—used on loopback interfaces automatically.

### Caveats Regarding OSPF Network Types over NBMA Networks

When configuring OSPF over Frame Relay, the OSPF network type concept can become a bit troublesome. In fact, many CCIE Routing and Switching lab preparation texts and lab books focus on the variety of combinations of OSPF network types used with Frame Relay for various interfaces/subinterfaces. The following list contains many of the key items you should check when looking at an OSPF configuration over Frame Relay, when the OSPF network types used on the various routers do not match:

- Make sure that the default Hello/Dead timers do not cause the Hello parameter check to fail. (See Table 9-3 for the defaults for each OSPF network type.)

- If one router expects a DR to be elected, and the other does not, the neighbors might come up and full LSAs be communicated. However, **show** command output might show odd information, and next-hop routers might not be reachable. So, make sure that all routers in the same NBMA subnet use an OSPF network type that either uses a DR or does not.

- If a DR is used, the DR and BDR must have a permanent virtual circuit (PVC) to every other router in the subnet. If not, routers will not be able to learn routes, because the DR must forward the LSU packets to each of the other routers, and in addition, the type 2 LSA originated by the DR for the common subnet will contain incomplete information. Routers that do not have a PVC to every other router must not be permitted to become a DR/BDR.

- If neighbors need to be configured statically, configuring the **neighbor** command on a single router is sufficient to bring up the OSPF adjacency with the configured neighbor. For clarity and stability, however, it is better to configure **neighbor** commands on both routers.

Two simple options exist for making OSPF work over Frame Relay—both of which do not require a DR and do not require **neighbor** commands. If the design allows for the use of point-to-point subinterfaces, use those and take the default OSPF network type of point-to-point, and no additional work is required. If multipoint subinterfaces are needed, or if the configuration must not use subinterfaces, adding the **ip ospf network point-to-multipoint** command on all the routers works, without requiring additional effort to manually define neighbors or worry about which router becomes the DR.

### Example of OSPF Network Types and NBMA

On NBMA networks with an OSPF network type that requires that a DR be elected, you must take care to make sure that the correct DR is elected. The reason is that the DR and BDR must each have a PVC connecting them to all the DROther routers and to each other. Otherwise, appropriate LSA flooding will not be possible and the type 2 LSA generated for the NBMA network might contain incomplete information, or there might even be multiple conflicting type 2 LSAs. So, with partial meshes, the election should be influenced by configuring the routers' priority and RIDs such that the hub site of a hub-and-spoke partial mesh becomes the DR. Figure 9-2 shows an example network for which R1 should be the only router allowed to become the DR or BDR.

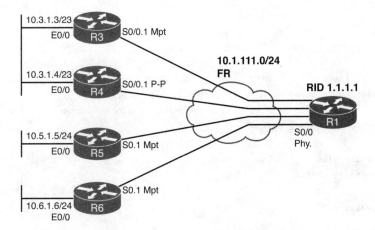

**Figure 9-2**  *Network Used in the Frame Relay Priority and Network Type Example*

Example 9-3 depicts the following scenarios relating to DR election in Figure 9-2:

- The R1, R3, and R5 configuration is correct for operating with the default OSPF network type nonbroadcast in a partial mesh.

- R6 has omitted the **ip ospf priority** interface subcommand, causing it to inadvisably become the DR.

- R4 will be used as an example of what not to do, in part to point out some interesting facts about OSPF **show** commands.

**Note**  Figure 9-2 and Example 9-3 do not depict a suggested design for Frame Relay and OSPF. With this topology, using point-to-point subinterfaces in all cases, using four small (/30) subnets, and defaulting to OSPF network type point-to-point would work well. Such a design, however, would not require any thought regarding the OSPF network type. So, this example is purposefully designed to provide a backdrop from which to show how the OSPF network types work.

Example 9-3 shows only the nondefault OSPF configuration settings; also, the routers have an obvious RID numbering scheme (1.1.1.1 for R1, 2.2.2.2 for R2, and so on).

**Example 9-3**  *Setting Priority on NBMA Networks*

```
! R1 configuration - the neighbor commands default to a priority value of 0,
! meaning R1's perception of that neighbor is priority 0.

router ospf 1
 log-adjacency-changes detail
 network 0.0.0.0 255.255.255.255 area 0
 neighbor 10.1.111.3
```

```
 neighbor 10.1.111.4
 neighbor 10.1.111.5
 neighbor 10.1.111.6


! R3 configuration - R3's interface priority is set to 0; R1 will use the higher
! of R3's announced priority 0 (based on R3's ip ospf priority interface
! subcommand) and the priority value on R1's neighbor command, which defaulted
! to 0. So, R3 will not ever become a DR/BDR.

interface Serial0/0.1 multipoint
 ip address 10.1.111.3 255.255.255.0
 ip ospf priority 0
 frame-relay interface-dlci 100


! R4 configuration - note from Figure 9-2 that R4 is using a point-to-point
! subinterface, with all defaults. This is not a typical use of a point-to-point
! subinterface, and is shown to make a few points later in the example.


router ospf 1
 network 0.0.0.0 255.255.255.255 area 0


! R5's configuration is equivalent to R3 in relation to the OSPF network type
! and its implications.

interface Serial0.1 multipoint
 ip address 10.1.111.5 255.255.255.0
 ip ospf priority 0
 frame-relay interface-dlci 100
!
router ospf 1
 network 0.0.0.0 255.255.255.255 area 0


! R6 configuration - R6 forgot to set the interface priority with the
! ip ospf priority 0 command, defaulting to priority 1.


router ospf 1
 network 0.0.0.0 255.255.255.255 area 0


! Below, the results of R6's default interface priority of 1 - R6, with RID
! 6.6.6.6, and an announced priority of 1, wins the DR election. Note that the
! command is issued on R1.


R1# show ip ospf neighbor
Neighbor ID      Pri    State          Dead Time    Address       Interface
6.6.6.6            1    FULL/DR        00:01:52     10.1.111.6    Serial0/0
3.3.3.3            0    FULL/DROTHER   00:01:46     10.1.111.3    Serial0/0
```

```
N/A                 0   ATTEMPT/DROTHER    -          10.1.111.4     Serial0/0
5.5.5.5             0   FULL/DROTHER    00:01:47      10.1.111.5     Serial0/0
```

```
! Next, R1's neighbor command was automatically changed to "priority 1" based on
! the Hello, with priority 1, that R1 received from R6. To prevent this dynamic
! reconfiguration, you could add an ip ospf priority 0 command under R6's s0/0.1
! interface.

R1# show run | beg router ospf 1
router ospf 1
 network 0.0.0.0 255.255.255.255 area 0
 neighbor 10.1.111.6 priority 1
 neighbor 10.1.111.3
 neighbor 10.1.111.4
 neighbor 10.1.111.5
! Lines omitted for brevity


! Below, R4 is OSPF network type "point to point," with Hello/dead of 10/40.
! R1's settings, based on Table 9-3, would be nonbroadcast, 30/120.


R4# show ip ospf int s 0/0.1
Serial0/0.1 is up, line protocol is up
  Internet Address 10.1.111.4/24, Area 0
  Process ID 1, Router ID 4.4.4.4, Network Type POINT_TO_POINT, Cost: 1562
  Transmit Delay is 1 sec, State POINT_TO_POINT,
  Timer intervals configured, Hello 10, Dead 40, Wait 40, Retransmit 5
! Lines omitted for brevity


! Below, R4 changes its network type to yet a different value, one that expects
! neighbor commands, but does not expect a DR to be used.


R4# conf t
Enter configuration commands, one per line.  End with CNTL/Z.
R4(config)# int s 0/0.1
R4(config-subif)# ip ospf network point-to-multipoint non-broadcast


! Next, R1 and R4 become neighbors now that the Hello parameters match. Note that
! R1 believes that R4 is DROther.


R1# show ip ospf neighbor

Neighbor ID    Pri   State          Dead Time   Address        Interface
! Lines omitted for brevity
4.4.4.4          1   FULL/DROTHER   00:01:56    10.1.111.4     Serial0/0


! Below, R4 agrees it is in a full state with R1, but does not list R1 as DR,
```

```
! because R4 is not using the concept of a DR at all due to R4's network type.

R4# sh ip ospf neigh
Neighbor ID     Pri   State           Dead Time   Address      Interface
1.1.1.1           0   FULL/ -         00:01:42    10.1.111.1   Serial0/0.1
```

In the following text, it is assumed that all **neighbor** statements define neighbors reachable over a single interface. If there are static neighbors configured that are reachable over different interfaces, the following text applies individually to each group of static neighbors reachable over a particular interface.

One of the important points from Example 9-3 is the use of the priority setting in the **neighbor** command. There is much confusion regarding its use. Somewhat surprisingly, the priority specified in the **neighbor** command *is never used* in DR/BDR elections. For that purpose, exclusively the interface priority configured by the **ip ospf priority** interface command is taken into account. However, if there are multiple **neighbor** statements configured and at least one of them has a nonzero priority specified in the statement (the default **neighbor** priority setting is 0 when unspecified), the router will first send Hello packets only to those neighbors with a nonzero priority. Only after DR/BDR elections have completed between these routers, the router will start sending Hello packets to all remaining neighbors. In consequence, if the priority setting in the **neighbor** command matches the interface priority of the neighbor, the router will first engage in DR/BDR elections with only those neighbors that have a chance of becoming DR/BDR. This optimization increases the chances that the DR and BDR roles will be taken up by appropriate routers, and prevents routers from competing in DR/BDR elections with neighbors that are not entitled to these roles.

The priorities specified in the **neighbor** commands do not need to match the real priorities of these neighbors, but if they differ, the router can engage in DR/BDR elections with neighbors not entitled to become a DR/BDR. In any case, though, real priorities of these neighbors as seen in their Hello packets will be used to complete the DR/BDR elections. Some IOS versions might even automatically update the priority in the **neighbor** statements in case a mismatch is detected; however, in recent IOS versions, the configuration is not updated automatically.

If all **neighbor** statements omit the priority setting, this optimization is not used, and all neighbors are contacted immediately. Also, if the neighbors are reachable over an interface whose priority has been set to 0 using the **ip ospf priority** command, the router will automatically remove all corresponding **neighbor** statements from the configuration. This behavior prevents the router from participating in any way in the DR/BDR elections (even though an advertised priority of 0 would suffice alone to prevent the router from ever becoming a DR or BDR), and it forces the router to wait for its neighbors to contact it. In this case, the router knows about no neighbors on its own, and is dependent on the DR and BDR contacting it thanks to their own **neighbor** statements.

Also note that, although neighbors must be statically configured for some network types, the **neighbor** command needs to be configured on only one router. R3 and R5, with correct working configurations, did not actually need a **neighbor** command.

Finally, it might seem that all is now fine between R1 and R4 by the end of the example, but even though the neighbors are fully adjacent, R4 cannot route packets to R3, R5, or R6 over the Frame Relay network. For example, R5 could have some routes that point to 10.1.111.4 (R4's Frame Relay IP address) as the next hop. However, because R5 is using a multipoint subinterface, R5 will not know what PVC to use to reach 10.1.111.4. In this case, the routers with multipoint subinterfaces would need to add **frame-relay map** commands. For example, R5 would need a **frame-relay map ip 10.1.111.4 100 broadcast** command, causing packets to next-hop 10.1.111.4 to go over DLCI 100 to R1, which would then route the packet on to R4. Keep in mind that R4's configuration is not a recommended configuration.

## SPF Calculation

So far, this chapter has covered a lot of ground related to the exchange of LSAs. Regardless of the OSPF network type and whether DRs are used, after a router has new or different information in its LSDB, it uses the Dijkstra SPF algorithm to examine the LSAs in the LSDB and derive the new tree of shortest paths to available destinations. The LSAs in the LSDB contain information to create a math equivalent of a figure of a network. This mathematical model has routers, links, costs for each link, and the current (up/down) status of each link. Figure 9-3 represents the SPF model of a sample network.

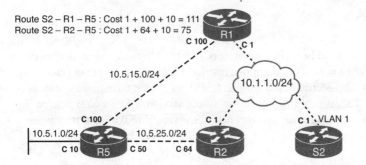

**Figure 9-3** *Single-Area SPF Calculation: Conceptual View*

In this simple network, humans can easily see the conclusion that the SPF algorithm will reach, even though the algorithm itself requires a couple of steps to arrive at the same conclusion. SPF on a router constructs least-cost paths from this router to all possible destinations, summing the costs for each outgoing interface along a path to a destination and picking the path with the lowest total cost. Found destinations and corresponding next hops on the least-cost paths toward these destinations are then placed into the routing table. For example, S2 calculates two possible routes to subnet 10.5.1.0/24, with the better route being out S2's VLAN 1 interface, with R2 as the next-hop router. Also note in Figure 9-3 that the cost values are per interface, and it is each outgoing interface's cost that SPF adds to come up with the total cost of the route.

### Steady-State Operation

Even after a network has stabilized, all routers in the same area have the exact same LSAs, and each router has chosen its best routes using SPF, the following is still true of routers running OSPF:

■ Each router sends Hellos, based on per-interface hello intervals.

■ Each router expects to receive Hellos from neighbors within the dead interval on each interface; if not, the neighbor is considered to have failed.

■ Each router originally advertising an LSA refloods each LSA (after incrementing its sequence number by 1) based on a per-LSA Link-State Refresh (LSRefresh) interval (default 30 minutes).

■ Each router expects to have its LSA refreshed within each LSA's MaxAge timer (default 60 minutes).

## OSPF Design and LSAs

This section covers two major topics:

■ OSPF design

■ OSPF LSA types

Although these might seem to be separate concepts, most OSPF design choices directly impact the LSA types in a network and impose restrictions on which neighbors can exchange those LSAs. This section starts with an OSPF design and terminology review, and then moves on to LSA types. Toward the end of the section, OSPF area types are covered, including how each variation changes how LSAs flow through the different types of OSPF stubby areas.

### OSPF Design Terms

OSPF design calls for grouping links into contiguous areas. Routers that connect to links in different areas are *Area Border Routers (ABR)*. ABRs must connect to area 0, the *backbone area*, and to one or more other areas as well. It is noteworthy to mention that RFC 2328 defines an ABR simply as a router "attached to multiple areas." While it does not explicitly state that one of these areas must be the backbone area 0, it nonetheless implicitly assumes it throughout its contents. This slight ambiguity has led different vendors to implement ABR functionality in slightly different ways. It is therefore strongly recommended to become familiar with RFC 3509, "Alternative Implementations of OSPF Area Border Routers," which explains in detail the Cisco approach to implementing ABR functionality. The key takeaway is that in the Cisco implementation, only a router that is *actively* attached to multiple areas (that is, has at least one active interface in these areas), *including the backbone area*, considers itself an ABR and performs the appropriate functions. A router actively attached to multiple areas but not to the backbone area does not consider itself an ABR and does not act like one.

*Autonomous System Boundary Routers (ASBR)* inject routes external to OSPF into the OSPF domain, having learned those routes from wide-ranging sources from the Border Gateway Protocol (BGP) on down to simple redistribution of static routes. Figure 9-4 shows the terms in the context of a simple OSPF design.

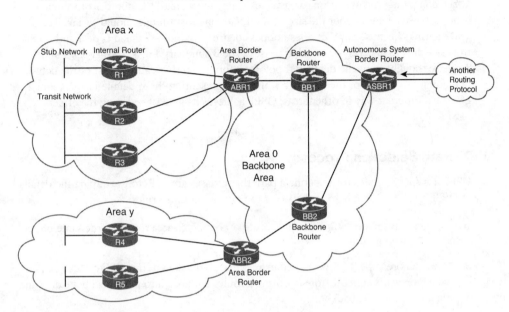

**Figure 9-4**   *OSPF Design Terminology*

Conceptually, an OSPF router keeps an independent and separate LSDB for each area to which it is connected. An internal router to an area has a single LSDB; an ABR has multiple separate LSDBs, one for each connected area (one of them must be the backbone area 0). By default, the contents of per-area LSDBs are completely isolated; that is, one LSDB does not leak into another. It is only the ABR role that is entitled to translate and carry information *in a controlled way* between LSDBs and thus between areas. When computing a routing table, SPF is run in each LSDB separately, and the results are combined in a single routing table subject to OSPF path preference rules. While this chapter uses the LSDB as a term to describe the entire link-state information maintained by the OSPF process (that is, the union of all per-area LSDBs) for simplicity reasons, it is important to keep in mind that in multiarea OSPF, ABRs maintain separate per-area LSDBs and run SPF in each of them independently, and then combine the results and use them to populate per-area LSDBs with condensed information about other areas.

Networks can use a single OSPF area, but using OSPF areas helps speed convergence and reduce overhead in an OSPF network. Using areas provides the following benefits:

- Generally smaller per-area LSDBs, requiring less memory.

- Faster SPF computation thanks to the sparser LSDB.

- A link failure in one area only requires a partial SPF computation in other areas.

- Routes can be summarized and filtered only at ABRs (and ASBRs). Having areas permits summarization, again shrinking the LSDB and improving SPF calculation performance.

When comparing the use of one area versus using many areas, the number of routers or subnets does not shrink, but the size of the LSDB on most routers should shrink. The LSDB shrinks because an ABR does not pass denser and more detailed type 1 and 2 LSAs from one area to another—instead, it passes type 3 summary LSAs. LSA types 1 and 2 can be thought of as the detailed topology information that causes most of the computing-intensive parts of the SPF algorithm. By representing these detailed type 1 and 2 LSAs in a different way in other areas, OSPF achieves its goal of reducing the effects of SPF.

## OSPF Path Selection Process

OSPF has specific rules for selecting a path that crosses areas. Before studying the details of OSPF LSAs, it might help at this point to understand those rules:

- OSPF always chooses an intra-area route over an inter-area route for the same prefix, regardless of metric.

- ABRs ignore type 3 LSAs learned in a nonbackbone area during SPF calculation, which prevents an ABR from choosing a route that goes into a nonbackbone area and then back into the backbone.

Note that these conditions can result in both asymmetric routing and suboptimal routing across multiarea OSPF networks. An example will be given in the section "Best-Path Side Effects of ABR Loop Prevention," later in this chapter. This fact must be considered in both the design and troubleshooting of OSPF networks.

## LSA Types

Table 9-4 lists the LSA types and their descriptions for reference; following the table, each type is explained in more detail, in the context of a working network. An important fact concerning all LSA types is that only a router that has originated a particular LSA is allowed to modify it or withdraw it. Other routers *must* process and flood this LSA within its defined flooding scope if they recognize the LSA's type and contents, but they *must not* ever change its contents, block it, or drop it before its maximum lifetime has expired. In other words, LSAs created by other routers are intangible and must be processed and forwarded unmodified. This requirement makes sure that all routers in an area have the same LSDB contents and have a consistent view of the network. It also brings along a strong limitation typical for all link-state routing protocols: Summarization and route filtering can be done in a very limited fashion, unlike in distance vector protocols, where summarization and route filtering can be performed at any point in the network.

**Table 9-4**  *OSPF LSA Types*

| LSA Type | Common Name | Description |
|---|---|---|
| 1 | Router | One per router per area, listing the router's RID and all interface IP addresses in that area. Represents stub networks as well. Flooded only within its area of origin. |
| 2 | Network | One per transit network. Created by the DR on the subnet, and represents the subnet and the router interfaces connected to the subnet. Flooded only within its area of origin. |
| 3 | Net Summary | Created by ABRs to represent networks present in one area when being advertised into another area. Defines the subnets in the origin area, and cost, but no topology data. Flooded only within its area of origin; reoriginated on ABRs. |
| 4 | ASBR Summary | Like a type 3 LSA, except it advertises a host route used to reach an ASBR. Flooded only within its area of origin; reoriginated on ABRs. |
| 5 | AS External | Created by ASBRs for external routes injected into OSPF. Flooded to all regular areas. |
| 6 | Group Membership | Defined for MOSPF; not supported by Cisco IOS. |
| 7 | NSSA External | Created by ASBRs inside an NSSA, instead of a type 5 LSA. Flooded only within its area of origin; converted to type 5 LSA on an ABR toward other areas. |
| 8 | External Attributes | Created by ASBRs during BGP-to-OSPF redistribution to preserve BGP attributes of redistributed networks. Not implemented in Cisco routers. |
| 9–11 | Opaque | Used as generic LSAs to allow for easy future extension of OSPF; for example, type 10 has been adapted for MPLS traffic engineering. These LSAs have different flooding scope: Type 9 has link-local flooding scope, type 10 has area-local flooding scope, type 11 has autonomous system flooding scope equivalent to the flooding scope of type 5 LSAs (not flooded into stubby areas and NSSAs). |

Before diving into the coverage of LSA types, two more definitions are needed:

■  **Transit network:** A network over which two or more OSPF routers have become neighbors and elected a DR so that traffic can transit from one to the other. An exception to this rule is a point-to-point interconnection between two routers: This interconnection is treated by OSPF as a combination of a point-to-point link and a stub IP network on this link. This is done to facilitate using unnumbered point-to-point links.

■ **Stub network:** A subnet on which a router has not formed any neighbor relationships.

Now on to the LSA types!

## LSA Types 1 and 2

Each router creates and floods a type 1 LSA for itself. These LSAs describe the router, its interfaces (in that area), and a list of neighboring routers (in that area) on each interface. The LSA itself is identified by a *link-state ID (LSID)* equal to that router's RID.

Type 2 LSAs represent a transit subnet for which a DR has been elected. The LSID is the DR's interface IP address on that subnet. Note that type 2 LSAs are not created for subnets on which no DR has been elected.

Armed with an LSDB with all the type 1 and 2 LSAs inside an area, a router's SPF algorithm is able to create a topological graph of the network, calculate the possible routes, and finally choose the best routes. For example, Figure 9-5 shows a sample internetwork that is used in several upcoming examples. Switches S1 and S2 in the figure are multilayer switches running OSPF, so for OSPF purposes, they are indistinguishable from routers. Figure 9-6 shows a graphical view of the type 1 and type 2 LSAs created in area 3.

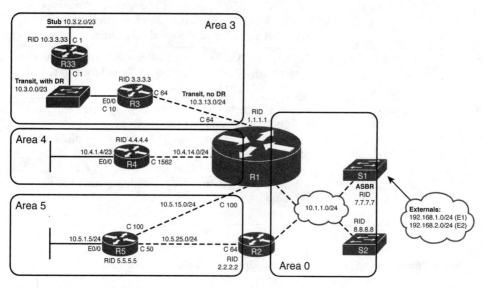

**Figure 9-5**  *Network Used in LSA Examples*

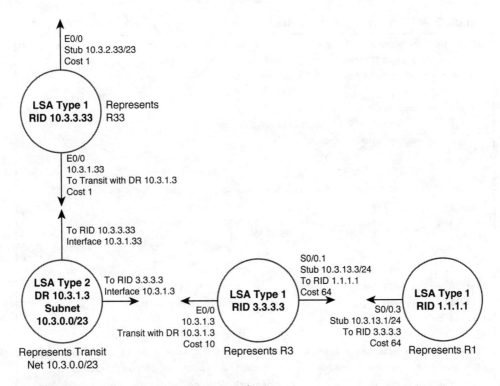

**Figure 9-6**  *Graph of Type 1 and 2 LSAs for Area 3*

For subnets without a DR, the type 1 LSAs hold enough information for the SPF algorithm to create the math model of the topology. For example, R1 and R3 use point-to-point subinterfaces and the OSPF point-to-point network type. SPF can match up the information shown in the type 1 LSAs for R1 and R3 in Figure 9-6 to know that the two routers are connected.

For transit networks with DRs, OSPF uses a type 2 LSA to model the subnet as a node in the SPF mathematical model. Because the SPF process treats the type 2 LSA as a node in the graph, this LSA is sometimes called a *pseudonode*. The type 2 LSA includes references to the RIDs of all routers that are currently neighbors of the DR on that subnet. That information, combined with the type 1 LSAs for each router connected to the subnet represented by the type 2 LSA, allows SPF to construct an accurate picture of the network.

Example 9-4 shows the LSAs in area 3 (Figures 9-5 and 9-6) through **show** commands. Be aware of a long-term glitch in the **show ip ospf database** output: The *Link ID* column is a misnomer; correctly, it should say *Link State ID.* This seemingly subtle difference is serious enough to warrant a mention: While Link State ID is a unique identifier of an entire LSA, a Link ID is a particular entry specifically in a type 1 LSA body that describes an adjacency to a neighboring object of a router. A single type 1 LSA identified by a single Link State ID can describe several adjacencies represented by several Link ID entries. These two terms are not interchangeable.

**Example 9-4**   *LSA Types 1 and 2 in Area 3*

```
! R3's LSDB is shown, with type 1 LSAs listed as "Router Link States" and type 2
! LSAs as "Net Link States." The command output shows a section for each LSA type,
! in sequential order. The Link ID column should correctly spell Link State ID.


R3# show ip ospf database
            OSPF Router with ID (3.3.3.3) (Process ID 1)
            Router Link States (Area 3)



Link ID          ADV Router       Age        Seq#        Checksum Link count
1.1.1.1          1.1.1.1          1203        0x80000025 0x0072C3 2
3.3.3.3          3.3.3.3          779         0x80000027 0x003FB0 3
10.3.3.33        10.3.3.33        899         0x80000020 0x002929 2


                 Net Link States (Area 3)
Link ID          ADV Router       Age        Seq#        Checksum
10.3.1.3         3.3.3.3          1290        0x8000001F 0x00249E
! Lines omitted for brevity


! Next, the specific LSA's link ID is included in the show command, listing detail
! for the one LSA type 2 inside area 3. Note that the "Link ID" is the DR's
! interface address on the subnet. The network keyword refers to the network LSAs
! (type 2 LSAs).


R3# show ip ospf database network 10.3.1.3
            OSPF Router with ID (3.3.3.3) (Process ID 1)
                Net Link States (Area 3)


Routing Bit Set on this LSA
LS age: 1304
Options: (No TOS-capability, DC)
LS Type: Network Links
Link State ID: 10.3.1.3 (address of Designated Router)
Advertising Router: 3.3.3.3
LS Seq Number: 8000001F
Checksum: 0x249E
Length: 32
Network Mask: /23
      Attached Router: 3.3.3.3
      Attached Router: 10.3.3.33


! Next, the type 1 LSA for R3 is listed. The link ID is the RID of R3. Note that
! the LSA includes reference to each stub and transit link connected to R3. The
```

```
! router keyword refers to the router LSAs (type 1 LSAs).


R3# show ip ospf database router 3.3.3.3
           OSPF Router with ID (3.3.3.3) (Process ID 1)
                Router Link States (Area 3)


  LS age: 804
  Options: (No TOS-capability, DC)
  LS Type: Router Links
  Link State ID: 3.3.3.3
  Advertising Router: 3.3.3.3
  LS Seq Number: 80000027
  Checksum: 0x3FB0
  Length: 60
  Number of Links: 3


! Note how each network object adjacent to R3 is described by a separate
! entry, each now being correctly labeled as Link ID.

    Link connected to: another Router (point-to-point)
     (Link ID) Neighboring Router ID: 1.1.1.1
     (Link Data) Router Interface address: 10.3.13.3
     Number of TOS metrics: 0
      TOS 0 Metrics: 64
    Link connected to: a Stub Network
     (Link ID) Network/subnet number: 10.3.13.0
     (Link Data) Network Mask: 255.255.255.0
     Number of TOS metrics: 0
      TOS 0 Metrics: 64


! Note that R3's LSA refers to a transit network next, based on its DR IP address;
! these lines allow OSPF to know that this router (R3) connects to the transit
! network whose type 2 LSA has LSID 10.3.1.3, derived from DR's IP address
! in that network.

    Link connected to: a Transit Network
     (Link ID) Designated Router address: 10.3.1.3
     (Link Data) Router Interface address: 10.3.1.3
     Number of TOS metrics: 0
      TOS 0 Metrics: 10


! Below, the routes from R3 and R1 to 10.3.2.0/23 are shown. Note the cost values
! for each reflect the cumulative costs of the outgoing interfaces used to reach
! the subnet - for instance, R3's cost is the sum of its outgoing interface cost
! (10) plus R33's outgoing interface cost (1). R1's cost is based on three outgoing
! links: R1 (cost 64), R3 (cost 10), and R33 (cost 1), for a total of 75. Also
```

```
! note that the time listed in the route is the time since this LSA first arrived
! at the router, even if the LSA has been refreshed due to the LSRefresh interval.

R3# show ip route ospf 1 | include 10.3.2.0
O       10.3.2.0/23 [110/11] via 10.3.1.33, 17:08:33, Ethernet0/0
R1# show ip route ospf | include 10.3.2.0
O       10.3.2.0/23 [110/75] via 10.3.13.3, 17:10:15, Serial0/0.3
```

The **show ip ospf database** command lists the LSAs in that router's LSDB, with LSA type 1 LSAs (router LSAs) first, then type 2 (network link states), continuing sequentially through the LSA types. Also note that the LSDB for area 3 should be identical on R33, R3, and R1. However, on R1, the **show ip ospf database** command lists all of R1's LSDB entries, including LSAs from other areas, so using an internal router to look at the LSDB might be the best place to begin troubleshooting a problem. Also note the costs for the routes on R3 and R1 at the end of the example—the SPF algorithm simply added the outgoing costs along the routes, from each router's perspective.

**Note**   To signify a network that is down, the appropriate type 1 or 2 LSA is either reoriginated and the disconnected network is removed from that LSA, or the entire LSA is prematurely aged by setting its age to 3600 seconds and flooding it, causing it to immediately expire from all LSDBs.

## LSA Type 3 and Inter-Area Costs

ABRs do not forward type 1 and 2 LSAs from one area to another. Instead, ABRs advertise type 3 LSAs into one area to represent subnets described in both the type 1 and 2 LSAs in another area. Each type 3 summary LSA describes a simple inter-area destination—the subnet, the mask, and the ABR's cost to reach that subnet, as shown in Figure 9-7.

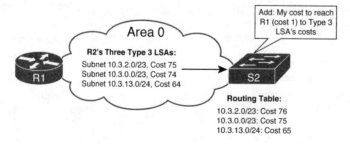

**Figure 9-7**   *Representation of Area 3 Subnets as Type 3 LSAs in Area 0*

Example 9-5 focuses on the three subnets inside area 3, looking at the type 3 summary LSAs created for those subnets by ABR R1. Note the example **show** commands on S2; S2 has identical area 0 LSDB entries as compared with R1.

**Example 9-5**  *LSA Type 3 Created by R1 for Area 3's Subnets*

```
! S2, internal to area 0, does not have the type 1 and 2 LSAs seen by R3 back in
! Example 9-4. However, type 3 LSAs (listed as "Summary Net Links") show all
! three subnets inside area 3. R1 is listed as the advertising router because it
! created the type 3 LSAs.


S2# show ip ospf database
! Lines omitted for brevity
            Summary Net Link States (Area 0)
Link ID        ADV Router      Age       Seq#         Checksum
10.3.0.0       1.1.1.1         257       0x80000001 0x00A63C
10.3.2.0       1.1.1.1         257       0x80000001 0x009A45
10.3.13.0      1.1.1.1         261       0x80000021 0x007747
! Lines omitted for brevity


! Below, note that the summary keyword is used to view type 3 LSAs. The metric
! reflects R1's cost to reach the subnet inside area 3.


S2# show ip ospf database summary 10.3.0.0
            OSPF Router with ID (8.8.8.8) (Process ID 1)
               Summary Net Link States (Area 0)


  Routing Bit Set on this LSA
  LS age: 341
  Options: (No TOS-capability, DC, Upward)
  LS Type: Summary Links(Network)
  Link State ID: 10.3.0.0 (summary Network Number)
  Advertising Router: 1.1.1.1
  LS Seq Number: 80000001
  Checksum: 0xA63C
  Length: 28
  Network Mask: /23
        TOS: 0   Metric: 74


! Next, S2's routes to all three subnets are listed. S2 calculates its cost
! based on its cost to reach R1, plus the cost listed in the type 3 LSA. For
! example, the cost (above) in the type 3 LSA for 10.3.0.0/23 is 74; S2 adds
! that to S2's cost to reach ABR R1 (cost 1), for a metric of 75.


S2# show ip route ospf | include 10.3
O IA    10.3.13.0/24 [110/65] via 10.1.1.1, 00:16:04, Vlan1
O IA    10.3.0.0/23 [110/75] via 10.1.1.1, 00:05:08, Vlan1
O IA    10.3.2.0/23 [110/76] via 10.1.1.1, 00:05:12, Vlan1
```

```
! Next, S2's cost to reach RID 1.1.1.1 is listed as cost 1.


S2# show ip ospf border-routers
OSPF Process 1 internal Routing Table
Codes: i - Intra-area route, I - Inter-area route

i 1.1.1.1 [1] via 10.1.1.1, Vlan1, ABR, Area 0, SPF 18
i 2.2.2.2 [1] via 10.1.1.2, Vlan1, ABR, Area 0, SPF 18
i 7.7.7.7 [1] via 10.1.1.3, Vlan1, ASBR, Area 0, SPF 18


! Below, the show ip ospf statistics command lists the number of SPF calculations.


R1# show ip ospf stat
OSPF process ID 1
-------------------------------------------

  Area 0: SPF algorithm executed 6 times
  Area 3: SPF algorithm executed 15 times
  Area 4: SPF algorithm executed 6 times
  Area 5: SPF algorithm executed 5 times
! Lines omitted for brevity
```

Example 9-5 shows how S2 calculated its cost to the area 3 subnets. Routers calculate the cost for a route to a subnet defined in a type 3 LSA by adding the following items:

**Key
Topic**

■   The calculated cost to reach the ABR that created and advertised the type 3 LSA

■   The cost as listed in the type 3 LSA

You can see the cost of the type 3 LSA with the **show ip ospf database summary** *link-id* command, and the cost to reach the advertising ABR with the **show ip ospf border-routers** command, as shown in Example 9-5.

The beauty of this two-step cost calculation process is that it allows a significant reduction in the number of SPF calculations. When a type 1 or 2 LSA changes in some way that affects the underlying routes—for example, a link failure—each router in the area runs SPF, but routers inside other areas do not. They only perform minor modification to their already computed shortest path trees—a process called a *partial run*, *partial SPF*, or *partial route calculation*.

For example, imagine that in Figure 9-5, R33's LAN interface cost increases from 1 to 10. R33 will originate a new type 1 LSA and flood it. All routers in area 3 will run a full SPF and will update the metric of the path toward the network 10.3.2.0/23. R1, being an ABR, will then flood an updated type 3 LSA regarding the network 10.3.2.0/23 into areas 0, 4, and 5, indicating the new cost of 84. All other routers in area 0 will install the updated LSA into their LSDB, add the indicated cost of 84 to their cost of reaching R1 as the ABR advertising the LSA, and use the updated cost as the total cost of reaching the 10.3.2.0/23 through R1. No full SPF run was required on any of the routers in area 0. The same would be valid for areas 4 and 5.

For a more complex scenario, imagine that R3's LAN interface fails. This event constitutes two topological changes to OSPF: R3's link to the transit network 10.3.0.0/23 is down, and because R3 was the DR in this network, the type 2 LSA it had originated is no longer valid because the interface on which it was DR became inoperable. R3 will therefore flood two updates. First, it will create and flood an updated type 1 LSA with an incremented sequence number that describes all R3's currently working links in area 3, leaving out the former link to the transit network that is no longer operable. Second, it will withdraw the type 2 LSA describing the transit network by setting its age to 3600 seconds without incrementing the sequence number and flooding it.

Upon receiving these updates, R1 will install the updated type 1 LSA from R3 into its area 3 LSDB and will flush the type 2 LSA regarding the transit network 10.3.0.0/23. After running the SPF in area 3 over the updated area 3 LSDB, R1 finds out that the network 10.3.0.0/23 no longer exists, and while the R33's type 1 LSA still exists in the LSDB, it is not reachable: There is no continuous sequence of type 1 and 2 LSAs pointing one to another that can be traversed to reach R33 from R1. As a result, networks 10.3.0.0/23 and 10.3.2.0/23 will be removed from the routing table on R1, so R1 will withdraw the type 3 LSAs about these two networks from areas 0, 4, and 5. Withdrawal of type 3 LSAs does not require a full SPF run. Instead, routers in these areas simply check whether there is another type 3 LSA concerning the same networks providing a backup path, and when they find there is none, they simply remove the affected networks from their routing tables.

Instead of flushing type 3 LSAs to indicate that the inter-area network is not reachable anymore, it is also possible to advertise an updated type 3 LSA regarding that network with the metric set to $2^{24}-1$, or 16,777,215. This metric value represents an infinite path cost, and routers will ignore such path. This approach is seldom used, however. RFC 2328 prefers premature aging instead.

Of particular importance is that partial calculations happen without any route summarization. With OSPF, route summarization does help reduce the overall number of routes that require SPF calculations, but route summarization is not required for partial calculations to occur.

Type 3 summary LSAs are flooded only within the area into which they were originated by ABRs. They do not cross area boundaries. Instead, ABRs compute an internal OSPF routing table for the backbone area using all types of LSAs received in the backbone area, and for each intra-area and inter-area route, they originate a new type 3 LSA to be flooded to their attached nonbackbone areas. For example, in Figure 9-5, R1 creates and floods a type 3 LSA on behalf of the network 10.3.2.0/23 in area 3 into the backbone area. R2 computes its internal routing table for the backbone area using all LSAs received through the backbone, including R1's summary LSA, and installs an inter-area route to 10.3.2.0/23 through R1. Subsequently, for all intra-area and inter-area routes, including the 10.3.2.0/23 in the backbone area, R2 will create and flood a separate type 3 LSA to its attached nonbackbone area 5.

The following are two important rules about originating and processing type 3 LSAs:

- An ABR uses only those type 3 LSAs that are received over a backbone area in its SPF calculation. Type 3 LSAs received over nonbackbone areas will be skipped during the ABR's SPF computation, though they are stored in the ABR's LSDB and flooded within that nonbackbone area as usual.

- When an ABR creates and floods type 3 LSAs to advertise networks from one area to another, only intra-area routes from nonbackbone areas are advertised into the backbone; both intra-area and inter-area routes are advertised from the backbone into nonbackbone areas.

The second rule is in fact only a direct consequence of the first rule. Because an ABR must not use type 3 LSAs received over a nonbackbone area when running SPF over the associated per-area LSDB, the SPF computation produces no inter-area routes related to that nonbackbone area. Consequently, no inter-area routes from a nonbackbone area can be advertised to the backbone because there are none. Nevertheless, these rules are often stated independently.

## LSA Types 4 and 5, and External Route Types 1 and 2

OSPF allows for two types of external routes, aptly named types 1 and 2. The type determines whether only the external metric is considered by SPF when picking the best routes (external type 2, or E2), or whether both the external and internal metrics are added together to compute the metric (external type 1, or E1). The choice of external metric types is always done by a network administrator, depending on the requirements. By default, Cisco routers use the E2 metric type in redistribution.

When an ASBR injects an external route, it creates a type 5 LSA for the subnet. The LSA lists the metric and the metric type. The ASBR then floods the type 5 LSA throughout all regular areas. Other routers process the LSA depending on the metric type. If the LSA contains the E1 metric, the total cost of reaching the external network is computed as the cost of reaching the ASBR, plus the E1 cost of the external network carried in the LSA. In other words, the E1 metric is added to the metric of the path between the calculating router and the ASBR to produce the total metric of the path. If there are multiple paths of reaching the same E1 external network, the path with the least total cost is used. If there are still multiple paths to the same network having the same least cost, all of them will be used.

If the LSA contains the E2 metric, this metric is used exactly as it is indicated in the LSA. No additional costs are ever summed with the E2 metric. This is because the E2 metric is *considered* to be orders of magnitude larger than any path cost inside the OSPF domain, or in other words, costs of paths inside the OSPF domain are considered to be negligible (that is, practically zero) in comparison to the E2 metric. If there are multiple paths of reaching the same E2 external network, the path with the lowest E2 metric is used. If there are still multiple paths to the same network with the same lowest E2 metric, the path through the closest ASBR is used. In case there are still multiple paths to the network, it follows that they must have the same lowest E2 metric and the same lowest metric of reaching the corresponding ASBRs, and all of them will be used.

Hence, the total cost of E1 external routes is computed as the cost of reaching the ASBR advertising the network, plus the E1 cost of the external network. The path with the least total cost is used; if there are multiple such paths, use them all. The total cost of E2 external routes is immediately the E2 cost of the external network. The path with the least E2 cost is used, and in case of a tie, the path having the least cost to an advertising ASBR is used; if there are still multiple paths, use them all. If there are both E1 and E2 routes to the same external network available, the E1 is always preferred to E2.

Both with E1 and E2 metric types, it is necessary to compute the metric to the ASBR advertising an external network. Within the same area where the ASBR resides, this is simply the least-cost path from the computing router to the ASBR that can be comfortably computed using type 1 and 2 LSAs. This topological information is not present in other areas, however, so without additional help, routers in other areas would not be able to compute their metric to reach the ASBR. Fortunately, what routers in other areas really need to know is only what ABR can be used to reach the ASBR, and what is the path cost between them. Therefore, when an ABR then floods the type 5 LSA into another area, the ABR creates a type 4 LSA, containing the ASBR's RID and the ABR's metric to reach the ASBR that created the type 5 LSA. Routers in other areas use the type 4 LSA to know what ASBRs in other areas exist, what ABRs can be used to reach them, and what is the distance of each ABR to a particular ASBR. For a router in a different area than an ASBR's, the total cost of reaching the ASBR through an ABR is then the sum of the cost between the router and an ABR in the router's area, plus the cost indicated in the type 4 LSA advertised by the ABR toward a particular ASBR. Whenever a cost of reaching an ASBR is therefore required, if the ASBR is in the same area as the computing router, it is computed using the type 1 and 2 LSAs in that area. If the ASBR is in a different area, the cost of reaching it is computed using the type 1 and 2 LSAs in the computing router's area toward an ABR, plus the cost from the ABR's type 4 LSA toward the ASBR. Rules concerning the evaluation of E1 and E2 routes explained earlier therefore hold for routers in all areas.

Note that a type 4 LSA concerning a particular ASBR is not required in the area where the ASBR resides. It is therefore never flooded into it. Only other areas require the type 4 LSA to be able to compute their metrics toward ASBRs and external networks behind them.

Figure 9-8 outlines the mechanics of how the LSAs are propagated, and how the metrics are calculated.

E1 routes by definition include the cost as assigned when the ASBR injected the route into OSPF, plus any cost inside the OSPF domain. To calculate the cost for the E1 route, a router inside a different area than the ASBR must use two steps to calculate the internal cost to ASBR, and a third step to add the external cost. For example, when R3, internal to area 3, calculates the cost to reach 192.168.1.0/24 (an E1 route), R3 adds the following:

- R3's calculated area 3 cost to reach ABR R1 (RID 1.1.1.1).

- R1's cost to reach the ASBR that advertised the route (S1, RID 7.7.7.7). R1 announces this cost in the LSA type 4 that describes R1's cost to reach ASBR 7.7.7.7.

- The external metric for the route, as listed in the type 5 LSA created by the ASBR.

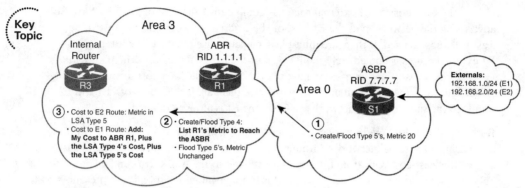

Note: Arrows Show Propagation of LSAs.

**Figure 9-8**  *LSA Types 4 and 5 Propagation and the Effect on Type 1 External Routes*

Example 9-6 shows the components of the metrics and LSAs for two external routes: 192.168.1.0/24 E1 with metric 20, and 192.168.2.0/24 E2, also with metric 20.

**Example 9-6**  *Calculating the Metric for External Types 1 and 2*

```
! R3 has learned the two type 5 LSAs.

R3# show ip ospf database | begin Type-5
            Type-5 AS External Link States


Link ID        ADV Router      Age       Seq#        Checksum Tag
192.168.1.0    7.7.7.7         1916      0x8000002B 0x0080EF 0
192.168.2.0    7.7.7.7         1916      0x80000028 0x00FEF2 0


! Next, the detail for E2 192.168.2.0 is listed, with "metric type" referring
! to the external route type E2. (192.168.1.0, not shown, is type 1.)


R3# show ip ospf database external 192.168.2.0
            OSPF Router with ID (3.3.3.3) (Process ID 1)
        Type-5 AS External Link States


  Routing Bit Set on this LSA
  LS age: 1969
  Options: (No TOS-capability, DC)
  LS Type: AS External Link
  Link State ID: 192.168.2.0 (External Network Number)
  Advertising Router: 7.7.7.7
  LS Seq Number: 80000028
  Checksum: 0xFEF2
  Length: 36
```

```
   Network Mask: /24
      Metric Type: 2 (Larger than any link state path)
      TOS: 0
      Metric: 20
      Forward Address: 0.0.0.0
      External Route Tag: 0

! Next, R1's advertised cost of 1 between itself and the ASBR is listed. Note
! that S1's RID (7.7.7.7) is listed, with the ABR that forwarded the LSA into
! area 3, R1 (RID 1.1.1.1) also listed.

R3# show ip ospf database asbr-summary
            OSPF Router with ID (3.3.3.3) (Process ID 1)
         Summary ASB Link States (Area 3)


      Routing Bit Set on this LSA
      LS age: 923
      Options: (No TOS-capability, DC, Upward)
      LS Type: Summary Links(AS Boundary Router)
      Link State ID: 7.7.7.7 (AS Boundary Router address)
      Advertising Router: 1.1.1.1
      LS Seq Number: 8000000A
      Checksum: 0x12FF
      Length: 28
      Network Mask: /0
        TOS: 0      Metric: 1


! Below, R3's calculated cost to R1 (64) and then to S1 (7.7.7.7) are listed. Note
! that the total of 65 is the cost 64 to reach the ABR, plus the cost 1 for the
! ABR to reach the ASBR.

R3# show ip ospf border-routers
OSPF Process 1 internal Routing Table
Codes: i - Intra-area route, I - Inter-area route

i 1.1.1.1 [64] via 10.3.13.1, Serial0/0.1, ABR, Area 3, SPF 30
I 7.7.7.7 [65] via 10.3.13.1, Serial0/0.1, ASBR, Area 3, SPF 30

! Below, each route is noted as E1 or E2, with the E1 route's metric including
! the external cost (20), plus cost to reach the ASBR (65).

R3# show ip route | include 192.168
O E1 192.168.1.0/24 [110/85] via 10.3.13.1, 00:50:34, Serial0/0.1
O E2 192.168.2.0/24 [110/20] via 10.3.13.1, 00:50:34, Serial0/0.1
```

## OSPF Design in Light of LSA Types

OSPF's main design trade-offs consist of choosing links for particular areas, with the goal of speeding convergence, reducing memory and computing resources, and keeping routing tables small through route summarization. For example, by using a larger number of areas, and the implied conversion of dense types 1 and 2 LSAs into sparser type 3 LSAs, the OSPF LSDBs can be made smaller. Also, link flaps in one area require SPF calculations only in that area, thanks to the partial calculation feature. Additionally, ABRs and ASBRs can be configured to summarize routes, reducing the number of Type 3 and Type 5 LSAs introduced into other areas as well. (Route summarization is covered in Chapter 11.)

The OSPF design goals to reduce convergence time, reduce overhead processing, and improve network stability can be reached using the core OSPF protocols and features covered so far. Another key OSPF design tool, stubby areas, will be covered next.

> **Note**    Before we move on, a comment is in order about the relative use of the word *summary* in OSPF. The typical uses within OSPF include the following:
>
> - Type 3 and 4 LSAs are called *summary* LSAs in the OSPF RFCs.
>
> - The term *LSA summary* refers to the LSA headers that identify LSAs and are sent inside DD packets.
>
> The term *summary* can also be used to refer to summary routes created with the **area range** and **summary-address** commands.

## Stubby Areas

The areas described so far allow OSPF to limit the complexity of the information stored in the LSDB, simplify and thus accelerate its processing, and optionally perform summarization. The visibility of networks (intra-area, inter-area, external) was not affected. Such areas that do not perform any automatic filtering on the type of accepted information are called *regular* areas. All areas described so far were regular areas.

OSPF can further reduce overhead by treating each area with one of several variations of rules, based on a concept called a *stubby area*. Stubby areas take advantage of the fact that, depending on the actual network topology, not all areas need to have knowledge about individual external networks. In particular, if a nonbackbone area does not contain any ASBRs and does not inject any external routes into the OSPF domain, any information about external networks (if present) must have come in through ABRs from other areas.

Knowing the particular external networks one by one, then, is useful only to a limited degree:

- Because to reach the external networks, a packet must still be routed through an ABR toward the area where the ASBR is located.

■ Because there is no ASBR in the current area, there can never be a possibility of the local ASBR providing a better path to any external network.

This is what forms the concept of a *stubby area*—an area that does not contain an ASBR and thus does not mediate an external connectivity to the entire OSPF domain. Such an area does not really benefit from knowing about individual external networks. The advantage of knowing the external networks one by one in an area without its own ASBR would be visible if there were multiple ABRs in the current area *and* multiple ASBRs in other areas. In this case, the knowledge of individual external networks would allow for choosing the least total cost path to each of the networks individually. In most other cases, however, the connectivity to external networks can be equivalently provided to a stubby area by replacing the list of external networks with a simple default route injected by the area's ABRs.

Therefore, if an area is configured as a stubby area, ABRs will stop advertising type 4 and 5 LSAs into this area. In addition, every internal router in a stubby area will ignore any received type 5 LSAs, and will not originate any such LSAs itself. As a result, no external networks or ASBRs will be known by any internal router in a stubby area. In addition, ABRs in a stubby area will automatically inject a default route into the area as a type 3 LSA. The connectivity to external networks reachable through other areas will be maintained thanks to the default routes through ABRs. As a result, internal routers will still be able to reach the external networks but their LSDBs will be sparser. The visibility of intra-area and inter-area networks in a stubby area is not affected in any way.

RFC 2328 is vague on the point of whether type 4 LSAs are also ignored upon arrival, but common sense dictates that type 4 LSAs are usable only in conjunction with type 5 LSAs, and because stubby areas explicitly prohibit the use of type 5 LSAs, the type 4 LSAs are useless in such areas and should be treated in the same way as type 5 LSAs.

To sum up, a stubby area is an area that does not contain an ASBR and is not intended to. Such an area can benefit from filtering out type 4 and 5 LSAs, replacing the list of all external networks with a default route. A stubby area can contain one or more ABRs. For example, the only way out of area 3 in Figure 9-5 is through the only ABR, R1. So, R1 could advertise a default route into area 3 instead of advertising any external type 5 LSAs.

Also in Figure 9-5, area 5 has two ABRs. If area 5 were a stubby area, both ABRs would inject default routes into the area. This configuration would work, but it might result in suboptimal routing. This is not really a limitation of OSPF. Replacing a set of routes with a default route is a form of route summarization, and route summarization always goes hand in hand with a certain loss of granularity in the available choices.

OSPF defines several different types of stubby areas. By definition, all stubby areas stop type 4 (ASBR summary) and type 5 (external) LSAs from being injected into them by the ABRs. However, depending on the variation, a stubby area might also prevent type 3 LSAs from being injected, causing the area to stop seeing individual inter-area routes as well. The other variation includes whether a router inside the stubby area can redistribute routes into OSPF, thereby injecting an external route. Table 9-5 lists the variations on stubby areas, and their names.

Note in Table 9-5 that all four stub area types stop type 4 and 5 LSAs from entering the area. When the name includes "totally," type 3 LSAs are also not passed into the area by ABRs except a type 3 LSA carrying the default route, significantly reducing the size of the LSDB. If the name includes "NSSA," it means that external routes can be redistributed into OSPF by routers inside the stubby area; note that the LSAs for these external routes would be type 7 because type 5 LSAs are still prohibited in such areas.

**Table 9-5**   *OSPF Stubby Area Types*

| Area Type | Stops Injection of Type 4/5 LSAs? | Stops Injection of Type 3 LSAs? | Allows Creation of Type 7 LSAs Inside the Area? |
|---|---|---|---|
| Stubby | Yes | No | No |
| Totally stubby (TS) | Yes | Yes | No |
| Not-so-stubby area (NSSA) | Yes | No | Yes |
| Totally NSSA (NSSA-TS) | Yes | Yes | Yes |

To configure stubby areas, all routers attached to the area must be configured with the exact same command for each stubby area type, as listed in Table 9-6. However, in areas that are totally stubby, non-ABRs should omit the **no-summary** keyword because the additional type 3 LSA filtering is performed only on ABRs.

**Table 9-6**   *Stub Area Configuration Options*

| Stub Type | Router OSPF Subcommand |
|---|---|
| NSSA | area *area-id* nssa |
| Totally NSSA | area *area-id* nssa no-summary |
| Stubby | area *area-id* stub |
| Totally stubby | area *area-id* stub no-summary |

NSSAs require a few comments. The motivation for NSSAs comes from the fact that while an area might not require knowing the full list of external networks reachable through other areas, it is nevertheless often necessary to inject a couple of external networks into the OSPF domain in such areas. If such an area was configured as a stubby area, external networks known in other areas would indeed not be advertised into it. However, because any external network is strictly prohibited in a stubby area, it would not be possible to configure route redistribution to inject the external routes. The NSSA type lifts the second limitation. An NSSA is still a stubby area in the sense that external routes from *other* areas are not advertised to it. However, an NSSA can hold an ASBR and perform external route injection. This external information is carried in type 7 LSAs to distinguish it from normal external routes in type 5 LSAs, which are still prohibited even in NSSAs. In addition, the ABR with the highest RID will perform a translation from type 7 LSA to type 5 LSA and thereby inject the external route to other areas. An NSSA is therefore a sensible compromise: It is allowed to inject external routing information and "upload" it to backbone and other regular areas, and yet it still does not "download" external routing information from the backbone or other areas, keeping its LSBD relatively small. The NSSA is also the only nonregular type of area into which a default route is not advertised automatically. To advertise a default route into an NSSA, ABRs must be configured with the **area** *area-id* **nssa default-information-originate** command. All other nonregular area types will inject a default route automatically, including totally NSSA (NSSA-TS).

Example 9-7, based on Figure 9-5, shows the results of the following configuration:

- Area 3 is configured as a totally NSSA.

- R3 will inject an external route to 192.168.21.0/24 as a type 7 LSA.

- Area 4 is configured as a totally stubby area.

- Area 5 is configured as simply stubby.

**Example 9-7**  *Stub Area Example*

```
! R3, in a totally NSSA area, knows intra-area routes (denoted with an "IA"
! near the front of the output line from show ip route), but the only
! inter-area route is the default route created and sent by R1, the ABR.


R3# show ip route ospf
     10.0.0.0/8 is variably subnetted, 3 subnets, 2 masks
O       10.3.2.0/23 [110/11] via 10.3.1.33, 00:00:00, Ethernet0/0
O*IA 0.0.0.0/0 [110/65] via 10.3.13.1, 00:00:00, Serial0/0.1


! Still on R3, the LSA type 3 summary, created by ABR R1, is shown first.
! Next, the External NSSA LSA type 7 LSA created by R3 is listed.


R3# show ip ospf database | begin Summary
        Summary Net Link States (Area 3)


Link ID         ADV Router      Age        Seq#        Checksum
0.0.0.0         1.1.1.1         704        0x80000004 0x00151A



        Type-7 AS External Link States (Area 3)


Link ID         ADV Router      Age        Seq#        Checksum Tag
192.168.21.0    3.3.3.3         17         0x80000003 0x00C12B 0
```

```
! R1, because it is attached to area 3, also has the R3-generated NSSA external
! LSA. Note the advertising router is R3, and it is an E2 external route.


R1# show ip ospf database nssa-external
          OSPF Router with ID (1.1.1.1) (Process ID 1)
        Type-7 AS External Link States (Area 3)


          Routing Bit Set on this LSA
          LS age: 188
          Options: (No TOS-capability, Type 7/5 translation, DC)
          LS Type: AS External Link
          Link State ID: 192.168.21.0 (External Network Number)
          Advertising Router: 3.3.3.3
          LS Seq Number: 80000003
          Checksum: 0xC12B
          Length: 36
          Network Mask: /24
            Metric Type: 2 (Larger than any link state path)
            TOS: 0
            Metric: 20
            Forward Address: 10.3.13.3
            External Route Tag: 0


! Below, the same command on R2, not in area 3, shows no type 7 LSAs. ABRs
! convert type 7 LSAs to type 5 LSAs before forwarding them into another area.


R2# show ip ospf database nssa-external


          OSPF Router with ID (2.2.2.2) (Process ID 2)

! Next, R2 does have a type 5 LSA for the subnet; R1 converts the type 7 to a type
! 5 before flooding it into other areas.


R2# show ip ospf database | begin Type-5
                Type-5 AS External Link States


Link ID          ADV Router       Age        Seq#          Checksum Tag
192.168.1.0      7.7.7.7          521        0x80000050 0x003615 0
192.168.2.0      7.7.7.7          521        0x8000004D 0x00B418 0
192.168.21.0     1.1.1.1          1778       0x80000019 0x006682 0


! Below, R4 is in a totally stubby area, with only one inter-area route.


R4# show ip route ospf
O*IA 0.0.0.0/0 [110/1563] via 10.4.14.1, 00:11:59, Serial0/0.1
```

```
! R5, in a stubby area, has several inter-area routes, but none of the
! external routes (e.g. 192.168.1.0). R5's default points to R2.


R5# show ip route ospf
10.0.0.0/8 is variably subnetted, 7 subnets, 3 masks
O IA    10.3.13.0/24 [110/115] via 10.5.25.2, 13:45:49, Serial0.2
O IA    10.3.0.0/23 [110/125] via 10.5.25.2, 13:37:55, Serial0.2
O IA    10.1.1.0/24 [110/51] via 10.5.25.2, 13:45:49, Serial0.2
O IA    10.4.0.0/16 [110/1613] via 10.5.25.2, 13:45:49, Serial0.2
O*IA 0.0.0.0/0 [110/51] via 10.5.25.2, 13:45:49, Serial0.2


! Below, R5's costs on its interfaces are shown. Note that
! the default route's metric (51) comes from the 50 below, plus an advertised
! cost of 1 in the summary (type 3) for default 0.0.0.0/0 generated by R2. R5
! simply chose to use the default route with the lower metric.


R5# sh ip ospf int brief
Interface    PID   Area          IP Address/Mask    Cost  State Nbrs F/C
Se0.1        1     5             10.5.15.5/24       64    P2P   1/1
Se0.2        1     5             10.5.25.5/24       50    P2P   1/1
Et0          1     5             10.5.1.5/24        10    DR    0/0

! Next, R2 changes the cost of its advertised summary from 1 to 15.


R2# conf t
Enter configuration commands, one per line.  End with CNTL/Z.
R2(config)# router ospf 2
R2(config-router)# area 5 default-cost 15


! Below, R5's metrics to both R1's and R2's default routes tie,
! so both are now in the routing table.


R5# show ip route ospf
! Lines omitted for brevity
O*IA 0.0.0.0/0 [110/65] via 10.5.25.2, 00:00:44, Serial0.2
                [110/65] via 10.5.15.1, 00:00:44, Serial0.1
```

The legend in the top of the output of a **show ip route** command lists several identifiers that pertain to OSPF. For example, the acronym "IA" refers to inter-area OSPF routes, E1 refers to external type 1 routes, and E2 refers to external type 2 routes. If using NSSAs, N1 refers to NSSA-external type 1 routes in NSSAs, and N2 refers to NSSA-external type 2. The differences are equivalent to differences between E1 and E2 routes.

## OSPF Path Choices That Do Not Use Cost

Under most circumstances, when an OSPF router runs the SPF algorithm and finds more than one possible route to reach a particular subnet, the router chooses the route with the least cost. However, OSPF does consider a few conditions other than cost when making this best-path decision. This short section explains the remaining factors that impact which route, or path, is considered best by the SPF algorithm.

### Choosing the Best Type of Path

As mentioned earlier, some routes are considered to be intra-area routes, some are inter-area routes, and two are types of external routes (E1/N1 and E2/N2). It is possible for a router to find multiple routes to reach a given subnet where the type of route (intra-area, inter-area, E1/N1, or E2/N2) is different. In these cases, RFC 2328 specifies that the router should ignore the costs and instead chooses the best route based on the following order of preference:

1. Intra-area routes

2. Inter-area routes

3. E1/N1 routes (the E1 and N1 routes are considered equivalent)

4. E2/N2 routes (the E2 and N2 routes are considered equivalent)

For example, if a router using OSPF finds one intra-area route for subnet 1 and one inter-area route to reach that same subnet, the router ignores the costs and simply chooses the intra-area route. Similarly, if a router finds one inter-area route, one E1/N1 route, and one E2/N2 route to reach the same subnet, that router chooses the inter-area route, again regardless of the cost for each route.

### Best-Path Side Effects of ABR Loop Prevention

The other item that affects OSPF best-path selection relates to some OSPF loop-avoidance features. Inside an area, OSPF uses Link State logic, but between areas, OSPF acts as a Distance Vector (DV) protocol. For example, the advertisement of a type 3 LSA from one area to another hides the topology in the original area from the second area, just listing a destination subnet, metric (cost), and the ABR through which the subnet can be reached—all DV concepts.

OSPF does not use all the traditional DV loop-avoidance features, but it does use some of the same underlying concepts, including Split Horizon. In OSPF's case, it applies Split Horizon for several types of LSAs so that information from an LSA is not advertised into one nonbackbone area and then advertised back into the backbone area. Figure 9-9 shows an example in which ABR1 and ABR2 both advertise type 3 LSAs into area 1, but then they both choose to not originate a type 3 LSA containing the same network back into area 0. This corresponds to one of the rules about type 3 LSA origination described earlier: From a nonbackbone area, only internal routes can be advertised into the backbone.

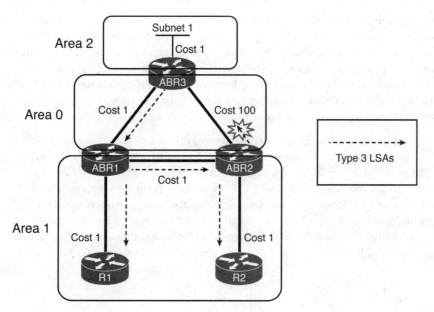

**Figure 9-9**  *Split Horizon per Area with OSPF*

The figure shows the propagation of some of the LSAs for subnet 1. ABR3 generates a type 3 LSA for subnet 1 and floods that LSA within area 0. ABR1 computes its routing table in area 0 and floods its own type 3 LSA for subnet 1 into area 1. However, when ABR2 gets this LSA from ABR1, ABR2 does not use it in its SPF computation because the only type 3 LSAs used in SPF by ABRs are those received over the backbone. In addition, no inter-area routes from nonbackbone areas can be advertised to backbone. These two rules prevent ABR2 from processing this LSA and advertising the contained network back into the backbone area. (To reduce clutter, the figure does not include arrowed lines for the opposite direction, in which ABR2 floods a type 3 LSA into area 1, and then ABR1 chooses not to flood a corresponding type 3 LSA back into area 0.)

Let's restate once again the rules regarding originating and processing type 3 LSAs on ABRs. First, when an ABR originates type 3 LSAs on behalf of known routes, it translates only intra-area routes from a nonbackbone area into type 3 LSAs and floods them into the backbone, and it translates both intra-area and inter-area routes from the backbone area into type 3 LSAs and floods them into nonbackbone areas. Second, when an ABR runs the SPF algorithm, it ignores all type 3 LSAs received over nonbackbone areas.

The first rule essentially makes sure that the only valid way of one area learning about routes in another area is through the backbone, and that the backbone is never fed a route that must have already traversed the backbone. An internal route begins its life as an intra-area route in some area. If that area is a nonbackbone area, an ABR will create a type 3 LSA on behalf of this network and flood it into the backbone. Other ABRs in the backbone will use these type 3 LSAs along with others to compute their routing tables, and they will create their own type 3 LSAs for both intra-area (internal to backbone) and inter-area (behind backbone) routes and flood them into their own attached nonbackbone areas.

The second rule makes sure that an ABR does not traverse a nonbackbone area to reach a network that is located in the backbone or in some other nonbackbone area. In other words, an ABR never uses a nonbackbone area to reach an inter-area network. Especially when a nonbackbone area has multiple ABRs and their mutual distance in the nonbackbone area is smaller than their distance in the backbone, one ABR could choose an inter area path over the nonbackbone area rather than through the backbone. The second rule prevents this. However, the consequences of this rule can be rather surprising.

For example, without this second rule, in the internetwork of Figure 9-10, router ABR2 would calculate a cost 3 path to subnet 1: from ABR2 to ABR1 inside area 1 and then from ABR1 to ABR3 in area 0. ABR2 would also calculate a cost 101 path to subnet 1, going from ABR2 through area 0 to ABR3. Clearly, the first of these two paths, with cost 3, is the least-cost path. However, ABRs use this additional loop-prevention rule, meaning that ABR2 ignores the type 3 LSA advertised by ABR1 for subnet 1. This behavior prevents ABR2 from choosing the path through ABR1, so in actual practice, ABR2 would find only one possible path to subnet 1: the path directly from ABR2 to ABR3.

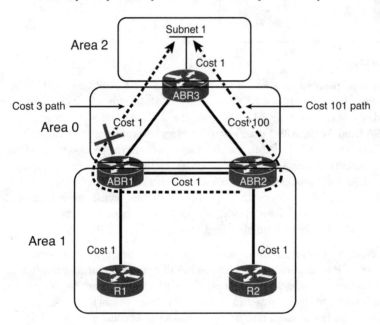

**Figure 9-10**  *Effect of ABR2 Ignoring Path to Subnet 1 Through Area 1*

It is important to notice that the link between ABR1 and ABR2 is squarely inside non-backbone area 1. If this link were in area 0, ABR2 would pick the best route to reach ABR3 as being ABR2 – ABR1 – ABR3, choosing the lower-cost route.

This loop-prevention rule has some even more interesting side effects for internal routers. Again in Figure 9-10, consider the routes calculated by internal Router R2 to reach subnet 1. R2 learns a type 3 LSA for subnet 1 from ABR1, with the cost listed as 2. To calculate the total cost for using ABR1 to reach subnet 1, R2 adds its cost to reach ABR1 (cost 2), totaling cost 4. Likewise, R2 learns a type 3 LSA for subnet 1 from ABR2, with cost 101.

R2 calculates its cost to reach ABR2 (cost 1) and adds that to 101 to arrive at cost 102 for this alternative route. As a result, R2 picks the route through ABR1 as the best route.

However, the story gets even more interesting with the topology shown in Figure 9-10. R2's next-hop router for the R2 – ABR2 – ABR1 – ABR3 path is ABR2. So, R2 forwards packets destined to subnet 1 to ABR2 next. However, as noted just a few paragraphs ago, ABR2's route to reach subnet 1 points directly to ABR3. As a result, packets sent by R2, destined to subnet 1, actually take the path from R2 – ABR2 – ABR3. As you can see, these decisions can result in arguably suboptimal routes, and even asymmetric routes, as would be the case in this particular example.

## OSPF Configuration

This section covers the core OSPF configuration commands, along with the OSPF configuration topics not already covered previously in the chapter. (If you happened to skip the earlier parts of this chapter, planning to review OSPF configuration, make sure to go back and look at the earlier examples in the chapter. These examples cover OSPF stubby area configuration, OSPF network types, plus OSPF **neighbor** and **priority** commands.)

Example 9-8 shows configuration for the routers in Figure 9-5, with the following design goals in mind:

- Proving that OSPF process IDs do not have to match on separate routers, though best practice recommends using the same process IDs across the network

- Using the **network** command to match interfaces, thereby triggering neighbor discovery inside network 10.0.0.0

- Configuring S1's RID as 7.7.7.7

- Setting priorities on the backbone LAN to favor S1 and S2 to become the DR/BDR

- Configuring a minimal dead interval of 1 second, with hello multiplier of 4, yielding a 250-ms hello interval on the backbone LAN

**Example 9-8**  *OSPF Configuration Basics and OSPF Costs*

```
! R1 !!!!!!!!!!!!!!!!!!!!!!!!!!!!!!!!!!!!!!!!!!!!!!!!!!!!!!!!!!!!!!!!!!!!!!!!!!!!!!!!!!!!
! R1 has been configured for a (minimal) 1-second dead interval, and 1/4-second
! (250 ms) hello interval based on 4 Hellos per 1-second dead interval.

interface FastEthernet0/0
 ip address 10.1.1.1 255.255.255.0
 ip ospf dead-interval minimal hello-multiplier 4

! R1 uses the same stub area configuration as in Example 9-7, with network
! commands matching based on the first two octets. Note that the network commands
! place each interface into the correct area.

router ospf 1
```

```
 area 3 nssa no-summary
 area 4 stub no-summary
 area 5 stub
 network 10.1.0.0 0.0.255.255 area 0
 network 10.3.0.0 0.0.255.255 area 3
 network 10.4.0.0 0.0.255.255 area 4
 network 10.5.0.0 0.0.255.255 area 5


! R2 !!!!!!!!!!!!!!!!!!!!!!!!!!!!!!!!!!!!!!!!!!!!!!!!!!!!!!!!!!!!!!!!!!!!!!!!!!!
! The R2 configuration also uses the Fast Hello feature, otherwise it
! would not match hello and dead intervals with R1. Also, OSPF on R2 is activated
! directly on interfaces using ip ospf process-id area area-id command that
! replaces
! the use of network commands. It is assumed that all interfaces are configured
! using this command so the router ospf section contains no network commands

interface FastEthernet0/0
 ip address 10.1.1.2 255.255.255.0
 ip ospf dead-interval minimal hello-multiplier 4
 ip ospf 2 area 0


! Below, R2 uses a different PID than R1, but the PID is only used locally.
! R1 and R2 will become neighbors. Also, all routers in a stubby area must be
! configured to be that type of stubby area; R2 does that for area 5 below.

router ospf 2
 area 5 stub


! R3 !!!!!!!!!!!!!!!!!!!!!!!!!!!!!!!!!!!!!!!!!!!!!!!!!!!!!!!!!!!!!!!!!!!!!!!!!!!!
! Note that R3's area 3 nssa no-summary command matches R1's area command.
! However, R3 should omit the no-summary keyword, because R3 is not an ABR.

router ospf 1
 area 3 nssa no-summary
 network 10.0.0.0 0.255.255.255 area 3


! R4 !!!!!!!!!!!!!!!!!!!!!!!!!!!!!!!!!!!!!!!!!!!!!!!!!!!!!!!!!!!!!!!!!!!!!!!!!!!!

router ospf 1
 area 4 stub no-summary
 network 10.0.0.0 0.255.255.255 area 4


! S1 !!!!!!!!!!!!!!!!!!!!!!!!!!!!!!!!!!!!!!!!!!!!!!!!!!!!!!!!!!!!!!!!!!!!!!!!!!!!
! S1 matches hello and dead intervals on the LAN. Also, it sets its OSPF
! priority to 255, the maximum value, hoping to become the DR.
```

```
interface Vlan1
 ip address 10.1.1.3 255.255.255.0
 ip ospf dead-interval minimal hello-multiplier 4
 ip ospf priority 255

! Below, S1 sets its RID manually, removing any reliance on an interface address.

router ospf 1
 router-id 7.7.7.7
 network 10.1.0.0 0.0.255.255 area 0

! S2 !!!!!!!!!!!!!!!!!!!!!!!!!!!!!!!!!!!!!!!!!!!!!!!!!!!!!!!!!!!!!!!!!!!!!!!!!!!!!!!!!!
! Below, S2 also matches timers, and sets its priority to 1 less than S1, hoping
! to be the BDR.

interface Vlan1
 ip address 10.1.1.4 255.255.255.0
 ip ospf dead-interval minimal hello-multiplier 4
 ip ospf priority 254
!
router ospf 1
 network 10.0.0.0 0.255.255.255 area 0
```

Note that R3 and R4 do not need the **no-summary** option on the **area** command; this parameter is only needed at the ABR, in this case R1. The parameters are shown here to stress the variations of stubby areas.

## OSPF Costs and Clearing the OSPF Process

Example 9-9 highlights a few details about clearing (restarting) the OSPF process, and looks at changes to OSPF costs. This example shows the following sequence:

1. R3's OSPF process is cleared, causing all neighbors to fail and restart.

2. R3's **log-adjacency-changes detail** configuration command (under **router ospf**) causes more detailed neighbor state change messages to appear.

3. R5 has tuned its cost settings with the **ip ospf cost 50** interface subcommand under S0.2 to prefer R2 over R1 for reaching the core.

4. R2 is configured to use a new reference bandwidth, changing its cost calculation per interface.

**Example 9-9**   *Changing RIDs, Clearing OSPF, and Modifying Cost Settings*

```
R3# clear ip ospf process
Reset ALL OSPF processes? [no]: y


! Above, all OSPF processes are cleared on R3. R3 has the log-adjacency-changes
! detail command configured, so that a message is generated at each state
! change, as shown below for neighbor R33 (RID 192.168.1.1). (Messages for
! other routers are omitted.)


00:02:46: %OSPF-5-ADJCHG: Process 1, Nbr 192.168.1.1 on Ethernet0/0 from FULL to
   DOWN,   Neighbor Down: Interface down or detached
00:02:53: %OSPF-5-ADJCHG: Process 1, Nbr 192.168.1.1 on Ethernet0/0 from DOWN to
   INIT,   Received Hello
00:02:53: %OSPF-5-ADJCHG: Process 1, Nbr 192.168.1.1 on Ethernet0/0 from INIT to
   2WAY, 2-Way Received
00:02:53: %OSPF-5-ADJCHG: Process 1, Nbr 192.168.1.1 on Ethernet0/0 from 2WAY to
   EXSTART,   AdjOK?
00:02:53: %OSPF-5-ADJCHG: Process 1, Nbr 192.168.1.1 on Ethernet0/0 from EXSTART
   to EXCHANGE, Negotiation Done
00:02:53: %OSPF-5-ADJCHG: Process 1, Nbr 192.168.1.1 on Ethernet0/0 from EXCHANGE
   to LOADING, Exchange Done
00:02:53: %OSPF-5-ADJCHG: Process 1, Nbr 192.168.1.1 on Ethernet0/0 from LOADING to
   FULL,   Loading Done


! Next R5 has costs of 50 and 64, respectively, on interfaces s0.2 and s0.1.

R5# show ip ospf int brief
Interface   PID   Area        IP Address/Mask    Cost   State   Nbrs F/C
Se0.2       1     5           10.5.25.5/24       50     P2P     1/1
Se0.1       1     5           10.5.15.5/24       64     P2P     1/1
Et0         1     5           10.5.1.5/24        10     DR      0/0


! Below, S0.1's cost was based on bandwidth of 1544 Kbps, using the formula
! 100,000 Kbps / bandwidth with bandwidth in Kbps.


R5# sh int s 0.1
Serial0.1 is up, line protocol is up
  Hardware is HD64570
  Internet address is 10.5.15.5/24
  MTU 1500 bytes, BW 1544 Kbit, DLY 20000 usec,
     reliability 255/255, txload 1/255, rxload 1/255
  Encapsulation FRAME-RELAY
  Last clearing of "show interface" counters never


! Next, R2's interface costs are shown, including the minimum cost 1 on Fa0/0.
```

```
R2# sho ip ospf int brief
Interface    PID   Area          IP Address/Mask   Cost  State Nbrs F/C
Fa0/0        2     0             10.1.1.2/24       1     BDR   3/3
Se0/0.5      2     5             10.5.25.2/24      64    P2P   1/1

! Below, R2 changes its reference bandwidth from the default of 100 Mbps to
! 10,000 Mbps. That in turn changes R2's calculated cost values to be 100 times
! larger than before. Note that IOS allows this setting to differ on the routers,
! but recommends against it.

R2# conf t
Enter configuration commands, one per line.  End with CNTL/Z.
R2(config)# router ospf 2
R2(config-router)# auto-cost reference-bandwidth 10000
% OSPF: Reference bandwidth is changed.
       Please ensure reference bandwidth is consistent across all routers.
R2# show ip ospf int brief
Interface    PID   Area          IP Address/Mask   Cost  State Nbrs F/C
Fa0/0        2     0             10.1.1.2/24       100   BDR   3/3
Se0/0.5      2     5             10.5.25.2/24      6476  P2P   1/1
```

While Examples 9-8 and 9-9 show some details, the following list summarizes how IOS chooses OSPF interface costs:

1. Set the cost per neighbor using the **neighbor** *neighbor* **cost** *value* command. (This is valid only on OSPF point-to-multipoint nonbroadcast network types.)

2. Set the cost per interface using the **ip ospf cost** *value* interface subcommand.

3. Allow the cost to default based on interface bandwidth and the OSPF Reference Bandwidth (Ref-BW) (default $10^5$ Kbps). The formula is Ref-BW / bandwidth (Kbps).

4. Default based on bandwidth, but change Ref-BW using the **auto-cost reference-bandwidth** value command within the OSPF process.

The only slightly tricky part of the cost calculation math is to keep the units straight, because the IOS interface bandwidth is kept in Kbps and the **auto-cost reference-bandwidth** command's units are Mbps. For example, on R5 in Example 9-9, the cost is calculated as 100 Mbps divided by 1544 Kbps, where 1544 Kbps is equal to 1.544 Mbps. The result is rounded down to the nearest integer, 64 in this case. On R2's Fa0/0 interface, the bandwidth is 100,000 Kbps, or 100 Mbps, making the calculation yield a cost of 1. After changing the reference bandwidth to 10,000, which means 10,000 Mbps, R2's calculated costs were 100 times larger.

> **Note** When choosing the best routes to reach a subnet, OSPF also considers whether a route is an intra-area route, inter-area route, E1/N1 route, or E2/N2 route. OSPF prefers intra-area over all the rest, then inter-area, then E1/N1, and finally E2/N2 routes. Under normal circumstances, routes to a single subnet should all be the same type; however, it is possible to have multiple route paths to reach a single subnet in the OSPF SPF tree, but with some of these routes being a different type. Example 11-7 in Chapter 11 demonstrates this.

### Alternatives to the OSPF network Command

As of Cisco IOS Software Release 12.3(11)T, OSPF configuration can completely omit the **network** command, instead relying on the **ip ospf** *process-id* **area** area-id interface subcommand. This new command enables OSPF on the interface and selects the area.

The **network** and **ip ospf area** commands have some minor differences when secondary IP addresses are used. With the **network** command, OSPF advertises stub networks for any secondary IP subnets that are matched by the command. ("Secondary subnet" is jargon that refers to the subnet in which a secondary IP address resides.) The **ip ospf area** interface subcommand causes any and all secondary subnets on the interface to be advertised as stub networks—unless the optional **secondaries none** parameter is included at the end of the command.

Regardless of the **network** or **ip ospf area** command, OSPF will always establish adjacencies over an interface only using the primary IP address. OSPF will never use secondary addresses to establish an adjacency.

## OSPF Filtering

Intra-routing protocol filtering presents some special challenges with link-state routing protocols like OSPF. Link-state protocols do not advertise routes—they advertise topology information. Also, SPF loop prevention relies on each router in the same area having an identical copy of the LSDB for that area. As mentioned in the section about LSA types, only the router that has originated an LSA is ever allowed to modify its contents. Filtering or changing LSA contents in transit could conceivably make the LSDBs differ on different routers, causing routing irregularities.

IOS supports three variations of what could loosely be categorized as OSPF route filtering. These three major types of OSPF filtering are as follows:

- **Filtering routes, not LSAs:** Using the **distribute-list in** command, a router can filter the routes that its SPF process is attempting to add to its routing table, without affecting the LSDB.

- **ABR type 3 LSA filtering:** A process of preventing an ABR from creating particular type 3 summary LSAs.

- **Using the area range no-advertise option:** Another process to prevent an ABR from creating specific type 3 summary LSAs.

Each of these three topics is discussed in sequence in the next few sections.

### Filtering Routes Using the distribute-list Command

For RIP and EIGRP, the **distribute-list** command can be used to filter incoming and outgoing routing updates. The process is straightforward, with the **distribute-list** command referring to ACLs or prefix lists. With OSPF, the **distribute-list in** command filters what ends up in the IP routing table, and only on the router on which the **distribute-list in** command is configured.

**Note**    The **redistribute** command, when used for route distribution between OSPF and other routing protocols, does control what enters and leaves the LSDB. Chapter 11 covers more on route redistribution.

The following rules govern the use of distribute lists for OSPF:

- The distribute list in the inbound direction applies to results of SPF—the routes to be installed into the router's routing table.

- The distribute list in the outbound direction applies only to redistributed routes and only on an ASBR; it selects which redistributed routes shall be advertised.

- The inbound logic does not filter inbound LSAs; it instead filters the routes that SPF chooses to add to that one router's routing table.

- If the distribute list includes the incoming interface parameter, the incoming interface is checked as if it were the outgoing interface of the route.

That last bullet could use a little clarification. For example, if R2 learns routes through RIP or EIGRP updates that enter R2's s0/0 interface, those routes typically use R2's s0/0 interface as the outgoing interface of the routes. The OSPF LSAs might have been flooded into a router on several interfaces, so an OSPF router checks the outgoing interface of the route as if it had learned about the routes through updates coming in that interface.

Example 9-10 shows an example of two distribute lists on R5 from Figure 9-5. The example shows two options to achieve the same goal. In this case, R5 will filter the route to 10.4.8.0/24 through R5's S0.2 subinterface (to R2). Later, it uses a **route-map** command to achieve the same result.

**Example 9-10**   *Filtering Routes with OSPF* **distribute-list** *Commands on R5*

```
! R5 has a route to 10.4.8.0/24 through R2 (10.5.25.2, s0.2)

R5# sh ip route ospf | incl 10.4.8.0
O IA    10.4.8.0/24 [110/1623] via 10.5.25.2, 00:00:28, Serial0.2

! Next, the distribute-list command refers to a prefix list that denies 10.4.8.0/24

ip prefix-list prefix-10-4-8-0 seq 5 deny 10.4.8.0/24
ip prefix-list prefix-10-4-8-0 seq 10 permit 0.0.0.0/0 le 32
!
router ospf 1
 distribute-list prefix prefix-10-4-8-0 in Serial0.2

! Below, note that R5's route through R2 is gone, but the LSDB is unchanged!

R5# sh ip route ospf |  incl 10.4.8.0

! Not shown: the earlier distribute-list command is removed.
! Below, note that the distribute-list command with the route-map option does not
! have an option to refer to an interface, so the route-map itself has been
! configured to refer to the advertising router's RID (2.2.2.2).

router ospf 1
 distribute-list route-map lose-10-4-8-0 in

! Next, ACL 48 matches the 10.4.8.0/24 prefix, with ACL 51 matching R2's RID.

access-list 48 permit 10.4.8.0
access-list 51 permit 2.2.2.2

! Below, the route map matches the prefix (based on ACL 48) and the advertising
! RID (ACL 51, matching R2's 2.2.2.2 RID). Clause 20 permits all other prefixes.

route-map lose-10-4-8-0 deny 10
 match ip address 48
 match ip route-source 51
route-map lose-10-4-8-0 permit 20

! Above, note the same results as the previous distribute list.
R5# sh ip route ospf | incl 10.4.8.0
```

Example 9-10 shows only two ways to filter the routes. The **distribute-list route-map** option allows a much greater variety of matching parameters, and much more detailed logic with route maps. For example, this example showed matching a prefix as well as the

RID that advertised the LSA to R5, namely 2.2.2.2 (R2). Refer to Chapter 11 for a more complete review of route maps and the **match** command.

> **Note**  Some earlier IOS releases allowed the router to not only filter the route as shown in Example 9-10 but also to replace the route with the next best route. Testing at Release 12.4 and beyond shows the behavior as shown in the example, with IOS simply not adding the route to the IP routing table.

## OSPF ABR LSA Type 3 Filtering

ABRs do not forward type 1 and 2 LSAs from one area into another, but instead create type 3 LSAs for each subnet defined in the type 1 and 2 LSAs. Type 3 LSAs do not contain detailed information about the topology of the originating area; instead, each type 3 LSA represents a subnet, and a cost from the ABR to that subnet. The earlier section "LSA Type 3 and Inter-Area Costs" covers the details and provides an example.

The *OSPF ABR type 3 LSA filtering* feature allows an ABR to filter type 3 LSAs at the point where the LSAs would normally be created. By filtering at the ABR, before the type 3 LSA is injected into another area, the requirement for identical LSDBs inside the area can be met, while still filtering LSAs.

To configure type 3 LSA filtering, you use the **area** *number* **filter-list prefix** *name* **in | out** command under **router ospf**. The referenced **prefix-list** is used to match the subnets and masks to be filtered. The **area** *number* and the **in | out** option of the **area filter-list** command work together, as follows:

■  When **in** is configured, IOS filters prefixes going into the configured area.

■  When **out** is configured, IOS filters prefixes coming out of the configured area.

Example 9-11 should clarify the basic operation. ABR R1 will use two alternative **area filter-list** commands, both to filter subnet 10.3.2.0/23, a subnet connected to R33 in Figure 9-5. Remember that R1 is connected to areas 0, 3, 4, and 5. The first **area filter-list** command shows filtering the LSA as it goes out of area 3; as a result, R1 will not inject the LSA into any of the other areas. The second case shows the same subnet being filtered going into area 0, meaning that the type 3 LSA for that subnet still gets into the area 4 and 5 LSDBs.

**Example 9-11**  *Type 3 LSA Filtering on R1 with the* **area filter-list** *Command*

```
! The command lists three lines of extracted output. One line is for the
! type 3 LSA in area 0, one is for area 4, and one is for area 5.

R1# show ip ospf data summary | include 10.3.2.0
     Link State ID: 10.3.2.0 (summary Network Number)
     Link State ID: 10.3.2.0 (summary Network Number)
     Link State ID: 10.3.2.0 (summary Network Number)
```

```
! Below, the two-line prefix list denies subnet 10.3.2.0/23, and then permits
! all others.


ip prefix-list filter-type3-10-3-2-0 seq 5 deny 10.3.2.0/23
ip prefix-list filter-type3-10-3-2-0 seq 10 permit 0.0.0.0/0 le 32


! Next, the area filter-list command filters type 3 LSAs going out of area 3.


R1# conf t
Enter configuration commands, one per line.  End with CNTL/Z.
R1(config)# router ospf 1
R1(config-router)# area 3 filter-list prefix filter-type3-10-3-2-0 out
R1(config-router)# ^Z


! Below, R1 no longer has any type 3 LSAs, in areas 0, 4, and 5. For
! comparison, this command was issued a few commands ago, listing 1 line
! of output for each of the other 3 areas besides area 3.


R1# show ip ospf data | include 10.3.2.0


! Below, the previous area filter-list command is replaced by the next command
! below, which filters type 3 LSAs going into area 0, with the same prefix list.


area 0 filter-list prefix filter-type3-10-3-2-0 in


! Next, only 2 type 3 LSAs for 10.3.2.0 are shown - the ones in areas 4 and 5.


R1# show ip ospf data | include 10.3.2.0
  Link State ID: 10.3.2.0 (summary Network Number)
  Link State ID: 10.3.2.0 (summary Network Number)


! Below, the configuration for filtering type 3 LSAs with the area range command,
! which is explained following this example. The existing area filter-list
! commands from earlier in this chapter have been removed at this point.


R1(config-router)# area 3 range 10.3.2.0 255.255.254.0 not-advertise
R1# show ip ospf data summary | include 10.3.2.0
R1#
```

## Filtering Type 3 LSAs with the area range Command

The third method to filter OSPF routes is to filter type 3 LSAs at an ABR using the **area range** command. The **area range** command performs route summarization at ABRs, telling a router to cease advertising smaller subnets in a particular address range, instead creating a single type 3 LSA whose address and prefix encompass the smaller subnets.

When the **area range** command includes the **not-advertise** keyword, not only are the smaller component subnets not advertised as type 3 LSAs, but the summary route is also not advertised as a type 3 LSA either. As a result, this command has the same effect as the **area filter-list** command with the **out** keyword, filtering the LSA from going out to any other areas. An example **area range** command is shown at the end of Example 9-11.

## Virtual Link Configuration

OSPF requires that each nonbackbone area be connected to the backbone area (area 0). OSPF also requires that the routers in each area have a contiguous intra-area path to the other routers in the same area, because without that path, LSA flooding inside the area would fail. However, in some designs, meeting these requirements might be a challenge. You can use OSPF *virtual links* to overcome these problems.

For example, in the top part of Figure 9-11, area 33 connects only to area 3, and not to area 0.

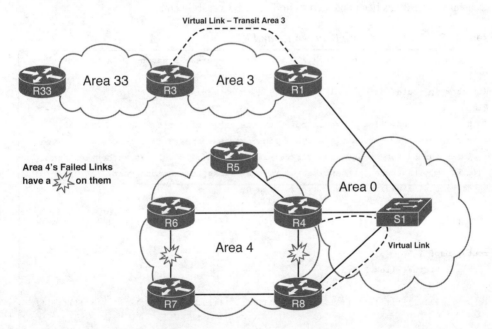

**Figure 9-11**  *Need for Virtual Links*

Key
Topic

One straightforward solution to area 33's lack of connection to the backbone area would be to combine areas 3 and 33 into a single area, but OSPF virtual links could solve the problem as well. An OSPF virtual link allows a pair of possibly remote routers to create a targeted OSPF session across the IP network. A virtual link between R3 and R1 gives area 33 a connection to area 0. Also note that R3 becomes an ABR, with a full copy of area 0's LSDB entries. A virtual link *is not a tunnel* for data packets; rather, it is a targeted session that allows two remote routers within a single area to become fully adjacent and synchronize their LSDBs. The virtual link is internally represented as an unnumbered point-to-point link between the two endpoint routers and exists in the backbone area, regardless of the area through which it is created. The area through which the virtual link is created is called a *transit area* and it *must* be a regular area: As no tunneling is involved, packets routed through this transit area are forwarded based on their true destination addresses, requiring the transit area to know all networks in the OSPF domain, intra-area, inter-area, and external. While the top part of Figure 9-11 simply shows a possibly poor OSPF area design, the lower part shows what could happen just because of a particular set of link failures. The figure shows several failed links that result in a *partitioned* area 4. As a result of the failures, R7 and R8 have no area 4 links connecting to the other three routers in area 4. A virtual link can be used to connect R4 and R8—the requirement being that both R4 and R8 connect to a common and working area—recombining the partitions through the virtual link. (A better solution than the virtual link in this particular topology might be to trunk on R4 and R8, create a small subnet through the LAN switch, and put it in area 4.)

Example 9-12 demonstrates a virtual link configuration between R33 and R1, as shown in Figure 9-11. Note that the virtual link cannot pass through a transit area that is a stubby area, so area 3 has been changed to no longer be a stubby area.

**Example 9-12**  *Virtual Link Between R3 and R1*

```
! R1 has not learned subnet 10.3.2.0 yet, because area 33 has no link to area 0.


R1# show ip route ospf | incl 10.3.2.0
R1#
! The area virtual link commands point to the other router's RID, and the
! transit area over which the virtual link exists - area 3 in this case. Note that
! timers can be set on the area virtual-link command, as well as authentication.
! It is important when authenticating virtual links to remember that
! the virtual links themselves are in area 0.


! R1 !!!!!!!!!!!!!!!!!!!!!!!!!!!!!!!!!!!!!!!!!!!!!!!!!!!!!!!!!!!!!!!!!!!!!!!!!!!!!!!!!

router ospf 1
  area 3 virtual-link 3.3.3.3


! R3 !!!!!!!!!!!!!!!!!!!!!!!!!!!!!!!!!!!!!!!!!!!!!!!!!!!!!!!!!!!!!!!!!!!!!!!!!!!!!!!!!

router ospf 1
  area 3 virtual-link 1.1.1.1

! Below, the status of the virtual link is listed.

R1# show ip ospf virtual-links
Virtual Link OSPF_VL0 to router 3.3.3.3 is up
  Run as demand circuit
  DoNotAge LSA allowed.
  Transit area 3, via interface Serial0/0.3, Cost of using 64
```

```
    Transmit Delay is 1 sec, State POINT_TO_POINT,
    Timer intervals configured, Hello 10, Dead 40, Wait 40, Retransmit 5
       Hello due in 00:00:02
       Adjacency State FULL (Hello suppressed)
       Index 3/6, retransmission queue length 0, number of retransmission 1
       First 0x0(0)/0x0(0) Next 0x0(0)/0x0(0)
       Last retransmission scan length is 1, maximum is 1
       Last retransmission scan time is 0 msec, maximum is 0 msec

! Because R1 and R3 are also sharing the same link, there is a neighbor
! relationship in area 3 that has been seen in the other examples, listed off
! interface s0/0.3. The new virtual link neighbor relationship is shown as well,
! with interface VL0 listed.


R1# show ip ospf nei
! Lines omitted for brevity
Neighbor ID     Pri   State         Dead Time   Address        Interface
3.3.3.3           0   FULL/ -           -        10.3.13.3      OSPF_VL0
3.3.3.3           0   FULL/ -       00:00:10     10.3.13.3      Serial0/0.3
! Below, subnet 10.3.2.0/23, now in area 33, is learned by R1 over the Vlink.
R1# show ip route ospf | incl 10.3.2.0
O IA    10.3.2.0/23 [110/75] via 10.3.13.3, 00:00:10, Serial0/0.3
```

## Configuring Classic OSPF Authentication

OSPF traditionally supported three authentication types: none, clear text, and MD5-based authentication. With the recent addition of SHA-1 to the list of supported hashes, the way to configure OSPF authentication differs based on what hashing function you intend to use. This section describes the classic way of configuring OSPF authentication that allows only the use of none, plain text, and MD5 authentication. The newer style of configuring OSPF authentication is described in the next section.

One of the keys to keeping classic OSPF authentication configuration straight is to remember that it differs significantly with RIPv2 and EIGRP, although some of the concepts are very similar. The basic rules for configuring OSPF authentication are as follows:

■ Three types are available: type 0 (none), type 1 (clear text), and type 2 (MD5).

■ Authentication is enabled per interface using the **ip ospf authentication** interface subcommand.

■ The default authentication is type 0 (no authentication).

■ The default can be redefined using the **area authentication** subcommand under **router ospf**.

■ The keys are always configured as interface subcommands.

■ Multiple MD5 keys with different key IDs are allowed per interface. This allows for graceful key migration where a new key can be added without disrupting the adjacencies. OSPF does it in a simple way: To sign *sent* packets, it always uses the key that was added as the last one to the interface (regardless of the key number). To authenticate the *received* packet, it uses the key ID that is indicated in the packet. If a neighbor is detected on an interface that uses a different key number than this router, OSPF enters a key migration phase in which it sends all packets as many times as how many keys are configured on the interface, and each packet is signed with a different key. The migration phase ends when all neighbors have migrated to the same key as the one used to sign sent packets by this router. This procedure is also called the *OSPF key rollover* procedure. Because plaintext passwords do not have key numbers, the key rollover is not available for plaintext authentication.

Table 9-7 lists the three OSPF authentication types, along with the commands to enable each type and the commands to define the authentication keys. Note that the three authentication types can be seen in the messages generated by the **debug ip ospf adj** command.

**Key Topic**

**Table 9-7**  *OSPF Authentication Types*

| Type | Meaning | Enabling Interface Subcommand | Authentication Key Configuration Interface Subcommand |
|------|---------|-------------------------------|-------------------------------------------------------|
| 0 | None | **ip ospf authentication null** | — |
| 1 | Clear text | **ip ospf authentication** | **ip ospf authentication-key** *key-value* |
| 2 | MD5 | **ip ospf authentication message-digest** | **ip ospf message-digest-key** *key-number* **md5** *key-value* |

Example 9-13 (again based on Figure 9-5) shows examples of type 1 and type 2 authentication configuration on Routers R1 and R2. (Note that S1 and S2 have been shut down for this example, but they would need the same configuration as shown on R1 and R2.) In this example, both R1 and R2 use their Fa0/0 interfaces, so their authentication configuration will be identical. As such, the example shows only the configuration on R1.

**Example 9-13**  *OSPF Authentication Using Only Interface Subcommands*

```
! The two ip ospf commands are the same on R1 and R2. The first enables
! type 1 authentication, and the other defines the simple text key.


interface FastEthernet0/0
 ip ospf authentication
 ip ospf authentication-key key-t1


! Below, the neighbor relationship formed, proving that authentication works.
```

```
R1# show ip ospf neighbor fa 0/0
Neighbor ID     Pri   State      Dead Time   Address      Interface
2.2.2.2          1    FULL/BDR   00:00:37    10.1.1.2     FastEthernet0/0

! Next, each interface's OSPF authentication type can be seen in the last line
! or two in the output of the show ip ospf interface command.

R1# show ip ospf int fa 0/0
! Lines omitted for brevity
  Simple password authentication enabled

! Below, both R1 and R2 change to use type 2 authentication. Note that the key
! must be defined with the "ip ospf message-digest-key" interface subcommand. Key
! chains are not supported.

interface FastEthernet0/0
 ip ospf authentication message-digest
 ip ospf message-digest-key 1 md5 key-t2

! Below, the command confirms type 2 (MD5) authentication, key number 1.

R1# show ip ospf int fa 0/0 | begin auth
! Lines omitted for brevity
Message digest authentication enabled
Youngest key id is 1
```

Example 9-13 shows two working examples of OSPF authentication, neither of which uses the **area** *area-id* **authentication** command **under router ospf**. Some texts imply that the **area authentication** command is required—in fact, it was required prior to Cisco IOS Software Release 12.0. In later IOS releases, the **area authentication** command simply tells the router to change that router's default OSPF authentication type for all interfaces in that area. Table 9-8 summarizes the effects and syntax of the **area authentication** router subcommand.

**Table 9-8**   *Effect of the* **area authentication** *Command on OSPF Interface Authentication Settings*

| area authentication Command | Interfaces in That Area Default to Use |
| --- | --- |
| <no command> | Type 0 |
| area *area-id* authentication | Type 1 |
| area *area-id* authentication message-digest | Type 2 |

The keys themselves are kept in clear text in the configuration, unless you add the **service password-encryption** global command to the configuration.

The last piece of authentication configuration relates to OSPF virtual links. Because virtual links have no underlying interface on which to configure authentication, authentication is configured on the **area virtual-link** command itself. Table 9-9 shows the variations of the command options for configuring authentication on virtual links. Note that beyond the base **area** *area-id* **virtual-link** *router-id* command, the parameters use similar keywords as compared with the equivalent interface subcommands.

**Table 9-9**  *Configuring OSPF Authentication on Virtual Links*

| Type | Command Syntax for Virtual Links |
|------|----------------------------------|
| 0 | **area** *area-id* **virtual-link** *router-id* **authentication null** |
| 1 | **area** *area-id* **virtual-link** *router-id* **authentication authentication-key** *key-value* |
| 2 | **area** *area-id* **virtual-link** *router-id* **authentication message-digest message-digest-key** *key-num* **md5** *key-value* |

### Configuring Extended Cryptographic OSPF Authentication

Starting with IOS Release 15.4(1)T, OSPF also supports the extended Secure Hash Algorithm Hash Message Authentication Code (SHA-HMAC) authentication as described in RFC 5709. The introduction of this feature brings along a change in how OSPF authentication is configured. To utilize the SHA-HMAC authentication, OSPF uses key chains similarly to EIGRP or RIPv2. In addition, the key chain definition has been enhanced to select a particular cryptographic algorithm for a particular key.

A number of facts to watch out for:

■ Each key in the key chain must have a cryptographic algorithm configured using a per-key **cryptographic-algorithm** command. Failure to do so will result in OSPF not using that key.

■ Each key in a key chain can be configured with the **send-lifetime** and **accept-lifetime** keywords to limit its usability to a particular timeframe. If multiple keys in the key chain are eligible to sign egress packets, the key with *the highest* key ID will be used. Be aware that this behavior differs from RIPv2 and EIGRP that select the key with *the lowest* key ID.

■ The key rollover procedure as used by classic OSPF is not used with key chains. To sign egress packets, OSPF will always use the valid key with the highest key ID in the key chain. To authenticate ingress packets, OSPF will try to use the key indicated in the received packet. There is no key migration phase of sending multiple OSPF packets signed with different valid keys.

■ The extended cryptographic authentication is enabled per interface using the **ip ospf authentication key-chain** *key-chain-name* interface subcommand using its extended syntax, referring to a particular key chain. Configuring the extended cryptographic authentication using the **area** OSPF process level command is not supported.

- Using the extended cryptographic authentication on virtual links is accomplished using the **area** *area-id* **virtual-link** *router-id* **key-chain** *key-chain-name* OSPF-level command.

- MD5 authentication is one of the supported cryptographic algorithms in key chains. An OSPF router configured for MD5 authentication using the classic commands will be able to interoperate with a router configured using the new key chain style, provided the cryptographic algorithm for the keys in the key chain is MD5. When the new key chain style configuration is used, passwords configured with the **ip ospf message-digest-key** commands will be ignored.

Example 9-14 shows the configuration of an OSPF router for extended cryptographic authentication.

**Example 9-14**  *Configuring Extended Cryptographic Authentication in OSPF*

```
! First the key chain OSPF is configured with a single key ID 1 and key-string
! set to CC1E. Note the added cryptographic-algorithm command and the set
! of available algorithms to choose from.

R1(config)# key chain OSPF
R1(config-keychain)# key 1
R1(config-keychain-key)# cryptographic-algorithm ?
  hmac-sha-1    HMAC-SHA-1 authentication algorithm
  hmac-sha-256  HMAC-SHA-256 authentication algorithm
  hmac-sha-384  HMAC-SHA-384 authentication algorithm
  hmac-sha-512  HMAC-SHA-512 authentication algorithm
  md5           MD5 authentication algorithm

R1(config-keychain-key)# cryptographic-algorithm hmac-sha-256
R1(config-keychain-key)# key-string CC1E
R1(config-keychain-key)# exit
R1(config-keychain)# exit


! On a particular interface, the ip ospf authentication command is enhanced
! with the key-chain keyword, allowing to reference a key chain.


R1(config)# interface gi0/0
R1(config-if)# ip ospf authentication ?
  key-chain       Use a key-chain for cryptographic authentication keys
  message-digest  Use message-digest authentication
  null            Use no authentication
  <cr>
R1(config-if)# ip ospf authentication key-chain OSPF


! The show ip ospf interface command shows the extended cryptographic
! authentication active on the interface at the end of the output.
```

```
R1(config-if)# do show ip ospf interface gi0/0
GigabitEthernet0/0 is up, line protocol is up
 ! Lines omitted for brevity.
 Neighbor Count is 1, Adjacent neighbor count is 1
    Adjacent with neighbor 10.0.12.2   (Backup Designated Router)
 Suppress hello for 0 neighbor(s)
 Cryptographic authentication enabled
    Sending SA: Key 1, Algorithm HMAC-SHA-256 - key chain OSPF
```

**Note**   OSPF authentication is a good place for tricky CCIE lab questions—ones that can be solved in a few minutes if you know all the intricacies.

## Protecting OSPF Routers with TTL Security Check

In addition to protecting OSPF communication with authentication, recent IOS implementations also offer protection against remote attacks by sending unicast-addressed OSPF packets possibly across the network to a victim router. Such packets can easily be generated on a common PC with appropriate software and targeted toward any router in the network. This type of attack can lead to, apart from other obvious results, greatly increased CPU load and subsequent denial of service if the attacker is sending an intense flow of OSPF packets with the goal of overloading the router's control plane. The TTL Security Check feature provides protection against this type of attack.

The idea behind the TTL Security Check is simple. If an IP packet is routed, its TTL header value is decremented. If all OSPF routers sent their packets with TTL set to 255, receiving an OSPF packet with its TTL less than 255 would be a clear indication that the packet originated outside the network segment over which it was received. Because OSPF communication is, with the notable exception of virtual links and sham links, always based on direct router-to-router communication, receiving an OSPF packet outside a virtual link or a sham link with its TTL less than 255 is a possible indication of a malicious activity. Such packets can be dropped.

TTL Security Check can be activated either on a per-interface basis using the **ip ospf ttl-security** interface level command, or globally for all interfaces in a particular OSPF process using the **ttl-security all-interfaces** command. If the TTL Security Check is activated on a per-process basis, individual interfaces can be exempted from TTL Security Check using the **ip ospf ttl-security disable** interface level command. When the TTL Security Check is active on a particular interface, all OSPF packets sourced by that interface have their TTL set to 255, and only packets received with a TTL of 255 are accepted.

Both these commands have an optional **hops** *hop-count* argument that allows relaxing the TTL Security Check. The *hop-count* is a value in the range of 1–254. Setting the *hop-count* to a particular value makes the TTL Security Check accept OSPF packets with their TTL in the range from 255 down to 255 minus *hop-count*. For example, using the **ttl-security all-interface hops 100** command enables OSPF to accept all packets with their TTL in the range from 255 down to 155, inclusive. Setting the *hop-count* to 254 effectively disables the TTL Security check; this can be used when gradually migrating to TTL Security Check. If the **hops** keyword is not specified, the value of 1 is automatically assumed. Using the **hops** *hop-count* command influences what OSPF packets will be accepted; it has no impact on the TTL of OSPF packets originated by the router, which will remain at 255.

The minimum *hop-count* value of 1 might be surprising, considering that OSPF packets sourced by directly connected neighbors will have their TTL set to 255, and there is no reason to allow OSPF packets with a TTL of 254. However, IOS-based Cisco routers exhibit a peculiar behavior in that they appear to decrement the TTL of received OSPF packets before handing them over to the OSPF process. For example, an OSPF packet received with a TTL of 255 will be processed by the OSPF process as having the TTL of 254. Similarly, an OSPF packet received with a TTL of 2 will be processed by the OSPF process having a TTL of 1. An exception applies to OSPF packets received with their TTL already set to 1—these are handed over to the OSPF process with their TTL unchanged. This behavior can be seen in the output of **debug ip ospf adj** when TTL Security Check drops a packet. The reason for this behavior was not known at the time of writing. A packet's TTL should not be checked or decremented if the packet is not to be routed and forwarded to another host (RFC 1812 Section 4.2.2.9 and contained references provide more information). In any case, this IOS behavior at least explains why the minimum allowed (and default) value of the *hop-count* argument is 1: The OSPF process will see the TTL to be 1 less than the original packet's TTL, so to accept OSPF packets from directly connected neighbors, the TTL Security Check must be instructed to accept packets with their apparent TTL of 254. To sum things up, whenever an OSPF packet is received by a router, its TTL is first decremented by 1 (this decrement is skipped if the packet's TTL is equal to 1), and the packet is then passed to OSPF and to TTL Security Check, which will act based on this decremented TTL value.

Neither the **ttl-security all-interface** nor the **ip ospf ttl-security** command has any impact on configured virtual or sham links. If virtual or sham links are also to be protected by TTL Security Check, the protection can be activated in the **area virtual-link ttl-security hops** or the **area sham-link ttl-security hops** command; in these commands, the *hop-count* argument is mandatory. Obviously, its value should be based on the longest possible intra-area path (in terms of number of routers) between the link endpoints.

When migrating to TTL Security Check, it is recommended to first activate it with an explicit *hop-count* of 254. This will make sure that the router's OSPF packets are already sent out with their TTL set to 255, without dropping neighbors' packets if they are not sent with a TTL of 255 yet. Interfaces toward routers that do not support the TTL Security Check shall be configured with the **ip ospf ttl-security disable** command. Afterward, the *hop-count* shall be set to the default value of 1.

## Tuning OSPF Performance

Apart from interface timers that define the Hello and Dead intervals, OSPF can be significantly tuned in several other aspects. This section covers selected features in OSPF that can be used to improve its performance.

### Tuning the SPF Scheduling with SPF Throttling

After a router receives an updated LSA, it needs to schedule its SPF to process the update. Because a topology change very often affects multiple routers, it is quite prudent to wait some time for more updated LSAs to arrive, and run the SPF only after this waiting period is over. This allows the SPF to process multiple updates in a single run. However, if the topology change is caused by a repetitive fault, such as a flapping link because of faulty connectors, frequently running SPF would put an unnecessary burden on the router. Therefore, if a router continuously keeps receiving updated LSAs, the delay before the upcoming SPF run should progressively grow to dampen the negative impact of the flapping in network. By default, Cisco routers will schedule an SPF run 5 seconds after receiving an updated LSA, and if an updated LSA arrives after this SPF run, the subsequent delay will grow up to 10 seconds.

The scheduling of SPF runs can be controlled by a feature called *SPF Throttling*. This feature defines a variable-length wait interval between two consecutive SPF runs. There are three parameters controlling this feature called *spf-start*, *spf-hold*, and *spf-max-wait*. The *spf-start* parameter defines the initial wait interval before an SPF computation, if the network has been stable for a prolonged period of time. The *spf-hold* parameter defines a wait time between subsequent SPF runs, and its value doubles for each consecutive SPF run. The *spf-max-wait* parameter is the maximum time between two SPF runs (that is, doubling the *spf-hold* value is capped at *spf-max-wait*), and also defines a period during which the network must be stable for the wait interval to be set back to *spf-start* and the *spf-hold* to its preconfigured value. If the network has been stable for the last *spf-hold* period but not for the entire *spf-max-wait* since the last SPF run, the wait interval returns to the *spf-start* value but the subsequent wait will still be set to twice the previous *spf-hold* value.

Instead of talking in general terms, let us demonstrate the behavior of SPF Throttling in a scenario. Assume that *spf-start* is set to 10 sec, *spf-hold* is 15 sec, and *spf-max-wait* is set to 100 sec. The network is assumed to have been stable for more than 100 seconds before the first update arrived.

- An updated LSA arrives at time T. The router schedules the nearest SPF run at T+10 and waits until this period expires.

- Another updated LSA arrives at time T+2. The router stores it in its LSDB and continues waiting.

- At T+10, the router runs the SPF and sets the next wait interval to 15 secs, the initial *spf-hold* value, meaning that if another updated LSA arrives within 15 secs since this SPF run, the nearest SPF will be run at T+25. The network will be considered stable if no topology change is detected within 100 seconds since this SPF run, that is, until T+110.

- One or more updated LSAs indeed arrive between T+10 and T+25. The router stores them in its LSDB and continues waiting.

- At T+25, the router runs the SPF and sets the next wait interval to twice the previous *spf-hold* value, that is, 30 sec. If another updated LSA arrives within 30 secs since this SPF run, the nearest SPF will be run at T+55. The network will be considered stable if no topology change is detected within 100 seconds since this SPF run, that is, until T+125.

- During the next 30 secs, no updated LSA arrives. The wait interval is reset back to *spf-start*, that is, 10 sec. The network is not considered stable, though, because 100 seconds since the last SPF have not elapsed yet; therefore, *spf-hold* remains at 30 secs.

- At T+80, an updated LSA arrives. The router schedules the nearest SPF run at T+90 and waits until this period expires.

- At T+90, the router runs the SPF and sets the next wait interval to twice the previous *spf-hold* value, that is, 60 sec. If another updated LSA arrives within 60 secs since this SPF run, the nearest SPF will be run at T+150. The network will be considered stable if no topology change is detected within 100 seconds since this SPF run, that is, until T+190.

- During the next 60 secs, no updated LSA arrives. The wait interval is reset back to *spf-start*, that is, 10 sec. The network is not considered stable, though, because 100 seconds since the last SPF have not elapsed yet; therefore, *spf-hold* remains at 60 secs.

- No updated LSA arrives till T+190. As a result, the network is considered stable and the *spf-hold* is set to its initial value of 15 secs. Any topology change detected after this moment will be handled equivalently to the beginning of this scenario.

The SPF Throttling feature is configured by a single **timers throttle spf** *spf-start spf-hold spf-max-wait* command in the **router ospf** section. All arguments are indicated in milliseconds. Current values can be also verified in the **show ip ospf** output, as indicated in Example 9-15. Although not shown, the **debug ip ospf spf statistic** command can be used to verify the current and next wait intervals.

**Example 9-15** *Configuring and Verifying SPF Throttling*

```
! First, the default values of SPF Throttling are displayed, then they are
! modified to match the description above, and their setting is verified again

R2(config)# do show ip ospf | i SPF
 Initial SPF schedule delay 5000 msecs
 Minimum hold time between two consecutive SPFs 10000 msecs
 Maximum wait time between two consecutive SPFs 10000 msecs
R2(config)# router ospf 2
R2(config-router)# timers throttle spf 10000 15000 100000
R2(config-router)# do show ip ospf | i SPF
 Initial SPF schedule delay 10000 msecs
 Minimum hold time between two consecutive SPFs 15000 msecs
 Maximum wait time between two consecutive SPFs 100000 msecs
```

## Tuning the LSA Origination with LSA Throttling

Another way to both speed OSPF convergence and prevent creating an excessive burden on the routers' CPUs is to control the rate at which a particular LSA might be reoriginated by its originating router. For this purpose, we will use the term "same LSA" to denote an LSA instance that has the same link-state ID, type, and originating router, but possibly updated contents. In Cisco IOS, this feature is called *LSA Throttling*.

The idea behind LSA Throttling is precisely the same as with SPF Throttling, together with the handling of the waiting interval. The mechanism is again driven by three values: *start-interval*, *hold-interval*, and *max-interval*. After a particular LSA has not been updated for more than *max-interval* and a need arises to create an updated version, it will be created and flooded after *start-interval*, and the next wait interval is set to the value of *hold-interval*. If the same LSA needs to be updated again within the wait interval since its last reorigination, its true origination and flooding will be postponed until the current wait interval expires, and after creating and flooding the updated LSA, the *hold-interval* is doubled and used as the next wait interval. This behavior will repeat itself during the next wait interval. The same LSA needs to be updated at least once, each time doubling the *hold-interval* and the resulting next wait interval in the process (the *hold-interval* is capped at *max-interval* if it grows over that value). If, during the next wait interval, the LSA does not need to be updated, the wait interval is set back to the *start-interval*; however, the *hold-interval* is still set to its potentially increased value. If the same LSA needs to be updated after the current wait interval has elapsed but before the *max-interval* elapses, its reorigination and flooding will be scheduled after *start-interval* but the next wait interval will be set to twice the previous *hold-time* value, effectively continuing with the exponentially growing hold times. The *hold-time* will be reset to its configured value only if the LSA was not required to be updated for the entire *max-interval* since its last update. Hence, the behavior of the wait interval is precisely the same as in the SPF Throttling and the scenario explained in the SPF Throttling would perfectly match the LSA Throttling behavior as well.

By default, Cisco routers are configured to originate an updated LSA immediately and delay its subsequent origination by 5 seconds and not to progressively increase this interval. That is, *start-interval* is 0, and *hold-interval* and *max-interval* are set to 5000 milliseconds.

The LSA Throttling feature is configured using a single **timers throttle lsa all** *start-interval hold-interval max-interval* command in OSPF configuration. The parameters are again expressed in milliseconds. Example 9-16 shows the use of this command along with the verification of its settings. Should a need arise to verify the LSA Throttling wait intervals, the **debug ip ospf database-timer rate-limit** command can be used.

**Example 9-16** *Configuring and Verifying LSA Throttling*

```
! First, the default values of LSA origination are displayed, then the LSA
! Throttling is configured and the setting is verified again

R1(config)# do show ip ospf | i LSA
```

```
 ! Output omitted
 Minimum LSA interval 5 secs
 Minimum LSA arrival 1000 msecs
 LSA group pacing timer 240 secs
 ! Output omitted
R1(config)# router ospf 1
R1(config-router)# timers throttle lsa all 10000 15000 100000
R1(config-router)# do show ip ospf | i LSA
 ! Output omitted
 Initial LSA throttle delay 10000 msecs
 Minimum hold time for LSA throttle 15000 msecs
 Maximum wait time for LSA throttle 100000 msecs
 Minimum LSA arrival 1000 msecs
 LSA group pacing timer 240 secs
 ! Output omitted
```

Apart from throttling the LSA origination, a router can also be configured to ignore the same LSA upon arrival if it appears to arrive too often. This throttling of arriving LSAs is configured using the **timers lsa arrival** *milliseconds* OSPF command. If two or more same LSAs arrive less than *milliseconds* apart, only the first one is accepted and the remaining LSAs are dropped. In effect, the same LSA is accepted only if it arrives more than *milliseconds* after the previous accepted one. The default setting is 1000 milliseconds and can be seen in the **show ip ospf** output in Example 9-16. Obviously, the value of the minimum LSA arrival interval should be smaller than the neighbors' initial hold interval in LSA Throttling. Otherwise, a neighbor would be allowed to send an updated LSA sooner than this router would be willing to accept it.

## Incremental SPF

Running full SPF every time a topology change is encountered always produces correct results. However, depending on the location of the topology change, the SPF recomputes even those parts of the shortest-path tree that have not been affected by the change. This can unnecessarily increase the CPU load and prolong convergence time. At the expense of maintaining more information in the shortest-path tree about transit nodes' parent and neighbor nodes (and slightly increased memory footprint as a consequence), the SPF calculation can be augmented so that after a topology change, only the affected part of the shortest-path tree is recalculated. This improvement to SPF is called *incremental SPF* and can be activated using the simple **ispf** command in the OSPF configuration, as shown in Example 9-17. There are no additional arguments or parameters to it, and the feature can be activated or deactivated on routers in the network individually. The benefit of incremental SPF computation varies. It is difficult to predict how significantly it speeds the SPF computation as that depends on the network topology and nature of the topology change. However, in general, the farther the topology change occurs from the computing router, the better the gain.

**Example 9-17**   *Configuring Incremental SPF*

```
! The state of Incremental SPF is displayed in the show ip ospf output

R1(config)# do show ip ospf | i Incremental
 Incremental-SPF disabled
R1(config)# router ospf 1
R1(config-router)# ispf
R1(config-router)# do show ip ospf | i Incremental
 Incremental-SPF enabled
R1(config-router)#
```

## OSPFv2 Prefix Suppression

In large and densely interconnected networks, a significant amount of space in LSDBs and resulting routing tables is occupied by transit link prefixes—that is, IP networks on inter-router links without end hosts. Most communication, however, occurs between end hosts located in nontransit networks. Also, for remote management purposes, network devices such as routers, switches, or access points are either assigned a loopback address that is subsequently advertised in OSPF, or they are located in a standalone management or other dedicated LAN/VLAN that can also be considered a nontransit network. Therefore, maintaining the transit link prefixes in LSDBs and routing tables is, at least from the connectivity standpoint, largely useless. Not advertising these prefixes can possibly save a significant amount of memory and CPU cycles without impairing the network connectivity.

RFC 6860 defines a method of hiding, or suppressing, the transit link prefixes in OSPF. Because OSPFv2 combines topology and addressing information in type 1 and 2 LSAs, meaning that some of the addressing information must be maintained in these LSAs (otherwise it would be impossible to construct them), the means of suppressing transit link prefixes are different for type 1 and for type 2 LSAs. Keep in mind that the goal of this mechanism is to suppress transit link *prefixes*, that is, the IP network addresses used on these links, not the transit links themselves. Transit links describe the connections between routers and must continue to be advertised; otherwise, SPF would be unable to construct the shortest-path tree.

Recall that a type 1 LSA describes a router and its adjacencies (links) to its neighboring objects. There are four possible link types that can be described by a type 1 LSA:

- **Point-to-point link to another router:** This is a transit link pointing toward the other router's RID. It contains no addressing information and will not be influenced by the prefix suppression mechanism.

- **Link to a transit network:** This is a transit link pointing toward the transit network's DR IP address. While it refers to an IP address of the DR, it contains no further addressing information such as network mask, and will not be influenced by the prefix suppression mechanism.

- **Stub network:** This entry describes the IP prefix used either in a true stub network or a prefix used on a point-to-point link to another router. A router can suppress all stub network entries in a type 1 LSA that correspond to IP prefixes used on point-to-point links.

- **Virtual link:** This is a virtual transit point-to-point link pointing toward a virtually adjacent router's RID. It contains no addressing information and will not be influenced by the prefix suppression mechanism.

Therefore, in type 1 LSAs, suppressing the transit link prefixes is accomplished by *omitting* stub network entries that contain prefixes on point-to-point interfaces to other routers.

Type 2 LSAs are somewhat more cumbersome to tweak. These LSAs describe a transit multiaccess network and all connected routers, and they include information from which the IP prefix used in this network can be calculated. Specifically, the Link State ID of a type 2 LSA is set to the IP address of the DR in the network, and the LSA body contains, among others, the network subnet mask. The IP prefix of the network can be computed by bitwise ANDing the Link State ID of the LSA and the netmask carried in its payload. Neither of these two fields can be removed from the type 2 LSA without making its format incompatible. Therefore, RFC 6860 uses a different approach: It suggests setting the netmask field to the value of 255.255.255.255—clearly an invalid mask for a multiaccess transit network. To routers that implement RFC 6860, a type 2 LSA advertising the netmask of 255.255.255.255 is a signal that the LSA contains no IP prefix information. Routers not implementing this RFC will install a host route toward that network's DR. While the advantage of saving routing table space is lost on such routers, no interoperability issues will be introduced. The support for prefix suppression can therefore be introduced gradually.

OSPFv3 has different LSA semantics; therefore, the prefix suppression in OSPFv3 works in a different manner, yet the results are identical. The differences will be explained later in the section "OSPFv3."

For OSPFv2, the prefix suppression can be activated for the entire router very easily by simply entering the **prefix-suppression** command in **router ospf** mode. This command will cause the router to suppress all prefixes on all its OSPF-enabled interfaces *except* loopbacks, secondary IP addresses, and prefixes on passive interfaces. Such prefixes are considered nontransit prefixes. The prefix suppression can also be configured on a per-interface basis using the **ip ospf prefix-suppression** interface command. Should a particular interface prefix be advertised even if the prefix suppression is activated globally, the interface can be exempted by using the **ip ospf prefix-suppression disable** command.

## OSPF Stub Router Configuration

First defined in RFC 3137 (now obsoleted by RFC 6987), and supported since Cisco IOS Software Release 12.2(4)T onward, the OSPF *stub router* feature (not to be confused with stubby areas) allows a router to either temporarily or permanently be prevented from becoming a transit router. In this context, a transit router is simply one to which packets are forwarded, with the expectation that the transit router will forward the packet to yet another router. Conversely, nontransit routers only forward packets to and from locally attached subnets.

Figure 9-12 shows one typical case in which a stub router might be useful.

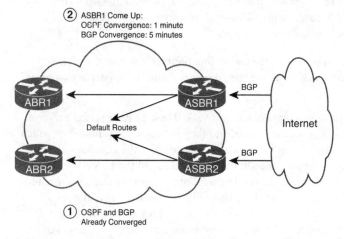

**Figure 9-12** *OSPF Stub Router*

Both ASBR1 and ASBR2 advertise defaults into the network, expecting to have the capability to route to the Internet through BGP-learned routes. In this case, ASBR2 is already up and fully converged. However, if ASBR1 reloads, when it comes back up, OSPF is likely to converge faster than BGP. As a result, ASBR1 will advertise its default route, and OSPF routers might send packets to ASBR1, but ASBR1 will end up discarding or misrouting the packets until BGP converges.

Using the stub router feature on the ASBRs solves the problem by making them advertise their own type 1 LSAs with an infinite metric (cost 16,777,215) for all transit-type adjacencies (point-to-point links, transit network links, virtual links); stub network adjacencies will continue to be advertised with their real interface metrics. This infinite metric can be advertised either for a configured time period or until BGP convergence is complete. To do so, under **router ospf**, the ASBRs would use either the **max-metric router-lsa on-startup** *announce-time* command or the **max-metric router-lsa on-startup wait-for-bgp** command. With the first version, the actual time period (in seconds) can be set. With the second, OSPF waits until BGP signals that convergence is complete or until 10 minutes pass, whichever comes first.

## OSPF Graceful Restart

In steady-state operation, OSPF can react to changes in the routing domain and reconverge quickly. This is one of OSPF's strengths as an interior gateway protocol (IGP). However, what happens when something goes really wrong is just as important as how things work under relatively stable conditions.

One of those "really wrong" things that sometimes happens is that a router requires a restart to its OSPF software process. Problems arising from this restart range from temporary outages in network connectivity to temporary routing loops. Considering that certain router platforms can continue to forward packets even while they restart, RFC 3623 describes a technique called Graceful OSPF Restart (GR) that allows a router to restart while its neighbors continue to forward packets to the restarting router as if it was up and running. This approach is sometimes called "routing through a failure," as opposed to "routing around a failure," which would be the usual OSPF's response to a router going down. Cisco implemented its own version of graceful restart in Cisco IOS prior to RFC 3623 that is called Non Stop Forwarding (NSF); as a result, Cisco IOS supports both NSF and GR versions of this feature. Nonetheless, to keep the differences in the CLI minimal, both NSF and GR are configured using **nsf** commands.

**Key Topic**

Two classes of devices are involved in GR/NSF. The router undergoing the graceful restart is said to be in the graceful *restart mode* (or simply in the restarting mode). Its directly connected neighbors are said to be in the *helper mode* during the graceful restart. Helper neighbors have important responsibilities during a router's graceful restart: In the absence of other changes to the LSDB, they must ignore its lack of Hellos for an indicated grace period, continue to consider it fully adjacent and report it as fully adjacent in their type 1 and 2 LSAs, and continue to consider it a DR for the segment if it was elected as the DR before the graceful restart. In a way, helper neighbors assist in pretending that the router undergoing a graceful restart is up and running. Every router can act as a helper provided that the support is available in the IOS. However, only routers with specific hardware support can perform the graceful restart themselves because of the obvious need to have forwarding hardware autonomous and independent from the main CPU. Therefore, Cisco uses two specific terms when talking about GR/NSF support: *NSF-aware* devices, which can act only as helper devices, and *NSF-capable* devices, which can act both as helpers and can also perform a graceful restart themselves. The NSF awareness is generally available across many IOS versions, even on low-end routers. NSF-capable devices are platforms such as Catalyst 6500 switches; router Series 7200, 7300, 7600, 10000, and 12000; ASR; and CRS.

Graceful restart takes advantage of the fact that modern router architectures use separate control and forwarding planes. It is possible to continue forwarding without loops while the routing process restarts, assuming that the following conditions are true:

- The router's hardware construction allows the control element, such as the CPU, the supervisor, or the route processor, to restart while the line cards continue to forward packets based on the last version of their forwarding database.

- The router whose OSPF process is restarting must notify its neighbors that the restart is going to take place by sending a "grace LSA," which is a type 9 opaque LSA with link-local flooding scope, containing the estimated duration of restart (the grace period), the reason of the restart, and on multiaccess networks, the IP address of the restarting router.

- The LSA database remains stable during the restart.

- All the neighbors support, and are configured for, graceful restart helper mode.

- The restart takes place within a specific grace period.

- During restart, the neighboring fully adjacent routers must operate in helper mode.

In Cisco devices, Cisco Express Forwarding (CEF), especially its hardware embodiment in multilayer switches and high-end routers, handles forwarding during graceful restart while OSPF rebuilds the RIB tables, provided that the preceding conditions are met. Both Cisco and IETF NSF awareness are enabled by default in Cisco IOS. Disabling it requires a routing process command for each NSF version, **nsf [cisco | ietf] helper disable**.

## OSPF Graceful Shutdown

In certain situations, it is necessary to take a router out of service while causing as little disruption as possible. This can be accomplished by a feature called Graceful Shutdown. The Graceful Shutdown feature allows an OSPF process to update the neighbors that the router is going down. Using a simple **shutdown** command in the **router ospf** mode, the router will immediately

- Drop all OSPF adjacencies

- Flush all LSAs it has originated (flood them with the age set to 3600 seconds)

- Send out Hello packets to its neighbors with the DR/BDR fields set to 0.0.0.0 and an empty neighbor list, prompting the neighbors' adjacency states to fall back to the Init state

- Stop sending and receiving OSPF packets

The Graceful Shutdown feature can also be configured on a per-interface basis using the **ip ospf shutdown** command. In that case, the procedure is slightly modified—the router will immediately

- Drop all OSPF adjacencies over that particular interface

- Flood updated LSAs that no longer include that particular interface and adjacencies through other interfaces, if any

- Send out Hellos over that particular interface to its neighbors with the DR/BDR fields set to 0.0.0.0 and an empty neighbor list, prompting the neighbors' adjacency states to fall back to the Init state

- Stop sending and receiving OSPF packets over that particular interface

Reverting to Graceful Shutdown can be accomplished by removing the **shutdown** or the **ip ospf shutdown** command from the configuration.

At the time of this writing, selected IOS versions have the **shutdown** command available in the **router ospf** configuration mode, but the command appears to be ineffective. When experimenting with this feature, make sure to use a recent IOS.

# OSPFv3

The good news about OSPFv3 is that OSPFv2 was a mature routing protocol when development began on OSPFv3. The bad news about OSPFv3 is that it is more complex in some ways than OSPFv2. But mostly the two protocols are simply *different* because of the differences in the underlying Layer 3 protocol. Fortunately, RFC 5340, which defines OSPFv3, goes into quite a bit of detail in describing these differences. (And this RFC is well worth a read to gain a better understanding of OSPFv3 than this chapter can provide.)

## Differences Between OSPFv2 and OSPFv3

OSPFv2 and OSPFv3 share many key concepts, including most of their basic operations and the concepts of neighbor relationships, areas, interface types, virtual links, metric calculations, and many others. However, you should understand the significant differences as well.

Key differences between OSPFv2 and OSPFv3 include the following:

- **Configured using interface commands:** Cisco IOS enables OSPFv3 using interface subcommands, instead of using the OSPFv2 method (using the **network** command in router configuration mode). To enable OSPFv3 process ID (PID) 1 and area 2 on a given interface, the basic command is simply **ipv6 ospf 1 area 2**. Issuing this command also creates the **ipv6 router ospf 1** command in global configuration mode.

- **Advertising multiple networks on an interface:** If multiple IPv6 addresses are configured on an interface, OSPFv3 advertises all the corresponding networks.

- **OSPFv3 RID must be set:** OSPFv3 can automatically set its 32-bit RID based on the configured IPv4 addresses, using the same rules for OSPFv2. If no IPv4 addresses are configured, however, OSPFv3 cannot automatically choose its RID. You must manually configure the RID before OSPFv3 will start. By comparison, an OSPFv2 RID is created automatically if any IP interfaces are configured on a router.

- **Flooding scope:** The scope for flooding LSAs is one of three specific types in OSPFv3:

  - **Link-local scope:** Used by the new LSA type, Link LSA.

  - **Area scope:** For LSAs flooded throughout a single OSPFv3 area. Used by Router, Network, Inter-Area Prefix, Inter-Area Router, and Intra-Area Prefix LSA types.

  - **AS scope:** LSAs of this type are flooded throughout the routing domain; this is used for AS External LSAs.

- **Multiple instances per link:** OSPFv3 supports multiple instances on a link. For example, suppose that you have four routers on an Ethernet segment: Routers A, B, 1, and 2. You want Routers A and B to form adjacencies (become neighbors), and Routers 1 and 2 to become neighbors, but you do not want Routers A and B to form neighborships with Routers 1 and 2. OSPFv3 supports this type of adjacency scoping. The range of instance numbers is 0–255, and the command format on the interface is, for example, **ipv6 ospf 1 area 0 instance 33**. The instance must match on all routers that are to become adjacent on a link.

■ **Terminology:** OSPFv3 uses the term *link* for what OSPFv2 calls a *network.*

■ **Sources packets from link-local addresses:** With the exception of virtual links, OSPFv3 uses link-local addresses for all communications between neighbors and sources packets from link-local addresses. On virtual links, OSPFv3 sources packets from a globally scoped IPv6 address.

■ **Authentication:** OSPFv2 natively supports three authentication types: null, simple password, and MD5. OSPFv3, however, does not itself provide authentication, because IPv6 covers this requirement with its internal support for AH and ESP protocols, as described in more detail later in this chapter.

■ **Networks in LSAs:** Whereas OSPFv2 expresses networks in LSAs as [address, mask], OSPFv3 expresses networks in LSAs as [prefix, prefix length]. The default route is expressed with a prefix length of 0.

## Virtual Links, Address Summarization, and Other OSPFv3 Features

Many OSPFv3 features are conceptually identical to OSPFv2 and differ only slightly in their configuration. Some of these features include the following:

■ Virtual links (which point to router IDs)

■ Address summarization by area

■ Address summarization in the routing process

■ Stub area configuration

■ NSSA configuration

■ Advertising, or not advertising, a summary using the **area range** [**advertise** | **not-advertise**] command

■ OSPF network types and interface configuration

■ Router priority configuration for multiaccess networks, to influence DR and BDR elections

■ Most OSPF **show** commands

## OSPFv3 LSA Types

Most LSA functionality in OSPFv3 is the same as that in OSPFv2, with a few changes in the LSA names. In addition, OSPFv3 has two additional LSA types. Table 9-10 briefly describes each of the LSA types in OSPFv3. Compare this table to Table 9-4 for a better perspective on how OSPFv2 and OSPFv3 LSA types are similar to and different from each other. Note that OSPFv3 LSA types are basically the same as OSPFv2 LSAs, except for their slightly different names and the additions of type 8 and 9 LSAs to OSPFv3.

**Table 9-10**  *OSPFv3 LSA Types*

| LSA Type | Common Name | Description | Flooding Scope |
|---|---|---|---|
| 1 | Router LSA | Describes a router and its links to its neighboring objects within one area. | Area |
| 2 | Network LSA | Generated by a DR to represent the multiaccess transit network and its connection to member routers. | Area |
| 3 | Inter-Area Prefix LSA | Originated by ABRs to describe inter-area networks in other areas. | Area |
| 4 | Inter-Area Router LSA | Originated by ABRs to advertise the existence of ASBRs in other areas. | Area |
| 5 | Autonomous System External LSA | Originated by an ASBR in a regular area to describe networks learned from other protocols (redistributed routes). | Autonomous System |
| 7 | NSSA LSA | Originated by an ASBR in an NSSA to describe networks learned from other protocols (redistributed routes). | Area |
| 8 | Link LSA | Advertises link-local address and prefix(es) of a router to all other routers on the link, as well as option information. Sent only if more than one router is present on a link. | Link |
| 9 | Intra-Area-Prefix LSA | Performs one of two functions:<br>■ Associates a list of IPv6 prefixes with a transit network by pointing to a Network LSA.<br>■ Associates a list of IPv6 prefixes with a router by pointing to a Router LSA. | Area |

LSA types 8 and 9 require a closer discussion. In OSPFv2, type 1 and 2 LSAs combine together topology and address semantics—a single LSA both describes a part of the topology (what is connected to whom) and the addresses being used in that part of the topology. If an address changes on a router, new type 1 and possibly type 2 LSAs have to be flooded. To other routers, these updated LSAs are indistinguishable from a topology change in which the router with the previous addresses "went away" and a new router with the new addresses "came in." As a result, all other routers will recompute the short-est-path tree, even though the network has stayed the same and the shortest-path tree has not changed; just the addressing was modified. OSPFv2 does not provide for clear separation of addressing and topology information, and as a result, the SPF is run more often than actually necessary.

OSPFv3 creators took their lesson and as they designed the new protocol, they decided to take the addressing information out from type 1 and 2 LSAs and move it to new, separate LSA types. This is how type 8 and 9 LSAs came to be. In OSPFv3, the type 1 and 2 LSAs no longer carry any addressing information. They only carry a description of topology adjacencies—what other object is a router or a multiaccess network connected to, using router RIDs as an address-independent way of referring to a neighboring object. IPv6 prefixes on individual interfaces of a router are carried in a type 9 LSA (Intra-Area-Prefix LSA) with the area flooding scope. Moreover, as IPv6 unicast routing uses link-local addresses as next-hop addresses, each router advertises its link-local address in a type 8 LSA (Link LSA) sent out the particular interface. Type 8 LSAs have the link flooding scope and are never flooded beyond the receiving neighbor on the link. Carrying the interface link-local addresses in type 9 LSAs would expose them to all routers in an area; while not harmful, it would be a waste of resources.

With this separation of topology and addressing information, OSPFv3 is significantly more efficient when it comes to scheduling an SPF run. If an interface address changes, only an updated Link LSA and Intra-Area-Prefix LSA will be originated and flooded. Because there is no change to the topology itself, type 1 and 2 LSAs will not change. Therefore, routers do not need to schedule a new SPF run but merely update the prefixes located in an already computed shortest-path tree. Only updated type 1 or 2 LSAs will trigger a new SPF.

## OSPFv3 in NBMA Networks

OSPFv3 operates in NBMA networks almost exactly like OSPFv2. In particular, each interface has an OSPF network type, with that network type dictating whether OSPFv3 needs to use a DR/BDR and whether at least one router needs to have an OSPF **neighbor** command configured. For example, when configuring Frame Relay with the IPv6 address on a physical interface or multipoint subinterface, the OSPF network type defaults to "nonbroadcast," which requires the use of a per-interface **ipv6 ospf neighbor** command:

```
R1(config-if)# ipv6 ospf neighbor fe80::1
```

Note that the address in the command must be a link-local address of the neighbor; other addresses will be rejected.

OSPFv3 neighbor relationships over NBMA networks take a relatively long time to form (a minute or two), even on high-speed media, as they do in OSPFv2. This delay can lead to confusion and can cause you to spend time troubleshooting a nonproblem.

Invariably, at some point in your studies (or lab exams), you will configure OSPFv2 or v3 over an NBMA network and forget to include a **neighbor** statement. As a result, neighbors will not form and you will have to troubleshoot the problem. A useful crutch you can use to help you remember that NBMA OSPF peers require **neighbor** statements is the saying, "*n*onbroadcast *n*eeds *n*eighbors."

For completeness, you should be aware that it is possible to get OSPF neighbors to form over an NBMA network without **neighbor** statements, if you change the interfaces' network types from their defaults. This is done using the **ipv6 ospf network** interface command, as it is in IPv4. The same rules apply for IPv6.

## Configuring OSPFv3 over Frame Relay

In IPv4 Frame Relay networks, you are likely to be familiar with mapping IP addresses to data-link connection identifier (DLCI) numbers. The configuration of **frame-relay map** statements is much the same in IPv6, but there are a couple of twists: First, there is no InverseARP for IPv6. All IPv6/DLCI mappings therefore have to be configured manually. Second, the mappings must be created both for the link-local and the global addresses of the neighbor's interface. Only the link-local mapping statement requires the **broadcast** keyword, though (and if a nonbroadcast or point-to-multipoint nonbroadcast network type is used, the **broadcast** keyword is not necessary). In Example 9-18, the far-end interface's IPv6 unicast address is 2001::207:85FF:FE80:7208 and its link-local address is FE80::207:85FF:FE80:7208. The DLCI number is 708.

**Example 9-18**  *Frame Relay Mapping for IPv6*

```
R1(config-if)# frame-relay map ipv6 FE80::207:85FF:FE80:7208 708 broadcast
R1(config-if)# frame-relay map ipv6 2001::207:85FF:FE80:7208 708
```

If you configure only the link-local mapping, OSPFv3 will be happy. The neighbors will come up, the routers will become fully adjacent, and their routing tables will fully populate, and even routing across the Frame Relay cloud will work, as the next hop is the link-local address of the appropriate neighbor. However, if you tried to contact the global IPv6 address of a neighbor, it would fail because of Frame Relay encapsulation failures.

As default link-local addresses derived by a modified EUI-64 procedure are strongly inconvenient to use, you might want to consider redefining the link-local addresses on the serial interfaces to some simple values, that is, FE80::1, FE80::2, and so on for individual routers using the **ipv6 address** *link-local-address* **link-local** interface command, and using them instead. During the Lab Exam, however, make sure that this modification is permitted.

## Enabling and Configuring OSPFv3

Enabling OSPFv3 on a Cisco router is straightforward if you have a good grasp of OSPFv2. After basic IPv6 addressing and reachability are configured and working, the OSPFv3 configuration process includes these steps:

**Step 1.**  Identify the desired links connected to each OSPFv3 router.

**Step 2.**  Determine the OSPF area design and the area to which each router link (interface) should belong.

**Step 3.**  Identify any special OSPF routing requirements, such as stub areas, address summarization, LSA filtering, and virtual links.

**Step 4.**   Configure OSPF on the interfaces.

**Step 5.**   Configure routing process commands, including a router ID on IPv6-only routers.

**Step 6.**   Verify OSPF configuration, routing tables, and reachability.

Figure 9-13 shows the network layout for this basic OSPFv3 routing example. Configuration details follow in Examples 9-19 and 9-20.

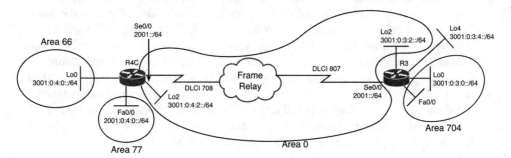

**Figure 9-13**   *Topology for Basic OSPFv3 Routing Configuration Examples 9-19 and 9-20*

**Example 9-19**   *Configuring OSPFv3 on Router R3*

```
R3# show run
Building configuration...
! Lines omitted for brevity
!
! IPv6 unicast routing must be enabled to configure IPv6 features:

ipv6 unicast-routing
ipv6 cef
!
interface Loopback0
 no ip address

! IPv6 addresses are assigned to each OSPFv3 interface:

 ipv6 address 3001:0:3::/64 eui-64

! Next OSPFv3 is enabled on the interface and the interface is assigned to an area:

 ipv6 ospf 1 area 704

! IPv6 OSPFv3 draws its router ID from the IPv4 loopback address on
! interface Loopback 1:

interface Loopback1
```

```
 ip address 10.3.3.6 255.255.255.0
!
interface Loopback2
 no ip address
 ipv6 address 3001:0:3:2::/64 eui-64

! Like IPv4, setting the network type of a loopback address to point-to-point
! makes the route to this loopback appear in R4C's routing table as a /64
! network rather than as a /128 network (a host route):

 ipv6 ospf network point-to-point
 ipv6 ospf 1 area 0

! Note that interface Loopback 4 will be added later. Its use will be covered
! in another example later in this chapter.

interface FastEthernet0/0
 no ip address
 speed auto

! Assign an IPv6 address and perform OSPFv3 configuration on the interface:

 ipv6 address 2001:0:3::/64 eui-64
 ipv6 ospf 1 area 704
!
interface Serial0/0
 bandwidth 128
 no ip address
 encapsulation frame-relay

! On the serial interface, first configure the IPv6 address:
 ipv6 address 2001::/64 eui-64

! Next must specify a neighbor, because the interface is
! NBMA (Frame Relay in this case).
! Like OSPFv2, OSPFv3 in Cisco IOS requires a neighbor statement at
! only one end of the link:

 ipv6 ospf neighbor FE80::207:85FF:FE80:71B8
 ipv6 ospf 1 area 0
 clock rate 128000
 no fair-queue
 cdp enable
```

```
! Because this is a frame-relay interface, map the link-local address of
! the next hop. This allows OSPFv3 neighbors to form:

 frame-relay map ipv6 FE80::207:85FF:FE80:71B8 807 broadcast

! Next, add a frame-relay map statement to the unicast address of
! the next hop on the serial link so that unicast IPv6 packets will
! reach their destination:

 frame-relay map ipv6 2001::207:85FF:FE80:71B8 807

! The ipv6 router ospf 1 global commands are created when OSPFv3 is
! enabled on the first interface:

ipv6 router ospf 1
 log-adjacency-changes
! Lines omitted for brevity
R3#
```

**Example 9-20**  *Configuring OSPFv3 on Router R4C*

```
R4C# show run
Building configuration...
! Lines omitted for brevity
ipv6 unicast-routing
ipv6 cef
!
interface Loopback0
 no ip address
 ipv6 address 3001:0:4::/64 eui-64
 ipv6 ospf 1 area 66
!
interface Loopback2
 no ip address
 ipv6 address 3001:0:4:2::/64 eui-64

! Like IPv4, setting the network type of a loopback address to point-to-point
! makes the route to this loopback appear in R3's routing table as a /64
! network rather than as a /128 network (a host route):

 ipv6 ospf network point-to-point
 ipv6 ospf 1 area 0
!
interface FastEthernet0/0
 no ip address
 speed 100
```

```
 full-duplex
 ipv6 address 2001:0:4::/64 eui-64
 ipv6 ospf 1 area 77
!
interface Serial0/0
 bandwidth 128
 no ip address
 encapsulation frame-relay

! Because the other neighbor has the neighbor statement, this side doesn't need
! one.

 ipv6 address 2001::/64 eui-64
 ipv6 ospf 1 area 0
 clock rate 128000
 no fair-queue
 cdp enable

! Here again, two frame-relay map statements are required:

 frame-relay map ipv6 FE80::207:85FF:FE80:7208 708 broadcast
 frame-relay map ipv6 2001::207:85FF:FE80:7208 708
!
ipv6 router ospf 1
! Here, we must specify the OSPFv3 router ID, because this router
! has no IPv4 interfaces:

 router-id 99.99.99.99
 log-adjacency-changes
! Lines omitted for brevity
R4C#
```

Note that this example configures several OSPF areas, so both intra-area and inter-area routes appear in the OSPFv3 routing tables. Routes with different network sizes and metrics will also be present. Example 9-21 confirms the OSPFv3 routing configuration by using **show** commands and ping tests.

**Example 9-21**   *Verifying OSPFv3 Configuration and Reachability*

```
! The show ipv6 interface brief command displays both
! the unicast and link-local addresses,
! which is useful during ping and traceroute testing:

R3# show ipv6 interface brief
FastEthernet0/0             [up/up]
    FE80::207:85FF:FE80:7208
    2001:0:3:0:207:85FF:FE80:7208
```

```
Serial0/0                     [up/up]
    FE80::207:85FF:FE80:7208
    2001::207:85FF:FE80:7208
Loopback0                     [up/up]
    FE80::207:85FF:FE80:7208
    3001:0:3:0:207:85FF:FE80:7208
Loopback1                     [up/up]
Loopback2                     [up/up]
    FE80::207:85FF:FE80:7208
    3001:0:3:2:207:85FF:FE80:7208
Loopback4                     [up/up]
    FE80::207:85FF:FE80:7208
    3001:0:3:4:207:85FF:FE80:7208
R3#

! The show ipv6 protocols command gives the best summary of
! OSPFv3 configuration by interface and OSPF area:

R3# show ipv6 protocols
IPv6 Routing Protocol is "connected"
IPv6 Routing Protocol is "static"
IPv6 Routing Protocol is "ospf 1"
  Interfaces (Area 0):
    Loopback2
    Serial0/0
  Interfaces (Area 704):
    Loopback0
    FastEthernet0/0
R3#

! Next we'll look at the OSPFv3 interfaces in more
! detail to view the corresponding settings:

R3# show ipv6 ospf interface
Loopback2 is up, line protocol is up
  Link Local Address FE80::207:85FF:FE80:7208, Interface ID 10
  Area 0, Process ID 1, Instance ID 0, Router ID 10.3.3.6
  Network Type POINT_TO_POINT, Cost: 1
  Transmit Delay is 1 sec, State POINT_TO_POINT,
  Timer intervals configured, Hello 10, Dead 40, Wait 40, Retransmit 5
  Index 1/1/4, flood queue length 0
  Next 0x0(0)/0x0(0)/0x0(0)
  Last flood scan length is 0, maximum is 0
  Last flood scan time is 0 msec, maximum is 0 msec
  Neighbor Count is 0, Adjacent neighbor count is 0
  Suppress hello for 0 neighbor(s)
```

```
Serial0/0 is up, line protocol is up
  Link Local Address FE80::207:85FF:FE80:7208, Interface ID 3
  Area 0, Process ID 1, Instance ID 0, Router ID 10.3.3.6
  Network Type NON_BROADCAST, Cost: 781
  Transmit Delay is 1 sec, State DR, Priority 1
  Designated Router (ID) 10.3.3.6, local address FE80::207:85FF:FE80:7208
  Backup Designated router (ID) 99.99.99.99, local address
    FE80::207:85FF:FE80:71B8
  Timer intervals configured, Hello 30, Dead 120, Wait 120, Retransmit 5
    Hello due in 00:00:05
  Index 1/3/3, flood queue length 0
  Next 0x0(0)/0x0(0)/0x0(0)
  Last flood scan length is 1, maximum is 6
  Last flood scan time is 0 msec, maximum is 0 msec
  Neighbor Count is 1, Adjacent neighbor count is 1
    Adjacent with neighbor 99.99.99.99  (Backup Designated Router)
  Suppress hello for 0 neighbor(s)
Loopback0 is up, line protocol is up
  Link Local Address FE80::207:85FF:FE80:7208, Interface ID 8
  Area 704, Process ID 1, Instance ID 0, Router ID 10.3.3.6
  Network Type LOOPBACK, Cost: 1
  Loopback interface is treated as a stub Host
FastEthernet0/0 is up, line protocol is up
  Link Local Address FE80::207:85FF:FE80:7208, Interface ID 2
  Area 704, Process ID 1, Instance ID 0, Router ID 10.3.3.6
  Network Type BROADCAST, Cost: 1
  Transmit Delay is 1 sec, State DR, Priority 1
  Designated Router (ID) 10.3.3.6, local address FE80::207:85FF:FE80:7208
  No backup designated router on this network
  Timer intervals configured, Hello 10, Dead 40, Wait 40, Retransmit 5
    Hello due in 00:00:06
  Index 1/1/1, flood queue length 0
  Next 0x0(0)/0x0(0)/0x0(0)
  Last flood scan length is 0, maximum is 0
  Last flood scan time is 0 msec, maximum is 0 msec
  Neighbor Count is 0, Adjacent neighbor count is 0
  Suppress hello for 0 neighbor(s)
R3#

! Now let's take a look at the IPv6 routing table's OSPF routes.
! Note the presence of two inter-area routes and one intra-area route.
! The intra-area route points to Loopback 0 on R4C, which is a /128 (host)
! route because Lo0 has the default network type for a loopback interface.
! The others are /64 routes because of their network types.

R3# show ipv6 route ospf
```

```
IPv6 Routing Table - 15 entries
Codes: C - Connected, L - Local, S - Static, R - RIP, B - BGP
       U - Per-user Static route
       I1 - ISIS L1, I2 - ISIS L2, IA - ISIS interarea, IS - ISIS summary
       O - OSPF intra, OI - OSPF inter, OE1 - OSPF ext 1, OE2 - OSPF ext 2
       ON1 - OSPF NSSA ext 1, ON2 - OSPF NSSA ext 2
       D   EIGRP, EX - EIGRP external
OI  2001:0:4::/64 [110/782]
     via FE80::207:85FF:FE80:71B8, Serial0/0
OI  3001:0:4::/64 [110/782]
     via FE80::207:85FF:FE80:71B8, Serial0/0
O   3001:0:4:2:207:85FF:FE80:71B8/128 [110/781]
     via FE80::207:85FF:FE80:71B8, Serial0/0
R3#


! A ping test proves reachability to an address on an inter-area route:


R3# ping 3001:0:4:2:207:85FF:FE80:71B8
Type escape sequence to abort.
Sending 5, 100-byte ICMP Echos to 3001:0:4:2:207:85FF:FE80:71B8,
    timeout is 2 seconds:
!!!!!
Success rate is 100 percent (5/5), round-trip min/avg/max = 28/29/32 ms
R3#
```

Next, Example 9-22 shows redistributing a new loopback interface into OSPFv3 on R3, filtered through a route map, to see the effect on R4C's routing table. Note the similarity in command syntax and output to OSPFv2.

**Example 9-22** *Redistributing a Connected Interface into OSPFv3*

```
! First create the Loopback 4 interface on R3:


R3# conf t
R3(config)# interface Loopback4
R3(config-if)# ipv6 address 3001:0:3:4::/64 eui-64


! Next, create a route map to select only this new
! loopback interface for redistribution:


R3(config-if)# route-map Con2OSPFv3
R3(config-route-map)# route-map Con2OSPFv3 permit 10
R3(config-route-map)# match interface loopback 4
R3(config-route-map)# exit
R3(config)# ipv6 router ospf 1
R3(config-rtr)# redistribute connected route-map Con2OSPFv3
R3(config-rtr)# end
```

```
R3# show ipv6 protocols
IPv6 Routing Protocol is "connected"
IPv6 Routing Protocol is "static"
IPv6 Routing Protocol is "ospf 1"
  Interfaces (Area 0):
   Loopback2
   Serial0/0
  Interfaces (Area 704):
   Loopback0
   FastEthernet0/0
  Redistribution:
   Redistributing protocol connected route-map Con2OSPFv3
R3#


! On R4 the new redistributed route on R3 appears as an OE2 route, because
! type E2 is the default for redistributed routes, and the default
! metric is 20, as in OSPFv2.

R4C# show ipv6 route ospf
IPv6 Routing Table - 14 entries
Codes: C - Connected, L - Local, S - Static, R - RIP, B - BGP
       U - Per-user Static route
       I1 - ISIS L1, I2 - ISIS L2, IA - ISIS interarea, IS - ISIS summary
       O - OSPF intra, OI - OSPF inter, OE1 - OSPF ext 1, OE2 - OSPF ext 2
       ON1 - OSPF NSSA ext 1, ON2 - OSPF NSSA ext 2
       D - EIGRP, EX - EIGRP external
OI  2001:0:3::/64 [110/782]
     via FE80::207:85FF:FE80:7208, Serial0/0
OI  3001:0:3:0:207:85FF:FE80:7208/128 [110/781]
     via FE80::207:85FF:FE80:7208, Serial0/0
O   3001:0:3:2::/64 [110/782]
     via FE80::207:85FF:FE80:7208, Serial0/0
OE2 3001:0:3:4::/64 [110/20]
     via FE80::207:85FF:FE80:7208, Serial0/0
R4C#


! Finally, verify reachability to the redistributed loopback interface:

R4C# ping 3001:0:3:4:207:85FF:FE80:7208
Type escape sequence to abort.
Sending 5, 100-byte ICMP Echos to 30001:0:3:4:207:85FF:FE80:7208, timeout is 2
  seconds:
!!!!!
Success rate is 100 percent (5/5), round-trip min/avg/max = 28/29/33 ms
R4C#
```

## OSPFv3 Authentication and Encryption

One area in which OSPFv3 is arguably simpler than OSPFv2, at the protocol operation level, is that it uses IPv6's native authentication support rather than implementing its own authentication mechanisms. OSPFv3 uses Authentication Header (AH), beginning with Cisco IOS Release 12.3(4)T, and Encapsulating Security Payload (ESP) protocols for authentication, beginning with Cisco IOS Release 12.4(9)T. Both of these features require a Crypto feature set in the router.

To enable IPv6 OSPF authentication using AH, issue the **ipv6 ospf authentication** command. To enable encryption using ESP, issue the **ipv6 ospf encryption** command. These are interface configuration commands. While regular IPsec allows combining AH and ESP, the use of authentication and encryption is mutually exclusive with OSPFv3 on a single interface—if you configure **ipv6 ospf authentication**, you cannot add **ipv6 ospf encryption** and vice versa. Note that ESP provides both encryption and authentication, so use of ESP is generally preferred.

Configuring OSPFv3 authentication or encryption requires selecting cryptographic algorithms for hashing or encryption, and supplying keys of appropriate length that are used during hashing (IPsec uses keyed hashing) and encryption. Together, the selected mode of operation plus the cryptographic algorithms and keys form a so-called security association that defines how packets should be protected by IPsec. A security association is identified by a number called the Security Parameter Index (SPI). Each OSPFv3 packet protected by IPsec carries the SPI number of the security association used to protect it, and the receiving router uses the SPI to identify the security association to process the packet to decrypt and authenticate it. While in common IPsec deployments, security associations are negotiated by the ISAKMP/IKE protocol, with OSPFv3, all these parameters must be specified manually and must match on all routers that mutually authenticate themselves or encrypt OSPFv3 packets sent to each other. In the Example 9-23, use of per-area and per-interface commands to configure encryption or authentication is shown; the authentication or encryption configured on an interface overrides the per-area configuration.

**Example 9-23** *Configuring IPsec Protection of OSPFv3*

```
! It is assumed that IPv6 and OSPFv3 have already been correctly configured on this
! router, therefore only the IPsec-related configuration is shown in this example
!
! The FastEthernet0/0 interface is configured with AH-based authentication

interface FastEthernet0/0
 ipv6 ospf auth ipsec spi 1000 sha1 8E63C2FF7E2997D7D26FD80E047C43A7FEEA9833

! The Serial1/0 interface is configured with ESP-based encryption and
! authentication. Because of the length of encryption and hashing keys, the command
! line is broken into two but in the configuration, it would be a single command
```

```
interface Serial1/0
 ipv6 ospf encryption ipsec spi 1001 esp aes-cbc 128
   DE7EC1FDF5BDC3367DB071BF090FFA2A sha1 6D8583145994287B6088A2D674E412A5F862DD5B


! Per-area configurations in OSPFv3 process 1: area 1 uses authentication,
! area 2 uses encryption and authentication. Line for area 2 is again broken into
! two

ipv6 router ospf 1
 area 1 authentication ipsec spi 1002 md5 7F0A8F0AE30CC9AB6F12E87C36D595C6
 area 2 encryption ipsec spi 1003 esp 3des
   0BEA0DDE40603346B44184599202BE5CAEE674CF26EA22C3 md5
   F93BBBB0A02512EA0565361947D0EAA1
```

It is noteworthy to mention that RFC 7166, "Supporting Authentication Trailer for OSPFv3," comes with an alternative approach to OSPFv3 authentication in a way similar to the OSPFv2 authentication, using an authentication trailer in OSPFv3 messages and not relying on IPsec infrastructure to provide authentication and encryption services. The support for this extension has been added in IOS Release 15.4(2)T and is called OSPF3 Authentication Trailer. The feature is configured in a way similar to OSPFv2 Extended Cryptographic Authentication, by defining a key chain with keys and explicit cryptographic algorithms and then referring to this key chain using the **ospfv3 authentication key-chain** *key-chain-name* interface command. The syntax of this command stems from the OSPFv3 address family mode described in the next section, but it can be used to secure OSPFv3 configured either for basic IPv6 or for address family operation. Obviously, this authentication mechanism does not provide encryption services and is not compatible with OSPFv3 IPsec-based authentication or encryption.

Here are key things to know about OSPFv3 authentication and encryption:

- OSPFv3 can use AH for authentication.

- OSPFv3 can use ESP for authentication and encryption.

- OSPFv3 can use authentication trailer for authentication.

- OSPFv3 IPsec-based authentication and encryption can be applied per area or per link (interface); per-link configuration is more secure because it creates more layers of security.

- Routers that directly exchange IPsec-protected OSPFv3 packets must use the same SPI number, AH or ESP mode, cryptographic algorithms, and keys for the encryption/decryption and authentication to succeed.

- Routers that directly exchange authentication trailer–protected OSPFv3 packets must use the same cryptographic algorithms, key IDs, and key strings for the authentication to succeed.

## OSPFv3 Address Family Support

The support of address families—a move toward OSPFv3 as a multiprotocol IGP—is a relatively new addition to OSPFv3 described in RFC 5838. When OSPFv3 was first specified, its authors made two important changes to its design in which OSPFv3 differs from OSPFv2 that ultimately made the address family support possible. First, the addressing information has been moved out from type 1 and 2 LSAs to separate LSA types 8 and 9 whose format is more flexible to carry different address formats, even though not in a single LSA because they lack an internal address family identifier. LSA types 3 (inter-area routes) and 5/7 (external routes) are also formatted similarly. Second, OSPFv3 was augmented with an instance ID that allows multiple OSPFv3 processes to communicate over the same link while remaining separate.

Authors of RFC 5838 suggested that the entire range of instance IDs can be effectively split into several categories for different address families. Table 9-11 documents this assignment.

**Table 9-11**   *Mapping of Instance IDs to Address Families*

| Instance ID Number | Address Family |
|---|---|
| 0 | Base IPv6 Unicast |
| 1–31 | IPv6 Unicast dependent on local policy |
| 32 | Base IPv6 Multicast |
| 33–63 | IPv6 Multicast dependent on local policy |
| 64 | Base IPv4 Unicast |
| 65–95 | IPv4 Unicast dependent on local policy |
| 96 | Base IPv4 Multicast |
| 97–127 | IPv4 Multicast dependent on local policy |
| 128–191 | Unassigned |
| 192–255 | Reserved for private use |

In effect, instance IDs have become address family identifiers. By reserving a range of instance IDs for particular address families, OSPFv3 can run in several instances in parallel while the instance ID will help distinguish the instances and the types of addresses that each instance advertises in its type 8 and 9 LSAs.

Multiple address family support in OSPFv3 works by OSPFv3 running a completely separate instance for each configured address family. If not specified explicitly, these instances will choose their base instance IDs automatically (0 for IPv6, 64 for IPv4), and will exchange packets, establish adjacencies, originate and flood LSAs, compute shortest-path trees, and populate routing tables completely independently of each other. There is no information shared between individual instances, even if they run under a single

OSPFv3 process. The instance ID carried in OSPFv3 packet headers will not only keep these two instances separate but will also serve as an identifier of the address family as none of the LSA types contains an internal indication of the address format.

In addition, the Options bitfield present in OSPFv3 Hellos, DD packets, and LSAs has a new AF-bit defined. This bit is set if the sending router supports the address family extension *and* the particular instance is not an IPv6 unicast instance according to Table 9-11. In other words, an OSPFv3 router supporting address families will keep this bit cleared for example IDs 0–31 that indicate IPv6 unicast address families, and will set it for all other instance IDs. If a router that sets the AF-bit for a particular (non-IPv6-unicast) instance receives an OSPFv3 packet in the same instance from a neighbor in which the AF-bit is cleared, it is an indication that the neighbor does not support address families and treats the instance just as a plain IPv6 unicast instance. As a result, the router will drop such packets and never establish an adjacency in that instance with the neighbor. Summing up this behavior, routers supporting address families will nicely establish adjacencies for an IPv6 unicast address family with non-AF-compliant neighbors running instance IDs 0–31. Beyond this range, only neighbors that mutually support address families will be able to establish an adjacency. This prevents possible traffic blackholing.

The encapsulation of OSPFv3 packets does not change with the introduction of address families. OSPFv3 packets are always encapsulated into IPv6 packets. To run OSPFv3, with or without address families, network interfaces must be configured for IPv6 operation. This is true even if running OSPFv3 in IPv4 address family mode only, advertising only IPv4 prefixes. Although LSAs will carry IPv4 prefixes, resulting OSPFv3 packets will still be encapsulated in IPv6. Also, because of the same reasons, a virtual link requires end-to-end IPv6 connectivity, which is by definition not available in non-IPv6 address families. Therefore, OSPFv3 with address families supports virtual links only for IPv6 unicast address families.

To the OSPFv3 protocol itself, the support for address families is a fairly simple extension without significantly changing any of the underlying protocol workings. The changed CLI in IOS only reflects the fact that while running a single OSPFv3 process, separate AF-related instances are started for each address family. Overall, the configuration is very similar to plain OSPFv3. Instead of an **ipv6 router ospf** section, the **router ospfv3** and appropriate **address-family** inside the **router ospfv3** section is configured. Interfaces are added by the **ospfv3** *process-id* { **ipv4** | **ipv6** } **area** *area-id* command instead of **ipv6 ospf** *process-id* **area** *area-id*. The following two examples are designed to show the differences between configuring a plain IPv4 and IPv6 OSPF (Example 9-24) and using a single OSPFv3 process with address families to accomplish the same (Example 9-25).

**Example 9-24**  *Dual OSPFv2 and OSPFv3 Configuration on a Router*

```
! This router has a number of interfaces configured with both IPv4 and IPv6.

! The usual loopback interface for OSPF RID and remote management

interface Loopback0
 ipv6 address 2001:DB8:0:FFFF::1/128
```

```
 ip address 10.255.255.1 255.255.255.255
 ipv6 ospf 1 area 0
 ip ospf 1 area 0


! An interface connected in a point-to-point fashion to a single neighboring
! router. OSPF network type is changed to point-to-point to avoid DR/BDR elections
! and LSA3 generation, saving resources and 40 seconds of waiting on link coming
! up.

interface FastEthernet0/0
 ipv6 address 2001:DB8:1:1::1/64
 ip address 10.1.1.1 255.255.255.0
 ipv6 ospf network point-to-point
 ip ospf network point-to-point
 ipv6 ospf 1 area 1
 ip ospf 1 area 1


! Another interface towards a router in the backbone area with shortened timers

interface Serial0/0/0
 ipv6 address 2001:DB8:0:1::1/64
 ip address 10.0.1.1 255.255.255.0
 ipv6 ospf hello-interval 1
 ip ospf hello-interval 1
 ipv6 ospf 1 area 0
 ip ospf 1 area 0


! Summarization for inter-area IPv4 routes

router ospf 1
 area 1 range 10.1.0.0 255.255.0.0


! Summarization for inter-area IPv6 routes

ipv6 router ospf 1
 area 1 range 2001:DB8:1::/48
```

**Example 9-25**  *Router Configured with OSPFv3 Using Address Families*

```
! The same router configured with OSPFv3 and address family support

! The usual loopback interface for OSPF RID and remote management

interface Loopback0
 ipv6 address 2001:DB8:0:FFFF::1/128
 ip address 10.255.255.1 255.255.255.255
```

```
 ospfv3 1 ipv6 area 0
 ospfv3 1 ipv4 area 0


! An interface connected in a point-to-point fashion to a single neighboring
! router. OSPF network type is changed to point-to-point to avoid DR/BDR elections
! and LSA2 generation, saving resources and 40 seconds of waiting on link coming
! up.

interface FastEthernet0/0
 ipv6 address 2001:DB8:1:1::1/64
 ip address 10.1.1.1 255.255.255.0
 ospfv3 network point-to-point ! Applies both to IPv4 and IPv6 AF
 ospfv3 1 ipv6 area 1
 ospfv3 1 ipv4 area 1


! Another interface towards a router in the backbone area with shortened timers


interface Serial0/0/0
 ipv6 address 2001:DB8:0:1::1/64
 ip address 10.0.1.1 255.255.255.0
 ospfv3 hello-interval 1 ! Applies both to IPv4 and IPv6 AF
 ospfv3 1 ipv6 area 0
 ospfv3 1 ipv4 area 0


! Summarization for inter-area IPv4 and IPv6 routes

router ospfv3 1
 address-family ipv4
   area 1 range 10.1.0.0 255.255.0.0
 !
 address-family ipv6
   area 1 range 2001:DB8:1::/48
```

Keep in mind that although the configuration gives off an impression of running a single
OSPFv3 process for both address families, in reality, there are two separate instances running under the single OSPFv3 process 1—one for IPv6 AF and the other for IPv4. Each
of them has its own independent LSDB, exchanges its own set of packets, establishes its
own adjacencies, and performs its own computations. By most measures, the memory
and CPU footprint are similar to running a separate OSPFv2 and OSPFv3 process. What
makes things different, though, is the fact that here, both IPv6 and IPv4 address families
are handled by OSPFv3 mechanisms.

## OSPFv3 Prefix Suppression

The idea behind the need for a prefix suppression feature was described in the section "OSPFv2 Prefix Suppression," earlier in this chapter, along with the description of how the mechanism works in OSPFv2. There is a similar mechanism for OSPFv3 as well, described in the same RFC 6860 as for OSPFv2, although its operation is much more simplified thanks to the type 8 and 9 LSAs that carry addressing information instead of LSA types 1 and 2. In OSPFv3, the prefix suppression works simply by omitting the suppressed transit link prefixes from type 8 and 9 LSAs.

For OSPFv3, the transit link prefix suppression is configured either on a per-process basis using the **prefix-suppression** command, or on per-interface basis using either the **ipv6 ospf prefix-suppression** or **ospfv3 prefix-suppression** command, depending on whether OSPFv3 is running in plain or in address family mode. If OSPFv3 address family mode is used, the prefix suppression can either be configured outside the address family, in which case it influences all address families, or it can be configured for a particular address family only. Just like in OSPFv2, prefix suppression applies to all configured interfaces except for loopbacks, passive interfaces, and secondary IP addresses in an IPv4 address family.

## OSPFv3 Graceful Shutdown

The Graceful Shutdown feature in OSPFv3 accomplishes the same goal as in OSPFv2, but the process is slightly modified. When an OSPFv3 process is gracefully shut down using the **shutdown** command, the router will

- Start sending out Hello packets with the router priority set to 0, dropping its DR/BDR role where applicable

- Stop accepting received Hello packets

- Flush all LSAs it has originated except a type 1 LSA

- Flood its type 1 LSA with all links in that LSA having the maximum cost of 65,535

- After the Dead interval expires and all neighbors are considered dead, flush its own type 1 LSA

- Stop sending and processing OSPFv3 packets

As opposed to the Graceful Shutdown procedure in OSPFv2, where the shutdown is practically immediate, OSPFv3 will perform the shutdown over the Dead interval until all neighbors are declared down. The shutdown is carried out in a more gradual fashion, by dropping the DR/BDR roles, withdrawing all attached, inter-area and redistributed prefixes, declaring the router as a stub router (by setting the costs of all links to 65,535), and finally flushing the router's own type 1 LSA entirely after all neighbors have gone down thanks to the Hello packets from neighbors being ignored as a part of the procedure.

# Foundation Summary

This section lists additional details and facts to round out the coverage of the topics in this chapter. Unlike most of the Cisco Press Exam Certification Guides, this "Foundation Summary" does not repeat information presented in the "Foundation Topics" section of the chapter. Please take the time to read and study the details in the "Foundation Topics" section of the chapter, as well as review items noted with a Key Topic icon.

Table 9-12 lists some of the key protocols regarding OSPF.

**Table 9-12**  *Protocols and Corresponding Standards for Chapter 9*

| Name | Standard |
| --- | --- |
| OSPF Version 2 | RFC 2328 |
| Alternative Implementations of OSPF Area Border Routers | RFC 3509 |
| The OSPF Opaque LSA Option | RFC 5250 |
| The OSPF Not-So-Stubby Area (NSSA) Option | RFC 3101 |
| OSPF Stub Router Advertisement | RFC 6987 |
| Traffic Engineering (TE) Extensions to OSPF Version 2 | RFC 3630 |
| Graceful OSPF Restart | RFC 3623 |
| OSPFv2 HMAC-SHA Cryptographic Authentication | RFC 5709 |
| OSPF for IPv6 | RFC 5340 |
| OSPFv3 Graceful Restart | RFC 5187 |
| Hiding Transit-Only Networks in OSPF | RFC 6860 |
| Support of Address Families in OSPFv3 | RFC 5838 |
| Supporting Authentication Trailer for OSPFv3 | RFC 7166 |

Table 9-13 lists some of the most popular IOS commands related to the topics in this chapter. Also, refer to Tables 9-7 through 9-9 for references to OSPF authentication commands.

**Table 9-13**  *Command Reference for Chapter 9*

| Command | Command Mode and Description |
|---|---|
| router ospf *process-id* | Global config; puts user in OSPF configuration mode for that PID. |
| ipv6 router ospf *process-id* | Global config; puts user in IPv6 OSPFv3 configuration mode for that PID. |
| router ospfv3 *process-id* | Global config; puts user in OSPFv3 address family configuration mode for that PID. |
| network *ip-address* [*wildcard-mask*] **area** *area* | OSPF config mode; defines matching parameters, compared to interface IP addresses, to pick interfaces on which to enable OSPF. |
| ip ospf *process-id* **area** *area-id* [secondaries none] | Interface config mode; alternative to the **network** command for enabling OSPF on an interface. |
| ipv6 ospf *process-id* **area** *area-id* | Interface config mode; enables IPv6 OSPFv3 on an interface. |
| ospfv3 *process-id* { **ipv4** \| **ipv6** } **area** *area-id* | Interface config mode; enable OSPFv3 in selected address family on an interface. |
| neighbor *ip-address* [**priority** *number*] [**poll-interval** *seconds*] [**cost** *number*] [**database-filter all**] | OSPF config mode; used when neighbors must be defined statically, it identifies the neighbor's IP address, priority, cost, and poll interval. |
| ipv6 ospf neighbor *ipv6-address* [**priority** *number*] [**poll-interval** *seconds*] [**cost** *number*] [**database-filter all**] | Interface config mode; used when neighbors must be defined statically for IPv6 OSPFv3, it identifies the neighbor's IPv6 address, priority, cost, and poll interval. |
| ospfv3 [ *process-id* [ **ipv4** \| **ipv6** ] ] neighbor *ipv6-address* [**priority** *number*] [**poll-interval** *seconds*] [**cost** *number*] [**database-filter all**] | Interface config mode; used when neighbors must be defined statically for OSPFv3 in address family mode, it identifies the neighbor's IPv6 address, priority, cost, and poll interval. |
| auto-cost reference-bandwidth *ref-bw* | OSPF config mode; changes the numerator in the formula to calculate the interface cost for all OSPF interfaces on that router. |
| router-id *ip-address* | OSPF config mode; statically sets the router ID. |
| log-adjacency-changes [detail] | OSPF subcommand; displays log messages when neighbor status changes. On by default. |

| Command | Command Mode and Description |
|---------|------------------------------|
| **passive-interface [default]** {*interface-type interface-number*} | OSPF config mode; causes OSPF to stop sending Hellos on the specified interface. OSPF will still advertise the subnet as a stub network. |
| **area** *area-id* **stub [no-summary]** | OSPF config mode; sets the area type to stub or totally stubby. |
| **area** *area-id* **nssa [no-redistribution] [default-information-originate [metric] [metric-type]] [no-summary]** | OSPF config mode; sets the area type to NSSA or totally NSSA. |
| **area** *area-id* **default-cost** *cost* | OSPF config mode; sets the cost of the default route created by ABRs and sent into stubby areas. |
| **area** *area-id* **nssa translate type7 suppress-fa** | OSPF config mode; sets an NSSA ABR to set the forwarding address to 0.0.0.0 for the type 5 LSAs it translates from type 7. |
| **area** *area-id* **range** *ip-address mask* **[advertise | not-advertise] [cost** *cost*] | OSPF config mode; summarizes routes into a larger prefix at ABRs. Optionally filters type 3 LSAs (**not-advertise** option). |
| **area** {*area-id*} **filter-list prefix** {*prefix-list-name* **in | out**} | OSPF config mode; filters type 3 LSA creation at ABR. |
| **distribute-list [***ACL***] | [route-map** *map-tag*] **in [***int-type* | *int-number*] | OSPF config mode; defines ACL or prefix list to filter what OSPF puts into the routing table. |
| **area** *area-id* **virtual-link** *router-id* **[authentication [message-digest | null | key-chain** *key-chain-name* **] ] [hello-interval** *seconds*] **[retransmit-interval** *seconds*] **[transmit-delay** *seconds*] **[dead-interval** *seconds*] **[[authentication-key** *key*] | **[message-digest-key** *key-id* **md5** *key*]] | OSPF config mode; creates a virtual link, with typical interface configuration settings to overcome the fact that the link is virtual. |
| **ip ospf authentication [ key-chain** *name* | **message-digest | null ]** | Interface subcommand; sets the authentication mode or refers to a key chain for extended cryptographic authentication. |
| **ip ospf authentication-key** *password* | Interface subcommand; sets the password for the classic plaintext authentication. |
| **ip ospf message-digest-key** *key-id* **md5** *key* | Interface subcommand; sets the password for the classic MD5 authentication. |

| Command | Command Mode and Description |
|---|---|
| ipv6 ospf authentication { null \| ipsec spi *spi authentication-algorithm key* } | Interface subcommand; sets the IPsec AH authentication algorithm and key for OSPFv3, or refers to a key chain for authentication trailer-based authentication. |
| ospfv3 authentication { null \| ipsec spi *spi authentication-algorithm key* \| key-chain *key-chain-name*} | |
| ipv6 ospf encryption { null \| ipsec spi *spi* esp { *encryption-algorithm key* \| null } *authentication-algorithm key* } | Interface subcommand; sets the IPsec ESP encryption and authentication algorithms and key for OSPFv3. |
| ospfv3 encryption { null \| ipsec spi *spi* esp { *encryption-algorithm key* \| null } *authentication-algorithm key* } | |
| ip ospf hello-interval *seconds* | Interface subcommand; sets the interval for periodic Hellos. |
| ipv6 ospf hello-interval *seconds* | |
| ospfv3 [ *process-id* [ ipv4 \| ipv6 ] ] hello-interval *seconds* | |
| ip ospf dead-interval {*seconds* \| minimal hello-multiplier *multiplier*} | Interface subcommand; defines the dead interval, or optionally the minimal dead interval of 1 second (not supported for OSPFv3). |
| ipv6 ospf dead-interval *seconds* | |
| ospfv3 [ *process-id* [ ipv4 \| ipv6 ] ] dead-interval *seconds* | |
| ip ospf name-lookup | Global command; causes the router to use DNS to correlate RIDs to host names for **show** command output. |
| ipv6 ospf name-lookup | |
| ip ospf cost *interface-cost* | Interface subcommand; sets the cost. |
| ipv6 ospf cost *interface-cost* | |
| ospfv3 [ *process-id* [ ipv4 \| ipv6 ] ] cost *interface-cost* | |
| ip ospf mtu-ignore | Interface subcommand; tells the router to ignore the check for equal MTUs that occurs when sending DD packets. |
| ipv6 ospf mtu-ignore | |
| ospfv3 [ *process-id* [ ipv4 \| ipv6 ] ] mtu-ignore | |

| Command | Command Mode and Description |
|---|---|
| **ip ospf network** {broadcast \| non-broadcast \| {point-to-multipoint [non-broadcast] \| point-to-point}} | Interface subcommand; sets the OSPF network type on an interface. |
| **ipv6 ospf network** {broadcast \| non-broadcast \| {point-to-multipoint [non-broadcast] \| point-to-point}} | |
| **ospfv3** [ *process-id* [ **ipv4** \| **ipv6** ] ] **network** {broadcast \| non-broadcast \| {point-to-multipoint [non-broadcast] \| point-to-point}} | |
| **ip ospf priority** *number-value* | Interface subcommand; sets the OSPF priority on an interface. |
| **ipv6 ospf priority** *number-value* | |
| **ospfv3** [ *process-id* [ **ipv4** \| **ipv6** ] ] **priority** *number-value* | |
| **ip ospf retransmit-interval** *seconds* | Interface subcommand; sets the time between LSA transmissions for adjacencies belonging to an interface. |
| **ipv6 ospf retransmit-interval** *seconds* | |
| **ospfv3** [ *process-id* [ **ipv4** \| **ipv6** ] ] **retransmit-interval** *seconds* | |
| **ip ospf transmit-delay** *seconds* | Interface subcommand; defines the estimated time expected for the transmission of an LSU. |
| **ipv6 ospf transmit-delay** *seconds* | |
| **ospfv3** [ *process-id* [ **ipv4** \| **ipv6** ] ] **transmit-delay** *seconds* | |
| **max-metric router-lsa** [on-startup {*announce-time* \| **wait-for-bgp**)] | OSPF config mode; configures a stub router, delaying the point at which it can become a transit router. |
| **show** { **ip ospf** \| **ipv6 ospf** \| **ospfv3** } **border-routers** | User mode; displays hidden routes for ABRs and ASBRs. |
| **show** { **ip ospf** \| **ipv6 ospf** \| **ospfv3** } [*process-id* [*area-id*]] **database** | User mode; has many options not shown here. Displays the OSPF LSDB. |
| **show** { **ip ospf** \| **ipv6 ospf** \| **ospfv3** } **neighbor** [*interface-type interface-number*] [*neighbor-id*] [**detail**] | User mode; lists information about OSPF neighbors. |
| **show** { **ip ospf** \| **ipv6 ospf** \| **ospfv3** } [*process-id*] **summary-address** | User mode; lists information about route summaries in OSPF. |
| **show** { **ip ospf** \| **ipv6 ospf** \| **ospfv3** } **virtual-links** | User mode; displays status and info about virtual links. |
| **show** { **ip ospf** \| **ipv6 ospf** \| **ospfv3** } **ospf** | User mode; displays all OSPF routes in the IP routing table. |

| Command | Command Mode and Description |
|---|---|
| show { ip ospf | ipv6 ospf | ospfv3 } interface [*interface-type interface-number*] [brief] | User mode; lists OSPF protocol timers and statistics per interface. |
| show { ip ospf | ipv6 ospf | ospfv3 } statistics [detail] | User mode; displays OSPF SPF calculation statistics. |
| clear { ip ospf | ipv6 ospf | ospfv3 } [*pid*] {process | redistribution | counters [neighbor [*neighbor-interface*] [*neighbor-id*]]} | Enable mode; restarts the OSPF process, clears redistributed routes, or clears OSPF counters. |
| debug { ip ospf | ipv6 ospf | ospfv3 } hello | Enable mode; displays messages regarding Hellos, including Hello parameter mismatches. |
| debug { ip ospf | ipv6 ospf | ospfv3 } adj | Enable mode; displays messages regarding adjacency changes. |

Table 9-14 summarizes many OSPF timers and their meaning.

**Table 9-14**  *OSPF Timer Summary*

| Timer | Meaning |
|---|---|
| MaxAge | The maximum time an LSA can be in a router's LSDB, without receiving a newer copy of the LSA, before the LSA is removed. Default is 3600 seconds. |
| LSRefresh | The timer interval per LSA on which a router refloods an identical LSA, except for a 1-larger sequence number, to prevent the expiration of MaxAge. Default is 1800 seconds. |
| Hello | Per interface; time interval between Hellos. Default is 10 or 30 seconds, depending on interface type. Broadcast and point-to-point use 10 seconds; NBMA and point-to-multipoint use 30 seconds. |
| Dead | Per interface; time interval in which a Hello should be received from a neighbor. If not received, the neighbor is considered to have failed. Default is four times Hello. |
| Wait | Per interface; set to the same number as the dead interval. Defines the time a router will wait to get a Hello asserting a DR after reaching a 2-Way state with that neighbor. |
| Retransmission | Per interface; the time between sending an LSU, not receiving an acknowledgment, and then resending the LSU. Default is 5 seconds. |

| Timer | Meaning |
|---|---|
| Inactivity | Countdown timer, per neighbor, used to detect when a neighbor has not been heard from for a complete dead interval. It starts equal to the dead interval, counts down, and is reset to be equal to the dead interval when each Hello is received. |
| Poll Interval | On NBMA networks, the period at which Hellos are sent to a neighbor when the neighbor is down. Default is 60 seconds. |
| Flood (Pacing) | Per interface; defines the interval between successive LSUs when flooding LSAs. Default is 33 ms. |
| Retransmission (Pacing) | Per interface; defines the interval between retransmitted packets as part of a single retransmission event. Default is 66 ms. |
| Lsa-group (Pacing) | Per OSPF process. LSA's LSRefresh intervals time out independently. This timer improves LSU reflooding efficiency by waiting, collecting several LSAs whose LSRefresh timers expire, and flooding all these LSAs together. Default is 240 seconds. |

Table 9-15 lists OSPF neighbor states and their meaning.

**Table 9-15**   *OSPF Neighbor States*

| State | Meaning |
|---|---|
| Down | No Hellos have been received from this neighbor for more than the dead interval. |
| Attempt | This router is sending Hellos to a manually configured neighbor. |
| Init | A Hello has been received from the neighbor, but it did not have the receiving router's RID in it. |
| 2-Way | A Hello has been received from the neighbor, and it has the receiving router's RID in it. This is a stable state for pairs of DROther neighbors. |
| ExStart | Currently negotiating the DD sequence numbers and master/slave logic used for DD packets. |
| Exchange | Finished negotiating and currently exchanging DD packets. |
| Loading | All DD packets exchanged, and currently pulling the complete LSDB entries with LSU packets. |
| Full | Neighbors are adjacent (fully adjacent), and should have identical LSDB entries for the area in which the link resides. Routing table calculations begin. |

Table 9-16 lists several key OSPF numeric values.

**Table 9-16**    *OSPF Numeric Ranges*

| Setting | Range of Values |
| --- | --- |
| Single interface cost | 1 to 65,535 ($2^{16} - 1$) |
| Complete route cost | 1 to 16,777,215 ($2^{24} - 1$) |
| Infinite route cost | 16,777,215 ($2^{24} - 1$) |
| Reference bandwidth (units: Mbps) | 1 to 4,294,967 |
| OSPF PID | 1 to 65,535 ($2^{16} - 1$) |
| LSA Age | 1 to 3600 seconds |

# Memory Builders

The CCIE Routing and Switching written exam, like all Cisco CCIE written exams, covers a fairly broad set of topics. This section provides some basic tools to help you exercise your memory about some of the broader topics covered in this chapter.

## Fill In Key Tables from Memory

Appendix E, "Key Tables for CCIE Study," on the CD in the back of this book, contains empty sets of some of the key summary tables in each chapter. Print Appendix E, refer to this chapter's tables in it, and fill in the tables from memory. Refer to Appendix F, "Solutions for Key Tables for CCIE Study," on the CD to check your answers.

## Definitions

Next, take a few moments to write down the definitions for the following terms:

LSDB, Dijkstra, link-state routing protocol, LSA, LSU, DD, Hello, LSAck, RID, neighbor state, neighbor, adjacent, fully adjacent, 2-Way, 224.0.0.5, 224.0.0.6, area, stub area type, network type, external route, E1 route, E2 route, Hello timer, dead time/interval, sequence number, DR, BDR, DROther, priority, LSA flooding, DR election, SPF calculation, partial SPF calculation, full SPF calculation, LSRefresh, hello time/interval, MaxAge, ABR, ASBR, internal router, backbone area, transit network, stub network, LSA type, stub area, NSSA, totally stubby area, totally NSSA area, virtual link, stub router, transit router, SPF algorithm, All OSPF DR Routers, All OSPF Routers, graceful restart, prefix suppression, address family, instance ID, graceful shutdown, flooding scope

Refer to the glossary to check your answers.

## Further Reading

Jeff Doyle's *Routing TCP/IP*, Volume I, Second Edition—every word a must for CCIE Routing and Switching.

*Cisco OSPF Command and Configuration Handbook*, by Dr. William Parkhurst, covers every OSPF-related command available in Cisco IOS at the time of that book's publication, with examples of each one.

The CCIE Routing and Switching v5.0 exam blueprint also mentions the OSPF IP Fast Reroute features. More information about them can be found on the Cisco website in the *IP Routing: OSPF Configuration Guide* for Cisco IOS Release 15S, specifically in the "OSPFv2 Loop-Free Alternate Fast Reroute" and "OSPF IPv4 Remote Loop-Free Alternate IP Fast Reroute" sections. Also, many Cisco Live! sessions cover these features, including "IP LFA (Loop-Free-Alternative): Architecture and Troubleshooting" (BRKRST-3020) and "Routed Fast Convergence" (BRKRST-3363), available at www.ciscolive365.com. At the time of writing, these features were supported only on service provider IOS, IOS-XE, and IOS-XR image builds and will not be present on the Lab exam. The Written exam might cover general properties of these features.

**Blueprint topics covered in this chapter:**

This chapter covers the following subtopics from the Cisco CCIE Routing and Switching written exam blueprint. Refer to the full blueprint in Table I-1 in the Introduction for more details on the topics covered in each chapter and their context within the blueprint.

- Describe a Basic IS-IS Network in a Single Area and a Single Topology

- Describe Neighbor Relationships

- Describe Network Types, Routing Levels, and Router Types

- Describe IS-IS Operations

- Describe Metrics and Wide Metrics

## CHAPTER 10

# IS-IS

This chapter covers IS-IS, the other link-state routing protocol covered by the CCIE Routing and Switching exam. Inclusion of the Intermediate System–to–Intermediate System (IS-IS) into the Routing and Switching track might be surprising, as IS-IS is more associated with service provider environments. Still, with the ever-increasing proliferation of IPv6, TRILL, and FabricPath, compounded with the intrinsic OSPFv3 complexity, IS-IS, with its inherent multiprotocol capability, simplicity, and general flexibility, is becoming more interesting, even for enterprise deployments.

## "Do I Know This Already?" Quiz

Table 10-1 outlines the major sections in this chapter and the corresponding "Do I Know This Already?" quiz questions.

**Table 10-1** *"Do I Know This Already?" Foundation Topics Section-to-Question Mapping*

| Foundation Topics Section | Questions Covered in This Section | Score |
|---|---|---|
| OSI Network Layer and Addressing | 1–4 | |
| Levels of Routing in OSI Networks | 5–7 | |
| IS-IS Metrics, Levels, and Adjacencies | 8–10 | |
| IS-IS Packet Types | 11–15 | |
| IS-IS Operation over Different Network Types | 16–20 | |
| Areas in IS-IS | 21–24 | |
| Authentication in IS-IS | 25–27 | |
| IPv6 Support in IS-IS | 28–29 | |
| Configuring IS-IS | 30–33 | |
| **Total Score** | | |

To best use this pre-chapter assessment, remember to score yourself strictly. You can find the answers in Appendix A, "Answers to the 'Do I Know This Already?' Quizzes." In all items, try to select all correct answers.

1. How many NSAP addresses are usually configured on a router?

   a. One per every active (up/up) interface with IS-IS configured

   b. One per every interface with IS-IS configured

   c. One per area

   d. One per node

2. What is the size of an NSAP address?

   a. Fixed length of 20 octets

   b. Fixed length of 32 octets

   c. Variable length ranging from 8 to 20 octets

   d. Variable length ranging from 16 to 32 octets

3. What is the common length of the System ID field?

   a. 8 octets

   b. 6 octets

   c. 4 octets

   d. 1 octet

   e. 4 bits

4. In the NSAP 49.0001.FF11.2233.4455.6600, what is the value of the System ID field?

   a. 49.0001

   b. FF11.2233

   c. FF11.2233.4455

   d. FF11.2233.4455.6600

   e. 2233.4455

   f. 2233.4455.6600

   g. 1122.3344.5566

5. In OSI terminology, intra-area routing is also called which of the following?

   a. L0 routing

   b. L1 routing

   c. L2 routing

   d. L3 routing

6. In OSI terminology, inter-area routing within a domain is also called which of the following?

   **a.** L0 routing

   **b.** L1 routing

   **c.** L2 routing

   **d.** L3 routing

7. In OSI terminology, interdomain routing is also called which of the following?

   **a.** L0 routing

   **b.** L1 routing

   **c.** L2 routing

   **d.** L3 routing

8. What is the range of metrics defined by the original IS-IS standard?

   **a.** 6 bits for interface metric, 10 bits for total metric

   **b.** 8 bits for interface metric, 16 bits for total metric

   **c.** 16 bits for interface metric, 32 bits for total metric

   **d.** 24 bits for interface metric, 32 bits for total metric

9. What is the width of metrics if wide metrics are activated?

   **a.** 24 bits for interface metric, 32 bits for total metric

   **b.** 16 bits for interface metric, 24 bits for total metric

   **c.** 32 bits for interface metric, 32 bits for total metric

   **d.** There is no concept of wide metrics in IS-IS.

10. Select the correct answer about the established adjacency type, assuming that the routers are directly connected.

   **a.** R1: L1L2, R2: L2, both in the same area. L2 adjacency will be created.

   **b.** R1: L1L2, R2: L2, both in the same area. L1 and L2 adjacencies will be created.

   **c.** R1: L1L2, R2: L1L2, each in a different area. L1 and L2 adjacencies will be created.

   **d.** R1: L1L2, R2: L1L2, each in a different area. L2 adjacency will be created.

   **e.** R1: L1, R2: L1L2, both in the same area. L1 and L2 adjacencies will be created.

   **f.** R1: L1, R2: L1L2, both in the same area. L1 adjacency will be created.

   **g.** R1: L1 R2: L1, each in a different area. No adjacency will be created.

   **h.** R1: L2 R2: L2, each in a different area. L2 adjacency will be created.

**11.** How many IIH types are sent in default configuration over a broadcast link?

   **a.** One; L1 IIH

   **b.** One; L2 IIH

   **c.** One; L1L2 IIH

   **d.** Two, L1 and L2 IIHs

**12.** Do the timers on neighboring IS-IS routers need to match?

   **a.** Yes

   **b.** Only on point-to-point links

   **c.** Only on broadcast links

   **d.** No

**13.** Which of the following fields can be used to identify an LSP?

   **a.** Area ID

   **b.** System ID

   **c.** NSEL

   **d.** Pseudonode ID

   **e.** Fragment

   **f.** SNPA

**14.** Can an LSP be fragmented?

   **a.** Yes. Any router can fragment any LSP according to its interface MTU.

   **b.** Yes, but only the originator of an LSP can fragment it.

   **c.** Yes, but only backbone routers can fragment an LSP (regardless of its originator).

   **d.** No. LSP packets cannot be fragmented.

**15.** Which packets are used to request or acknowledge an LSP?

   **a.** IIH

   **b.** SNPA

   **c.** CSNP

   **d.** PSNP

**16.** Which of the following states are valid adjacency states in IS-IS?

   **a.** Down

   **b.** Init

   **c.** 2Way

   **d.** Exchange

   **e.** Full

   **f.** Up

**17.** How is a Backup DIS elected in IS-IS?

   **a.** By its priority

   **b.** By its SNPA

   **c.** By its System ID

   **d.** There is no Backup DIS in IS-IS.

**18.** What is the DIS election based on?

   **a.** Interface priority

   **b.** Uptime

   **c.** System ID

   **d.** SNPA

   **e.** IP address

**19.** Does the IS priority of 0 have any special significance?

   **a.** No

   **b.** Yes. The router will not participate in DIS elections.

   **c.** Yes. The router will not be considered by others during their SPF run.

   **d.** Yes. The router will act as an area boundary router.

**20.** How many DISs are going to be elected on a common broadcast segment with ten routers in default IS-IS configuration if the router adjacencies have been fully established?

   **a.** Only one. A DIS function is shared between L1 and L2.

   **b.** Two, one for L1 and one for L2, each level having a different router as the DIS.

   **c.** Two, one for L1 and one for L2, with the same router winning DIS in both levels.

   **d.** None. IS-IS treats all links as point-to-point by default.

**21.** It is possible to renumber, merge, or split areas in IS-IS without network disruption.

    **a.** False

    **b.** True

**22.** What IPv4/IPv6 prefixes are advertised in an L1 LSP?

    **a.** Directly attached networks

    **b.** Networks from a router's own area

    **c.** Networks from other areas

    **d.** Redistributed networks if redistribution into L1 is configured

**23.** What IPv4/IPv6 prefixes are advertised in an L2 LSP?

    **a.** Directly attached networks

    **b.** Networks from a router's own area

    **c.** Networks from other areas

    **d.** Redistributed networks

**24.** In what mode must a backbone router operate if all other routers in its own area are L1-only routers?

    **a.** L1-only

    **b.** L1L2

    **c.** L2-only

    **d.** As the area is a totally stubby area, the level setting on the backbone router is irrelevant.

**25.** Which statements are true about authentication in IS-IS?

    **a.** All packet types are always authenticated by a common password.

    **b.** P2P IIH packets can be authenticated independently for each level.

    **c.** LAN IIH packets can be authenticated independently for each level.

    **d.** Each of LSP, CSNP, and PSNP packet types can be authenticated by an independent password.

    **e.** IIH packets can be authenticated independently from LSP+CSNP+PSNP packets.

    **f.** If authentication is configured, LSP+CSNP+PSNP packets are authenticated by a common password for both levels.

    **g.** If authentication is configured, LSP+CSNP+PSNP packets can be authenticated in each level independently.

**26.** What authentication mechanisms are currently available for IS-IS?

  **a.** Plaintext

  **b.** AES

  **c.** 3DES

  **d.** MD5

**27.** Which statements are true about authentication in IS-IS?

  **a.** If using key chains, key numbers must match, even with the plaintext authentication method.

  **b.** If using key chains, key numbers do not need to match, even with the MD5 authentication method.

  **c.** Authentication password for L1 LSP+CSNP+PSNP must match only between directly connected neighbors.

  **d.** Authentication password for L1 LSP+CSNP+PSNP must match across the area.

  **e.** Authentication password for L1 LSP+CSNP+PSNP must match across the domain.

  **f.** Authentication password for L2 LSP+CSNP+PSNP must match only between directly connected neighbors.

  **g.** Authentication password for L2 LSP+CSNP+PSNP must match across the area.

  **h.** Authentication password for L2 LSP+CSNP+PSNP must match across the domain.

**28.** Which statements are true about IPv6 support in IS-IS?

  **a.** When IPv6 support is activated, IS-IS packets are sent to the FF02::2 multicast IPv6 address.

  **b.** Separate LSPs are generated for IPv4 and IPv6 prefixes.

  **c.** IPv4 and IPv6 prefixes can coexist in a single LSP.

  **d.** Separate NSAP/NET addresses have to be configured for IPv4 and IPv6 IS-IS instances.

  **e.** A single IS-IS process advertises both IPv4 and IPv6 routes.

  **f.** The System ID of an IS-IS router has to be derived from its IPv6 loopback address.

**29.** Which statements are true regarding advertising a local interface's IPv6 prefix in IS-IS?

    **a.** The **address-family ipv6** section must be created in **router isis** mode before IS-IS can start advertising IPv6 prefixes.

    **b.** The **ip router isis** command in interface configuration mode applies both to IPv4 and IPv6 prefixes configured on the interface.

    **c.** The **prefix** command in the **address-family ipv6** section of the **router isis** mode can be used to advertise locally connected prefixes.

    **d.** The **ipv6 router isis** command in interface configuration mode is used to advertise that interface's IPv6 prefixes.

**30.** Which values can be used to manually derive a System ID for an IS-IS router?

    **a.** Any arbitrary value as long as it is unique

    **b.** Any router's MAC address

    **c.** Any router's IP address after an appropriate transliteration

    **d.** None of these answers applies; Cisco routers derive a System ID automatically.

**31.** How can the logging of neighbor state changes be activated for an IS-IS process?

    **a.** The logging is activated automatically; no action is necessary.

    **b.** **log-adjacency-changes all** command in **router isis** mode

    **c.** **isis log-neighbor-changes** command in global configuration mode

    **d.** **isis neighbor log-changes** command in interface configuration mode

**32.** How can a local interface's IPv4 prefix be advertised in IS-IS?

    **a.** Using the **network** command in **router isis** mode

    **b.** Using the **ip router isis** command in interface configuration mode

    **c.** Using the **passive-interface** command in **router isis** mode

    **d.** No command is necessary; IS-IS automatically advertises IPv4 prefixes of all local interfaces on a router.

**33.** How can summarization be configured in IS-IS?

    **a.** Using the **summary-address** command in **router isis** mode for IPv4 prefixes

    **b.** Using the **summary-prefix** command in the **address-family ipv6** section of the **router isis** mode for IPv6 prefixes

    **c.** Using the **isis summary** command in interface mode for both IPv4 and IPv6 prefixes

    **d.** IS-IS does not support summarization.

# Foundation Topics

IS-IS is covered in this chapter in more depth than the CCIE Routing and Switching exam blueprint officially requires. Considering, however, the perceived "otherworldliness" of IS-IS, we felt it was necessary to provide a significantly larger overview of Open Systems Interconnection (OSI) protocol operations with particular focus on IS-IS, to put things into perspective, and to show you that some ideas from OSI networks on which IS-IS is also based can be found, in a certain modification, in our TCP/IP environments. It is natural for us humans to treat a nonmainstream, different approach to things with a reserved attitude, and if you are relatively new to IS-IS, you will very probably have this feeling of "why did they do it so differently?" more often than not. Nevertheless, try to keep an open, unbiased mind. Discovering and learning about different ways to do things can be extremely enlightening.

IS-IS is a link-state routing protocol originally specified in ISO/IEC standard 10589:2002, and initially created for OSI networks. Internally, it uses the same Dijkstra Shortest Path First (SPF) algorithm as Open Shortest Path First (OSPF). The true dependence of IS-IS on OSI protocols and principles is remarkably low, though. IS-IS uses so-called Network Service Access Point (NSAP) addressing, described in the following section, to identify individual routers, their area memberships, and their adjacencies, and is designed to provide Level 1 (intra-area) and Level 2 (inter-area) routing according to OSI routing hierarchies. Apart from that, however, there is little OSI-specific left. IS-IS does not run over any network layer protocol; instead, it encapsulates its messages directly into data-link frames. Adjacency and addressing information in IS-IS messages is encoded as Type-Length-Value (TLV) records, thereby providing excellent flexibility and extendability. Enhancing IS-IS for a new address family is a matter of defining new TLVs to carry the desired addressing information along the existing topology information, without requiring any changes to the underlying protocol operations or message formats. Based on these characteristics, IS-IS is best described as being protocol-agnostic. RFC 1195 specified how the original IS-IS for OSI networks can be extended to support IP routing along with OSI routing in a single IS-IS instance, coining the term Integrated IS-IS. Since then, IS-IS development and further extensions have been strongly driven by the IETF in numerous RFCs.

The chapter begins with a light introduction into OSI networks and focuses on NSAP addressing in these networks that is retained by IS-IS. After discussing the routing levels, IS-IS is introduced in greater detail, its packet types are discussed, and link-state database is explained. We then have a look at the IS-IS operation on point-to-point and broadcast links; discuss the multiarea routing in IS-IS, authentication, and IPv6 support; and end with a commented configuration example. The chapter predominantly focuses on explaining the principles and fundamentals of IS-IS. Its configuration is relatively simple, and while shown in a relatively extensive way, the CCIE Routing and Switching blueprint itself focuses more on the "Describe" aspect of IS-IS, rather than "Configure, Maintain, Operate, and Troubleshoot."

Originally, IS-IS started as a routing protocol for ISO OSI networks and is naturally influenced in its fundamental aspects by the OSI approach to networking. Therefore, to understand IS-IS well, it is important to review the key concepts of OSI networks first.

## OSI Network Layer and Addressing

Whenever the *OSI* acronym is mentioned, a person working in networking immediately thinks of the OSI Reference Model developed by the International Standards Organization. The OSI Reference Model is common knowledge among networkers, and no doubt every well-prepared CCIE candidate could talk about it even in his sleep. It is somewhat less known, however, that ISO also created protocol specifications for individual layers of this reference model, and many of those protocols are actually implemented and in use. While they have never been anywhere near TCP/IP's popularity and adoption (for several reasons not to be discussed here), ISO OSI protocols have been nonetheless widely implemented, for example, in telecommunications equipment and networks and in aviation. The OSI Reference Model and related protocols were developed independently of the TCP/IP protocol suite, and TCP/IP creators never intended to follow the OSI Reference Model. As a result, many aspects of OSI networks are foreign to network professionals who have been in touch only with TCP/IP networks. While it might be tempting to approach these differences with distrust or contempt, it is best to keep an open mind without biases or preconceptions.

**Key Topic**

ISO OSI terminology is significantly different. In ISO-speak, as many authors call it, there are no hosts or routers. Instead, the term *End System (ES)* is used for a host, and the term *Intermediate System (IS)* is used for a router. The term *System* alone describes a network node. Also, the term *Circuit* stands for interface, and the term *Domain* stands for autonomous system. Hence, an end-to-end communication between two End Systems (hosts) in a Domain (autonomous system) involves zero or more Intermediate Systems (routers) interconnected by Circuits (interfaces). We will introduce a couple of other terms later in the chapter.

The network layer specification of the OSI Reference Model that is concerned with end-to-end communication between two ES entities calls for two basic services: connectionless-mode and connection-mode network layer communication. The connectionless mode of operation is identical to the way that IP operates, as a pure datagram service without any prior session establishments. In OSI networks, the Layer 3 network protocol that provides a connectionless communication between ES entities is called ConnectionLess-mode Network Protocol (CLNP) and is specified in ISO/IEC 8473-1:1998. The ITU-T republished its specification in the X.233 recommendation. The CLNP protocol is to OSI networks what IPv4/IPv6 are to TCP/IP networks. The set of services provided by CLNP is called ConnectionLess Network Services, or simply CLNS. We will be seeing a number of commands, mostly of the **show clns...** format, that refer to a router's operation in OSI connectionless mode, including IS-IS. For connection-oriented mode in OSI networks, an adaptation of the X.25 protocol is used. There is no analogous connection-oriented network layer protocol in TCP/IP networks.

End-to-end communication requires addressing on the network layer. The addressing used in OSI networks, both in connectionless and connection-oriented mode, is called *NSAP addressing*, with the acronym standing for Network Service Access Point representing an address of a particular network service on a particular network node in the network. This form of addressing is defined in its basic form in ISO/IEC 8348, and the ITU-T republished this standard in its X.213 recommendation. Further details of NSAP addressing are specified in the IS-IS ISO/IEC 10589:2002 standard. This chapter explains the NSAP addressing by combining knowledge from both standards.

NSAP addressing bears many differences to addressing in TCP/IP networks. An NSAP address is assigned to the *entire network node*, not to its individual interfaces. A single node requires only one NSAP address in a common setup, regardless of how many network interfaces it uses. As a result, NSAP addressing does not have the notion of per-interface subnets similar to IP subnets. An approximate analogy can be created in an IPv6 network by assigning each node a global IPv6 address to its loopback interface only, leaving all physical network interfaces running only with IPv6 link-local addresses, and running a routing protocol over all loopbacks and physical links to allow all nodes to learn about each other's global address and the path toward it.

Figure 10-1 shows the basic format of an NSAP address.

| IDP | | DSP | | |
|---|---|---|---|---|
| AFI | IDI | HO-DSP | System ID | SEL |

**Figure 10-1**  *NSAP Address Format*

At a high level, an NSAP address consists of two parts:

- The Initial Domain Part (IDP)

- The Domain Specific Part (DSP)

The internal format and length of these two parts are variable to a large extent and depend on the actual application in which the NSAP addressing is used. As a result, an NSAP address has a variable length.

The IDP itself consists of two fields: the Authority and Format Identifier (AFI) and the Initial Domain Identifier (IDI). The AFI value (1 octet in the range of 00 to FF) indicates the format of the remaining address fields. The IDI field has a variable length depending on the address format indicated by AFI and might even be omitted. Together, the AFI and IDI indicate the routing domain (the autonomous system) in which the node is located.

The format of DSP is again dependent on the particular address format. However, at least in a general approach, the DSP consists of a variable-length High-Order Domain Specific Part (HO-DSP) that identifies the part (or an *area*) of the domain in which the node is located. This field can be further structured into subfields. The System ID is the unique identifier of the node itself. While NSAP allows this field to be from 1 to 8 octets long, all current implementations fix the length of the System ID field to 6 octets. Finally, the

SEL field, also called an NSAP Selector or NSEL, is a 1-octet-long field that identifies the particular service in or above the network layer on the destination node that should process the datagram. A rough analogy in the IP world would be the particular protocol above IP, or the transport port.

Table 10-2 lists some of the most often used NSAP address formats.

**Table 10-2**  *Selected NSAP Address Formats*

| AFI | Meaning | IDI Length and Contents | HO-DSP Length and Contents |
|---|---|---|---|
| 39 | Use of Data Country Code (ISO 3166) | 2 octets; numeric country code according to ISO 3166 | 10 octets; area number |
| 45 | Use of international phone numbers (ITU-T E.164) | 8 octets; international phone number according to E.164 | 4 octets; area number |
| 47 | Use of International Code Designator (ISO 6523) | 2 octets; international organization code according to ISO 6523 | 10 octets; area number |
| 49 | Locally defined format (private addressing; free format) | Formally not present | Between 0 and 12 octets; area number |

In each of these AFI types, the HO-DSP (the area number) can be further internally structured; however, these details are not relevant at this point. In typical IS-IS deployments, the addressing uses the AFI of 49 in which the length and meaning of the HO-DSP field are entirely up to the administrator. While this system of addressing might be perceived as complex and possibly cumbersome, it is nonetheless very flexible and adaptable to various enumeration approaches.

The minimum size of an NSAP address is 8 octets—with only AFI, System ID, and SEL fields present. The maximum NSAP address size is 20 octets.

The SEL octet deserves a special mention. As mentioned earlier, it is used to address the datagram to a particular service at the destination node. As an example, the SEL value of 22 or 1D indicates the OSI TP4 transport layer protocol (different vendors appear to use different SEL values); the value of 2F indicates a GRE IP-over-CLNP tunneling. Specifically, if the value of the SEL octet is 0, no particular service is being addressed, and the entire NSAP address simply identifies the destination node itself without referring to any particular service on that node. An NSAP address in which the SEL octet is set to 0 is called a Network Entity Title (NET), and this is the address that is configured on the node. Configuration of NETs will be a mandatory part of IS-IS configuration.

To summarize, NSAP addresses can be thought to contain, in a single instance, information about the destination's autonomous system, area, unique identifier, and even the requested upper-layer service.

The written format of NSAP addresses uses hexadecimal digits separated into groups of one or more octets by a dot. Usually, the AFI value (1 octet; 2 hexadecimal digits) is immediately separated by a dot for better readability, with the remainder of the NSAP address simply written in two-octet groups, for example, 49.0001.1234.5678.3333.00. In this address, the AFI is 49, signifying a local address; the 0001 is the area number; the 1234.5678.3333 is the System ID of the node; and the trailing 00 is the SEL value, making this NSAP address also a NET. The use of the dot, however, is arbitrary, as long as it separates groups of integer octet length. Therefore, all the following notations represent the same address:

> 49.0001.1234.5678.3333.00
>
> 4900.0112.3456.7833.3300
>
> 49.00.01.12.34.56.78.33.33.00
>
> 49000112.34.5678.33.3300
>
> 49000112345678333300

Whenever any of these NSAP addresses is configured on a Cisco router, it rewrites the address into the notation used in the first line.

An NSAP address is often easier to read from right to left. In the NSAP address 49.0001.1234.5678.3333.00, the rightmost octet is the SEL value (00), the following six octets are the System ID (1234.5678.3333), followed by other HO-DSP octets (0001), IDI (not present in this NSAP) and ending with the leftmost octet, the AFI (49).

To visualize a network using NSAP addressing, consider the topology shown in Figure 10-2.

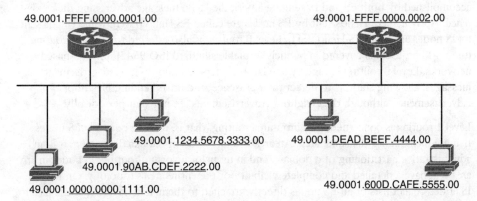

**Figure 10-2**  *Network with NSAP Addressing*

Addressing in Figure 10-2 again uses the local NSAP space, indicated by the AFI value of 49. For better readability, the System ID portion of the NSAP address has been underlined in the figure. Note that all nodes in the network are in the same area, 0001. Each node has a unique System ID. As there is no concept of a subnet, routing between the two networks is accomplished by each IS assembling a list of all attached ES nodes and advertising it to its neighbors.

Individual interfaces are not assigned their own addresses at the network layer. However, their Layer 2 addresses are used in the same way as TCP/IP networks use them: When a packet is routed, it is encapsulated into a frame addressed to the next directly attached hop identified by its Layer 2 address. In OSI networks, a Layer 2 address of an interface is called a Sub Network Point of Attachment (SNPA).

Finally, for purposes of distinguishing between interfaces of the same node, an IS enumerates its interfaces by a locally significant 1-octet number called the Local Circuit ID, which increments by 1 with every interface added to the IS-IS instance beginning with 0 on Cisco routers.

## Levels of Routing in OSI Networks

Routing in OSI networks has a concept of hierarchies, or *levels*, depending on the network scope in which the routing is performed. Four levels of routing are defined:

- **Level 0 routing:** Routing between two ES nodes on the same link, or between an ES node and its nearest IS

- **Level 1 routing:** Routing between ES nodes in a single area of a domain

- **Level 2 routing:** Routing between ES nodes in different areas of a domain

- **Level 3 routing:** Routing between ES nodes in different domains

Level 0 routing is concerned with the way that an ES (end node) discovers its nearest IS (gateway), and conversely, how an IS knows which ES nodes are connected to it. This is accomplished by both ES and IS sending a periodic Hello message advertising their existence. Aptly named, Hellos sent by ES nodes are called ES Hello (ESH), while Hellos sent by IS nodes are called IS Hello (ISH). Level 0 routing is also referred to as ES-IS routing (the ES-IS protocol is covered in publicly available standard ISO 9542). In IPv6-based networks, Level 0 routing is vaguely similar to routers sending Router Advertisement messages, allowing stations to detect their presence, and hosts sending Neighbor Advertisements, although the Neighbor Advertisements are not sent periodically.

Level 1 routing is concerned with intra-area routing, that is, routing between ES nodes that are members of the same area. An area is understood in the usual meaning: It is an administrative partitioning of a domain, and in terms of link-state routing, IS nodes in an area will have a detailed and complete visibility of the entire area's topology. On Level 1, IS nodes collect lists of all ES nodes directly attached to them, and advertise these lists to each other to learn the placement of all ES nodes.

Level 2 routing is concerned with inter-area routing within the same domain, that is, routing between ES nodes that reside in different areas of the same domain. On Level 2, IS nodes do not advertise the list of connected ES nodes anymore. Instead, in this level, IS nodes exchange area prefixes to learn how to reach particular areas. If a Level 1 IS determines that the packet's destination ES is in a different area, it will forward the packet toward the nearest IS capable of Level 2 routing, regardless of the destination area. The packet will then be forwarded by Level 2–capable IS nodes until it reaches the area with the destination ES where it will again be forwarded by Level 1 IS nodes. Hence, Level 1 routing can be described as routing by System ID, while Level 2 routing can be described as routing by area prefix. Level 2 routing constitutes the backbone of a domain, providing communication between individual areas of the domain. Level 1 and Level 2 routing are provided by the IS-IS routing protocol (ISO 10589), which is the focus of this chapter.

Level 3 routing is concerned with interdomain routing. In a TCP/IP world, this is a fairly direct analogy of inter-autonomous system routing provided by Border Gateway Protocol (BGP). In OSI networks, the original intended routing protocol was Inter Domain Routing Protocol (IDRP, ISO 10747). However, with BGP being a multiprotocol interdomain routing protocol also capable of carrying information about NSAP addresses, today's OSI networks are replacing IDRP with BGP.

IS-IS provides Level 1 and Level 2 routing. Level 0 and Level 3 routing are provided by different mechanisms and are not relevant for TCP/IP networks.

## IS-IS Metrics, Levels, and Adjacencies

IS-IS metrics are assigned to individual interfaces (links). The original IS-IS specification defines four types of metrics:

- **Default:** Required to be supported by all IS-IS implementations; usually relates to the bandwidth of the link (higher value represents a slower link)

- **Delay:** Relates to the transit delay on the link

- **Expense:** Relates to the monetary cost of carrying data through the link

- **Error:** Relates to the residual bit error rate of the link

Each of these metrics is intended to be evaluated independently in the SPF calculation, effectively resulting in four independent shortest-path trees (and thus routing tables), each one computed according to a particular metric. Most IS-IS implementations today support only the default metric.

Cisco IS-IS implementation assigns all interfaces the default metric of 10, regardless of their bandwidth. Contrary to OSPF implementation, Cisco IOS does not automatically recalculate an interface's bandwidth into its IS-IS metric. It is up to the administrator to configure different interface metrics if necessary using the **isis metric** *metric* [ *level* ] per-interface command. Other types of metrics can be configured but are advertised as unsupported in IS-IS advertisements.

The original IS-IS specification and RFC 1195 define any single interface (link) and attached network metric to be 6 bits wide, resulting in the range of 1–63, and the complete path metric as 10 bits wide in the range of 1–1023. At the time IS-IS was defined, these metric widths were considered adequate. Today's requirements, however, call for a much wider range of metrics. Therefore, in RFC 3784 (now RFC 5305), so-called *wide metrics* were introduced, allowing for a 24-bit width for the interface metric and a 32-bit width for the entire path metric. The same RFC also defines a set of information elements augmenting the wide metrics for use in MPLS Traffic Engineering applications. The original metrics were retroactively named *narrow metrics*. It is strongly recommended to use wide metrics whenever available and supported; however, all routers in an area must use the same type of metrics.

IS-IS routers operate on each routing level independently. For each routing level, be it Level 1 or Level 2, an IS-IS router establishes separate adjacencies with its neighbors running on the same level, and maintains a separate link-state database. A router config ured for Level 1 routing establishes adjacencies only with those neighbors that are also configured for Level 1 routing. Similarly, a router configured for Level 2 routing creates adjacencies only with neighbors also configured for Level 2 routing. A Level 1–only router will not establish an adjacency to a Level 2–only router. Two neighboring routers configured for both Level 1 and Level 2 routing will create two independent adjacencies, one for each level. In addition, as each router belongs to a single area (recall that only a single NET is usually configured on a router, and the NET carries the area identifier), Level 1 adjacencies are created only between routers with the same area identifier. Table 10-3 documents the resulting adjacency for different combinations of neighboring rout-ers' levels.

Key
Topic

**Table 10-3**   *Adjacencies Between Routers*

| 1st Neighbor's Level | 2nd Neighbor's Level | Resulting Adjacency |
| --- | --- | --- |
| Level 1 only | Level 1 only | Level 1 if area matches |
| Level 1 only | Level 1 + 2 | Level 1 if area matches |
| Level 1 only | Level 2 only | No adjacency |
| Level 1 + 2 | Level 1 + 2 | Level 1 if area matches<br>Level 2 |
| Level 1 + 2 | Level 2 only | Level 2 |
| Level 2 only | Level 2 only | Level 2 |

IS-IS routers maintain a separate link-state database for each routing level they operate on. For each enabled level, a router originates and floods a Link State PDU (LSP; not to be confused with Label Switched Path, which is an unrelated term from MPLS using the same acronym). An LSP is similar to an OSPF Link State Update packet with one or more Link State Advertisements. IS-IS routers use Level 1 and Level 2 LSPs to describe their adjacencies on that particular level. As a result, a Level 1 link-state database contains only Level 1 LSPs describing only Level 1 adjacencies of their respective originating routers. Similarly, a Level 2 link-state database contains only Level 2 LSPs describing only Level 2 adjacencies of their originating routers. Contents of a Level 1 link-state database are exchanged only over Level 1 adjacencies, and Level 2 link-state database contents are exchanged over Level 2 adjacencies only. Illustratively, albeit slightly imprecisely, IS-IS can be thought as running a separate instance (or a process) on each routing level. While individual LSPs never leak between Level 1 and Level 2 databases, routing information computed using a particular link-state database can be injected in a very controlled way into the other database. Rules of doing that will be discussed further in the chapter.

## IS-IS Packet Types

IS-IS defines four basic types of packets:

- Hello packet

- Link State PDU

- Complete Sequence Numbers PDU

- Partial Sequence Numbers PDU

To ease the understanding, we will often be comparing IS-IS packet types to OSPF packet types, drawing on their similarities and differences, assuming that the reader is already well-acquainted with OSPF packets, their purpose, and contents. However, OSPF and IS-IS have been developed independently, and any comparisons here are used only to highlight similarities and differences, and should not suggest in any way that one protocol tries to mimic, more or less successfully, the other.

### Hello Packets

Key
Topic

Hello packets, also denoted as IIH (IS-IS Hello), are used to perform the usual task of detecting neighboring routers (and also their loss), verifying bidirectional visibility, establishing and maintaining adjacencies, and electing a Designated IS (DIS—similar to a Designated Router in OSPF). On broadcast-type interfaces, IS-IS routers use separate Hello packet types for L1 and L2 adjacencies. On point-to-point type interfaces, for efficiency reasons, a single L1L2 Hello, also called a point-to-point Hello, is used. Each router sends Hello packets every 10 seconds by default; the interval can be configured in the range of 1 to 65535 seconds using a per-interface **isis hello-interval** *seconds* [ *level* ] command for a particular routing level. Instead of defining a Hold timer directly, a Hello multiplier value is used to compute the Hold time as the Hello value multiplied by the Hello multiplier value. The default Hello multiplier value is 3, resulting in a Hold time of 30 seconds. The multiplier value can be changed by a per-interface **isis hello-multiplier** *multiplier* [ *level* ] command. As opposed to OSPF, timers do not need to match on neighboring routers.

On a DIS, the individual timers are *always* one-third of the configured timers (with default settings)—a DIS sends Hellos every 10/3=3.333 seconds, and the Hold interval is 30/3=10 seconds. With settings changed to a Hello time of 6 seconds and a Hello multiplier of 4, for example, a DIS would then send Hello packets every 6/3=2 seconds, and advertise a Hold interval of 24/3=8 seconds. This is done to detect a DIS or its outage more readily.

> **Note**   There are three types of Hello: Level 1 Hello, Level 2 Hello (both used on broad-cast networks), and L1L2 Hello (used on point-to-point interfaces). Hellos are sent every 10 seconds by default. The hold time is 30 seconds by default, and is computed using the Hello timer and Hello multiplier value as Hello time × Hello multiplier. On a DIS, timers are always set to one-third of the configured values. Timers do not need to match between routers.

## Link State PDUs

A Link State Protocol Data Unit (LSP) is used to advertise the routing information. An LSP is vaguely similar to an OSPF Link State Update packet containing one or more Link State Advertisements. There are, however, notable differences between OSPF LSU/LSA and IS-IS LSP.

In OSPF, the smallest standalone element of the link-state database is an LSA (note that LSA is not a packet itself). There are several types of LSAs in OSPF, each one of which describes a different type of a network object. In IS-IS, the smallest standalone element of the link-state database is an entire LSP. There are no different types of LSPs to describe different network objects; instead, these are described by distinct Type-Length-Value (TLV) records inside an LSP's variably sized payload.

Similar to OSPF LSAs that are uniquely identified by their type and Link-State ID, IS-IS LSPs are also uniquely identified by a number that consists of three parts:

- **System ID** of the router that originated this LSP (6 octets; taken from the router's NET address)

- **Pseudonode ID** that differentiates between the LSP describing the router itself and the LSPs for multiaccess networks in which the router is a Designated IS (1 octet)

- **LSP Number** denoting the fragment number of this LSP (1 octet). The LSP Number is also called simply the Fragment Number or Fragment for short.

We will denote this triplet of System ID + Pseudonode ID + LSP Number as LSPID. For LSPs that describe routers themselves, the Pseudonode ID is always set to 0. The meaning of Pseudonode LSP and Pseudonode IDs will be explained later in the chapter. For each routing level, a router originates a standalone LSP, that is, separate LSPs are originated for Level 1 and for Level 2, depending on what levels the router operates at.

To distinguish between various versions of the same LSP, each LSP has a sequence number—a 32-bit unsigned integer starting at 0x00000001 and ending at 0xFFFFFFFF. Each modification to an LSP is accompanied by incrementing its sequence number. If two LSPs with the same LSPID have a different sequence number, the LSP with the higher sequence number is more recent. This is similar to LSA sequence numbers in OSPF, although LSA sequence numbers start at 0x80000001 ($-2^{31}+1$) and end at 0x7FFFFFFF ($2^{31}-1$). In contrast to OSPF, which is able to handle the wrapover of the sequence number gracefully, IS-IS has no such facility. If the sequence number of an LSP reaches the maximum value, the originating router must be turned off for enough time to allow the LSP to expire, or its System ID must be changed. While this might sound like a serious flaw, even if a new version of an LSP was originated every second, it would take more than 136 years to reach the maximum sequence number—clearly a time that is beyond any reasonable router lifespan. IS-IS implementations also throttle down the LSP origination to avoid rapid increases of the sequence number.

Each LSP has a Remaining Lifetime value associated with it. When originated, the Remaining Lifetime is set to 1200 seconds (20 minutes), and is decreased. IS-IS routers refresh their self-originated LSPs every 15 minutes. If the LSP's Remaining Lifetime decreases to 0, the router will delete the LSP's body from the link-state database, keep only its header, and advertise the empty LSP with the Remaining Lifetime set to 0. Flooding an empty LSP with the Remaining Lifetime set to 0 is called an *LSP purge*. Router purging an LSP will not flush the LSP from its link-state database just yet, though. The expired LSP can be purged from the link-state database after an additional time called ZeroAgeLifetime set to 60 seconds. This is done to ensure that the LSP's header is retained until the purged LSP has been safely propagated to all neighbors. Cisco routers, however, appear to hold the empty LSP header for another 20 minutes.

Because IS-IS messages are encapsulated directly into Layer 2 frames whose maximum payload size—the Maximum Transmission Unit (MTU)—is limited, IS-IS must implement its own fragmentation functions for LSPs whose size exceeds the MTU. This fragmentation is accomplished in a relatively straightforward way. Each LSP consists of a fixed-size header and a variable-size body that contains one or more TLV records that carry the actual addressing and topological information. If putting all TLV records into a single LSP would cause it to exceed the MTU, the router will simply create multiple LSPs. Each of them will carry a particular subset of the TLV records to be advertised so that the MTU is not exceeded. These LSPs are identified with the same System and Pseudonode ID, and with an increasing LSP Number as the fragment number, starting from 0. An important fact is that this fragmentation is performed only by the router that originates the LSP. After the LSP is flooded, it must not be modified by any other router, and also not be defragmented and/or refragmented. A consequence of this rule is that across the entire flooding scope of the LSP (an area for a Level 1 LSP, or all Level 2 routers and their interconnections for a Level 2 LSP), the MTU on interfaces must be identical. If this requirement cannot be met, IS-IS routers must be manually configured to keep each LSP not bigger than the smallest MTU.

To illustrate the facts about LSPs, consider the topology shown in Figure 10-3.

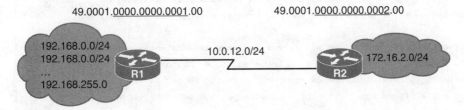

**Figure 10-3**  *Sample Network Requiring LSP Fragmentation*

Two routers, R1 and R2, are interconnected by a serial point-to-point link. R1 is connected to 256 different LANs, and R2 is connected to a single LAN. Example 10-1 shows and
explains the output of several **show** commands on R1.

Key
Topic

**Example 10-1**  *Link-State Database Contents and LSPs on R1*

```
! The show isis hostname on R1 displays the numerical System ID and the related
! hostname of the router with that ID. This mapping of hostnames to their
! System IDs is carried in LSPs along with addressing and adjacency information.


R1# show isis hostname
Level  System ID       Dynamic Hostname  (notag)
     * 0000.0000.0001 R1
 1     0000.0000.0002 R2


! The show isis database shows the contents of the link-state database.
! Because both routers have been configured as Level 1 routers, only a single
! database for Level 1 is displayed. Notice that in the output, the router
! automatically substitutes the numerical System ID for the router's hostname
! to make the output easily readable.


R1# show isis database


IS-IS Level-1 Link State Database:
LSPID                 LSP Seq Num  LSP Checksum  LSP Holdtime    ATT/P/OL
R1.00-00            * 0x00000002   0x4BD3        676             0/0/0
R1.00-01            * 0x00000002   0xF403        708             0/0/0
R1.00-02            * 0x00000003   0xF86B        643             0/0/0
R2.00-00              0x00000003   0x449C        574             0/0/0


! According to the output above, there are four LSPs in R1's link-state database,
! three originated by R1 and carrying information about R1, the other originated
! by R2. Each LSP is identified by the triplet SystemID.PseudonodeID-Fragment
! in the LSPID column. Also notice the sequence number and holdtime of each LSP.
! For LSPs that describe routers, the Pseudonode ID is always 0. Because R1 has
! a high number of directly connected networks to advertise, it needs to create
! three fragments of its LSP. On R2, all information it needs to advertise about
! itself fits into a single LSP. Entries in the show isis database output marked
! with the asterisk sign are the LSPs the router has originated itself.


! To see the LSP contents, we will check the show isis database detail output.
! R1's LSPs will be significantly abbreviated. Note the individual entries
! contained in LSPs: Information about the area the router is in, Network Layer
! Protocol ID field specifying the list of supported Layer3 protocols, Hostname,
! Router management IP address, directly connected IP networks, and neighboring IS
```

```
R1# show isis database detail

IS-IS Level-1 Link State Database:
LSPID                    LSP Seq Num  LSP Checksum  LSP Holdtime     ATT/P/OL
R1.00-00               * 0x00000003  0x49D4         957              0/0/0
  Area Address: 49.0001
  NLPID:        0xCC
  Hostname: R1
  IP Address:   192.168.0.1
  Metric: 10        IP 10.0.12.0 255.255.255.0
  Metric: 10        IP 192.168.0.0 255.255.255.0
  Metric: 10        IP 192.168.1.0 255.255.255.0
<output omitted>
  Metric: 10        IP 192.168.116.0 255.255.255.0
  Metric: 10        IP 192.168.117.0 255.255.255.0
R1.00-01               * 0x00000003  0xF204         950              0/0/0
  Metric: 10        IP 192.168.118.0 255.255.255.0
  Metric: 10        IP 192.168.119.0 255.255.255.0
<output omitted>
  Metric: 10        IP 192.168.236.0 255.255.255.0
  Metric: 10        IP 192.168.237.0 255.255.255.0
R1.00-02               * 0x00000004  0xF66C         872              0/0/0
  Metric: 10        IP 192.168.238.0 255.255.255.0
  Metric: 10        IP 192.168.239.0 255.255.255.0
<output omitted>
  Metric: 10        IP 192.168.254.0 255.255.255.0
  Metric: 10        IP 192.168.255.0 255.255.255.0
  Metric: 10        IS R2.00
R2.00-00                 0x00000004  0x429D         872              0/0/0
  Area Address: 49.0001
  NLPID:        0xCC
  Hostname: R2
  IP Address:   172.16.2.1
  Metric: 10        IP 10.0.12.0 255.255.255.0
  Metric: 10        IP 172.16.2.0 255.255.255.0
  Metric: 10        IS R1.00


! Note the straightforward readability of the LSPs. A directly connected network
! is marked by an "IP" label. A neighboring router is marked by an "IS" label
! and identified by its System ID and Pseudonode ID. All metrics default to 10.
```

In OSPF, a router originates possibly numerous LSAs of different types:

■  One type 1 LSA describing the router itself

■  One type 2 LSA for each multiaccess network in which this router is a designated router (DR)

■  One type 3 LSA for each inter-area prefix

■  One type 4 LSA for each autonomous system boundary router (ASBR) located in a different area if this router is an area border router (ABR)

■  One type 5 or type 7 LSA for each redistributed network if the router is an ASBR

Each of these LSA instances has its type, unique ID, sequence number, and age, and must be uniquely identified, flooded, acknowledged, refreshed, aged, and flushed. In IS-IS, a router on a particular routing level generates only a single (although possibly fragmented) LSP containing all relevant information related to that router in one place:

■  Adjacencies to neighboring routers or networks (similar to type 1 LSAs)

■  Intra-area and inter-area prefixes (similar to prefix information collected from type 1, 2, and 3 LSAs)

■  External prefixes (similar to type 5/7 LSAs)

Type 4 LSA is not mentioned here, as there is no similar type of information present in IS-IS LSPs.

Regarding type 2 LSA, in OSPF, this LSA carries two vital pieces of information:

■  The address and netmask of a multiaccess network (address information)

■  A list of connected routers to this network (topological information)

In IS-IS, the address information about all networks, both point-to-point and multiaccess, is contained in the LSP of each router connected to that network. The topological information about the network itself and the list of connected routers are contained in a so-called Pseudonode LSP generated by the DIS on the multiaccess network. An IS-IS router on a particular routing level therefore generates one LSP describing itself and all relevant topological information, plus one more Pseudonode LSP for each network it is a DIS in. Behavior of IS-IS on broadcast networks will be described in further detail in the section "IS-IS Operation over Broadcast Links," later in this chapter.

An LSP has a unique identifier as a whole, and can only be flooded, requested, acknowledged, refreshed, aged, and flushed as a whole. Therefore, with any topological or addressing change, affected routers regenerate their entire LSPs and flood them. While the reorigination and flooding of an entire LSP, even if only one TLV record needs to be changed, can be perceived as inefficient, the maintenance of the link-state database is significantly more simple: While in OSPF, each router needs to age and refresh each LSA it has originated (possibly many), each IS-IS router originates only a single LSP (plus Pseudonode LSPs if it is a DIS), and has therefore only a single or a few self-originated

LSPs to age and refresh. This saving is especially visible on inter-area and external prefix information, for which there can be hundreds or thousands of LSAs, one for each prefix. Additionally, the link-state database in IS-IS is more compact, as instead of individual LSAs, all information is grouped into LSPs.

Another difference between LSUs/LSAs and LSPs concerns their internal format with particular regard to extensibility. In OSPF, individual LSA types are strongly optimized toward the particular type of information they carry. That allows for efficient memory usage and their optimized processing. At the same time, however, it complicates adding new types of information, such as new address families, into existing LSA types. One of the reasons for the creation of OSPFv3, a new version of OSPF for IPv6, was the inability to carry IPv6 information in any of the basic OSPFv2 LSA types. While new types of information can be advertised using OSPFv2 Opaque LSAs (type 9, 10, and 11), an OSPFv2 router must nonetheless advertise its capability to store and forward Opaque LSAs to be sent these LSAs. OSPFv3 has been made more flexible in this aspect, as a router accepts even those LSAs whose type is unknown for possible further flooding. On the other hand, IS-IS encodes all topological and addressing information in Type-Length-Value records (the specification of IS-IS uses the term Code instead of Type). While slightly less efficient in terms of memory and processing, this approach allows extensibility from day zero: A router will process those TLV records it recognizes and ignore the records it does not support. The inclusion of the Length field allows a router to skip those records whose Type (and thus its content size) is not recognized.

> **Note**   LSP packets are used to carry topological and addressing information in IS-IS. An LSP describes its originator, its adjacencies to neighboring network objects, and related addressing. Each LSP is uniquely identified by the **SystemID.PseudonodeID-LSPNumber**. Each LSP has a sequence number, starting at 0x00000001 and ending at 0xFFFFFFFF. The lifespan of an LSP is limited by its Remaining Lifetime timer set to 1200 seconds and decreasing. After this timer expires, a router is required to wait at least another ZeroAgeLifetime (60 seconds) before flushing the LSP. LSPs are refreshed by default every 900 seconds. Separate LSPs are originated for Level 1 and Level 2.

## Complete and Partial Sequence Numbers PDUs

Complete Sequence Numbers PDU (CSNP) and Partial Sequence Numbers PDU (PSNP) packets are used to synchronize link-state databases. The *sequence numbers* term in names of these messages refers to the *range of LSPID values*, that is, about a *set of LSPs* these packets carry information about, and has no relation to the sequence numbers in individual LSP packets.

CSNP packets are very similar in their function to OSPF Database Description Packets. The purpose of CSNP packets is to advertise a complete list of LSPs in the sender's link-state database. Receivers of CSNP packets can compare their link-state database contents to the list of LSPs in the CSNP and perform appropriate action—flood a newer or missing LSP if they have one, or request an LSP if they find it missing in their own database.

If the sender's link-state database contains so many LSPs that listing them all in a single CSNP packet would cause it to exceed the MTU, multiple CSNPs are sent. For this purpose, the individual LSPIDs to be advertised are first sorted as integer numbers in ascending order. Each CSNP contains information about the Start LSPID and End LSPID that is described by this CSNP. The full range of possible LSPIDs starts with the value of **0000.0000.0000**.00-00 (the bold part is the System ID, the following octet is the Pseudonode ID, and the octet following the dash is the LSP Number ID), and ends with the value of **FFFF.FFFF.FFFF.FF-FF**. If all LSPs can be listed in a single CSNP, the Start and End LSPIDs will use these respective values. If it is necessary to send more CSNPs, the first CSNP will have the **0000.0000.0000**.00-00 as the Start LSPID, and the End LSPID will be set to the LSPID of the last entry in this CSNP. In the following CSNPs, the Start and End LSPIDs will be set to the respective LSPIDs of the first and last entry, sorted in ascending order. The last CSNP will have the value of **FFFF.FFFF.FFFF.FF-FF** as the End LSPID. This sorting of LSPIDs into ascending number and CSNPs sequentially listing all LSPIDs from the allowable range are the reasons for calling these PDUs Sequence Numbers PDUs. Note that CSNPs list only LSPIDs, but they do not contain LSP bodies.

**Key Topic**

On point-to-point links, CSNP packets are exchanged usually only during initial adjacency buildup; on broadcast networks, CSNP packets are originated periodically by the DIS.

PSNP packets are functionally similar to OSPF Link State Request and Link State Acknowledgment packets. Using PSNP, a router can either request a particular LSP or acknowledge its arrival. A single PSNP can request or acknowledge multiple LSPs. As a PSNP is intended to request or acknowledge individual LSPs by their LSPIDs, there are no Start or End LSPID fields present in PSNPs. As we will learn later, PSNP on point-to-point links are used both to request an LSP and acknowledge it. On broadcast networks, PSNP packets are used only to request an LSP. Acknowledgments on broadcast networks are accomplished by CSNP messages sent by Designated ISs.

**Note**   CSNP and PSNP packets are used to facilitate link-state database synchronization. CSNP packets contain a list of all LSPs in a sender's link-state database, allowing the recipient to compare this list to the index of its own link-state database. PSNP packets are used to request an LSP or acknowledge its successful arrival.

## IS-IS Operation over Different Network Types

Contrary to OSPF, which recognizes several network types, IS-IS natively supports only broadcast and point-to-point network types. Running IS-IS over Ethernet networks, as well as over HDLC, PPP, GRE tunnels, and point-to-point Frame Relay or ATM subinterfaces, works right out of the box. However, IS-IS has no special provisions to correctly operate over partially meshed data link layer technologies such as hub-and-spoke Frame Relay. Running IS-IS over such networks can result in partial visibility and incomplete routing tables. Recommended practice dictates that you configure such networks using point-to-point subinterfaces and run IS-IS over these point-to-point links.

It is noteworthy to mention that what IS-IS calls broadcast links should much better be called *multiaccess* links. The reason is that IS-IS is not really concerned about the capability of the data link layer technology to replicate broadcasts and multicasts but rather to create a communication environment in which multiple neighbors can be reached over the same interface, and each router can talk to each other router on the link. While we will adhere to the terminology specified in the IS-IS standard by using the term *broadcast*, the true meaning is more relevant to the term *multiaccess*.

IS-IS is much simpler in terms of adjacency states than OSPF with its eight states. In IS-IS, there are only three possible adjacency states:

Key
Topic

- **Down:** The initial state. No IIHs have been received from the neighbor.

- **Initializing:** IIHs have been received from the neighbor, but it is not certain that the neighbor is properly receiving this router's IIHs.

- **Up:** IIHs have been received from the neighbor, and it is certain that the neighbor is properly receiving this router's IIHs.

The way of verifying whether the two adjacent routers can hear each other differs on point-to-point and broadcast links. Also, the synchronization and flooding procedure is different on these two network types. The sections that follow examine these behaviors more closely.

## IS-IS Operation over Point-to-Point Links

On point-to-point interfaces, IS-IS expects to detect a single neighbor, bring up an adjacency, and then synchronize link-state databases.

The original IS-IS specification assumed that an adjacency could be brought up as soon as a point-to-point IIH was received from the neighbor. There was no verification of a bidirectional visibility between the two routers. This naïve approach led to problems if the point-to-point link was not capable of successfully carrying packets in both directions between the same pair of routers and their interfaces. Therefore, in RFC 3373 (now RFC 5303), a three-way handshake method for IS-IS adjacencies over point-to-point links was defined, and this method has now been universally adopted by major IS-IS implementors.

Before exploring the three-way handshake in closer detail, first recall from the section about OSI addressing that each router assigns a locally significant single octet number to each interface, and this number is called the Local Circuit ID. Local Circuit IDs on point-to-point interfaces appear only in IIH packets and are only used for detection of a change in identity at the other end of a link. On a broadcast link, the Local Circuit ID is used as the Pseudonode ID if the router acts as a DIS on that interface. Hence, the Local Circuit ID is required to be truly unique only for broadcast interfaces on which the router is a DIS, as this number is advertised in LSPs as the Pseudonode ID. Local Circuit IDs of broadcast and point-to-point interfaces do not clash; therefore, the same number can be reused both for broadcast and point-to-point interfaces. Example 10-2 shows how these IDs are displayed on point-to-point interfaces. Being a 1-octet quantity, it would appear that the Local Circuit ID limits a router to at most 256 interfaces. To support more than 256 point-to-point interfaces, the three-way handshake also introduces an Extended Local Circuit ID that is 4 octets long. Similar to a Local Circuit ID, it is assigned automatically to all interfaces on a router, and is used exclusively in the three-way handshake procedure.

**Example 10-2** *Local Circuit ID and Extended Local Circuit ID*

```
! The show clns interface on R2 displays vital information used by IS-IS
! in its operation. The clns keyword refers to Connection Less Network Services,
! the namespace in which CLNP would operate. The following output show Serial0/0/1
! interface before activating the three-way handshake utilizing Extended Local
! Circuit ID.

R2# show clns interface s0/0/1
Serial0/0/1 is up, line protocol is up
  Checksums enabled, MTU 1500, Encapsulation HDLC
  ERPDUs enabled, min. interval 10 msec.
  CLNS fast switching enabled
  CLNS SSE switching disabled
  DEC compatibility mode OFF for this interface
  Next ESH/ISH in 32 seconds
  Routing Protocol: IS-IS
    Circuit Type: level-1-2
    Interface number 0x2, local circuit ID 0x101
    Neighbor System-ID: R1
    Level-1 Metric: 10, Priority: 64, Circuit ID: R2.01
    Level-1 IPv6 Metric: 10
    Number of active level-1 adjacencies: 1
    Next IS-IS Hello in 4 seconds
    if state UP


! The Local Circuit ID here is set to 0x101. While this number is actually wider
! than 1 octet, this is just Cisco's internal implementation that enumerates
! point-to-point interfaces with Local Circuit IDs starting with 256 (0x100) while
! broadcast interfaces are enumerated starting with 0x0. While on wire, only the
! least significant octet of the ID is advertised, thereby apparently reusing the
! same number for broadcast and point-to-point interfaces, this approach allows
! a router to keep unique internal IDs internally.


! After activating the three-way handshake using isis three-way-handshake ietf
! command, the show clns interface also indicates the Extended Local Circuit ID:

R2# show clns interface s0/0/1
Serial0/0/1 is up, line protocol is up
  Checksums enabled, MTU 1500, Encapsulation HDLC
  ERPDUs enabled, min. interval 10 msec.
```

```
CLNS fast switching enabled
CLNS SSE switching disabled
DEC compatibility mode OFF for this interface
Next ESH/ISH in 19 seconds
Routing Protocol: IS-IS
  Circuit Type: level-1-2
  Interface number 0x2, local circuit ID 0x101
  Neighbor Extended Local Circuit ID: 0x0
  Neighbor System-ID: R1
  Level-1 Metric: 10, Priority: 64, Circuit ID: R2.01
  Level-1 IPv6 Metric: 10
  Number of active level-1 adjacencies: 1
  Next IS-IS Hello in 7 seconds
  if state UP
```

The three-way-handshake method is based on each router on a point-to-point link advertising an adjacency state TLV in its IIH packets that contains the following fields:

- **Adjacency Three Way State:** This is the state of adjacency as seen by the sending router.

- **Extended Local Circuit ID:** This is the ID of the sending router's interface.

- **Neighbor System ID:** This value is set to the ID of the neighboring router whose IIHs have been successfully received.

- **Neighbor Extended Local Circuit ID:** This value is set to the Extended Local Circuit ID field value from the neighbor's IIH packets.

Early implementations of the three-way handshake included only the Adjacency Three Way State field in the adjacency state TLV, and omitted all other fields described here. The logic of the three-way handshake was very simple. Consider two routers, Router A and Router B, both assumed to have not received an IIH from each other yet, and both treating the adjacency to be in the Down state:

1. If Router A receives an IIH from Router B with the Adjacency Three Way State set to Down, it is clear that Router A can hear Router B. It is not certain, though, whether Router B can hear Router A. Router A will start sending its IIH with the Adjacency Three Way State set to Initializing to tell Router B it can hear it.

2. When Router B receives an IIH from Router A with the Adjacency Three Way State set to Initializing, it knows that these IIHs are effectively sent in response to its own IIH, and that Router A is in fact telling Router B it can hear it. Router B is now certain that bidirectional communication is possible. Therefore, it starts sending its IIH with the Adjacency Three Way State set to Up.

3. When Router A receives an IIH from Router B with the Adjacency Three Way State set to Up, it knows Router B can hear it. Router A is now also certain that bidirectional communication is possible and starts sending its IIH with the Adjacency Three Way State set to Up, concluding the three-way handshake.

A slight variant of this sequence of steps would occur if both routers transmitted IIHs with the Adjacency Three Way State set to Down at the same time, both replied to each other with the State set to Initialize, and both arrived at the Up state simultaneously.

This simple method is in fact the default three-way handshake method used by Cisco on point-to-point interfaces, and can be configured using the **isis three-way-handshake cisco** interface command.

The simple approach is effective and works nicely in well-behaved cases; however, there are a few types of network failures in which the simple mechanism falls short. For example, if the transmission is running over a Frame Relay or ATM virtual circuit, it is possible to reconfigure the virtual circuit to be switched toward a different neighbor than before, without the actual (sub)interface going down and up. Other physical and data link layer technologies can exhibit the same behavior. Effectively, the change in the connectivity will go unnoticed if both routers continue to advertise that the adjacency state is Up. Another mode of failure is concerned with technologies in which the Rx and Tx directions are independent, such as in fiber technologies. In case of miswiring, it is possible that the Tx fiber connects to a different router than the Rx fiber. In certain topologies, this can lead to routers arriving to the Up state but sending packets to a different router than the one they hear the IIH from. Also, if a point-to-point link to a neighbor was moved from one of its interfaces to another, under certain circumstances, this change could go unnoticed.

Therefore, the adjacency state TLV was augmented with the Extended Local Circuit ID, Neighbor System ID, and Neighbor Extended Local Circuit ID fields to carry additional information about the neighbor's identity and interface. Their usage is fairly straightforward. Again, consider Router A and Router B connected with a point-to-point link. If no IIH from Router B has been received yet, Router A will be sending its IIH with only the Extended Local Circuit ID present, set to Router A's outgoing interface ID. The remaining Neighbor fields will not be present. When an IIH from Router B arrives and is accepted, Router A will put Router B's System ID into the Neighbor System ID field, put Router B's Extended Local Circuit ID into the Neighbor Extended Local Circuit ID field, and continue sending IIHs to Router B using these values. Using this information, Router B can verify whether Router A indeed hears B on the link (by comparing the indicated Neighbor System ID from the received IIH with its own System ID) and whether Router B can *speak* to Router A over the same interface it *hears* Router A on (by comparing the indicated Neighbor Extended Local Circuit ID from the received IIH with the ingress interface ID).

With these fields in place, an IIH that carries a three-way adjacency state TLV is accepted only if one of the following conditions is met:

Key
Topic

- The Neighbor System ID and Neighbor Extended Local Circuit ID are not present (typical at the beginning of the adjacency buildup, or the neighbor implements only the early version of the three-way handshake).

- The Neighbor System ID matches the receiving router's System ID and the Neighbor Extended Local Circuit ID matches the receiving interface's ID.

If these conditions are not met, the incoming IIH is silently dropped. Hence, these rules form an IIH acceptance check (in fact, one of many in IS-IS).

The operation of the three-way handshake with these additional fields is precisely the same as with the early implementation described previously—with the addition that every received IIH is subject to the acceptance check described previously. If the IIH does not pass the check, it is silently dropped, as if it never arrived. Therefore, the three-way handshake logic as described in the three previous steps changes simply by replacing all occurrences of *"receives IIH"* with *"receives and accepts IIH."*

This three-way handshake method can be configured using the **isis three-way-handshake ietf** interface command. It is noteworthy to mention that because the IETF three-way handshake method also accepts IIH packets with the adjacency TLV containing only the Adjacency Three Way State field without the other fields, it is also backward compatible with the Cisco early implementation. Hence, each router on a point-to-point link can use a different method and still successfully negotiate the adjacency with its neighbor. Naturally, using the same method on both routers is preferred, and if both routers support the IETF three-way handshake method, it should be used instead of the earlier implementation.

**Key Topic**

After the adjacency is declared as Up, routers will attempt to synchronize their link-state databases. This is accomplished in a somewhat heavyweight way: Both routers will *mark* all their LSPs for flooding over the point-to-point link; plus they send CSNP packets to each other. Because the IS-IS standard assumes that the actual transmission of LSPs marked for flooding is driven by a periodically scheduled process, it is possible that the CSNP packets are exchanged before the LSP transmission takes place. If a router learns from the received CSNP that its neighbor already has an LSP that is scheduled to be sent, the router will *unmark* the LSP, removing it from the set of LSPs to be flooded. This way, only the LSPs missing from the neighbor's database will be sent to it. In addition, if a router learns from the received CSNP that the neighbor has LSPs that are newer or unknown, it will request them using a PSNP packet. Note that neither of these is necessary, as both routers nonetheless initially set up all their LSPs to be flooded across the link, without the aid of CSNP or PSNP packets. The *initial* sending of CSNPs to compare the link-state databases and PSNPs to request missing or updated entries increases the resiliency of the synchronization process but is not strictly necessary: Without these packets, routers will simply exchange the full link-state database.

**Key Topic**

Importantly, though, every LSP sent over a point-to-point link, whether during the initial database synchronization or anytime later when it is updated or purged, must be acknowledged, and this is done using PSNP or CSNP packets. Because the IS-IS specification says that CSNP packets are not periodically exchanged on point-to-point links, each sent LSP must be acknowledged by a corresponding PSNP from the neighbor. Interestingly, though, *if* the neighbor was also sending periodic CSNPs (which the IS-IS specification does not explicitly prohibit!), they would be also accepted as valid acknowledgments. Some vendors implement periodic CSNPs even on point-to-point links to further increase the reliability of the flooding process. Cisco routers by default do not use periodic CSNPs on point-to-point interfaces, but if required, they can be activated using the **isis csnp-interval** *interval* [ *level* ] interface command with a nonzero interval value for a particular routing level.

## IS-IS Operation over Broadcast Links

On broadcast links, IS-IS shares many traits with OSPF. The basic operation is similar: Routers must create adjacencies, synchronize their databases, and keep them synchronized.

On Ethernet networks, IS-IS packets are encapsulated into IEEE 802.2 Logical Link Control (LLC) formatted frames with Destination Service Access Point (DSAP) and Source Service Access Point (SSAP) fields set to 0xFE. All Level 1 IS-IS packets are sent to the multicast MAC address 0180.c200.0014, while all Level 2 IS-IS packets use the 0180.c200.0015 as their destination MAC address.

Detecting neighbors is again performed by IIH packets. In a fashion similar to OSPF, an IS-IS router lists the MAC addresses (or better said, SNPAs) of all neighboring routers it hears on a broadcast interface in its IIH packet sent through that interface. If a router receives an IIH from a neighbor and finds its own SNPA indicated in the IIH, it knows that the routers can see each other, and can move the adjacency to the Up state. If IIH packets from a neighbor do not contain the receiving router's SNPA, the adjacency is kept in the Initializing state. OSPF performs a similar operation, but it lists Router IDs of heard routers in its Hello packets.

Similar to OSPF, which elects a designated router (DR) and a backup designated router (BDR) on each broadcast network, IS-IS also elects one Designated IS for each broadcast network. IS-IS has no concept of a backup DIS, and in fact, it does not need it, as we shall see later. A DIS is elected based on these criteria:

**Key Topic**

- The router with the highest interface priority.

- In case of a tie, the router with the highest SNPA.

- In case the SNPAs are not comparable, the router with the highest System ID. This rule is used on Frame Relay and ATM physical interfaces and multipoint subinterfaces, which are treated as broadcast interfaces by IS-IS. On these interfaces, each router can see itself and a particular neighbor on the same virtual circuit (VC) identified by the same Data Link Connection Identifier (DLCI) or Virtual Path Identifier/Virtual Channel Identifier (VPI/VCI) (that is, this router's and the neighbor's SNPA appear to be the same), and in addition, there can be multiple VCs terminated under a single interface, so it is ambiguous which VC ID should be used as the SNPA.

The interface priority is a number in the range of 0 to 127 configurable using a per-interface **isis priority** *priority* [ *level* ] command. The entire range is usable; no number in this range has a special meaning. 0 is a valid priority as well, and it does exclude a router from participating in DIS elections. In addition, DIS elections in IS-IS are preemptive: Whenever a router is connected that has a higher priority than the current DIS, or the same priority and higher SNPA (or in case the SNPA is not comparable as described before, the same priority and higher System ID), it will take over the DIS role. The DIS elections are effectively performed with each received IIH. Thus, the DIS role is not influenced by the order that routers were started or connected to a segment, and is deterministic.

As mentioned previously, two routers on a broadcast segment become adjacent as soon as it is verified that they can hear each other, and the adjacency state is put into the Up state. Note that in this process, there is no distinction whether any of these routers is the DIS. In other words, in IS-IS, all routers on a common broadcast segment become fully adjacent, regardless of which is the DIS. This is different from OSPF, in which only the DR and BDR become fully adjacent to all other routers on a broadcast segment. In IS-IS, every router can send an LSP on the broadcast link and all others are allowed to accept it. In OSPF, a DRother router can send an LSU/LSA only to the DR and BDR, and the DR will in turn forward it back to remaining routers on the segment, effectively working as a relay. As the DIS is not doing any similar relaying, you might wonder—what it the purpose of DIS, then?

A DIS is responsible for two important operations:

- Helping routers on a broadcast segment to synchronize

- Representing the broadcast segment in the link-state database as a standalone object—the Pseudonode

**Key Topic**

Synchronization of IS-IS routers on a broadcast network is surprisingly simple. The DIS creates and sends a CSNP packet in regular intervals (10 seconds by default) on the segment. This CSNP packet lists all LSPs present in the DIS's link-state database. Other routers on the segment receive this CSNP and compare it to the index of their own link-state database. Possible results of this comparison are as follows (the term *router* here refers to any other router on the segment that receives and processes a CSNP packet from DIS):

- The router has an LSP with the same LSPID in its link-state database, with the same sequence number. No action needs to be performed; this is a confirmation that both the router and the DIS have the same LSP.

- The router does not have an LSP with the indicated LSPID in its link-state database, or the LSP's sequence number on DIS is higher. The router needs to download the LSP from the DIS by creating a PSNP requesting the LSP in question and forwarding it onto the segment. The DIS will receive the PSNP and flood the requested LSP.

- The router has an LSP with the same LSPID in its link-state database but its sequence number on the DIS is lower, or the DIS does not advertise this LSPID. The router needs to update the DIS simply by flooding the LSP on the network right away.

**Key Topic**

Note the simplicity of this mechanism. The DIS is not a relay of LSPs; rather, it is a reference point of comparison. If a router misses an LSP known by the DIS, or if the LSP is older than the one known by the DIS, the router will request the newer LSP through PSNP and the DIS will flood it. If the PSNP or the LSP gets lost during transmission, the process will simply repeat itself. Conversely, if a router knows about a newer LSP than the one known by the DIS, or if the DIS seems to miss it completely, the router will simply flood the LSP onto the network. No explicit acknowledgment by the DIS is sent.

If the LSP has arrived, the DIS will advertise it in its next periodic CSNP, and this CSNP serves as an implicit acknowledgment. If the DIS does not advertise the LSP even after the router has flooded it, it must have been lost in transit, and the router will simply flood it again. If a router learns about a new LSP, it will flood it onto the segment, and will expect the DIS to advertise this LSP in its subsequent CSNPs (if not, it refloods the LSP). If another router on the segment did not receive this LSP, it will learn about it from CSNPs and will request it from the DIS. PSNPs are used on broadcast networks only to request LSPs, not to acknowledge them. This way, full synchronization is achieved between all routers on a broadcast segment by a mechanism considerably simpler than in OSPF.

Another responsibility of the DIS is to represent the broadcast network in the link-state database so that the topological model of the network is simpler. Consider Figure 10-4.

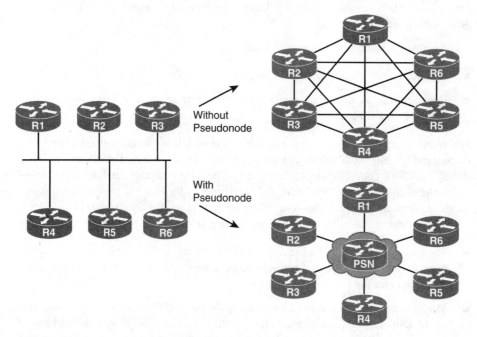

**Figure 10-4**   *Use of Pseudonode in IS-IS*

Without a pseudonode, this network of six routers on a broadcast segment would be represented in the link-state database as the "dense" fully meshed topology on the upper right. Each of the six routers would need to create five entries in its LSP, point-ing toward each other router on the segment. The link-state database would, just for this single network, contain 6*5=30 links. Generally, with N routers on a single broadcast network, there would be N(N–1) links, their count growing quadratically with the num-ber of routers. That would cause an increased memory footprint and a possibly slower SPF computation.With a pseudonode, the broadcast network itself is represented as a node—more specifically, a *pseudo*node—in the topology, as shown in the lower right. The resulting topological model is much more simple and natural: Each router claims it is connected to the broadcast network represented by the pseudonode (which it truly is), and the network also claims connectivity to every attached router. In this model, there are only 6*2=12 links (each router advertising a link to the network; the network advertising a link to each router). This is exactly what OSPF accomplishes with its LSA2.

To exist as a pseudonode in a link-state database, a broadcast network must have its own LSP. It is the responsibility of the DIS to originate and flood the Pseudonode LSP on behalf of the broadcast network. Recall that each LSP is identified by a triplet of System ID, Pseudonode ID, and LSP Fragment Number. Also recall that an IS-IS router internally enumerates its interfaces using a 1-octet value called the Local Circuit ID. In case of router LSPs, the System ID carries the ID of the router and the Pseudonode ID is set to 0. In case of network LSPs (that is, Pseudonode LSPs), the System ID is the ID of the DIS, and the Pseudonode ID is set to the Local Circuit ID of the DIS's interface in the network. Refer to Figure 10-5 and Example 10-3.

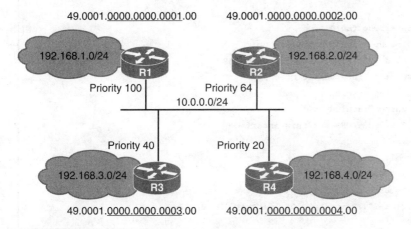

**Figure 10-5**  *DIS Elections on a Broadcast Segment*

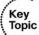

**Example 10-3**  *DIS, Pseudonode LSP, and Its Contents*

```
! On R1, show isis hostname is used to check the mapping of hostnames to System IDs


R1# show isis hostname
Level  System ID       Dynamic Hostname  (notag)
     * 0000.0000.0001 R1
1      0000.0000.0002 R2
1      0000.0000.0003 R3
1      0000.0000.0004 R4


! To verify IS-IS neighbor adjacencies, show isis neighbors is useful


R1# show isis neighbors
```

```
System Id     Type Interface   IP Address      State Holdtime Circuit Id
R4            L1   Fa0/0        10.0.0.4        UP    26       R1.02
R3            L1   Fa0/0        10.0.0.3        UP    29       R1.02
R2            L1   Fa0/0        10.0.0.2        UP    27       R1.02
```

```
! Using show isis neighbors detail would also show information about each router's
! SNPA and configured priority. We omit the output for brevity purposes.


! According to Figure 10-5, R1 has the highest configured priority using
! isis priority 100 command on its Fa0/0 interface, and so should become
! the DIS. This can be confirmed in the show clns interface fa0/0 output.
! Note the DR ID indeed says that it is R1. Also note that the Local Circuit ID
! is set to 0x2, and it becomes the Pseudonode ID


R1# show clns interface fa0/0
FastEthernet0/0 is up, line protocol is up
  Checksums enabled, MTU 1497, Encapsulation SAP
  ERPDUs enabled, min. interval 10 msec.
  CLNS fast switching enabled
  CLNS SSE switching disabled
  DEC compatibility mode OFF for this interface
  Next ESH/ISH in 7 seconds
  Routing Protocol: IS-IS
    Circuit Type: level-1-2
    Interface number 0x1, local circuit ID 0x2
    Level-1 Metric: 10, Priority: 100, Circuit ID: R1.02
    DR ID: R1.02
    Level-1 IPv6 Metric: 10
    Number of active level-1 adjacencies: 3
    Next IS-IS LAN Level-1 Hello in 1 seconds


! The show isis database on R1 lists 5 LSPs - one for each router, plus one
! Pseudonode LSP that is recognizable by its Pseudonode ID being non-zero:
! it is R1.02-00. Notice that as explained earlier, its LSPID consists of
! System ID set to that of DIS, in this case, R1; Pseudonode ID set to the
! Local Circuit ID of DIS's interface, in this case, 0x2; and the Fragment 0.


R1# show isis database


IS-IS Level-1 Link State Database:
LSPID                   LSP Seq Num  LSP Checksum  LSP Holdtime    ATT/P/OL
R1.00-00              * 0x00000003   0x1481        624             0/0/0
R1.02-00              * 0x00000003   0x67C9        729             0/0/0
R2.00-00                0x00000002   0x583A        626             0/0/0
R3.00-00                0x00000002   0x9AF3        678             0/0/0
R4.00-00                0x00000002   0xDCAD        730             0/0/0
```

```
! To see the contents of LSPs, show isis database detail is issued.
! Note that each router advertises the common network 10.0.0.0/24 in its LSP,
! and also, that each router advertises a connectivity to the common network
! by referencing only the Pseudonode LSP R1.02 as an "IS", and not each other's
! LSP. The Pseudonode LSP only contains the list of routers connected to the network.

R1# show isis database detail

IS-IS Level-1 Link State Database:
LSPID                   LSP Seq Num  LSP Checksum  LSP Holdtime    ATT/P/OL
R1.00-00              * 0x00000003   0x1481        527             0/0/0
  Area Address: 49.0001
  NLPID:         0xCC
  Hostname: R1
  IP Address:    192.168.1.1
  Metric: 10        IP 10.0.0.0 255.255.255.0
  Metric: 10        IP 192.168.1.0 255.255.255.0
  Metric: 10        IS R1.02
R1.02-00             * 0x00000003   0x67C9        632             0/0/0
  Metric: 0         IS R1.00
  Metric: 0         IS R4.00
  Metric: 0         IS R3.00
  Metric: 0         IS R2.00
R2.00-00               0x00000002   0x583A        528             0/0/0
  Area Address: 49.0001
  NLPID:         0xCC
  Hostname: R2
  IP Address:    192.168.2.1
  Metric: 10        IP 10.0.0.0 255.255.255.0
  Metric: 10        IP 192.168.2.0 255.255.255.0
  Metric: 10        IS R1.02
R3.00-00               0x00000002   0x9AF3        580             0/0/0
  Area Address: 49.0001
  NLPID:         0xCC
  Hostname: R3
  IP Address:    192.168.3.1
  Metric: 10        IP 10.0.0.0 255.255.255.0
  Metric: 10        IP 192.168.3.0 255.255.255.0
  Metric: 10        IS R1.02
R4.00-00               0x00000002   0xDCAD        631             0/0/0
  Area Address: 49.0001
  NLPID:         0xCC
  Hostname: R4
  IP Address:    192.168.4.1
```

```
Metric: 10        IP 10.0.0.0 255.255.255.0
Metric: 10        IP 192.168.4.0 255.255.255.0
Metric: 10        IS R1.02
```

Finally, the router acting as a DIS shortens its own Hello and Hold time to just one-third of the configured values. This is done to allow other routers to detect its failure more rapidly. If a DIS fails, another router will be elected in its place, but because there is no additional adjacency buildup necessary (all routers on the segment are already fully adjacent), a DIS switchover is merely related to replacing the old Pseudonode LSP originated by the previous DIS with a new LSP from the newly elected DIS and remaining routers updating their LSPs to point toward the new Pseudonode LSP. Relative simplicity of this process is the reason why IS-IS does not have a concept of a backup DIS—it does not really need it.

## Areas in IS-IS

The concept of routing levels in OSI networks is crucial to understanding inter-area routing in IS-IS, so it is worth revisiting.

Figure 10-6 shows the structure of an NSAP address, this time with added information about how IS-IS interprets it. Because only a single NSAP address is assigned to a node, and the NSAP address contains the domain and area identifier, the entire node with all its interfaces belongs only to a single area.

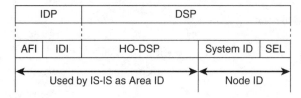

**Figure 10-6**  *NSAP Address as Interpreted by IS-IS*

Because routers are also usually assigned a single NSAP address, they also belong to a single area only. It is in fact possible to configure up to three different NSAP addresses on an IS-IS router in a single IS-IS instance, provided that the System ID in all NSAP addresses is identical and the NSAP addresses differ only in their Area ID. A router with multiple NSAP addresses will nonetheless maintain only a single link-state database, causing all configured areas to merge together. This behavior is useful when splitting, joining, or renumbering areas. For example, when you are renumbering an area, all routers are first added a second NSAP address with the new Area ID and then the old NSAP address is removed—without causing any adjacencies between routers to flap. Similarly, when you are joining two areas, routers in an annexed area are given the new NSAP with the same Area ID as the area into which they are being joined, and afterward, the old NSAP is removed. Splitting an area again uses a similar approach—first add the new NSAP address to all routers, and afterward, remove the former NSAP address. These changes can be done without disruptions to network operation, which is an obvious advantage.

Multiple NSAP addresses on an IS-IS instance are nonetheless used only during network changes, and in stable operation, there should be only a single NSAP address configured per IS-IS process. Necessarily, area boundaries are then placed on links. It is important to mention that IS-IS uses the entire high-order part of the NSAP address up to the start of System ID as the area identifier, although it covers much more information. This is logical, though: Nodes in a single area must obviously be addressed using the same NSAP format, the same initial domain identifier, and the same internal area number (high-order domain specific part). Any difference in these octets would signify that the addressing format is different (and hence incomparable to any other), or the domain (that is, the autonomous system) is different, or the internal area numbering differs. To provide the necessary isolation of information between areas, IS-IS routers maintain separate and independent Level 1 (L1 in short) and Level 2 (L2 in short) link-state databases, and do not allow LSPs from one database to ever leak into the other.

L1 routing is a process of intra-area routing, that is, delivering packets between stations located in the same area. If OSI protocols such as CLNP were in use, routers would collect NSAP addresses of their directly attached end hosts and advertise them in their routing updates simply as other adjacencies. With IP protocols, each L1 router advertises its *directly connected IP networks* in its L1 LSP. A very important fact is that two interconnected neighboring L1 routers configured with different areas will never establish an adjacency. Compounded with the fact that L1 and L2 link-state databases do not leak LSPs to each other, these rules together make sure that L1 routers keep the intra-area information contained and never leak it to another area.

L2 routing is a process of inter-area routing, that is, delivering packets between stations located in different areas. If OSI protocols were in use, routers would *not* collect nor advertise end host NSAP addresses. Instead, routers would only advertise their area IDs in their L2 LSPs. Because to reach an end host with a particular NSAP, the area described in the NSAP must first be reached; therefore, L2 routing in OSI networks would be concerned only with area IDs. L2 routers therefore form a backbone of a multiarea domain, and for this backbone to operate correctly, it must be contiguous and pervade all areas within the domain. Sometimes, the backbone as the set of L2 routers is also called an L2 subdomain. With IP protocols, IP addresses do not carry embedded area information like NSAP addresses. Therefore, the logic of populating L2 LSPs with IP networks is slightly different. Each L2 router advertises its *directly connected IP networks* to achieve contiguous IP connectivity in the backbone, *plus all other L1 routes from its own area with appropriate metrics*, to advertise IP networks present in particular areas. Thus, while LSPs are never leaked between L1 and L2 link-state databases, on L2 routers, IP routing information computed from the router's L1 link-state database is injected into its L2 LSP. In other words, IP routing information flows from L1 into L2. There is no opposite flow of routing information; that is, no IP networks are injected from L2 into L1 unless specifically configured. L2 routers establish adjacencies regardless of their areas. Thus, the entire L2 subdomain becomes aware of all IP networks in the domain, forming a true backbone between areas.

Areas in OSPF cannot be directly likened to IS-IS areas, because the visibility and behavior of IS-IS routers within an area depend on the routing level enabled on those routers. L1 routers in an area have no L2 link-state database and therefore have no information about other areas that is carried by L2 routers. From this viewpoint, L1 routers in an area have a visibility identical to routers in an OSPF Totally Stubby Area—they see their own area but nothing more. Yet, an L1 router can still perform redistribution from external sources, and these redistributed networks will be visible both in that area and uptaken by L2 routers into the backbone. Therefore, L1 routers in an area behave more as if they were in an OSPF Not So Stubby-Totally Stubby (NSSA-TS) area.

L2 routers disrespect area boundaries when it comes to creating adjacencies and flooding link-state database contents. They create adjacencies with other L2 routers regardless of the area ID, and share all information present in their L2 link-state databases. Therefore, the entire L2 subdomain across all areas in the entire domain can be likened to a single OSPF backbone area.

IS-IS on Cisco routers defaults to L1L2 operation, meaning that both L1 and L2 routing are enabled by default.

Figure 10-7 presents an example network containing three areas. Each router emulates a LAN on its loopback interface, using an address in the form 10.<Area>.<Router>.1/24; for example, R4 is located in area 49.0002, and its loopback is thus 10.2.4.1/24. Links between routers inside an area are addressed as 10.<Area>.<Ri><Rj>.0/24; for example, a link between R6 and R7 in area 49.0003 is addressed using 10.3.67.0/24. Addresses on inter-area links are shown in the figure. Importantly, Routers R2 – R3 – R4 – R6 are configured as L1L2 routers and form a contiguous backbone that crosses all areas in the domain. Note that because R5 is not an L2-enabled router, if the link between R3 and R4 failed, the backbone would become discontiguous. R5, even though physically interconnecting R3 and R4, has no information from the L2 subdomain (the backbone), and is not capable of routing packets between different areas because it does not know about other areas.

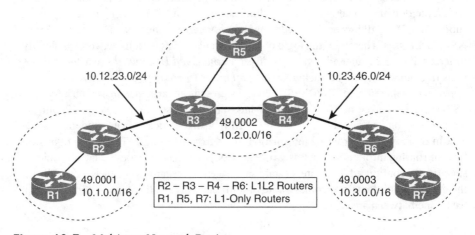

**Figure 10-7**  *Multiarea Network Design*

Example 10-4 shows R1's IS-IS link-state database and routing table. Note the default administrative distance of 115 for all IS-IS-learned routes.

**Example 10-4**  *R1's Link-State Database in a Multiarea Network*

```
! Area 49.0001 contains two routers, R1 and R2. R1 is configured as L1-only router.
! On R1, show isis database displays only two L1 LSPs, one for each router. Also
! note that because R1 is limited to L1 operation, it does not maintain any L2
! LSPs, either originated by itself or downloaded from R2.


R1# show isis database

IS-IS Level-1 Link State Database:
LSPID                  LSP Seq Num  LSP Checksum  LSP Holdtime      ATT/P/OL
R1.00-00             * 0x00000020   0x2207        841               0/0/0
R2.00-00               0x00000020   0xCC8A        506               1/0/0


! Notice that in the last column denoted ATT/P/OL, the ATT flag of R2 is set to 1.
! This means R2 is actively attached to backbone, and is therefore a prospective
! area border router to handle traffic destined to other areas. Details will
! be described later.


! The show isis database detail shows us the contents of L1 LSPs. Note that each
! L1 LSP contains IP addresses of networks directly attached to the router that
! originated the LSP. In R2's LSP, the inter-area link is also advertised.


R1# show isis database detail

IS-IS Level-1 Link State Database:
LSPID                  LSP Seq Num  LSP Checksum  LSP Holdtime      ATT/P/OL
R1.00-00             * 0x00000020   0x2207        828               0/0/0
  Area Address: 49.0001
  NLPID:        0xCC
  Hostname: R1
  IP Address:   10.1.1.1
  Metric: 10        IP 10.1.12.0 255.255.255.0
  Metric: 10        IP 10.1.1.0 255.255.255.0
  Metric: 10        IS R2.00
R2.00-00               0x00000020   0xCC8A        493               1/0/0
  Area Address: 49.0001
  NLPID:        0xCC
  Hostname: R2
  IP Address:   10.1.2.1
  Metric: 10        IP 10.12.23.0 255.255.255.0
  Metric: 10        IP 10.1.12.0 255.255.255.0
```

```
    Metric: 10        IP 10.1.2.0 255.255.255.0
    Metric: 10        IS R1.00


! The routing table on R1 shows the usual list of directly connected networks,
! plus the list of other networks in area 49.0001, all listed as L1. Note that
! R1 installed a default route towards R2, though in R2's LSP, there is no
! explicit default route advertised.


R1# show ip route
Codes: C - connected, S - static, R - RIP, M - mobile, B - BGP
       D - EIGRP, EX - EIGRP external, O - OSPF, IA - OSPF inter area
       N1 - OSPF NSSA external type 1, N2 - OSPF NSSA external type 2
       E1 - OSPF external type 1, E2 - OSPF external type 2
       i - IS-IS, su - IS-IS summary, L1 - IS-IS level-1, L2 - IS-IS level-2
       ia - IS-IS inter area, * - candidate default, U - per-user static route
       o - ODR, P - periodic downloaded static route


Gateway of last resort is 10.1.12.2 to network 0.0.0.0


     10.0.0.0/24 is subnetted, 4 subnets
C       10.1.12.0 is directly connected, Serial0/0/0
i L1    10.1.2.0 [115/20] via 10.1.12.2, Serial0/0/0
C       10.1.1.0 is directly connected, Loopback0
i L1    10.12.23.0 [115/20] via 10.1.12.2, Serial0/0/0
i*L1 0.0.0.0/0 [115/10] via 10.1.12.2, Serial0/0/0
```

**Key Topic**

A couple of facts from this example deserve mention. We have not yet discussed the rightmost column in **show isis database** output, where three flags, ATT, P, and OL, are displayed. These flags are called ATTached, Partition repair, and Overload flags. The ATT flag is especially relevant to inter-area routing. When an L1L2 router performs its L2 SPF calculation and determines that it can reach other areas besides its own (note that LSPs also carry the area ID of their originating routers), it sets the ATT flag in its L1 LSP, effectively saying "I have a working attachment to other areas, so I can do inter-area routing." L1-only routers in the area can use any router whose ATT bit is set in its L1 LSP to reach other areas. Because no IP addressing information flows down from L2 into L1, L1-only routers have no knowledge about prefixes in other areas. Reaching them can therefore be accomplished by means of a default route, and this is exactly what L1-only routers do: They automatically install a default route toward their nearest L1L2 router whose ATT bit is set into their routing table. Note in Example 10-4, R1 installed a default route toward R2, although L2 does not advertise such a route in its LSP. What R1 did was to look at other routers' LSPs, and from the available routers advertising their ATT bit set, choose the closest one and inject a default route toward that router into its routing table. If R2 loses connection to R3 and, as a result, its L2 SPF computation shows that the only L2 routers it can reach are from its own area, it clears the ATT bit and floods the updated L1 LSP. That will cause R1 to remove the default route pointing toward R2 from its routing table.

The Partition repair bit indicates whether the router is capable of an optional feature that allows healing a partitioned area over the L2 subdomain—functionality similar to an OSPF virtual link. The Partition repair function was never widely implemented, and Cisco routers do not support it; hence they always set the P bit to 0.

Finally, the Overload bit was originally intended to signal that the router is, for whatever reason, unable to store all LSPs in its memory, and that its link-state database is overloaded. Running SPF over an incomplete link-state database will produce an incomplete routing table, and routing packets over this router to distant networks could result in routing loops or traffic blackholing. Therefore, if a router's LSP has the O bit set, the SPF computation on other routers will ignore this router when computing shortest paths to other routers and their networks. However, the SPF will still take the directly attached networks of this router into account because these continue to be reachable. In other words, if the O bit set is on an LSP, the SPF calculation will ignore all "IS" adjacencies indicated in the LSP, but it will continue to process the end system adjacencies, such as "IP," that denote directly attached networks. The router will thus not be used as a transit router to other routers, but it still will be considered as a router usable to reach its own directly connected networks.

Today, the use cases of the O bit have evolved beyond its original meaning and intention. As it can also be set or cleared by a configuration command, it is very useful when, say, a router needs to be taken out of service for maintenance without causing major disruption to the network. Instead of simply shutting the router down, setting the O bit first will make other routers immediately recalculate their routing tables, computing alternate paths (if such paths exist) that do not traverse this router. The network converges on alternate paths much sooner than it would take if the router was simply taken offline and other routers needed to wait for its Hold timer to expire. Also, the O bit is very useful if a new router is to be attached to a network, its routing table populated by IS-IS and its behavior verified, without actually having the network route the packets through the new router. When you set the O bit, the new router can be plugged into the network and have its IS-IS converge, without actually altering paths in the network. Yet another important application of the O bit is to allow the router to settle its adjacencies after reboot and wait for some time to stabilize while already running IS-IS and populating its routing table, before becoming a transit router. This feature is especially important with BGP that can converge significantly slower than IS-IS, and routing packets through a router right after it has rebooted and converged in IS-IS—without waiting for its BGP peerings to come up and synchronize with the peers—could again result in temporary traffic black holes. It is possible to configure the router so that after a reboot, it sets the O bit and clears it either after a predefined time period, or when BGP signals it has converged. This particular use of the O bit is documented nicely in RFC 3277.

Now check R2. Example 10-5 shows a series of outputs.

**Example 10-5**   *R2's Link-State Database in a Multiarea Network*

**Key Topic**

```
! First, show ip route isis is issued on R2, showing a series of L1 and L2 routes.
! As an L1L2 router, R2 knows about all networks in the domain, both internal and
! inter-area.

R2# show ip route isis
     10.0.0.0/24 is subnetted, 14 subnets
i L1    10.1.1.0 [115/20] via 10.1.12.1, Serial0/0/1
i L2    10.2.3.0 [115/20] via 10.12.23.3, Serial0/0/0
i L2    10.2.4.0 [115/30] via 10.12.23.3, Serial0/0/0
i L2    10.2.5.0 [115/30] via 10.12.23.3, Serial0/0/0
i L2    10.3.7.0 [115/50] via 10.12.23.3, Serial0/0/0
i L2    10.3.6.0 [115/40] via 10.12.23.3, Serial0/0/0
i L2    10.2.45.0 [115/30] via 10.12.23.3, Serial0/0/0
i L2    10.2.34.0 [115/20] via 10.12.23.3, Serial0/0/0
i L2    10.2.35.0 [115/20] via 10.12.23.3, Serial0/0/0
i L2    10.23.46.0 [115/30] via 10.12.23.3, Serial0/0/0
i L2    10.3.67.0 [115/40] via 10.12.23.3, Serial0/0/0

! Issuing the show isis database on R2 will reveal that R2 maintains two link-state
! databases, one for L1 and another for L2. The L1 database contents are identical
! to the L1 database on R1 shown in Example 10-4 so no further comments are needed.
! In its L2 database, R2 keeps an LSP from each L2-enabled router in the domain.

R2# show isis database

IS-IS Level-1 Link State Database:
LSPID               LSP Seq Num  LSP Checksum  LSP Holdtime    ATT/P/OL
R1.00-00            0x00000034   0xF91B        584             0/0/0
R2.00-00          * 0x00000039   0x9AA3        1193            1/0/0
IS-IS Level-2 Link State Database:
LSPID               LSP Seq Num  LSP Checksum  LSP Holdtime    ATT/P/OL
R2.00-00          * 0x00000036   0xF6A2        823             0/0/0
R3.00-00            0x00000044   0x98F1        539             0/0/0
R4.00-00            0x0000003B   0xD3B9        899             0/0/0
R6.00-00            0x00000035   0x4BD4        918             0/0/0

! To see the contents of L2 database, the show isis database l2 detail command
! is used. Note in the following output that each the L2 LSP of each router
! contains both its directly connected networks along with all L1 networks
! in that router's area. For example, R2 advertises the network 10.1.1.0/24
! even though that network is an L1 network learned from R1 (see the routing table
! above) but which is nonetheless a network internal to R2's area. The metric
! of each L1 network advertised in L2 LSPs corresponds to the router's L1 total
! metric towards that network. Each L2-enabled router becomes a representative
```

```
! for its area, advertising all its internal networks. This is nicely seen
! on R3's and R4's LSPs.

R2# show isis database l2 detail

IS-IS Level-2 Link State Database:
LSPID                 LSP Seq Num  LSP Checksum  LSP Holdtime    ATT/P/OL
R2.00-00            * 0x00000036   0xF6A2        800             0/0/0
  Area Address: 49.0001
  NLPID:        0xCC
  Hostname: R2
  IP Address:   10.1.2.1
  Metric: 10        IS R3.00
  Metric: 20        IP 10.1.1.0 255.255.255.0
  Metric: 10        IP 10.1.2.0 255.255.255.0
  Metric: 10        IP 10.1.12.0 255.255.255.0
  Metric: 10        IP 10.12.23.0 255.255.255.0
R3.00-00              0x00000044   0x98F1        516             0/0/0
  Area Address: 49.0002
  NLPID:        0xCC
  Hostname: R3
  IP Address:   10.2.3.1
  Metric: 10        IS R2.00
  Metric: 10        IS R4.00
  Metric: 10        IP 10.2.3.0 255.255.255.0
  Metric: 20        IP 10.2.4.0 255.255.255.0
  Metric: 20        IP 10.2.5.0 255.255.255.0
  Metric: 10        IP 10.2.34.0 255.255.255.0
  Metric: 10        IP 10.2.35.0 255.255.255.0
  Metric: 20        IP 10.2.45.0 255.255.255.0
  Metric: 10        IP 10.12.23.0 255.255.255.0
  Metric: 20        IP 10.23.46.0 255.255.255.0
R4.00-00              0x0000003B   0xD3B9        875             0/0/0
  Area Address: 49.0002
  NLPID:        0xCC
  Hostname: R4
  IP Address:   10.2.4.1
  Metric: 10        IS R3.00
  Metric: 10        IS R6.00
  Metric: 20        IP 10.2.3.0 255.255.255.0
  Metric: 10        IP 10.2.4.0 255.255.255.0
  Metric: 20        IP 10.2.5.0 255.255.255.0
  Metric: 10        IP 10.2.34.0 255.255.255.0
  Metric: 20        IP 10.2.35.0 255.255.255.0
  Metric: 10        IP 10.2.45.0 255.255.255.0
  Metric: 20        IP 10.12.23.0 255.255.255.0
```

```
  Metric: 10         IP 10.23.46.0 255.255.255.0
R6.00-00                 0x00000035  0x4BD4       893              0/0/0
  Area Address: 49.0003
  NLPID:        0xCC
  Hostname: R6
  IP Address:   10.3.6.1
  Metric: 10         IS R4.00
  Metric: 10         IP 10.3.6.0 255.255.255.0
  Metric: 20         IP 10.3.7.0 255.255.255.0
  Metric: 10         IP 10.3.67.0 255.255.255.0
  Metric: 10         IP 10.23.46.0 255.255.255.0
```

Identical L2 link-state database contents would be displayed on any L2-enabled router in
this network. Example 10-5 shows how the IP routing information flow between routing
levels works. An L1 router advertises only its directly connected networks in its L1 LSP.
An L2 router advertises both its directly connected networks and all L1 networks (that is,
networks internal to the router's area) in its L2 LSP. In fact, looking at any L2 LSP in isolation, you do not even know which prefix is directly connected to the router and which
one is an L1 prefix "uptaken" into L2—they are both advertised in the same manner.

Checking any L1L2 router's L2 link-state database would produce the same results as
shown previously, and checking R7 would be very similar to what we have already
seen on R1. The only slightly more interesting router is R5, which is the focus on
Example 10-6.

**Example 10-6**  *R5's Link-State Database in a Multiarea Network*

```
! R5 being an L1-only router has only L1 link-state database containing 3 LSPs,
! one for each router in area 49.0002. Notice that on R3's and R4's LSP, the ATT
! bit is set because both R3 and R4 can reach other areas than 49.0002 after
! running their L2 SPF calculation. The detailed LSP listing shows the ordinary L1
! LSP contents, each router advertising its directly connected networks.

R5# show isis database

IS-IS Level-1 Link State Database:
LSPID              LSP Seq Num  LSP Checksum  LSP Holdtime    ATT/P/OL
R3.00-00           0x00000042   0xDBD5        555             1/0/0
R4.00-00           0x00000039   0x0586        829             1/0/0
R5.00-00         * 0x0000003A   0xBDB9        1154            0/0/0

R5# show isis database detail

IS-IS Level-1 Link State Database:
LSPID              LSP Seq Num  LSP Checksum  LSP Holdtime    ATT/P/OL
R3.00-00           0x00000042   0xDBD5        543             1/0/0
  Area Address: 49.0002
```

```
  NLPID:         0xCC
  Hostname: R3
  IP Address:    10.2.3.1
  Metric: 10        IP 10.2.34.0 255.255.255.0
  Metric: 10        IP 10.12.23.0 255.255.255.0
  Metric: 10        IP 10.2.35.0 255.255.255.0
  Metric: 10        IP 10.2.3.0 255.255.255.0
  Metric: 10        IS R5.00
  Metric: 10        IS R4.00
R4.00-00              0x00000039  0x0586       816          1/0/0
  Area Address: 49.0002
  NLPID:         0xCC
  Hostname: R4
  IP Address:    10.2.4.1
  Metric: 10        IP 10.2.45.0 255.255.255.0
  Metric: 10        IP 10.2.34.0 255.255.255.0
  Metric: 10        IP 10.23.46.0 255.255.255.0
  Metric: 10        IP 10.2.4.0 255.255.255.0
  Metric: 10        IS R3.00
  Metric: 10        IS R5.00
R5.00-00            * 0x0000003A  0xBDB9      1140          0/0/0
  Area Address: 49.0002
  NLPID:         0xCC
  Hostname: R5
  IP Address:    10.2.5.1
  Metric: 10        IP 10.2.35.0 255.255.255.0
  Metric: 10        IP 10.2.45.0 255.255.255.0
  Metric: 10        IP 10.2.5.0 255.255.255.0
  Metric: 10        IS R3.00
  Metric: 10        IS R4.00

! Because both R3 and R4 indicate the ATT bit and R5 is equally distant from both
! of them, it installs a default route towards both R3 and R4. Note once again
! that the default route is not advertised explicitly; the ATT bit serves as an
! implicit advertisement instead.

R5# show ip route isis
     10.0.0.0/24 is subnetted, 8 subnets
i L1    10.2.3.0 [115/20] via 10.2.35.3, Serial0/0/0
i L1    10.2.4.0 [115/20] via 10.2.45.4, Serial0/0/1
i L1    10.12.23.0 [115/20] via 10.2.35.3, Serial0/0/0
i L1    10.2.34.0 [115/20] via 10.2.45.4, Serial0/0/1
                  [115/20] via 10.2.35.3, Serial0/0/0
i L1    10.23.46.0 [115/20] via 10.2.45.4, Serial0/0/1
i*L1 0.0.0.0/0 [115/10] via 10.2.45.4, Serial0/0/1
                  [115/10] via 10.2.35.3, Serial0/0/0
```

R5's behavior is strongly reminiscent of the OSPF Totally Stubby Area. Such an area has no information about external (redistributed) and inter-area networks. All networks outside the area are reachable through a default route advertised by the ABRs. If the area 49.0002 was running OSPF, the routing table on R5 would be very similar; in particular, there would be two default routes, one through R3 and the other through R4. Because, however, R5 can be configured to redistribute external networks into an IS-IS L1 link state database, its behavior ultimately resembles an OSPF NSSA TS area operation. Regarding redistribution, external networks are by default injected into L2 but can be configured to be injected into L1 or both L1 and L2 on a router. If an external route is redistributed to L1, all other routers in the same area will see the route as an L1 IS-IS route. Each L1L2 backbone router in that area will add this route along with other L1 routes into its L2 LSP. In other words, when "uptaking" L1 routes into L2 on backbone routers, they do not discriminate between internal L1 networks and external networks in the area that have been redistributed as L1 routes.

Multiple areas in a domain are nowadays created primarily for the purpose of address summarization. In OSPF, summarization of networks in an area would be configured on ABRs. In case of IS-IS, area summarization should be configured on each L1L2 router in the area. While configuration examples will be shown later, it is worthy to mention that in IS-IS, area summarization is configured simply by the **summary-address** command inside the **router isis** section, and this command applies equally when summarizing intra-area networks during their L1-to-L2 "uptake" and to redistributed routes.

## Authentication in IS-IS

Key
Topic

IS-IS authentication is configured in a somewhat peculiar way: IIH packets are authenticated independently of LSP, CSNP, and PSNP packets. While somewhat surprising, this is a result of how IS-IS operates. Authentication information is added to IS-IS packets as an additional TLV record containing the authentication information. In particular with LSPs, recall the general rule in link-state routing protocols that LSP packets originated by one router must not be modified by any other router. The consequence is that for L1 LSPs, all routers within the area must use the same *area password*—the *level-1 authentication password*, while for L2 LSPs, all L2-enabled routers within the L2 subdomain must use the same *domain password*—the *level-2 authentication password*, to authenticate LSPs. If a single area or domain password was used to authenticate all packets, however, all routers in the area or in the backbone would be using the same password, which can be considered a security drawback. Therefore, to authenticate adjacencies themselves, IS-IS allows you to separately authenticate IIH packets.

Table 10-4 explains how individual packets are authenticated in IS-IS depending on their type and level, and what commands can be used to activate this authentication. The table uses an abbreviation—the **auth** keyword is a shorthand of **authentication**, to save space. Nevertheless, all commands will be accepted exactly as shown, with the **auth** expanding to its full spelling. Also, because the authentication support has evolved in IOS over time, some IS-IS deployments might still be using an old, deprecated form of authentication commands. They are indicated as well but should not be used anymore.

**Table 10-4**  *Authentication of IS-IS Packets*

| Packet | Level | Command | Old Command |
|---|---|---|---|
| LAN IIH | Level 1 | Interface:<br>isis auth mode { text \| md5 } level-1<br>isis auth key-chain *name* level-1 | Interface:<br>isis password *text* level-1 |
| LAN IIH | Level 2 | Interface:<br>isis auth mode { text \| md5 } level-2<br>isis auth key-chain *name* level-2 | Interface:<br>isis password *text* level-2 |
| P2P IIH | N/A | Interface:<br>isis auth mode { text \| md5 }<br>isis auth key-chain *name* | Interface:<br>isis password *text* |
| LSP<br>CSNP<br>PSNP | Level 1 | IS-IS process:<br>auth mode { text \| md5 } level-1<br>auth key-chain *name* level-1 | IS-IS process:<br>area-password *text* |
| LSP<br>CSNP<br>PSNP | Level 2 | IS-IS process:<br>auth mode { text \| md5 } level-2<br>auth key-chain *name* level-2 | IS-IS process:<br>domain-password *text* |

In all indicated commands in Table 10-4, if the **level-1** or **level-2** keyword is omitted from a command where it is currently indicated, the corresponding authentication type will be activated for both levels.

Authentication in IS-IS can be activated independently for IIH and independently for non-IIH (LSP, CSNP, PSNP) packets. IIH authentication is configured on interfaces and applies only to IIH packets exchanged with directly connected neighbors. Therefore, different interfaces of a router can use different IIH passwords. However, if non-IIH packets are to be authenticated, the same type of authentication and the same password must be configured on all routers in an area if L1 non-IIH authentication is used, or on all L2 routers in the domain if L2 non-IIH authentication is used. This behavior is unique to IS-IS: While IIH can be authenticated on each interface independently, authentication of non-IIH packets must be consistent across the entire area for L1, and across the entire domain for L2.

Key Topic

It is important to understand the consequences of failed authentication independently for IIH and non-IIH packets. If IIH packets received from a neighboring router fail authentication, no adjacency will be created between this router and the neighbor. As a result, these routers will not accept LSP, CSNP, or PSNP packets from each other, as these packets are accepted only from routers in the Up adjacency state. In other words, if IIH packets fail authentication, the routers will be completely prevented from communicating in

IS-IS even if the non-IIH packets themselves passed the authentication or did not require the authentication.

If IIH packets pass the authentication but the non-IIH packets fail it, the routers will be in the Up adjacency state but they will not be able to synchronize their link-state databases.

Understandably, the best course of action is to either authenticate all IS-IS packets on a given level or to not authenticate any of them. If configuration simplicity is required, both IIH and non-IIH packets can be authenticated using the same password. If security is a major concern, different passwords for L1 IIH, L2 IIH, L1 non-IIH, and L2 non-IIH packets can be configured. (Mind the scope: The same password must be used in the entire area for L1 non-IIH packets and in the entire domain for L2 non-IIH packets; IIH packets can use different passwords on a per-interface and per-level basis.)

The original IS-IS standard specifies only plaintext authentication. RFC 3567 (now RFC 5304) defines a cryptographic authentication for IS-IS, currently using the MD5 hash. Somewhat surprisingly, though, even if the MD5 hash is used and the authentication is configured using key chains, the key IDs (key numbers) are not carried along with the authentication information in IS-IS packets. This is different from RIP, EIGRP, or OSPF, where the number of the key used to sign the packet is indicated in the packet so that the same key can be used by the receiving router to verify the packet's authentication. In IS-IS, key numbers are not advertised and can differ between routers. If the key strings match, regardless of the key number, the authentication will succeed. Of course, in the case of the MD5 hash, the MD5 is computed over the entire packet, not just over the password, so the packet itself must not be altered during transit if the authentication is to be successful.

# IPv6 Support in IS-IS

IS-IS is a true multiprotocol routing protocol in the sense that it does not require any particular Layer 3 protocol to carry its packets, and in a single instance, it can carry information about destinations described by different address families. Previous examples of link-state database contents have shown that the LSPs advertise adjacencies to other routers along with adjacencies to directly connected networks—in other words, the LSPs already contain descriptions of adjacencies of different types. In the same way, IPv6 prefixes can be advertised in a similar way along with IPv4 addresses. Rules about advertising IPv6 prefixes in L1 and L2 LSPs are identical to those for IPv4: In an L1 LSP, a router advertises all its directly connected IPv6 networks. In an L2 LSP, a router advertises all its directly connected IPv6 networks, all L1 IPv6 networks from within its own area (internal or redistributed into L1), and all networks it redistributes itself, possibly summarizing them if summarization is configured. It is not necessary to start an additional IS-IS process to carry IPv6 routes along with IPv4. Instead, the existing IS-IS process is simply instructed to advertise IPv6 routes along with other information it is already advertising. This makes IS-IS a very interesting protocol for those networks that do not run IS-IS yet and need to migrate to a new routing protocol to support their newly deployed IPv6. As they need to start a new routing protocol for IPv6, IS-IS comes into consideration just like OSPFv3 or EIGRP for IPv6. And because IS-IS is actually capable of handling both

IPv4 and IPv6 in the same instance, without running two independent processes, moving to IS-IS altogether might be an option worth considering.

Consider the network back in Figure 10-7, with Routers R3, R4, and R5 configured with IPv6 addresses. Links between routers in area 49.0002 will be using the IPv6 addressing convention 2001:DB8:2:<R*i*><R*j*>::/64, and loopbacks will be using the 2001:DB8:2:<Router>::/64 convention. After activating IS-IS for IPv6 as well, R5's L1 link-state database and routing table are examined in Example 10-7.

**Example 10-7**  *R5's Link-State Database in a Multiarea Network with IPv4 and IPv6*

```
! After configuring IPv6 on all three routers in area 49.0002 and activating IS-IS
! to also carry IPv6 prefixes, the show isis database does not show any visible
! change. There are still only 3 LSPs.


R5# show isis database


IS-IS Level-1 Link State Database:
LSPID               LSP Seq Num  LSP Checksum  LSP Holdtime    ATT/P/OL
R3.00-00            0x0000005B   0x14F1        1003            1/0/0
R4.00-00            0x0000004F   0x7C54        1003            1/0/0
R5.00-00          * 0x00000052   0x288F        1009            0/0/0


! Looking into the LSP details, the change is immediately visible. The NLPID field
! that lists the supported Layer3 protocols on the originating router now contains
! two values: 0xCC (IPv4) and 0x8E (IPv6). Furthermore, LSPs now contain all
! directly connected IPv4 networks along with IPv6 networks and adjacent routers.


R5# show isis database detail


IS-IS Level-1 Link State Database:
LSPID               LSP Seq Num  LSP Checksum  LSP Holdtime    ATT/P/OL
R3.00-00            0x0000005B   0x14F1        997             1/0/0
  Area Address: 49.0002
  NLPID:        0xCC 0x8E
  Hostname: R3
  IP Address:   10.2.3.1
  Metric: 10        IP 10.2.34.0 255.255.255.0
  Metric: 10        IP 10.12.23.0 255.255.255.0
  Metric: 10        IP 10.2.35.0 255.255.255.0
  Metric: 10        IP 10.2.3.0 255.255.255.0
  IPv6 Address: 2001:DB8:2:3::1
  Metric: 10        IPv6 2001:DB8:2:34::/64
  Metric: 10        IPv6 2001:DB8:2:35::/64
  Metric: 10        IPv6 2001:DB8:2:3::/64
  Metric: 10        IS R5.00
  Metric: 10        IS R4.00
```

```
R4.00-00                    0x0000004F   0x7C54        998              1/0/0
   Area Address: 49.0002
   NLPID:         0xCC 0x8E
   Hostname: R4
   IP Address:   10.2.4.1
   Metric: 10         IP 10.2.45.0 255.255.255.0
   Metric: 10         IP 10.2.34.0 255.255.255.0
   Metric: 10         IP 10.23.46.0 255.255.255.0
   Metric: 10         IP 10.2.4.0 255.255.255.0
   IPv6 Address: 2001:DB8:2:4::1
   Metric: 10         IPv6 2001:DB8:2:45::/64
   Metric: 10         IPv6 2001:DB8:2:34::/64
   Metric: 10         IPv6 2001:DB8:2:4::/64
   Metric: 10         IS R5.00
   Metric: 10         IS R3.00
R5.00-00                  * 0x00000052   0x288F       1002              0/0/0
   Area Address: 49.0002
   NLPID:         0xCC 0x8E
   Hostname: R5
   IP Address:   10.2.5.1
   Metric: 10         IP 10.2.35.0 255.255.255.0
   Metric: 10         IP 10.2.45.0 255.255.255.0
   Metric: 10         IP 10.2.5.0 255.255.255.0
   IPv6 Address: 2001:DB8:2:5::1
   Metric: 10         IPv6 2001:DB8:2:35::/64
   Metric: 10         IPv6 2001:DB8:2:45::/64
   Metric: 10         IPv6 2001:DB8:2:5::/64
   Metric: 10         IS R4.00
   Metric: 10         IS R3.00


! The routing table on R5 is populated as usual. Note that the default route
! has been injected towards routers with the ATT bit set in the same way IPv4
! default route was injected in previous examples.

R5# show ipv6 route isis
IPv6 Routing Table - 11 entries
Codes: C - Connected, L - Local, S - Static, R - RIP, B - BGP
       U - Per-user Static route, M - MIPv6
       I1 - ISIS L1, I2 - ISIS L2, IA - ISIS interarea, IS - ISIS summary
       O - OSPF intra, OI - OSPF inter, OE1 - OSPF ext 1, OE2 - OSPF ext 2
       ON1 - OSPF NSSA ext 1, ON2 - OSPF NSSA ext 2
       D - EIGRP, EX - EIGRP external
I1   ::/0 [115/10]
     via FE80::3, Serial0/0/0
     via FE80::4, Serial0/0/1
```

```
I1  2001:DB8:2:3::/64 [115/20]
       via FE80::3, Serial0/0/0
I1  2001:DB8:2:4::/64 [115/20]
       via FE80::4, Serial0/0/1
I1  2001:DB8:2:34::/64 [115/20]
       via FE80::3, Serial0/0/0
       via FE80::4, Serial0/0/1
```

## Configuring IS-IS

Using the topology shown previously in Figure 10-7, the following examples will show the configuration of selected individual routers. Only the relevant configuration parts will be shown along with specific comments.

There are a few general comments about the configuration. The NET, that is, an NSAP address with the SEL octet set to 0, is constructed using AFI=49; HO-DSP of 0001, 0002, or 0003 depending on the area; and System ID equal to 0000.0000.000<Router> depending on the router, thereby making it unique. Because the System ID is 6 octets long, it would be also possible to use one of the MAC addresses of the router as the System ID, ensuring its uniqueness. Another way of deriving a unique System ID is taking an IP address, preferably a loopback address, and performing the following transliteration (the address is just an example):

10.1.255.42 → 010.001.255.042 → 010001255042 → 0100.0125.5042

Any approach of creating a System ID is viable as long as the resulting System IDs are unique. Recall that a System ID of an L1-only router must be unique within its area; the System ID of an L2-enabled router must be unique in the entire domain. Ideally, the System IDs should be unique across the domain, regardless of the enabled routing level.

Each router in the following examples is configured using **metric-style wide**; this is the recommended setting for all new deployments. Also, on all routers, the **log-adjacency-changes all** command is added to have IOS print logging messages about an IS-IS router coming up or down. This command is not added automatically.

First, Example 10-8 shows the configuration and IS-IS operation on R1.

**Example 10-8**  *R1 Configuration and Verification*

```
! On R1, IS-IS adjacency to R2 will be authenticated. This is the key chain.

key chain ISISAuth
 key 1
   key-string S3cretP4ss

! Interfaces are configured with IPv4 addresses, and ip router isis is used
! to add them to IS-IS. There is no network command in IS-IS.

interface Loopback0
```

```
 ip address 10.1.1.1 255.255.255.0
 ip router isis


! On S0/0/0 interface, MD5 authentication of IIH is configured, and IETF three-way
! handshake method is activated. Note that the authentication configured on an
! interface affects only the IIH packets. Non-IIH packet authentication must be
! configured in the router isis section.

interface Serial0/0/0
 description => To R2 <=
 ip address 10.1.12.1 255.255.255.0
 ip router isis
 isis authentication mode md5
 isis authentication key-chain ISISAuth
 isis three-way-handshake ietf


! In IS-IS configuration, the NET is configured, and the router is put into L1-only
! mode. Authentication of non-IIH packets is configured, and wide metrics are used.

router isis
 net 49.0001.0000.0000.0001.00
 is-type level-1
 authentication mode md5
 authentication key-chain ISISAuth
 metric-style wide
 log-adjacency-changes all


! In the show isis database detail, note that the use of wide metrics is indicated
! adjacencies to other routers denoted as IS-Extended instead of just IS. Also
! note that LSPs also carry authentication information (its presence is indicated
! by the Auth: entries).


R1# show isis database detail

IS-IS Level-1 Link State Database:
LSPID                 LSP Seq Num   LSP Checksum   LSP Holdtime      ATT/P/OL
R1.00-00            * 0x0000000E    0x7A4E         551               0/0/0
  Auth:         Length: 17
  Area Address: 49.0001
  NLPID:        0xCC
  Hostname: R1
  IP Address:   10.1.1.1
  Metric: 10        IP 10.1.12.0/24
  Metric: 10        IP 10.1.1.0/24
  Metric: 10        IS-Extended R2.00
R2.00-00              0x00000013    0x1E24         1123              1/0/0
```

```
Auth:          Length: 17
Area Address: 49.0001
NLPID:         0xCC
Hostname: R2
IP Address:    10.1.2.1
Metric: 10          IP 10.1.12.0/24
Metric: 0           IP 10.1.2.0/24
Metric: 10          IS-Extended R1.00
```

As seen from Example 10-8, interfaces are added to IS-IS directly by configuring them with the **ip router isis** command. IS-IS has no **network** command; therefore, per-interface configuration is the way of adding networks and interfaces into IS-IS. Because R1 is a purely internal router not intended to be a part of backbone, only Level 1 routing operation is configured; by default, Cisco routers operate as L1L2 routers.

Example 10-9 shows the configuration of R2.

**Example 10-9**  *R2 Configuration and Verification*

```
! On R2, IS-IS adjacency to R1 will be authenticated. This is the key chain.

key chain ISISAuth
 key 1
   key-string S3cretP4ss

! The Lo0 interface does not have any IS-IS related command but in router isis,
! it is declared as passive. This will cause the network from Lo0 to be advertised
! in IS-IS but the interface will be passive (no adjacencies will be established
! over it).

interface Loopback0
 ip address 10.1.2.1 255.255.255.0

! Interface towards R3 is an inter-area link, therefore, it does not make sense
! to even try to establish L1 adjacency over it. Therefore, the isis circuit-type
! command is used to allow only L2 packets to be sent over it. Also, in L2, metric
! of this interface set to 100.

interface Serial0/0/0
 description => To R3 <=
 ip address 10.12.23.2 255.255.255.0
 ip router isis
 isis circuit-type level-2-only
 isis metric 100 level-2

! Interface towards R1 is configured with IIH authentication and IETF three-way
! handshake.
```

```
interface Serial0/0/1
 description => To R1 <=
 ip address 10.1.12.2 255.255.255.0
 ip router isis
 isis authentication mode md5
 isis authentication key-chain ISISAuth
 isis three-way-handshake ietf
```

! In IS-IS configuration, the NET is configured, followed by authentication
! activated only for L1 non-IIH packets. Non-IIH packets in L2 adjacencies will
! not be authenticated. Because no **isis is-type** command is used, R2 acts as L1L2
! router which is the default setting on Cisco routers. The **summary-address** command
! is used to summarize L1 networks when injecting them into L2.

```
router isis
 net 49.0001.0000.0000.0002.00
 authentication mode md5 level-1
 authentication key-chain ISISAuth level-1
 metric-style wide
 log-adjacency-changes all
 summary-address 10.1.0.0 255.255.0.0
 passive-interface Loopback0
```

! Of particular notice on R2 is its L2 database. Note that thanks to summarization
! configured on R2 (and on other L2-enabled routers as well), the L2 LSPs contain
! only the summarized prefixes. L2 LSPs received from R3 and R4 also contain
! summarized IPv6 prefixes, although R2 does not process these IPv6 prefixes
! as it is not configured for IPv6 operation.

R2# **show isis database l2 detail**

IS-IS Level-2 Link State Database:

| LSPID | LSP Seq Num | LSP Checksum | LSP Holdtime | ATT/P/OL |
|-------|-------------|--------------|--------------|----------|
| R2.00-00 | * 0x0000005C | 0x5694 | 1160 | 0/0/0 |

```
  Area Address: 49.0001
  NLPID:       0xCC
  Hostname: R2
  IP Address:  10.1.2.1
  Metric: 100      IP 10.12.23.0/24
  Metric: 100      IS-Extended R3.00
  Metric: 0        IP 10.1.0.0/16
```

| R3.00-00 |   0x0000007A | 0xF333 | 416 | 0/0/0 |
|----------|--------------|--------|-----|-------|

```
  Area Address: 49.0002
  NLPID:       0xCC 0x8E
  Hostname: R3
  IP Address:  10.2.3.1
```

```
    Metric: 100         IP 10.12.23.0/24
    IPv6 Address: 2001:DB8:2:3::1
    Metric: 100         IS-Extended R2.00
    Metric: 10          IS-Extended R4.00
    Metric: 10          IP 10.2.0.0/16
    Metric: 10          IPv6 2001:DB8::/32
  R4.00-00              0x00000065   0x1AF8        426            0/0/0
    Area Address: 49.0002
    NLPID:              0xCC 0x8E
    Hostname: R4
    IP Address:   10.2.4.1
    Metric: 100         IP 10.23.46.0/24
    IPv6 Address: 2001:DB8:2:4::1
    Metric: 100         IS-Extended R6.00
    Metric: 10          IS-Extended R3.00
    Metric: 10          IP 10.2.0.0/16
    Metric: 10          IPv6 2001:DB8::/32
  R6.00-00              0x00000057   0x664A        579            0/0/0
    Area Address: 49.0003
    NLPID:              0xCC
    Hostname: R6
    IP Address:   10.3.6.1
    Metric: 100         IP 10.23.46.0/24
    Metric: 100         IS-Extended R4.00
    Metric: 10          IP 10.3.0.0/16

! Finally, the tidy IPv4 routing table on R2. Note the discard route to Null0
! installed for the summarized 10.1.0.0/16 prefix.

R2# show ip route isis
      10.0.0.0/8 is variably subnetted, 8 subnets, 2 masks
i L2    10.2.0.0/16 [115/110] via 10.12.23.3, Serial0/0/0
i L2    10.3.0.0/16 [115/220] via 10.12.23.3, Serial0/0/0
i L1    10.1.1.0/24 [115/20] via 10.1.12.1, Serial0/0/1
i su    10.1.0.0/16 [115/0] via 0.0.0.0, Null0
i L2    10.23.46.0/24 [115/210] via 10.12.23.3, Serial0/0/0
```

On R2, the routing level of the entire router was not modified, causing this router to operate as an L1L2 router. This setting is crucial. If the router was limited to L1 operation only, it would be unable to establish L2 adjacency to R3, which is in a different area. On the other hand, if R2 was configured for L2 operation only, R1 operating as an L1-only router would be unable to establish adjacency with R2. Therefore, R2 must operate as an L1L2 router, and this is a general rule for all backbone (that is, L2-enabled) routers: If they are to provide inter-area routing services to other L1-only routers in their area, they must operate in L1L2 mode.

The behavior of **passive-interface** to actually advertise the Lo0's network without using the **ip router isis** command on Lo0 in Example 10-9 might be surprising, but there is a logic to it. If an interface should not be added to IS-IS, the entire IS-IS configuration will simply not refer to it in any place, neither by **ip router isis** on that interface nor in the **router isis** section by declaring it as passive. If the network from the interface shall be advertised but the interface should remain passive, simply referring to it by the **passive-interface** command is signal enough to IS-IS to know that the interface's network should be advertised even though the interface itself should disallow creating any adjacencies over it. And finally, if the interface is intended to operate as an active interface, it shall be configured with the **ip router isis** command. This behavior is also shared by EIGRP for IPv6. It is important to mention that configuring **passive-interface default** will cause all local interfaces' networks to be advertised in IS-IS.

The use of **isis circuit-type** command in the Serial0/0/0 interface deserves a mention. If a router is configured for L1L2 operation, it will by default try to establish both L1 and L2 adjacencies over all active IS-IS interfaces. Recall that an IS-IS router originates separate LSP, CSNP, and PSNP packets independently for L1 and L2, and if the interface is a broadcast interface, also separate L1 and L2 IIHs will be originated. If it is known that an interface should be used to establish only L1 or only L2 adjacencies, it is possible to limit its operation only to the selected level. That will prevent the router from sending and processing packets of a different routing level over that interface. In Example 10-9, the interface Serial0/0/0 is connected to a router in a different area; therefore, it makes no sense to even attempt establishing L1 adjacencies. Therefore, the **isis circuit-type level-2-only** command was used on the Serial0/0/0 interface to limit its operation to Level 2 only.

Regarding authentication, older Cisco CLIs supported only a plaintext authentication using the per-interface **isis password** command for IIH authentication, and **area-password** and **domain-password** commands in **router isis** configuration to activate authentication for L1 (area) and L2 (domain) non-IIH packets. Passwords were specified directly on the command line, and key chains were not supported. These commands are obsolete and should not be used anymore. The per-interface **isis authentication** and per-process **authentication** commands support optional **level-1** and **level-2** keywords to specify the desired level for which the authentication should be activated. If not specified, both levels are authenticated.

Example 10-10 shows the configuration of R3.

**Example 10-10**  *R3 Configuration*

```
! The Lo0 interface is configured with IPv4 and IPv6 addresses, and IS-IS is
! activated for both IPv4 and IPv6 using ip router isis and ipv6 router isis

ipv6 unicast-routing
!
interface Loopback0
 ip address 10.2.3.1 255.255.255.0
 ip router isis
```

```
 ipv6 address 2001:DB8:2:3::1/64
 ipv6 router isis

! Interfaces S0/0/0, S0/0/1, and S0/1/0 are configured similarly. To aid,
! readability the link-local IPv6 address on the interface is also modified. The
! S0/0/1 interface connects to R2 in a different area, therefore IS-IS is
! configured to operate only in L2 mode on this interface.

interface Serial0/0/0
 description => To R4 <=
 ip address 10.2.34.3 255.255.255.0
 ip router isis
 ipv6 address FE80::3 link-local
 ipv6 address 2001:DB8:2:34::3/64
 ipv6 router isis
!
interface Serial0/0/1
 description => To R2 <=
 ip address 10.12.23.3 255.255.255.0
 ip router isis
 isis circuit-type level-2-only
 isis metric 100 level-2
!
interface Serial0/1/0
 description => To R5 <=
 ip address 10.2.35.3 255.255.255.0
 ip router isis
 ipv6 address FE80::3 link-local
 ipv6 address 2001:DB8:2:35::3/64
 ipv6 router isis

! The IS-IS configuration on R3 should be, for the most part, fairly obvious.
! The only new section is the address-family ipv6 section in which specific
! settings for IPv6 operation are configured. Here, area summarization is
! configured. You do not need to create this section just to make IS-IS work for IPv6.

router isis
 net 49.0002.0000.0000.0003.00
 metric-style wide
 log-adjacency-changes all
 summary-address 10.2.0.0 255.255.0.0
 !
 address-family ipv6
  summary-prefix 2001:DB8:2::/32
```

```
    exit-address-family


! We omit the view into R3's link-state database at this point, as the L2 database
! contents are identical to the contents already displayed for R2.
```

Note that unlike other IGP protocols, IS-IS does not use a separate process configuration section for its IPv6 operation. The **router isis** section is universal for all address families supported by IS-IS. If IS-IS shall advertise an interface's IPv6 address, that interface shall be configured with the **ipv6 router isis** command. The **address-family ipv6** subsection in the IS-IS configuration has been specifically created in this example to configure IPv6-specific operations of IS-IS—in this case, intra-area prefix summarization when advertising the networks into L2.

Example 10-11 shows a selected set of diagnostic commands on R3 that are useful to verify the IS-IS operation on an L1L2 router.

**Example 10-11**    *IS-IS Diagnostic Commands on R3*

```
! The show clns command shows a brief but useful information about this router's
! NET and mode of Integrated IS-IS operation


R3# show clns
Global CLNS Information:
  4 Interfaces Enabled for CLNS
  NET: 49.0002.0000.0000.0003.00
  Configuration Timer: 60, Default Holding Timer: 300, Packet Lifetime 64
  ERPDU's requested on locally generated packets
  Running IS-IS in IP/IPv6-only mode (CLNS forwarding not allowed)


! There is a series of commands to display neighbors - most of these commands
! in fact display the same information, just formatted differently.
! show clns is-neighbors show information about neighboring routers running IS-IS.
! The optional detail keyword provides more detailed information.


R3# show clns is-neighbors

System Id       Interface   State  Type Priority  Circuit Id    Format
R2              Se0/0/1     Up     L2   0          00            Phase V
R5              Se0/1/0     Up     L1   0          00            Phase V
R4              Se0/0/0     Up     L1L2 0 /0       01            Phase V


R3# show clns is-neighbors detail

System Id       Interface   State  Type Priority  Circuit Id    Format
R2              Se0/0/1     Up     L2   0          00            Phase V
  Area Address(es): 49.0001
  IP Address(es):  10.12.23.2*
```

```
   Uptime: 01:07:59
   NSF capable
R5              Se0/1/0    Up     L1   0        00              Phase V
   Area Address(es): 49.0002
   IP Address(es):  10.2.35.5*
   IPv6 Address(es): FE80::5
   Uptime: 01:51:39
   NSF capable
R4              Se0/0/0    Up     L1L2 0 /0     01              Phase V
   Area Address(es): 49.0002
   IP Address(es):  10.2.34.4*
   IPv6 Address(es): FE80::4
   Uptime: 05:15:33
   NSF capable

! The show clns neighbors is very similar. This command is capable of displaying
! the SNPA of the neighbor; for HDLC and PPP, only a textual description is shown,
! as these protocols do not have a concept of a SNPA. This command also supports
! the optional detail keyword (not shown here).

R3# show clns neighbors

System Id       Interface   SNPA        State  Holdtime  Type  Protocol
R2              Se0/0/1     *HDLC*       Up     26        L2    IS-IS
R5              Se0/1/0     *HDLC*       Up     23        L1    IS-IS
R4              Se0/0/0     *HDLC*       Up     24        L1L2  IS-IS

! Details about IS-IS operation on an interface can be shown using
! show clns interface command.

R3# show clns interface s0/0/0
Serial0/0/0 is up, line protocol is up
   Checksums enabled, MTU 1500, Encapsulation HDLC
   ERPDUs enabled, min. interval 10 msec.
   CLNS fast switching enabled
   CLNS SSE switching disabled
   DEC compatibility mode OFF for this interface
   Next ESH/ISH in 14 seconds
   Routing Protocol: IS-IS
     Circuit Type: level-1-2
     Interface number 0x1, local circuit ID 0x100
     Neighbor System-ID: R4
     Level-1 Metric: 10, Priority: 64, Circuit ID: R4.01
     Level-1 IPv6 Metric: 10
     Number of active level-1 adjacencies: 1
     Level-2 Metric: 10, Priority: 64, Circuit ID: R3.00
```

```
     Level-2 IPv6 Metric: 10
     Number of active level-2 adjacencies: 1
     Next IS-IS Hello in 526 milliseconds
     if state UP


! Finally, the show isis neighbors shows the usual list of IS-IS neighbors.
! You may find this command superfluous; in fact, it did not exist for quite
! some time, and show clns commands shown above were used instead. This command
! also supports the optional detail keyword (not shown here).


R3# show isis neighbors

System Id      Type Interface   IP Address     State Holdtime Circuit Id
R2             L2   Se0/0/1      10.12.23.2     UP    22       00
R5             L1   Se0/1/0      10.2.35.5      UP    24       00
R4             L1L2 Se0/0/0      10.2.34.4      UP    27       01
```

Finally, Example 10-12 shows the configuration of R5. It is not necessary to show other routers. R4 is similar to R3, R6 is similar to R2, and R7 is similar to R1.

**Example 10-12** *R5 Configuration and Verification*

```
! The Lo0 interface is configured with IPv4 and IPv6 addresses, and IS-IS is
! activated for both IPv4 and IPv6 using ip router isis and ipv6 router isis

ipv6 unicast-routing
!
interface Loopback0
 ip address 10.2.5.1 255.255.255.0
 ip router isis
 ipv6 address 2001:DB8:2:5::1/64
 ipv6 router isis
!
interface Serial0/0/0
 description => To R3 <=
 ip address 10.2.35.5 255.255.255.0
 ip router isis
 ipv6 address FE80::5 link-local
 ipv6 address 2001:DB8:2:35::5/64
 ipv6 router isis
!
interface Serial0/0/1
 description => To R4 <=
 ip address 10.2.45.5 255.255.255.0
 ip router isis
 ipv6 address FE80::5 link-local
 ipv6 address 2001:DB8:2:45::5/64
```

```
 ipv6 router isis
!
router isis
 net 49.0002.0000.0000.0005.00
 is-type level-1
 metric-style wide
 log-adjacency-changes all


! Following is a couple of diagnostic commands. By this moment, you should be
! able to read all displayed information without further comments.


R5# show isis database detail

IS-IS Level-1 Link State Database:
LSPID                   LSP Seq Num  LSP Checksum  LSP Holdtime    ATT/P/OL
R3.00-00                0x00000084   0xF1E0        562             1/0/0
  Area Address: 49.0002
  NLPID:        0xCC 0x8E
  Hostname: R3
  IP Address:   10.2.3.1
  Metric: 10        IP 10.2.34.0/24
  Metric: 10        IP 10.2.35.0/24
  Metric: 10        IP 10.2.3.0/24
  IPv6 Address: 2001:DB8:2:3::1
  Metric: 10        IPv6 2001:DB8:2:34::/64
  Metric: 10        IPv6 2001:DB8:2:35::/64
  Metric: 10        IPv6 2001:DB8:2:3::/64
  Metric: 10        IS-Extended R5.00
  Metric: 10        IS-Extended R4.00
R4.00-00                0x00000078   0xB00F        961             1/0/0
  Area Address: 49.0002
  NLPID:        0xCC 0x8E
  Hostname: R4
  IP Address:   10.2.4.1
  Metric: 10        IP 10.2.45.0/24
  Metric: 10        IP 10.2.34.0/24
  Metric: 10        IP 10.2.4.0/24
  IPv6 Address: 2001:DB8:2:4::1
  Metric: 10        IPv6 2001:DB8:2:45::/64
  Metric: 10        IPv6 2001:DB8:2:34::/64
  Metric: 10        IPv6 2001:DB8:2:4::/64
  Metric: 10        IS-Extended R5.00
  Metric: 10        IS-Extended R3.00
R5.00-00              * 0x00000083   0xCEE8        921             0/0/0
  Area Address: 49.0002
  NLPID:        0xCC 0x8E
```

```
    Hostname: R5
    IP Address:    10.2.5.1
    Metric: 10         IP 10.2.35.0/24
    Metric: 10         IP 10.2.45.0/24
    Metric: 10         IP 10.2.5.0/24
    IPv6 Address: 2001:DB8:2:5::1
    Metric: 10         IPv6 2001:DB8:2:35::/64
    Metric: 10         IPv6 2001:DB8:2:45::/64
    Metric: 10         IPv6 2001:DB8:2:5::/64
    Metric: 10         IS-Extended R3.00
    Metric: 10         IS-Extended R4.00


R5# show ip route isis
    10.0.0.0/24 is subnetted, 6 subnets
i L1    10.2.3.0 [115/20] via 10.2.35.3, Serial0/0/0
i L1    10.2.4.0 [115/20] via 10.2.45.4, Serial0/0/1
i L1    10.2.34.0 [115/20] via 10.2.45.4, Serial0/0/1
                 [115/20] via 10.2.35.3, Serial0/0/0
i*L1 0.0.0.0/0 [115/10] via 10.2.45.4, Serial0/0/1
                 [115/10] via 10.2.35.3, Serial0/0/0


R5# show ipv6 route isis
I1   ::/0 [115/10]
     via FE80::4, Serial0/0/1
     via FE80::3, Serial0/0/0
I1   2001:DB8:2:3::/64 [115/20]
     via FE80::3, Serial0/0/0
I1   2001:DB8:2:4::/64 [115/20]
     via FE80::4, Serial0/0/1
I1   2001:DB8:2:34::/64 [115/20]
     via FE80::4, Serial0/0/1
     via FE80::3, Serial0/0/0
```

# Foundation Summary

This section lists additional details and facts to round out the coverage of the topics in this chapter. Unlike most of the Cisco Press Exam Certification Guides, this "Foundation Summary" does not repeat information presented in the "Foundation Topics" section of the chapter. Please take the time to read and study the details in the "Foundation Topics" section of the chapter, as well as review items noted with a Key Topic icon.

Table 10-5 lists some of the key protocols regarding IS-IS.

**Table 10-5**   *Protocols and Corresponding Standards for Chapter 10*

| Name | Standard |
|---|---|
| Information technology—Telecommunications and information exchange between systems—Intermediate System–to–Intermediate System intra-domain routeing information exchange protocol for use in conjunction with the protocol for providing the connectionless-mode network service | ISO/IEC 10589:2002 |
| Use of OSI IS-IS for Routing in TCP/IP and Dual Environments | RFC 1195 |
| Intermediate System–to–Intermediate System (IS-IS) Transient Blackhole Avoidance | RFC 3277 |
| Recommendations for Interoperable Networks using Intermediate System to Intermediate System (IS-IS) | RFC 3719 |
| Recommendations for Interoperable IP Networks using Intermediate System–to–Intermediate System (IS-IS) | RFC 3787 |
| Dynamic Hostname Exchange Mechanism for IS-IS | RFC 5301 |
| Three-Way Handshake for IS-IS Point-to-Point Adjacencies | RFC 5303 |
| IS-IS Cryptographic Authentication | RFC 5304 |
| IS-IS Extensions for Traffic Engineering | RFC 5305 |
| Routing IPv6 with IS-IS | RFC 5308 |

Table 10-6 lists some of the most popular IOS commands related to the topics in this chapter.

**Table 10-6**   *Command Reference for Chapter 10v*

| Command | Command Mode and Description |
|---|---|
| **router isis** [ area-tag ] | Global config; starts the IS-IS process and puts the user into its configuration. The optional *area-tag* is a process ID used when running multiple IS-IS processes, and is not related to area ID in NSAP/NET. |

| Command | Command Mode and Description |
|---------|------------------------------|
| net *network-entity-title* | IS-IS config mode; defines Network Entity Title for the IS-IS process. A maximum of three NETs can be defined, one on a line, for purposes of area renumbering, splitting, or joining. If multiple NET commands are configured, their System ID parts must match. |
| is-type { level-1 \| level-1-2 \| level-2-only } | IS-IS config mode; limits the router to a selected routing level operation. If omitted, **level-1-2** is assumed. |
| authentication mode { text \| md5 } [ level-1 \| level-2 ] | IS-IS config mode; configures the authentication mode for non-IIH packets. If no level is specified, authentication applies to both levels. |
| authentication key-chain *key-chain-name* [ level-1 \| level-2 ] | IS-IS config mode; defines the key chain to be used to authenticate non-IIH packets. If no level is specified, authentication applies to both levels. |
| metric-style { narrow \| transition \| wide } [ level-1 \| level-1-2 \| level-2 ] | IS-IS config mode; configures the metric type used in a particular routing level. The **transition** option is used when transitioning between narrow and wide metrics. If omitted, narrow metrics for both levels are used. |
| passive-interface *interface-type interface-number* \| default | IS-IS config mode; defines an interface as passive and automatically advertises its connected network. |
| summary-address *ip-address mask* [ level-1 \| level-1-2 \| level-2 ] [ metric *metric* ] | IS-IS config mode; defines summarization of IPv4 networks during their injection into a particular routing level. If not specified, **level-2** and metric 0 are used. |
| address-family ipv6 | IS-IS config mode; enters a submode for IPv6 settings. |
| summary-prefix *ipv6-prefix/prefix-length* [ level-1 \| level-1-2 \| level-2 ] | IS-IS IPv6 AF submode; defines summarization of IPv6 networks during their injection into a particular routing level. If not specified, **level-2** is used. |
| protocol shutdown | IS-IS config mode; allows you to stop the IS-IS process entirely without removing it from the configuration. The process can be started again by removing this command. |
| ip router isis [ *area-tag* ] | Interface subcommand; activates an interface in IS-IS and advertises the connected IPv4 subnet. The optional *area-tag* selects the particular IS-IS process. |
| ipv6 router isis [ *area-tag* ] | Interface subcommand; activates an interface in IS-IS and advertises the connected IPv6 subnet. The optional *area-tag* selects the particular IS-IS process. |
| isis circuit-type { level-1 \| level-1-2 \| level-2-only } | Interface subcommand; limits the IS-IS operation on the interface to the specified routing level. |
| isis metric *metric* [ level-1 \| level-2 ] | Interface subcommand; defines the interface metric. If the level is omitted, applies to both levels. |

| Command | Command Mode and Description |
|---|---|
| isis hello-interval *seconds* [ level-1 \| level-2 ] | Interface subcommand; defines the hello interval in range of 1 to 65535. If the level is omitted, applies to both levels. On point-to-point interfaces, configuring the level has no effect because a single IIH is used for both levels. |
| isis hello-multiplier *multiplier* [ level-1 \| level-2 ] | Interface subcommand; defines the multiplier to compute the resulting Hold time, in the range 3 to 1000. If the level is omitted, applies to both levels. On point-to-point interfaces, configuring the level has no effect because a single IIH is used for both levels. |
| isis priority *priority* [ level-1 \| level-2 ] | Interface subcommand; defines the priority for DIS elections in the range 0 to 127. If the level is omitted, applies to both levels. |
| isis authentication mode { text \| md5 } [ level-1 \| level-2 ] | Interface subcommand; configures the authentication mode for IIH packets. If no level is specified, authentication applies to both levels. |
| isis authentication key-chain *key-chain-name* [ level-1 \| level-2 ] | Interface subcommand; defines the key chain to be used to authenticate IIH packets. If no level is specified, authentication applies to both levels. |
| isis three-way-handshake { cisco \| ietf } | Interface subcommand; activates the three-way handshake on point-to-point interfaces. The **cisco** method is default (does not carry information about the neighbor identity); **ietf** is preferred. |
| isis network point-to-point | Interface subcommand; allows treating a broadcast link with just two routers (that is, a fiber Ethernet between two routers) as a point-to-point link, bypassing the DIS election and pseudonode origination. |
| isis protocol shutdown | Interface subcommand; allows deactivating IS-IS on the interface without deconfiguring it. |
| show clns | Displays CLNS-related information about the router, including NET and IS-IS mode of operation. |
| show clns neighbors [ detail ] | Displays all CLNS neighbors, ES and IS, and related information. |
| show clns is-neighbors [ detail ] | Displays CLNS IS neighbors and related information. |
| show clns interface *interface-name interface-type* | Displays CLNS-related interface information. |
| show isis neighbors [ detail ] | Displays IS-IS neighbors and related information. |

Table 10-7 summarizes important IS-IS timers and their meanings.

**Table 10-7**    *IS-IS Timer Summary*

| Timer | Meaning |
|---|---|
| MaxAge, a.k.a. RemainingLifetime | The maximum remaining lifetime of an LSP without receiving a newer copy of the LSP, before the LSP expires. Default is 1200 seconds. |
| ZeroAgeLifetime | The minimum time an LSP must be retained in the link-state database after expiring or initiating an LSP purge. Default is 60 seconds. |
| Hello | Per interface; time interval between Hellos. Default is 10 seconds. Independent for L1 and L2 Hellos on broadcast interfaces. |
| Hold | Per interface; time interval in which a Hello should be received from a neighbor. If not received, the neighbor is considered to have failed. Default is three times Hello. |
| CSNP Interval | Per interface; defines the time interval between sending consecutive CSNP packets if the router is a DIS on that interface. Defaults to 10 seconds. |

Table 10-8 lists IS-IS neighbor states and their meanings.

**Table 10-8**    *IS Neighbor States*

| State | Meaning |
|---|---|
| Down | The initial state. No IIHs have been received from the neighbor. |
| Init | IIHs have been received from the neighbor, but it is not certain that the neighbor is properly receiving this router's IIH. |
| Up | IIHs have been received from the neighbor, and it is certain that the neighbor is properly receiving this router's IIH. |

Table 10-9 lists OSI acronyms and their meanings.

**Table 10-9**    *OSI Terminology*

| Term | Meaning |
|---|---|
| System | Network node. |
| End System (ES) | End node; host. |
| Intermediate System (IS) | Intermediate node; router. |
| Domain | Autonomous system. |

| Term | Meaning |
|------|---------|
| Circuit | Interface; working interconnection to another host or a router. |
| Local Circuit ID | Internal enumeration of circuits by a router, 1 octet. |
| Extended Local Circuit ID | Internal enumeration of point-to-point circuits for three-way handshaking purpose, 4 octets. |
| Network Service Access Point (NSAP) | Layer 3 address of a node. |
| Network Entity Title | NSAP address in which the SEL octet is set to 0; identifies the node itself without addressing any particular network service. |
| Initial Domain Part (IDP) | High-order octets of an NSAP address identifying its format and the domain in which the node is located. |
| Domain Specific Part (DSP) | Low-order octets of an NSAP address identifying the area, individual host, and network service that is being addressed. |
| Authority and Format ID (AFI) | The most significant octet of NSAP address; identifies the format of the address. |
| Initial Domain ID (IDI) | A part of the NSAP address following the AFI identifying the domain. |
| High-Order Domain Specific Part (HO-DSP) | A part of the NSAP address following the IDI (if any) identifying the internal partitioning of the domain. |
| System ID | Identifier of the network node, 6 octets. |
| NSAP Selector (NSEL, SEL) | Identifier of the network service on the node, 1 octet. |
| Sub Network Point of Attachment (SNPA) | Layer 2 address relevant to an interface (if any). |
| Designated IS (DIS) | Designated router on a broadcast segment. |
| Network Layer Protocol ID (NLPID) | Supported Layer 3 protocol (address family) on a router. |

# Memory Builders

The CCIE Routing and Switching written exam, like all Cisco CCIE written exams, covers a fairly broad set of topics. This section provides some basic tools to help you exercise your memory about some of the broader topics covered in this chapter.

## Fill In Key Tables from Memory

Appendix E, "Key Tables for CCIE Study," on the CD in the back of this book, contains empty sets of some of the key summary tables in each chapter. Print Appendix E, refer to this chapter's tables in it, and fill in the tables from memory. Refer to Appendix F, "Solutions for Key Tables for CCIE Study," on the CD to check your answers.

## Definitions

Next, take a few moments to write down the definitions for the following terms:

ES, IS, domain, circuit, NLPID, SNPA, NSAP, NET, IDP, DSP, AFI, IDI, HO-DSP, SEL, TLV, Level 1 routing, Level 2 routing, IIH, ISH, LSP, CSNP, PSNP, LSP fragmentation, three-way handshake, pseudonode, DIS, area, Level 2 subdomain, backbone, ATTached bit, Overload bit

Refer to the glossary to check your answers.

## Further Reading

Jeff Doyle's *Routing TCP/IP*, Volume I, Second Edition; every word a must for CCIE Routing and Switching.

Jeff Doyle's *OSPF and IS-IS: Choosing an IGP for Large-Scale Networks* is yet another book specifically devoted to these two routing protocols, and—as can be expected—it is a great book to read.

*IS-IS and OSPF: A Comparative Anatomy*: A presentation available online by Dave Katz under this title is a great introduction into both protocols and a very nice comparison of their common and different features.

Another in-depth comparison of OSPF and IS-IS can be found in an Internet draft available online with the filename *draft-bhatia-manral-diff-isis-ospf-01.txt*.

**Blueprint topics covered in this chapter:**

This chapter covers the following subtopics from the Cisco CCIE Routing and Switching written exam blueprint. Refer to the full blueprint in Table I-1 in the Introduction for more details on the topics covered in each chapter and their context within the blueprint.

- Manual Summarization and Autosummarization

- Route Redistribution

- Default Routing

- Performance Routing

- Troubleshooting Complex Layer 3 Problems

# IGP Route Redistribution, Route Summarization, Default Routing, and Troubleshooting

This chapter covers several topics related to the use of multiple internal gateway protocol (IGP) routing protocols. IGPs can use default routes to pull packets toward a small set of routers, with those routers having learned routes from some external source. IGPs can use route summarization with a single routing protocol, but it is often used at redistribution points between IGPs as well. Route redistribution by definition involves moving routes from one routing source to another. This chapter takes a look at each topic.

New to the qualification exam blueprint are a number of troubleshooting topics. One of them, troubleshooting complex Layer 3 problems, is covered in this chapter. The goal is to provide you with a process and tools to troubleshoot these types of problems.

For perspective, note that this chapter includes coverage of Routing Information Protocol version 2 (RIPv2) redistribution topics. Even though RIPv2 has been removed from the CCIE Routing and Switching qualifying exam blueprint, you might still see exam questions on redistribution involving RIPv2. Therefore, this chapter includes coverage of that topic.

## "Do I Know This Already?" Quiz

Table 11-1 outlines the major headings in this chapter and the corresponding "Do I Know This Already?" quiz questions.

**Table 11-1**   *"Do I Know This Already?" Foundation Topics Section-to-Question Mapping*

| Foundation Topics Section | Questions Covered in This Section | Score |
|---|---|---|
| Route Maps, Prefix Lists, and Administrative Distance | 1–2 | |
| Route Redistribution | 3–6 | |
| Route Summarization | 7 | |
| Default Routes | 8 | |
| Troubleshooting Layer 3 Problems | 9–10 | |
| Performance Routing | 11–12 | |
| Total Score | | |

To best use this pre-chapter assessment, remember to score yourself strictly. You can find the answers in Appendix A, "Answers to the 'Do I Know This Already?' Quizzes."

1.  A route map has several clauses. A route map's first clause has a **permit** action configured. The **match** command for this clause refers to an ACL that matches route 10.1.1.0/24 with a **permit** action, and matches route 10.1.2.0/24 with a **deny** action. If this route map is used for route redistribution, which of the following are true?

    a.  The route map will attempt to redistribute 10.1.1.0/24.

    b.  The question does not supply enough information to determine whether 10.1.1.0/24 is redistributed.

    c.  The route map will not attempt to redistribute 10.1.2.0/24.

    d.  The question does not supply enough information to determine whether 10.1.2.0/24 is redistributed.

2.  Which of the following routes would be matched by this prefix list command: **ip prefix-list fred permit 10.128.0.0/9 ge 20?**

    a.  10.1.1.0 255.255.255.0

    b.  10.127.1.0 255.255.255.0

    c.  10.200.200.192 255.255.255.252

    d.  10.128.0.0 255.255.240.0

    e.  None of these answers is correct.

3.  A router is using the following configuration to redistribute routes. This router has several working interfaces with IP addresses in network 10.0.0.0, and has learned some network 10 routes with EIGRP and some with OSPF. Which of the following is true about the redistribution configuration?

```
router eigrp 1
 network 10.0.0.0
 redistribute ospf 2
!
router ospf 2
 network 10.0.0.0 0.255.255.255 area 3
 redistribute eigrp 1 subnets

R1# show ip route 10.0.0.0
Routing entry for 10.0.0.0/24, 5 known subnets
  Attached (2 connections)
  Redistributing via eigrp 1

O E1     10.6.11.0 [110/84] via 10.1.6.6, 00:21:52, Serial0/0/0.6
O E2     10.6.12.0 [110/20] via 10.1.6.6, 00:21:52, Serial0/0/0.6
C        10.1.6.0 is directly connected, Serial0/0/0.6
O IA     10.1.2.0 [110/65] via 10.1.1.5, 00:21:52, Serial0/0/0.5
C        10.1.1.0 is directly connected, Serial0/0/0.5
```

    **a.** EIGRP will not advertise any additional routes because of redistribution.

    **b.** OSPF will not advertise any additional routes because of redistribution.

    **c.** Routes redistributed into OSPF will be advertised as E1 routes.

    **d.** The **redistribute ospf 2** command would be rejected because of missing parameters.

**4.** Examine the following router configuration and excerpt from its IP routing table. Which routes could be redistributed into OSPF?

```
router eigrp 1
 network 12.0.0.0
router ospf 2
 redistribute eigrp 1 subnets
 network 13.0.0.0 0.255.255.255 area 3
An excerpt from the routing table is shown next:
C        12.1.6.0 is directly connected, Serial0/0/0.6
D        12.0.0.0/8 [90/2172416] via 13.1.1.1, 00:01:30, Serial0/0/0.5
C        13.1.1.0 is directly connected, Serial0/0/0.5
```

    **a.** 12.1.6.0

    **b.** 12.0.0.0

    **c.** 13.1.1.0

    **d.** None of these answers is correct.

**5.** Two corporations merged. The network engineers decided to redistribute between one company's EIGRP network and the other company's OSPF network, using two mutually redistributing routers (R1 and R2) for redundancy. Assume that as many defaults as is possible are used for the redistribution configuration. Assume that one of the subnets in the OSPF domain is 10.1.1.0/24. Which of the following is true about a possible suboptimal route to 10.1.1.0/24 on R1—a route that sends packets through the EIGRP domain, and through R2 into the OSPF domain?

    **a.** The suboptimal routes will occur unless the configuration filters routes at R1.

    **b.** R1's administrative distance must be manipulated, such that OSPF routes have an administrative distance less than EIGRP's default of 90.

    **c.** EIGRP prevents the suboptimal routes by default.

    **d.** Using route tags is the only way to prevent the suboptimal routes.

6.  Which of the following statements is true about the type of routes created when redistributing routes?

    a.  Routes redistributed into OSPF default to be external type 2.

    b.  Routes redistributed into EIGRP default to external, but can be set to internal with a route map.

    c.  Routes redistributed into RIP are external by default.

    d.  Routes redistributed into OSPF by a router in an NSSA area default to be external type 1.

7.  Which of the following is not true about route summarization?

    a.  The advertised summary is assigned the same metric as the lowest-metric component subnet.

    b.  The router does not advertise the summary when its routing table does not have any of the component subnets.

    c.  The router does not advertise the component subnets.

    d.  Summarization, when used with redistribution, prevents all cases of suboptimal routes.

8.  Which of the following is/are true regarding the **default-information originate** router subcommand?

    a.  It is not supported by EIGRP.

    b.  It causes OSPF to advertise a default route, but only if a static route to 0.0.0.0/0 is in that router's routing table.

    c.  The **always** keyword in the **default-information originate** command, when used for OSPF, means that OSPF will originate a default route even if no default route exists in its own IP routing table.

    d.  None of the other answers is correct.

9.  An EIGRP router is showing intermittent reachability to 172.30.8.32/27. Which command(s) reveals the source by which this prefix is being advertised to the local router?

    a.  show ip protocols

    b.  show ip route eigrp

    c.  show ip eigrp neighbor

    d.  show ip eigrp topology 172.30.8.32

    e.  show ip route 172.30.8.32

**10.** You suspect that a routing loop exists in your network because a subnet is intermittently reachable. What is the most specific way to determine that a routing loop is the cause?

   **a.** ping

   **b.** traceroute

   **c.** debug ip packet detail

   **d.** debug ip routing

   **e.** show ip protocols

**11.** What routing optimization feature exists to change existing routing parameters of an IGP such that it will add new prefixes and manipulate overall data forwarding at the network's edge?

   **a.** Overlay transport virtualization

   **b.** OSPFv3

   **c.** Enhanced traffic selection

   **d.** Performance Routing (PfR)

**12.** What solution is used to ensure that rogue devices cannot be used to poison the manipulation of route optimization through adding dynamic static routes to the routing information base of a given border router?

   **a.** MD5

   **b.** Key chains

   **c.** Clear text password

   **d.** SHA1

## Foundation Topics

# Route Maps, Prefix Lists, and Administrative Distance

Route maps, IP prefix lists, and administrative distance (AD) must be well understood to do well with route redistribution topics on the CCIE Routing and Switching written exam. This section focuses on the tools themselves, followed by coverage of route redistribution.

## Configuring Route Maps with the route-map Command

Route maps provide programming logic similar to the If/Then/Else logic seen in other programming languages. A single route map has one or more **route-map** commands in it, and routers process **route-map** commands in sequential order based on sequence numbers. Each **route-map** command has underlying matching parameters, configured with the aptly named **match** command. (To match all packets, the **route-map** clause simply omits the **match** command.) Each **route-map** command also has one or more optional **set** commands that you can use to manipulate information—for example, to set the metric for some redistributed routes. The general rules for route maps are as follows:

- Each **route-map** command must have an explicitly configured name, with all commands that use the same name being part of the same route map.

- Each **route-map** command has an action (**permit** or **deny**).

- Each **route-map** command in the same route map has a unique sequence number, allowing deletion and insertion of single **route-map** commands.

- When a route map is used for redistribution, the route map processes routes taken from the then-current routing table.

- The route map is processed sequentially based on the sequence numbers.

- After a particular route is matched by the route map, it is not processed beyond that matching **route-map** command (specific to route redistribution).

- When a route is matched in a **route-map** statement, if the **route-map** command has a **permit** parameter, the route is redistributed (specific to route redistribution).

- When a route is matched in a **route-map** statement, if the **route-map** statement has a **deny** parameter, the route is not redistributed (specific to route redistribution).

Route maps can be confusing at times, especially when using the **deny** option on the **route-map** command. To help make sure that the logic is clear before getting into redistribution, Figure 11-1 shows a logic diagram for an example route map. (This example is contrived to demonstrate some nuances of route map logic; a better, more efficient route map could be created to achieve the same results.) In the figure, R1 has eight loopback interfaces configured to be in class A networks 32 through 39. Figure 11-1 shows how the contrived **route-map picky** would process the routes.

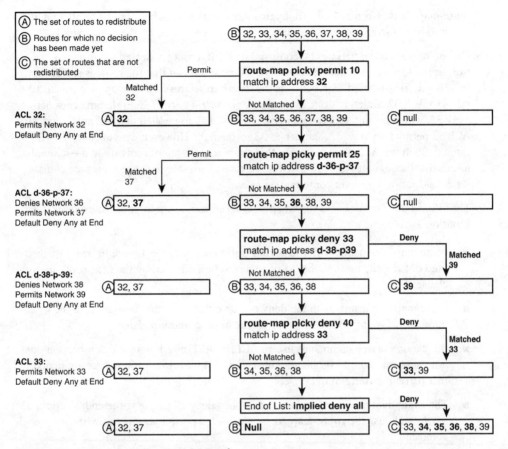

**Figure 11-1**  *Route Map Logic Example*

First, a few clarifications about the meaning of Figure 11-1 are in order. The top of the figure begins with the set of connected networks (32 through 39), labeled with a "B," which is the set of routes still being considered for redistribution. Moving down the figure, four separate **route-map** commands sit inside this single route map. Each **route-map** clause (the clause includes the underlying **match** and **set** commands) in turn moves routes from the list of possible routes ("B") to either the list of routes to redistribute ("A") or the list to not redistribute ("C"). By the bottom of the figure, all routes will be noted as either to be redistributed or not to be redistributed.

The route map chooses to redistribute a route only if the **route-map** command has a **permit** option; the only time a **route-map** clause chooses to *not redistribute* a route is when the clause has a **deny** option. Ignoring the matching logic for a moment, the first two **route-map** commands (sequence numbers 10 and 25) use the **permit** option. As a result of those clauses, routes are either added to the list of routes to redistribute ("A") or left in the list of candidate routes ("B"). The third and fourth clauses (sequence numbers 33 and 40) use the **deny** option, so those clauses cause routes to be either added to the list of routes to not redistribute ("C") or left in the list of candidate routes ("B"). In effect, after a

**route-map** clause has matched a route, that route is flagged either as to be redistributed or as not to be redistributed, and the route is no longer processed by the route map.

One point that can sometimes be confused is that if a route is denied by an access control list (ACL) used by a **match** command, it does not mean that the route is prevented from being redistributed. For example, the **match ip address 32** command in clause 10 refers to ACL 32, which has one explicit *access control entry (ACE)* that matches network 32, with a **permit** action. Of course, ACL 32 has an implied deny all at the end, so ACL 32 permits network 32, and denies 33 through 39. However, denying networks 33 through 39 in the ACL does not mean that those routes are not redistributed—it simply means that those routes do not match **route-map** clause 10, so those routes are eligible for consideration by a later **route-map** clause.

The following list summarizes the key points about route map logic when used for redistribution:

**Key
Topic**

- ■ **route-map** commands with the **permit** option either cause a route to be redistributed or leave the route in the list of routes to be examined by the next **route-map** clause.

- ■ **route-map** commands with the **deny** option either filter the route or leave the route in the list of routes to be examined by the next **route-map** clause.

- ■ If a clause's **match** commands use an ACL, an ACL match with the **deny** action does not cause the route to be filtered. Instead, it just means that route does not match that particular **route-map** clause.

- ■ The **route-map** command includes an implied deny all clause at the end; to configure a permit all, use the **route-map** command, with a **permit** action, but without a **match** command.

### Route Map match Commands for Route Redistribution

Route maps use the **match** command to define the fields and values used for matching the routes being processed. If more than one **match** command is configured in a single **route-map** clause, a route is matched only if all the **match** commands' parameters match the route. The logic in each **match** command itself is relatively straightforward. Table 11-2 lists the **match** command options when used for IGP route redistribution.

**Table 11-2**    match *Command Options for IGP Redistribution*

| match Command | Description |
|---|---|
| **match interface** *interface-type interface-number* [*... interface-type interface-number*] | Looks at outgoing interface of routes |
| **\*match ip address** {[*access-list-number* \| *access-list-name*] \| *prefix-list prefix-list-name*} | Examines route prefix and prefix length |

| match Command | Description |
|---|---|
| *match ip next-hop {*access-list-number* \| *access-list-name*} | Examines route's next-hop address |
| *match ip route-source {*access-list-number* \| *access-list-name*} | Matches advertising router's IP address |
| match metric *metric-value* [+ – *deviation*] | Matches route's metric exactly, or optionally a range of metrics (plus/minus the configured deviation) |
| match route-type {internal \| external [type-1 \| type-2] \| level-1 \| level-2} | Matches route type |
| match tag *tag-value* [...*tag-value*] | Tag must have been set earlier |

*Can reference multiple numbered and named ACLs on a single command.

### Route Map set Commands for Route Redistribution

When used for redistribution, route maps have an implied action—either to allow the route to be redistributed or to filter the route so that it is not redistributed. As described earlier in this chapter, that choice is implied by the **permit** or **deny** option in the **route-map** command. Route maps can also change information about the redistributed routes by using the **set** command. Table 11-3 lists the **set** command options when used for IGP route redistribution.

**Table 11-3**   set *Command Options for IGP Redistribution*

| set Command | Description |
|---|---|
| set level {level-1 \| level-2 \| level-1-2 \| stub-area \| backbone} | Defines database(s) into which the route is redistributed |
| set metric *metric-value* | Sets the route's metric for OSPF, RIP, and IS-IS |
| set metric *bandwidth delay reliability loading mtu* | Sets the IGRP/EIGRP route's metric values |
| set metric-type {internal \| external \| type-1 \| type-2} | Sets the type of route for IS-IS and OSPF |
| set tag *tag-value* | Sets the unitless tag value in the route |

## IP Prefix Lists

IP prefix lists provide mechanisms to match two components of an IP route:

- The route prefix (the subnet number)

- The prefix length (the subnet mask)

The **redistribute** command cannot directly reference a prefix list, but a route map can refer to a prefix list by using the **match** command.

A prefix list itself has similar characteristics to a route map. The list consists of one or more statements with the same text name. Each statement has a sequence number to allow deletion of individual commands, and insertion of commands into a particular sequence position. Each command has a **permit** or **deny** action—but because it is used only for matching packets, the **permit** or **deny** keyword just implies whether a route is matched (**permit**) or not (**deny**). The generic command syntax is as follows:

```
ip prefix-list list-name [seq seq-value] {deny network/length | permit
  network/length}[ge ge-value] [le le-value]
```

The sometimes tricky and interesting part of working with prefix lists is that the meaning of the *network/length*, *ge-value*, and *le-value* parameters changes depending on the syntax. The *network/length* parameters define the values to use to match the route prefix. For example, a *network/length* of 10.0.0.0/8 means "any route that begins with a 10 in the first octet and has a /8 mask." The **ge** and **le** options are used for comparison to the prefix length—in other words, to the number of binary 1s in the subnet mask. For example, **ge 20 le 22** matches only routes whose masks are /20, /21, or /22. So, prefix list logic can be summarized into a two-step comparison process for each route:

1. The *route's prefix* must be within the range of addresses implied by the **prefix-list** command's *network/length* parameters.

2. The *route's prefix length* must match the *range of prefixes* implied by the **prefix-list** command.

The potentially tricky part of the logic relates to knowing the range of prefix lengths checked by this logic. The range is defined by the *ge-value* and *le-value* parameters, which stand for *greater-than-or-equal-to* and *less-than-or-equal-to*. Table 11-4 formalizes the logic, including the default values for *ge-value* and *le-value*. In the table, note that *conf-length* refers to the prefix length configured in the *network/prefix* (required) parameter, and *route-length* refers to the prefix length of a route being examined by the prefix list.

**Table 11-4**   *LE and GE Parameters on IP Prefix List, and the Implied Range of Prefix Lengths*

| Prefix List Parameters | Range of Prefix Lengths |
|---|---|
| Neither | *conf-length = route-length* |
| Only **le** | *conf-length <= route-length <= le-value* |
| Only **ge** | *ge-value <= route-length <= 32* |
| Both **ge** and **le** | *ge-value <= route-length <= le-value* |

Several examples can really help nail down prefix list logic. The following routes will be examined by a variety of prefix lists, with the routes numbered for easier reference:

1. 10.0.0.0/8

2. 10.128.0.0/9

3. 10.1.1.0/24

4. 10.1.2.0/24

5. 10.128.10.4/30

6. 10.128.10.8/30

Next, Table 11-5 shows the results of seven different one-line prefix lists applied to these six example routes. The table lists the matching parameters in the **prefix-list** commands, omitting the first part of the commands. The table explains which of the six routes would match the listed prefix list and why.

**Table 11-5**  *Example Prefix Lists Applied to the List of Routes*

| prefix-list Command Parameters | Routes Matched | Results |
|---|---|---|
| 10.0.0.0/8 | 1 | Without **ge** or **le** configured, both the prefix (10.0.0.0) and length (8) must be an exact match. |
| 10.128.0.0/9 | 2 | Without **ge** or **le** configured, the prefix (10.128.0.0) and length (9) must be an exact match; only the second route in the list is matched by this prefix list. |
| 10.0.0.0/8 ge 9 | 2–6 | The 10.0.0.0/8 means "all routes whose first octet is 10," effectively representing an address range. The prefix length must be between 9 and 32, inclusive. |
| 10.0.0.0/8 ge 24 le 24 | 3, 4 | The 10.0.0.0/8 means "all routes whose first octet is 10," and the prefix range is 24 to 24—meaning only routes with prefix length 24. |
| 10.0.0.0/8 le 28 | 1–4 | The prefix length needs to be between 8 and 28, inclusive. |
| 0.0.0.0/0 | None | 0.0.0.0/0 means "match all prefixes, with prefix length of exactly 0." So, it would match all routes' prefixes but none of their prefix lengths. Only a default route would match this prefix list. |
| 0.0.0.0/0 le 32 | All | The range implied by 0.0.0.0/0 is all IPv4 addresses. The **le 32** then implies any prefix length between 0 and 32, inclusive. This is the syntax for "match all" prefix list logic. |

## Administrative Distance

A single router can learn routes using multiple IP routing protocols, as well as through connected and static routes. When a router learns a particular route from multiple sources, the router cannot use the metrics to determine the best route, because the metrics are based on different units. So, the router uses each route's *administrative distance (AD)* to determine which is best, with the lower number being better. Table 11-6 lists the default AD values for the various routing sources.

**Table 11-6**  *Administrative Distances*

| Route Type | Administrative Distance |
|---|---|
| Connected | 0 |
| Static | 1 |
| EIGRP summary route | 5 |
| EBGP | 20 |
| EIGRP (internal) | 90 |
| IGRP | 100 |
| OSPF | 110 |
| IS-IS | 115 |
| RIP | 120 |
| EIGRP (external) | 170 |
| iBGP | 200 |
| Unreachable | 255 |

The defaults can be changed by using the **distance** command. The command differs among all three IGPs covered in this book. The generic versions of the **distance** router subcommand for RIP, Enhanced Interior Gateway Routing Protocol (EIGRP), and Open Shortest Path First (OSPF), respectively, are as follows:

```
distance distance
distance eigrp internal-distance external-distance
distance ospf {[intra-area dist1] [inter-area dist2] [external dist3]}
```

As you can see, EIGRP and OSPF can set a different AD depending on the type of route as well, whereas RIP cannot. You can also use the **distance** command to set a router's view of the AD per route, as is covered later in this chapter.

# Route Redistribution

Although using a single routing protocol throughout an enterprise might be preferred, many enterprises use multiple routing protocols because of business mergers and acquisitions, organizational history, or in some cases for technical reasons. Route redistribution allows one or more routers to take routes learned through one routing protocol and advertise those routes through another routing protocol so that all parts of the internetwork can be reached.

To perform redistribution, one or more routers run both routing protocols, with each routing protocol placing routes into that router's routing table. Then, each routing protocol can take all or some of the other routing protocol's routes from the routing table and advertise those routes. This section begins by looking at the mechanics of how to perform simple redistribution on a single router, and ends with a discussion of tools and issues that matter most when redistributing on multiple routers.

## Mechanics of the redistribute Command

The **redistribute** router subcommand tells one routing protocol to take routes from another routing protocol. This command can simply redistribute all routes or, by using matching logic, redistribute only a subset of the routes. The **redistribute** command also supports actions for setting some parameters about the redistributed routes—for example, the metric.

The full syntax of the **redistribute** command is as follows:

```
redistribute protocol [process-id] [level-1 | level-1-2 | level-2] [as-number]
[metric metric-value] [metric-type type-value] [match {internal | external 1 |
   external 2}] [tag tag-value] [route-map map-tag] [subnets]
```

The **redistribute** command identifies the routing source from which routes are taken, and the **router** command identifies the routing process into which the routes are advertised. For example, the **redistribute eigrp 1** command tells the router to *take routes from* EIGRP process 1; if that command were under **router rip**, the routes would be redistributed into RIP, enabling other RIP routers in the network to see some or all routes coming from EIGRP AS 1.

The **redistribute** command has a lot of other parameters as well, most of which will be described in upcoming examples. The first few examples use the network shown in Figure 11-2. In this network, each IGP uses a different class A network just to make the results of redistribution more obvious. Also note that the numbering convention is such that each of R1's connected WAN subnets has 1 as the third octet, and each LAN subnet off R3, R4, and R5 has 2 as the third octet.

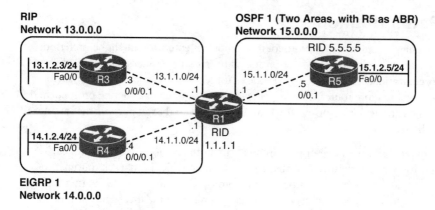

**Figure 11-2** *Sample Network for Default Route Examples*

## Redistribution Using Default Settings

The first example configuration meets the following design goals:

- R1 redistributes between each pair of IGPs—RIP, EIGRP, and OSPF.

- Default metrics are used whenever possible; when required, the metrics are configured on the **redistribute** command.

- Redistribution into OSPF uses the nondefault **subnets** parameter, which causes subnets to be advertised into OSPF.

- All other settings use default values.

Example 11-1 shows R1's configuration for each routing protocol, along with **show** commands from all four routers to highlight the results of the redistribution.

**Example 11-1** *Route Redistribution with Minimal Options*

```
! EIGRP redistributes from OSPF (process ID 1) and RIP. EIGRP must
! set the metric, as it has no default values. It also uses the
! no auto-summary command so that subnets will be redistributed into
! EIGRP.
router eigrp 1
redistribute ospf 1 metric 1544 5 255 1 1500
redistribute rip metric 1544 5 255 1
network 14.0.0.0
no auto-summary
! OSPF redistributes from EIGRP (ASN 1) and RIP. OSPF defaults the
! metric to 20 for redistributed IGP routes. It must also use the
! subnets option in order to redistribute subnets.
router ospf 1
router-id 1.1.1.1
redistribute eigrp 1 subnets
```

```
redistribute rip subnets
network 15.0.0.0 0.255.255.255 area 0
! RIP redistributes from OSPF (process ID 1) and EIGRP (ASN 1). RIP
! must set the metric, as it has no default values. It also uses the
! no auto-summary command so that subnets will be redistributed into
! EIGRP.
router rip
version 2
redistribute eigrp 1 metric 2
redistribute ospf 1 metric 3
network 13.0.0.0
no auto-summary
! R1 has a connected route (x.x.1.0) in networks 13, 14, and 15, as well as
! an IGP-learned route (x.x.2.0).
R1# show ip route
! lines omitted for brevity
     10.0.0.0/24 is subnetted, 1 subnets
C       10.1.1.0 is directly connected, FastEthernet0/0
     13.0.0.0/24 is subnetted, 2 subnets
C       13.1.1.0 is directly connected, Serial0/0/0.3
R       13.1.2.0 [120/1] via 13.1.1.3, 00:00:07, Serial0/0/0.3
     14.0.0.0/24 is subnetted, 2 subnets
D       14.1.2.0 [90/2172416] via 14.1.1.4, 00:58:20, Serial0/0/0.4
C       14.1.1.0 is directly connected, Serial0/0/0.4
     15.0.0.0/24 is subnetted, 2 subnets
O IA    15.1.2.0 [110/65] via 15.1.1.5, 00:04:25, Serial0/0/0.5
C       15.1.1.0 is directly connected, Serial0/0/0.5
```

```
! R3 learned two routes each from nets 14 and 15.
! Compare the metrics set on R1's RIP redistribute command to the metrics below.
R3# show ip route rip
     14.0.0.0/24 is subnetted, 2 subnets
R       14.1.2.0 [120/2] via 13.1.1.1, 00:00:19, Serial0/0/0.1
R       14.1.1.0 [120/2] via 13.1.1.1, 00:00:19, Serial0/0/0.1
     15.0.0.0/24 is subnetted, 2 subnets
R       15.1.2.0 [120/3] via 13.1.1.1, 00:00:19, Serial0/0/0.1
R       15.1.1.0 [120/3] via 13.1.1.1, 00:00:19, Serial0/0/0.1
```

```
! R4 learned two routes each from nets 13 and 15.
! EIGRP injected the routes as external (EX), which are considered AD 170.
R4# show ip route eigrp
     13.0.0.0/24 is subnetted, 2 subnets
D EX    13.1.1.0 [170/2171136] via 14.1.1.1, 00:09:57, Serial0/0/0.1
D EX    13.1.2.0 [170/2171136] via 14.1.1.1, 00:09:57, Serial0/0/0.1
     15.0.0.0/24 is subnetted, 2 subnets
D EX    15.1.2.0 [170/2171136] via 14.1.1.1, 01:00:27, Serial0/0/0.1
D EX    15.1.1.0 [170/2171136] via 14.1.1.1, 01:00:27, Serial0/0/0.1
```

```
! R5 learned two routes each from nets 13 and 14.
```

```
! OSPF by default injected the routes as external type 2, cost 20.
R5# show ip route ospf
      13.0.0.0/24 is subnetted, 2 subnets
O E2    13.1.1.0 [110/20] via 15.1.1.1, 00:36:12, Serial0/0.1
O E2    13.1.2.0 [110/20] via 15.1.1.1, 00:36:12, Serial0/0.1
      14.0.0.0/24 is subnetted, 2 subnets
O E2    14.1.2.0 [110/20] via 15.1.1.1, 00:29:56, Serial0/0.1
O E2    14.1.1.0 [110/20] via 15.1.1.1, 00:36:12, Serial0/0.1
! As a backbone router, OSPF on R1 created type 5 LSAs for the four E2 subnets.
! If R1 had been inside an NSSA stub area, it would have created type 7 LSAs.
R5# show ip ospf data | begin Type-5
        Type-5 AS External Link States

Link ID         ADV Router       Age        Seq#        Checksum Tag
13.1.1.0        1.1.1.1          1444       0x80000002 0x000785 0
13.1.2.0        1.1.1.1          1444       0x80000002 0x00FB8F 0
14.1.1.0        1.1.1.1          1444       0x80000002 0x00F991 0
14.1.2.0        1.1.1.1          1444       0x80000002 0x00EE9B 0
```

Metrics must be set through configuration when redistributing into RIP and EIGRP, whereas OSPF uses default values. In the example, the two **redistribute** commands under **router rip** used hop counts of 2 and 3 just so that the metrics could be easily seen in the **show ip route** command output on R3. The EIGRP metric in the **redistribute** command must include all five metric components, even if the last three are ignored by EIGRP's metric calculation (as they are by default). The **redistribute rip metric 1544 5 255 1 1500** command lists EIGRP metric components of bandwidth, delay, reliability, load, and MTU, in order. OSPF defaults to cost 20 when redistributing from an IGP, and 1 when redistributing from BGP.

The **redistribute** command redistributes only routes in that router's current IP routing table. When redistributing from a given routing protocol, the **redistribute** command takes routes listed in the IP routing table as being learned from that routing protocol. Interestingly, the **redistribute** command can also pick up connected routes. For example, R1 has an OSPF route to 15.1.2.0/24, and a connected route to 15.1.1.0/24. However, R3 (RIP) and R4 (EIGRP) redistribute both of these routes—the OSPF-learned route and one connected route—as a result of their respective **redistribute ospf** commands. As it turns out, the **redistribute** command causes the router to use the following logic to choose which routes to redistribute from a particular IGP protocol:

**1.** Take all routes in my routing table that were learned by the routing protocol from which routes are being redistributed.

**2.** Take all connected subnets matched by that routing protocol's **network** commands.

Example 11-1 shows several instances of exactly how this two-part logic works. For example, R3 (RIP) learns about connected subnet 14.1.1.0/24, because RIP redistributes from EIGRP, and R1's EIGRP **network 14.0.0.0** command matches that subnet.

The **redistribute** command includes a **subnets** option, but only OSPF needs to use it. By default, when redistributing into OSPF, OSPF redistributes only routes for classful networks, ignoring subnets. By including the **subnets** option, OSPF redistributes subnets as well. The other IGPs redistribute subnets automatically; however, if at a network boundary, the RIP or EIGRP **auto-summary** setting would still cause summarization to use the classful network. In Example 11-1, if either RIP or EIGRP had used **auto-summary**, each redistributed network would show just the classful networks. For example, if RIP had configured **auto-summary** in Example 11-1, R3 would have a route to networks 14.0.0.0/8 and 15.0.0.0/8, but no routes to subnets inside those class A networks.

## Setting Metrics, Metric Types, and Tags

Cisco IOS provides three mechanisms for setting the metrics of redistributed routes, as follows:

1. Call a route map from the **redistribute** command, with the route map using the **set metric** command. This method allows different metrics for different routes.

2. Use the **metric** option on the **redistribute** command. This sets the same metric for all routes redistributed by that **redistribute** command.

3. Use the **default-metric** command under the **router** command. This command sets the metric for all redistributed routes whose metric was not set by either of the other two methods.

The list implies the order of precedence if more than one method defines a metric. For example, if a route's metric is set by all three methods, the route map's metric is used. If the metric is set on the **redistribute** command and there is a **default-metric** command as well, the setting on the **redistribute** command takes precedence.

The **redistribute** command also allows a setting for the *metric-type* option, which really refers to the route type. For example, routes redistributed into OSPF must be OSPF external routes, but they can be either external type 1 (E1) or type 2 (E2) routes. Table 11-7 summarizes the defaults for metrics and metric types.

**Table 11-7**  *Default Metrics and Route Metric Types in IGP Route Redistribution*

| IGP into Which Routes Are Redistributed | Default Metric | Default (and Possible) Metric Types |
|---|---|---|
| RIP | None | RIP has no concept of external routes |
| EIGRP | None | External |
| OSPF | 20/1* | E2 (E1 or E2) |
| IS-IS | 0 | L1 (L1, L2, L1/L2, or external) |

* OSPF uses cost 20 when redistributing from an IGP, and cost 1 when redistributing from BGP.

## Redistributing a Subset of Routes Using a Route Map

Route maps can be referenced by any **redistribute** command. The route map can actually let all the routes through, setting different route attributes (for example, metrics) for different routes. Or it might match some routes with a **deny** clause, which prevents the route from being redistributed. (Refer to Figure 11-1 for a review of route map logic.)

Figure 11-3 and Example 11-2 show an example of mutual redistribution between EIGRP and OSPF, with some routes being either filtered or changed using route maps.

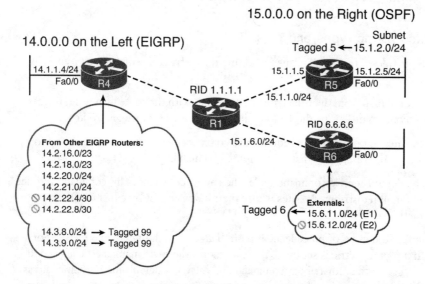

**Figure 11-3** *OSPF and EIGRP Mutual Redistribution Using Route Maps*

The following list details the requirements for redistribution from OSPF into EIGRP. These requirements use R1's perspective, because it is the router doing the redistribution.

- Routes with next-hop address 15.1.1.5 (R5) should be redistributed, with route tag **5**.

- E1 routes sourced by R6 (RID 6.6.6.6) should be redistributed, and assigned a route tag of 6.

- No other routes should be redistributed.

The requirements for redistributing routes from EIGRP into OSPF are as follows, again from R1's perspective:

- Routes beginning with 14.2, and with masks /23 and /24, should be redistributed, with metric set to 300.

- Other routes beginning with 14.2 should not be redistributed.

- Routes beginning with 14.3 should be redistributed, with route tag 99.

- No other routes should be redistributed.

Most of the explanation of the configuration is provided in the comments in Example 11-2, with a few additional comments following the example.

**Example 11-2**  *Route Redistribution Using Route Maps*

```
! No metrics are set on the redistribute commands; either the default metric
! is used, or the route maps set the metrics. The default-metric command
! sets the unused EIGRP metric parameters to "1" because something must be
! configured, but the values are unimportant.
router eigrp 1
redistribute ospf 1 route-map ospf-into-eigrp
network 14.0.0.0
default-metric 1544 5 1 1 1
no auto-summary
! While this configuration strives to use other options besides the options
! directly on the redistribute command, when used by OSPF, you must still
! include the subnets keyword for OSPF to learn subnets from other IGPs.
router ospf 1
router-id 1.1.1.1
redistribute eigrp 1 subnets route-map eigrp-into-ospf
network 15.0.0.0 0.255.255.255 area 0
! ACL A-14-3-x-x matches all addresses that begin 14.3. ACL A-15-1-1-5 matches
! exactly IP address 15.1.1.5. ACL A-6-6-6-6 matches exactly address 6.6.6.6.
ip access-list standard A-14-3-x-x
 permit 14.3.0.0 0.0.255.255
ip access-list standard A-15-1-1-5
permit 15.1.1.5
ip access-list standard A-6-6-6-6
permit 6.6.6.6
! The prefix lists matches prefixes in the range 14.2.0.0 through 14.2.255.255,
! with prefix length 23 or 24.
ip prefix-list e-into-o seq 5 permit 14.2.0.0/16 ge 23 le 24
! route-map ospf-into-eigrp was called by the redistribute command under router
! eigrp, meaning that it controls redistribution from OSPF into EIGRP.
! Clause 10 matches OSPF routes whose next hop is 15.1.1.5, which is R5's serial
! IP address. R1's only route that meets this criteria is 15.1.2.0/24. This route
! will be redistributed because the route-map clause 10 has a permit action.
! The route tag is also set to 5.
route-map ospf-into-eigrp permit 10
match ip next-hop A-15-1-1-5
set tag 5
! Clause 15 matches OSPF routes whose LSAs are sourced by router with RID 6.6.6.6,
! namely R6, and also have metric type E1. R6 sources two external routes, but
! only 15.6.11.0/24 is E1. The route is tagged 6.
route-map ospf-into-eigrp permit 15
match ip route-source A-6-6-6-6
match route-type external type-1
```

```
set tag 6
! route-map eigrp-into-ospf was called by the redistribute command under router
! ospf, meaning that it controls redistribution from EIGRP into OSPF.
! Clause 10 matches using a prefix list, which in turn matches prefixes that begin
! with 14.2, and which have either a /23 or /24 prefix length. By implication, it
! does not match prefix length /30. The metric is set to 300 for these routes.
route-map eigrp-into-ospf permit 10
match ip address prefix-list e-into-o
set metric 300
! Clause 18 matches routes that begin 14.3. They are tagged with a 99.
route-map eigrp-into-ospf permit 18
match ip address A-14-3-x-x
set tag 99
! Next, the example shows the routes that could be redistributed, and then
! shows the results of the redistribution, pointing out which routes were
! redistributed. First, the example shows, on R1, all routes that R1 could
! try to redistribute into EIGRP.
R1# show ip route 15.0.0.0
Routing entry for 15.0.0.0/24, 5 known subnets
Attached (2 connections)
Redistributing via eigrp 1


O E1    15.6.11.0 [110/84] via 15.1.6.6, 00:21:52, Serial0/0/0.6
O E2    15.6.12.0 [110/20] via 15.1.6.6, 00:21:52, Serial0/0/0.6
C       15.1.6.0 is directly connected, Serial0/0/0.6
O IA    15.1.2.0 [110/65] via 15.1.1.5, 00:21:52, Serial0/0/0.5
C       15.1.1.0 is directly connected, Serial0/0/0.5
! R4 sees only two of the five routes from 15.0.0.0, because only two matched
! either of
! the route-map clauses. The other three routes matched the default deny clause.
R4# show ip route 15.0.0.0
Routing entry for 15.0.0.0/24, 2 known subnets
Redistributing via eigrp 1
D EX    15.6.11.0 [170/2171136] via 14.1.1.1, 00:22:21, Serial0/0/0.1
D EX    15.1.2.0 [170/2171136] via 14.1.1.1, 00:22:21, Serial0/0/0.1
! Still on R4, the show ip eigrp topology command displays the tag. This command
! filters the output so that just one line of output lists the tag values.
R4# sho ip eigrp topo 15.1.2.0 255.255.255.0 | incl tag
        Administrator tag is 5 (0x00000005)
R4# sho ip eigrp topo 15.6.11.0 255.255.255.0 | incl tag
        Administrator tag is 6 (0x00000006)
! Next, the example shows the possible routes that could be redistributed from
! EIGRP into OSPF.
! The next command (R1) lists all routes that could be redistributed into OSPF.
R1# show ip route 14.0.0.0
Routing entry for 14.0.0.0/8, 10 known subnets
```

```
      Attached (1 connections)
      Variably subnetted with 3 masks
      Redistributing via eigrp 1, ospf 1


D        14.3.9.0/24 [90/2297856] via 14.1.1.4, 00:34:48, Serial0/0/0.4
D        14.3.8.0/24 [90/2297856] via 14.1.1.4, 00:34:52, Serial0/0/0.4
D        14.1.2.0/24 [90/2172416] via 14.1.1.4, 00:39:27, Serial0/0/0.4
C        14.1.1.0/24 is directly connected, Serial0/0/0.4
D        14.2.22.8/30 [90/2297856] via 14.1.1.4, 00:35:49, Serial0/0/0.4
D        14.2.20.0/24 [90/2297856] via 14.1.1.4, 00:36:12, Serial0/0/0.4
D        14.2.21.0/24 [90/2297856] via 14.1.1.4, 00:36:08, Serial0/0/0.4
D        14.2.16.0/23 [90/2297856] via 14.1.1.4, 00:36:34, Serial0/0/0.4
D        14.2.22.4/30 [90/2297856] via 14.1.1.4, 00:35:53, Serial0/0/0.4
D        14.2.18.0/23 [90/2297856] via 14.1.1.4, 00:36:23, Serial0/0/0.4
```

```
! Next, on R5, note that the two /30 routes beginning with 14.2 were correctly
! prevented from getting into OSPF. It also filtered the redistribution of the
! two routes that begin with 14.1. As a result, R5 knows only 6 routes in
! network 14.0.0.0, whereas R1 had 10 subnets of that network it could have
! redistributed. Also below, note that the /23 and /24 routes inside 14.2 have
! metric 300.
R5# show ip route 14.0.0.0
Routing entry for 14.0.0.0/8, 6 known subnets
   Variably subnetted with 2 masks


O E2    14.3.9.0/24 [110/20] via 15.1.1.1, 00:22:41, Serial0/0.1
O E2    14.3.8.0/24 [110/20] via 15.1.1.1, 00:22:41, Serial0/0.1
O E2    14.2.20.0/24 [110/300] via 15.1.1.1, 00:22:41, Serial0/0.1
O E2    14.2.21.0/24 [110/300] via 15.1.1.1, 00:22:41, Serial0/0.1
O E2    14.2.16.0/23 [110/300] via 15.1.1.1, 00:22:41, Serial0/0.1
O E2    14.2.18.0/23 [110/300] via 15.1.1.1, 00:22:41, Serial0/0.1
! The show ip ospf database command confirms that the route tag was set
! correctly.
R5# show ip ospf data external 14.3.8.0 | incl Tag
External Route Tag: 99
```

**Note**  Route maps have an implied **deny** clause at the end of the route map. This implied **deny** clause matches all packets. As a result, any routes not matched in the explicitly configured **route-map** clauses match the implied **deny** clause, and are filtered. Both route maps in the example used the implied **deny** clause to actually filter the routes.

## Mutual Redistribution at Multiple Routers

When multiple routers redistribute between the same two routing protocol domains, several potential problems can occur. One type of problem occurs on the redistributing routers, because those routers will learn a route to most subnets through both routing protocols. That router uses the AD to determine the best route when comparing the best routes from each of the two routing protocols; this typically results in some routes using suboptimal paths. For example, Figure 11-4 shows a sample network, with R3 choosing its AD 110 OSPF route to 10.1.2.0/24 over the probably better AD 120 RIP route.

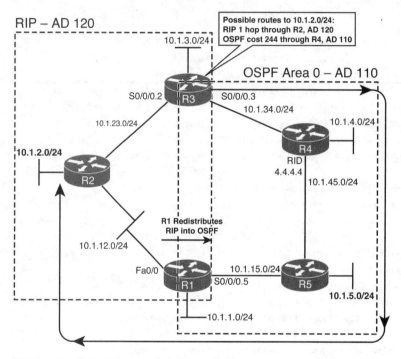

**Figure 11-4**  *OSPF and RIP Redistribution*

**Note**  The OSPF configuration for this network matches only the interfaces implied by the OSPF box in Figure 11-4. RIP does not have a *wildcard-mask* option in the **network** command, so R1's and R3's **network** commands will match all of their interfaces, as all are in network 10.0.0.0.

In Figure 11-4, R3 learns of subnet 10.1.2.0/24 through RIP updates from R2. Also, R1 learns of the subnet with RIP and redistributes the route into OSPF, and then R3 learns of a route to 10.1.2.0/24 through OSPF. R3 chooses the route with the lower administrative distance; with all default settings, OSPF's AD of 110 is better that RIP's 120.

If both R1 and R3 mutually redistribute between RIP and OSPF, the suboptimal route problem would occur on either R1 or R3 for each RIP subnet, all depending on timing.

Example 11-3 shows the redistribution configuration, along with R3 having the suboptimal route shown in Figure 11-4. However, after R1's fa0/0 interface flaps, R1 now has a suboptimal route to 10.1.2.0/24, but R3 has an optimal route.

**Example 11-3**  *Suboptimal Routing at Different Redistribution Points*

```
! R1's related configuration follows:
router ospf 1
 router-id 1.1.1.1
 redistribute rip subnets
 network 10.1.15.1 0.0.0.0 area 0
!
router rip
 redistribute ospf 1
 network 10.0.0.0
 default-metric 1
! R3's related configuration follows:
router ospf 1
 router-id 3.3.3.3
 redistribute rip subnets
 network 10.1.34.3 0.0.0.0 area 0
!
router rip
 redistribute ospf 1
 network 10.0.0.0
 default-metric 1
! R3 begins with an AD 110 OSPF route, and not a RIP route, to 10.1.2.0/24.
R3# sh ip route | incl 10.1.2.0
O E2    10.1.2.0 [110/20] via 10.1.34.4, 00:02:01, Serial0/0/0.4
! R1 has a RIP route to 10.1.2.0/24, and redistributes it into OSPF, causing R3
! to learn an OSPF route to 10.1.2.0/24.
R1# sh ip route | incl 10.1.2.0
R       10.1.2.0 [120/1] via 10.1.12.2, 00:00:08, FastEthernet0/0
! Next, R1 loses its RIP route to 10.1.2.0/24, causing R3 to lose its OSPF route.
R1# conf t
Enter configuration commands, one per line.  End with CNTL/Z.
R1(config)# int fa 0/0
R1(config-if)# shut
! R3 loses its OSPF route, but can then insert the RIP route into its table.
R3# sh ip route | incl 10.1.2.0
R       10.1.2.0 [120/1] via 10.1.23.2, 00:00:12, Serial0/0/0.2
! Not shown: R1 brings up its fa0/0 again
! However, R1 now has the suboptimal route to 10.1.2.0/24, through OSPF.
R1# sh ip route | incl 10.1.2.0
O E2    10.1.2.0 [110/20] via 10.1.15.5, 00:00:09, Serial0/0/0.5
```

The key concept behind this seemingly odd example is that a redistributing router processes only the current contents of its IP routing table. When this network first came up, R1 learned its RIP route to 10.1.2.0/24, and redistributed into OSPF, *before* R3 could do the same. So, R3 was faced with the choice of putting the AD 110 (OSPF) or AD 120 (RIP) route into its routing table, and R3 chose the lower AD OSPF route. Because R3 never had the RIP route to 10.1.2.0/24 in its routing table, R3 could not redistribute that RIP route into OSPF.

Later, when R1's fa0/0 failed (as shown in Example 11-3), R3 had time to remove the OSPF route and add the RIP route for 10.1.2.0/24 to its routing table—which then allowed R3 to redistribute that RIP route into OSPF, causing R1 to have the suboptimal route.

To solve this type of problem, the redistributing routers must have some awareness of which routes came from the other routing domain. In particular, the lower-AD routing protocol needs to decide which routes came from the higher-AD routing protocol, and either use a different AD for those routes or filter the routes. The next few sections show a few different methods of preventing this type of problem.

### Preventing Suboptimal Routes by Setting the Administrative Distance

One simple and elegant solution to the problem of suboptimal routes on redistributing routers is to flag the redistributed routes with a higher AD. A route's AD is not advertised by the routing protocol. However, a single router can be configured such that it assigns different AD values to different routes, which then impacts that one router's choice of which routes end up in that router's routing table. For example, back in Figure 11-4 and Example 11-3, R3 could have assigned the OSPF-learned route to 10.1.2.0/24, an AD higher than 120, thereby preventing the original problem.

Figure 11-5 shows a more complete example, with a route from the RIP domain (10.1.2.0/24) and another from the OSPF domain (10.1.4.0/24). Redistributing Router R3 will learn the two routes both from RIP and OSPF. When you configure R3's logic to treat OSPF internal routes with default AD 110, and OSPF external routes with AD 180 (or any other value larger than RIP's default of 120), R3 will choose the optimal path for both RIP and OSPF routes.

Example 11-4 shows how to configure both R1 and R3 to use a different AD for external routes by using the **distance ospf external 180** command, under the **router ospf** process.

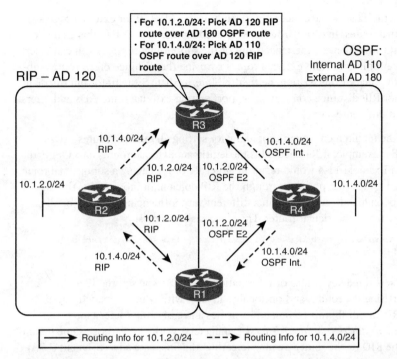

**Figure 11-5** *Effect of Differing ADs for Internal and External Routes*

**Example 11-4** *Preventing Suboptimal Routes with the* **distance** *Router Subcommand*

```
! Both R1's and R3's configurations look like they do in Example 11-3's, but with
! the addition of the distance command.
router ospf 1
distance ospf external 180
! R3 has a more optimal RIP route to 10.1.2.0/24, as does R1.
R3# sh ip route | incl 10.1.2.0
R       10.1.2.0 [120/1] via 10.1.23.2, 00:00:19, Serial0/0/0.2
! R1 next...
R1# show ip route | incl 10.1.2.0_
R       10.1.2.0 [120/1] via 10.1.12.2, 00:00:11, FastEthernet0/0
! R1 loses its next-hop interface for the RIP route, so now its OSPF route, with
! AD 180, is its only and best route to 10.1.2.0/24.
R1# conf t
Enter configuration commands, one per line.  End with CNTL/Z.
R1(config)# int fa 0/0
R1(config-if)# shut
R1(config-if)# do sh ip route | incl 10.1.2.0
O E2    10.1.2.0 [180/20] via 10.1.15.5, 00:00:05, Serial0/0/0.5
```

EIGRP supports the exact same concept by default, using AD 170 for external routes and 90 for internal routes. In fact, if EIGRP were used instead of OSPF in this example, neither R1 nor R3 would have experienced any of the suboptimal routing. You can reset EIGRP's distance for internal and external routes by using the **distance eigrp** router subcommand. (At the time of this writing, neither the Intermediate System–to–Intermediate System [IS-IS] nor RIP **distance** commands support setting external route ADs and internal route ADs to different values.)

In some cases, the requirements might not allow for setting all external routes' ADs to another value. For example, if R4 injected some legitimate external routes into OSPF, the configuration in Example 11-4 would result in either R1 or R3 having a suboptimal route to those external routes that pointed through the RIP domain. In those cases, the **distance** router subcommand can be used in a different way, influencing some of or all the routes that come from a particular router. The syntax is as follows:

```
distance {distance-value ip-address {wildcard-mask} [ip-standard-list]
    [ip-extended-list]
```

This command sets three key pieces of information: the AD to be set, the IP address of the router advertising the routes, and optionally, an ACL with which to match routes. With RIP, EIGRP, and IS-IS, this command identifies a neighboring router's interface address using the *ip-address wildcard-mask* parameters. With OSPF, those same parameters identify the RID of the router owning (creating) the link-state advertisement (LSA) for the route. The optional ACL then identifies the subset of routes for which the AD will be set. The logic boils down to something like this:

> Set this AD value for all routes, learned from a router that is defined by the IP address and wildcard mask, and for which the ACL permits the route.

Example 11-5 shows how the command could be used to solve the same suboptimal route problem on R1 and R3, while not causing suboptimal routing for other external routes. The design goals are summarized as follows:

- Set a router's local AD for its OSPF routes for subnets in the RIP domain to a value of 179, thereby making the RIP routes to those subnets better than the OSPF routes to those same subnets.

- Do not set the AD for any other routes.

**Example 11-5** *Using the* **distance** *Command to Reset Particular Routes' ADs*

```
! R1 config. Note that the command refers to 3.3.3.3, which is R3's RID. Other
! commands not related to resetting the AD are omitted. Of particular importance,
! the distance command on R1 refers to R3's OSPF RID, because R3 created the OSPF
! LSAs that we are trying to match--the LSAs created when R3 injected the
! routes redistributed from RIP.
router ospf 1
 distance 179 3.3.3.3 0.0.0.0 only-rip-routes
!
ip access-list standard only-rip-routes
```

```
  permit 10.1.12.0
  permit 10.1.3.0
  permit 10.1.2.0
  permit 10.1.23.0
! R3 config. Note that the command refers to 1.1.1.1, which is R1's RID. Other
! commands not related to resetting the AD are omitted. Also, the only-rip-routes
! ACL is identical to R1's only-rip-routes ACL.
router ospf 1
distance 179 1.1.1.1 0.0.0.0 only-rip-routes
```

## Preventing Suboptimal Routes by Using Route Tags

Another method of preventing suboptimal routing on the redistributing routers is to simply filter the problematic routes. Using subnet 10.1.2.0/24 as an example again, R3 could use an incoming **distribute-list** command to filter the OSPF route to 10.1.2.0/24, allowing R3 to use its RIP route to 10.1.2.0/24. R1 would need to perform similar route filtering as well to prevent its suboptimal route.

Performing simple route filtering based on IP subnet number works, but the redistributing routers will need to be reconfigured every time subnets change in the higher-AD routing domain. The administrative effort can be improved by adding *route tagging* to the process. When you tag all routes taken from the higher-AD domain and advertised into the lower-AD domain, the **distribute-list** command can make a simple check for that tag. Figure 11-6 shows the use of this idea for subnet 10.1.2.0/24.

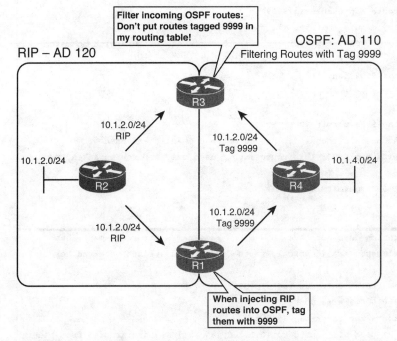

**Figure 11-6**  *Filtering with Reliance on Route Tags*

Route tags are simply unitless integer values in the data structure of a route. These tags, typically either 16 or 32 bits long depending on the routing protocol, allow a router to imply something about a route that was redistributed from another routing protocol. For example, R1 can tag its OSPF-advertised route to 10.1.2.0/24 with a tag—say, 9999. OSPF does not define what a tag of 9999 means, but the OSPF protocol includes the tag field in the LSA so that it can be used for administrative purposes. Later, R3 can filter routes based on their tag, solving the suboptimal route problem.

Figure 11-6 and Example 11-6 depict an example of route tagging and route filtering, used to solve the same old problem with suboptimal routes. R1 and R3 tag all redistributed RIP routes with tag 9999 as they enter the OSPF domain, and then R1 and R3 filter incoming OSPF routes based on the tags. This design works well because R1 can tag all redistributed RIP routes, thereby removing the need to change the configuration every time a new subnet is added to the RIP domain. (Note that both R1 and R3 will tag routes injected from RIP into OSPF as 9999, and both will then filter OSPF-learned routes with tag 9999. Figure 11-6 just shows one direction to keep the figure less cluttered.)

**Example 11-6**   *Using Route Tags and Distribute Lists to Prevent Suboptimal Routes at Redistributing Routers*

```
! R1 config. The redistribute command calls the route map that tags routes taken
! from RIP as 9999. distribute-list looks at routes learned in OSPF that were
! earlier tagged by R3.
router ospf 1
redistribute rip subnets route-map tag-rip-9999
network 10.1.15.1 0.0.0.0 area 0
distribute-list route-map check-tag-9999 in
! Clause 10, a deny clause, matches all tagged 9999 routes--so those
! routes are filtered. Clause 20 permits all other routes, because with no match
! subcommand, the clause is considered to "match all."
route-map check-tag-9999 deny 10
match tag 9999
!
route-map check-tag-9999 permit 20
! tag-rip-9999 matches all routes (it has no match command), and then
! tags them all with tag 9999. This route-map is used only for routes taken from
! RIP into OSPF.
route-map tag-rip-9999 permit 10
set tag 9999
! R3 Config
! The R3 configuration does not have to use the same names for route maps, but
! the essential elements are identical, so the route maps are not repeated here.
router ospf 1
redistribute rip subnets route-map tag-rip-9999
network 10.1.34.3 0.0.0.0 area 0
distribute-list route-map check-tag-9999 in
! R3 (shown) and R1 have RIP routes to 10.1.2.0, as well as other routes from the
```

```
! RIP domain. Also, note that the OSPF LSDB shows the tagged values on the routes.
R3# show ip route | incl 10.1.2.0
R         10.1.2.0 [120/1] via 10.1.23.2, 00:00:26, Serial0/0/0.2
R3# sh ip ospf data | begin Type-5
                 Type-5 AS External Link States

Link ID          ADV Router       Age          Seq#          Checksum Tag
10.1.1.0         1.1.1.1          834          0x80000006 0x00CE86 9999
10.1.1.0         3.3.3.3          458          0x80000003 0x0098B7 9999
10.1.2.0         1.1.1.1          834          0x80000006 0x00C390 9999
10.1.2.0         3.3.3.3          458          0x80000003 0x008DC1 9999
! lines omitted for brevity
! Next, the unfortunate side effect of filtering the routes--R3 does not have an
! alternative route to RIP subnets, although OSPF internal routers (like R4
! in Figure 11-6) will.
R3# conf t
Enter configuration commands, one per line.  End with CNTL/Z.
R3(config)# int s0/0/0.2
R3(config-subif)# shut
R3(config-subif)# ^Z
R3# sh ip route | incl 10.1.2.0
R3#
```

The last few lines of the example show the largest negative of using route filtering to prevent the suboptimal routes. When R3 loses connectivity to R2, R3 does not use the alternate route through the OSPF domain. R3's filtering of those routes occurs regardless of whether R3's RIP routes are available or not. As a result, using a solution that manipulates the AD might ultimately be the better solution to this suboptimal-routing problem.

## Using Metrics and Metric Types to Influence Redistributed Routes

A different set of issues can occur for a router that is internal to a single routing domain, like R4 and R5 in Figure 11-4. The issue is simple—with multiple redistributing routers, an internal router learns multiple routes to the same subnet, so it must pick the best route. As covered earlier in the chapter, the redistributing routers can set the metrics; by setting those metrics with meaningful values, the internal routers can be influenced to use a particular redistribution point.

Interestingly, internal routers might not use metric as their first consideration when choosing the best route. For example, an OSPF internal router will first take an intra-area route over an inter-area route, regardless of their metrics. Table 11-8 lists the criteria an internal router will use when picking the best route, before considering the metrics of the different routes.

**Key Topic**

**Table 11-8**  *IGP Order of Precedence for Choosing Routes Before Considering the Metric*

| IGP | Order of Precedence of Metric |
|-----|-------------------------------|
| RIP | No other considerations |
| EIGRP | Internal, then external |
| OSPF | Intra-area, inter-area, E1, then E2* |
| IS-IS | L1, L2, external |

* For E2 routes whose metric ties, OSPF also checks the cost to the advertising ASBR.

To illustrate some of these details, Example 11-7 focuses on R4 and its routes to 10.1.2.0/24 and 10.1.5.0/24 from Figure 11-4. The example shows the following, in order:

1.  R1 and R3 advertise 10.1.2.0/24 as an E2 route, metric 20. R4 uses the route through R3, because R4's cost to reach ASBR R3 is lower than its cost to reach ASBR R1.

2.  After changing R1 to advertise redistributed routes into OSPF as E1 routes, R4 uses the E1 routes through R1, even though the metric is larger than the E2 route through R3.

3.  R4 uses it higher-metric intra-area route to 10.1.5.0/24 through R5. Then, the R4-R5 link fails, causing R4 to use the OSPF external E2 route to 10.1.5.0/24—the route that leads through the RIP domain and back into OSPF through the R3-R2-R1-R5 path.

**Example 11-7**  *Demonstration of the Other Decision Criteria for Choosing the Best Routes*

```
! R4 has E2 routes to all the subnets in the RIP domain, and they all point to R3.
R4# sh ip route ospf
10.0.0.0/24 is subnetted, 10 subnets
O        10.1.15.0 [110/128] via 10.1.45.5, 00:03:23, Serial0/0/0.5
O E2     10.1.12.0 [110/20] via 10.1.34.3, 00:03:23, Serial0/0/0.3
O E2     10.1.3.0 [110/20] via 10.1.34.3, 00:03:23, Serial0/0/0.3
O E2     10.1.2.0 [110/20] via 10.1.34.3, 00:03:23, Serial0/0/0.3
O E2     10.1.1.0 [110/20] via 10.1.34.3, 00:03:23, Serial0/0/0.3
O        10.1.5.0 [110/65] via 10.1.45.5, 00:03:23, Serial0/0/0.5
O E2     10.1.23.0 [110/20] via 10.1.34.3, 00:03:23, Serial0/0/0.3
! R4 chose the routes through R3 instead of R1 due to the lower cost to R3.
R4# show ip ospf border-routers
OSPF Process 1 internal Routing Table
Codes: i - Intra-area route, I - Inter-area route

i 1.1.1.1 [128] via 10.1.45.5, Serial0/0/0.5, ASBR, Area 0, SPF 13
i 3.3.3.3 [64] via 10.1.34.3, Serial0/0/0.3, ASBR, Area 0, SPF 13
! (Not Shown): R1 is changed to redistribute RIP routes as E1 routes by
! adding the metric-type 1 option on the redistribute command on R1.
```

```
! R4 picks routes through R1 because they are E1 routes, even though the metric
! (148) is higher than the routes through R3 (cost 20)
R4# show ip route ospf
10.0.0.0/24 is subnetted, 10 subnets
O E1    10.1.2.0 [110/148] via 10.1.45.5, 00:00:11, Serial0/0/0.5
! lines omitted for brevity
! R4's route to 10.1.5.0/24 below is intra-area, metric 65
R4# show ip route | incl 10.1.5.0
O       10.1.5.0 [110/65] via 10.1.45.5, 00:04:48, Serial0/0/0.5
! (Not Shown): R4 shuts down link to R5
! R4's new route to 10.1.5.0/24 is E2, learned from R3, with metric 20
R4# show ip route | incl 10.1.5.0\
O E2    10.1.5.0 [110/20] via 10.1.34.3, 00:10:52, Serial0/0/0.3
```

# Route Summarization

Route summarization creates a single route whose numeric range, as implied by the prefix/prefix length, is larger than the one or more smaller component routes. For example, 10.1.0.0/16 is a summary route that includes component subnets 10.1.1.0/24, 10.1.4.132/30, and any other subnets with the range 10.1.0.0 through 10.1.255.255.

**Note**   I use the term *component route* to refer to a route whose range of IP addresses is a subset of the range specified by a summary route; however, I have not seen this term in other reference materials from Cisco.

The following list details some of the key features that the three IGPs covered in this book have in common with regard to how route summarization works (by default):

■   The advertised summary is assigned the same metric as the currently lowest-metric component subnet.

■   The router does not advertise the component subnets.

■   The router does not advertise the summary when its routing table does not have any of the component subnets.

■   The summarizing router creates a local route to the summary, with destination null0, to prevent routing loops.

■   Summary routes reduce the size of routing tables and topology databases, indirectly improving convergence.

■   Summary routes decrease the amount of specific information in routing tables, sometimes causing suboptimal routing.

Figure 11-7 depicts the suboptimal-routing side effect when using route summarization. It also depicts the effect of using a summary to null0 on the summarizing router.

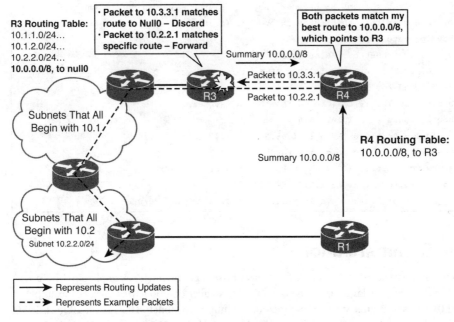

**Figure 11-7**    *Route Summarization Suboptimal Routing and Routing to Null0*

In Figure 11-7, R4 learned two paths to summary route 10.0.0.0/8, and picked the route through R3 based on the metric. Because R4 does not have a route for 10.2.2.0/24, R4 then sends any packets to that subnet based on its route to network 10.0.0.0/8, through R3. So, although subnets like 10.2.2.0/24 might be topologically closer to R4 through R1, R4 sends the packets through the scenic, suboptimal route through R3.

Also note that R4's summary route to 10.0.0.0/8 matches packets for which the component subnet does not exist anywhere in the network. In that case, routers like R4 forward the packets based on the larger summary, but when the packet reaches the router that created the summary, the packet is discarded by the summarizing router because of its null route. For example, Figure 11-7 shows R4 forwarding a packet destined to 10.3.3.1 to R3. R3 does not have a more specific route than its route to 10.0.0.0/8, with next-hop interface null0. As a result, R3 discards the packet.

The sections that follow provide a few details about summarization with each routing protocol.

## EIGRP Route Summarization

EIGRP provides the easiest and most straightforward rules for summarizing routes as compared with RIPv2, OSPF, and IS-IS. To summarize routes, the **ip summary-address eigrp** *as-number network-address subnet-mask* [*admin-distance*] command is placed under an interface. If any of the component routes are in that router's routing table, EIGRP advertises the summary route *out* that interface. The summary is defined by the *network-address subnet-mask* parameters.

One of the more interesting features of the EIGRP summary is the ability to set the AD of the summary route. The AD is not advertised with the route. The summarizing router, however, uses the configured AD to determine whether the null route for the summary should be put into its routing table. The EIGRP AD for summary routes defaults to 5.

## OSPF Route Summarization

All OSPF routers in the same area must have identical link-state databases (LSDB) after flooding is complete. As a result, all routers in the same OSPF area must have the same summary routes, and must be missing the same component subnets of each summary. To make that happen, OSPF allows route summarization only as routes are injected into an area, either by an Area Border Router ABR (inter-area routes) or by an Autonomous System Boundary Router ASBR (external routes).

OSPF uses two different configuration commands to create the summary routes, depending on whether the summary is for inter-area or external routes. Table 11-9 lists the two commands. Both commands are configured under **router ospf**.

**Table 11-9**  *OSPF Route Summarization Commands*

| Where Used | Command |
|---|---|
| ASBR | **summary-address** {{*ip-address mask*} \| {*prefix mask*}} [**not-advertise**] [**tag** *tag*] |
| ABR | **area** *area-id* **range** *ip-address mask* [**advertise** \| **not-advertise**] [**cost** *cost*] |

The commands have a couple of important attributes. First, the **area range** command specifies an area; this area is the area in which the component subnets reside, with the summary being advertised into *all other areas*. Also, the **area range** command can set the cost for the summary route, instead of using the lowest cost of all component routes. Also, the **not-advertise** keyword can essentially be used to filter the subnets implied by the summary, as covered in Chapter 9, "OSPF."

The **summary-address** command summarizes external routes as they are injected into OSPF as an ASBR. The cost can be assigned, and the routes can be filtered using the **not-advertise** keyword.

# Default Routes

Routers forward packets using a default route when there are no specific routes that match a packet's destination IP address in the IP routing table. Routing protocols can advertise default routes, with each router choosing the best default route to list as that router's *gateway of last resort*. This section covers how a router can create a default route and then cause an IGP to advertise the default route.

In addition to the advertisement of default routes, each router can use one of two options for how the default route is used. As described in Chapter 6, "IP Forwarding (Routing)," each router's configuration includes either the (default) **ip classless** command or the **no ip classless** command. With **ip classless**, if a packet's destination does not match a specific route in the IP routing table, the router uses the default route. With **no ip classless**, the router first checks to see whether any part of the destination address's classful network is in the routing table. If so, that router will not use the default route for forwarding that packet.

**Note**   The topic of default routing requires discussion of the configuration on one router, plus configuration of the other routers using the same IGP. For this section, I will call the router with the default routing configuration the "local" router and other routers using the same IGP "other" routers.

Cisco IOS supports five basic methods of advertising default routes with IGPs, four of which are covered here. One method for advertising a default route is for one routing protocol to redistribute another routing protocol's default route. Because route redistribution has already been covered heavily, this section of the chapter covers other methods. Of the other four methods, not all are supported by all IGPs, as you can see in Table 11-10.

Key
Topic

**Table 11-10**   *Four Methods for Learning Default Routes*

| Feature | RIP | EIGRP | OSPF |
|---|---|---|---|
| Static route to 0.0.0.0, with the **redistribute static** command | Yes | Yes | No |
| The **default-information originate** command | Yes | No | Yes |
| The **ip default-network** command | Yes | Yes | No |
| Using summary routes | No | Yes | No |

Interestingly, when a router learns of multiple default routes, using any of these methods, it will use the usual process for choosing the best route: administrative distance, route type (per Table 11-8, earlier in this chapter), and lowest metric, in that order.

**Note**   Table 11-10 has details that might be difficult to memorize. To make it easier, you could start by ignoring the use of summary static routes, because it is not recommended by Cisco. Then, note that RIP supports the other three methods, whereas EIGRP supports two methods and OSPF supports only one—with EIGRP and OSPF not supporting any of the same options.

Figure 11-8 shows a sample network used with all the default route examples, in which R1 is the local router that configures the default routing commands.

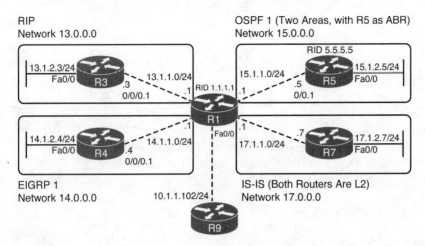

RIP
Network 13.0.0.0

OSPF 1 (Two Areas, with R5 as ABR)
Network 15.0.0.0

EIGRP 1
Network 14.0.0.0

IS-IS (Both Routers Are L2)
Network 17.0.0.0

**Figure 11-8**   *Sample Network for Default Route Examples*

## Using Static Routes to 0.0.0.0, with redistribute static

Routers consider a route to 0.0.0.0/0 as a default route. RIP and EIGRP support redistribution of static routes, including such a default static route. The rules and conditions for redistributing static defaults into RIP and EIGRP are as follows:

- The static **ip route 0.0.0.0 0.0.0.0** and **redistribute static** commands need to be configured on the same local router.

- The metric must be defaulted or set, using the same methods covered earlier in this chapter.

- The **redistribute** command can refer to a **route map**, which examines all static routes (not just the default).

- EIGRP treats the default route as an external route by default, with default AD 170.

- This method is not supported by OSPF.

Example 11-8 shows how R1 can inject defaults through RIP to R3 and through EIGRP to R4. The EIGRP configuration refers to a **route map** that examines all static routes, matching only static default routes. If other static routes existed, EIGRP would not advertise those routes based on the route map.

**Example 11-8**   *Static Default Route with Route Redistribution*

```
! R1 Config--note that ip classless is configured, but it does not impact the
! advertisement of the static route at all.
router eigrp 1
 redistribute static route-map just-default
 network 10.0.0.0
 network 14.0.0.0
 default-metric 1544 10 1 1 1
```

```
!
router rip
 version 2
 redistribute static
 network 13.0.0.0
 default-metric 1
!
ip classless
! The static route is configured next, followed by the prefix list that matches
! the default route, and the route map that refers to the prefix list.
ip route 0.0.0.0 0.0.0.0 10.1.1.102
!
ip prefix-list zero-prefix seq 5 permit 0.0.0.0/0
!
route-map just-default permit 10
 match ip address prefix-list zero-prefix
!
route-map just-default deny 20
```

```
! Next, R3, the RIP router, lists R1 (13.1.1.1) as its gateway of last resort,
! based on the RIP route to 0.0.0.0/0, next hop 13.1.1.1.
R3# sh ip route
! Lines omitted for brevity
Gateway of last resort is 13.1.1.1 to network 0.0.0.0


     13.0.0.0/24 is subnetted, 2 subnets
C       13.1.1.0 is directly connected, Serial0/0/0.1
C       13.1.2.0 is directly connected, FastEthernet0/0
R*   0.0.0.0/0 [120/1] via 13.1.1.1, 00:00:12, Serial0/0/0.1
```

```
! Next, R4, the EIGRP router, lists R1 (14.1.1.1) as its gateway of last resort,
! based on the EIGRP route to 0.0.0.0/0, next hop 14.1.1.1. Note that the default
! points to 0.0.0.0/0, AD 170, as it is an external route, due to the EX listed
! in the output of the show ip route command.
R4# sh ip route
! lines omitted for brevity
Gateway of last resort is 14.1.1.1 to network 0.0.0.0


D    10.0.0.0/8 [90/2172416] via 14.1.1.1, 00:01:30, Serial0/0/0.1
     14.0.0.0/24 is subnetted, 2 subnets
C       14.1.2.0 is directly connected, FastEthernet0/0
C       14.1.1.0 is directly connected, Serial0/0/0.1
D*EX 0.0.0.0/0 [170/2172416] via 14.1.1.1, 00:01:30, Serial0/0/0.1
```

## Using the default-information originate Command

OSPF does not support redistribution of statically defined default routes. Instead, OSPF requires the **default-information originate** router subcommand, which essentially tells OSPF to redistribute any default routes found in the routing table, either static routes or routes from another routing protocol. The following list summarizes the default routing features when using the **default-information originate** command with OSPF:

■ Redistributes any default route (0.0.0.0/0) in the routing table.

■ The command can set the metric and metric type directly, with OSPF defaulting to cost 1 and type E2.

■ OSPF allows the use of the **always** keyword, which means that a default is sourced regardless of whether a default route is in the routing table.

■ Not supported by EIGRP.

■ Supported by RIP, with some differences. (Refer to the text following Example 11-9 for an explanation of the differences.)

Example 11-9 shows an example of using the **default-information originate** command with OSPF. In this case, R1 has learned a route to 0.0.0.0/0 through BGP from R9 in Figure 11-8.

**Example 11-9**   *Static Default Route with Route Redistribution*

```
router ospf 1
network 15.0.0.0 0.255.255.255 area 0
default-information originate
! R5 has a default route, defaulting to type E2, cost 1. It as advertised as a
! type 5 LSA.
R5# show ip route ospf
O*E2 0.0.0.0/0 [110/1] via 15.1.1.1, 00:18:07, Serial0/0.1
R5# sh ip ospf data | begin Type-5
                Type-5 AS External Link States

Link ID          ADV Router      Age      Seq#        Checksum Tag
0.0.0.0          1.1.1.1         1257     0x80000001 0x008C12 1
```

As mentioned earlier, RIP does support the **default-information originate** command; however, the command behaves slightly differently in RIP than it does in OSPF. With RIP, this command creates and advertises a default route if either no default route exists or a default route was learned from another routing protocol. However, if a static route to 0.0.0.0/0 is in the local routing table, the **default-information originate** command does *not* cause RIP to inject a default. The reason behind this behavior is that RIP already supports redistribution of static routes, so **redistribute static** should be used in that case.

## Using the ip default-network Command

RIP and EIGRP can inject default routes by using the **ip default-network** command. To do so, the following must be true on the local router:

■ The local router must configure the **ip default-network** *net-number* command, with *net-number* being a classful network number.

■ The classful network must be in the local router's IP routing table, through any means.

■ For EIGRP only, the classful network must be advertised by the local router into EIGRP, again through any means.

■ This method is not supported by OSPF.

When using the **ip default-network** command, RIP and EIGRP differ in how they advertise the default. RIP advertises a route to 0.0.0.0/0, but EIGRP flags its route to the classful network as a candidate default route. Because EIGRP flags these routes as candidates, EIGRP must then also be advertising those classful networks. However, because RIP does not flag the classful network as a candidate default route, RIP does not actually have to advertise the classful network referenced in the **ip default-network** command.

Example 11-10 shows the key difference between RIP and EIGRP with regard to the **ip default-network** command. In this case, R1 will advertise about classful network 10.0.0.0 using EIGRP because of the **auto-summary** command.

**Example 11-10**  *Static Default Route with Route Redistribution*

```
! EIGRP will advertise classful network 10.0.0.0/8 due to its network command,
! matching R1's fa0/0 interface, and the auto-summary command. Also, R1 must have
! a route to classful network 10.0.0.0/8, in this case due to a static route.
! RIP will not advertise classful network 10.0.0.0/8, but it will still be able
! to inject a default route based on the ip default-network command.
router eigrp 1
network 10.0.0.0
network 14.0.0.0
auto-summary
!
router rip
version 2
network 13.0.0.0
!
ip classless
ip default-network 10.0.0.0
ip route 10.0.0.0 255.0.0.0 10.1.1.102
! On R3, RIP learns a route to 0.0.0.0/0 as its default.
R3# show ip route rip
R*    0.0.0.0/0 [120/1] via 13.1.1.1, 00:00:19, Serial0/0/0.1
! On R4, note that EIGRP learned a route to 10.0.0.0/8, shown with a * that
```

```
! flags the route as a candidate default route.
R4# show ip route
! lines omitted for brevity
      ia  IS-IS inter area, * - candidate default, U - per-user static route
      o - ODR, P - periodic downloaded static route

Gateway of last resort is 14.1.1.1 to network 10.0.0.0

D*   10.0.0.0/8 [90/2172416] via 14.1.1.1, 00:05:35, Serial0/0/0.1
     14.0.0.0/24 is subnetted, 2 subnets
C       14.1.2.0 is directly connected, FastEthernet0/0
C       14.1.1.0 is directly connected, Serial0/0/0.1
```

## Using Route Summarization to Create Default Routes

Generally speaking, route summarization combines smaller address ranges into a small number of larger address ranges. From that perspective, 0.0.0.0/0 is the largest possible summary, because it includes all possible IPv4 addresses. And, as it turns out, EIGRP route summarization supports summarizing the 0.0.0.0/0 supernet, effectively creating a default route.

Because route summarization causes a null route to be created for the summary, some Cisco documentation advises against using route summarization to create a default route. For example, in Figure 11-8, imagine that R9 is owned by this network's ISP, and R1 learns a default route (0.0.0.0/0) through EBGP from R9. However, when R1 configures an EIGRP default route using route summarization, R1 will also create a local route to 0.0.0.0/0 as well, but with destination null0. The EBGP route has a higher AD (20) than the EIGRP summary route to null0 (AD 5), so R1 will now replace its BGP-learned default route with the summary route to null0—preventing R1 from being able to send packets to the Internet.

Route summarization can still be used to create default routes with the proper precautions. The following list details a few of the requirements and options:

■ The local router creates a local summary route, destination null0, using AD 5 (EIGRP), when deciding whether its route is the best one to add to the local routing table.

■ EIGRP advertises the summary to other routers as AD 90 (internal).

■ This method is not supported by RIP and OSPF.

■ To overcome the caveat of EIGRP's default route being set to null by having a low AD, set the AD higher (as needed) with the **ip summary-address** command.

Example 11-11 lists a sample configuration on R1 again, this time creating summary routes to 0.0.0.0/0 for EIGRP.

**Example 11-11**   *EIGRP Configuration for Creating Default Summary Routes*

```
! EIGRP route summarization is done under s0/0/0.4, the subnet connected to R4. In
! this example, the AD was changed to 7 (default 5) just to show how to change the
! AD. To avoid the problem with the default route to null0 on R1, the AD should
! have been set higher than the default learned via BGP.
interface Serial0/0/0.4 point-to-point
ip address 14.1.1.1 255.255.255.0
ip summary-address eigrp 1 0.0.0.0 0.0.0.0 7
! In this example, R1 has two sources for a local route to 0.0.0.0/0: EIGRP
! (AD 7, per the ip summary-address command), and BGP from R9
! (AD 20). R1 installs the EIGRP route based on the lowest AD.
R1# show ip route eigrp
     14.0.0.0/8 is variably subnetted, 3 subnets, 2 masks
D       14.1.2.0/24 [90/2172416] via 14.1.1.4, 00:01:03, Serial0/0/0.4
D       14.0.0.0/8 is a summary, 05:53:19, Null0
D*   0.0.0.0/0 is a summary, 00:01:08, Null0
```
```
! Next, R4's EIGRP route shows AD 90, instead of the AD 7 configured at R1. AD is
! a local parameter--R4 uses its default AD of 90 for internal routes.
R4# show ip route eigrp
D*   0.0.0.0/0 [90/2172416] via 14.1.1.1, 00:01:14, Serial0/0/0.1
```

# Performance Routing (PfR)

Cisco Systems began experimenting with routing protocols that could make best route selection based on variable parameters like load and bandwidth as early as the 1980s. The Cisco-proprietary routing protocol EIGRP was the first attempt at this approach, expanding route selection criteria. EIGRP gave us the "K Values" that we could select to make dynamic changes to the selection process. The problem with this approach was that the dynamic nature of the circuits connecting neighbors resulted in what could only be described as unstable links and adjacencies based on network load and traffic utilization. So the advised best practice became to simply turn off the K values that impacted network stability.

Not satisfied with this, Cisco continued to research other protocol enhancements. These efforts ultimately culminated in the creation of Optimized Edge Routing (OER). This technology gave us the capability to perform prefix-based route optimizations. Now this is not to be confused with what is currently referred to as Performance Routing (PfR). We will start at the beginning and work our way forward to PfR.

OER promised many things; among those promises was the ability to extend the capabilities of routers to more optimally route traffic. In OER, the network performance criteria use to manipulate traffic was limited. Specifically, OER relied on packet loss, response time, path availability, and traffic load distribution to make its decisions. Each of these criteria was a significant deviation from how typical routing protocols operate and could be used to significantly enhance network performance. But we have to realize that as technology advances, so do the needs of modern networks. Herein lay the Achilles heel of OER.

Modern networks benefited greatly from the more granular control that OER brought to the table, but one element was missing from OER. Keep in mind that we described optimized edge routing as a "Prefix-based Route Optimization" enhancement. But modern networks needed something even more capable, something that would take application-specific needs into account, not just route and prefix information. Thus, Performance Routing was introduced.

PfR was built on OER's foundation and extended its capabilities to include route optimization criteria that could be based on application type, application performance requirements, as well as the traditional network performance criteria available in OER. In light of this fundamental enhancement to the protocol, the decision to change the name from OER (a "Prefix-based Route Optimization" protocol) to Performance Routing (an "Application Path Optimization" protocol) made perfect sense. Despite these feature enhancements and the expanded deployment options we now have available to us, the fundamental operation of PfR is still identical to OER. By this we are referring to what is commonly called the OER Phases wheel.

## Performance Routing Operational Phases

Cisco created the idea of the Phases Wheel to help illustrate and explain the operation of OER/PfR. The problem with this notion is the fact that in operation these phases are not so easy to identify, and the lines between them become somewhat blurred and hard to recognize. What we will do in this section is look at each of the five phases and attempt to quantify what the goal of each is. I personally feel that this is the best method for using this multiphased approach to describe this technology and how it operates. However, after the configurations have been applied and we begin to look at what is happening in a working deployment, we will make reference to these different phases in a loose context. The key point to remember at this juncture of our discussion is the fact that each of these phases makes a repeating cycle, thus the term "phases wheel," that will run constantly after OER has been configured and enabled on our network devices.

- **Profile Phase:** Learn flows that have high latency and throughput sometimes referred to as the "Learning" phase. Traffic that is being "profiled or learned" is referred to as a traffic class. The list of all monitored traffic classes (MTC) is referred to as an MTC list.

- **Measure Phase:** Collect and compute performance metrics for the traffic identified in the MTC list.

- **Apply Policy Phase:** Create low and high thresholds to define in-policy and out-of-policy (OOP) performance categories.

- **Control Phase:** Influence traffic by manipulating routing or by using policy-based routing (PBR).

■ **Verify Phase:** After controls have been introduced, OER will verify OOP event performance and make necessary adjustments to bring back in-policy performance.

When we understand that each of these phases constantly repeats, we clearly see that the process is designed to be constantly adjusting. In a way, this is no different than the finite state machine (FSM) process that runs between adjacent neighbors like those found in OSPF or EIGRP, but instead of a neighbor peering status, we are checking to see whether the network needs optimizing or whether a decision to optimize made previously is still valid.

The "phases wheel" is not the only logical construct that we have to get our minds around when it comes to understanding PfR. There are a number of classifications, capabilities, and roles that need to be discussed before we move on.

## Performance Routing Concepts

There are three primary interface types that we will need to understand to configure PfR. These interface types are defined based on their roles in the PfR environment. These roles are used to identify whether interfaces are used to forward packets out of the network or into the network. Each of these interface types is required in a topology to correctly deploy PfR:

■ **Internal Interfaces:** These interfaces are used to connect to the internal network and will always be the interfaces used for communication with the device in the infrastructure that is designated as the control plane manager for the performance routing environment. This device is known as the Master Controller. We will cover this device in greater detail in a subsequent section.

■ **External Interfaces:** These are the physical interfaces that are used to transmit packets out of the local network. There must be at least two interfaces identified as external interfaces to successfully deploy OER. These are the interfaces where prefixes and exit link performance will be monitored.

■ **Local Interfaces:** These are interfaces that are used in the formation of the control plane mechanism that drives the OER process. Specifically, this interface defines the source interface that will be used to communicate to the Master Controller we mentioned earlier.

## Authentication

The next section discusses the physical and logical roles associated with the component elements found in a typical PfR deployment. Suffice it to say that the component devices, one of which is the Master Controller we have alluded to and the routers it controls, all work in concert to optimize network performance. We have to realize that these communications all serve to change existing routing parameters, add new prefixes, and manipulate overall network performance at the network's edge. This translates into handing over network control to the Master Controller. For our discussions, a Master Controller will be a router that will manage all optimization decisions. Simply put, it will control what happens at the periphery of the local domain. However, handing over control to a device brings with it some level of risk. The foremost risk is that the newly created control plane mechanism could be leveraged by an unauthorized party or parties.

In an effort to mitigate this level of risk, Performance Routing incorporates mandatory authentication. Specifically, communication between the Master Controller and its slave devices is protected by key-chain authentication. This authentication key must be configured on all devices involved in the process before communications can be established. The key chain is created under the global configuration mode on each device to include the Master Controller. Thus far, we have been careful to avoid discussing device roles, because it is more important for us to understand the fundamental concepts at this juncture rather than the actual operational roles fulfilled by each device. Now that we have a firm grasp of these concepts, we will move into a more detailed discussion about how OER accomplishes optimization and what specific tasks are accomplished by devices assuming different operational roles.

## Performance Routing Operational Roles

Cisco PfR requires two primary components—a Master Controller and one or more border routers. The Master Controller is the decision maker, whereas the border routers are network edge devices with exit interfaces. These exit interfaces can be used to connect with the Internet or as outbound links to other network resources.

### Master Controller (MC)

In any PfR environment, there will be a single device that manages all aspects of PfR operations. The job of the MC is to maintain communication and authenticate the sessions with the border routers. The Master Controller will monitor outbound traffic flows and then apply policies to optimize routing for network prefixes and exit links. Even though the MC manages all aspects of PfR, it must be noted that it is not necessary for the MC to be in the forwarding path taken by the network traffic, but it must be reachable by the border routers. A single MC can support up to ten individual border routers or up to 20 managed exit interfaces (external interfaces).

This device can be configured in multiple fashions based on network size.

The simplest configuration is where the MC and the border router are running on a single device. This configuration is used most often in small office or home office networks that have multihomed connectivity to the Internet. In these environments, it must be noted that authentication is still required for PfR to function. Another very common topology employed in branch office networks is to have the master control coreside on one of multiple border routers. Figure 11-9 illustrates these MC deployments.

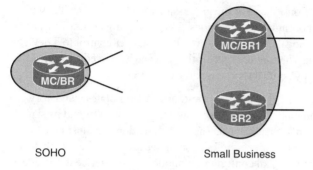

SOHO                    Small Business

**Figure 11-9**   *Colocated MC/BR Deployments*

Figure 11-10 illustrates that the third method of deployment for an MC is a standalone MC. This design is the most common, because it distributes CPU and resource utilization more evenly and can be found in medium to large enterprises. The benefits of being able to spread the control aspects of Performance Routing to multiple devices along the edge of the local network is where most organizations see a real return when using a technology like PfR.

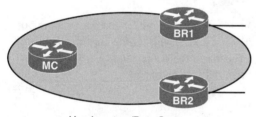

Headquarters/Data Center

**Figure 11-10**   *Sample Network for Standalone MC Deployment*

## Border Router

In the context of PfR, a border router is a router with one or more interfaces serving as exit links to either ISP, in the case of multihoming, or to other attached networks. The border router is where all policy decisions and routing changes will be enforced. It is the border router, under the control of the MC, that participates in prefix monitoring. It is the individual border routers that report prefix and transit link measurements back to the MC, where policy decisions are made. The MC will then instruct the appropriate border router to enforce any selected policy changes by injecting a preferred route to alter the course of packet flow in the network. Remember that the border router process we are describing can be, and often will be, enabled on the same router running the Master Controller process in small environments.

At this juncture in our discussion about performance routing, we have only really discussed the fundamental theory behind how it operates. We have been careful to avoid getting very detailed about device roles and how they are to be assigned. In the next section, we will begin to narrow our focus and start using our new understanding of the basic elements we have discussed thus far to practice PfR deployment while expanding our knowledge of the operation of the protocol to critical observation and testing.

## PfR Basic Configuration

Figure 11-11 illustrates the topology that we are going to work with in this section. We will perform all the basic tasks necessary to configure a working PfR topology. In this section, however, our primary focus will be to simply create the MC and BRs illustrated in Figure 11-11. In doing so, we will explore the commands necessary to establish the peering and exchange of communication that we have discussed; now we will start making the theoretical concepts tangible.

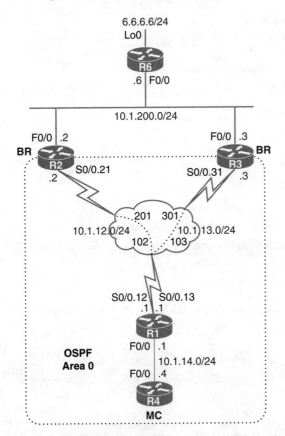

**Figure 11-11**  *Sample Network for Basic PfR Configuration*

## Configuration of the Master Controller

First we will look at the most basic configuration commands necessary to create a Master Controller. Note that the majority of the Performance Routing configuration is actually done on this particular component.

**Step 1.**   Create the authentication key chain.

As we mentioned in the previous section, PfR requires authentication before
it will even operate, and the method employed by the protocol to do this is
the MD5 key chain/key-string approach. This configuration is made under the
global configuration context of all devices that will fulfill operational roles
as they are defined in PfR; this includes the MC and all BRs. We will wait to
configure the key chains on the BRs in our topology until we reach the border
router subtopic in this section. In our topology, R4 is our MC, so it is on that
device that we will be working. The following example shows the MC configuration:

```
R4# conf t
R4(config)# key chain PFR_AUTH
R4(config-keychain)# key 1

R4(config-keychain-key)# key-string CISCO
R4(config-keychain-key)# end
!
!We can see the detail about the key chain we just configured via the
!show key chain !command.
!
R4# show key chain
Key-chain PFR_AUTH:
    key 1 -- text "CISCO"
        accept lifetime (always valid) - (always valid) [valid now]
        send lifetime (always valid) - (always valid) [valid now]
```

Now that we have the key chain configured, we can move to the next step of
the Master Controller configuration process.

**Step 2.**   Enable the PfR process.

This is accomplished with one simple command; however, there are several
available configuration options available:

```
R4# conf t
R4(config)# pfr master
R4(config-pfr-mc)#
!!!!!!!!!!!!!!!!!!!!!!!!!!!!!!!!!!!!!!!!!!!!!!!!!!!!!!!!!!!!!!!!!!!!!!!!!!!!!!!!!
!!!!!!!!!!!!!!!!!!!
!Observe that we are now inside the PfR master controller
!configuration context. At this point it is worthwhile for us to
!explore the array of commands that we have available to us in this
!mode. We can do that simply by using "?".
!!!!!!!!!!!!!!!!!!!!!!!!!!!!!!!!!!!!!!!!!!!!!!!!!!!!!!!!!!!!!!!!!!!!!!!!!!!!!!!!!
!!!!!!!!!!!!!!!!!!!
R4(config-pfr-mc)# ?
PFR master controller configuration commands:
  active-probe             Manually create an active probe for a known
                           target
```

| | |
|---|---|
| api | OER API related configuration |
| application | Define application |
| backoff | Specify backoff timer parameters |
| border | Enter OER managed border router configuration submode |
| default | Set a command to its defaults |
| delay | Specify delay parameters |
| exit | Exit from OER master controller configuration submode |
| holddown | Specify hold-down timer parameter |
| jitter | Specify jitter parameters |
| keepalive | Specify keepalive interval |
| learn | Enter prefix and traffic class learning submode |
| logging | Event Logging |
| loss | Specify loss parameters |
| max | Specify the upper limit |
| max-range-utilization | Configure the maximum range for utilization of all exits |
| mode | Specify OER operating mode settings |
| mos | Specify mos parameters |
| no | Negate a command or set its defaults |
| periodic | Specify periodic rotation timer value |
| policy-rules | Name of oer-map defining OER policy |
| port | Specify tcp port number for OER communication |
| resolve | Specify OER policy resolver settings |
| shutdown | Disable OER master controller functionality |
| traceroute | Configure Traceroute global parameters |
| unreachable | Specify unreachable parameters |

There are only 26 commands available under this configuration context, and 3 of them are "exit," "shutdown," and "no." That leaves 23 commands relevant to the configuration of the Master Controller. Before we have finished this example, we will have discussed each and every one of these commands, to include what role they play, and to describe how they can be manipulated to obtain desired outcomes or performances. The point we are trying to make here is that there is not only a finite range of commands, but also the true point of fact is that there are only a handful of commands. To be honest, there are about as many commands to be found in PfR as there are in RIP. This should help to alleviate any concerns regarding the operational complexity of this protocol.

Thus far, we have created the authentication key chain and enabled PfR, but without border routers and internal and external interfaces, our MC is worthless. So we need to move on to the next step of our configuration and discussion.

**Step 3.**    Designate internal/external interfaces.

The MC needs something to control, and based on our discussions these controlled devices are referred to as border routers. It is the border routers that host the internal and external interfaces. The interesting point that we need to make at this point is that even though the interfaces exist on the discreet BR, we must designate which interfaces are which on the MC. Yes, it is the MC that tells the BR which of its interfaces are considered internal or external. This configuration is made on the MC under the "config-pfr-mc" configuration context. To do this, we will first use the **border** command on the MC to enter the Master Controller border router configuration mode. We will use the loopback 0 addresses of our border routers to identify them, and remember we are required to use the key chain we created. We will start with the BR 2.2.2.2 (R2) as seen here:

```
R4(config-pfr-mc)# border 2.2.2.2 key-chain PFR_AUTH
R4(config-pfr-mc-br)#
!
!!!!!!!!!!!!!!!!!!!!!!!!!!!!!!!!!!!!!!!!!!!!!!!!!!!!!!!!!!!!!!!!!!!!!!!!!!!!!
!!!!!!!!!!!!!!!!!
!!It is under this context that we will specify and designate the
!!interface roles for R2. This is done via the interface command:
!!!!!!!!!!!!!!!!!!!!!!!!!!!!!!!!!!!!!!!!!!!!!!!!!!!!!!!!!!!!!!!!!!!!!!!!!!!!!
!!!!!!!!!!!!!!!!!
!
R4(config-pfr-mc-br)# interface Serial0/0.21 internal
R4(config-pfr-mc-br)# interface FastEthernet0/0 external
R4(config-pfr-mc-br-if)# exit
R4(config-pfr-mc-br)# exit
!
!!!!!!!!!!!!!!!!!!!!!!!!!!!!!!!!!!!!!!!!!!!!!!!!!!!!!!!!!!!!!!!!!!!!!!!!!!!!!
!!!!!!!!!!!!!!!!!
!!Now we know that we have two BRs R2 and R3 so this configuration will
!!need to be repeated for R3 on the MC.
!!!!!!!!!!!!!!!!!!!!!!!!!!!!!!!!!!!!!!!!!!!!!!!!!!!!!!!!!!!!!!!!!!!!!!!!!!!!!
!!!!!!!!!!!!!!!!!
!
R4(config-pfr-mc)# border 3.3.3.3 key-chain OER_AUTH
R4(config-pfr-mc-br)# interface Serial0/0.31 internal
R4(config-pfr-mc-br)# interface FastEthernet0/0 external
R4(config-pfr-mc-br-if)# exit
R4(config-pfr-mc-br)# exit
!
!!!!!!!!!!!!!!!!!!!!!!!!!!!!!!!!!!!!!!!!!!!!!!!!!!!!!!!!!!!!!!!!!!!!!!!!!!!!!
!!!!!!!!!!!!!!!!!
!!This has created the master border configuration on R4.
!!We know that we have not made
```

```
!!any configuration on the border routers so we should not expect this
!!to create a working configuration. We can however still use the show
!!oer master border command on
!!R4 to look at the status of the MC to BR relationship.
!!!!!!!!!!!!!!!!!!!!!!!!!!!!!!!!!!!!!!!!!!!!!!!!!!!!!!!!!!!!!!!!!!!!!!!!!!!!!!!!!
!!!!!!!!!!!!!!!!!
!
R4(config-pfr-mc)# do show oer master border
Border          Status    UP/DOWN          AuthFail  Version
3.3.3.3         INACTIVE DOWN                    0   0.0
2.2.2.2         INACTIVE DOWN                    0   0.0
R4(config-pfr-mc)#
```

## Configuration of the Border Router

We will move now to R2 and create the basic configuration necessary to enable it as a BR in our topology.

**Step 1.**    Create the authentication key chain.

As we mentioned in the previous section, PfR requires authentication before it will even operate, and the method employed by the protocol to do this is the MD5 key chain/key-string approach. We will make this configuration under the global configuration context of R2 as seen here:

```
R4(config-pfr-mc)# border 2.2.2.2 key-chain PFR_AUTH
R4(config-pfr-mc-br)#
!
!!!!!!!!!!!!!!!!!!!!!!!!!!!!!!!!!!!!!!!!!!!!!!!!!!!!!!!!!!!!!!!!!!!!!!!!!!!!!!!!!
!!!!!!!!!!!!!!!!!
!!It is under this context that we will specify and designate the
!!interface roles for
!!R2. This is done via the interface command:
!!!!!!!!!!!!!!!!!!!!!!!!!!!!!!!!!!!!!!!!!!!!!!!!!!!!!!!!!!!!!!!!!!!!!!!!!!!!!!!!!
!!!!!!!!!!!!!!!!!
!
R4(config-pfr-mc-br)# interface Serial0/0.21 internal
R4(config-pfr-mc-br)# interface FastEthernet0/0 external
R4(config-pfr-mc-br-if)# exit
R4(config-pfr-mc-br)# exit
!
!!!!!!!!!!!!!!!!!!!!!!!!!!!!!!!!!!!!!!!!!!!!!!!!!!!!!!!!!!!!!!!!!!!!!!!!!!!!!!!!!
!!!!!!!!!!!!!!!!!
!!Now we know that we have two BRs R2 and R3 so this configuration
!! will need to be repeated for R3 on the MC.
!!!!!!!!!!!!!!!!!!!!!!!!!!!!!!!!!!!!!!!!!!!!!!!!!!!!!!!!!!!!!!!!!!!!!!!!!!!!!!!!!
!!!!!!!!!!!!!!!!!
!
R4(config-pfr-mc)# border 3.3.3.3 key-chain PFR_AUTH
```

**Step 2.**   Enable the PfR process.

In this instance, we are going to enable the PfR process on R2, but we will actually be activating the BR process as seen here:

```
R2# conf t
R2(config)# pfr border
R2(config-pfr-br)# master 1.1.1.1 key-chain OER_AUTH
R2(config-pfr-br)#
```

**Step 3.**   Specify the local interface.

We employed the use of the loopback 0 addresses for BRs when we made the configuration on the MC. We will need to ensure that the BRs source their TCP sessions to the MC using these addresses as well. This is where we will specify the local interface. The local interface is the interface used by the BRs to communicate to the MC; this process is demonstrated here:

```
R2(config-pfr-br)# local loopback0
R2(config-pfr-br)#
```

## Task Completion on R3

We will need to configure the same setup parameters on R3 to have two working BRs in our topology. Remember, we need one MC and at least two external interfaces. These interfaces can be on a single BR or distributed across multiple BRs. Rather than apply these configurations in a stage approach, we will simply get R3 up and running as a BR, as illustrated in the configuration that follows and move to the MC to conduct verifications:

```
R3# conf t
Enter configuration commands, one per line.  End with CNTL/Z.
R3(config)# key chain PFR_AUTH
R3(config-keychain)# key 1
R3(config-keychain-key)# key-string CISCO
R3(config-keychain-key)# exit
R3(config-keychain)# exit
R3(config)#
R3(config)# pfr border
R3(config-pfr-br)# master 4.4.4.4 key-chain OER_AUTH
R3(config-pfr-br)# local loopback0
R3(config-pfr-br)# logging
R3(config-pfr-br)# port 3950
R3(config-pfr-br)# end
R3#
%OER_BR-5-NOTICE: MC 4.4.4.4 UP
```

The following output on R4 is provided to the console by the logging feature under the PfR process we enabled:

```
R4#
%PFR_MC-5-NOTICE: BR 2.2.2.2 UP
%PFR_MC-5-NOTICE: BR 2.2.2.2 IF Fa0/0 UP
%PFR_MC-5-NOTICE: BR 2.2.2.2 IF Se0/0.21 UP
%PFR_MC-5-NOTICE: BR 2.2.2.2 Active
R4#
%PFR_MC-5-NOTICE: BR 3.3.3.3 UP
%PFR_MC-5-NOTICE: BR 3.3.3.3 IF Fa0/0 UP
%PFR_MC-5-NOTICE: BR 3.3.3.3 IF Se0/0.31 UP
%PFR_MC-5-NOTICE: BR 3.3.3.3 Active
```

The behavior we are observing is very important. Note that, as we have discussed previously, we need two external interfaces before the MC process will become active. We can see the MC process come "up" on R4 after we have two external interfaces. Observe that this requires both BRs to be operational in our topology.

```
%PFR_MC-5-NOTICE: MC Active
```

# Troubleshooting Complex Layer 3 Issues

In troubleshooting, perhaps the easiest way to find the source of most problems is through the **show run** command or variations of it. Therefore, as in Chapter 3, "Spanning Tree Protocol," we'll institute a simple "no **show run**" rule in this section that will force you to use your knowledge of more in-depth troubleshooting commands in the Cisco IOS portion of this section.

In addition, you can expect that the issues that you'll face in this part of the written exam will need more than one command or step to isolate and resolve. You will need strong mastery of the commands associated with the Layer 3 protocols tested in the CCIE Routing & Switching track, and especially of OSPF, EIGRP, and BGP troubleshooting commands. Those topics are addressed in other chapters in this book, and you should know them well before going into the exam.

In this section, focus on the process first and then on specific techniques. We also provide a table of several of the more subtle types of Layer 3 problems that you're likely to encounter and describe ways of isolating those problems using Cisco IOS commands. Because there are so many possible causes of trouble at Layer 3, we won't spend these pages on specific examples. Although you might become good at solving specific problems through examples, this section focuses more on the approach than on specific examples because the approach and tools will get you through many more situations than a few specific examples would.

## Layer 3 Troubleshooting Process

You can expect that many difficulties that appear at Layer 3 are not really Layer 3 problems at all, but rather are the result of troubles in other layers of the protocol stack. Here are some examples of issues at other layers that can impact Layer 3 protocols in subtle or misleading ways:

- An MTU mismatch on a link

- A unidirectional link

- A duplex mismatch

- A link with a high error rate in one or both directions

- Layer 2 configuration issues

- Access list (ACL or VACL) filtering with unintended consequences (don't forget that implicit **deny!**)

- Security policy that blocks required traffic

- A TTL setting that's too low for Layer 3 protocol operation

- Two or more Layer 3 subnets configured in the same VLAN, which is especially problematic with Layer 3 protocols that use broadcast or multicast traffic to form adjacencies

From the standpoint of troubleshooting techniques, two basic stack-based approaches come into play, depending on what type of issue you're facing. The first is the climb-the-stack approach, where you begin at Layer 1 and work your way up until you find the problem. Alternatively, you can start at Layer 7 and work your way down; however, in the context of the CCIE Routing and Switching exams, the climb-the-stack approach generally makes more sense.

The second approach is often referred to as the divide-and-conquer method. With this technique, you start in the middle of the stack (usually where you see the problem; in this case we'll assume Layer 3) and work your way down or up the stack from there until you find the problem. In the interest of time, which is paramount in an exam environment, the divide-and-conquer approach usually provides the best results. In that vein, let's start by looking at some basic Layer 3 configuration items that can break routing protocols if they're incorrectly configured.

First, consider any field in the IP packet header that has configuration options. Some fields in the IP header to check are these:

- Mismatched subnet masks within a subnet.

- A too-short TTL can cause some routing protocol adjacencies (specifically eBGP) to fail to form, or stop IP communications from taking place across a path with multiple Layer 3 hops.

- An MTU too low on a link can cause large packets to be dropped.

- An MTU mismatch on a link can cause large packets to be dropped on the low-MTU end when they arrive.

- Multicast traffic is not supported, disabled, or rate-limited on one or more links.

- An overloaded link can result in packet loss, long latency, and jitter.

- QoS configuration can cause packet loss, especially of keepalives.

After you've gotten past these core IP issues, you can begin to look for more in-depth issues at Layer 3. These are likely to be specific to routing protocol configuration or operation. However, in keeping with the scope of this section, we won't consider simpler, one-command issues such as adjacencies failing to form or authentication failures. These issues are covered in the earlier chapters of this book. Some of the common sources of problems in routing include the following:

- Incorrect split-horizon configuration. This is challenging to find quickly because the result is usually that most routes are propagated correctly, but some are not propagated.

- Incorrect redistribution configuration, especially with multiple points of redistribution or mutual redistribution. Incorrectly configured filtering or a lack of filtering can cause routing loops.

- Protocols not advertising routes when they appear to be configured to do so.

- Protocols not redistributing routes when they appear to be configured to do so.

- Incorrect route filtering because of incorrect masks applied in an access list or prefix list.

- EIGRP stuck-in-active (SIA) issues.

- Incorrect summarization.

- Administrative distance manipulation causing fundamental routing rules to be superseded.

- Metric calculations configured differently on different routers (particularly affecting metric calculations in OSPF or mismatched EIGRP k values).

- Metric manipulation on a router.

- NAT configuration with unintended consequences.

- Policy-based routing configuration issues or unintended consequences.

- Interface damping activity causing intermittent or flapping operation.

- Mismatched timer settings, which sometimes result in adjacencies flapping.

When you're troubleshooting Layer 3 issues, it's a good idea to start with the basics: Verify reachability, verify that the correct path is being used, and check the routing table carefully. Make sure that routes are being learned through the correct protocols and from the correct neighbors. Then look for deeper issues.

## Layer 3 Protocol Troubleshooting and Commands

In addition to the myriad protocol-specific troubleshooting commands that you've learned in previous chapters, this section addresses commands that can help you isolate problems through a solid understanding of the information they present. We'll use a variety of command output examples to illustrate the key parameters you should understand. Note that this section doesn't address Layer 2–specific commands because Chapter 3 covers those areas in the troubleshooting section.

### IP Routing Processes

The **show ip protocols** command reveals a great deal of helpful information, as shown in Example 11-12. Comments are inserted between lines and begin with an exclamation point for clarity.

**Example 11-12**   show ip protocols *Command*

```
Rush1# show ip protocols
Routing Protocol is "eigrp 1"
! Note the AS number.
  Outgoing update filter list for all interfaces is not set
  Incoming update filter list for all interfaces is not set
! Note the filter list, which would be specified in these two lines.
Outgoing routes in Serial0/0.4 will have 1 added to metric if on list 11
! This is an example of metric manipulation, which can have unintended
! consequences.
  Default networks flagged in outgoing updates
  Default networks accepted from incoming updates
  EIGRP metric weight K1=0, K2=0, K3=1, K4=0, K5=0
  EIGRP maximum hopcount 100
! These two lines show configuration options that must match throughout
! the EIGRP AS 1 domain for correct EIGRP operation.
  EIGRP maximum metric variance 1
  Redistributing: eigrp 1
! Provides details of redistribution, including less obvious sources
! of redistribution such as connected and static routes.
  EIGRP NSF-aware route hold timer is 240s
  Automatic network summarization is not in effect
  Maximum path: 4
  Routing for Networks:
    172.31.0.0
! The list of networks being advertised can provide clues to routing
! problems.
  Routing Information Sources:
    Gateway          Distance       Last Update
    172.31.14.2           90        2d18h
  Distance: internal 90 external 170
```

```
! Administrative distances are shown. In most cases these should
! match from router to router within a routing domain. Watch for
! non-default AD settings.

Routing Protocol is "ospf 1"
! Note the process ID.
  Outgoing update filter list for all interfaces is not set
  Incoming update filter list for all interfaces is not set
  Router ID 150.1.1.1
  It is an area border router
  Number of areas in this router is 2. 2 normal 0 stub 0 nssa
Details of areas and area types, as well as the router's role (ABR).
  Maximum path: 4
  Routing for Networks:
    144.222.100.0 0.0.0.255 area 0
    144.254.254.0 0.0.0.255 area 0
    150.1.1.0 0.0.0.255 area 1
  Routing Information Sources:
    Gateway         Distance      Last Update
    150.1.3.129          110      2d20h
    150.1.1.1            110      2d20h
  Distance: (default is 110)

Routing Protocol is "bgp 200"
  Outgoing update filter list for all interfaces is not set
  Incoming update filter list for all interfaces is not set
  IGP synchronization is disabled
  Automatic route summarization is disabled
! These two lines show important information about fundamentals of BGP
! configuration.
  Neighbor(s):
    Address         FiltIn FiltOut DistIn DistOut Weight RouteMap
    172.31.14.2
  Maximum path: 1
  Routing Information Sources:
    Gateway         Distance      Last Update
  Distance: external 20 internal 200 local 200
```

Next, consider what interface statistics from a router can point toward the source of trouble in Layer 3 protocols. Example 11-13 shows settings and statistics on a serial interface, with comments as in the previous example. In this example, we show two interface **show** commands (**show interfaces** and **show ip interface**) for the same interface, to illustrate the differences between them and the significance of a small difference in a command. Example 11-14 examines the differences between these commands on an Ethernet interface to show the difference between serial Frame Relay interfaces and Ethernet interfaces.

**Example 11-13**   show interfaces *and* show ip interface *Commands*

```
RDXC# show interfaces s0/0.4
Serial0/0.4 is up, line protocol is up
  Hardware is PowerQUICC Serial
  Internet address is 172.31.14.1/30
  MTU 1500 bytes, BW 1544 Kbit, DLY 20000 usec,
     reliability 255/255, txload 1/255, rxload 1/255
! Reliability shows that the link is not experiencing any receive errors.
! Remember to check the other end of the link, because this parameter
! shows only inbound errors.
! The txload and rxload parameters indicate that the link is not near its
! load limits in either direction.
  Encapsulation FRAME-RELAY
  Last clearing of "show interface" counters never
RDXC# sh ip int s0/0.4
Serial0/0.4 is up, line protocol is up
  Internet address is 172.31.14.1/30
  Broadcast address is 255.255.255.255
  Address determined by non-volatile memory
  MTU is 1500 bytes
! MTU configuration can affect protocol operation.
  Helper address is not set
  Directed broadcast forwarding is disabled
  Multicast reserved groups joined: 224.0.0.10
! Multicast is enabled and operating on the interface.
  Outgoing access list is not set
  Inbound  access list is not set
  Proxy ARP is enabled
  Local Proxy ARP is disabled
! Proxy ARP configuration affects protocol operation through an
! interface.
  Security level is default
  Split horizon is enabled
! Split horizon affects distance-vector routing protocol operation.
  ICMP redirects are always sent
  ICMP unreachables are always sent
  ICMP mask replies are never sent
  IP fast switching is enabled
  IP fast switching on the same interface is enabled
  IP Flow switching is disabled
  IP CEF switching is disabled
  IP Fast switching turbo vector
  IP multicast fast switching is enabled
  IP multicast distributed fast switching is disabled
  IP route-cache flags are Fast
```

```
  Router Discovery is disabled
  IP output packet accounting is disabled
  IP access violation accounting is disabled
  TCP/IP header compression is disabled
  RTP/IP header compression is disabled
  Policy routing is disabled
  Network address translation is disabled
! NAT can adversely affect many protocols if the appropriate exceptions
! aren't made.
  WCCP Redirect outbound is disabled
  WCCP Redirect inbound is disabled
  WCCP Redirect exclude is disabled
  BGP Policy Mapping is disabled
```

Along the same lines as Example 11-13, Example 11-14 shows the same **show** commands on an Ethernet interface with the appropriate annotations.

**Example 11-14**   show interfaces *and* show ip interface *Commands on Fast Ethernet*

```
R9# show interfaces fa0/0
FastEthernet0/0 is up, line protocol is up
  Hardware is PQUICC_FEC, address is 000b.be90.5907 (bia 000b.be90.5907)
  Internet address is 204.12.1.9/24
  MTU 1500 bytes, BW 100000 Kbit/sec, DLY 100 usec,
     reliability 255/255, txload 1/255, rxload 1/255
! Key interface settings and statistics. See Example 11-13 for more details.
  Encapsulation ARPA, loopback not set
  Keepalive set (10 sec)
  Full-duplex, 100Mb/s, 100BaseTX/FX
! Details of speed and duplex settings, which must be configured
! appropriately or unexpected consequences will develop.
  ARP type: ARPA, ARP Timeout 04:00:00
  Last input 00:00:11, output 00:00:08, output hang never
  Last clearing of "show interface" counters never
  Input queue: 0/75/0/0 (size/max/drops/flushes); Total output drops: 0
! The queuing stats include drops, which can cause L3 protocol problems.
  Queueing strategy: fifo
  Output queue: 0/40 (size/max)
  5 minute input rate 0 bits/sec, 0 packets/sec
  5 minute output rate 0 bits/sec, 0 packets/sec
     992849 packets input, 114701010 bytes
     Received 992541 broadcasts, 0 runts, 0 giants, 0 throttles
     0 input errors, 0 CRC, 0 frame, 0 overrun, 0 ignored
! On a healthy Ethernet interface, this is what you should see. A large
! number for any of these metrics usually indicates a Layer 1 problem
! or a Layer 2 configuration issue such as a duplex mismatch.
     0 watchdog
```

```
        0 input packets with dribble condition detected
        785572 packets output, 89170479 bytes, 0 underruns
        3 output errors, 0 collisions, 3 interface resets
        2 unknown protocol drops
        0 babbles, 0 late collision, 0 deferred
        3 lost carrier, 0 no carrier
        0 output buffer failures, 0 output buffers swapped out
! Depending on how many input and output packets the interface
! shows, and when the interface timers were last reset, the stats
! shown on these lines can indicate Layer 1 or Layer 2 problems.
R9# show ip interface fa0/0
FastEthernet0/0 is up, line protocol is up
  Internet address is 204.12.1.9/24
  Broadcast address is 255.255.255.255
  Address determined by setup command
  MTU is 1500 bytes
! Remaining output is omitted because it duplicates that in
! Example 11-13 from this point onward
```

Among the other useful troubleshooting commands in diagnosing Layer 3 problems are the following:

- **show ip nat translations**
- **show ip access-list**
- **show ip interface brief**
- **show dampening**
- **show logging**
- **show policy-map**
- **traceroute**
- **ping** (and extended **ping**)
- **show route-map**
- **show standby**
- **show vrrp**
- **show track**
- **show ip route** *prefix*

In your use of **show** commands, don't overlook the amount of information available in the **show ip route** command and its more detailed variant, **show ip route** *prefix*. For example, you can use the **show ip route 172.31.14.0** command to learn detailed information about the 172.31.14.0 network, including its next hop and other pertinent information. Example 11-15 shows a sample of that output.

**Example 11-15**  *Displaying Detailed Information for a Prefix*

```
Routing entry for 172.31.14.0/30
  Known via "eigrp 1", distance 90, metric 1024000, type internal
  Redistributing via eigrp 1
  Last update from 172.31.24.1 on Serial0/0.4, 01:23:40 ago
  Routing Descriptor Blocks:
  * 172.31.24.1, from 172.31.24.1, 01:23:40 ago, via Serial0/0.4
      Route metric is 1024000, traffic share count is 1
      Total delay is 40000 microseconds, minimum bandwidth is 64 Kbit
      Reliability 255/255, minimum MTU 1500 bytes
      Loading 1/255, Hops 1
```

Note the details that this command provides for an individual prefix in the routing table under the Routing Descriptor Blocks. The same command for an OSPF route includes information on key items such as the type of route (that is, inter-area or intra-area) that can be helpful in troubleshooting.

Another command that yields considerable detail is the extended **ping** command. Example 11-16 shows the variety of configuration options it provides. Of particular note is this command's ability to test using multiple protocols including IPv4 and IPv6, to sweep a range of packet sizes to test for MTU-related issues, to permit testing with various ToS values in the packet headers, and to specify the source interface to help determine the source of routing issues.

**Example 11-16**  *Using the Extended* ping *Command*

```
R8# ping
Protocol [ip]:
Target IP address: 192.10.1.8
Repeat count [5]: 100
Datagram size [100]:
Timeout in seconds [2]:
Extended commands [n]: y
Source address or interface: fastethernet0/0
Type of service [0]: 3
Set DF bit in IP header? [no]:
Validate reply data? [no]:
Data pattern [0xABCD]:
Loose, Strict, Record, Timestamp, Verbose[none]:
Sweep range of sizes [n]: y
Sweep min size [36]:
Sweep max size [18024]:
Sweep interval [1]:
Type escape sequence to abort.
Sending 1798900, [36..18024]-byte ICMP Echos to 192.10.1.8, timeout is 2 seconds:
Packet sent with a source address of 192.10.1.8
```

```
!!!!!!!!!!!!!!!!!!!!!!!!!!!!!!!!!!!!!!!!!!!!!!!!!!!!!!!!!!!!!!!!!!!!!!!!!!
 [output omitted]
!!!!!!!!!!!!!!!!!!!!!!!!!!!!!!!!!!!!!!!!!!!!!!!!!!!!!!!!!!!!!!!!!!!!!!!!!
Success rate is 100 percent (3565/3565), round-trip min/avg/max = 1/4/76 ms
```

The idea of using the ping utility is to see whether the path to a destination prefix is operational, and thanks to the echo reply mechanism, we know that both the send and receive paths are okay. However, if there are problems, ping cannot be used to find where the problems might exist in the infrastructure; for that, we need to rely on the traceroute utility.

If you execute the **traceroute** command on a route, that device will send IP packets toward the destination with a Time To Live (TTL) value that will increment up to the defined maximum specified hop count. This is 30 by default. Typically, each router in the path toward the destination decrements the TTL field by 1 unit while it forwards these packets. When a router in the middle of the path finds a packet with TTL = 1, it responds with an Internet Control Message Protocol (ICMP) "time exceeded" message to the source. This message lets the source know that the packet traversed that particular router as a hop.

The TTL for the initial User Datagram Protocol (UDP) datagram probe is set to 1 in the basic traceroute utility. The destination UDP port of the initial datagram probe is set to 33434 by default. The source UDP port of the initial datagram probe is randomized and has logical operator OR with 0x8000 (ensures a minimum source port of 0x8000). These steps illustrate what happens when the UDP datagram is launched:

**Step 1.**   The UDP datagram is sent with TTL = 1, destination UDP port = 33434, and the source port randomized.

**Step 2.**   The UDP destination port is incremented, the source UDP port is randomized, and the second datagram is dispatched. (This process is repeated for up to three probes. For each of the probes sent, a "TTL exceeded" message is received, which is used to build a step-by-step path to the destination host.)

The TTL is incremented, and this cycle repeats with incremental destination port numbers if the ICMP "time exceeded" message is received. You can also get one of these messages:

■   An ICMP type 3, code 3 ("destination unreachable," "port unreachable") message, which indicates that a host has been reached

■   A "host unreachable," "net unreachable," "maximum TTL exceeded," or "timeout" type of message, which means that the probe is resent

Cisco routers send UDP probe packets with a random source port and an incremental destination port (to distinguish the different probes). Cisco routers send the ICMP message "time exceeded" back to the source from where the UDP/ICMP packet was received. We can see how to employ the extended version of **traceroute** in Example 11-17.

**Example 11-17**    *Using the Extended* traceroute *Command*

```
Router A> enable
Router A# traceroute
Protocol [ip]:
Target IP address: 192.168.40.2
Source address: 172.16.23.2
Numeric display [n]:
Timeout in seconds [3]:
Probe count [3]:
Minimum Time to Live [1]:
Maximum Time to Live [30]:
Port Number [33434]:
Loose, Strict, Record, Timestamp, Verbose[none]:
Type escape sequence to abort.
Tracing the route to 192.168.40.2

  1 172.31.20.2 16 msec 16 msec 16 msec
  2 172.20.10.2 28 msec 28 msec 32 msec
  3 192.168.40.2 32 msec 28 msec *
```

The extended **traceroute** command can be used to see what path packets take to get to a destination. The command can also be used to check routing at the same time. This is helpful for when you troubleshoot routing loops, or for when you determine where packets are getting lost. You can use the extended **ping** command to determine the type of connectivity problem, and then use the extended **traceroute** command to narrow down where the problem occurs.

A "time exceeded" error message indicates that an intermediate communication server has seen and discarded the packet. A "destination unreachable" error message indicates that the destination node has received the probe and discarded it because it could not deliver the packet. If the timer goes off before a response comes in, traceroute prints an asterisk (*). The command terminates when any of these happens, the destination responds, the maximum TTL is exceeded, or the user interrupts the trace with the escape sequence. In Cisco routers, the codes for a **traceroute** command reply are

- ! — success
- * — time out
- N — network unreachable
- H — host unreachable
- P — protocol unreachable
- A — admin denied
- Q — source quench received (congestion)
- ? — unknown (any other ICMP message)

These commands make it easier for us to actually interpret the results of our traceroute test and should not be overlooked when learning how to use this utility.

Perhaps the most powerful Cisco IOS troubleshooting tools are the array of **debug** commands that Cisco provides. The most appropriate **debug** command for tracking down Layer 3 problems is **debug ip routing**, which reveals a great deal about the Layer 3 environment. Although this command might be of limited help in the qualification exam, understanding what it can provide in the way of information is especially helpful for lab exam preparation, where you will use this command and its IPv6 sibling, **debug ipv6 routing**, extensively. Example 11-18 shows some **debug ip routing** output to show the information it provides.

**Example 11-18**   *Output from the* **debug ip routing** *Command*

```
R2# debug ip routing
R2#
May 25 22:03:03.664: %DUAL-5-NBRCHANGE: IP-EIGRP(0) 1: Neighbor 172.31.24.1
  (Serial0/0.4) is down: peer restarted
! An EIGRP neighbor in AS 1 went down because it was restarted.
May 25 22:03:03.664: RT: delete route to 172.31.14.0 via 172.31.24.1, eigrp metric
  [90/1024000]
May 25 22:03:03.664: RT: no routes to 172.31.14.0
May 25 22:03:03.664: RT: NET-RED 172.31.14.0/30
May 25 22:03:03.668: RT: NET-RED queued, Queue size 1
May 25 22:03:03.668: RT: delete subnet route to 172.31.14.0/30
! The route to 172.31.14.0 was removed from the routing table.
May 25 22:03:03.668: RT: NET-RED 172.31.14.0/30
May 25 22:03:03.668: RT: NET-RED queued, Queue size 2
May 25 22:03:03.672: destroy peer: 172.31.24.1
May 25 22:03:05.071: %DUAL-5-NBRCHANGE: IP-EIGRP(0) 1: Neighbor 172.31.24.1
  (Serial0/0.4) is up: new adjacency
! The EIGRP neighbor came back up.
May 25 22:03:05.668: RT: add 172.31.14.0/30 via 172.31.24.1, eigrp metric
  [90/1024000]
May 25 22:03:05.668: RT: NET-RED 172.31.14.0/30
! The route to 172.31.14.0 was restored to the routing table.
May 25 22:03:05.668: RT: NET-RED queued, Queue size 1
```

Not shown in this example, but particularly helpful, is what happens if a route or a set of routes is flapping because of a loop. You'll see a consistent set of learn/withdraw messages from each routing source, usually quite evenly timed, indicating the loop's presence. The **ping** and **traceroute** commands are usually your first clue to a loop.

If you need to dig really deep into a particular issue, you can use the **debug ip packet detail** *acl* command to filter the IP packet debugging function through an access list. Create an access list that filters all but the specific information you're seeking; otherwise, you'll get so much information that it's difficult, at best, to interpret. At worst, it can cause the router to hang or reboot.

## Approaches to Resolving Layer 3 Issues

In this final section of the chapter, we present a table with several generalized types of issues and ways of approaching them, including the relevant Cisco IOS commands. Table 11-11 summarizes these techniques.

**Table 11-11**  *Troubleshooting Approach and Commands*

| Problem | Approach | Helpful IOS Commands |
|---|---|---|
| Intermittent reachability to a subnet. | Use **ping** to gather information. | show interface |
|  | Verify that the route(s) exist in the routing tables. Find where the routing information stops or becomes unstable. | show ip interface<br><br>ping |
|  | Eliminate Layer 1 issues with **show interface** commands. | traceroute<br><br>show ip route *prefix* |
|  | Use **traceroute** to verify the path. | debug ip routing |
| Redistributed routes do not make it to all the desired routers. | Verify the maximum number of hops (EIGRP) configured using the **metric hopcount** *x* EIGRP subcommand. | show ip protocols<br><br>show ip route |
|  | Check split horizon configuration in a multipoint network. | show ip interface |
| A router does not appear to be advertising prefixes that it should be configured to advertise. | Verify configuration using **show ip protocols**. | show ip protocols<br><br>show ip interface |
|  | Verify summarization. | show ip route |
|  | Check metrics and administrative distance. | show ip route *prefix* |
|  | Check interface filters. | show route-map |
|  | Check route maps. |  |
|  | Check for split-horizon issues. |  |

## Foundation Summary

This section lists additional details and facts to round out the coverage of the topics in this chapter. Unlike most of the Cisco Press Exam Certification Guides, this "Foundation Summary" does not repeat information presented in the "Foundation Topics" section of the chapter. Please take the time to read and study the details in the "Foundation Topics" section of the chapter, as well as review items noted with a Key Topic icon.

Table 11-12 lists some of the most relevant Cisco IOS commands related to the topics in this chapter. Also refer to Tables 11-2 and 11-3 for the **match** and **set** commands.

**Table 11-12**  *Command Reference for Chapter 11*

| Command | Command Mode and Description |
| --- | --- |
| **redistribute** *protocol* [*process-id*] {**level-1** \| **level-1-2** \| **level-2**} [*as-number*] [**metric** *metric-value*] [**metric-type** *type-value*] [**match** {**internal** \| **external 1** \| **external 2**}] [**tag** *tag-value*] [**route-map** *map-tag*] [**subnets**] | Router config mode; defines the routing protocol from which to take routes, several matching parameters, and several things that can be marked on the redistributed routes. |
| **ip prefix-list** *list-name* [**seq** *seq-value*] {**deny** *network/length* \| **permit** *network/length*} [**ge** *ge-value*] [**le** *le-value*] | Global config mode; defines members of a prefix list that match a prefix (subnet) and prefix length (subnet mask). |
| **ip prefix-list** *list-name sequence-number* **description** *text* | Global config; sets a description to a line in a prefix list. |
| **distance** *value* {*ip-address* {*wildcard-mask*}} [*ip-standard-list*] [*ip-extended-list*] | Router config mode; identifies the route source, and an optional ACL to define a subnet of routes, for which this router's AD is changed. Influences the selection of routes by selectively overriding the default AD. |
| **distance eigrp** *internal-distance external-distance* | EIGRP config; sets the AD for all internal and external routes. |
| **distance ospf** {[**intra-area** *dist1*] [**inter-area** *dist2*] [**external** *dist3*]} | OSPF config; sets the AD for all intra-area, inter-area, and external routes. |
| **ip summary-address eigrp** *as-number network-address subnet-mask* [*admin-distance*] | Interface mode; configures an EIGRP route summary. |
| **ip summary-address rip** *ip-address ip-network-mask* | Interface mode; configures a RIP route summary. |
| **area** *area-id* **range** *ip-address mask* [**advertise** \| **not-advertise**] [**cost** *cost*] | OSPF mode; configures an OSPF summary between areas. |
| **summary-address** {{*ip-address mask*} \| {*prefix mask*}} [**not-advertise**] [**tag** *tag*] | OSPF mode; configures an OSPF summary of external routes. |

| Command | Command Mode and Description |
|---|---|
| **ip default-network** *network-number* | Global config; sets a network from which to derive default routes. |
| **default-information originate** [**route-map** *map-name*] | IS-IS config; tells IS-IS to advertise a default route if it is in the routing table. |
| **default-information originate** [**always**] [**metric** *metric-value*] [**metric-type** *type-value*] [**route-map** *map-name*] | OSPF config; tells OSPF to advertise a default route, either if it is in the routing table or always. |
| **ip route** *prefix mask* {*ip-address* \| *interface-type interface-number* [*ip-address*]} [*distance*] [*name*] [**permanent**] [**tag** *tag*] | Global config; used to create static IP routes, including static routes to 0.0.0.0 0.0.0.0, which denotes a default route. |
| **debug ip routing** | Enables displaying output of all IPv4 routing table events for troubleshooting purposes. |
| **debug ipv6 routing** | Enables displaying output of all IPv6 routing table events for troubleshooting purposes. |
| **debug** | Provides many protocol-specific debug functions for indicating routing protocol events (such as debug ip ospf neighbor events, as one example). |
| **ping** | Allows extended testing of reachability using packets of different sizes, ToS values, and other variables for testing reachability issues, with a specified source interface for testing routing-related reachability issues. |
| **traceroute** | Similar to the extended **ping** command, provides extended traceroute capability. |
| **show ip route** [*prefix*] | Provides specific routing information for individual IPv4 prefixes present in the routing table. |
| **pfr** | Enables a PfR process and configures a router as a PfR border router or as a PfR Master Controller. |
| **show pfr border defined** | Displays all applications that are defined to be monitored by a PfR border router. |
| **show pfr master defined** | Displays all applications that are defined on a PfR Master Controller. |
| **show pfr master nbar application** | Displays information about the status of an application identified using Network-Based Application Recognition (NBAR) for each PfR border router. |

## Memory Builders

The CCIE Routing and Switching written exam, like all Cisco CCIE written exams, covers a fairly broad set of topics. This section provides some basic tools to help you exercise your memory about some of the broader topics covered in this chapter.

### Fill In Key Tables from Memory

Appendix E, "Key Tables for CCIE Study," on the CD in the back of this book, contains empty sets of some of the key summary tables in each chapter. Print Appendix E, refer to this chapter's tables in it, and fill in the tables from memory. Refer to Appendix F, "Solutions for Key Tables for CCIE Study," on the CD to check your answers.

### Definitions

Next, take a few moments to write down the definitions for the following terms:

> default route, route redistribution, external route, aggregate route, route map, IP prefix list, summary route, component route, gateway of last resort

Refer to the glossary to check your answers.

### Further Reading

*Routing TCP/IP*, Volume I, Second Edition, by Jeff Doyle and Jennifer DeHaven Carroll

*CCIE Practical Studies*, Volume II, by Karl Solie and Leah Lynch

"Troubleshooting IP Routing Protocols," www.ciscopress.com/bookstore/product.asp?isbn=1587050196

The first 11 chapters of this book cover the portion of technologies, protocols, and considerations required to be prepared to pass the 400-101 CCIE Routing and Switching written exam. While these chapters supply the detailed information, most people need more preparation than simply reading the first 11 chapters of this book. This chapter details a set of tools and a study plan to help you complete your preparation for the exams.

This short chapter has two main sections. The first section lists the exam preparation tools useful at this point in the study process. The second section lists a suggested study plan now that you have completed all the earlier chapters in this book.

**Note** Appendix E, "Key Tables for CCIE Study," and Appendix F, "Solutions for Key Tables for CCIE Study," exist as soft-copy appendices on the CD included in the back of this book.

## CHAPTER 12

# Final Preparation

## Tools for Final Preparation

This section lists some information about the available tools and how to access the tools.

### Pearson Cert Practice Test Engine and Questions on the CD

The CD in the back of the book includes the Pearson Cert Practice Test engine—software that displays and grades a set of exam-realistic multiple-choice questions. Using the Pearson Cert Practice Test engine, you can either study by going through the questions in Study Mode, or take a simulated (timed) CCIE Routing and Switching Written Exam.

The installation process requires two major steps. The CD in the back of this book has a recent copy of the Pearson Cert Practice Test engine. The practice exam—the database of CCIE Routing and Switching exam questions—is not on the CD.

**Note**  The cardboard CD case in the back of this book includes the CD and a piece of paper. The paper lists the activation key for the practice exam associated with this book. *Do not lose the activation key.*

### Install the Software from the CD

The software installation process is pretty routine as compared with other software installation processes. To be complete, the following steps outline the installation process:

**Step 1.**   Insert the CD into your PC.

**Step 2.**   The software that automatically runs is the Cisco Press software to access and use all CD-based features, including the exam engine and the CD-only appendices. From the main menu, click the option to **Install the Exam Engine**.

**Step 3.**   Respond to Windows prompts as with any typical software installation process.

The installation process will give you the option to activate your exam with the activation code supplied on the paper in the CD sleeve. This process requires that you establish a Pearson website login. You will need this login to activate the exam, so please do register when prompted. If you already have a Pearson website login, there is no need to register again. Just use your existing login.

## Activate and Download the Practice Exam

After the exam engine is installed, you should then activate the exam associated with this book (if you did not do so during the installation process) as follows:

**Step 1.** Start the Pearson Cert Practice Test (PCPT) software from the Windows **Start** menu or from your desktop shortcut icon.

**Step 2.** To activate and download the exam associated with this book, from the **My Products** or **Tools** tab, click the **Activate** button.

**Step 3.** At the next screen, enter the activation key from the paper inside the cardboard CD holder in the back of the book. After it is entered, click the **Activate** button.

**Step 4.** The activation process will download the practice exam. Click **Next**, and then click **Finish.**

After the activation process is completed, the **My Products** tab should list your new exam. If you do not see the exam, make sure that you have selected the **My Products** tab on the menu. At this point, the software and practice exam are ready to use. Simply select the exam and click the **Use** button.

To update a particular exam that you have already activated and downloaded, simply select the **Tools** tab and click the **Update Products** button. Updating your exams will ensure that you have the latest changes and updates to the exam data.

If you want to check for updates to the Pearson Cert Practice Test exam engine software, simply select the **Tools** tab and click the **Update Application** button. This will ensure that you are running the latest version of the software engine.

## Activating Other Exams

The exam software installation process, and the registration process, only has to happen once. Then, for each new exam, only a few steps are required. For example, if you buy another new Cisco Press Official Cert Guide or Pearson IT Certification Cert Guide, extract the activation code from the CD sleeve in the back of that book—you don't even need the CD at this point. From there, all you have to do is start the exam engine (if not still up and running), and perform Steps 2 through 4 from the previous list.

### Premium Edition

In addition to the free practice exam provided on the CD-ROM, you can purchase additional exams with expanded functionality directly from Pearson IT Certification. The Premium Edition of this title contains an additional two full practice exams as well as an eBook (in both PDF and ePub format). In addition, the Premium Edition title also has remediation for each question to the specific part of the eBook that relates to that question.

Because you have purchased the print version of this title, you can purchase the Premium Edition at a deep discount. There is a coupon code in the CD sleeve that contains a one-time use code as well as instructions for where you can purchase the Premium Edition.

To view the Premium Edition product page, go to www.informit.com/title/ 9780133481648.

## The Cisco Learning Network

Cisco provides a wide variety of CCIE Routing and Switching preparation tools at a Cisco Systems website called the Cisco Learning Network. This site includes a large variety of exam preparation tools, including sample questions, forums on each Cisco exam, learning video games, and information about each exam.

To reach the Cisco Learning Network, go to www.cisco.com/go/learningnetwork, or just search for "Cisco Learning Network." You will need to use the login that you created at www.cisco.com. If you don't have such a login, you can register for free. To register, simply go to www.cisco.com, click **Register** at the top of the page, and supply the requested information.

## Memory Tables

Like most Official Cert Guides from Cisco Press, this book purposefully organizes information into tables and lists for easier study and review. Rereading these tables can be very useful before the exam. However, it is easy to skim over the tables without paying attention to every detail, especially when you remember having seen the table's contents when reading the chapter.

Instead of simply reading the tables in the various chapters, this book's Appendices E and F give you another review tool. Appendix E lists partially completed versions of many of the tables from the book. You can open Appendix F (a PDF on the CD that comes with this book) and print the appendix. For review, you can attempt to complete the tables. This exercise can help you focus on the review. It also exercises the memory connectors in your brain; plus it makes you think about the information without as much information, which forces a little more contemplation about the facts.

Appendix F, also a PDF located on the CD, lists the completed tables to check yourself. You can also just refer to the tables as printed in the book.

## Chapter-Ending Review Tools

Chapters 1–11 have several features in the "Foundation Summary" sections at the end of the chapter. You might have already worked through these in each chapter. It can also be useful to use these tools again as you make your final preparations for the exam.

# Suggested Plan for Final Review/Study

This section lists a suggested study plan from the point at which you finish reading the last chapter of Volume 2 of this book, until you take the 400-101 CCIE Routing and Switching written exam. Certainly, you can ignore this plan, use it as is, or just take suggestions from it.

The plan uses three steps:

**Step 1.**   **Review Key Topics and DIKTA Questions:** You can use the table that lists the key topics in each chapter, or just flip through the pages looking for key topics. Also, reviewing the "Do I Know This Already?" (DIKTA) questions from the beginning of the chapter can be helpful for review.

**Step 2.**   **Complete Memory Tables:** Open Appendix E on the CD and print the entire appendix, or print the tables by major part. Then complete the tables.

**Step 3.**   **Use the Pearson Cert Practice Test Engine to Practice:** The Pearson Cert Practice Test engine on the CD can be used to study using a bank of unique exam-realistic questions available only with this book.

## Using the Exam Engine

The Pearson Cert Practice Test engine on the CD includes a database of questions created specifically for this book. The Pearson Cert Practice Test engine can be used either in study mode or practice exam mode, as follows:

■   **Study mode:** Study mode is most useful when you want to use the questions for learning and practicing. In study mode, you can select options like randomizing the order of the questions and answers, automatically viewing answers to the questions as you go, testing on specific topics, and many other options.

■   **Practice Exam mode:** This mode presents questions in a timed environment, providing you with a more exam-realistic experience. It also restricts your ability to see your score as you progress through the exam and view answers to questions as you are taking the exam. These timed exams not only allow you to study for the actual 400-101 CCIE Routing and Switching written exam, but they also help you simulate the time pressure that can occur on the actual exam.

When doing your final preparation, you can use study mode, practice exam mode, or both. However, after you have seen each question a couple of times, you will likely start to remember the questions, and the usefulness of the exam database might go down. So, consider the following options when using the exam engine:

■ Use this question database for review. Use study mode to study the questions by chapter, just as with the other final review steps listed in this chapter. Plan on getting another exam (possibly from the Premium Edition) if you want to take additional simulated exams.

■ Save the question database, not using it for review during your review of each book part. Save it until the end so that you will not have seen the questions before. Then, use practice exam mode to simulate the exam.

Picking the correct mode from the exam engine's user interface is pretty obvious. The following steps show how to move to the screen from which to select study or practice exam mode:

**Step 1.**   Click the **My Products** tab if you are not already in that screen.

**Step 2.**   Select the exam that you want to use from the list of available exams.

**Step 3.**   Click the **Use** button.

When you take these actions, the engine should display a window from which you can choose **Study Mode** or **Practice Exam Mode**. When in study mode, you can further choose the book chapters, limiting the questions to those explained in the specified chapters of the book.

## Summary

The tools and suggestions listed in this chapter have been designed with one goal in mind: to help you develop the skills required to pass the 400-101 CCIE Routing and Switching written exam. This book has been developed from the beginning to not just tell you the facts but also to help you learn how to apply the facts. No matter what your experience level leading up to taking the exams, it is our hope that the broad range of preparation tools, and even the structure of the book, will help you pass the exam with ease. We hope you do well on the exam.

# Answers to the "Do I Know This Already?" Quizzes

## Chapter 1

1. C and E
2. A
3. C
4. B and C
5. B and C
6. B
7. A, B, and D
8. C
9. C
10. D
11. C
12. D

## Chapter 2

1. A and D
2. A and B
3. C
4. B
5. A
6. A
7. A and B
8. A, B, and C
9. A, C, and D
10. C

## Chapter 3

1. B
2. C
3. A and C
4. B and C
5. C
6. D
7. C, D, and F
8. E
9. A, B, and C
10. C
11. E

## Chapter 4

1. D
2. C
3. D
4. A and D
5. A
6. C and D
7. B
8. A and B
9. B
10. C
11. A

## Chapter 5

1. C and D
2. A and E
3. B and D
4. D
5. D
6. D
7. B and D
8. A and C
9. C and E
10. A
11. A
12. A, B, C, and D
13. E
14. A
15. B

## Chapter 6

1. C
2. C
3. B
4. C, D, and E
5. B and D
6. A
7. E
8. E
9. C
10. C
11. A and C

## Chapter 7

1. A, B, and C
2. A
3. B and C
4. A
5. A and E
6. A, B, D, and E
7. B and D

## Chapter 8

1. C and D
2. A, C, E, and H
3. B, D, F, and G
4. D
5. A, C, and D
6. A, B, C, D, and G
7. C, D, E, F, and G
8. A, C, and D
9. C and E
10. C, D, E, F, and G
11. A, B, C, D, E, F, and G
12. A
13. B
14. C
15. B
16. B
17. A
18. A
19. B, C, D, and F
20. B, C, and E
21. B
22. D

**23.** B

**24.** C

**25.** B, D, and E

**26.** C, D, and F

**27.** C and E

**28.** A and C

**29.** B, D, and F

**30.** A, B, and C

**31.** B and C

# Chapter 9

**1.** B and C

**2.** A and C

**3.** C

**4.** B and D

**5.** A

**6.** C and D

**7.** A and B

**8.** B

**9.** B and D

**10.** A and E

**11.** C and F

**12.** A

**13.** A, D, and E

**14.** B, C, and D

**15.** C and E

**16.** B, E, and F

# Chapter 10

**1.** D

**2.** C

**3.** B

**4.** G

**5.** B

**6.** C

**7.** D

**8.** A

**9.** A

**10.** A, D, F, G, and H

**11.** D

**12.** D

**13.** B, D, and E

**14.** B

**15.** C and D

**16.** A, B, and F

**17.** D

**18.** A, C, and D

**19.** A

**20.** C

**21.** B

**22.** A and D

**23.** A, B, and D

**24.** B

**25.** C, E, and G

**26.** A and D

**27.** B, D, and H

**28.** C and E

**29.** D

**30.** A, B, and C

**31.** B

**32.** B and C

**33.** A and B

# Chapter 11

1. A and D

2. C and D

3. A

4. A and B

5. C

6. A

7. D

8. A and C

9. B, D, and E

10. D

11. D

12. B

# CCIE Exam Updates

## EIGRP RID on IPv6-enabled Routers

Each IPv4 and IPv6 EIGRP instance must be assigned a 4B-long Router ID (RID) in order to run. If the RID is not configured manually, an EIGRP process tries to choose its RID first as the highest IPv4 address from among non-shutdown Loopback interfaces, and if no such Loopback interfaces are available, as the highest IPv4 address from among all remaining non-shutdown interfaces. On routers running pure IPv6 without any IPv4 (IPv6-only routers), the automatic RID selection will not work as these routers have no IPv4 addresses configured to choose from. As a result, on IPv6-only routers, each IPv6 EIGRP process must be configured with a unique RID manually, otherwise it will be unable to start and operate. This is accomplished in the IPv6 EIGRP process configuration using the **eigrp router-id** command followed by the RID in dotted-decimal format.

Over time, reader feedback enables Cisco Press to gauge which topics give our readers the most problems when taking the exams. Additionally, Cisco might make small changes in the breadth of exam topics or in the emphasis of certain topics. To assist readers with those topics, the author creates new materials clarifying and expanding upon those troublesome exam topics.

Each IPv4 and IPv6 EIGRP instance must have a RID assigned in order to run. On routers running pure IPv6 without any IPv4 (IPv6-only routers), the automatic RID selection will not work as it has no IPv4 addresses available to choose from. As a result, on IPv6-only routers, each IPv6 EIGRP process must be configured with a unique RID manually, otherwise it will be unable to start and operate.

The document you are viewing is Version 1.0 of this appendix and there are no updates. You can check for an updated version at www.ciscopress.com/title/9781587143960.

# Index

# F

# G

# J-K

key chains, 337
K-values, 364

# L

L4 port algorithm, 285
LACNIC (Latin American and Caribbean Internet Addresses Registry), 207
LACP (Link Aggregation Control Protocol), 159-161
LANs
  DRs, 469
    *election process, 471-472*
    *optimizing, 470-471*
  switch forwarding behavior, 19
Layer 2
  frame rewrites, 273
  troubleshooting, 161-169, 175-176
    *with CDP, 163-165*
    *with LLDP, 165-167*
    *show interfaces command, 167-169*
Layer 3
  MLS interfaces, 291
  troubleshooting, 695
    *debug commands, 694*
    *extended ping command, 691-692*
    *extended traceroute command, 693-694*
    *show commands, 690-691*
    *show interfaces command, 688-690*
    *show ip interface command, 688-690*
    *show ip protocols command, 686-687*
Length field (Ethernet), 15, 18
Level 0 routing, 576

Level 1 routing, 576
Level 2 routing, 576-577
Level 3 routing, 577
Link Aggregation, 154-161
  load balancing, 154-156
link-state database (IS-IS) in multiarea networks, 603-608
link-state routing protocols, 317-318
  IS-IS
    *adjacencies, 578-579, 587*
    *broadcast links, 587*
    *DIS, 579*
    *IPv6 support, 610-613*
    *metrics, 577-578*
    *NSAP addressing, 571*
    *over broadcast links, 592-598*
    *over point-to-point links, 587-592*
    *packets, 579-586*
    *System IDs, creating, 613*
  migration strategy, 299-308
    *activating new IGP, 300-301*
    *deactivating current IGPs, 301-303*
    *verifying working database contents, 301*
  OSPF, 464-466
    *ABRs, 480*
    *ASBRs, 481*
    *best path selection, 502-505*
    *configuring, 505-507*
    *costs, 507-510*
    *DRs, 469*
    *external routes, 492-495*
    *GR, 530-532*
    *Graceful Shutdown, 532*
    *incremental SPF, 527-528*
    *LSA Throttling, 526-527*
    *messages, 461-462*
    *neighbor states, 462-464*
    *network types, 473*

# M

# P

packets. *See also* IP routing

  EIGRP, 368-374. *See also* RTP (Reliable Transport Protocol)

  *ACK packets, 372-373*

  *format, 368-371*

  *Hello packets, 372*

  *Query packets, 374*

  *Reply packets, 374*

  *SIA-Query packets, 374*

  *SIA-Reply packets, 374*

  *TLVs, 369*

  *Update packets, 373*

  forwarding process, 271-272

  *fast switching, 272-273*

  IGRP, Update packets, 357-358

  IS-IS, 579-586

  *authentication, 608-610*

  *CSNP packets, 585-586*

  *Hello packets, 579-580*

  *LSPs, 580-585*

  *PSNP packets, 585-586*

PAgP (Port Aggregation Protocol), 159-161

Partition repair flag (LSPs), 603

passive interfaces (EIGRP), 431-432

Passive state (EIGRP), 381

passive-interface command, 431-432

passwords, VTP, 87

PAT (Port Address Translation), 211-212

  configuring, 212-214

path selection

  influencing with interface metrics, 368

  OSPF, 482

  *best path selection, 502-505*

  *path choices not using cost, 502*

path-vector routing protocols, 317

PBR (Policy-Based Routing), 296-299

  logic, 296

  SDM templates, 299

  set commands, 296-299

  specifying matching criteria, 296

Pearson Cert Practice Test engine, 700-705

  installing, 700-702

  practice exam, downloading, 702

Pending state (EIGRP), 378

Per-AF Interface configuration mode (EIGRP), 415

Per-AF Topology configuration mode (EIGRP), 416-417

per-destination load sharing, 282-283

performance

  Cisco IOS IP SLA, 249-250

  OSPF

  *LSA Throttling, 526-527*

  *SPF Throttling, 524-525*

per-packet load sharing, 282

PfR (Performance Routing), 672-683

  authentication, 674-675

  border routers, 676-677

  *configuring, 681-683*

  configuring, 677

  external interfaces, 674

  internal interfaces, 674

  local interfaces, 674

  MC, 675-676

  *configuring, 677-681*

  operational roles, 675

  phases wheel, 673-674

phases wheel (PfR), 673-674

PID (process ID), 465

pinouts, RJ-45, 8-9

point-to-multipoint networks, 473

point-to-multipoint nonbroadcast networks, 473

# Q

# W

# X-Y-Z

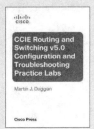

# CCIE Routing and Switching v5.0 Official Cert Guide, Volume 2

## Fifth Edition

Narbik Kocharians, CCIE No. 12410
Terry Vinson, CCIE No. 35347

**Cisco Press**

800 East 96th Street

Indianapolis, Indiana 46240 USA

# CCIE Routing and Switching v5.0 Official Cert Guide, Volume 2, Fifth Edition

Narbik Kocharians, CCIE No. 12410
Terry Vinson, CCIE No. 35347

Published by:
Cisco Press
800 East 96th Street
Indianapolis, IN 46240 USA

Printed in the United States of America

First Printing November 2014

Library of Congress Control Number: 2014950779

ISBN-13: 978-1-58714-491-2

ISBN-10: 1-58714-491-3

## Warning and Disclaimer

## Trademark Acknowledgments

## Special Sales

For information about buying this title in bulk quantities, or for special sales opportunities (which may include electronic versions; custom cover designs; and content particular to your business, training goals, marketing focus, or branding interests), please contact our corporate sales department at corpsales@pearsoned.com or (800) 382-3419.

For government sales inquiries, please contact governmentsales@pearsoned.com.

For questions about sales outside the U.S., please contact international@pearsoned.com.

## Feedback Information

At Cisco Press, our goal is to create in-depth technical books of the highest quality and value. Each book is crafted with care and precision, undergoing rigorous development that involves the unique expertise of members from the professional technical community.

Readers' feedback is a natural continuation of this process. If you have any comments regarding how we could improve the quality of this book, or otherwise alter it to better suit your needs, you can contact us through email at feedback@ciscopress.com. Please make sure to include the book title and ISBN in your message.

We greatly appreciate your assistance.

**Publisher:** Paul Boger

**Associate Publisher:** Dave Dusthimer

**Business Operation Manager, Cisco Press:** Jan Cornelssen

**Executive Editor:** Brett Bartow

**Managing Editor:** Sandra Schroeder

**Senior Development Editor:** Christopher Cleveland

**Senior Project Editor:** Tonya Simpson

**Copy Editor:** John Edwards

**Technical Editor(s):** Dave Burns, Sean Wilkins

**Editorial Assistant:** Vanessa Evans

**Cover Designer:** Mark Shirar

**Composition:** Tricia Bronkella

**Indexer:** Tim Wright

**Proofreader:** Chuck Hutchinson

**Americas Headquarters**
Cisco Systems, Inc.
170 West Tasman Drive
San Jose, CA 95134-1706
USA
www.cisco.com
Tel: 408 526-4000
800 553-NETS (6387)
Fax: 408 527-0883

**Asia Pacific Headquarters**
Cisco Systems, Inc.
168 Robinson Road
#28-01 Capital Tower
Singapore 068912
www.cisco.com
Tel: +65 6317 7777
Fax: +65 6317 7799

**Europe Headquarters**
Cisco Systems International BV
Haarlerbergpark
Haarlerbergweg 13-19
1101 CH Amsterdam
The Netherlands
www-europe.cisco.com
Tel: +31 0 800 020 0791
Fax: +31 0 20 357 1100

Cisco has more than 200 offices worldwide. Addresses, phone numbers, and fax numbers are listed on the Cisco Website at www.cisco.com/go/offices.

## About the Authors

**Narbik Kocharians**, CCIE No. 12410 (Routing and Switching, Security, SP), is a Triple CCIE with more than 32 years of experience in the IT industry. He has designed, implemented, and supported numerous enterprise networks. Narbik is the president of Micronics Training, Inc. (www.Micronicstraining.com), where he teaches CCIE R&S and SP boot camps.

**Terry Vinson**, CCIE No. 35347 (Routing and Switching, Data Center), is a seasoned instructor with nearly 25 years of experience teaching and writing technical courses and training materials. Terry has taught and developed training content, as well as provided technical consulting for high-end firms in the north Virginia/Washington, D.C. area. His technical expertise lies in the Cisco arena with a focus on all routing and switching technologies as well as the latest data center technologies, including Nexus switching, unified computing, and storage-area networking (SAN) technologies. Terry currently teaches for CCIE R&S and Data Center Bootcamps for Micronics Training, Inc. and enjoys sailing and game design in his "free time."

# About the Technical Reviewers

**David Burns** has in-depth knowledge of routing and switching technologies, network security, and mobility. He is currently a senior systems engineering manager for Cisco, leading the engineering team covering cable/MSO and content service providers in the United States. In July 2008, Dave joined Cisco as a lead systems engineer in several areas, including Femtocell, Datacenter, MTSO, and security architectures, working for a U.S.-based SP Mobility account. He came to Cisco from a large U.S.-based cable company, where he was a senior network and security design engineer. Dave held various roles before joining Cisco during his ten-plus years in the industry, working in SP operations, SP engineering, SP architecture, enterprise IT, and U.S. military intelligence communications engineering. He holds various sales and industry/Cisco technical certifications, including the CISSP, CCSP, CCDP, and two associate-level certifications. Dave recently passed the CCIE Security Written exam and is currently preparing for the CCIE Security Lab. Dave is a big advocate of knowledge transfer and sharing and has a passion for network technologies, especially as they relate to network security. Dave has been a speaker at Cisco Live on topics such as Femtocell (IP mobility) and IPS (security). Dave earned his Bachelor of Science degree in telecommunications engineering technology from Southern Polytechnic State University, Georgia, where he currently serves as a member of the Industry Advisory Board for the Computer & Electrical Engineering Technology School. Dave also earned a Master of Business Administration (MBA) degree from the University of Phoenix.

**Sean Wilkins** is an accomplished networking consultant for SR-W Consulting and has been in the field of IT since the mid 1990s, working with companies such as Cisco, Lucent, Verizon, and AT&T as well as several other private companies. Sean currently holds certifications with Cisco (CCNP/CCDP), Microsoft (MCSE), and CompTIA (A+ and Network+). He also has a Master of Science degree in information technology with a focus in network architecture and design, a Master of Science in organizational management, a Master's Certificate in network security, a Bachelor of Science in computer networking, and an Associate of Applied Science in computer information systems. In addition to working as a consultant, Sean spends most of his time as a technical writer and editor for various companies. Check out his work at his author website, www.infodispersion.com.

## Dedications

**From Narbik Kocharians:**

I would like to dedicate this book to my wife, Janet, for her love, encouragement, and continuous support, and to my dad, for his words of wisdom.

**From Terry Vinson:**

I would like to dedicate this book to my father, who has taught me many things in life and include the one thing I've tried to live by: "Never give up on your dreams. Hard work and diligence will see you through so long as you never give up." So it is with all my love, respect, and admiration that I dedicate this to you.

# Acknowledgments

**From Narbik Kocharians:**

First, I would like to thank God for giving me the opportunity and ability to write, teach, and do what I truly enjoy doing. Also, I would like to thank my family, especially my wife of 29 years, Janet, for her constant encouragement and help. She does such an amazing job of interacting with students and handling all the logistics of organizing classes as I focus on teaching. I also would like to thank my children, Chris, Patrick, Alexandra, and my little one Daniel, for their patience.

A special thanks to Mr. Brett Bartow for his patience with our constantly changing deadlines. It goes without saying that the technical editors and reviewers did a phenomenal job; thank you very much. Finally, I would like to thank all my students, who inspire me every day, and you, for reading this book.

**From Terry Vinson:**

The opportunity to cooperate on the new edition of this book has been an honor and privilege beyond words for me. I have to thank Narbik for approaching me with the opportunity and for all his support and mentoring over the years. If it were not for him, I would not be where I am today. Additionally, I would like to thank all the fine people at Cisco Press for being so cool and understanding over the last few months. Among those people, I want to specifically thank Brett Bartow, whose patience has been almost infinite (yet I managed to tax it), David Burns, and Sean Wilkins for their incredible suggestions and devotion to making sure that I stayed on track. Last but not least among the Cisco Press crew there is Christopher Cleveland, who diligently nudged, kicked, and all-out shoved when necessary to see that things got done.

Personally, I need to thank my wife, Sheila. She has been the difference I was looking for in my life, the impetus to try to do more and to get up each day and try to make myself a better person, a better engineer, and a better instructor. Without her, I would not have the life I have come to love so much.

Finally, I want to thank my students and Micronics Training for giving me the opportunity to do what I enjoy every day. Thanks for all your questions, patience, and unbridled eagerness to learn. You guys are absolutely stellar examples of why this industry is like no other on the planet.

# Contents at a Glance

## Part VIII    Appendixes

## CD-Only

# Contents

# Icons Used in This Book

## Command Syntax Conventions

The conventions used to present command syntax in this book are the same conventions used in the IOS Command Reference. The Command Reference describes these conventions as follows:

- **Boldface** indicates commands and keywords that are entered literally as shown. In actual configuration examples and output (not general command syntax), boldface indicates commands that are manually input by the user (such as a **show** command).

- *Italic* indicates arguments for which you supply actual values.

- Vertical bars (|) separate alternative, mutually exclusive elements.

- Square brackets ([ ]) indicate an optional element.

- Braces ({ }) indicate a required choice.

- Braces within brackets ([{ }]) indicate a required choice within an optional element.

# Introduction

The Cisco Certified Internetwork Expert (CCIE) certification might be the most challenging and prestigious of all networking certifications. It has received numerous awards and certainly has built a reputation as one of the most difficult certifications to earn in all of the technology world. Having a CCIE certification opens doors professionally, typically results in higher pay, and looks great on a résumé.

Cisco currently offers several CCIE certifications. This book covers the version 5.0 exam blueprint topics of the written exam for the CCIE Routing and Switching certification. The following list details the currently available CCIE certifications at the time of this book's publication; check www.cisco.com/go/ccie for the latest information. The certifications are listed in the order in which they appear on the web page:

- CCDE
- CCIE Collaboration
- CCIE Data Center
- CCIE Routing & Switching
- CCIE Security
- CCIE Service Provider
- CCIE Service Provider Operations
- CCIE Wireless

Each of the CCDE and CCIE certifications requires the candidate to pass both a written exam and a one-day, hands-on lab exam. The written exam is intended to test your knowledge of theory, protocols, and configuration concepts that follow good design practices. The lab exam proves that you can configure and troubleshoot actual gear.

## Why Should I Take the CCIE Routing and Switching Written Exam?

The first and most obvious reason to take the CCIE Routing and Switching written exam is that it is the first step toward obtaining the CCIE Routing and Switching certification. Also, you cannot schedule a CCIE lab exam until you pass the corresponding written exam. In short, if you want all the professional benefits of a CCIE Routing and Switching certification, you start by passing the written exam.

The benefits of getting a CCIE certification are varied, among which are the following:

- Better pay
- Career-advancement opportunities
- Applies to certain minimum requirements for Cisco Silver and Gold Channel Partners, as well as those seeking Master Specialization, making you more valuable to Channel Partners

- Better movement through the problem-resolution process when calling the Cisco TAC

- Prestige

- Credibility for consultants and customer engineers, including the use of the Cisco CCIE logo

The other big reason to take the CCIE Routing and Switching written exam is that it recertifies an individual's associate-, professional-, and expert-level Cisco certifications, regardless of his or her technology track. Recertification requirements do change, so please verify the requirements at www.cisco.com/go/certifications.

# CCIE Routing and Switching Written Exam 400-101

The CCIE Routing and Switching written exam, at the time of this writing, consists of a two-hour exam administered at a proctored exam facility affiliated with Pearson VUE (www.vue.com/cisco). The exam typically includes approximately 100 multiple-choice questions. No simulation questions are currently part of the written exam.

As with most exams, everyone wants to know what is on the exam. Cisco provides general guidance as to topics on the exam in the CCIE Routing and Switching written exam blueprint, the most recent copy of which can be accessed from www.cisco.com/go/ccie.

Cisco changes both the CCIE written and lab blueprints over time, but Cisco seldom, if ever, changes the exam numbers. However, exactly this change occurred when the CCIE Routing and Switching blueprint was refreshed for v5.0. The previous written exam for v4.0 was numbered as 350-001; the v5.0 written exam is identified by 400-101.

The CCIE Routing and Switching written exam blueprint 5.0, as of the time of publication, is listed in Table I-1. Table I-1 also lists the chapters that cover each topic.

**Table I-1**  *CCIE Routing and Switching Written Exam Blueprint*

| Topics | Book Volume | Book Chapter |
| --- | --- | --- |
| **1.0 Network Principles** | | |
| *1.1 Network theory* | | |
| 1.1.a Describe basic software architecture differences between IOS and IOS XE | | |
| 1.1.a (i) Control plane and Forwarding plane | 1 | 1 |
| 1.1.a (ii) Impact to troubleshooting and performances | 1 | 1 |
| 1.1.a (iii) Excluding specific platform's architecture | 1 | 1 |
| 1.1.b Identify Cisco Express Forwarding concepts | | |
| 1.1.b (i) RIB, FIB, LFIB, adjacency table | 1 | 6 |
| 1.1.b (ii) Load-balancing hash | 1 | 6 |

| Topics | Book Volume | Book Chapter |
|---|---|---|
| 1.1.b (iii) Polarization concept and avoidance | 1 | 6 |
| 1.1.c Explain general network challenges | | |
| 1.1.c (i) Unicast flooding | 1 | 4 |
| 1.1.c (ii) Out-of-order packets | 1 | 4 |
| 1.1.c (iii) Asymmetric routing | 1 | 4 |
| 1.1.c (iv) Impact of micro-burst | 1 | 4 |
| 1.1.d Explain IP operations | | |
| 1.1.d (i) ICMP unreachable, redirect | 1 | 4 |
| 1.1.d (ii) IPv4 options, IPv6 extension headers | 1 | 4 |
| 1.1.d (iii) IPv4 and IPv6 fragmentation | 1 | 4 |
| 1.1.d (iv) TTL | 1 | 4 |
| 1.1.d (v) IP MTU | 1 | 4 |
| 1.1.e Explain TCP operations | | |
| 1.1.e (i) IPv4 and IPv6 PMTU | 1 | 4 |
| 1.1.e (ii) MSS | 1 | 4 |
| 1.1.e (iii) Latency | 1 | 4 |
| 1.1.e (iv) Windowing | 1 | 4 |
| 1.1.e (v) Bandwidth delay product | 1 | 4 |
| 1.1.e (vi) Global synchronization | 1 | 4 |
| 1.1.e (vii) Options | 1 | 4 |
| 1.1.f Explain UDP operations | | |
| 1.1.f (i) Starvation | 1 | 4 |
| 1.1.f (ii) Latency | 1 | 4 |
| 1.1.f (iii) RTP/RTCP concepts | 1 | 4 |
| *1.2 Network implementation and operation* | | |
| 1.2.a Evaluate proposed changes to a network | | |
| 1.2.a (i) Changes to routing protocol parameters | 1 | 7–10 |
| 1.2.a (ii) Migrate parts of a network to IPv6 | 1 | 4 |
| 1.2.a (iii) Routing protocol migration | 1 | 6 |
| 1.2.a (iv) Adding multicast support | 2 | 8 |
| 1.2.a (v) Migrate Spanning Tree Protocol | 1 | 3 |

| Topics | Book Volume | Book Chapter |
|---|---|---|
| 1.2.a (vi) Evaluate impact of new traffic on existing QoS design | 2 | 3, 4, 5 |
| *1.3 Network troubleshooting* | | |
| 1.3.a Use IOS troubleshooting tools | | |
| 1.3.a (i) debug, conditional debug | 1 | 4 |
| 1.3.a (ii) ping, traceroute with extended options | 1 | 4 |
| 1.3.a (iii) Embedded packet capture | 2 | 9 |
| 1.3.a (iv) Performance monitor | 1 | 5 |
| 1.3.b Apply troubleshooting methodologies | | |
| 1.3.b (i) Diagnose the root cause of networking issue (analyze symptoms, identify and describe root cause) | 1 | 11 |
| 1.3.b (ii) Design and implement valid solutions according to constraints | 1 | 11 |
| 1.3.b (iii) Verify and monitor resolution | 1 | 11 |
| 1.3.c Interpret packet capture | | |
| 1.3.c (i) Using Wireshark trace analyzer | 2 | 9 |
| 1.3.c (ii) Using IOS embedded packet capture | 2 | 9 |
| **2.0 Layer 2 Technologies** | | |
| *2.1 LAN switching technologies* | | |
| 2.1.a Implement and troubleshoot switch administration | | |
| 2.1.a (i) Managing MAC address table | 1 | 1 |
| 2.1.a (ii) errdisable recovery | 1 | 3 |
| 2.1.a (iii) L2 MTU | 1 | 1 |
| 2.1.b Implement and troubleshoot Layer 2 protocols | | |
| 2.1.b (i) CDP, LLDP | 1 | 3 |
| 2.1.b (ii) UDLD | 1 | 3 |
| 2.1.c Implement and troubleshoot VLAN | | |
| 2.1.c (i) Access ports | 1 | 2 |
| 2.1.c (ii) VLAN database | 1 | 2 |
| 2.1.c (iii) Normal, extended VLAN, voice VLAN | 1 | 2 |

| Topics | Book Volume | Book Chapter |
|---|---|---|
| 2.1.d Implement and troubleshoot trunking | | |
| 2.1.d (i) VTPv1, VTPv2, VTPv3, VTP pruning | 1 | 2 |
| 2.1.d (ii) dot1Q | 1 | 2 |
| 2.1.d (iii) Native VLAN | 1 | 2 |
| 2.1.d (iv) Manual pruning | 1 | 2 |
| 2.1.e Implement and troubleshoot EtherChannel | | |
| 2.1.e (i) LACP, PAgP, manual | 1 | 3 |
| 2.1.e (ii) Layer 2, Layer 3 | 1 | 3 |
| 2.1.e (iii) Load balancing | 1 | 3 |
| 2.1.e (iv) EtherChannel misconfiguration guard | 1 | 3 |
| 2.1.f Implement and troubleshoot spanning tree | | |
| 2.1.f (i) PVST+/RPVST+/MST | 1 | 3 |
| 2.1.f (ii) Switch priority, port priority, path cost, STP timers | 1 | 3 |
| 2.1.f (iii) PortFast, BPDU Guard, BPDU Filter | 1 | 3 |
| 2.1.f (iv) Loop Guard, Root Guard | 1 | 3 |
| 2.1.g Implement and troubleshoot other LAN switching technologies | | |
| 2.1.g (i) SPAN, RSPAN, ERSPAN | 1 | 1 |
| 2.1.h Describe chassis virtualization and aggregation technologies | | |
| 2.1.h (i) Multichassis | 1 | 1 |
| 2.1.h (ii) VSS concepts | 1 | 1 |
| 2.1.h (iii) Alternative to STP | 1 | 1 |
| 2.1.h (iv) Stackwise | 1 | 1 |
| 2.1.h (v) Excluding specific platform implementation | 1 | 1 |
| 2.1.i Describe spanning-tree concepts | | |
| 2.1.i (i) Compatibility between MST and RSTP | 1 | 3 |
| 2.1.i (ii) STP dispute, STP Bridge Assurance | 1 | 3 |
| 2.2 Layer 2 multicast | | |
| 2.2.a Implement and troubleshoot IGMP | | |
| 2.2.a (i) IGMPv1, IGMPv2, IGMPv3 | 2 | 7 |
| 2.2.a (ii) IGMP snooping | 2 | 7 |

| Topics | Book Volume | Book Chapter |
|---|---|---|
| 2.2.a (iii) IGMP querier | 2 | 7 |
| 2.2.a (iv) IGMP filter | 2 | 7 |
| 2.2.a (v) IGMP proxy | 2 | 7 |
| 2.2.b Explain MLD | 2 | 8 |
| 2.2.c Explain PIM snooping | 2 | 8 |
| *2.3 Layer 2 WAN circuit technologies* | | |
| 2.3.a Implement and troubleshoot HDLC | 2 | 6 |
| 2.3.b Implement and troubleshoot PPP | | |
| 2.3.b (i) Authentication (PAP, CHAP) | 2 | 6 |
| 2.3.b (ii) PPPoE | 2 | 6 |
| 2.3.b (iii) MLPPP | 2 | 6 |
| 2.3.c Describe WAN rate-based Ethernet circuits | | |
| 2.3.c (i) Metro and WAN Ethernet topologies | 2 | 6 |
| 2.3.c (ii) Use of rate-limited WAN Ethernet services | 2 | 6 |
| **3.0 Layer 3 Technologies** | | |
| *3.1 Addressing technologies* | | |
| 3.1.a Identify, implement, and troubleshoot IPv4 addressing and subnetting | | |
| 3.1.a (i) Address types, VLSM | 1 | 4 |
| 3.1.a (ii) ARP | 1 | 4 |
| 3.1.b Identify, implement, and troubleshoot IPv6 addressing and subnetting | | |
| 3.1.b (i) Unicast, multicast | 1 | 4 |
| 3.1.b (ii) EUI-64 | 1 | 4 |
| 3.1.b (iii) ND, RS/RA | 1 | 4 |
| 3.1.b (iv) Autoconfig/SLAAC, temporary addresses (RFC 4941) | 1 | 4 |
| 3.1.b (v) Global prefix configuration feature | 1 | 4 |
| 3.1.b (vi) DHCP operations | 1 | 4 |
| 3.1.b (vii) SLAAC/DHCPv6 interaction | 2 | 10 |
| 3.1.b (viii) Stateful, stateless DHCPv6 | 1 | 4 |
| 3.1.b (ix) DHCPv6 prefix delegation | 1 | 4 |

| Topics | Book Volume | Book Chapter |
|---|---|---|
| *3.2 Layer 3 multicast* | | |
| 3.2.a Troubleshoot reverse path forwarding | | |
| 3.2.a (i) RPF failure | 2 | 8 |
| 3.2.a (ii) RPF failure with tunnel interface | 2 | 8 |
| 3.2.b Implement and troubleshoot IPv4 protocol-independent multicast | | |
| 3.2.b (i) PIM dense mode, sparse mode, sparse-dense mode | 2 | 8 |
| 3.2.b (ii) Static RP, auto-RP, BSR | 2 | 8 |
| 3.2.b (iii) Bidirectional PIM | 2 | 8 |
| 3.2.b (iv) Source-specific multicast | 2 | 8 |
| 3.2.b (v) Group-to-RP mapping | 2 | 8 |
| 3.2.b (vi) Multicast boundary | 2 | 8 |
| 3.2.c Implement and troubleshoot multicast source discovery protocol | | |
| 3.2.c (i) Intra-domain MSDP (anycast RP) | 2 | 8 |
| 3.2.c (ii) SA filter | 2 | 8 |
| 3.2.d Describe IPv6 multicast | | |
| 3.2.d (i) IPv6 multicast addresses | 2 | 7 |
| 3.2.d (ii) PIMv6 | 2 | 8 |
| *3.3 Fundamental routing concepts* | | |
| 3.3.a Implement and troubleshoot static routing | 1 | 6 |
| 3.3.b Implement and troubleshoot default routing | 1 | 7–11 |
| 3.3.c Compare routing protocol types | | |
| 3.3.c (i) Distance vector | 1 | 7 |
| 3.3.c (ii) Link state | 1 | 7 |
| 3.3.c (iii) Path vector | 1 | 7 |
| 3.3.d Implement, optimize, and troubleshoot administrative distance | 1 | 11 |
| 3.3.e Implement and troubleshoot passive interface | 1 | 7–10 |
| 3.3.f Implement and troubleshoot VRF Lite | 2 | 11 |
| 3.3.g Implement, optimize, and troubleshoot filtering with any routing protocol | 1 | 11 |

| Topics | Book Volume | Book Chapter |
|---|---|---|
| 3.3.h Implement, optimize, and troubleshoot redistribution between any routing protocol | 1 | 11 |
| 3.3.i Implement, optimize, and troubleshoot manual and autosummarization with any routing protocol | 1 | 7–10 |
| 3.3.j Implement, optimize, and troubleshoot Policy-Based Routing | 1 | 6 |
| 3.3.k Identify and troubleshoot suboptimal routing | 1 | 11 |
| 3.3.l Implement and troubleshoot bidirectional forwarding detection | 1 | 11 |
| 3.3.m Implement and troubleshoot loop-prevention mechanisms | | |
| 3.3.m (i) Route tagging, filtering | 1 | 11 |
| 3.3.m (ii) Split Horizon | 1 | 7 |
| 3.3.m (iii) Route Poisoning | 1 | 7 |
| 3.3.n Implement and troubleshoot routing protocol authentication | | |
| 3.3.n (i) MD5 | 1 | 7–10 |
| 3.3.n (ii) Key-chain | 1 | 7–10 |
| 3.3.n (iii) EIGRP HMAC SHA2-256bit | 1 | 8 |
| 3.3.n (iv) OSPFv2 SHA1-196bit | 1 | 9 |
| 3.3.n (v) OSPFv3 IPsec authentication | 1 | 9 |
| 3.4 RIP (v2 and v6) | | |
| 3.4.a Implement and troubleshoot RIPv2 | 1 | 7 |
| 3.4.b Describe RIPv6 (RIPng) | 1 | 7 |
| 3.5 EIGRP (for IPv4 and IPv6) | | |
| 3.5.a Describe packet types | | |
| 3.5.a (i) Packet types (hello, query, update, and so on) | 1 | 8 |
| 3.5.a (ii) Route types (internal, external) | 1 | 8 |
| 3.5.b Implement and troubleshoot neighbor relationship | | |
| 3.5.b (i) Multicast, unicast EIGRP peering | 1 | 8 |
| 3.5.b (ii) OTP point-to-point peering | 1 | 8 |

| Topics | Book Volume | Book Chapter |
|---|---|---|
| 3.5.b (iii) OTP route-reflector peering | 1 | 8 |
| 3.5.b (iv) OTP multiple service providers scenario | 1 | 8 |
| 3.5.c Implement and troubleshoot loop-free path selection | | |
| 3.5.c (i) RD, FD, FC, successor, feasible successor | 1 | 8 |
| 3.5.c (ii) Classic metric | 1 | 8 |
| 3.5.c (iii) Wide metric | 1 | 8 |
| 3.5.d Implement and troubleshoot operations | | |
| 3.5.d (i) General operations | 1 | 8 |
| 3.5.d (ii) Topology table, update, query, active, passive | 1 | 8 |
| 3.5.d (iii) Stuck in active | 1 | 8 |
| 3.5.d (iv) Graceful shutdown | 1 | 8 |
| 3.5.e Implement and troubleshoot EIGRP stub | | |
| 3.5.e (i) Stub | 1 | 8 |
| 3.5.e (ii) Leak-map | 1 | 8 |
| 3.5.f Implement and troubleshoot load balancing | | |
| 3.5.f (i) equal-cost | 1 | 8 |
| 3.5.f (ii) unequal-cost | 1 | 8 |
| 3.5.f (iii) add-path | 1 | 8 |
| 3.5.g Implement EIGRP (multi-address) named mode | | |
| 3.5.g (i) Types of families | 1 | 8 |
| 3.5.g (ii) IPv4 address-family | 1 | 8 |
| 3.5.g (iii) IPv6 address-family | 1 | 8 |
| 3.5.h Implement, troubleshoot, and optimize EIGRP convergence and scalability | | |
| 3.5.h (i) Describe fast convergence requirements | 1 | 8 |
| 3.5.h (ii) Control query boundaries | 1 | 8 |
| 3.5.h (iii) IP FRR/fast reroute (single hop) | 1 | 8 |
| 3.5.h (iv) Summary leak-map | 1 | 8 |
| 3.5.h (v) Summary metric | 1 | 8 |
| 3.6 OSPF (v2 and v3) | | |

| Topics | Book Volume | Book Chapter |
|---|---|---|
| **3.6.a Describe packet types** | | |
| 3.6.a (i) LSA types (1, 2, 3, 4, 5, 7, 9) | 1 | 9 |
| 3.6.a (ii) Route types (N1, N2, E1, E2) | 1 | 9 |
| 3.6.b Implement and troubleshoot neighbor relationship | 1 | 9 |
| **3.6.c Implement and troubleshoot OSPFv3 address-family support** | | |
| 3.6.c (i) IPv4 address-family | 1 | 9 |
| 3.6.c (ii) IPv6 address-family | 1 | 9 |
| **3.6.d Implement and troubleshoot network types, area types, and router types** | | |
| 3.6.d (i) Point-to-point, multipoint, broadcast, nonbroadcast | 1 | 9 |
| 3.6.d (ii) LSA types, area type: backbone, normal, transit, stub, NSSA, totally stub | 1 | 9 |
| 3.6.d (iii) Internal router, ABR, ASBR | 1 | 9 |
| 3.6.d (iv) Virtual link | 1 | 9 |
| 3.6.e Implement and troubleshoot path preference | 1 | 9 |
| **3.6.f Implement and troubleshoot operations** | | |
| 3.6.f (i) General operations | 1 | 9 |
| 3.6.f (ii) Graceful shutdown | 1 | 9 |
| 3.6.f (iii) GTSM (Generic TTL Security Mechanism) | 1 | 9 |
| **3.6.g Implement, troubleshoot, and optimize OSPF convergence and scalability** | | |
| 3.6.g (i) Metrics | 1 | 9 |
| 3.6.g (ii) LSA throttling, SPF tuning, fast hello | 1 | 9 |
| 3.6.g (iii) LSA propagation control (area types, ISPF) | 1 | 9 |
| 3.6.g (iv) IP FRR/fast reroute (single hop) | 1 | 9 |
| 3.6.g (v) LFA/loop-free alternative (multihop) | 1 | 9 |
| 3.6.g (vi) OSPFv3 prefix suppression | 1 | 9 |
| *3.7 BGP* | | |
| **3.7.a Describe, implement, and troubleshoot peer relationships** | | |
| 3.7.a (i) Peer-group, template | 2 | 1 |

| Topics | Book Volume | Book Chapter |
|---|---|---|
| 3.7.a (ii) Active, passive | 2 | 1 |
| 3.7.a (iii) States, timers | 2 | 1 |
| 3.7.a (iv) Dynamic neighbors | 2 | 1 |
| 3.7.b Implement and troubleshoot iBGP and iBGP | | |
| 3.7.b (i) eBGP, iBGP | 2 | 1 |
| 3.7.b (ii) 4-byte AS number | 2 | 1 |
| 3.7.b (iii) Private AS | 2 | 1 |
| 3.7.c Explain attributes and best-path selection | 2 | 1 |
| 3.7.d Implement, optimize, and troubleshoot routing policies | | |
| 3.7.d (i) Attribute manipulation | 2 | 2 |
| 3.7.d (ii) Conditional advertisement | 2 | 2 |
| 3.7.d (iii) Outbound route filtering | 2 | 2 |
| 3.7.d (iv) Communities, extended communities | 2 | 2 |
| 3.7.d (v) Multihoming | 2 | 2 |
| 3.7.e Implement and troubleshoot scalability | | |
| 3.7.e (i) Route-reflector, cluster | 2 | 2 |
| 3.7.e (ii) Confederations | 2 | 2 |
| 3.7.e (iii) Aggregation, AS set | 2 | 2 |
| 3.7.f Implement and troubleshoot multiprotocol BGP | | |
| 3.7.f (i) IPv4, IPv6, VPN address-family | 2 | 2 |
| 3.7.g Implement and troubleshoot AS path manipulations | | |
| 3.7.g (i) Local AS, allow AS in, remove private AS | 2 | 2 |
| 3.7.g (ii) Prepend | 2 | 2 |
| 3.7.g (iii) Regexp | 2 | 2 |
| 3.7.h Implement and troubleshoot other features | | |
| 3.7.h (i) Multipath | 2 | 2 |
| 3.7.h (ii) BGP synchronization | 2 | 2 |
| 3.7.h (iii) Soft reconfiguration, route refresh | 2 | 2 |

| Topics | Book Volume | Book Chapter |
|---|---|---|
| **3.7.i Describe BGP fast convergence features** | | |
| 3.7.i (i) Prefix-independent convergence | 2 | 2 |
| 3.7.i (ii) Add-path | 2 | 2 |
| 3.7.i (iii) Next-hop address tracking | 2 | 2 |
| *3.8 IS-IS (for IPv4 and IPv6)* | | |
| **3.8.a Describe basic IS-IS network** | | |
| 3.8.a (i) Single area, single topology | 1 | 10 |
| 3.8.b Describe neighbor relationship | 1 | 10 |
| **3.8.c Describe network types, levels, and router types** | | |
| 3.8.c (i) NSAP addressing | 1 | 10 |
| 3.8.c (ii) Point-to-point, broadcast | 1 | 10 |
| 3.8.d Describe operations | 1 | 10 |
| **3.8.e Describe optimization features** | | |
| 3.8.e (i) Metrics, wide metric | 1 | 10 |
| **4.0 VPN Technologies** | | |
| *4.1 Tunneling* | | |
| **4.1.a Implement and troubleshoot MPLS operations** | | |
| 4.1.a (i) Label stack, LSR, LSP | 2 | 11 |
| 4.1.a (ii) LDP | 2 | 11 |
| 4.1.a (iii) MPLS ping, MPLS traceroute | 2 | 11 |
| **4.1.b Implement and troubleshoot basic MPLS L3VPN** | | |
| 4.1.b (i) L3VPN, CE, PE, P | 2 | 11 |
| 4.1.b (ii) Extranet (route leaking) | 2 | 11 |
| **4.1.c Implement and troubleshoot encapsulation** | | |
| 4.1.c (i) GRE | 2 | 10 |
| 4.1.c (ii) Dynamic GRE | 2 | 10 |
| 4.1.c (iii) LISP encapsulation principles supporting EIGRP OTP | 1 | 8 |
| **4.1.d Implement and troubleshoot DMVPN (single hub)** | | |
| 4.1.d (i) NHRP | 2 | 10 |
| 4.1.d (ii) DMVPN with IPsec using preshared key | 2 | 10 |

| Topics | Book Volume | Book Chapter |
|---|---|---|
| 4.1.d (iii) QoS profile | 2 | 10 |
| 4.1.d (iv) Pre-classify | 2 | 10 |
| 4.1.e Describe IPv6 tunneling techniques | | |
| 4.1.e (i) 6in4, 6to4 | 2 | 8 |
| 4.1.e (ii) ISATAP | 2 | 8 |
| 4.1.e (iii) 6RD | 2 | 8 |
| 4.1.e (iv) 6PE/6VPE | 2 | 8 |
| 4.1.g Describe basic Layer 2 VPN: wireline | | |
| 4.1.g (i) L2TPv3 general principles | 2 | 10 |
| 4.1.g (ii) AToM general principles | 2 | 11 |
| 4.1.h Describe basic L2VPN—LAN services | | |
| 4.1.h (i) MPLS-VPLS general principles | 2 | 10 |
| 4.1.h (ii) OTV general principles | 2 | 10 |
| 4.2 Encryption | | |
| 4.2.a Implement and troubleshoot IPsec with preshared key | | |
| 4.2.a (i) IPv4 site to IPv4 site | 2 | 10 |
| 4.2.a (ii) IPv6 in IPv4 tunnels | 2 | 10 |
| 4.2.a (iii) Virtual Tunneling Interface (VTI) | 2 | 10 |
| 4.2.b Describe GET VPN | 2 | 10 |
| 5.0 Infrastructure Security | | |
| 5.1 Device security | | |
| 5.1.a Implement and troubleshoot IOS AAA using local database | 2 | 9 |
| 5.1.b Implement and troubleshoot device access control | | |
| 5.1.b (i) Lines (VTY, AUX, console) | 1 | 5 |
| 5.1.b (ii) SNMP | 1 | 5 |
| 5.1.b (iii) Management plane protection | 2 | 9 |
| 5.1.b (iv) Password encryption | 1 | 5 |
| 5.1.c Implement and troubleshoot control plane policing | 2 | 9 |

| Topics | Book Volume | Book Chapter |
|---|---|---|
| *6.1 System management* | | |
| 6.1.a Implement and troubleshoot device management | | |
| 6.1.a (i) Console and VTY | 1 | 5 |
| 6.1.a (ii) Telnet, HTTP, HTTPS, SSH, SCP | 1 | 5 |
| 6.1.a (iii) (T)FTP | 1 | 5 |
| 6.1.b Implement and troubleshoot SNMP | | |
| 6.1.b (i) v2c, v3 | 1 | 5 |
| 6.1.c Implement and troubleshoot logging | | |
| 6.1.c (i) Local logging, syslog, debug, conditional debug | 1 | 5 |
| 6.1.c (ii) Timestamp | 2 | 6 |
| *6.2 Quality of service* | | |
| 6.2.a Implement and troubleshoot end-to-end QoS | | |
| 6.2.a (i) CoS and DSCP mapping | 2 | 3 |
| 6.2.b Implement, optimize, and troubleshoot QoS using MQC | | |
| 6.2.b (i) Classification | 2 | 3 |
| 6.2.b (ii) Network-Based Application Recognition (NBAR) | 2 | 3 |
| 6.2.b (iii) Marking using IP precedence, DSCP, CoS, ECN | 2 | 3 |
| 6.2.b (iv) Policing, shaping | 2 | 5 |
| 6.2.b (v) Congestion management (queuing) | 2 | 4 |
| 6.2.b (vi) HQoS, subrate Ethernet link | 2 | 3, 4, 5 |
| 6.2.b (vii) Congestion avoidance (WRED) | 2 | 4 |
| 6.2.c Describe layer 2 QoS | | |
| 6.2.c (i) Queuing, scheduling | 2 | 4 |
| 6.2.c (ii) Classification, marking | 2 | 2 |
| *6.3 Network services* | | |
| 6.3.a Implement and troubleshoot first-hop redundancy protocols | | |
| 6.3.a (i) HSRP, GLBP, VRRP | 1 | 5 |
| 6.3.a (ii) Redundancy using IPv6 RS/RA | 1 | 5 |

| Topics | Book Volume | Book Chapter |
|---|---|---|
| 6.4.e Identify performance routing (PfR) | | |
| 6.4.e (i) Basic load balancing | 1 | 11 |
| 6.4.e (ii) Voice optimization | 1 | 11 |

To give you practice on these topics, and pull the topics together, Edition 5 of the *CCIE Routing and Switching v5.0 Official Cert Guide, Volume 2* includes a large set of CD questions that mirror the types of questions expected for the Version 5.0 blueprint. By their very nature, these topics require the application of the knowledge listed throughout the book. This special section of questions provides a means to learn and practice these skills with a proportionally larger set of questions added specifically for this purpose.

These questions will be available to you in the practice test engine database, whether you take full exams or choose questions by category.

## About the *CCIE Routing and Switching v5.0 Official Cert Exam Guide, Volume 2*, Fifth Edition

This section provides a brief insight into the contents of the book, the major goals, and some of the book features that you will encounter when using this book.

## Book Organization

This volume contains six major parts. Beyond the chapters in these parts of the book, you will find several useful appendixes gathered in Part VIII.

Following is a description of each part's coverage:

- **Part I, "IP BGP Routing" (Chapters 1 and 2):** This part focuses on the details of BGP (Chapter 1), with Chapter 2 looking at BGP path attributes and how to influence BGP's choice of best path.

- **Part II, "QoS" (Chapters 3–5):** This part covers the more popular QoS tools, including some MQC-based tools, as well as several older tools, particularly FRTS. The chapters include coverage of classification and marking (Chapter 3), queuing and congestion avoidance (Chapter 4), plus shaping, policing, and link efficiency (Chapter 5).

- **Part III, "Wide-Area Networks" (Chapter 6):** The WAN coverage has been shrinking over the last few revisions to the CCIE R&S written exam. Chapter 6 includes some brief coverage of PPP and Frame Relay. Note that the previous version (V4.0) and current version (V5.0) of the blueprint include another WAN topic, MPLS, which is covered in Part VI, Chapter 11.

- **Part IV, "IP Multicast" (Chapters 7 and 8):** Chapter 7 covers multicast on LANs, including IGMP and how hosts join multicast groups. Chapter 8 covers multicast WAN topics.

- **Part V, "Security" (Chapters 9 and 10):** Given the CCIE tracks for both Security and Voice, Cisco has a small dilemma regarding whether to cover those topics on CCIE Routing and Switching, and if so, in how much detail. This part covers a variety of security topics appropriate for CCIE Routing and Switching. This chapter focuses on switch and router security.

- **Part VI, "Multiprotocol Label Switching (MPLS)" (Chapter 11):** As mentioned in the WAN section, the CCIE R&S exam's coverage of MPLS has been growing over the last two versions of the blueprint. This chapter focuses on enterprise-related topics such as core MPLS concepts and MPLS VPNs, including basic configuration.

- **Part VII, "Final Preparation" (Chapter 12):** This part provides a set of tools and a study plan to help you complete your preparation for the exams.

- **Part VIII, "Appendixes":**

  Appendix A, "Answers to the 'Do I Know This Already?' Quizzes": This appendix lists answers and explanations for the questions at the beginning of each chapter.

  Appendix B, "CCIE Exam Updates": As of the first printing of the book, this appendix contains only a few words that reference the web page for this book at www.ciscopress.com/title/9781587144912. As the blueprint evolves over time, the authors will post new materials at the website. Any future printings of the book will include the latest newly added materials in printed form inside Appendix B. If Cisco releases a major exam update, changes to the book will be available only in a new edition of the book and not on this site.

**NOTE**    Appendixes C through F and the Glossary are in printable, PDF format on the CD.

(CD-only) Appendix C, "Decimal-to-Binary Conversion Table": This appendix lists the decimal values 0 through 255, with their binary equivalents.

(CD-only) Appendix D, "IP Addressing Practice": This appendix lists several practice problems for IP subnetting and finding summary routes. The explanations to the answers use the shortcuts described in the book.

(CD-only) Appendix E, "Key Tables for CCIE Study": This appendix lists the most important tables from the core chapters of the book. The tables have much of the content removed so that you can use them as an exercise. You can print the PDF and then fill in the table from memory, checking your answers against the completed tables in Appendix F.

(CD-only) Appendix F, "Solutions for Key Tables for CCIE Study"

(CD-only) Glossary: The Glossary contains the key terms listed in the book.

# Book Features

The core chapters of this book have several features that help you make the best use of your time:

- **"Do I Know This Already?" Quizzes:** Each chapter begins with a quiz that helps you to determine the amount of time you need to spend studying that chapter. If you score yourself strictly, and you miss only one question, you might want to skip the core of the chapter and move on to the "Foundation Summary" section at the end of the chapter, which lets you review facts and spend time on other topics. If you miss more than one, you might want to spend some time reading the chapter or at least reading sections that cover topics about which you know you are weaker.

- **Foundation Topics:** These are the core sections of each chapter. They explain the protocols, concepts, and configurations for the topics in that chapter.

- **Foundation Summary:** The "Foundation Summary" section of this book departs from the typical features of the "Foundation Summary" section of other Cisco Press Exam Certification Guides. This section does not repeat any details from the "Foundation Topics" section; instead, it simply summarizes and lists facts related to the chapter but for which a longer or more detailed explanation is not warranted.

- **Key topics:** Throughout the "Foundation Topics" section, a Key Topic icon has been placed beside the most important areas for review. After reading a chapter, when doing your final preparation for the exam, take the time to flip through the chapters, looking for the Key Topic icons, and review those paragraphs, tables, figures, and lists.

- **Fill In Key Tables from Memory:** The more important tables from the chapters have been copied to PDF files available on the CD as Appendix E. The tables have most of the information removed. After printing these mostly empty tables, you can use them to improve your memory of the facts in the table by trying to fill them out. This tool should be useful for memorizing key facts. The CD-only Appendix F contains the completed tables so that you can check your work.

- **CD-based practice exam:** The companion CD contains multiple-choice questions and a testing engine. The CD includes 200 questions unique to the CD. As part of your final preparation, you should practice with these questions to help you get used to the exam-taking process, as well as to help refine and prove your knowledge of the exam topics.

- **Special question section for the "Implement Proposed Changes to a Network" section of the Blueprint:** To provide practice and perspectives on these exam topics, a special section of questions has been developed to help you prepare for these new types of questions.

- **Key terms and Glossary:** The more important terms mentioned in each chapter are listed at the end of each chapter under the heading "Definitions." The Glossary, found on the CD that comes with this book, lists all the terms from the chapters. When studying each chapter, you should review the key terms, and for those terms about which you are unsure of the definition, you can review the short definitions from the Glossary.

- **Further Reading:** Most chapters include a suggested set of books and websites for additional study on the same topics covered in that chapter. Often, these references will be useful tools for preparation for the CCIE Routing and Switching lab exam.

**Blueprint topics covered in this chapter:**

This chapter covers the following subtopics from the Cisco CCIE Routing and Switching written exam blueprint. Refer to the full blueprint in Table I-1 in the Introduction for more details on the topics covered in each chapter and their context within the blueprint.

- Next Hop

- Peering

- Troubleshooting a BGP Route That Will Not Install in the Routing Table

- MP-BGP

## CHAPTER 1

# Fundamentals of BGP Operations

This chapter covers what might be the single most important topic on both the CCIE Routing and Switching written and lab exams—Border Gateway Protocol (BGP) Version 4. This chapter focuses on how BGP accomplishes its fundamental tasks:

1. Forming neighbor relationships

2. Injecting routes into BGP from some other source

3. Exchanging those routes with other routers

4. Placing routes into IP routing tables

All of these BGP topics have close analogies with those of BGP's IGP cousins, but of course there are many differences in the details.

This chapter focuses on how BGP performs its central role as a routing protocol.

## "Do I Know This Already?" Quiz

Table 1-1 outlines the major headings in this chapter and the corresponding "Do I Know This Already?" quiz questions.

**Table 1-1** *"Do I Know This Already?" Foundation Topics Section-to-Question Mapping*

| Foundation Topics Section | Questions Covered in This Section | Score |
|---|---|---|
| Building BGP Neighbor Relationships | 1–3 | |
| Building the BGP Table | 4–8 | |
| Building the IP Routing Table | 9–12 | |
| Total Score | | |

To best use this pre-chapter assessment, remember to score yourself strictly. You can find the answers in Appendix A, "Answers to the 'Do I Know This Already?' Quizzes."

1.  Into which of the following neighbor states must a neighbor stabilize before BGP Update messages can be sent?

    a.  Active

    b.  Idle

    c.  Connected

    d.  Established

2.  BGP neighbors check several parameters before the neighbor relationship can be completed. Which of the following is not checked?

    a.  That the neighbor's router ID is not duplicated with other routers

    b.  That the **neighbor** command on one router matches the update source IP address on the other router

    c.  If eBGP, that the **neighbor** command points to an IP address in a connected network

    d.  That a router's **neighbor remote-as** command refers to the same autonomous system number (ASN) as in the other router's **router bgp** command (assuming that confederations are not used)

3.  A group of BGP routers, some with iBGP and some with eBGP connections, all use loopback IP addresses to refer to each other in their **neighbor** commands. Which of the following statements are false regarding the configuration of these peers?

    a.  IBGP peers require a **neighbor** *ip-address* **ibgp-multihop** command for the peer to become established.

    b.  eBGP peers require a **neighbor** *ip-address* **ebgp-multihop** command for the peer to become established.

    c.  eBGP and iBGP peers cannot be placed into the same peer group.

    d.  For eBGP peers, a router's BGP router ID must be equal to the IP address listed in the eBGP neighbor's **neighbor** command.

4.  A router has routes in the IP routing table for 20.0.0.0/8, 20.1.0.0/16, and 20.1.2.0/24. BGP on this router is configured with the **no auto-summary** command. Which of the following is true when using the BGP **network** command to cause these routes to be injected into the BGP table?

    a.  The **network 20.0.0.0** command would cause all three routes to be added to the BGP table.

    b.  The **network 20.0.0.0 mask 255.0.0.0** command would cause all three routes to be added to the BGP table.

    c.  The **network 20.1.0.0 mask 255.255.0.0** command would cause 20.1.0.0/16 and 20.1.2.0/24 to be added to the BGP table.

    d.  The **network 20.0.0.0** command would cause only 20.0.0.0/8 to be added to the BGP table.

5.  A router has configured redistribution of EIGRP routes into BGP using the command **redistribute eigrp 1 route-map fred**. This router's BGP configuration includes the **no auto-summary** command. Which of the following are true?

    a.  **route-map fred** can consider for redistribution routes listed in the IP routing table as EIGRP-learned routes.

    b.  **route-map fred** can consider for redistribution routes in the IP routing table listed as connected routes, but only if those interfaces are matched by EIGRP 1's **network** commands.

    c.  **route-map fred** can consider for redistribution routes that are listed in the EIGRP topology table as successor routes but that are not in the IP routing table because a lower administrative distance (AD) route from a competing routing protocol exists.

    d.  **route-map fred** can consider for redistribution routes listed in the IP routing table as EIGRP-learned routes, but only if those routes also have at least one feasible successor route.

6.  Using BGP, R1 has learned its best route to 9.1.0.0/16 from R3. R1 has a neighbor connection to R2, over a point-to-point serial link using subnet 8.1.1.4/30. R1 has **auto-summary** configured. Which of the following is true regarding what R1 advertises to R2?

    a.  R1 advertises only 9.0.0.0/8 to R2, and not 9.1.0.0/16.

    b.  If the **aggregate-address 9.0.0.0 255.0.0.0** BGP subcommand is configured, R1 advertises only 9.0.0.0/8 to R2, and not 9.1.0.0/16.

    c.  If the **network 9.0.0.0 mask 255.0.0.0** BGP subcommand is configured, R1 advertises only 9.0.0.0/8 to R2, and not 9.1.0.0/16.

    d.  None of the other answers is correct.

**7.** Which of the following statements are false regarding what routes a BGP router can advertise to a neighbor? (Assume that no confederations or route reflectors are in use.)

    **a.** To advertise a route to an eBGP peer, the route cannot have been learned from an iBGP peer.

    **b.** To advertise a route to an iBGP peer, the route must have been learned from an eBGP peer.

    **c.** The NEXT_HOP IP address must respond to a **ping** command.

    **d.** Do not advertise routes if the neighboring router's AS is in the AS_PATH.

    **e.** The route must be listed as **valid** in the output of the **show ip bgp** command.

**8.** Several different routes were injected into BGP through various methods on R1. Those routes were then advertised through iBGP to R2. R2 summarized the routes using the **aggregate-address summary-only** command, and then advertised through eBGP to R3. Which of the following are true about the ORIGIN path attribute of these routes?

    **a.** The routes injected using the **network** command on R1 have an ORIGIN value of IGP.

    **b.** The routes injected using the **redistribute ospf** command on R1 have an ORIGIN value of IGP.

    **c.** The routes injected using the **redistribute** command on R1 have an ORIGIN value of EGP.

    **d.** The routes injected using the **redistribute static** command on R1 have an ORIGIN value of incomplete.

    **e.** If the **as-set** option was not used, the summary route created on R2 has an ORIGIN code of IGP.

**9.** Which of the following statements is true regarding the use of BGP synchronization?

    **a.** With BGP synchronization enabled, a router can add an iBGP-learned route to its IP routing table only if that same prefix is also learned through eBGP.

    **b.** With BGP synchronization enabled, a router cannot consider an iBGP-learned route as a "best" route to that prefix unless the NEXT_HOP IP address matches an IGP route in the IP routing table.

    **c.** BGP synchronization can be safely disabled when the routers inside a single AS either create a full mesh of BGP peers or create a hub-and-spoke to the router that learns the prefix through eBGP.

    **d.** None of the other answers is correct.

**10.** Which of the following statements are true regarding the operation of BGP confederations?

    **a.** Confederation eBGP connections act like normal (nonconfederation) eBGP connections with regard to the need for the **neighbor ebgp-multihop** command for nonadjacent neighbor IP addresses.

    **b.** iBGP-learned routes are advertised over confederation eBGP connections.

    **c.** A full mesh of iBGP peers inside a confederation sub-AS is not required.

    **d.** None of the other answers is correct.

**11.** R1 is BGP peered to R2, R3, R4, and R5 inside ASN 1, with no other peer connections inside the AS. R1 is a route reflector, serving R2 and R3 only. Each router also has an eBGP connection, through which it learns the following routes: 1.0.0.0/8 by R1, 2.0.0.0/8 by R2, 3.0.0.0/8 by R3, 4.0.0.0/8 by R4, and 5.0.0.0/8 by R5. Which of the following are true regarding the propagation of these routes?

    **a.** NLRI 1.0.0.0/8 is forwarded by R1 to each of the other routers.

    **b.** NLRI 2.0.0.0/8 is sent by R2 to R1, with R1 forwarding only to R3.

    **c.** NLRI 3.0.0.0/8 is sent by R3 to R1, with R1 forwarding to R2, R4, and R5.

    **d.** NLRI 4.0.0.0/8 is sent by R4 to R1, but R1 does not forward the information to R2 or R3.

    **e.** NLRI 5.0.0.0/8 is sent by R5 to R1; R1 reflects the route to R2 and R3, but not to R4.

**12.** R1 is in confederation ASN 65001; R2 and R3 are in confederation ASN 65023. R1 is peered to R2, and R2 is peered to R3. These three routers are perceived to be in AS 1 by eBGP peers. Which of the following is true regarding the configuration of these routers?

    **a.** Each of the three routers has a **router bgp 1** command.

    **b.** Both R2 and R3 need a **bgp confederation peers 65001** BGP subcommand.

    **c.** R1 needs a **bgp confederation identifier 1** BGP subcommand.

    **d.** Both R2 and R3 need a **bgp confederation identifier 65023** BGP subcommand.

# Foundation Topics

Like Interior Gateway Protocols (IGP), BGP exchanges topology information for routers to eventually learn the best routes to a set of IP prefixes. Unlike IGPs, BGP does not use a metric to select the best route among alternate routes to the same destination. Instead, BGP uses several BGP *path attributes (PA)* and an involved decision process when choosing between multiple possible routes to the same subnet.

BGP uses the BGP *autonomous system path (AS_PATH)* PA as its default metric mechanism when none of the other PAs has been overly set and configured. Generally speaking, BGP uses PAs to describe the characteristics of a route; this introduces and explains a wide variety of BGP PAs. The AS_PATH attribute lists the path, as defined by a sequence of *autonomous system numbers (ASN)* through which a packet must pass to reach a prefix. Figure 1-1 shows an example.

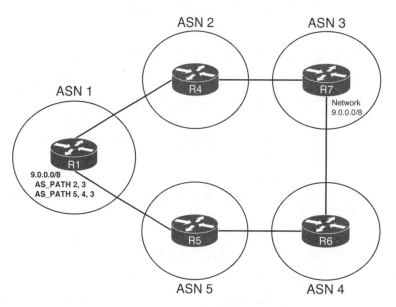

**Figure 1-1**   *BGP AS_PATHs and Path Vector Logic*

Figure 1-1 shows a classic case of how BGP uses *path vector* logic to choose routes. In the figure, R1 learns of two AS_PATHs by which to reach 9.0.0.0/8—through ASNs 2-3 and through ASNs 5-4-3. If none of the routers has used routing policies to influence other PAs that influence BGP's choice of which route is best, R1 will choose the shortest AS_PATH—in this case, AS_PATH 2-3. In effect, BGP treats the AS_PATH as a vector, and the length of the vector (the number of ASNs in the path) determines the best route. With BGP, the term *route* still refers to traditional hop-by-hop IP routes, but the term *path* refers to the sequence of autonomous systems used to reach a particular destination.

This chapter follows a similar sequence as several of the IGP chapters. First, the text focuses on neighbor relationships, followed by how BGP exchanges routing information with its neighbors. The chapter ends with a section covering how BGP adds IP routes to a router's IP routing table based on the BGP topology table.

## Building BGP Neighbor Relationships

BGP neighbors form a TCP connection with each neighbor, sending BGP messages over the connections—culminating in *BGP Update* messages that contain the routing information. Each router explicitly configures its neighbors' IP addresses, using these definitions to tell a router with which IP addresses to attempt a TCP connection. Also, if a router receives a TCP connection request (to BGP port 179) from a source IP address that is not configured as a BGP neighbor, the router rejects the request.

After the TCP connection is established, BGP begins with BGP *Open* messages. After a pair of BGP Open messages has been exchanged, the neighbors have reached the *established* state, which is the stable state of two working BGP peers. At this point, BGP Update messages can be exchanged.

This section examines many of the details about protocols and configuration for BGP neighbor formation. If you are already familiar with BGP, Table 1-2 summarizes some of the key facts found in this section.

**Key Topic**

**Table 1-2**  *BGP Neighbor Summary Table*

| BGP Feature | Description and Values |
|---|---|
| TCP port | 179 |
| Setting the keepalive interval and hold time (using the **bgp timers** *keepalive holdtime* router subcommand or **neighbor timers** command, per neighbor) | Default to 60 and 180 seconds; define time between keepalives and time for which silence means that the neighbor has failed |
| What makes a neighbor internal BGP (iBGP)? | Neighbor is in the same AS |
| What makes a neighbor external BGP (eBGP)? | Neighbor is in another AS |
| How is the BGP router ID (RID) determined? | In order: The **bgp router-id** command The highest IP of an up/up loopback at the time that the BGP process starts The highest IP of another up/up interface at the time that the BGP process starts |
| How is the source IP address used to reach a neighbor determined? | Defined with the **neighbor update-source** command; or, by default, uses the outgoing interface IP address for the route used to reach the neighbor |

| BGP Feature | Description and Values |
|---|---|
| How is the destination IP address used to reach a neighbor determined? | Explicitly defined in the **neighbor** command |
| Auto-summary* | Off by default, enabled with the **auto-summary** router subcommand |
| Neighbor authentication | MD5 only, using the **neighbor password** command |

* Cisco changed the IOS default for BGP **auto-summary** to be disabled as of Cisco IOS Software Release 12.3.

## Internal BGP Neighbors

A BGP router considers each neighbor to be either an *internal BGP (iBGP)* peer or an *external BGP (eBGP)* peer. Each BGP router resides in a single AS, so neighbor relationships are either with other routers in the same AS (iBGP neighbors) or with routers in other autonomous systems (eBGP neighbors). The two types of neighbors differ only slightly in regard to forming neighbor relationships, with more significant differences in how the type of neighbor (iBGP or eBGP) impacts the BGP update process and the addition of routes to the routing tables.

iBGP peers often use loopback interface IP addresses for BGP peering to achieve higher availability. Inside a single AS, the physical topology often has at least two routes between each pair of routers. If BGP peers use an interface IP address for their TCP connections, and that interface fails, there still might be a route between the two routers, but the underlying BGP TCP connection will fail. Anytime two BGP peers have more than one route through which they can reach the other router, peering using loopbacks makes the most sense.

Several examples that follow demonstrate BGP neighbor configuration and protocols, beginning with Example 1-1. The example shows some basic BGP configuration for iBGP peers R1, R2, and R3 in AS 123, with the following features, based on Figure 1-2.

- The three routers in ASN 123 will form iBGP neighbor relationships with each other (full mesh).

- R1 will use the **bgp router-id** command to configure its RID, rather than use a loopback.

- R3 uses a **peer-group** configuration for neighbors R1 and R2. This allows fewer configuration commands, and improves processing efficiency by having to prepare only one set of outbound Update packets for the peer group. (Identical Updates are sent to all peers in the peer group.)

- The R1-R3 relationship uses BGP MD5 authentication, which is the only type of BGP authentication supported in Cisco IOS.

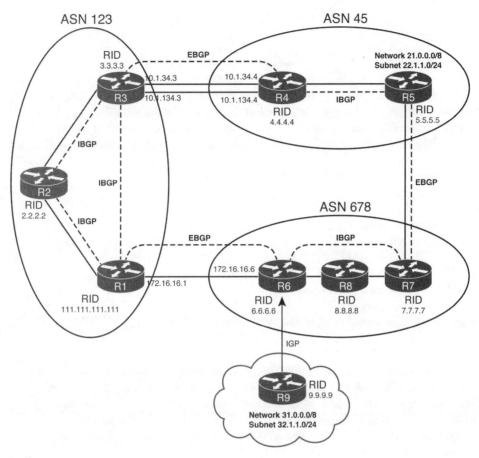

**Figure 1-2**    *Sample Network for BGP Neighbor Configuration*

**Example 1-1**    *Basic iBGP Configuration of Neighbors*

```
! R1 Config—R1 correctly sets its update-source to 1.1.1.1 for both R2 and R3,
! in order to match the R2 and R3 neighbor commands. The first three highlighted
! commands below were not typed, but added automatically as defaults by IOS 12.3
! in fact, IOS 12.3 docs imply that the defaults of sync and auto-summary at
! IOS 12.2 has changed to no sync and no auto-summary as of IOS 12.3. Also, R1
! knows that neighbors 2.2.2.2 and 3.3.3.3 are iBGP because their remote-as values
! match R1's router BGP command.
interface Loopback1
 ip address 1.1.1.1 255.255.255.255
!
router bgp 123
 no synchronization
 bgp router-id 111.111.111.111
 bgp log-neighbor-changes
 neighbor 2.2.2.2 remote-as 123
```

```
 neighbor 2.2.2.2 update-source Loopback1
 neighbor 3.3.3.3 remote-as 123
 neighbor 3.3.3.3 password secret-pw
 neighbor 3.3.3.3 update-source Loopback1
 no auto-summary
! R3 Config—R3 uses a peer group called "my-as" for combining commands related
! to R1 and R2. Note that not all parameters must be in the peer group: R3-R2 does
! not use authentication, but R3-R1 does, so the neighbor password command was
! not placed inside the peer group, but instead on a neighbor 1.1.1.1 command.
interface Loopback1
 ip address 3.3.3.3 255.255.255.255
!
router bgp 123
 no synchronization
 bgp log-neighbor-changes
 neighbor my-as peer-group
 neighbor my-as remote-as 123
 neighbor my-as update-source Loopback1
 neighbor 1.1.1.1 peer-group my-as
 neighbor 1.1.1.1 password secret-pw
 neighbor 2.2.2.2 peer-group my-as
 no auto-summary
! Next, R1 has two established peers, but the fact that the status is "established"
! is implied by not having the state listed on the right side of the output, under
! the heading State/PfxRcd. Once established, that column lists the number of
! prefixes learned via BGP Updates received from each peer. Note also R1's
! configured RID, and the fact that it is not used as the update source.
R1# show ip bgp summary
BGP router identifier 111.111.111.111, local AS number 123
BGP table version is 1, main routing table version 1
Neighbor        V    AS MsgRcvd MsgSent   TblVer  InQ OutQ Up/Down  State/PfxRcd
2.2.2.2         4   123      59      59        0    0    0 00:56:52           0
3.3.3.3         4   123      64      64        0    0    0 00:11:14           0
```

A few features in Example 1-1 are particularly important. First, note that the configuration does not overtly define peers as iBGP or eBGP. Instead, each router examines its own ASN as defined in the **router bgp** command, and compares that value to the neighbor's ASN listed in the **neighbor remote-as** command. If they match, the peer is iBGP; if not, the peer is eBGP.

R3 in Example 1-1 shows how to use the **peer-group** construct to reduce the number of configuration commands. BGP peer groups do not allow any new BGP configuration settings; they simply allow you to group BGP neighbor configuration settings into a group, and then apply that set of settings to a neighbor using the **neighbor peer-group** command. Additionally, BGP builds one set of Update messages for the peer group, applying routing policies for the entire group—rather than one router at a time—thereby reducing some BGP processing and memory overhead.

## External BGP Neighbors

The physical topology between eBGP peers is often a single link, mainly because the connection is between different companies in different autonomous systems. As a result, eBGP peering can simply use the interface IP addresses for redundancy, because if the link fails, the TCP connection will fail because there is no longer an IP route between the peers. For example, in Figure 1-2, the R1-R6 eBGP peering uses interface IP addresses defined in the **neighbor** commands.

When IP redundancy exists between two eBGP peers, the eBGP **neighbor** commands should use loopback IP addresses to take advantage of that redundancy. For example, two parallel links exist between R3 and R4. With **neighbor** commands that reference loopback addresses, either of these links could fail, but the TCP connection would remain. Example 1-2 shows additional configuration for the network in Figure 1-2, showing the use of loopbacks between R3 and R4, and interface addresses between R1 and R6.

**Example 1-2**   *Basic eBGP Configuration of Neighbors*

```
! R1 Config -This example shows only commands added since Example 1-1.
router bgp 123
 neighbor 172.16.16.6 remote-as 678
! R1 does not have a neighbor 172.16.16.6 update-source command configured. R1
! uses its s0/0/0.6 IP address, 172.16.16.1, because R1's route to 172.16.16.6
! uses s0/0/0.6 as the outgoing interface, as seen below.
R1# show ip route 172.16.16.6
Routing entry for 172.16.16.0/24
  Known via "connected", distance 0, metric 0 (connected, via interface)
  Routing Descriptor Blocks:
  * directly connected, via Serial0/0/0.6
      Route metric is 0, traffic share count is 1
R1# show ip int brief | include 0/0/0.6
Serial0/0/0.6                172.16.16.1     YES manual up              up
! R3 Config—Because R3 refers to R4's loopback (4.4.4.4), and R4 is an eBGP
! peer, R3 and R4 have added the neighbor ebgp-multihop command to set TTL to 2.
! R3's update source must be identified as its loopback in order to match
! R4's neighbor 3.3.3.3 commands.
router bgp 123
 neighbor 4.4.4.4 remote-as 45
 neighbor 4.4.4.4 update-source loopback1
 neighbor 4.4.4.4 ebgp-multihop 2
! R3 now has three working neighbors. Also note the three TCP connections, one for
! each BGP peer. Note that because R3 is listed using a dynamic port number, and
! R4 as using port 179, R3 actually initiated the TCP connection to R4.
R3# show ip bgp summary
BGP router identifier 3.3.3.3, local AS number 123
BGP table version is 1, main routing table version 1
```

```
Neighbor        V    AS MsgRcvd MsgSent    TblVer   InQ OutQ Up/Down   State/PfxRcd
1.1.1.1         4   123    247     247         0     0    0 03:14:49          0
2.2.2.2         4   123    263     263         0     0    0 03:15:07          0
4.4.4.4         4    45     17      17         0     0    0 00:00:11          0
R3# show tcp brief
TCB        Local Address          Foreign Address          (state)
649DD08C   3.3.3.3.179            2.2.2.2.43521            ESTAB
649DD550   3.3.3.3.179            1.1.1.1.27222            ESTAB
647D928C   3.3.3.3.21449          4.4.4.4.179              ESTAB
```

The eBGP configurations differ from iBGP configuration in a couple of small ways. First, the **neighbor remote-as** commands refer to a different AS than does the **router bgp** command, which implies that the peer is an eBGP peer. Second, R3 had to configure the **neighbor 4.4.4.4 ebgp-multihop 2** command (and R4 with a similar command) or the peer connection would not have formed. For eBGP connections, Cisco IOS defaults the IP packet's TTL field to a value of 1, based on the assumption that the interface IP addresses will be used for peering (like R1-R6 in Example 1-2). In this example, if R3 had not used multihop, it would have sent packets to R4 with TTL 1. R4 would have received the packet (TTL 1 at that point) and then attempted to route the packet to its loopback interface—a process that would decrement the TTL to 0, causing R4 to drop the packet. So, even though the router is only one hop away, think of the loopback as being on the other side of the router, requiring that extra hop.

## Checks Before Becoming BGP Neighbors

Similar to IGPs, BGP checks certain requirements before another router can become a neighbor, reaching the BGP established state. Most of the settings are straightforward; the only tricky part relates to the use of IP addresses. The following list describes the checks that BGP performs when forming neighbor relationships:

**Key Topic**

1. The router must receive a TCP connection request with a source address that the router finds in a BGP **neighbor** command.

2. A router's ASN (on the **router bgp** *asn* command) must match the neighboring router's reference to that ASN with its **neighbor remote-as** *asn* command. (This requirement is not true of confederation configurations.)

3. The BGP RIDs of the two routers must not be the same.

4. If configured, MD5 authentication must pass.

Figure 1-3 shows the first three items in the list graphically, with R3 initiating a BGP TCP connection to R1. The circled numbers 1, 2, and 3 in the figure correspond to the item numbers in the previous list. Note that R1's check at Step 2 uses the **neighbor** command R1 identified as part of Step 1.

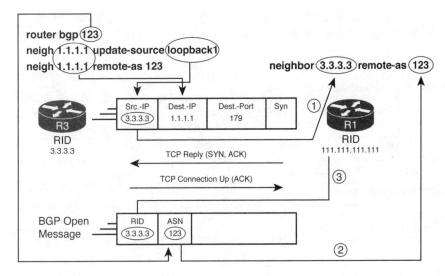

Note: R3's Loopback IP Address is 3.3.3.3

**Figure 1-3**  *BGP Neighbor Parameter Checking*

In Figure 1-3, R3 initiates a TCP connection with its update source IP address (3.3.3.3) as the source address of the packet. The first check occurs when R1 receives the first packet, looks at the source IP address of the packet (3.3.3.3), and finds that address in a **neighbor** command. The second check has R1 comparing R3's stated ASN (in R3's BGP Open message) to R1's **neighbor** command it identified at Step 1. Step 3 checks to ensure that the BGP RIDs are unique, with the BGP Open message stating the sender's BGP RID.

While the check at Step 1 might seem intuitive, interestingly, the reverse bit of logic does not have to be true for the neighbors to come up. For example, if R1 did not have a **neighbor 3.3.3.3 update-source 1.1.1.1** command, the process shown in Figure 1-3 would still work. Succinctly put, only one of the two routers' update source IP addresses needs to be in the other router's **neighbor** command for the neighbor to come up. Examples 1-1 and 1-2 showed the correct update source on both routers, and that makes good sense, but it works with only one of the two.

BGP uses a *keepalive timer* to define how often that router sends BGP keepalive messages, and a *Hold timer* to define how long a router will wait without receiving a keepalive message before resetting a neighbor connection. The Open message includes each router's stated keepalive timer. If they do not match, each router uses the lower of the values for each of the two timers, respectively. *Mismatched settings do not prevent the routers from becoming neighbors.*

## BGP Messages and Neighbor States

The desired state for BGP neighbors is the established state. In that state, the routers have formed a TCP connection, and they have exchanged Open messages, with the parameter checks having passed. At this point, topology information can be exchanged using Update messages. Table 1-3 lists the BGP neighbor states, along with some of their characteristics. Note that if the IP addresses mismatch, the neighbors settle into an active state.

**Table 1-3**  *BGP Neighbor States*

| State | Listen for TCP? | Initiate TCP? | TCP Up? | Open Sent? | Open Received? | Neighbor Up? |
|---|---|---|---|---|---|---|
| Idle | No | | | | | |
| Connect | Yes | | | | | |
| Active | Yes | Yes | | | | |
| Open sent | Yes | Yes | Yes | Yes | | |
| Open confirm | Yes | Yes | Yes | Yes | Yes | |
| Established | Yes | Yes | Yes | Yes | Yes | Yes |

## BGP Message Types

BGP uses four basic messages. Table 1-4 lists the message types and provides a brief description of each.

**Table 1-4**  *BGP Message Types*

| Message | Purpose |
|---|---|
| Open | Used to establish a neighbor relationship and exchange basic parameters. |
| Keepalive | Used to maintain the neighbor relationship, with nonreceipt of a keepalive message within the negotiated Hold timer causing BGP to bring down the neighbor connection. (The timers can be configured with the **bgp timers** *keepalive holdtime* subcommand or the **neighbor** [*ip-address* \| *peer-group-name*] **timers** *keepalive holdtime* BGP subcommand.) |
| Update | Used to exchange routing information, as covered more fully in the next section. |
| Notification | Used when BGP errors occur; causes a reset to the neighbor relationship when sent. |

## Purposefully Resetting BGP Peer Connections

Example 1-3 shows how to reset neighbor connections by using the **neighbor shutdown** command and, along the way, shows the various BGP neighbor states. The example uses Routers R1 and R6 from Figure 1-2, as configured in Example 1-2.

**Example 1-3**  *Examples of Neighbor States (Continued)*

```
! R1 shuts down R6's peer connection. debug ip bgp shows moving to a down state,
! which shows as "Idle (Admin)" under show ip bgp summary.
R1# debug ip bgp
BGP debugging is on for address family: BGP IPv4
R1# conf t
Enter configuration commands, one per line.  End with CNTL/Z.
R1(config)# router bgp 123
R1(config-router)# neigh 172.16.16.6 shutdown
R1#
*Mar  4 21:01:45.946: BGP: 172.16.16.6 went from Established to Idle
*Mar  4 21:01:45.946: %BGP-5-ADJCHANGE: neighbor 172.16.16.6 Down Admin. shutdown
*Mar  4 21:01:45.946: BGP: 172.16.16.6 closing
R1# show ip bgp summary | include 172.16.16.6
172.16.16.6    4    678    353    353    0   0   0 00:00:06 Idle (Admin)
! Next, the no neighbor shutdown command reverses the admin state. The various
! debug messages (with some omitted) list the various states. Also note that the
! final message is the one log message in this example that occurs due to the
! default configuration of bgp log-neighbor-changes. The rest are the result of
! a debug ip bgp command.
R1# conf t
Enter configuration commands, one per line.  End with CNTL/Z.
R1(config)# router bgp 123
R1(config-router)# no neigh 172.16.16.6 shutdown
*Mar  4 21:02:16.958: BGP: 172.16.16.6 went from Idle to Active
*Mar  4 21:02:16.958: BGP: 172.16.16.6 open active, delay 15571ms
*Mar  4 21:02:29.378: BGP: 172.16.16.6 went from Idle to Connect
*Mar  4 21:02:29.382: BGP: 172.16.16.6 rcv message type 1, length (excl. header) 26
*Mar  4 21:02:29.382: BGP: 172.16.16.6 rcv OPEN, version 4, holdtime 180 seconds
*Mar  4 21:02:29.382: BGP: 172.16.16.6 went from Connect to OpenSent
*Mar  4 21:02:29.382: BGP: 172.16.16.6 sending OPEN, version 4, my as: 123,
  holdtime 180    seconds
*Mar  4 21:02:29.382: BGP: 172.16.16.6 rcv OPEN w/ OPTION parameter len: 16
BGP: 172.16.16.6 rcvd OPEN w/ remote AS 678
*Mar  4 21:02:29.382: BGP: 172.16.16.6 went from OpenSent to OpenConfirm
*Mar  4 21:02:29.382: BGP: 172.16.16.6 send message type 1, length (incl. header)
  45
*Mar  4 21:02:29.394: BGP: 172.16.16.6 went from OpenConfirm to Established
*Mar  4 21:02:29.398: %BGP-5-ADJCHANGE: neighbor 10.16.16.6 Up
```

All BGP neighbors can be reset with the **clear ip bgp** * EXEC command, which, like the **neighbor shutdown** command, resets the neighbor connection, closes the TCP connection to that neighbor, and removes all entries from the BGP table learned from that neighbor. The **clear** command will be shown in the rest of the chapter as needed, including in coverage of how to clear just some neighbors.

> **Note**   The **clear** command can also be used to implement routing policy changes without resetting the neighbor completely, using a feature called *soft reconfiguration*, as covered in the Chapter 2 section, "Soft Reconfiguration."

## Building the BGP Table

The BGP *topology table*, also called the BGP *Routing Information Base (RIB)*, holds the *network layer reachability information (NLRI)* learned by BGP, as well as the associated PAs. An NLRI is simply an IP prefix and prefix length. This section focuses on the process of how BGP injects NLRI into a router's BGP table, followed by how routers advertise their associated PAs and NLRI to neighbors.

> **Note**   Technically, BGP does not advertise routes; rather, it advertises PAs plus a set of NLRI that shares the same PA values. However, most people simply refer to NLRI as *BGP prefixes* or *BGP routes*. This book uses all three terms. However, because there is a distinction between a BGP route in the BGP table and an IP route in the IP routing table, the text takes care to refer to the BGP table or IP routing table to distinguish the two tables.

### Injecting Routes/Prefixes into the BGP Table

Unsurprisingly, an individual BGP router adds entries to its local BGP table by using the same general methods used by IGPs: by using the **network** command, by hearing the topology information through an Update message from a neighbor, or by redistributing from another routing protocol. The next few sections show examples of how a local BGP router adds routes to the BGP table by methods other than learning them from a BGP neighbor.

### BGP network Command

This section, and the next section, assumes that the BGP **no auto-summary** command has been configured. Note that as of the Cisco IOS Software Release 12.3 Mainline, **no auto-summary** is the default; earlier releases defaulted to use **auto-summary**. Following that, the section "Impact of Auto-Summary on Redistributed Routes and the network Command," later in this chapter, discusses the impact of the **auto-summary** command on both the **network** command and the **redistribute** command.

The BGP **network** router subcommand differs significantly from the **network** command used by IGPs. The BGP **network** command instructs that router's BGP process to do the following:

**Key Topic**

Look for a route in the router's current IP routing table that exactly matches the parameters of the **network** command; if the IP route exists, put the equivalent NLRI into the local BGP table.

With this logic, connected routes, static routes, or IGP routes could be taken from the IP routing table and placed into the BGP table for later advertisement. When the router removes that route from its IP routing table, BGP then removes the NLRI from the BGP table, and notifies neighbors that the route has been withdrawn.

Note that the IP route must be matched exactly when the **no auto-summary** command is configured or used by default.

Table 1-5 lists a few of the key features of the BGP **network** command, whose generic syntax is

```
network {network-number [mask network-mask]} [route-map map-tag]
```

**Table 1-5**  *Key Features of the BGP* network *Command*

| Feature | Implication |
|---|---|
| No mask is configured | Assumes the default classful mask. |
| Matching logic with **no auto-summary** configured | An IP route must match both the prefix and prefix length (mask). |
| Matching logic with **auto-summary** configured | If the **network** command lists a classful network, it matches if any subnets of the classful network exist. |
| NEXT_HOP of BGP route added to the BGP table* | Uses next hop of IP route. |
| Maximum number injected by the **network** command into one BGP process | Limited by NVRAM and RAM. |
| Purpose of the **route-map** option on the **network** command | Can be used to filter routes and manipulate PAs, including NEXT_HOP*. |

*NEXT_HOP is a BGP PA that denotes the next-hop IP address that should be used to reach the NLRI.

Example 1-4 shows a sample **network** command as implemented on R5 of Figure 1-4 (R5's BGP neighbors have been shut down so that the BGP table shows only BGP table entries created by the **network** commands on R5). In Example 1-4, R5 uses two **network** commands to add 21.0.0.0/8 and 22.1.1.0/24 to its BGP table.

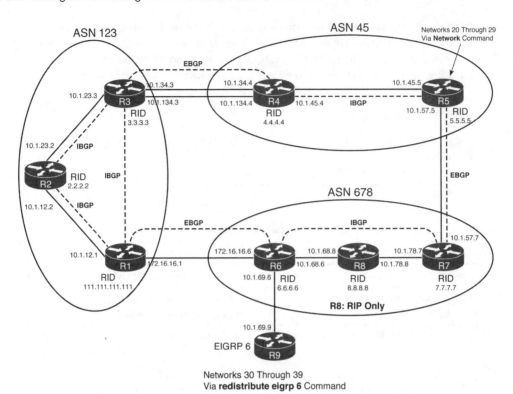

**Figure 1-4**  *Sample BGP Network, with IP Addresses*

**Example 1-4**  *Examples of Populating the BGP Table Through the* **network** *Command*

```
! On R5, the network commands specifically match prefixes 21.0.0.0/8 and
! 22.1.1.0/24. The omission of the mask on the first command implies the associated
! classful mask of 255.0.0.0, as the IP address listed (21.0.0.0) is a class A
! address.
router bgp 45
 no synchronization
 bgp log-neighbor-changes
 network 21.0.0.0
 network 22.1.1.0 mask 255.255.255.0
! The neighbor commands are not shown, as they are not pertinent to the topics
! covered in this example.
! Next, the two routes matched by the network commands are indeed in the IP
! routing table. Note that the route to 21.0.0.0/8 is a connected route, and the
! route to 22.1.1.0/24 is a static route.
R5# show ip route | incl 21 | 22
C      21.0.0.0/8 is directly connected, Loopback20
       22.0.0.0/24 is subnetted, 1 subnets
S      22.1.1.0 [1/0] via 10.1.5.9
! Below, the prefixes have been added to the BGP table. Note that the NEXT_HOP
```

```
! PA has been set to 0.0.0.0 for the route (21.0.0.0/8) that was taken from a
! connected route, with the NEXT_HOP for 22.1.1.0/24 matching the IP route.
R5# show ip bgp
BGP table version is 38, local router ID is 5.5.5.5
Status codes: s suppressed, d damped, h history, * valid, > best, i - internal,
              r RIB-failure, S Stale
Origin codes: i - IGP, e - EGP, ? - incomplete

   Network          Next Hop          Metric LocPrf Weight Path
*> 21.0.0.0         0.0.0.0                0          32768 i
*> 22.1.1.0/24      10.1.5.9               0          32768 i
```

## Redistributing from an IGP, Static, or Connected Route

The BGP **redistribute** subcommand can redistribute static, connected, and IGP-learned routes. This section covers a few nuances that are unique to BGP.

BGP does not use the concept of calculating a metric for each alternate route to reach a particular prefix. Instead, BGP uses a stepwise decision process that examines various PAs to determine the best route. As a result, redistribution into BGP does not require any consideration of setting metrics. However, a router might need to apply a route map to the redistribution function to manipulate PAs, which in turn affects the BGP decision process. If a metric is assigned to a route injected into BGP, BGP assigns that metric value to the BGP *Multi-Exit Discriminator (MED)* PA, which is commonly referred to as *metric*.

**Note**  Although this point is not unique to BGP, keep in mind that redistribution from an IGP causes two types of routes to be taken from the routing table—those learned by the routing protocol and those connected routes for which that routing protocol matches with a **network** command.

Example 1-5 shows R6 (from Figure 1-4) filling its BGP table through route redistribution from Enhanced IGRP (EIGRP) process 6 (as configured in Example 1-5 with the **router eigrp 6** command) and redistributing a single static route. EIGRP on R6 learns routes only for networks 30 through 39. The goals of this example are as follows:

- Redistribute EIGRP routes for networks 31 and 32.

- Redistribute the static route to network 34, and set the MED (metric) to 9.

- Do not accidentally redistribute the connected routes that are matched by EIGRP's **network** commands.

- Use the Cisco IOS Release 12.3 default setting of **no auto-summary**.

Example 1-5 shows the mistake of accidentally redistributing additional routes—the connected subnets of network 10.0.0.0 matched by EIGRP **network** commands. Later in the example, a route map is added to prevent the problem.

**Example 1-5**   *Example of Populating the BGP Table Through Redistribution*

```
! R6 redistributes EIGRP 6 routes and static routes below, setting the metric on
! redistributed static routes to 9. Note that EIGRP 6 matches subnets 10.1.68.0/24
! and 10.1.69.0/24 with its network command.
router bgp 678
 redistribute static metric 9
 redistribute eigrp 6
!
router eigrp 6
 network 10.0.0.0
!
ip route 34.0.0.0 255.255.255.0 null0
! Commands unrelated to populating the local BGP table are omitted.
! R6 has met the goal of injecting 31 and 32 from EIGRP, and 34 from static.
! It also accidentally picked up two subnets of 10.0.0.0/8 because EIGRP's network
! 10.0.0.0 command matched these connected subnets.
R6# show ip bgp
BGP table version is 1, local router ID is 6.6.6.6
Status codes: s suppressed, d damped, h history, * valid, > best, i - internal,
              r RIB-failure, S Stale
Origin codes: i - IGP, e - EGP, ? - incomplete
   Network          Next Hop          Metric LocPrf Weight Path
*> 10.1.68.0/24     0.0.0.0                0          32768 ?
*> 10.1.69.0/24     0.0.0.0                0          32768 ?
*> 31.0.0.0         10.1.69.9         156160          32768 ?
*> 32.1.1.0/24      10.1.69.9         156160          32768 ?
*> 34.0.0.0/24      0.0.0.0                9          32768 ?
! Below, note the metrics for the two EIGRP routes. The show ip bgp command output
! above shows how BGP assigned the MED (metric) that same value.
R6# show ip route eigrp
     32.0.0.0/24 is subnetted, 1 subnets
D       32.1.1.0 [90/156160] via 10.1.69.9, 00:12:17, FastEthernet0/0
D    31.0.0.0/8 [90/156160] via 10.1.69.9, 00:12:17, FastEthernet0/0
! Below, the redistribute eigrp command has been changed to the following, using
! a route map to only allow routes in networks in the 30s.
redist eigrp 6 route-map just-30-something
! The route map and ACLs used for the filtering are shown next. As a result, the
! two subnets of 10.0.0.0/8 will not be redistributed into the BGP table.
R6# show route-map
route-map just-30-something, permit, sequence 10
  Match clauses:
    ip address (access-lists): permit-30-39
  Set clauses:
  Policy routing matches: 0 packets, 0 bytes
R6# show access-list
```

```
Standard IP access list permit-30-39
    10 permit 32.0.0.0, wildcard bits 7.255.255.255 (1538 matches)
    20 permit 30.0.0.0, wildcard bits 1.255.255.255 (1130 matches)
```

Also note that the NEXT_HOP PA for each route either matches the next hop of the redistributed route or is 0.0.0.0 for connected routes and routes to null0.

### Impact of Auto-Summary on Redistributed Routes and the network Command

As it does with IGPs, the BGP **auto-summary** command causes a classful summary route to be created if any component subnet of that summary exists. However, unlike IGPs, the BGP **auto-summary** router subcommand causes BGP to summarize only those routes *injected because of redistribution on that router*. BGP **auto-summary** does not look for classful network boundaries in the topology, and it does not look at routes already in the BGP table. It simply looks for routes injected into the BGP because of the **redistribute** and **network** commands on that same router.

The logic differs slightly based on whether the route is injected with the **redistribute** command or the **network** command. The logic for the two commands is summarized as follows:

- **redistribute:** If any subnets of a classful network would be redistributed, do not redistribute, but instead redistribute a route for the classful network.

- **network:** If a **network** command lists a classful network number, with the classful default mask or no mask, and any subnets of the classful network exist, inject a route for the classful network.

While the preceding definitions are concise for study purposes, a few points deserve further emphasis and explanation. First, for redistribution, the **auto-summary** command causes the redistribution process to inject only classful networks into the local BGP table, and no subnets. The **network** command, with **auto-summary** configured, still injects subnets based on the same logic already described in this chapter. In addition to that logic, if a **network** command matches the classful network number, BGP injects the classful network, as long as at least any one subnet of that classful network exists in the IP routing table.

Example 1-6 shows an example that points out the impact of the **auto-summary** command. The example follows these steps on Router R5 from Figure 1-2:

1. 10.15.0.0/16 is injected into BGP because of the **redistribute** command.

2. Auto-summary is configured, BGP is cleared, and now only 10.0.0.0/8 is in the BGP table.

3. Auto-summary and redistribution are disabled.

4. The **network 10.0.0.0** command, **network 10.12.0.0 mask 255.254.0.0** command, and **network 10.14.0.0 mask 255.255.0.0** command are configured. Only the last of these three commands exactly matches a current route, so only that route is injected into BGP.

5. Auto-summary is enabled, causing 10.0.0.0/8 to be injected, as well as the original 10.14.0.0/16 route.

**Example 1-6**  *Auto-Summary Impact on Routing Tables*

```
! R5 has shut down all neighbor connections, so the output of show ip bgp only
! shows routes injected on R5.
! Step 1 is below. Only 10.15.0.0/16 is injected by the current configuration. Note
! that the unrelated lines of output have been removed, and route-map only15 only
! matches 10.15.0.0/16.
R5# show run | be router bgp
router bgp 5
 no synchronization
 redistribute connected route-map only15
 no auto-summary
! Below, note the absence of 10.0.0.0/8 as a route, and the presence of
! 10.15.0.0/16,
! as well as the rest of the routes used in the upcoming steps.
R5# show ip route 10.0.0.0
Routing entry for 10.0.0.0/8, 4 known subnets
  Attached (4 connections)
  Redistributing via eigrp 99, bgp 5
  Advertised by bgp 5 route-map only15
C       10.14.0.0/16 is directly connected, Loopback10
C       10.15.0.0/16 is directly connected, Loopback10
C       10.12.0.0/16 is directly connected, Loopback10
C       10.13.0.0/16 is directly connected, Loopback10
! Only 10.15.0.0/16 is injected into BGP.
R5# show ip bgp
BGP table version is 2, local router ID is 5.5.5.5
Status codes: s suppressed, d damped, h history, * valid, > best, i - internal,
              r RIB-failure, S Stale
Origin codes: i - IGP, e - EGP, ? - incomplete

   Network          Next Hop           Metric LocPrf Weight Path
*> 10.15.0.0/16     0.0.0.0                 0         32768 ?
! Next, step 2, where auto-summary is enabled. Now, 10.15.0.0/16 is no longer
! injected into BGP, but classful 10.0.0.0/8 is.
R5# conf t
Enter configuration commands, one per line.  End with CNTL/Z.
R5(config)# router bgp 5
R5(config-router)# auto-summary
R5(config-router)# ^Z
R5# clear ip bgp *
R5# show ip bgp
```

```
BGP table version is 2, local router ID is 5.5.5.5
Status codes: s suppressed, d damped, h history, * valid, > best, i - internal,
              r RIB-failure, S Stale
Origin codes: i - IGP, e - EGP, ? - incomplete


   Network          Next Hop          Metric LocPrf Weight Path
*> 10.0.0.0         0.0.0.0                0            32768 ?
! Now, at step 3, no auto-summary disables automatic summarization, redistribution is
! disabled, and at step 4, the network commands are added. Note that 10.12.0.0/15 is
! not injected, as there is no exact match, nor is 10.0.0.0/8, as there is no exact
! match. However, 10.14.0.0/16 is injected due to the exact match of the prefix and
! prefix length.
R5# conf t
Enter configuration commands, one per line.  End with CNTL/Z.
R5(config)# router bgp 5
R5(config-router)# no auto-summary
R5(config-router)# no redist conn route-map only15
R5(config-router)# no redist connected
R5(config-router)# network 10.0.0.0
R5(config-router)# network 10.12.0.0 mask 255.254.0.0
R5(config-router)# network 10.14.0.0 mask 255.255.0.0
R5(config-router)# ^Z
R5# clear ip bgp *
R5# sh ip bgp | begin network
   Network          Next Hop          Metric LocPrf Weight Path
*> 10.14.0.0/16     0.0.0.0                0            32768 i
! Finally, auto-summary is re-enabled (not shown in the example).
! 10.14.0.0/16 is still an exact match, so it is
! still injected. 10.0.0.0/8 is also injected because of the network 10.0.0.0
! command.
R5# sh ip bgp | begin network
   Network          Next Hop          Metric LocPrf Weight Path
*  10.0.0.0         0.0.0.0                0            32768 i
*  10.14.0.0/16     0.0.0.0                0            32768 i
```

## Manual Summaries and the AS_PATH Path Attribute

As covered in the last several pages, a router can add entries to its BGP table using the **network** command and route redistribution. Additionally, BGP can use manual route summarization to advertise summary routes to neighboring routers, causing the neighboring routers to learn additional BGP routes. BGP manual summarization with the **aggregate-address** command differs significantly from using the **auto-summary** command. It can summarize based on any routes in the BGP table, creating a summary of any prefix length. It does not always suppress the advertisement of the component subnets, although it can be configured to do so.

The aggregate route must include the AS_PATH PA, just like it is required for every other NLRI in the BGP table. However, to fully understand what this command does, you need to take a closer look at the AS_PATH PA.

The AS_PATH PA consists of up to four different components, called *segments*, as follows:

- AS_SEQ (short for AS Sequence)

- AS_SET

- AS_CONFED_SEQ (short for AS Confederation Sequence)

- AS_CONFED_SET

The most commonly used segment is called AS_SEQ. AS_SEQ is the idea of AS_PATH as shown back in Figure 1-1, with the PA representing all ASNs, in order, through which the route has been advertised.

However, the **aggregate-address** command can create a summary route for which the AS_SEQ must be null. When the component subnets of the summary route have differing AS_SEQ values, the router simply can't create an accurate representation of AS_SEQ, so it uses a null AS_SEQ. However, this action introduces the possibility of creating routing loops, because the contents of AS_PATH, specifically AS_SEQ, are used so that when a router receives an update, it can ignore prefixes for which its own ASN is listed.

The AS_PATH AS_SET segment solves the problem when the summary route has a null AS_SEQ. The AS_SET segment holds an unordered list of all the ASNs in all the component subnets' AS_SEQ segments.

Example 1-7 shows an example in which the router does use a null AS_SEQ for a summary route, and then the same summary with the **as-set** option creating the AS_SET segment.

**Example 1-7**   *Route Aggregation and the* as-set *Option*

```
! Note that R3's routes to network 23 all have the same AS_PATH except one new
! prefix, which has an AS_PATH that includes ASN 678. As a result, R3 will
! create a null AS_SEQ for the summary route.
R3# show ip bgp | include 23
*> 23.3.0.0/20      4.4.4.4                              0 45 i
*> 23.3.16.0/20     4.4.4.4                              0 45 i
*> 23.3.32.0/19     4.4.4.4                              0 45 i
*> 23.3.64.0/18     4.4.4.4                              0 45 i
*> 23.3.128.0/17    4.4.4.4                              0 45 i
*> 23.4.0.0/16      4.4.4.4                              0 45 678 i
! The following command is now added to R3's BGP configuration:
aggregate-address 23.0.0.0 255.0.0.0 summary-only
```

```
! Note: R3 will not have a BGP table entry for 23.0.0.0/8; however, R3 will
! advertise this summary to its peers, because at least one component subnet
! exists.
! R1 has learned the prefix, NEXT_HOP 3.3.3.3 (R3's update source IP address for
! R1), but the AS_PATH is now null because R1 is in the same AS as R3.
! (Had R3-R1 been an eBGP peering, R3 would have prepended its own ASN.)
! Note that the next command is on R1.
```

```
R1# sh ip bgp | begin Network
   Network          Next Hop          Metric LocPrf Weight Path
*>i21.0.0.0         3.3.3.3                0    100      0 45 i
*>i23.0.0.0         3.3.3.3                0    100      0 i
```

```
! Next, R1 displays the AGGREGATOR PA, which identifies R3 (3.3.3.3) and its AS
! (123) as the aggregation point at which information is lost. Also, the phrase
! "atomic-aggregate" refers to the fact that the ATOMIC_AGGREGATE PA has also
! been set; this PA simply states that this NLRI is a summary.
```

```
R1# show ip bgp 23.0.0.0
BGP routing table entry for 23.0.0.0/8, version 45
Paths: (1 available, best #1, table Default-IP-Routing-Table)
Flag: 0x800
  Advertised to update-groups:
     2
  Local, (aggregated by 123 3.3.3.3), (received & used)
     3.3.3.3 (metric 2302976) from 3.3.3.3 (3.3.3.3)
       Origin IGP, metric 0, localpref 100, valid, internal, atomic-aggregate, best
```

```
! R6, in AS 678, receives the summary route from R1, but the lack of information
! in the current AS_PATH allows R6 to learn of the route, possibly causing
! a routing loop. (Remember, one of the component subnets, 23.4.0.0/16, came from
! ASN 678.)
```

```
R6# sh ip bgp nei 172.16.16.1 received-routes | begin Network
   Network          Next Hop          Metric LocPrf Weight Path
*> 21.0.0.0         172.16.16.1                         0 123 45 i
*> 23.0.0.0         172.16.16.1                         0 123 i
```

```
! The R3 configuration is changed as shown next to use the as-set option.
```

```
R3# aggregate-address 23.0.0.0 255.0.0.0 summary-only as-set
! R1 now has the AS_SET component of the AS_PATH PA, which includes an unordered
! list of all autonmous systems from all the component subnets' AS_PATHs on R3.
```

```
R1# sh ip bgp | begin Network
   Network          Next Hop          Metric LocPrf Weight Path
*>i21.0.0.0         3.3.3.3                0    100      0 45 i
*>i23.0.0.0         3.3.3.3                0    100      0 {45,678} i
```

```
! R6 does receive the 23.0.0.0 prefix from R1, then checks the AS_SET PA, notices
! its own ASN (678), and ignores the prefix to avoid a loop.
```

```
R6# sh ip bgp nei 172.16.16.1 received-routes | begin Network
   Network          Next Hop          Metric LocPrf Weight Path
*> 21.0.0.0         172.16.16.1                         0 123 45 i
```

**Note**  AS_PATH includes the AS_CONFED_SEQ and AS_CONFED_SET segments as well, which are covered later, in the section "Confederations."

The following list summarizes the actions taken by the **aggregate-address** command when it creates a summary route:

Key Topic

- It does not create the summary if the BGP table does not currently have any routes for NLRI inside the summary.

- If all the component subnets are withdrawn from the aggregating router's BGP table, it also then withdraws the aggregate. (In other words, the router tells its neighbors that the aggregate route is no longer valid.)

- It sets the NEXT_HOP address of the summary, as listed in the local BGP table, as 0.0.0.0.

- It sets the NEXT_HOP address of the summary route, as advertised to neighbors, to the router's update source IP address for each neighbor, respectively.

- If the component subnets inside the summary all have the same AS_SEQ, it sets the new summary route's AS_SEQ to be exactly like the AS_SEQ of the component subnets.

- If the AS_SEQ of the component subnets differs in any way, it sets the AS_SEQ of the new summary route to null.

- When the **as-set** option has been configured, the router creates an AS_SET segment for the aggregate route, but only if the summary route's AS_SEQ is null.

- As usual, if the summary is advertised to an eBGP peer, the router prepends its own ASN to the AS_SEQ before sending the Update.

- It suppresses the advertisement of all component subnets if the **summary-only** keyword is used, advertises all of them if the **summary-only** keyword is omitted, or advertises a subset if the **suppress-map** option is configured.

Example 1-7 shows R3 from Figure 1-4 summarizing 23.0.0.0/8. R3 advertises the summary with ASN 123 as the only AS in the AS_SEQ, because some component subnets have AS_PATHs of 45, and others have 678 45. As a result, R3 uses a null AS_SEQ for the aggregate. The example goes on to show the impact of the **as-set** option.

**Note**  Summary routes can also be added through another method. First, the router would create a static route, typically with destination of interface null0. Then, the prefix/length can be matched with the **network** command to inject the summary. This method does not filter any of the component subnets.

Table 1-6 summarizes the key topics regarding summarization using the **aggregate-address**, **auto-summary**, and **network** commands.

**Key Topic**

**Table 1-6**  *Summary: Injecting Summary Routes in BGP*

| Command | Component Subnets Removed | Routes It Can Summarize |
|---|---|---|
| **auto-summary** (with redistribution) | All | Only those injected into BGP on that router using the **redistribute** command |
| **aggregate-address** | All, none, or a subset | Any prefixes already in the BGP table |
| **auto-summary** (with the **network** command) | None | Only those injected into BGP on that router using the **network** command |

## Adding Default Routes to BGP

The final method covered in this chapter for adding routes to a BGP table is to inject default routes into BGP. Default routes can be injected into BGP in one of three ways:

- By injecting the default using the **network** command

- By injecting the default using the **redistribute** command

- By injecting a default route into BGP using the **neighbor** *neighbor-id* **default-originate** [**route-map** *route-map-name*] BGP subcommand

When you inject a default route into BGP using the **network** command, a route to 0.0.0.0/0 must exist in the local routing table, and the **network 0.0.0.0** command is required. The default IP route can be learned through any means, but if it is removed from the IP routing table, BGP removes the default route from the BGP table.

Injecting a default route through redistribution requires an additional configuration command—**default-information originate**. The default route must first exist in the IP routing table; for example, a static default route to null0 could be created. Then, the **redistribute static** command could be used to redistribute that static default route. However, in the special case of the default route, Cisco IOS also requires the **default-originate** BGP subcommand.

Injecting a default route into BGP by using the **neighbor** *neighbor-id* **default-originate** [**route-map** *route-map-name*] BGP subcommand does not add a default route to the local BGP table; instead, it causes the advertisement of a default to the specified neighbor. In fact, this method does not even check for the existence of a default route in the IP routing table by default, but it can. With the **route-map** option, the referenced route map examines the entries in the IP routing table (not the BGP table); if a route map **permit** clause is matched, the default route is advertised to the neighbor. Example 1-8 shows just such an example on R1, with **route-map check-default** checking for the existence of a default route before R1 would originate a default route to R3.

**Example 1-8**   *Originating a Default Route to a Neighbor with the* **neighbor default-**
**originate** *Command*

```
! The pertinent parts of the R1 configuration are listed next, with the route map
! matching an IP route to 0.0.0.0/0 with a permit action, enabling the
! advertisement of a default route to neighbor 3.3.3.3 (R3).
router bgp 123
 neighbor 3.3.3.3 remote-as 123
 neighbor 3.3.3.3 update-source Loopback1
 neighbor 3.3.3.3 default-originate route-map check-default
!
ip route 0.0.0.0 0.0.0.0 Null0
!
ip prefix-list def-route seq 5 permit 0.0.0.0/0
!
route-map check-default permit 10
 match ip address prefix-list def-route
! R1 indeed has a default route, as seen below.
R1# show ip route | include 0.0.0.0/0
S*    0.0.0.0/0 is directly connected, Null0
! R3 now learns a default route from R1, as seen below.
R3# show ip bgp | begin Network
   Network          Next Hop            Metric LocPrf Weight Path
*>i0.0.0.0           1.1.1.1                      100      0 i
```

## ORIGIN Path Attribute

Depending on the method used to inject a route into a local BGP table, BGP assigns one
of three BGP ORIGIN PA codes: IGP, EGP, or incomplete. The ORIGIN PA provides a
general descriptor as to how a particular NLRI was first injected into a router's BGP table.
The **show ip bgp** command includes the three possible values in the legend at the top of
the command output, listing the actual ORIGIN code for each BGP route at the far right
of each output line. Table 1-7 lists the three ORIGIN code names, the single-letter abbreviation used by Cisco IOS, and the reasons why a route is assigned a particular code.

**Key
Topic**

The ORIGIN codes and meanings hide a few concepts that many people find counterintuitive. First, routes redistributed into BGP from an IGP actually have an ORIGIN code of
incomplete. Also, do not confuse EGP with eBGP; an ORIGIN of EGP refers to Exterior
Gateway Protocol, the very old and deprecated predecessor to BGP. In practice, the EGP
ORIGIN code should not be seen today.

**Table 1-7**   *BGP ORIGIN Codes*

| ORIGIN Code | Cisco IOS Notation | Used for Routes Injected Because of the Following Commands |
|---|---|---|
| IGP | i | **network**, **aggregate-address** (in some cases), and **neighbor default-originate** commands. |
| EGP | e | Exterior Gateway Protocol (EGP). No specific commands apply. |
| Incomplete | ? | **redistribute**, **aggregate-address** (in some cases), and **default-information originate** command. |

The rules regarding the ORIGIN codes used for summary routes created with the **aggregate-address** command can also be a bit surprising. The rules are summarized as follows:

- If the **as-set** option is not used, the aggregate route uses ORIGIN code i.

- If the **as-set** option is used, and all component subnets being summarized use ORIGIN code i, the aggregate has ORIGIN code i.

- If the **as-set** option is used, and at least one of the component subnets has an ORIGIN code ?, the aggregate has ORIGIN code ?.

**Note**   The BGP ORIGIN PA provides a minor descriptor for the origin of a BGP table entry, which is used as part of the BGP decision process.

### Advertising BGP Routes to Neighbors

The previous section focused on the tools that BGP can use to inject routes into a local router's BGP table. BGP routers take routes from the local BGP table and advertise a subset of those routes to their BGP neighbors. This section continues to focus on the BGP table because the BGP route advertisement process takes routes from the BGP table and sends them to neighboring routers, where the routes are added to the neighbors' BGP tables. Later, the final major section in the chapter, "Building the IP Routing Table," focuses on the rules regarding how BGP places routes into the IP routing table.

### BGP Update Message

After a BGP table has a list of routes, paths, and prefixes, the router needs to advertise the information to neighboring routers. To do so, a router sends BGP Update messages to its neighbors. Figure 1-5 shows the general format of the BGP Update message.

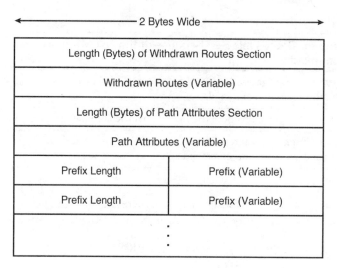

**Figure 1-5**  *BGP Update Message Format*

Each Update message has three main parts:

■   The Withdrawn Routes field enables BGP to inform its neighbors about failed routes.

■   The Path Attributes field lists the PAs for each route. NEXT_HOP and AS_PATH are sample values for this field.

■   The Prefix and Prefix Length fields define each individual NLRI.

The central concept in an individual Update message is the set of PAs. Then, all the prefixes (NLRIs) that share the exact same set of PAs and PA values are included at the end of the Update message. If a router needs to advertise a set of NLRIs, and each NLRI has a different setting for at least one PA, separate Update messages will be required for each NLRI. However, when many routes share the same PAs—typical of prefixes owned by a particular ISP, for example—multiple NLRIs are included in a single Update. This reduces router CPU load and uses less link bandwidth.

## Determining the Contents of Updates

A router builds the contents of its Update messages based on the contents of its BGP table. However, the router must choose which subset of its BGP table entries to advertise to each neighbor, with the set likely varying from neighbor to neighbor. Table 1-8 summarizes the rules about which routes BGP does *not* include in routing updates to each neighbor; each rule is described more fully following the table.

**Table 1-8**  *Summary of Rules Regarding Which Routes BGP Does Not Include in an Update*

| iBGP and/or eBGP | Routes Not Taken from the BGP Table |
|---|---|
| Both | Routes that are not considered "best" |
| Both | Routes matched by a **deny** clause in an outbound BGP filter |
| iBGP | iBGP-learned routes* |

*This rule is relaxed or changed as a result of using route reflectors or confederations.

BGP only advertises a route to reach a particular subnet (NLRI) if that route is considered to be the best route. If a BGP router learns of only one route to reach a particular prefix, the decision process is very simple. However, when choosing between multiple paths to reach the same prefix, BGP determines the best route based on a lengthy BGP decision process, as discussed in the Chapter 2 section, "The BGP Decision Process." Assuming that none of the routers has configured any routing policies that impact the decision process, the decision tree reduces to a four-step process that is mainly composed of tie-breakers, as follows:

1. Choose the route with the shortest AS_PATH.

2. If AS_PATH length is a tie, prefer a single eBGP-learned route over one or more iBGP routes.

3. If the best route has not yet been chosen, choose the route with the lowest IGP metric to the NEXT_HOP of the routes.

4. If the IGP metric ties, choose the iBGP-learned route with the lowest BGP RID of the advertising router.

Additionally, BGP rules out some routes from being considered best based on the value of the NEXT_HOP PA. For a route to be a candidate to be considered best, the NEXT_HOP must be either

■ 0.0.0.0, as the result of the route being injected on the local router.

■ Reachable according to that router's current IP routing table. In other words, the NEXT_HOP IP address must match a route in the routing table.

Because the NEXT_HOP PA is so important with regard to BGP's choice of its best path to reach each NLRI, this section summarizes the logic and provides several examples. The logic is separated into two parts based on whether the route is being advertised to an iBGP or eBGP peer. By default, when sending to an eBGP peer, the NEXT_HOP is changed to an IP address on the advertising router—specifically, to the same IP address the router used as the source IP address of the BGP Update message, for each respective neighbor. When sending to an iBGP peer, the default action is to leave the NEXT_HOP PA unchanged. Both of these default behaviors can be changed through the commands listed in Table 1-9.

**Table 1-9**   *Conditions for Changing the NEXT_HOP PA*

| Type of Neighbor | Default Action for Advertised Routes | Command to Switch to Other Behavior |
|---|---|---|
| iBGP | Do not change the NEXT_HOP | **Neighbor... next-hop-self** |
| eBGP | Change the NEXT_HOP to the update source IP address | **Neighbor... next-hop-unchanged** |

Note that the NEXT_HOP PA cannot be set through a route map; the only way to change the NEXT_HOP PA is through the methods listed in Table 1-9.

### Example: Impact of the Decision Process and NEXT_HOP on BGP Updates

The next several examples together show a sequence of events regarding the propagation of network 31.0.0.0/8 by BGP throughout the network of Figure 1-4. R6 originated the routes in the 30s (as in Example 1-4) by redistributing EIGRP routes learned from R9. The purpose of this series of examples is to explain how BGP chooses which routes to include in Updates under various conditions.

The first example, Example 1-9, focuses on the commands used to examine what R6 sends to R1, what R1 receives, and the resulting entries in R1's BGP table. The second example, Example 1-10, then examines those same routes propagated from R1 to R3, including problems related to R1's default behavior of not changing the NEXT_HOP PA of those routes. Finally, Example 1-11 shows the solution of R1's use of the **neighbor 3.3.3.3 next-hop-self** command, and the impact that has on the contents of the BGP Updates in AS 123.

**Example 1-9**   *R6 Sending the 30s Networks to R1 Using BGP*

```
! R6 has injected the three routes listed below; they were not learned from
! another BGP neighbor. Note all three show up as >, meaning they are the best
! (and only in this case) routes to the destination NLRIs.
R6# show ip bgp
BGP table version is 5, local router ID is 6.6.6.6
Status codes: s suppressed, d damped, h history, * valid, > best, i - internal,
              r RIB-failure, S Stale
Origin codes: i - IGP, e - EGP, ? - incomplete

   Network          Next Hop            Metric LocPrf Weight Path
*> 31.0.0.0         10.1.69.9           156160         32768 ?
*> 32.0.0.0         0.0.0.0                            32768 i
*> 32.1.1.0/24      10.1.69.9           156160         32768 ?
! R6 now lists the routes it advertises to R1—sort of. This command lists R6's
! BGP table entries that are intended to be sent, but R6 can (and will in this
! case) change the information before advertising to R1. Pay particular attention
```

```
! to the Next Hop column, versus upcoming commands on R1. In effect, this command
! shows R6's current BGP table entries that will be sent to R1, but it shows them
! before R6 makes any changes, including NEXT_HOP.
R6# show ip bgp neighbor 172.16.16.1 advertised-routes
BGP table version is 5, local router ID is 6.6.6.6
Status codes: s suppressed, d damped, h history, * valid, > best, i - internal,
              r RIB-failure, S Stale
Origin codes: i - IGP, e - EGP, ? - incomplete


   Network          Next Hop           Metric LocPrf Weight Path
*> 31.0.0.0         10.1.69.9          156160         32768 ?
*> 32.0.0.0         0.0.0.0                           32768 i
*> 32.1.1.0/24      10.1.69.9          156160         32768 ?
Total number of prefixes 3
! The next command (R1) lists the info in the received BGP update from R6. Note
! that the NEXT_HOP is different; R6 changed the NEXT_HOP before sending the
! update, because it has an eBGP peer connection to R1, and eBGP defaults to set
! NEXT_HOP to itself. As R6 was using 172.16.16.6 as the IP address from which to
! send BGP messages to R1, R6 set NEXT_HOP to that number. Also note that R1 lists
! the neighboring AS (678) in the Path column at the end, signifying the AS_PATH
! for the route.
R1# show ip bgp neighbor 172.16.16.6 received-routes
BGP table version is 7, local router ID is 111.111.111.111
Status codes: s suppressed, d damped, h history, * valid, > best, i - internal,
              r RIB-failure, S Stale
Origin codes: i - IGP, e - EGP, ? - incomplete


   Network          Next Hop           Metric LocPrf Weight Path
*> 31.0.0.0         172.16.16.6        156160          0 678 ?
*> 32.0.0.0         172.16.16.6             0          0 678 i
*> 32.1.1.0/24      172.16.16.6        156160          0 678 ?
Total number of prefixes 3
! The show ip bgp summary command lists the state of the neighbor until the
! neighbor becomes established; at that point, the State/PfxRcd column lists the
! number of NLRIs (prefixes) received (and still valid) from that neighbor.
R1# show ip bgp summary | begin Neighbor
Neighbor       V    AS MsgRcvd MsgSent   TblVer  InQ OutQ Up/Down  State/PfxRcd
2.2.2.2        4   123      55      57        7    0    0 00:52:30        0
3.3.3.3        4   123      57      57        7    0    0 00:52:28        3
172.16.16.6    4   678      53      51        7    0    0 00:48:50        3
! R1 has also learned of these prefixes from R3, as seen below. The routes through
! R6 have one AS in the AS_PATH, and the routes through R3 have two autonmous
! systems, so the routes through R6 are best. Also, the iBGP routes have an "i" for
! "internal" just before the prefix.
```

```
R1# show ip bgp
BGP table version is 7, local router ID is 111.111.111.111
Status codes: s suppressed, d damped, h history, * valid, > best, i - internal,
              r RIB-failure, S Stale
Origin codes: i - IGP, e - EGP, ? - incomplete

   Network          Next Hop           Metric LocPrf Weight Path
*  i31.0.0.0        3.3.3.3                 0    100      0 45 678 ?
*>                  172.16.16.6        156160               0 678 ?
*  i32.0.0.0        3.3.3.3                 0    100      0 45 678 i
*>                  172.16.16.6             0               0 678 i
*  i32.1.1.0/24     3.3.3.3                 0    100      0 45 678 ?
*>                  172.16.16.6        156160               0 678 ?
```

Example 1-9 showed examples of how you can view the contents of the actual Updates
sent to neighbors (using the **show ip bgp neighbor advertised-routes** command) and the
contents of Updates received from a neighbor (using the **show ip bgp neighbor received-
routes** command). RFC 1771 suggests that the BGP RIB can be separated into components for received Updates from each neighbor and sent Updates for each neighbor. Most
implementations (including Cisco IOS) keep a single RIB, with notations as to which
entries were sent and received to and from each neighbor.

**Note**   For the **received-routes** option to work, the router on which the command is used
must have the **neighbor** *neighbor-id* **soft-reconfiguration inbound** BGP subcommand
configured for the other neighbor.

These **show ip bgp neighbor** commands with the **advertised-routes** option list the BGP
table entries that will be advertised to that neighbor. However, note that any changes to
the PAs inside each entry are not shown in the command output. For example, the **show
ip bgp neighbor 172.16.16.1 advertised-routes** command on R6 listed the NEXT_HOP
for 31/8 as 10.1.69.9, which is true of that entry in R6's BGP table. R6 then changes the
NEXT_HOP PA before sending the actual Update, with a NEXT_HOP of 172.16.16.6.

By the end of Example 1-9, R1 knows of both paths to each of the three prefixes in the
30s (AS_PATH 678 and 45-678), but has chosen the shortest AS_PATH (through R6) as
the best path in each case. Note that the > in the **show ip bgp** output designates the
routes as R1's best routes. Next, Example 1-10 shows some possibly surprising results on
R3 related to its choices of best routes.

**Example 1-10**   *Examining the BGP Table on R3*

```
! R1 now updates R3 with R1's "best" routes
R1# show ip bgp neighbor 3.3.3.3 advertised-routes | begin Network
   Network          Next Hop           Metric LocPrf Weight Path
*> 31.0.0.0         172.16.16.6        156160               0 678 ?
*> 32.0.0.0         172.16.16.6             0               0 678 i
```

```
*> 32.1.1.0/24      172.16.16.6         156160            0 678 ?
Total number of prefixes 3
! R3 received the routes, but R3's best routes to each prefix point back to
! R4 in AS 45, with AS_PATH 45-678, which is a longer path. The route through R1
! cannot be "best" because the NEXT_HOP was sent unchanged by iBGP neighbor R1.

R3# show ip bgp
BGP table version is 7, local router ID is 3.3.3.3
Status codes: s suppressed, d damped, h history, * valid, > best, i - internal,
              r RIB-failure, S Stale
Origin codes: i - IGP, e - EGP, ? - incomplete

   Network          Next Hop          Metric LocPrf Weight Path
*> 31.0.0.0         4.4.4.4                               0 45 678 ?
*  i                172.16.16.6       156160    100       0 678 ?
*> 32.0.0.0         4.4.4.4                               0 45 678 i
*  i                172.16.16.6            0    100       0 678 i
*> 32.1.1.0/24      4.4.4.4                               0 45 678 ?
*  i                172.16.16.6       156160    100       0 678 ?
! Proof that R3 cannot reach the next-hop IP address is shown next.
R3# ping 172.16.16.6

Type escape sequence to abort.
Sending 5, 100-byte ICMP Echos to 172.16.16.6, timeout is 2 seconds:
.....
Success rate is 0 percent (0/5)
```

Example 1-10 points out a quirk with some terminology in the **show ip bgp** command output, as well as an important design choice with BGP. First, the command output lists * as meaning valid; however, that designation simply means that the route is a candidate for use. Before the route can be actually used and added to the IP routing table, the NEXT_HOP must also be reachable. In some cases, routes that the **show ip bgp** command considers "valid" might not be usable routes, with Example 1-10 showing just such an example.

Each BGP route's NEXT_HOP must be reachable for a route to be truly valid. With all default settings, an iBGP-learned route has a NEXT_HOP IP address of the last eBGP router to advertise the route. For example, R3's route to 31.0.0.0/8 through R1 lists R6's IP address (172.16.16.6) in the NEXT_HOP field. Unfortunately, R3 does not have a route for 172.16.16.6, so that route cannot be considered "best" by BGP.

There are two easy choices to solve the problem:

- Make the eBGP neighbor's IP address reachable by advertising that subnet into the IGP.

- Use the **next-hop-self** option on the **neighbor** command that points to iBGP peers.

The first option typically can be easily implemented. Because many eBGP neighbors use interface IP addresses on their **neighbor** commands, the NEXT_HOP exists in a subnet directly connected to the AS. For example, R1 is directly connected to 172.16.16.0/24, so R1 could simply advertise that connected subnet into the IGP inside the AS.

However, this option might be problematic when loopback addresses are used for BGP neighbors. For example, if R1 had been configured to refer to R6's 6.6.6.6 loopback IP address, and it was working, R1 must have a route to reach 6.6.6.6. However, it is less likely that R1 would already be advertising a route to reach 6.6.6.6 into ASN 123.

The second option causes the router to change the NEXT_HOP PA to one of its own IP addresses—an address that is more likely to already be in the neighbor's IP routing table, which works well even if using loopbacks with an eBGP peer. Example 1-11 points out such a case, with R1 using the **neighbor next-hop-self** command, advertising itself (1.1.1.1) as the NEXT_HOP. As a result, R3 changes its choice of best routes, because R3 has a route to reach 1.1.1.1, overcoming the "NEXT_HOP unreachable" problem.

Example 1-11 points out how an iBGP peer can set NEXT_HOP to itself. However, it's also a good example of how BGP decides when to advertise routes to iBGP peers. The example follows this sequence, with the command output showing evidence of these events:

1. The example begins like the end of Example 1-10, with R1 advertising routes with R6 as the next hop, and with R3 not being able to use those routes as best routes.

2. Because R3's best routes are eBGP routes (through R4), R3 is allowed to advertise those routes to R2.

3. R1 then changes its configuration to use NEXT_HOP SELF.

4. R3 is now able to treat the routes learned from R1 as R3's best routes.

5. R3 can no longer advertise its best routes to these networks to R2, because the new best routes are iBGP routes.

**Example 1-11**  *R3 Advertises the 30s Networks to R2, and Then R3 Withdraws the Routes*

```
! (Step 1): At this point, R3 still believes its best route to all three prefixes
! in the 30s is through R4; as those are eBGP routes, R3 advertises all three
! routes to iBGP peer R2, as seen next.
R3# show ip bgp neighbor 2.2.2.2 advertised-routes
BGP table version is 7, local router ID is 3.3.3.3
Status codes: s suppressed, d damped, h history, * valid, > best, i - internal,
              r RIB-failure, S Stale
Origin codes: i - IGP, e - EGP, ? - incomplete

   Network          Next Hop            Metric LocPrf Weight Path
*> 31.0.0.0         4.4.4.4                            0 45 678 ?
*> 32.0.0.0         4.4.4.4                            0 45 678 i
*> 32.1.1.0/24      4.4.4.4                            0 45 678 ?
```

```
Total number of prefixes 3
! (Step 2) R2 lists the number of prefixes learned from R3 next (3).
```

```
R2# show ip bgp summary | begin Neighbor
Neighbor        V    AS MsgRcvd MsgSent    TblVer  InQ OutQ Up/Down   State/PfxRcd
1.1.1.1         4   123     212     210        7    0    0 03:27:59       3
3.3.3.3         4   123     213     211        7    0    0 03:28:00       3
! (Step 3) R1 now changes to use next-hop-self to peer R3.
```

```
R1# conf t
Enter configuration commands, one per line.  End with CNTL/Z.
R1(config)# router bgp 123
R1(config-router)# neigh 3.3.3.3 next-hop-self
! (Step 4) R3 now lists the routes through R1 as best, because the new
! NEXT_HOP is R1's update source IP address, 1.1.1.1, which is reachable by R3.
```

```
R3# show ip bgp
BGP table version is 10, local router ID is 3.3.3.3
Status codes: s suppressed, d damped, h history, * valid, > best, i - internal,
              r RIB-failure, S Stale
Origin codes: i - IGP, e - EGP, ? - incomplete

   Network          Next Hop          Metric LocPrf Weight Path
*  31.0.0.0         4.4.4.4                             0 45 678 ?
*>i                 1.1.1.1           156160    100     0 678 ?
*  32.0.0.0         4.4.4.4                             0 45 678 i
*>i                 1.1.1.1                0    100     0 678 i
*  32.1.1.0/24      4.4.4.4                             0 45 678 ?
*>i                 1.1.1.1           156160    100     0 678 ?
! (Step 5) First, note above that all three "best" routes are iBGP routes, as noted
! by the "i" immediately before the prefix. R3 only advertises "best" routes, with
! the added requirement that it must not advertise iBGP routes to other iBGP peers.
! As a result, R3 has withdrawn the routes that had formerly been sent to R2.
```

```
R3# show ip bgp neighbor 2.2.2.2 advertised-routes

Total number of prefixes 0
! The next command confirms on R2 that it no longer has any prefixes learned from
! R3.
```

```
R2# show ip bgp summary | begin Neighbor
Neighbor        V    AS MsgRcvd MsgSent    TblVer  InQ OutQ Up/Down   State/PfxRcd
1.1.1.1         4   123     213     211        7    0    0 03:28:44       3
3.3.3.3         4   123     214     211        7    0    0 03:28:46       0
```

### Summary of Rules for Routes Advertised in BGP Updates

The following list summarizes the rules dictating which routes a BGP router sends in its Update messages:

■   Send only the best route listed in the BGP table.

■   To iBGP neighbors, do not advertise paths learned from other iBGP neighbors.

■   Do not advertise suppressed or dampened routes.

■   Do not advertise routes filtered through configuration.

The first two rules have been covered in some depth in this section. The remaining rules are outside the scope of this book.

# Building the IP Routing Table

So far, this chapter has explained how to form BGP neighbor relationships, how to inject routes into the BGP table, and how BGP routers choose which routes to propagate to neighboring routers. Part of that logic relates to how the BGP decision process selects a router's best route to each prefix, with the added restriction that the NEXT_HOP must be reachable before the route can be considered as a best route.

This section completes the last step in BGP's ultimate goal—adding the appropriate routes to the IP routing table. In its simplest form, BGP takes the already identified best BGP routes for each prefix and adds those routes to the IP routing table. However, there are some additional restrictions, mainly related to administrative distance (AD) (for eBGP and iBGP routes) and BGP synchronization (iBGP routes only). The sections that follow detail the exceptions.

## Adding eBGP Routes to the IP Routing Table

Cisco IOS Software uses simple logic when determining which eBGP routes to add to the IP routing table. The only two requirements are as follows:

■   The eBGP route in the BGP table is considered to be a "best" route.

■   If the same prefix has been learned through another IGP or through static routes, the AD for BGP external routes must be lower than the ADs for other routing source(s).

By default, Cisco IOS considers eBGP routes to have AD 20, which gives eBGP routes a better (lower) AD than any other dynamic routing protocol's default AD (except for the AD 5 of EIGRP summary routes). The rationale behind the default is that eBGP-learned routes should never be prefixes from within an AS. Under normal conditions, eBGP-learned prefixes should seldom be seen as IGP-learned routes as well, but when they are, the BGP route would win by default.

BGP sets the AD differently for eBGP routes, iBGP routes, and for local (locally injected) routes—with defaults of 20, 200, and 200, respectively. These values can be overridden in two ways, both consistent with the coverage of AD in Chapter 9, "Device and Network Security":

- By using the **distance bgp** *external-distance internal-distance local-distance* BGP subcommand, which allows the simple setting of AD for eBGP-learned prefixes, iBGP-learned prefixes, and prefixes injected locally, respectively

- By changing the AD using the **distance** *distance {ip-address {wildcard-mask}} [ip-standard-list | ip-extended-list]* BGP subcommand

With BGP, the IP address and wildcard mask refer to the IP address used on the **neighbor** command for that particular neighbor, not the BGP RID or NEXT_HOP of the route. The ACL examines the BGP routes received from the neighbor, assigning the specified AD for any routes matching the ACL with a permit action.

Finally, a quick note is needed about the actual IP route added to the IP routing table. The route contains the exact same prefix, prefix length, and next-hop IP address as listed in the BGP table—even if the NEXT_HOP PA is an IP address that is not in a connected network. As a result, the IP forwarding process might require a recursive route lookup. Example 1-12 shows such a case on R3, where the three BGP routes each list a next hop of 1.1.1.1, which happens to be a loopback interface on R1. As you can see from Figure 1-4, R3 and R1 have no interfaces in common. The route to 1.1.1.1 lists the actual next-hop IP address to which a packet would be forwarded.

**Example 1-12**  *R3 Routes with Next Hop 1.1.1.1, Requiring Recursive Route Lookup*

```
! Packets forwarded to 31.0.0.0/8 match the last route, with next-hop 1.1.1.1; R3
! then finds the route that matches destination 1.1.1.1 (the first route), finding
! the appropriate next-hop IP address and outgoing interface.
R3# show ip route | incl 1.1.1.1
D       1.1.1.1 [90/2809856] via 10.1.23.2, 04:01:44, Serial0/0/1
B       32.1.1.0/24 [200/156160] via 1.1.1.1, 00:01:00
B       32.0.0.0/8 [200/0] via 1.1.1.1, 00:01:00
B       31.0.0.0/8 [200/156160] via 1.1.1.1, 00:01:00
```

## Backdoor Routes

Having a low default AD (20) for eBGP routes can cause a problem in some topologies. Figure 1-6 shows a typical case, in which Enterprise 1 uses its eBGP route to reach network 99.0.0.0 in Enterprise 2. However, the two enterprises want to use the OSPF-learned route through the leased line between the two companies.

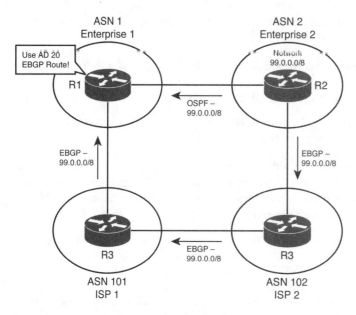

**Figure 1-6**   *Need for BGP Backdoor Routes*

R1 uses its eBGP route to reach 99.0.0.0 because eBGP has a lower AD (20) than OSPF (110). One solution would be to configure the **distance** command to lower the AD of the OSPF-learned route. However, BGP offers an elegant solution to this particular problem through the use of the **network backdoor** command. In this case, if R1 configures the **network 99.0.0.0 backdoor** router BGP subcommand, the following would occur:

- R1 would use the local AD (default 200) for the eBGP-learned route to network 99.0.0.0.

- R1 does not advertise 99.0.0.0 with BGP.

Given that logic, R1 can use a **network backdoor** command for each prefix for which R1 needs to use the private link to reach Enterprise 2. If the OSPF route to each prefix is up and working, R1 uses the OSPF (AD 110) route over the eBGP-learned (AD 20) route through the Internet. If the OSPF route is lost, the two companies can still communicate through the Internet.

## Adding iBGP Routes to the IP Routing Table

Cisco IOS has the same two requirements for adding iBGP routes to the IP routing table as it does for eBGP routes:

- The route must be the best BGP route.

- The route must be the best route (according to the AD) in comparison with other routing sources.

Additionally, for iBGP-learned routes, IOS considers the concept of *BGP synchronization*.

With BGP synchronization (often called *sync*) disabled using the **no synchronization** command, BGP uses the same logic for iBGP routes as it does for eBGP routes regarding which routes to add to the IP routing table. However, enabling BGP sync (with the **synchronization** BGP subcommand) prevents a couple of problems related to IP routing. Figure 1-7 shows the details of just such a problem. In this case, sync was inappropriately disabled in ASN 678, creating a black hole.

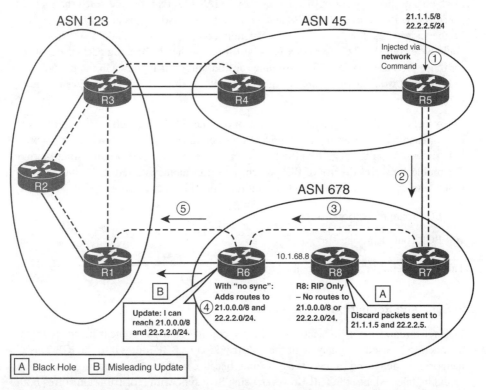

**Figure 1-7**   *Problem: Routing Black Hole Because of Not Using BGP Sync*

The following list takes a sequential view of what occurs within BGP in Figure 1-7:

1. R5 adds two prefixes (21.0.0.0/8 and 22.2.2.0/24) into its BGP table using two **network** commands.

2. R5 advertises the prefixes to R7, but does not redistribute the routes into its IGP.

3. R7 advertises the prefixes to R6.

4. R6, with synchronization disabled, considers the routes as "best," so R6 adds the routes to its routing table.

5. R6 also advertises the two prefixes to R1.

Two related problems (labeled A and B in the figure) actually occur in this case. The routing *black hole* occurs because R8 does not have a route to either of the prefixes advertised by BGP. R8 is not running BGP—a common occurrence for a router that does not directly connect to an eBGP peer. R7 did not redistribute those two prefixes into the IGP; as a result, R8 cannot route packets for those prefixes. R6, and possibly routers in AS 123, try to forward packets destined to the two prefixes through AS 678, but R8 discards the packets—hence the black hole.

The second related problem, labeled B, occurs at Step 5. R6 exacerbated the routing black-hole problem by advertising to another AS (AS 123) that it could reach the prefixes. R6 considers its routes to 21.0.0.0/8 and 22.2.2.0/24 as "best" routes in its BGP table, so R6 then advertises those routes to R1. Depending on the topology and PA settings, R1 could have considered these routes as its best routes—thereby sending packets destined for those prefixes into AS 678. (Assuming the configuration as shown in the previous examples, R1 would actually believe the one AS_PATH through R3 to AS 45 as the best path.)

The solutions to these problems are varied, but all the solutions result in the internal routers (for example, R8) learning the routes to these prefixes, thereby removing the black hole and removing the negative effect of advertising the route. The original solution to this problem involves the use of BGP synchronization, along with redistributing BGP routes into the IGP. However, two later solutions provide better options today:

■   BGP route reflectors

■   BGP confederations

The next several sections cover all of these options.

## Using Sync and Redistributing Routes

BGP synchronization is best understood when considered in the context in which it was intended to be used—namely, with the redistribution of BGP routes into the IGP. This method is seldom used by ISPs today, mainly because of the large number of routes that would be injected into the IGP. However, using BGP sync with redistribution solves both problems related to the routing black hole.

The key to understanding BGP sync is to know that redistribution solves the routing black-hole problem, and sync solves the problem of advertising a black-hole route to another AS. For example, to solve the routing black-hole problem, R7 redistributes the two prefixes into RIP (from Figure 1-7). R8 then has routes to those prefixes, solving the black-hole problem.

Sync logic on R6 controls the second part of the overall problem, regulating the conditions under which R6 advertises the prefixes to other eBGP peers (like R1). Sync works by controlling whether a BGP table entry can be considered "best"; keep in mind that a route in the BGP table must be considered to be "best" before it can be advertised to another BGP peer. The BGP sync logic controls that decision as follows:

**Key Topic**

> Do not consider an iBGP route in the BGP table as "best" unless the exact prefix was learned through an IGP and is currently in the routing table.

Sync logic essentially gives a router a method to know whether the non-BGP routers inside the AS should have the ability to route packets to the prefix. Note that the route must be IGP-learned because a static route on R6 would not imply anything about what other routers (like R8) might or might not have learned. For example, using Figure 1-7 again, after R6 learns the prefixes through RIP, RIP will place the routes in its IP routing table. At that point, the sync logic on R6 can consider those same BGP-learned prefixes in the BGP table as candidates to be best routes. If chosen as best, R6 can then advertise the BGP routes to R1.

Example 1-13 shows the black hole occurring from R6's perspective, with sync disabled on R6 using the **no synchronization** BGP subcommand. Following that, the example shows R6's behavior after R7 has begun redistributing BGP routes into RIP, with sync enabled on R6.

**Example 1-13**   *Comparing the Black Hole (No Sync) and Solution (Sync)*

```
! R6 has a "best" BGP route to 21.0.0.0/8 through R7 (7.7.7.7), but a trace
! command shows that the packets are discarded by R8 (10.1.68.8).
R6# show ip bgp | begin Network
   Network          Next Hop          Metric LocPrf Weight Path
*  21.0.0.0         172.16.16.1                      0 123 45 i
*>i                 7.7.7.7                0    100   0 45 i
*  22.2.2.0/24      172.16.16.1                      0 123 45 i
*>i                 7.7.7.7                0    100   0 45 i
R6# trace 21.1.1.5
Type escape sequence to abort.
Tracing the route to 21.1.1.5

  1 10.1.68.8 20 msec 20 msec 20 msec
  2 10.1.68.8 !H  *  !H
! R7 is now configured to redistribute BGP into RIP.
R7# conf t
Enter configuration commands, one per line.  End with CNTL/Z.
R7(config)# router rip
R7(config-router)# redist bgp 678 metric 3
! Next, R6 switches to use sync, and the BGP process is cleared.
R6# conf t
Enter configuration commands, one per line.  End with CNTL/Z.
R6(config)# router bgp 678
R6(config-router)# synchronization
R6(config-router)# ^Z
R6# clear ip bgp *
```

```
! R6's BGP table entries now show "RIB-failure," a status code that can mean
! (as of some 12.2T IOS releases) that the prefix is known via an IGP. 21.0.0.0/8
! is shown to be included as a RIP route in R6's routing table. Note also that R6
! considers the BGP routes through R7 as the "best" routes; these are still
! advertised to R1.
R6# show ip bgp
BGP table version is 5, local router ID is 6.6.6.6
Status codes: s suppressed, d damped, h history, * valid, > best, i - internal,
              r RIB-failure, S Stale
Origin codes: i - IGP, e - EGP, ? - incomplete

   Network          Next Hop         Metric LocPrf Weight Path
r  21.0.0.0         172.16.16.1                        0 123 45 i
r>i                 7.7.7.7               0    100      0 45 i
r  22.2.2.0/24      172.16.16.1                        0 123 45 i
r>i                 7.7.7.7               0    100      0 45 i
R6# show ip route | incl 21.0.0.0
R    21.0.0.0/8 [120/4] via 10.1.68.8, 00:00:15, Serial0/0.8
! R6 considers the routes through R7 as the "best" routes; these are still
! advertised to R1, even though they are in a "RIB-failure" state.
R6# show ip bgp neighbor 172.16.16.1 advertised-routes | begin Network
   Network          Next Hop         Metric LocPrf Weight Path
r>i21.0.0.0         7.7.7.7               0    100      0 45 i
r>i22.2.2.0/24      7.7.7.7               0    100      0 45 i
```

**Note** Sync includes an additional odd requirement when OSPF is used as the IGP. If the OSPF RID of the router advertising the prefix is a different number than the BGP router advertising that same prefix, sync still does not allow BGP to consider the route to be the best route. OSPF and BGP use the same priorities and logic to choose their RIDs. However, when using sync, it makes sense to explicitly configure the RID for OSPF and BGP to be the same value on the router that redistributes from BGP into OSPF.

### Disabling Sync and Using BGP on All Routers in an AS

A second method to overcome the black-hole issue is to simply use BGP to advertise all the BGP-learned prefixes to all routers in the AS. Because all routers know the prefixes, sync can be disabled safely. The downside is the introduction of BGP onto all routers, and the addition of iBGP neighbor connections between each pair of routers. (In an AS with N routers, N(N–1)/2 neighbor connections will be required.) With large autonomous systems, BGP performance and convergence time can degrade as a result of the large number of peers.

BGP needs the full mesh of iBGP peers inside an AS because BGP does not advertise iBGP routes (routes learned from one iBGP peer) to another iBGP peer. This additional restriction helps prevent routing loops, but it then requires a full mesh of iBGP peers—otherwise, only a subset of the iBGP peers would learn each prefix.

BGP offers two tools (confederations and route reflectors) that reduce the number of peer connections inside an AS, prevent loops, and allow all routers to learn about all prefixes. These two tools are covered next.

## Confederations

An AS using BGP confederations, as defined in RFC 5065, separates each router in the AS into one of several confederation subautonomous systems. Peers inside the same sub-AS are considered to be *confederation iBGP peers*, and routers in different subautonomous systems are considered to be *confederation eBGP peers*.

Confederations propagate routes to all routers, without a full mesh of peers inside the entire AS. To do so, confederation eBGP peer connections act like true eBGP peers in some respects. In a single sub-AS, the confederation iBGP peers must be fully meshed, because they act exactly like normal iBGP peers—in other words, they do not advertise iBGP routes to each other. However, confederation eBGP peers act like eBGP peers in that they can advertise iBGP routes learned inside their confederation sub-AS into another confederation sub-AS.

Confederations prevent loops inside a confederation AS by using the AS_PATH PA. BGP routers in a confederation add the subautonomous systems into the AS_PATH as part of an AS_PATH segment called the AS_CONFED_SEQ. (The AS_PATH consists of up to four different components, called segments—AS_SEQ, AS_SET, AS_CONFED_SEQ, and AS_CONFED_SET; see the earlier section "Manual Summaries and the AS_PATH Path Attribute" for more information on AS_SEQ and AS_SET.)

**Note**   The terms *AS* and *sub-AS* refer to the concept of an autonomous system and sub-autonomous system. *ASN* and *sub-ASN* refer to the actual AS numbers used.

Just as the AS_SEQ and AS_SET components help prevent loops between autonomous systems, AS_CONFED_SEQ and AS_CONFED_SET help prevent loops within confederation autonomous systems. Before confederation eBGP peers can advertise an iBGP route into another sub-AS, the router must make sure that the destination sub-AS is not already in the AS_PATH AS_CONFED_SEQ segment. For example, in Figure 1-8, the routers in sub-ASN 65001 learn some routes and then advertise those routes to sub-ASNs 65002 and 65003. Routers in these two sub-ASNs advertise the routes to each other. However, they never re-advertise the routes to routers in sub-ASN 65001 because of AS_CONFED_SEQ, as shown in parentheses inside the figure.

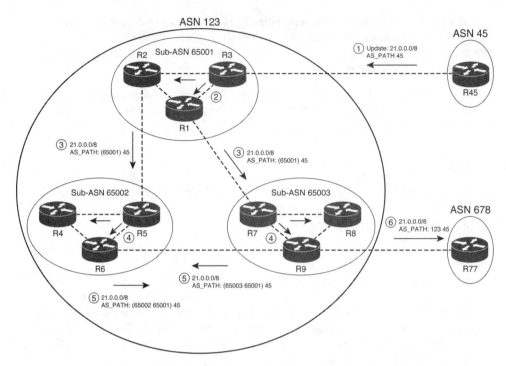

**Figure 1-8**  *AS_PATH Changes in a Confederation*

Figure 1-8 depicts a detailed example, with the steps in the following list matching the steps outlined in circled numbers in the figure:

1. 21.0.0.0/8 is injected by R45 and advertised through eBGP to AS 123. This route has an AS_PATH of 45.

2. R3 advertises the prefix through its two iBGP connections; however, because of iBGP rules inside the sub-AS, R1 and R2 do not attempt to advertise this prefix to each other.

3. Routers in sub-AS 65001 use eBGP-like logic to advertise 21.0.0.0/8 to their confederation eBGP peers, but first they inject their own sub-AS into the AS_PATH AS_CONFED_SEQ segment. (This part of the AS_PATH is displayed inside parentheses in the output of the **show ip bgp** command, as shown in the figure.)

4. The same process as in Step 2 occurs in the other two subautonomous systems, respectively.

5. R6 and R9 advertise the route to each other after adding their respective ASNs to the AS_CONFED_SEQ.

6. R9 advertises the prefix through a true eBGP connection after removing the sub-AS portion of the AS_PATH.

By the end of these steps, all the routers inside ASN 123 have learned of the 21.0.0.0/8 prefix. Also, ASN 678 (R77 in this case) learned of a route for that same prefix—a route that would work and would not have the black-hole effect. In fact, from ASN 678's perspective, it sees a route that appears to be through ASNs 123 and 45. Also note that routers in sub-AS 65002 and 65003 will not advertise the prefix back into sub-AS 65001 because AS 65001 is already in the confederation AS_PATH.

The choice of values for sub-ASNs 65001, 65002, and 65003 is not coincidental in this case. ASNs 64512 through 65535 are *private ASNs*, meant for use in cases where the ASN will not be advertised to the Internet or other autonomous systems. By using private ASNs, a confederation can hopefully avoid the following type of problem. Imagine that sub-AS 65003 instead used ASN 45. The AS_PATH loop check examines the entire AS_PATH. As a result, the prefixes shown in Figure 1-8 would never be advertised to sub-AS 45, and in turn would not be advertised to ASN 678. Using private ASNs would prevent this problem.

The following list summarizes the key topics regarding confederations:

**Key Topic**

- Inside a sub-AS, full mesh is required, because full iBGP rules are in effect.

- The confederation eBGP connections act like normal eBGP connections in that iBGP routes are advertised—as long as the AS_PATH implies that such an advertisement would not cause a loop.

- Confederation eBGP connections also act like normal eBGP connections regarding Time to Live (TTL), because all packets use a TTL of 1 by default. (TTL can be changed with the **neighbor ebgp-multihop** command.)

- Confederation eBGP connections act like iBGP connections in every other regard— for example, the NEXT_HOP is not changed by default.

- Confederation ASNs are not considered part of the length of the AS_PATH when a router chooses the best routes based on the shortest AS_PATH.

- Confederation routers remove the confederation ASNs from the AS_PATH in Updates sent outside the confederation; therefore, other routers do not know that a confederation was used.

## Configuring Confederations

Configuring confederations requires only a few additional commands beyond those already covered in this chapter. However, migrating to use confederations can be quite painful. The problem is that the true ASN will no longer be configured on the **router bgp** command, but instead on the **bgp confederation identifier** BGP subcommand. So, BGP will simply be out of service on one or more routers while the migration occurs. Table 1-10 lists the key confederation commands and their purpose.

**Key Topic**

**Table 1-10** *BGP Subcommands Used for Confederations*

| Purpose | Command |
|---|---|
| Define a router's sub-AS | **router bgp** *sub-as* |
| Define the true AS | **bgp confederation identifier** *asn* |
| Identify a neighboring AS as another sub-AS | **bgp confederation peers** *sub-asn* |

Example 1-14 shows a simple configuration for the topology in Figure 1-9.

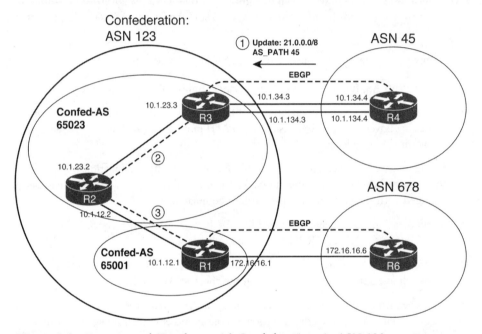

**Figure 1-9**   *Internetwork Topology with Confederations in ASN 123*

In this internetwork topology, R1 is in sub-AS 65001, with R2 and R3 in sub-AS 65023. In this case, R1 and R3 will not be neighbors. The following list outlines the sequence of events to propagate a prefix:

1. R3 will learn prefix 21.0.0.0/8 through eBGP from AS 45 (R4).

2. R3 will advertise the prefix through iBGP to R2.

3. R2 will advertise the prefix through confederation eBGP to R1.

**Example 1-14**   *Confederation Inside AS 123 (Continued)*

```
! R1 Configuration. Note the sub-AS in the router bgp command, and the true AS in
! the bgp confederation identifier command. Also note the neighbor ebgp-multihop
! command for confederation eBGP peer R2, as they are using loopbacks. Also, sync
! is not needed now that the confederation has been created.
```

```
router bgp 65001
 no synchronization
 bgp router-id 111.111.111.111
 bgp confederation identifier 123
 bgp confederation peers 65023
 neighbor 2.2.2.2 remote-as 65023
 neighbor 2.2.2.2 ebgp-multihop 2
 neighbor 2.2.2.2 update-source Loopback1
 neighbor 2.2.2.2 next-hop-self
 neighbor 172.16.16.6 remote-as 678
! R2 Configuration. Note the bgp confederation peers 65001 command. Without it,
! R2 would think that neighbor 1.1.1.1 was a true eBGP connection, and remove
! the confederation AS_PATH entries before advertising to R1.
router bgp 65023
 no synchronization
 bgp confederation identifier 123
 bgp confederation peers 65001
 neighbor 1.1.1.1 remote-as 65001
 neighbor 1.1.1.1 ebgp-multihop 2
 neighbor 1.1.1.1 update-source Loopback1
 neighbor 3.3.3.3 remote-as 65023
 neighbor 3.3.3.3 update-source Loopback1
! R3 Configuration. Note that R3 does not need a bgp confederation peers command,
! as it does not have any confederation eBGP peers.
router bgp 65023
 no synchronization
 bgp log-neighbor-changes
 bgp confederation identifier 123
 neighbor 2.2.2.2 remote-as 65023
 neighbor 2.2.2.2 update-source Loopback1
 neighbor 2.2.2.2 next-hop-self
 neighbor 4.4.4.4 remote-as 45
 neighbor 4.4.4.4 ebgp-multihop 2
 neighbor 4.4.4.4 update-source Loopback1
! R1 has received the 21.0.0.0/8 prefix, with sub-AS 65023 shown in parentheses,
! and true AS 45 shown outside the parentheses. R1 has also learned the same
! prefix via AS 678 and R6. The route through the sub-AS is best because it is the
! shortest AS_PATH; the shortest AS_PATH logic ignores the confederation sub-
! autonomous systems.
R1# show ip bgp | begin Network
   Network          Next Hop            Metric LocPrf Weight Path
*> 21.0.0.0         3.3.3.3                  0    100      0 (65023) 45 i
*                   172.16.16.6                            0 678 45 i
*> 22.2.2.0/24      3.3.3.3                  0    100      0 (65023) 45 i
*                   172.16.16.6                            0 678 45 i
! R6 shows its received update from R1, showing the removed sub-AS, and the
```

```
! inclusion of the true AS, AS 123.
R6# show ip bgp neighbor 172.16.16.1 received-routes | begin Network
   Network          Next Hop          Metric LocPrf Weight Path
r  21.0.0.0         172.16.16.1                        0 123 45 i
r  22.2.2.0/24      172.16.16.1                        0 123 45 i
```

## Route Reflectors

Route reflectors (RR) achieve the same result as confederations: They remove the need
for a full mesh of iBGP peers, allow all iBGP routes to be learned by all iBGP routers in
the AS, and prevent loops. In an iBGP design using RRs, a partial mesh of iBGP peers
is defined. Some routers are configured as RR servers; these servers are allowed to learn
iBGP routes from their clients and then advertise them to other iBGP peers. The example
in Figure 1-10 shows the key terms and some of the core logic used by an RR; note that
only the RR server itself uses different logic, with clients and nonclients acting as normal
iBGP peers.

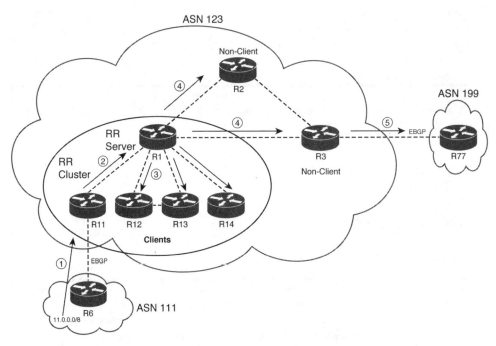

**Figure 1-10**  *Basic Flow Using a Single RR, Four Clients, and Two Nonclients*

Figure 1-10 shows how prefix 11.0.0.0/8 is propagated through the AS, using the following
steps:

**1.**  R11 learns 11.0.0.0/8 using eBGP.

**2.**  R11 uses normal iBGP rules and sends an Update to R1.

3.  R1 reflects the routes by sending Updates to all other clients.

4.  R1 also reflects the routes to all nonclients.

5.  Nonclients use non-RR rules, sending an Update over eBGP to R77.

Only the router acting as the RR uses modified rules; the other routers (clients and non-clients) are not even aware of the RR, nor do they change their operating rules. Table 1-11 summarizes the rules for RR operation, which vary based on from what type of BGP peer the RR receives the prefix. The table lists the sources from which a prefix can be learned, and the types of other routers to which the RR will reflect the prefix information.

**Table 1-11** *Types of Neighbors to Which Prefixes Are Reflected*

| Location from Which a Prefix Is Learned | Are Routes Advertised to Clients? | Are Routes Advertised to Nonclients? |
|---|---|---|
| Client | Yes | Yes |
| Nonclient | Yes | No |
| eBGP | Yes | Yes |

The one case in which the RR does not reflect routes is when the RR receives a route from a nonclient, with the RR not reflecting that route to other nonclients. The perspective behind that logic is that RRs act like normal iBGP peers with nonclients and with eBGP neighbors—in other words, the RR does not forward iBGP-learned routes to other nonclient iBGP peers. The difference in how the RR behaves relates to when a client sends the RR a prefix or when the RR decides to reflect a prefix to the clients.

One (or more) RR servers, and their clients, create a single RR cluster. A BGP design using RRs can consist of

■  Clusters with multiple RRs in a cluster

■  Multiple clusters, although using multiple clusters makes sense only when physical redundancy exists as well

With multiple clusters, at least one RR from a cluster must be peered with at least one RR in each of the other clusters. Typically, all RRs are peered directly, creating a full mesh of RR iBGP peers among RRs. Also, if some routers are nonclients, they should be included in the full mesh of RRs. Figure 1-11 shows the concept, with each RR fully meshed with the other RRs in other clusters, as well as with the nonclient.

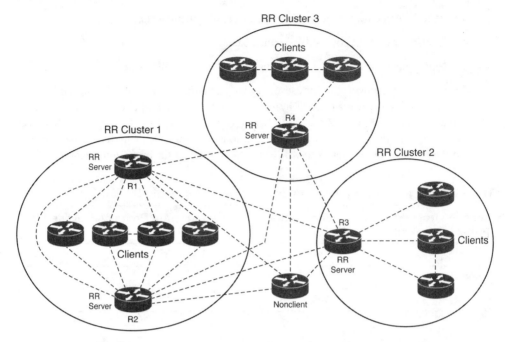

**Figure 1-11**   *Multiple RR Clusters with Full Mesh Among RRs and Nonclients*

If you consider the logic summary in Table 1-11 compared to Figure 1-11, it appears that routing loops are not only possible but probable with this design. However, the RR feature uses several tools to prevent loops, as follows:

- **CLUSTER_LIST:** RRs add their *cluster ID* into a BGP PA called the CLUSTER_LIST before sending an Update. When receiving a BGP Update, RRs discard received prefixes for which their cluster ID already appears. As with AS_PATH for confederations, this prevents RRs from looping advertisements between clusters.

- **ORIGINATOR_ID:** This PA lists the RID of the first iBGP peer to advertise the route into the AS. If a router sees its own BGP ID as the ORIGINATOR_ID in a received route, it does not use or propagate the route.

- **Only advertise the best routes:** RRs reflect routes only if the RR considers the route to be a "best" route in its own BGP table. This further limits the routes reflected by the RR. (It also has a positive effect compared with confederations in that an average router sees fewer, typically useless, redundant routes.)

Example 1-15 shows a simple example of using RRs. The design uses two clusters, with two RRs (R9 and R2) and two clients (R1 and R3). The following list outlines the sequence of events to propagate a prefix, as shown in Figure 1-12:

**1.** R3 learns prefix 21.0.0.0/8 through eBGP from AS 45 (R4).

**2.** R3 advertises the prefix through iBGP to R2 using normal logic.

3. R2, an RR, receiving a prefix from an RR client, reflects the route through iBGP to R9—a nonclient as far as R2 is concerned.

4. R9, an RR, receiving an iBGP route from a nonclient, reflects the route to R1, its RR client.

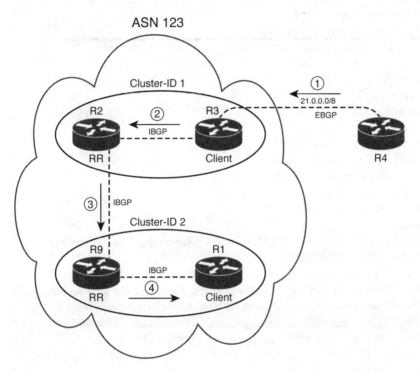

**Figure 1-12**  *Modified AS 123 Used in RR Example 1-15*

**Example 1-15**  *RR Configuration for AS 123, Two RRs, and Two Clients*

```
! R3 Configuration. The RR client has no overt signs of being a client; the
! process is completely hidden from all routers except RRs. Also, do not forget
! that one of the main motivations for using RRs is to allow sync to be disabled.
router bgp 123
 no synchronization
 neighbor 2.2.2.2 remote-as 123
 neighbor 2.2.2.2 update-source Loopback1
 neighbor 2.2.2.2 next-hop-self
 neighbor 4.4.4.4 remote-as 45
 neighbor 4.4.4.4 ebgp-multihop 255
 neighbor 4.4.4.4 update-source Loopback1
! R2 Configuration. The cluster ID would default to R2's BGP RID, but it has been
! manually set to "1," which will be listed as "0.0.0.1" in command output. R2
! designates 3.3.3.3 (R3) as a client.
router bgp 123
```

```
 no synchronization
 bgp cluster-id 1
 neighbor 3.3.3.3 remote-as 123
 neighbor 3.3.3.3 update-source Loopback1
 neighbor 3.3.3.3 route-reflector-client
 neighbor 9.9.9.9 remote-as 123
 neighbor 9.9.9.9 update-source Loopback1
```

```
! R9 Configuration. The configuration is similar to R2, but with a different
! cluster ID.
router bgp 123
 no synchronization
 bgp router-id 9.9.9.9
 bgp cluster-id 2
 neighbor 1.1.1.1 remote-as 123
 neighbor 1.1.1.1 update-source Loopback2
 neighbor 1.1.1.1 route-reflector-client
 neighbor 2.2.2.2 remote-as 123
 neighbor 2.2.2.2 update-source Loopback2
 no auto-summary
! The R1 configuration is omitted, as it contains no specific RR configuration,
! as is the case with all RR clients.
! The 21.0.0.0/8 prefix has been learned by R3, forwarded over iBGP as normal to
! R2. Then, R2 reflected the prefix to its only other peer, R9. The show ip bgp
! 21.0.0.0 command shows the current AS_PATH (45); the iBGP originator of the
! route (3.3.3.3), and the iBGP neighbor from which it was learned ("from
! 2.2.2.2"); and the cluster list, which currently has R2's cluster (0.0.0.1).
! The next output is from R9.
R9# show ip bgp 21.0.0.0
BGP routing table entry for 21.0.0.0/8, version 3
Paths: (1 available, best #1, table Default-IP-Routing-Table)
Flag: 0x820
  Advertised to update-groups:
     2
  45
    3.3.3.3 (metric 2300416) from 2.2.2.2 (2.2.2.2)
      Origin IGP, metric 0, localpref 100, valid, internal, best
      Originator: 3.3.3.3, Cluster list: 0.0.0.1
! RR R9 reflected the prefix to its client (R1), as seen next. Note the changes
! compared to R9's output, with iBGP route being learned from R9 ("from 9.9.9.9"),
! and the cluster list now including cluster 0.0.0.2, as added by R9.
```

```
R1# sho ip bgp 21.0.0.0
BGP routing table entry for 21.0.0.0/8, version 20
Paths: (1 available, best #1, table Default-IP-Routing-Table)
  Not advertised to any peer
  45
```

```
3.3.3.3 (metric 2302976) from 9.9.9.9 (9.9.9.9)
  Origin IGP, metric 0, localpref 100, valid, internal, best
    Originator: 3.3.3.3, Cluster list: 0.0.0.2, 0.0.0.1
```

# Multiprotocol BGP

Now we need to discuss the existence of an extension to the BGP-4 protocol. This extension allows the advertisement of customer Virtual Private Network (VPN) routes between provider edge (PE) devices that were injected into customer edge (CE) devices. These prefixes can be learned through a number of dynamic methods to include standard BGP-4, EIGRP, OSPF, or static routes.

We are required to run Multiprotocol BGP (MP-BGP) only within the service provider cloud. As such, each MP-BGP session is an internal BGP session. The session is considered internal because of the fact that the session is formed between two routers that belong to the same autonomous system.

MP-iBGP is required within the MPLS/VPN architecture because the BGP update needs to carry more information than just an IPv4 address. As an example, in the case of the Multiprotocol Label Switching (MPLS) L3 VPNs, the update must communicate the VPN IPv4 address, MPLS label information, and extended or standard BGP communities.

**Key Topic**

As mentioned, the actual nature of these extensions to the BGP is to provide additional capabilities that allow BGP to carry more information than just the IPv4 address and the typical BGP attributes. As we have discussed thus far, when a BGP session is established between two peers, an OPEN message exchanges initial BGP parameters, such as the ASN. In BGP, the OPEN message is used to communicate other parameters, one of which is Capabilities. This optional parameter is used to define which capabilities the peer can understand and execute; among these capabilities is multiprotocol extensions. It is through the application of multiprotocol extensions that the ability to exchange addresses other than standard IPv4 addresses was introduced into BGP. This process required the creation of some additional Optional attributes needed to provide enhanced functionality in the management and injection of these non-IPv4 addresses.

Specifically, MP-BGP employs two new Optional nontransitive attributes:

- Multiprotocol Reachable NLRI (MP_REACH_NLRI) announces new multiprotocol routes.

- Multiprotocol Unreachable NLRI (MP_UNREACH_NLRI) serves to revoke the routes previously announced by MP_REACH_NLRI.

We need to take a closer look at each of these to better understand the fundamental operation of MP-BGP itself.

MP_REACH_NLRI communicates a set of reachable prefixes together with their next-hop information. The second attribute, MP_UNREACH_NLRI, carries the set of unreachable destinations. For two BGP speakers to exchange multiprotocol data, they must agree on these capabilities during their capabilities exchange.

When a PE router sends an MP-iBGP update to other PE routers, the MP_REACH_NLRI attribute contains one or more triples. Table 1-12 outlines the values defined by these triples.

**Table 1-12**   *MP-BGP Attributes*

| Purpose | Command |
|---|---|
| Address family information | The address family information identifies the Network layer protocol that is being carried within the Update. |
| Next-hop information | The next-hop information is the next-hop address of the next router in the path to the destination. |
| NLRI (network layer reachability information) | The NLRI manages the addition or withdrawal of multiprotocol routes and the next-hop address, and the NLRI prefixes must be in the same address family. |

## Configuration of Multiprotocol BGP

The configuration of MP-BGP is accomplished by following several steps and various configuration commands in many different configuration contexts. This process is slightly more complicated than the typical BGP configuration processes that we have followed thus far in our discussions. This added complexity and syntax change were created to support the need of the protocol to support multiple PE-to-PE sessions across the service provider cloud as well as to support the possibility that the customer might want to run eBGP as his CE-PE protocol of choice.

In our previous discussion, we covered how the MP-BGP specification defined the concept of an address family and that this was created to allow BGP to carry protocols other than IPv4. Address families come in many forms. As an example, in MPLS/VPN deployments, the address family is called the VPN-IPv4 address and is much longer than a standard IPv4 address. Additionally, we have to also realize that by default, when MP-BGP is activated, it will automatically carry IPv4 unicast routes; this behavior can be problematic in situations where we do not want this to take place. Situations like this can arise in our infrastructure when we only want to communicate applications or protocol-specific addresses like those characteristic to Layer 3 VPNs, to name a few. To alter this behavior, we can disable the automatic advertisement of IPv4 unicast prefixes. Example 1-16 shows the syntax of this command.

**Example 1-16**   bgp default ipv4-unicast *Command*

```
R1(config)# router bgp 1
R1(config-router)# no bgp default ipv4-unicast
```

The next step in the configuration of MP-iBGP is to define and activate the BGP sessions between PE routers. Just to illustrate the versatility of the command syntax, observe that some of these configurations carry VPN-IPv4 routes, some only IPv4 routes, and others carry VPN-IPv4 and IPv4 routes. The type of BGP session and the specification of which routes the peering sessions will carry are controlled through the use of the address families that we have been discussing. Notice also that each of the BGP configurations manages what routes will be redistributed into and out of BGP. This behavior is best described as *context-based routing*.

To accomplish this, we must configure a BGP address family for each Virtual Routing and Forwarding (VRF) configured on the PE router and a separate address family to carry no IPv4 routes between PE routers. The initial BGP process, the portion of the configuration that cites no address family specifications, becomes the default address family. This default context becomes the "catch all" where any non-VRF-based or IPv4-specific sessions can be configured. Any prefixes learned or advertised in this default address family will be injected into the global routing table. As such, it must be noted that the configuration of these BGP sessions is exactly the same as the standard BGP configuration we have discussed up to this point, with the exception that the session needs to be activated. The **neighbor** command controls the activation of the session, as shown in Example 1-17.

**Example 1-17**  *BGP Standard IPv4 Configuration*

```
R1(config)# router bgp 1
R1(config-router)# neighbor 194.22.15.3 remote-as 1
R1(config-router)# neighbor 194.22.15.3 update-source loopback0
R1(config-router)# neighbor 194.22.15.3 activate
```

The BGP process activates the MP-iBGP session that carries non-IPv4 prefixes through the use of a protocol-specific address family. This configuration creates a routing context for exchanging these non-IPv4 prefixes. Example 1-18 illustrates this command syntax and the relevant commands needed to configure the MP-iBGP session between Routers R1 and R2.

**Example 1-18**  *Address Family Configuration*

```
R1(config)# router bgp 1
R1(config-router)# address-family ?
  ipv4    Address family
  vpnv4   Address family

R1(config-router)# address-family vpnv4
R1(config-router)# neighbor 194.22.15.3 activate
```

Key
Topic

In Example 1-18, notice that the VPNv4 address family configuration requires only one command. This is because the BGP neighbor configuration commands need to be entered under the global BGP process, and therefore need to be activated to carry non-IPv4 prefixes.

The configuration of the VPNv4 address family also adds a further command to the BGP configuration to support the MP-BGP-specific extended community attributes. This command will be added by the IOS by default and is necessary because it instructs BGP to advertise the extended community attributes. Example 1-19 provides the syntax of this command.

**Example 1-19**  *Enabling Extended Community Support*

```
R1(config-router)# neighbor 194.22.15.3 send-community ?
  both      Send Standard and Extended Community attributes
  extended  Send Extended Community attribute
  standard  Send Standard Community attribute
  <cr>
```

**Key Topic**

The default behavior is to send only the extended community attribute. If the network design requires the standard community attribute to be attached to these non-IPv4 prefixes, this behavior can be changed through the **neighbor 194.22.15.3 send-community both** command.

We now need to advertise these non-IPv4 routes across the service provider cloud. For the purposes of our discussions, we will explore this syntax using numerous VPNv4 configurations. Note that MP-iBGP communicates these routes across the MP-iBGP sessions running between PE routers. To this end, the routing context must be configured under the BGP process to communicate to BGP which VRF prefixes it needs to advertise.

This is accomplished through the address family configuration under the BGP process, using the IPv4 option of the **address-family** command, as illustrated in Example 1-18. Each VRF needs to be configured under the BGP process using its own address family. Also, these prefixes must be redistributed into BGP if they are to be advertised across the service provider cloud.

Example 1-20 illustrates how this is accomplished using VPNv4 address families to illustrate the syntax used.

**Example 1-20**  *MP-BGP Redistribution Between VRFs*

```
hostname R1
!
ip vrf VPN_A
 rd 1:100
 route-target export 100:100
 route-target import 100:100
!
ip vrf VPN_B
 rd 1:200
 route-target export 100:200
 route-target import 100:200
!
interface loopback0
 ip address 194.22.15.2 255.255.255.255
!
interface serial0
```

```
ip vrf forwarding VPN_A
 ip address 10.2.1.5 255.255.255.252
!
interface serial1
ip vrf forwarding VPN_B
 ip address 195.12.2.5 255.255.255.252
!
router rip
 version 2
 !
address-family ipv4 vrf VPN_A
 version 2
 redistribute bgp 1 metric 1
 network 10.0.0.0
 no auto-summary
exit-address-family
!
address-family ipv4 vrf VPN_B
 version 2
 redistribute bgp 1 metric 1
 network 195.12.2.0
 no auto-summary
exit-address-family
!
router bgp 1
 no bgp default ipv4-unicast
 neighbor 194.22.15.3 remote-as 1
 neighbor 194.22.15.3 update-source loopback0
 neighbor 194.22.15.3 activate
 neighbor 194.22.15.1 remote-as 1
 neighbor 194.22.15.1 update-source loopback0
 !
address-family ipv4 vrf VPN_A
 redistribute rip metric 1
 no auto-summary
 no synchronization
exit-address-family
!
address-family ipv4 vrf VPN_B
 redistribute rip metric 1
 no auto-summary
 no synchronization
exit-address-family
!
address-family vpnv4
```

```
  neighbor 194.22.15.3 activate
  neighbor 194.22.15.3 send-community extended
  neighbor 194.22.15.1 activate
  neighbor 194.22.15.1 send-community extended
 exit-address-family
```

# Foundation Summary

This section lists additional details and facts to round out the coverage of the topics in this chapter. Unlike most of the Cisco Press Exam Certification Guides, this "Foundation Summary" does not repeat information presented in the "Foundation Topics" section of the chapter. Please take the time to read and study the details in the "Foundation Topics" section of the chapter, as well as review items noted with a Key Topic icon.

Table 1-13 lists some of the key RFCs for BGP.

**Table 1-13**   *Protocols and Standards for Chapter 1*

| Topic | Standard |
|---|---|
| BGP-4 | RFC 4271 |
| BGP Confederations | RFC 5065 |
| BGP Route Reflection | RFC 4456 |
| MD5 Authentication | RFC 2385 |

Table 1-14 lists the BGP path attributes mentioned in this chapter and describes their purpose.

**Table 1-14**   *BGP Path Attributes*

| Path Attribute | Description | Characteristics |
|---|---|---|
| AS_PATH | Lists ASNs through which the route has been advertised | Well-known Mandatory |
| NEXT_HOP | Lists the next-hop IP address used to reach an NLRI | Well-known Mandatory |
| AGGREGATOR | Lists the RID and ASN of the router that created a summary NLRI | Optional Transitive |
| ATOMIC_AGGREGATE | Tags a summary NLRI as being a summary | Well-known Discretionary |
| ORIGIN | Value implying from where the route was taken for injection into BGP: i(IGP), e(EGP), or ? (incomplete information) | Well-known Mandatory |
| ORIGINATOR_ID | Used by RRs to denote the RID of the iBGP neighbor that injected the NLRI into the AS | Optional Nontransitive |
| CLUSTER_LIST | Used by RRs to list the RR cluster IDs to prevent loops | Optional Nontransitive |

Table 1-15 lists and describes the methods to introduce entries into the BGP table.

**Table 1-15**    *Summary: Methods to Introduce Entries into the BGP Table*

| Method | Summary Description |
|---|---|
| **network** command | Advertises a route into BGP. Depends on the existence of the configured network/subnet in the IP routing table. |
| Redistribution | Takes IGP, static, or connected routes; metric (MED) assignment is not required. |
| Manual summarization | Requires at least one component subnet in the BGP table; options for keeping all component subnets, suppressing all from advertisement, or suppressing a subset from being advertised. |
| **default-information originate** command | Requires a default route in the IP routing table, plus the **redistribute** command. |
| **neighbor default-originate** command | With the optional route map, requires the route map to match the IP routing table with a permit action before advertising a default route. Without the route map, the default is always advertised. |

Table 1-16 lists some of the most popular Cisco IOS commands related to the topics in this chapter.

**Table 1-16**    *Command Reference for Chapter 1*

| Command | Command Mode and Description |
|---|---|
| **address-family vpnv4** | BGP mode; allows the creation of the MP-BGP session necessary to form the VPNv4 session between PE devices |
| **aggregate-address** *address mask* [**as-set**] [**summary-only**] [**suppress-map** *map-name*] [**advertise-map** *map-name*] [**attribute-map** *map-name*] | BGP mode; summarizes BGP routes, suppressing all/none/some of the component subnets |
| **auto-summary** | BGP mode; enables automatic summarization to classful boundaries of locally injected routes |
| **bgp client-to-client reflection** | BGP mode; on by default, tells an RR server to reflect routes learned from a client to other clients |
| **bgp cluster-id** *cluster-id* | BGP mode; defines a nondefault RR cluster ID to an RR server |

| Command | Command Mode and Description |
|---|---|
| bgp confederation identifier *as-number* | BGP mode; for confederations, defines the ASN used for the entire AS as seen by other autonomous systems |
| bgp confederation peers *as-number* [... *as-number*] | BGP mode; for confederations, identifies which neighboring ASNs are in other confederation subautonomous systems |
| bgp log-neighbor-changes | BGP mode; on by default, it tells BGP to create log messages for significant changes in BGP operation |
| bgp router-id *ip-address* | BGP mode; defines the BGP router ID |
| default-information originate | BGP mode; required to allow a static default route to be redistributed into BGP |
| default-metric *number* | BGP mode; sets the default metric assigned to routes redistributed into BGP; normally defaults to the IGP metric for each route |
| distance bgp *external-distance internal-distance local-distance* | BGP mode; defines the administrative distance for eBGP, iBGP, and locally injected BGP routes |
| neighbor {*ip-address* \| *peer-group-name*} default-originate [route-map *map-name*] | BGP mode; tells the router to add a default route to the BGP Update sent to this neighbor, under the conditions set in the optional route map |
| neighbor {*ip-address* \| *peer-group-name*} description *text* | BGP mode; adds a descriptive text reference in the BGP configuration |
| neighbor {*ip-address* \| *peer-group-name*} ebgp-multihop [*ttl*] | BGP mode; for eBGP peers, sets the TTL in packets sent to this peer to something larger than the default of 1 |
| neighbor *ip-address* \| *peer-group-name* next-hop-self | BGP mode; causes IOS to reset the NEXT_HOP PA to the IP address used as the source address of Updates sent to this neighbor |
| neighbor {*ip-address* \| *peer-group-name*} password *string* | BGP mode; defines the key used in an MD5 hash of all BGP messages to this neighbor |
| neighbor *ip-address* peer-group *peer-group-name* | BGP mode; associates a neighbor's IP address as part of a peer group |
| neighbor *peer-group-name* peer-group | BGP mode; defines the name of a peer group |
| neighbor {*ip-address* \| *peer-group-name*} remote-as *as-number* | BGP mode; defines the AS of the neighbor |
| neighbor {*ip-address* \| *peer-group-name*} shutdown | BGP mode; administratively shuts down a neighbor, stopping the TCP connection |

| Command | Command Mode and Description |
|---------|------------------------------|
| neighbor [*ip-address* \| *peer-group-name*] timers *keepalive holdtime* | BGP mode; sets the two BGP timers, just for this neighbor |
| neighbor {*ip-address* \| *ipv6-address* \| *peer-group-name*} update-source *interface-type interface-number* | BGP mode; defines the source IP address used for BGP messages sent to this neighbor |
| network {*network-number* [mask *network-mask*] [route-map *map-tag*] | BGP mode; causes IOS to add the defined prefix to the BGP table if it exists in the IP routing table |
| router bgp *as-number* | Global command; defines the ASN and puts the user in BGP mode |
| synchronization | BGP mode; enables BGP synchronization |
| timers bgp *keepalive holdtime* | BGP mode; defines BGP timers for all neighbors |
| show ip bgp [*network*] [*network-mask*] [longer-prefixes] [prefix-list *prefix-list-name* \| route-map *route-map-name*] [shorter prefixes mask-length] | Exec mode; lists details of a router's BGP table |
| show ip bgp injected-paths | Exec mode; lists routes locally injected into BGP |
| show ip bgp neighbors [*neighbor-address*] [received-routes \| routes \| advertised-routes \| {paths *regexp*} \| dampened-routes \| *received prefix-filter*] | Exec mode; lists information about routes sent and received to particular neighbors |
| show ip bgp peer-group [*peer-group-name*] [summary] | Exec mode; lists details about a particular peer group |
| show ip bgp summary | Exec mode; lists basic statistics for each BGP peer |

# Memory Builders

The CCIE Routing and Switching written exam, like all Cisco CCIE written exams, covers a fairly broad set of topics. This section provides some basic tools to help you exercise your memory about some of the broader topics covered in this chapter.

## Fill In Key Tables from Memory

Appendix E, "Key Tables for CCIE Study," on the CD in the back of this book, contains empty sets of some of the key summary tables in each chapter. Print Appendix E, refer to this chapter's tables in it, and fill in the tables from memory. Refer to Appendix F, "Solutions for Key Tables for CCIE Study," on the CD, to check your answers.

## Definitions

Next, take a few moments to write down the definitions for the following terms:

path attribute, BGP table, BGP Update, established, iBGP, eBGP, EGP, BGP, peer group, eBGP multihop, autonomous system, AS number, AS_PATH, ORIGIN, NLRI, NEXT_HOP, MULTI_EXIT_DISC, LOCAL_PREF, routing black hole, synchronization, confederation, route reflector, confederation identifier, sub-AS, route reflector server, route reflector client, route reflector nonclient, confederation AS, confederation eBGP, weight

Refer to the glossary to check your answers.

## Further Reading

*Routing TCP/IP, Volume II*, by Jeff Doyle and Jennifer DeHaven Carrol

*Cisco BGP-4 Command and Configuration Handbook*, by William R. Parkhurst

*Internet Routing Architectures*, by Bassam Halabi

*Troubleshooting IP Routing Protocols*, by Zaheer Aziz, Johnson Liu, Abe Martey, and Faraz Shamim

Almost every reference can be reached from the Cisco BGP support page at www.cisco.com/en/US/partner/tech/tk365/tk80/tsd_technology_support_sub-protocol_home.html. Requires a Cisco.com username/password.

**Blueprint topics covered in this chapter:**

This chapter covers the following topics from the Cisco CCIE Routing and Switching written exam blueprint:

- Implement IPv4 BGP synchronization, attributes, and other advanced features

- Fast convergence

## CHAPTER 2

# BGP Routing Policies

This chapter examines the tools available to define Border Gateway Protocol (BGP) routing policies. A BGP routing policy defines the rules used by one or more routers to impact two main goals: filtering routes and influencing which routes are considered the best routes by BGP.

BGP filtering tools are mostly straightforward, with the exception of AS_PATH filtering. AS_PATH filters use regular expressions to match the AS_PATH path attribute (PA), making the configuration challenging. Beyond that, most of the BGP filtering concepts are directly comparable to IGP filtering concepts.

The other topics in this chapter explain routing policies that focus on impacting the BGP decision process. The decision process itself is first outlined, followed by explanations of how each step in the process can be used to impact which routes are considered best by BGP.

## "Do I Know This Already?" Quiz

Table 2-1 outlines the major headings in this chapter and the corresponding "Do I Know This Already?" quiz questions.

**Table 2-1** *"Do I Know This Already?" Foundation Topics Section-to-Question Mapping*

| Foundation Topics Section | Questions Covered in This Section | Score |
|---|---|---|
| Route Filtering and Route Summarization | 1–4 | |
| BGP Path Attributes and the BGP Decision Process | 5–7 | |
| Configuring BGP Policies | 8–12 | |
| BGP Communities | 13, 14 | |
| Total Score | | |

To best use this pre-chapter assessment, remember to score yourself strictly. You can find the answers in Appendix A, "Answers to the 'Do I Know This Already?' Quizzes."

1. A BGP policy needs to be configured to filter all the /20 prefixes whose first two octets are 20.128. Which of the following answers would provide the correct matching logic for the filtering process, matching only the described subnets and no others?

   a. access-list 1 deny 20.128.0.0 0.0.255.255

   b. access-list 101 deny ip 20.128.0.0 0.0.255.255 host 255.255.240.0

   c. ip prefix-list 1 deny 20.128.0.0/16 eq 20

   d. ip prefix-list 2 deny 20.128.0.0/16 ge 20 le 20

2. Router R1 has a working BGP implementation, advertising subnets of 1.0.0.0/8 to neighbor 2.2.2.2 (R2). A route map named fred has been configured on R1 to filter all routes in network 1.0.0.0. R1 has just added the **router bgp** subcommand **neighbor 2.2.2.2 route-map fred out**. No other commands have been used afterward. Which of the following answers, taken as the next step, would allow proper verification of whether the filter indeed filtered the routes?

   a. The **show ip bgp neighbor 2.2.2.2 advertised-routes** command on R1 will no longer list the filtered routes.

   b. The **show ip bgp neighbor 2.2.2.2 advertised-routes** command on R1 will reflect the filtered routes by listing them with a code of **r**, meaning "RIB failure."

   c. The filtering will not occur, and cannot be verified, until R1 issues a **clear ip bgp 2.2.2.2** command.

   d. None of the **show ip bgp** command options on R1 will confirm whether the filtering has occurred.

3. A router needs to match routes with AS_PATHs that include 333, as long as it is not the first ASN in the AS_PATH, while not matching AS_PATHs that include 33333. Which of the following syntactically correct commands could be a part of the complete configuration to match the correct AS_PATHs?

   a. ip filter-list 1 permit ^.*_333_

   b. ip filter-list 2 permit .*333_

   c. ip filter-list 3 permit .*_333.*$

   d. ip filter-list 4 permit _333_$

   e. ip filter-list 5 permit ^.*_333_.*$

**4.** R1 and R2 are working BGP peers. The following output of the **show ip bgp** command shows the entries learned by R1 from R2. It also shows some configuration that was added later on R1. After the appropriate **clear** command is used to make the new configuration take effect, which of the following entries should R1 have in its BGP table?

```
Network            Next Hop Metric       LocPrf  Weight  Path
*>i11.10.0.0/16    2.2.2.2  4294967294   100      0 4 1   33333 10    200 44 i
*>i11.11.0.0/16    2.2.2.2  4294967294   100      0 4 1   33333 10    200 44 i
*>i11.12.0.0/16    2.2.2.2  4294967294   100      0 4 1   404      303 202    i
! New config shown next
router bgp 1
neighbor 2.2.2.2 distribute-list 1 in
access-list 1 permit 11.8.0.0 0.3.255.255
```

   **a.** 11.10.0.0/16

   **b.** 11.11.0.0/16

   **c.** 11.12.0.0/16

   **d.** 11.8.0.0/14

   **e.** None of the listed prefixes

**5.** Which of the following is true regarding BGP path attribute types?

   **a.** The BGP features using well-known attributes must be included in every BGP Update.

   **b.** Optional attributes do not have to be implemented by the programmers that are creating a particular BGP implementation.

   **c.** Nontransitive attributes cannot be advertised into another AS.

   **d.** Discretionary attributes contain sensitive information; Updates should be encoded with MD5 for privacy.

**6.** Which of the following items in the BGP decision tree occur after the check of the AS_PATH length?

   **a.** Best ORIGIN code

   **b.** LOCAL_PREF

   **c.** MED

   **d.** Whether the next hop is reachable

7. Which of the following steps in the BGP decision process consider a larger value to be the better value?

   a. ORIGIN

   b. LOCAL_PREF

   c. WEIGHT

   d. MED

   e. IGP metric to reach the next hop

8. Which of the following is not advertised to BGP neighbors?

   a. WEIGHT

   b. MED

   c. LOCAL_PREF

   d. ORIGIN

9. The following shows the output of the **show ip bgp** command on R1. Which BGP decision tree step determined which route was best? (Assume that the next-hop IP address is reachable.)

```
Network            Next Hop   Metric      LocPrf Weight Path
*> 11.10.0.0/16   10.1.2.3   4294967294    100     0 4 1  33333 10 200 44 i
*  i               2.2.2.2    4294967294    100     0 4 1  33333 10 200 44 i
*  i               2.2.2.2    4294967294    100     0 4 1  404 505 303 202 i
```

   a. Largest Weight

   b. Best ORIGIN code

   c. Lowest MED

   d. Largest LOCAL_PREF

   e. Better neighbor type

   f. None of the answers is correct.

**10.** The following shows the output of the **show ip bgp** command on R1. Which BGP decision tree step determined which route was best? (Assume that the NEXT_HOP IP address is reachable.)

```
Network            Next Hop    Metric  LocPrf  Weight  Path
*   11.10.0.0/16   10.1.2.3         3     120      10   4 1  33333 10 200 44 ?
*>i                2.2.2.2          1     130      30   4 33333 10 200 44 i
*  i                2.2.2.2          2     110      20   4 1  404 505 303 202 ?
```

   **a.** Largest Weight

   **b.** Best ORIGIN code

   **c.** Lowest MED

   **d.** Largest LOCAL_PREF

   **e.** Better Neighbor Type

   **f.** None of the answers is correct.

**11.** The following exhibit lists commands that were typed using a text editor and later pasted into config mode on Router R1. At the time, R1 had a working eBGP connection to several peers, including 3.3.3.3. R1 had learned of several subnets of networks 11.0.0.0/8 and 12.0.0.0/8 through neighbors besides 3.3.3.3. After being pasted, a **clear** command was issued to pick up the changes. Which of the following statements is true regarding the AS_PATH of the routes advertised by R1 to 3.3.3.3?

```
router bgp 1
 neighbor 3.3.3.3 route-map zzz out
ip prefix-list match11 seq 5 permit 11.0.0.0/8 le 32
route-map zzz permit 10
 match ip address prefix-list match11
 set as-path prepend 1 1 1
```

   **a.** No changes would occur, because the configuration would be rejected because of syntax errors.

   **b.** Routes to subnets inside network 11.0.0.0/8 would contain three consecutive 1s, but no more, in the AS_PATH.

   **c.** Routes to subnets inside 11.0.0.0/8 would contain at least four consecutive 1s in the AS_PATH.

   **d.** Routes to subnets inside 12.0.0.0/8 would have no 1s in the AS_PATH.

   **e.** Routes to subnets inside 12.0.0.0/8 would have one additional 1 in the AS_PATH.

**12.** Which of the following must occur or be configured for BGP to mark multiple iBGP routes in the BGP table—entries for the exact same destination prefix/length—as the best routes?

**a.** Inclusion of the **maximum-paths** *number* command under router BGP, with a setting larger than 1.

**b.** Inclusion of the **maximum-paths ibgp** *number* command under router BGP, with a setting larger than 1.

**c.** Multiple routes that tie for all BGP decision process comparisons up through checking a route's ORIGIN code.

**d.** BGP cannot consider multiple routes in the BGP table for the exact same prefix as best routes.

**13.** Which of the following special BGP COMMUNITY values, when set, imply that a route should not be forwarded outside a confederation AS?

**a.** LOCAL_AS

**b.** NO_ADVERT

**c.** NO_EXPORT

**d.** NO_EXPORT_SUBCONFED

**14.** When BGP peers have set and sent COMMUNITY values in BGP Updates, which of the following is true?

**a.** The BGP decision process adds a check for the COMMUNITY just before the check for the shortest AS_PATH length.

**b.** The lowest COMMUNITY value is considered best by the BGP decision process, unless the COMMUNITY is set to one of the special reserved values.

**c.** The COMMUNITY does not impact the BGP decision process directly.

**d.** None of the other answers is correct.

# Foundation Topics

## Route Filtering and Route Summarization

This section focuses on four popular tools used to filter BGP routes:

- Distribution lists

- Prefix lists

- AS_PATH filter lists

- Route maps

Additionally, the **aggregate-address** command can be used to filter component subnets of a summary route. This section covers these five options. (Filtering using special BGP COMMUNITY values will be covered at the end of the chapter in the section "BGP Communities.")

The four main tools have the following features in common:

**Key
Topic**

- All can filter incoming and outgoing Updates, per neighbor or per peer group.

- Peer group configurations require Cisco IOS Software to process the routing policy against the Update only once, rather than once per neighbor.

- The filters cannot be applied to a single neighbor that is configured as part of a peer group; the filter must be applied to the entire peer group, or the neighbor must be reconfigured to be outside the peer group.

- Each tool's matching logic examines the contents of the BGP Update message, which includes the BGP PAs and network layer reachability information (NLRI).

- If a filter's configuration is changed, a **clear** command is required for the changed filter to take effect.

- The **clear** command can use the soft reconfiguration option to implement changes without requiring BGP peers to be brought down and back up.

The tools differ in what they can match in the BGP Update message. Table 2-2 outlines the commands for each tool and the differences in how they can match NLRI entries in an Update.

> **Note**  Throughout the book, the *wildcard mask* used in ACLs is abbreviated *WC mask*.

**Table 2-2**   *NLRI Filtering Tools*

| BGP Subcommand | Commands Referenced by neighbor Command | What Can Be Matched |
|---|---|---|
| **neighbor distribute-list** (standard ACL) | **access-list, ip access-list** | Prefix, with WC mask |
| **neighbor distribute-list** (extended ACL) | **access-list, ip access-list** | Prefix and prefix length, with WC mask for each |
| **neighbor prefix-list** | **ip prefix-list** | Exact or "first *N*" bits of prefix, plus range of prefix lengths |
| **neighbor filter-list** | **ip as-path access-list** | AS_PATH contents; all NLRIs whose AS_PATHs are matched are considered to be a match |
| **neighbor route-map** | **route-map** | Prefix, prefix length, AS_PATH, and/or any other PA matchable within a BGP route map |

This section begins by covering filtering through the use of matching NLRI, distribute lists, prefix lists, and route maps. From there, it moves on to describe how to use BGP filter lists to match AS_PATH information to filter NLRI entries from routing updates.

## Filtering BGP Updates Based on NLRI

One difference between BGP distribute lists and IGP distribute lists is that a BGP distribute list can use an extended ACL to match against both the prefix and the prefix length. When used with IGP filtering tools, ACLs called from distribute lists cannot match against the prefix length. Example 2-1 shows how an extended ACL matches the prefix with the source address portion of the ACL commands, and matches the prefix length (mask) using the destination address portion of the ACL commands.

The matching logic used by **prefix-list** and **route-map** commands works just the same for BGP as it does for IGPs. For example, both commands have an implied **deny** action at the end of the list, which can be overridden by matching all routes with the final entry in the **prefix-list** or **route-map** command.

Figure 2-1 shows the important portions of the network used for Example 2-1. The example shows a prefix list, distribute list, and a route map performing the same logic to filter based on NLRI. In this case, the four routers in AS 123 form a full mesh. R3 will learn a set of prefixes from AS 45, and then filter the same two prefixes (22.2.2.0/24 and 23.3.16.0/20) from being sent in Updates to each of R3's three neighbors—in each case using a different tool.

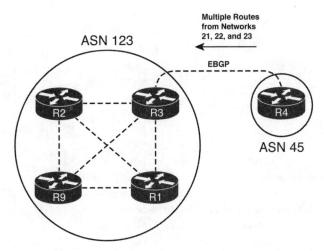

**Figure 2-1**  *iBGP Full Mesh in AS 123 with Routes Learned from AS 45*

**Example 2-1**  *Route Filtering on R3 with Route Maps, Distribution Lists, and Prefix Lists*

```
! R3 Configuration. Only the commands related to filtering are shown. Note that
! BGP Updates to R1 and R2 are filtered at this point; filtering to R9 will be
! added later in the example.
router bgp 123
 neighbor 1.1.1.1 route-map rmap-lose-2 out
 neighbor 2.2.2.2 distribute-list lose-2 out
! This ACL matches exactly for a prefix of 23.3.16.0 and 22.2.2.0, as well as
! exactly matching masks 255.255.240.0 and 255.255.255.0, respectively.
ip access-list extended lose-2
 deny    ip host 23.3.16.0 host 255.255.240.0
 deny    ip host 22.2.2.0 host 255.255.255.0
 permit ip any any
! The prefix list matches the exact prefixes and prefix lengths; the omission of
! any ge or le parameter means each line matches only that exact prefix. Also, the
! third line matches all prefixes, changing the default action to permit.
ip prefix-list prefix-lose-2 seq 5 deny 22.2.2.0/24
ip prefix-list prefix-lose-2 seq 10 deny 23.3.16.0/20
ip prefix-list prefix-lose-2 seq 15 permit 0.0.0.0/0 le 32
! The route map refers to ACL lose-2, passing routes that are permitted
! by the ACL, and filtering all others. The two filtered routes are actually
! filtered by the implied deny clause at the end of the route map: Because the ACL
! matches those two prefixes with a deny action, they do not match clause 10 of the
! route map, and are then matched by the implied deny clause.
route-map rmap-lose-2 permit 10
 match ip address lose-2
! Next, R3 has seven prefixes, with the two slated for filtering highlighted.
R3# show ip bgp | begin Network
```

```
      Network           Next Hop          Metric LocPrf Weight Path
 *> 21.0.0.0           4.4.4.4                         0 45 i
 *> 22.2.2.0/24        4.4.4.4                         0 45 i
 *> 23.3.0.0/20        4.4.4.4                         0 45 i
 *> 23.3.16.0/20       4.4.4.4                         0 45 i
 *> 23.3.32.0/19       4.4.4.4                         0 45 i
 *> 23.3.64.0/18       4.4.4.4                         0 45 i
 *> 23.3.128.0/17      4.4.4.4                         0 45 i
Total number of prefixes 7
! The next command shows what entries R3 will advertise to R1. Note that the
! correct two prefixes have been removed, with only five prefixes listed. The same
! results could be seen for the Update sent to R2, but it is not shown here.
R3# show ip bgp neighbor 1.1.1.1 advertised-routes | begin Network
      Network           Next Hop          Metric LocPrf Weight Path
 *> 21.0.0.0           4.4.4.4                         0 45 i
 *> 23.3.0.0/20        4.4.4.4                         0 45 i
 *> 23.3.32.0/19       4.4.4.4                         0 45 i
 *> 23.3.64.0/18       4.4.4.4                         0 45 i
 *> 23.3.128.0/17      4.4.4.4                         0 45 i
Total number of prefixes 5
! Next, R3 adds an outbound prefix list for neighbor R9 (9.9.9.9). However,
! afterwards, R3 still believes it should send all seven prefixes to R9.
R3# conf t
Enter configuration commands, one per line.  End with CNTL/Z.
R3(config)# router bgp 123
R3(config-router)# neigh 9.9.9.9 prefix-list prefix-lose-2 out
R3(config-router)# ^Z
R3# show ip bgp neighbor 9.9.9.9 advertised-routes | begin Network
      Network           Next Hop          Metric LocPrf Weight Path
 *> 21.0.0.0           4.4.4.4                         0 45 i
 *> 22.2.2.0/24        4.4.4.4                         0 45 i
 *> 23.3.0.0/20        4.4.4.4                         0 45 i
 *> 23.3.16.0/20       4.4.4.4                         0 45 i
 *> 23.3.32.0/19       4.4.4.4                         0 45 i
 *> 23.3.64.0/18       4.4.4.4                         0 45 i
 *> 23.3.128.0/17      4.4.4.4                         0 45 i
Total number of prefixes 7
! Instead of the clear ip bgp 9.9.9.9 command, which would close the BGP neighbor
! and TCP connection to R9, R3 uses the clear ip bgp 9.9.9.9 out or clear ip bgp *
! soft command to perform a soft reconfiguration. Now R3 filters the correct two
! prefixes.
R3# clear ip bgp 9.9.9.9 out
R3# show ip bgp neighbor 9.9.9.9 advertised-routes | begin Network
      Network           Next Hop          Metric LocPrf Weight Path
 *> 21.0.0.0           4.4.4.4                         0 45 i
 *> 23.3.0.0/20        4.4.4.4                         0 45 i
```

```
*> 23.3.32.0/19     4.4.4.4                              0 45 i
*> 23.3.64.0/18     4.4.4.4                              0 45 i
*> 23.3.128.0/17    4.4.4.4                              0 45 i
Total number of prefixes 5
```

### Route Map Rules for NLRI Filtering

The overall logic used by route maps to filter NLRIs is relatively straightforward: The Update is compared to the route map and the route is filtered (or not) based on the first-matching clause. However, route maps can cause a bit of confusion on a couple of points; the next several pages point out some of the potential confusing points with regard to route maps when they are used to filter BGP routes.

Both the route map and any referenced ACL or prefix list have **deny** and **permit** actions configured, so it is easy to confuse the context in which they are used. The **route-map** command's action—either **deny** or **permit**—defines whether an NLRI is filtered (**deny**) or allowed to pass (**permit**). The **permit** or **deny** action in an ACL or prefix list implies whether an NLRI matches the **route map** clause (**permit** by the ACL/prefix list) or does not match (**deny** in the ACL/prefix list).

For example, **route-map rmap-lose-2 permit 10** from Example 2-1 matched all NLRIs except the two prefixes that needed to be filtered based on named ACL lose-2. The matched routes—all the routes that do not need to be filtered in this case—were then advertised, because clause 10 had a **permit** action configured. The route map then filtered the other two routes by virtue of the implied **deny all** logic at the end of the route map.

Alternatively, the route map could have just as easily used a beginning clause of **route-map rmap-lose-2 deny 10**, with the matching logic only matching the two prefixes that needed to be filtered—in that case, the first clause would have filtered the two routes because of the **deny** keyword in the **route-map** command. Such a route map would then require a second clause that matched all routes, with a **permit** action configured. (To match all NLRIs in a route map, simply omit the **match** command from that **route map** clause. In this case, adding just the command **route-map rmap-lose-2 20**, with no sub-commands, would match all remaining routes and allow them to be advertised.)

### Soft Reconfiguration

The end of Example 2-1 shows a BGP feature called *soft reconfiguration*. Soft reconfiguration allows a BGP peer to reapply its routing policies without closing a neighbor connection. To reapply the policies, Cisco IOS uses the **clear** command with either the **soft**, **in**, or **out** options, as shown in the following generic **clear** command syntax:

```
clear ip bgp {* | neighbor-address | peer-group-name} [soft [in | out]]
```

The **soft** option alone reapplies the policy configuration for both inbound and outbound policies, whereas the inclusion of the **in** or **out** keyword limits the reconfiguration to the stated direction.

Cisco IOS supports soft reconfiguration for sent Updates automatically, but BGP must be configured to support soft reconfiguration for inbound Updates. To support soft reconfiguration, BGP must remember the actual sent and received BGP Update information for each neighbor. The **neighbor** *neighbor-id* **soft-reconfiguration inbound** command causes the router to keep a copy of the received Updates from the specified neighbor. (IOS keeps a copy of sent Updates automatically.) With these Updates available, BGP can simply reapply the changed filtering policy to the Update without closing the neighbor connection.

Clearing the neighbor is required to pick up the changes to routing policies that impact Updates sent and received from neighbors. All such changes can be implemented using soft reconfiguration. However, for configuration changes that impact the local injection of routes into the BGP table, soft reconfiguration does not help. The reason is that soft reconfiguration simply reprocesses Updates, and features that inject routes into BGP through the **redistribute** or **network** commands are not injected based on Update messages.

## Comparing BGP Prefix Lists, Distribute Lists, and Route Maps

Prefix lists and distribute lists both use their matching logic on the BGP Update's NLRI. However, a prefix list allows more flexible matching of the prefix length because it can match a range of prefixes that extends to a maximum length of less than 32. For example, the command **ip prefix-list test1 permit 10.0.0.0/8 ge 16 le 23** matches a range of prefix lengths, but the same logic using an ACL as a distribute list takes several more lines, or a tricky wildcard mask.

For many BGP filtering tasks, route maps do not provide any benefit over prefix lists, ACLs, and AS_PATH filter lists. If the desired policy is only to filter routes based on matching prefixes/lengths, a route map does not provide any additional function over using a distribute list or prefix list directly. Similarly, if the goal of the policy is to filter routes just based on matching with an AS_PATH filter, the route map does not provide any additional function as compared to calling an AS_PATH filter directly using the **neighbor filter-list** command.

However, only route maps can provide the following two functions for BGP routing policy configurations:

- Matching logic that combines multiples of the following: prefix/length, AS_PATH, or other BGP PAs

- The setting of BGP PAs for the purpose of manipulating BGP's choice of which route to use

Many of the features for manipulating the choice of best routes by BGP, as covered later in this chapter, use route maps for that purpose.

## Filtering Subnets of a Summary Using the aggregate-address Command

Manual BGP route summarization, using the **aggregate-address** BGP router subcommand, provides the flexibility to allow none, all, or a subset of the summary's component subnets to be advertised out of the BGP table. By allowing some and not others, the **aggregate-address** command can in effect filter some routes. The filtering options on the **aggregate-address** command are as follows:

- Filtering all component subnets of the summary from being advertised, by using the **summary-only** keyword

- Advertising all the component subnets of the summary, by *omitting* the **summary-only** keyword

- Advertising some and filtering other component subnets of the summary, by omitting the **summary-only** keyword and referring to a route map using the **suppress-map** keyword

The logic behind the **suppress-map** option can be a little tricky. This option requires reference to a route map, with any component subnets matching a route map **permit** clause being *suppressed*—in other words, routes permitted by the route map are filtered and not advertised. The router does not actually remove the suppressed route from its local BGP table; however, it does suppress the advertisement of those routes.

Example 2-2 shows how the **suppress-map** option works, with a summary of 23.0.0.0/8 and a goal of allowing all component subnets to be advertised except 23.3.16.0/20.

**Example 2-2**  *Filtering Routes Using the* **aggregate-address suppress-map** *Command*

```
! The first command below lists all BGP routes in network 23.
R3# sh ip bgp neigh 1.1.1.1 advertised-routes | include 23
*> 23.3.0.0/20      4.4.4.4                          0 45 i
*> 23.3.16.0/20     4.4.4.4                          0 45 i
*> 23.3.32.0/19     4.4.4.4                          0 45 i
*> 23.3.64.0/18     4.4.4.4                          0 45 i
*> 23.3.128.0/17    4.4.4.4                          0 45 i
*> 23.4.0.0/16      4.4.4.4                          0 45 678 i
! The ACL below matches 23.3.16.0/20 with a permit clause, and denies all other
! routes (default). The route-map uses a permit clause and references
! access-list permit-1. The logic means that the one route permitted by the ACL
! will be suppressed. Note also that the summary-only keyword was not used
! on the aggregate-address command, allowing the subnets to also be advertised.
ip access-list extended permit-1
 permit ip host 23.3.16.0 host 255.255.240.0
!
route-map suppress-1 permit 10
 match ip address permit-1
!
```

```
router bgp 123
 aggregate-address 23.0.0.0 255.0.0.0 as-set suppress-map suppress-1
! Below, R3 (after a clear ip bgp * soft command) no longer advertises the route.
R3# sh ip bgp neigh 1.1.1.1 advertised-routes | include 23.3.16.0
R3#
! Note the "s" on the left side of the show ip bgp command output for the
! suppressed route. The route remains in the table; it is simply no longer
! advertised outside the router.
R3# sh ip bgp neigh 1.1.1.1 advertised-routes | include 23
*> 23.3.0.0/20      4.4.4.4                              0 45 i
s> 23.3.16.0/20     4.4.4.4                              0 45 i
*> 23.3.32.0/19     4.4.4.4                              0 45 i
*> 23.3.64.0/18     4.4.4.4                              0 45 i
*> 23.3.128.0/17    4.4.4.4                              0 45 i
*> 23.4.0.0/16      4.4.4.4                              0 45 678 i
```

## Filtering BGP Updates by Matching the AS_PATH PA

To filter routes by matching the AS_PATH PA, Cisco IOS uses AS_PATH filters. The overall configuration structure is similar to BGP distribute lists and prefix lists, with the matching logic specified in a list and the logic being applied with a **neighbor** command. The main two steps are as follows:

1. Configure the AS_PATH filter using the **ip as-path access-list** *number* {**permit** | **deny**} *regex* command.

2. Enable the AS_PATH filter using the **neighbor** *neighbor-id* **filter-list** *as-path-filter-number* {**in** | **out**} command.

Based on these commands, Cisco IOS examines the AS_PATH PA in the sent or received Updates for the stated neighbor. NLRIs whose AS_PATHs match with a **deny** action are filtered.

AS_PATH filters use *regular expressions* (abbreviated *regex*) to apply powerful matching logic to the AS_PATH. To match the AS_PATH contents, the regex need to match values, delimiters, and other special characters. For example, the AS_PATH itself has several components, called *segments*, which, when present, require slightly different matching logic within a regex. The next few sections take a closer look at both regex and AS_PATHs, followed by some examples of using AS_PATH filters.

### The BGP AS_PATH and AS_PATH Segment Types

RFC 1771 describes four types of AS_PATH segments held inside the AS_PATH PA (see Table 2-3). The most common segment is called AS_SEQUENCE, which is an ordered list of all the autonomous systems through which the route has passed. The AS_SEQUENCE segment lists the most recently added ASN as the first ASN; this value is also the leftmost entry when looking at **show** commands, and is considered to be the first ASN for the regex matching logic.

Because the most recently added ASN is the first ASN in the AS_SEQUENCE segment, the process of adding the ASN before advertising routes to external BGP (eBGP) peers is called *AS_PATH prepending*. For example, Figure 2-2 shows a sample network in which a route is injected inside AS 1, advertised to AS 4, and then advertised to AS 123.

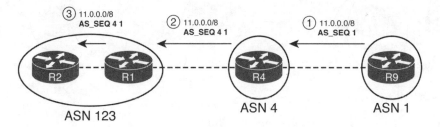

**Figure 2-2**   *AS_PATH (AS_SEQUENCE) Prepending*

The other three AS_PATH segment types come into play when using confederations and route summarization. Table 2-3 lists and briefly describes all four types.

**Table 2-3**   *AS_PATH Segment Types*

| Component | Description | Delimiters Between ASNs | Character Enclosing the Segment |
|---|---|---|---|
| AS_SEQUENCE | An ordered list of ASNs through which the route has been advertised | Space | None |
| AS_SET | An unordered list of ASNs through which the route has been advertised | Comma | {} |
| AS_CONFED_SEQ[1] | Like AS_SEQ, but holds only confederation ASNs | Space | () |
| AS_CONFED_SET[1] | Like AS_SET, but holds only confederation ASNs | Comma | {} |

[1] *Not advertised outside the confederation.*

Figure 2-3 shows an example of AS_SET in which R4 summarizes some routes using the **aggregate-address... as-set** command. As a result of including the **as-set** keyword, R4 creates an AS_SET segment in the AS_PATH of the aggregate route. Note that the AS_SET segment is shown in brackets, and it is listed in no particular order. These facts are all important to the process of AS_PATH filtering.

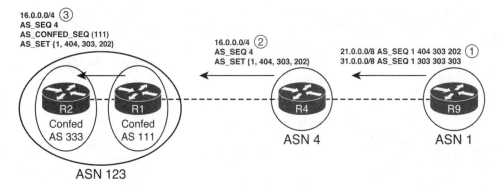

**Figure 2-3** *AS_SET and AS_CONFED_SEQ Example*

Also note the addition of the AS_CONFED_SEQ segment by R1 in Figure 2-3. Confederation ASNs are used to prevent loops inside the confederation. Because these ASNs will be removed before advertising the route outside the full AS, the confederation ASNs are kept inside a different segment—the AS_CONFED_SEQ segment. Finally, if a route is aggregated inside a confederation, the AS_CONFED_SET segment holds the confederation ASNs with the same logic as used by the AS_SET segment type, but keeps them separate for easy removal before advertising the routes outside the confederation. Example 2-3 provides sample **show ip bgp** command output showing an AS_SET and AS_CONFED_SEQ. The output shows R2's AS_PATH for the route shown in Figure 2-3.

**Example 2-3** *AS_PATH on R2: AS_CONFED_SEQ, AS_SEQUENCE, and AS_SET*

```
! The AS_CONFED_SEQ is (111), enclosed in parentheses. The AS_SEQUENCE only
! contains 4, with no enclosing characters. The AS_SET created by R4 when
! summarizing 16.0.0.0/4 is {1,404,303,202}, enclosed in brackets.
R2# show ip bgp | include 16.0.0.0
*> 16.0.0.0/4      10.1.14.4           0    100      0 (111) 4
   {1,404,303,202} i
```

## Using Regular Expressions to Match AS_PATH

A Cisco IOS AS_PATH filter has one or more configured lines, with each line requiring a regex. The logic is then applied as follows:

**Key Topic**

1.  The regex of the first line in the list is applied to the AS_PATH of each route.

2.  For matched NLRIs, the NLRI is passed or filtered based on that AS_PATH filter's configured **permit** or **deny** action.

3.  For unmatched NLRIs, Steps 1 and 2 are repeated, using the next line in the AS_PATH filter, analyzing all NLRIs yet to be matched by this list.

4.  Any NLRI not matched explicitly is filtered.

Regexs contain literal strings as well as metacharacters. The *metacharacters* allow matching using wildcards, matches for different delimiters, and other special operations. Table 2-4 lists the regex metacharacters that are useful for IOS AS_PATH filters.

**Table 2-4**  *Regex Metacharacters Useful for AS_PATH Matching*

| Metacharacter | Meaning |
| --- | --- |
| ^ | Start of line |
| $ | End of line |
| \| | Logical OR applied between the preceding and succeeding characters[1] |
| _ | Any delimiter: blank, comma, start of line, or end of line[2] |
| . | Any single character |
| ? | Zero or one instance of the preceding character |
| * | Zero or more instances of the preceding character |
| + | One or more instances of the preceding character |
| (*string*) | Parentheses combine enclosed string characters as a single entity when used with ?, *, or + |
| [*string*] | Creates a wildcard for which any of the single characters in the string can be used to match that position in the AS_PATH |

[1] *If preceded by a value in parentheses, the logic applies to the preceding string listed inside the parentheses, and not just to the preceding character.*

[2] *This character is an underscore.*

When the regular expression is applied to a BGP route, Cisco IOS searches the AS_PATH for the first instance of the first item in the regex; from that point forward, it processes the rest of the AS_PATH sequentially. For example, consider two routes, one with an AS_PATH with only an AS_SEQ, set to 12 34 56 and another route with an AS_SEQ of 78 12 34 56. A regular expression of **12_34_56** matches both routes, because IOS looks for the first occurrence of AS 12 and then searches sequentially. However, a regular expression of **^12_34_56** would match only the first route. The second AS_PATH (78 12 34 56) would not match because the regex would immediately match on the ^ (start of line) and then search sequentially—finding AS 78 next, which does not match the regex.

Although Table 2-4 provides a useful reference, Table 2-5 provides a number of examples of using these metacharacters, with explanations of what they match. Take special note of the wording in the explanations. Phrases like "ASN 303" and "ASN beginning with 303" differ in that the first phrase means exactly 303, and not 3031, 30342, and so on, whereas the second phrase would match any of these values.

**Table 2-5**  *Sample AS_PATH Regex and Their Meanings*

| Sample Regex | What Type of AS_PATH It Would Match |
| --- | --- |
| .* | All AS_PATHs (useful as a final match to change the default from **deny** to **permit**). |
| ^$ | Null (empty)—used for NLRIs originated in the same AS. |

| Sample Regex | What Type of AS_PATH It Would Match |
|---|---|
| ^123$ | An AS_PATH with only one AS, ASN 123. |
| ^123 | An AS_PATH whose first ASN begins with or is 123; includes 123, 1232, 12354, and so on. |
| ^123. | An AS_PATH whose first ASN is one of two things: a four-digit number that begins with 123, or a number that begins with ASN 123 and is followed by a delimiter before the next ASN. (It does not match an AS_PATH of only ASN 123, because the period does not match the end-of-line.) |
| ^123+ | An AS_PATH whose first ASN begins with 123, with 1233, or is 12333. For example, it includes ASNs 1231 and 12331 because it does not specify what happens after the +. |
| ^123+_ | An AS_PATH whose first ASN is one of three numbers: 123, 1233, or 12333. It does not match 1231 and 12331, for example, because it requires a delimiter after the last 3. |
| ^123* | An AS_PATH whose first ASN begins with 12, 123, or 1233, or is 12333. Any character can follow these values, because the regex does not specify anything about the next character. For example, 121 would match because the * can represent 0 occurrences of "3". 1231 would match with * representing 1 occurrence of 3. |
| ^123*_ | An AS_PATH whose first ASN begins with 12, 123, or 1233, or is 12333. It does not include matches for 121, 1231, and 12331, because the next character must be a delimiter. |
| ^123? | An AS_PATH whose first ASN begins with either 12 or 123. |
| ^123_45$ | An AS_PATH with two autonomous systems, beginning with 123 and ending with 45. |
| ^123_.*_45$ | An AS_PATH beginning with AS 123 and ending in AS 45, with at least one other AS in between. |
| ^123_.*45 | An AS_PATH beginning with AS 123, with zero or more intermediate ASNs and delimiters, and ending with any AS whose last two digits are 45 (including simply AS 45). |
| (^123_45$)\|(^123_.*_45$) | An AS_PATH beginning with 123 and ending with AS 45, with zero or more other ASNs between the two. |
| ^123_45$\|^123_.*_45$ | (Note: This is the same as the previous example, but without the parentheses.) Represents a common error in attempting to match AS_PATHs that begin with ASN 123 and end with ASN 45. The problem is that the \| is applied to the previous character ($) and next character (^), as opposed to everything before and after the \|. |
| ^123(_[0..9]+)*_45 | Another way to match an AS_PATH beginning with 123 and ending with AS 45. |

| Sample Regex | What Type of AS_PATH It Would Match |
|---|---|
| ^{123 | The AS_PATH begins with an AS_SET or AS_CONFED_SET, with the first three numerals of the first ASN being 123. |
| [(\|303.*[)] | Find the AS_CONFED_SEQ, and match if the first ASN begins with 303. |

### Example: Matching AS_PATHs Using AS_PATH Filters

NLRI filtering with AS_PATH filters uses two commands:

```
ip as-path access-list access-list-number {permit | deny} as-regexp
neighbor {ip-address | peer-group-name} filter-list access-list-number {in | out}
```

Figure 2-4 shows a sample internetwork used in many of the upcoming examples, two of which show the use of AS_PATH filtering.

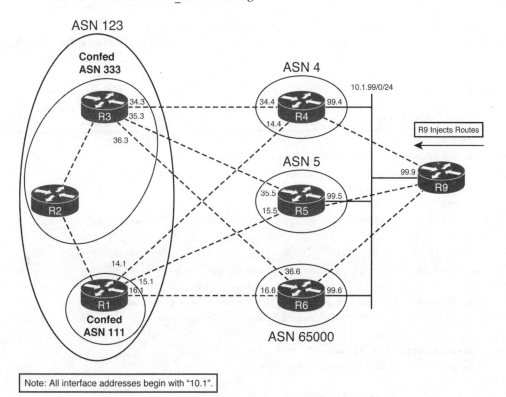

**Figure 2-4**  *Network Used for AS_PATH Filter Examples*

Example 2-4 shows an AS_PATH filter in which routes are filtered going from R4 to R3. Filtering the outbound Update on R4 will be shown first, followed by filtering of inbound Updates on R3. In both cases, the goal of the filter is as follows:

Filter routes in R4's BGP table whose ASN begins with AS 1, has three additional ASNs of any value, and ends with ASN 44.

The two NLRIs matching these criteria are 11.0.0.0/8 and 12.0.0.0/8.

**Example 2-4**   *AS_PATH Filtering of Routes Sent from R4 to R3*

```
! R4 learned its best routes to 11.0.0.0/8 and 12.0.0.0/8 from R9 (10.1.99.9), plus
! two other routers. Only the routes learned from R9, with NEXT_HOP 10.1.99.9,
! match the AS_PATH criteria for this example.
R4# show ip bgp
BGP table version is 9, local router ID is 4.4.4.4
Status codes: s suppressed, d damped, h history, * valid, > best, i-internal,
              r RIB-failure, S Stale
Origin codes: i-IGP, e-EGP, ?-incomplete

   Network          Next Hop         Metric LocPrf Weight Path
*  11.0.0.0         10.1.14.1                         0 123 5 1 33333 10 200 44 i
*                   10.1.34.3                         0 123 5 1 33333 10 200 44 i
*>                  10.1.99.9              0           0 1 33333 10 200 44 i
*  12.0.0.0         10.1.14.1                         0 123 5 1 33333 10 200 44 i
*                   10.1.34.3                         0 123 5 1 33333 10 200 44 i
*>                  10.1.99.9              0           0 1 33333 10 200 44 i
! lines omitted for brevity
! R4 currently advertises four routes to R3, as shown next.
R4# show ip bgp neighbor 10.1.34.3 advertised-routes | begin Network
   Network          Next Hop         Metric LocPrf Weight Path
*> 11.0.0.0         10.1.99.9              0           0 1 33333 10 200 44 i
*> 12.0.0.0         10.1.99.9              0           0 1 33333 10 200 44 i
*> 21.0.0.0         10.1.99.9              0           0 1 404 303 202 i
*> 31.0.0.0         10.1.99.9              0           0 1 303 303 303 i
! R4's new AS_PATH filter is shown next. The first line matches AS_PATHs beginning
! with ASN 1, and ending in 44, with three ASNs in between. The second line matches
! all other AS_PATHs, with a permit action-essentially a permit all at the end. The
! list is then enabled with the neighbor filter-list command, for outbound Updates
! sent to R3 (10.1.34.3).
ip as-path access-list 34 deny ^1_.*_.*_.*_44$
ip as-path access-list 34 permit .*
router bgp 4
neighbor 10.1.34.3 filter-list 34 out
! After soft reconfiguration, R4 no longer advertises the routes to networks
! 11 and 12.
R4# clear ip bgp * soft
```

```
R4# show ip bgp neighbor 10.1.34.3 advertised-routes | begin Network
   Network          Next Hop          Metric LocPrf Weight Path
*> 21.0.0.0         10.1.99.9              0              0 1 404 303 202 i
*> 31.0.0.0         10.1.99.9              0              0 1 303 303 303 i
Total number of prefixes 2
```

! Not shown: R4's **neighbor filter-list** command is now removed, and soft
! reconfiguration used to restore the Updates to their unfiltered state.
! R3 lists its unfiltered received Update from R4. Note that R4's ASN was added
! by R4 before sending the Update.

```
R3# show ip bgp neighbor 10.1.34.4 received-routes | begin Network
   Network          Next Hop          Metric LocPrf Weight Path
*  11.0.0.0         10.1.34.4                        0 4 1 33333 10 200 44 i
*  12.0.0.0         10.1.34.4                        0 4 1 33333 10 200 44 i
*  21.0.0.0         10.1.34.4                        0 4 1 404 303 202 i
*  31.0.0.0         10.1.34.4                        0 4 1 303 303 303 i
```

! R3 uses practically the same AS_PATH filter, except that it must look for ASN
! 4 as the first ASN.

**ip as-path access-list 34 deny ^4_1_.*_.*_.*_44$**
**ip as-path access-list 34 permit .***
**router bgp 333**
 **neighbor 10.1.34.4 filter-list 34 in**

! The **show ip as-path-access-list** command shows the contents of the list.

```
R3# show ip as-path-access-list 34
AS path access list 34
    deny ^4_1_.*_.*_.*_44$
    permit .*
```

! To test the logic of the regex, the **show ip bgp** command can be used, with the
! pipe (|) and the **include** option. That parses the command output based on the
! regex at the end of the **show** command. However, note that some things matchable
! using an AS_PATH filter are not in the **show** command output-for example, the
! beginning or end of line cannot be matched with a ^ or $, respectively.
! These metacharacters must be omitted for this testing trick to work.

```
R3# show ip bgp neighbor 10.1.34.4 received-routes | include 4_1_.*_.*_.*_44
*  11.0.0.0         10.1.34.4                        0 4 1 33333 10 200 44 i
*  12.0.0.0         10.1.34.4                        0 4 1 33333 10 200 44 i
```

! After a **clear**, it first appears that the routes were not filtered, as they
! still show up in the output below.

**R3# clear ip bgp * soft**

```
R3# show ip bgp neighbor 10.1.34.4 received-routes | begin Network
   Network          Next Hop          Metric LocPrf Weight Path
*  11.0.0.0         10.1.34.4                        0 4 1 33333 10 200 44 i
*  12.0.0.0         10.1.34.4                        0 4 1 33333 10 200 44 i
*  21.0.0.0         10.1.34.4                        0 4 1 404 303 202 i
*  31.0.0.0         10.1.34.4                        0 4 1 303 303 303 i
```

```
! However, R3 does not show the routes shown in the received Update from R4 in
! the BGP table; the routes were indeed filtered.
R3# show ip bgp | begin Network
   Network          Next Hop          Metric LocPrf Weight Path
*  11.0.0.0         10.1.36.6                            0 65000 1 33333 10 200 44 i
* i                 10.1.15.5              0    100      0 (111) 5 1 33333 10 200 44 i
*>                  10.1.35.5                            0 5 1 33333 10 200 44 i
*  12.0.0.0         10.1.36.6                            0 65000 1 33333 10 200 44 i
* i                 10.1.15.5              0    100      0 (111) 5 1 33333 10 200 44 i
*>                  10.1.35.5                            0 5 1 33333 10 200 44 i
! lines omitted for brevity
```

The explanations in Example 2-4 cover most of the individual points about using filter lists to filter NLRIs based on the AS_PATH. The example also depicts a couple of broader issues regarding the Cisco IOS BGP **show** commands:

Key Topic

- The **show ip bgp neighbor** *neighbor-id* **advertised-routes** command displays the routes actually sent—in other words, this command reflects the effects of the filtering by omitting the filtered routes from the output.

- The **show ip bgp neighbor** *neighbor-id* **received-routes** command displays the routes actually received from a neighbor, never omitting routes from the output, even if the router locally filters the routes on input.

- Output filter lists are applied before the router adds its own ASN to the AS_PATH. (See Example 2-4's AS_PATH filter on R4 for an example.)

There are also a couple of ways to test regex without changing the routing policy. Example 2-4 showed one example using the following command:

```
show ip bgp neighbor 10.1.34.4 received-routes | include 4_1_.*_.*_.*_44
```

This command parses the entire command output using the regex after the **include** keyword. However, note that this command looks at the ASCII text of the command output, meaning that some special characters (like beginning-of-line and end-of-line characters) do not exist. For example, Example 2-4 left out the caret (^) in the regex, because the text output of the **show** command does not include a ^.

The other method to test a regex is to use the **show ip bgp regexp** *expression* command. This command parses the AS_PATH variables in a router's BGP table, including all special characters, allowing all aspects of the regex to be tested. However, the **regexp** option of the **show ip bgp** command is not allowed with the **received-routes** or **advertised-routes** option.

While Example 2-4 shows BGP using the **neighbor filter-list** command, the AS_PATH filter list can also be referenced in a route map using the **match as-path** *list-number* command. In that case, the route map then can be called using the **neighbor route-map** command.

## Matching AS_SET and AS_CONFED_SEQ

Example 2-5 shows how to use a BGP filter list to match the AS_SET and AS_CONFED_ SEQ segment types. Figure 2-5 depicts the specifics of the example. In this case, R4 summarizes 16.0.0.0/4, creating an AS_SET entry for the summary and advertising it to R1 and R3. R1 and R3 in turn advertise the route to R2; R1's route includes an AS_ CONFED_SEQ, because R1 and R2 are confederation eBGP peers.

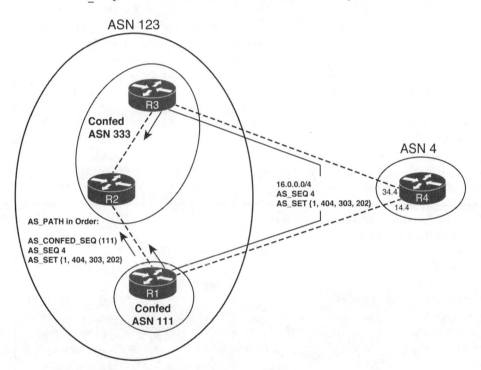

**Figure 2-5**   *Generating AS_SET and AS_CONFED_SEQ*

Example 2-5 shows two different sample filters, as follows:

■   Filtering routes with ASN 303 anywhere inside the AS_SET

■   Filtering based on the AS_CONFED_SEQ of only ASN 111 to begin the AS_PATH

**Example 2-5**   *AS_PATH Filtering of Routes Sent from R4 to R3*

```
! The next command shows R2's BGP table before filtering is enabled. R2 has five
! routes with AS_CONFED_SEQ of (111), all learned from R1. R2 also learned the
! same NLRI from R3, with the related AS_PATH not including the beginning
```

```
! AS_CONFED_SEQ of (111), because R3 is in the same confederation sub-AS as R2.
R2# sh ip bgp | begin Network
   Network         Next Hop        Metric LocPrf Weight Path
*  i11.0.0.0       10.1.35.5            0    100      0 5 1 33333 10 200 44 i
*>                 10.1.15.5            0    100      0 (111) 5 1 33333 10 200 44 i
*  i12.0.0.0       10.1.35.5            0    100      0 5 1 33333 10 200 44 i
*>                 10.1.15.5            0    100      0 (111) 5 1 33333 10 200 44 i
*  i16.0.0.0/4     10.1.34.4            0    100      0 4 {1,404,303,202} i
*>                 10.1.14.4            0    100      0 (111) 4 {1,404,303,202} i
*  i21.0.0.0       10.1.34.4            0    100      0 4 1 404 303 202 i
*>                 10.1.15.5            0    100      0 (111) 5 1 404 303 202 i
*  i31.0.0.0       10.1.34.4            0    100      0 4 1 303 303 303 i
*>                 10.1.15.5            0    100      0 (111) 5 1 303 303 303 i
! R2 will use AS_PATH access-list 1 to find routes that begin with AS_CONFED_SEQ
! of 111. Note that the "(" must be matched by enclosing it in square brackets, as
! the "(" itself and the ")" are metacharacters, and would otherwise be
! interpreted as a metacharacter. Without the "[(]" to begin the regex, the
! AS_PATH filter would not match.
R2# show ip as-path-access-list 1
AS path access list 1
    deny ^[(]111
    permit .*
! R2 filters incoming routes from both peers, and performs a soft reconfig.
R2(config)# router bgp 333
R2(config-router)# neigh 1.1.1.1 filter-list 1 in
R2(config-router)# neigh 3.3.3.3 filter-list 1 in
R2# clear ip bgp * soft
! Now all routes with AS_CONFED_SEQ of 111 beginning the AS_PATH are gone.
R2# sh ip bgp | begin Network
   Network         Next Hop        Metric LocPrf Weight Path
*>i11.0.0.0        10.1.35.5            0    100      0 5 1 33333 10 200 44 i
*>i12.0.0.0        10.1.35.5            0    100      0 5 1 33333 10 200 44 i
*>i16.0.0.0/4      10.1.34.4            0    100      0 4 {1,404,303,202} i
*>i21.0.0.0        10.1.34.4            0    100      0 4 1 404 303 202 i
*>i31.0.0.0        10.1.34.4            0    100      0 4 1 303 303 303 i
! Not shown-R2's switches to using AS_PATH filter-list 2 instead for peer R3
! only, and soft reconfiguration is applied.
! The next command shows the contents
! of the new filter for inbound Updates from R3. Because the "{" and "}" are not
! metacharacters, they can simply be typed directly into the regex. AS_PATH
! access-list 2 matches an AS_SET anywhere in the AS_PATH, as long as 303
! resides anywhere inside the AS_SET.
```

```
R2# show ip as-path-access-list 2
AS path access list 2
    deny {.*303.*}
    permit .*
! The next command is a test to show routes received by R2 from R3 that happen to
! have 303 anywhere in the AS_PATH. Remember, filtered routes are still
! displayed when viewing the BGP table with the received-routes option.
R2# show ip bgp neighbor 3.3.3.3 received-routes | include 303
* i16.0.0.0/4      10.1.34.4            0    100      0 4 {1,404,303,202} i
* i21.0.0.0        10.1.34.4            0    100      0 4 1 404 303 202 i
* i31.0.0.0        10.1.34.4            0    100      0 4 1 303 303 303 i
! R2 has filtered the route with 303 in the AS_SET, but it did not filter the
! routes with 303 in the AS_SEQ.
R2# sh ip bgp | include 10.1.34.4
* i21.0.0.0        10.1.34.4            0    100      0 4 1 404 303 202 i
* i31.0.0.0        10.1.34.4            0    100      0 4 1 303 303 303 i
```

**Note**   While AS_SET and AS_CONFED_SET are both unordered lists, when applying regex logic, Cisco IOS uses the order listed in the output of the **show ip bgp** command.

# BGP Path Attributes and the BGP Decision Process

BGP path attributes define different characteristics about the NLRI(s) associated with a PA. For example, the AS_PATH PA lists the ASNs through which the NLRI has been advertised. Some BGP PAs impact the *BGP decision process* by which a router chooses the best path among multiple known routes to the same NLRI. This section explains the BGP decision process and introduces several new PAs and other BGP features that impact that process.

## Generic Terms and Characteristics of BGP PAs

Each BGP PA can be described as either a *well-known* or *optional* PA. These terms refer to whether a particular implementation of BGP software must support the PA (well-known) or support for the PA is not required (optional).

Well-known PAs are either one of the following:

■ **Mandatory:** The PA must be in every BGP Update.

■ **Discretionary:** The PA is not required in every BGP Update.

These classifications relate not to the capabilities of a BGP implementation, but rather to whether a particular feature has been configured or used by default. For example, the ATOMIC_AGGREGATE PA is a well-known discretionary PA. That means that all implementations of BGP must understand this PA, but a particular router adds this PA only at its discretion, in this case by a router that creates a summary route. Conversely, the AS_PATH PA is a well-known mandatory PA, and as such must be included in every BGP Update.

BGP classifies optional PAs into one of two other categories that relate to a router's behavior when the router's BGP implementation does not understand the PA:

- **Transitive:** The router should silently forward the PA to other routers without needing to consider the meaning of the PA.

- **Nontransitive:** The router should remove the PA so that it is not propagated to any peers.

Table 2-6 summarizes these classification terms and definitions.

Key Topic

**Table 2-6** *Definitions of Path Attribute Classification Terms*

| Term | All BGP Software Implementations Must Support It | Must Be Sent in Each BGP Update | Silently Forwarded If Not Supported |
|---|---|---|---|
| Well-known mandatory | Yes | Yes | — |
| Well-known discretionary | Yes | No | — |
| Optional transitive | No | — | Yes |
| Optional nontransitive | No | — | No |

The BGP PAs that have been mentioned so far in this book provide several good examples of the meanings behind the terms given in Table 2-6. Those PAs are summarized in Table 2-7, along with their characteristics.

**Table 2-7** *BGP Path Attributes Covered So Far and Their Characteristics*

| Path Attribute | Description | Characteristics |
|---|---|---|
| AS_PATH | Lists ASNs through which the route has been advertised | Well-known mandatory |
| NEXT_HOP | Lists the next-hop IP address used to reach an NLRI | Well-known mandatory |
| AGGREGATOR | Lists the RID and ASN of the router that created a summary NLRI | Optional transitive |
| ATOMIC_AGGREGATE | Tags a summary NLRI as being a summary | Well-known discretionary |
| ORIGIN | Value implying from where the route was taken for injection into BGP; i (IGP), e (EGP), or ? (incomplete information) | Well-known mandatory |

| Path Attribute | Description | Characteristics |
| --- | --- | --- |
| ORIGINATOR_ID | Used by RRs to denote the RID of the iBGP neighbor that injected the NLRI into the AS | Optional nontransitive |
| CLUSTER_LIST | Used by RRs to list the RR cluster IDs in order to prevent loops | Optional nontransitive |

Additions to BGP can be defined through the creation of new optional PAs, without requiring a new baseline RFC and a bump to a new version for BGP. The last two PAs in Table 2-7 list two such examples, both of which were added by RFC 1966 for the route reflectors feature.

## The BGP Decision Process

The BGP decision process uses some of the PAs listed in Table 2-7, as well as several others. This section focuses on the decision process as an end to itself, with only brief explanations of new features or PAs. Following that, the text explains the details of some of the PAs that have not yet been covered in the book, as well as some other details that affect the BGP decision process.

When a BGP router learns multiple routes to the same NLRI, it must choose a single best route to reach that NLRI. BGP does not rely on a single concept like an IGP metric, but rather provides a rich set of tools that can be manipulated to affect the choice of routes. The following list defines the core of the BGP decision process to choose routes. Three additional tiebreaker steps are listed later in this section.

1. **Is the NEXT_HOP reachable?** Many texts, as well as RFC 1771, mention the fact that if a router does not have a route to the NEXT_HOP PA for a route, it should be rejected in the decision process.

2. **Highest administrative weight:** This is a Cisco-proprietary feature. The administrative weight can be assigned to each NLRI locally on a router, and the value cannot be communicated to another router. The higher the value, the better the route.

3. **Highest LOCAL_PREF PA:** This well-known discretionary PA can be set on a router inside an AS, and distributed inside the AS only. As a result, this feature can be used by all BGP routers in one AS to choose the same exit point from their AS for a particular NLRI. The higher the value, the better the route.

4. **Locally injected routes:** Pick the route injected into BGP locally (using the **network** command, redistribution, or route summarization). (This step is seldom needed, and is sometimes omitted from other BGP references.)

5. **Shortest AS_PATH length:** The shorter the AS_PATH length, the better the route. The length calculation ignores both AS_CONFED_SET and AS_CONFED_SEQ, and treats an AS_SET as one ASN, regardless of the number of ASNs in the AS_SET.

It counts each ASN in the AS_SEQUENCE as one. (This step is ignored if the **bgp bestpath as-path ignore** command is configured.)

6.   **ORIGIN PA:** IGP (I) routes are preferred over EGP (E) routes, which are in turn preferred over incomplete (?) routes.

7.   **Smallest Multi-Exit Discriminator (MED) PA:** Traditionally, this PA allows an ISP with multiple peer connections to a customer AS to tell the customer AS which of the peer connections is best for reaching a particular NLRI. The smaller the value, the better the route.

8.   **Neighbor Type:** Prefer external BGP (eBGP) routes over internal BGP (iBGP). For this step, treat confederation eBGP as equal to iBGP.

9.   **IGP metric for reaching the NEXT_HOP:** IGP metrics for each NLRI's NEXT_HOP are compared. The lower the value, the better the route.

### Clarifications of the BGP Decision Process

The goal of this nine-step decision process is to determine the one best route to reach each NLRI. These steps do not attempt to find multiple equal routes, and install equal routes into the IP routing table, until a later step—even if the **maximum-paths** router subcommand has been configured to some number higher than the default of 1. The goal is to find the one best route to each NLRI.

First, you probably noticed that the list starts with NEXT_HOP reachability. I debated whether to include this step at all. Certainly, the statement at Step 1 is true. However, one could argue that this concept is not related to choosing between multiple useful routes, because it is really a restriction as to which routes could be used, thereby being candidates to become the best route. I decided to include it in the list for a couple of reasons: It is prominently mentioned in the corresponding parts of RFC 1771, and it is part of the decision process listed in both *Internet Routing Architectures* (Halabi) and *Routing TCP/IP*, Volume II (Doyle and Carroll). It is an important point, and worth memorizing.

**Key Topic**

If a step determines the best route for an NLRI, BGP does not bother with the remaining steps. For example, imagine that R1 has five routes to 9.0.0.0/10, two with AS_PATH length 3 and the others with AS_PATH length 5. The decision process did not determine a best route before reaching Step 4 (AS_PATH length). Step 4's logic can determine that two routes are better than the others because they have a shorter AS_PATH length. BGP typically chooses the first-learned valid route as best. For any new alternate routes for the same prefix, BGP applies the BGP decision process to the currently best and new route.

BGP applies this process to each unique NLRI. When overlapping NLRIs exist—for example, 130.1.0.0/16, 130.2.0.0/16, and 130.0.0.0/12—BGP attempts to find the best route for each specific prefix/prefix length.

### Three Final Tiebreaker Steps in the BGP Decision Process

It is possible for BGP to fail to determine a best path to an NLRI using Steps 1 through 9, so BGP includes the following tiebreakers. These values would not typically be manipulated in a routing policy to impact the decision process.

**10.** Keep the oldest eBGP route. If the routes being compared are eBGP, and one of the paths is currently the best path, retain the existing best path. This action reduces eBGP route flaps.

**11.** Choose the smallest neighbor router ID (RID). Use the route whose next-hop router RID is the smallest. Only perform this step if **bgp bestpath compare-routerid** is configured.

**12.** Smallest neighbor ID. To get to this step, the local router has at least two neighbor relationships with a single other router. For this atypical case, the router now prefers the route advertised by the lowest neighbor ID, as listed in that router's neighbor commands.

**Note**   The decision for eBGP routes can reach Step 11 if at Step 10 the formerly best route fails and BGP is comparing two other alternate routes.

**Note**   For those of you more familiar with BGP, hopefully the lists describing the BGP decision process bring to mind the details you have learned in the past. For those of you less familiar with BGP, you might begin to feel a little overwhelmed by the details of the process. The lists are useful for study and memorization after you understand the background and details, which will be forthcoming in just a few pages. However, a few other general details need to be introduced before you get to the details at each step of the decision process. Hang in there!

### Adding Multiple BGP Routes to the IP Routing Table

The BGP decision process has an impact on whether BGP adds multiple routes for a single NLRI to the IP routing table. The following statements summarize the logic:

■ If the best path for an NLRI is determined in Steps 1 through 9, BGP adds only one BGP route to the IP routing table—the best route, of course.

■ If the best path for an NLRI is determined after Step 9, BGP considers placing multiple BGP routes into the IP routing table.

■ Even if multiple BGP routes are added to the IP routing table, BGP still chooses only one route per NLRI as the best route; that best route is the only route to that NLRI that BGP will advertise to neighbors.

The section "The maximum-paths Command and BGP Decision Process Tiebreakers," later in this chapter, details the restrictions.

## Mnemonics for Memorizing the Decision Process

Many people do not bother to memorize the BGP decision process steps. However, memorizing the list is very useful for both the CCIE Routing and Switching written and lab exams. This section provides a set of mnemonic devices to aid you in memorizing the list. Please feel free to learn the mnemonic or skip to the next heading, at your discretion.

Table 2-8 is part of the practice effort to memorize the BGP decision tree.

**Table 2-8**   *BGP Decision Process Mnemonic: N WLLA OMNI*

| Trigger Letter | Short Phrase | Which Is Better? |
|---|---|---|
| N | Next hop: reachable? | — |
| W | Weight | Bigger |
| L | LOCAL_PREF | Bigger |
| L | Locally injected routes | Locally injected is better than iBGP/eBGP learned |
| A | AS_PATH length | Smaller |
| O | ORIGIN | Prefer ORIGIN code I over E, and E over ? |
| M | MED | Smaller |
| N | Neighbor Type | Prefer eBGP over iBGP |
| I | IGP metric to NEXT_HOP | Smaller |

The first mnemonic step is to memorize the nine trigger letters—single letters that, after being memorized, should hopefully trigger your memory to recall some short phrase that describes the logic of each decision point. Of course, memorizing nine seemingly random letters is not easy. So, memorize them as three groups:

N

WLLA

OMNI

**Note**   The nine letters are organized as shown here for several reasons. First, the single letter N, for Step 1, is purposefully separated from the other two groups because it can be argued that this step is not really part of the decision process. OMNI was separated because it is a commonly known English language prefix. And WLLA was just left over after designating OMNI.

After memorizing the trigger letter groups, you should exercise correlating the triggers to the short phrases listed in Table 2-8. (The CD contains memory-builder versions of the tables, including Table 2-8, which you can print and use for this practice if you like.)

Simply write down the nine trigger letters, and exercise your memory by writing out the short phrase associated with each letter. I'd recommend practicing as the first thing you do when you pick up the book for your next reading/study session, and do it for 5 minutes, and typically after a few rounds you will have it memorized.

Of these nine steps, I find also that most people have difficulty correlating the I to the phrase "IGP metric to reach the NEXT_HOP"; in case it helps, memorize also that the first and last of the nine items relate to NEXT_HOP. Based on that fact, and the fact that the trigger letter I implies IGP, maybe the two facts together might trigger your memory.

After you can essentially re-create the first two columns of Table 2-8 from memory, memorize the fact that the first two quantitative decision points use bigger-is-better logic and the rest use smaller-is-better logic. By doing so, you do not have to memorize which specific feature uses which type of logic. As long as you can write down the entire list, you can easily find the first two with quantitative comparisons (specifically Steps 2 and 3, WEIGHT and LOCAL_PREF, respectively).

Finally, Steps 10 and 11 are left to you to simply memorize. Remember that **maximum-paths** comes into play only if the first eight points do not determine a best route.

## Configuring BGP Policies

BGP policies include route filters as well as tools that modify PAs and other settings that impact the BGP decision process. This section examines the Cisco IOS tools used to implement routing policies that impact the BGP decision process, covering the tools in the same order as the decision process.

### Background: BGP PAs and Features Used by Routing Policies

Before getting into each individual step of the decision process, it is important to have a handy reference for the features the process manipulates, and the command output on routers that will reflect the changes made by each step. First, Table 2-9 summarizes the BGP PAs and other features used in the BGP decision process.

**Table 2-9** *Proprietary Features and BGP Path Attributes That Affect the BGP Decision Process*

| PA/Other | Description | BGP PA Type |
|---|---|---|
| NEXT_HOP | Lists the next-hop IP address used to reach an NLRI. | Well-known mandatory |
| Weight[1] | Local Cisco-proprietary setting, not advertised to any peers. Bigger is better. | — |
| LOCAL_PREF | Communicated inside a single AS. Bigger is better; range 0 through $2^{32} - 1$. | Well-known discretionary |
| AS_PATH length | The number of ASNs in the AS_SEQ, plus 1 if an AS_SET exists. | Well-known mandatory |

| PA/Other | Description | BGP PA Type |
|---|---|---|
| ORIGIN | Value implying that the route was injected into BGP; I (IGP), E (EGP), or ? (incomplete information). | Well-known mandatory |
| MULTI_EXIT_DISC (MED) | Multi-Exit Discriminator. Set and advertised by routers in one AS, impacting the BGP decision of routers in the other AS. Smaller is better. | Optional nontransitive |
| Neighbor Type[1] | The type of BGP neighbor from which a route was learned. Confederation eBGP is treated as iBGP for the decision process. | — |
| IGP metric to reach NEXT_HOP[1] | Smaller is better. | — |
| BGP RID[1] | Defines a unique identifier for a BGP router. Smaller is better. | — |

[1] *This value is not a BGP PA.*

Next, Figure 2-6 shows an example of the **show ip bgp** command. Note that the locations of most of the variables used for the BGP decision process are given in the output.

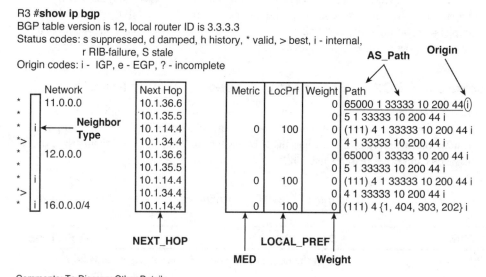

**Figure 2-6**  *Locating Key BGP Decision Features in the* **show ip bgp** *Command*

The **show ip bgp** command lists most of the settings that impact the decision process, but it does not list the advertising router's RID, the IGP metric to reach the NEXT_HOP, or the neighbor ID that advertised the route. Two other commands do supply these three missing pieces of information. Example 2-6 shows the output of one of those commands, the **show ip bgp 16.0.0.0** command, which lists the advertising router's RID and neighbor ID. The IGP metric, of course, is given by the **show ip route** command.

**Example 2-6**  *Output of the* **show ip bgp 16.0.0.0** *Command on R3*

```
! Two routes to 16.0.0.0 are listed. The "from z.z.z.z" phrases identify the
! neighbor ID that advertised the route. The "(y.y.y.y)" output that follows lists
! the RID of that same router. Also, note that the
! output first identifies entry #2 as the best one, indicated by that entry (on the
! last line of output) also listing the word "best."
R3# sh ip bgp 16.0.0.0
BGP routing table entry for 16.0.0.0/4, version 8
Paths: (2 available, best #2, table Default-IP-Routing-Table)
  Advertised to update-groups:
     1         2
  (111) 4 {1,404,303,202}, (aggregated by 4 4.4.4.4), (received & used)
    10.1.14.4 (metric 3193856) from 2.2.2.2 (2.2.2.2)
      Origin IGP, metric 0, localpref 100, valid, confed-internal
  4 {1,404,303,202}, (aggregated by 4 4.4.4.4), (received & used)
    10.1.34.4 from 10.1.34.4 (4.4.4.4)
Origin IGP, metric 0, localpref 100, valid, external, best* i11.0.0.0
```

Armed with the BGP decision process steps, the definitions for the PAs that impact the process, and a good reference for where you need to look to see the values, the next several sections take a tour of the BGP decision process. Each successive heading examines the decision process steps, in sequence.

## Step 1: NEXT_HOP Reachable

This decision step simply prevents BGP from making the poor choice of accepting a BGP route as best, even though that router cannot possibly forward packets to the next-hop router.

Routing policies do not typically attempt to change a NEXT_HOP address to impact a routing choice. However, the NEXT_HOP can be changed by using either the **neighbor** *neighbor-id* **next-hop-self** command (the default for eBGP peers) or the **neighbor** *neighbor-id* **next-hop-unchanged** command (the default for iBGP peers). If **next-hop-self** is used, the NEXT_HOP is set to the IP address used as the source of the BGP Update sent to that neighbor. If **next-hop-unchanged** is used, the NEXT_HOP is not changed.

## Step 2: Administrative Weight

The *weight*, more fully titled *administrative weight*, allows a single router to examine inbound BGP Updates and decide which routes to prefer. The weight is not a BGP PA, but simply a Cisco-proprietary setting on a local router. In fact, it cannot be included in a BGP Update sent to another router, because there is no place in the Update message to include the weight. Table 2-10 summarizes the key topics regarding BGP weight.

Key Topic

**Table 2-10**   *Key Features of Administrative Weight*

| Feature | Description |
|---|---|
| Is it a PA? | No; Cisco-proprietary feature |
| Purpose | Identifies a single router's best route |
| Scope | In a single router only |
| Default | 0 for learned routes, 32,768 for locally injected routes |
| Changing the defaults | Not supported |
| Range | 0 through 65,535 ($2^{16} - 1$) |
| Which is best? | Bigger values are better |
| Configuration | Through the **neighbor route-map in** command or the **neighbor weight** command (if a route is matched by both commands, IOS uses the weight specified in the route map) |

Figure 2-7 shows an updated version of Figure 2-4 that is used in the next example. Compared to Figure 2-4, Figure 2-7 shows the three routers in AS 123 as a full mesh of iBGP peers, with no confederations.

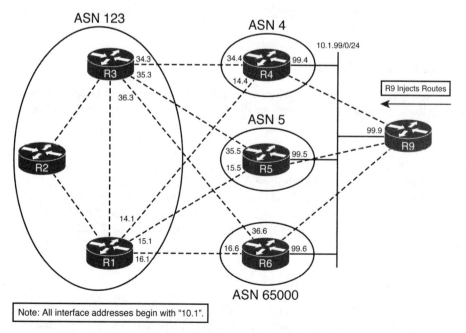

**Figure 2-7**   *Sample Network: AS 123 Without Confederations*

In Example 2-7, R1 sets the weight for NLRIs learned from R4, R5, and R6. The configuration shows both methods of configuring weight:

■ Routes learned from R4 are set to weight 4 by using the **neighbor weight** command.

■ Routes learned from R5 are set to weight 200 if ASN 200 is in the AS_PATH, by using a route map.

**Example 2-7**  *Setting BGP Administrative Weight on R1*

```
! The commands below list only commands that were added to the existing R1
! configuration. All routes from R4 (10.1.14.4) will now be weight 4, and those
! matching clause 10 of the route-map, from R5 (10.1.15.5), will be weight 200.
router bgp 123
 neighbor 10.1.14.4 weight 4
 neighbor 10.1.15.5 route-map set-weight-200 in
! The AS_PATH ACL matches any AS_PATH that includes ASN 200. Note that the
! route-map requires a second permit clause with no match or set, otherwise all
! routes not matched by clause 10 will be filtered.
ip as-path access-list 5 permit _200_
!
route-map set-weight-200 permit 10
 match as-path 5
 set weight 200
!
route-map set-weight-200 permit 20
! The changes are reflected below. Note also that both networks 11 and 12 have
! weights of 200, so those routes were chosen as the best paths.
R1# sh ip bgp | begin Network
   Network          Next Hop         Metric LocPrf Weight Path
*  11.0.0.0         10.1.14.4        4294967294           4 4 1 33333 10 200 44 i
* i                 10.1.36.6        4294967294    100    0 65000 1 33333 10 200 44 i
*                   10.1.16.6        4294967294           0 65000 1 33333 10 200 44 i
*>                  10.1.15.5        4294967294        200 5 1 33333 10 200 44 i
*  12.0.0.0         10.1.14.4        4294967294           4 4 1 33333 10 200 44 i
* i                 10.1.36.6        4294967294    100    0 65000 1 33333 10 200 44 i
*                   10.1.16.6        4294967294           0 65000 1 33333 10 200 44 i
*>                  10.1.15.5        4294967294        200 5 1 33333 10 200 44 i
```

Of particular importance in the example is the fact that the route map includes clause 20, with a **permit** action and no **match** or **set** commands. The **neighbor route-map** command creates an implied filtering decision. Any route matched by a **permit** clause in the route map is implied to be allowed through, and routes matched by a **deny** clause will be filtered. Route maps use an implied **deny all** at the end of the route map for any unmatched routes. By including a final clause with just a **permit** keyword, the route map changes to use **permit all** logic, thereby passing all routes.

## Step 3: Highest Local Preference (LOCAL_PREF)

The BGP LOCAL_PREF PA allows routers in an AS with multiple exit points to choose which exit point is used to reach a particular NLRI. To do so, the router that is the desired exit point sets the LOCAL_PREF for its eBGP route for that NLRI to a relatively high value and then advertises that route through iBGP. The other routers in the same AS can learn of multiple routes to reach the NLRI, but they will choose the route with the higher LOCAL_PREF as the best route.

Table 2-11 summarizes the key topics regarding LOCAL_PREF.

**Table 2-11**   *Key Features of LOCAL_PREF*

| Feature | Description |
|---|---|
| PA? | Yes, well-known, discretionary |
| Purpose | Identifies the best exit point from the AS to reach the NLRI |
| Scope | Throughout the AS in which it was set, including confederation sub-ASs |
| Default | 100 |
| Changing the default | Using the **bgp default local-preference <0-4294967295>** BGP subcommand |
| Range | 0 through 4,294,967,295 ($2^{32} - 1$) |
| Which is best? | Higher values are better |
| Configuration | Through the **neighbor route-map** command; **in** option is required for Updates from an eBGP peer |

Figure 2-8 shows a typical example of using LOCAL_PREF. In this case, the engineers for AS 123 want to use R1 to forward packets to 11.0.0.0/8, but use R3 to forward packets to 12.0.0.0/8. If either route fails, the other router should be used instead.

Example 2-8 shows the configuration used on R1 and R3 to implement the following routing policy:

- AS 123 routers should use R1 to reach 11.0.0.0/8.

- AS 123 routers should use R3 to reach 12.0.0.0/8.

- R1 can use any of its three routes to reach 11.0.0.0/8, and R3 can use any of its three routes to reach 12.0.0.0/8.

To meet these design goals, R1 and R3 will set LOCAL_PREF to values higher than the default of 100.

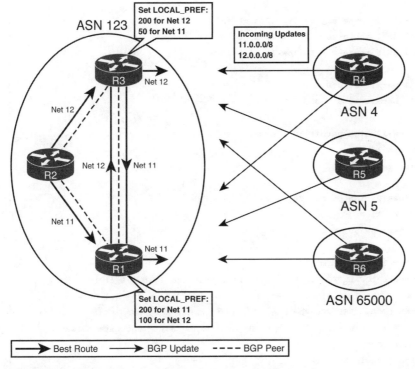

**Figure 2-8**  *Typical Use of LOCAL_PREF to Influence Exit Point from AS 123*

**Example 2-8**  *LOCAL_PREF Directing Packets for 11/8 Out R1 and Packets for 12/8 Out R3*

```
! R1 Config-only the relevant configuration is shown. The same route-map is
! called for incoming Updates from R4, R5, and R6. Note that the route-map
! includes a permit clause 20 with no match or set commands to permit
! any routes not specified in clause 10 to pass without changes. The route-map
! allows the LOCAL_PREF for 12.0.0.0/8 to default (100).
router bgp 123
 neighbor 10.1.14.4 route-map 11-high-12-default in
 neighbor 10.1.15.5 route-map 11-high-12-default in
 neighbor 10.1.16.6 route-map 11-high-12-default in
!
access-list 11 permit 11.0.0.0
!
route-map 11-high-12-default permit 10
 match ip address 11
 set local-preference 200
!
route-map 11-high-12-default permit 20
! R3 Config-Same general concept as R1, but the 12.0.0.0/8 route is assigned
! LOCAL_PREF 200, and 11.0.0.0/8 is assigned LOCAL_PREF 50.
```

```
router bgp 123
 neighbor 10.1.34.4 route-map 11-low-12-high in
 neighbor 10.1.35.5 route-map 11-low-12-high in
 neighbor 10.1.36.6 route-map 11-low-12-high in
!
access-list 11 permit 11.0.0.0
access-list 12 permit 12.0.0.0
!
route-map 11-low-12-high permit 10
 match ip address 12
 set local-preference 200
!
route-map 11-low-12-high permit 20
 match ip address 11
 set local-preference 50
!
route-map 11-low-12-high permit 30
! R3 now shows the LOCAL_PREF values. R3's best route to 12.0.0.0 is the one it
! learned from R4 (10.1.34.4). Its best route to 11.0.0.0 is the only one of the
! 4 routes with LOCAL_PREF 200-the one learned from R1. Note also that the
! administrative weights are all tied at 0; otherwise, BGP might have chosen a
! different best route.
R3# show ip bgp | begin Network
   Network          Next Hop         Metric LocPrf Weight Path
*  11.0.0.0         10.1.36.6        4294967294    50      0 65000 1 33333 10 200 44 i
*>i                 10.1.14.4        4294967294   200      0 4 1 33333 10 200 44 i
*                   10.1.35.5        4294967294    50      0 5 1 33333 10 200 44 i
*                   10.1.34.4        4294967294    50      0 4 1 33333 10 200 44 i
*  12.0.0.0         10.1.36.6        4294967294   200      0 65000 1 33333 10 200 44 i
*                   10.1.35.5        4294967294   200      0 5 1 33333 10 200 44 i
*>                  10.1.34.4        4294967294   200      0 4 1 33333 10 200 44 i
R3# show ip bgp 11.0.0.0
! lines omitted for brevity
   4 1 33333 10 200 44, (received & used)
     10.1.14.4 (metric 2681856) from 1.1.1.1 (1.1.1.1)
       Origin IGP, metric 4294967294, localpref 200, valid, internal, best
! lines omitted for brevity
! Because R3's best route to 11.0.0.0/8 is through R1, R3 does not advertise that
! iBGP route to R2. Similarly, R1's best route to 12.0.0.0/8 is through R3, so R1
! does not advertise its best route to 12.0.0.0/8, again because it is an iBGP
! route. As a result, R2 receives only one route to each of the two networks.
R2# show ip bgp | begin Network
   Network          Next Hop         Metric LocPrf Weight Path
*>i11.0.0.0         10.1.14.4        4294967294   200      0 4 1 33333 10 200 44 i
*>i12.0.0.0         10.1.34.4        4294967294   200      0 4 1 33333 10 200 44 i
```

This example does meet the stated design goals, but note that one design goal states that it does not matter which of the three eBGP routes R1 and R3 use to reach their assigned prefixes. Interestingly, R1 did not choose its best BGP route to network 11.0.0.0/8 based on LOCAL_PREF, nor did R3 choose its best route to 12.0.0.0/8 based on LOCAL_PREF. Note that R1 and R3 had three routes that tied based on LOCAL_PREF. In this case, their decisions happened to fall all the way to Step 10—the lowest advertising BGP RID. As a result, R3 chose the route through R4 (RID 4.4.4.4) instead of R5 (RID 5.5.5.5) or R6 (RID 6.6.6.6).

Had R1 or R3 wanted to impact which of the three eBGP routers to use to reach their respective NLRI, the route map could have been changed to match routes from each neighbor and set the LOCAL_PREF to different high values. For example, the LOCAL_PREF could be set to 204, 205, and 206 for R4, R5, and R6, respectively, thereby making R3 choose to use the route through R6 if 12.0.0.0/8 was learned from each of the three eBGP peers. To match, the **match ip next-hop** or **match ip route-source** command could be used, or a different route map could simply be used per neighbor.

## Step 4: Choose Between Locally Injected Routes Based on ORIGIN PA

This logic step is seldom used, but it is a valid part of the BGP decision process. To appreciate why it is so seldom needed, consider the following: BGP assigns a weight of 32,768 to routes locally injected into BGP. As a result, a router would have already picked a locally injected route as best because of its high weight.

Two general cases can occur that cause a router to use the logic for this step. The first case is unlikely. A router must locally inject an NLRI, learn the same NLRI from a neighbor, and use an inbound **route-map** to set the weight of that received NLRI to the same value as the locally injected route. That only occurs in lab experiments.

The second case occurs when a router attempts to inject routes locally through multiple methods, and the same NLRI is injected from two different sources. For example, imagine that R1 injects a route to network 123.0.0.0/8 because of both a **network 123.0.0.0** command and a **redistribute connected** command. Both routes would have default weights of 32,768, and both would default to the same LOCAL_PREF. The two routes would then be compared at this step, with the ORIGIN code determining which route is best.

The logic for the second (and only likely) case to use this step in the decision process can be reduced to the following:

> When the same NLRI is locally injected into BGP from multiple methods, pick the route with the better ORIGIN PA.

The only hard part is memorizing the ORIGIN codes, and that "I" is better than "E" is better than "?".

## Step 5: Shortest AS_PATH

Routers can easily determine the shortest AS_PATH length by using a few rules that define how to account for all four parts of the AS_PATH—the AS_SEQ, AS_SET,

AS_CONFED_SEQ, and AS_CONFED_SET. Additionally, routing policies can change the number of ASNs in the AS_PATH. Table 2-12 summarizes the key topics regarding AS_PATH length.

**Key Topic**

**Table 2-12**  *Features That Impact the Total Number of ASs in the AS_PATH Length Calculation*

| Feature | Description |
| --- | --- |
| AS_SET | Regardless of actual length, it counts as a single ASN. |
| Confederations | AS_CONFED_SEQ and AS_CONFED_SET do not count in the calculation. |
| **aggregate-address** command | If the component subnets have different AS_PATHs, the summary route has only the local AS in the AS_SEQ; otherwise, the AS_SEQ contains the AS_SEQ from the component subnets. Also, the presence/absence of the **as-set** command option determines whether the AS_SET is included. |
| **neighbor remove-private-as** command | Used by a router attached to a private AS (64512–65535), causing the router to remove the private ASN used by the neighboring AS. |
| **neighbor local-as no-prepend** command | Allows a router to use a different AS than the one on the **router bgp** command; with the **no-prepend** option, the router does not prepend any ASN when sending eBGP Updates to this neighbor. |
| AS_PATH prepending | Using a **neighbor route-map** in either direction, the route map can use the **set as-path prepend** command to prepend one or more ASNs into the AS_SEQ. |
| **bgp bestpath as-path ignore** command | Removes the AS_PATH length step from the decision tree for the local router. |

The typical logic at this step simply requires the router to calculate the number of ASNs in the AS_SEQ, and add 1 if an AS_SET exists. However, the table mentions several other features that impact what ASNs are used and whether an eBGP peer adds an ASN. These additional features are covered next before moving on to Step 5 of the BGP decision process.

## Removing Private ASNs

Private ASNs (64,512–65,535) should not be used in AS_PATHs advertised into the Internet beyond a single ISP. One purpose of this private range is to conserve the ASN space by assigning private ASNs to customers that only connect to that single ISP. Then, the ISP can simply remove the private ASN before advertising any routes for that customer outside its network.

Figure 2-9 shows the typical case for using a private AS. While the concept is relatively simple, the configuration details can be a bit surprising.

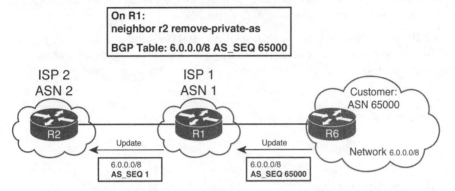

**Figure 2-9**    *Typical Use of Private ASNs and the* **neighbor remove-private-as** *Command*

Following Figure 2-9 from right to left, here are the key topics:

- R6, inside the private AS, does not require any special commands.

- R1, acting as a router in the sole ISP to which ASN 65000 is connected, lists private AS 65000 in its BGP table for any routes learned from R6.

- R1 needs the command **neighbor R2 remove-private-as** under router BGP, telling R1 to remove any private ASNs from AS_PATHs advertised to Router R2.

Cisco IOS has several restrictions regarding whether a private AS is removed as a protection against causing routing loops:

- Private ASNs can be removed only at the point of sending an eBGP Update.

- If the current AS_SEQ contains both private and public ASNs, the private ASNs will not be removed.

- If the ASN of the eBGP peer is in the current AS_PATH, the private ASNs will not be removed, either.

This feature works with confederations as well, with the same restrictions being applied to the AS_CONFED_SEQ.

## AS_PATH Prepending and Route Aggregation

The concept and motivation behind the AS_PATH prepend feature is simple—impact the AS_PATH length decision step by increasing the length of the AS_PATH. To do so, a router simply configures a route map and refers to it with a **neighbor route-map** command, with the route map using the **set as-path prepend** *asn1 asn2...* command. As a result, the route map prepends additional ASNs to the AS_SEQUENCE.

Any ASN can be prepended, but in practice, it makes the most sense to prepend the local router's ASN. The reason is that prepending some other ASN prevents that route from being advertised into that AS—a scenario that might not be intended. Also, if the AS_PATH needs to be lengthened by more than one ASN, the **set** command can repeat the same ASN multiple times, as shown in Example 2-9.

Figure 2-10 shows a design depicting the use of AS_PATH prepending. R6 correctly prepends its own ASN 4 for routes advertised to R1 (in the top part of the figure). R6 also causes problems by prepending ASN 2 for the route sent to R3 (in the lower part of the figure).

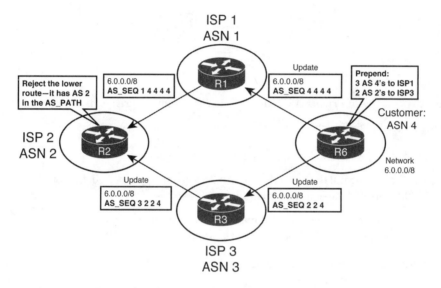

**Figure 2-10** *Options for Prepending ASNs*

While AS_PATH prepending lengthens the AS_PATH, route aggregation can actually decrease the AS_PATH length. Route aggregation (summarization) with the BGP **aggregate-address** command impacts the AS_PATH length in a couple of ways:

■ The router checks the component subnets' AS_PATH AS_SEQ values. If all the component subnets' AS_SEQ values are identical, the aggregate route uses that same AS_SEQ.

■ If the component subnets' AS_SEQ values differ, the aggregating router uses a null AS_SEQ for the aggregate. (When advertised to an eBGP peer, the router does prepend its local ASN, as normal.) Of course, this process shortens the AS_PATH length.

Additionally, the **aggregate-address** command with the **as-set** option can lengthen the AS_PATH length calculation as well. When a router uses this command with the **as-set** option, and the aggregate empties out the AS_SEQ as described in the previous paragraph, the router adds an AS_SET segment to the AS_PATH. (Conversely, if the aggregate does not empty the AS_SEQ, the router does not create the AS_SET, as it is not needed for loop prevention in that case.) The AS_SET includes all ASNs of all component subnets.

The BGP AS_PATH length calculation counts the entire AS_SET as 1, regardless of the actual length.

Example 2-9 shows examples of both AS_PATH prepending and route aggregation on the AS_PATH length. In the example, the familiar network of Figure 2-7 is used. The following features are used in the example:

- R4 prepends route 11.0.0.0/8 with three additional ASN 4s, using an outbound route map, before advertising routes into AS 123.

- R4 and R5 both summarize 16.0.0.0/4, but R4 uses the **as-set** option and R5 does not.

As a result of the second item, R3 learns both summaries, but treats the summary from R5 as better, because the AS_SET in R4's route counts as one ASN in the AS_PATH length calculation.

**Example 2-9**  *AS_PATH Prepending and an Examination of Route Summarization and AS_PATH Length*

```
! R4's configuration shows the route-map called add3-4s for its neighbor commands
! for R1 (10.1.14.1) and R3 (10.1.34.3). The route-map matches 11.0.0.0/8,
! prepending three additional ASN 4s. The normal process of prepending the local AS
! before advertising over eBGP peer connection adds the 4th instance of ASN 4. As
! usual, the route-map needs a null final clause with a permit so that the rest
! of the routes are not affected.
router bgp 4
 aggregate-address 16.0.0.0 240.0.0.0 as-set
 neighbor 10.1.14.1 route-map add3-4s out
 neighbor 10.1.34.3 route-map add3-4s out
!
ip prefix-list match11 seq 5 permit 11.0.0.0/8
!
route-map add3-4s permit 10
 match ip address prefix-list match11
 set as-path prepend 4 4 4
!
route-map add3-4s permit 20
! Below, first focus on 11.0.0.0/8. The highlighted route with NEXT_HOP 10.1.34.4
! (R4) has four consecutive 4s in the AS_PATH, showing the effects of the prepending
! on R4. The route through 10.1.35.5 ends up being best based on the tiebreaker
! at Step 9.
! Next, look at 16.0.0.0/4. The route through 10.1.34.4 is considered
! to be AS_PATH length 2, but the length through 10.1.35.5 is only 1. The
```

```
! route to 16.0.0.0/4 through NEXT_HOP 10.1.35.5 is chosen over the route through
! 10.1.15.5 because it is eBGP, versus iBGP for the route through 10.1.15.5.
R3# show ip bgp | begin Network
   Network          Next Hop        Metric LocPrf Weight Path
*  11.0.0.0         10.1.36.6       4294967294          0 65000 1 33333 10 200 44 i
* i                 10.1.16.6       4294967294          0 65000 1 33333 10 200 44 i
*                   10.1.34.4       4294967294          0 4 4 4 4 1 33333 10 200 44 i
*>                  10.1.35.5       4294967294          0 5 1 33333 10 200 44 i
*  16.0.0.0/4       10.1.34.4       4294967294          0 4 {1,404,303,202} ?
*>                  10.1.35.5       4294967294          0 5 i
* i                 10.1.15.5       4294967294          0 5 i
```

## Step 6: Best ORIGIN PA

The well-known mandatory BGP ORIGIN PA characterizes a route based on how it was injected into BGP. The ORIGIN is either IGP (i), EGP (e), or incomplete (?).

The actual BGP decision process for the ORIGIN code is quite simple. First, an ORIGIN of EGP (e) should not occur today, because EGP is not even supported in current IOS revisions. So, the logic reduces to the following:

**Key Topic**

If the set of routes to reach a single NLRI includes only one route of ORIGIN code IGP (i), and all the others as incomplete (?), the route with ORIGIN i is the best route.

BGP routing policies can set the ORIGIN code explicitly by using the **set origin** route map subcommand, although the earlier steps in the BGP decision process are typically better choices for configuring BGP policies. BGP determines the ORIGIN code based on the method used to inject the routes, along with the options used with the **aggregate-address** command.

Chapter 1's section, "ORIGIN Path Attribute," describes more detail about the ORIGIN PA and how NLRIs are assigned an ORIGIN code.

## Step 7: Smallest Multi-Exit Discriminator

The purpose of the MED (or MULTI_EXIT_DISC) is to allow routers in one AS to tell routers in a neighboring AS how good a particular route is. In fact, because of how MED works, it is often called the *BGP metric*, even though it is not close to the top of the BGP decision process. Figure 2-11 shows a classic case for the use of MED, where a customer has two links connecting it to a single ISP. The ISP, aware of its best routes for 11.0.0.0/8 and 12.0.0.0/8, can set MED so that the customer routes packets to the eBGP peer that is closest to the destination network.

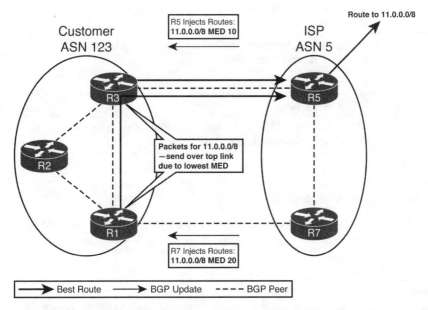

**Figure 2-11**  *Typical Use of MED*

The ISP, knowing its best route to reach 11.0.0.0/8 is through R5, configures R5 to set a low MED for that prefix and R7 to set a higher MED for the same prefix. As a result, the BGP routers in customer AS 123 choose the route through the top peer connection. The customer could then use the route through the lower link to R7 if the top connection failed.

Figure 2-11 shows the classic topology—a customer using a single ISP but with multiple links to the ISP. Many customers want redundant ISPs as well, or at least connections to multiple autonomous systems controlled by a single, large ISP. MED can also be used in such cases, but it requires the multiple ISPs or multiple ASs in the same ISP to use the same policy when determining the MED values to set. For example, two ISPs might agree that because one ISP has more link bandwidth to a certain range of BGP prefixes, that ISP will set a lower MED for those NLRIs.

Table 2-13 summarizes the key topics regarding MED.

**Table 2-13**  *Key Features of MED*

| Feature | Description |
|---|---|
| Is it a PA? | Yes, optional nontransitive |
| Purpose | Allows an AS to tell a neighboring AS the best way to forward packets into the first AS |
| Scope | Advertised by one AS into another, propagated inside the AS but not sent to any other ASs |
| Default | 0 |

| Feature | Description |
|---|---|
| Changing the default | Using the **bgp bestpath med missing-as-worst** BGP subcommand; sets it to the maximum value |
| Range | 0 through 4,294,967,295 ($2^{32} - 1$) |
| Which is best? | Smaller is better |
| Configuration | Through the **neighbor route-map out** command, using the **set metric** command inside the route map |

## Configuring MED: Single Adjacent AS

Example 2-10 shows a sample MED configuration that matches Figure 2-11, with R5 and R7 setting the MED for 11.0.0.0/8 to 10 and 20, respectively.

**Example 2-10**  *Classical MED Example Between Two ASs*

```
! The pertinent R5 configuration follows. R5 simply matches 11.0.0.0/8 and sets
! the metric to 10. The route-map includes a default permit any clause at the end
! to avoid affecting other routes.
router bgp 5
 neighbor 10.1.35.3 route-map set-med out
!
ip prefix-list 11 seq 5 permit 11.0.0.0/8
!
route-map set-med permit 10
 match ip address prefix-list 11
 set metric 10
route-map set-med permit 20
! R7's configuration is not shown, but it is basically the same regarding the
! setting of the MED. However, R7 sets the MED to 20.
```
```
! R1 lists routes with R5 (10.1.35.5) and R7 (10.1.17.7) as NEXT_HOP; the route
! through R5 is best due to the lower MED.
R1# show ip bgp | begin Network
   Network          Next Hop          Metric LocPrf Weight Path
*>i11.0.0.0         10.1.35.5             10    100      0 5 1 33333 10 200 44 i
*                   10.1.17.7             20             0 5 1 33333 10 200 44 i
*> 12.0.0.0         10.1.35.5                            0 5 1 33333 10 200 44 i
* i                 10.1.17.7              0    100      0 5 1 33333 10 200 44 i
```
```
! R3 sees only the MED 10 route. R1's best route to NEXT_HOP 10.1.35.5 is through
! R3, so R1 did not advertise its best route to 11.0.0.0/8 to iBGP peer R3.
R3# show ip bgp | begin Network
   Network          Next Hop          Metric LocPrf Weight Path
*> 11.0.0.0         10.1.35.5             10             0 5 1 33333 10 200 44 i
*> 12.0.0.0         10.1.35.5                            0 5 1 33333 10 200 44 i
* i                 10.1.17.7              0    100      0 5 1 33333 10 200 44 i
```

**Key Topic**

It is important that both R5 and R7 set the MED for 11.0.0.0/8. If R5 had set the MED to 10, and R7 had done nothing, the router through R7 would have been the best route. R1 and R3 would have used their assumed default setting of 0 for the MED for the route through R1 and R7, and as with IGP metrics, smaller is better with MED. A better default for MED can be set by using the **bgp bestpath med missing-as-worst** BGP subcommand, which resets a router's default MED to the largest possible MED value, instead of the lowest. Note that it is important that all routers in the same AS either use the default of 0 or configure this command; otherwise, routing choices will be affected.

### Configuring MED: Multiple Adjacent Autonomous Systems

By default, a Cisco router ignores MED when the multiple routes to a single NLRI list different neighboring ASNs. This default action makes sense—normally you would not expect two different neighboring ISPs to have chosen to work together to set MEDs. To override this default and consider the MED in all cases, a router needs to configure the **bgp always-compare-med** BGP subcommand. If used on one router, all routers inside the same AS should also use the **bgp always-compare-med** command, or routing loops can result.

Additionally, some Cisco documents imply that the internal BGP decision process for the MED might be different depending on the order of the entries in the BGP table. Interestingly, BGP lists the table entries from newest (most recently learned) to oldest in the output of the **show ip bgp** and **show ip bgp** *prefix* commands. Depending on that order, in some cases in which the competing routes for the same NLRI have different MEDs from different autonomous systems, the order of the entries impacts the final choice of the best route. In part, the difference results from the fact that Cisco IOS (by default) processes the list sequentially—which means that it processes the first pair of routes (newest), picks the best of those two, then compares that one with the next newest, and so on.

Cisco solved this nondeterministic behavior for the MED processing problem by creating an alternative process for analyzing and making the MED decision. With this new process, BGP processes the routes per adjacent AS, picking the best from each neighboring AS and then comparing those routes. This logic provides a deterministic choice based on MED—in other words, it removes the possibility of BGP picking a different route based on the order of the routes in the BGP table. To enable this enhanced logic, add the **bgp deterministic-med** command to the routers in the same AS. In fact, Cisco recommends this setting for all new BGP implementations.

### The Scope of MED

The MED PA is not intended to be advertised outside the AS that heard the MED in an incoming BGP Update. Typically, and as shown in the examples in this section, the MED can be set in an outbound route map by a router in one AS to influence the BGP decision process in another AS. So, the MED value is set by routers in one AS and learned by routers in another AS. However, after reaching the other AS, the MED is advertised inside the AS, but not outside the AS. For example, in Figure 2-11, R5 and R7 set the MED and advertise it into AS 123. However, if routers in AS 123 had any other eBGP connections to other ASNs, they would advertise the NLRI, but they would not include the MED value.

MED can also be set through inbound route maps, although that is not the intended design with which to use MED. When you set MED through an inbound route map, the MED is indeed set. The router can advertise the MED to iBGP peers. However, the MED is still not advertised outside the local AS.

### Step 8: Prefer Neighbor Type eBGP over iBGP

This step is rather simple and needs very little elucidation. Keeping in mind that the goal is a single best route for each NLRI, this decision point simply looks to see whether a single eBGP route exists. If so, that route is chosen. If multiple eBGP routes exist, this decision point cannot determine the best route.

Interestingly, BGP uses this decision point frequently when two or more enterprise routers connect to the same ISP. Each border BGP router in the enterprise receives the same prefixes with the same AS_PATH lengths from the ISP, and then these border BGP routers advertise these routes to their iBGP peers. So, each enterprise border router knows of one eBGP route to reach each prefix, and one or more iBGP routes to the same prefix learned from that enterprise's other border routers. With no routing policies configured, the routes tie on all decision points up to this one, including AS_PATH length, because all the prefixes were learned from the same neighboring ISP. The decision process reaches this step, at which point the one eBGP route is picked as the best route.

### Step 9: Smallest IGP Metric to the NEXT_HOP

This step again requires little explanation. The router looks for the route that would be used to reach the NEXT_HOP listed in each BGP table entry for a particular prefix. It is mentioned here just to complete the list.

### The maximum-paths Command and BGP Decision Process Tiebreakers

The goal of the BGP decision tree is to find the one best BGP route to each NLRI, from that router's perspective. That router then considers only its best routes for advertising to other routers, restricting those routes based on AS_PATH loop prevention and routing policy configuration. That router also attempts to add that best route, and that best route only, to its IP routing table. In fact, as long as another routing source has not found a route to the same prefix, with a better administrative distance, the best BGP route is placed into that router's routing table.

If BGP has not chosen a best route for a particular NLRI after Steps 0 through 8, multiple routes tie for being the best route. At this point, BGP needs to make two important decisions:

■ **Which route is best?** BGP uses two tiebreakers, discussed next, to determine which route is best.

- **Whether to add multiple BGP routes for that NLRI to the IP routing table:** BGP considers the setting of the **maximum-paths** command to make this decision, as described after the discussion of Steps 10 and 11.

Even if BGP adds to the IP routing table multiple BGP routes to the same prefix, it still picks only one as the best route in the BGP table.

## Step 10: Lowest BGP Router ID of Advertising Router (with One Exception)

The first tiebreaker is to pick the route with the lowest RID. The logic is actually two steps, as follows:

1. Examine the eBGP routes only, picking the route advertised by the router with the lowest RID.

2. If only iBGP routes exist, pick the route advertised by the router with the lowest RID.

These straightforward rules are followed in some cases, but not in some others. The exception to this rule occurs when BGP already has a best route to the NLRI, but it has learned new BGP information from other routers, including a new BGP route to reach a previously known prefix. The router then applies its BGP decision process again to decide whether to change its opinion of which route is best for that NLRI. If the decision process does not determine a best route by this step, this step uses the following default logic:

> If the existing best route is an eBGP route, do not replace the existing best route, even if the new route has a smaller RID.

The reasoning is that replacing the route could result in route flaps, so keeping the same route is fine. This behavior can be changed so that the lowest RID is always used, by configuring the **bgp bestpath compare-routerid** BGP subcommand. Note that this exception only applies to eBGP routes. If the currently best route is an iBGP route, the decision is simply based on the lowest advertising router's RID.

## Step 11: Lowest Neighbor ID

If Step 10 did not break the tie, the router has at least two **neighbor** commands that point to the same router, and that router happens to have the lowest RID of all current neighbors advertising the NLRI in question. Typically, if redundancy exists between two routers, the configuration uses loopback interfaces, a single **neighbor** command, and the **neighbor ebgp-multihop** command if the neighbor is an eBGP neighbor. However, using a pair (or more) of **neighbor** commands pointing to a single neighboring router is a valid configuration option; this final tiebreaker provides a way to break ties for this case.

At this point, the router looks at the IP addresses on the **neighbor** commands corresponding to all the neighbors from which the route was received, and it picks the lowest neighbor IP address. Note that, as usual, it considers all routes again at this step, so it might not pick the neighboring router with the lowest RID at this point.

### The BGP maximum-paths Command

BGP defaults the **maximum-paths** command to a setting of 1; in other words, only the BGP best route in the BGP table could possibly be added to the IP routing table. However, BGP will consider adding multiple entries to the IP routing table, for the same NLRI, under certain conditions—conditions that differ based on whether the best route is an eBGP route or an iBGP route.

First, consider eBGP routes. The following rules determine if and when a router will add multiple eBGP routes to the IP routing table for a single NLRI:

**Key Topic**

1. BGP must have had to use a tiebreaker (Step 10 or 11) to determine the best route.

2. The **maximum-paths** *number* command must be configured to something larger than the default of 1.

3. Only eBGP routes whose adjacent ASNs are the same ASN as the best route are considered as candidates.

4. If more candidates exist than that called for with the **maximum-paths** command, the tiebreakers of Steps 10 and 11 determine the ones to use.

Although the list is detailed, the general idea is that the router can trust multiple routes, but only if the packets end up in the same adjacent AS. Also, BGP must restrict itself to not use multipath if the best route was found through Steps 1 through 9 of the decision process, because forwarding based on another route could cause loops.

Next, consider iBGP routes. The rules for iBGP have some similarities with eBGP, and a few differences, as follows:

**Key Topic**

1. Same rule as eBGP rule 1.

2. The **maximum-paths ibgp** *number* command defines the number of possible IP routes, instead of the **maximum-paths** *number* command used for eBGP.

3. Only iBGP routes with differing NEXT_HOP settings are considered as candidates.

4. Same rule as eBGP rule 4.

The rationale is similar to eBGP with regard to most of the logic. Additionally, it does not help to add multiple IP routes if the NEXT_HOP settings are equal, so BGP performs that additional check.

Finally, the **maximum-paths eibgp** *number* command seemingly would apply to both iBGP and eBGP routes. However, this command applies only when MPLS is in use. Table 2-14 summarizes the key commands related to BGP multipath.

**Key Topic**

**Table 2-14**   *BGP* **maximum-paths** *Command Options*

| Command | Conditions for Use |
| --- | --- |
| **maximum-paths** *number* | eBGP routes only |
| **maximum-paths ibgp** *number* | iBGP routes only |
| **maximum-paths eibgp** *number* | Both types, but MPLS only |

# BGP Communities

The BGP COMMUNITY PA provides a mechanism by which to group routes so that routing policies can be applied to all the routes with the same community. By marking a set of routes with the same COMMUNITY string, routers can look for the COMMUNITY string and then make policy decisions—like setting some PA that impacts the BGP decision process or simply filtering the routes. BGP communities are powerful in that they allow routers in one AS to communicate policy information to routers that are one or more autonomous systems distant. In fact, because the COMMUNITY PA is an optional transitive PA, it can pass through autonomous systems that do not even understand the COMMUNITY PA and then still be useful at another downstream AS.

Figure 2-12 shows an example of one way in which communities can be used. The goal with this design is to have the engineers in ASNs 4 and 5 work together to decide which of them has the best route to reach each prefix, and then somehow tell the routers in ASN 123. That might sound familiar—that is exactly the motivation behind using MED, as shown in Figure 2-11. However, MED is relatively far into the BGP decision process, even after the shortest AS_PATH. A better design might be to set the COMMUNITY PA and then let the routers in ASN 123 react to the COMMUNITY string and set LOCAL_PREF based on that value, because LOCAL_PREF is considered early in the BGP decision process.

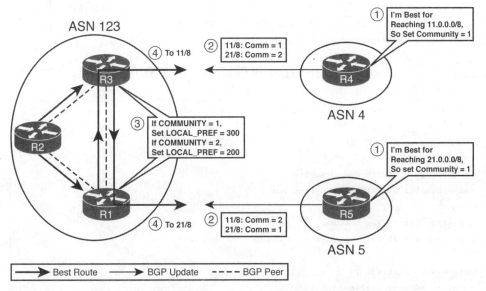

**Figure 2-12**  *Using COMMUNITY to Augment Routing Policies*

Figure 2-12 depicts the following steps:

1.  The engineers at AS 4 and AS 5 agree as to which prefixes are best reached by each AS.

2.  They then configure outbound route maps on their respective neighbor connections to AS 123, setting COMMUNITY to 1 for routes for which they are the best path, and setting COMMUNITY to 2 for some other routes.

3. R1 and R3 receive the Updates, match the NLRI based on the COMMUNITY, and set LOCAL_PREF to a large value for routes whose COMMUNITY was set to 1.

4. The LOCAL_PREF settings impact the BGP choice for the best routes.

This design includes several advantages over some of the options covered earlier in the chapter. It includes the best aspects of using LOCAL_PREF, helping AS 123 decide which neighboring AS to use to reach each prefix. However, it puts the choice of which routes should be reached through AS 4 and AS 5 into the hands of the folks running AS 4 and AS 5. If the AS 4 or AS 5 topology changes, link speeds increase, or other changes occur, the route maps that set the COMMUNITY in AS 4 and AS 5 can be changed accordingly. No changes would be required inside AS 123, because it already simply looks at the COMMUNITY string. Assuming that AS 123 is an enterprise, and AS 4 and AS 5 are ISPs, the ISPs can make one set of changes and impact the routing choices of countless customers.

Example 2-11 shows the configuration matching the scenario of Figure 2-12. The configuration follows mostly familiar commands and reasoning, with two additional features:

■ R4 and R5 (AS 4 and AS 5) must use the **neighbor send-community** BGP subcommand, which tells BGP to include the COMMUNITY PA in the Update. Without that command, the Update does not even include the COMMUNITY PA.

■ R1 and R3 (AS 123) need to match NLRIs based on the received COMMUNITY values, so they must configure *community lists* that match the COMMUNITY by using the **ip community-list** command.

**Example 2-11**  *Setting COMMUNITY and Reacting to COMMUNITY to Set LOCAL_PREF*

```
! R4 must add the neighbor send-community command, otherwise it will not include
! the COMMUNITY PA in Updates sent to R3. The route-map matches 11/8, and sets
! COMMUNITY to 1, and matches 21/8 and sets COMMUNITY to 2.
router bgp 4
 neighbor 10.1.34.3 send-community both
 neighbor 10.1.34.3 route-map comm out
!
ip prefix-list 11 seq 5 permit 11.0.0.0/8
ip prefix-list 21 seq 5 permit 21.0.0.0/8
!
route-map comm permit 10
 match ip address prefix-list 11
 set community 1
!
route-map comm permit 20
 match ip address prefix-list 21
 set community 2
!
route-map comm permit 30
```

```
! R5 has essentially the same configuration, except that R5 sets COMMUNITY to 1
! for 21/8 and to 2 for 11/8-the opposite of R4.
router bgp 5
 neighbor 10.1.15.1 send-community
 neighbor 10.1.15.1 route-map comm out
!
ip prefix-list 11 seq 5 permit 11.0.0.0/8
ip prefix-list 21 seq 5 permit 21.0.0.0/8
!
route-map comm permit 10
 match ip address prefix-list 11
 set community 2
!
route-map comm permit 20
 match ip address prefix-list 21
 set community 1
!
route-map comm permit 30
```

```
! R3 Config: Next, R3 matches on the received COMMUNITY strings and sets
! LOCAL_PREF using a route-map called react-to-comm. The only way to match the
! COMMUNITY is to refer to an ip community-list, which then has the matching
! parameters.
router bgp 123
 neighbor 10.1.34.4 route-map react-to-comm in
!
ip community-list 1 permit 1
ip community-list 2 permit 2
!
route-map react-to-comm permit 10
 match community 1
 set local-preference 300
!
route-map react-to-comm permit 20
 match community 2
 set local-preference 200
!
route-map react-to-comm permit 30
! Not shown-R1 Config. R1's config matches R3's in every way, except for the
! fact that the inbound route-map is applied for the neighbor command pointing
! to R5 (10.1.15.5).
! R3 chooses its best path to 11/8 with NEXT_HOP of R4 (10.1.34.4), as a result
! of R3's assignment of LOCAL_PREF 300, which in turn was a result of the Update
! from R4 listing 11/8 as COMMUNITY 1. R3's best route to 12/8 points to NEXT_HOP
! R5 (10.1.15.1), which happens to point back through R1, because R1 received an
! Update from R5 for 21/8 listing COMMUNITY 1, and then set LOCAL_PREF to 300.
R3# show ip bgp | begin Network
```

```
   Network          Next Hop            Metric LocPrf Weight Path
*> 11.0.0.0         10.1.34.4         4294967294    300     0 4 1 33333 10 200 44 i
*  i12.0.0.0        10.1.15.5         4294967294    100     0 5 1 33333 10 200 44 i
*>                  10.1.34.4         4294967294            0 4 1 33333 10 200 44 i
*>i21.0.0.0         10.1.15.5         4294967294    300     0 5 1 404 303 202 i
*                   10.1.34.4         4294967294    200     0 4 1 404 303 202 i
! R3 now lists its BGP table entries that have COMMUNITY settings that include
! 1 or 2. Note that both commands only list the routes learned directly from R4.
! If R1 had configured a neighbor 3.3.3.3 send-community command, R3 would have
! additional entries using COMMUNITY strings 1 and 2. However, for this design,
! the COMMUNITY strings do not need to be advertised to iBGP peers inside AS 123,
! as R1 and R3 have already reacted to the communities to set the LOCAL_PREF.
R3# show ip bgp community 1
BGP table version is 37, local router ID is 3.3.3.3
Status codes: s suppressed, d damped, h history, * valid, > best, i-internal,
              r RIB-failure, S Stale
Origin codes: i-IGP, e-EGP, ?-incomplete


   Network          Next Hop            Metric LocPrf Weight Path
*> 11.0.0.0         10.1.34.4         4294967294    300     0 4 1 33333 10 200 44 i
R3# show ip bgp community 2 | begin Network
   Network          Next Hop            Metric LocPrf Weight Path
*  21.0.0.0         10.1.34.4         4294967294    200     0 4 1 404 303 202 i
! The COMMUNITY can be seen with the show ip bgp prefix command, as seen below.
! Note that the route learned from R1 (1.1.1.1) does not list a COMMUNITY, as R1
! did not configure a neighbor 3.3.3.3 send-community command.
R3# show ip bgp 21.0.0.0
BGP routing table entry for 21.0.0.0/8, version 35
Paths: (3 available, best #1, table Default-IP-Routing-Table)
Multipath: eBGP
  Advertised to update-groups:
     2
  5 1 404 303 202, (received & used)
    10.1.15.5 (metric 2681856) from 1.1.1.1 (1.1.1.1)
      Origin IGP, metric 4294967294, localpref 300, valid, internal, best
  4 1 404 303 202
    10.1.34.4 from 10.1.34.4 (4.4.4.4)
      Origin IGP, metric 4294967294, localpref 200, valid, external
      Community: 2
  4 1 404 303 202, (received-only)
    10.1.34.4 from 10.1.34.4 (4.4.4.4)
      Origin IGP, metric 4294967294, localpref 100, valid, external
      Community: 2
```

## Matching COMMUNITY with Community Lists

Cisco originally created communities as a proprietary feature, treating the 32-bit COMMUNITY as a decimal value (as shown in Example 2-11). When the COMMUNITY PA was added to the BGP standard RFC 1997, the 32-bit COMMUNITY was formatted as AA:NN, where AA is a 16-bit number to potentially represent an ASN and NN represents a value as set by that ASN. However, the COMMUNITY PA remained a 32-bit number.

Cisco routers can use either the original format or the RFC 1997 format for the COMMUNITY PA. By default, **show** commands list the decimal value; to use the AA:NN format, you should configure the global command **ip bgp-community new-format**. Also, the **set** command, as used with route maps, can use either the old decimal format or the newer AA:NN format. However, the absence or presence of the **ip bgp-community new-format** command dictates whether the output of a **show route-map** command lists the values as decimal or as AA:NN, respectively. For this reason, in practice it makes sense to choose and use a single format, typically the newer format, today.

The COMMUNITY PA also supports multiple entries. For example, the **set community 10 20 30** command, applied within a route map, would actually create a COMMUNITY with all three values. In that case, any existing COMMUNITY value would be replaced with 10, 20, and 30. However, the **set community 10 20 30 additive** command would add the values to the existing COMMUNITY string.

As a result of the multi-entry COMMUNITY, and as a result of the literal ":" inside the COMMUNITY string when using the new format, Cisco IOS requires some more sophisticated matching capabilities as compared with IP ACLs. For example, community lists can list multiple values on the same **ip community-list** command; to match such a command, the COMMUNITY must include all the values. (The COMMUNITY values are unordered, so the order in which the values are listed in the community list does not matter.) Also, extended community lists (numbered 100–199) allow matching of the COMMUNITY PA with regular expressions. Table 2-15 summarizes some of the key topics related to community lists.

Key Topic

**Table 2-15**  *Comparing Standard and Extended Community Lists*

| Feature | Standard | Extended |
|---|---|---|
| List numbers | 1–99 | 100–199 |
| Can match multiple communities in a single command? | Yes | Yes |
| Can match the COMMUNITY PA with regular expressions? | No | Yes |
| More than 16 lines in a single list? | No | Yes |

Example 2-12 shows a few sample community lists just to show the logic. In the example, R4 has set multiple COMMUNITY values for prefixes 11/8 and 12/8. The **show ip bgp community-list** *list-number* command is then used to show whether a match would

be made. This command lists the entries of the BGP table that match the associated
COMMUNITY PA, much like the **show ip bgp regex** command examines the
AS_PATH PA.

**Example 2-12**  *Matching with IP Community Lists*

```
R3# show ip community-list
Community standard list 2
    permit 0:1234
Community standard list 3
    permit 0:1212 8:9
Community (expanded) access list 111
   permit 0:12.*
! 11/8's COMMUNITY string is listed next, followed by 12/8's COMMUNITY string.
R3# show ip bgp 11.0.0.0 | include Community
      Community: 0:1212 0:1234 8:9 8:12 12:9 12:13
R3# show ip bgp 12.0.0.0 | include Community
      Community: 0:1212 8:12 8:13
! List 2 should match only 11/8, and not 12/8, as only 11/8 has 0:1234 as one of
! the values.
R3# show ip bgp community-list 2 | begin Network
   Network          Next Hop          Metric LocPrf Weight Path
*> 11.0.0.0         10.1.34.4         4294967294         0 4 1 33333 10 200 44 i
! Both 11/8 and 12/8 match the 0:1212 listed in list 3, but list 3 has two
! values configured. The list uses a logical AND between the entries, and only
! 11/8 has matching values for both communities.
R3# show ip bgp community-list 3 | begin Network
   Network          Next Hop          Metric LocPrf Weight Path
*> 11.0.0.0         10.1.34.4         4294967294         0 4 1 33333 10 200 44 i
! List 111 matches any COMMUNITY string with one entry beginning with 0:12,
! followed by any additional characters. 11/8 matches due to the 0:1234, and 12/8
! matches due to the 0:1212. COMMUNITY values 0:12, 0:123, and other would also
! have matched.
R3# show ip bgp community-list 111 | begin Network
   Network          Next Hop          Metric LocPrf Weight Path
*> 11.0.0.0         10.1.34.4         4294967294         0 4 1 33333 10 200 44 i
*> 12.0.0.0         10.1.34.4         4294967294         0 4 1 33333 10 200 44 i
```

## Removing COMMUNITY Values

In some cases, a routing policy might need to remove one string from the COMMUNITY
PA or even delete the entire COMMUNITY PA. This also can be accomplished with a
route map, using the **set** command. Removing the entire COMMUNITY is relatively
simple: Include the **set community none** command in a **route-map** clause, and all
routes matched by that clause will have their COMMUNITY PA removed. For example,
Example 2-11 lists a **route-map react-to-comm** route map on each router. In that design,

after the received COMMUNITY string on R1 and R3 was used to match the correct routes and set the LOCAL_PREF values, the COMMUNITY PA was no longer needed. The revised route map in Example 2-13 simply removes the COMMUNITY at that point.

**Example 2-13**  *Removing the Entire COMMUNITY PA After It Is No Longer Needed*

```
route-map react-to-comm permit 10
 match community 1
 set local-preference 300
 set community none
!
route-map react-to-comm permit 20
 match community 2
 set local-preference 200
 set community none
!
route-map react-to-comm permit 30
```

A route map can also remove individual COMMUNITY strings by using the **set comm-list** *community-list-number* **delete** command. This command tells the route map to match routes based on the community list and then delete the COMMUNITY strings listed in the community list. (The referenced community list can contain only one COMMUNITY string per **ip community-list** command in this case.)

## Filtering NLRIs Using Special COMMUNITY Values

Routers can use route maps to filter NLRIs from being added to the BGP table or from being sent in Updates to other routers. These route maps can match a BGP route's COMMUNITY by using the **match community** {*standard-list-number* | *expanded-list-number* | *community-list-name* [**exact**]} command, which in turn references a community list.

Additionally, BGP includes several reserved values for the COMMUNITY PA that allow route filtering to occur, but with less effort than is required with community lists and route maps. These special COMMUNITY values, after they are set, affect the logic used by routers when making decisions about to which BGP peers they will advertise the route. The values are listed in Table 2-16.

Key
Topic

**Table 2-16**  *COMMUNITY Values Used Specifically for NLRI Filtering*

| Name | Value | Meaning |
|------|-------|---------|
| NO_EXPORT | FFFF:FF01 | Do not advertise outside this AS. It can be advertised to other confederation autonomous systems. |
| NO_ADVERT | FFFF:FF02 | Do not advertise to any other peer. |
| LOCAL_AS[1] | FFFF:FF03 | Do not advertise outside the local confederation sub-AS. |

[1] *LOCAL_AS is the Cisco term; RFC 1997 defines this value as NO_EXPORT_SUBCONFED.*

A route with COMMUNITY NO_EXPORT is not advertised outside an AS. This value can be used to prevent an AS from being a transit AS for a set of prefixes. For example, a router in AS 1 could advertise an eBGP route into AS 2 with NO_EXPORT set. The routers inside AS 2 would then advertise the route inside AS 2 only. By not advertising the route outside AS 2, AS 2 cannot become a transit AS for that prefix. Note that the routers inside AS 2 do not have to configure a route map to prevent the route from exiting AS 2. However, the iBGP peers inside AS 2 must enable COMMUNITY using the **neighbor send-community** command.

The LOCAL_AS COMMUNITY value performs a similar function as NO_EXPORT, put just inside a single confederation sub-AS.

The NO_ADVERT COMMUNITY string might seem a bit unusual at first glance. However, it allows one router to advertise a prefix to a peer, with the intent that the peer will not advertise the route.

Finally, there are a few operational considerations to note regarding these COMMUNITY values. First, a router receiving any of these special communities can match them using an **ip community-list** command with obvious keywords for all three values. Additionally, a router can use a route map to match and then remove these COMMUNITY strings—in effect, ignoring the dictate to limit the scope of advertisement of the routes. Finally, routes with these settings can be seen with commands like **show ip bgp community no-export**, with similar options NO_ADVERT and LOCAL_AS.

## Fast Convergence Enhancements

For the purpose of communicating routes and prefixes on the Internet, BGP has been selected for its special characteristics and capabilities, despite many of its inherent drawbacks. BGP is massive in administrative scale and as such it is complex and difficult to master, but above all, it is exceedingly slow to converge. Point in fact: One of the reasons that BGP has been so widely adopted for the Internet is its slowness to converge. However, as the landscapes of networks have changed over the years with the adoption of burgeoning technologies like L3 VPNs, we find ourselves in a unique position. We now have an essential reliance on BGP because of its unparalleled route exchange capacity, but the slowness to converge has become a liability in the network infrastructure. Faced with this dilemma, it was necessary to make modifications to how the BGP code operates in the context of IOS.

To better understand what these modifications are, we will start with an analysis of how the protocol's finite state machine operates. Specifically, we will start by looking at what happens when a BGP peering relationship goes down. In this scenario, we have to point out that even though the IP routing table will represent that the neighbor is not reachable, the underlying BGP process will not reinitiate the convergence process until such time that either the TCP session times out or until the BGP session hold-down timer expires. This process can take up to 3 minutes by default.

The reliance on these session timers is not the only element in the BGP process that translates into slow convergence. We also must recognize that BGP only provides updates to its neighbors periodically using an interval based on the peering type: iBGP peers receive updates every 5 seconds, whereas eBGP peers are updated only every 30 seconds.

Finally, we need to look at BGP's reliance on the underlying interior gateway protocol that is used to resolve next-hop reachability. We know that typically any interior gateway routing protocol will detect changes in the network and reconverge very quickly; in fact they will and can reconverge on a new route far faster than BGP can. This issue is compounded when we consider that BGP will only verify next-hop reachability every 60 seconds.

It does not take long to see that each of these elements quickly combines to create a "perfect storm" of delays that had to be overcome. Now that we understand the nature of the problem, we can better understand the fast convergence optimization made to BGP.

## Fast External Neighbor Loss Detection

One of the first modifications to the behavior of BGP in the context of IOS was the advent of fast external fall-over. In this mode of operation, the eBGP session between directly connected eBGP neighbors will be torn down the moment that the connected subnet between the peers is lost. This will result in the immediate flushing of BGP routes, and BGP will immediately begin looking at alternate routes. This feature is not a new advent in the context of IOS, and it is enabled by default in IOS Release 10.0 and later.

## Internal Neighbor Loss Detection

This is a new enhancement made to IOS that started in IOS Release 12.0. Whereas fast external fall-over only works for the detection of neighbor loss between eBGP peers and allows IOS to immediately begin reconvergence between those peers, when it comes to internal neighbors, we had no such tools. Until the advent of fast-peering deactivation, an iBGP session could only be optimized through the reduction of keepalive and holdtime values.

Now with the **neighbor fall-over** command, we can alter the behavior between iBGP peers without the added CPU strain of increased keepalive traffic. Now the moment that the IP address of the BGP peer is removed from the routing table, the BGP session with the peer will be torn down, thus resulting in immediate convergence.

Note that we must consider the characteristics of the underlying interior gateway protocol when we use this solution. The IGP protocol must be able to find an alternative route to the BGP peer immediately. If the slightest interruption exists between the moments the original route to the BGP peer is lost and a new route is inserted in the IP routing table, the BGP session would already be disconnected.

Note that hold-down or delay in BGP session deactivation is not used.

## EBGP Fast Session Deactivation

BGP fast session deactivation works on all BGP sessions. You can use it to quickly detect failures of eBGP sessions established between loopback interfaces of eBGP peers or to detect eBGP neighbor loss when you disable fast external fall-over.

Fast external fall-over is a global setting, whereas the fast session deactivation is configured per neighbor. You can thus disable fast external fall-over with the **no bgp fast-external-fallover** router configuration command and retain the quick response to interface failures for a selected subset of eBGP.

The eBGP fast session deactivation is identical to the iBGP use case described previously and is implemented through the **neighbor fall-over** command. You can even reflect the rule that the BGP peer has to be directly connected with a **route-map** command that matches only connected subnets.

# Foundation Summary

This section lists additional details and facts to round out the coverage of the topics in this chapter. Unlike most Cisco Press Exam Certification Guides, this book does not repeat information listed in the "Foundation Topics" section of the chapter. Please take the time to read and study the details in this section of the chapter, as well as review the items in the "Foundation Topics" section noted with a Key Topic icon.

Table 2-17 lists some of the RFCs for BGP whose concepts were covered in this chapter.

**Table 2-17**  *Protocols and Standards for Chapter 2*

| Topic | Standard |
|---|---|
| BGP-4 | RFC 4271 |
| The NOPEER Community | RFC 3765 |
| BGP Route Reflection | RFC 4456 |
| BGP Communities | RFC 1997 |

Table 2-18 lists some of the relevant Cisco IOS commands related to the topics in this chapter.

**Table 2-18**  *Command Reference for Chapter 2*

| Command | Command Mode and Description |
|---|---|
| bgp always-compare-med | BGP mode; tells the router to compare MED even if the neighboring ASNs are different |
| bgp bestpath med confed | BGP mode; tells the router to consider MED for choosing routes through different confederation sub-ASs |
| bgp bestpath med missing-as-worst | BGP mode; resets the default MED from 0 to the maximum (232 − 1) |
| bgp default local-preference *number* | BGP mode; sets the default LOCAL_PREF value |
| bgp deterministic-med | BGP mode; tells IOS to process MED logic based on neighboring AS, rather than on the order in which the routes were learned |
| bgp maxas-limit *number* | BGP mode; tells the router to discard routes whose AS_PATH length exceeds this setting |
| clear ip bgp {* \| *neighbor-address* \| *peer-group-name*} [soft [in \| out]] | EXEC mode; clears the BGP process, or neighbors, optionally using soft reconfiguration |

| Command | Command Mode and Description |
|---|---|
| distribute-list *acl-number* \| prefix *list-name* in \| out | BGP mode; defines a BGP distribution list (ACL or prefix list) for filtering routes |
| ip as-path access-list *access-list-number* {permit \| deny} *as-regexp* | Global config; creates entries in AS_PATH access lists used in matching existing AS_PATH values |
| ip bgp-community new-format | Global config; tells IOS to display and interpret the COMMUNITY PA in the RFC 1997 format, AA:NN |
| ip community-list {standard \| standard *list-name* {deny \| permit} [*community-number*] [*AA:NN*] [internet] [local-AS] [no-advertise] [no-export]} \| {*expanded* \| expanded *list-name* {deny \| permit} *regexp*} | Global config; creates entries in a community list used in matching existing COMMUNITY values |
| maximum-paths *number* | BGP mode; sets the number of eBGP routes that can be added to the IP routing table |
| maximum-paths eibgp *number* [import *number*] | BGP mode; sets the number of eBGP and iBGP routes that can be added to the IP routing table when using MPLS |
| maximum-paths ibgp *number* | BGP mode; sets the number of iBGP routes that can be added to the IP routing table |
| neighbor {*ip-address* \| *peer-group-name*} distribute-list {*access-list-number* \| *expanded-list-number* \| *access-list-name* \| *prefix-list-name*} {in \| out} | BGP mode; identifies a distribute list used to filter NLRIs being sent to or received from the neighbor |
| neighbor {*ip-address* \| *peer-group-name*} filter-list *access-list-number* {in \| out} | BGP mode; identifies an AS_PATH access list used to filter NLRIs by matching the AS_PATH PA |
| neighbor {*ip-address* \| *peer-group-name*} local-as *as-number* [no-prepend] | BGP mode; defines an alternate ASN to be prepended in the AS_PATH of sent eBGP Updates, instead of the ASN listed in the **router bgp** command |
| neighbor {*ip-address* \| *peer-group-name*} prefix-list {*prefix-list-name* \| *clns-filter-expr-name* \| *clns-filter-set-name*} {in \| out} | BGP mode; identifies an IP prefix list used to filter NLRIs being sent to or received from the neighbor |
| neighbor {*ip-address* \| *peer-group-name*} remove-private-as | BGP mode; used with eBGP peers, removes any private ASNs from the AS_PATH under certain conditions |
| neighbor {*ip-address* \| *peer-group-name*} route-map *map-name* {in \| out} | BGP mode; defines a route map and direction for applying routing policies to BGP Updates |

| Command | Command Mode and Description |
|---|---|
| neighbor *ip-address* **route-reflector-client** | BGP mode; used on the RR server, identifies a neighbor as an RR client |
| neighbor {*ip-address* \| *peer-group-name*} **send-community** [**both** \| **standard** \| **extended**] | BGP mode; causes the router to include the COMMUNITY PA in Updates sent to this neighbor |
| neighbor {*ip-address* \| *peer-group-name*} **soft-reconfiguration** [**inbound**] | BGP mode; enables soft reconfiguration of Updates |
| neighbor {*ip-address* \| *peer-group-name*} **unsuppress-map** *route-map-name* | BGP mode; allows a router to identify previously suppressed routes and no longer suppress them |
| neighbor {*ip-address* \| *peer-group-name*} **weight** *number* | BGP mode; sets the BGP weight for all routes learned from the neighbor |
| network *ip-address* **backdoor** | BGP mode; identifies a network as a backdoor route, considering it to have the same administrative distance as iBGP routes |
| show ip bgp quote-regexp *regexp* | EXEC mode; displays BGP table entries whose AS_PATH PA is matched by the stated regex |
| show ip bgp regexp *regexp* | EXEC mode; displays BGP table entries whose AS_PATH PA is matched by the stated regex |
| show ip community-list [*standard-community-list-number* \| *extended-community-list-number* \| *community-list-name*] [**exact-match**] | EXEC mode; lists the contents of configured IP community lists |
| show ip bgp community *community-number* [**exact**] | EXEC mode; lists BGP table entries that include the listed COMMUNITY |
| show ip bgp filter-list *access-list-number* | EXEC mode; lists the contents of AS_PATH access lists |
| neighbor *ip-address* **fall-over** [**route-map** *map-name*] | BGP mode; eBGP session between directly connected eBGP neighbors will be torn down the moment the connected subnet between the peers is lost |

Table 2-19 lists the route map **match** and **set** commands pertinent to defining BGP routing policies.

**Table 2-19**  *Route Map* **match** *and* **set** *Commands for BGP*

| Command | Function |
|---|---|
| match as-path *path-list-number* | References an **ip as-path access-list** command to examine the AS_PATH |
| match community {*standard-list-number* \| *expanded-list-number* \| *community-list-name* [**exact**]} | References an **ip community-list** command to examine the COMMUNITY PA |
| match ip address {*access-list-number* [*access-list-number ...* \| *access-list-name ...*] | References an IP access list to match based on NLRI |
| match ip address prefix-list *prefix-list-name* [*prefix-list-name ...*]} | References an IP prefix list to match based on NLRI |
| match tag *tag-value* [*... tag-value*] | Matches a previously set route tag |
| set as-path prepend *as-path-string* | Adds the listed ASNs to the beginning of the AS_PATH |
| set comm-list *community-list-number* \| *community-list-name* **delete** | Removes individual strings from the COMMUNITY PA as matched by the referenced community list |
| set community {*community-number* [**additive**] [*well-known-community*] \| **none**} | Sets, replaces, adds to, or deletes the entire COMMUNITY |
| set ip next-hop *ip-address* [*... ip-address*] [**peer-address**] | With the peer address option, resets the NEXT_HOP PA to be the sender's IP address used to send Updates to a neighbor |
| set local-preference *number-value* | Sets the LOCAL_PREF PA |
| set metric *metric-value* | Inbound only; sets the MULTI_EXIT_DISC PA |
| set origin {**igp** \| **egp** *as-number* \| **incomplete**} | Sets the ORIGIN PA value |
| set weight *number* | Sets the proprietary administrative weight value |

# Memory Builders

The CCIE Routing and Switching written exam, like all Cisco CCIE written exams, covers a fairly broad set of topics. This section provides some basic tools to help you exercise your memory about some of the broader topics covered in this chapter.

## Fill In Key Tables from Memory

First, take the time to print Appendix E, "Key Tables for CCIE Study," which contains empty sets of some of the key summary tables from the "Foundation Topics" section of this chapter. Then, simply fill in the tables from memory. Refer to Appendix F, "Solutions for Key Tables for CCIE Study," on the CD, to check your answers.

## Definitions

Next, take a few moments to write down the definitions for the following terms:

NLRI, soft reconfiguration, AS_PATH access list, AS_PATH prepending, regular expression, AS_SEQUENCE, AS_SET, well-known mandatory, well-known discretionary, optional transitive, optional nontransitive, AS_PATH, NEXT_HOP, AGGREGATOR, ATOMIC AGGREGATE, ORIGINATOR_ID, CLUSTER_LIST, ORIGIN, administrative weight, LOCAL_PREF, AS_PATH length, MULTI_EXIT_DISC (MED), Neighbor Type, BGP decision process, private AS, COMMUNITY, LOCAL_AS, NO_EXPORT, NO_ADVERT, NO_EXPORT_SUBCONFED

## Further Reading

*Routing TCP/IP, Volume II*, by Jeff Doyle and Jennifer DeHaven Carrol

*Cisco BGP-4 Command and Configuration Handbook*, by William R. Parkhurst

*Internet Routing Architectures*, by Bassam Halabi

*Troubleshooting IP Routing Protocols*, by Zaheer Aziz, Johnson Liu, Abe Martey, and Faraz Shamim

Almost every reference can be reached from the Cisco BGP support page at www.cisco.com/en/US/partner/tech/tk365/tk80/tsd_technology_support_sub-protocol_home.html. Requires a Cisco.com username/password.

For the oddities of BGP table sequence impacting the MED-related best-path choice, refer to the following Cisco resource: www.cisco.com/en/US/partner/tech/tk365/technologies_tech_note09186a0080094925.shtml.

**Blueprint topics covered in this chapter:**

This chapter covers the following subtopics from the Cisco CCIE Routing and Switching written exam blueprint. Refer to the full blueprint in Table I-1 in the Introduction for more details on the topics covered in each chapter and their context within the blueprint.

- Modular QoS CLI (MQC)

- Network-Based Application Recognition (NBAR)

- QoS Classification

- QoS Marking

- Cisco AutoQoS

## CHAPTER 3

# Classification and Marking

The goal of classification and marking tools is to simplify the classification process of other quality of service (QoS) tools by performing complicated classification steps as few times as possible. For example, a classification and marking tool might examine the source IP address of packets, incoming Class of Service (CoS) settings, and possibly TCP or UDP port numbers. Packets matching all those fields might have their IP Precedence (IPP) or DiffServ Code Points (DSCP) field marked with a particular value. Later, other QoS tools—on the same router/switch or a different one—can simply look for the marked field when making a QoS decision, rather than having to perform the detailed classification again before taking the desired QoS action.

## "Do I Know This Already?" Quiz

Table 3-1 outlines the major headings in this chapter and the corresponding "Do I Know This Already?" quiz questions.

**Table 3-1**  *"Do I Know This Already?" Foundation Topics Section-to-Question Mapping*

| **Foundation Topics Section** | **Questions Covered in This Section** | **Score** |
|---|---|---|
| Fields That Can Be Marked for QoS Purposes | 1–4 | |
| Cisco Modular QoS CLI | 5–7 | |
| Classification and Marking Tools | 8–10 | |
| AutoQoS | 11 | |
| Total Score | | |

To best use this pre-chapter assessment, remember to score yourself strictly. You can find the answers in Appendix A, "Answers to the 'Do I Know This Already?' Quizzes."

1. According to the DiffServ RFCs, which PHB defines a set of three DSCPs in each service class, with different drop characteristics for each of the three DSCP values?

    a. Expedited Forwarding

    b. Class Selector

    c. Assured Forwarding

    d. Multi-class-multi-drop

2.  Which of the following are true about the location of DSCP in the IP header?

    a.  High-order 6 bits of ToS byte/DS field.

    b.  Low-order 6 bits of ToS byte.

    c.  Middle 6 bits of ToS byte.

    d.  Its first 3 bits overlap with IP Precedence.

    e.  Its last 3 bits overlap with IP Precedence

3.  Imagine that a packet is marked with DSCP CS3. Later, a QoS tool classifies the packet. Which of the following classification criteria would match the packet, assuming that the marking had not been changed from the original CS3 marking?

    a.  Match on DSCP CS3

    b.  Match on precedence 3

    c.  Match on DSCP AF32

    d.  Match on DSCP AF31

    e.  Match on DSCP decimal 24

4.  Imagine that a packet is marked with AF31. Later, a QoS tool classifies the packet. Which of the following classification criteria would match the packet, assuming that the marking had not been changed from the original AF31 marking?

    a.  Match on DSCP CS3

    b.  Match on precedence 3

    c.  Match on DSCP 24

    d.  Match on DSCP 26

    e.  Match on DSCP 28

5.  Examine the following output from a router that shows a user adding configuration to a router. Which of the following statements is true about the configuration?

    ```
    Router(config)# class-map fred
    Router(config-cmap)# match dscp EF
    Router(config-cmap)# match access-group 101
    ```

    a.  Packets that match both DSCP EF and ACL 101 will match the class.

    b.  Packets that match either DSCP EF or ACL 101 will match the class.

    c.  Packets that match ACL 101 will match the class, because the second **match** command replaces the first.

    d.  Packets will only match DSCP EF because the first match exits the class map.

6.  Router R1 is configured with the following three class maps. Which class map(s) would match an incoming frame whose CoS field is set to 3, IP Precedence is set to 2, and DSCP is set to AF21?

```
class-map match-all c1
  match cos 3 4
class-map match-any c2
  match cos 2 3
  match cos 1
class-map match-all c3
  match cos 3 4
  match cos 2
```

   a.  c1

   b.  c2

   c.  c3

   d.  All of these answers are correct.

7.  Examine the following example of commands typed in configuration mode to create a class map. Assuming that the **class fred** command was used inside a policy map, and the policy map was enabled on an interface, which of the following would be true with regard to packets classified by the class map?

```
Router(config)# class-map fred
Router(config-cmap)# match ip dscp ef
Router(config-cmap)# match ip dscp af31
```

   a.  Match packets with both DSCP EF and AF31

   b.  Match packets with either DSCP EF or AF31

   c.  Match all packets that are neither EF nor AF31

   d.  Match no packets

   e.  Match packets with precedence values of 3 and 5

8.  The **service-policy output fred** command is found in Router R1's configuration under Frame Relay subinterface s0/0.1. Which of the following could be true about this CB Marking policy map?

   a.  The policy map can classify packets using class maps that match based on the DE bit.

   b.  The policy map can refer to class maps that match based on DSCP.

   c.  The policy map can set CoS.

   d.  The policy map can set CLP.

   e.  The policy map can set DE.

**9.** Which of the following is true regarding the listed configuration steps?

```
Router(config)# class-map barney
Router(config-cmap)# match protocol http url "this-here.jpg"
Router(config-cmap)# policy-map fred
Router(config-pmap)# class barney
Router(config-pmap-c)# set dscp af21
Router(config-pmap-c)# interface fa0/0
Router(config-if)# service-policy output fred
```

   **a.** If not already configured, the **ip cef** global command is required.

   **b.** The configuration does not use NBAR because the **match nbar** command was not used.

   **c.** The **service-policy** command would be rejected because **match protocol** is not allowed as an output function.

   **d.** None of these answers are correct.

**10.** In which mode(s) can the **qos pre-classify** command be issued on a router?

   **a.** In crypto map configuration mode

   **b.** In GRE tunnel configuration mode

   **c.** In point-to-point subinterface configuration mode

   **d.** Only in physical interface configuration mode

   **e.** In class map configuration mode

   **f.** In global configuration mode

**11.** Which of the following statements about Cisco AutoQoS are true?

   **a.** It can be used only on switches, not routers.

   **b.** It makes QoS configuration quicker, easier, and cheaper.

   **c.** AutoQoS can be used to configure quality of service for voice, video, and other types of data.

   **d.** AutoQoS commands are applied at the interface.

   **e.** AutoQoS must be disabled before its settings can be modified.

## Foundation Topics

This chapter has three major sections. The chapter begins by examining the fields that can be marked by the classification and marking (C&M) tools. Next, the chapter covers the mechanics of the Cisco IOS Modular QoS CLI (MQC), which is used by all the IOS QoS tools that begin with the words "Class-Based." Finally, the C&M tools are covered, with most of the content focused on the most important C&M tool, Class-Based Marking (CB Marking).

# Fields That Can Be Marked for QoS Purposes

The IP header, LAN trunking headers, Frame Relay header, and ATM cell header all have at least one field that can be used to perform some form of QoS marking. This section lists and defines those fields, with the most significant coverage focused on the IP header IP Precedence (IPP) and Differentiated Services Code Point (DSCP) fields.

## IP Precedence and DSCP Compared

The IP header is defined in RFC 791, including a 1-byte field called the Type of Service (ToS) byte. The ToS byte was intended to be used as a field to mark a packet for treatment with QoS tools. The ToS byte itself was further subdivided, with the high-order 3 bits defined as the *IP Precedence (IPP)* field. The complete list of values from the ToS byte's original IPP 3-bit field, and the corresponding names, is provided in Table 3-2.

**Table 3-2**  *IP Precedence Values and Names*

| Name | Decimal Value | Binary Value |
|------|---------------|--------------|
| Routine | Precedence 0 | 000 |
| Priority | Precedence 1 | 001 |
| Immediate | Precedence 2 | 010 |
| Flash | Precedence 3 | 011 |
| Flash Override | Precedence 4 | 100 |
| Critic/Critical | Precedence 5 | 101 |
| Internetwork Control | Precedence 6 | 110 |
| Network Control | Precedence 7 | 111 |

Bits 3 through 6 of the ToS byte included flag fields that were toggled on or off to imply a particular QoS service. The final bit (bit 7) was not defined in RFC 791. The flags were not used very often, so in effect, the ToS byte's main purpose was to hold the 3-bit IPP field.

A series of RFCs collectively called *Differentiated Services (DiffServ)* came along later. DiffServ needed more than 3 bits to mark packets, so DiffServ standardized a redefinition of the ToS byte. The ToS byte itself was renamed the *Differentiated Services (DS) field*, and IPP was replaced with a 6-bit field (high-order bits 0–5) called the *Differentiated Services Code Point (DSCP)* field. Later, RFC 3168 defined the low-order 2 bits of the DS field for use with the QoS *Explicit Congestion Notification (ECN)* feature. Figure 3-1 shows the ToS byte's format with the pre-DiffServ and post-DiffServ definition of the field.

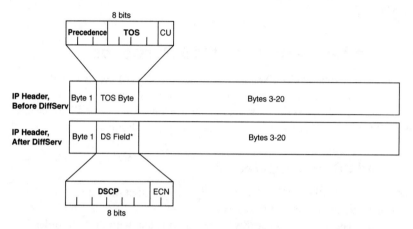

**Figure 3-1** *IP ToS Byte and DS Field Compared*

C&M tools often mark DSCP or IPP because the IP packet remains intact as it is forwarded throughout an IP network. The other possible marking fields reside inside Layer 2 headers, which means that the headers are discarded when forwarded by a Layer 3 process. Thus, the latter cannot be used to carry QoS markings beyond the current hop.

## DSCP Settings and Terminology

Several DiffServ RFCs suggest a set of values to use in the DSCP field and an implied meaning for those settings. For example, RFC 3246 defines a DSCP of decimal 46, with a name *Expedited Forwarding (EF)*. According to that RFC, packets marked as EF should be given queuing preference so that they experience minimal latency, but the packets should be policed to prevent them from taking over a link and preventing any other types of traffic from exiting an interface during periods when this high-priority traffic reaches or exceeds the interface bandwidth. These suggested settings, and the associated QoS behavior recommended when using each setting, are called *Per-Hop Behaviors (PHB)* by DiffServ. (The particular example listed in this paragraph is called the Expedited Forwarding PHB.)

### Class Selector PHB and DSCP Values

IPP overlaps with the first 3 bits of the DSCP field because the DS field is simply a redefinition of the original ToS byte in the IP header. Because of this overlap, RFC 2475 defines a set of DSCP values and PHBs, called *Class Selector (CS)* PHBs that provide backward compatibility with IPP. A C&M feature can set a CS DSCP value, and if another router or switch just looks at the IPP field, the value will make sense from an IPP perspective. Table 3-3 lists the CS DSCP names and values, and the corresponding IPP values and names.

**Table 3-3**   *Default and Class Selector DSCP Values*

| DSCP Class Selector Names | Binary DSCP Values | IPP Binary Values | IPP Names |
|---|---|---|---|
| Default/CS0* | 000000 | 000 | Routine |
| CS1 | 001000 | 001 | Priority |
| CS2 | 010000 | 010 | Immediate |
| CS3 | 011000 | 011 | Flash |
| CS4 | 100000 | 100 | Flash Override |
| CS5 | 101000 | 101 | Critical |
| CS6 | 110000 | 110 | Internetwork Control |
| CS7 | 111000 | 111 | Network Control |

*The terms "CS0" and "Default" both refer to a binary DSCP of 000000, but most Cisco IOS commands allow only the keyword "default" to represent this value.

Besides defining eight DSCP values and their text names, the CS PHB also suggests a simple set of QoS actions that should be taken based on the CS values. The CS PHB simply states that packets with larger CS DSCPs should be given better queuing preference than packets with lower CS DSCPs.

## Assured Forwarding PHB and DSCP Values

The *Assured Forwarding (AF)* PHB (RFC 2597) defines four classes for queuing purposes, along with three levels of drop probability inside each queue. To mark packets and distinguish into which of four queues a packet should be placed, along with one of three drop priorities inside each queue, the AF PHB defines 12 DSCP values and their meanings. The names of the AF DSCPs conform to the following format:

AF*xy*

where $x$ implies one of four queues (values 1 through 4) and $y$ implies one of three drop priorities (values 1 through 3).

The AF PHB suggests that the higher the value of $x$ in the DSCP name AF*xy*, the better the queuing treatment a packet should get. For example, packets with AF11 DSCPs should get worse queuing treatment than packets with AF23 DSCP values. Additionally, the AF PHB suggests that the higher the value of $y$ in the DSCP name AF*xy*, the worse the drop treatment for those packets. (Treating a packet worse for drop purposes means that the packet has a higher probability of being dropped.) For example, packets with

AF11 DSCPs should get better drop treatment than packets with AF23 DSCP values. Table 3-4 lists the names of the DSCP values, the queuing classes, and the implied drop likelihood.

**Table 3-4**   *Assured Forwarding DSCP Values—Names, Binary Values, and Decimal Values*

| Queue Class | Low Drop Probability | Medium Drop Probability | High Drop Probability |
|---|---|---|---|
| | Name/Decimal/Binary | Name/Decimal/Binary | Name/Decimal/Binary |
| 1 | AF11/10/001010 | AF12/12/001100 | AF13/14/001110 |
| 2 | AF21/18/010010 | AF22/20/010100 | AF23/22/010110 |
| 3 | AF31/26/011010 | AF32/28/011100 | AF33/30/011110 |
| 4 | AF41/34/100010 | AF42/36/100100 | AF43/38/100110 |

The text AF PHB names do not follow the "bigger-is-better" logic in all cases. For example, the name AF11 represents a decimal value of 10, and the name AF13 represents a decimal DSCP of 14. However, AF11 is "better" than AF13, because AF11 and AF13 are in the same queuing class, but AF11 has a lower probability of being dropped than AF13.

The binary version of the AF DSCP values shows the patterns of the values. The first 3 bits of the binary DSCP values designate the queuing class (bits 0 through 2 counting left to right), and the next 2 bits (bits 3 and 4) designate the drop preference. As a result, queuing tools that operate only on IPP can still react to the AF DSCP values, essentially making the AF DSCPs backward compatible with non-DiffServ nodes for queuing purposes.

**Note**   To convert from the AF name to the decimal equivalent, you can use a simple formula. If you think of the AF values as AF$xy$, the formula is

$8x + 2y$ = decimal value

For example, AF41 gives you a formula of (8 * 4) + (2 * 1) = 34.

## Expedited Forwarding PHB and DSCP Values

RFC 2598 defines the *Expedited Forwarding (EF)* PHB, which was described briefly in the introduction to this section. This RFC defines a very simple pair of PHB actions:

■   Queue EF packets so that they get scheduled quickly, to give them low latency.

■   Police the EF packets so that they do not consume all bandwidth on the link or starve other queues.

The DSCP value defined for EF is named EF, with decimal value 46, binary value 101110.

## Non-IP Header Marking Fields

As IP packets pass through an internetwork, the packet is encapsulated in a variety of other headers. In several cases, these other headers have QoS fields that can be used for classification and marking.

### Ethernet LAN Class of Service

Ethernet supports a 3-bit QoS marking field, but the field only exists when the Ethernet header includes either an 802.1Q or ISL trunking header. IEEE 802.1Q defines its QoS field as the 3 most-significant bits of the 2-byte *Tag Control* field, calling the field the *user-priority bits*. ISL defines the 3 least-significant bits from the 1-byte *User* field, calling this field the *Class of Service (CoS)*. Generally speaking, most people (and most IOS commands) refer to these fields as *CoS*, regardless of the type of trunking. Figure 3-2 shows the general location of the CoS field inside ISL and 802.1P headers.

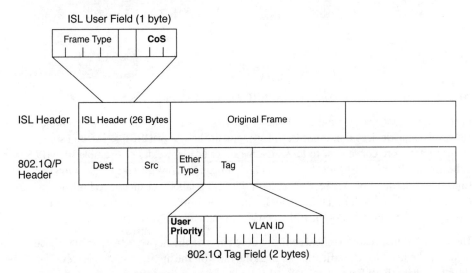

**Figure 3-2**  *LAN CoS Fields*

### WAN Marking Fields

Frame Relay and ATM support a single bit that can be set for QoS purposes, but these single bits are intended for a very strict use related to drop probability. Frames or cells with these bits set to 1 are considered to be better candidates to be dropped than frames or cells without the bit set to 1. Named the Frame Relay *Discard Eligibility (DE)* bit and the ATM *Cell Loss Priority (CLP)* bit, these bits can be set by a router, or by an ATM or Frame Relay switch. Router and switch drop features can then be configured to more aggressively drop frames and cells that have the DE or CLP bit set, respectively.

MPLS defines a 3-bit field called the *MPLS Experimental (EXP)* bit that is intended for general QoS marking. Often, C&M tools are used on the edge of MPLS networks to remap DSCP or IPP values to MPLS Experimental bit values to provide QoS inside the MPLS network.

## Locations for Marking and Matching

Figure 3-3 shows a sample network, with notes about the locations of the QoS fields.

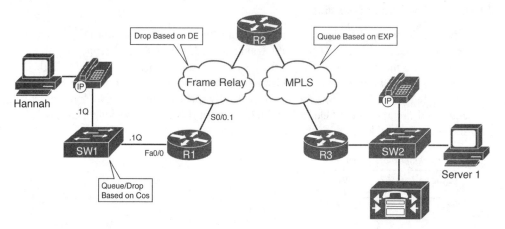

**Figure 3-3**    *Sample Network Showing Non-IP Markable QoS Fields*

In such a network, the IPP and DSCP inside the IP packet remain intact from end to end. However, some devices might not be able to look at the IPP or DSCP fields, and some might find it more convenient to look at some other header field. For example, an MPLS Label Switch Router (LSR) inside the MPLS cloud can be configured to make QoS decisions based on the 3-bit MPLS EXP field in the MPLS label, but unable to look at the encapsulated IP header and DSCP field. In such cases, QoS tools might need to be configured on edge devices to look at the DSCP and then mark a different field.

The non-IP header markable fields exist in only parts of the network. As a result, those fields can be used for classification or marking only on the appropriate interfaces. The rules for where these fields (CoS, DE, CLP, EXP) can be used are as follows:

- **For classification:** On ingress only, and only if the interface supports that particular header field

- **For marking:** On egress only, and only if the interface supports that particular header field

For example, if CB Marking were to be configured on R1's fa0/0.1 802.1Q subinterface, it could classify incoming frames based on their CoS values, and mark outgoing frames with a CoS value. However, on ingress, it could not mark CoS, and on egress, it could not classify based on CoS. Similarly, on that same fa0/0.1 subinterface, CB Marking could neither classify nor mark based on a DE bit, CLP bit, or MPLS EXP bits, because these headers never exist on Ethernet interfaces.

Table 3-5 summarizes the QoS marking fields.

**Key Topic**

**Table 3-5**  *Marking Field Summary*

| Field | Location | Length |
|---|---|---|
| IP Precedence (IPP) | IP header | 3 bits |
| IP DSCP | IP header | 6 bits |
| DS field | IP header | 1 byte |
| ToS byte | IP header | 1 byte |
| CoS | ISL and 802.1Q header | 3 bits |
| Discard Eligible (DE) | Frame Relay header | 1 bit |
| Cell Loss Priority (CLP) | ATM cell header | 1 bit |
| MPLS Experimental | MPLS header | 3 bits |

# Cisco Modular QoS CLI

For many years and over many IOS releases, Cisco added QoS features and functions, each of which used its own separate set of configuration and exec commands. Eventually, the number of different QoS tools and different QoS commands got so large that QoS configuration became a big chore. Cisco created the *Modular QoS CLI (MQC)* to help resolve these problems, by defining a common set of configuration commands to configure many QoS features in a router or switch.

MQC is not a totally new CLI, different from IOS configuration mode, for configuring QoS. Rather, it is a method of categorizing IOS classification, marking, and related actions into logical groupings to unify the command-line interface. MQC defines a new set of configuration commands—commands that are typed in using the same IOS CLI, in configuration mode. However, after you understand MQC, you typically need to learn only one new command to know how to configure any additional MQC-based QoS tools. You can identify MQC-based tools by the name of the tool; they all begin with the phrase "Class-Based" (abbreviated CB for this discussion). These tools include CB Marking, CB Weighted Fair Queuing (CBWFQ), CB Policing, CB Shaping, and CB Header Compression.

## Mechanics of MQC

MQC separates the classification function of a QoS tool from the action (PHB) that the QoS tool wants to perform. To do so, there are three major commands with MQC, with several subordinate commands:

- The **class-map** command defines the matching parameters for classifying packets into service classes.

- The PHB actions (marking, queuing, and so on) are configured under a **policy-map** command.

- The policy map is enabled on an interface by using a **service-policy** command.

Figure 3-4 shows the general flow of commands.

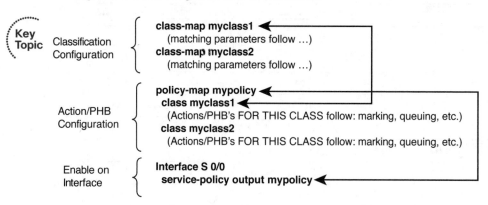

**Figure 3-4**   *MQC Commands and Their Correlation*

In Figure 3-4, the network's QoS policy calls for treating packets in one of two categories, called *QoS service classes*. (The actual types of packets that are placed into each class are not shown, to keep the focus on the general flow of how the main commands work together.) Classifying packets into two classes calls for the use of two **class-map** commands. Each **class-map** command would be followed by a **match** subcommand, which defines the actual parameters that are compared to the frame/packet header contents to match packets for classification.

For each class, some QoS action (PHB) needs to be performed; this action is configured using the **policy-map** command. Under a single policy map, multiple classes can be referenced; in Figure 3-4, the two classes are myclass1 and myclass2. Inside the single policy called mypolicy, under each of the two classes myclass1 and myclass2, you can configure separate QoS actions. For example, you could apply different markings to packets in myclass1 and myclass2 at this point. Finally, when the **service-policy** command is applied to an interface, the QoS features are enabled either inbound or outbound on that interface.

The next section takes a much closer look at packet classification using class maps. Most of the discussion of policy maps will be included when specifically covering CB Marking configuration later in the chapter.

## Classification Using Class Maps

MQC-based tools classify packets using the **match** subcommand inside an MQC class map. The following list details the rules surrounding how class maps work for matching and classifying packets:

- The **match** command has many options for matching packets, including QoS fields, ACLs, and MAC addresses.

- Class-map names are case sensitive.

- The **match protocol** command means that IOS uses Network-Based Application Recognition (NBAR) to perform that match.

- The **match any** command matches any packet—in other words, any and all packets.

Example 3-1 shows a simple CB Marking configuration, with comments focused on the classification configuration. Note that the names and logic match Figure 3-4.

**Example 3-1**  *Basic CB Marking Example*

```
! CEF is required for CB Marking. Without it, the class map and policy map
! configuration would be allowed, but the service-policy command would be rejected.
ip cef
! The first class map matches all UDP/RTP packets with UDP ports between 16384 and
! 32767 (the 2nd number is added to the first to get the end of the range.) The
! second class map matches any and all packets.
class-map match-all myclass1
  match ip rtp 16384 16383
class-map match-all myclass2
  match any
! The policy map calls each of the two class maps for matching. The set command
! implies that the PHB is marking, meaning that this is a CB Marking config.
policy-map mypolicy
  class myclass1
    set dscp EF
  class myclass2
    set dscp default
! The policy map processes packets leaving interface fa0/0.
interface Fastethernet0/0
 service-policy output mypolicy
```

With Example 3-1, each packet leaving interface fa0/0 will match one of the two classes. Because the policy map uses a **set dscp** command in each class, and all packets happen to match either myclass1 or myclass2, each packet will leave the interface marked either with DSCP EF (decimal 46) or default (decimal 0). (If the matching logic was different and some packets match neither myclass1 nor myclass2, those packets would not be marked, and would retain their existing DSCP values.)

## Using Multiple match Commands

In some cases, a class map might need to examine multiple items in a packet to decide whether the packet should be part of that class. Class maps can use multiple **match** commands, and even nest class maps inside other class maps, to achieve the desired combination of logic. The following list summarizes the key points regarding these more complex matching options:

- Up to four (CoS and IPP) or eight (DSCP) values can be listed on a single **match cos**, **match precedence**, or **match dscp** command, respectively. If any of the values are found in the packet, the statement is matched.

- If a class map has multiple **match** commands in it, the **match-any** or **match-all** (default) parameter on the **class-map** command defines whether a logical OR or a logical AND (default) is used between the **match** commands, respectively.

- The **match class** *name* command refers to another class map by name, nesting the named class map's matching logic; the **match class** *name* command is considered to match if the referenced class map also results in a match.

Example 3-2 shows several examples of this more complicated matching logic, with notations inside the example of what must be true for a class map to match a packet.

**Example 3-2**   *Complex Matching with Class Maps*

```
! class-map example1 uses match-all logic (default), so this class map matches
! packets that are permitted by ACL 102, and that also have an IP precedence of 5.
class-map match-all example1
  match access-group 102
  match precedence 5
! class-map example2 uses match-any logic, so this class map matches packets that
! are permitted by ACL 102, or have DSCP AF21, or both.
class-map match-any example2
  match access-group 102
  match dscp AF21
! class-map example3 matches no packets, due to a common mistake—the two match
! commands use a logical AND between them due to the default match-all argument,
! meaning that a single packet must have DSCP 0 and DSCP 1, which is impossible.
! class-map example4 shows how to correctly match either DSCP 0 or 1.
class-map match-all example3
  match dscp 0
  match dscp 1
!
class-map match-any example4
  match dscp 0 1
! class-map i-am-nesting refers to class-map i-am-nested through the match class
! i-am-nested command. The logic is explained after the example.
class-map match-all i-am-nested
  match access-group 102
  match precedence 5
!
class-map match-any i-am-nesting
  match class i-am-nested
  match cos 5
```

The trickiest part of Example 3-2 is how the class maps can be nested, as shown at the end. **class-map i-am-nesting** uses OR logic between its two **match** commands, meaning "I will match if the CoS is 5, or if **class-map i-am-nested** matches the packet, or both."

When combined with the match-all logic of the **i-am-nested** class map, the logic matches the following packets/frames:

Packets that are permitted by ACL 102, AND marked with precedence 5

or

frames with CoS 5

### Classification Using NBAR

NBAR classifies packets that are normally difficult to classify. For example, some applications use dynamic port numbers, so a statically configured **match** command, matching a particular UDP or TCP port number, simply could not classify the traffic. NBAR can look past the UDP and TCP header, and refer to the host name, URL, or MIME type in HTTP requests. (This deeper examination of the packet contents is sometimes called *deep packet inspection*.) NBAR can also look past the TCP and UDP headers to recognize application-specific information. For example, NBAR allows recognition of different Citrix application types, and allows searching for a portion of a URL string.

NBAR itself can be used for a couple of different purposes. Independent of QoS features, NBAR can be configured to keep counters of traffic types and traffic volume for each type. For QoS, NBAR can be used by CB Marking to match difficult-to-match packets. Whenever the MQC **match protocol** command is used, IOS is using NBAR to match the packets. Table 3-6 lists some of the more popular uses of the **match protocol** command and NBAR.

**Table 3-6**  *Popular Fields Matchable by CB Marking Using NBAR*

| Field | Comments |
|---|---|
| RTP audio versus video | RTP uses even-numbered UDP ports from 16,384 to 32,768. The odd-numbered port numbers are used by RTCP for call control traffic. NBAR allows matching the even-numbered ports only, for classification of voice payload into a different service class from that used for voice signaling. |
| Citrix applications | NBAR can recognize different types of published Citrix applications. |
| Host name, URL string, MIME type | NBAR can also match URL strings, including the host name and the MIME type, using regular expressions for matching logic. |
| Peer-to-peer applications | NBAR can find file-sharing applications like KaZaa, Morpheus, Grokster, and Gnutella. |

# Classification and Marking Tools

The final major section of this chapter covers CB Marking, with a brief mention of a few other, less popular marking tools.

## Class-Based Marking (CB Marking) Configuration

As with the other QoS tools whose names begin with the phrase "Class-Based," you will use MQC commands to configure CB Marking. The following list highlights the key points regarding CB Marking configuration and logic:

- CB Marking requires CEF (enabled using the **ip cef** global command).

- Packets are classified based on the logic in MQC class maps.

- An MQC policy map refers to one or more class maps using the **class** *class-map-name* command; packets classified into that class are then marked.

- CB Marking is enabled for packets either entering or exiting an interface using the MQC **service-policy in | out** *policy-map-name* interface subcommand.

- A CB Marking policy map is processed sequentially; after a packet has matched a class, it is marked based on the **set** command(s) defined for that class.

- You can configure multiple **set** commands in one class to set multiple fields, for example, to set both DSCP and CoS.

- Packets that do not explicitly match a defined class are considered to have matched a special class called *class-default*.

- For any class inside the policy map for which there is no **set** command, packets in that class are not marked.

Table 3-7 lists the syntax of the CB Marking **set** command, showing the familiar fields that can be set by CB Marking. Table 3-8 lists the key **show** commands available for CB Marking.

**Table 3-7**   set *Configuration Command Reference for CB Marking*

| Command | Function |
|---|---|
| set [ip] precedence *ip-precedence-value* | Marks the value for IP Precedence for IPv4 and IPv6 packets if the **ip** parameter is omitted; sets only IPv4 packets if the **ip** parameter is included |
| set [ip] dscp *ip-dscp-value* | Marks the value for IP DSCP for IPv4 and IPv6 packets if the **ip** parameter is omitted; sets only IPv4 packets if the **ip** parameter is included |
| set cos *cos-value* | Marks the value for CoS |
| set qos-group *group-id* | Marks the group identifier for the QoS group |
| set atm-clp | Sets the ATM CLP bit |
| set fr-de | Sets the Frame Relay DE bit |

**Table 3-8** *EXEC Command Reference for CB Marking*

| Command | Function |
|---|---|
| **show policy-map** *policy-map-name* | Lists configuration information about a policy map |
| **show policy-map** *interface-spec* [input \| output] [**class** *class-name*] | Lists statistical information about the behavior of a policy map when enabled on an interface |

## CB Marking Example

The first CB Marking example uses the network shown in Figure 3-5. Traffic was generated in the network to make the **show** commands more meaningful. Two G.711 voice calls were completed between R4 and R1 using *Foreign Exchange Station (FXS)* cards on these two routers, with *Voice Activity Detection (VAD)* disabled. Client1 performed an FTP get of a large file from Server1, and downloaded two large HTTP objects, named important.jpg and not-so.jpg. Finally, Client1 and Server1 held a Microsoft NetMeeting conference, using G.723 for the audio and H.263 for the video.

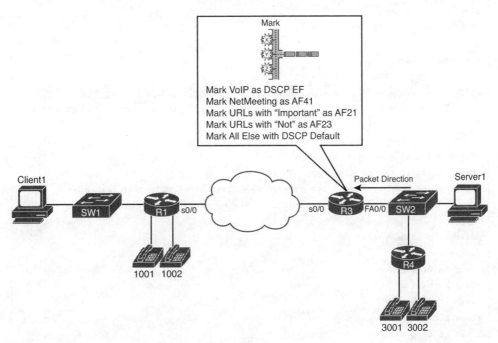

**Figure 3-5** *Sample Network for CB Marking Examples*

The following criteria define the requirements for marking the various types of traffic for Example 3-3:

■ VoIP payload is marked with DSCP EF.

■ NetMeeting video traffic is marked with DSCP AF41.

- Any HTTP traffic whose URL contains the string "important" anywhere in the URL is marked with AF21.

- Any HTTP traffic whose URL contains the string "not-so" anywhere in the URL is marked with AF23.

- All other traffic is marked with DSCP Default (0).

Example 3-3 lists the annotated configuration, including the appropriate **show** commands.

**Example 3-3**   *CB Marking Example 1, with* **show** *Command Output*

```
ip cef
! Class map voip-rtp uses NBAR to match all RTP audio payload, but not the video
! or the signaling.
class-map voip-rtp
 match protocol rtp audio
! Class map http-impo matches all packets related to downloading objects whose
! name contains the string "important," with any text around it. Similar logic
! is used for class-map http-not.
class-map http-impo
 match protocol http url "*important*"
!
class-map http-not
 match protocol http url "*not-so*"
! Class map NetMeet matches two RTP subtypes—one for G.723 audio (type 4) and
! one for H.263 video (type 34). Note the match-any logic so that if either is
! true, a match occurs for this class map.
class-map match-any NetMeet
 match protocol rtp payload-type 4
 match protocol rtp payload-type 34
! policy-map laundry-list calls each of the class maps. Note that the order
! listed here is the order in which the class commands were added to the policy
! map.
policy-map laundry-list
 class voip-rtp
  set ip dscp EF
 class NetMeet
  set ip dscp AF41
 class http-impo
  set ip dscp AF21
 class http-not
  set ip dscp AF23
 class class-default
  set ip DSCP default
! Above, the command class class-default is only required if some nondefault action
! needs to be taken for packets that are not explicitly matched by another class.
```

```
! In this case, packets not matched by any other class fall into the class-default
! class, and are marked with DSCP Default (decimal 0). Without these two commands,
! packets in this class would remain unchanged.
!!!!!!!!!!!!!!!!!!!!!!!!!!!!!!!!!!!!!!!!!!!!!!!!!!!!!!!!!!!!!!!!!!!!!!!!!!!!!!!!!!!!!!!!
!!!
! Below, the policy map is enabled for input packets on fa0/0.
interface Fastethernet 0/0
service-policy input laundry-list
! The command show policy-map laundry-list simply restates the configuration.
R3# show policy-map laundry-list
  Policy Map laundry-list
    Class voip-rtp
      set ip dscp 46
    Class NetMeet
      set ip dscp 34
    Class http-impo
      set ip dscp 18
    Class http-not
      set ip dscp 22
    Class class-default
      set ip dscp 0
! The command show policy-map interface lists statistics related to MQC features.
! Several stanzas of output were omitted for brevity.
R3# show policy-map interface fastethernet 0/0 input
  Fastethernet0/0

  Service-policy input:     laundry-list

    Class-map: voip-rtp (match-all)
      35268 packets, 2609832 bytes
      5 minute offered rate     59000 bps, drop rate 0 bps
      Match: protocol rtp audio
      QoS Set
        ip dscp 46
            Packets marked 35268

    Class-map: NetMeet (match-any)
      817 packets, 328768 bytes
      5 minute offered rate     19000 bps, drop rate 0 bps
      Match: protocol rtp payload-type 4
            protocol rtp payload-type 34
      QoS Set
        ip dscp 34
            Packets marked 817

! omitting stanza of output for class http-impo
```

```
! omitting stanza of output for class http-not

   Class-map: class-default (match-all)
      33216 packets, 43649458 bytes
      5 minute offered rate      747000 bps, drop rate 0 bps
      Match: any
      QoS Set
        ip dscp 0
Packets marked 33301
```

Example 3-3 includes several different classification options using the **match** command, including the matching of Microsoft NetMeeting traffic. NetMeeting uses RTP for the video flows, and by default uses G.723 for audio and H.323 for video. To match both the audio and video for NetMeeting, a class map that matches either of the two RTP payload subtypes for G.723 and H.263 is needed. So, class map **NetMeet** uses match-any logic, and matches on RTP payload types 4 (G.723) and 34 (H.263). (For more background information on RTP payload types, refer to www.cisco.com/en/US/products/ps6616/products_white_paper09186a0080110040.shtml.)

The **show policy-map interface** command provides statistical information about the number of packets and bytes that have matched each class in the policy maps. The generic syntax is as follows:

**show policy-map interface** *interface-name* [**vc** [*vpi/*] *vci*] [**dlci** *dlci*]
   [**input** | **output**] [**class** *class-name*]

The end of Example 3-3 shows a sample of the command, which lists statistics for marking. If other MQC-based QoS features were configured, statistics for those features would also be displayed. As you can see from the generic command, the **show policy-map interface** command allows you to select just one interface, either input or output, and even select a single class inside a single policy map for display.

The **load-interval** interface subcommand can also be useful when looking at any QoS tool's statistics. The **load-interval** command defines the time interval over which IOS measures packet and bit rates on an interface. With a lower load interval, the statistics change more quickly; with a larger load interval, the statistics change more slowly. The default setting is 5 minutes, and it can be lowered to 30 seconds.

Key
Topic

Example 3-3 also shows a common oversight with QoS configuration. Note that the first class in **policy-map laundry-list** is **class voip-rtp**. Because that class map matches all RTP audio, it matches the Microsoft NetMeeting audio stream as well, so the NetMeeting audio is not matched by class **NetMeet** that follows. If the first two classes (**voip-rtp** and **NetMeet**) called in the policy map had been reversed, the NetMeeting audio would have been correctly matched in the **NetMeet** class, and all other audio would have been marked as part of the **voip-rtp** class.

## CB Marking of CoS and DSCP

Example 3-4 shows how a router might be configured for CB Marking when an attached
LAN switch is performing QoS based on CoS. In this case, R3 looks at frames coming in its fa0/0 interface, marking the DSCP values based on the incoming CoS settings.
Additionally, R3 looks at the DSCP settings for packets exiting its fa0/0 interface toward
the switch, setting the CoS values in the 802.1Q header. The actual values used on R3's
fa0/0 interface for classification and marking are as follows:

■ Frames entering with CoS 5 will be marked with DSCP EF.

■ Frames entering with CoS 1 will be marked with DSCP AF11.

■ Frames entering with any other CoS will be marked DSCP 0.

■ Packets exiting with DSCP EF will be marked with CoS 5.

■ Packets exiting with DSCP AF11 will be marked with CoS 1.

■ Packets exiting with any other DSCP will be marked with CoS 0.

**Example 3-4**  *Marking DSCP Based on Incoming CoS, and Vice Versa*

```
! The class maps each simply match a single CoS or DSCP value.
class-map cos1
 match cos 1
!
class-map cos5
 match cos 5
!
class-map AF11
 match dscp af11
!
class-map EF
 match dscp EF
! This policy map will map incoming CoS to a DSCP value
policy-map map-cos-to-dscp
 class cos1
  set DSCP af11
 class cos5
  set ip DSCP EF
 class class-default
  set ip dscp default
! This policy map will map incoming DSCP to outgoing CoS. Note that the DSCP
! value is not changed.
policy-map map-dscp-to-cos
 class AF11
  set cos 1
 class EF
  set cos 5
```

```
  class class-default
    set cos 0
!!!!!!!!!!!!!!!!!!!!!!!!!!!!!!!!!!!!!!!!!!!!!!!!!!!!!!!!!!!!!!!!!!!!!!!!!!!!!!!!!!!!
! The policy maps are applied to an 802.1q subinterface.
interface FastEthernet0/0.1
 encapsulation dot1Q 102
 service-policy input map-cos-to-dscp
 service-policy output map-dscp-to-cos
!
interface FastEthernet0/0.2
 encapsulation dot1Q 2 native
```

The QoS policy requires two policy maps in this example. Policy map **map-cos-to-dscp** matches CoS values for frames entering R3's fa0/0.1 interface, and marks DSCP values, for packets flowing right to left in Figure 3-5. Therefore, the policy map is enabled on input of R3's fa0/0.1 interface. Policy map **map-dscp-to-cos** matches DSCP values for packets exiting R3's fa0/0.1 interface, and marks the corresponding CoS value. Therefore, the policy map was enabled on the output of R3's fa0/0.1 interface. Neither policy map could be applied on the WAN interface, because only interfaces configured for 802.1Q accept **service-policy** commands that reference policy maps that either classify or mark based on CoS.

Note that you cannot enable a **policy-map** that refers to CoS on interface fa0/0.2 in this example. That subinterface is in the native VLAN, meaning that no 802.1Q header is used.

## Network-Based Application Recognition

CB Marking can make use of NBAR's powerful classification capabilities through the **match protocol** subcommand. Example 3-5 shows a configuration for CB Marking and NBAR in which the following requirements are met:

- Any HTTP traffic whose URL contains the string "important" anywhere in the URL is marked with AF21.

- Any HTTP traffic whose URL contains the string "not-so" anywhere in the URL is marked with DSCP default.

- All other traffic is marked with AF11.

Example 3-5 shows the configuration, along with a few NBAR-related **show** commands.

**Example 3-5**  *CB Marking Based on URLs, Using NBAR for Classification*

```
ip cef
! The "*" in the url string is a wildcard meaning "0 or more characters."
class-map http-impo
     match protocol http url "*important*"
class-map http-not
     match protocol http url "*not-so*"
```

```
! The policy map lists the three classes in order, setting the DSCP values.
policy-map http
 class http-impo
  set dscp AF21
 !
 class http-not
  set dscp default
 !
 class class-default
  set DSCP AF11
! The ip nbar protocol discovery command may or may not be required—see the notes
! following this example.
interface fastethernet 0/0
 ip nbar protocol-discovery
 service-policy input http
! The show ip nbar command only displays statistics if the ip nbar
! protocol-discovery command is applied to an interface. These statistics are
! independent of those created by CB Marking. This example shows several of
! the large number of options on the command.
R3# show ip nbar protocol-discovery interface fastethernet 0/0 stats packet-count
   top-n 5
   FastEthernet0/0

                                 Input                    Output
            Protocol             Packet Count             Packet Count
   ------------------------  ------------------------  ------------------------
            http                 721                      428
            eigrp                635                      0
            netbios              199                      0
            icmp                 1                        1
            bgp                  0                        0
            unknown              46058                    63
            Total                47614                    492
```

**Key Topic**

**Note**    Before the 12.2T/12.3 IOS releases, the **ip nbar protocol-discovery** command was required on an interface before using a **service-policy** command that used NBAR matching. With 12.2T/12.3 train releases, this command is no longer required.

The use of the **match protocol** command implies that NBAR will be used to match the packet.

Unlike most other IOS features, NBAR can be upgraded without changing to a later IOS version. Cisco uses a feature called *Packet Description Language Modules (PDLM)* to define new protocols that NBAR should match. When Cisco decides to add one or more new protocols to the list of protocols that NBAR should recognize, it creates and compiles a PDLM. You can then download the PDLM from Cisco, copy it into Flash memory, and add the **ip nbar pdlm** *pdlm-name* command to the configuration, where *pdlm-name* is the name of the PDLM file in Flash memory. NBAR can then classify based on the protocol information from the new PDLM.

## CB Marking Design Choices

The intent of CB Marking is to simplify the work required of other QoS tools by marking packets of the same class with the same QoS marking. For other QoS tools to take advantage of those markings, packets should generally be marked as close to the ingress point of the packet as possible. However, the earliest possible point might not be a trusted device. For example, in Figure 3-5 (the figure upon which Examples 3-3 and 3-4 are based), Server1 could set its own DSCP and even CoS if its network interface card (NIC) supported trunking. However, trusting the server administrator might or might not be desirable. So, the following rule summarizes how to choose the best location to perform marking:

Mark as close to the ingress edge of the network as possible, but not so close to the edge that the marking is made by an untrusted device.

Cisco QoS design guide documents make recommendations not only as to where to perform marking, but also as to which CoS, IPP, and DSCP values to set for certain types of traffic. Table 3-9 summarizes those recommendations.

**Table 3-9**  *RFC-Recommended Values for Marking*

| Type of Traffic | CoS | IPP | DSCP |
|---|---|---|---|
| Voice payload | 5 | 5 | EF |
| Video payload | 4 | 4 | AF41 |
| Voice/video signaling | 3 | 3 | CS3 |
| Mission-critical data | 3 | 3 | AF31, AF32, AF33 |
| Transactional data | 2 | 2 | AF21, AF22, AF23 |
| Bulk data | 1 | 1 | AF11, AF12, AF13 |
| Best effort | 0 | 0 | BE |
| Scavenger (less than best effort) | 0 | 0 | 2, 4,6 |

Also note that Cisco recommends not to use more than four or five different service classes for data traffic. When you use more classes, the difference in behavior between the various classes tends to blur. For the same reason, do not give too many data service classes high-priority service.

## Marking Using Policers

Traffic policers measure the traffic rate for data entering or exiting an interface, with the goal of determining whether a configured *traffic contract* has been exceeded. The contract has two components: a *traffic rate*, configured in bits/second, and a *burst size*, configured as a number of bytes. If the traffic is within the contract, all packets are considered to have *conformed* to the contract. However, if the rate or burst exceeds the contract, some packets are considered to have *exceeded* the contract. QoS actions can be taken on both categories of traffic.

The simplest form of policing enforces the traffic contract strictly by forwarding conforming packets and discarding packets that exceed the contract. However, both IOS policers allow a compromise action in which the policer *marks down* packets instead of dropping them. To mark down the packet, the policer re-marks a QoS field, typically IPP or DSCP, with a value that makes the packet more likely to be discarded downstream. For example, a policer could re-mark AF11 packets that exceed a contract with a new DSCP value of AF13, but not discard the packet. By doing so, the packet still passes through the router, but if the packet experiences congestion later in its travels, it is more likely to be discarded than it would have otherwise been. (Remember, DiffServ suggests that AF13 is more likely to be discarded than AF11 traffic.)

When marking requirements can be performed by using CB Marking, CB Marking should be used instead of either policer. However, if a requirement exists to mark packets based on whether they conform to a traffic contract, marking with policers must be used. Chapter 5, "Shaping, Policing, and Link Fragmentation," covers CB policing, with an example of the syntax it uses for marking packets.

## QoS Pre-Classification

With unencrypted, unencapsulated traffic, routers can match and mark QoS values, and perform ingress and egress actions based on markings, by inspecting the IP headers. However, what happens if the traffic is encrypted? If we encapsulate traffic inside a VPN tunnel, the original headers and packet contents are unavailable for inspection. The only thing we have to work with is the ToS byte of the original packet, which is automatically copied to the tunnel header (in IPsec transport mode, in tunnel mode, and in GRE tunnels) when the packet is encapsulated. But features like NBAR are broken when we are dealing with encapsulated traffic.

The issue that arises from this inherent behavior of tunnel encapsulation is the inability of a router to take egress QoS actions based on encrypted traffic. To mitigate this limitation, Cisco IOS includes a feature called QoS pre-classification. This feature can be enabled on VPN endpoint routers to permit the router to make egress QoS decisions based on the original traffic, before encapsulation, rather than just the encapsulating tunnel header. QoS pre-classification works by keeping the original, unencrypted traffic in memory until the egress QoS actions are taken.

You can enable QoS pre-classification in tunnel interface configuration mode, virtual-template configuration mode, or crypto map configuration mode by issuing the **qos pre-classify** command. You can view the effects of pre-classification using several **show** commands, which include **show interface** and **show crypto-map**.

Table 3-10 lists the modes in which you apply the **qos pre-classify** command.

**Table 3-10**  *Where to Use the* qos pre-classify *Command*

| Configuration Command Under Which qos pre-classify Is Configured | VPN Type |
| --- | --- |
| interface tunnel | GRE and IPIP |
| interface virtual-template | L2F and L2TP |
| crypto map | IPsec |

## Policy Routing for Marking

Policy routing provides the capability to route a packet based on information in the packet besides the destination IP address. The policy routing configuration uses route maps to classify packets. The **route-map** clauses include **set** commands that define the route (based on setting a next-hop IP address or outgoing interface).

Policy routing can also mark the IPP field, or the entire ToS byte, using the **set** command in a route map. When you use policy routing for marking purposes, the following logic sequence is used:

1.  Packets are examined as they enter an interface.

2.  A route map is used to match subsets of the packets.

3.  Mark either the IPP or entire ToS byte using the **set** command.

4.  The traditional policy routing function of using the **set** command to define the route might also be configured, but it is not required.

Policy routing should be used to mark packets only in cases where CB Marking is not available, or when a router needs to both use policy routing and mark packets entering the same interface.

## AutoQoS

AutoQoS is a macro that helps automate class-based quality of service (QoS) configuration. It creates and applies QoS configurations based on Cisco best-practice recommendations. Using AutoQoS provides the following benefits:

■  Simpler QoS deployment.

■  Less operator error, because most steps are automated.

■  Cheaper QoS deployment because less staff time is involved in analyzing network traffic and determining QoS configuration.

■  Faster QoS deployment because there are dramatically fewer commands to issue.

■  Companies can implement QoS without needing an in-depth knowledge of QoS concepts.

There are two flavors—AutoQoS for VoIP and AutoQoS for the Enterprise—as discussed in the following sections.

## AutoQoS for VoIP

AutoQoS for VoIP is supported on most Cisco switches and routers, and provides QoS configuration for voice and video applications. It is enabled on individual interfaces, but creates both global and interface configurations. When enabled on access ports, AutoQoS uses Cisco Discovery Protocol (CDP) to detect the presence or absence of a Cisco phone or softphone, and configures the interface QoS appropriately. When enabled on uplink or trunk ports, it trusts the COS or DSCP values received and sets up the interface QoS.

### AutoQoS VoIP on Switches

AutoQoS assumes that switches will have two types of interfaces: user access and uplink. It also assumes that a user access interface might or might not have an IP phone connected to it. There is no need to enable QoS globally. After it is enabled for any interface, the command starts a macro that globally enables QoS, configures interface ingress and egress queues, configures class maps and policy maps, and applies the policy map to the interface.

AutoQoS is enabled for an access interface by the interface-level command **auto qos voip** {**cisco-phone** | **cisco-softphone**}. When you do this, the switch uses CDP to determine whether a Cisco phone or softphone is connected to the interface. If one is not found, the switch marks all traffic down to DSCP 0 and treats it as best effort. This is the default behavior for a normal trunk port. If a phone is found, the switch then trusts the QoS markings it receives. On the ingress interface, the following traffic is put into the priority, or expedite, queue:

■ Voice and video control traffic

■ Real-time video traffic

■ Voice traffic

■ Routing protocol traffic

■ Spanning-tree BPDU traffic

All other traffic is placed in the normal ingress queue. On the egress side, voice is placed in the priority queue. The remaining traffic is distributed among the other queues, depending on the number and type of egress queues supported by that particular switch or switch module.

AutoQoS is enabled for an uplink port by the interface-level command **auto qos voip trust**. When this command is given, the switch trusts the COS values received on a Layer 2 port and the DSCP values received on a Layer 3 port.

The AutoQoS macro also creates quite a bit of global configuration in the switch. It generates too much to reproduce here, but the following list summarizes the configuration created:

- Globally enables QoS.

- Creates COS-to-DCSP mappings and DSCP-to-COS mappings. As the traffic enters the switch, the frame header containing the COS value is removed. The switch uses the COS value in the frame header to assign a DSCP value to the packet. If the packet exits a trunk port, the internal DSCP value is mapped back to a COS value.

- Enables priority or expedite ingress and egress queues.

- Creates mappings of COS values to ingress and egress queues and thresholds.

- Creates mappings of DSCP values to ingress and egress queues and thresholds.

- Creates class maps and policy maps to identify, prioritize, and police voice traffic. Applies those policy maps to the interface.

For best results, enable AutoQoS before configuring any other QoS on the switch. You can then go back and modify the default configuration if needed to fit your specific requirements.

## AutoQoS VoIP on Routers

The designers of AutoQoS assumed that routers would be connecting to downstream switches or the WAN, rather than user access ports. Therefore, the VoIP QoS configuration is simpler. The command to enable it is **auto qos voip [trust]**. Make sure that the interface bandwidth is configured before giving this command. If you change it later, the QoS configuration will not change. When you issue the **auto qos voip** command on an individual data circuit, the configuration it creates differs depending on the bandwidth of the circuit itself. Compression and fragmentation are enabled on links of 768 kbps bandwidth and lower. They are not enabled on links faster than 768 kbps. The router additionally configures traffic shaping and applies an AutoQoS service policy regardless of the bandwidth.

When you issue the command on a serial interface with a bandwidth of 768 kbps or less, the router changes the interface encapsulation to PPP. It creates a PPP Multilink interface and enables Link Fragmentation and Interleave (LFI) on the interface. Serial interfaces with a configured bandwidth greater than 768 kbps keep their configured encapsulation, and the router merely applies an AutoQoS service policy to the interface.

If you use the **trust** keyword in the command, the router creates class maps that group traffic based on its DSCP values. It associates those class maps with a created policy map and assigns it to the interface. You would use this keyword when QoS markings are assigned by a trusted device.

If you do not use the **trust** keyword, the router creates access lists that match voice and video data and call control ports. It associates those access lists with class maps with a created policy map that marks the traffic appropriately. Any traffic not matching those access lists is marked with DSCP 0. You would use this command if the traffic either arrives at the router unmarked or arrives marked by an untrusted device.

### Verifying AutoQoS VoIP

Displaying the running configuration shows all the mappings, class and policy maps, and interface configurations created by the AutoQoS VoIP macro. Use the following commands to get more specific information:

- **show auto qos:** Displays the interface AutoQoS commands

- **show mls qos:** Has several modifiers that display queuing and COS/DSCP mappings

- **show policy-map interface:** Verifies the actions of the policy map on each interface specified

## AutoQoS for the Enterprise

AutoQoS for the Enterprise is supported on Cisco routers. The main difference between it and AutoQoS VoIP is that it automates the QoS configuration for VoIP plus other network applications, and is meant to be used for WAN links. It can be used for Frame Relay and ATM subinterfaces only if they are point-to-point links. It detects the types and amounts of network traffic and then creates policies based on that. As with AutoQoS for VoIP, you can modify those policies if you desire. There are two steps to configuring Enterprise AutoQoS. The first step discovers the traffic, and the second step provides the recommended QoS configuration.

### Discovering Traffic for AutoQoS Enterprise

The command to enable traffic discovery is **auto discovery qos [trust]** and is issued at the interface, DLCI, or PVC configuration level. Make sure that Cisco Express Forwarding (CEF) is enabled, that the interface bandwidth is configured, and that no QoS configuration is on the interface before giving the command. Use the **trust** keyword if the traffic arrives at the router already marked, and if you trust those markings, because the AutoQoS policies will use those markings during the configuration stage.

Traffic discovery uses NBAR to learn the types and amounts of traffic on each interface where it is enabled. You should run it long enough for it to gather a representative sample of your traffic. The router will classify the traffic collected into one of ten classes. Table 3-11 shows the classes, the DSCP values that will be mapped to each if you use the **trust** option in the command, and sample types of traffic that NBAR will map to each. Note that the traffic type is not a complete list, but is meant to give you a good feel for each class.

**Table 3-11** *AutoQoS for the Enterprise Classes and DSCP Values*

| Class | DSCP/PHB Value | Traffic Types |
|---|---|---|
| Routing | CS6 | EIGRP, OSPF |
| VoIP | EF (46) | RTP Voice Media |
| Interactive video | AF41 | RTP Video Media |
| Streaming video | CS4 | Real Audio, Netshow |
| Control | CS3 | RTCP, H323, SIP |
| Transactional | AF21 | SAP, Citrix, Telnet, SSH |
| Bulk | AF11 | FTP, SMTP, POP3, Exchange |
| Scavenger | CS1 | Peer-to-peer applications |
| Management | CS2 | SNMP, Syslog, DHCP, DNS |
| Best effort | All others | All others |

### Generating the AutoQoS Configuration

When the traffic discovery has collected enough information, the next step is to issue the **auto qos** command on the interface. This runs a macro that creates templates based on the traffic collected, creates class maps to classify that traffic, and creates a policy map to allocate bandwidth and mark the traffic. The router then automatically applies the policy map to the interface. In the case of a Frame Relay DLCI, the router applies the policy map to a Frame Relay map class, and then applies that class to the DLCI. You can optionally turn off NBAR traffic collection with the **no auto discovery qos** command.

### Verifying AutoQoS for the Enterprise

As with AutoQoS VoIP, displaying the running configuration will show all the mappings, class and policy maps, and interface configurations created by the AutoQoS macro. Use the following commands to get more specific information:

- **show auto discovery qos**: Lists the types and amounts of traffic collected by NBAR
- **show auto qos**: Displays the class maps, policy maps, and interface configuration generated by the AutoQoS macro
- **show policy-map interface**: Displays each policy map and the actual effect it had on the interface traffic

# Foundation Summary

This section lists additional details and facts to round out the coverage of the topics in this chapter. Unlike most of the Cisco Press Exam Certification Guides, this "Foundation Summary" does not repeat information presented in the "Foundation Topics" section of the chapter. Please take the time to read and study the details in the "Foundation Topics" section of the chapter, as well as review items noted with a Key Topic icon.

Table 3-12 lists the various **match** commands that can be used for MQC tools like CB Marking.

**Table 3-12**  match *Configuration Command Reference for MQC Tools*

| Command | Function |
|---------|----------|
| **match [ip] precedence** *precedence-value* [*precedence-value precedence-value precedence-value*] | Matches precedence in IPv4 packets when the **ip** parameter is included; matches IPv4 and IPv6 packets when the **ip** parameter is missing. |
| **match access-group** {*access-group* \| **name** *access-group-name*} | Matches an ACL by number or name. |
| **match any** | Matches all packets. |
| **match class-map** *class-map-name* | Matches based on another class map. |
| **match cos** *cos-value* [*cos-value cos-value cos-value*] | Matches a CoS value. |
| **match destination-address mac** *address* | Matches a destination MAC address. |
| **match fr-dlci** *dlci-number* | Matches a particular Frame Relay DLCI. |
| **match input-interface** *interface-name* | Matches an ingress interface. |
| **match ip dscp** [*ip-dscp-value ip-dscp-value ip-dscp-value ip-dscp-value ip-dscp-value ip-dscp-value ip-dscp-value ip-dscp-value*] | Matches DSCP in IPv4 packets when the **ip** parameter is included; matches IPv4 and IPv6 packets when the **ip** parameter is missing. |
| **match ip rtp** *starting-port-number port-range* | Matches the RTP's UDP port-number range, even values only. |
| **match mpls experimental** *number* | Matches an MPLS Experimental value. |
| **match mpls experimental topmost** *value* | When multiple labels are in use, matches the MPLS EXP field in the topmost label. |
| **match not** *match-criteria* | Reverses the matching logic. In other words, things matched by the matching criteria do *not* match the class map. |

| Command | Function |
|---|---|
| match packet length {max *maximum-length-value* [min *minimum-length-value*] \| min *minimum-length-value* [max *maximum-length-value*]} | Matches packets based on the minimum length, maximum length, or both. |
| match protocol citrix app *application-name-string* | Matches NBAR Citrix applications. |
| match protocol http [url *url-string* \| host *hostname- string* \| mime *MIME-type*] | Matches a host name, URL string, or MIME type. |
| match protocol *protocol-name* | Matches NBAR protocol types. |
| match protocol rtp [audio \| video \| payload-type *payload-string*] | Matches RTP audio or video payload, based on the payload type. Also allows explicitly specifying payload types. |
| match qos-group *qos-group-value* | Matches a QoS group. |
| match source-address mac *address-destination* | Matches a source MAC address. |

Table 3-13 lists AutoQoS and QoS verification commands.

**Table 3-13**   *AutoQoS and QoS Verification Commands*

| Command | Function |
|---|---|
| auto qos voip {cisco-phone \| cisco-softphone} | Enables AutoQoS VoIP on a switch access interface |
| auto qos voip trust | Enables AutoQoS VoIP on a switch uplink interface |
| auto qos voip [trust] | Enables AutoQoS VoIP on a router interface |
| auto discovery qos [trust] | Enables NBAR traffic discovery for AutoQoS Enterprise |
| auto qos | Enables AutoQoS Enterprise on an interface |
| show auto qos | Displays the interface AutoQoS commands |
| show mls qos | Displays queueing and COS/DSCP mappings |
| show policy-map interface | Displays the interface queuing actions caused by the policy map |
| show auto discovery qos | Displays the traffic collected by NBAR |
| show auto qos | Displays the configuration generated by the AutoQoS macro |

Table 3-14 lists the RFCs related to DiffServ.

**Table 3-14**  *DiffServ RFCs*

| RFC | Title | Comments |
|-----|-------|----------|
| 2474 | Definition of the Differentiated Services Field (DS Field) in the IPv4 and IPv6 Headers | Contains the details of the 6-bit DSCP field in an IP header |
| 2475 | An Architecture for Differentiated Service | The core DiffServ conceptual document |
| 2597 | Assured Forwarding PHB Group | Defines a set of 12 DSCP values and a convention for their use |
| 3246 | An Expedited Forwarding PHB | Defines a single DSCP value as a convention for use as a low-latency class |
| 3260 | New Terminology and Clarifications for DiffServ | Clarifies, but does not supersede, existing DiffServ RFCs |

# Memory Builders

The CCIE Routing and Switching written exam, like all Cisco CCIE written exams, covers a fairly broad set of topics. This section provides some basic tools to help you exercise your memory about some of the broader topics covered in this chapter.

## Fill In Key Tables from Memory

Appendix E, "Key Tables for CCIE Study," on the CD in the back of this book, contains empty sets of some of the key summary tables in each chapter. Print Appendix E, refer to this chapter's tables in it, and fill in the tables from memory. Refer to Appendix F, "Solutions for Key Tables for CCIE Study," on the CD, to check your answers.

## Definitions

Next, take a few moments to write down the definitions for the following terms:

IP Precedence, ToS byte, Differentiated Services, DS field, Per-Hop Behavior, Assured Forwarding, Expedited Forwarding, Class Selector, Class of Service, Differentiated Services Code Point, User Priority, Discard Eligible, Cell Loss Priority, MPLS Experimental bits, class map, policy map, service policy, Modular QoS CLI, Class-Based Marking, Network-Based Application Recognition, QoS preclassification, AutoQoS

Refer to the glossary to check your answers.

## Further Reading

*Cisco QoS Exam Certification Guide*, by Wendell Odom and Michael Cavanaugh

*End-to-End QoS Network Design*, by Tim Szigeti and Christina Hattingh

"The Enterprise QoS SRND Guide," posted at www.cisco.com/en/US/docs/solutions/Enterprise/WAN_and_MAN/QoS_SRND/QoS-SRND-Book.html, provides great background and details for real-life QoS deployments.

**Blueprint topics covered in this chapter:**

This chapter covers the following subtopics from the Cisco CCIE Routing and Switching written exam blueprint. Refer to the full blueprint in Table I-1 in the Introduction for more details on the topics covered in each chapter and their context within the blueprint.

- Class-Based Weighted Fair Queuing (CBWFQ)

- Low-Latency Queuing (LLQ)

- Modified Deficit Round-Robin (MDRR)

- Weighted Random Early Detection (WRED)

- Random Early Detection (RED)

- Weighted Round-Robin (WRR)

- Shaped Round-Robin (SRR)

- Resource Reservation Protocol (RSVP)

## CHAPTER 4

# Congestion Management and Avoidance

Congestion management, commonly called *queuing*, refers to how a router or switch manages packets or frames while they wait to exit a device. With routers, the waiting occurs when IP forwarding has been completed, so the queuing is always considered to be output queuing. LAN switches often support both output queuing and input queuing, where input queuing is used for received frames that are waiting to be switched to the switch's output interfaces.

*Congestion avoidance* refers to the logic used when deciding if and when packets should be dropped as a queuing system becomes more congested. This chapter covers a wide variety of Cisco IOS queuing tools, along with the most pervasive congestion avoidance tool, namely weighted random early detection (WRED).

## "Do I Know This Already?" Quiz

Table 4-1 outlines the major headings in this chapter and the corresponding "Do I Know This Already?" quiz questions.

**Table 4-1** *"Do I Know This Already?" Foundation Topics Section-to-Question Mapping*

| Foundation Topics Section | Questions Covered in This Section | Score |
|---|---|---|
| Cisco Router Queuing Concepts | 1 | |
| Queuing Tools: CBWFQ and LLQ | 2–3 | |
| Weighted Random Early Detection | 4–5 | |
| Modified Deficit Round-Robin | 6 | |
| LAN Switch Congestion Management and Avoidance | 7–8 | |
| RSVP | 9 | |
| Total Score | | |

To best use this pre-chapter assessment, remember to score yourself strictly. You can find the answers in Appendix A, "Answers to the 'Do I Know This Already?' Quizzes."

**1.** What is the main benefit of the hardware queue on a Cisco router interface?

    **a.** Prioritizes latency-sensitive packets so that they are always scheduled next

    **b.** Reserves a minimum amount of bandwidth for particular classes of traffic

    **c.** Provides a queue in which to hold a packet so that, as soon as the interface is available to send another packet, the packet can be sent without requiring an interrupt to the router CPU

    **d.** Allows configuration of a percentage of the remaining link bandwidth, after allocating bandwidth to the LLQ and the class-default queue

**2.** Examine the following configuration snippet. If a new class, called class3, is added to the policy map, which of the following commands could be used to reserve 25 kbps of bandwidth for the class?

```
policy-map fred
 class class1
  priority 20
 class class2
  bandwidth 30
!
interface serial 0/0
 bandwidth 100
 service-policy output fred
```

    **a.** priority 25

    **b.** bandwidth 25

    **c.** bandwidth percent 25

    **d.** bandwidth remaining-percent 25

**3.** Examine the following configuration snippet. How much bandwidth does Cisco IOS assign to class2?

```
policy-map fred
 class class1
  priority percent 20
 class class2
  bandwidth remaining percent 20
interface serial 0/0
 bandwidth 100
 service-policy output fred
```

    **a.** 10 kbps

    **b.** 11 kbps

    **c.** 20 kbps

    **d.** 21 kbps

    **e.** Not enough information to tell

4. Which of the following impacts the percentage of packet discards when using WRED, when the current average queue depth is between the minimum and maximum thresholds?

   a. The **bandwidth** command setting on the interface

   b. The mark probability denominator (MPD)

   c. The exponential weighting constant

   d. The congestive discard threshold

5. Which of the following commands, under an interface like s0/0, would enable WRED and tell it to use IP Precedence (IPP) when choosing its default traffic profiles?

   a. **random-detect**

   b. **random-detect precedence-based**

   c. **random-detect dscp-based**

   d. **random-detect precedence 1 20 30 40**

6. On a Catalyst 3560 switch, interface fa0/1 has been configured for SRR scheduling, and fa0/2 has been configured for SRR scheduling with a priority queue. Which of the following is true regarding interface fa0/2?

   a. It must be configured with the **priority-queue out** command.

   b. The last parameter (*w4*) of the **srr-queue bandwidth share** *w1 w2 w3 w4* command must be 0.

   c. Only CoS 5 frames can be placed into queue 1, the expedite queue.

   d. Only DSCP EF frames can be placed into queue 1, the expedite queue.

7. In modified deficit round-robin, what is the function of QV?

   a. Sets the ratio of bandwidth to be sent from each queue on each pass through the queues

   b. Sets the absolute bandwidth for each queue on each pass through the queues

   c. Sets the number of bytes removed from each queue on each pass through the queues

   d. Identifies the MDRR priority queue

**8.** The Cisco 3560 switch uses SRR and WTD for its queuing and congestion management methods. How many ingress queues and egress queues can be configured on each port of a 3560 switch, and how many priority queues are configurable on ingress and egress?

   **a.** One ingress queue, four egress queues; one priority queue on each side

   **b.** One ingress queue, four egress queues; one priority queue on the egress side

   **c.** Two ingress queues, four egress queues; one priority queue on the egress side

   **d.** Two ingress queues, four egress queues; one priority queue on each side

**9.** What interface command would configure RSVP to reserve up to one-quarter of a 100-Mbps link, but only allow each individual flow to use 1 Mbps?

   **a.** **ip rsvp bandwidth 25000 1000**

   **b.** **ip rsvp-bandwidth 25 1**

   **c.** **rsvp bandwidth 100 2500**

   **d.** **ip rsvp bandwidth 25 1**

# Foundation Topics

## Cisco Router Queuing Concepts

Cisco routers can be configured to perform *fancy queuing* for packets that are waiting to exit an interface. For example, if a router receives 5 Mbps of traffic every second for the next several seconds, and all that traffic needs to exit a T1 serial link, the router can't forward all the traffic. So, the router places the packets into one or more *software queues*, which can then be managed—thus impacting which packets get to leave next and which packets might be discarded.

### Software Queues and Hardware Queues

Although many network engineers already understand queuing, many overlook some of the details behind the concepts of a hardware queue and a software queue associated with each physical interface. The queues created on an interface by the popularly known queuing tools are called *software queues*, as these queues are implemented in software. However, when the queuing scheduler picks the next packet to take from the software queues, the packet does not move directly out the interface. Instead, the router moves the packet from the interface software queue to a small hardware FIFO (first-in, first-out) queue on each interface. Cisco calls this separate, final queue either the *transmit queue* (Tx queue) or *transmit ring* (Tx ring), depending on the model of the router; generically, these queues are called *hardware queues*.

Hardware queues provide the following features:

**Key Topic**

- When an interface finishes sending a packet, the next packet from the hardware queue can be encoded and sent out the interface, without requiring a software interrupt to the CPU—ensuring full use of interface bandwidth.

- Always use FIFO logic.

- Cannot be affected by IOS queuing tools.

- IOS automatically shrinks the length of the hardware queue to a smaller length than the default when a queuing tool is present.

- Short hardware queue lengths mean packets are more likely to be in the controllable software queues, giving the software queuing more control of the traffic leaving the interface.

The only function of a hardware queue that can be manipulated is the length of the queue. Example 4-1 shows how to see the current length of the queue and how to change the length.

**Example 4-1**  *Tx Queue Length: Finding and Changing the Length*

```
! The example begins with only FIFO queuing on the interface. For this
! router, it defaults to a TX queue length 16.
R3# show controllers serial 0/0
Interface Serial0/0
! about 30 lines omitted for brevity
tx_limited=0(16)
! lines omitted for brevity
! Next, the TX ring is set to length 1.
! (The smallest recommended value is 2.)
R3# conf t
Enter configuration commands, one per line.  End with CNTL/Z.
R3(config)# int s 0/0
R3(config-if)# tx-ring-limit 1
R3(config-if)# ^Z
```

## Queuing on Interfaces Versus Subinterfaces and Virtual Circuits

IOS queuing tools can create and manage software queues associated with a physical interface, and then the packets drain into the hardware queue associated with the interface. Additionally, queuing tools can be used in conjunction with traffic shaping. Traffic-shaping tools delay packets to ensure that a class of packets does not exceed a defined traffic rate. While delaying the packets, the shaping function queues the packets—by default in a FIFO queue. Depending on the type of shaping tool in use, various queuing tools can be configured to manage the packets delayed by the shaping tool.

Chapter 5, "Shaping, Policing, and Link Fragmentation," covers traffic shaping, including how to use queuing tools with shapers. The queuing coverage in this chapter focuses on the implementation of software queuing tools directly on the physical interface.

## Comparing Queuing Tools

Cisco IOS provides a wide variety of queuing tools. The upcoming sections of this chapter describe several different IOS queuing tools, with a brief summary ending the section on queuing. Table 4-2 summarizes the main characteristics of different queuing tools that you will want to keep in mind while comparing each successive queuing tool.

Key
Topic

**Table 4-2**  *Key Comparison Points for Queuing Tools*

| Feature | Definition |
| --- | --- |
| Classification | The ability to look at packet headers to choose the right queue for each packet |
| Drop policy | The rules used to choose which packets to drop as queues begin to fill |

| Feature | Definition |
|---------|------------|
| Scheduling | The logic used to determine which packet should be dequeued next |
| Maximum number of queues | The number of unique classes of packets for a queuing tool |
| Maximum queue length | The maximum number of packets in a single queue |

## Queuing Tools: CBWFQ and LLQ

This section hits the highlights of the modern queuing tools in Cisco IOS and covers detailed configuration for the more popular tools—specifically, class-based weighted fair queuing (CBWFQ) and low-latency queuing (LLQ). Because the CCIE Routing and Switching exam blueprint no longer includes the priority queuing (PQ) and custom queuing (CQ) legacy queuing methods, they are not covered in this book. Furthermore, WFQ is covered only in the context of CBWFQ and not as a standalone feature.

Cisco created CBWFQ and LLQ using some of the best concepts from the legacy queuing methods PQ and CQ, as well as WFQ, while adding several additional features. CBWFQ reserves bandwidth for each queue, and provides the ability to use WFQ concepts for packets in the default (class-default) queue. LLQ adds to CBWFQ the concept of a priority queue, but unlike legacy PQ, LLQ prevents the high-priority queue from starving other queues. Additionally, both CBWFQ and LLQ use Modular QoS CLI (MQC) for configuration, which means that they have robust classification options, including Network-Based Application Recognition (NBAR).

CBWFQ and LLQ use almost identical configuration; the one major difference is whether the **bandwidth** command (CBWFQ) or the **priority** command (LLQ) is used to configure the tool. Because both tools use MQC, both use class maps for classification and policy maps to create a set of classes to be used on an interface. The classes defined in the policy map each define a single queue; as a result, the terms *queue* and *class* are often used interchangeably when working with LLQ and CBWFQ.

CBWFQ and LLQ support 64 queues/classes. The maximum queue length can be changed, with the maximum possible value and the default length varying based on the model of router and the amount of memory installed. They both also have one special queue called the *class-default queue*. This queue exists even if it is not configured. If a packet does not match any of the explicitly configured classes in a policy map, IOS places the packet into the class-default class/queue. CBWFQ settings can be configured for the class-default queue.

The sections that follow cover the details of CBWFQ and then LLQ.

## CBWFQ Basic Features and Configuration

The CBWFQ scheduler guarantees a minimum percentage of a link's bandwidth to each class/queue. If all queues have a large number of packets, each queue gets the percentage bandwidth implied by the configuration. However, if some queues are empty and do not need their bandwidth for a short period, the bandwidth is proportionally allocated across the other classes. (Cisco does not publish the details of how CBWFQ achieves these functions.)

Table 4-3 summarizes some of the key features of CBWFQ.

**Table 4-3** *CBWFQ Functions and Features*

| CBWFQ Feature | Description |
|---|---|
| Classification | Classifies based on anything that MQC commands can match |
| Drop policy | Tail drop or WRED, configurable per queue |
| Number of queues | 64 |
| Maximum queue length | Varies based on router model and memory |
| Scheduling inside a single queue | FIFO on 63 queues; FIFO or WFQ on class-default queue[1] |
| Scheduling among all queues | Result of the scheduler provides a percentage of guaranteed bandwidth to each queue |

[1] Cisco 7500 series routers support FIFO or WFQ in all the CBWFQ queues.

Table 4-4 lists the key CBWFQ commands that were not covered in Chapter 3, "Classification and Marking."

**Table 4-4** *Command Reference for CBWFQ*

| Command | Mode and Function |
|---|---|
| **bandwidth** {*bandwidth-kbps* \| **percent** *percent*} | Class subcommand; sets literal or percentage bandwidth for the class |
| **bandwidth** {remaining percent *percent*} | Class subcommand; sets percentage of remaining bandwidth for the class |
| **queue-limit** *queue-limit* | Class subcommand; sets the maximum length of a CBWFQ queue |
| **fair-queue** [queue-limit *queue-value*] | Class subcommand; enables WFQ in the class (class-default only) |

Example 4-2 shows a simple CBWFQ configuration that uses the class-default queue. The configuration was created on R3 in Figure 4-1, using the following requirements:

- All VoIP payload traffic is placed in a queue.

- All other traffic is placed in another queue.

- Give the VoIP traffic 50 percent of the bandwidth.

- WFQ should be used on the non-VoIP traffic.

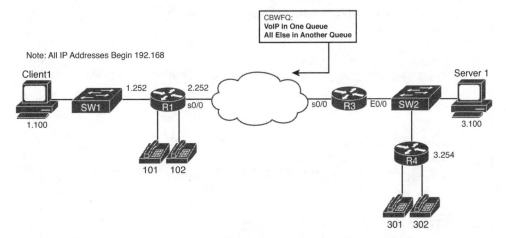

**Figure 4-1**  *Network Used with CBWFQ and LLQ Configuration Examples*

**Example 4-2**  *CBWFQ with VoIP in One Queue, Everything Else in Class-Default*

```
! The class map matches on UDP/RTP header and RTP port numbers.
class-map match-all voip-rtp
  match ip rtp 16384 16383
! Next, the policy map uses the bandwidth command to reserve 64 kbps for the class
! voip-rtp. Class-default gets some of the leftover bandwidth by default.
policy-map queue-voip
  class voip-rtp
    bandwidth 64
  class class-default
    fair-queue
! The interface's bandwidth 128 command is used as the basis for the limit on the
! amount of bandwidth that can be allocated in the policy map queue-voip.
! The load-interval command sets how often counters are updated. Also, note
! that the policy-map is enabled for output; input is not allowed on routers for
! policy maps that perform queuing.
interface Serial0/0
 encapsulation frame-relay
 load-interval 30
 bandwidth 128
```

```
 service-policy output queue-voip
! This command lists counters, reserved bandwidth, maximum queue length (listed
! as max threshold), and a reminder that WFQ is used in the class-default queue.
R3# show policy-map int s 0/0
 Serial0/0

  Service-policy output:     queue-voip

    Class-map: voip-rtp (match-all)
      136435 packets, 8731840 bytes
      30 second offered rate 51000 bps, drop rate 0 bps
      Match:      ip rtp 16384 16383
      Weighted Fair Queueing
        Output Queue: Conversation 265
        Bandwidth 64 (kbps) Max Threshold 64 (packets)
        (pkts matched/bytes matched) 48550/3107200
        (depth/total drops/no-buffer drops) 14/0/0


    Class-map: class-default (match-any)
      1958 packets, 1122560 bytes
      30 second offered rate 59000 bps, drop rate 0 bps
      Match: any
      Weighted Fair Queueing
        Flow Based Fair Queueing
        Maximum Number of Hashed Queues 256
        (total queued/total drops/no-buffer drops) 15/0/0
! This command just lists the configuration in a concise manner.
R3# show policy-map
  Policy Map queue-voip
    Class voip-rtp
      Weighted Fair Queueing
              Bandwidth 64 (kbps) Max Threshold 64 (packets)
    Class class-default
      Weighted Fair Queueing
Flow based Fair Queueing Max Threshold 64 (packets)
```

## Defining and Limiting CBWFQ Bandwidth

In previous versions of Cisco IOS Software, the system checks a CBWFQ policy map
to ensure that it does not allocate too much bandwidth. These older versions of IOS
perform the check when the **service-policy output** command was added; if the policy
map defined too much bandwidth for that interface, the **service-policy** command was
rejected. IOS defined the allowed bandwidth based on two interface subcommands: the
**bandwidth** command and the reserved bandwidth that was implied by the **max-reserved-
bandwidth** command. The nonreservable bandwidth was meant for overhead traffic.

In the IOS 15 code releases, the **max-reserved-bandwidth** command does not have any effect on the queuing system. IOS does not even check a policy map's total reservation parameters against the **max-reserved-bandwidth** settings. What's more, these versions of IOS even notify you of this fact. IOS allows a policy map to allocate bandwidth based on the **int-bw**. In other words, on an interface with **int-bw** of 256 (256 kbps), the policy map could allocate the entire 256 kbps of bandwidth.

The bandwidth can also be defined as percentages using either the **bandwidth percent** or **bandwidth remaining percent** command. When you use percentages, it is easier to ensure that a policy map does not attempt to allocate too much bandwidth.

The two percentage-based **bandwidth** command options work in slightly different ways. Figure 4-2 shows the concept for each.

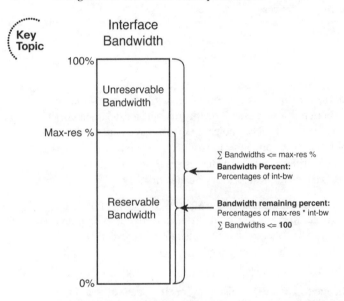

**Figure 4-2**  *Bandwidth Percent and Bandwidth Remaining Percent Concepts*

The **bandwidth percent** *bw-percent* command sets a class's reserved bandwidth as a percentage of **int-bw**. For example, in Example 4-2, if the **bandwidth percent 50** command had been used instead of **bandwidth 64**, the voip-rtp class would have used 50% × 128 kbps, or 64 kbps.

The **bandwidth remaining percent** *bw-percent* command sets a class's reserved bandwidth as a percentage of remaining bandwidth.

**Note**  Using the **bandwidth remaining percent** command is particularly useful with LLQ and will be explained in that context later in the chapter. The reason is that the remaining bandwidth calculation is changed by the addition of LLQ.

Note that in a single policy map, only one of the three variations of the **bandwidth** command can be used. Table 4-5 summarizes the three methods for reserving bandwidth with CBWFQ.

**Table 4-5**    *Reference for CBWFQ Bandwidth Reservation*

| Method | Amount of Bandwidth Reserved by the bandwidth Command | The Sum of Values in a Single Policy Map Must Be <= ... |
|---|---|---|
| Explicit bandwidth | As listed in commands | **max-res** × **int-bw** |
| Percent | A percentage of the **int-bw** | **max-res** setting |
| Remaining percent | A percentage of the reservable bandwidth (**int-bw** × **max-res**) | 100 |

## Low-Latency Queuing

Low-latency queuing sounds like the best queuing tool possible, just based on the name. What packet wouldn't want to experience low latency? As it turns out, for delay (latency) sensitive traffic, LLQ is indeed the queuing tool of choice. LLQ looks and acts just like CBWFQ in most regards, except it adds the capability for some queues to be configured as low-latency queues. LLQ schedules these specific queues as strict-priority queues. In other words, LLQ always services packets in these priority queues first.

LLQ lingo can sometimes be used in a couple of different ways. With a single policy map that has at least one low-latency queue, the policy map might be considered to be implementing LLQ, while at the same time, that one low-latency queue is often called "the LLQ." Sometimes, a single low-latency queue is even called "the PQ" as a reference to the legacy PQ-like behavior, or even a "priority queue."

While LLQ adds a low-latency queue to CBWFQ, it also prevents the queue starvation that occurs with legacy PQ. LLQ actually *polices* the PQ based on the configured bandwidth. In effect, the bandwidth given to an LLQ priority queue is both the guaranteed minimum and policed maximum. (You might recall from Chapter 3 that the DiffServ Expedited Forwarding PHB formally defines the priority queuing and policing PHBs.) As a result, the packets that make it out of the queue experience low latency, but some might be discarded to prevent starving the other queues.

Figure 4-3 depicts the scheduler logic for LLQ. Note that the PQ logic is shown, but with the policer check as well.

LLQ configuration requires one more command in addition to the commands used for CBWFQ configuration. Instead of using the **bandwidth** command on a class, use the **priority** command:

```
priority {bandwidth-kbps | percent percentage} [burst]
```

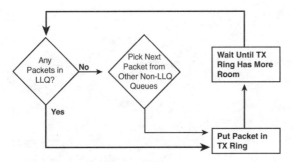

**Figure 4-3**  *LLQ Scheduler Logic*

This **class** subcommand enables LLQ in the class, reserves bandwidth, and enables the policing function. You can also configure the burst size for the policer with this command, but the default setting of 20 percent of the configured bandwidth is typically a reasonable choice.

Example 4-3 shows a sample LLQ configuration, using the following criteria. Like Example 4-2, the LLQ policy is applied to R3's s0/0 interface from Figure 4-1:

■  R3's s0/0 bandwidth is 128 kbps.

■  Packets will already have been marked with good Differentiated Services Code Point (DSCP) values.

■  VoIP payload is already marked DSCP EF and should be LLQed with 58 kbps of bandwidth.

■  AF41, AF21, and AF23 traffic should get 22, 20, and 8 kbps, respectively.

■  All other traffic should be placed into class class-default, which should use WRED and WFQ.

**Example 4-3**  *LLQ for EF; CBWFQ for AF41, AF21, AF23; and All Else*

```
! The class maps used by the queue-on-dscp are not shown, but the names imply what
! each class map has been configured to match. Note the priority 58 command makes
! class dscp-ef an LLQ.
policy-map queue-on-dscp
  class dscp-ef
    priority 58
  class dscp-af41
   bandwidth 22
  class dscp-af21
   bandwidth 20
   random-detect dscp-based
  class dscp-af23
   bandwidth 8
   random-detect dscp-based
```

```
      class class-default
        fair-queue
        random-detect dscp-based
! max-res has to be raised or the policy map would be rejected.
interface Serial0/0
 bandwidth 128
 encapsulation frame-relay
 load-interval 30
 max-reserved-bandwidth 85
 service-policy output queue-on-dscp
! Below, for class dscp-ef, note the phrase "strict priority," as well as the
! computed policing burst of 1450 bytes (20% of 58 kbps and divided by 8 to convert
! the value to a number of bytes.)
R3# show policy-map queue-on-dscp
      Policy Map queue-on-dscp
      Class dscp-ef
         Weighted Fair Queueing
              Strict Priority
              Bandwidth 58 (kbps) Burst 1450 (Bytes)
! lines omitted for brevity
! Note the statistics below. Any packets dropped due to the policer would show
! up in the last line below.
R3# show policy-map interface s 0/0 output class dscp-ef
 Serial0/0
  Service-policy output: queue-on-dscp
    Class-map: dscp-ef (match-all)
      227428 packets, 14555392 bytes
      30 second offered rate 52000 bps, drop rate 0 bps
      Match: ip dscp ef
      Weighted Fair Queueing
        Strict Priority
        Output Queue: Conversation 40
        Bandwidth 58 (kbps) Burst 1450 (Bytes)
        (pkts matched/bytes matched) 12194/780416
 (total drops/bytes drops) 0/0
```

## Defining and Limiting LLQ Bandwidth

The LLQ **priority** command provides two syntax options for defining the bandwidth of an LLQ—a simple explicit amount or bandwidth as a percentage of interface bandwidth. (There is no remaining bandwidth equivalent for the **priority** command.) However, unlike the **bandwidth** command, both the explicit and percentage versions of the **priority** command can be used inside the same policy map.

IOS still limits the amount of bandwidth in an LLQ policy map, with the actual bandwidth from both LLQ classes (with **priority** commands) and non-LLQ classes (with **bandwidth** commands) not being allowed to exceed **max-res × int-bw**. Although the math is easy, the details can get confusing, especially because a single policy map could have one queue configured with **priority** *bw*, another with **priority percent** *bw*, and others with one of the three versions of the **bandwidth** command. Figure 4-4 shows an example with three versions of the commands.

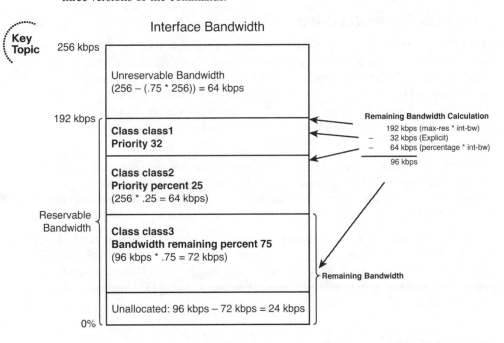

**Figure 4-4**  *Priority, Priority Percent, and Bandwidth Remaining Percent*

The figure shows both versions of the **priority** command. Class1 has an explicit **priority 32** command, which reserves 32 kbps. Class2 has a **priority percent 25** command, which, when applied to the interface bandwidth (256 kbps), gives class2 64 kbps.

The most interesting part of Figure 4-4 is how IOS views the remaining-bandwidth concept when **priority** queues are configured. IOS subtracts the bandwidth reserved by the priority commands as well. As a result, a policy map can essentially allocate nonpriority classes based on percentages of the leftover (remaining) bandwidth, with those values totaling 100 (100 percent).

## LLQ with More Than One Priority Queue

LLQ allows multiple queues/classes to be configured as priority queues. This begs the question, "Which queue gets scheduled first?" As it turns out, LLQ actually places the packets from multiple LLQs into a single internal LLQ. So, packets in the different configured priority queues still get scheduled ahead of nonpriority queues, but they are serviced based on their arrival time for all packets in any of the priority queues.

**Key Topic**

So why use multiple priority queues? The answer is *policing*. By policing traffic in one class at one speed, and traffic in another class at another speed, you get more granularity for the policing function of LLQ. For example, if you are planning for video and voice, you can place each into a separate LLQ and get low-latency performance for both types of traffic, but at the same time prevent video traffic from consuming the bandwidth engineered for voice and vice versa.

## Miscellaneous CBWFQ/LLQ Topics

CBWFQ and LLQ allow a policy map to either allocate bandwidth to the class-default class, or not. When a **bandwidth** command is configured under **class class-default**, the class is indeed reserved that minimum bandwidth. (IOS will not allow the **priority** command in **class-default**.) When **class class-default** does not have a **bandwidth** command, IOS internally allocates any unassigned bandwidth among all classes. As a result, **class class-default** might not get much bandwidth unless the class is configured a minimum amount of bandwidth using the **bandwidth** command.

This chapter's coverage of guaranteed bandwidth allocation is based on the configuration commands. In practice, a policy map might not have packets in all queues at the same time. In that case, the queues get more than their reserved bandwidth. IOS allocates the extra bandwidth proportionally to each active class's bandwidth reservation.

Finally, IOS uses queuing only when congestion occurs. IOS considers congestion to be occurring when the hardware queue is full; that generally happens when the offered load of traffic is far less than the clock rate of the link. So, a router could have a **service-policy out** command on an interface, with LLQ configured, but the LLQ logic would be used only when the hardware queue is full.

## Queuing Summary

Table 4-6 summarizes some of the key points regarding the IOS queuing tools covered in this chapter.

**Key Topic**

**Table 4-6**   *Queuing Protocol Comparison*

| Feature | CBWFQ | LLQ |
|---|---|---|
| Includes a strict-priority queue | No | Yes |
| Polices priority queues to prevent starvation | No | Yes |
| Reserves bandwidth per queue | Yes | Yes |
| Includes robust set of classification fields | Yes | Yes |
| Classifies based on flows | Yes[1] | Yes[1] |
| Supports RSVP | Yes | Yes |
| Maximum number of queues | 64 | 64 |

[1] WFQ can be used in the class-default queue or in all CBWFQ queues in 2900 Series routers running 15.3 code.

# Weighted Random Early Detection

When a queue is full, IOS has no place to put newly arriving packets, so it discards them. This phenomenon is called *tail drop*. Often, when a queue fills, several packets are tail dropped at a time, given the bursty nature of data packets.

Tail drop can have an overall negative effect on network traffic, particularly TCP traffic. When packets are lost, for whatever reason, TCP senders slow their rate of sending data. When tail drops occur and multiple packets are lost, the TCP connections slow even more. Also, most networks send a much higher percentage of TCP traffic than UDP traffic, meaning that the overall network load tends to drop after multiple packets are tail dropped.

Interestingly, overall throughput can be improved by discarding a few packets as a queue begins to fill, rather than waiting for the larger impact of tail drops. Cisco created *weighted random early detection (WRED)* specifically for the purpose of monitoring queue length and discarding a percentage of the packets in the queue to improve overall network performance. As a queue gets longer and longer, WRED begins to discard more packets, hoping that a small reduction in offered load that follows might be just enough to prevent the queue from filling.

WRED uses several numeric settings when making its decisions. First, WRED uses the measured *average queue depth* when deciding whether a queue has filled enough to begin discarding packets. WRED then compares the average depth to a minimum and maximum queue threshold, performing different discard actions depending on the outcome. Table 4-7 lists the actions.

When the average queue depth is very low or very high, the actions are somewhat obvious, although the term *full drop* in Table 4-7 might be a bit of a surprise. When the average depth rises above the maximum threshold, WRED discards all new packets. Although this action might seem like tail drop, technically it is not, because the actual queue might not be full. So, to make this fine distinction, WRED calls this action category *full drop*.

**Key Topic**

**Table 4-7**   *WRED Discard Categories*

| Average Queue Depth Versus Thresholds | Action | WRED Name for Action |
|---|---|---|
| Average < minimum threshold | No packets dropped. | No drop |
| Minimum threshold < average depth < maximum threshold | A percentage of packets dropped. Drop percentage increases from 0 to a maximum percent as the average depth moves from the minimum threshold to the maximum. | Random drop |
| Average depth > maximum threshold | All new packets discarded; similar to tail drop. | Full drop |

When the average queue depth is between the two thresholds, WRED discards a percentage of packets. The percentage grows linearly as the average queue depth grows from the minimum threshold to the maximum, as depicted in Figure 4-5 (which shows WRED's default settings for IPP 0 traffic).

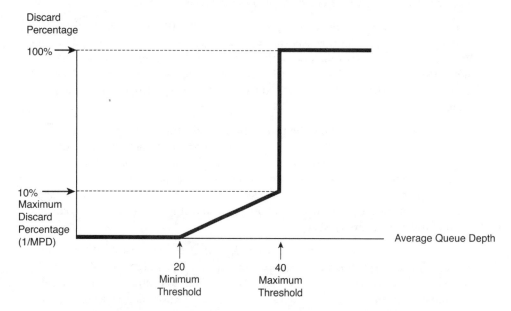

**Figure 4-5**  *WRED Discard Logic with Defaults for IPP 0*

The last of the WRED numeric settings that affect its logic is the *mark probability denominator (MPD)*, from which the maximum percentage of 10 percent is derived in Figure 4-5. IOS calculates the discard percentage used at the maximum threshold based on the simple formula 1/MPD. In the figure, an MPD of 10 yields a calculated value of 1/10, meaning that the discard rate grows from 0 percent to 10 percent as the average queue depth grows from the minimum threshold to the maximum. Also, when WRED discards packets, it randomly chooses the packets to discard.

## How WRED Weights Packets

WRED gives preference to packets with certain IP Precedence (IPP) or DSCP values. To do so, WRED uses different traffic profiles for packets with different IPP and DSCP values. A WRED *traffic profile* consists of a setting for three key WRED variables: the minimum threshold, the maximum threshold, and the MPD. Figure 4-6 shows just such a case, with two WRED traffic profiles (for IPP 0 and IPP 3).

As Figure 4-6 illustrates, IPP 3's minimum threshold was higher than for IPP 0. As a result, IPP 0 traffic will be discarded earlier than IPP 3 packets. Also, the MPD is higher for IPP 3, resulting in a lower discard percentage (based on the formula discard percentage = 1/MPD).

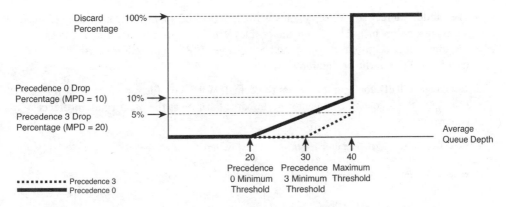

**Figure 4-6**  *Example WRED Profiles for Precedences 0 and 3*

Table 4-8 lists the IOS default WRED profile settings for various DSCP values. You might recall from Chapter 3 that Assured Forwarding DSCPs whose names end in 1 (for example, AF21) should get better WRED treatment than those settings that end in 2 (for example, AF32). The IOS defaults listed in Table 4-8 achieve that goal by setting lower minimum thresholds for the appropriate AF DSCPs.

**Table 4-8**  *Cisco IOS Software Default WRED Profiles for DSCP-Based WRED*

| DSCP | Minimum Threshold | Maximum Threshold | MPD | 1/MPD |
|------|-------------------|-------------------|-----|-------|
| AFx1 | 33 | 40 | 10 | 10% |
| AFx2 | 28 | 40 | 10 | 10% |
| AFx3 | 24 | 40 | 10 | 10% |
| EF   | 37 | 40 | 10 | 10% |

## WRED Configuration

Because WRED manages drops based on queue depth, WRED must be configured alongside a particular queue. However, most queuing mechanisms do not support WRED; as a result, WRED can be configured only in the following locations:

- On a physical interface (with FIFO queuing)

- For a non-LLQ class inside a CBWFQ policy map

- For an ATM VC

To use WRED directly on a physical interface, IOS actually disables all other queuing mechanisms and creates a single FIFO queue. WRED then manages the queue with regard to drops. For CBWFQ, WRED is configured in a class inside a policy map, in the same location as the **bandwidth** and **priority** commands discussed earlier in this chapter.

The **random-detect** command enables WRED, either under a physical interface or under a class in a policy map. This command enables WRED to use IPP, and not DSCP. The **random-detect dscp-based** command both enables WRED and tells it to use DSCP for determining the traffic profile for a packet.

To change WRED configuration from the default WRED profile for a particular IPP or DSCP, use the following commands, in the same location as the other **random-detect** command:

```
random-detect precedence precedence min-threshold max-threshold
   [mark-prob-denominator]
random-detect dscp dscpvalue min-threshold max-threshold
   [mark-probability-denominator]
```

Finally, calculation of the rolling average queue depth can be affected through configuring a parameter called the *exponential weighting constant*. A low exponential weighting constant means that the old average is a small part of the calculation, resulting in a more quickly changing average. The setting can be changed with the following command, although changing it is not recommended:

```
random-detect exponential-weighting-constant exponent
```

Note that earlier, Example 4-4 showed basic WRED configuration inside some classes of a CBWFQ configuration.

## Modified Deficit Round-Robin

Modified deficit round-robin (MDRR) is a queuing feature implemented only in the Cisco 12000 Series router family. Because the 12000 Series does not support CBWFQ and LLQ, MDRR serves in place of these features. Its main claims to fame are better fairness than legacy queuing methods such as priority queuing and custom queuing, and that it supports a priority queue (like LLQ). For the CCIE Routing and Switching qualifying exam, you must understand how MDRR works at the conceptual level, but you don't need to know how to configure it.

MDRR allows classifying traffic into seven round-robin queues (0–6), with one additional priority queue. When no packets are placed into the priority queue, MDRR normally services its queues in a round-robin approach, cycling through each queue once per cycle. With packets in the priority queue, MDRR has two options for how to include the priority queue in the queue service algorithm:

■ Strict priority mode

■ Alternate mode

Strict priority mode serves the priority queue whenever traffic is present in that queue. The benefit is, of course, that this traffic gets the first service regardless of what is going on in the other queues. The downside is that it can lead to queue starvation in other queues if there is always traffic in the priority queue. In this mode, the priority queue also can get more than the configured bandwidth percentage, because this queue is served more than once per cycle.

In contrast, alternate mode serves the priority queue in between serving each of the other queues. Let's say that five queues are configured: 0, 1, 2, 3, and the priority queue (P). Assuming that there is always traffic in each queue, here is how it would be processed: 0, P, 1, P, 2, P, 3, P, and so on. The result is that queue starvation in nonpriority queues does not occur, because each queue is being served. The drawback of this mode is that it can cause jitter and additional latency for the traffic in the priority queue, compared to strict priority mode.

Two terms in MDRR, unique to this queuing method, help to differentiate MDRR from other queuing tools:

■ Quantum value (QV)

■ Deficit

**Key Topic**

MDRR supports two types of scheduling, one of which uses the same general algorithm as the legacy CQ feature in Cisco IOS routers (other than the 12000 Series). MDRR removes packets from a queue until the quantum value (QV) for that queue has been removed. The QV quantifies a number of bytes and is used much like the byte count is used by the CQ scheduler. MDRR repeats the process for every queue, in order from 0 through 7, and then repeats this round-robin process. The end result is that each queue gets some percentage bandwidth of the link.

MDRR deals with the CQ scheduler's problem by treating any "extra" bytes sent during a cycle as a "deficit." If too many bytes were taken from a queue, next time around through the queues, the number of extra bytes sent by MDRR is subtracted from the QV. In effect, if more than the QV is sent from a queue in one pass, that many fewer bytes are taken in the next pass. As a result, averaged over many passes through the cycle, the MDRR scheduler provides an exact bandwidth reservation.

Figure 4-7 shows an example of how MDRR works. In this case, MDRR is using only two queues, with QVs of 1500 and 3000, respectively, and with all packets at 1000 bytes in length.

Some discussion of how to interpret Figure 4-7 can help you digest what is going on. The figure shows the action during the first round-robin pass in the top half of the figure, and the action during the second pass in the lower half of the figure. The example begins with six packets (labeled P1 through P6) in queue 1, and six packets (labeled P7 through P12) in queue 2. Each arrowed line to the right sides of the queues, pointing to the right, represents the choice by MDRR to send a single packet.

When a queue first fills, the queue's deficit counter (DC) is set to the QV for that queue, which is 1500 for queue 1 and 3000 for queue 2. In Figure 4-7, MDRR begins by taking one packet from queue 1, decrementing the DC to 500, and deciding that the DC is still greater than 0. Therefore, MDRR takes a second packet from queue 1, decrementing the DC to –500. MDRR then moves on to queue 2, taking three packets, after which the deficit counter (DC) for queue 2 has decremented to 0.

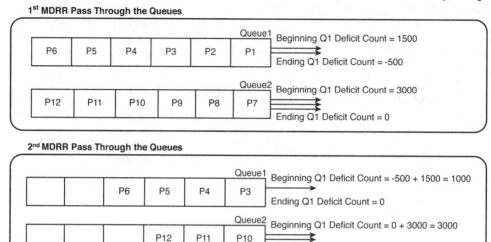

**Figure 4-7**  *MDRR: Making Up Deficits*

That concludes the first round-robin pass through the queues. MDRR has taken 2000 bytes from queue 1 and 3000 bytes from queue 2, giving the queues 40 percent and 60 percent of link bandwidth, respectively.

In the second round-robin pass, shown in the lower half of Figure 4-7, the process begins by MDRR adding the QV for each queue to the DC for each queue. Queue 1's DC becomes 1500 + (–500), or 1000, to begin the second pass. During this pass, MDRR takes P3 from queue 1, decrements DC to 0, and then moves on to queue 2. After taking three more packets from queue 3, decrementing queue 2's DC to 0, MDRR completes the second pass. Over these two round-robin passes, MDRR has taken 3000 bytes from queue 1 and 6000 bytes from queue 2—which is the same ratio as the ratio between the QVs. In other words, MDRR has exactly achieved the configured bandwidth ratio between the two queues.

The deficit feature of MDRR provides a means that, over time, gives each queue a guaranteed bandwidth based on the following formula:

$$\frac{\text{QV for Queue X}}{\text{Sum of All QVs}}$$

For additional examples of the operation of the MDRR deficit feature, refer to www.cisco.com/warp/public/63/toc_18841.html. Alternatively, you can go to Cisco.com and search for "Understanding and Configuring MDRR and WRED on the Cisco 12000 Series Internet Router."

# LAN Switch Congestion Management and Avoidance

This section looks at the ingress and egress queuing features on Cisco 3560 switches.

## Cisco Switch Ingress Queuing

Cisco 3560 switches perform both ingress and egress queuing. They have two ingress queues, one of which can be configured as a priority queue. The ingress queues in the Cisco 3560 use a method called *weighted tail drop*, or WTD, to set discard thresholds for each queue.

This section addresses the details of ingress queuing features.

The 3560 packet scheduler uses a method called *shared round-robin (SRR)* to control the rates at which packets are sent from the ingress queues to the internal switch fabric. In shared mode, SRR shares the bandwidth between the two queues according to the weights that you configure. Bandwidth for each queue is guaranteed, but it is not limited. If one queue is empty and the other has packets, that queue is allowed to use all the bandwidth. SRR uses weights that are relative rather than absolute—only the ratios affect the frequency of dequeuing. SRR's shared operation is much like CBWFQ configured for percentages rather than bandwidth.

If you plan to configure ingress queuing on your switches, you must determine the following:

- Which traffic to put in each queue. By default, COS 5 traffic is placed in queue 2, and all other traffic is in queue 1. Traffic can also be mapped to queues based on DSCP value.

- Whether some traffic needs priority treatment. If so, you will need to configure one of the queues as a priority queue.

- How much bandwidth and buffer space to allocate to each queue to achieve the traffic split you need.

- Whether the default WTD thresholds are appropriate for your traffic. The default treatment is to drop packets when the queue is 100 percent full. Each queue can have three different points, or thresholds, at which it drops traffic.

### Creating a Priority Queue

Either of the two ingress queues can be configured as a priority queue. You would usually use a priority queue for voice traffic to ensure that it is forwarded ahead of other traffic to reduce latency. To enable ingress priority queuing, use the **mls qos srr-queue input priority-queue** *queue-id* **bandwidth** *weight* command. The *weight* parameter defines the percentage of the link's bandwidth that can be consumed by the priority queue when there is competing traffic in the nonpriority queue.

For example, consider a case with queue 2 as the priority queue, with a configured bandwidth of 20 percent. If frames have been coming in only queue 1 for a while and then some frames arrive in queue 2, the scheduler would finish servicing the current frame from queue 1 but then immediately start servicing queue 2. It would take frames from queue 2 up to the bandwidth configured with the *weight* command. It would then share the remaining bandwidth between the two queues.

Example 4-4 begins by showing the default CoS-to-input-queue and DSCP-to-input-queue assignments. The defaults include the mapping of CoS 5 to queue 2 and drop threshold 1, and CoS 6 to queue 1, threshold 1. The example then shows the configuration of queue 2 as a priority queue, and the mapping of CoS 6 to input queue 2.

**Example 4-4** *Mapping Traffic to Input Queues and Creating a Priority Queue*

```
sw2# show mls qos maps cos-input-q
  Cos-inputq-threshold map:
               cos:  0   1   2   3   4   5   6   7
               ------------------------------------
  queue-threshold:  1-1 1-1 1-1 1-1 1-1 2-1 1-1 1-1
!
sw2# show mls qos maps dscp-input-q
  Dscp-inputq-threshold map:
     d1 :d2    0     1     2     3     4     5     6     7     8     9
     -----------------------------------------------------------------
      0 :     01-01 01-01 01-01 01-01 01-01 01-01 01-01 01-01 01-01 01-01
      1 :     01-01 01-01 01-01 01-01 01-01 01-01 01-01 01-01 01-01 01-01
      2 :     01-01 01-01 01-01 01-01 01-01 01-01 01-01 01-01 01-01 01-01
      3 :     01-01 01-01 01-01 01-01 01-01 01-01 01-01 01-01 01-01 01-01
      4 :     02-01 02-01 02-01 02-01 02-01 02-01 02-01 02-01 01-01 01-01
      5 :     01-01 01-01 01-01 01-01 01-01 01-01 01-01 01-01 01-01 01-01
      6 :     01-01 01-01 01-01 01-01
!
sw2# conf t
sw2(config)# mls qos srr-queue input cos-map queue 2 6
!
sw2(config)# mls qos srr-queue input priority-queue 2 bandwidth 20
!
sw2# show mls qos maps cos-input-q
Cos-inputq-threshold map:
               cos:  0   1   2   3   4   5   6   7
               ------------------------------------
  queue-threshold:  1-1 1-1 1-1 1-1 1-1 2-1 2-1 1-1
```

Next, you will allocate the ratio by which to divide the ingress buffers to the two queues using the **mls qos srr-queue input buffers** *percentage1 percentage2* command. By default, 90 percent of the buffers are assigned to queue 1 and 10 percent to queue 2. In addition, you need to configure the bandwidth percentage for each queue. This sets the frequency at which the scheduler takes packets from the two buffers, using the **mls qos srr-queue input bandwidth** *weight1 weight2* command. The default bandwidth values are 4 and 4, which divides traffic evenly between the two queues. (Although the command uses the **bandwidth** keyword, the parameters are just relative weightings and do not represent any particular bit rate.) These two commands, together, determine how much data the switch can buffer and send before it begins dropping packets.

When QoS is enabled on a Cisco 3560 switch, the default ingress queue settings are as follows:

- Queue 2 is the priority queue.

- Queue 2 is allocated 10 percent of the interface bandwidth.

- CoS 5 traffic is placed in queue 2.

### Cisco 3560 Congestion Avoidance

The Cisco 3560 uses a congestion avoidance method known as *weighted tail drop*, or WTD. WTD is turned on by default when QoS is enabled on the switch. It creates three thresholds per queue, based on CoS value, for tail drop when the associated queue reaches a particular percentage.

Because traffic in the priority queue is usually UDP traffic, you will probably leave that at the default of dropping at 100 percent. But in the other queue, you might want to drop less business-critical traffic more aggressively than others. For example, you can configure threshold 1 so that it drops traffic with CoS values of 0–3 when the queue reaches 40 percent full, threshold 2 so that it drops traffic with CoS 4 and 5 at 60 percent full, and finally threshold 3 drops CoS 6 and 7 traffic only when the queue is 100 percent full. The behavior of threshold 3 cannot be changed; it always drops traffic when the queue is 100 percent full. Figure 4-8 shows this behavior.

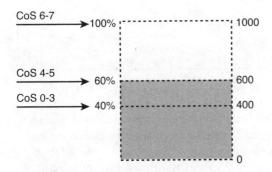

**Figure 4-8**  *WTD Configuration in Graphical Form*

Because WTD is configurable separately for all six queues in the 3560 (two ingress, four egress), a great deal of granularity is possible in 3560 configuration (maybe even *too* much!).

Notice in Example 4-4 that each CoS and DSCP is mapped by default to drop threshold 1. If you are trusting CoS, and thus queue traffic based on the received CoS value, use the command **mls qos srr-queue input cos-map threshold** *threshold-id cos1 ... cos8* to assign specific CoS values to a specific threshold. If you trust DSCP, use the command **mls qos srr-queue input dscp-map threshold** *threshold-id dscp1 ... dscp8* to assign up to eight DSCP values to a threshold. To configure the tail drop percentages for each threshold, use the command **mls qos srr-queue input threshold** *queue-id threshold-percentage1 threshold-percentage2*. Example4-5 builds on the configuration in Example 4-4, adding configuration of the buffers, bandwidth, and drop thresholds.

**Example 4-5** *Configuring Ingress Queue Buffers, Bandwidth, and Drop Thresholds*

```
!Configure the buffers for input interface queues 1 and 2
sw2(config)# mls qos srr-queue input buffers 80 20
!
!Configure the relative queue weights
sw2(config)# mls qos srr-queue input bandwidth 3 1
!
!Configure the two WTD thresholds for queue 1, and map traffic to each
!threshold based on its CoS value
sw2(config)# mls qos srr-queue input threshold 1 40 60
sw2(config)# mls qos srr-queue input cos-map threshold 1 0 1 2 3
sw2(config)# mls qos srr-queue input cos-map threshold 2 4 5
sw2(config)# mls qos srr-queue input cos-map threshold 3 6 7
!
!Verify the configuration
sw2# show mls qos input-queue
Queue      :      1       2
-----------------------------------------------
buffers    :     80      20
bandwidth  :      3       1
priority   :      0      20
threshold1:      40     100
threshold2:      60     100
```

With the configuration in Examples 4-4 and 4-5, the switch will place traffic with CoS values of 5 and 6 into queue 2, which is a priority queue. It will take traffic from the priority queue based on its weight configured in the **priority-queue bandwidth** statement. It will then divide traffic between queues 1 and 2 based on the relative weights configured in the **input bandwidth** statement. Traffic in queue 1 has WTD thresholds of 40, 60, and 100 percent. Traffic with CoS values 0–3 are in threshold 1, with a WTD drop percent of 40. Traffic with CoS values 4 and 5 are in threshold 2, with a WTD drop percent of 60. CoS values 6 and 7 are in threshold 3, which has a nonconfigurable drop percent of 100.

**Note**   The ingress QoS commands are given at the global configuration mode, so they apply to all interfaces.

## Cisco 3560 Switch Egress Queuing

The concepts of egress queuing are similar to ingress. There are four queues per interface rather than two, but you can configure which CoS and DCSP values are mapped to those queues, the relative weight of each queue, and the drop thresholds of each. You can configure a priority queue, but it must be queue 1. WTD is used for the queues, and thresholds can be configured as with ingress queuing. One difference between the two is that many of the egress commands are given at the interface, whereas the ingress commands were global.

A key difference between the ingress and egress queues is that the 3560 has a shaping feature that slows egress traffic. This can help prevent some types of denial of service (DoS) attacks and provides the means to implement subrate speed for Metro Ethernet implementations.

The Cisco 3560 uses a relatively simple classification scheme, assuming that you consider only what happens when the forwarding decision has been made. These switches make most internal QoS decisions based on an *internal DSCP* setting. The internal DSCP is determined when the frame is forwarded. So, when a frame has been assigned an internal DSCP and an egress interface, the following logic determines into which of the four interface output queues the frame is placed:

**Key Topic**

1. The frame's internal DSCP is compared to a global DSCP-to-CoS map to determine a CoS value.

2. The per-interface CoS-to-queue map determines the queue for a frame based on the assigned CoS.

This section focuses on the scheduler, assuming that frames have been classified and placed into the four output queues. In particular, the 3560 has two options for the scheduler, both using the acronym SRR: shared round-robin and shaped round-robin. The key differences between the two schedulers is that while both help to prevent queue starvation when a priority queue exists, the shaped option also rate-limits (shapes) the queues so that they do not exceed the configured percentage of the link's bandwidth.

To see the similarities and differences, it is helpful to think about both options without a PQ and with two scenarios: first, with all four queues holding plenty of frames, and second, with only one queue holding frames.

In the first case, with all four output queues holding several frames, both shared and shaped modes work the same. Both use the configuration of weights for each queue, with the queues serviced proportionally based on the weights. The following two commands configure the weights, depending on which type of scheduling is desired on the interface:

```
srr-queue bandwidth share weight1 weight2 weight3 weight4
srr-queue bandwidth shape weight1 weight2 weight3 weight4
```

For example, with the default weights of 25 for each queue in shared mode, still assuming that all four queues contain frames, the switch would service each queue equally.

The two schedulers' operations differ, however, when the queues are not all full. Consider a second scenario, with frames only in one queue with a weight of 25 (default) in that queue. With shared scheduling, the switch would keep servicing this single queue with that queue getting all the link's bandwidth. However, with shaped scheduling, the switch would purposefully wait to service the queue, not sending any data out the interface so that the queue would receive only its configured percentage of link bandwidth—25 percent in this scenario.

Next, consider the inclusion of queue 1 as the priority queue. First, consider a case where queues 2, 3, and 4 all have frames, queue 1 has no frames, and then some frames arrive in the egress PQ. The switch completes its servicing of the current frame but then transitions over to serve the PQ. However, instead of starving the other queues, while all the queues have frames waiting to exit the queues, the scheduler limits the bandwidth used for the PQ to the configured bandwidth. However, this limiting queues the excess rather than discarding the excess. (In this scenario, the behavior is the same in both shaped and shared mode.)

Finally, to see the differences between shared and shaped modes, imagine that the PQ still has many frames to send, but queues 2, 3, and 4 are now empty. In shared mode, the PQ would send at full line rate. In shaped mode, the switch would simply not service the PQ part of the time so that its overall rate would be the bandwidth configured for that queue.

Hopefully, these examples help demonstrate some of the similarities and differences between the SRR scheduler in shaped and shared modes. The following list summarizes the key points:

- Both shared and shaped mode scheduling attempt to service the queues in proportion to their configured bandwidths when more than one queue holds frames.

- Both shared and shaped mode schedulers service the PQ as soon as possible if at first the PQ is empty but then frames arrive in the PQ.

- Both shared and shaped mode schedulers prevent the PQ from exceeding its configured bandwidth when all the other queues have frames waiting to be sent.

- The shaped scheduler never allows any queue, PQ or non-PQ, to exceed its configured percentage of link bandwidth, even if that means that link sits idle.

**Note**   The 3560 supports the ability to configure shared mode scheduling on some queues, and shaped mode on others, on a single interface. The difference in operation is that the queues in shaped mode never exceed their configured bandwidth setting.

Mapping DSCP or CoS values to queues is done in global configuration mode, as with ingress queuing. Each interface belongs to one of two egress *queue-sets*. Buffer and

WTD threshold configurations are done in global configuration mode for each queue-set. Bandwidth weights, shaped or shared mode, and priority queuing are configured per interface.

Example 4-6 shows an egress queue configuration. Buffers and the WTD thresholds for one of the queues are changed for queue-set 1. Queue-set 1 is assigned to an interface, which then has sharing configured for queue 2 with a new command: **srr-queue band-width share** *weight1 weight2 weight3 weight4*. Shaping is configured for queues 3 and 4 with the similar command **srr-queue bandwidth shape** *weight1 weight2 weight3 weight4*. Queue 1 is configured as a priority queue. When you configure the priority queue, the switch ignores any bandwidth values assigned to the priority queue in the **share** or **shape** commands. The 3560 also gives the ability to rate-limit the interface bandwidth with the command **srr-queue bandwidth limit** *percent*. In this example, the interface is limited by default to using 75 percent of its bandwidth.

**Example 4-6**  *Egress Queue Configuration*

```
sw2(config)# mls qos queue-set output 1 buffers 40 20 30 10
!
sw2(config)# mls qos queue-set output 1 threshold 2 40 60 100 100
!
sw2(config)# int fa 0/2
sw2(config-if)# queue-set 1
sw2(config-if)# srr-queue bandwidth share 10 10 1 1
sw2(config-if)# srr-queue bandwidth shape 10 0 20 20
sw2(config-if)# priority-queue out
!
sw2# show mls qos int fa 0/2 queueing
FastEthernet0/2
Egress Priority Queue : enabled
Shaped queue weights (absolute) :  10 0 20 20
Shared queue weights  :  10 10 1 1
The port bandwidth limit : 75   (Operational Bandwidth:75.0)
The port is mapped to qset : 1
```

# Resource Reservation Protocol (RSVP)

RSVP is an IETF protocol that is unique among the quality of service (QoS) methods in that it can reserve end-to-end resources for the length of the data flow. The QoS techniques covered so far allocate bandwidth or prioritize traffic at an individual router or switch interface. The actual treatment of a packet can vary from router to router based on the interface congestion when the packet arrives and on each router's configuration. Previous techniques are concerned with providing quality of service to individual frames or packets, rather than traffic flows.

When RSVP is used, each RSVP-enabled router along the path reserves bandwidth and the requested QoS for the duration of that flow. Reservations are made on a flow-by-flow basis, so each has its own reservation. In addition, reservations are unidirectional; one is made from source to destination, and another must be made from destination back to the source. RSVP is typically used in networks that have limited bandwidth and frequent congestion. It is most appropriate for traffic that cannot tolerate much delay or packet loss, such as voice and video.

## RSVP Process Overview

Some applications and devices are RSVP aware and initiate their own reservations. More typically, the gateways act in proxy for the devices, creating a reserved path between them. Figure 4-9 shows how a reservation is created. Reservations are made per direction per flow; a flow is identified in RSVP by a destination IP address, protocol ID, and destination port. One reservation is made from terminating to originating gateway, and another reservation is made from originating to terminating gateway.

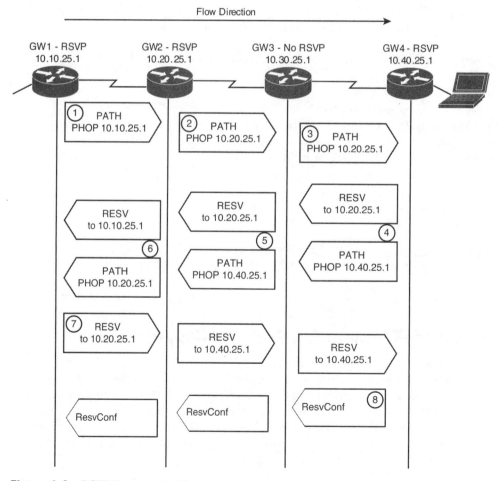

**Figure 4-9**  *RSVP Reservation Process*

In Figure 4-9, neither endpoint application is RSVP aware. The RSVP reservation setup proceeds as follows:

1.  Router GW1 receives the first packet in a flow that needs a reservation made for it. GW1 sends an RSVP PATH message toward the destination IP address. PATH messages contain the IP address of the previous hop (PHOP) so that return messages can follow the same path back. They also describe the bandwidth and QoS needs of the traffic.

2.  The next-hop router, GW2, is configured with RSVP. It records the previous-hop information and forwards the PATH message on. Notice that it inserts its IP address as the previous hop. The destination address is unchanged.

3.  The third router, GW3, does not have RSVP configured. The PATH message looks just like an IP packet to this router, and it will route the message untouched toward the destination, just as it would any IP packet.

4.  When the fourth router, GW4, receives the PATH message, it replies with a reservation (RESV) message to the previous-hop address listed in the PATH message. This RESV message requests the needed QoS. If any router along the way does not have sufficient resources, it returns an error message and discards the RSVP message. GW4 also initiates a PATH message toward GW1, to reserve resources in the other direction.

5.  The RESV and PATH messages again look like normal IP packets to GW3, the non-RSVP router, so it just routes the packets toward GW2. No resources are reserved on this gateway.

6.  GW2 receives the RESV message and checks to see whether it can supply the requested resources. If the check succeeds, it creates a reservation for that flow, and then forwards the RESV message to the previous-hop IP address listed in the PATH message it received earlier. When the other PATH message arrives, GW2 processes it and sends it on to GW1.

7.  When GW1 receives the RESV message, it knows that its reservation has succeeded. However, a reservation must be made in each direction for QoS to be provided to traffic flowing in both directions.

8.  GW1 responds to the second PATH message with an RESV message, which proceeds through the network as before. When GW4 receives the RESV message, resources have been reserved in both directions. GW4 responds with a ResvConf message, confirming the reservation.

Data transmission has been delayed during the exchange of messages. When GW1 receives the ResvConf message, it knows that reservations have been made in both directions. Traffic can now proceed. RSVP will send periodic refresh messages along the call path, enabling it to dynamically adjust to network changes.

## Configuring RSVP

Before configuring RSVP, decide how much bandwidth to allocate per flow and how much total bandwidth to allow RSVP to use, per interface. Remember to allow bandwidth for all other applications that will use that interface.

RSVP must be configured on each router that will create reservations, and at each interface the traffic will traverse. It is enabled at the interface configuration mode with the **ip rsvp bandwidth** *total-kbps single-flow-kbps* command. If you do not specify the total bandwidth to reserve, the router reserves 75 percent of the interface bandwidth. If no flow value is specified, any flow can reserve the entire bandwidth.

To set the DSCP value for RSVP control messages, use the interface command **ip rsvp signalling dscp** *dscp-value.*

It is not necessary to configure RSVP on every single router within the enterprise. Because RSVP messages are passed through non-RSVP-enabled routers, it can be used selectively. You might enable it in sections of the network prone to congestion, such as areas with low bandwidth. In the core of the network, where bandwidth is higher, you might rely on LLQ/CBWFQ to handle the traffic. This helps in scaling RSVP, cutting down on the number of routers that must track each session and be involved in RSVP messaging.

Figure 4-10 shows a network with remote sites connecting to a core IP WAN. The core might be enterprise owned or it might be a service provider's multiprotocol packet label switched (MPLS) network, for example. The remote site links are all T1 and carry both voice and data. WAN interfaces of the remote site routers are all configured for RSVP. Bandwidth will be reserved when they send data between each other. When traffic goes across the core IP WAN, reservations will be made on the WAN interfaces of the edge routers based on resources available on the remote site routers. The core will not participate in RSVP, so other means of QoS must be done there.

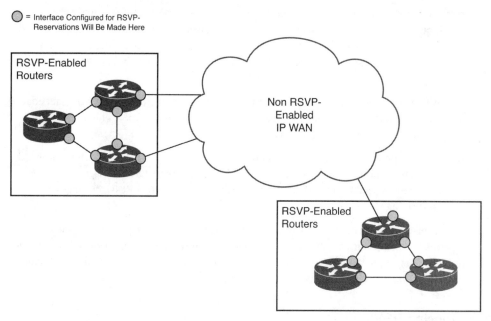

**Figure 4-10**   *Using RSVP in a Larger Network*

## Using RSVP for Voice Calls

RSVP reserves resources, but it is up to each router to implement the appropriate QoS techniques to deliver those resources. Low-latency queuing (LLQ) is the QoS mechanism typically used for voice, putting voice in a priority queue with guaranteed but policed bandwidth. This is part of the DiffServ model of QoS. However, RSVP has its own set of queues that it puts reserved traffic into by default. These queues have a low weight, but they are not prioritized. What is needed is a way to put reserved voice traffic into the low-latency queue.

By default, RSVP uses weighted fair queuing (WFQ) to provide its QoS. When using LLQ with class-based weighted fair queuing (CBWFQ), disable RSVP's use of WFQ with the interface command **ip rsvp resource-provider none**. Also, by default, RSVP will attempt to process every packet (not just voice traffic). Turn this off with the interface command **ip rsvp data-packet classification none**. LLQ and CBWFQ should be configured as usual. RSVP will then reserve bandwidth for voice calls, and the gateway's QoS processes will place voice traffic into the priority queue.

> **Note** When you are using LLQ, the priority queue size includes Layer 2 overhead. RSVP's bandwidth statement does not take Layer 2 overhead into consideration. Therefore, when using both LLQ and RSVP, be sure to set the RSVP bandwidth equal to the Priority Queue minus the Layer 2 overhead.

Example 4-7 shows RSVP configured on an interface. This interface uses CBWFQ with an LLQ, so RSVP is configured appropriately.

**Example 4-7** *Configuring RSVP*

```
R4(config)# int s0/1/0
R4(config-if)# ip rsvp bandwidth 128 64
R4(config-if)# ip rsvp signalling dscp 40
R4(config-if)# ip rsvp resource-provider none
R4(config-if)# ip rsvp data-packet classification none
R4(config-if)# service-policy output LLQ
!
!The next two commands verify the interface RSVP
!configuration.
R4# show ip rsvp interface
interface    allocated  i/f max  flow max sub max
Se0/1/0      0          128K     64K      0
!
R4# show ip rsvp interface detail
 Se0/1/0:
   Interface State: Down
   Bandwidth:
     Curr allocated: 0 bits/sec
```

```
        Max. allowed (total): 128K bits/sec
        Max. allowed (per flow): 64K bits/sec
        Max. allowed for LSP tunnels using sub-pools: 0 bits/sec
        Set aside by policy (total): 0 bits/sec
     Admission Control:
        Header Compression methods supported:
           rtp (36 bytes-saved), udp (20 bytes-saved)
     Traffic Control:
        RSVP Data Packet Classification is OFF
        RSVP resource provider is: none
     Signalling:
        DSCP value used in RSVP msgs: 0x28
        Number of refresh intervals to enforce blockade state: 4
        Number of missed refresh messages: 4
        Refresh interval: 30
     Authentication: disabled
```

# Foundation Summary

Please take the time to read and study the details in the "Foundation Topics" section of the chapter, as well as review the items in the "Foundation Topics" section noted with a Key Topic icon.

# Memory Builders

The CCIE Routing and Switching written exam, like all Cisco CCIE written exams, covers a fairly broad set of topics. This section provides some basic tools to help you exercise your memory about some of the broader topics covered in this chapter.

## Fill In Key Tables from Memory

Appendix E, "Key Tables for CCIE Study," on the CD in the back of this book, contains empty sets of some of the key summary tables in each chapter. Print Appendix E, refer to this chapter's tables in it, and fill in the tables from memory. Refer to Appendix F, "Solutions for Key Tables for CCIE Study," on the CD, to check your answers.

## Definitions

Next, take a few moments to write down the definitions for the following terms:

> class-based weighted fair queuing, low-latency queuing, weighted round-robin, modified deficit round-robin, shared round-robin, shared mode, shaped mode, WTD, WRR, quantum value, alternate mode, tail drop, full drop, priority queue, sequence number, finish time, modified tail drop, scheduler, queue starvation, strict priority, software queue, hardware queue, remaining bandwidth, maximum reserved bandwidth, actual queue depth, average queue depth, minimum threshold, maximum threshold, mark probability denominator, exponential weighting constant, expedite queue, DSCP-to-CoS map, DSCP-to-threshold map, internal DSCP, differentiated tail drop, AutoQoS, RSVP

Refer to the glossary to check your answers.

## Further Reading

*Cisco QoS Exam Certification Guide*, Second Edition, by Wendell Odom and Michael Cavanaugh.

*Cisco Catalyst QoS: Quality of Service in Campus Networks*, by Mike Flanagan, Richard Froom, and Kevin Turek.

Cisco.com includes a great deal more information on the very detailed aspects of 3560 QoS configuration, including SRR and WTD, at www.cisco.com/en/US/partner/docs/ switches/lan/catalyst3560/software/release/12.2_52_se/configuration/guide/swqos.html.

**Blueprint topics covered in this chapter:**

This chapter covers the following subtopics from the Cisco CCIE Routing and Switching written exam blueprint. Refer to the full blueprint in Table I-1 in the Introduction for more details on the topics covered in each chapter and their context within the blueprint.

- Marking
- Shaping
- Policing
- Hierarchical QoS
- Troubleshooting Quality of Service (QoS)

# Shaping, Policing, and Link Fragmentation

Traffic-shaping tools delay packets exiting a router so that the overall bit rate does not exceed a defined shaping rate. This chapter covers the concepts behind IOS traffic shaping mechanisms like Class-Based Shaping (CB Shaping).

Traffic policers measure bit rates for packets either entering or exiting an interface. If the defined rate is exceeded, the policer either discards enough packets so that the rate is not exceeded or marks some packets such that the packets are more likely to be discarded later. This chapter covers the concepts and configuration behind Class-Based Policing (CB Policing), with a brief mention of committed access rate (CAR).

## "Do I Know This Already?" Quiz

Table 5-1 outlines the major headings in this chapter and the corresponding "Do I Know This Already?" quiz questions.

**Table 5-1** *"Do I Know This Already?" Foundation Topics Section-to-Question Mapping*

| Foundation Topics Section | Questions Covered in This Section | Score |
|---|---|---|
| Traffic-Shaping Concepts | 1–2 | |
| Generic Traffic Shaping | 3 | |
| Class-Based Shaping Configuration | 4–5 | |
| Policing Concepts and Configuration | 6–7 | |
| QoS Troubleshooting and Commands | 8 | |
| Total Score | | |

To best use this pre-chapter assessment, remember to score yourself strictly. You can find the answers in Appendix A, "Answers to the 'Do I Know This Already?' Quizzes."

1. When does Class-Based Shaping add tokens to its token bucket, and how many tokens does it add when Bc and Be are both set to something larger than 0?

   a. Upon the arrival of each packet, a pro-rated portion of Bc is added to the token bucket.

   b. Upon the arrival of each packet, a pro-rated portion of Bc + Be is added to the token bucket.

   c. At the beginning of each time interval, Bc worth of tokens are added to the token bucket.

   d. At the beginning of each time interval, Bc + Be worth of tokens are added to the token bucket.

   e. None of the answers is correct.

2. If shaping was configured with a rate of 128 kbps and a Bc of 3200 bits, what value would be calculated for Tc?

   a. 125 ms

   b. 125 sec

   c. 25 ms

   d. 25 sec

   e. Shaping doesn't use a Tc.

   f. Not enough information is provided to tell.

3. Which of the following statements about Generic Traffic Shaping are true?

   a. The configuration can be created once and then used for multiple interfaces.

   b. It is not supported on ATM interfaces.

   c. It must be configured under each individual interface or subinterface where shaping is required.

   d. You can specify which traffic will be shaped and which will not.

   e. It supports adaptive traffic shaping.

**4.** Which of the following commands, when typed in the correct configuration mode, enables CB Shaping to be 128 kbps?

   **a.** shape average 128000 8000 0

   **b.** shape average 128 8000 0

   **c.** shape average 128000

   **d.** shape peak 128000 8000 0

   **e.** shape peak 128 8000 0

   **f.** shape peak 128000

**5.** Examine the following configuration, noting the locations of the comment lines labeled point 1, point 2, and so on. Assume that a correctly configured policy map that implements CBWFQ, called **queue-it**, is also configured but not shown. To enable CBWFQ for the packets queued by CB Shaping, what command is required, and at what point in the configuration is the command required?

```
policy-map shape-question
! point 1
 class class-default
! point 2
   shape average 256000 5120
! point 3
interface serial 0/0
! point 4
   service-policy output shape-question
! point 5
interface s0/0.1 point-to-point
! point 6
   ip address 1.1.1.1
! point 7
```

   **a.** service-policy queue-it, at point 1

   **b.** service-policy queue-it, at point 3

   **c.** service-policy queue-it, at point 5

   **d.** shape queue service-policy queue-it, at point 1

   **e.** shape queue service-policy queue-it, at point 3

   **f.** shape queue service-policy queue-it, at point 6

**6.** Which of the following commands, when typed in the correct configuration mode, enables CB Policing at 128 kbps, with no excess burst?

   **a.** police 128000 conform-action transmit exceed-action transmit violate-action drop

   **b.** police 128 conform-action transmit exceed-action transmit violate-action drop

   **c.** police 128000 conform-action transmit exceed-action drop

   **d.** police 128 conform-action transmit exceed-action drop

   **e.** police 128k conform-action transmit exceed-action drop

**7.** Which of the following features of CB Policing are not supported by CAR?

   **a.** The capability to categorize packets as conforming, exceeding, and violating a traffic contract

   **b.** The capability to police all traffic at one rate, and subsets of that same traffic at other rates

   **c.** The capability to configure policing using MQC commands

   **d.** The capability to police input or output packets on an interface

**8.** To troubleshoot a suspected QoS issue, you need to see the QoS policy configured on an interface along with which queues are filling up and dropping packets. Which of the following commands will display that information?

   **a.** show policy-map interface *interface*

   **b.** show queue *interface*

   **c.** show queue-list interface *interface*

   **d.** show ip policy interface *interface*

# Foundation Topics

## Traffic-Shaping Concepts

Traffic shaping prevents the bit rate of the packets exiting an interface from exceeding a configured shaping rate. To do so, the shaper monitors the bit rate at which data is being sent. If the configured rate is exceeded, the shaper delays packets, holding the packets in a *shaping queue*. The shaper then releases packets from the queue such that, over time, the overall bit rate does not exceed the shaping rate.

Traffic shaping solves two general types of problems that can occur in multiaccess networks. First, if a service provider purposefully discards any traffic on a VC when the traffic rate exceeds the committed information rate (CIR), it makes sense for the router to not send traffic faster than the CIR.

Egress blocking is the second type of problem for which shaping provides some relief. *Egress blocking* occurs when a router sends data into an ATM service, and the egress switch has to queue the data before it can be sent out to the router on the other end of the VC. For example, when a T1-connected router sends data, it must be sent at T1 speed. If the router on the other end of the VC has a link clocked at 256 kbps, the frames/cells will start to back up in the output queue of the egress switch. Likewise, if that same T1 site has VCs to 20 remote sites, and each remote site uses a 256-kbps link, when all 20 remote sites send at about the same time, frames/cells will be queued, waiting to exit the WAN egress switch to the T1 router. In this case, shaping can be used to essentially prevent egress queuing, moving the packets back into a queue in the router, where they can then be manipulated with fancy queuing tools.

### Shaping Terminology

Routers can send bits out an interface only at the physical clock rate. To average sending at a lower rate, the router has to alternate between sending packets and being silent. For example, to average sending at a packet rate of half the physical link speed, the router should send packets half of the time and not send packets the other half of the time. Over time, it looks like a staccato series of sending and silence. Figure 5-1 shows a graph of what happens when a router has a link with a clock rate of 128 kbps and a shaper configured to shape traffic to 64 kbps.

Figure 5-1 shows the sending rate and implies quite a bit about how Cisco IOS implements shaping. A shaper sets a static time interval, called *Tc*. Then, it calculates the number of bits that can be sent in the Tc interval such that, over time, the number of bits/second sent matches the shaping rate.

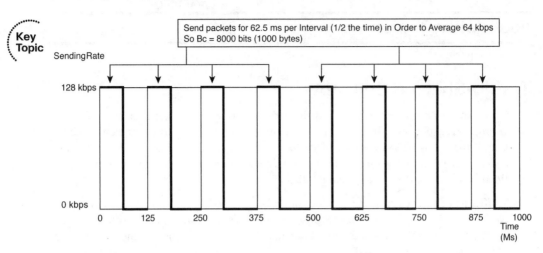

**Figure 5-1** *Mechanics of Traffic Shaping—128-kbps Access Rate, 64-kbps Shaped Rate*

The number of bits that can be sent in each Tc is called the *committed burst (Bc)*. In Figure 5-1, an 8000-bit Bc can be sent in every 125-ms Tc to achieve a 64-kbps average rate. In other words, with a Tc of 125 ms, there will be eight Tc intervals per second. If Bc bits (8000) are sent each Tc, eight sets of 8000 bits will be sent each second, resulting in a rate of 64,000 bps.

Because the bits must be encoded on the link at the clock rate, the 8000 bits in each interval require only 62.5 ms (8000/128,000) to exit the interface onto the link. The graph shows the results: The interface sends at the line rate (access rate) for 62.5 ms, and then waits for 62.5 ms, while packets sit in the shaping queue.

Table 5-2 lists the terminology related to this shaping model. Note in particular that the term *CIR* refers to the traffic rate for a VC based on a business contract, and *shaping rate* refers to the rate configured for a shaper on a router.

**Table 5-2** *Shaping Terminology*

| Term | Definition |
|------|------------|
| Tc | Time interval, measured in milliseconds, over which the committed burst (Bc) can be sent. With many shaping tools, Tc = Bc/CIR. |
| Bc | Committed burst size, measured in bits. This is the amount of traffic that can be sent during the Tc interval. Typically defined in the traffic contract. |
| CIR | Committed information rate, in bits per second, which defines the rate of a VC according to the business contract. |
| Shaped rate | The rate, in bits per second, to which a particular configuration wants to shape the traffic. It might or might not be set to the CIR. |
| Be | Excess burst size, in bits. This is the number of bits beyond Bc that can be sent after a period of inactivity. |

## Shaping with an Excess Burst

To accommodate bursty data traffic, shapers implement a concept by which, after a period in which an interface sends relatively little data compared to its CIR, more than Bc bits can be sent in one or more time intervals. This concept is called *excess burst (Be)*. When using a Be, the shaper can allow, in addition to the Bc bits per Tc, Be extra bits to be sent. Depending on the settings, it might take one time interval to send the extra bits, or it might require multiple time intervals. Figure 5-2 shows a graph of the same example in Figure 5-1, but with a Be also equal to 8000 bits. In this case, the Be extra bits are all sent in the first time interval after the relative inactivity.

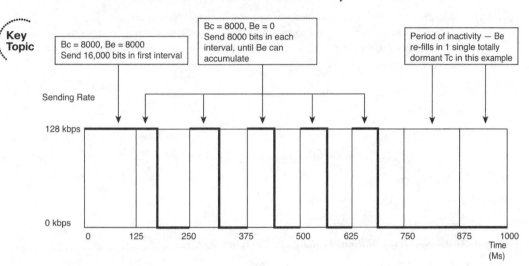

**Key Topic**

**Figure 5-2**  *Bc and Be, After a Period of Inactivity*

In the first interval, traffic shaping can send a total of 16,000 bits (Bc + Be bits). On a 128-kbps link, assuming a 125-ms Tc, all 125 ms is required to send 16,000 bits. In this particular case, after a period of inactivity, R1 sends continuously for the entire first interval. In the second interval, the shaper allows the usual Bc bits to be sent. In effect, with these settings, the shaper allows 187.5 ms of consecutive sending after a period of low activity.

## Underlying Mechanics of Shaping

Shapers apply a simple formula to the Tc, Bc, and shaping rate parameters:

**Key Topic**

Tc = Bc/shaping rate

For example, in Figures 5-1 and 5-2, if the shaping rate (64 kbps) and the Bc (8000 bits) were both configured, the shaper would then calculate the Tc as 8000/64,000 = 0.125 seconds. Alternatively, if the rate and Tc had been configured, the shaper would have calculated Bc as Bc = rate * Tc (a simple derivation of the formula listed earlier), or 64 kbps * 0.125 s = 8000 bits. (CB Shaping uses default values in some cases, as described in the configuration sections of this chapter.)

Traffic shaping uses a *token bucket* model to manage the shaping process. First, consider the case in which the shaper is not using Be. Imagine a bucket of size Bc, with the bucket filled with tokens at the beginning of each Tc. Each token lets the shaper buy the right to send 1 bit. So, at the beginning of each Tc, the shaper has the ability to release Bc worth of bits.

Shapers perform two main actions related to the bucket:

**1.**   Refill the bucket with new tokens at the beginning of each Tc.

**2.**   Spend tokens to gain the right to forward packets.

Step 1 describes how the bucket is filled with Bc tokens to start each interval. Figure 5-3 shows a visual representation of the process. Note that if some of the tokens from the previous time interval are still in the bucket, some of the new tokens spill over the side of the bucket and are wasted.

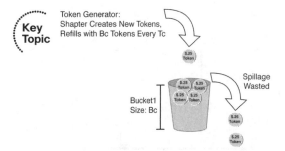

**Figure 5-3**   *Mechanics of Filling the Shaping Token Bucket*

Step 2 describes how the shaper spends the tokens. The shaper has to take tokens from the bucket equal to the number of bits in a packet to release that packet for transmission. For example, if the packet is 1000 bits long, the shaper must remove 1000 tokens from the bucket to send that packet. When traffic shaping tries to send a packet, and the bucket does not have enough tokens in it to buy the right to send the packet, traffic shaping must wait until the next interval, when the token bucket is refilled.

Traffic shaping implements Be by making the single token bucket bigger, with no other changes to the token-bucket model. In other words, only Bc tokens are added each Tc, and tokens must still be consumed to send packets. The key difference using Be (versus not using Be) is that when some of the tokens are left in the bucket at the end of the time interval, and Bc tokens are added at the beginning of the next interval, more than Bc tokens are in the bucket—therefore allowing a larger burst of bits in this new interval.

## Generic Traffic Shaping

In older versions of IOS, there was a concept of Generic Traffic Shaping (GTS) that functioned as a simple form of traffic shaping that was supported on most router interfaces but could not be used with flow switching. GTS was configured and applied to an interface or subinterface. In its basic configuration, it shaped all traffic leaving the interface. You could modify that behavior with an access list, permitting the traffic to be shaped and denying any traffic that should be passed through unshaped. We will entertain how this feature functioned in the IOS Release 12 train, to better understand how IOS Release 15 code's implementation of QoS mechanisms has changed.

GTS was enabled for all interface traffic with this interface-level command:

```
traffic-shape rate shaped-rate [Bc] [Be] [buffer-limit]
```

In this command, the shaped rate was specified in bps, the Bc was in bits, and the Be was in bits. The buffer limit set the maximum size of the queue buffer and was specified in bps. Only the shaped rate was required. If you did not specify the Bc or the Be, both would have been set to one-quarter of the shaped rate by default.

To limit the types of traffic that would be shaped, you could configure an access list that permitted that traffic and denied all other traffic. Then you would apply it to the GTS with the following command:

```
traffic-shape group access-list-number shaped-rate {Bc} {Be}
```

Example 5-1 shows a GTS example where Internet Control Message Protocol (ICMP) traffic would have been shaped to only 500 kbps. An access list was first created and then GTS was configured on the interface. The example also shows the output verification for this legacy command set.

**Example 5-1**   *Generic Traffic Shaping*

```
! Access list 101 permits ICMP.  All other traffic is denied by default.
access-list 101 permit icmp any any
!
! Generic Traffic Shaping is configured on the interface. The access list
! is associated with the shaping.  A CIR of 500 kbps is specified, but no
! Bc or Be.
interface fa 0/0
 traffic-shape group 101 500000
!
! The shaping configuration is verified. Note that the router has added a
! Bc and Be of 12 kb each. It has also calculated a Tc of 24 ms. This
! command also shows that shaping is not currently active.
R3# show traffic-shape fa 0/0

Interface   Fa0/0
    Access  Target Byte  Sustain  Excess    Interval  Increment  Adapt
VC  List    Rate   Limit bits/int bits/int  (ms)      (bytes)    Active
-   101     500000 3000  12000    12000     24        1500       -
!
! Once shaping is active, the statistics and queue information is shown in
!  the following two commands.
```

```
Router# show traffic-shape statistics
         Acc.    Queue   Packets  Bytes      Packets   Bytes      Shaping
I/F      List    Depth   Delayed  Delayed                         Active
Fa0/0    101     24      10542    14753352 10252       14523964   yes


Router# show traffic-shape queue
Traffic queued in shaping queue on FastEthernet0/0
 Traffic shape group: 101
  Queueing strategy: weighted fair
  Queueing Stats: 10/1000/64/0 (size/max total/threshold/drops)
     Conversations  2/3/32 (active/max active/max total)
     Reserved Conversations 0/0 (allocated/max allocated)
     Available Bandwidth 500 kilobits/sec

 (depth/weight/total drops/no-buffer drops/interleaves) 4/32384/0/0/0
 Conversation 16, linktype: ip, length: 1514
 source: 10.2.2.2, destination: 10.1.1.4, id: 0x014D, ttl: 255, prot: 1

 (depth/weight/total drops/no-buffer drops/interleaves) 6/32384/0/0/0
 Conversation 15, linktype: ip, length: 1514
 source: 10.2.2.2, destination: 10.1.1.3, id: 0x0204, ttl: 255, prot: 1
```

# Class-Based Shaping

Class-Based Shaping (CB Shaping) is the Cisco-recommended way to configure traffic shaping. It allows you to create class maps and policy maps once and then reuse them for multiple interfaces, rather than redoing the entire configuration under each individual interface. This lessens the likelihood of operator error or typos. CB Shaping also provides more granular control over the QoS operation.

Class-Based Shaping implements all the core concepts described so far in this chapter, plus several other important features. First, it allows several Cisco IOS queuing tools to be applied to the packets delayed by the shaping process. At the same time, it allows fancy queuing tools to be used on the interface software queues. It also allows classification of packets, so that some types of packets can be shaped at one rate, a second type of packet can be shaped at another rate, while allowing a third class of packets to not be shaped at all.

The only new MQC command required to configure CB Shaping is the **shape** command. The "Foundation Summary" section, later in this chapter, provides a CB Shaping command reference, in Table 5-10:

**shape** [**average** | **peak**] *mean-rate* [[*burst-size*] [*excess-burst-size*]]

CB Shaping can be implemented for output packets only, and it can be associated with either a physical interface or a subinterface.

To enable CB Shaping, the **service-policy output** command is configured under either the interface or the subinterface, with the referenced policy map including the **shape** command.

Example 5-2 shows a simple CB Shaping configuration that uses the following criteria:

- Interface clock rate is 128 kbps.

- Shape all traffic at a 64-kbps rate.

- Use the default setting for Tc.

- Shape traffic exiting subinterface s0/0.1.

- The software queuing on s0/0 will use WFQ (the default).

- The shaping queue will use FIFO (the default).

**Example 5-2**  *CB Shaping of All Traffic Exiting S0/0.1 at 64 kbps*

```
! Policy map shape-all places all traffic into the class-default class, matching
! all packets. All packets will be shaped to an average of 64 kbps. Note the
! units are in bits/second, so 64000 means 64 kbps.
policy-map shape-all
  class class-default
    shape average 64000
! The physical interface will not show the fair-queue command, but it is
! configured by default, implementing WFQ for interface s0/0/0 software queuing.
interface serial0/0/0
 bandwidth 128
! Below, CB Shaping has been enabled for all packets forwarded out s0/0/0.1.
interface serial0/0/0.1
 service-policy output shape-all
! Refer to the text after this example for more explanations of this next command.
R3# show policy-map interface s0/0/0.1
 Serial0/0/0.1

  Service-policy output: shape-all

    Class-map: class-default (match-any)
      1 packets, 328 bytes
      5 minute offered rate 0000 bps, drop rate 0000 bps
      Match: any
      Queueing
      queue limit 64 packets
      (queue depth/total drops/no-buffer drops) 0/0/0
      (pkts output/bytes output) 1/328
      shape (average) cir 64000, bc 256, be 256
      target shape rate 64000
```

The configuration itself is relatively straightforward. The **shape-all** policy map matches all packets in a single class (class-default) and is enabled on s0/0.1. So, all packets exiting s0/0.1 will be shaped to the defined rate of 64 kbps.

The output of the **show policy-map interface s0/0/0.1** command shows the settings for all the familiar shaping concepts, but it uses slightly different terminology. CB Shaping defaults to a Bc and Be of 256 bits each.

The CB Shaping **shape** command requires the shaping rate to be set. However, Bc and Be can be omitted, and Tc cannot be set directly. As a result, CB Shaping calculates some or all of these settings. CB Shaping calculates the values differently based on whether the shaping rate exceeds 320 kbps. Table 5-3 summarizes the rules.

**Table 5-3**  *CB Shaping Calculation of Default Variable Settings*

| Variable | Rate <= 320 kbps | Rate > 320 kbps |
| --- | --- | --- |
| Bc | 8000 bits | Bc = shaping rate * Tc |
| Be | Be = Bc = 8000 | Be = Bc |
| Tc | Tc = Bc/shaping rate | 25 ms |

### Tuning Shaping for Voice Using LLQ and a Small Tc

Example 5-2 in the previous section shows default settings for queuing for the interface software queues (WFQ) and for the shaping queue (FIFO). Example 5-3 shows an alternative configuration that works better for voice traffic by using low-latency queuing (LLQ) for the shaped traffic. Also, the configuration forces the Tc down to 10 ms, which means that each packet will experience only a short delay waiting for the beginning of the next Tc. By keeping Tc to a small value, the LLQ logic applied to the shaped packets does not have to wait nearly as long to release packets from the PQ, as compared with the default Tc settings.

The revised requirements, as compared with Example 5-2, are as follows:

■ Enable LLQ to support a single G.729 voice call.

■ Shape to 96 kbps—less than the clock rate (128 kbps), but more than the CIR of the VC.

■ Tune Tc to 10 ms.

**Example 5-3**  *CB Shaping on R3, 96-kbps Shape Rate, with LLQ for Shaping Queues*

```
class-map match-all voip-rtp
  match ip rtp 16384 16383
! queue-voip implements a PQ for VoIP traffic, and uses WFQ in the default class.
policy-map queue-voip
  class voip-rtp
```

```
   priority 32
 class class-default
  fair-queue
! shape-all shapes all traffic to 96 kbps, with Bc of 960. Tc is calculated as
! 960/96000 or 10 ms. Also note the service-policy queue-voip command. This applies
! policy map queue-voip to all packets shaped by the shape command.
policy-map shape-all
 class class-default
  shape average 96000 960
  service-policy queue-voip
!
interface serial0/0.1
 service-policy output shape-all
! Note the Interval is now listed as 10 ms. Also, note the detailed stats for LLQ
! are also listed at the end of the command.
R3# show policy-map interface serial 0/0.1
 Serial0/0.1

  Service-policy output: shape-all

    Class-map: class-default (match-any)
      5189 packets, 927835 bytes
      30 second offered rate 91000 bps, drop rate 0 bps
      Match: any
      Traffic Shaping
            Target/Average  Byte   Sustain   Excess    Interval  Increment
              Rate          Limit  bits/int  bits/int  (ms)      (bytes)
            96000/96000     1200   960       960       10        120


      Adapt   Queue    Packets   Bytes    Packets   Bytes     Shaping
      Active  Depth                       Delayed   Delayed   Active
       —       17       5172      910975   4002      831630    yes


    Service-policy : queue-voip
      Class-map: voip-rtp (match-all)
        4623 packets, 295872 bytes
        30 second offered rate 25000 bps, drop rate 0 bps
        Match: ip rtp 16384 16383
        Weighted Fair Queueing
          Strict Priority
          Output Queue: Conversation 24
          Bandwidth 32 (kbps) Burst 800 (Bytes)
          (pkts matched/bytes matched) 3528/225792
          (total drops/bytes drops) 0/0


      Class-map: class-default (match-any)
        566 packets, 631963 bytes
```

```
        30 second offered rate 65000 bps, drop rate 0 bps
        Match: any
        Weighted Fair Queueing
          Flow Based Fair Queueing
          Maximum Number of Hashed Queues 16
(total queued/total drops/no-buffer drops) 17/0/0
```

Example 5-3 shows how to use LLQ against the packets shaped by CB Shaping by calling an LLQ policy map with the **service-policy** command. Note that the command syntax (**service-policy queue-voip**) does not include the **output** keyword; the output direction is implied. Figure 5-4 shows the general idea behind what is happening in the configuration.

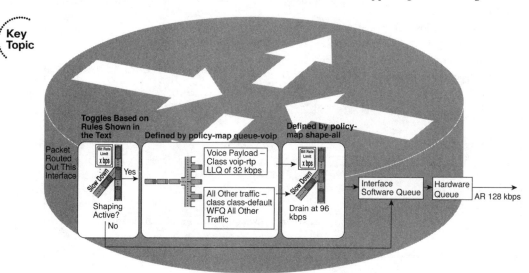

**Figure 5-4**  *Interaction Between Shaping Policy Map* **shape-all** *and Queuing Policy Map* **queue-voip**

Scanning Figure 5-4 from left to right, CB Shaping must make the first decision after a packet has been routed out the subinterface. CB Shaping first needs to decide whether shaping is active; if it is, CB Shaping should put the packet into a shaping queue. If it is not active, the packet can move right on to the appropriate interface software queue. Shaping becomes active only when a single packet exceeds the traffic contract; it becomes inactive again when all the shaping queues are drained.

Assuming that a packet needs to be delayed by CB Shaping, the LLQ logic of **policy-map queue-voip** determines into which of the two shaping queues the packet should be placed. Later, when CB Shaping decides to release the next packet (typically when the next Tc begins), LLQ determines which packets are taken next. This example has only two queues, one of which is an LLQ, so packets are always taken from the LLQ if any are present in that queue.

When a packet leaves one of the two shaping queues, it drains into the interface software queues. For routers with many VCs on the same physical interface, the VCs compete for the available interface bandwidth. Examples 5-1 and 5-2 both defaulted to use WFQ on the interface. However, LLQ or class-based weighted fair queuing (CBWFQ) could have been used on the interface in addition to its use on the shaping function, simply by adding a **service-policy output policy-map-name** command under s0/0.

> **Note**  When one policy map refers to another, as in Example 5-3, the configurations are sometimes called "hierarchical" policy maps. Other times, they are called "nested" policy maps. Or, you can just think of it as how CBWFQ and LLQ can be configured for the shaping queues.

## Configuring Shaping by Bandwidth Percent

The **shape** command allows the shaping rate to be stated as a percentage of the setting of the interface or subinterface **bandwidth** setting. Configuring based on a simple percentage of the bandwidth command setting seems obvious at first. However, you should keep in mind the following facts when configuring the **shape** command based on percentage of interface bandwidth:

Key Topic

- The **shape percent** command uses the bandwidth of the interface or subinterface under which it is enabled.

- Subinterfaces do not inherit the bandwidth setting of the physical interface, so if it is not set through the **bandwidth** command, it defaults to 1544.

- The Bc and Be values are configured as a number of milliseconds; the values are calculated as the number of bits that can be sent at the configured shaping rate, in the configured time period.

- Tc is set to configure the Bc value, which is in milliseconds.

Example 5-4 shows a brief example of CB Shaping configuration using percentages, including explanations of the points from the preceding list.

**Example 5-4**  *Shaping Based on Percent*

```
! With s0/0.1 bandwidth of 128, the rate is 50% * 128, or 64 kbps. At 64 kbps, 8000
! bits can be sent in the configured 125-ms time interval (64000 * 0.125 = 8000).
! Note that the ms parameter in the shape command is required after the Bc
! (shown) or Be (not shown), otherwise the command is rejected. Not shown: The
! Tc was set to 125 ms, the exact value configured for Bc.
policy-map percent-test
  class class-default
   shape average percent 50 125 ms
interface Serial0/1
 bandwidth 128
 service-policy output percent-test
```

## CB Shaping to a Peak Rate

The **shape average** command has been used in all the examples so far. However, the command **shape peak** *mean-rate* is also allowed, which implements slightly different behavior as compared with **shape average** for the same configured rate. The key actions of the **shape peak** *mean-rate* command are summarized as follows:

- It calculates (or defaults) Bc, Be, and Tc the same way as the **shape average** command.

- It refills Bc + Be tokens (instead of just Bc tokens) into the token bucket for each time interval.

This logic means that CB Shaping gets the right to send the committed burst, and the excess burst, every time period. As a result, the actual shaping rate is as follows:

Shaping_rate = configured_rate (1 + Be/Bc)

For example, the **shape peak 64000** command, with Bc and Be defaulted to 8000 bits each, results in an actual shaping rate of 128 kbps, based on the following formula:

64 (1 + 8000/8000) = 128

## Adaptive Shaping

Adaptive shaping configuration requires only a minor amount of effort compared to the topics covered so far. To configure it, just add the **shape adaptive** *min-rate* command under the **shape** command. Example 5-5 shows a short example.

**Example 5-5**   *Adaptive CB Shaping Configuration*

```
policy-map shape-all
  class class-default
    shape average 96000 9600
    shape adaptive 32000
```

# Policing Concepts and Configuration

Class-Based Policing (CB Policing) performs different internal processing than the older, alternative policer in Cisco router IOS, namely committed access rate (CAR). This section focuses on CB Policing, starting with concepts and then covering configuration details.

## CB Policing Concepts

CB Policing is enabled for packets either entering or exiting an interface, or those entering or exiting a subinterface. It monitors, or *meters*, the bit rate of the combined packets; when a packet pushes the metered rate past the configured policing rate, the policer takes action against that packet. The most aggressive action is to discard the packet. Alternately, the policer can simply re-mark a field in the packet. This second option allows the packets through, but if congestion occurs at later places during a marked-down packet's journey, it is more likely to be discarded.

Table 5-4 lists the keywords used to imply the policer's actions.

**Table 5-4**   *Policing Actions Used in CB Policing*

| Command Option | Mode and Function |
| --- | --- |
| drop | Drops the packet |
| set-dscp-transmit | Sets the DSCP and transmits the packet |
| set-prec-transmit | Sets the IP Precedence (0 to 7) and sends the packet |
| set-qos-transmit | Sets the QoS Group ID (1 to 99) and sends the packet |
| set-clp-transmit | Sets the ATM CLP bit (ATM interfaces only) and sends the packet |
| transmit | Sends the packet |

CB Policing categorizes packets into two or three categories, depending on the style of policing, and then applies one of these actions to each category of packet. The categories are *conforming* packets, *exceeding* packets, and *violating* packets. The CB Policing logic that dictates when packets are placed into a particular category varies based on the type of policing. The next three sections outline the types of CB Policing logic.

### Single-Rate, Two-Color Policing (One Bucket)

Single-rate, two-color policing is the simplest option for CB Policing. This method uses a single policing rate with no excess burst. The policer will then use only two categories (*conform* and *exceed*), defining a different action on packets of each type. (Typically, the conform action is to transmit the packet, with the exceed action either being to drop the packet or mark it down.)

While this type of policing logic is often called *single-rate, two-color* policing, it is sometimes called *single-bucket, two-color* policing because it uses a single token bucket for internal processing. Like shaping's use of token buckets, the policer's main logic relates to filling the bucket with tokens and then spending the tokens. Over time, the policer refills the bucket according to the policing rate. For example, policing at 96 kbps, over the course of 1 second, adds 12,000 tokens to the bucket. (A token represents a byte with policers, so 12,000 tokens is 96,000 bits' worth of tokens.)

CB Policing does not refill the bucket based on a time interval. Instead, CB Policing reacts to the arrival of a packet by replenishing a prorated number of tokens into the bucket. The number of tokens is defined by the following formula:

(Current_packet_arrival_time - Previous_packet_arrival_time) x Police_rate

8

**Note**   Note that a token represents the right to send 1 byte, so the formula includes the division by 8 to convert the units to bytes instead of bits.

The idea behind the formula is simple—essentially, a small number of tokens are replenished before each packet is policed; the end result is that tokens are replenished at the policing rate. For example, for a police rate of 128 kbps, the policer should replenish 16,000 tokens per second. If 1 second has elapsed since the previous packet arrived, CB Policing would replenish the bucket with 16,000 tokens. If 0.1 second has passed since the previous packet had arrived, CB Policing would replenish the bucket with 0.1 second's worth of tokens, or 1600 tokens. If 0.01 second had passed, CB Policing would replenish 160 tokens at that time.

The policer then considers whether it should categorize the newly arrived packet as either conforming or exceeding the traffic contract. The policer compares the number of bytes in the packet (represented here as $Xp$, with "p" meaning "packet") to the number of tokens in the token bucket (represented here as $Xb$, with "b" meaning "bucket"). Table 5-5 shows the decision logic, along with whether the policer spends/removes tokens from the bucket.

**Table 5-5**   *Single-Rate, Two-Color Policing Logic for Categorizing Packets*

| Category | Requirements | Tokens Drained from Bucket |
|---|---|---|
| Conform | If $Xp <= Xb$ | $Xp$ tokens |
| Exceed | If $Xp > Xb$ | None |

As long as the overall bit rate does not exceed the policing rate, the packets will all conform. However, if the rate is exceeded, as tokens are removed for each conforming packet, the bucket will eventually empty—causing some packets to exceed the contract. Over time, tokens are added back to the bucket, so some packets will conform. After the bit rate lowers below the policing rate, all packets will again conform to the contract.

### Single-Rate, Three-Color Policer (Two Buckets)

When you want the policer to police at a particular rate, but to also support a Be, the policer uses two token buckets. It also uses all three categories for packets—conform, exceed, and violate. Combining those concepts together, such policing is typically called *single-rate, three-color policing.*

As before, CB Policing fills the buckets in reaction to packet arrival. (For lack of a better set of terms, this discussion calls the first bucket the Bc bucket, because it is Bc in size, and the other one the Be bucket, because it is Be in size.) CB Policing fills the Bc bucket just like a single-bucket model. However, if the Bc bucket has any tokens left in it, some will spill; these tokens then fill the Be bucket. Figure 5-5 shows the basic process.

Refill Bytes Upon Arrival of Packet, per Formula:
(New_packet_arrival_time - previous_packet_arrival_time) * Policed_rate / 8

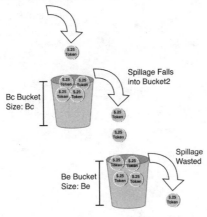

**Figure 5-5**   *Refilling Dual Token Buckets with CB Policing*

After filling the buckets, the policer then determines the category for the newly arrived packet, as shown in Table 5-6. In this case, $Xbc$ is the number of tokens in the Bc bucket, and $Xbe$ is the number in the Be bucket.

**Table 5-6**   *Single-Rate, Three-Color Policing Logic for Categorizing Packets*

| Category | Requirements | Tokens Drained from Bucket |
|----------|-------------|---------------------------|
| Conform | $Xp <= Xbc$ | $Xp$ tokens from the Bc bucket |
| Exceed | $Xp > Xbc$ and $Xp <= Xbe$ | $Xp$ tokens from the Be bucket |
| Violate | $Xp > Xbc$ and $Xp > Xbe$ | None |

## Two-Rate, Three-Color Policer (Two Buckets)

The third main option for CB Policing uses two separate policing rates. The lower rate is the previously discussed committed information rate (CIR), and the higher, second rate is called the *peak information rate (PIR)*. Packets that fall under the CIR conform to the traffic contract. Packets that exceed the CIR, but fall below PIR, are considered to exceed the contract. Finally, packets beyond the PIR are considered to violate the contract.

The key difference between the single-rate and dual-rate three-color policers is that the dual-rate method essentially allows sustained excess bursting. With a single-rate, three-color policer, an excess burst exists, but the burst is sustained only until the Be bucket empties. A period of relatively low activity has to occur to refill the Be bucket. With the dual-rate method, the Be bucket does not rely on spillage when filling the Bc bucket, as depicted in Figure 5-6. (Note that these buckets are sometimes called the CIR and PIR buckets with dual-rate policing.)

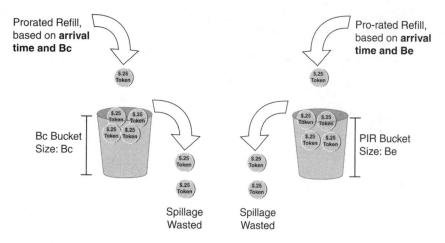

**Figure 5-6** *Refilling CIR and PIR Dual Token Buckets*

The refilling of the two buckets based on two different rates is very important. For example, imagine that you set a CIR of 128 kbps (16 kilobytes/second) and a PIR of 256 kbps (32 KBps). If 0.1 second passed before the next packet arrived, the CIR bucket would be replenished with 1600 tokens (1/10 of 1 second's worth of tokens, in bytes), while the PIR bucket would be replenished with 3200 tokens. So, there are more tokens to use in the PIR bucket, as compared to the CIR bucket.

Next, the policer categorizes the packet. The only difference in logic as compared with the single-rate, three-color policer is highlighted in Table 5-7, specifically related to how tokens are consumed for conforming packets.

**Table 5-7**  *Two-Rate, Three-Color Policing Logic for Categorizing Packets*

| Category | Requirements | Tokens Drained from Bucket |
|----------|--------------|----------------------------|
| Conform | $Xp <= Xbc$ | $Xp$ tokens from the Bc bucket and $Xp$ tokens from the Be bucket |
| Exceed | $Xp > Xbc$ and $Xp <= Xbe$ | $Xp$ tokens from the Be bucket |
| Violate | $Xp > Xbc$ and $Xp > Xbe$ | None |

While Table 5-7 does outline each detail, the underlying logic might not be obvious from the table. In effect, by filling the Be bucket based on the higher PIR, but also draining tokens from the Be bucket for packets that conform to the lower CIR, the Be bucket has tokens that represent the difference between the two rates.

## Class-Based Policing Configuration

CB Policing uses the familiar Modular QoS CLI (MQC) commands for configuration. As a result, a policy map can police all packets using the convenient class-default class, or it can separate traffic into classes, apply different policing parameters to different classes of traffic, or even simply not police some classes.

The **police** command configures CB Policing inside a policy map. On the **police** command, you define the policing rate in bps, the **Bc** in bytes, and the **Be** in bytes, along with the actions for each category:

```
police bps burst-normal burst-max conform-action action exceed-action action
  [violate-action action]
```

### Single-Rate, Three-Color Policing of All Traffic

Example 5-6 shows how to police all traffic, with criteria as follows:

- Create a single-rate, three-color policing configuration.

- All traffic is policed at 96 kbps at ingress.

- Bc of 1 second's worth of traffic is allowed.

- Be of 0.5 second's worth of traffic is allowed.

- The conform, exceed, and violate actions should be to forward, mark down to DSCP 0, and discard, respectively.

**Example 5-6**   *Single-Rate, Three-Color CB Policing at 96 kbps*

```
! The police command sets the rate (in bps), Bc and Be (in bytes), and the three
! actions.
policy-map police-all
  class class-default
! note: the police command wraps around to a second line.
  police cir 96000 bc 12000 be 6000 conform-action transmit exceed-action set-dscp-
    transmit 0 violate-action drop
!
interface Serial1/0
 encapsulation frame-relay
 service-policy input police-all
! The show command below lists statistics for each of the three categories.
ISP-edge# show policy-map interface s 1/0
 Serial1/0
  Service-policy input: police-all

    Class-map: class-default (match-any)
      8375 packets, 1446373 bytes
      30 second offered rate 113000 bps, drop rate 15000 bps
```

```
Match: any
police:
    cir 96000 bps, conform-burst 12000, excess-burst 6000
    conformed 8077 packets, 1224913 bytes; action: transmit
    exceeded 29 packets, 17948 bytes; action: set-dscp-transmit 0
    violated 269 packets, 203512 bytes; action: drop
    conformed 95000 bps, exceed 0 bps violate 20000 bps
```

The **police** command defines a single rate, but the fact that it is a three-color policing configuration, and not a two-color configuration, is not obvious at first glance. To configure a single-rate, three-color policer, you need to configure a violate action or explicitly set Be to something larger than 0.

## Policing a Subset of the Traffic

One of the advantages of CB Policing is the ability to perform policing per class. Example 5-7 shows CB Policing with HTTP traffic classified and policed differently than the rest of the traffic, with the following criteria:

■   Police web traffic at 80 kbps at ingress to the ISP-edge router. Transmit conforming and exceeding traffic, but discard violating traffic.

■   Police all other traffic at 16 kbps at ingress to the ISP-edge router. Mark down exceeding and violating traffic to DSCP 0.

■   For both classes, set Bc and Be to 1 second's worth and 0.5 second's worth of traffic, respectively.

**Key Topic**

**Example 5-7**   *CB Policing 80 kbps for Web Traffic, 16 kbps for the Rest with Markdown to Be, at ISP-Edge Router*

```
class-map match-all match-web
  match protocol http
! The new policy map uses the new class to match http, and class-default to
! match all other traffic.
policy-map police-web
  class match-web
     police cir 80000 bc 10000 be 5000 conform-action transmit exceed-action
       transmit
violate-action drop
  class class-default
     police cir 16000 bc 2000 be 1000 conform-action transmit exceed-action
set-dscp-transmit 0 violate-action set-dscp-transmit 0
!
interface Serial1/0
 encapsulation frame-relay
 service-policy input police-web
```

## CB Policing Defaults for Bc and Be

If you do not configure a Bc value on the **police** command, CB Policing configures a default value equivalent to the bytes that could be sent in 1/4 second at the defined policing rate. The formula is as follows:

$$Bc = \frac{(CIR * 0.25 \text{ second})}{8 \text{ bits/byte}} = \frac{CIR}{32}$$

The only part that might not be obvious is the division by 8 on the left—that is simply for the conversion from bits to bytes. The math reduces to CIR/32. Also, if the formula yields a number less than 1500, CB Policing uses a Bc of 1500.

If the **police** command does not include a Be value, the default Be setting depends on the type of policing. Table 5-8 summarizes the details.

**Table 5-8**   *Setting CB Policing Bc and Be Defaults*

| Type of Policing Configuration | Telltale Signs in the police Command | Defaults |
|---|---|---|
| Single-rate, two-color | No **violate-action** configured | Bc = CIR/32; Be = 0 |
| Single-rate, three-color | **violate-action** is configured | Bc = CIR/32; Be = Bc |
| Dual-rate, three-color | PIR is configured | Bc = CIR/32; Be = PIR/32 |

## Configuring Dual-Rate Policing

Dual-rate CB Policing requires the same MQC commands, but with slightly different syntax on the **police** command, as shown here:

```
police {cir cir} [bc conform-burst] {pir pir} [be peak-burst]
  [conform-action action [exceed-action action [violate-action action]]]
```

Note that the syntax of this command requires configuration of both the CIR and a PIR because the curly brackets mean that the parameter is required. The command includes a place to set the Bc value and the Be value as well, plus the same set of options for conform, exceed, and violate actions. For example, if you wanted to perform dual-rate policing, with a CIR of 96 kbps and a PIR of 128 kbps, you would simply use a command like **police cir 96000 pir 128000**, with optional settings of Bc and Be, plus the settings for the actions for each of the three categories.

## Multi-Action Policing

When CB Policing re-marks packets instead of discarding them, the design might call for marking more than one field in a packet. Marking multiple fields in the same packet with CB Policing is called *multi-action policing*.

The **police** command uses a slightly different syntax to implement multi-action policing. By omitting the actions from the command, the **police** command places the user into a policing subconfiguration mode in which the actions can be added through separate commands (the **conform-action**, **exceed-action**, and **violate-action** commands). To configure multiple actions, one of these three **action** commands would be used more than once, as shown in Example 5-8, which marks DSCP 0 and sets FR DE for packets that violate the traffic contract.

**Example 5-8**   *Multi-Action Policing*

```
R3# conf t
Enter configuration commands, one per line.  End with CNTL/Z.
R3(config)# policy-map testpol1
R3(config-pmap)# class class-default
! This command implements dual-rate policing as well, but it is not required
R3(config-pmap-c)# police 128000 256000
R3(config-pmap-c-police)# conform-action transmit
R3(config-pmap-c-police)# exceed-action transmit
R3(config-pmap-c-police)# violate-action set-dscp-transmit 0
R3(config-pmap-c-police)# violate-action set-frde-transmit
```

## Policing by Percentage

As it does with the **shape** command, Cisco IOS supports configuring policing rates as a percentage of link bandwidth. The Bc and Be values are configured as a number of milliseconds, from which IOS calculates the actual Bc and Be values based on how many bits can be sent in that many milliseconds. Example 5-9 shows an example of a dual-rate policing configuration using the **percentage** option.

**Example 5-9**   *Configuring Percentage-Based Policing*

```
R3# show running-config
! Portions omitted for Brevity
 policy-map test-pol6
  class class-default
    police cir percent 25 bc 500 ms pir percent 50 be 500 ms conform transmit exceed
      transmit      violate drop
!
interface serial0/0
 bandwidth 256
 service-policy output test-pol6
! The output below shows the configured percentage for the rate and the time for
! Bc and Be, with the calculated values immediately below.
R3# show policy-map interface s0/0
! lines omitted for brevity
      police:
          cir 25 % bc 500 ms
```

```
        cir 64000 bps, bc 4000 bytes
        pir 50 % be 500 ms
        pir 128000 bps, be 8000 bytes
! lines omitted
```

## Committed Access Rate

CAR implements single-rate, two-color policing. As compared with that same option in CB Policing, CAR and CB Policing have many similarities. They both can police traffic either entering or exiting an interface or subinterface; they can both police subsets of that traffic based on classification logic; and they both set the rate in bps, with Bc and Be configured as a number of bytes.

CAR differs from CB Policing regarding four main features, as follows:

- CAR uses the **rate-limit** command, which is not part of the MQC set of commands.

- CAR has a feature called *cascaded* or *nested* **rate-limit** commands, which allows multiple **rate-limit** commands on an interface to process the same packet.

- CAR does support Be; however, even in this case, it still supports only conform and exceed categories, and never supports a third (violate) category.

- When CAR has a Be configured, the internal logic used to determine which packets conform and exceed differs as compared with CB Policing.

CAR puts most parameters on the **rate-limit** command, which is added under an interface or subinterface:

```
rate-limit {input | output} [access-group [rate-limit] acl-index] bps burst-
   normal burst-max conform-action conform-action exceed-action exceed-action
```

Example 5-10 shows an example CAR configuration for perspective. The criteria for the CAR configuration in Example 5-10 are as follows:

- All traffic is policed at 96 kbps at ingress to the ISP-edge router.

- Bc of 1 second's worth of traffic is allowed.

- Be of 0.5 second's worth of traffic is allowed.

- Traffic that exceeds the contract is discarded.

- Traffic that conforms to the contract is forwarded with Precedence reset to 0.

**Example 5-10**    *CAR at 96 kbps at ISP-Edge Router*

```
! The rate-limit command omits the access-group option, meaning that it has no
! matching parameters, so all packets are considered to match the command. The rest
! of the options simply match the requirements.
interface Serial1/0.1 point-to-point
```

```
ip address 192.168.2.251 255.255.255.0
! note: the rate-limit command wraps around to a second line.
 rate-limit input 96000 12000 18000 conform-action set-prec-transmit 0
   exceed-action drop
 frame-relay interface-dlci 103
! The output below confirms the parameters, including matching all traffic.
ISP-edge# show interfaces s 1/0.1 rate-limit
  Input
    matches: all traffic
      params:  96000 bps, 12000 limit, 18000 extended limit
      conformed 2290 packets, 430018 bytes; action: set-prec-transmit 0
      exceeded 230 packets, 67681 bytes; action: drop
      last packet: 0ms ago, current burst: 13428 bytes
last cleared 00:02:16 ago, conformed 25000 bps, exceeded 3000 bps
```

To classify traffic, CAR requires the use of either a normal access control list (ACL) or a *rate-limit ACL*. A rate-limit ACL can match Multiprotocol Label Switching (MPLS) Experimental bits, IP Precedence, or MAC Address. For other fields, an IP ACL must be used. Example 5-11 shows an example in which CAR polices three different subsets of traffic using ACLs for matching the traffic, as well as limiting the overall traffic rate. The criteria for this example are as follows (note that CAR allows only policing rates that are multiples of 8 kbps):

■   Police all traffic on the interface at 496 kbps, but before sending this traffic on its way...

■   Police all web traffic at 400 kbps.

■   Police all FTP traffic at 160 kbps.

■   Police all VoIP traffic at 200 kbps.

■   Choose Bc and Be so that Bc has 1 second's worth of traffic and Be provides no additional burst capability over Bc.

**Example 5-11**   *Cascaded CAR* **rate-limit** *Commands, with Subclassifications*

```
! ACL 101 matches all HTTP traffic
! ACL 102 matches all FTP traffic
! ACL 103 matches all VoIP traffic
interface s 0/0
rate-limit input 496000 62000 62000 conform-action continue exceed-action drop
rate-limit input access-group 101 400000 50000 50000 conform-action transmit
  exceed-action drop
rate-limit input access-group 102 160000 20000 20000 conform-action transmit
  exceed-action drop
rate-limit input access-group 103 200000 25000 25000 conform-action transmit
  exceed-action drop
```

The CAR configuration refers to IP ACLs to classify the traffic, using three different IP ACLs in this case. ACL 101 matches all web traffic, ACL 102 matches all FTP traffic, and ACL 103 matches all VoIP traffic.

Under subinterface S0/0.1, four **rate-limit** commands are used. The first sets the rate for all traffic, dropping traffic that exceeds 496 kbps. However, the conform action is "continue." This means that packets conforming to this statement will be compared to the next **rate-limit** statements, and when matching a statement, some other action will be taken. For example, web traffic matches the second **rate-limit** command, with a resulting action of either transmit or drop. VoIP traffic would be compared with the next three **rate-limit** commands before matching the last one. As a result, all traffic is limited to 496 kbps, and three particular subsets of traffic are prevented from taking all the bandwidth.

CB Policing can achieve the same effect of policing subsets of traffic by using nested policy maps.

# Hierarchical Queuing Framework (HQF)

Thus far we have discussed the deployment of our quality of service mechanism through the use of the MQC. It is the MQC that provides a means to configure QoS using a generic command-line interface to all types of interfaces and protocols. MQC is important because it is the mechanism of choice used to configure HQF for queuing and shaping.

HQF is a logical engine used to support QoS features. The HQF hierarchy is a tree structure that is built using policy maps. When data passes through an interface using HQF, the data is classified so that it traverses the branches of the tree. Data arrives at the top of the tree and is classified on one of the leaves. Data then traverses down the hierarchy (tree) until it is transmitted out the interface at the root (trunk).

Example 5-12 illustrates how to build a QoS hierarchy.

**Example 5-12**  *QoS Hierarchy*

```
policy-map class
 class c1
  bandwidth 14
 class c2
  bandwidth 18

policy-map map1
 class class-default
  shape average 64000
  service-policy class

policy-map map2
 class class-default
  shape average 96000
```

```
map-class frame-relay fr1
 service-policy output map1

map-class frame fr2
 service-policy output map2

interface serial4/1
 encapsulation frame-relay
 frame-relay interface-dlci 16
  class fr1
 frame-relay interface-dlci 17
  class fr2
```

The command-line entries in Example 5-15 act to create a structured application of QoS mechanisms; the nature of this structure can be seen in Figure 5-7.

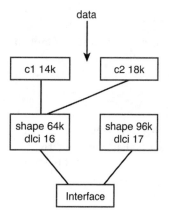

**Figure 5-7**   *HQF Tree Structure*

Now that we understand what the structure looks like, we need to underline the main benefits of the structure. QoS Hierarchical Queuing Framework allows for faster deployment of QoS queuing and shaping in large-scale networks. Furthermore, it also enables consistent queuing behavior that can be applied with a common MQC across all main Cisco IOS Software releases, making implementation of QoS easier and transparent regardless of the Cisco IOS Software release being used.

HQF has built-in functionality that supports both distributed and nondistributed implementations, providing consistency of QoS feature behavior across all software-forwarding hardware, thus making implementation of QoS easier and transparent, regardless of the platform being used. This consistency of behavior we are describing results in accelerated delivery of feature enhancements and new QoS features in different Cisco IOS Software releases through different hardware deployments. In addition, advantages of HQF include multiple levels of packet scheduling and support for integrated Class-Based Shaping and queuing, as well as the ability to apply fair queuing and drop policies on a per-class basis.

These benefits are all made possible in the context of HQF because of new functionality that has been introduced. These features include the placement of hierarchical policies with queuing features situated at every level of the HQF structure. This translates into the ability to apply Class-Based Queuing to any traffic class in the parent or child level of a hierarchical policy while simultaneously creating discrete service levels for different sessions or subscribers.

In Example 5-13, we see that traffic belonging to class parent-c2 has more scheduling time than class parent-c1.

**Example 5-13**    *QoS Hierarchy*

```
policy-map class
 class c1
  bandwidth 14
 class c2
  bandwidth 18

policy-map map1
 policy-map child
 class child-c1
  bandwidth 400
 class child-c2
  bandwidth 400

policy-map parent
 class parent-c1
  bandwidth 1000
  service-policy child
 class parent-c2
  bandwidth 2000
  service-policy child
```

There are a number of behavioral changes that are also part of HFQ that sets it apart from traditional MQC. These changes are discussed in the following sections.

## Flow-Based Fair-Queuing Support in Class-Default

The fair-queuing behavior for the class-default class is flow based. This is a change from the weighted fair queuing (WFQ) behavior in previous releases. With flow-based fair queuing, the flow queues in the class-default class are scheduled equally instead of by weight based on the IP Precedence bits.

### Default Queuing Implementation for Class-Default

When you do not explicitly configure the class-default class in a policy map, its default queuing behavior is first in, first out (FIFO). You can configure the **bandwidth**, **fair-queue**, or **service-policy** commands in the class-default class to achieve different queuing behaviors.

### Class-Default and Bandwidth

The bandwidth assigned to the class-default class is the unused interface bandwidth not consumed by user-defined classes. By default, the class-default class receives a minimum of 1 percent of the interface bandwidth.

### Default Queuing Implementation for Shape Class

When you configure the **shape** command in a class, the default queuing behavior for the shape queue is FIFO instead of weighted fair queuing (WFQ). You can configure the **bandwidth**, **fair-queue**, or **service-policy** commands in shape class to achieve different queuing behaviors.

### Policy Map and Interface Bandwidth

In HQF, a policy map can reserve up to 100 percent of the interface bandwidth. If you do not assign an explicit bandwidth guarantee to the class-default class, you can assign a maximum of 99 percent of the interface bandwidth to user-defined classes and reserve the other 1 percent for the class-default class.

If you are migrating to Cisco IOS Release 12.4(20)T and the configured policy map allocates 100 percent of the bandwidth to the user-defined classes, an error message appears in the console after booting the HQF image. The message indicates that the allocated bandwidth exceeds the allowable amount, and the service policy is rejected. In HQF, you must reconfigure the policy to account for the minimum 1 percent bandwidth guaranteed for the class-default. Then you can apply a service policy to the interface.

### Per-Flow Queue Limit in Fair Queue

In HQF, when you enable fair queuing, the default per-flow queue limit is 1/4 of the class queue limit. If you do not enable the queue limit in a class, the default per-flow queue limit is 16 packets (1/4 of 64).

### Oversubscription Support for Multiple Policies on Logical Interfaces

When you attach a shaping policy to multiple logical interfaces including a subinterface, and the sum of the shape rate exceeds the physical interface bandwidth, congestion at the physical interface results in back pressure to each logical interface policy. This back pressure causes each policy to reduce the output rate to its fair share of the interface bandwidth.

### Shaping on a GRE Tunnel

In HQF, you can apply the shaping to a generic routing encapsulation (GRE) tunnel by using a hierarchical service policy after encapsulation. This means that the shape rate is based on packets with tunnel encapsulation and L2 encapsulation.

When configuring the shape feature in the parent policy applied to the tunnel interface, you can use the class-default class only. You cannot configure a user-defined class in the parent policy.

Some QoS deployments include a service policy with queuing features applied at the tunnel or a virtual interface and a service policy with queuing features applied at the physical interface. You can apply a service policy with queuing features only at one of these interfaces.

### Nested Policy and Reference Bandwidth for Child-Policy

In HQF, when you configure a nested policy with a child queuing policy under a parent shaping class, the reference bandwidth for the child queuing policy is taken from the following: minimum (parent shaper rate, parent class's implicit/explicit bandwidth guarantee). When you do not define bandwidth for the parent class, the interface bandwidth divides equally among all parent classes as the implicit bandwidth guarantee.

### Handling Traffic Congestion on an Interface Configured with Policy Map

If an interface configured with a policy map is full of heavy traffic, the implicitly defined policer allows the traffic as defined in the **bandwidth** statement of each traffic class. The policer is activated whenever there is traffic congestion on an interface.

## QoS Troubleshooting and Commands

QoS problems are almost all administrator related and typically result from one of three causes:

- A lack of proper prior planning for the QoS requirements of your network, resulting in an improper QoS configuration

- Failure to track changes in network applications and network traffic, resulting in an outdated QoS configuration

- A lack of good network documentation (or a failure to check that documentation before adding a device or application to the network)

The focus of this section is to provide you with a set of Cisco IOS–based tools, beyond the more common ones that you already know, as well as some guidance on the troubleshooting process for QoS issues that you might encounter. In the CCIE R&S lab exam, you will encounter an array of troubleshooting situations that require you to have mastered fast, efficient, and thorough troubleshooting skills. In the written exam, you'll need a different set of skills (mainly the knowledge of troubleshooting techniques that are specific to Cisco routers and switches, and the ability to interpret the output of various **show** commands and possibly **debug** output). You can also expect to be given an example along with a problem statement. You will need to quickly narrow the question down to possible solutions and then pinpoint the final solution.

You should expect, as in all CCIE exams, that the easiest or most direct ways to a solution might be unavailable to you. In troubleshooting, perhaps the easiest way to the source of most problems is through the **show run** command or variations on it. Therefore, we'll institute a simple "no **show run**" rule in this section that will force you to use your knowledge of more in-depth troubleshooting commands in the Cisco IOS portion of this section.

In addition, you can expect that the issues that you'll face in this part of the written exam will need more than one command or step to isolate and resolve.

## Troubleshooting Slow Application Response

You have a QoS policy enabled in your network, but users have begun complaining about slow response to a particular application. First, examine your policy to ensure that you are allocating enough bandwidth for that application. Check the bandwidth, latency, and drop requirements for the application, and then look at your documentation to see whether your policy supplies these.

If it does, you might want to verify the response time using IP service-level agreements (SLA). IP SLA was explained in Volume 1, Chapter 5, "IP Services." Set it up on the routers or switches closest to the traffic source and destination, using the application's destination port number. Schedule it to run, and then verify the results with the **show ip sla statistics** command. If the response time is indeed slow but your documentation shows that you have properly set up the policy, check that the QoS policy is configured on each hop in the network. In a large network, you should have a management tool that allows you to check QoS configuration and operation. If you are doing it manually, however, the **show policy-map** command displays your configured policy maps, and **show class-map** displays the associated class maps. The **show policy-map interface** command is a great way to see which policies are applied at which interfaces, and what actions they are taking.

For example, suppose that your users are complaining about Citrix response times. Your documentation shows that the network's QoS policy has the following basic settings:

- **Voice queue:** Prioritize and allocate bandwidth

- **Citrix queue:** Allocate bandwidth to typical Citrix ports such as 1494 and 2512

- **Web queue:** Allocate limited bandwidth to ports 80 and 443

- **Default queue:** Allocate bandwidth to all other traffic

The network performed well until a popular new Internet video came out that was streamed over port 80. The administrator who created the QoS policy didn't realize that Citrix also uses ports 80 and 443. The **show policy-map interface** command showed that web queue was filling up, so Citrix traffic was being delayed or dropped along with the normal Internet traffic. You could pinpoint this by turning on Network-Based Application Recognition (NBAR) to learn what types of traffic are traversing the interfaces. Use the **show ip nbar protocol-discovery** command to see the traffic types found.

One solution is to classify Citrix traffic using NBAR rather than port numbers. Classification using NBAR is explained in Chapter 3, "Classification and Marking."

## Troubleshooting Voice and Video Problems

Introducing voice/video over IP into the network is the impetus for many companies to institute QoS. Cisco has made this easy with the AutoQoS function for voice. Adding video is trickier because it has the latency constraints of voice, but can handle drops better. Plus, streaming one-way video uses bandwidth differently than interactive video, so your QoS policy must allow for that.

If you are experiencing poor voice or video quality, you can check several QoS-related items on both switches and routers:

- Verify that QoS is enabled and that either AutoQoS or manual policies are configured. The **show mls qos** command will tell you whether QoS is enabled.

- Examine the QoS policy maps and class maps to ensure correct configuration with the **show policy-map** and **show class-map** commands. Verify that voice and video are classified correctly and guaranteed appropriate bandwidth.

- Examine the results of the service policy using the **show policy-map interface** command.

- Possibly use IP SLA between various pairs of devices to narrow down the problem location.

Troubleshooting techniques unique to switches include the following:

- Make sure an expedite (or priority) queue has been enabled both for ingress and egress traffic. Use the **show mls qos input-queue** command for ingress queues and the **show mls qos** *interface* **queueing** command for egress queues.

- Make sure that the correct traffic is being mapped into the correct queues. For input queues, the command is **show mls qos maps cos-input-q**. On a 3560 switch, CoS 5 is mapped to ingress queue 2 by default, so if queue 1 is your priority queue and you have not changed the default mapping, that will be a problem. For egress queues, the command is **show mls qos maps cos-output-q**. On egress queues, CoS 5 is mapped to queue 1 by default.

- Make sure that the CoS values are being mapped to the correct internal Differentiated Services Code Point (DSCP) values, and that the DSCP values are in turn being mapped back to the correct class of service (CoS) values. For CoS-to-DSCP mapping, use the **show mls qos maps cos-dscp** command. For DSCP-to-CoS mapping, use the **show mls qos maps dscp-cos** command. (See Chapter 4, "Congestion Management and Avoidance," for a review of switch queuing and examples of output from these commands.)

Routers have some other troubleshooting spots:

- Viewing the CoS-to-DSCP mapping on a router is easier than on a switch because it uses just one command: **show mls qos maps**.

- If traffic shaping is enabled on a WAN interface, make sure that the time interval (Tc) is tuned down to 10 ms. Otherwise you might induce too much latency, resulting in bad voice and video quality. You can use the **show traffic-shape** command to determine this setting.

- If your WAN service provider has different levels of service, make sure that your voice and video traffic are marked correctly to map to its queue.

## Other QoS Troubleshooting Tips

Even networks with properly configured QoS can run into problems that are, at least indirectly, caused by QoS. One issue that especially shows up in networks where people and offices move frequently is because of either a lack of documentation or a network administrator not checking the documentation.

Suppose, for example, that you have a switch that was dedicated to user ports but some of the users have moved to a different location. You now need some ports for printers or servers. All the switch ports are set up with AutoQoS for voice, and with input and egress expedite queues. If the administrator just connects a printer or server to one of those ports, performance will not be optimal. There is only one type of traffic going through those ports, so only one ingress and one egress queue are needed. Also, there is no need to introduce the latency, however minimal, involved in attempting to map the nonexistent input CoS to a queue. The port should be reconfigured as a data port, with just one queue. A quick way to remove all configuration from an interface is to use the global command **default interface** *interface*.

Network applications change, and a network set up for good QoS operation today might need something different tomorrow. Monitor your network traffic and QoS impact. Review the monitoring results periodically. Consider whether any policy changes will be necessary before introducing a new application into the network, or upgrading an existing one.

## Approaches to Resolving QoS Issues

In this final section of the chapter, we present a table with several generalized types of issues and ways of approaching them, including the relevant Cisco IOS commands. Table 5-9 summarizes these techniques.

**Table 5-9**   *Troubleshooting Approach and Commands*

| Problem | Approach | Helpful IOS Commands |
|---|---|---|
| Troubleshooting possible QoS misconfiguration on either a router or a switch (commands common to both) | Verify that QoS is enabled.<br><br>Verify the class map configuration.<br><br>Verify the policy map configuration.<br><br>Verify the operation of the service policy. | **show mls qos**<br><br>**show class-map**<br><br>**show policy-map**<br><br>**show policy-map interface** *interface* |
| Possible switch QoS misconfiguration | Use **show** commands to determine how interface input and egress queuing are configured. | **show mls qos input-queue**<br><br>**show mls qos interface** *interface* **queueing**<br><br>**show mls qos maps cos-input-q**<br><br>**show mls qos maps cos-output-q**<br><br>**show mls qos maps cos-dscp**<br><br>**show mls qos maps dscp-cos** |
| Possible router QoS misconfiguration | Use **show** commands to determine how queuing is configured. | **show mls qos maps**<br><br>**show traffic-shape** |

# Foundation Summary

This section lists additional details and facts to round out the coverage of the topics in this chapter. Unlike most of the Cisco Press Exam Certification Guides, this "Foundation Summary" does not repeat information presented in the "Foundation Topics" section of the chapter. Please take the time to read and study the details in the "Foundation Topics" section of the chapter, as well as review items noted with a Key Topic icon.

Table 5-10 lists commands related to CB Shaping.

**Table 5-10**   *Class-Based and Generic Shaping Command Reference*

| Command | Mode and Function |
|---|---|
| **traffic-shape rate** shaped-rate [*Bc*] [*Be*] [*buffer-limit*] | Interface command to enable Generic Traffic Shaping |
| **shape** [**average** \| **peak**] mean-rate [[*burst-size*] [*excess-burst-size*]] | Class configuration mode; enables shaping for the class |
| **shape** [**average** \| **peak**] **percent** *percent* [[*burst- size*] [*excess-burst-size*]] | Enables shaping based on percentage of bandwidth |
| **shape adaptive** *min-rate* | Enables the minimum rate for adaptive shaping |
| **shape fecn-adapt** | Causes reflection of BECN bits after receipt of an FECN |
| **service-policy** {**input** \| **output**} *policy-map-name* | Interface or subinterface configuration mode; enables CB Shaping on the interface |
| **shape max-buffers** number-of-buffers | Sets the maximum queue length for the default FIFO shaping queue |
| **show policy-map** *policy-map-name* | Lists configuration information about all MQC-based QoS tools |
| **show policy-map** *interface-spec* [**input** \| **output**] [**class** *class-name*] | Lists statistical information about the behavior of all MQC-based QoS tools |

Table 5-11 provides a command reference for CB Policing.

**Table 5-11**   *Class-Based Policing Command Reference*

| Command | Mode and Function |
|---|---|
| **police** *bps burst-normal burst-max* **conform-action** *action* **exceed-action** *action* [**violate-action** *action*] | **policy-map** class subcommand; enables policing for the class |
| **police cir percent** *percent* [**bc** *conform-burst-in-msec*] [**pir percent** *percent*] [**be** *peak-burst-in-msec*] [**conform-action** *action* [**exceed-action** *action* [**violate-action** *action*]]] | **policy-map** class subcommand; enables policing using percentages of bandwidth |

| Command | Mode and Function |
|---|---|
| police {cir *cir*} [bc *conform-burst*] {pir *pir*} [be *peak-burst*] [conform-action *action* [exceed-action *action* [violate-action *action*]]] | policy-map class subcommand; enables dual-rate policing |
| service-policy {input \| output} *policy-map-name* | Enables CB Policing on an interface or subinterface |

# Memory Builders

The CCIE Routing and Switching written exam, like all Cisco CCIE written exams, covers a fairly broad set of topics. This section provides some basic tools to help you exercise your memory about some of the broader topics covered in this chapter.

## Fill In Key Tables from Memory

Appendix E, "Key Tables for CCIE Study," on the CD in the back of this book, contains empty sets of some of the key summary tables in each chapter. Print Appendix E, refer to this chapter's tables in it, and fill in the tables from memory. Refer to Appendix F, "Solutions for Key Tables for CCIE Study," on the CD, to check your answers.

## Definitions

Next, take a few moments to write down the definitions for the following terms:

Tc, Bc, Be, CIR, GTS shaping rate, policing rate, token bucket, Bc bucket, Be bucket, adaptive shaping, BECN, ForeSight, ELMI, mincir, map class, marking down, single-rate two-color policer, single-rate three-color policer, dual-rate three-color policer, conform, exceed, violate, traffic contract, dual token bucket, PIR, nested policy maps, multi-action policing

Refer to the glossary to check your answers.

## Further Reading

*Cisco QoS Exam Certification Guide*, by Wendell Odom and Michael Cavanaugh

*Cisco IOS Quality of Service Solutions Configuration Guide*, www.cisco.com/en/US/docs/ios/qos/configuration/guide/12_4/qos_12_4_book.html

**Blueprint topics covered in this chapter:**

This chapter covers the following topics from the Cisco CCIE Routing and Switching written exam blueprint:

- HDLC
- PPP
- Ethernet WAN

## CHAPTER 6

# Wide-Area Networks

This chapter covers several protocols and details about two of the most commonly used data link layer protocols in wide-area networks (WAN): Point-to-Point Protocol (PPP) and Ethernet WAN.

## "Do I Know This Already?" Quiz

Table 6-1 outlines the major headings in this chapter and the corresponding "Do I Know This Already?" quiz questions.

**Table 6-1** *"Do I Know This Already?" Foundation Topics Section-to-Question Mapping*

| Foundation Topics Section | Questions Covered in This Section | Score |
|---|---|---|
| Point-to-Point Protocol | 1–3 | |
| PPPoE | 4, 5 | |
| Metro-Ethernet | 6 | |
| Total Score | | |

To best use this pre-chapter assessment, remember to score yourself strictly. You can find the answers in Appendix A, "Answers to the 'Do I Know This Already?' Quizzes."

1. Imagine that a PPP link failed and has just recovered. Which of the following features is negotiated last?

   a. CHAP authentication

   b. RTP header compression

   c. Looped link detection

   d. Link Quality Monitoring

**2.** Interfaces s0/0, s0/1, and s1/0 are up and working as part of a multilink PPP bundle that connects to another router. The multilink interface has a bandwidth setting of 1536. When a 1500-byte packet is routed out the multilink interface, which of the following determines out which link the packet will flow?

   **a.** The current CEF FIB and CEF load-balancing method.

   **b.** The current fast-switching cache.

   **c.** The packet is sent out one interface based on round-robin scheduling.

   **d.** One fragment is sent over each of the three links.

**3.** R1 and R2 connect over a leased line, with each interface using its s0/1 interface. When configuring CHAP to use a locally defined name and password, which of the following statements are false about the commands and configuration mode in which they are configured?

   **a.** The **encapsulation ppp** interface subcommand

   **b.** The **ppp authentication chap** interface subcommand

   **c.** The **username** *R1* **password** *samepassword* global command on R1

   **d.** The **username** *R2* **password** *samepassword* interface subcommand on R2

**4.** At a minimum, what command must be entered on the PPPoE server to support remote connections from clients?

   **a.** **ip dhcp**

   **b.** **ip address**

   **c.** **no virtual-reassembly**

   **d.** **ip unnumbered**

   **e.** **ip peer default ip address**

**5.** PPP headers add how much additional overhead to each frame?

   **a.** 4 bytes

   **b.** 6 bytes

   **c.** 8 bytes

   **d.** No overhead is added.

**6.** Which one of the following architectural requirements is not part of the VPLS forwarding operation?

   **a.** Autodiscovery of provider edges

   **b.** Signaling of pseudo-wires used to connect to VSIs

   **c.** Loop prevention

   **d.** Static configuration of the provider edge

   **e.** MAC address withdrawal

# Foundation Topics

## Layer 2 Protocols

The two most popular Layer 2 protocols used on point-to-point links are *High-Level Data Link Control (HDLC)* and *Point-to-Point Protocol (PPP)*. The ISO standard for the much older HDLC does not include a Type field, so the Cisco HDLC implementation adds a Cisco-proprietary 2-byte Type field to support multiple protocols over an HDLC link. It is this Cisco-proprietary version of HDLC that is the default serial interface encapsulation used on Cisco routers.

### HDLC

The default serial encapsulation on Cisco routers is Cisco HDLC, so it does not need to be explicitly configured on the router. As a result, the encapsulation type is not displayed in the configuration.

With a back-to-back serial connection, the router connected to the data communications equipment (DCE) end of the cable provides the clock signal for the serial link. The **clockrate** command in the interface configuration mode enables the router at the DCE end of the cable (R1, in this example) to provide the clock signal for the serial link. Issue the **show controllers** command to determine which end of the cable is connected to the serial interface.

In Example 6-1, the DCE end of the cable is connected to R1, and the data terminal equipment (DTE) end is connected to R2. The clock rate is now part of the default configuration of our serial interfaces, and will be applied automatically. However, it is still necessary to understand that you can manipulate this value on a case-by-case basis, depending on the environment in which your devices are installed.

**Example 6-1**  *HDLC Configuration*

```
! First we will apply the ip address to R1
! and "no shut" the interface
R1(config)# interface serial0/0
R1(config-if)# ip address 10.1.12.1 255.255.255.0
R1(config-if)# no shut
R1(config-if)#
! Now we will do the same for R2
R2# conf t
R2(config)# interface serial0/0
R2(config-if)# ip address 10.1.12.2 255.255.255.0
R2(config-if)# no shut
```

There are only a few commands that we need to utilize to verify this configuration:

■ **show controllers**

■ **ping**

■ **show interface**

The output shown in Example 6-2 illustrates the results of these commands used in this sample configuration.

**Example 6-2**   *HDLC Configuration*

```
! Show controllers on R1:
R1# show controllers serial 0/0
Interface Serial0/0
Hardware is GT96K
DCE 530, clock rate 2000000
! ---- Output Omitted ----
!
! Now for the Ping test from R1 to R2:
!
R1# ping 10.1.12.2

Type escape sequence to abort.
Sending 5, 100-byte ICMP Echos to 10.1.12.2, timeout is 2 seconds:
!!!!!
Success rate is 100 percent (5/5), round-trip min/avg/max = 1/2/4 ms
R1#
!
! Lastly we will look at the output of the show interface serial 0/0 command on R1:
!
R1# show interface serial 0/0
Serial0/0 is up, line protocol is up
  Hardware is GT96K Serial
  Internet address is 10.1.12.1/24
  MTU 1500 bytes, BW 1544 Kbit/sec, DLY 20000 usec,
     reliability 255/255, txload 1/255, rxload 1/255
  Encapsulation HDLC, loopback not set
!
! Notice that the above output indicates that we are running HDLC Encapsulation
!
  Keepalive set (10 sec)
  CRC checking enabled
  Last input 00:00:01, output 00:00:02, output hang never
  Last clearing of "show interface" counters never
  Input queue: 0/75/0/0 (size/max/drops/flushes); Total output drops: 0
  Queueing strategy: weighted fair
```

```
Output queue: 0/1000/64/0 (size/max total/threshold/drops)
    Conversations  0/1/256 (active/max active/max total)
    Reserved Conversations 0/0 (allocated/max allocated)
    Available Bandwidth 1158 kilobits/sec
5 minute input rate 0 bits/sec, 0 packets/sec
5 minute output rate 0 bits/sec, 0 packets/sec
    129 packets input, 8280 bytes, 0 no buffer
    Received 124 broadcasts, 0 runts, 0 giants, 0 throttles
    0 input errors, 0 CRC, 0 frame, 0 overrun, 0 ignored, 0 abort
    133 packets output, 8665 bytes, 0 underruns
    0 output errors, 0 collisions, 7 interface resets
    0 unknown protocol drops
    0 output buffer failures, 0 output buffers swapped out
    0 carrier transitions
    DCD=up  DSR=up  DTR=up  RTS=up  CTS=up
```

## Point-to-Point Protocol

PPP, defined in RFC 1661, includes an architected Protocol field, plus a long list of rich features. Table 6-2 points out some of the key comparison points of these two protocols.

**Table 6-2**  *HDLC and PPP Comparisons*

| Feature | HDLC | PPP |
| --- | --- | --- |
| Error detection? | Yes | Yes |
| Error recovery? | No | Yes* |
| Standard Protocol Type field? | No | Yes |
| Defaults on IOS serial links? | Yes | No |
| Supports synchronous and asynchronous links? | No | Yes |

* Cisco IOS defaults to not use the reliable PPP feature, which enables PPP to perform error recovery.

PPP framing (RFC 1662) defines the use of a simple HDLC header and trailer for most parts of the PPP framing, as shown in Figure 6-1. PPP simply adds the Protocol field and optional Padding field to the original HDLC framing. (The Padding field allows PPP to ensure that the frame has an even number of bytes.)

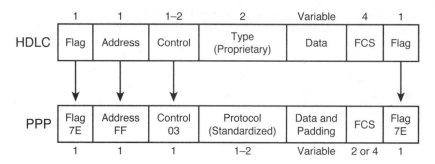

**Figure 6-1**    *HDLC and PPP Framing Compared*

## PPP Link Control Protocol

PPP standards can be separated into two broad categories—those features unrelated to any specific Layer 3 protocol and those specific to a Layer 3 protocol. The PPP *Link Control Protocol (LCP)* controls the features independent of any specific Layer 3 protocol. For each Layer 3 protocol supported by PPP, PPP defines a *Network Control Protocol (NCP)*. For example, the PPP Internet Protocol Control Protocol (IPCP) defines PPP features for IP, such as dynamic address assignment.

When a PPP serial link first comes up—for example, when a router senses the Clear to Send (CTS), Data Send Read (DSR), and Data Carrier Detect (DCD) leads come up at the physical layer—LCP begins parameter negotiation with the other end of the link. For example, LCP controls the negotiation of which authentication methods to attempt, and in what order, and then allows the authentication protocol (for example, Challenge Handshake Authentication Protocol) to complete its work. After all LCP negotiation has completed successfully, LCP is considered to be "up." At that point, PPP begins each Layer 3 Control Protocol.

Table 6-3 lists and briefly describes some of the key features of LCP. Following that, several of the key LCP features are covered in more detail.

**Table 6-3**    *PPP LCP Features*

| Function | Description |
| --- | --- |
| Link Quality Monitoring (LQM) | LCP exchanges statistics about the percentage of frames received without any errors; if the percentage falls below a configured value, the link is dropped. |
| Looped link detection | Each router generates and sends a randomly chosen magic number. If a router receives its own magic number, the link is looped and might be taken down. |
| Layer 2 load balancing | Multilink PPP (MLP) balances traffic by fragmenting each frame into one fragment per link, and sending one fragment over each link. |
| Authentication | Supports CHAP and PAP. |

## Basic LCP/PPP Configuration

PPP can be configured with a minimal number of commands, requiring only an **encapsulation ppp** command on each router on opposite ends of the link. Example 6-3 shows a simple configuration with basic PPP encapsulation, plus the optional LQM and CHAP authentication features. For this configuration, Routers R3 and R4 connect to each other's s0/1/0 interfaces.

**Example 6-3**  *PPP Configuration with LQM and CHAP*

```
! R3 configuration is first. The username/password could be held in a AAA server,
! but is shown here as a local username/password. The other router (R4) sends
! its name "R4" with R3 being configured with that username and password setting.
username R4 password 0 rom838
!!!!!!!!!!!!!!!!!!!!!!!!!!!!!!!!!!!!!!!!!!!!!!!!!!!!!!!!!!!!!!!!!!!!!!!!!!!!!!!!!!!!!!!!
! The LQM percentage is set with the ppp quality command. CHAP simply needs to be
! enabled, with this router reacting to the other router's host name as stated in
! the CHAP messages.
interface Serial0/1/0
 ip address 10.1.34.3 255.255.255.0
 encapsulation ppp
 ppp quality 80
 ppp authentication chap
! R4 configuration is next. The configuration is mostly a mirror image of R3.
username R3 password 0 rom838
!
interface Serial0/1/0
 ip address 10.1.34.4 255.255.255.0
 encapsulation ppp
 ppp quality 70
 ppp authentication chap
! Next, on R3, the show command lists the phrase "LCP Open," implying that LCP has
! completed negotiations. On the next line, two NCPs (CDPCP and IPCP) are listed.
R3# show int s 0/1/0
Serial0/1/0 is up, line protocol is up
  Hardware is GT96K Serial
  Internet address is 10.1.34.3/24
  MTU 1500 bytes, BW 1544 Kbit, DLY 20000 usec,
     reliability 255/255, txload 1/255, rxload 1/255
  Encapsulation PPP, LCP Open
  Open: CDPCP, IPCP, loopback not set
  Keepalive set (10 sec)
! (The following debug output has been shortened in several places.) The link was
! shut/no shut after issuing the debug ppp negotiation command. The first messages
! state a configuration request, listing CHAP for authentication, that LQM should
! be used, and with the (default) setting of using magic numbers to detect loops.
```

```
*Apr 11 14:48:14.795: Se0/1/0 PPP: Phase is ESTABLISHING, Active Open
*Apr 11 14:48:14.795: Se0/1/0 LCP: O CONFREQ [Closed] id 186 len 23
*Apr 11 14:48:14.795: Se0/1/0 LCP:    AuthProto CHAP (0x0305C22305)
*Apr 11 14:48:14.795: Se0/1/0 LCP:    QualityType 0xC025 period 1000
(0x0408C025000003E8)
*Apr 11 14:48:14.795: Se0/1/0 LCP:    MagicNumber 0x13403093 (0x050613403093)
*Apr 11 14:48:14.807: Se0/1/0 LCP: State is Open
! LCP completes, with authentication occurring next. In succession below, the
! challenge is issued in both directions ("O" means "output," "I" means "Input").
! Following that, the response is made, with the hashed value. Finally, the
! confirmation is sent ("success"). Note that by default the process occurs in
! both directions.
*Apr 11 14:48:14.807: Se0/1/0 PPP: Phase is AUTHENTICATING, by both
*Apr 11 14:48:14.807: Se0/1/0 CHAP: O CHALLENGE id 85 len 23 from "R3"
*Apr 11 14:48:14.811: Se0/1/0 CHAP: I CHALLENGE id 41 len 23 from "R4"
*Apr 11 14:48:14.811: Se0/1/0 CHAP: Using hostname from unknown source
*Apr 11 14:48:14.811: Se0/1/0 CHAP: Using password from AAA
*Apr 11 14:48:14.811: Se0/1/0 CHAP: O RESPONSE id 41 len 23 from "R3"
*Apr 11 14:48:14.815: Se0/1/0 CHAP: I RESPONSE id 85 len 23 from "R4"
*Apr 11 14:48:14.819: Se0/1/0 CHAP: O SUCCESS id 85 len 4
*Apr 11 14:48:14.823: Se0/1/0 CHAP: I SUCCESS id 41 len 4
*Apr 11 14:48:14.823: Se0/1/0 PPP: Phase is UP
```

## Multilink PPP

Multilink PPP, abbreviated as MLP, MP, or MLPPP, defines a method to combine multiple parallel serial links at Layer 2. The original motivation for MLP was to combine multiple ISDN B-channels without requiring any Layer 3 load balancing; however, MLP can be used to load-balance traffic across any type of point-to-point serial link.

MLP balances traffic by fragmenting each data link layer frame, either based on the number of parallel links or on a configured fragmentation delay. MLP then sends the fragments over different links. For example, with three parallel links, MLP fragments each frame into three fragments and sends one over each link. To allow reassembly on the receiving end, MLP adds a header (either 4 or 2 bytes) to each fragment. The header includes a Sequence Number field as well as Flag bits designating the beginning and ending fragments.

MLP can be configured using either multilink interfaces or virtual templates. Example 6-4 shows an MLP multilink interface with two underlying serial interfaces. Following the configuration, the example shows some interface statistics that result from a ping from one router (R4) to the other router (R3) across the MLP connection.

**Example 6-4**  *MLP Configuration and Statistics with Multilink Interfaces—R3*

```
! All Layer 3 parameters are configured on the multilink interface. The
! serial links are associated with the multilink interface using the ppp
! multilink group commands.
interface Multilink1
 ip address 10.1.34.3 255.255.255.0
 encapsulation ppp
 ppp multilink
 ppp multilink group 1
!
interface Serial0/1/0
 no ip address
 encapsulation ppp
 ppp multilink group 1
!
interface Serial0/1/1
 no ip address
 encapsulation ppp
 ppp multilink group 1
! Below, the interface statistics reflect that each of the two serial links sends
! the same number of packets, one fragment of each original packet. Note that the
! multilink interface shows roughly the same number of packets, but the bit rate
! matches the sum of the bit rates on the two serial interfaces. These stats
! reflect the fact that the multilink interface shows prefragmentation
! counters, and the serial links show post-fragmentation counters.
R3# sh int s 0/1/0
Serial0/1/0 is up, line protocol is up
! lines omitted for brevity
   5 minute input rate 182000 bits/sec, 38 packets/sec
   5 minute output rate 182000 bits/sec, 38 packets/sec
      8979 packets input, 6804152 bytes, 0 no buffer
      8977 packets output, 6803230 bytes, 0 underruns
R3# sh int s 0/1/1
Serial0/1/1 is up, line protocol is up
! lines omitted for brevity
   5 minute input rate 183000 bits/sec, 38 packets/sec
   5 minute output rate 183000 bits/sec, 38 packets/sec
      9214 packets input, 7000706 bytes, 0 no buffer
      9213 packets output, 7000541 bytes, 0 underruns
R3# sh int multilink1
Multilink1 is up, line protocol is up
! lines omitted for brevity
   Hardware is multilink group interface
   Internet address is 10.1.34.3/24
```

```
MTU 1500 bytes, BW 3088 Kbit, DLY 100000 usec,
    reliability 255/255, txload 31/255, rxload 30/255
Encapsulation PPP, LCP Open, multilink Open
Open: CDPCP, IPCP, loopback not set
5 minute input rate 374000 bits/sec, 40 packets/sec
5 minute output rate 377000 bits/sec, 40 packets/sec
    9385 packets input, 14112662 bytes, 0 no buffer
    9384 packets output, 14243723 bytes, 0 underruns
```

## MLP Link Fragmentation and Interleaving

The term *Link Fragmentation and Interleaving (LFI)* refers to a type of Cisco IOS QoS tool that prevents small, delay-sensitive packets from having to wait on longer, delay-insensitive packets to be completely serialized out an interface. To do so, LFI tools fragment larger packets, and then send the delay-sensitive packet after just a portion of the original, longer packet. The key elements include fragmentation, the ability to interleave parts of one packet between fragments of another packet, and a queuing scheduler that interleaves the packets. Figure 6-2 depicts the complete process. A 1500-byte packet is fragmented and a 60-byte packet is interleaved between the fragments by the queuing scheduler after the first two fragments.

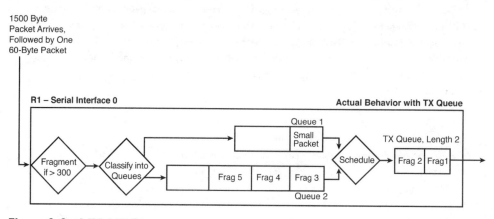

**Figure 6-2**   *MLP LFI Concept*

MLP supports LFI, the key elements of which are detailed in the following list:

■   The **ppp multilink interleave** interface subcommand tells the router to allow interleaving.

■   The **ppp multilink fragment-delay** $x$ command defines the fragment size indirectly, based on the following formula. Note that the unit for the delay parameter is milliseconds, so the units for the interface bandwidth must also be converted.

size = $x$ * bandwidth

■   MLP LFI can be used with only one link or with multiple links.

- The queuing scheduler on the multilink interface determines the next packet to send; as a result, many implementations use LLQ to always interleave delay-sensitive traffic between fragments.

Example 6-5 shows an updated version of the configuration in Example 6-2, with LFI enabled.

**Example 6-5**  *MLP LFI with LLQ to Interleave Voice*

```
! The fragment delay is set to 10 ms, so the fragments will be of size (256,000 *
! .01 second) = 2560 bits = 320 bytes. The ppp multilink interleave command allows
! the queuing tool to interleave packets between fragments of other packets, and
! the referenced policy map happens to use LLQ to interleave voice packets.
interface Multilink1
 bandwidth 256
 ip address 10.1.34.3 255.255.255.0
 encapsulation ppp
 ppp multilink
 ppp multilink group 1
 ppp multilink fragment-delay 10
 ppp multilink8 interleave
 service-policy output queue-on-dscp
```

## PPP Compression

PPP can negotiate to use Layer 2 payload compression, TCP header compression, and/ or RTP header compression. Each type of compression has pros and cons, with the most obvious relating to what is compressed, as shown in Figure 6-3.

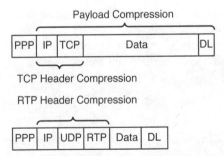

**Figure 6-3**  *Fields Compressed with Compression Features*

Comparing payload compression and header compression, payload compression works best with longer packet lengths, and header compression with shorter packet lengths. Header compression takes advantage of the predictability of headers, achieving a compression ratio for the header fields around 10:1 to 20:1. However, when the data inside the packet is much larger than the header, saving some bytes with header compression might be only a small reduction in the overall bandwidth required, making payload compression more appealing.

### PPP Layer 2 Payload Compression

Cisco IOS Software supplies three different payload compression options for PPP, namely, Lempel-Ziv Stacker (LZS), Microsoft Point-to-Point Compression (MPPC), and Predictor. Stacker and MPPC both use the same underlying Lempel-Ziv (LZ) compression algorithm, with Predictor using an algorithm called Predictor. LZ uses more CPU and less memory in comparison to Predictor, and LZ typically results in a better compression ratio.

Table 6-4 summarizes some of the key topics regarding payload compression. Note that of the three options, only LZS is supported on Frame Relay and HDLC links. Also note that for payload compression when using ATM–to–Frame Relay Service Interworking, MLP must be used; as a result, all payload compression types supported by PPP are also supported for Interworking.

**Table 6-4**   *Point-to-Point Payload Compression Tools: Feature Comparison*

| Feature | Stacker | MPPC | Predictor |
|---|---|---|---|
| Uses LZ algorithm? | Yes | Yes | No |
| Uses Predictor algorithm? | No | No | Yes |
| Supported on HDLC? | Yes | No | No |
| Supported on PPP? | Yes | Yes | Yes |
| Supported on Frame Relay? | Yes | No | No |
| Supports ATM and ATM–to–Frame Relay Service Interworking (using MLP)? | Yes | Yes | Yes |

Configuring payload compression simply requires a matching **compress** command under each interface on each end of the link(s), with matching parameters for the type of compression. After compression is configured, PPP starts the Compression Control Protocol (CCP), which is another NCP, to perform the compression negotiations and manage the compression process.

### Header Compression

PPP supports two styles of IP header compression: TCP header compression and RTP header compression. (Figure 6-3 shows the headers compressed by each.)

Voice and video flows use the RTP encapsulation shown at the bottom of Figure 6-3. Voice flows, particularly for low-bit-rate codecs, have very small data fields. For example, with G.729, the packet is typically 60 bytes, with 40 bytes of the 60 bytes being the IP/UDP/RTP headers. RTP header compression compresses the IP/UDP/RTP headers (40 bytes) into 2 or 4 bytes. With G.729 in use, RTP header compression reduces the required bandwidth by more than 50 percent.

TCP header compression compresses the combined IP and TCP headers, a combined 40 bytes, into 3 or 5 bytes. For TCP packets with small payloads, the saving can be significant; the math is similar to the RTP compression example in the previous paragraph. However, TCP header compression might not be worth the CPU and memory expense for larger packets. For example, for a 1500-byte packet, compressing the 40 bytes of the header into 3 bytes reduces the packet size by only about 2 percent.

Header compression can be configured using a pair of legacy commands, or it can be configured using Modular QoS CLI (MQC) commands. The legacy commands are **ip tcp header-compression [passive]** and **ip rtp header-compression [passive]**, used under the serial (PPP) or multilink (MLP) interfaces on each end of the link. PPP reacts to this command by using IPCP to negotiate to enable each type of compression. (If you use the **passive** keyword, that router waits for the other router to initiate the IPCP negotiation.) With this style of configuration, all TCP flows and/or all RTP flows using the link are compressed.

Example 6-6 shows the alternative method using an MQC policy map to create class-based header compression. In the example, TCP header compression is applied only to the class that holds Telnet traffic. As a result, TCP header compression is applied to the packets that are most likely to benefit from TCP compression, without wasting CPU and memory to compress larger packets. (Recall that Telnet sends one keystroke per TCP segment, unless **service nagle** is configured, making Telnet highly inefficient by default.)

**Example 6-6**   *MQC Class-Based Header Compression*

```
! RTP compression is enabled in the voice class, TCP header compression in the
! critical data class, and no compression in the class-default class.
policy-map cb-compression
 class voice
 bandwidth 82
 compress header ip rtp
 class critical
 bandwidth 110
 compress header ip tcp
!
interface Multilink1
 bandwidth 256
 service-policy output cb-compression
```

## PPPoE

PPP over Ethernet (PPPoE) provides the capability to connect hosts on a network over a simple bridging device to a remote aggregation concentrator. PPPoE is the predominant access protocol in broadband networks worldwide. PPPoE typically is deployed with a software stack housed on the end-customer's (subscriber's) PC. This software allows the network service provider to "own" the customer as the PPP session runs from the customer PC to the service provider network.

PPPoE provides an emulated (and optionally authenticated) point-to-point link across a shared medium, typically a broadband aggregation network such as those found in DSL service providers. In fact, a very common scenario is to run a PPPoE client on the customer side, which connects to and obtains its configuration from the PPPoE server (head-end router) at the ISP side.

## Server Configuration

Example 6-7 demonstrates the very first step that must be taken at the ISP end. It is here that we will create a Broadband Aggregation (BBA) group that will handle incoming PPPoE connections. For the purposes of our discussion, we will name the bba-group **BBA-Group** and bind it to a virtual template that we will create later.

**Example 6-7** *Virtual Template Configuration*

```
ISP(config)# bba-group pppoe BBA-GROUP
ISP(config-bba-group)# virtual-template 1
```

Another useful option would be to apply PPPoE session limits just as a protective measure. To limit the number of sessions established based on the associated MAC addresses, you would enter the following, for example:

```
ISP(config-bba-group)# sessions per-mac limit 2
```

In this scenario, we will specify a limit of 2. This will allow a new session to be established immediately if the prior session has been dropped or is waiting to expire.

The next important step will be to create the virtual template, the one we mentioned previously, that will service the client-facing interface:

```
ISP(config)# interface virtual-template 1
```

When a PPPoE client initiates a session with this router, the router will dynamically create a virtual interface. This interface will act as the placeholder for the point-to-point connection spawned by this process.

To operate properly, the virtual template will need two components: an IP address and a pool of IP addresses that will be used to issue negotiated addresses to clients. This process, illustrated in Example 6-8, would have to be considered the absolute basic elements needed to create an operational process.

**Example 6-8** *PPPoE Basic Configuration*

```
ISP(config-if)# ip address 10.0.0.1 255.255.255.0
ISP(config-if)# peer default ip address pool PPOE_POOL
```

Now we will need to define the range of addresses that will be issued as part of the pool. To configure the local IP pool named **PPPOE-POOL** with the starting and ending addresses of an IP range, you would enter the following in global configuration mode:

```
ISP(config)# ip local pool PPPOE_POOL 10.0.0.2 10.0.0.254
```

The final step is to enable the PPPoE group on the interface facing the client, as shown in Example 6-9.

**Example 6-9**   *PPPoE Enabling the PPPoE Group*

```
ISP(config)# interface f0/0
ISP(config-if)# no ip address
ISP(config-if)# pppoe enable group MyGroup
ISP(config-if)# no shutdown
```

**Key Topic**

Note that this interface is not configured with an IP address; in this case, the addressing will be issued by the virtual template that we configured previously.

### Client Configuration

Compared to the server configuration, creating a client is far less complicated. First, we will create a dialer interface to handle the PPPoE connection and then associate it with the physical interface that will be used to provide transport.

Creating the PPPoE dialer interface configuration can be seen in Example 6-10.

**Example 6-10**   *PPPoE Dialer Interface*

```
CPE(config)# interface dialer1
CPE(config-if)# dialer pool 1
CPE(config-if)# encapsulation ppp
CPE(config-if)# ip address negotiated
```

The **ip address negotiated** command tells the client to use an IP address provided by the PPPoE server.

**Key Topic**

As part of this process, the PPP header adds 8 bytes of overhead to each frame. This could be problematic in situations where we might have packets close to the default Ethernet MTU of 1500 bytes, and to manage this eventuality, we will need to lower the MTU of the specific dialer interface to 1492 to avoid fragmentation. Example 6-11 demonstrates this as well as shows how to assign the ISP interface to our newly created PPPoE dial group.

**Example 6-11**   *PPPoE Session Limits*

```
CPE(config-if)# mtu 1492
CPE(config-if)# exit
CPE(config)# interface f0/0
CPE(config-if)# no ip address
CPE(config-if)# pppoe-client dial-pool-number 1
CPE(config-if)# no shutdown
!!!!!!!!!!!!!!!!!!!!!!!!!!!!!!!!!!!!!!!!!!!!!!!!!!!!!!!!!!!!!!!!!!!!!!!!!!!!!!!!!!!!!
!!!If all is well, you should see a notification indicating the PPPoE session has
!!!successfully formed:
```

```
!!!!!!!!!!!!!!!!!!!!!!!!!!!!!!!!!!!!!!!!!!!!!!!!!!!!!!!!!!!!!!!!!!!!!!!!!!!!!!!!!!!!!!!!!!!!!
%DIALER-6-BIND: Interface Vi1 bound to profile Di1
%LINK-3-UPDOWN: Interface Virtual-Access1, changed state to up
%LINEPROTO-5-UPDOWN: Line protocol on Interface Virtual-Access1, changed
state to up
```

We can verify that interface Dialer1 has negotiated an IP address from the ISP router through the commands found in Example 6-12.

**Example 6-12**  *PPPoE Verification*

```
CPE# show ip interface brief
Interface                 IP-Address      OK? Method Status               Protocol
FastEthernet0/0           unassigned      YES manual up                   up
[...]
Virtual-Access1           unassigned      YES unset  up                   up
Dialer1                   10.0.0.2        YES IPCP   up                   up
!!!!!!!!!!!!!!!!!!!!!!!!!!!!!!!!!!!!!!!!!!!!!!!!!!!!!!!!!!!!!!!!!!!!!!!!!!!!!!!!!!!!!!!
!!!!
!!! show pppoe session shows our PPPoE session with the ISP router terminated on
!!! Dialer0, via FastEthernet0/0:
!!!!!!!!!!!!!!!!!!!!!!!!!!!!!!!!!!!!!!!!!!!!!!!!!!!!!!!!!!!!!!!!!!!!!!!!!!!!!!!!!!!!!!!
!!!
CPE# show pppoe session
 1 client session

Uniq ID  PPPoE  RemMAC          Port                   Source   VA       State
         SID    LocMAC                                          VA-st
N/A      16     ca00.4843.0008  Fa0/0                  Di1      Vi1      UP
                ca01.4843.0008                                  UP
```

## Authentication

Now we need to consider the fact that at this point, anyone can connect through PPPoE. This is a less-than-satisfactory situation because we will need to restrict access to trusted clients. To accomplish this, we will configure authentication. This is probably the most prudent course of action available. As we discussed previously, PPP can use PAP or CHAP to authenticate clients, with the latter heavily preferred. To explore the authentication option in the context of PPPoE, we will configure our ISP router with a local user account named **PPP** and the password **PPPpassword**. This process can be seen in the output of Example 6-13.

**Example 6-13**  *PPPoE Authentication*

```
ISP(config)# username PPP password PPPpassword
!!!!!!!!!!!!!!!!!!!!!!!!!!!!!!!!!!!!!!!!!!!!!!!!!!!!!!!!!!!!!!!!!!!!!!!!!!!!!!!!!!!
!!! Next we enforce CHAP authentication on our virtual template
!!!!!!!!!!!!!!!!!!!!!!!!!!!!!!!!!!!!!!!!!!!!!!!!!!!!!!!!!!!!!!!!!!!!!!!!!!!!!!!!!!!
ISP(config)# interface virtual-template 1
ISP(config-if)# ppp authentication chap callin
!!!!!!!!!!!!!!!!!!!!!!!!!!!!!!!!!!!!!!!!!!!!!!!!!!!!!!!!!!!!!!!!!!!!!!!!!!!!!!!!!!!
!!! This will terminate our client session, as we can see from the logs on CPE:
!!!!!!!!!!!!!!!!!!!!!!!!!!!!!!!!!!!!!!!!!!!!!!!!!!!!!!!!!!!!!!!!!!!!!!!!!!!!!!!!!!!
%DIALER-6-UNBIND: Interface Vi1 unbound from profile Di1
%LINK-3-UPDOWN: Interface Virtual-Access1, changed state to down
%LINEPROTO-5-UPDOWN: Line protocol on Interface Virtual-Access1, changed state to
  down
!!!!!!!!!!!!!!!!!!!!!!!!!!!!!!!!!!!!!!!!!!!!!!!!!!!!!!!!!!!!!!!!!!!!!!!!!!!!!!!!!!!
!!! To reestablish the connection from CPE, we'll need to enter the proper
!!! credentials:
!!!!!!!!!!!!!!!!!!!!!!!!!!!!!!!!!!!!!!!!!!!!!!!!!!!!!!!!!!!!!!!!!!!!!!!!!!!!!!!!!!!
CPE(config)# interface dialer 1
CPE(config-if)# ppp chap password MyPassword
!!!!!!!!!!!!!!!!!!!!!!!!!!!!!!!!!!!!!!!!!!!!!!!!!!!!!!!!!!!!!!!!!!!!!!!!!!!!!!!!!!!
!!! We should see the PPPoE session come back up a few seconds later after
!!! successfully authenticating. debug ppp authentication can be used on the ISP
!!! router to monitor the CHAP exchange:
!!!!!!!!!!!!!!!!!!!!!!!!!!!!!!!!!!!!!!!!!!!!!!!!!!!!!!!!!!!!!!!!!!!!!!!!!!!!!!!!!!!
ppp50 PPP: Using vpn set call direction
ppp50 PPP: Treating connection as a callin
ppp50 PPP: Session handle[E800003A] Session id[50]
ppp50 PPP: Authorization required
ppp50 CHAP: O CHALLENGE id 1 len 24 from "ISP"
ppp50 CHAP: I RESPONSE id 1 len 24 from "CPE"
ppp50 PPP: Sent CHAP LOGIN Request
ppp50 PPP: Received LOGIN Response PASS
Vi1.1 PPP: Sent LCP AUTHOR Request
Vi1.1 PPP: Sent IPCP AUTHOR Request
Vi1.1 LCP: Received AAA AUTHOR Response PASS
Vi1.1 IPCP: Received AAA AUTHOR Response PASS
Vi1.1 CHAP: O SUCCESS id 1 len 4
```

# Ethernet WAN

After you've spent so much time learning about the various capabilities and features of Ethernet technologies, it should come as no surprise that industry trends have pushed this technology from the typical local-area deployment and into the arena of wide-area networks. As early as ten years ago, WAN technologies included a short list of protocols and features that included Frame Relay, ATM, and Synchronous Optical Network (SONET). Today the ever-increasing demand for bandwidth between geographically isolated environments has created a new breed of interconnectivity solutions that utilize Ethernet and Ethernet features at their core. This list includes but is not limited to technologies like Virtual Private LAN Services (VPLS), Multi-Protocol Label Switching (MPLS), Any-Transport Over MPLS (ATOM), Dot1Q-in-Dot1Q Tunnels (QnQ Tunnels), and Metro-Ethernet.

These technologies create "borderless networks"; that is, networks where a service can be turned up anywhere and at any time. Furthermore, these technologies provide LAN-like user performance normally only found in headquarter offices. All this is accomplished through the primary technology: Ethernet Wide-Area Networks (EWAN).

Ethernet has evolved from just a LAN technology to a scalable, cost-effective, and manageable WAN solution for businesses of all sizes. Ethernet offers numerous cost and operational advantages over conventional WAN solutions. Ethernet Wide-Area Networks maintain the high bandwidth and simplicity of Layer 2 Ethernet, and the flat network design makes the connected sites appear as a single logical network and simplifies connectivity back to the headquarters and between remote sites.

For the purposes of our discussions, we will first look at Virtual Private LAN Services (VPLS), which is designed to deliver Layer 2 connectivity to all endpoints in the EWAN configuration and then move to another service type called Metro-Ethernet. Both of these technologies are often simply referred to as Layer 2 VPNs and, more often than not, will use MPLS as an enabling technology.

## VPLS

VPLS enables the carriers to bring the various WAN connections (over either IP or MPLS networks) together as a single logical Ethernet network where quality of service (QoS) levels can be defined to ensure that audio or video applications get their required bandwidth.

Very simply, VPLS is an architecture that allows MPLS networks to provide multipoint Ethernet LAN services, often referred to as Transparent LAN Service (TLS). A multipoint network service is one that allows a customer edge (CE) endpoint or node to communicate directly with all other CE nodes associated with the multipoint service. By contrast, using a point-to-point network service such as ATM, the end customer typically designates one CE node to be the hub to which all spoke sites are connected. In this scenario, if a spoke site needs to communicate with another spoke site, it must communicate through the hub, and this requirement can introduce transmission delay.

To provide multipoint Ethernet capability, the IETF VPLS drafts describe the concept of linking virtual Ethernet bridges using MPLS Pseudo-Wires (PW). As a VPLS forwards Ethernet frames at Layer 2, the operation of VPLS is exactly the same as that found within IEEE 802.1 bridges in that VPLS will self-learn the source MAC address to port associations, and frames are forwarded based upon the destination MAC address. If the destination address is unknown, or is a broadcast or multicast address, the frame is flooded to all ports associated with the virtual bridge. Although the forwarding operation of VPLS is relatively simple, the VPLS architecture needs to be able to perform other operational functions, such as

- Autodiscover other provider edges (PE) associated with a particular VPLS instance

- Signaling of PWs to interconnect VPLS virtual switch instances (VSI)

- Loop avoidance

- MAC address withdrawal

## Metro-Ethernet

Ethernet on the metropolitan-area network (MAN) can be used as pure Ethernet, Ethernet over MPLS, or Ethernet over Dark Fiber, but regardless of the transport medium, we have to recognize that in network deployments requiring medium-distance backhaul or metropolitan (in the same city) connectivity, this Ethernet WAN technology is king. Why do we have so many different types of Metro-E solutions? The answer is that each has advantages and disadvantages. As an example, pure Ethernet-based deployments are cheaper but less reliable and scalable, and are usually limited to small-scale or experimental deployments. Dark Fiber–based deployments are useful when there is an existing infrastructure already in place, whereas solutions that are MPLS based are costly but highly reliable and scalable, and as such are used typically by large corporations.

We will focus briefly on the idea of employing Metro-Ethernet by using MPLS because of the fact that MPLS figures so prominently in our CCIE R&S written studies. An MPLS-based Metro-Ethernet network uses MPLS in the service provider's network. The subscriber will get an Ethernet interface on copper (for example, 100BASE-TX) or fiber (such as 100BASE-FX). The customer's Ethernet packet is transported over MPLS, and the service provider network uses Ethernet again as the underlying technology to transport MPLS. So MPLS-based Metro-E is effectively Ethernet over MPLS over Ethernet.

Label Distribution Protocol (LDP) signaling can be used to provide site-to-site signaling for the inner label (VC label) and Resource Reservation Protocol-Traffic Engineering (RSVP-TE), or LDP can be used to provide the network signaling for the outer label.

It should also be noted that a typical Metro-Ethernet system has a star network or mesh network topology, with individual routers or servers interconnected through cable or fiber-optic media. This is important when it becomes necessary to troubleshoot Metro-Ethernet solutions.

# Foundation Summary

This section lists additional details and facts to round out the coverage of the topics in this chapter. Unlike most Cisco Press Exam Certification Guides, this book does not repeat information listed in the "Foundation Topics" section of the chapter. Please take the time to read and study the details in this section of the chapter, as well as review the items in the "Foundation Topics" section noted with a Key Topic icon.

Table 6-5 lists the key protocols covered in this chapter.

**Table 6-5**  *Protocols and Standards for Chapter 6*

| Topic | Standard |
|---|---|
| Point-to-Point Protocol (PPP) | RFC 1661 |
| PPP in HDLC-like Framing | RFC 1662 |
| PPP Internet Protocol Control Protocol (IPCP) | RFC 1332 |
| IP Header Compression over PPP | RFC 3544 |
| PPP Multilink Protocol (MLP) | RFC 1990 |
| PPPoE | RFC 2684 |
| Virtual Private LAN Service (VPLS) | RFC 4762 |
| Metro-Ethernet (GMPLS) | RFC 6004 |

Table 6-6 lists the Cisco IOS commands related to serial links, as covered in this chapter.

**Table 6-6**  *Command Reference for Chapter 6*

| Command | Mode and Function |
|---|---|
| **interface virtual-template** *number* | Global mode; creates a virtual template interface for MLP and moves the user into virtual template configuration mode |
| **ppp authentication** {*protocol1* [*protocol2...*]} [**if-needed**] [*list-name* \| **default**] [**callin**] [**one-time**] [**optional**] | Interface mode; defines the authentication protocol (PAP, CHAP, EAP) and other parameters |
| **ppp multilink** [**bap**] | Interface mode; enables MLP on an interface |
| **ppp multilink fragment-delay** *delay-max* | Interface mode; defines the fragment size based on the delay and interface bandwidth |
| **ppp multilink group** *group-number* | Interface mode; associates a physical interface to a multilink interface |
| **ppp multilink interleave** | Interface mode; allows the queuing scheduled to interleave packets between fragments of another packet |

| Command | Mode and Function |
| --- | --- |
| compress [predictor \| stac \| mppc [ignore-pfc]] | Interface mode; configures payload compression |
| ip rtp header-compression [passive] | Interface mode; enables RTP header compression |
| ip tcp header-compression [passive] | Interface mode; enables TCP header compression |
| compression header ip [rtp \| tcp] | Class configuration mode; enables RTP or TCP header compression inside an MQC class |
| ppp quality *percentage* | Interface mode; enables LQM monitoring at the stated percentage |
| debug ppp negotiation | Enables debugging that shows the various stages of PPP negotiation |

See Chapter 5, "Shaping, Policing, and Link Fragmentation," for more information about the **class-map, policy-map,** and **service-policy** commands.

# Memory Builders

The CCIE Routing and Switching written exam, like all Cisco CCIE written exams, covers a fairly broad set of topics. This section provides some basic tools to help you exercise your memory about some of the broader topics covered in this chapter.

## Fill In Key Tables from Memory

First, take the time to print Appendix E, "Key Tables for CCIE Study," on the CD, which contains empty sets of some of the key summary tables from the "Foundation Topics" section of this chapter. Then, simply fill in the tables from memory. Refer to Appendix F, "Solutions for Key Tables for CCIE Study," also on the CD, to check your answers.

## Definitions

Next, take a few moments to write down the definitions for the following terms:

PPP, MLP, LCP, NCP, IPCP, CDPCP, MLP, PPPoE LFI, CHAP, PAP, LFI, Layer 2 payload compression, TCP header compression, RTP header compression, VC, PVC, SVC, DTE, DCE, access rate, access link, Service Interworking, Using Multilink PPP (MLP)

Refer to the glossary to check your answers.

# Further Reading

www.cisco.com/c/en/us/td/docs/ios-xml/ios/bbdsl/configuration/15-mt/bba-15-mt-book.html

http://tools.ietf.org/html/draft-ietf-l2vpn-vpls-ldp-09

**Blueprint topics covered in this chapter:**

This chapter covers the following subtopics from the Cisco CCIE Routing and Switching written exam blueprint. Refer to the full blueprint in Table I-1 in the Introduction for more details on the topics covered in each chapter and their context within the blueprint.

■    IP Multicast

## CHAPTER 7

# Introduction to IP Multicasting

IP multicast concepts and protocols are an important part of the CCIE Routing and Switching written exam. Demand for IP multicast applications has increased dramatically over the last several years. Almost all major campus networks today use some form of multicasting. This chapter covers why multicasting is needed, the fundamentals of multicast addressing, and how multicast traffic is distributed and controlled over a LAN.

## "Do I Know This Already?" Quiz

Table 7-1 outlines the major headings in this chapter and the corresponding "Do I Know This Already?" quiz questions.

**Table 7-1** *"Do I Know This Already?" Foundation Topics Section-to-Question Mapping*

| Foundation Topics Section | Questions Covered in This Section | Score |
| --- | --- | --- |
| Why Do You Need Multicasting? | 1 | |
| Multicast IP Addresses | 2–4 | |
| Managing Distribution of Multicast Traffic with IGMP | 5–6 | |
| LAN Multicast Optimizations | 7 | |
| Total Score | | |

To best use this pre-chapter assessment, remember to score yourself strictly. You can find the answers in Appendix A, "Answers to the 'Do I Know This Already?' Quizzes."

1. Which of the following reasons for using IP multicasting are valid for one-to-many applications?

   a. Multicast applications use connection-oriented service.

   b. Multicast uses less bandwidth than unicast.

   c. A multicast packet can be sent from one source to many destinations.

   d. Multicast eliminates traffic redundancy.

**2.** Which of the following statements is true of a multicast address?

    **a.** Uses a Class D address that can range from 223.0.0.0 to 239.255.255.255

    **b.** Uses a subnet mask ranging from 8 bits to 24 bits

    **c.** Can be permanent or transient

    **d.** Can be entered as an IP address on an interface of a router only if the router is configured for multicasting

**3.** Which of the following multicast addresses are reserved and not forwarded by multicast routers?

    **a.** 224.0.0.1 and 224.0.0.13

    **b.** 224.0.0.9 and 224.0.1.39

    **c.** 224.0.0.10 and 224.0.1.40

    **d.** 224.0.0.5 and 224.0.0.6

**4.** From the following pairs of Layer 3 multicast addresses, select a pair that will use the same Ethernet multicast MAC address of 0x0100.5e4d.2643.

    **a.** 224.67.26.43 and 234.67.26.43

    **b.** 225.77.67.38 and 235.77.67.38

    **c.** 229.87.26.43 and 239.87.26.43

    **d.** 227.77.38.67 and 238.205.38.67

**5.** From the following statements, select the true statement(s) regarding IGMP Query messages and IGMP Report messages.

    **a.** Hosts, switches, and routers originate IGMP Membership Report messages.

    **b.** Hosts, switches, and routers originate IGMP Query messages.

    **c.** Hosts originate IGMP Query messages and routers originate IGMP Membership messages.

    **d.** Hosts originate IGMP Membership messages and routers originate IGMP Query messages.

    **e.** Hosts and switches originate IGMP Membership messages and routers originate IGMP Query messages.

6.  Seven hosts and a router on a multicast LAN network are using IGMPv2. Hosts 5, 6, and 7 are members of group 226.5.6.7, and the other four hosts are not. Which of the following answers is/are true about how the router will respond when Host 7 sends an IGMPv2 Leave message for the group 226.5.6.7?

    a.  Sends an IGMPv2 General Query to multicast destination address 224.0.0.1

    b.  Sends an IGMPv2 Group-Specific Query to multicast destination address 224.0.0.1

    c.  Sends an IGMPv2 General Query to multicast destination address 226.5.6.7

    d.  Sends an IGMPv2 Group-Specific Query to multicast destination address 226.5.6.7

    e.  First sends an IGMPv2 Group-Specific Query to multicast destination address 226.5.6.7, and then sends an IGMPv2 General Query to multicast destination address 224.0.0.1

7.  Which of the following statements is/are true regarding CGMP and IGMP snooping?

    a.  CGMP and IGMP snooping are used to constrain the flooding of multicast traffic in LAN switches.

    b.  CGMP is a Cisco-proprietary protocol and uses the well-known Layer 2 multicast MAC address 0x0100.0cdd.dddd.

    c.  IGMP snooping is preferable in a mixed-vendor environment; however, if implemented using Layer 2–only LAN switches, it can cause a dramatic reduction in switch performance.

    d.  CGMP is simple to implement, and in CGMP only routers send CGMP messages, while switches only listen for CGMP messages.

    e.  All of these answers are correct.

## Foundation Topics

# Why Do You Need Multicasting?

"Necessity is the mother of all invention," a saying derived from Plato's *Republic*, holds very true in the world of technology. In the late 1980s, Dr. Steve Deering was working on a project that required him to send a message from one computer to a group of computers across a Layer 3 network. After studying several routing protocols, Dr. Deering concluded that the functionality of the routing protocols could be extended to support "Layer 3 multicasting." This concept led to more research, and in 1991, Dr. Deering published his doctoral thesis, "Multicast Routing in a Datagram Network," in which he defined the components required for IP multicasting, their functions, and their relationships with each other.

The most basic definition of IP multicasting is as follows:

> Sending a message from a single source to selected multiple destinations across a Layer 3 network in one data stream.

If you want to send a message from one source to one destination, you could send a unicast message. If you want to send a message from one source to all the destinations on a local network, you could send a broadcast message. However, if you want to send a message from one source to selected multiple destinations spread across a routed network in one data stream, the most efficient method is IP multicasting.

Demand for multicast applications is increasing with the advent of such applications as audio and video web content; broadcasting TV programs, radio programs, and concerts over the Internet; communicating stock quotes to brokers; transmitting a corporate message to employees; and transmitting data from a centralized warehouse to a chain of retail stores. Success of one-to-many multicast applications has created a demand for the second generation of multicast applications that are referred to as "many-to-many" and "many-to-few," in which there are many sources of multicast traffic. Examples of these types of applications include playing games on an intranet or the Internet and conducting interactive audio and video meetings. The primary focus of this chapter and the next chapter is to help you understand concepts and technologies required for implementing one-to-many multicast applications.

## Problems with Unicast and Broadcast Methods

Why not use unicast or broadcast methods to send a message from one source to many destinations? Figure 7-1 shows a video server as a source of a video application and the video data that needs to be delivered to a group of receivers—H2, H3, and H4—two hops away across a WAN link.

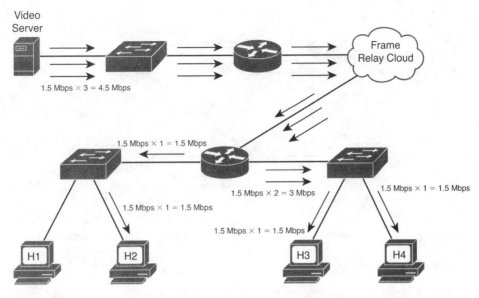

**Figure 7-1**   *Unicast*

The unicast method requires that the video application send one copy of each packet to every group member's unicast address. To support full-motion, full-screen viewing, the video stream requires approximately 1.5 Mbps of bandwidth for each receiver. If only a few receivers exist, as shown in Figure 7-1, this method works fine but still requires $n \times$ 1.5 Mbps of bandwidth, where $n$ is the number of receiving hosts.

Figure 7-2 shows that as the number of receivers grows into the hundreds or thousands, the load on the server to create and send copies of the same data also increases, and replicated unicast transmissions consume a lot of bandwidth within the network. For 100 users, as indicated in the upper-left corner of Figure 7-2, the bandwidth required to send the unicast transmission increases to 150 Mbps. For 1000 users, the bandwidth required would increase to 1.5 Gbps.

You can see from Figure 7-2 that the unicast method is not scalable. Figure 7-3 shows that the broadcast method requires transmission of data only once, but it has some serious issues. First, as shown in Figure 7-3, if the receivers are in a different broadcast domain from the sender, routers need to forward broadcasts. However, forwarding broadcasts might be the worst possible solution, because broadcasting a packet to all hosts in a network can waste bandwidth and increase processing load on all the network devices if only a small group of hosts in the network actually needs to receive the packet.

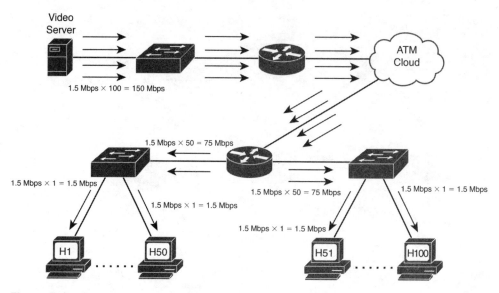

**Figure 7-2** *Unicast Does Not Scale to Large Numbers of Receivers*

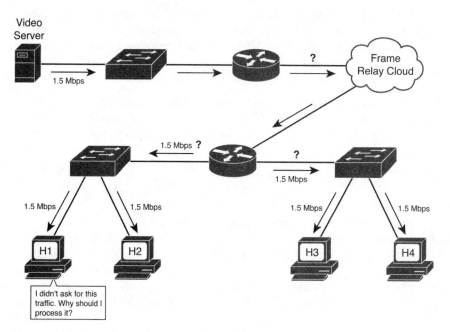

**Figure 7-3** *Broadcast Wastes Bandwidth and Increases Processing Load on the CPU*

## How Multicasting Provides a Scalable and Manageable Solution

The six basic requirements for supporting multicast across a routed network are as follows:

■ A designated range of Layer 3 addresses that can only be used by multicast applications must exist. A network administrator needs to install a multicast application on a multicast server using a Layer 3 multicast address from the designated range.

■ A multicast address must be used only as a destination IP address and specifically not as a source IP address. Unlike a unicast IP packet, a destination IP address in a multicast packet does not specify a recipient's address but rather signifies that the packet is carrying multicast traffic for a specific multicast application.

■ The multicast application must be installed on all the hosts in the network that need to receive the multicast traffic for the application. The application must be installed using the same Layer 3 multicast address that was used on the multicast server. This is referred to as *launching an application* or *joining a group*.

■ All hosts that are connected to a LAN must use a standard method to calculate a Layer 2 multicast address from the Layer 3 multicast address and assign it to their network interface cards (NIC). For example, if multiple routers are connected to an Ethernet segment and all of them are using the Open Shortest Path First (OSPF) routing protocol, all the routers on their Ethernet interfaces will also be listening to the Layer 2 multicast address 0x0100.5e00.0005 in addition to their Burned-In Addresses (BIA). This Layer 2 multicast address 0x0100.5e00.0005 is calculated from the multicast Layer 3 address 224.0.0.5, which is reserved for the OSPF routing protocol.

■ There must be a mechanism by which a host can dynamically indicate to the connected router whether it would like to receive the traffic for the installed multicast application. The Internet Group Management Protocol (IGMP) provides communication between hosts and a router connected to the same subnet. The Cisco Group Management Protocol (CGMP) or IGMP snooping helps switches learn which hosts have requested to receive the traffic for a specific multicast application and to which switch ports these hosts are connected.

■ There must be a multicast routing protocol that allows routers to forward multicast traffic from multicast servers to hosts without overtaxing network resources. Some of the multicast routing protocols are Distance Vector Multicast Routing Protocol (DVMRP), Multicast Open Shortest Path First (MOSPF), and Protocol Independent Multicast dense mode (PIM-DM) and sparse mode (PIM-SM).

This chapter discusses the first five bulleted items, and Chapter 8, "IP Multicast Routing," covers the multicast routing protocols.

Figure 7-4 shows how multicast traffic is forwarded in a Layer 3 network. The purpose of this illustration is to give you an overview of how multicast traffic is forwarded and received by selected hosts.

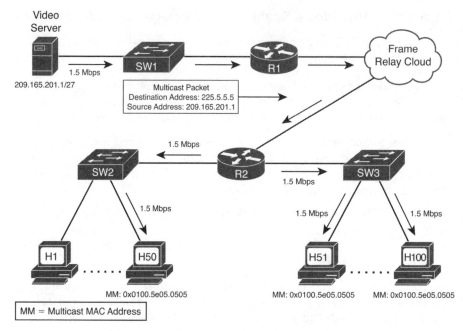

**Figure 7-4** *How Multicast Delivers Traffic to Selected Users*

Assume that a video multicast application was installed on the video server using the special Layer 3 multicast address 225.5.5.5. Hosts 1 to 50, located across a WAN link, are not interested at this time in receiving traffic for this application. Hosts 51 to 100 are interested in receiving traffic for this application and launch this application on their PCs. When the host launches the application, the host *joins the group*, which means that the host now wants to receive multicast packets sent to 225.5.5.5. Hosts 51 to 100 join group 225.5.5.5 and indicate to R2 their desire to receive traffic for this multicast application by using IGMP. The multicast application calculates the Layer 2 multicast address 0x0100.5e05.0505 from the Layer 3 multicast address 225.5.5.5, and NICs of hosts 51 to 100 are listening to this address in addition to their BIAs.

A multicast routing protocol is configured on R1 and R2 so that they can forward the multicast traffic. R2 has one WAN link connected to the Frame Relay cloud and two Ethernet links connected to two switches, SW2 and SW3. R2 knows that it has hosts on both Ethernet links that would like to receive multicast traffic for the group 225.5.5.5 because these hosts have indicated their desire to receive traffic for the group using IGMP. Both switches have also learned on which ports they have hosts that would like to receive the multicast traffic for this application by using either CGMP or IGMP snooping.

A multicast packet travels from the video server over the Ethernet link to R1, and R1 forwards a single copy of the multicast packet over the WAN link to R2. When R2 receives a multicast packet on the WAN link with the destination address 225.5.5.5, it makes a copy of the packet and forwards a copy on each Ethernet link. Because it is a multicast packet for the group (application) 225.5.5.5, R2 calculates the Layer 2 destination multicast address of 0x0100.5e05.0505 and uses it as the destination MAC address on each packet it forwards to both switches. When the switches receive these packets, they forward them on appropriate ports to hosts. When the hosts receive the packets, their NICs compare the destination MAC address with the multicast MAC address they are listening to, and because they match, inform the higher layers to process the packet.

You can see from Figure 7-4 that the multicast traffic is sent once over the WAN links and is received by the hosts that have requested it. Should additional hosts request to receive the same multicast traffic, neither the multicast server nor the network resources would incur any additional burden, as shown in Figure 7-5.

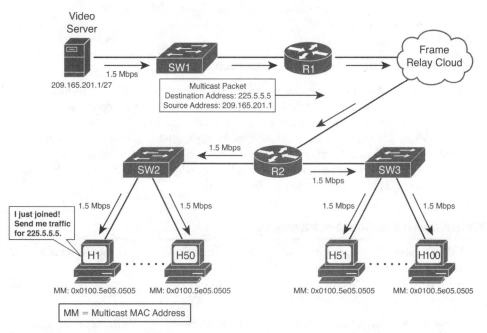

**Figure 7-5**    *Multicasting Is Scalable*

Assume that hosts 1 to 50 have also indicated their desire to receive traffic for the multicast group 225.5.5.5 using IGMP. R2 is already forwarding the traffic to both switches. Either CGMP or IGMP snooping can help SW2 (shown in Figure 7-5) learn that hosts 1 to 50 have also requested the multicast traffic for the group so that it can start forwarding the multicast traffic on ports connected to hosts 1 to 50. The additional 50 users are now receiving multicast traffic, and the load on the multicast server, load on other network devices, and demand for bandwidth on the WAN links remain the same. The load on SW2 shown in Figure 7-5 increases because it has to make 50 more copies of the multicast traffic and forward it on 50 more ports; however, it is now operating at the same level as the other switch. You can see that IP multicast is scalable.

Although multicast offers many advantages, it also has some disadvantages. Multicast is UDP based and hence unreliable. Lack of TCP windowing and "slow start" mechanisms can result in network congestion. Some multicast protocol mechanisms occasionally generate duplicate packets and deliver packets out of order.

# Multicast IP Addresses

Multicast applications always use a multicast IP address. This multicast address represents the multicast application and is referred to as a multicast *group*. Unlike a unicast IP address, which uniquely identifies a single IP host, a multicast address used as a destination address on an IP packet signifies that the packet is carrying traffic for a specific multicast application. For example, if a multicast packet is traveling over a network with a destination address 225.5.5.5, it is proclaiming to the network devices that, "I am carrying traffic for the multicast application that uses multicast group address 225.5.5.5; do you want it?" A multicast address is never assigned to a network device, so it is never used as a source address. The source address on a multicast packet, or any IP packet, should always be a unicast address.

## Multicast Address Range and Structure

The Internet Assigned Numbers Authority (IANA) has assigned class D IP addresses to multicast applications. The first 4 bits of the first octet for a class D address are always 1110. IP multicast addresses range from 224.0.0.0 through 239.255.255.255. As these addresses are used to represent multicast groups (applications) and not hosts, there is no need for a subnet mask for multicast addresses because they are not hierarchical. In other words, there is only one requirement for a multicast address: The first 4 bits of the first octet must be 1110. The last 28 bits are unstructured.

## Well-Known Multicast Addresses

IANA controls the assignment of IP multicast addresses. To preserve multicast addresses, IANA is reluctant to assign individual IP multicast addresses to new applications without a good technical justification. However, IANA has assigned individual IP multicast addresses to popular network protocols.

IANA has assigned several ranges of multicast IP addresses for specific types of reasons. Those types are as follows:

- Permanent multicast groups, in the range 224.0.0.0–224.0.1.255

- Addresses used with Source-Specific Multicast (SSM), in the range 232.0.0.0–232.255.255.255

- GLOP addressing, in the range 233.0.0.0–233.255.255.255

- Private multicast addresses, in the range 239.0.0.0–239.255.255.255

This section provides some insights into each of these four types of reserved IP multicast addresses. The rest of the multicast addresses are referred to as *transient* groups, which are covered later in this chapter in the section "Multicast Addresses for Transient Groups."

## Multicast Addresses for Permanent Groups

IANA has reserved two ranges of permanent multicast IP addresses. The main distinction between these two ranges of addresses is that the first range is used for packets that should not be forwarded by routers, and the second group is used when packets should be forwarded by routers.

The range of addresses used for local (not routed) purposes is 224.0.0.0 through 224.0.0.255. These addresses should be somewhat familiar from the routing protocol discussions earlier in the book. For example, the 224.0.0.5 and 224.0.0.6 IP addresses used by OSPF fit into this first range of permanent addresses. Other examples include the IP multicast destination address of 224.0.0.1, which specifies that all multicast-capable hosts on a local network segment should examine this packet. Similarly, the IP multicast destination address of 224.0.0.2 on a packet specifies that all multicast-capable routers on a local network segment should examine this packet.

The range of permanent group addresses used when the packets should be routed is 224.0.1.0 through 224.0.1.255. This range includes 224.0.1.39 and 224.0.1.40, which are used by Cisco-proprietary Auto-Rendezvous Point (Auto-RP) protocols (covered in Chapter 8). Table 7-2 shows some of the well-known addresses from the permanent address range.

Key Topic

**Table 7-2**  *Some Well-Known Reserved Multicast Addresses*

| Address | Usage |
| --- | --- |
| 224.0.0.1 | All multicast hosts |
| 224.0.0.2 | All multicast routers |
| 224.0.0.4 | DVMRP routers |
| 224.0.0.5 | All OSPF routers |
| 224.0.0.6 | OSPF designated routers |
| 224.0.0.9 | RIPv2 routers |
| 224.0.0.10 | EIGRP routers |
| 224.0.0.13 | PIM routers |
| 224.0.0.22 | IGMPv3 |
| 224.0.0.25 | RGMP |
| 224.0.1.39 | Cisco-RP-Announce |
| 224.0.1.40 | Cisco-RP-Discovery |

### Multicast Addresses for Source-Specific Multicast Applications and Protocols

IANA has allocated the range 232.0.0.0 through 232.255.255.255 for SSM applications and protocols. The purpose of these applications is to allow a host to select a source for the multicast group. SSM makes multicast routing efficient, allows a host to select a better-quality source, and helps network administrators minimize multicast denial of service (DoS) attacks.

### Multicast Addresses for GLOP Addressing

IANA has reserved the range 233.0.0.0 through 233.255.255.255 (RFC 3180), called GLOP addressing, on an experimental basis. It can be used by anyone who owns a registered autonomous system number (ASN) to create 256 global multicast addresses that can be owned and used by the entity. IANA reserves addresses to ensure global uniqueness of addresses; for similar reasons, each autonomous system should be using an assigned unique ASN.

By using a value of 233 for the first octet, and by using the ASN for the second and third octets, a single autonomous system can create globally unique multicast addresses as defined in the GLOP addressing RFC. For example, the autonomous system using registered ASN 5663 could convert ASN 5663 to binary (0001011000011111). The first 8 bits, 00010110, equals 22 in decimal notation, and the last 8 bits, 00011111, equals 31 in decimal notation. Mapping the first 8 bits to the second octet and the last 8 bits to the third octet in the 233 range addresses, the entity that owns the ASN 5663 is automatically allocated the address range 233.22.31.0 through 233.22.31.255.

**Note**   GLOP is not an acronym and does not stand for anything. One of the authors of RFC 2770, David Meyer, started referring to this range of addresses as "GLOP" addressing, and since then the range has been identified by the name GLOP addressing.

### Multicast Addresses for Private Multicast Domains

The last of the reserved multicast address ranges mentioned here is the range of *administratively scoped* addresses. IANA has assigned the range 239.0.0.0 through 239.255.255.255 (RFC 2365) for use in private multicast domains, much like the IP unicast ranges defined in RFC 1918, namely, 10.0.0.0/8, 172.16.0.0/12, and 192.168.0.0/16. IANA will not assign these administratively scoped multicast addresses to any other protocol or application. Network administrators are free to use multicast addresses in this range; however, they must configure their multicast routers to ensure that multicast traffic in this address range does not leave their multicast domain boundaries.

## Multicast Addresses for Transient Groups

When an enterprise wants to use globally unique unicast addresses, it needs to get a block of addresses from its ISP or from IANA. However, when an enterprise wants to use a multicast address for a global multicast application, it can use any multicast address that is not part of the well-known permanent multicast address space covered in the previous sections. These remaining multicast addresses are called *transient groups* or *transient multicast addresses*. This means that the entire Internet must share the transient multicast addresses; they must be dynamically allocated when needed and must be released when no longer in use.

Because these addresses are not permanently assigned to any application, they are called transient. Any enterprise can use these multicast addresses without requiring any registration or permission from IANA, but the enterprise is expected to release these multicast addresses after their use. At the time of this writing, there is no standard method available for using the transient multicast addresses. However, a great deal of work is being done by IETF to define and implement a standard method for dynamically allocating multicast addresses.

## Summary of Multicast Address Ranges

Table 7-3 summarizes various multicast address ranges and their use.

Key
Topic

**Table 7-3**  *Multicast Address Ranges and Their Use*

| Multicast Address Range | Usage |
|---|---|
| 224.0.0.0 to 239.255.255.255 | This range represents the entire IPv4 multicast address space. It is reserved for multicast applications. |
| 224.0.0.0 to 224.0.0.255 | This range is part of the permanent groups. Addresses from this range are assigned by IANA for network protocols on a local segment. Routers do not forward packets with destination addresses used from this range. |
| 224.0.1.0 to 224.0.1.255 | This range is also part of the permanent groups. Addresses from this range are assigned by IANA for the network protocols that are forwarded in the entire network. Routers forward packets with destination addresses used from this range. |
| 232.0.0.0 to 232.255.255.255 | This range is used for SSM applications. |
| 233.0.0.0 to 233.255.255.255 | This range is called the GLOP addressing. It is used for automatically allocating 256 multicast addresses to any enterprise that owns a registered ASN. |
| 239.0.0.0 to 239.255.255.255 | This range is used for private multicast domains. These addresses are called administratively scoped addresses. |
| Remaining ranges of addresses in the multicast address space | Addresses from these ranges are called transient groups. Any enterprise can allocate a multicast address from the transient groups for a global multicast application and should release it when the application is no longer in use. |

## Mapping IP Multicast Addresses to MAC Addresses

Assigning a Layer 3 multicast address to a multicast group (application) automatically generates a Layer 2 multicast address. Figure 7-6 shows how a multicast MAC address is calculated from a Layer 3 multicast address. The MAC address is formed using an IEEE-registered OUI of 01005E, then a binary 0, and then the last 23 bits of the multicast IP address. The method is identical for Ethernet and Fiber Distributed Data Interface (FDDI).

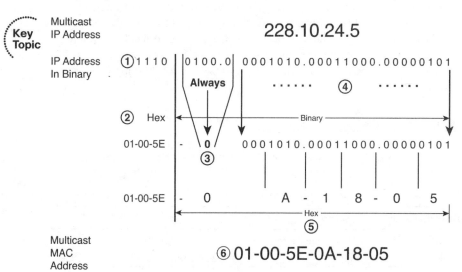

**Figure 7-6**  *Calculating a Multicast Destination MAC Address from a Multicast Destination IP Address*

To understand the mechanics of this process, use the following six steps, which are referenced by number in Figure 7-6:

**Step 1.**    Convert the IP address to binary. Notice the first 4 bits; they are always 1110 for any multicast IP address.

**Step 2.**    Replace the first 4 bits 1110 of the IP address with the 6 hexadecimal digits (or 24 bits) 01-00-5E as multicast OUI, in the total space of 12 hexadecimal digits (or 48 bits) for a multicast MAC address.

**Step 3.**    Replace the next 5 bits of the binary IP address with one binary 0 in the multicast MAC address space.

**Step 4.**    Copy the last 23 bits of the binary IP address in the last 23-bit space of the multicast MAC address.

**Step 5.**    Convert the last 24 bits of the multicast MAC address from binary to 6 hexadecimal digits.

**Step 6.**    Combine the first 6 hexadecimal digits 01-00-5E with the last 6 hexadecimal digits, calculated in Step 5, to form a complete multicast MAC address of 12 hexadecimal digits.

Unfortunately, this method does not provide a unique multicast MAC address for each multicast IP address, because only the last 23 bits of the IP address are mapped to the MAC address. For example, the IP address 238.10.24.5 produces exactly the same MAC address, 0x01-00-5E-0A-18-05, as 228.10.24.5. In fact, because 5 bits from the IP address are always mapped to 0, 25 (32) different class D IP addresses produce exactly the same MAC address. IETF points out that the chances of two multicast applications on the same LAN producing the same MAC address are very low. If it happens accidentally, a packet from a different IP multicast application can be identified at Layer 3 and discarded; however, network administrators should be careful when they implement multicast applications so that they can avoid using IP addresses that produce identical MAC addresses.

## Managing Distribution of Multicast Traffic with IGMP

Refer to Figure 7-4. Assume that R2 has started receiving multicast traffic from the server. R2 has to make a decision about forwarding this traffic on the Ethernet links. R2 needs to know the answers to the following questions:

- Is there any host connected to any of my Ethernet links that has shown interest in receiving this traffic?

- If none of the hosts has shown any interest in receiving this traffic, why should I forward it on the Ethernet links and waste bandwidth?

- If any host has shown interest in receiving this traffic, where is it located? Is it connected to one of my Ethernet links or to both?

As you can see, a mechanism is required for hosts and a local router to communicate with each other. The IGMP was designed to enable communication between a router and connected hosts.

Not only do routers need to know out which LAN interface to forward multicast packets, but switches also need to know on which ports they should forward the traffic. By default, if a switch receives a multicast frame on a port, it will flood the frame throughout the VLAN, just like it would do for a broadcast or unknown unicast frame. The reason is that switches will never find a multicast MAC address in their Content Addressable Memory (CAM) table, because a multicast MAC address is never used as a source address.

A switch's decision to flood multicast frames means that if any host or hosts in a VLAN request to receive the traffic for a multicast group, all the remaining hosts in the same VLAN, whether or not they have requested to receive the traffic for the multicast group, will receive the multicast traffic. This behavior is contrary to one of the major goals of multicast design, which is to deliver multicast traffic to only those hosts that have requested it, while maximizing bandwidth efficiency. To forward traffic more efficiently in Figure 7-4, SW2 and SW3 need to know the answers to the following questions:

- Should I forward this multicast traffic on all the ports in this VLAN or only on specific ports?

- If I should forward this multicast traffic on specific ports of a VLAN, how will I find those port numbers?

Three different tools, namely CGMP, IGMP snooping, and RGMP, allow switches to optimize their multicast forwarding logic by answering these kinds of questions. These topics are covered in more depth later in the chapter. For now, this section focuses on how routers and hosts use IGMP to make sure that the router knows whether it should forward multicasts out the router's LAN interfaces.

## Joining a Group

Before a host can receive any multicast traffic, a multicast application must be installed and running on that host. The process of installing and running a multicast application is referred to as *launching an application* or *joining a multicast group*. After a host joins a group, the host software calculates the multicast MAC address, and its NIC then starts listening to the multicast MAC address, in addition to its BIA.

Before a host (or a user) can join a group, the user needs to know what groups are available and how to join them. For enterprise-scale multicast applications, the user can simply find a link on a web page and click it, prompting the user's multicast client application to start working with the correct multicast address—totally hiding the multicast address details. Alternately, for an internally developed multicast application, the multicast address can be preconfigured on the client application. For example, a user might be required to log on to a server and authenticate with a name and a password; if the user is authenticated, the multicast application automatically installs on the user's PC, which means that the user has joined the multicast group. When the user no longer wants to use the multicast application, the user must leave the group. For example, the user can simply close the multicast application to leave the group.

The process by which a human discovers which multicast IP address to listen for and join can be a challenge, particularly for multicast traffic on the Internet. The problem is similar to when you have a satellite or digital cable TV system at home: You might have literally thousands of channels, but finding the channel that has the show you want to watch might require a lot of surfing through the list of channels and time slots. For IP multicast, a user needs to discover what applications he might want to use, and the multicast IP addresses used by the applications. A lot of work remains to be done in this area, but some options are available. For example, online TV program guides and web-based schedules advertise events that will use multicast groups and specify who to contact if you want to see the event, lecture, or concert. Tools like Session Description Protocol (SDP) and Service Advertising Protocol (SAP) also describe multicast events and advertise them. However, a detailed discussion of the different methods, their limitations, and procedures for using them is beyond the scope of this book. The rest of the discussion in this section assumes that hosts have somehow learned about a multicast group.

## Internet Group Management Protocol

IGMP has evolved from the Host Membership Protocol, described in Dr. Steve Deering's doctoral thesis, to IGMPv1 (RFC 1112), to IGMPv2 (RFC 2236), to the latest, IGMPv3 (RFC 3376). IGMP messages are sent in IP datagrams with IP protocol number 2, with the IP Time-to-Live (TTL) field set to 1. IGMP packets pass only over a LAN and are not forwarded by routers, because of their TTL field values.

The two most important goals of IGMP are as follows:

■ To inform a local multicast router that a host wants to receive multicast traffic for a specific group

■ To inform local multicast routers that a host wants to leave a multicast group (in other words, the host is no longer interested in receiving the multicast group traffic)

Multicast routers use IGMP to maintain information for each router interface about which multicast group traffic they should forward and which hosts want to receive it.

The following section examines IGMPv2 in detail and introduces important features of IGMPv3. In the figures that show the operation of IGMP, Layer 2 switches are not shown because IGMP is used for communication between hosts and routers. Later in the chapter, the sections "Cisco Group Management Protocol," "IGMP Snooping," and "Router-Port Group Management Protocol" discuss the operation of multicasting at Layer 2.

IGMP is automatically enabled when multicast routing and PIM are configured on a router. The version can be changed on an interface-by-interface basis. Version 2 is the current default version.

## IGMP Version 2

Figure 7-7 shows the 8-octet format of an IGMPv2 message.

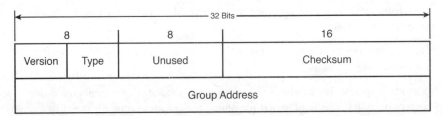

**Figure 7-7**  *IGMPv2 Message Format*

IGMPv2 has four fields, which are defined as follows:

■ **Type:** 8-bit field that is one of four message types defined by IGMPv2:

■ **Membership Query (Type code = 0x11):** Used by multicast routers to discover the presence of group members on a subnet. A General Membership Query message sets the Group Address field to 0.0.0.0. A Group-Specific Query sets the Group Address field to the address of the group being queried. It is sent by a router after it receives the IGMPv2 Leave Group message from a host.

■ **Version 1 Membership Report (Type code = 0x12):** Used by IGMPv2 hosts for backward compatibility with IGMPv1.

- **Version 2 Membership Report (Type Code = 0x16):** Sent by a group member to inform the router that at least one group member is present on the subnet.

- **Leave Group (Type code = 0x17):** Sent by a group member if it was the last member to send a Membership Report to inform the router that it is leaving the group.

- **Maximum Response Time:** 8-bit field included only in Query messages. The units are 1/10 of a second, with 100 (10 seconds) being the default. The values range from 1 to 255 (0.1 to 25.5 seconds).

- **Checksum:** Carries the 16-bit checksum computed by the source. The IGMP checksum is computed over the entire IP payload, not just over the first 8 octets, even though IGMPv2 messages are only 8 bytes in length.

- **Group Address:** Set to 0.0.0.0 in General Query messages and to the group address in Group-Specific messages. Membership Report messages carry the address of the group being reported in this field; Leave Group messages carry the address of the group being left in this field.

IGMPv2 supports complete backward compatibility with IGMPv1. The IGMPv2 Type codes 0x11 and 0x12 match the type codes for IGMPv1 for the Membership Query and Membership Report messages. This enables IGMPv2 hosts and routers to recognize IGMPv1 messages when IGMPv1 hosts or routers are on the network.

One of the primary reasons for developing IGMPv2 was to provide a better Leave mechanism to shorten the leave latency compared to IGMPv1. IGMPv2 has the following features:

Key
Topic

- **Leave Group messages:** Provide hosts with a method for notifying routers that they want to leave the group.

- **Group-Specific Query messages:** Permit the router to send a query for a specific group instead of all groups.

- **Maximum Response Time field:** A field in Query messages that permits the router to specify the MRT. This field allows for tuning the response time for the Host Membership Report. This feature can be useful when a large number of groups are active on a subnet and you want to decrease the burstiness of the responses by spreading the responses over a longer period of time.

- **Querier election process:** Provides the method for selecting the preferred router for sending Query messages when multiple routers are connected to the same subnet.

IGMPv2 helps reduce surges in IGMPv2 Solicited Report messages sent by hosts in response to IGMPv2 Query messages by allowing the network administrator to change the Query Response Interval. Setting the MRT, which ranges from 0.1 to 25.5 seconds, to a value slightly longer than 10 seconds spreads the hosts' collective IGMPv2 Solicited Report messages over a longer time period, resulting in more uniform consumption of subnet bandwidth and router resources. The unit of measurement for the MRT is 0.1 second. For example, a 3-second MRT is expressed as 30.

A multicast host can send an IGMP Report in response to a Query or simply send a Report when the host's application first comes up. The IGMPv2 router acting as the IGMPv2 querier sends general IGMP Query messages every 60 seconds. The operations of IGMPv2 General Query messages and Report messages are covered next.

### IGMPv2 Host Membership Query Functions

As illustrated in Figure 7-8, multicast routers send IGMPv2 Host Membership Query messages out LAN interfaces to determine whether a multicast group member is on any interface. Routers send these messages every Query Interval, which is 60 seconds by default. Host Membership Queries use a destination IP address and MAC address of 224.0.0.1 and 01-00-5e-00-00-01, with the source IP address and MAC address of the router's interface IP address and BIA, respectively. IGMPv2 Queries use a TTL of 1 to prevent the packet from being routed.

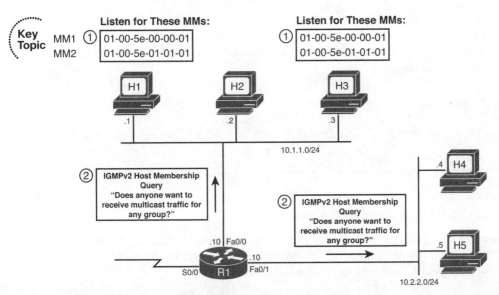

**Figure 7-8**  *IGMPv2 Host Membership Query Process*

The details of the two steps are as follows:

1.  Hosts H1 and H3 join multicast group 226.1.1.1. The hosts prepare to receive messages sent to both 226.1.1.1 (the joined group) and 224.0.0.1 (the address to which IGMPv2 Queries will be sent). The Join causes these hosts to calculate the two multicast MAC (MM) addresses, 01-00-5e-01-01-01 (from 226.1.1.1) and 01-00-5e-00-00-01 (from 224.0.0.1), and then listen for frames sent to these two MMs.

2.  R1 periodically sends an IGMPv2 Host Membership Query out each LAN interface, looking for any host interested in receiving packets for any multicast group. After sending IGMPv2 Queries, R1 expects any host that has joined any group to reply with an IGMPv2 Report.

At this point, Router R1 still does not know whether any hosts need to receive any multi-cast traffic. The next section covers how the hosts respond with IGMP Report messages to inform R1 of their interest in receiving multicast packets.

## IGMPv2 Host Membership Report Functions

Hosts use IGMPv2 Host Membership Report messages to reply to IGMP Queries and communicate to a local router for which multicast groups they want to receive traffic.

In IGMPv2, a host sends a Host Membership Report under the following two conditions:

- When a host receives an IGMPv2 Query from a local router, it is supposed to send an IGMPv2 Host Membership Report for all the multicast groups for which it wants to receive multicast traffic. This Report is called an IGMPv2 Solicited Host Membership Report.

- When a host joins a new group, the host immediately sends an IGMPv2 Host Membership Report to inform a local router that it wants to receive multicast traffic for the group it has just joined. This Report is called an IGMPv2 Unsolicited Host Membership Report.

**Note** The term *Solicited Host Membership Report* is not defined in RFC 2236. It is used in this book to specify whether the IGMPv2 Report was sent in response to a Query (solicited).

### IGMPv2 Solicited Host Membership Report

Figure 7-9 shows the operation of the IGMPv2 Solicited Host Membership Report process and the Report Suppression mechanism. Figure 7-9 picks up the example from Figure 7-8, in which Router R1 had sent an IGMPv2 Query.

If many hosts have launched multicast applications and if all of them respond to the Host Membership Query, unnecessary bandwidth and router resources would be used to process all the redundant reports. A multicast router needs to receive only one report for each application on each of its LAN interfaces. It forwards multicast traffic on an inter-face whether 1 user or 200 users belong to a given multicast group.

The Report Suppression mechanism helps to solve these problems. It uses the IGMPv2 Maximum Response Time (MRT) timer to suppress many of the unnecessary IGMP Reports. This timer is called the *Query Response Interval*. In other words, when any host receives an IGMPv2 Query, it has a maximum of the configured MRT to send the IGMP Report if it wants to receive multicast traffic for that application. Each host picks a random time between 0 and the MRT and starts a timer. When this timer expires, the host will send a Host Membership report—but only if it has not already heard another host send a report for its group. This is called *Report Suppression* and is designed to reduce redundant reports.

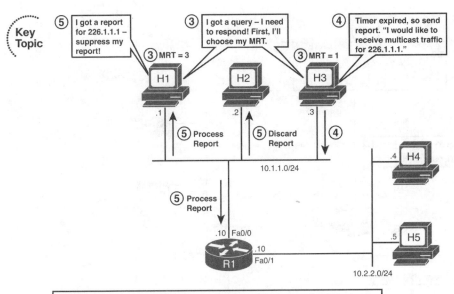

**Figure 7-9**  *IGMPv2 Solicited Host Membership Report and Report Suppression Processes*

The following three steps describe the sequence of events for the IGMPv2 Solicited Host Membership Report and Report Suppression mechanism shown in Figure 7.9:

**3.**  Assume that H1 and H3 have received an IGMPv2 Query (as shown in Step 2 of Figure 7-8). Because both H1 and H3 have joined the group 226.1.1.1, they need to send an IGMPv2 Solicited Host Membership Report. Furthermore, assume that H1 and H3 have randomly picked an MRT of 3 seconds and 1 second, respectively.

**4.**  H3's timer expires in 1 second; it prepares and sends the IGMPv2 Solicited Host Membership Report with the TTL value of 1. H3 uses the destination IP address 226.1.1.1 and its source IP address 10.1.1.3, the destination MAC address 01-00-5e-01-01-01 calculated from the Layer 3 address 226.1.1.1, and its BIA as the source address. By using the group address of 226.1.1.1, H3 is telling the multicast router, "I would like to receive multicast traffic for group 226.1.1.1."

**5.**  Hosts H1, H2, and R1 see the IGMPv2 Solicited Host Membership Report, but only H1 and R1 process the Report. H2 discards the frame sent because it is not listening to that multicast MAC address. H1 realizes that H3's Report is for the same multicast group as 226.1.1.1. Therefore, H1, suppresses its own Report and does not send it.

R1 has now received the IGMPv2 Solicited Host Membership Report on its fa0/0 interface requesting traffic for multicast group 226.1.1.1, but it has not received a Host Membership Report on its fa0/1 interface. Figure 7-10 shows that R1 has started forwarding multicast traffic for group 226.1.1.1 on its fa0/0 interface.

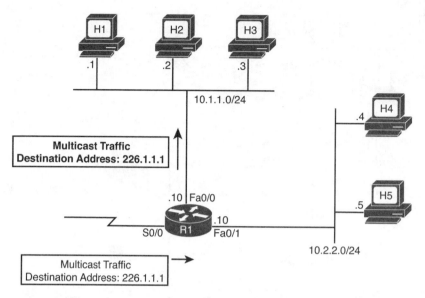

**Figure 7-10**   *R1 Forwarding Traffic for Group 226.1.1.1 on Its Fa0/0 Interface*

## IGMPv2 Unsolicited Host Membership Report

In IGMPv2, a host does not have to wait for a Host Membership Query message from the router. Hosts can send an IGMPv2 Unsolicited Host Membership Report anytime a user launches a multicast application. This feature reduces the waiting time for a host to receive traffic for a multicast group. For example, Figure 7-11 shows that a user has launched a multicast application that uses 226.1.1.1 on H4. H4 sends an IGMPv2 Unsolicited Host Membership Report, and R1 then starts forwarding traffic for 226.1.1.1 on its fa0/1 interface.

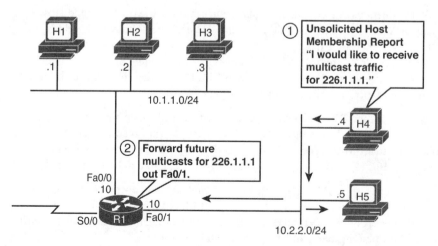

**Figure 7-11**   *H4 Sends IGMPv2 Unsolicited Host Membership Report*

## IGMPv2 Leave Group and Group-Specific Query Messages

The IGMPv2 Leave Group message is used to significantly reduce the leave latency, while the IGMPv2 Group-Specific Query message prevents a router from incorrectly stopping the forwarding of packets on a LAN when a host leaves a group. In IGMPv2, when a host leaves a group, it sends an IGMPv2 Leave message. When an IGMPv2 router receives a Leave message, it immediately sends a Group-Specific Query for that group. The Group-Specific Query asks only whether any remaining hosts still want to receive packets for that single multicast group. As a result, the router quickly knows whether to continue to forward traffic for that multicast group.

The main advantage of IGMPv2 over IGMPv1 is IGMPv2's shorter leave latency. An IGMPv1 router takes, by default, 3 minutes to conclude that the last host on the subnet has left a group and no host on the subnet wants to receive traffic for the group. Meanwhile, the IGMPv1 router continues forwarding the group traffic on the subnet and wastes bandwidth. On the other hand, an IGMPv2 router concludes in 3 seconds that no host on the subnet wants to receive traffic for a group and stops forwarding it on the subnet.

**Note**   IGMPv2 RFC 2236 recommends that a host sends a Leave Group message only if the leaving member was the last host to send a Membership Report in response to a Query. However, most IGMPv2 vendor operating systems have implemented the Leave Group processing by always sending a Leave Group message when any host leaves the group.

Figure 7-12 shows the operation of the IGMPv2 Leave process and the IGMP Group-Specific Query. In Figure 7-12, hosts H1 and H3 are currently members of group 226.1.1.1; H1 wants to leave the group.

The following three steps, referenced in Figure 7-12, describe the sequence of events for the IGMPv2 Leave mechanism when H1 leaves:

1.  H1 sends an IGMPv2 Leave Group message. The destination address is 224.0.0.2, the well-known address for All Multicast Routers to inform all routers on the subnet that "I don't want to receive multicast traffic for 226.1.1.1 anymore."

2.  R1 sends a Group-Specific Query. Routers do not keep track of hosts that are members of the group, only the group memberships that are active. Because H1 has decided to leave 226.1.1.1, R1 needs to make sure that no other hosts off this interface still need to receive packets for group 226.1.1.1. Therefore, R1 sends a Group-Specific Query using 226.1.1.1 as the destination address on the packet so that only hosts that are members of this group will receive the message and respond. Through this message, R1 is asking any remaining hosts on the subnet, "Does anyone want to receive multicast traffic for 226.1.1.1?"

3.  H3 sends a Membership Report. H3 hears the Group-Specific Query and responds with an IGMPv2 Membership Report to inform the routers on the subnet that it is still a member of group 226.1.1.1 and would like to keep receiving traffic for group 226.1.1.1.

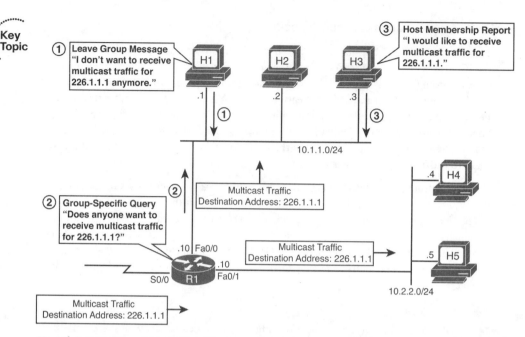

**Figure 7-12**   *How Group-Specific Queries Work with the IGMPv2 Leave Process*

**Note**   The Report Suppression mechanism explained earlier for the General Group Query is also used for the Group-Specific Query.

IGMPv2 routers repeat the process of Step 2 in this example each time they receive a Leave message. In the next example, H3 is the only remaining member of group 226.1.1.1 on the subnet. Figure 7-13 shows what happens when H3 also wants to leave the group.

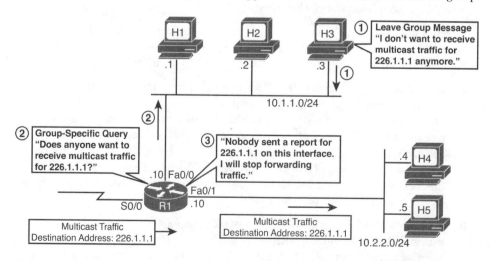

**Figure 7-13**   *IGMPv2 Leave Process—No Response to the Group-Specific Query*

The following three steps, referenced in Figure 7-13, describe the sequence of events for the IGMPv2 Leave mechanism when H3 leaves:

1.  H3 sends an IGMPv2 Leave Group message. The destination address on the packet is 224.0.0.2 to inform all routers on the subnet that "I don't want to receive multicast traffic for 226.1.1.1 anymore."

2.  When R1 receives the Leave Group message from H3, it sends a Group-Specific Query to determine whether any hosts are still members of group 226.1.1.1. R1 uses 226.1.1.1 as the destination address on the packet.

3.  Because there are now no remaining members of 226.1.1.1 on the subnet, R1 does not receive a response to the Group-Specific Query. As a result, R1 stops forwarding multicasts for 226.1.1.1 out its fa0/0 interface.

Step 3 of this example provides a nice backdrop from which to describe the concepts of a *Last Member Query Interval* and a *Last Member Query Count*. These values determine how long it takes a router to believe that all hosts on a LAN have left a particular group. By default, routers use an MRT of 10 (1 second) for Group-Specific Queries. Because a router should receive a response to a Group-Specific Query in that amount of time, the router uses the MRT value as the value of the Last Member Query Interval. So, the router uses the following process:

**Key Topic**

1.  Send a Group-Specific Query in response to an IGMP Leave.

2.  If no Report is received within the Last Member Query Interval, repeat Step 1.

3.  Repeat Step 1 the number of times defined by the value of the Last Member Query Count.

The Last Member Query Count is the number of consecutive Group-Specific Queries a router will send before it concludes that there are no active members of the group on a subnet. The default value for the Last Member Query Count is 2. So the leave latency is typically less than 3 seconds, compared to up to 3 minutes with IGMPv1.

## IGMPv2 Querier

IGMPv2 defines a querier election process that is used when multiple routers are connected to a subnet. When IGMPv2 routers start, they each send an IGMPv2 General Query message to the well-known All Hosts group 224.0.0.1. When an IGMPv2 router receives a General Query message, it compares the source IP address of the General Query message with its own interface address. The router with the lowest IP address on the subnet is elected as the IGMP querier. The nonquerier routers do not send queries but monitor how frequently the querier is sending general IGMPv2 Queries. When the elected querier does not send a query for two consecutive Query Intervals plus one half of one Query Response Interval, it is considered to be dead, and a new querier is elected. RFC 2236 refers to this time interval as the *Other Querier Present Interval*. The default value for the Other Querier Present Interval is 255 seconds, because the default General IGMPv2 Query Interval is 125 seconds and the default Query Response Interval is 10 seconds.

## IGMPv2 Timers

Table 7-4 summarizes important timers used in IGMPv2, their usage, and default values.

Key
Topic

**Table 7-4**   *Important IGMPv2 Timers*

| Timer | Usage | Default Value |
|---|---|---|
| Query Interval | A time period between General Queries sent by a router. | 60 seconds |
| Query Response Interval | The maximum response time for hosts to respond to the periodic general Queries. | 10 seconds; can be between 0.1 and 25.5 seconds |
| Group Membership Interval | A time period during which, if a router does not receive an IGMP Report, the router concludes that there are no more members of the group on the subnet. | 260 seconds |
| Other Querier Present Interval | A time period during which, if the IGMPv2 nonquerier routers do not receive an IGMP Query from the querier router, the nonquerier routers conclude that the querier is dead. | 255 seconds |
| Last Member Query Interval | The maximum response time inserted by IGMPv2 routers into the Group-Specific Queries and the time period between two consecutive Group-Specific Queries sent for the same group. | 1 second |
| Version 1 Router Present Timeout | A time period during which, if an IGMPv2 host does not receive an IGMPv1 Query, the IGMPv2 host concludes that there are no IGMPv1 routers present and starts sending IGMPv2 messages. | 400 seconds |

## IGMP Version 3

In October 2002, RFC 3376 defined specifications for IGMPv3, which is a major revision of the protocol. To use the new features of IGMPv3, last-hop routers have to be updated, host operating systems have to be modified, and applications have to be specially designed and written. This section does not examine IGMPv3 in detail; instead, it summarizes IGMPv3's major features.

In IGMPv2, when a host makes a request to join a group, a multicast router forwards the traffic for the group to the subnet regardless of the source IP address of the packets. In very large networks, such as an Internet broadcast, this can cause problems. For example, assume that a multimedia conference is in session. A group member decides to maliciously disturb the session by sending talking or music to the same group. Although multimedia applications allow a user to mute any of the other members, it does not stop the unwanted traffic from being delivered to the host. In addition, if a group of hackers decides to flood a company's network with bogus high-bandwidth data using the same multicast group address that the company's employees have joined, it can create a DoS attack for the company by overwhelming low-speed links. Neither IGMPv1 nor IGMPv2 has a mechanism to prevent such an attack.

IGMPv3 allows a host to filter incoming traffic based on the source IP addresses from which it is willing to receive packets, through a feature called *Source-Specific Multicast (SSM)*. SSM allows a host to indicate interest in receiving packets only from specific source addresses, or from all but specific source addresses, sent to a particular multicast address. Figure 7-14 shows the basic operation of the IGMPv3 Membership Report process.

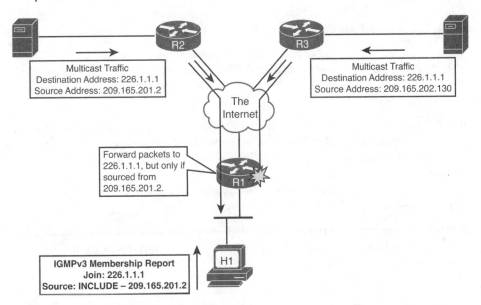

**Figure 7-14** *IGMPv3 Membership Report*

In Figure 7-14, the multicast traffic for the group 226.1.1.1 is available from two sources. R1 receives traffic from both the sources. H1 prepares an IGMPv3 Membership Report using the destination address 224.0.0.22, specially assigned by IANA for the IGMPv3 Membership Report. The message type is 0x22 (defined in RFC 3376), with a note "Source–INCLUDE—209.165.201.2," which means, "I would like to join multicast group 226.1.1.1, but only if the group traffic is coming from the source 209.165.201.2."

Cisco has designed URL Rendezvous Directory (URD) and IGMP v3lite to use the new features of IGMPv3 until IGMPv3 applications are available and operating systems are updated. A detailed discussion of URD and IGMP v3lite is beyond the scope of this book. IGMPv3 is compatible with IGMPv1 and IGMPv2.

**Note**   The following URL provides more information on IGMPv3, URD, and IGMP v3lite: www.cisco.com/en/US/docs/ios/ipmulti/configuration/guide/12_4/imc_12_4_book.html.

# IGMPv1 and IGMPv2 Interoperability

IGMPv2 is designed to be backward compatible with IGMPv1. RFC 2236 defines some special interoperability rules. The next two sections explore the following interoperability scenarios:

- "IGMPv2 Host and IGMPv1 Routers": Defines how an IGMPv2 host should behave in the presence of an IGMPv1 router on the same subnet.

- "IGMPv1 Host and IGMPv2 Routers": Defines how an IGMPv2 router should behave in the presence of an IGMPv1 host on the same subnet.

## IGMPv2 Host and IGMPv1 Routers

When a host sends the IGMPv2 Report with the message type 0x16, which is not defined in IGMPv1, a version 1 router would consider 0x16 an invalid message type and ignore it. Therefore, a version 2 host must send IGMPv1 Reports when a version 1 router is active. But how does an IGMPv2 host detect the presence of an IGMPv1 router on the subnet?

IGMPv2 hosts determine whether the querying router is an IGMPv1 or IGMPv2 host based on the value of the MRT field of the periodic general IGMP Query. In IGMPv1 Queries, this field is 0, whereas in IGMPv2, it is nonzero and represents the MRT value. When an IGMPv2 host receives an IGMPv1 Query, it knows that the IGMPv1 router is present on the subnet and marks the interface as an IGMPv1 interface. The IGMPv2 host then stops sending IGMPv2 messages.

Whenever an IGMPv2 host receives an IGMPv1 Query, it starts a 400-second Version 1 Router Present Timeout timer. This timer is reset whenever it receives an IGMPv1 Query. If the timer expires, which indicates that there are no IGMPv1 routers present on the subnet, the IGMPv2 host starts sending IGMPv2 messages.

## IGMPv1 Host and IGMPv2 Routers

IGMPv2 routers can easily determine whether any IGMPv1 hosts are present on a LAN based on whether any hosts send an IGMPv1 Report message (type 0x12) or IGMPv2 Report message (type 0x16). Like IGMPv1 routers, IGMPv2 routers send periodic IGMPv2 General Queries. An IGMPv1 host responds normally because IGMPv2 General Queries are very similar in format to IGMPv1 Queries—except for the second octet, which is ignored by IGMPv1 hosts. So, an IGMPv2 router will examine all Reports to find out whether any IGMPv1 hosts exist on a LAN.

**Note** If IGMPv2 hosts are also present on the same subnet, they would send IGMPv2 Membership Reports. However, IGMPv1 hosts do not understand IGMPv2 Reports and ignore them; they do not trigger Report Suppression in IGMPv1 hosts. Therefore, sometimes an IGMPv2 router receives both an IGMPv1 Report and an IGMPv2 Report in response to a General Query.

While an IGMPv2 router knows that an IGMPv1 host is present on a LAN, the router ignores Leave messages and the Group-Specific Queries triggered by receipt of the Leave messages. This is necessary because if an IGMPv2 router responds to a Leave Group message with a Group-Specific Query, IGMPv1 hosts will not understand it and thus ignore the message. When an IGMPv2 router does not receive a response to its Group-Specific Query, it might erroneously conclude that nobody wants to receive traffic for the group and thus stop forwarding it on the subnet. So with one or more IGMPv1 hosts listening for a particular group, the router essentially suspends the optimizations that reduce leave latency.

IGMPv2 routers continue to ignore Leave messages until the IGMPv1-Host-Present Countdown timer expires. RFC 2236 defines that when IGMPv2 routers receive an IGMPv1 Report, they must set an IGMPv1-host-present countdown timer. The timer value should be equal to the Group Membership Interval, which defaults to 180 seconds in IGMPv1 and 260 seconds in IGMPv2. (Group Membership Interval is a time period during which, if a router does not receive an IGMP Report, the router concludes that there are no more members of the group on a subnet.)

# Comparison of IGMPv1, IGMPv2, and IGMPv3

Table 7-5 compares the important features of IGMPv1, IGMPv2, and IGMPv3.

**Table 7-5**   *Comparison of IGMPv1, IGMPv2, and IGMPv3*

| Feature | IGMPv1 | IGMPv2 | IGMPv3 |
|---|---|---|---|
| First Octet Value for the Query Message | 0x11 | 0x11 | 0x11 |
| Group Address for the General Query | 0.0.0.0 | 0.0.0.0 | 0.0.0.0 |
| Destination Address for the General Query | 224.0.0.1 | 224.0.0.1 | 224.0.0.1 |
| Default Query Interval | 60 seconds | 125 seconds | 125 seconds |
| First Octet Value for the Report | 0x12 | 0x16 | 0x22 |
| Group Address for the Report | Joining multicast group address | Joining multicast group address | Joining multicast group address and source address |
| Destination Address for the Report | Joining multicast group address | Joining multicast group address | 224.0.0.22 |
| Is Report Suppression Mechanism Available? | Yes | Yes | No |

| Feature | IGMPv1 | IGMPv2 | IGMPv3 |
|---|---|---|---|
| Can Maximum Response Time Be Configured? | No, fixed at 10 seconds | Yes, 0 to 25.5 seconds | Yes, 0 to 53 minutes |
| Can a Host Send a Leave Group Message? | No | Yes | Yes |
| Destination Address for the Leave Group Message | — | 224.0.0.2 | 224.0.0.22 |
| Can a Router Send a Group-Specific Query? | No | Yes | Yes |
| Can a Host Send Source- and Group-Specific Reports? | No | No | Yes |
| Can a Router Send Source- and Group-Specific Queries? | No | No | Yes |
| Rule for Electing a Querier | None (depends on multicast routing protocol) | Router with the lowest IP address on the subnet | Router with the lowest IP address on the subnet |
| Compatible with Other Versions of IGMP? | No | Yes, only with IGMPv1 | Yes, with both IGMPv1 and IGMPv2 |

## LAN Multicast Optimizations

This final major section of this chapter introduces the basics of three tools that optimize the flow of multicast over a LAN. Specifically, this section covers the following topics:

- Cisco Group Management Protocol (CGMP)

- IGMP snooping

- Router-Port Group Management Protocol (RGMP)

### Cisco Group Management Protocol

IGMP helps routers to determine how to distribute multicast traffic. However, IGMP works at Layer 3, and switches do not understand IGMP messages. Switches, by default, flood multicast traffic to all the hosts in a broadcast domain, which wastes bandwidth. Figure 7-15 illustrates the problem.

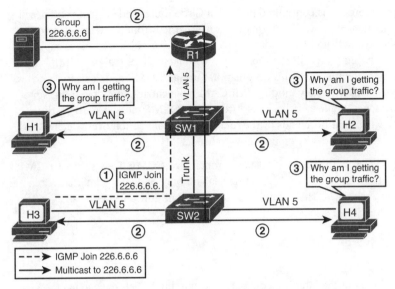

**Figure 7-15**  *Switches Flood Multicast Traffic*

Hosts H1, H2, H3, H4, and R1 are all in the same broadcast domain of VLAN 5. The following three steps, referenced in Figure 7-15, describe the sequence of events when H3 sends an IGMP Join message:

1. H3 sends an IGMP Join message for group 226.6.6.6.

2. R1 forwards the group traffic to SW1. The destination MAC address on the frame is 0x0100.5e06.0606. SW1 cannot find this address in its CAM table because it is never used by any device as a source address. Therefore, SW1 starts forwarding the group traffic to H1, H2, and SW2 because the group traffic is for VLAN 5. Similarly, SW2 starts forwarding the group traffic to H3 and H4.

3. All the hosts, H1 to H4, receive the group traffic, but only H3 requested it. H3 requested the group traffic and has started receiving it. However, H1, H2, and H4 did not ask for the group traffic, and they are flooded by switches with the group traffic.

In this illustration, only four hosts are shown in the broadcast domain of VLAN 5. What happens if a broadcast domain is flat and has hundreds of users? If a single host joins a multicast group, all the hosts would be flooded with the group traffic whether or not they have requested the group traffic. The goal of multicasting is to deliver the group traffic to only those hosts that have requested it and maximize the use of bandwidth.

There are two popular methods for helping Layer 2 switches determine how to distribute the multicast traffic to hosts:

■ CGMP, which is Cisco proprietary and discussed throughout the rest of this section.

■ IGMP snooping, discussed in the next section.

CGMP, a Layer 2 protocol, is configured on both a Cisco router and switches and permits the router to communicate Layer 2 information it has learned from IGMP to switches. A multicast router knows the MAC addresses of the multicast hosts, and the groups to which they listen, based on IGMP communication with hosts. The goal of CGMP is to enable the router to communicate this information through CGMP messages to switches so that switches can dynamically modify their CAM table entries. Only the routers produce CGMP messages, while switches only listen to the CGMP messages. To do this, CGMP must be enabled at both ends of the router-switch connection over which CGMP is operating, because both devices must know to use CGMP.

Layer 3 switches, such as the Cisco 3560, act as routers for CGMP. They serve as CGMP servers only. On these switches, CGMP can be enabled only on Layer 3 interfaces that connect to Layer 2 switches. The following commands configure a router or a Layer 3 switch interface for CGMP:

```
int fa 0/1
 ip cgmp
```

On a Layer 3 switch, use the interface command **no switchport** before enabling CGMP.

The destination address on the CGMP messages is always the well-known CGMP multicast MAC address 0x0100.0cdd.dddd. The use of the multicast destination MAC address on the CGMP messages forces switches to flood the message through all the ports so that all the switches in a network receive the CGMP messages. The important information in the CGMP messages is one or more pairs of MAC addresses:

- Group Destination Address (GDA)

- Unicast Source Address (USA)

The following five steps describe the general process of CGMP. Later, these steps are explained using a detailed example.

1.  When a CGMP-capable router gets connected to the switch, it sends a CGMP Join message with the GDA set to 0 and the USA set to its own MAC address. The CGMP-capable switch now knows that a multicast router is connected to the port on which it received the router's CGMP message. The router repeats the message every 60 seconds. A router can also tell the switch that it no longer participates in CGMP by sending a CGMP Leave message with the GDA set to 0 and the USA set to its own MAC address.

2.  When a host joins a group, it sends an IGMP Join message. Normally, a multicast router examines only Layer 3 information in the IGMP Join message, and the router does not have to process any Layer 2 information. However, when CGMP is configured on a router, the router also examines the Layer 2 destination and source MAC addresses of the IGMP Join message. The source address is the unicast MAC address of the host that sent the IGMP Join message. The router then generates a CGMP Join message that includes the multicast MAC address associated with the multicast IP address (to the GDA field of the CGMP join) and the unicast MAC address of the

host (to the USA field of the CGMP message). The router sends the CGMP Join message using the well-known CGMP multicast MAC address 0x0100.0cdd.dddd as the destination address.

3.   When switches receive a CGMP Join message, they search in their CAM tables for the port number associated with the host MAC address listed in the USA field. Switches create a new CAM table entry (or use an existing entry if it was already created before) for the multicast MAC address listed in the GDA field of the CGMP Join message, add the port number associated with the host MAC address listed in the USA field to the entry, and forward the group traffic on the port.

4.   When a host leaves a group, it sends an IGMP Leave message. The router learns the host's unicast MAC address (USA) and the IP multicast group it has just left. Because the Leave messages are sent to the All Multicast Routers MAC address 0x0100.5e00.0002 and not to the multicast group address the host has just left, the router calculates the multicast MAC address (GDA) from the IP multicast group the host has just left. The router then generates a CGMP Leave message, copies the multicast MAC address it has just calculated in the GDA field and unicast MAC address in the USA field of the CGMP Leave message, and sends it to the well-known CGMP multicast MAC address.

5.   When switches receive a CGMP Leave message, they again search for the port number associated with the host MAC address listed in the USA field. Switches remove this port from the CAM table entry for the multicast MAC address listed in the GDA field of the CGMP Leave message and stop forwarding the group traffic on the port.

Thus, CGMP helps switches send group traffic to only those hosts that want it, which helps to avoid wasted bandwidth.

Figures 7-16, 7-17, and 7-18 show a complete example of how routers and switches use CGMP in response to a host joining and then leaving a group. Figure 7-16 begins the example by showing a router's reaction to an IGMP Report, which is to send a CGMP Join to the switches on a LAN. The following two steps, referenced in Figure 7-16, describe the sequence of events when H3 sends an IGMP Join message:

1.   H3 sends an IGMP Join message for 226.6.6.6. At Layer 2, H3 uses 0x0100.5e06.0606 (the multicast MAC address associated with 226.6.6.6) as the destination address of a frame and its own BIA 0x0006.7c11.1103 as the source MAC address.

2.   R1 generates a CGMP Join message. When a CGMP-capable router receives an IGMP Join message, it generates a Layer 2 CGMP Join message. The destination address on the frame is the well-known multicast MAC address 0x0100.0cdd.dddd, which is understood only by Cisco switches but is forwarded by all switches. R1 sets the GDA to the group MAC address 0x0100.5e06.0606 and sets the USA to H3's MAC address 0x0006.7c11.1103, which communicates to switches that "A host with the USA 0x0006.7c11.1103 has requested multicast traffic for the GDA 0x0100.5e06.0606, so map your CAM tables accordingly." This message is received by both switches.

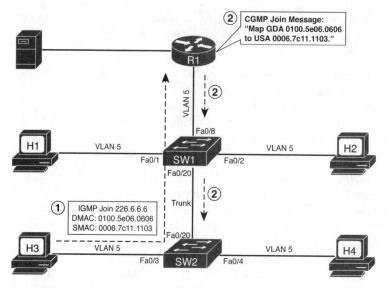

**Figure 7-16** *CGMP Join Message Process*

SW1 and SW2 search their CAM table entries and find that a host with the USA 0x0006.7c11.1103 is located on their port number fa0/20 and fa0/3, respectively. Figure 7-17 shows that SW1 and SW2 have mapped the GDA 0x0100.5e06.0606 to their port numbers fa0/20 and fa0/3, respectively.

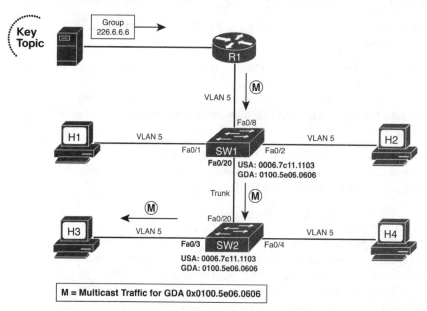

**Figure 7-17** *Switches Map GDA to Port Numbers and Don't Flood All the Hosts in a Broadcast Domain*

When R1 forwards multicast traffic with GDA 0x0100.5e06.0606 to SW1, as shown in Figure 7-17, SW1 searches its CAM table and notices that this traffic should be forwarded only on port fa0/20. Therefore, only SW2 receives the group traffic. Similarly, SW2 searches its CAM table and forwards the group traffic only on its port fa0/3, and only H3 receives the group traffic.

CGMP optimizes the forwarding of IGMP traffic as well. Although not shown in the figures, assume that H1 sends an IGMP Join message for 226.6.6.6. R1 will send another CGMP Join message, and SW1 will add the GDA 0x0100.5e06.0606 to its port fa0/1 also. When a router sends IGMP General Queries, switches forward them to host members who have joined any group, for example, H1 and H3. When hosts send IGMP Reports, switches forward them to the members of the group and the router.

The final step of the example, shown in Figure 7-18, demonstrates what happens when H3 leaves the group. Note that for this example, H1 has also joined the same multicast group.

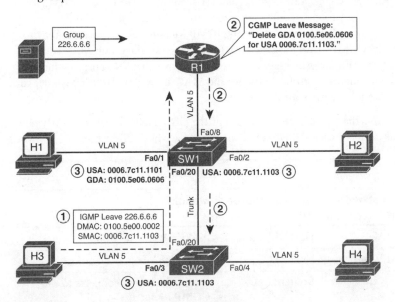

**Figure 7-18** *CGMP Leave Message Process*

The following three steps, referenced in Figure 7-18, describe the sequence of events when H3 sends an IGMP Leave message:

1. H3 sends an IGMP Leave message for 226.6.6.6. At Layer 2, H3 uses the All Multicast Routers MAC address 0x0100.5e00.0002 as the destination address and its own BIA 0x0006.7c11.1103 as the source address.

2. R1 generates a CGMP Leave message. When a CGMP-capable router receives an IGMP Leave message, it generates a Layer 2 CGMP Leave message. The destination address on the frame is the well-known multicast MAC address 0x0100.0cdd.dddd. R1 calculates the group MAC address 0x0100.5e06.0606 from the Layer 3 address 226.6.6.6 and sets the GDA to that value. It sets the USA to H3's MAC unicast MAC

address of 0x0006.7c11.1103. This Leave message communicates to switches that "A host with the USA 0x0006.7c11.1103 does not want to receive multicast traffic for GDA 0x0100.5e06.0606, so update your CAM tables accordingly." This message is received by both switches.

3. Switches update their CAM table entries. SW1 and SW2 search their CAM table entries and find that a host with the USA 0x0006.7c11.1103 is located on their port numbers fa0/20 and fa0/3, respectively. Figure 7-18 shows that SW1 and SW2 have removed the GDA 0x0100.5e06.0606 from their port numbers fa0/20 and fa0/3, respectively.

H1 is still a member of the group 226.6.6.6, so R1 keeps forwarding the traffic with GDA 0x0100.5e06.0606 to SW1, as shown in Figure 7-18. SW1 searches its CAM table and finds that this traffic should be forwarded only on port fa0/1. Therefore, only H1 receives the group traffic.

Continuing the example further, now assume that H1 sends an IGMP Leave message for 226.6.6.6. R1 will send a Group-Specific Query for 226.6.6.6. Because no host is currently a member of this group, R1 does not receive any IGMP Membership Reports for the group. R1 sends the CGMP Leave message with the GDA set to the group MAC address and the USA set to 0. This message communicates to switches that "No hosts are interested in receiving the multicast group traffic for the MAC address 0x0100.5e06.0606, so remove all the CAM table entries for this group."

Table 7-6 summarizes the possible combinations of the GDA and the USA in CGMP messages and the meanings of each. The first five messages have been discussed.

**Key Topic**

**Table 7-6**   *CGMP Messages*

| Type | Group Destination Address | Unicast Source Address | Meaning |
|------|---------------------------|------------------------|---------|
| Join | Group MAC | Host MAC | Add USA port to group |
| Leave | Group MAC | Host MAC | Delete USA port from group |
| Join | Zero | Router MAC | Learn which port connects to the CGMP router |
| Leave | Zero | Router MAC | Release CGMP router port |
| Leave | Group MAC | Zero | Delete the group from the CAM |
| Leave | Zero | Zero | Delete all groups from the CAM |

The last Leave message in Table 7-6, Delete All Groups, is used by the router for special maintenance functions. For example, when the **clear ip cgmp** command is entered at the router for clearing all the CGMP entries on the switches, the router sends the CGMP Leave message with GDA set to 0 and USA set to 0. When switches receive this message, they delete all group entries from the CAM tables.

## IGMP Snooping

What happens if your network has non-Cisco switches? You cannot use CGMP because it is Cisco proprietary. IGMP snooping can be used for a multivendor switched network to control distribution of multicast traffic at Layer 2. IGMP snooping requires the switch software to eavesdrop on the IGMP conversation between multicast hosts and the router. The switch examines IGMP messages and learns the location of multicast routers and group members.

> **Note**  Many Cisco switches support IGMP snooping, including the 3560 switches used in the CCIE Routing and Switching lab exam.

The following three steps describe the general process of IGMP snooping. Later, these steps are explained in detail.

**Key Topic**

1. To detect whether multiple routers are connected to the same subnet, Cisco switches listen to the following routing protocol messages to determine on which ports routers are connected:

   - IGMP General Query message with GDA 01-00-5e-00-00-01

   - OSPF messages with GDA 01-00-5e-00-00-05 or 01-00-5e-00-00-06

   - Protocol Independent Multicast (PIM) version 1 and Hot Standby Routing Protocol (HSRP) Hello messages with GDA 01-00-5e-00-00-02

   - PIMv2 Hello messages with GDA 01-00-5e-00-00-0d

   - Distance Vector Multicast Routing Protocol (DVMRP) Probe messages with GDA 01-00-5e-00-00-04

   As soon as the switch detects router ports in a VLAN, they are added to the port list of all GDAs in that VLAN.

2. When the switch receives an IGMP Report on a port, its CPU looks at the GDA, creates an entry in the CAM table for the GDA, and adds the port to the entry. The router port is also added to the entry. The group traffic is now forwarded on this port and the router port. If other hosts send their IGMP Reports, the switch adds their ports to the group entry in the CAM table and forwards the group traffic on these ports.

3. Similarly, when the switch receives an IGMP Leave message on a port, its CPU looks at the GDA, removes the port from the group entry in the CAM table, and does not forward the group traffic on the port. The switch checks whether this is the last nonrouter port for the GDA. If it is not the last nonrouter port for the GDA, which means that there is at least one host in the VLAN that wants the group traffic, the switch discards the Leave message; otherwise, it sends the Leave message to the router.

Thus, IGMP snooping helps switches send group traffic to only those hosts that want it and helps to avoid wasted bandwidth.

For efficient operations, IGMP snooping requires hardware filtering support in a switch so that it can differentiate between IGMP Reports and actual multicast traffic. The switch CPU needs to see IGMP Report messages (and Multicast Routing Protocol messages) because the IGMP snooping process requires the CPU. However, the forwarding of multicast frames does not require the CPU, instead requiring only a switch's forwarding ASICs. Older switches, particularly those that have no Layer 3 awareness, could not identify a packet as IGMP; these switches would have overburdened their CPUs by having to send all multicasts to the CPU. Most of today's more modern switches support enough Layer 3 awareness to recognize IGMP so that IGMP snooping does not overburden the CPU.

IGMP snooping is enabled by default on the Cisco 3560 switches used in the lab, and most other Layer 3 switches. The exact VLANs it snoops on can be controlled, as well as timers. The following configuration assumes that IGMP snooping has been disabled. It reenables snooping, disables it for VLAN 20, and reduces the last-member query interval from the default of 1000 seconds to 500 seconds. In addition, because VLAN 22 is connected only to hosts, it enables the switch to immediately remove a port when an IGMP Leave is received. Notice that commands are given globally.

```
sw2(config)# ip igmp snooping
sw2(config)# no ip igmp snooping vlan 20
sw2(config)# ip igmp snooping last-member-query-interval 500
sw2(config)# ip igmp snooping vlan 22 immediate-leave
```

**Note**  CGMP was a popular Cisco switch feature in years past because IGMP implementations on some switches would have required too much work. Today, many of the Cisco current switch product offerings do not even support CGMP, in deference to IGMP snooping, or support it only for connecting to lower-end Layer 2 switches.

Figure 7-19 shows an example of the IGMP snooping process.

The following three steps, referenced in Figure 7-19, describe the sequence of events when H1 and H2 send IGMP Join messages:

1. H1 sends an IGMP Join message for 226.6.6.6. At Layer 2, H1 uses the multicast MAC address 0x0100.5e06.0606 (the MAC for group 226.6.6.6) as the destination address and uses its own BIA 0x0006.7c11.1101 as the source address. SW1 receives the packet on its fa0/1 port and, noticing that it is an IGMP packet, forwards the packet to the switch CPU. The CPU uses the information to set up a multicast forwarding table entry, as shown in the CAM table that includes the port numbers 0 for CPU, 1 for H1, and 8 for R1. Notice that the CAM table lists two entries for the same destination MAC address 0x0100.5e06.0606—one for the IGMP frames for port 0 and the other for the non-IGMP frames for ports 1 and 8. The CPU of the switch instructs the switching engine to not forward any non-IGMP frames to port 0, which is connected to the CPU.

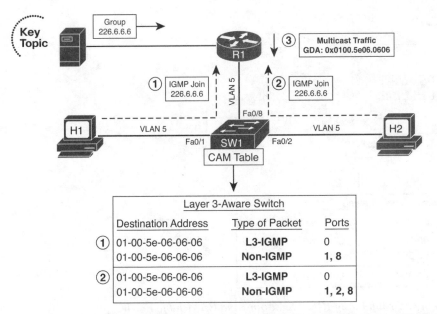

**Figure 7-19**  *Joining a Group Using IGMP Snooping and CAM Table Entries*

2.  H2 sends an IGMP Join message for 226.6.6.6. At Layer 2, H2 uses the multicast MAC address 0x0100.5e06.0606 as the destination address and uses its own BIA 0x0006.7c11.1102 as the source address. SW1 receives the packet on its fa0/2 port, and its switching engine examines the packet. The process of analyzing the packet, as described in Step 1, is repeated and the CAM table entries are updated as shown.

3.  Router R1 forwards the group traffic. R1 is receiving multicast traffic for group 226.6.6.6 and starts forwarding the traffic to SW1. SW1 starts receiving the multicast traffic on its port fa0/8. The switching engine would examine the packet and determine that this is a non-IGMP packet, search its CAM table, and determine that it should forward the packet on ports fa0/1 and fa0/2.

Compared to CGMP, IGMP snooping is less efficient in maintaining group information. In Figure 7-20, when R1 periodically sends IGMP General Queries to the All Hosts group, 224.0.0.1 (GDA 0x0100.5e00.0001), SW1 intercepts the General Queries and forwards them through all ports in VLAN 5. In CGMP, because of communication from the router through CGMP messages, the switch knows exactly on which ports multicast hosts are connected and, therefore, forwards IGMP General Queries only on those ports. Also, in IGMP snooping, when hosts send IGMP Reports, the switch must intercept them to maintain GDA information in the CAM table. As a result, the hosts do not receive each other's IGMP Report, which breaks the Report Suppression mechanism and forces each host to send an IGMP Report. However, the switch sends only one IGMP Report per group to the router. In CGMP, the switch does not have to intercept IGMP Reports, because maintaining group information in the switch is not dependent on examining IGMP packets from hosts; instead, the switch uses CGMP messages from the router.

Figure 7-20 shows the Leave process for IGMP snooping.

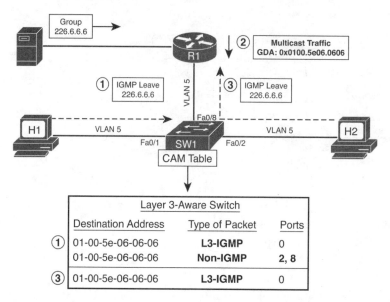

**Figure 7-20** *Leaving a Group Using IGMP Snooping and CAM Table Entries*

The following three steps, referenced in Figure 7-20, describe the sequence of events when H1 and H2 send IGMP Leave messages:

1. H1 sends an IGMP Leave message for 226.6.6.6, but SW1 does not forward it to Router R1 in this case. At Layer 2, H1 uses the All Multicast Routers MAC address 0x0100.5e00.0002 as the destination address and uses its own BIA 0x0006.7c11.1101 as the source address. SW1 captures the IGMP Leave message on its fa0/1 port, and its switching engine examines the packet. The switch sends an IGMP General Query on port fa0/1 to determine whether there are any other hosts that are members of this group on the port. (This feature was designed to protect other hosts if they are connected to the same switch port using a hub.) If an IGMP Report is received on port fa0/1, the switch discards the Leave message received from H1. Because, in this example, there is only one host connected to port fa0/1, the switch does not receive any IGMP Report and deletes the port fa0/1 from the CAM table entry, as shown in Figure 7-20. H2 connected with port fa0/2 is still a member of the group, and its port number is in the CAM table entry. Hence, SW1 does not forward the IGMP Leave message to the router.

2. Router R1 continues forwarding the group traffic. R1 continues forwarding multicast traffic for group 226.6.6.6 to SW1 because R1 did not even know that H1 left the group. Based on the updated CAM table entry for the group shown in Figure 7-20, SW1 now forwards this traffic only on port fa0/2.

3. H2 sends an IGMP Leave message for 226.6.6.6, and SW1 does forward it to Router R1 in this case. At Layer 2, H2 uses the All Multicast Routers MAC address 0x0100.5e00.0002 as the destination address and uses its own BIA 0x0006.7c11.1102 as the source address. Again, SW1 captures the IGMP Leave message on its fa0/2 port, and its switching engine examines the packet. The switch sends an IGMP

General Query on port fa0/2 to determine whether there are any other hosts that are members of this group on the port. Because, in this example, there is only one host connected to port fa0/2, the switch does not receive any IGMP Report and deletes the port fa0/2 from the CAM table entry. After SW1 deletes the port, it realizes that this was the last nonrouter port for the CAM table entry for 0x0100.5e06.0606. Therefore, SW1 deletes the CAM table entry for this group, as shown in Figure 7-20, and forwards the IGMP Leave message to R1, which sends an IGMP Group-Specific Query and, when no hosts respond, stops forwarding traffic for 226.6.6.6 toward SW1.

IGMP snooping becomes more complicated when multiple multicast routers are used and many LAN switches are interconnected through high-speed trunks. Also, CGMP and IGMP snooping control distribution of multicast traffic only on ports where hosts are connected. They do not provide any control mechanism for ports where routers are connected. The next section briefly examines how Router-Port Group Management Protocol (RGMP) helps switches control distribution of multicast traffic on ports where routers are connected.

## Router-Port Group Management Protocol

RGMP is a Layer 2 protocol that enables a router to communicate to a switch which multicast group traffic the router does and does not want to receive from the switch. By being able to restrict the multicast destinations that a switch forwards to a router, a router can reduce its overhead. In fact, RGMP was designed to help routers reduce overhead when they are attached to high-speed LAN backbones. It is enabled at the interface configuration mode using the simple command **ip rgmp**.

Although RGMP is Cisco proprietary, oddly enough it cannot work concurrently with Cisco-proprietary CGMP. When RGMP is enabled on a router or a switch, CGMP is silently disabled; if CGMP is enabled on a router or a switch, RGMP is silently disabled. Note also that while it is proprietary, RGMP is published as informational RFC 3488.

RGMP works well in conjunction with IGMP snooping. In fact, IGMP snooping would typically learn the ports of all multicast routers by listening for IGMP and multicast routing protocol traffic. In some cases, some routers might not want all multicast traffic, so RGMP provides a means to reduce the unwanted traffic. The subtle key to the need for RGMP when using IGMP snooping is to realize this important fact about IGMP snooping:

> IGMP snooping helps switches control distribution of multicast traffic on ports where multicast hosts are connected, but it does not help switches control distribution of multicast traffic on ports where multicast routers are connected.

For example, consider the simple network shown in Figure 7-21. SW2 has learned of Routers R3 and R4 with IGMP snooping, so it forwards multicasts sent to all multicast groups out to both R3 and R4.

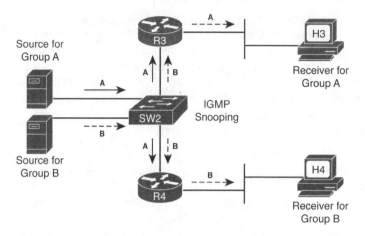

**Figure 7-21**   *IGMP Snooping Without RGMP*

As you can see from Figure 7-21, R3 needs to receive traffic only for group A, and R4 needs to receive traffic only for group B. However, IGMP snooping causes the switch to forward all multicast packets to each router. To combat that problem, RGMP can be used by a router to tell the switch to only forward packets for particular multicast groups. For example, Figure 7-22 shows the same network as Figure 7-21, but with RGMP snooping. In this case, RGMP Join messages are enabled in both the routers and the switch, with the results shown in Figure 7-22.

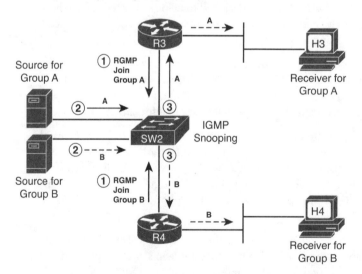

**Figure 7-22**   *More Efficient Forwarding with RGMP Added to IGMP Snooping*

Figure 7-22 shows the following three main steps, with the first step showing the RGMP function with the RGMP Join message. The Join message allows a router to identify the groups for which the router wants to receive traffic:

1.  R3 sends an RGMP Join for group A, and R4 sends an RGMP Join for group B. As a result, SW2 knows to forward multicasts for group A only to R3, and for group B only to R4.

2.  The sources send a packet to groups A and B, respectively.

3.  SW2 forwards the traffic for group A only to R3 and the packets for group B only to R4.

While Figure 7-22 shows just one example and one type of RGMP message, RGMP includes four different messages. All the RGMP messages are generated by a router and are sent to the multicast IP address 224.0.0.25. The following list describes the four RGMP messages:

■   When RGMP is enabled on a router, the router sends RGMP Hello messages by default every 30 seconds. When the switch receives an RGMP Hello message, it stops forwarding all multicast traffic on the port on which it received the Hello message.

■   When the router wants to receive traffic for a specific multicast group, the router sends an RGMP Join *G* message, where *G* is the multicast group address, to the switch. When the switch receives an RGMP Join message, it starts forwarding the requested group traffic on the port on which it received the Hello message.

■   When the router does not want to receive traffic for a formerly RGMP-joined specific multicast group, the router sends an RGMP Leave *G* message, where *G* is the multicast group address, to the switch. When the switch receives an RGMP Leave message, it stops forwarding the group traffic on the port on which it received the Hello message.

■   When RGMP is disabled on the router, the router sends an RGMP Bye message to the switch. When the switch receives an RGMP Bye message, it starts forwarding all IP multicast traffic on the port on which it received the Hello message.

## IGMP Filtering

As we have discussed earlier in this chapter, IGMP snooping is a protocol that learns and maintains multicast group membership at the Layer 2 level. IGMP snooping looks at IGMP traffic to decide which ports should be allowed to receive multicast traffic from certain sources and for certain groups. This information is used to forward multicast traffic to only interested ports. The main benefit of IGMP snooping is to reduce flooding of packets.

Another enhancement that works in unison with IGMP Snooping is IGMP filtering. IGMP filtering allows users to configure filters on a switch virtual interface (SVI), a per-port, or a per-port per-VLAN basis to control the propagation of IGMP traffic through the network. By managing the IGMP traffic, IGMP filtering provides the capability to manage IGMP snooping, which in turn optimizes the forwarding of multicast traffic.

When an IGMP packet is received, IGMP filtering uses the filters configured by the user to determine whether the IGMP packet should be discarded or allowed to be processed by the existing IGMP snooping code. With an IGMP version 1 or version 2 packet, the entire packet is discarded. With an IGMPv3 packet, the packet will be rewritten to remove message elements that were denied by the filters.

IGMP traffic filters control the access of a port to multicast traffic. Access can be restricted based on the following:

- Which multicast groups or channels can be joined on a given port. Keep in mind that channels are joined by IGMPv3 hosts that specify both the group and the source of the multicast traffic.

- Maximum number of groups or channels allowed on a specific port or interface (regardless of the number of hosts requesting service).

- IGMP protocol versions (for example, disallow all IGMPv1 messages).

When an IGMP filtering command is configured, a user policy is applied to a Layer 3 SVI interface, a Layer 2 port, or a particular VLAN on a Layer 2 trunk port. The Layer 2 port can be an access port or a trunk port. The IGMP filtering features will work only if IGMP snooping is enabled (either on the interface or globally). Thus it is important to keep in mind that this is a supplementary feature to IGMP snooping and not a standalone option.

Typically, IGMP filters are applied on access switches that are connected to end-user devices. Additionally, there are three different types of IGMP filters: IGMP group and channel access control, several IGMP groups and channels limit, and an IGMP minimum version. These filters are configurable and operate differently on different types of ports:

- Per SVI

- Per port

- Per VLAN basis on a trunk port

You can configure filters separately for each VLAN passing through a trunk port.

## IGMP Proxy

An IGMP proxy enables hosts in a unidirectional link routing (UDLR) environment that are not directly connected to a downstream router to join a multicast group sourced from an upstream network.

Figure 7-23 illustrates a sample topology that shows a UDLR scenario.

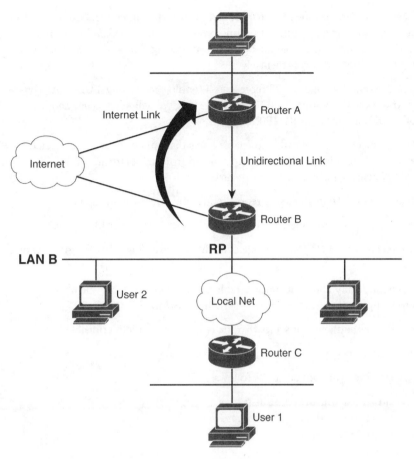

**Figure 7-23**  *UDLR Scenario*

Before you can see how this optimization improves multicast performance, you need to explore what a UDL routing scenario actually is. UDL creates a scenario that would normally be an issue for standard multicast and unicast routing protocols because of the fact that these routing protocols forward data on interfaces from which they have received routing control information. This model works only on bidirectional links for most existing routing protocols like those that we have discussed thus far; however, some networks use broadcast satellite links, which are by their very nature unidirectional. For networks that use broadcast satellite links, accomplishing two-way communication over broadcast satellite links presents a problem in terms of discovering and sharing knowledge of a network topology through traditional protocols like OSPF or Enhanced Interior Gateway Routing Protocol (EIGRP). This impacts Protocol Independent Multicast (PIM) operation because of PIM reliance on these protocols.

Specifically, in unicast routing, when a router receives an update message on an interface for a prefix, it forwards data for destinations that match that prefix out that same interface. This is the case in distance vector routing protocols like EIGRP. Similarly, in multicast routing, when a router receives a Join message for a multicast group on an interface, it forwards copies of data destined for that group out that same interface. Based on these principles, existing unicast and multicast routing protocols cannot be supported over UDLs. UDLR was designed to enable the operation of routing protocols over UDLs without changing the routing protocols themselves.

The topology illustrated in Figure 7-23 represents a topology involving a UDL that you need to use to work with multicast and IGMP. To do this, we will need to use another multicast optimization known as IGMP Proxy.

The IGMP proxy mechanism is needed to enable hosts that are not directly connected to a downstream device to join a multicast group sourced from an upstream network. In this scenario, the following sequence of events occurs:

1. User 1 sends an IGMP membership report requesting interest in group G.

2. Router C sends a PIM Join message hop by hop to the RP (Router B).

3. Router B receives the PIM Join message and adds a forwarding entry for group G on LAN B.

4. Router B periodically checks its mroute table and proxies the IGMP membership report to its upstream UDL device across the Internet link.

5. Router A creates and maintains a forwarding entry on the unidirectional link (UDL).

To make this feature work, you will need to apply configuration on each end of the UDL.

You will start with the upstream device as follows:

```
sw2(config)# interface gigabitethernet 0/0/0
sw2(config)# ip address 10.1.1.1 255.255.255.0
sw2(config)# ip pim dense-mode
sw2(config)#!
sw2(config)# interface gigabitethernet 1/0/0
sw2(config)# ip address 10.2.1.1 255.255.255.0
sw2(config)# ip pim dense-mode
sw2(config)# ip igmp unidirectional-link
sw2(config)#!
sw2(config)# interface gigabitethernet 2/0/0
sw2(config)# ip address 10.3.1.1 255.255.255.0
```

The remaining configuration would need to be applied on the downstream device:

```
sw3(config)# ip pim rp-address 10.5.1.1 5
sw3(config)# access-list 5 permit 239.0.0.0 0.255.255.255
sw3(config)#!
sw3(config)# interface loopback 0
sw3(config)# ip address 10.7.1.1 255.255.255.0
sw3(config)# ip pim dense-mode
sw3(config)# ip igmp helper-address udl ethernet 0
sw3(config)# ip igmp proxy-service
```

```
sw3(config)#!
sw3(config)# interface gigabitethernet 0/0/0
sw3(config)# ip address 10.2.1.2 255.255.255.0
sw3(config)# ip pim dense-mode
sw3(config)# ip igmp unidirectional-link
sw3(config)#!
sw3(config)# interface gigabitethernet 1/0/0
sw3(config)# ip address 10.5.1.1 255.255.255.0
sw3(config)# ip pim sparse-mode
sw3(config)# ip igmp mroute-proxy loopback 0
sw3(config)#!
sw3(config)# interface gigabitethernet 2/0/0
sw3(config)# ip address 10.6.1.1 255.255.255.0
```

**Note**  For more information on UDLR, see the "Configuring Unidirectional Link Routing" documentation at Cisco.com or visit the following URL: http://tinyurl.com/CiscoUDLR.

# Foundation Summary

This section lists additional details and facts to round out the coverage of the topics in this chapter. Unlike most of the Cisco Press Exam Certification Guides, this "Foundation Summary" does not repeat information presented in the "Foundation Topics" section of the chapter. Please take the time to read and study the details in the "Foundation Topics" section of the chapter, as well as review items noted with a Key Topic icon.

Table 7-7 lists some of the key protocols and facts regarding IGMP.

**Table 7-7**  *Protocols and Standards for Chapter 7*

| Name | Standard |
| --- | --- |
| GLOP Addressing in 233/8 | RFC 3180 |
| Administratively Scoped IP Multicast | RFC 2365 |
| IGMP version 0 | RFC 988 |
| Host Extensions for IP Multicasting [IGMPv1] | RFC 1112 |
| Internet Group Management Protocol, Version 2 | RFC 2236 |
| Internet Group Management Protocol, Version 3 | RFC 3376 |
| Multicast Listener Discovery (MLD) for IPv6 | RFC 2710 |
| Cisco Systems Router-Port Group Management Protocol (RGMP) | RFC 3488 |

Configuring multicasting on a Cisco router is relatively easy. You must first configure a multicast routing protocol on a Cisco router. The multicast routing protocols are covered in the next chapter, which also presents all the important configuration commands in the "Foundation Summary" section.

# Memory Builders

The CCIE Routing and Switching written exam, like all Cisco CCIE written exams, covers a fairly broad set of topics. This section provides some basic tools to help you exercise your memory about some of the broader topics covered in this chapter.

## Fill In Key Tables from Memory

Appendix E, "Key Tables for CCIE Study," on the CD in the back of this book, contains empty sets of some of the key summary tables in each chapter. Print Appendix E, refer to this chapter's tables in it, and fill in the tables from memory. Refer to Appendix F, "Solutions for Key Tables for CCIE Study," on the CD, to check your answers.

## Definitions

Next, take a few moments to write down the definitions for the following terms:

> multicasting, multicast address range, multicast address structure, permanent multicast group, source-specific addresses, GLOP addressing, administratively scoped addresses, transient multicast group, multicast MAC address, joining a group, IGMP, MRT, Report Suppression mechanism, IGMPv2 Host Membership Query, IGMPv2 Leave, IGMPv2 Group-Specific Query, IGMPv2 Host Membership Report, SSM, querier election, CGMP, IGMP snooping, RGMP

Refer to the glossary to check your answers.

## Further Reading

Beau Williamson, *Developing IP Multicast Networks*, Volume I, Cisco Press, 2000.

# References in This Chapter

"Multicast in a Campus Network: CGMP and IGMP Snooping (Document ID 10559)," www.cisco.com/en/US/products/hw/switches/ps708/products_tech_note-09186a00800b0871.shtml

Router-Port Group Management Protocol, www.cisco.com/en/US/docs/ios/12_1t/12_1t5/feature/guide/dtrgmp.html

"Configuring Unidirectional Link Routing," www.cisco.com/c/en/us/td/docs/ios/12_2/ip/configuration/guide/fipr_c/1cfudlr.html

**Blueprint topics covered in this chapter:**

This chapter covers the following subtopics from the Cisco CCIE Routing and Switching written exam blueprint. Refer to the full blueprint in Table I-1 in the Introduction for more details on the topics covered in each chapter and their context within the blueprint.

■ Protocol Independent Multicast (PIM) sparse mode

■ Multicast Source Discovery Protocol (MSDP)

■ Interdomain multicast routing

■ PIM Auto-Rendezvous Point (Auto-RP), unicast rendezvous point (RP), and BootStrap Router (BSR)

■ Implement multicast tools, features, and source-specific multicast (SSM)

■ IPv6 Multicast Operation

## CHAPTER 8

# IP Multicast Routing

In Chapter 7, "Introduction to IP Multicasting," you learned how a multicast router communicates with hosts and then decides whether to forward or stop the multicast traffic on a subnet. But how does a multicast router receive the group traffic? How is the multicast traffic forwarded from a source so that all the group users receive it? This chapter provides answers to those questions.

This chapter first defines the multicast routing problem by identifying the difference between unicast and multicast routing. It then provides an overview of the basic design concepts of multicast routing protocols, and shows how they solve multicast routing problems. Next, the chapter covers the operations of the Protocol Independent Multicast routing protocol in dense mode (PIM-DM) and sparse mode (PIM-SM). The chapter also covers the basic functions of Distance Vector Multicast Routing Protocol (DVMRP) and Multicast OSPF (MOSPF) as well as IPv6 Multicast Operation.

## "Do I Know This Already?" Quiz

Table 8-1 outlines the major headings in this chapter and the corresponding "Do I Know This Already?" quiz questions.

**Table 8-1**  *"Do I Know This Already?" Foundation Topics Section-to-Question Mapping*

| Foundation Topics Section | Questions Covered in This Section | Score |
|---|---|---|
| Multicast Routing Basics | 1 | |
| Dense-Mode Routing Protocols | 2–4 | |
| Sparse-Mode Routing Protocols | 5–8 | |
| IPv6 Multicast PIM | 9–10 | |
| Total Score | | |

To best use this pre-chapter assessment, remember to score yourself strictly. You can find the answers in Appendix A, "Answers to the 'Do I Know This Already?' Quizzes."

1. When a multicast router receives a multicast packet, which one of the following tasks will it perform first?

   a. Examine the IP multicast destination address on the packet, consult the multicast routing table to determine the next-hop address, and forward the packet through appropriate interface(s).

   b. Depending on the multicast routing protocol configured, either forward the packet on all the interfaces or forward the packet on selected interfaces except the one on which the packet was received.

   c. Determine the interface this router would use to send packets to the source of the packet, and decide whether the packet arrived in that interface or not.

   d. Send a Prune message to its upstream neighbor if it does not have any directly connected group members or active downstream routers.

2. A PIM router receives a PIM Assert message on a LAN interface. Which of the following statements is (are) true about the response of the router?

   a. The router does not have to take any action.

   b. If the router is configured with the PIM-DM routing protocol, it will process the Assert message; otherwise, it will ignore it.

   c. If the router is configured with the PIM-SM routing protocol, it will process the Assert message; otherwise, it will ignore it.

   d. The router will send a PIM Assert message.

3. When a PIM-DM router receives a Graft message from a downstream router after it has sent a Prune message to its upstream router for the same group, which of the following statements is (are) true about its response?

   a. It will send a Graft message to the downstream router and a Prune message to the upstream router.

   b. It will send a Prune message to the downstream router and a Graft message to the upstream router.

   c. It will reestablish adjacency with the upstream router.

   d. It will send a Graft message to the upstream router.

4. On Router R1, the **show ip mroute 239.5.130.24** command displays **Serial2, Prune/ Dense, 00:01:34/00:01:26** for the (S,G) entry under the outgoing interface list. Which of the following statements provide correct interpretation of this information?

   a. Router R1 has sent a Prune message on its Serial2 interface to its upstream router 1 minute and 34 seconds ago.

   b. Router R1 will send a Graft message on its Serial2 interface to its upstream router after 1 minute and 26 seconds.

   c. Router R1 received a Prune message on its Serial2 interface from its downstream router 1 minute and 34 seconds ago.

   d. Router R1 will send a Prune message on its Serial2 interface to its upstream router after 1 minute and 26 seconds.

   e. Router R1 will forward the traffic for the group on its Serial2 interface after 1 minute and 26 seconds.

5. From the following statements, select the true statement(s) regarding when a PIM-SM RP router will send the unicast PIM Register-Stop messages to the first-hop DR.

   a. If the RP has no need for the traffic

   b. If the RP is already receiving traffic on the shared tree

   c. When the RP begins receiving multicast traffic through SPT from the source

   d. When the RP sends multicast traffic through SPT to the downstream router

6. R1, a PIM-SM router, sends an (S,G) RP-bit Prune to its upstream neighbor. Assume that all the PIM-SM routers in the network are using the Cisco default **spt-threshold** value. Which of the following statements is (are) true about the status of different routers in the PIM-SM network at this time?

   a. At R1, the root-path tree and shortest-path tree diverge.

   b. R1 is switching over from shortest-path tree to root-path tree.

   c. R1 is switching over from root-path tree to shortest-path tree.

   d. At R1, the RPF neighbor for the (S,G) entry is different from the RPF neighbor of the (*,G) entry.

**7.** In a PIM-SM LAN network using Auto-RP, one of the routers is configured to send Cisco-RP-Announce and Cisco-RP-Discovery messages. All the routers show all the interfaces with correct PIM neighbors in sparse mode. However, the network administrator is puzzled by inconsistent RP mapping information shown on many routers. Some routers show correct RP mappings, but many leaf routers do not show any RP mappings. Which of the following statements represent(s) the most likely cause(s) for the above problem?

   **a.** The links between the leaf routers and the mapping agent are congested.

   **b.** All the interfaces of all the routers are configured with the command **ip pim sparse-mode**.

   **c.** The leaf routers are configured with a static RP address using an **override** option.

   **d.** The RPF check on the leaf routers is failing.

**8.** PIM-SM Router R1 has two interfaces listed, s0/0 and fa0/0, in its (*,G) entry for group 227.7.7.7 in its multicast routing table. Assuming that nothing changes in that (*,G) entry in the next 10 minutes, which of the following could be true?

   **a.** R1 is sending PIM Join messages toward the RP.

   **b.** R1 does not need to send Join messages toward the RP as long as the RP is continuing to forward multicasts for group 227.7.7.7 to R1.

   **c.** R1 is receiving PIM Join messages periodically on one or both of interfaces s0/0 and fa0/0.

   **d.** R1 is receiving IGMP Report messages periodically on interface fa0/0.

   **e.** The RP has been sending PIM Prune messages to R1 periodically, but R1 has been replying with PIM Reject messages because it still needs to receive the packets.

**9.** MLD uses what three types of messages?

   **a.** Query

   **b.** Null

   **c.** Report

   **d.** Done

**10.** Which of the following list of IPv6 addresses is used to represent an embedded RP address in IPv6?

   **a.** FE7E:0240:2001:2:2:2:0:1

   **b.** F17E:0240:2001:2:2:2:0:1

   **c.** FF7E:0240:2001:2:2:2:0:1

   **d.** F07E:0240:2001:2:2:2:0:1

# Foundation Topics

## Multicast Routing Basics

The main function of any routing protocol is to help routers forward a packet in the right direction, causing the packet to keep moving closer to its desired destination and ultimately reaching its destination. To forward a unicast packet, a router examines the packet's destination address, finds the next-hop address from the unicast routing table, and forwards the packet through the appropriate interface. A unicast packet is forwarded along a single path from the source to the destination.

The top part of Figure 8-1 shows how a router can easily make a decision about forwarding a unicast packet by consulting its unicast routing table. However, when a router receives a multicast packet, as shown at the bottom of Figure 8-1, it cannot forward the packet because multicast IP addresses are not listed in the unicast routing table. Also, routers often have to forward multicast packets out multiple interfaces to reach all receivers. These requirements make the multicast forwarding process more complex than unicast forwarding.

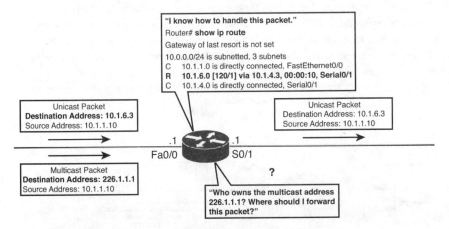

**Figure 8-1**  *Multicast Routing Problem*

Figure 8-1 shows that the router has received a multicast packet with the destination address 226.1.1.1. The destination address represents a dynamically changing group of recipients, not any one recipient's address. How can the router find out where these users are? Where should the router forward this packet?

An analogy can help you to better understand the difficulty of multicast routing. Assume that you want to send party invitations through the mail, but instead of creating dozens of invitations, you create only one. Before mailing the invitation, you put a destination address on it, "This envelope contains my party invitation," and then drop it in a mailbox. When the postal system examines the destination address on your envelope, where should it deliver your envelope? And because it is only one invitation, does the postal system need to make copies? Also, how can the postal system figure out to which addresses to deliver the copies? By contrast, if IP multicast were the post office, it would know who you want to invite to the party, know where they are located, and make copies of the invitation and deliver them all to the correct addresses.

The next few sections discuss solutions for forwarding multicast traffic and controlling the distribution of multicast traffic in a routed network.

## Overview of Multicast Routing Protocols

Routers can forward a multicast packet by using either a *dense-mode multicast routing protocol* or a *sparse-mode multicast routing protocol*. This section examines the basic concepts of multicast forwarding using dense mode, the Reverse Path Forwarding (RPF) check, and multicast forwarding using sparse mode, all of which help to solve the multicast routing problem.

### Multicast Forwarding Using Dense Mode

Dense-mode routing protocols assume that the multicast group application is so popular that every subnet in the network has at least one receiver wanting to receive the group traffic. Therefore, the design of a dense-mode routing protocol instructs the router to forward the multicast traffic on all the configured interfaces, with some exceptions to prevent looping. For example, a multicast packet is never forwarded out the interface on which it was received. Figure 8-2 shows how a dense-mode routing protocol receives a multicast on one interface, and then forwards copies out all other interfaces.

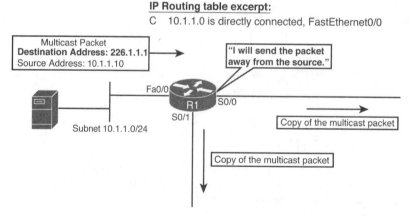

**Figure 8-2**   *R1 Forwarding a Multicast Packet Using a Dense-Mode Routing Protocol*

Figure 8-2 shows the dense-mode logic on R1, with R1 *flooding* copies of the packet out all interfaces except the one on which the packet was received. Although Figure 8-2 shows only one router, other routers can receive these multicasts and repeat the same process. All subnets will receive a copy of the original multicast packet.

Dense-mode protocols assume that all subnets need to receive a copy of the packets; however, dense-mode protocols do allow routers to ask to not receive traffic sent to a particular multicast group. Dense-mode routers typically do not want to receive multicast packets for a particular group if both of the following are true:

- The router does not have any active downstream routers that need packets for that group.

- The router does not know of any hosts on directly connected subnets that have joined that group.

When both of these conditions are true, the router needs to inform its upstream router not to send traffic for the group, which it does by using a special message called a Prune message. The mechanics of how dense-mode routers communicate with each other are discussed in detail in the PIM-DM section, later in this chapter.

DVMRP, PIM-DM, and MOSPF are the dense-mode routing protocols discussed in this chapter, with most of the attention being paid to PIM-DM.

## Reverse Path Forwarding Check

Routers cannot simply use logic by which they receive a multicast packet and then forward a copy of it out all other interfaces, without causing multicast packets to loop around the internetwork. To prevent such loops, routers do not forward multicasts out the same interface on which they were received. Multicast routers use a *Reverse Path Forwarding (RPF) check* to prevent loops. The RPF check adds this additional step to a dense-mode router's forwarding logic:

Look at the source IP address of the multicast packet. If my route that matches the source lists an outgoing interface that is the actual interface on which the packet was received, the packet passes the RPF check. If not, do not replicate and forward the packet.

Figure 8-3 shows an example in which R3 uses the RPF check on two separate copies of the same original multicast packet. Host S1 sends a multicast packet, with R1 flooding it to R2 and R3. R2 receives its copy, and floods it as well. As a result, R3 receives the same packet from two routers: on its s0/0 interface from R2 and on its s0/1 interface from R1. Without the RPF check, R3 would forward the packet it got from R1 to R2, and vice versa, and begin the process of looping packets. With this same logic, R1 and R2 also keep repeating the process. This duplication creates multicast routing loops and generates multicast storms that waste bandwidth and router resources.

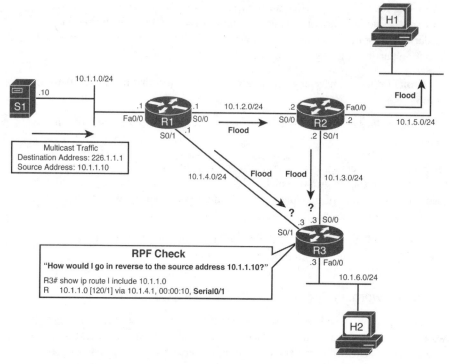

**Figure 8-3** *R3 Performs the RPF Check*

A multicast router does not forward any multicast packet unless the packet passes the RPF check. In Figure 8-3, R3 has to decide whether it should accept the multicast packets coming from R1 and R2. R3 makes this decision by performing the RPF check, described in detail as follows:

1. R3 examines the source address of each incoming multicast packet, which is 10.1.1.10. The source address is used in the RPF check of Step 2.

2. R3 determines the reverse path interface based on its route used to forward packets to 10.1.1.10. In this case, R3's route to 10.1.1.0/24 is matched, and it lists an outgoing interface of s0/1, making s0/1 R3's RPF interface for IP address 10.1.1.10.

3. R3 compares the reverse path interface determined in Step 2 with the interface on which the multicast packet arrived. If they match, it accepts the packet and forwards it; otherwise, it drops the packet. In this case, R3 floods the packet received on s0/1 from R1, but it ignores the packet received on s0/0 from R2.

The RPF check implements a strategy by which routers accept packets that arrive over the shortest path, and discard those that arrive over longer routes. Multicast routing protocols cannot use the destination address to help routers forward a packet, because that address represents the group traffic. So, multicast routing protocols use the RPF check to determine whether the packet arrived at the router using the shortest-path route from the source to the router. If it did, multicast routing protocols accept the packet and forward it; otherwise, they drop the packet and thereby avoid routing loops and duplication.

Different multicast routing protocols determine their RPF interfaces in different ways, as follows:

■ Distance Vector Multicast Routing Protocol (DVMRP) maintains a separate multicast routing table and uses it for the RPF check.

■ Protocol Independent Multicast (PIM) and Core-Based Tree (CBT) generally use the unicast routing table for the RPF check, as shown in Figure 8-3.

■ PIM and CBT can also use the DVMRP route table, the Multiprotocol Border Gateway Protocol (MP-BGP) route table, or statically configured multicast route(s) for the RPF check.

■ Multicast OSPF does not use the RPF check, because it computes both forward and reverse shortest-path source-rooted trees by using the Dijkstra algorithm.

## Multicast Forwarding Using Sparse Mode

A dense-mode routing protocol is useful when a multicast application is so popular that you need to deliver the group traffic to almost all the subnets of a network. However, if the group users are located on a few subnets, a dense-mode routing protocol will still flood the traffic in the entire internetwork, wasting bandwidth and resources of routers. In those cases, a sparse-mode routing protocol, such as PIM-SM, could be used to help reduce the waste of network resources.

The fundamental difference between dense-mode and sparse-mode routing protocols relates to their default behavior. By default, dense-mode protocols keep forwarding the group traffic unless a downstream router sends a message stating that it does not want that traffic. Sparse-mode protocols do not forward the group traffic to any other router unless it receives a message from that router requesting copies of packets sent to a particular multicast group. Λ downstream router requests to receive the packets only for one of two reasons:

■ The router has received a request to receive the packets from some downstream router.

■ A host on a directly connected subnet has sent an Internet Group Management Protocol (IGMP) Join message for that group.

Figure 8-4 shows an example of what must happen with PIM-SM before a host (H2 in this case) can receive packets sent by host S1 to multicast group address 226.1.1.1. The PIM sparse-mode operation begins with the packet being forwarded to a special router called the *rendezvous point (RP)*. When the group traffic arrives at an RP, unlike the dense-mode design, the RP does not automatically forward the group traffic to any router; the group traffic must be specifically requested by a router.

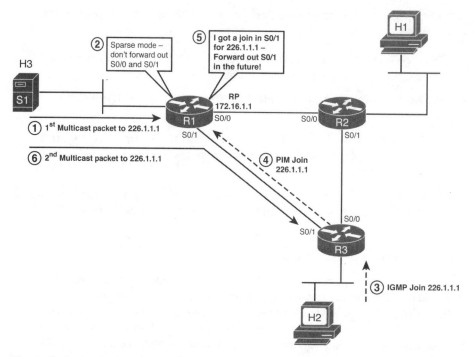

**Figure 8-4** *R1 Forwarding a Multicast Packet Using a Sparse-Mode Routing Protocol*

**Note** Throughout this chapter, the solid arrowed lines in the figures represent multicast packets, with dashed arrowed lines representing PIM and IGMP messages.

Before you look at the numbered steps in Figure 8-4, consider the state of this internetwork. PIM-SM is configured on all the routers, R1 is selected as an RP, and in all three routers, the IP address 172.16.1.1 of R1 is configured statically as the RP address. Usually, a loopback interface address is used as an RP address and the loopback network is advertised in the unicast routing protocol so that all the routers learn how to locate an RP. At this point, R1, as the RP, can receive multicast packets sent to 226.1.1.1, but it will not forward them.

The following list describes the steps shown in Figure 8-4:

1.  Host S1 sends a multicast to the RP, with destination address 226.1.1.1.

2.  R1 chooses to ignore the packet, because no routers or local hosts have told the RP (R1) that they want to receive copies of multicast packets.

3.  Host H2 sends an IGMP Join message for group 226.1.1.1.

4.  R3 sends a PIM Join message to the RP (R1) for address 226.1.1.1.

5. R1's logic now changes, so future packets sent to 226.1.1.1 will be forwarded by R1 out s0/1 to R3.

6. Host S1 sends a multicast packet to 226.1.1.1, and R1 forwards it out s0/1 to R3.

In a PIM-SM network, it is critical for all the routers to somehow learn the IP address of an RP. One option in a small network is to statically configure the IP address of an RP in every router. Later in the chapter, the section "Dynamically Finding RPs and Using Redundant RPs" covers how routers can dynamically discover the IP address of the RP.

The example in Figure 8-4 shows some of the savings in using a sparse-mode protocol like PIM-SM. R2 has not received any IGMP Join messages on its LAN interface, so it does not send any request to the RP to forward the group traffic. As a result, R1 does not waste link bandwidth on the link from R1 to R2. R3 will not forward multicasts to R2 either in this case.

**Note**    In Figure 8-4, R3 first performs its RPF check by using the IP address of the RP rather than the IP address of the source of the packet, because it is receiving the group traffic from the RP. If the RPF check succeeds, R3 forwards the traffic on its LAN.

## Multicast Scoping

Multicast scoping confines the forwarding of multicast traffic to a group of routers, for administrative, security, or policy reasons. In other words, multicast scoping is the practice of defining boundaries that determine how far multicast traffic will travel in your network. The following sections discuss two methods of multicast scoping:

■  TTL scoping

■  Administrative scoping

### TTL Scoping

With TTL scoping, routers compare the time to live (TTL) value on a multicast packet with a configured TTL value on each outgoing interface. A router forwards the multicast packet only on those interfaces whose configured TTL value is less than or equal to the TTL value of the multicast packet. In effect, TTL scoping resets the TTL value at which the router discards multicasts from the usual value of 0 to some higher number. Figure 8-5 shows an example of a multicast router with various TTL threshold values configured on its interfaces.

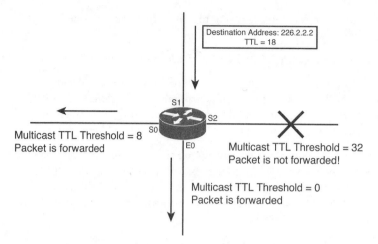

**Figure 8-5**   *Multicast Scoping Using TTL Thresholds*

In Figure 8-5, a multicast packet arrives on the s1 interface with a TTL of 18. The router decreases the packet's TTL by 1 to 17. Assume that the router is configured with a dense-mode routing protocol on all four interfaces and the RPF check succeeds—in other words, the router will want to forward a copy of the packet on each interface. The router compares the remaining TTL of the packet, which is now 17, with the TTL threshold of each outgoing interface. If the packet's TTL is higher than or equal to the interface TTL, it forwards a copy of the packet on that interface; otherwise, it does not forward it. On a Cisco router, the default TTL value on all the interfaces is 0.

On the s0 and s2 interfaces in Figure 8-5, the network administrator has configured the TTL as 8 and 32, respectively. A copy of the packet is forwarded on the s0 and e0 interfaces because their TTL thresholds are less than 17. However, the packet is not forwarded on the s2 interface because its TTL threshold is 32, which is higher than 17.

TTL scoping has some weaknesses. First, it is difficult to implement in a large and complex network, because estimating correct TTL thresholds on many routers and many interfaces so that the network correctly confines only the intended sessions becomes an extremely demanding task. Another problem with TTL scoping is that a configured TTL threshold value on an interface applies to all multicast packets. If you want flexibility for some multicast sessions, you have to manipulate the applications to alter the TTL values when packets leave the servers.

## Administrative Scoping

Recall from Chapter 7 that administratively scoped multicast addresses are private addresses in the range 239.0.0.0 to 239.255.255.255. They can be used to set administrative boundaries to limit the forwarding of multicast traffic outside of a domain. It requires manual configuration. You can configure and apply a filter on a router's interface so that multicast traffic with group addresses in the private address range is not allowed to enter or exit the interface.

**Note**  This chapter assumes that you have read Chapter 7 or are thoroughly familiar with the operation of IGMP; if neither is true, read Chapter 7 before continuing with this chapter.

# Dense-Mode Routing Protocols

There are three dense-mode routing protocols:

- Protocol Independent Multicast Dense Mode (PIM-DM)

- Distance Vector Multicast Routing Protocol (DVMRP)

- Multicast Open Shortest Path First (MOSPF)

This section covers the operation of PIM-DM in detail and provides an overview of DVMRP and MOSPF.

## Operation of Protocol Independent Multicast Dense Mode

Protocol Independent Multicast (PIM) defines a series of protocol messages and rules by which routers can provide efficient forwarding of multicast IP packets. PIM previously existed as a Cisco-proprietary protocol, although it has been offered as an experimental protocol through RFCs 2362, 3446, and 3973. The PIM specifications spell out the rules mentioned in the earlier examples in this chapter—things like the RPF check, the PIM dense-mode logic of flooding multicasts until routers send Prune messages, and the PIM sparse-mode logic of not forwarding multicasts anywhere until a router sends a Join message. This section describes the PIM-DM protocols in more detail.

PIM gets its name from its ability to use the unicast IP routing table for its RPF check—independent of whatever unicast IP routing protocol(s) was used to build the unicast routing table entries. In fact, the name "PIM" really says as much about the two other dense-mode protocols—DVMRP and MOSPF—as it does about PIM. These other two protocols do not use the unicast IP routing table for their RPF checks, instead building their own independent tables. PIM simply relies on the unicast IP routing table, independent of which unicast IP routing protocol built a particular entry in the routing table.

### Forming PIM Adjacencies Using PIM Hello Messages

PIM routers form adjacencies with neighboring PIM routers for the same general reasons, and with the same general mechanisms, as many other routing protocols. PIMv2, the current version of PIM, sends Hello messages every 30 seconds (default) on every interface on which PIM is configured. By receiving Hellos on the same interface, routers discover neighbors, establish adjacency, and maintain adjacency. PIMv2 Hellos use IP protocol number 103 and reserved multicast destination address 224.0.0.13, called the All-PIM-Routers multicast address. The Hello messages contain a Holdtime value, typically three times the sender's PIM hello interval. If the receiver does not receive a Hello message from the sender during the Holdtime period, it considers the sending neighbor to be dead.

> **Note**   The older version, PIMv1, does not use Hellos, instead using a PIM Query message. PIMv1 messages are encapsulated in IP packets with protocol number 2 and use the multicast destination address 224.0.0.2.

As you will see in the following sections, establishing and maintaining adjacencies with directly connected neighbors are very important for the operation of PIM. A PIM router sends other PIM messages only on interfaces on which it has known active PIM neighbors.

## Source-Based Distribution Trees

Dense-mode routing protocols are suitable for dense topology in which there are many multicast group members relative to the total number of hosts in a network. When a PIM-DM router receives a multicast packet, it first performs the RPF check. If the RPF check succeeds, the router forwards a copy of the packet to all the PIM neighbors except the one on which it received the packet. Each PIM-DM router repeats the process and floods the entire network with the group traffic. Ultimately, the packets are flooded to all leaf routers that have no downstream PIM neighbors.

The logic described in the previous paragraph actually describes the concepts behind what PIM calls a *source-based distribution tree*. It is also sometimes called a *shortest-path tree (SPT)* or simply a *source tree*. The tree defines a path between the source host that originates the multicast packets and all subnets that need to receive a copy of the multicasts sent by that host. The tree uses the source as the root, the routers as the nodes in the tree, and the subnets connected to the routers as the branches and leaves of the tree. Figure 8-3, earlier in the chapter, shows the concept behind an SPT.

The configuration required on the three routers in Figure 8-3 is easy: Just add the global command **ip multicast-routing** on each router and the interface command **ip pim dense-mode** on all the interfaces of all the routers.

PIM-DM might have a different source-based distribution tree for each combination of source and multicast group, because the SPT will differ based on the location of the source and the locations of the hosts listening for each multicast group address. The notation (S,G) refers to a particular SPT, or to an individual router's part of a particular SPT, where S is the source's IP address and G is the multicast group address. For example, the (S,G) notation for the example in Figure 8-3 would be written as (10.1.1.10, 226.1.1.1).

Example 8-1 shows part of the (S,G) SPT entry on R3, from Figure 8-3, for the (10.1.1.0, 226.1.1.1) SPT. Host S1 is sending packets to 226.1.1.1, and host H2 sends an IGMP Join message for the group 226.1.1.1. Example 8-1 shows R3's multicast configuration and a part of its multicast routing table, as displayed using the **show ip mroute** command.

**Example 8-1**    *Multicast Configuration and Route Table Entry*

```
R3(config)# ip multicast-routing
R3(config)# int fa0/0
R3(config-if)# ip pim dense-mode
R3(config-if)# int s0/1
R3(config-if)# ip pim dense-mode
!
R3# show ip mroute
 (10.1.1.10/32, 226.1.1.1), 00:00:12/00:02:48, flags: CT
  Incoming interface: Serial0/1, RPF nbr 10.1.4.1
  Outgoing interface list:
FastEthernet0/0, Forward/Dense, 00:00:12/00:00:00
```

The interpretation of the multicast routing information shown in Example 8-1 is as follows:

- The shaded line shows that the (S,G) entry for (10.1.1.10/32, 226.1.1.1) has been up for 12 seconds, and that if R3 does not forward an (S,G) packet in 2 minutes and 48 seconds, it will expire. Every time R3 forwards a packet using this entry, the timer is reset to 3 minutes.

- The C flag indicates that R3 has a directly connected group member for 226.1.1.1. The T flag indicates that the (S,G) traffic is forwarded on the shortest-path tree.

- The incoming interface for the group 226.1.1.1 is s0/1, and the RPF neighbor (the next-hop IP address to go in the reverse direction toward the source address 10.1.1.10) is 10.1.4.1.

- The group traffic is forwarded out on the fa0/0 interface. This interface has been in the forwarding state for 12 seconds. The second timer is listed as 00:00:00, because it cannot expire with PIM-DM, as this interface will continue to forward traffic until pruned.

**Note**    The multicast routing table flags mentioned in this list, as well as others, are summarized in Table 8-7 in the "Foundation Summary" section of this chapter.

The next two sections show how PIM-DM routers use information learned from IGMP to dynamically expand and contract the source-based distribution trees to satisfy the needs of the group users.

## Prune Message

PIM-DM creates a new SPT when a source first sends multicast packets to a new multicast group address. The SPT includes all interfaces except RPF interfaces, because PIM-DM assumes that all hosts need to receive a copy of each multicast packet. However, some subnets might not need a copy of the multicasts, so PIM-DM defines a process by which routers can remove interfaces from an SPT by using PIM Prune messages.

For example, in Figure 8-3, hosts H1 and H2 need a copy of the multicast packets sent to 226.1.1.1. However, as shown, when R2 gets the multicast from R1, R2 then forwards the multicasts to R3. As it turns out, R3 is dropping the packets for the group traffic from 10.1.1.10, sent to 226.1.1.1, because those packets fail R3's RPF check. In this case, R3 can cause R2 to remove its s0/1 interface from its outgoing interface list for (10.1.1.10, 226.1.1.1) by sending a Prune message to R2. As a result, R2 will not forward the multi-casts to R3, thereby reducing the amount of wasted bandwidth.

**Note**  The term *outgoing interface list* refers to the list of interfaces in a forwarding state, listed for an entry in a router's multicast routing table.

The following is a more formal definition of a PIM Prune message:

Key
Topic

The PIM Prune message is sent by one router to a second router to cause the second router to remove the link on which the Prune is received from a particular (S,G) SPT.

Figure 8-6 shows the same internetwork and example as Figure 8-3, but with R3's Prune messages sent to R2.

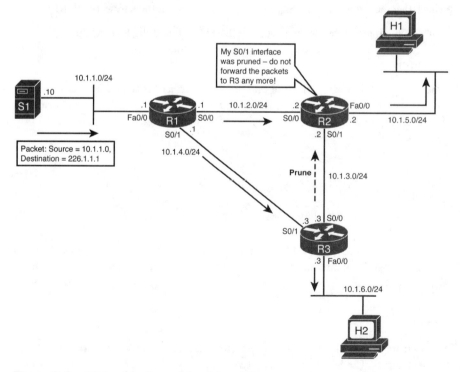

**Figure 8-6**  *R3 Sends a Prune Message to R2*

As a result of the Prune message from R3 to R2, R2 will prune its s0/1 interface from the SPT for (10.1.1.10, 226.1.1.1). Example 8-2 shows the multicast route table entry for R2 in Figure 8-6, with the line that shows the pruned state highlighted.

**Example 8-2**   *Multicast Route Table Entry for the Group 226.1.1.1 for R2*

```
(10.1.1.10/32, 226.1.1.1), 00:00:14/00:02:46, flags: CT
 Incoming interface: Serial0/0, RPF nbr 10.1.2.1
 Outgoing interface list:
   FastEthernet0/0, Forward/Dense, 00:00:14/00:00:00
   Serial0/1, Prune/Dense, 00:00:08/00:02:52
```

Most of the information shown in Example 8-2 is similar to the information shown in Example 8-1. Notice the Serial0/1 information shown under the outgoing interface list. It shows that this interface was pruned 8 seconds ago because R3 sent a Prune message to R2. This means that, at this time, R2 is not forwarding traffic for 226.1.1.1 on its s0/1 interface.

Because PIM-DM's inherent tendency is to flood traffic through an internetwork, the pruned s0/1 interface listed in Example 8-2 will be changed back to a forwarding state after 2 minutes and 52 seconds. In PIM-DM, when a router receives a Prune message on an interface, it starts a (default) 3-minute Prune timer, counting down to 0. When the Prune timer expires, the router changes the interface to a forwarding state again. If the downstream router does not want the traffic, it can again send a Prune message. This feature keeps a downstream router aware that the group traffic is available on a particular interface from the upstream neighbor.

**Note**   PIMv2 offers a better solution to maintaining the pruned state of an interface, using State Refresh messages. These messages are covered later in the chapter, in the section "Steady-State Operation and the State Refresh Message."

Note that a multicast router can have more than one interface in the outgoing interface list, but it can have only one interface in the incoming interface list. The only interface in which a router will receive and process multicasts from a particular source is the RPF interface. Routers still perform an RPF check, with the incoming interface information in the beginning of the **show ip mroute** output stating the RPF interface and neighbor.

### PIM-DM: Reacting to a Failed Link

When links fail, or any other changes affect the unicast IP routing table, PIM-DM needs to update the RPF interfaces based on the new unicast IP routing table. Because the RPF interface can change, (S,G) entries might also need to list different interfaces in the outgoing interface list. This section describes an example of how PIM-DM reacts.

Figure 8-7 shows an example in which the link between R1 and R3, originally illustrated in Figure 8-6, has failed. After the unicast routing protocol converges, R3 needs to update its RPF neighbor IP address from 10.1.4.1 (R1) to 10.1.3.2 (R2). Also in this case, H1 has issued an IGMP Leave message.

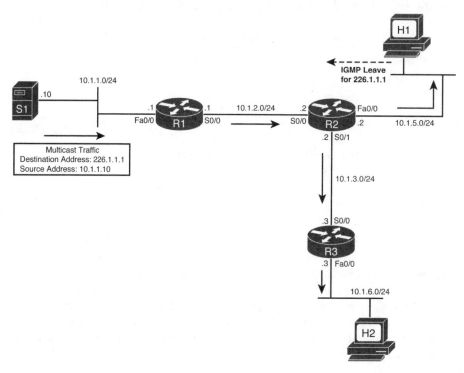

**Figure 8-7** *Direct Link Between R1 and R3 Is Down, and Host H1 Sends an IGMP Leave Message*

Example 8-3 shows the resulting multicast route table entry for R3 in Figure 8-7. Note that the RPF interface and neighbor IP address have changed to point to R2.

**Example 8-3** *Multicast Route Table Entry for the Group 226.1.1.1 for R3*

```
(10.1.1.10/32, 226.1.1.1), 00:02:16/00:01:36, flags: CT
  Incoming interface: Serial0/0, RPF nbr 10.1.3.2
  Outgoing interface list:
    FastEthernet0/0, Forward/Dense, 00:02:16/00:00:00
```

Example 8-3 shows how R3's view of the (10.1.1.10, 226.1.1.1) SPT has changed. However, R2 had pruned its s0/1 interface from that SPT, as shown in Figure 8-6. So, R2 needs to change its s0/1 interface back to a forwarding state for SPT (10.1.1.10, 226.1.1.1). Example 8-4 shows the resulting multicast route table entry for (10.1.1.10, 226.1.1.1) in R2.

**Example 8-4**   *Multicast Route Table Entry for the Group 226.1.1.1 for R2*

```
(10.1.1.10/32, 226.1.1.1), 00:03:14/00:02:38, flags: T
  Incoming interface: Serial0/0, RPF nbr 10.1.2.1
  Outgoing interface list:
  Serial0/1, Forward/Dense, 00:02:28/00:00:00
```

**Note**   R2 changed its s0/1 to a forwarding state because of a PIM Graft message sent by R3. The upcoming section "Graft Message" explains the details.

In Example 8-4, notice the outgoing interface list for R2. R2 has now removed interface fa0/0 from the outgoing interface list and stopped forwarding traffic on the interface because it received no response to the IGMP Group-Specific query for group 226.1.1.1. As a result, R2 has also removed the C flag (C meaning "connected") from its multicast routing table entry for (10.1.1.10, 226.1.1.1). Additionally, R2 forwards the traffic on its s0/1 interface toward R3 because R3 is still forwarding traffic on its fa0/0 interface and has not sent a Prune message to R2.

## Rules for Pruning

This section explains two key rules that a PIM-DM router must follow to decide when it can request a prune. Before you learn another example of how PIM-DM reacts to changes in an internetwork, a couple of new multicast terms must be defined. To simplify the wording, the following statements define *upstream router* and *downstream router* from the perspective of a router named R1.

■ R1's upstream router is the router from which R1 receives multicast packets for a particular SPT.

■ R1's downstream router is a router to which R1 forwards some multicast packets for a particular SPT.

For example, R1 is R2's upstream router for the packets that S1 is sending to 226.1.1.1 in Figure 8-7. R3 is R2's downstream router for those same packets, because R2 sends those packets to R3.

PIM-DM routers can choose to send a Prune message for many reasons, one of which was covered earlier with regard to Figure 8-6. The main reasons are summarized here:

■ When receiving packets on a non-RPF interface.

■ When a router realizes that both of the following are true:

  ■ No locally connected hosts in a particular group are listening for packets.

  ■ No downstream routers are listening for the group.

This section shows the logic behind the second reason for sending prunes. At this point in the explanation of Figure 8-6 and Figure 8-7, the only host that needs to receive packets sent to 226.1.1.1 is H2. What would the PIM-DM routers in this network do if H2 leaves group 226.1.1.1? Figure 8-8 shows just such an example, with H2 sending an IGMP Leave message for group 226.1.1.1. Figure 8-8 shows how PIM-DM uses this information to dynamically update the SPT.

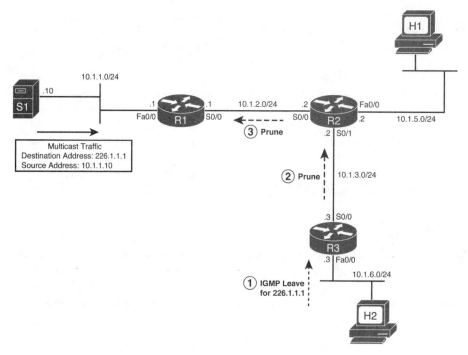

**Figure 8-8**   *R3 and R2 Sending Prune Messages*

Figure 8-8 shows three steps, with the logic in Steps 2 and 3 being similar but very im--portant:

**1.**   H2 leaves the multicast group by using an IGMP Leave message.

**2.**   R3 uses an IGMP Query to confirm that no other hosts on the LAN want to receive traffic for group 226.1.1.1. So, R3 sends a Prune, referencing the (10.1.1.10, 226.1.1.1) SPT, out its RPF interface R2.

**3.**   R2 does not have any locally connected hosts listening for group 226.1.1.1. Now, its only downstream router has sent a Prune for the SPT with source 10.1.1.10, group 226.1.1.1. Therefore, R2 has no reason to need packets sent to 226.1.1.1 anymore. So, R2 sends a Prune, referencing the (10.1.1.10, 226.1.1.1) SPT, out its RPF interface R1.

After the pruning is complete, both R3 and R2 will not be forwarding traffic sent to 226.1.1.1 from source 10.1.1.10. In the routers, the **show ip mroute** command shows that fact using the P (prune) flag, which means that the router has completely pruned itself from that particular (S,G) SPT.

Example 8-5 shows R3's command output with a null outgoing interface list.

**Example 8-5**   *Multicast Route Table Entry for the Group 226.1.1.1 for R3*

```
(10.1.1.10/32, 226.1.1.1), 00:03:16/00:01:36, flags: PT
  Incoming interface: Serial0/0, RPF nbr 10.1.3.2
    Outgoing interface list: Null
```

After all the steps in Figure 8-8 have been completed, R1 also does not need to send packets sent by 10.1.1.10 to 226.1.1.1 out any interfaces. After receiving a Prune message from R2, R1 has also updated its outgoing interface list, which shows that there is only one outgoing interface and that it is in the pruned state at this time. Example 8-6 shows the details.

**Example 8-6**   *Multicast Route Table Entry for the Group 226.1.1.1 for R1*

```
(10.1.1.10/32, 226.1.1.1), 00:08:35/00:02:42, flags: CT
  Incoming interface: FastEthernet0/0, RPF nbr 0.0.0.0
  Outgoing interface list:
    Serial0/0, Prune/Dense, 00:00:12/00:02:48
```

Of particular interest in the output, R1 has also set the C flag, but for R1 the C flag does not indicate that it has directly connected group members. In this case, the combination of a C flag and an RPF neighbor of 0.0.0.0 indicates that the connected device is the source for the group.

In reality, there is no separate Prune message and Join message; instead, PIM-DM and PIM-SM use a single message called a Join/Prune message. A Prune message is actually a Join/Prune message with a group address listed in the Prune field, and a Join message is a Join/Prune message with a group address listed in the Join field.

### Steady-State Operation and the State Refresh Message

As mentioned briefly earlier in the chapter, with PIM-DM, an interface stays pruned only for 3 minutes by default. Prune messages list a particular source and group [in other words, a particular (S,G) SPT]. Whenever a router receives a Prune message, it finds the matching (S,G) SPT entry and marks the interface on which the Prune message was received as "pruned." However, it also sets a Prune timer, default 3 minutes, so that after 3 minutes, the interface is placed into a forwarding state again.

So, what happens with PIM-DM and pruned links? Well, the necessary links are pruned, and 3 minutes later they are added back. More multicasts flow, and the links are pruned. Then they are added back. And so on. So, when Cisco created PIM V2 (published as experimental RFC 3973), it included a feature called *state refresh*. State Refresh messages can prevent this rather inefficient behavior in PIM-DM version 1 of pruning and automatically unpruning interfaces.

Figure 8-9 shows an example that begins with the same state as the network described at the end of the preceding section, where the link between R1 and R2 and the link between

R2 and R3 have been pruned. Almost 3 minutes have passed, and the links are about to be added to the SPT again because of the expiration of the Prune timers.

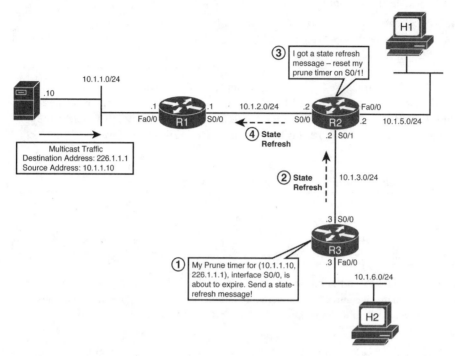

**Figure 8-9**  *How PIM-DM Version 2 Uses State Refresh Messages*

The PIM State Refresh message can be sent, just before a neighbor's Prune timer expires, to keep the interface in a pruned state. In Figure 8-9, the following steps do just that:

1. R3 monitors the time since it sent the last Prune to R2. Just before the Prune timer expires, R3 decides to send a State Refresh message to R2.

2. R3 sends the State Refresh message to R2, referencing SPT (10.1.1.10, 226.1.1.1).

3. R2 reacts by resetting its Prune timer for the interface on which it received the State Refresh message.

4. Because R2 had also pruned itself by sending a Prune message to R1, R2 also uses State Refresh messages to tell R1 to leave its s0/0 interface in a pruned state.

As long as R3 keeps sending a State Refresh message before the Prune timer on the upstream router (R2) expires, the SPT will remain stable, and there will not be the periodic times of flooding of more multicasts for that (S,G) tree. Note that the State Refresh timer has a default value of 60 seconds. Sending of a State Refresh message is not tied to the expiration of the Prune timer as the text implies.

## Graft Message

When new hosts join a group, routers might need to change the current SPT for a particular (S,G) entry. With PIM-DM, one option could be to wait on the pruned links to expire. For example, in Figure 8-9, R3 could simply quit sending State Refresh messages, and within 3 minutes at most, R3 would be receiving the multicast packets for some (S,G) SPT again. However, waiting on the (default) 3-minute Prune timer to expire is not very efficient. To allow routers to "unprune" a previously pruned interface from an SPT, PIM-DM includes the *Graft* message, which is defined as follows:

Key
Topic

A router sends a Graft message to an upstream neighbor—a neighbor to which it had formerly sent a Prune message—causing the upstream router to put the link back into a forwarding state [for a particular (S,G) SPT].

Figure 8-10 shows an example that uses the same ongoing example network. The process shown in Figure 8-10 begins in the same state as described at the end of the preceding section. Neither host H1 nor H2 has joined group 226.1.1.1, and R2 and R3 have been totally pruned from the (10.1.1.10, 226.1.1.1) SPT. Referring to Figure 8-10, R1's s0/0 interface has been pruned from the (S,G) SPT, so R2 and R3 are not receiving the multicasts sent by server S1 to 226.1.1.1. The example then begins with host H2 joining group 226.1.1.1 again.

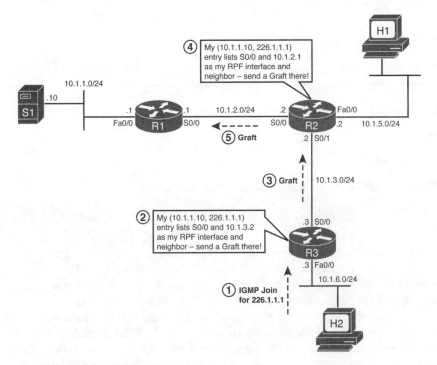

**Figure 8-10**  *R3 and R2 Send Graft Messages*

Without the Graft message, host H2 would have to wait for as much as 3 minutes before it would receive the group traffic. However, with the following steps, as listed in Figure 8-10, H2 will receive the packets in just a few seconds:

1. Host H2 sends an IGMP Join message.

2. R3 looks for the RPF interface for its (S,G) state information for the group 226.1.1.1 (see earlier Example 8-5), which shows the incoming interface as s0/0 and RPF neighbor as 10.1.3.2 for the group.

3. R3 sends the Graft message out s0/0 to R2.

4. R2 now knows it needs to be receiving messages from 10.1.1.10, sent to 226.1.1.1. However, R2's (S,G) entry also shows a P flag, meaning that R2 has pruned itself from the SPT. So, R2 finds its RPF interface and RPF neighbor IP address in its (S,G) entry, which references interface s0/0 and Router R1.

5. R2 sends a graft to R1.

At this point, R1 immediately puts its s0/0 back into the outgoing interface list, as does R2, and now H2 receives the multicast packets. Note that R1 also sends a Graft Ack message to R2 in response to the Graft message, and R2 sends a Graft Ack in response to R3's Graft message as well.

## LAN-Specific Issues with PIM-DM and PIM-SM

This section covers three small topics related to operations that only matter when PIM is used on LANs:

■ Prune Override

■ Assert messages

■ Designated routers

Both PIM-DM and PIM-SM use these features in the same way.

### Prune Override

In both PIM-DM and PIM-SM, the Prune process on multiaccess networks operates differently from how it operates on point-to-point links. The reason for this difference is that when one router sends a Prune message on a multiaccess network, other routers might not want the link pruned by the upstream router. Figure 8-11 shows an example of this problem, along with the solution through a PIM Join message that is called a *Prune Override*. In this figure, R1 is forwarding the group traffic for 239.9.9.9 on its fa0/0 interface, with R2 and R3 receiving the group traffic on their e0 interfaces. R2 does not have any connected group members, and its outgoing interface list would show null. The following list outlines the steps in logic shown in Figure 8-11, in which R3 needs to send a Prune Override:

1. R2 sends a Prune for group 239.9.9.9 because R2 has a null outgoing interface list for the group.

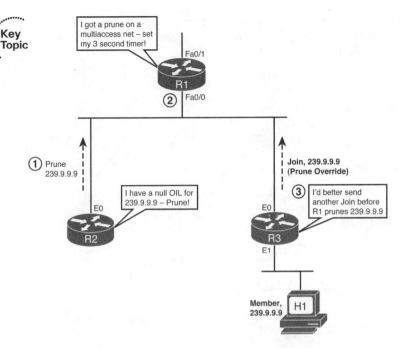

**Figure 8-11** *Prune Override*

> **2.** R1, realizing that it received the Prune on a multiaccess network, knows that other routers might still want to get the messages. So, instead of immediately pruning the interface, R1 sets a 3-second timer that must expire before R1 will prune the interface.
>
> **3.** R3 also receives the Prune message sent by R2, because Prune messages are multicast to the All-PIM-Routers group address 224.0.0.13. R3 still needs to get traffic for 239.9.9.9, so R3 sends a Join message on its e0 interface.
>
> **4.** (Not shown in Figure 8-11) R1 receives the Join message from R3 before removing its LAN interface from the outgoing interface list. As a result, R1 does not prune its Fa0/0 interface.

This process is called *Prune Override* because R3 overrides the Prune sent by R2. The Prune Override is actually a Join message, sent by R3 in this case. The message itself is no different from a normal Join. As long as R1 receives a Join message from R3 before its 3-second timer expires, R3 continues to receive traffic without interruption.

## Assert Message

The final PIM-DM message covered in this chapter is the PIM Assert message. The Assert message is used to prevent wasted effort when more than one router attaches to the same LAN. Rather than sending multiple copies of each multicast packet onto the LAN, the PIM Assert message allows the routers to negotiate. The winner gets the right to be responsible for forwarding multicasts onto the LAN.

Figure 8-12 shows an example of the need for the Assert message. R2 and R3 both attach to the same LAN, with H1 being an active member of the group 227.7.7.7. Both R2 and R3 are receiving the group traffic for 227.7.7.7 from the source 10.1.1.10.

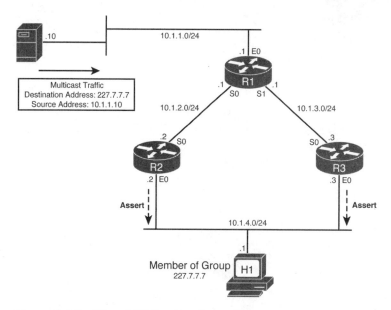

**Figure 8-12**   *R2 and R3 Sending Assert Messages*

The goal of the Assert message is to assign the responsibility of forwarding group traffic on the LAN to the router that is closest to the source. When R2 and R3 receive group traffic from the source on their s0 interfaces, they forward it on their e0 interfaces. Both of them have their s0 interfaces in the incoming interface list and e0 interfaces in the out-going interface list. Now, R2 and R3 receive a multicast packet for the group on their e0 interfaces, which will cause them to send an Assert message to resolve who should be the forwarder.

The Assert process picks a winner based on the routing protocol and metric used to find the route to reach the unicast address of the source. In this example, that means that R2 or R3 will win based on the routes they each use to reach 10.1.1.10. R2 and R3 send and receive Assert messages that include their respective administrative distances of the routing protocols used to learn the route that matches 10.1.1.10, as well as the metric for those routes. The routers on the LAN compare their own routing protocol administrative distance and metrics to those learned in the Assert messages. The winner of the Assert process is determined as follows:

**Key
Topic**

1. The router advertising the lowest administrative distance of the routing protocol used to learn the route wins.

2. If a tie occurs, the router with the lowest advertised routing protocol metric for that route wins.

3. If a tie occurs, the router with the highest IP address on that LAN wins.

### Designated Router

PIM Hello messages are also used to elect a designated router (DR) on a multiaccess network. A PIM-DM or PIM-SM router with the highest IP address becomes the DR for the link. This behavior should be easy to remember because it is very much like the operation of how an OSPF DR router is elected using the highest router-id or RID.

The PIM DR concept applies mainly when IGMPv1 is used. IGMPv1 does not have a mechanism to elect a querier. That is to say that IGMPv1 has no way to decide which of the many routers on a LAN should send IGMP Queries. When IGMPv1 is used, the PIM DR is used as the IGMP Querier. IGMPv2 can directly elect a querier (the router with the lowest IP address), so the PIM DR is not used as the IGMP Querier when IGMPv2 is used.

Note that on a LAN, one router might win the Assert process for a particular (S,G) SPT, while another might become the IGMP Querier (PIM DR for IGMPv1, IGMP Querier for IGMPv2). The winner of the Assert process is responsible for forwarding multicasts onto the LAN, whereas the IGMP Querier is responsible for managing the IGMP process by being responsible for sending IGMP Query messages on the LAN. Note also that the IGMPv2 Querier election chooses the lowest IP address, and the Assert process uses the highest IP address as a tiebreaker, making it slightly more likely that different routers are chosen for each function.

### Summary of PIM-DM Messages

This section concludes the coverage of PIM-DM. Table 8-2 lists the key PIM-DM messages covered in this chapter, along with a brief definition of their use.

**Table 8-2** *Summary of PIM-DM Messages*

| PIM Message | Definition |
| --- | --- |
| Hello | Used to form neighbor adjacencies with other PIM routers, and to maintain adjacencies by monitoring for received Hellos from each neighbor. Also used to elect a PIM DR on multiaccess networks. |
| Prune | Used to ask a neighboring router to remove the link over which the Prune flows from that neighboring router's outgoing interface list for a particular (S,G) SPT. |
| State Refresh | Used by a downstream router, sent to an upstream router on an RPF interface, to cause the upstream router to reset its Prune timer. This allows the downstream router to maintain the pruned state of a link, for a particular (S,G) SPT. |
| Assert | Used on multiaccess networks to determine which router wins the right to forward multicasts onto the LAN, for a particular (S,G) SPT. |

| PIM Message | Definition |
|---|---|
| Prune Override (Join) | On a LAN, a router can multicast a Prune message to its upstream routers. Other routers on the same LAN, wanting to prevent the upstream router from pruning the LAN, immediately send another Join message for the (S,G) SPT. (The Prune Override is not actually a Prune Override message— it is a Join. This is the only purpose of a Join message in PIM-DM, per RFC 3973.) |
| Graft/Graft-Ack | When a pruned link needs to be added back to an (S,G) SPT, a router sends a Graft message to its RPF neighbor. The RPF neighbor acknowledges with a Graft-Ack. |

The next two short sections introduce two other dense-mode protocols, DVMRP and MOSPF.

## Distance Vector Multicast Routing Protocol

RFC 1075 describes Version 1 of DVMRP. DVMRP has many versions. The operation of DVMRP is similar to PIM-DM. The major differences between PIM-DM and DVMRP are defined as follows:

- Cisco IOS does not support a full implementation of DVMRP; however, it does support connectivity to a DVMRP network.

- DVMRP uses its own distance vector routing protocol that is similar to RIPv2. It sends route updates every 60 seconds and considers 32 hops as infinity. Use of its own routing protocol adds more overhead to DVMRP operation compared to PIM-DM.

- DVMRP uses Probe messages to find neighbors using the All DVMRP Routers group address 224.0.0.4.

- DVMRP uses a truncated broadcast tree, which is similar to an SPT with some links pruned.

## Multicast Open Shortest Path First

MOSPF is defined in RFC 1584, "Multicast Extensions to OSPF," which is an extension to the OSPFv2 unicast routing protocol. The MOSPF RFC, 1584, has been changed to historic status, so MOSPF implementations are unlikely today. For perspective, the basic operation of MOSPF is described here:

- MOSPF uses the group membership link-state advertisement (LSA), Type 6, which it floods throughout the originating router's area. As with unicast OSPF, all MOSPF routers in an area must have identical link-state databases so that every MOSPF router in an area can calculate the same SPT.

- The SPT is calculated "on demand," when the first multicast packet for the group arrives.

- Through the SPF calculation, all the routers know where the attached group members are, based on the group membership LSAs.

- After the SPF calculation is completed, entries are made into each router's multicast forwarding table.

- Just like unicast OSPF, the SPT is loop free, and every router knows the upstream interface and downstream interfaces. As a result, an RPF check is not required.

- Obviously, MOSPF can only work with the OSPF unicast routing protocol. MOSPF is suitable for small networks. As more hosts begin to source multicast traffic, routers must perform a higher number of Dijkstra algorithm computations, which demands an increasing level of router CPU resources.

**Note**   Cisco IOS does not support MOSPF.

# Sparse-Mode Routing Protocols

There are two sparse-mode routing protocols:

- Protocol Independent Multicast Sparse Mode (PIM-SM)

- Core-Based Tree (CBT)

This section covers the operation of PIM-SM.

## Operation of Protocol Independent Multicast Sparse Mode

PIM-SM works with a completely opposite strategy from that of PIM-DM, although the mechanics of the protocol are not exactly opposite. PIM-SM assumes that no hosts want to receive multicast packets until they specifically ask to receive them. As a result, until a host in a subnet asks to receive multicasts for a particular group, multicasts are never delivered to that subnet. With PIM-SM, downstream routers must request to receive multicasts using PIM Join messages. Also, after they are receiving those messages, the downstream router must continually send Join messages to the upstream router; otherwise, the upstream router stops forwarding, putting the link in a pruned state. This process is opposite to that used by PIM-DM, in which the default is to flood multicasts, with downstream routers needing to continually send Prunes or State Refresh messages to keep a link in a pruned state.

PIM-SM makes the most sense with a small percentage of subnets that need to receive packets sent to any multicast group.

## Similarities Between PIM-DM and PIM-SM

PIM-SM has many similarities to PIM-DM. Like PIM-DM, PIM-SM uses the unicast routing table to perform RPF checks—regardless of what unicast routing protocol populated the table. (Like PIM-DM, the "protocol independent" part of the PIM acronym comes from the fact that PIM-SM is not dependent on any particular unicast IP routing protocol.) In addition, PIM-SM also uses the following mechanisms that are used by PIM-DM:

- PIM Neighbor discovery through exchange of Hello messages.

- Recalculation of the RPF interface when the unicast routing table changes.

- Election of a DR on a multiaccess network. The DR performs all IGMP processes when IGMPv1 is in use on the network.

- The use of Prune Overrides on multiaccess networks.

- Use of Assert messages to elect a designated forwarder on a multiaccess network. The winner of the Assert process is responsible for forwarding unicasts onto that subnet.

**Note**   The preceding list was derived, with permission, from *Routing TCP/IP*, Volume II, by Jeff Doyle and Jennifer DeHaven Carroll.

These mechanisms are described in the section "Operation of Protocol Independent Multicast Dense Mode," earlier in this chapter, and thus are not repeated in this section.

## Sources Sending Packets to the Rendezvous Point

PIM-SM uses a two-step process to initially deliver multicast packets from a particular source to the hosts wanting to receive packets. Later, the process is improved beyond these initial steps. The steps for the initial forwarding of multicasts with PIM-SM are as follows:

**Key Topic**

1. Sources send the packets to a router called the rendezvous point (RP).

2. The RP sends the multicast packets to all routers/hosts that have registered to receive packets for that group. This process uses a shared tree.

**Note**   In addition to these two initial steps, routers with local hosts that have sent an IGMP Join message for a group can go a step further, joining the source-specific tree for a particular (S,G) SPT.

This section describes the first of these two steps, in which the source sends packets to the RP. To make that happen, the router connected to the same subnet as the source host must register with the RP. The RP accepts the registration only if the RP knows of any routers or hosts that need to receive a copy of those multicasts.

Figure 8-13 shows an example of the registration process in which the RP knows that no hosts currently want the IP multicasts sent to group 228.8.8.8—no matter which source is sending them. All routers are configured identically with the global command **ip multicast-routing** and the interface command **ip pim sparse-mode** on all their physical interfaces. Also, all routers have statically configured R3 as the RP by using the global command **ip pim rp-address 10.1.10.3**. This includes R3; a router knows that it is an RP when it sees its interface address listed as an RP address. Usually, a loopback interface address is used as an RP address. The loopback network 10.1.10.3/32 of R3 is advertised in the unicast routing protocol so that all the routers know how to reach the RP. The configuration for R3 is shown in Example 8-7. The other routers have the same multicast configuration, without the loopback interface.

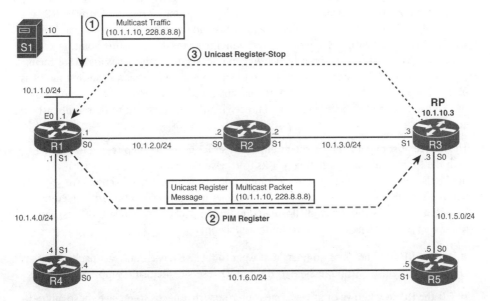

**Figure 8-13** *Source Registration Process When RP Has Not Received a Request for the Group from Any PIM-SM Router*

**Example 8-7** *Multicast Sparse-Mode and RP Configuration on R3*

```
ip multicast-routing
ip pim rp-address 10.1.10.3
!
interface Loopback2
 ip address 10.1.10.3 255.255.255.255
 ip pim sparse-mode
!
interface Serial0
```

```
  ip pim sparse-mode
 !
interface Serial1
  ip pim sparse-mode
```

The following three steps, referenced in Figure 8-13, describe the sequence of events for the Source Registration process when the RP has not received a request for the group from any PIM-SM router because no host has yet joined the group.

1. Host S1 begins sending multicasts to 228.8.8.8, and R1 receives those multicasts because it connects to the same LAN.

2. R1 reacts by sending unicast PIM Register messages to the RP. The Register messages are unicasts sent to the RP IP address, 10.1.10.3 in this case.

3. R3 sends unicast Register-Stop messages back to R1 because R3 knows that it does not have any need to forward packets sent to 228.8.8.8.

In this example, the router near the source (R1) is attempting to register with the RP, but the RP tells R1 not to bother anymore, because no one wants those multicast messages. R1 has not forwarded any of the native multicast messages at this point, in keeping with the PIM-SM strategy of not forwarding multicasts until a host has asked for them. However, the PIM Register message shown in Figure 8-13 encapsulates the first multicast packet. As will be seen in Figure 8-14, the encapsulated packet would be forwarded by the RP had any senders been interested in receiving the packets sent to that multicast group.

The source host might keep sending multicasts, so R1 needs to keep trying to register with the RP in case some host finally asks to receive the packets. So, when R1 receives the Register-Stop messages, it starts a 1-minute Register-Suppression timer. Five seconds before the timer expires, R1 sends another Register message with a flag set, called the Null-Register bit, without any encapsulated multicast packets. As a result of this additional Register message, one of two things will happen:

- If the RP still knows of no hosts that want to receive these multicast packets, it sends another Register-Stop message to R1, and R1 resets its Register-Suppression timer.

- If the RP now knows of at least one router/host that needs to receive these multicast packets, it does not reply to this briefer Register message. As a result, R1, when its timer expires, again sends its multicast packets to R3 (RP) encapsulated in PIM Register messages.

## Joining the Shared Tree

So far, this section on PIM-SM has explained the beginnings of the registration process, by which a router near the source of multicast packets registers with the RP. Before completing that discussion, however, the concept of the shared tree for a multicast group, also called the *root-path tree (RPT)*, must be explained. As mentioned earlier, PIM-SM initially causes multicasts to be delivered in a two-step process: First, packets are sent from the source to the RP, and then the RP forwards the packets to the subnets that have hosts that need a copy of those multicasts. PIM-SM uses this shared tree in the second part of the process.

The RPT is a tree, with the RP at the root that defines over which links multicasts should be forwarded to reach all required routers. One such tree exists for each multicast group that is currently active in the internetwork. So, after the multicast packets sent by each source are forwarded to the RP, the RP uses the RPT for that multicast group to determine where to forward these packets.

PIM-SM routers collectively create the RPT by sending PIM Join messages toward the RP. PIM-SM routers choose to send a Join under two conditions:

**Key Topic**

- When a PIM-SM router receives a PIM Join message on any interface other than the interface used to route packets toward the RP

- When a PIM-SM router receives an IGMP Membership Report message from a host on a directly connected subnet

Figure 8-14 shows an example of the PIM-SM join process, using the same network as Figure 8-12 but with H1 joining group 228.8.8.8. The routers react to the IGMP Join by sending a Join toward the RP, to become part of the shared SPT (*,228.8.8.8).

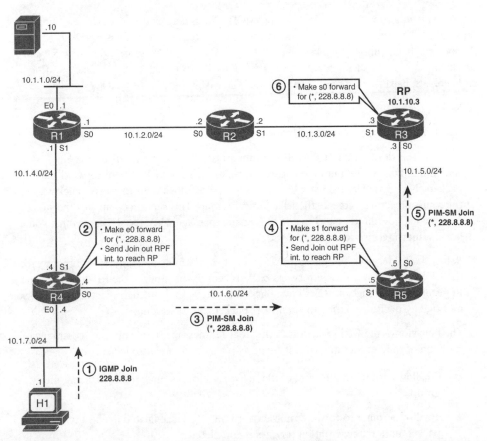

**Figure 8-14** *Creating a Shared Tree for (*,228.8.8.8)*

Figure 8-14 shows how H1 causes a shared tree (*,228.8.8.8) to be created, as described in the following steps:

**1.**   H1 sends an IGMP Join message for the group 228.8.8.8.

**2.**   R4 realizes that it needs to ask the RP for help, specifically asking the RP to forward packets destined to 228.8.8.8. So, R4 sends a PIM Join for the shared tree for group 228.8.8.8 toward the RP. R4 also puts its e0 interface into a forwarding state for the RPT for group 228.8.8.8.

**3.**   R5 receives the Join on its s1 interface, so R5 puts its s1 interface in a forwarding state for the shared tree [represented by (*,228.8.8.8)]. R5 also knows it needs to forward the Join toward the RP.

**4.**   R5 sends the Join toward the RP.

**5.**   R3, the RP, puts its s0 interface in a forwarding state for the (*,288.8.8.8) shared tree.

By the end of this process, the RP knows that at least one host wants packets sent to 228.8.8.8. The RPT for group 228.8.8.8 is formed with R3's s0 interface, R5's s1 interface, and R4's e0 interface.

**Note**   The notation (*,G) represents a single RPT. The * represents a wildcard, meaning "any source," because the PIM-SM routers use this shared tree regardless of the source of the packets. For example, a packet sent from any source IP address, arriving at the RP and destined to group 228.8.8.8, would cause the RP to use its (*,228.8.8.8) multicast routing table entries, because these entries are part of the RPT for group 228.8.8.8.

### Completion of the Source Registration Process

So far in this description of PIM-SM, a source (10.1.1.10) sent packets to 228.8.8.8, as shown in Figure 8-13—but no one cared at the time, so the RP did not forward the packets. Next, you learned what happens when a host does want to receive packets, with the routers reacting to create the RPT for that group. This section completes the story by showing how an RP reacts to a PIM Register message when the RP knows that some hosts want to receive those multicasts.

When the RP receives a Register message for an active multicast group—in other words, the RP believes that it should forward packets sent to the group—the RP does not send a Register-Stop message, as was shown back in Figure 8-13. Instead, it reacts to the Register message by deencapsulating the multicast packet and forwarding it.

The behavior of the RP in reaction to the Register message points out the second major function of the Register message. Its main two functions are as follows:

**Key Topic**

■   To allow a router to inform the RP that it has a local source for a particular multicast group

■   To allow a router to forward multicasts to the RP, encapsulated inside a unicast packet, until the registration process is completed

To show the complete process, Figure 8-15 shows an example. In the example, host H1 has already joined group 228.8.8.8, as shown in Figure 8-14. The following steps match those identified in Figure 8-15. Note that Step 3 represents the forwarding of the multicasts that were encapsulated inside Register messages at Step 2.

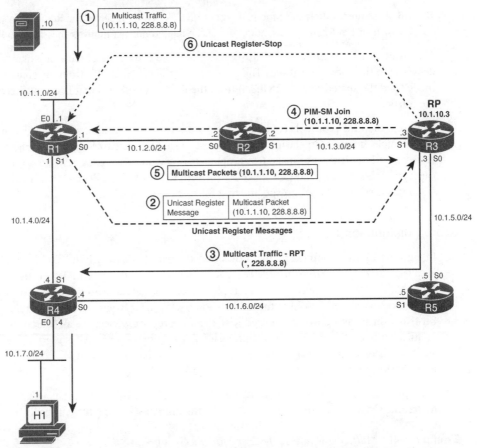

**Figure 8-15** *Source Registration When the RP Needs to Receive Packets Sent to That Group*

1. Host S1 sends multicasts to 228.8.8.8.

2. Router R1 encapsulates the multicasts, sending them inside Register messages to the RP, R3.

3. R3, knowing that it needs to forward the multicast packets, deencapsulates the packets and sends them toward H1. (This action allows R1 and R3 to distribute the multicasts while the registration process completes.) R5 forwards the group traffic to R4 and R4 forwards it on its LAN.

4. R3 joins the SPT for source 10.1.1.10, group 228.8.8.8, by sending a PIM-SM Join message for group (10.1.1.10, 228.8.8.8) toward the source 10.1.1.10.

5. When R1 and R2 receive the PIM-SM Join message from R3 requesting the group traffic from the source, they start forwarding group traffic toward the RP. At this point, R3 (the RP) now receives this traffic on the SPT from the source. However, R1 is also still sending the Register messages with encapsulated multicast packets to R3.

6. R3 sends unicast Register-Stop messages to R1. When R1 receives the Register-Stop messages from R3, it stops sending the encapsulated unicast Register messages to R3.

The process might seem like a lot of trouble, but at the end of the process, multicasts are delivered to the correct locations. The process uses the efficient SPT from the source to the RP and the shared tree (*,228.8.8.8) from the RP to the subnets that need to receive the traffic.

Note that the PIM protocols could have just let a router near the source, such as R1 in this example, continue to encapsulate multicasts inside the unicast Register messages. However, it is inefficient to make R1 encapsulate every multicast packet, make R3 deencapsulate every packet, and then make R3 forward the traffic. So, PIM-SM has the RP, R3 in this case, join the group-specific tree for that (S,G) combination.

### Shared Distribution Tree

In Figure 8-15, the group traffic that flows over the path from the RP (R3) to R5 to R4 is called a *shared distribution tree*. It is also called a *root-path tree (RPT)* because it is rooted at the RP. If the network has multiple sources for the same group, traffic from all the sources would first travel to the RP (as shown with the traffic from host S1 in Figure 8-14) and then travel down this shared RPT to all the receivers. Because all sources in the multicast group use a common shared tree, a wildcard notation of (*,G) is used to identify an RPT, where * represents all sources and G represents the multicast group address. The RPT for the group 228.8.8.8 shown in Figure 8-14 would be written as (*,228.8.8.8).

Example 8-8 shows the multicast route table entry for R4 in Figure 8-15. On a Cisco router, the **show ip mroute** command displays the multicast route table entries.

**Example 8-8**   *Multicast Route Table Entry for the Group 228.8.8.8 for R4*

```
(*, 228.8.8.8), 00:00:08/00:02:58, RP 10.1.10.3, flags: SC
 Incoming interface: Serial0, RPF nbr 10.1.6.5
 Outgoing interface list:
   Ethernet0, Forward/Sparse, 00:00:08/00:02:52
```

The interpretation of the information shown in Example 8-8 is as follows:

- The first line shows that the (*,G) entry for the group 228.8.8.8 was created 8 seconds ago, and if R4 does not forward group packets using this entry in 2 minutes and 58 seconds, it will expire. Every time R4 forwards a packet, the timer is reset to 3 minutes. This entry was created because R4 received an IGMP Join message from H1.

- The RP for this group is 10.1.10.3 (R3). The S flag indicates that this group is using the sparse-mode (PIM-SM) routing protocol. The C flag indicates that R4 has a directly connected group member for 228.8.8.8.

- The incoming interface for this (*,228.8.8.8) entry is s0 and the RPF neighbor is 10.1.6.5. Note that for the SPT, the RPF interface is chosen based on the route to reach the RP, not the route used to reach a particular source.

- Group traffic is forwarded out on the Ethernet0 interface. In this example, Ethernet0 was added to the outgoing interface list because an IGMP Report message was received on this interface from H1. This interface has been in the forwarding state for 8 seconds. The Prune timer indicates that if an IGMP Join is not received again on this interface within the next 2 minutes and 52 seconds, it will be removed from the outgoing interface list.

## Steady-State Operation by Continuing to Send Joins

To maintain the forwarding state of interfaces, PIM-SM routers must send PIM Join messages periodically. If a router fails to send Joins periodically, PIM-SM moves interfaces back to a pruned state.

PIM-SM routers choose to maintain the forwarding state on links based on two general criteria:

**Key Topic**

- A downstream router continues to send PIM Joins for the group.
- A locally connected host still responds to IGMP Query messages with IGMP Report messages for the group.

Figure 8-16 shows an example in which R5 maintains the forwarding state of its link to R3 based on both of these reasons. H2 has also joined the shared tree for 228.8.8.8. H1 had joined earlier, as shown in Figures 8-14 and 8-15.

Example 8-9 shows the multicast route table entry for R5 in Figure 8-16, with these two interfaces in a forwarding state.

**Example 8-9**  *Multicast Route Table Entry for the Group 228.8.8.8 for R5*

```
(*,228.8.8.8), 00:00:05/00:02:59, RP 10.1.10.3, flags: SC
  Incoming interface: Serial0, RPF nbr 10.1.5.3
  Outgoing interface list:
    Serial1, Forward/Sparse, 00:01:15/00:02:20
    Ethernet0, Forward/Sparse, 00:00:05/00:02:55
```

In Example 8-9, two interfaces are listed in the outgoing interface list. The s1 interface is listed because R5 has received a PIM-SM Join message from R4. In PIM-SM, the downstream routers need to keep sending PIM-SM Join messages every 60 seconds to the upstream router. When R5 receives another PIM-SM Join from R4 on its s1 interface, it resets the Prune timer to the default value of 3 minutes. If R5 does not receive a PIM-SM Join from R4 before R5's Prune timer on that interface expires, R5 places its s1 interface in a pruned state and stops forwarding the traffic on the interface.

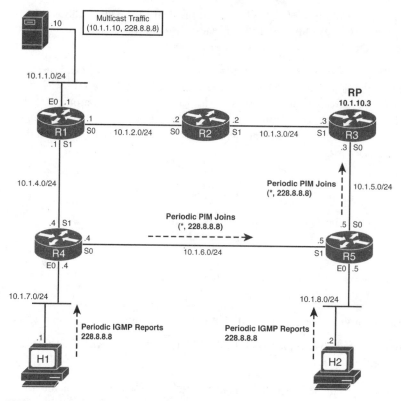

**Figure 8-16**  *Host H2 Sends an IGMP Join Message*

By contrast, R5's e0 interface is listed as forwarding in R5's outgoing interface list because R5 has received an IGMP Join message from H2. Recall from Chapter 7 that a multicast router sends an IGMP general query every 60 seconds on its LAN interfaces. It must receive at least one IGMP Report/Join message as a response for a group; otherwise, it stops forwarding the group traffic on the interface. When R5 receives another IGMP Report message on its e0 interface, it resets the Prune timer for the entry to the default value of 3 minutes.

Note also that on R5, the receipt of the PIM Join from R4, or the IGMP Report on e0, triggers R5's need to send the PIM Join toward the RP.

### Examining the RP's Multicast Routing Table

In the current state of the ongoing example, as last shown in Figure 8-16, the RP (R3) has joined the SPT for source 10.1.1.10, group 228.8.8.8. The RP also is the root of the shared tree for group 228.8.8.8. Example 8-10 shows both entries in R3's multicast route table.

**Example 8-10**    *Multicast Route Table Entry for the Group 228.8.8.8 for R3*

```
(*,228.8.8.8), 00:02:27/00:02:59, RP 10.1.10.3, flags: S
  Incoming interface: Null, RPF nbr 0.0.0.0
  Outgoing interface list:
    Serial0, Forward/Sparse, 00:02:27/00:02:33
(10.1.1.10/32, 228.8.8.8), 00:02:27/00:02:33, flags: T
  Incoming interface: Serial1, RPF nbr 10.1.3.2,
  Outgoing interface list:
  Outgoing interface list: Null
```

The first entry shows the shared tree, as indicated by the S flag. Notice the incoming interface is Null because R3, as RP, is the root of the tree. Also, the RPF neighbor is listed as 0.0.0.0 for the same reason. In other words, it shows that the shared-tree traffic for the group 228.8.8.8 has originated at this router and it does not depend on any other router for the shared-tree traffic.

The second entry shows the SPT entry on R3 for multicast group 228.8.8.8, source 10.1.1.10. The T flag indicates that this entry is for an SPT, and the source is listed at the beginning of that same line (10.1.1.10). The incoming interface is s1 and the RPF neighbor for the source address 10.1.1.10 is 10.1.3.2.

As you can see, an RP uses the SPT to pull the traffic from the source to itself and uses the shared tree to push the traffic down to the PIM-SM routers that have requested it.

### Shortest-Path Tree Switchover

PIM-SM routers could continue forwarding packets through the PIM-SM two-step process, whereby sources send packets to the RP, and the RP sends them to all other routers using the RPT. However, one of the most fascinating aspects of PIM-SM operations is that each PIM-SM router can build the SPT between itself and the source of a multicast group and take advantage of the most efficient path available from the source to the router. In Figure 8-16, R4 is receiving the group traffic from the source through the path R1-R2-R3-R5-R4. However, it is obvious that it would be more efficient for R4 to receive the group traffic directly from R1 on R4's s1 interface.

In the section "Completion of the Source Registration Process," earlier in this chapter, you saw that the PIM-SM design allows an RP to build an SPT between itself and the router that is directly connected with the source (also called the source DR) to pull the group traffic. Similarly, the PIM-SM design also allows any other PIM-SM router to build an SPT between the router and the source DR. This feature allows a PIM-SM router to avoid using the inefficient path, such as the one used by R4 in Figure 8-16. Also, after the router starts receiving the group traffic over the SPT, it can send a Prune message to the upstream router of the shared tree to stop forwarding the traffic for the group.

The question is, when should a router switch over from RPT to SPT? RFC 2362 for PIM-SM specifies that "The recommended policy is to initiate the switch to the SP-tree after receiving a significant number of data packets during a specified time interval from a particular source." What number should be considered as a significant number? The RFC does not specify that. Cisco routers, by default, switch over from the RPT to the source-specific SPT after they receive the first packet from the shared tree.

> **Note**  You can change this behavior by configuring the global command **ip pim spt-threshold** *rate* on any router for any group. After the traffic rate exceeds the stated rate (in kbps), the router joins the SPT. The command impacts the behavior only on the router(s) on which it is configured.

If a router is going to switch to SPT, why join the RPT first? In PIM-SM, a router does not know the IP address of a source until it receives at least one packet for the group from the source. After it receives one packet on the RPT, it can learn the IP address of a source, and initialize a switchover to the SPT for that (source,group) combination.

With the default Cisco PIM-SM operation, when multicast packets begin arriving on R4's s0 interface through the shared tree, R4 attempts to switch to the SPT for source 10.1.1.10. Figure 8-17 shows the general steps.

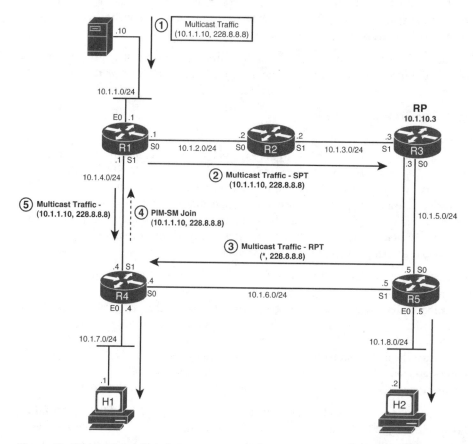

**Figure 8-17**  *R4 Initializing Switchover from RPT to SPT by Sending a PIM-SM Join to R1*

The first three steps in Figure 8-17 are as follows:

1.  The source (S1,10.1.1.10) sends a multicast packet to the first-hop Router R1.

2.  R1 forwards the packet to the RP (R3).

3.  The RP forwards the packet to R4 through the shared tree.

At Step 3, R4 learned that the source address of the multicast group 228.8.8.8 is 10.1.1.10. So, besides forwarding the packet at Step 3, R4 can use that information to join the SPT for group 228.8.8.8, from source 10.1.1.10, using the following steps from Figure 8-17:

4.  R4 consults its unicast routing table, finds the next-hop address and outgoing interface it would use to reach source 10.1.1.10, and sends the PIM-SM Join message out that interface (s1) to R1. This PIM-SM Join message is specifically for the SPT of (10.1.1.10,228.8.8.8). The Join travels hop by hop until it reaches the source DR.

5.  As a result of the Join, R1 places its s1 interface in a forwarding state for SPT (10.1.1.10,228.8.8.8). So, R1 starts forwarding multicasts from 10.1.1.10 to 228.8.8.8 out its s1 interface as well.

R4 now has a multicast routing table entry for the SPT, as shown in Example 8-11.

**Example 8-11**  *Multicast Route Table Entry for the Group 228.8.8.8 for R4*

```
(*,228.8.8.8), 00:02:36/00:02:57, RP 10.1.10.3, flags: SCJ
 Incoming interface: Serial0, RPF nbr 10.1.6.5
 Outgoing interface list:
   Ethernet0, Forward/Sparse, 00:02:36/00:02:13
(10.1.1.10/32, 228.8.8.8), 00:00:23/00:02:33, flags: CJT
 Incoming interface: Serial1, RPF nbr 10.1.4.1,
 Outgoing interface list:
 Ethernet0, Forward/Sparse, 00:00:23/00:02:37
```

In Example 8-11, you see two entries for the group. The J flag (for join) on both the entries indicates that the traffic was switched from RPT to SPT, and now the (S,G) entry will be used for forwarding multicast packets for the group. Notice that the incoming interfaces for the (*,G) entry and (S,G) entry are different.

## Pruning from the Shared Tree

When a PIM-SM router has joined a more efficient SPT, it might not need to receive multicast packets over the RPT anymore. For example, when R4 in Figure 8-17 notices that it is receiving the group traffic over RPT and SPT, it can and should ask the RP to stop sending the traffic.

To stop the RP from forwarding traffic to a downstream router on the shared tree, the downstream router sends a PIM-SM Prune message to the RP. The Prune message references the (S,G) SPT, which identifies the IP address of the source. Essentially, this prune means the following to the RP:

> Stop forwarding packets from the listed source IP address, to the listed group address, down the RPT.

For example, in Figure 8-18, which continues the example shown in Figure 8-17, R4 sends a Prune out its s0 interface toward R5. The Prune lists (S,G) entry (10.1.1.10,228.8.8.8), and it sets a bit called the RP-tree bit (RPT-bit). By setting the RPT-bit in the Prune message, R4 informs R5 (the upstream router) that it has switched to SPT and the Prune message is for the redundant traffic for the group 228.8.8.8, from 10.1.1.10, that R4 is receiving on the shared tree.

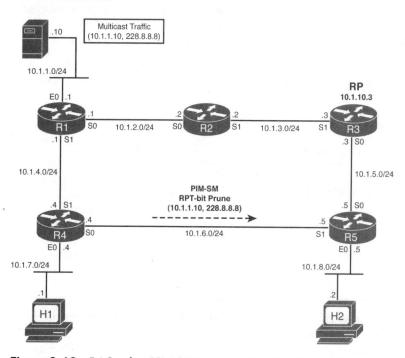

**Figure 8-18**    *R4 Sends a PIM-SM Prune with RP Bit Set to R5*

To stop the packets from being sent over the RPT to R4, R5 must prune its interface s1 in the RPT (*, 228.8.8.8). R5 can go on to join the SPT for (10.1.1.10,228.8.8.8) as well.

This concludes the coverage of the operations of PIM-SM. The next section covers some details about how routers can learn the IP address of the PIM RP.

## Dynamically Finding RPs and Using Redundant RPs

In a PIM-SM network, every router must somehow learn the IP address of an RP. A PIM-SM router can use one of the following three methods to learn the IP address of an RP:

**Key Topic**

■ With Unicast RP, the RP address is statically configured on all the PIM-SM routers (including the RP) with the Cisco IOS global command **ip pim rp-address** *address*. This is the method used for the five-router topology shown in Figure 8-18.

- The Cisco-proprietary Auto-RP protocol can be used to designate the RP and advertise its IP address so that all PIM-SM routers can learn its IP address automatically.

- A standard BootStrap Router (BSR) protocol can be used to designate the RP and advertise its IP address so that all the PIM-SM routers can learn its IP address automatically.

Additionally, because PIM-SM relies so heavily on the RP, it makes sense to have redundant RPs. Cisco IOS offers two methods of providing redundant RPs, which are also covered in this section:

- Anycast RP using the Multicast Source Discovery Protocol (MSDP)

- BootStrap Router (BSR)

## Dynamically Finding the RP Using Auto-RP

Static RP configuration is suboptimal under the following conditions:

- When an enterprise has a large number of PIM-SM routers and the enterprise wants to use many different RPs for different groups, it becomes time consuming and cumbersome to statically configure the IP addresses of many RPs for different groups on all the routers.

- When an RP fails or needs to be changed because a new RP is being installed, it becomes extremely difficult in a statically configured PIM-SM domain to switch over to an alternative RP without considerable downtime.

Auto-RP provides an alternative in which routers dynamically learn the unicast IP address used by each RP. Auto-RP uses a two-step process, which is shown in Figure 8-19 and Figure 8-20. In the first step, the RP sends RP-Announce messages to the reserved multicast address 224.0.1.39, stating that the router is an RP. The RP-Announce message also allows the router to advertise the multicast groups for which it is the RP, thereby allowing some load balancing of the RP workload among different routers. The RP continues to send these RP-Announce messages every minute.

For example, Figure 8-19 shows R3 as an RP that uses Auto-RP. R3 supports all multicast groups in this case. The RP-Announce message is shown as Step 1, to link it with Step 2 in Figure 8-20.

The second step for Auto-RP requires that one router be configured as a mapping agent. The mapping agent is usually the same router that was selected as an RP, but can be a different PIM-SM router. The mapping agent learns all the RPs and the multicast groups they each support. Then, the mapping agent multicasts another message, called RP-Discovery, that identifies the RP for each range of multicast group addresses. This message goes to reserved multicast address 224.0.1.40. It is this RP-Discovery message that actually informs the general router population as to which routers they should use as RPs.

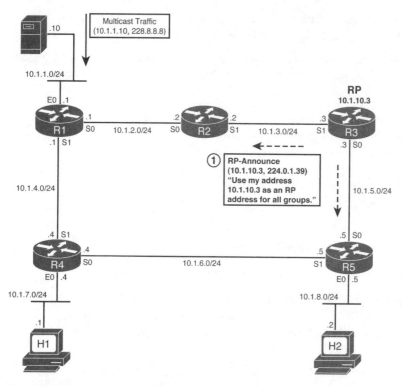

**Figure 8-19**  *R3 Sends RP-Announce Messages*

For example, in Figure 8-20, R2 is configured as a mapping agent. To receive all RP-Announce messages, R2 locally joins the well-known Cisco-RP-Announce multicast group 224.0.1.39. In other words, the mapping agent has become a group member for 224.0.1.39 and is listening for the group traffic. When R2 receives the RP-Announce packets shown in Figure 8-19, it examines the packet, creates group-to-RP mappings, and maintains this information in its cache, as shown in Figure 8-20.

At first glance, the need for the mapping agent might not be obvious. Why not just let the RPs announce themselves to all the other routers? Well, if Auto-RP supported only one RP, or even only one RP to support each multicast group, the mapping agent would be a waste of effort. However, to support RP redundancy—in other words, to support multiple RPs that can act as RP for the same multicast group—the Auto-RP mapping agent decides which RP should be used to support each group at the moment. To do so, the mapping agent selects the router with the highest IP address as an RP for the group. (Note that you can also configure multiple mapping agents, for redundancy.)

As soon as Cisco routers are configured with PIM-SM and Auto-RP, they automatically join the well-known Cisco-RP-Discovery multicast group 224.0.1.40. That means that they are listening to the group address 224.0.1.40, and when they receive a 224.0.1.40 packet, they learn group-to-RP mapping information and maintain it in their cache. When a PIM-SM router receives an IGMP Join message for a group or PIM-SM Join message from a downstream router, it checks the group-to-RP mapping information in its cache. Then it can proceed as described throughout the PIM-SM explanations in this chapter, using that RP as the RP for that multicast group.

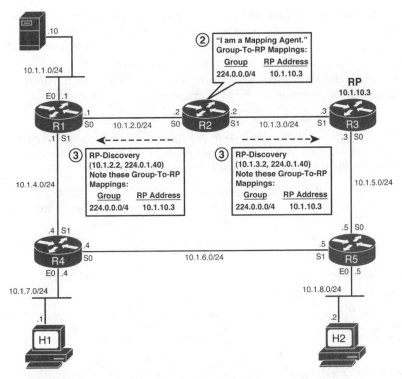

**Figure 8-20**  *R2 Creates Group-to-RP Mappings and Sends Them in RP-Discovery Messages*

The following list summarizes the steps used by Auto-RP:

1. Each RP is configured to use Auto-RP and to announce itself and its supported multicast groups through RP-Announce messages (224.0.1.39).

2. The Auto-RP mapping agent, which might or might not also be an RP router, gathers information about all RPs by listening to the RP-Announce messages.

3. The mapping agent builds a mapping table that lists the currently best RP for each range of multicast groups, with the mapping agent picking the RP with the highest IP address if multiple RPs support the same multicast groups.

4. The mapping agent sends RP-Discover messages to 224.0.1.40 advertising the mappings.

5. All routers listen for packets sent to 224.0.1.40 to learn the mapping information and find the correct RP to use for each multicast group.

Auto-RP creates a small chicken-and-egg problem in that the purpose of Auto-RP is to find the RPs, but to get the RP-Announce and RP-Discovery messages, PIM-SM routers would need to send a Join toward the RP, which they do not know yet. To overcome this problem, one option is to use a variation of PIM called *sparse-dense mode.* In PIM sparse-dense mode, a router uses PIM-DM rules when it does not know the location of the RP and PIM-SM rules when it does know the location of the RP. So, under normal conditions with Auto-RP, the routers would use dense mode long enough to learn the group-to-RP mappings from the mapping agent, and then switch over to sparse mode. However, if any other multicast traffic occurred before the routers learned of the RPs using Auto-RP, the multicast packets would be forwarded using dense-mode rules. This can result in extra network traffic. PIM sparse-dense mode is configured per interface using the **ip pim sparse-dense-mode** interface subcommand.

To avoid unnecessary dense-mode flooding, configure each router as an *Auto-RP Listener* and use sparse-mode on the interface. When you enable this feature, only Auto-RP traffic (groups 224.0.1.39 and 224.0.1.40) is flooded out all sparse-mode interfaces. You configure this feature with the global command **ip pim autorp listener**.

Example 8-12 shows the configuration for Routers R1, R2, and R3 from Figure 8-20. R1 is a normal multicast router using Auto-RP Listener, R2 is an Auto-RP mapping agent, and R3 is an RP.

**Example 8-12**  *Configuring Auto-RP*

```
!R1 Configuration (Normal MC Router)
ip multicast-routing
!
interface Serial0
 ip pim sparse-mode ! Repeat this command on each MC interface
!
ip pim autorp listener


!R2 Configuration (Auto-RP Mapping Agent)
ip multicast-routing
!
!The following command designates this router an Auto-RP Mapping Agent
!Optionally a source interface could be added
ip pim send-rp-discovery scope 10
!
interface Serial0
 ip pim sparse-mode ! Repeat this command on each MC interface


!R3 Configuration (Auto-RP Rendezvous Point)
ip multicast-routing
!
interface Loopback0
 ip address 10.1.10.3 255.255.255.255
 ip pim sparse-mode !Must be configured on source interface
!
interface Serial0
 ip pim sparse-mode ! Repeat this command on each MC interface
```

```
!
!The following command designates this router an Auto-RP RP
ip pim send-rp-announce loopback0 scope 10
```

### Dynamically Finding the RP Using BSR

Cisco provided the proprietary Auto-RP feature to solve a couple of specific problems. PIM Version 2, which came later, provided a different solution to the same problem, namely the BootStrap Router (BSR) feature. From a very general perspective, BSR works similarly to Auto-RP. Each RP sends a message to another router, which collects the group-to-RP mapping information. That router then distributes the mapping information to the PIM routers. However, any examination of BSR beyond that level of detail shows that these two tools do differ in many ways.

It is helpful to first understand the concept of the bootstrap router, or BSR router, before thinking about the RPs. One router acts as BSR, which is similar to the mapping agent in Auto-RP. The BSR receives mapping information from the RPs, and then it advertises the information to other routers. However, there are some specific differences between the actions of the BSR, and their implications, and the actions of the Auto-RP mapping agent:

■ The BSR router does not pick the best RP for each multicast group; instead, the BSR router sends all group-to-RP mapping information to the other PIM routers inside bootstrap messages.

■ PIM routers each independently pick the currently best RP for each multicast group by running the same hash algorithm on the information in the bootstrap message.

■ The BSR floods the mapping information in a bootstrap message sent to the all-PIM-routers multicast address (224.0.0.13).

■ The flooding of the bootstrap message does not require the routers to have a known RP or to support dense mode. (This will be described in more detail in the next few pages.)

Figure 8-21 shows an example, described next, of how the BSR floods the bootstrap message. PIMv2 creates specific rules for BSR bootstrap messages, stating that PIM routers should flood these messages. PIM-SM routers flood bootstrap messages out all non-RPF interfaces, which in effect guarantees that at least one copy of the message makes it to every router. Note that this logic is not dependent on a working dense- or sparse-mode implementation. As a result, BSR overcomes the chicken-and-egg problem of Auto-RP.

For example, in Figure 8-21, imagine that R4's s1 interface is its RPF interface to reach R2, and R5's RPF interface to reach R2 is its s0 interface. So, they each forward the bootstrap messages at Step 3 of Figure 8-21. However, because R4 receives the bootstrap message from R5 on one of R4's non-RPF interfaces, R4 discards the packet, thereby preventing loops. R5 also does not forward the bootstrap message any farther for the same basic reasons.

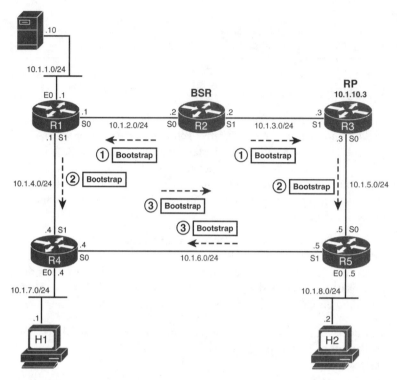

**Figure 8-21** *BSR Flooding Bootstrap Messages*

The other important part of BSR operation is for each candidate RP (c-RP) to inform the BSR router that it is an RP and to identify the multicast groups it supports. This part of the process with BSR is simple if you keep in mind the following point:

> All PIM routers already know the unicast IP address of the BSR based on the earlier receipt of bootstrap messages.

So, the c-RPs simply send unicast messages, called c-RP advertisements, to the BSR. These c-RP advertisements include the IP address used by the c-RP, and the groups it supports.

The BSR feature supports redundant RPs and redundant BSRs. As mentioned earlier, the bootstrap message sent by the BSR router includes all candidate RPs, with each router using the same hash algorithm to pick the currently best RP for each multicast group. The mapping information can list multiple RPs that support the same group addresses.

Additionally, multiple BSR routers can be configured. In that case, each candidate BSR (c-BSR) router sends bootstrap messages that include the priority of the BSR router and its IP address. The highest-priority BSR wins, or if a tie occurs, the highest BSR IP address wins. Then, the winning BSR, called the preferred BSR, continues to send bootstrap messages, while the other BSRs monitor those messages. If the preferred BSR's bootstrap messages cease, the redundant BSRs can attempt to take over.

Configuring BSR is similar to configuring Auto-RP. At a minimum, you need to tell a router that it is a candidate RP or candidate BSR, and which interface to use for the source of its messages. You can optionally tie an access list with the command to limit the groups for which the router will be the RP, or specify a preference to control the election among multiple BSRs.

Example 8-13 shows the configuration of a BSR and an RP.

**Example 8-13**  *Configuring a BSR and an RP*

```
!On the BSR (R2 in Figure 8-21)
ip multicast-routing
!
interface Loopback0
 ip pim sparse-mode !Must be configured on source interface
!
interface Serial0
 ip pim sparse-mode ! Repeat this command on each MC interface
!
!The following command configures the router as a candidate BSR with source
!interface of Lo0 and a priority of 0 (default)
ip pim bsr-candidate Loopback0 0


!On the RP (R3 in Figure 8-21)
ip multicast-routing
!
interface Loopback2
ip address 10.1.10.3 255.25.255.255
 ip pim sparse-mode !Must be configured on source interface
!
interface Serial0
 ip pim sparse-mode ! Repeat this command on each MC interface
!
!The following command configures the router as a candidate RP with source
!interface Lo2
ip pim rp-candidate Loopback2
```

## Anycast RP with MSDP

The final tool covered here for finding a router's RP is called Anycast RP with Multicast Source Discovery Protocol (MSDP). Anycast RP is actually an implementation feature more than a new feature with new configuration commands. As will be explained in the upcoming pages, Anycast RP can actually use static RP configuration, Auto-RP, and BSR.

The key differences between using Anycast RP and using either Auto-RP or BSR relate to how the redundant RPs are used. The differences are as follows:

■ **Without Anycast RP:** RP redundancy allows only one router to be the active RP for each multicast group. Load sharing of the collective work of the RPs is accomplished by using one RP for some groups and another RP for other groups.

■ **With Anycast RP:** RP redundancy and load sharing can be achieved with multiple RPs concurrently acting as the RP for the same group.

The way Anycast RP works is to have each RP use the same IP address. The RPs must advertise this address, typically as a /32 prefix, with its IGP. Then, the other methods of learning an RP—static configuration, Auto-RP, and BSR—all view the multiple RPs as a single RP. At the end of the process, any packets sent to "the" RP are routed per IGP routes to the closest RP. Figure 8-22 shows an example of the process.

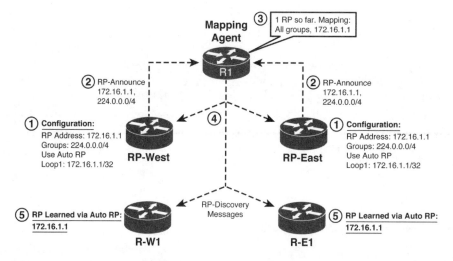

**Figure 8-22**  *Learning the RP Address with Anycast RP*

Figure 8-22 shows a design using two RPs (RP-East and RP-West) along with Auto-RP. The steps shown in the figure are as follows:

1. Both RPs are configured with 172.16.1.1/32, and configured to use that IP address for RP functions. In this case, both are configured to be the RP for all multicast groups.

2. Both RPs act as normal for Auto-RP by sending RP-Announce messages to 224.0.1.39.

3. The Auto-RP mapping agent builds its mapping table with a single entry, because it cannot tell the difference between the two RPs, because both use IP address 172.16.1.1.

4. The Auto-RP mapping agent acts as normal, sending an RP-Discovery message to 224.0.1.40. It includes (in this case) a single mapping entry: All groups map to 172.16.1.1.

**5.** All the routers, including Routers R-W1 and R-E1, learn through Auto-RP that the single RP for all groups is 172.16.1.1.

The last step described in the list brings the discussion to the main benefit of Anycast RP. At this point, the core Auto-RP function of advertising the IP address of the RP is complete. Of course, the IP address exists on two routers in Figure 8-22, but it could be more than that in other designs. Because of the IGP routes, when routers in the western part of the network (like R-W1) send packets to the RP at 172.16.1.1, they are actually sending the packets to RP-West. Likewise, when routers in the eastern part of the network (like R-E1) send packets to the RP (172.16.1.1), they are actually sending the packets to RP-East. This behavior is only achieved by using the Anycast RP implementation option beyond simply using Auto-RP.

The two biggest benefits of this design with Anycast RP are as follows:

**Key Topic**

- Multiple RPs share the load for a single multicast group.

- Recovery after a failed RP happens quickly. If an RP fails, multicast traffic is only interrupted for the amount of time it takes the IGP to converge to point to the other RP sharing the same IP address.

### Interdomain Multicast Routing with MSDP

The design of Anycast RP can create a problem because each individual RP builds its own shared tree, but any multicast source sends packets to only one of the RPs. For example, Figure 8-23 shows the same network as Figure 8-22, but now with a multicast source in the western part of the network. The routers in the west side of the figure receive the packets as distributed by RP-West through its shared tree. However, the routers in RP-East's shared tree do not get the packets because RP-East never gets the packet sent by the server in the west side.

In Figure 8-23, East and West are two *multicast domains*. In this case, they are part of the same company, but multicast domains might also belong to different companies, or different ISPs. The solution to this problem is for the RPs to tell each other about all known sources by using MSDP. When a PIM router registers a multicast source with its RP, the RP uses MSDP to send messages to peer RPs. These *Source Active (SA)* messages list the IP addresses of each source for each multicast group, and are sent as unicasts over a TCP connection maintained between peer RPs. MSDP peers must be statically configured, and RPs must have routes to each of their peers and to the sources. Typically, Border Gateway Protocol (BGP) or Multicast BGP (MBGP) is used for this routing.

In Figure 8-23, RP-West could use MSDP to tell RP-East about the multicast source for 226.1.1.1 at unicast IP address 172.16.5.5. Then, RP-East would flood that information to any other MSDP peers. The receiver in its domain can then join the SPT of source 172.16.5.5, group 226.1.1.1, just as it would have done if it had received the multicast traffic directly from 172.16.5.5. If an RP has no receivers for a multicast group, it caches the information for possible later use. MSDP RPs continue to send SA messages every 60 seconds, listing all of its groups and sources. An RP can also request an updated list by using an SA request message. The peer responds with an SA response message.

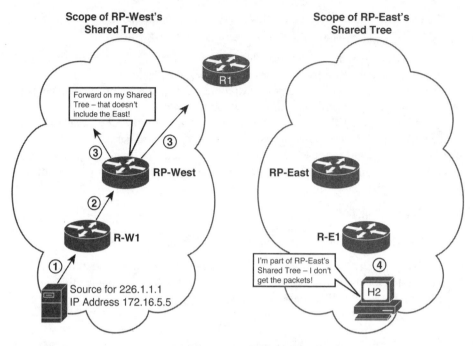

**Figure 8-23**   *Anycast RP Problem (Later Solved with MSDP)*

To use MSDP, first configure either Auto-RP or BSR. If running MSDP between routing domains, make sure that BGP is configured and there are routes to the MSDP peer. Then you can specify the MSDP peers on each router. Example 8-14 builds on Example 8-13. In Example 8-14, BSR is already configured. Routers RP-East and RP-West are then configured as MSDP peers with each other, using the **ip msdp peer** *address* command. BGP has also been configured between the two routers. The configuration is verified with the **show ip msdp peer** command on RP-West and the **show ip pim rp** command on RP-East. Note that RP-East shows RP-West as the RP for multicast group 226.1.1.1 from Figure 8-23.

**Example 8-14**   *Configuring Interdomain MC Routing with MSDP*

```
!RP-East Configuration

interface Loopback2
 ip address 10.1.10.3 255.255.255.255
 ip pim sparse-mode
!
ip multicast-routing
ip pim rp-candidate Loopback2
```

```
ip msdp peer 172.16.1.1
```

```
!RP-West Configuration
interface Loopback0
 ip address 172.16.1.1 255.255.255.255
 ip pim sparse-mode
!
ip multicast-routing
ip pim rp-candidate Loopback0
ip msdp peer 10.1.10.3 connect-source Loopback0
!
```

```
RP-West# show ip msdp peer
MSDP Peer 10.1.10.3 (?), AS 65001
  Connection status:
    State: Listen, Resets: 0, Connection source: Loopback0 (172.16.1.1)
    Uptime(Downtime): 00:30:18, Messages sent/received: 0/0
    Output messages discarded: 0
    Connection and counters cleared 00:30:18 ago
  SA Filtering:
    Input (S,G) filter: none, route-map: none
    Input RP filter: none, route-map: none
    Output (S,G) filter: none, route-map: none
    Output RP filter: none, route-map: none
  SA-Requests:
    Input filter: none
  Peer ttl threshold: 0
  SAs learned from this peer: 0
  Input queue size: 0, Output queue size: 0
!
```

```
RP-East# show ip pim rp
Group: 226.1.1.1, RP: 172.16.1.1, v2, uptime 00:23:56, expires 00:03:09
```

## Summary: Finding the RP

This section covers the concepts behind four separate methods for finding the RP. Three are specific configuration features, namely static configuration, Auto-RP, and BSR. The fourth, Anycast RP, actually uses any of the first three methods, but with the design that includes having the RPs use the same unicast IP address to achieve better redundancy features. Table 8-3 summarizes the methods of finding the RP with PIM-SM.

**Table 8-3**   *Comparison of Methods of Finding the RP*

| Method | RP Details | Mapping Info | Redundant RP Support? | Load Sharing of One Group? |
|---|---|---|---|---|
| Static | Simple reference to unicast IP address. | — | No | No |
| Auto-RP | Sends RP-Announce to 224.0.1.39; relies on sparse-dense mode. | Mapping agent sends through RP-Discovery to 224.0.1.40 | Yes | No |
| BSR | Sends c-RP advertisements as unicasts to BSR IP address; does not need sparse-dense mode. | Sends bootstrap messages flooded over non-RPF path | Yes | No |
| Anycast RP | Each RP uses identical IP addresses. | Can use Auto-RP or BSR normal processes | Yes | Yes |

## Bidirectional PIM

PIM-SM works efficiently with a relatively small number of multicast senders. However, in cases with a large number of senders and receivers, PIM-SM becomes less efficient. Bidirectional PIM addresses this relative inefficiency by slightly changing the rules used by PIM-SM.

To appreciate bidirectional PIM, a brief review of PIM-SM's normal operations is useful. While many variations can occur, the following general steps can be used by PIM-SM:

1. The RP builds a shared tree, with itself as the root, for forwarding multicast packets.

2. When a source first sends multicasts, the router nearest the source forwards the multicasts to the RP, encapsulated inside a PIM Register message.

3. The RP joins the source-specific tree for that source by sending a PIM Join toward that source.

4. Later, the routers attached to the same LANs as the receivers can send a PIM Join toward the source to join the SPT for that source.

With bidirectional PIM, the last three steps in this list are not performed. Bidirectional PIM instead follows these steps:

1. As with normal PIM-SM, the RP builds a shared tree, with itself as the root, for forwarding multicast packets.

2. When a source sends multicasts, the router receiving those multicasts does not use a PIM Register message. Instead, it forwards the packets in the opposite direction of the shared tree, back up the tree toward the RP. This process continues for all multicast packets from the source.

3. The RP forwards the multicasts through the shared tree.

4. All packets are forwarded per Steps 2 and 3. The RP does not join the source tree for the source, and the leaf routers do not join the SPT, either.

The name "bidirectional" comes from Step 2, in which the router near the source forwards packets back up the tree toward the RP. The other direction in the tree is used at Step 3, with the RP forwarding multicasts using the shared tree.

## Comparison of PIM-DM and PIM-SM

One of the most confusing parts of the PIM-DM and PIM-SM designs is that it appears that if sources keep sending, and receivers keep listening, there is no difference between the end results of the end-user multicast packet flow using these two options. After PIM-SM completes its more complicated processes, the routers near the receivers have all joined the SPT to the source, and the most efficient forwarding paths are used for each (S,G) tree.

Although its underlying operation is a bit more complicated, PIM-SM tends to be the more popular option today. PIM-SM's inherent strategy of not forwarding multicasts until hosts request them makes it more efficient during times of low usage. When the numbers of senders and receivers increase, PIM-SM quickly moves to use the SPT—the same SPT that would have been derived using PIM-DM. As such, PIM-SM has become a more popular option for most enterprise implementations today. It has also become a popular option for interdomain multicast as well.

Table 8-4 summarizes the important features of PIM-DM and PIM-SM.

**Key Topic**

**Table 8-4**   *Comparison of PIM-DM and PIM-SM*

| Feature | PIM-DM | PIM-SM |
|---|---|---|
| Destination address for Version 1 Query messages, and IP protocol number | 224.0.0.2 and 2 | 224.0.0.2 and 2 |
| Destination address for Version 2 Hello messages, and IP protocol number | 224.0.0.13 and 103 | 224.0.0.13 and 103 |
| Default interval for Query and Hello messages | 30 seconds | 30 seconds |
| Default Holdtime for Versions 1 and 2 | 90 seconds | 90 seconds |
| Rule for electing a designated router on a multiaccess network | Router with the highest IP address on the subnet | Router with the highest IP address on the subnet |

| Feature | PIM-DM | PIM-SM |
|---|---|---|
| Main design principle | A router automatically receives the traffic. If it does not want the traffic, it has to say no (send a Prune message) to its sender. | Unless a router specifically makes a request to an RP, it does not receive multicast traffic. |
| SPT or RPT? | Uses only SPT | First uses RPT and then switches to SPT |
| Uses Join/Prune messages? | Yes | Yes |
| Uses Graft and Graft-Ack messages? | Yes | No |
| Uses Prune Override mechanism? | Yes | Yes |
| Uses Assert message? | Yes | Yes |
| Uses RP? | No | Yes |
| Uses source registration process? | No | Yes |

## Source-Specific Multicast

The multicast scenarios we've discussed so far use Internet Standard Multicast (ISM). With ISM, receivers join an MC group without worrying about the source of the multicast. In very large networks, such as television video or the Internet, this can lead to problems such as the following:

- **Overlapping multicast IP addresses:** With a limited number of multicast addresses and a large amount of multicasts, multiple streams might use the same address. Receivers will then get the stream they wanted plus any others using that address. Hopefully, the application will drop the unwanted multicast, but it has used up network resources unnecessarily.

- **Denial of service attacks:** If an attacker acts as a source sending traffic to a known multicast address, that traffic is then forwarded through the network to all receivers in the group. Enough traffic could interrupt the actual stream and overburden network routers and switches.

- **Deployment complexity:** The deployment of RPs, Auto-RP, BSR, and MSDP can get complex in a very large network with many sources and receivers.

Source Specific Multicast (SSM) is a solution to those limitations. SSM receivers know the unicast IP address of their source, and specify it when they join a group. With SSM, receivers subscribe to an (S,G) channel, giving both the source address and the multicast group address. This helps relieve the problems listed previously:

- Because each stream, or channel, is identified by the combination of a unicast source and multicast group address, overlapping group addresses are okay. Hosts only receive traffic from their specified sources.

- Denial of service attacks are more difficult because an attacker has to know both the source and group addresses, and the path to their source has to pass RPF checks through the network.

- RPs are not needed to keep track of which sources are active, because source addresses are already known. In addition, SSM can be deployed in a network already set up for PIM-SM. Only edge routers nearest the hosts need to be configured for SSM.

SSM uses IGMP Version 3, which was briefly described in Chapter 7. To configure basic SSM, you enable it globally with the **ip pim ssm {default | range** *access-list*} command. The multicast address range of 232.0.0.0 through 232.255.255.255 has been designated by IANA as the SSM range. The keyword **default** permits the router to forward all multicasts in that range. You can limit the multicast groups by defining them in an access list and using the **range** keyword.

You must also enable IGMPv3 under each interface with the **ip igmp version 3** command. Example 8-15 shows a router configured for SSM. Notice that PIM—either sparse mode or sparse-dense mode—must also be enabled under each interface.

**Example 8-15**  *Configuring SSM and IGMPv3*

```
ip multicast-routing
!
interface FastEthernet0/0
 ip pim sparse-mode
 ip igmp version 3
!
ip pim ssm default
```

# Implementing IPv6 Multicast PIM

It is necessary to explicitly enable multicast routing for any IPv6 environment through the global configuration command **ipv6 multicast-routing**. The results of this command can be observed on all IPv6-enabled interfaces on a given device, which are then automatically enabled for all IPv6-enabled interfaces. This default configuration of each IPv6 interface assumes the IPv6 PIM, and it does not appear in the interface configuration. When PIMv6 is enabled on an interface, that interface always operates in sparse mode. PIM-SM uses unicast routing to provide reverse-path information for multicast tree building, but it is not dependent on any particular unicast routing protocol.

It is possible to disable PIM on a given interface through the **no ipv6 pim** command under the interface configuration context.

We will run OSPFv3 in our lab to create a functional IPv6 multicast environment. We will then observe the possible behaviors associated with IPv6 and multicast packet delivery in the topology illustrated in Figure 8-24.

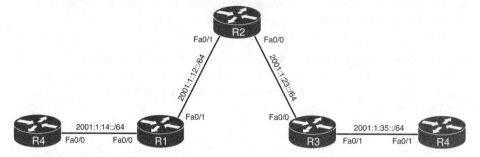

**Figure 8-24** *IPv6 Multicast Topology*

To enable IPv6 multicast routing on all the devices outlined in Figure 8-24, use the commands found in Example 8-16.

**Example 8-16** *Basic IPv6 Multicast Configuration*

```
R4# conf t
Enter configuration commands, one per line.  End with CNTL/Z.
R4(config)# ipv6 multicast-routing
!
R1# conf t
Enter configuration commands, one per line.  End with CNTL/Z.
R1(config)# ipv6 multicast-routing
!
R2# conf t
Enter configuration commands, one per line.  End with CNTL/Z.
R2(config)# ipv6 multicast-routing
!
R3# conf t
Enter configuration commands, one per line.  End with CNTL/Z.
R3(config)# ipv6 multicast-routing
!
R5# conf t
Enter configuration commands, one per line.  End with CNTL/Z.
R5(config)# ipv6 multicast-routing
```

This is the first stage where the multicast behavior of IPv6 shows its differences from IPv4 multicast routing. Notice immediately the formation of tunnels on each of these devices through the console messages. Example 8-17 illustrates this situation and shows how to verify the situation by looking specifically at the tunnels that are formed dynamically.

**Example 8-17**  *IPv6 Multicast Tunnel Verification*

```
R1(config)#
*Mar  9 17:22:57.754: %LINEPROTO-5-UPDOWN: Line protocol on Interface Tunnel0,
  changed state to up
R1(config)#
!!!!!!!!!!!!!!!!!!!!!!!!!!!!!!!!!!!!!!!!!!!!!!!!!!!!!!!!!!!!!!!!!!!!!!!!!!!!!!!!!!!
!!We can look at the statistics for these tunnels by:
!!!!!!!!!!!!!!!!!!!!!!!!!!!!!!!!!!!!!!!!!!!!!!!!!!!!!!!!!!!!!!!!!!!!!!!!!!!!!!!!!!!
R1# show int tunnel 0
Tunnel0 is up, line protocol is up
  Hardware is Tunnel
  MTU 1514 bytes, BW 9 Kbit/sec, DLY 500000 usec,
      reliability 255/255, txload 1/255, rxload 1/255
  Encapsulation TUNNEL, loopback not set
  Keepalive not set
  Tunnel source 2001:1:1:1::1 (Loopback0), destination UNKNOWN
  Tunnel protocol/transport PIM/IPv6
  Tunnel TTL 255
  Tunnel is transmit only
  Tunnel transmit bandwidth 8000 (kbps)
  Tunnel receive bandwidth 8000 (kbps)
  Last input never, output never, output hang never
  Last clearing of "show interface" counters never
  Input queue: 0/75/0/0 (size/max/drops/flushes); Total output drops: 0
  Queueing strategy: fifo
  Output queue: 0/0 (size/max)
  5 minute input rate 0 bits/sec, 0 packets/sec
  5 minute output rate 0 bits/sec, 0 packets/sec
     0 packets input, 0 bytes, 0 no buffer
     Received 0 broadcasts, 0 runts, 0 giants, 0 throttles
     0 input errors, 0 CRC, 0 frame, 0 overrun, 0 ignored, 0 abort
     0 packets output, 0 bytes, 0 underruns
     0 output errors, 0 collisions, 0 interface resets
     0 unknown protocol drops
     0 output buffer failures, 0 output buffers swapped out
R1#
```

Note that the tunnel is up, and that it is using the Tunnel Mode of PIM and IPv6 protocol
for transit. Additionally, to observe these neighbor relationships, we can use the **show
ipv6 pim neighbors** command, as demonstrated in Example 8-18.

**Example 8-18**  *PIM Neighbor Verification*

```
R4# show ipv6 pim neighbor
Neighbor Address              Interface           Uptime    Expires DR pri Bidir

FE80::1                       FastEthernet0/1     00:06:46  00:01:27 1      B
!!!!!!!!!!!!!!!!!!!!!!!!!!!!!!!!!!!!!!!!!!!!!!!!!!!!!!!!!!!!!!!!!!!!!!!!!!!!!!!!!!!
R1# show ipv6 pim neighbor
Neighbor Address              Interface           Uptime    Expires DR pri Bidir

FE80::2                       FastEthernet0/0     00:06:53  00:01:20 1 (DR) B
FE80::4                       FastEthernet0/1     00:07:23  00:01:19 1 (DR) B
!!!!!!!!!!!!!!!!!!!!!!!!!!!!!!!!!!!!!!!!!!!!!!!!!!!!!!!!!!!!!!!!!!!!!!!!!!!!!!!!!!!
R2# show ipv6 pim neighbor
Neighbor Address              Interface           Uptime    Expires DR pri Bidir

FE80::1                       FastEthernet0/0     00:07:24  00:01:16 1      B
FE80::3                       FastEthernet0/1     00:06:53  00:01:20 1 (DR) B
!!!!!!!!!!!!!!!!!!!!!!!!!!!!!!!!!!!!!!!!!!!!!!!!!!!!!!!!!!!!!!!!!!!!!!!!!!!!!!!!!!!
R3# show ipv6 pim neighbor
Neighbor Address              Interface           Uptime    Expires DR pri Bidir

FE80::5                       FastEthernet0/0     00:07:05  00:01:36 1 (DR) B
FE80::2                       FastEthernet0/1     00:07:32  00:01:39 1      B
!!!!!!!!!!!!!!!!!!!!!!!!!!!!!!!!!!!!!!!!!!!!!!!!!!!!!!!!!!!!!!!!!!!!!!!!!!!!!!!!!!!
R5# show ipv6 pim neighbor
Neighbor Address              Interface           Uptime    Expires DR pri Bidir

FE80::3                       FastEthernet0/0     00:08:06  00:01:33 1      B
```

Observe that the neighbor relationships form using the "link-local" addresses and that we still elect DRs. These values can be manipulated in similar fashion to those in IPv4.

## Designated Priority Manipulation

By directly manipulating the **dr-priority** value, you can manually designate what router on a given link will assume the role of the designated router. In topology shown in Figure 8-24, you will change the value of the **dr-priority** on R5 to ensure that it becomes the designated router, using the highest possible value to accomplish this, as shown in Example 8-19.

**Example 8-19**  *Designated Priority Manipulation*

```
R3# conf t
Enter configuration commands, one per line.  End with CNTL/Z.
R5(config)# int f0/0
R5(config-if)# ipv6 pim dr-priority ?
  <0-4294967295>  Hello DR priority, preference given to larger value

R5(config-if)# ipv6 pim dr-priority 4294967295
R5(config-if)# exit
!!!!!!!!!!!!!!!!!!!!!!!!!!!!!!!!!!!!!!!!!!!!!!!!!!!!!!!!!!!!!!!!!!!!!!!!!!!!!!!!!!!
!!Upon completion of this task we can observe the fact that R3 is now the DR for
!!the segment in question via the show ipv6 pim neighbor command:
!!!!!!!!!!!!!!!!!!!!!!!!!!!!!!!!!!!!!!!!!!!!!!!!!!!!!!!!!!!!!!!!!!!!!!!!!!!!!!!!!!!
!!!!!
R3# show ipv6 pim neighbor
Neighbor Address          Interface          Uptime     Expires DR pri Bidir

FE80::5                   FastEthernet0/0    00:20:53   00:01:36 1       B
FE80::2                   FastEthernet0/1    00:21:19   00:01:16 1       B
!!!!!!!!!!!!!!!!!!!!!!!!!!!!!!!!!!!!!!!!!!!!!!!!!!!!!!!!!!!!!!!!!!!!!!!!!!!!!!!!!!!
!!In this instance we do not see a value of (DR) which would indicate that this
!!device is serving as the DR. We can see this on R5.
!!!!!!!!!!!!!!!!!!!!!!!!!!!!!!!!!!!!!!!!!!!!!!!!!!!!!!!!!!!!!!!!!!!!!!!!!!!!!!!!!!!
R5# show ipv6 pim neighbor
Neighbor Address          Interface          Uptime     Expires DR pri Bidir

FE80::3                   FastEthernet0/0    00:23:25   00:01:20 4294967295 (DR) B
!!!!!!!!!!!!!!!!!!!!!!!!!!!!!!!!!!!!!!!!!!!!!!!!!!!!!!!!!!!!!!!!!!!!!!!!!!!!!!!!!!!
!!As expected we see that R3 is the DR for the segment connected to Fa0/0.
!!!!!!!!!!!!!!!!!!!!!!!!!!!!!!!!!!!!!!!!!!!!!!!!!!!!!!!!!!!!!!!!!!!!!!!!!!!!!!!!!!!
```

## PIM6 Hello Interval

As covered in the discussion of PIM for IPv4, the PIM process begins when the router establishes a PIM neighbor adjacency by sending PIM hello messages. Hello messages are sent periodically at the interval of 30 seconds. When all neighbors have replied, the PIM software chooses the router with the highest priority on each LAN segment as the designated router (DR). The DR priority is based on a DR priority value as we saw previously, but that information is contained in the PIM hello message. Additionally, if the DR priority value is not supplied by all routers, or if the priorities match, the highest IP address is used to elect the DR.

The hello message also contains a holdtime value, which is typically 3.5 times the hello interval. If this holdtime expires without a subsequent hello message from its neighbor, the device detects a PIM failure on that link.

For added security, you can configure an MD5 hash value that the PIM software uses to authenticate PIM hello messages with PIM neighbors. Example 8-20 observes this behavior by manipulating the hello-interval period and exploring the affects this has in our environment.

**Example 8-20**  *PIMv6 Hello Interval*

```
R3# conf t
Enter configuration commands, one per line.  End with CNTL/Z.
R3(config)# int f0/0
R3(config-if)# ipv6 pim hello-interval ?
  <1-3600>  Hello interval in seconds

R3(config-if)# ipv6 pim hello-interval 5
!!!!!!!!!!!!!!!!!!!!!!!!!!!!!!!!!!!!!!!!!!!!!!!!!!!!!!!!!!!!!!!!!!!!!!!!!!!!!!!!!!
!!The simple show command reveals the parameters of the PIM adjacency on the
!!interface in question.
!!!!!!!!!!!!!!!!!!!!!!!!!!!!!!!!!!!!!!!!!!!!!!!!!!!!!!!!!!!!!!!!!!!!!!!!!!!!!!!!!!
R3# show ipv6 pim interface fastEthernet 0/0
Interface        PIM Nbr   Hello  DR
                     Count Intvl Prior

FastEthernet0/0    on   1     5     4294967295
    Address: FE80::3
    DR     : this system
!!!!!!!!!!!!!!!!!!!!!!!!!!!!!!!!!!!!!!!!!!!!!!!!!!!!!!!!!!!!!!!!!!!!!!!!!!!!!!!!!!
!!!!!
!!You can clearly see the 30 second default value if you look at the same output
!!for FastEthernet0/1 on R3.
!!!!!!!!!!!!!!!!!!!!!!!!!!!!!!!!!!!!!!!!!!!!!!!!!!!!!!!!!!!!!!!!!!!!!!!!!!!!!!!!!!
R3# show ipv6 pim interface fastEthernet 0/1
Interface        PIM Nbr   Hello  DR
                     Count Intvl Prior

FastEthernet0/1    on   1     30    1
    Address: FE80::3
    DR     : this system
```

Note that you can also clearly see the DR status.

## IPv6 Sparse-Mode Multicast

When it comes to multicast operation, IPv6 supports a few options when it comes to designating an RP. These options included static assignment, IPv6 BSR, and the Embedded RP approach. We will observe each of these in our multicast lab environment starting with static assignment. Note that IPv6 multicast does not support Auto-RP or dense mode operation.

## IPv6 Static RP

This operation is no different that its IPv4 counterpart. You simply assign an RP, but you do it through an IPv6 address. You will assign R2 to be the RP in the topology presented in Figure 8-25. Example 8-21 shows the command syntax.

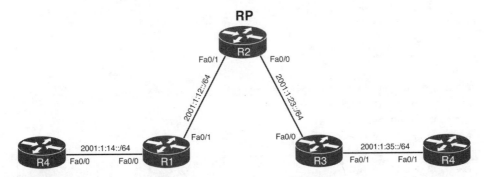

**Figure 8-25**  *IPv6 Static RP Multicast Topology*

**Example 8-21**  *IPv6 Static RP Configuration and Verification*

```
R4# conf t
Enter configuration commands, one per line.  End with CNTL/Z.
R4(config)# ipv6 pim rp-address 2001:2:2:2::2
!!!!!!!!!!!!!!!!!!!!!!!!!!!!!!!!!!!!!!!!!!!!!!!!!!!!!!!!!!!!!!!!!!!!!!!!!!!!!!!!!!!!!!!!!
R1# conf t
Enter configuration commands, one per line.  End with CNTL/Z.
R1(config)# ipv6 pim rp-address 2001:2:2:2::2
!!!!!!!!!!!!!!!!!!!!!!!!!!!!!!!!!!!!!!!!!!!!!!!!!!!!!!!!!!!!!!!!!!!!!!!!!!!!!!!!!!!!!!!!!
R2# conf t
Enter configuration commands, one per line.  End with CNTL/Z.
R2(config)# ipv6 pim rp-address 2001:2:2:2::2
!!!!!!!!!!!!!!!!!!!!!!!!!!!!!!!!!!!!!!!!!!!!!!!!!!!!!!!!!!!!!!!!!!!!!!!!!!!!!!!!!!!!!!!!!
R3# conf t
Enter configuration commands, one per line.  End with CNTL/Z.
R3(config)# ipv6 pim rp-address 2001:2:2:2::2
!!!!!!!!!!!!!!!!!!!!!!!!!!!!!!!!!!!!!!!!!!!!!!!!!!!!!!!!!!!!!!!!!!!!!!!!!!!!!!!!!!!!!!!!!
```

```
R5# conf t
Enter configuration commands, one per line.  End with CNTL/Z.
R5(config)# ipv6 pim rp-address 2001:2:2:2::2
```

In this task, you are statically assigning R2 to act as the IPv6 RP for the multicast topology. This configuration is most simply confirmed by checking the status of the **show ipv6 pim range-list** command on all devices in the network, as shown in Example 8-22.

**Example 8-22**   *IPv6 Range-List Verification*

```
R4# show ipv6 pim range-list
Static SSM Exp: never Learnt from : ::
  FF33::/32 Up: 01:19:06
  FF34::/32 Up: 01:19:06
  FF35::/32 Up: 01:19:06
  FF36::/32 Up: 01:19:06
  FF37::/32 Up: 01:19:06
  FF38::/32 Up: 01:19:06
  FF39::/32 Up: 01:19:06
  FF3A::/32 Up: 01:19:06
  FF3B::/32 Up: 01:19:06
  FF3C::/32 Up: 01:19:06
  FF3D::/32 Up: 01:19:06
  FF3E::/32 Up: 01:19:06
  FF3F::/32 Up: 01:19:06
Static SM RP: 2001:2:2:2::2 Exp: never Learnt from : ::
  FF00::/8 Up: 00:04:28
```

Example 8-23 shows that an additional verification step for this configuration would be to generate multicast traffic from a device in the topology, and verify that it registers with R2.

**Example 8-23**   *IPv6 Multicast Ping Test*

```
R4# ping FF08::1 r 10
Output Interface: FastEthernet0/1
Type escape sequence to abort.
Sending 10, 100-byte ICMP Echos to FF08::1, timeout is 2 seconds:
Packet sent with a source address of 2001:1:14::4

Request 0 timed out
Request 1 timed out
Request 2 timed out
Request 3 timed out
Request 4 timed out
Request 5 timed out
Request 6 timed out
```

```
Request 7 timed out
Request 8 timed out
Request 9 timed out
Success rate is 0 percent (0/10)
0 multicast replies and 0 errors.
```

You see that you are not getting any successful responses, but that is to be expected because you have no devices interested in being receivers for this group. You can look at R2 to see whether there is an (S,G) pair for the group FF08::1 in its routing table, as illustrated in Example 8-24.

**Example 8-24**   *IPv6 Multicast Routing Table Verification*

```
R2# sh ipv6 mroute
Multicast Routing Table
Flags: D - Dense, S - Sparse, B - Bidir Group, s - SSM Group,
       C - Connected, L - Local, I - Received Source Specific Host Report,
       P - Pruned, R - RP-bit set, F - Register flag, T - SPT-bit set,
       J - Join SPT
Timers: Uptime/Expires
Interface state: Interface, State

(2001:1:14::4, FF08::1), 00:00:22/00:03:07, flags: SP
  Incoming interface: FastEthernet0/0
  RPF nbr: FE80::1
  Outgoing interface list: Null
```

Note that we see the (S,G) pair and that it is sparse-mode and pruned (for lack of interested receivers).

## IPv6 BSR

We will start again in the current topology by removing our static IPv6 RP address configurations. Now we will look to create an environment where the RP is elected dynamically. This will be accomplished by making R1 and R3 candidate RPs, and R2 the bootstrap router. We will not walk through the removal of the static RP mappings, but suffice it to say that we will simply use the **no** form of the **ipv6 pim rp-address** command on each device, as is done in Example 8-25. With that completed, we will now make R2 the BSR.

**Example 8-25**   *Remove Static IPv6 RP Assignment and Apply BSR*

```
R2(config)#
R2(config)# no ipv6 pim rp-address 2001:2:2:2::2
R2(config)#!
R2(config)# ipv6 pim bsr candidate bsr 2001:2:2:2::2
!!!!!!!!!!!!!!!!!!!!!!!!!!!!!!!!!!!!!!!!!!!!!!!!!!!!!!!!!!!!!!!!!!!!!!!!!!!!!!!!!!!!
```

```
!!Now that R2 has been configured to act as the BSR we will make R1 and R3
!!candidate RPs
!!!!!!!!!!!!!!!!!!!!!!!!!!!!!!!!!!!!!!!!!!!!!!!!!!!!!!!!!!!!!!!!!!!!!!!!!!!!!!!!!!!
R1# conf t
Enter configuration commands, one per line.  End with CNTL/Z.
R1(config)# ipv6 pim bsr candidate rp 2001:1:1:1::1


R3# conf t
Enter configuration commands, one per line.  End with CNTL/Z.
R3(config)# ipv6 pim bsr candidate rp 2001:3:3:3::3
```

You will first confirm that all devices agree on the group-to-RP mappings through the
**show ipv6 pim range-list** command, as demonstrated in Example 8-26.

**Example 8-26**  *BSR Verification Procedures*

```
R4# show ipv6 pim range-list | be BSR
BSR SM RP: 2001:1:1:1::1 Exp: 00:01:44 Learnt from : 2001:2:2:2::2
  FF00::/8 Up: 00:02:38
BSR SM RP: 2001:3:3:3::3 Exp: 00:01:44 Learnt from : 2001:2:2:2::2
  FF00::/8 Up: 00:01:45
!!!!!!!!!!!!!!!!!!!!!!!!!!!!!!!!!!!!!!!!!!!!!!!!!!!!!!!!!!!!!!!!!!!!!!!!!!!!!!!!!!!
R1# show ipv6 pim range-list | be BSR
BSR SM RP: 2001:1:1:1::1 Exp: 00:01:49 Learnt from : 2001:2:2:2::2
  FF00::/8 Up: 00:04:33
BSR SM RP: 2001:3:3:3::3 Exp: 00:01:49 Learnt from : 2001:2:2:2::2
  FF00::/8 Up: 00:03:40
!!!!!!!!!!!!!!!!!!!!!!!!!!!!!!!!!!!!!!!!!!!!!!!!!!!!!!!!!!!!!!!!!!!!!!!!!!!!!!!!!!!
R2# show ipv6 pim range-list | be BSR
BSR SM RP: 2001:1:1:1::1 Exp: 00:02:26 Learnt from : 2001:2:2:2::2
  FF00::/8 Up: 00:04:56
BSR SM RP: 2001:3:3:3::3 Exp: 00:02:26 Learnt from : 2001:2:2:2::2
  FF00::/8 Up: 00:04:04
!!!!!!!!!!!!!!!!!!!!!!!!!!!!!!!!!!!!!!!!!!!!!!!!!!!!!!!!!!!!!!!!!!!!!!!!!!!!!!!!!!!
R3# show ipv6 pim range-list | be BSR
BSR SM RP: 2001:1:1:1::1 Exp: 00:01:58 Learnt from : 2001:2:2:2::2
  FF00::/8 Up: 00:05:25
BSR SM RP: 2001:3:3:3::3 Exp: 00:01:58 Learnt from : 2001:2:2:2::2
  FF00::/8 Up: 00:04:32
!!!!!!!!!!!!!!!!!!!!!!!!!!!!!!!!!!!!!!!!!!!!!!!!!!!!!!!!!!!!!!!!!!!!!!!!!!!!!!!!!!!
R5# show ipv6 pim range-list | be BSR
```

```
BSR SM RP: 2001:1:1:1::1 Exp: 00:01:33 Learnt from : 2001:2:2:2::2
  FF00::/8 Up: 00:05:50
BSR SM RP: 2001:3:3:3::3 Exp: 00:01:33 Learnt from : 2001:2:2:2::2
  FF00::/8 Up: 00:04:57
```

You see that the devices agree on the possible RPs in the topology, and that they have been "learned" from the BSR (2002:2:2:2::2). To check the topology, you will generate IPv6 multicast traffic on R4, the results of which can be seen in Example 8-27.

**Example 8-27** *IPv6 Ping Verification*

```
R4# ping FF08::1 repeat 10
Output Interface: FastEthernet0/1
Type escape sequence to abort.
Sending 10, 100-byte ICMP Echos to FF08::1, timeout is 2 seconds:
Packet sent with a source address of 2001:1:14::4

Request 0 timed out
Request 1 timed out
Request 2 timed out
Request 3 timed out
Request 4 timed out
Request 5 timed out
Request 6 timed out
Request 7 timed out
Request 8 timed out
Request 9 timed out
Success rate is 0 percent (0/10)
0 multicast replies and 0 errors.
!!!!!!!!!!!!!!!!!!!!!!!!!!!!!!!!!!!!!!!!!!!!!!!!!!!!!!!!!!!!!!!!!!!!!!!!!!!!!!!!
!!Now you will look to see if we can find the S,G entry in the multicast routing
!!table of R1 and R3.
!!!!!!!!!!!!!!!!!!!!!!!!!!!!!!!!!!!!!!!!!!!!!!!!!!!!!!!!!!!!!!!!!!!!!!!!!!!!!!!!
R1# show ipv6 mroute
Multicast Routing Table
Flags: D - Dense, S - Sparse, B - Bidir Group, s - SSM Group,
       C - Connected, L - Local, I - Received Source Specific Host Report,
       P - Pruned, R - RP-bit set, F - Register flag, T - SPT-bit set,
       J - Join SPT
Timers: Uptime/Expires
Interface state: Interface, State

(2001:1:14::4, FF08::1), 00:02:28/00:01:01, flags: SPFT
  Incoming interface: FastEthernet0/1
  RPF nbr: FE80::4
  Outgoing interface list: Null
```

```
!!!!!!!!!!!!!!!!!!!!!!!!!!!!!!!!!!!!!!!!!!!!!!!!!!!!!!!!!!!!!!!!!!!!!!!!!!!!!!!!!!!
R3# show ipv6 mroute
Multicast Routing Table
Flags: D - Dense, S - Sparse, B - Bidir Group, s - SSM Group,
       C - Connected, L - Local, I - Received Source Specific Host Report,
       P - Pruned, R - RP-bit set, F - Register flag, T - SPT-bit set,
       J - Join SPT
Timers: Uptime/Expires
Interface state: Interface, State

(2001:1:14::4, FF08::1), 00:04:05/00:03:05, flags: SP
  Incoming interface: FastEthernet0/1
  RPF nbr: FE80::2
  Outgoing interface list: Null
```

You see the (S,G) pair as you would expect. Now you will look closer at the different
components of the topology. Starting with the BSR, you will look to see what RP candidates are announcing their presence to the R2. You expect to see R1 and R3 appearing in
this list, the results of which are shown in Example 8-28.

**Example 8-28**  *Observing the IPv6 BSR RP-Cache*

```
R2# show ipv6 pim bsr rp-cache
PIMv2 BSR C-RP Cache


BSR Candidate RP Cache


Group(s) FF00::/8, RP count 2
  RP 2001:1:1:1::1 SM
     Priority 192, Holdtime 150
     Uptime: 00:14:28, expires: 00:02:03
  RP 2001:3:3:3::3 SM
     Priority 192, Holdtime 150
     Uptime: 00:13:36, expires: 00:01:56
!!!!!!!!!!!!!!!!!!!!!!!!!!!!!!!!!!!!!!!!!!!!!!!!!!!!!!!!!!!!!!!!!!!!!!!!!!!!!!!!!!!
!!On R3, one of our C-RPs, we clearly see the parameters being announced to the
!!Boot Strap Router.
!!!!!!!!!!!!!!!!!!!!!!!!!!!!!!!!!!!!!!!!!!!!!!!!!!!!!!!!!!!!!!!!!!!!!!!!!!!!!!!!!!!
R3# show ipv6 pim bsr candidate-rp
PIMv2 C-RP information
  Candidate RP: 2001:3:3:3::3 SM
       All Learnt Scoped Zones, Priority 192, Holdtime 150
       Advertisement interval 60 seconds
       Next advertisement in 00:00:25
```

The next section covers the concept of the "embedded RP."

## Multicast Listener Discovery (MLD)

Thus far in the discussions regarding IPv6 multicast routing, you have not seen a single successful multicast ping. This is because you have not assigned any host for any of the tested groups. You will correct this issue now, by making R5's FastEthernet0/0 interface join the multicast group FF08::1, as shown in Example 8-29.

**Example 8-29**  *Enable MLD Joins to IPv6 Multicast Groups*

```
R5# conf t
Enter configuration commands, one per line.  End with CNTL/Z.
R5(config)# int f0/0
R5(config-if)# ipv6 mld join-group FF08::1
```

In a nutshell, IPv6 multicast replaces IGMP with Multicast Listener Discovery Protocol. For the best comparison of features, you can consider that MLDv1 is similar to IGMP Version 2, while MLDv2 is similar to IGMP Version 3. That means that MLDv2 will support Source Specific Multicast in IPv6 networks.

Using MLD, hosts can indicate they want to receive multicast transmissions for select groups. Just like in IGMP, it is the elected queriers that are responsible for managing the flow of multicast traffic in the network through the use of MLD. These messages are carried inside Internet Control Message Protocol (ICMP); however, it must be noted that these messages are link-local in scope, and each has the router alert option set.

MLD uses three types of messages: Query, Report, and Done. The Done message is like the Leave message in IGMP Version 2. It indicates that a host no longer wants to receive the multicast transmission. This triggers a Query to check for any more receivers on the segment.

Configuration options for MLD will be very similar to configuration tasks we needed to master for IGMP. You can limit the number of receivers with the **ipv6 mld limit** command. If you want the interface to "permanently" subscribe, you can use the **ipv6 mld join-group** command. Also, as in IGMP, there are several timers you can manipulate for the protocol's mechanics.

Configuring IPv6 multicast routing with the **ipv6 multicast-routing** global configuration command automatically configures Protocol Independent Multicast on all active interfaces. This also includes the automatic configuration of MLD. Example 8-30 demonstrates what this would look like in our environment.

**Example 8-30**  *IPv6 PIM Join Verification*

```
R3# show ipv6 pim interface
Interface          PIM  Nbr    Hello  DR
                        Count  Intvl  Prior


Tunnel2            off  0      30     1
   Address: FE80::211:21FF:FEDF:8360
   DR      : not elected
```

```
Loopback0            on    0    30     1
   Address: FE80::211:21FF:FEDF:8360
   DR     : this system
VoIP-Null0           off   0    30     1
   Address: ::
   DR     : not elected
FastEthernet0/0      on    1    5      4294967295
   Address: FE80::3
   DR     : this system
FastEthernet0/1      on    1    30     1
   Address: FE80::3
   DR     : this system
Serial0/0            off   0    30     1
   Address: ::
   DR     : not elected
Serial0/1            off   0    30     1
   Address: ::
   DR     : not elected
Tunnel0              off   0    30     1
   Address: FE80::211:21FF:FEDF:8360
   DR     : not elected
Tunnel1              off   0    30     1
   Address: FE80::211:21FF:FEDF:8360
   DR     : not elected
Tunnel3              off   0    30     1
   Address: FE80::211:21FF:FEDF:8360
   DR     : not elected
```

Notice that PIM is enabled on all interfaces that you have manually configured in this scenario. With this complete, you need to take a closer look at MLD. This is done by using the **show ipv6 mld interface fa0/0** command, as shown in Example 8-31.

**Example 8-31** *Enabling PIM for IPv6 at the Interface Level*

```
R3# show ipv6 mld interface fa0/0
FastEthernet0/0 is up, line protocol is up
  Internet address is FE80::3/10
  MLD is enabled on interface
  Current MLD version is 2
  MLD query interval is 125 seconds
  MLD querier timeout is 255 seconds
  MLD max query response time is 10 seconds
  Last member query response interval is 1 seconds
  MLD activity: 8 joins, 0 leaves
  MLD querying router is FE80::3 (this system)
```

Note how similar MLD is to IGMP. Now that you have an interested host in the environment, you need to see what candidate RP registered the MLD Join message coming from R5. Based on what you know about RP election and BSR, the candidate with the highest IP address should have registered the (*,G) for FF08::1. You will first look at R1, however, just to verify that the Join is not in the multicast routing table there:

```
R1# show ipv6 mroute
No mroute entries found
```

Now look at R3, where you would expect to see the (*,G) entry, as verified in Example 8-32.

**Example 8-32**  *Verifying the IPv6 Routing Table with BSR Enabled*

```
R3# show ipv6 mroute
Multicast Routing Table
Flags: D - Dense, S - Sparse, B - Bidir Group, s - SSM Group,
       C - Connected, L - Local, I - Received Source Specific Host Report,
       P - Pruned, R - RP-bit set, F - Register flag, T - SPT-bit set,
       J - Join SPT
Timers: Uptime/Expires
Interface state: Interface, State


(*, FF08::1), 00:24:13/never, RP 2001:3:3:3::3, flags: SCJ
  Incoming interface: Tunnel3
  RPF nbr: 2001:3:3:3::3
  Immediate Outgoing interface list:
    FastEthernet0/0, Forward, 00:24:13/never
!!!!!!!!!!!!!!!!!!!!!!!!!!!!!!!!!!!!!!!!!!!!!!!!!!!!!!!!!!!!!!!!!!!!!!!!!!!!!!!!!!!!
!!Now that there is an interested host in the topology for FF08::1 we should be
!!able to successfully ping the group from R4.
!!!!!!!!!!!!!!!!!!!!!!!!!!!!!!!!!!!!!!!!!!!!!!!!!!!!!!!!!!!!!!!!!!!!!!!!!!!!!!!!!!!!
R4# ping FF08::1 repeat 10
Output Interface: FastEthernet0/1
Type escape sequence to abort.
Sending 10, 100-byte ICMP Echos to FF08::1, timeout is 2 seconds:
Packet sent with a source address of 2001:1:14::4

Reply to request 0 received from 2001:1:35::5, 24 ms
Reply to request 1 received from 2001:1:35::5, 0 ms
Reply to request 1 received from 2001:1:35::5, 4 ms
Reply to request 2 received from 2001:1:35::5, 0 ms
Reply to request 3 received from 2001:1:35::5, 0 ms
Reply to request 4 received from 2001:1:35::5, 0 ms
Reply to request 5 received from 2001:1:35::5, 0 ms
Reply to request 6 received from 2001:1:35::5, 0 ms
```

```
Reply to request 7 received from 2001:1:35::5, 0 ms
Reply to request 8 received from 2001:1:35::5, 0 ms
Reply to request 9 received from 2001:1:35::5, 0 ms
Success rate is 100 percent (10/10), round-trip min/avg/max = 0/2/24 ms
11 multicast replies and 0 errors.
```

Before moving on, you want to look at what traffic is traversing R2. The **show ipv6 pim traffic** command, illustrated in Example 8-33, will show the packets and messages that we have been discussing.

**Example 8-33** *Verification of IPv6 Traffic Counters*

```
R3# show ipv6 pim traffic
PIM Traffic Counters
Elapsed time since counters cleared: 02:59:09

                                    Received        Sent
Valid PIM Packets                      830          2054
Hello                                  725          2212
Join-Prune                               0            20
Data Register                            7             -
Null Register                           12             0
Register Stop                            0            15
Assert                                   0             0
Bidir DF Election                        0             0


Errors:
Malformed Packets                                      0
Bad Checksums                                          0
Send Errors                                            0
Packet Sent on Loopback Errors                       362
Packets Received on PIM-disabled Interface             0
Packets Received with Unknown PIM Version              0


Lastly we will look at the nature of the tunnels we have seen and discussed:
R3# show ipv6 pim tunnel
Tunnel0*
  Type  : PIM Encap
  RP    : Embedded RP Tunnel
  Source: 2001:3:3:3::3
Tunnel1*
  Type  : PIM Encap
  RP    : 2001:1:1:1::1
  Source: 2001:3:3:3::3
```

```
Tunnel2*
  Type  : PIM Encap
  RP    : 2001:3:3:3::3*
  Source: 2001:3:3:3::3
Tunnel3*
  Type  : PIM Decap
  RP    : 2001:3:3:3::3*
  Source:  -
```

## Embedded RP

Embedded RP is a handy feature that enables the identity of the RP to be embedded as part of the multicast group address. Any multicast router that sees this specific group address can extract the RP's identity and begin to use it for the shared tree immediately. This requires the identity of the RP to be explicitly configured on the device that will be used as the actual RP. No other configuration is required because all other routers in the domain will dynamically learn the RP address from the group address itself. However, an issue surfaces when you try to embed a 128-bit RP address into a 128-bit group address while leaving space for the group identity.

To accomplish the embedding of the RP address in the 128-bit multicast group address, you need to follow a few rules:

- **Rule 1:** You must indicate that the multicast group contains an embedded RP by setting the first 8 bits to all 1s. As such, we are saying that an embedded RP multicast address would always begin with FF70::/12 or 1111 1111 0111.

- **Rule 2:** You need numeric designations to specify a scope associated with the given address range, where the selected scope appears like so: FF7x. The value of "x" indicates the nature of the address in question. The following list shows your options:

  - **1:** Interface-Local scope
  - **2:** Link-Local scope
  - **4:** Admin-Local scope
  - **5:** Site-Local scope
  - **8:** Organization-Local scope
  - **E:** Global scope

- **Rule 3:** Isolate the three values from the RP address itself. These three values are

  - RP interface ID
  - Prefix length in hex
  - RP prefix

When we create the embedded RP address, the individual components mentioned in the preceding list are organized in the following pattern:

FF7<*Scope*>:0<*RP interface ID*><*Hex prefix length*>:<*64-bit RP prefix*>:<*32-bit group ID*>:<*1–F*>

We will execute this feature in the topology shown in Figure 8-26.

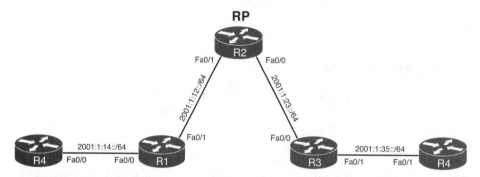

**Figure 8-26**  *IPv6 RP Advertisement Through Embedded RP Topology*

First, you must isolate the values you need to construct the Embedded RP group. You will use the address 2001:2:2:2::2/64 as the address, which means that

■ The RP interface ID is 2 (taken from ::2).

■ The prefix length is 64, which converts to 40 in hexadecimal.

■ The RP prefix is 2001:2:2:2.

Next, you define the scope. You want the scope to be global, so you will use "E." The 32-bit group ID will most commonly be "0" but it could be other values. With these values isolated and defined, we can construct the embedded RP address like so:

FF7<*Scope*>:0<*RP interface ID*><*Hex prefix length*>:<*64-bit RP prefix*>:<*32-bit group ID*>:<*1–F*>

FF7E:0240:2001:2:2:2:0:1

You will arbitrarily select the value of 1 as the last digit. So in this topology, you would have R5 or any of the routers join this group: FF7E:240:2001:2:2:2:0:1. This is accomplished by following the configuration and verification procedures shown in Example 8-34.

**Example 8-34**  *Embedded RP Configuration*

```
R5(config)# int f0/0
R5(config-if)# ipv6 mld join-group FF7E:240:2001:2:2:2:0:1
!!!!!!!!!!!!!!!!!!!!!!!!!!!!!!!!!!!!!!!!!!!!!!!!!!!!!!!!!!!!!!!!!!!!!!!!!!!!!!!!!!!!!!!!!
!!Remember, you need to notify R2 that it is the RP. You will do that via the
!!static RP method
```

```
!!!!!!!!!!!!!!!!!!!!!!!!!!!!!!!!!!!!!!!!!!!!!!!!!!!!!!!!!!!!!!!!!!!!!!!!!!!!!!!!!!!!!
R2# conf t
R2(config)# ipv6 pim rp-address 2001:2:2:2::2
!!!!!!!!!!!!!!!!!!!!!!!!!!!!!!!!!!!!!!!!!!!!!!!!!!!!!!!!!!!!!!!!!!!!!!!!!!!!!!!!!!!!!
!!Next, you will go to R4 and test by pinging the group FF7E:240:2001:2:2:2:0:1
!!!!!!!!!!!!!!!!!!!!!!!!!!!!!!!!!!!!!!!!!!!!!!!!!!!!!!!!!!!!!!!!!!!!!!!!!!!!!!!!!!!!!
R4# ping FF7E:240:2001:2:2:2:0:1 repeat 10
Output Interface: FastEthernet0/1
Type escape sequence to abort.
Sending 10, 100-byte ICMP Echos to FF7E:240:2001:2:2:2:0:1, timeout is 2 seconds:
Packet sent with a source address of 2001:1:14::4

Reply to request 0 received from 2001:1:35::5, 20 ms
Reply to request 1 received from 2001:1:35::5, 0 ms
Reply to request 1 received from 2001:1:35::5, 16 ms
Reply to request 2 received from 2001:1:35::5, 0 ms
Reply to request 3 received from 2001:1:35::5, 0 ms
Reply to request 4 received from 2001:1:35::5, 0 ms
Reply to request 5 received from 2001:1:35::5, 0 ms
Reply to request 6 received from 2001:1:35::5, 0 ms
Reply to request 7 received from 2001:1:35::5, 0 ms
Reply to request 8 received from 2001:1:35::5, 0 ms
Reply to request 9 received from 2001:1:35::5, 0 ms
Success rate is 100 percent (10/10), round-trip min/avg/max = 0/3/20 ms
11 multicast replies and 0 errors.
```

You can see that the configuration is working, and you can also verify that R2 is the RP being used by executing the command illustrated in Example 8-35.

**Example 8-35**  *Verification of the Multicast Routing Table with Embedded RP Enabled*

```
R2# show ipv6 mroute
Multicast Routing Table
Flags: D - Dense, S - Sparse, B - Bidir Group, s - SSM Group,
       C - Connected, L - Local, I - Received Source Specific Host Report,
       P - Pruned, R - RP-bit set, F - Register flag, T - SPT-bit set,
       J - Join SPT
Timers: Uptime/Expires
Interface state: Interface, State

(*, FF7E:240:2001:2:2:2:0:1), 00:02:29/00:03:00, RP 2001:2:2:2::2, flags: S
  Incoming interface: Tunnel2
  RPF nbr: 2001:2:2:2::2
```

```
    Immediate Outgoing interface list:
      FastEthernet0/1, Forward, 00:02:29/00:03:00


(2001:1:14::4, FF7E:240:2001:2:2:2:0:1), 00:01:25/00:03:03, flags: ST
  Incoming interface: FastEthernet0/0
  RPF nbr: FE80::1
  Immediate Outgoing interface list:
    FastEthernet0/1, Forward, 00:01:25/00:03:00
```

You can see that the identity of the RP is being communicated by embedding it into the group address itself. You can verify this directly by using the command illustrated in Example 8-36.

**Example 8-36**  *Identifying the RP Through the Embedded RP on a Router*

```
R3# show ipv6 pim group-map FF7E:240:2001:2:2:2::/96
IP PIM Group Mapping Table
(* indicates group mappings being used)


FF7E:240:2001:2:2:2::/96*
  SM, RP: 2001:2:2:2::2
  RPF: Fa0/1,FE80::2
  Info source: Embedded
  Uptime: 00:07:25, Groups: 1
```

This represents the local Multicast Listener Discovery information used to discriminate the embedded RP information.

## Foundation Summary

This section lists additional details and facts to round out the coverage of the topics in this chapter. Unlike most of the Cisco Press Exam Certification Guides, this "Foundation Summary" does not repeat information presented in the "Foundation Topics" section of the chapter. Please take the time to read and study the details in the "Foundation Topics" section of the chapter, as well as review items noted with a Key Topic icon.

Table 8-5 lists the protocol standards referenced in this chapter.

**Table 8-5**  *RFC Reference for Chapter 8*

| RFC | What It Defines |
| --- | --- |
| 3973 | PIM-DM |
| 3618 | MSDP |
| 3446 | Anycast RP |
| 4601 | PIM-SM |
| 1584 | Multicast Extensions to OSPF |
| 4604, 4607, 4608 | Source Specific Multicast |
| 3810 | Multicast Listener Discovery Version 2 (MLDv2) |
| 2710 | Multicast Listener Discovery for IPv6 |

Table 8-6 lists some of the most common Cisco IOS commands related to the topics in this chapter and Chapter 7.

**Table 8-6**  *Command Reference for Chapters 7 and 8*

| Command | Command Mode and Description |
| --- | --- |
| ip multicast-routing | Global mode; required first command on Cisco routers to use multicasting. |
| ip msdp peer *address* | Interface config mode; configures the router as an MSDP peer. |
| ip pim dense-mode* | Interface config mode; configures the interface to use PIM-DM routing protocol. |
| ip pim sparse-mode* | Interface config mode; configures the interface to use PIM-SM routing protocol. |
| ip pim sparse-dense-mode* | Interface config mode; configures the interface to use PIM-SM routing protocol for a group if the RP address is known; otherwise, uses PIM-DM routing protocol. |

| Command | Command Mode and Description |
|---------|------------------------------|
| ip pim ssm {default | range *access-list*} | Global config mode; enables Source Specific Multicast and specifies the multicast groups that the router will forward traffic for. |
| ip igmp version {1 | 2 | 3} | Interface config mode; sets the IGMP version on an interface. The default is 2. |
| ip igmp query-interval *seconds* | Interface config mode; changes the interval for IGMP queries sent by the router from the default 60 seconds. |
| ip igmp query-max-response-time *seconds* | Interface config mode; changes the Max Response Time advertised in IGMP Queries from the default of 10 seconds for IGMPv2 and IGMPv3. |
| ip igmp join-group *group-address* | Interface config mode; configures a router to join a multicast group. The group-address is a multicast IP address in four-part dotted-decimal notation. |
| ip multicast boundary *access-list* [*filter-autorp*] | Interface config mode; configures an interface as a multicast boundary for administrative scoping. A numbered or named access list controls the range of group addresses affected by the boundary. (Optional) **filter-autorp** filters Auto-RP messages denied by the boundary ACL. |
| ip multicast ttl-threshold *ttl-value* | Interface config mode; configures an interface as a multicast boundary for TTL scoping. Time-to-Live value represents number of hops, ranging from 0 to 255. The default value is 0, which means that all multicast packets are forwarded out the interface. |
| ip cgmp | Interface config mode; enables support for CGMP on an interface. |
| ip pim version {1 | 2} | Interface config mode; sets the PIM version on an interface. The default is 2. |
| ip pim query-interval *seconds* | Interface config mode; changes the interval for PIMv2 Hello or PIMv1 Router Query messages from the default 30 seconds. |
| ip pim spt-threshold {kbps | infinity} [group-list *access-list-number*] | Global mode; specifies the incoming rate for the multicast traffic for a PIM-SM router to switch from RPT to SPT. The default is to switch after the first multicast packet is received. If the **group-list** option is used, the command parameters are applied only to the groups permitted by the access list; otherwise, they are applied to all groups. |

| Command | Command Mode and Description |
|---|---|
| **ip pim rp-address** [*access-list*] [**override**] | Global mode; statically configures the IP address of an RP, where *rp-address* is a unicast IP address in four-part, dotted notation. (Optional) *access-list* represents a number or name of an access list that defines for which multicast groups the RP should be used. (Optional) **override** indicates that if there is a conflict, the RP configured with this command prevails over the RP learned dynamically by Auto-RP or any other method. |
| **ip pim send-rp-announce** *interface-type interface-number* **scope** *ttl-value* [**group-list** *access-list*] [**interval** *seconds*] | Global mode; configures the router to be an RP, and the router sends RP-Announce messages using the Auto-RP method for the interface address selected. Scope represents the TTL. (Optional) **group-list** defines the multicast groups for which this router is RP. (Optional) **interval** changes the announcement frequency from the default 60 seconds. |
| **ip pim send-rp-discovery** [*interface-type interface-number*] **scope** *ttl-value* | Global mode; configures the router to be a mapping agent, and the router sends RP-Discovery messages using the Auto-RP method. **scope** represents the TTL. (Optional) The IP address of the interface specified is used as the source address for the messages. The default is to use the IP address of the interface on which the message is sent as the source address. |
| **ip pim rp-announce-filter rp-list** *access-list* **group-list** *access-list* | Global mode; configures a mapping agent to filter RP-Announce messages coming from specific RPs. **rp-list** *access-list* specifies a number or name of a standard access list that specifies that this filter is only for the RP addresses permitted in this ACL. **group-list** *access-list* specifies a number or name of a standard access list that describes permitted group addresses. The filter defines that only the group range permitted in the **group-list** *access-list* should be accepted from the RP-Announcements received from the RP addresses permitted by the **rp-list** *access-list*. |
| **show ip igmp groups** [*group-name* | *group-address* | *interface-type interface-number*] [**detail**] | User mode; displays the list of multicast groups for which the router has directly connected group members, learned through IGMP. |
| **show ip mroute** [*group-address* | *group-name*] [*source-address* | *source-name*] [*interface-type interface-number*] [**summary**] [**count**] [**active** *kbps*] | User mode; displays the contents of the IP multicast routing table. |

| Command | Command Mode and Description |
|---|---|
| **show ip pim neighbor** [*interface-type interface-number*] | User mode; displays the list of neighbors discovered by PIM. |
| **show ip pim rp** [mapping [elected \| in-use] \| **metric**] [*rp-address*] | User mode; displays the active RPs associated with multicast groups. |
| **show ip rpf** {*source-address* \| *source-name*} [*metric*] | User mode; displays the information IP multicasting routing uses to perform the RPF check. |
| **clear ip cgmp** [*interface-type interface-number*] | Enable mode; the router sends a CGMP Leave message and instructs the switches to clear all group entries they have cached. |
| **debug ip igmp** | Enable mode; displays IGMP messages received and sent, and IGMP-host-related events. |
| **debug ip pim** | Enable mode; displays PIM messages received and sent, and PIM-related events. |

[*] When you configure any one of these commands on a LAN interface, IGMPv2 is automatically enabled on the interface.

Table 8-7 summarizes important flags displayed in an mroute entry when you use the **show ip mroute** command.

**Table 8-7** mroute *Flags*

| Flag | Description |
|---|---|
| D (dense) | Entry is operating in dense mode. |
| S (sparse) | Entry is operating in sparse mode. |
| C (connected) | A member of the multicast group is present on the directly connected interface. |
| L (local) | The router itself is a member of the multicast group. |
| P (pruned) | Route has been pruned. |
| R (RP-bit set) | Indicates that the (S,G) entry is pointing toward the RP. The RP is typically in a pruned state along the shared tree after a downstream router has switched to SPT for a particular source. |
| F (register flag) | Indicates that the software is registering for a multicast source. |
| T (SPT-bit set) | Indicates that packets have been received on the shortest-path source tree. |

| Flag | Description |
|------|-------------|
| J (join SPT) | This flag has meaning only for sparse-mode groups. For (*,G) entries, the J flag indicates that the rate of traffic flowing down the shared tree has exceeded the SPT-Threshold set for the group. This calculation is done once a second. On Cisco routers, the default SPT-Threshold value is 0 kbps. When the J flag is set on the (*,G) entry and the router has a directly connected group member denoted by the C flag, the next (S,G) packet received down the shared tree will trigger a switchover from RPT to SPT for source S and group G. For (S,G) entries, the J flag indicates that the entry was created because the router has switched over from RPT to SPT for the group. When the J flag is set for the (S,G) entries, the router monitors the traffic rate on SPT and switches back to RPT for this source if the traffic rate on the source tree falls below the group's SPT-Threshold for more than 1 minute. |

# Memory Builders

The CCIE Routing and Switching written exam, like all Cisco CCIE written exams, covers a fairly broad set of topics. This section provides some basic tools to help you exercise your memory about some of the broader topics covered in this chapter.

## Fill In Key Tables from Memory

Appendix E, "Key Tables for CCIE Study," on the CD in the back of this book, contains empty sets of some of the key summary tables in each chapter. Print Appendix E, refer to this chapter's tables in it, and fill in the tables from memory. Refer to Appendix F, "Solutions for Key Tables for CCIE Study," on the CD, to check your answers.

## Definitions

Next, take a few moments to write down the definitions for the following terms:

dense-mode protocol, RPF check, sparse-mode protocol, RP, multicast scoping, TTL scoping, administrative scoping, PIM-DM, PIM Hello message, designated router, source-based distribution tree, multicast state information, Join/Prune message, upstream router, downstream router, Graft message, Graft Ack message, Prune Override, Assert message, DVMRP, MOSPF, PIM-SM, source DR, source registration, shared distribution tree, shortest-path tree switchover, PIM-SM (S,G), RP-bit Prune, Auto-RP, BSR, SSM, MSDP, MLD, IPv6 mroute, embedded RP, IPv6 BSR, MLD Limiting

Refer to the glossary to check your answers.

## Further Reading

*Developing IP Multicast Networks*, Volume I, by Beau Williamson (Cisco Press, 2000).

*Interdomain Multicast Solutions Guide*, by Cisco Systems, Inc. (Cisco Press, 2003).

**Blueprint topics covered in this chapter:**

This chapter covers the following subtopics from the Cisco CCIE Routing and Switching written exam blueprint. Refer to the full blueprint in Table I-1 in the Introduction for more details on the topics covered in each chapter and their context within the blueprint.

- Access Lists

- Zone-Based Firewall and Classic IOS Firewall

- Unicast Reverse Path Forwarding

- IP Source Guard

- Authentication, Authorization, and Accounting (router configuration)

- Control-Plane Policing (CoPP)

- Secure Shell (SSH)

- 802.1X

- Device Access Control

- IPv6 First Hop Security

- RA Guard

- DHCP Guard

- Binding Table

- Device Tracking

- ND Inspection

- Source Guard

- PACL

## CHAPTER 9

# Device and Network Security

Over the years, the CCIE program has expanded to add several CCIE certifications besides the Routing and Switching track. As a result, some topics previously covered in the Routing and Switching exam have been removed, or shortened, because they are more appropriate for another CCIE track. For example, the CCIE Routing and Switching track formerly covered voice to some degree, but the CCIE Voice track now covers voice to a much deeper level.

The topics in this chapter are certainly covered in more detail in the CCIE Security written and lab exams. However, because security has such an important role in networks, and because many security features relate specifically to router and switch operations, some security details remain within the CCIE Routing and Switching track. This chapter covers many of the core security features related to routers and switches.

## "Do I Know This Already?" Quiz

Table 9-1 outlines the major headings in this chapter and the corresponding "Do I Know This Already?" quiz questions.

**Table 9-1** *"Do I Know This Already?" Foundation Topics Section-to-Question Mapping*

| Foundation Topics Section | Questions Covered in This Section | Score |
|---|---|---|
| Router and Switch Device Security | 1–3 | |
| Layer 2 Security | 4–7 | |
| Layer 3 Security | 8, 9 | |
| Total Score | | |

To best use this pre-chapter assessment, remember to score yourself strictly. You can find the answers in Appendix A, "Answers to the 'Do I Know This Already?' Quizzes."

1. Consider the following configuration commands, which will be pasted into a router's configuration. Assuming that no other AAA configuration or other security-related configuration exists before pasting in this configuration, which of the following is true regarding the process and sequences for authentication of a user attempting to enter privileged mode?

```
enable secret fred
enable authentication wilma
username barney password betty
aaa new-model
aaa authentication enable default group radius enable
aaa authentication enable wilma group fred local
aaa authentication login default group radius local
aaa authentication login fred line group radius none
radius-server host 10.1.1.1 auth-port 1812 acct-port 1646
radius-server host 10.1.1.2 auth-port 1645 acct-port 1646
radius-server key cisco
aaa group server radius fred
server 10.1.1.3 auth-port 1645 acct-port 1646
server 10.1.1.4 auth-port 1645 acct-port 1646
line con 0
 password cisco
 login authentication fred
line vty 0 4
 password cisco
```

   a. The user will only need to supply a password of fred without a username.

   b. The RADIUS server at either 10.1.1.1 or 10.1.1.2 must approve the username/password supplied by the user.

   c. The RADIUS server at 10.1.1.3 is checked first; if no response, the server at 10.1.1.4 is checked.

   d. None of these answers is correct.

2. Using the same exhibit and conditions as Question 1, which of the following is true regarding the process and sequences for authentication of a user attempting to log in through the console?

   a. A simple password of cisco will be required.

   b. The user will supply a username/password, which will be authenticated if either server 10.1.1.1 or 10.1.1.2 returns a RADIUS message approving the user.

   c. The username/password is presented to the RADIUS server at 10.1.1.3 first; if no response, the server at 10.1.1.4 is checked next.

   d. None of these answers is correct.

**3.** Using the same exhibit and conditions as Question 1, which of the following is true regarding the process and sequences for authentication of a user attempting to log in through Telnet?

   **a.** A simple password of cisco will be required.

   **b.** The router will attempt authentication with RADIUS server 10.1.1.1 first. If no response, then 10.1.1.2; if no response, it will require password cisco.

   **c.** The router will attempt authentication with RADIUS server 10.1.1.1 first. If no response, then 10.1.1.2; if no response, it will require a username/password of barney/betty.

   **d.** The username/password is presented to the RADIUS server at 10.1.1.3 first; if no response, the server at 10.1.1.4 is checked next.

   **e.** If neither 10.1.1.1 nor 10.1.1.2 responds, the user cannot be authenticated and is rejected.

   **f.** None of the other answers is correct.

**4.** Which of the following are considered best practices for Layer 2 security?

   **a.** Inspect ARP messages to prevent hackers from causing hosts to create incorrect ARP table entries.

   **b.** Enable port security.

   **c.** Put all management traffic in VLAN 1, but no user traffic.

   **d.** Configure DTP to use the auto setting.

   **e.** Shut down unused ports.

**5.** Assuming a Cisco 3560 switch, which of the following is true regarding the port security feature?

   **a.** The default maximum number of MACs allowed to be reached on an interface is three.

   **b.** Sticky-learned MAC addresses are automatically added to the startup configuration after they are learned the first time.

   **c.** Dynamic (nonsticky)–learned MAC addresses are added to the running configuration, but they can be saved using the **copy run start** command.

   **d.** A port must be set to be a static access or trunking port for port security to be allowed on the interface.

   **e.** None of the other answers is correct.

6. Which of the following is true regarding the use of IEEE 802.1X for LAN user authentication?

   a. The EAPoL protocol is used between the authenticator and authentication server.

   b. The supplicant is client software on the user's device.

   c. A switch acts in the role of 802.1X authentication server.

   d. The only traffic allowed to exit a currently unauthenticated 802.1X port is 802.1X-related messages.

7. The following ACE is typed into configuration mode on a router: **access-list 1 permit 10.44.38.0 0.0.3.255**. If this statement had instead used a different mask, with nothing else changed, which of the following choices for mask would result in a match for source IP address 10.44.40.18?

   a. 0.0.1.255

   b. 0.0.5.255

   c. 0.0.7.255

   d. 0.0.15.255

8. An enterprise uses a registered class A network. A smurf attack occurs from the Internet, with the enterprise receiving lots of ICMP Echoes, destined to subnet broadcast address 9.1.1.255, which is the broadcast address of an actual deployed subnet (9.1.1.0/24) in the enterprise. The packets all have a source address of 9.1.1.1. Which of the following tools might help mitigate the effects of the attack?

   a. Ensure that the **no ip directed-broadcast** command is configured on the router interfaces connected to the 9.1.1.0/24 subnet.

   b. Configure an RPF check so that the packets would be rejected based on the invalid source IP address.

   c. Routers will not forward packets to subnet broadcast addresses, so there is no need for concern in this case.

   d. Filter all packets sent to addresses in subnet 9.1.1.0/24.

9. Which of the following statements is true regarding the router Cisco IOS Software TCP intercept feature?

   a. Always acts as a proxy for incoming TCP connections, completing the client-side connection, and only then creating a server-side TCP connection.

   b. Can monitor TCP connections for volume and for incomplete connections, as well as serve as a TCP proxy.

   c. If enabled, must operate on all TCP connection requests entering a particular interface.

   d. None of the other answers is correct.

# Foundation Topics

## Router and Switch Device Security

Securing access to a router or switch command-line interface (CLI) is one of the first steps in securing a routed/switched network. Cisco includes several basic mechanisms appropriate for protecting devices in a lab, as well as more robust security features appropriate for devices deployed in production environments. Additionally, these same base authentication features can be used to authenticate dial Point-to-Point Protocol (PPP) users. The first section of this chapter examines each of these topics.

### Simple Password Protection for the CLI

Figure 9-1 provides a visual reminder of some hopefully familiar details about how users can reach a router's CLI user mode, and move into enable (privileged) mode using the **enable** command.

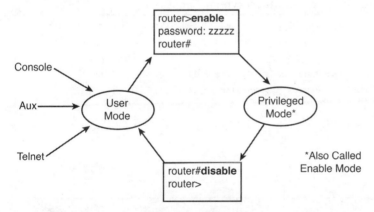

**Figure 9-1**   *Router User and Enable Modes*

Figure 9-1 shows three methods to reach user mode on a router. The figure also applies to Cisco IOS–based switches, except that Cisco switches do not have auxiliary ports.

Cisco IOS can be configured to require simple password protection for each of the three methods to access user mode. To do so, the **login** line subcommand is used to tell Cisco IOS to prompt the user for a password, and the **password** command defines the password. The configuration mode implies for which of the three access methods the password should be required. Example 9-1 shows a simple example.

**Example 9-1**   *Simple User Mode CLI Password Protection*

```
! The login and password commands under line con 0 tell the router to supply a
! password prompt, and define the password required at the console port,
! respectively.
line con 0
 login
 password fred
!
! The login and password commands under line vty 0 15 tell the router to supply a
! password prompt, and define the password required at the vty lines, respectively.
line vty 0 15
 login
 password barney
```

These passwords are stored as clear text in the configuration, but they can be encrypted by including the **service password-encryption** global command. Example 9-2 shows the results of adding this command.

**Example 9-2**   *Using the* service password-encryption *Command*

```
! The service password-encryption global command causes all existing clear-text
! passwords in the running config to be encrypted.
service password-encryption
! The "7" in the password commands means that the following value is the
! encrypted password per the service password-encryption command.
line con 0
 password 7 05080F1C2243
 login
line vty 0 4
 password 7 00071A150754
 login
```

Note that when the **service password-encryption** command is added to the configuration, all clear-text passwords in the running configuration are changed to an encrypted value. The passwords in the startup configuration are not changed until the **copy running-config startup-config** (or **write memory** for all you fellow old-timers out there) command has been used to save the configuration. Also, after you disable password encryption (**no service password-encryption**), passwords are not automatically decrypted. Instead, Cisco IOS waits for a password to be changed before listing the password in its unencrypted form.

Note that the encryption used by the **service password-encryption** command is weak. Publicly available tools can decrypt the password. The encryption is useful to prevent the curious from logging in to a router or switch, but it provides no real protection against a hacker with even modest ability.

### Better Protection of Enable and Username Passwords

The password required by the **enable** command can be defined by either the **enable password** *pw* command or the **enable secret** *pw* command. If both are configured, the **enable exec** command only accepts the password defined in the **enable secret** command.

The password in the **enable password** command follows the same encryption rules as login passwords, only being encrypted if the **service password-encryption** command is configured. However, the **enable secret** password is not affected by **service password-encryption**. Example 9-3 shows how Cisco IOS represents this subtle difference in how the password values are stored.

**Key Topic**

**Example 9-3**  *Differences in Hashed/Encrypted Enable Passwords*

```
! The enable password lists a 7 in the output to signify an encrypted value
! per the service password-encryption command; the
! enable secret command lists a 5, signifying an MD5-hashed value.
service password-encryption
!
enable secret 5 $1$GvDM$ux/PhTwSscDNOyNIyr5Be/
enable password 7 070C285F4D064B
```

### Using Secure Shell Protocol

Example 9-1 showed how to require a password for Telnet access through the vty lines. Telnet has long been used to manage network devices; however, Telnet traffic is sent in clear text. Anyone able to sniff that traffic would see your password and any other information sent during the Telnet session. Secure Shell (SSH) is a much more secure way to manage your routers and switches. It is a client/server protocol that encrypts the traffic in and out through the vty ports.

Cisco routers and switches can act as SSH clients by default, but must be configured to be SSH servers. That is, they can use SSH when connecting *to* another device, but require configuration before allowing devices to connect through SSH to them. They also require some method of authenticating the client. This can be either a local username and password, or authentication with a AAA server (AAA is detailed in the next section).

There are two versions of SSH. SSH version 2 is an IETF standard that is more secure than version 1. Version 1 is more vulnerable to man-in-the-middle attacks, for example. Cisco devices support both types of connections, but you can specify which version to use.

Telnet is enabled by default, but configuring even a basic SSH server requires several steps:

**Step 1.**  Ensure that your IOS supports SSH. You need a K9 image for this.

**Step 2.**  Configure a host name, unless this was done previously.

**Step 3.**  Configure a domain name, unless this was done previously.

**Step 4.**  Configure a client authentication method.

**Step 5.**    Tell the router or switch to generate the Rivest, Shamir, and Adelman (RSA) keys that will be used to encrypt the session.

**Step 6.**    Specify the SSH version, if you want to use version 2.

**Step 7.**    Disable Telnet on the VTY lines.

**Step 8.**    Enable SSH on the VTY lines.

Example 9-4 shows a router being configured to act as an SSH server.

**Example 9-4**    *SSH Configuration*

```
router(config)# hostname R3
R3(config)# ip domain-name CCIE2B
R3(config)# username cisco password Cisco
R3(config)# crypto key generate rsa
The name for the keys will be: R3.CCIE2B
Choose the size of the key modulus in the range of 360 to 2048 for your
  General Purpose Keys. Choosing a key modulus greater than 512 may take
  a few minutes.
How many bits in the modulus [512]: 1024
% Generating 1024 bit RSA keys ...[OK]


R3(config)#
*May 22 02:06:51.923: %SSH-5-ENABLED: SSH 1.99 has been enabled
R3(config)# ip ssh version 2
!
R3(config)# line vty 0 4
R3(config-line)# transport input none
R3(config-line)# transport input ssh
R3(config-line)#^Z
!
R3# show ip ssh
SSH Enabled - version 2.0
Authentication timeout: 120 secs; Authentication retries: 3
```

## User Mode and Privileged Mode AAA Authentication

The term *authentication, authorization, and accounting (AAA)* refers to a variety of common security features. This section focuses on the first "A" in AAA—authentication—and how it is used to manage access to a router or IOS switch's user mode and privileged mode.

The strongest authentication method to protect the CLI is to use a TACACS+ or RADIUS server. The *Cisco Secure Access Control Server (ACS)* is a Cisco Systems software product that can be installed on UNIX, Linux, and several Windows platforms, holding the set of usernames and passwords used for authentication. The routers and switches then need to receive the username and password from the user, send it as encrypted traffic to the server, and receive a reply—either accepting or rejecting the user. Table 9-2 summarizes some of the key facts about RADIUS and TACACS+.

**Table 9-2**  *Comparing RADIUS and TACACS+ for Authentication*

|  | RADIUS | TACACS+ |
|---|---|---|
| Scope of Encryption: packet payload or just the password | Password only | Entire payload |
| Layer 4 Protocol | UDP | TCP |
| Well-Known Port/IOS Default Port Used for Authentication | 1812/1645[1] | 49/49 |
| Standard or Cisco-Proprietary | RFC 2865 | Proprietary |

[1] RADIUS originally defined port 1645 as the well-known port, which was later changed to port 1812.

### Using a Default Set of Authentication Methods

AAA authentication configuration includes commands by which a set of authentication methods is defined. A single *authentication method* is exactly what it sounds like—a way to authenticate a user. For example, one method is to ask a RADIUS server to authenticate a login user; another is to let a router look at a set of locally defined **username** commands. A set of configuration methods represents an ordered list of authentication methods, each of which is tried in order until one of the methods returns an authentication response, either accepting or rejecting the user.

The simplest AAA configuration defines a default set of authentication methods used for all router or switch logins, plus a second set of default authentication methods used by the **enable** command. The defined default login authentication methods apply to all login access—console, Telnet, and aux (routers only). The default authentication methods used by the **enable** command simply dictate what Cisco IOS does when a user types the **enable** command. The overall configuration uses the following general steps:

**Step 1.**  Enable AAA authentication with the **aaa new-model** global command.

**Step 2.**  If using RADIUS or TACACS+, define the IP address(es) and encryption keys used by the server(s) by using the **radius-server host**, **radius-server key**, **tacacs-server host**, and **tacacs-server key** commands.

**Step 3.**  Define the default set of authentication methods used for all CLI access by using the **aaa authentication login default** command.

**Step 4.**  Define the default set of authentication methods used for enable-mode access by using the **aaa authentication enable default** command.

Example 9-5 shows a sample router configuration using these commands. In this case, two RADIUS servers are configured. One of the servers uses the Cisco IOS default port of 1645, and the other uses the reserved well-known port 1812. Per the following configuration, this router attempts the following authentication:

■ When a login attempt is made, Cisco IOS attempts authentication using the first RADIUS server; if there's no response, IOS tries the second RADIUS server; if there's no response, the user is allowed in (authentication mode **none**).

■ When any user issues the **enable** command, the router tries the RADIUS servers, in order; if none of the RADIUS servers replies, the router will accept the single username/password configured on the router of **cisco/cisco**.

**Example 9-5** *Example AAA Configuration for Login and Enable*

```
! The next command shows that the enable secret password is still configured,
! but it will not be used. The username command defines a user/password that
! will be used for enable authentication if the RADIUS servers are not reachable.
! Note that the 0 in the username command means the password is not encrypted.
R1# show running-config
! lines omitted for brevity
enable secret 5 $1$GvDM$ux/PhTwSscDNOyNIyr5Be/
username cisco password 0 cisco
! Next, AAA is enabled, and the default enable and login authentication is
! defined.
aaa new-model
aaa authentication enable default group radius local
aaa authentication login default group radius none
! Next, the two RADIUS servers are configured. The port numbers were omitted when
! the radius-server host 10.1.1.2 command was issued, and IOS filled in its
! default. Similarly, radius-server host 10.1.1.1 auth-port 1812 was issued,
! with IOS adding the accounting port number default into the command.
radius-server host 10.1.1.1 auth-port 1812 acct-port 1646
radius-server host 10.1.1.2 auth-port 1645 acct-port 1646
radius-server key cisco
! Before adding AAA configuration, both the console and vtys had both the login
! and password commands as listed in Example 9-1. The act of enabling AAA
! deleted the login command, which now by default uses the settings on global
! command aaa authentication login default. The passwords remaining below would
! be used only if the aaa authentication login command listed a method of "line."
line con 0
 password cisco
line vty 0 4
 password cisco
```

## Using Multiple Authentication Methods

AAA authentication allows a reference to multiple servers and to multiple authentication methods so that a user can be authenticated even if one authentication method is not working. The **aaa authentication** command supports up to four methods on a single command. Additionally, there is no practical limit to the number of RADIUS or TACACS+ servers that can be referenced in a RADIUS or TACACS+ server group. The logic used by Cisco IOS when using these methods is as follows:

- Use the first listed method first; if that method does not respond, move on to the next, and then the next, and so on until a method responds. Use the first-responding-method's decision (allow or reject).

- If a method refers to a set of more than one server, try the first server, with "first" being based on the order of the commands in the configuration file. If no response, move on to the next sequential server, and so on, until a server responds. Use the first-responding-server's decision (allow or reject).

- If no response occurs for any method, reject the request.

For example, Example 9-5 listed RADIUS servers 10.1.1.1 and 10.1.1.2, in that order, so those servers would be checked in that same order. If neither replies, the next method would be used—**none** for login sessions (meaning automatically allow the user in) and **local** (meaning authenticate based on configured **username** commands).

Table 9-3 lists the authentication methods allowed for login and enable (privileged EXEC) mode, along with a brief description.

**Table 9-3**  *Authentication Methods for Login and Enable*

| Method | Meaning |
|---|---|
| **group radius** | Use the configured RADIUS servers. |
| **group tacacs+** | Use the configured TACACS+ servers. |
| **aaa group server ldap** | Defines the AAA server group with a group name and enters LDAP server group configuration mode. |
| **group** *name* | Use a defined group of either RADIUS or TACACS+ servers. |
| **enable** | Use the enable password, based on **enable secret** or **enable password** commands. |
| **line**[1] | Use the password defined by the **password** command in **line** configuration mode. |
| **local** | Use **username** commands in the local configuration; treats the username as case insensitive, but the password as case sensitive. |
| **local-case** | Use **username** commands in the local configuration; treats both the username and password as case sensitive. |
| **none** | No authentication required; user is automatically authenticated. |

[1] Cannot be used for enable authentication.

### Groups of AAA Servers

By default, Cisco IOS automatically groups RADIUS and TACACS+ servers configured with the **radius-server host** and **tacacs-server host** commands into groups, aptly named *radius* and *tacacs+*. The **aaa authentication** command includes the keywords **group radius** or **group tacacs+** to refer to these default groups. By default, all defined RADIUS servers end up in the radius group, and all defined TACACS+ servers end up in the tacacs+ group.

In some cases, particularly with larger-scale dial implementations, a design might call for the separation of different sets of RADIUS or TACACS+ servers. To do so, servers can be grouped by name. Example 9-6 shows an example configuration with two servers in a RADIUS group named fred, and shows how the **aaa authentication** command can refer to the group.

**Example 9-6**   *Configuring a RADIUS Server Group*

```
! The next three commands create RADIUS group fred. Note that the servers are
! configured inside AAA group config mode, using the server subcommand. Note that
! IOS added the auth-port and acct-port parameters automatically.
R1(config)# aaa group server radius fred
R1(config-group)# server 10.1.1.3 auth-port 1645 acct-port 1646
R1(config-group)# server 10.1.1.4 auth-port 1645 acct-port 1646
! To use group fred instead of the default group, the aaa authentication
! commands need to refer to group fred, as shown next.
aaa new-model
aaa authentication enable default group fred local
aaa authentication login default group fred none
```

### Overriding the Defaults for Login Security

The console, vty, and aux (routers only) lines can override the use of the default login authentication methods. To do so, in line configuration mode, the **login authentication** *name* command is used to point to a named set of configuration methods. Example 9-7 shows a named group of configuration methods called **for-console**, **for-vty**, and **for-aux**, with each applied to the related login method. Each of the named groups defines a different set of authentication methods. Example 9-7 shows an example that implements the following requirements:

- **console:** Try the RADIUS servers, and use the line password if no response.

- **vty:** Try the RADIUS servers, and use local usernames/passwords if no response.

- **aux:** Try the RADIUS servers, and do not authenticate if no response.

**Example 9-7**   *Overriding the Default Login Authentication Method*

```
! The configuration shown here has been added to the configuration from earlier
! examples.
aaa authentication login for-console group radius line
aaa authentication login for-vty group radius local
aaa authentication login for-aux group radius
! The methods are enabled below with the login authentication commands. Note that
! the local passwords still exist on the console and vtys; for the console,
! that password would be used (based on the line keyword in the aaa
! authentication command above) if the RADIUS servers are all nonresponsive.
! However, the vty password command would not be used by this configuration.
line con 0
 password 7 14141B180F0B
 login authentication for-console
line aux 0
 login authentication for-aux
line vty 0 4
 password 7 104D000A0618
 login authentication for-vty
```

## PPP Security

PPP provides the capability to use Password Authentication Protocol (PAP) and Challenge Handshake Authentication Protocol (CHAP) for authentication, which is particularly useful for dial applications. The default authentication method for CHAP/PAP is the reliance on a locally configured set of **username** *name* **password** *password* commands.

Cisco IOS supports the use of AAA authentication for PPP using the same general set of commands as used for login authentication. The configuration steps are as follows:

**Key Topic**

**Step 1.**   Just as with login authentication, enable AAA authentication with the **aaa new-model** global command.

**Step 2.**   Just as with login authentication, if used, configure RADIUS and/or TACACS+ servers, using the same commands and syntax as used for login and enable authentication.

**Step 3.**   Similar to login authentication, define PPP to use a default set of authentication methods with the **aaa authentication ppp default** command. (The only difference is that the **ppp** keyword is used instead of **login**.)

**Step 4.**   Similar to login authentication, use the **aaa authentication ppp** *list-name method1* [*method2...*] command to create a named group of methods that can be used instead of the default set.

**Step 5.** To use a named group of authentication methods instead of the default set, use the **ppp authentication** {*protocol1* [*protocol2...*]} *list-name* command. For example, the **ppp authentication chap fred** command references the authentication methods defined by the **aaa authentication ppp fred** command.

## Layer 2 Security

The Cisco SAFE Blueprint document (available at www.cisco.com/go/safe) suggests a wide variety of best practices for switch security. In most cases, the recommendations depend on one of three general characterizations of the switch ports, as follows:

■ **Unused ports:** Switch ports that are not yet connected to any device—for example, switch ports that are pre-cabled to a faceplate in an empty cubicle

■ **User ports:** Ports cabled to end-user devices, or any cabling drop that sits in some physically unprotected area

■ **Trusted ports or trunk ports:** Ports connected to fully trusted devices, like other switches known to be located in an area with good physical security

The following list summarizes the best practices that apply to both unused and user ports. The common element between these types of ports is that a malicious person can gain access after getting inside the building, without having to gain further access behind the locked door to a wiring closet or data center.

■ Disable unneeded dynamic protocols like Cisco Discovery Protocol (CDP) and Dynamic Trunking Protocol (DTP).

■ Disable trunking by configuring these ports as access ports.

■ Enable BPDU Guard and Root Guard to prevent STP attacks and keep a stable STP topology.

■ Use either Dynamic ARP Inspection (DAI) or private VLANs to prevent frame sniffing.

■ Enable port security to at least limit the number of allowed MAC addresses, and possibly restrict the port to use only specific MAC addresses.

■ Use 802.1X user authentication.

■ Use DHCP snooping and IP Source Guard to prevent DHCP DoS and man-in-the-middle attacks.

Besides the preceding recommendations specifically for unused ports and user ports, the Cisco SAFE Blueprint makes the following additional recommendations:

■ For any port (including trusted ports), consider the general use of private VLANs to further protect the network from sniffing, including preventing routers or L3 switches from routing packets between devices in the private VLAN.

■ Configure VTP authentication globally on each switch to prevent DoS attacks.

- Disable unused switch ports and place them in an unused VLAN.

- Avoid using VLAN 1.

- For trunks, do not use the native VLAN.

The rest of this section's coverage of switch security addresses the points in these two lists of best practices, with the next subsection focusing on best practices for unused and user ports (based on the first list), and the following subsection focusing on the general best practices for unused and user ports (based on the second list).

## Switch Security Best Practices for Unused and User Ports

The first three items in the list of best practices for unused and user ports are mostly covered in earlier chapters. For a brief review, Example 9-8 shows an example configuration on a Cisco 3560 switch, with each of these items configured and noted. In this example, fa0/1 is a currently unused port. CDP has been disabled on the interface, but it remains enabled globally, on the presumption that some ports still need CDP enabled. DTP has been disabled as well, and STP Root Guard and BPDU Guard are enabled.

**Example 9-8**   *Disabling CDP and DTP and Enabling Root Guard and BPDU Guard*

```
! The cdp run command keeps CDP enabled globally, but it has been disabled on
! fa0/1, the unused port.
cdp run
int fa0/0
 no cdp enable
! The switchport mode access interface subcommand prevents the port from trunking,
! and the switchport nonegotiate command prevents any DTP messages
! from being sent or processed.
 switchport mode access
 switchport nonegotiate
! The last two interface commands enable Root Guard and BPDU Guard, per interface,
! respectively. BPDU Guard can also be enabled for all ports with PortFast
! enabled by configuring the spanning-tree portfast bpduguard enable global
! command.
 spanning-tree guard root
 spanning-tree bpduguard enable
```

### Port Security

Switch port security monitors a port to restrict the number of MAC addresses associated with that port in the Layer 2 switching table. It can also enforce a restriction for only certain MAC addresses to be reachable out the port.

To implement port security, the switch adds more logic to its normal process of examining incoming frames. Instead of automatically adding a Layer 2 switching table entry for the source MAC and port number, the switch considers the port security configuration and whether it allows that entry. By preventing MACs from being added to the switch table, port security can prevent the switch from forwarding frames to those MACs on a port.

Port security supports the following key features:

■ Limiting the number of MACs that can be associated with the port

■ Limiting the actual MAC addresses associated with the port, based on three methods:

   ■ Static configuration of the allowed MAC addresses

   ■ Dynamic learning of MAC addresses, up to the defined maximum, where dynamic entries are lost upon reload

   ■ Dynamic learning but with the switch saving those entries in the configuration (called *sticky learning*)

Port security protects against a couple of types of attacks. After a switch's forwarding table fills, the switch times out older entries. When the switch receives frames destined for those MACs that are no longer in the table, the switch floods the frames out all ports. An attacker could cause the switch to fill its switching table by sending lots of frames, each with a different source MAC, forcing the switch to time out the entries for most of or all the legitimate hosts. As a result, the switch floods legitimate frames because the destination MACs are no longer in the content-addressable memory (CAM), allowing the attacker to see all the frames.

An attacker could also claim to be the same MAC address as a legitimate user by simply sending a frame with that same MAC address. As a result, the switch would update its switching table and send frames to the attacker, as shown in Figure 9-2.

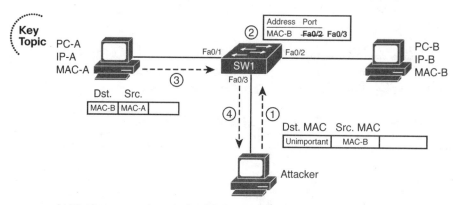

1. Attacker sources frame using PC-B's actual MAC.
2. SW1 updates its MAC address table.
3. Another frame is sent to destination MAC-B.
4. SW1 forwards frame to attacker.

**Figure 9-2**  *Claiming to Use Another Host's MAC Address*

Port security prevents both styles of these attacks by limiting the number of MAC addresses and by limiting MACs to particular ports. Port security configuration requires just a few configuration steps, all in interface mode. The commands are summarized in Table 9-4.

**Table 9-4**   *Port Security Configuration Commands*

| Command | Purpose |
|---|---|
| **switchport mode** {**access** \| **trunk**} | Port security requires that the port be statically set as either access or trunking |
| **switchport port-security** [**maximum** *value*] | Enables port security on an interface, and optionally defines the number of allowed MAC addresses on the port (default 1) |
| **switchport port-security mac-address** *mac-address* [**vlan** {*vlan-id* \| {**access** \| **voice**}} | Statically defines an allowed MAC address, for a particular VLAN (if trunking), and for either the access or voice VLAN |
| **switchport port-security mac-address sticky** | Tells the switch to remember the dynamically learned MAC addresses |
| **switchport port-security** [**aging**] [**violation** {**protect** \| **restrict** \| **shutdown**}] | Defines the Aging timer and actions taken when a violation occurs |

Of the commands in Table 9-4, only the first two are required for port security. With just those two commands, a port allows the first-learned MAC address to be used, but no others. If that MAC address times out of the CAM, another MAC address can be learned on that port, but only one is allowed at a time.

The next two commands in the table allow for the definition of MAC addresses. The third command statically defines the permitted MAC addresses, and the fourth command allows for sticky learning. Sticky learning tells the switch to learn the MACs dynamically, but then add the MACs to the running configuration. This allows port security to be enabled and the existing MAC addresses to be learned, but then have them locked into the configuration as static entries simply by saving the running configuration. (Note that the **switchport port-security maximum** *x* command would be required to allow more than one MAC address, with *x* being the maximum number.)

The last command in the table tells the switch what to do when violations occur. The *protect* option simply tells the switch to perform port security. The *restrict* option tells it to also send Simple Network Management Protocol (SNMP) traps and issue log messages regarding the violation. Finally, the *shutdown* option puts the port in an err-disabled state, and requires a **shutdown/no shutdown** combination on the port to recover the port's forwarding state.

Example 9-9 shows a sample configuration, based on Figure 9-3. In the figure, Server 1 and Server 2 are the only devices that should ever be connected to interfaces Fast Ethernet 0/1 and 0/2, respectively. In this case, a rogue device has attempted to connect to fa0/1.

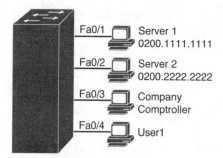

**Figure 9-3** *Port Security Configuration Example*

**Example 9-9** *Using Port Security to Define Correct MAC Addresses Connected to Particular Interfaces*

```
! FA0/1 has been configured to use a static MAC address, defaulting to allow
! only one MAC address.
interface FastEthernet0/1
 switchport mode access
 switchport port-security
 switchport port-security mac-address 0200.1111.1111
! FA0/2 has been configured to use a sticky-learned MAC address, defaulting to
! allow only one MAC address.
interface FastEthernet0/2
 switchport mode access
 switchport port-security
 switchport port-security mac-address sticky
! FA0/1 shows as err-disabled, as a device that was not 0200.1111.1111 tried to
! connect. The default violation mode is shutdown, as shown. It also lists the
! fact that a single MAC address is configured, that the maximum number of MAC
! addresses is 1, and that there are 0 sticky-learned MACs.
fred# show port-security interface fastEthernet 0/1
Port Security              : Enabled
Port Status                : Err-Disabled
Violation Mode             : Shutdown
Aging Time                 : 0 mins
Aging Type                 : Absolute
SecureStatic Address Aging : Disabled
Maximum MAC Addresses      : 1
Total MAC Addresses        : 1
Configured MAC Addresses   : 1
Sticky MAC Addresses       : 0
Last Source Address:Vlan   : f0f7.5538.f7a1:1
Security Violation Count   : 1
! FA0/2 shows as SecureUp, meaning that port security has not seen any violations
! on this port. Note also at the end of the stanza that the security violations
! count is 0. It lists the fact that one sticky MAC address has been learned.
```

```
fred# show port-security interface fastEthernet 0/2
Port Security              : Enabled
Port Status                : SecureUp
Violation Mode             : Shutdown
Aging Time                 : 0 mins
Aging Type                 : Absolute
SecureStatic Address Aging : Disabled
Maximum MAC Addresses      : 1
Total MAC Addresses        : 1
Configured MAC Addresses   : 1
Sticky MAC Addresses       : 0
Last Source Address:Vlan   : 0
Security Violation Count   : 0
Security Violation count : 0
! Note the updated configuration in the switch. Due to the sticky option, the
! switch added the last shown configuration command.
fred# show running-config
(Lines omitted for brevity)
interface FastEthernet0/2
 switchport mode access
 switchport port-security
 switchport port-security mac-address sticky
 switchport port-security mac-address sticky 0200.2222.2222
```

Key
Topic

The final part of the example shows that sticky learning updated the running configuration. The MAC address is stored in the running configuration, but it is stored in a command that also uses the **sticky** keyword, differentiating it from a truly statically configured MAC. Note that the switch does not automatically save the configuration in the startup config file.

## Dynamic ARP Inspection

A switch can use DAI to prevent certain types of attacks that leverage the use of IP Address Resolution Protocol (ARP) messages. To appreciate just how those attacks work, you must keep in mind several detailed points about the contents of ARP messages. Figure 9-4 shows a simple example with the appropriate usage of ARP messages, with PC-A finding PC-B's MAC address.

The ARP message itself does not include an IP header. However, it does include four important addressing fields: the source MAC and IP address of the sender of the message, and the target MAC and IP address. For an ARP request, the target IP lists the IP address whose MAC needs to be found, and the target MAC Address field is empty, as that is the missing information. Note that the ARP reply (a LAN unicast) uses the source MAC field to imply the MAC address value. For example, PC-B sets the source MAC inside the ARP message to its own MAC address and the source IP to its own IP address.

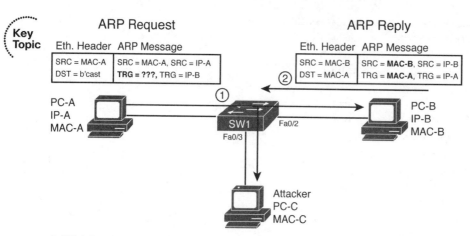

**Figure 9-4**   *Normal Use of ARP, Including Ethernet Addresses and ARP Fields*

An attacker can form a man-in-the-middle attack in a LAN by creative use of *gratuitous ARPs*. A gratuitous ARP occurs when a host sends an ARP reply, without even seeing an ARP request, and with a broadcast destination Ethernet address. The more typical ARP reply in Figure 9-4 shows the ARP reply as a unicast, meaning that only the host that sent the request will learn an ARP entry; by broadcasting the gratuitous ARP, all hosts on the LAN will learn an ARP entry.

While gratuitous ARPs can be used to good effect, they can also be used by an attacker. The attacker can send a gratuitous ARP, claiming to be an IP address of a legitimate host. All the hosts in the subnet (including routers and switches) update their ARP tables, pointing to the attacker's MAC address—and then later sending frames to the attacker instead of to the true host. Figure 9-5 depicts the process.

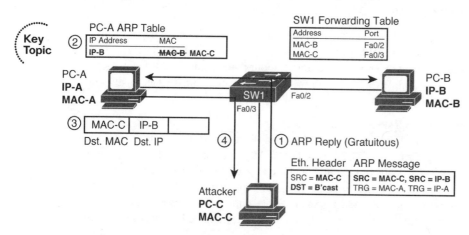

**Figure 9-5**   *Man-in-the-Middle Attack Using Gratuitous ARPs*

The steps shown in Figure 9-5 can be explained as follows:

1. The attacker broadcasts gratuitous ARP listing IP-B, but with MAC-C as the source IP and MAC.

2. PC-A updates its ARP table to list IP-B's associated address as MAC-C.

3. PC-A sends a frame to IP-B, but with destination MAC MAC-C.

4. SW1 forwards the frame to MAC-C, which is the attacker.

The attack results in other hosts, like PC-A, sending frames meant for IP-B to MAC address MAC-C—the attacker's PC. The attacker then simply forwards another copy of each frame to PC-B, becoming a man in the middle. As a result, the user can continue to work and the attacker can gain a much larger amount of data.

Switches use DAI to defeat ARP attacks by examining the ARP messages and then filtering inappropriate messages. DAI considers each switch port to be either untrusted (the default) or trusted, performing DAI messages only on untrusted ports. DAI examines each ARP request or reply (on untrusted ports) to decide whether it is inappropriate; if inappropriate, the switch filters the ARP message. DAI determines whether an ARP message is inappropriate by using the following logic:

**Key Topic**

Step 1. If an ARP reply lists a source IP address that was not DHCP-assigned to a device off that port, DAI filters the ARP reply.

Step 2. DAI uses additional logic like Step 1, but uses a list of statically defined IP/MAC address combinations for comparison.

Step 3. For a received ARP reply, DAI compares the source MAC address in the Ethernet header to the source MAC address in the ARP message. These MACs should be equal in normal ARP replies; if they are not, DAI filters the ARP message.

Step 4. Like Step 3, but DAI compares the destination Ethernet MAC and the target MAC listed in the ARP body.

Step 5. DAI checks for unexpected IP addresses listed in the ARP message, such as 0.0.0.0, 255.255.255.255, multicasts, and so on.

Table 9-5 lists the key Cisco 3560 switch commands used to enable DAI. DAI must first be enabled globally. At that point, all ports are considered to be untrusted by DAI. Some ports, particularly ports connected to devices in secure areas (ports connecting servers, other switches, and so on), need to be explicitly configured as trusted. Then, additional configuration is required to enable the different logic options. For example, DHCP snooping needs to be enabled before DAI can use the DHCP snooping binding database to perform the logic in Step 1 in the preceding list. Optionally, you can configure static IP addresses, or perform additional validation (per the last three points in the preceding list) using the **ip arp inspection validate** command.

**Key Topic**

**Table 9-5** *Cisco IOS Switch Dynamic ARP Inspection Commands*

| Command | Purpose |
|---|---|
| ip arp inspection vlan *vlan-range* | Global command to enable DAI on this switch for the specified VLANs. |
| [no] ip arp inspection trust | Interface subcommand that enables (with the **no** option) or disables DAI on the interface. Defaults to enabled after the **ip arp inspection** global command has been configured. |
| ip arp inspection filter *arp-acl-name* vlan *vlan-range* [static] | Global command to refer to an ARP ACL that defines static IP/MAC addresses to be checked by DAI for that VLAN (Step 2 in the preceding list). |
| ip arp inspection validate {[src-mac] [dst-mac] [ip]} | Enables additional optional checking of ARP messages (per Steps 3–5 in the preceding list). |
| ip arp inspection limit {rate *pps* [burst interval *seconds*] | none} | Limits the ARP message rate to prevent DoS attacks carried out by sending a large number or ARPs. |

Because DAI causes the switch to perform more work, an attacker could attempt a DoS attack on a switch by sending large numbers of ARP messages. DAI automatically sets a limit of 15 ARP messages per port per second to mitigate that risk; the settings can be changed using the **ip arp inspection limit** interface subcommand.

## DHCP Snooping

DHCP snooping prevents the damage inflicted by several attacks that use DHCP. DHCP snooping causes a switch to examine DHCP messages and filter those considered to be inappropriate. DHCP snooping also builds a table of IP address and port mappings, based on legitimate DHCP messages, called the *DHCP snooping binding table*. The DHCP snooping binding table can then be used by DAI and by the IP Source Guard feature.

Figure 9-6 shows a man-in-the-middle attack that leverages DHCP. The legitimate DHCP server sits at the main site, whereas the attacker sits on the local LAN, acting as a DHCP server.

The following steps explain how the attacker's PC can become a man in the middle in Figure 9-6:

**Step 1.** PC-B requests an IP address using DHCP.

**Step 2.** The attacker PC replies and assigns a good IP/mask, but using its own IP address as the default gateway.

**Step 3.** PC-B sends data frames to the attacker, thinking that the attacker is the default gateway.

**Step 4.** The attacker forwards copies of the packets, becoming a man in the middle.

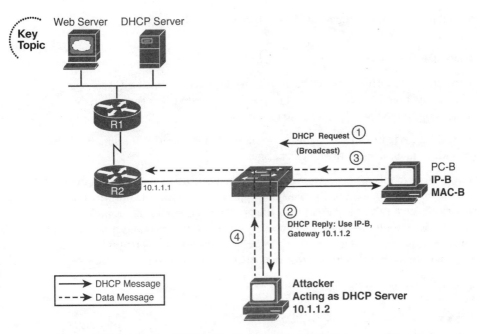

**Figure 9-6**  *Man-in-the-Middle Attack Using DHCP*

> **NOTE**  PC-B will use the first DHCP reply, so with the legitimate DHCP server only reachable over the WAN, the attacker's DHCP response should be the first response received by PC-B.

DHCP snooping defeats such attacks for ports that it considers to be untrusted. DHCP snooping allows all DHCP messages on trusted ports, but it filters DHCP messages on untrusted ports. It operates based on the premise that only DHCP clients should exist on untrusted ports; as a result, the switch filters incoming DHCP messages that are only sent by servers. So, from a design perspective, unused and unsecured user ports would be configured as untrusted to DHCP snooping.

DHCP snooping also needs to examine the DHCP client messages on untrusted ports, because other attacks can be made using DHCP client messages. DHCP servers identify clients based on their stated *client hardware address* as listed in the DHCP request. A single device could pose as multiple devices by sending repeated DHCP requests, each with a different DHCP client hardware address. The legitimate DHCP server, thinking that the requests are from different hosts, assigns an IP address for each request. The DHCP server will soon assign all IP addresses available for the subnet, preventing legitimate users from being assigned an address.

For untrusted ports, DHCP snooping uses the following general logic for filtering the packets:

**Key Topic**

1. It filters all messages sent exclusively by DHCP servers.

2. The switch checks DHCP *release* and *decline* messages against the DHCP snooping binding table. If the IP address in those messages is not listed with the port in the DHCP snooping binding table, the messages are filtered.

3. Optionally, it compares a DHCP request's client hardware address value with the source MAC address inside the Ethernet frame.

Of the three entries in this list, the first takes care of the fake DHCP server man-in-the-middle attack shown in Figure 9-6. The second item prevents an attacking host from releasing a legitimate host's DHCP lease, then attempting to request an address and be assigned the same IP address—thereby taking over any existing connections from the original host. Finally, the last item in the list prevents the DoS attack whereby a host attempts to allocate all the IP addresses that the DHCP server can assign in the subnet.

Table 9-6 lists the key configuration commands for configuring DHCP snooping on a Cisco 3560 switch.

**Table 9-6**  *Cisco IOS Switch Dynamic ARP Inspection Commands*

| Command | Purpose |
|---------|---------|
| **ip dhcp snooping vlan** *vlan-range* | Global command to enable DHCP snooping for one or more VLANs |
| [**no**] **ip dhcp snooping trust** | Interface command to enable or disable a trust level on an interface; the **no** version (enabled) is the default |
| **ip dhcp snooping binding** *mac-address* **vlan** *vlan-id ip-address* **interface** *interface-id* **expiry** *seconds* | Global command to add static entries to the DHCP snooping binding database |
| **ip dhcp snooping verify mac-address** | Interface subcommand to add the optional check of the Ethernet source MAC address to be equal to a DHCP request's client ID |
| **ip dhcp snooping limit rate** *rate* | Sets the maximum number of DHCP messages per second to mitigate DoS attacks |

## IP Source Guard

The Cisco IOS switch IP Source Guard feature adds one more check to the DHCP snooping logic. When enabled along with DHCP snooping, IP Source Guard checks the source IP address of received packets against the DHCP snooping binding database. Alternatively, it checks both the source IP and source MAC addresses against that same database. If the entries do not match, the frame is filtered.

IP Source Guard is enabled using interface subcommands. To check just the source IP address, use the **ip verify source** interface subcommand; alternatively, the **ip verify source port-security** interface subcommand enables checking of both the source IP and MAC addresses. Optionally, you can use the **ip source binding** *mac-address* **vlan** *vlan-id ip-address* **interface** *interface-id* global command to create static entries that will be used in addition to the DHCP snooping binding database.

To better appreciate this feature, consider the example DHCP snooping binding database shown in Example 9-10. DHCP snooping is enabled globally, and IP Source Guard is enabled on interface Fa0/1. Note that each of the database entries lists the MAC address and IP address, VLAN, and interface. These entries were gleaned from ports untrusted by DHCP snooping, with the DHCP snooping feature building these entries based on the source MAC address and source IP address of the DHCP requests.

**Example 9-10**  *Sample DHCP Snooping Binding Database*

```
SW1(config)# ip dhcp snooping
!
SW1(config)# interface FastEthernet0/1
SW1(config-if)# switchport access vlan 3
SW1(config-if)# ip verify source
!
SW1# show ip dhcp snooping binding
Mac Address          Ip Address        Lease(sec)  Type           VLAN  Interface
------------------   ---------------   ----------  -------------  ----  ---------------
02:00:01:02:03:04    172.16.1.1        3412        dhcp-snooping  3     FastEthernet0/1
02:00:AA:BB:CC:DD    172.16.1.2        4916        dhcp-snooping  3     FastEthernet0/2
```

Because IP Source Guard was enabled using the **ip verify source** command under interface fa0/1, the only packets allowed coming into interface fa0/1 would be those with source IP address 172.16.1.1.

### 802.1X Authentication Using EAP

Switches can use IEEE 802.1X to perform user authentication, rather than the types of device authentication performed by many of the other features described in this section. User authentication requires the user to supply a username and password, verified by a RADIUS server, before the switch will enable the switch port for normal user traffic. Requiring a username and password prevents the attacker from simply using someone else's PC to attack the network without first breaking the 802.1X authentication username and password.

IEEE 802.1X defines some of the details of LAN user authentication, but it also uses the Extensible Authentication Protocol (EAP), an Internet standard (RFC 3748), as the underlying protocol used for authentication. EAP includes the protocol messages by which the user can be challenged to provide a password, as well as flows that create one-time passwords (OTP) per RFC 2289. Figure 9-7 shows the overall flow of LAN user authentication, without the details behind each message.

 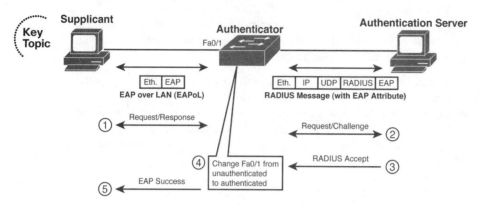

**Figure 9-7**  *802.1X for LAN User Authentication*

Figure 9-7 introduces a couple of general concepts plus several new terms. First, EAP messages are encapsulated directly inside an Ethernet frame when sent between the 802.1X *supplicant* (user device) and the 802.1X *authenticator* (switch). These frames are called *EAP over LAN (EAPoL)* frames. However, RADIUS expects the EAP message as a data structure called a *RADIUS attribute*, with these attributes sitting inside a normal RADIUS message. To support the two protocols, the switch translates between EAPoL and RADIUS for messages that need to flow between the supplicant and authentication server.

The rest of Figure 9-7 shows a simplistic view of the overall authentication flow. The switch and supplicant create an OTP using a temporary key, with the switch then forwarding the authentication request to the authentication server. The switch, as authenticator, must be aware of the results (Step 3), because the switch has a duty to enable the port after it is authenticated.

The 802.1X roles shown in Figure 9-7 are summarized as follows:

- **Supplicant:** The 802.1X driver that supplies a username/password prompt to the user and sends/receives the EAPoL messages

- **Authenticator:** Translates between EAPoL and RADIUS messages in both directions, and enables/disables ports based on the success/failure of authentication

- **Authentication server:** Stores usernames/passwords and verifies that the correct values were submitted before authenticating the user

802.1X switch configuration resembles the AAA configuration covered in the section "Using a Default Set of Authentication Methods," earlier in this chapter. The switch configuration treats 802.1X user authentication as another option for AAA authentication, using the following steps:

**Key Topic**

**Step 1.** As with other AAA authentication methods, enable AAA with the **aaa new-model** global command.

**Step 2.** As with other configurations using RADIUS servers, define the RADIUS server(s) IP address(es) and encryption key(s) using the **radius-server host** and **radius-server key** commands.

**Step 3.** Similar to login authentication configuration, define the 802.1X authentication method (RADIUS only today) using the **aaa authentication dot1x default** command or, for multiple groups, the **aaa authentication dot1x group** *name* global command.

**Step 4.** Enable 802.1X globally using the **dot1x system-auth-control** global command.

**Step 5.** Set each interface to use one of three operational settings using the **authentication port-control {auto | force-authorized | force-unauthorized}** interface subcommand:

■ Using 802.1X (**auto**)

■ Not using 802.1X, but the interface is automatically authorized (**force-authorized**) (default)

■ Not using 802.1X, but the interface is automatically unauthorized (**force-unauthorized**)

Example 9-11 shows a simple 802.1X configuration on a Cisco 3560 switch. The example shows a reasonable configuration based on Figure 9-3 earlier in the chapter, with servers off ports fa0/1 and fa0/2, and two users off ports fa0/3 and fa0/4. Also, consider fa0/5 as an unused port. Note that at the time of this writing, RADIUS is the only available authentication method for 802.1X in the Cisco 3560 switches.

**Example 9-11** *Example Cisco 3560 802.1X Configuration*

```
! The first three commands enable AAA, define that 802.1x should use the RADIUS
! group comprised of all defined RADIUS servers, and enable 802.1X globally.
aaa new-model
aaa authentication dot1x default group radius
dot1x system-auth-control
continues
! Next, commands shown previously are used to define the default radius group.
! These commands are unchanged compared to earlier examples.
radius-server host 10.1.1.1 auth-port 1812 acct-port 1646
radius-server host 10.1.1.2 auth-port 1645 acct-port 1646
radius-server key cisco
! The server ports (fa0/1 and fa0/2), inside a secure datacenter, do not require
! 802.1x authentication.
```

```
int fa0/1
 authentication port-control force-authorized
int fa0/2
 authentication port-control force-authorized
! The client ports (fa0/3 and fa0/4) require 802.1x authentication.
int fa0/3
 authentication port-control auto
int fa0/4
 authentication port-control auto
! The unused port (fa0/5) is configured to be in a permanently unauthorized
! state until the authentication port-control command is reconfigured for this
! port. As such, the port will only allow CDP, STP, and EAPoL frames.
int fa0/5
 authentication port-control force-unauthorized
```

## Storm Control

Cisco IOS for Catalyst switches supports rate-limiting traffic at Layer 2 using the **storm-control** commands. Storm control can be configured to set rising and falling thresholds for each of the three types of port traffic: unicast, multicast, and broadcast. Each rate limit can be configured on a per-port basis.

You can configure storm control to operate on each traffic type based on either packet rate or a percentage of the interface bandwidth. You can also specify rising and falling thresholds for each traffic type. If you don't specify a falling threshold, or if the falling threshold is the same as the rising threshold, the switch port will forward all traffic up to the configured limit and will not wait for that traffic to pass a specified falling threshold before forwarding it again.

When any of the configured thresholds is passed, the switch can take any of three additional actions, also on a per-port basis. The first, and the default, is that the switch can rate-limit by discarding excess traffic according to the configured command(s) and take no further action. The other two actions include performing the rate-limiting function and either shutting down the port or sending an SNMP trap.

Let's say that we have the following goals for a storm-control configuration:

- Limit broadcast traffic to 100 packets per second. When broadcast traffic drops back to 50 packets per second, begin forwarding broadcast traffic again.

- Limit multicast traffic to 0.5 percent of the 100-Mbps interface rate, or 500 kbps. When multicast traffic drops back to 400 kbps, begin forwarding multicast traffic again.

- Limit unicast traffic to 80 percent of the 100-Mbps interface rate, or 80 Mbps. Forward all unicast traffic up to this limit.

- When any of these three conditions occurs and results in rate-limiting, send an SNMP trap.

The configuration that results is shown in Example 9-12.

**Example 9-12**   *Storm Control Configuration Example*

```
Cat3560(config)# interface FastEthernet0/10
Cat3560(config-if)# storm-control broadcast level pps 100 50
Cat3560(config-if)# storm-control multicast level 0.50 0.40
Cat3560(config-if)# storm-control unicast level 80.00
Cat3560(config-if)# storm-control action trap
Cat3560(config-if)# end
Cat3560# show storm-control fa0/10 unicast
Interface  Filter State  Upper       Lower       Current
---------  ------------  ----------- ----------- ----------
Fa0/10     Forwarding    80.00%      80.00%      0.00%
Cat3560# show storm-control fa0/10 broadcast
Interface  Filter State  Upper       Lower       Current
---------  ------------  ----------- ----------- ----------
Fa0/10     Forwarding    100 pps     50 pps      0 pps
Cat3560# show storm-control fa0/10 multicast
Interface  Filter State  Upper       Lower       Current
---------  ------------  ----------- ----------- ----------
Fa0/10     Forwarding    0.50%       0.40%       0.00%
Jun 10 14:24:47.595: %STORM_CONTROL-3-FILTERED: A Multicast storm detected on
    Fa0/10. A packet filter action has been applied on the interface.
! The preceding output indicates that the multicast storm threshold was
! exceeded and the switch took the action of sending
! an SNMP trap to indicate this condition.
```

**Key Topic**

One important caveat about storm control is that it supports only physical ports. The configuration commands are available on EtherChannel (port-channel) interfaces, but they have no effect.

## General Layer 2 Security Recommendations

Recall that the beginning of the "Layer 2 Security" section, earlier in this chapter, outlined the Cisco SAFE Blueprint recommendations for user and unused ports and some general recommendations. The general recommendations include configuring VTP authentication globally on each switch, putting unused switch ports in an unused VLAN, and simply not using VLAN 1. The underlying configuration for each of these general recommendations is covered in Chapter 2, "BGP Routing Policies."

Additionally, Cisco recommends not using the native VLANs on trunks. The reason is that in some cases, an attacker on an access port might be able to hop from its access port VLAN to a trunk's native VLAN by sending frames that begin with multiple 802.1Q headers. This attack has been proven to be ineffective against Cisco switches. However, the attack takes advantage of unfortunate sequencing of programming logic in how a switch processes frames, so best practices call for not using native VLANs on trunks anyway. Simply put, by following this best practice of not using the native VLAN, even if an attacker managed to hop VLANs, if there are no devices inside that native VLAN, no damage could be inflicted. In fact, Cisco goes on to suggest using a different native VLAN for each trunk, to further restrict this type of attack.

The last general Layer 2 security recommendation covered in this chapter is to consider the use of private VLANs to further restrict traffic. As covered in Chapter 2, private VLANs restrict hosts on some ports from sending frames directly to each other. Figure 9-8 shows the allowed flows as dashed lines. The absence of a line between two devices means that private VLANs would prevent them from communicating. For example, PC1 and PC2 are not allowed to send frames to one another.

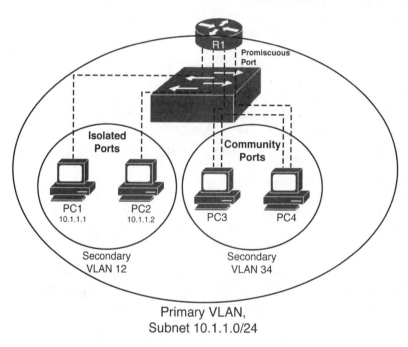

**Figure 9-8**  *Private VLAN Allowed Flows*

Private VLANs are created with some number of promiscuous ports in the primary VLAN, with other isolated and community ports in one or more secondary VLANs. Isolated ports can send frames only to promiscuous ports, whereas community ports can send frames to promiscuous ports and other community ports in the same secondary VLAN.

Private VLANs could be applied generally for better security by making user ports isolated, only allowing them access to promiscuous ports like routers, servers, or other network services. However, other, more recent additions to Cisco switches, such as DHCP snooping, DAI, and IP Source Guard, are typically better choices.

If private VLANs are used, Cisco also recommends additional protection against a trick by which an attacker can use the default gateway to overcome the protections provided by private VLANs. For example, in Figure 9-8, PC1 could send a frame with R1's destination MAC address but with PC2's destination IP address (10.1.1.2). The switch forwards the frame to R1 because R1's port is promiscuous. R1 then routes the packet to PC2, effectively getting around the private VLAN intent. To solve such a problem, the router simply needs an inbound access control list (ACL) on its LAN interface that denies traffic whose source and destination IP addresses are in the same local connected subnet. In this example, an **access-list 101 deny ip 10.1.1.0. 0.0.0.255 10.1.1.0 0.0.0.255** command would prevent this attack. (Of course, a few **permit** clauses would also be appropriate for the ACL.)

## Layer 3 Security

The Cisco SAFE Blueprint also lists several best practices for Layer 3 security. The following list summarizes the key Layer 3 security recommendations from the SAFE Blueprint:

1.  Enable secure Telnet access to a router user interface, and consider using Secure Shell (SSH) instead of Telnet.

2.  Enable SNMP security, particularly adding SNMPv3 support.

3.  Turn off all unnecessary services on the router platform.

4.  Turn on logging to provide an audit trail.

5.  Enable routing protocol authentication.

6.  Enable the CEF forwarding path to avoid using flow-based paths like fast switching.

Additionally, RFCs 2827 and 3704 outline other recommended best practices for protecting routers, Layer 3 forwarding (IP routing), and the Layer 3 control plane (routing protocols). RFC 2827 addresses issues with the use of the IP Source and Destination fields in the IP header to form some kind of attack. RFC 3704 details some issues related to how the tools of RFC 2827 can be best deployed over the Internet. Some of the details from those RFCs are as follows:

1.  If a company has registered a particular IP prefix, packets with a source address inside that prefix should not be sent into that autonomous system from the Internet.

2.  Packets should never have anything but a valid unicast source IP address, so packets with source IP addresses of loopback (127.0.0.1), 127.x.x.x, broadcast addresses, multicast addresses, and so on should be filtered.

3.  Directed (subnet) broadcasts should not be allowed unless a specific need exists.

4.  Packets for which no return route exists to the source IP address of the packet should be discarded (reverse-path-forwarding [RPF] check).

This section does not attempt to cover every portion of Layer 3 security, given the overall purpose of this book. The remainder of this chapter first provides some reference information regarding IP ACLs, which of course are often used to filter packets. This section ends with coverage of some of the more common Layer 3 attacks and how Layer 3 security can mitigate those attacks.

## IP Access Control List Review

A relatively deep knowledge of IP ACL configuration and use is assumed to be prerequisite knowledge for readers of this book. In fact, many of the examples in the earlier sections of the book did not take the space required to explain the detailed logic of ACLs used in the examples. However, some reference information, as well as statements regarding some of the rules and practices regarding IP ACLs, is useful for general CCIE Routing and Switching exam study. Those details are presented in this section.

First, Table 9-7 lists the majority of the Cisco IOS commands related to IP ACLs.

**Table 9-7**   *IP ACL Command Reference*

| Command | Configuration Mode and Description |
| --- | --- |
| **access-list** *access-list-number* {**deny** \| **permit**} *source* [*source-wildcard*] [**log**] | Global command for standard numbered access lists. |
| **access-list** *access-list-number* [**dynamic** *dynamic-name* [**timeout** *minutes*]] {**deny** \| **permit**} *protocol source source-wildcard destination destination-wildcard* [**precedence** *precedence*] [**tos** *tos*] [**log** \| **log-input**] [**time-range** *time-range-name*] [**fragments**] | Generic syntax used with a wide variety of protocols. The options beginning with **precedence** are also included for TCP, UDP, and ICMP. |
| **access-list** *access-list-number* [**dynamic** *dynamic-name* [**timeout** *minutes*]] {**deny** \| **permit**} **tcp** *source source-wildcard* [*operator* [*port*]] *destination destination-wildcard* [*operator* [*port*]] [**established**] | Version of **access-list** command with TCP-specific parameters; identical options exist for UDP, except for the **established** keyword. |
| **access-list** *access-list-number* {**deny** \| **permit**} **icmp** *source source-wildcard destination destination-wildcard* [*icmp-type* [*icmp-code*] \| *icmp-message*] | Version of **access-list** command to match ICMP packets. |
| **access-list** *access-list-number* **remark** *text* | Defines a remark. |
| **ip access-list** {**standard** \| **extended**} *access-list-name* | Global command to create a named ACL. |
| [*sequence-number*] **permit** \| **deny** *protocol source source-wildcard destination destination-wildcard* [**precedence** *precedence*] [**tos** *tos*] [**log** \| **log-input**] [**time-range** *time-range-name*] [**fragments**] | Named ACL subcommand used to define an individual entry in the list; similar options for TCP, UDP, ICMP, and others. |

| Command | Configuration Mode and Description |
|---|---|
| ip access-group {*number* \| *name* [in \| out]} | Interface subcommand to enable access lists. |
| access-class *number* \| *name* [in \| out] | Line subcommand for standard or extended access lists. |
| ip access-list resequence *access-list-name starting-sequence-number increment* | Global command to redefine sequence numbers for a crowded ACL. |
| show ip interface [*type number*] | Includes a reference to the access lists enabled on the interface. |
| show access-lists [*access-list-number* \| *access-list-name*] | Shows details of configured access lists for all protocols. |
| show ip access-list [*access-list-number* \| *access-list-name*] | Shows IP access lists. |

## ACL Rule Summary

Cisco IOS processes the *Access Control Entries (ACE)* of an ACL sequentially, either permitting or denying a packet based on the first ACE matched by that packet in the ACL. For an individual ACE, all the configured values must match before the ACE is considered a match. Table 9-8 lists several examples of named IP ACL **permit** and **deny** commands that create an individual ACE, along with their meanings.

**Key Topic**

**Table 9-8**   *Examples of ACL ACE Logic and Syntax*

| Access List Statement | What It Matches |
|---|---|
| deny ip any host 10.1.1.1 | IP packets with any source IP and destination IP = 10.1.1.1 only. |
| deny tcp any gt 1023 host 10.1.1.1 eq 23 | IP packets with a TCP header, with any source IP, a source TCP port greater than (**gt**) 1023, plus a destination IP of 10.1.1.1 and a destination TCP port of 23. |
| deny tcp any host 10.1.1.1 eq 23 | Same as previous example except that any source port matches, as that parameter was omitted. |
| deny tcp any host 10.1.1.1 eq telnet | Same results as the previous example; the syntax uses the **telnet** keyword instead of port 23. |
| deny udp 1.0.0.0 0.255.255.255 lt 1023 any | A packet with a source address in network 1.0.0.0/8, using UDP with a source port less than 1023, with any destination IP address. |

The Port Number field is only matchable when the protocol type in an extended IP ACL ACE is UDP or TCP. In these cases, the port number is positional in that the source port matching parameter occurs right after the source IP address, and the destination port parameter occurs right after the destination IP address. Several examples were included in Table 9-8. Table 9-9 summarizes the matching logic used to match UDP and TCP ports.

**Table 9-9**  *IP ACE Port Matching*

| Keyword | Meaning |
| --- | --- |
| gt | Greater than |
| lt | Less than |
| eq | Equals |
| ne | Not equal |
| range x-y | Range of port numbers, inclusive |

ICMP does not use port numbers, but it does include different message types, and some of those even include a further message code. The IP ACL commands allow these to be matched using a rather long list of keywords, or with the numeric message type and message code. Note that these parameters are also positional, following the destination IP address. For example, the named ACL command **permit icmp any any echo-reply** is correct, but the command **permit icmp any echo-reply any** is syntactically incorrect and would be rejected.

Several other parameters can also be checked. For example, the IP precedence bits can be checked, as well as the entire ToS byte. The **established** parameter matches if the TCP header has the ACK flag set—indicative of any TCP segment except the first segment of a new connection setup. (The **established** keyword will be used in an example later in the chapter.) Also, the **log** and **log-input** keywords can be used to tell Cisco IOS to generate periodic log messages when the ACE is matched—one message on initial match and one every 5 minutes afterward. The **log-input** option includes more information than the **log** option, specifically information about the incoming interface of the packet that matched the ACE.

For ACL configuration, several facts need to be kept in mind. First, standard ACLs can only match the source IP address field. Numbered standard ACLs are identified with ACL numbers of either 1–99 or 1300–1999, inclusive. Extended numbered IP ACLs range from 100 to 199 and 2000 to 2699, again inclusive. Additionally, newly configured ACEs in numbered IP ACLs are always added at the end of the existing ACL, and ACEs in numbered IP ACLs cannot be deleted one at a time. As a result, to insert a line into the middle of a numbered ACL, the entire numbered ACL might need to be deleted (using the **no access-list** *number* global command) and then reconfigured. Named ACLs overcome that problem by using an implied or explicit sequence number, with Cisco IOS listing and processing the ACEs in an ACL in sequence number order.

### Wildcard Masks

ACEs use *wildcard masks* (WC masks) to define the portion of the IP address that should be examined. WC masks represent a 32-bit number, with the mask's 0 bits telling Cisco IOS that those corresponding bits in the IP address must be compared when performing the matching logic. The binary 1s in the WC mask tell Cisco IOS that those bits do not need to be compared; as a result, these bits are often called "don't care" bits. Table 9-10 lists several example WC masks and the implied meanings.

**Table 9-10**  *Sample Access List Wildcard Masks*

| Wildcard Mask | Description |
| --- | --- |
| 0.0.0.0 | The entire IP address must match. |
| 0.0.0.255 | Just the first 24 bits must match. |
| 0.0.255.255 | Just the first 16 bits must match. |
| 0.255.255.255 | Just the first 8 bits must match. |
| 255.255.255.255 | Automatically considered to match because all 32 bits are "don't care" bits. |
| 0.0.15.255 | Just the first 20 bits must match. |
| 0.0.3.255 | Just the first 22 bits must match. |
| 17.44.97.33 | A valid WC mask, it means match all bits except bits 4, 8, 11, 13, 14, 18, 19, 24, 27, and 32. |

That last entry is unlikely to be useful in an actual production network, but unlike IP subnet masks, the WC mask does not have to list a single unbroken set of 0s and another unbroken string of 1s. A much more likely WC mask is one that matches a particular mask or prefix length. To find a WC mask to match hosts in a known prefix, use the following simple math: In decimal, subtract the subnet mask from 255.255.255.255. The result is the "right" WC mask to match that prefix length. For example, a subnet mask of 255.255.255.0, subtracted from 255.255.255.255, gives you 0.0.0.255 as a WC mask. This mask only checks the first 24 bits—which in this case is the network and subnet part of the address. Similarly, if the subnet mask is 255.255.240.0, subtracting from 255.255.255.255 gives you 0.0.15.255.

## General Layer 3 Security Considerations

This section explains a few of the more common ways to avoid Layer 3 attacks.

### Smurf Attacks, Directed Broadcasts, and RPF Checks

A smurf attack occurs when a host sends a large number of ICMP Echo Requests with some atypical IP addresses in the packet. The destination address is a *subnet broadcast address*, also known as a *directed broadcast address*. Routers forward these packets based on normal matching of the IP routing table, until the packet reaches a router connected to the destination subnet. This final router then forwards the packet onto the LAN as a LAN broadcast, sending a copy to every device. Figure 9-9 shows how the attack develops.

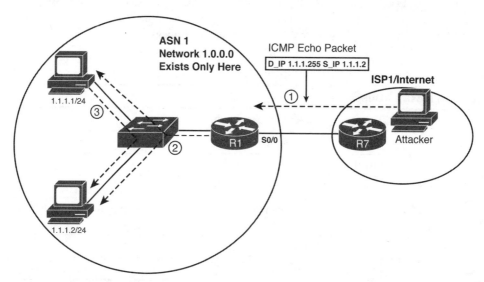

1. Attacker sends packet destined to subnet broadcast, source 1.1.1.2 (for secondary attack).
2. R1 forwards packet as LAN broadcast.
3. R1 replies with ICMP echo reply packet sent to 1.1.1.2.

**Figure 9-9**  *Smurf Attack*

The other feature of a smurf attack is that the source IP address of the packet sent by the attacker is the IP address of the attacked host. For example, in Figure 9-9, many hosts can receive the ICMP Echo Request at Step 2. All those hosts then reply with an Echo Reply, sending it to 10.1.1.2—the address that was the source IP address of the original ICMP Echo at Step 1. Host 10.1.1.2 receives a potentially large number of packets.

Several solutions to this problem exist. First, as of Cisco IOS Software Release 12.0, IOS defaults each interface to use the **no ip directed-broadcast** command, which prevents the router from forwarding the broadcast onto the LAN (Step 2 in Figure 9-9). Also, a unicast Reverse-Path-Forwarding (uRPF) check could be enabled using the **ip verify unicast source reachable-via** {**rx** | **any**} [**allow-default**] [**allow-self-ping**] [*list*] interface subcommand. This command tells Cisco IOS to examine the source IP address of incoming packets on that interface. (Cisco Express Forwarding [CEF] must be enabled for uRPF to work.) Two styles of check can be made with this command:

■ **Strict RPF:** Using the **rx** keyword, the router checks to see whether the matching route uses an outgoing interface that is the same interface on which the packet was received. If not, the packet is discarded. (An example scenario using Figure 9-9 will be explained shortly.)

- **Loose RPF:** Using the **any** keyword, the router checks for any route that can be used to reach the source IP address.

The command can also ignore default routes when it performs the check (default) or use default routes when performing the check by including the **allow-default** keyword. Also, although not recommended, the command can trigger a ping to the source to verify connectivity. Finally, the addresses for which the RPF check is made can be limited by a referenced ACL. In the following example, both CEF and uRPF are enabled on R1 in Figure 9-9:

```
R1(config)# ip cef
R1(config)# int s 0/0
R1(config-if)# ip verify unicast source reachable-via rx allow-default
```

Now, because R1 in Figure 9-9 uses strict uRPF on s0/0, it would notice that its route to reach 1.1.1.2 (the source IP address of the packet at Step 1) did not refer to s0/0 as the outgoing interface—thereby discarding the packet. However, with loose RPF, R1 would have found a connected route that matched 1.1.1.2, so it would have allowed the packet through. Finally, given that AS1 should never receive packets with source addresses in network 1.0.0.0, as it owns that entire class A network, R1 could simply use an inbound ACL to discard any packets sourced from 1.0.0.0/8 as they enter s0/0 from the Internet.

Fraggle attacks use similar logic as smurf attacks, but instead of ICMP, fraggle attacks use the UDP Echo application. These attacks can be defeated using the same options as listed for smurf attacks.

## Inappropriate IP Addresses

Besides smurf and fraggle attacks, other attacks involve the use of what can be generally termed inappropriate IP addresses, both for the source IP address and destination IP address. By using inappropriate IP addresses, the attacker can remain hidden and elicit cooperation of other hosts to create a distributed denial of service (DDoS) attack.

One of the Layer 3 security best practices is to use ACLs to filter packets whose IP addresses are not appropriate. For example, the smurf attack listed a valid source IP address of 1.1.1.2, but packets with that source address should never enter AS1 from the Internet. The Internet Assigned Numbers Authority (IANA) manages the assignment of IP prefix ranges. It lists the assigned ranges in a document found at www.iana.org/assignments/ipv4-address-space. A router can then be configured with ACLs that prevent packets based on known assigned ranges and on known unassigned ranges. For example, in Figure 9-9, an enterprise router should never need to forward a packet onto the Internet if that packet has a source IP address from another company's registered IP prefix. In the smurf attack case, such an ACL used at the attacker's ISP would have prevented the first packet from getting to AS1.

Routers should also filter packets that use IP addresses that should be considered bogus or inappropriate. For example, a packet should never have a broadcast or multicast source IP address in normal use. Also, an enterprise router should never receive a packet from an ISP with that packet's source IP address being a private network per RFC 1918. Additionally, that same router should not receive packets sourced from IP addresses in ranges currently unallocated by IANA. These types of IP addresses are frequently called *bogons*, which is a derivation of the word bogus.

Creating an ACL to match these bogon IP addresses is not particularly difficult, but it does require a lot of administrative effort, particularly to update it based on changes to IANA's assigned prefixes. You can use freeware called the Router Audit Tool (RAT) that makes recommendations for router security, including bogon ACLs. You can also use the Cisco IOS *AutoSecure* feature, which automatically configures ACLs to prevent the use of such bogus IP addresses.

### TCP SYN Flood, the Established Bit, and TCP Intercept

A TCP SYN flood is an attack directed at servers by initiating large numbers of TCP connections, but not completing the connections. Essentially, the attacker initiates many TCP connections, each with only the TCP SYN flag set, as usual. The server then sends a reply (with TCP SYN and ACK flags set)—but then the attacker simply does not reply with the expected third message in the three-way TCP connection setup flow. The server consumes memory and resources while waiting on its timeouts to occur before clearing up the partially initialized connections. The server might also reject additional TCP connections, and load balancers in front of a server farm might unbalance the load of actual working connections as well.

Stateful firewalls can prevent TCP SYN attacks. Both the Cisco ASA Firewall and the Cisco IOS Firewall feature set (discussed in the next section) can be used to do this. The impact of TCP SYN attacks can be reduced or eliminated by using a few other tools in Cisco IOS.

One way to prevent SYN attacks is to simply filter packets whose TCP header shows only the SYN flag set—in other words, filter all packets that are the first packet in a new TCP connection. In many cases, a router should not allow TCP connections to be established by a client on one side to a server on the other, as shown in Figure 9-10. In these cases, filtering the initial TCP segment prevents the SYN attack.

Cisco IOS ACLs cannot directly match the TCP SYN flag. However, an ACE can use the **established** keyword, which matches TCP segments that have the ACK flag set. The **established** keyword essentially matches all TCP segments except the very first TCP segment in a new connection. Example 9-13 shows the configuration that would be used on R1 to deny new connection requests from the Internet into the network on the left.

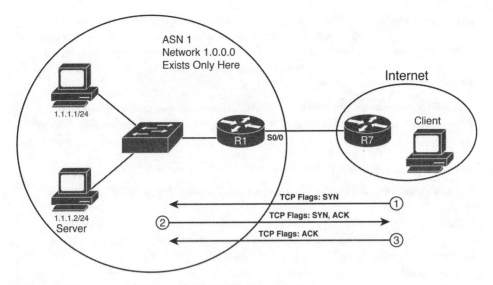

**Figure 9-10**   *Example Network: TCP Clients in the Internet*

**Example 9-13**   *Using an ACL with the* established *Keyword*

```
! The first ACE matches TCP segments that are not the first segment, and permits
! them. The second ACE matches all TCP segments between the same set of IP
! addresses, but because all non-initial segments have already been matched, the
! second ACE only matches the initial segments.
ip access-list extended prevent-syn
 permit tcp any 1.0.0.0 0.255.255.255 established
 deny tcp any 1.0.0.0 0.255.255.255
 permit (whatever)
!
interface s0/0
 ip access-group prevent-syn in
```

The ACL works well when clients outside a network are not allowed to make TCP connections into the network. However, in cases where some inbound TCP connections are allowed, this ACL cannot be used. Another Cisco IOS feature, called *TCP intercept*, provides an alternative that allows TCP connections into the network, but monitors those TCP connections for TCP SYN attacks.

TCP intercept operates in one of two different modes. In *watch mode*, it keeps state information about TCP connections that match a defined ACL. If a TCP connection does not complete the three-way handshake within a particular time period, TCP intercept sends a TCP reset to the server, cleaning up the connection. It also counts the number of new connections attempted over time, and if a large number occurs in 1 second ("large" defaulting to 1100), the router temporarily filters new TCP requests to prevent a perceived SYN attack.

In *intercept mode*, the router replies to TCP connection requests instead of forwarding them to the actual server. Then, if the three-way handshake completes, the router creates a TCP connection between itself and the server. At that point, the router knits the two connections together. This takes more processing and effort, but it provides better protection for the servers.

Example 9-14 shows an example using TCP intercept configuration, in watch mode, plus a few changes to its default settings. The example allows connections from the Internet into AS1 in Figure 9-10.

**Example 9-14**   *Configuring TCP Intercept*

```
! The following command enables TCP intercept for packets matching ACL
! match-tcp-from-internet. Also, the mode is set to watch, rather than the
! default of intercept. Finally, the watch timeout has been reset from the
! default of 30 seconds; if the TCP connection remains incomplete as of the
! 20-second mark, TCP intercept resets the connection.
ip tcp intercept list match-tcp-from-internet
ip tcp intercept mode watch
ip tcp intercept watch-timeout 20
! The ACL matches packets sent into 1.0.0.0/8 that are TCP. It is referenced by
! the ip tcp intercept-list command listed above.
ip access-list extended match-tcp-from-internet
 permit tcp any 1.0.0.0 0.255.255.255
! Note below that the ACL is not enabled on any interfaces.
interface s0/0
! Note: there is no ACL enabled on the interface!
```

## Classic Cisco IOS Firewall

In some cases, access-list filtering might be enough to control and secure a router interface. However, as attackers have become more sophisticated, Cisco has developed better tools to deal with threats. The challenge, as always, is to make security features relatively transparent to network users while thwarting attackers. The Cisco IOS Firewall is one of those tools.

The classic IOS Firewall relies on *Context-Based Access Control (CBAC)*. CBAC is a function of the firewall feature set in Cisco IOS. It takes access-list filtering a step or two further by providing dynamic inspection of traffic that you specify as it traverses the router. It does this based on actual protocol commands, such as the FTP **get** command—not simply on Layer 4 port numbers. Based on where the traffic originates, CBAC decides what traffic should be permitted to cross the firewall. When it sees a session initiate on the trusted network for a particular protocol, which would normally be blocked inbound based on other filtering methods, CBAC creates temporary openings in the firewall to permit the corresponding inbound traffic to enter from the untrusted network. It permits only the desired traffic, rather than opening the firewall to all traffic for a particular protocol.

CBAC works on TCP and UDP traffic, and it supports protocols such as FTP that require multiple, simultaneous sessions or connections. You would typically use CBAC to protect your internal network from external threats by configuring it to inspect inbound traffic from the outside world for those protocols. With CBAC, you configure the following:

- Protocols to inspect

- Interfaces on which to perform the inspection

- Direction of the traffic to inspect, per interface

### TCP Versus UDP with CBAC

TCP has clear-cut connections, so CBAC (and other stateful inspection and filtering methods) can handle it rather easily. However, CBAC works at a deeper level than simply protocols and port numbers. For example, with FTP traffic, CBAC recognizes and inspects the specific FTP control-channel commands to decide when to open and close the temporary firewall openings.

By comparison to TCP, UDP traffic is connectionless and therefore more difficult to handle. CBAC manages UDP by approximating based on factors such as whether the source and destination addresses and ports of UDP frames are the same as those that came recently, and their relative timing. You can configure a global idle timeout that CBAC uses to determine whether a segment arrived "close enough" in time to be considered part of the same flow. You can also configure other timeouts, including protocol-specific timeouts for TCP and UDP traffic.

### Cisco IOS Firewall Protocol Support

When using CBAC, an IOS firewall can inspect a long list of protocols, and more are added over time. Common protocols that CBAC can inspect include the following:

- Any generic TCP session, regardless of application layer protocol

- All UDP "sessions"

- FTP

- SMTP

- TFTP

- H.323 (NetMeeting, ProShare, and so on)

- Java

- CU-SeeMe

- UNIX R commands (**rlogin**, **rexec**, **rsh**, and so on)

- RealAudio

- Sun RPC

- SQL*Net

- StreamWorks

- VDOLive

## Cisco IOS Firewall Caveats

As powerful as CBAC is for dynamic inspection and filtering, however, it has some limitations. You should be aware of a few restrictions and caveats about how CBAC works:

- CBAC comes after access-list filters are applied to an interface. If an access list blocks a particular type of traffic on an interface where you are using CBAC to inspect inbound traffic, that traffic will be denied before CBAC sees it.

- CBAC cannot protect against attacks that originate inside your network, where most attacks originate.

- CBAC works only on protocols that you specify it should inspect, leaving all other filtering to access lists and other filtering methods.

- To inspect traffic other than TCP- and UDP-transported traffic, you must configure a named inspection rule.

- CBAC does not inspect traffic destined to or originated from the firewall router itself, only traffic that traverses the firewall router.

- CBAC has restrictions on handling encrypted traffic. See the link in the "Further Reading" section, later in this chapter, for more details.

## Cisco IOS Firewall Configuration Steps

Although configuring CBAC is not difficult, it does involve several steps, which are as follows:

**Step 1.** Choose an interface ("inside" or "outside").

**Step 2.** Configure an IP access list that denies all traffic to be inspected.

**Step 3.** Configure global timeouts and thresholds using the **ip inspect** commands.

**Step 4.** Define an inspection rule and an optional rule-specific timeout value using the **ip inspect name** *protocol* commands, for example, **ip inspect name actionjackson ftp timeout 3600.**

**Step 5.** Apply the inspection rule to an interface, for example, in interface configuration mode, **ip inspect actionjackson in.**

**Step 6.** Apply the access list to the same interface as the inspection rule, but in the opposite direction (inbound or outbound.)

Example 9-15 shows a router with one interface into the internal network and one interface into the external network. CBAC will be used on the external interface. This router has been configured to inspect all ICMP, TCP, and UDP traffic, using the inspection list CLASSIC_FW. TCP and UDP sessions will time out after 30 seconds, but ICMP sessions will time out after only 10 seconds. The access list IOS_FW permits routing traffic but denies all traffic that will be inspected by CBAC. The inspection rule is applied to the external interface, outbound. The access list is applied to that same interface, inbound. All TCP, UDP, and ICMP traffic bound out of the serial interface toward a host in the external network will be tracked. If an answering packet arrives, it will be allowed through via a dynamic entry in access list IOS_FW. Any external hosts that try to establish a session with an internal host will be blocked by access list IOS_FW, however.

The IOS firewall's operation is verified with the **show ip inspect sessions** command. Note that one Telnet session has been established.

**Example 9-15** *Configuring Classic IOS Firewall with CBAC*

```
ip inspect name CLASSIC_FW icmp timeout 10
ip inspect name CLASSIC_FW tcp timeout 30
ip inspect name CLASSIC_FW udp timeout 30
!
ip access-list extended IOS_FW
 permit eigrp any any
 deny    tcp any any
 deny    udp any any
 deny    icmp any any
!
interface Serial0/0
 ip address 192.168.1.3 255.255.255.0
 ip access-group IOS_FW in
 ip inspect CLASSIC_FW out
!
R2# show ip inspect sessions
Established Sessions
 Session 47699CFC (10.1.1.2:11003)=>(172.16.1.10:23) tcp SIS_OPEN
```

CBAC is a powerful IOS firewall feature set option that you should understand at the functional level before attempting the CCIE Routing and Switching qualifying exam. See the "Further Reading" section, later in this chapter, for a link to more information and configuration details on CBAC.

## Cisco IOS Zone-Based Firewall

You can see from Example 9-15 that configuring even a simple classic IOS firewall can be complex. Also, classic IOS inspection policies apply to all traffic on the interface; you can't apply different policies to different groups of users.

Zone-based firewall (ZFW), available in IOS Release 12.4(6)T or later, changes that. The concept behind zone-based firewalls is similar to that used by appliance firewalls. Router interfaces are placed into security zones. Traffic can travel freely between interfaces in the same zone, but is blocked by default from traveling between zones. Traffic is also blocked between interfaces that have been assigned to a security zone and those that have not. You must explicitly apply a policy to allow traffic between zones. Zone policies are configured using the Class-Based Policy Language (CPL), which is similar to the Modular QoS Command-Line Interface (MQC) in its use of class maps and policy maps. Class maps let you configure highly granular policies if needed. A new class and policy map type, the *inspect* type, is introduced for use with zone-based firewalls.

> **NOTE** The MQC, class maps, and policy maps are explained in Chapter 3, "Classification and Marking."

ZFW enables the inspection and control of multiple protocols, including the following:

- HTTP and HTTPS

- SMTP, Extended SMTP (ESMTP), POP3, and IMAP

- Peer-to-peer applications, with the ability to use heuristics to track port hopping

- Instant-messaging applications (AOL, Yahoo!, and MSN as of this writing)

- Remote Procedure Calls (RPC)

Follow these steps to configure ZFW:

**Step 1.** Decide the zones you will need, and create them on the router.

**Step 2.** Decide how traffic should travel between the zones, and create zone-pairs on the router.

**Step 3.** Create class maps to identify the interzone traffic that must be inspected by the firewall.

**Step 4.** Assign policies to the traffic by creating policy maps and associating class maps with them.

**Step 5.** Assign the policy maps to the appropriate zone-pair.

**Step 6.** Assign interfaces to zones. An interface can be assigned to only one security zone.

To help you understand these steps, consider the network shown in Figure 9-11. Router Branch1 has two interfaces: a serial WAN interface and an Ethernet LAN interface. This is a simple example but one common in small branch offices where an IOS firewall might be used. The LAN interface will be placed in one zone, the LAN zone, and the WAN interface will be placed into the WAN zone.

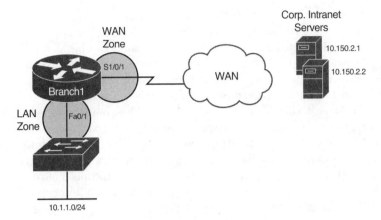

**Figure 9-11**  *Cisco IOS Zone-Based Firewall*

In this example, the network administrators have decided to apply the following policies to traffic from the LAN zone going through the WAN zone:

■  Only traffic from the LAN subnet is allowed.

■  HTTP traffic to corporate web-based intranet servers is allowed.

■  All other HTTP traffic is allowed but policed to 1 Mbps.

■  ICMP is blocked.

■  For all other traffic, the TCP and UDP timeouts must be lowered to 300 seconds.

For traffic initiated in the WAN zone and destined for the LAN zone, only SSH from the corporate management network is allowed.

So, you can see that you must configure two zones: LAN and WAN. The router automatically creates a zone for traffic to itself, called the *self zone*. By default, all traffic is allowed to and from this zone, but that can be configured. In this example, firewall policies will be applied to traffic from the LAN to the WAN zone, and also to traffic from the WAN to the LAN zone. Therefore, you need two zone pairs: LAN-to-WAN and WAN-to-LAN. To configure zones, use the global command **zone security** *name*. To configure zone pairs, use the global command **zone-pair security** *name* **source** *source-zone-name* **destination** *destination-zone-name*. Example 9-16 shows Steps 1 and 2: the zone and zone pair configuration.

**Example 9-16**  *Configuring ZFW Zones and Zone Pairs*

```
Branch1(config)# zone security LAN
Branch1(config-sec-zone)# description LAN zone
!
Branch1(config)# zone security WAN
Branch1(config-sec-zone)# description WAN zone
!
Branch1(config)# zone-pair security Internal source LAN destination WAN
Branch1(config)# zone-pair security External source WAN destination LAN
```

The next step is to create class maps to identify the traffic. Four class maps will be needed: three for the specific types of traffic that will have custom policies and one for all other traffic from the LAN. The router automatically creates a default class, but all traffic in this class is dropped. Example 9-17 shows access lists LAN_Subnet, which permits all traffic from the LAN subnet, and Web_Servers, which permits traffic to the corporate intranet web servers. Note that class map Corp_Servers matches both the access list Web_Servers and the HTTP protocol with a **match-all** statement. Thus, both the access list and the protocol type must be matched for the class map to have a hit. Likewise, class map Other_HTTP matches both the HTTP protocol and access list LAN_Subnet to permit only HTTP traffic from the local subnet. Class map ICMP matches only the ICMP protocol; because that traffic will be dropped, there is no need to have the router also check the source IP address. The router will use Network-Based Application Recognition (NBAR) to match HTTP and ICMP traffic.

**Example 9-17** *Configuring ZFW Class Maps*

```
Branch1(config)# ip access-list extended LAN_Subnet
Branch1(config-ext-nacl)# permit ip 10.1.1.0 0.0.0.255 any
!
Branch1(config-ext-nacl)# ip access-list extended Web_Servers
Branch1(config-ext-nacl)# permit tcp 10.1.1.0 0.0.0.255 host 10.150.2.1
Branch1(config-ext-nacl)# permit tcp 10.1.1.0 0.0.0.255 host 10.150.2.2
!
Branch1(config-ext-nacl)# class-map type inspect match-all Corp_Servers
Branch1(config-cmap)# match access-group name Web_Servers
Branch1(config-cmap)# match protocol http
!
Branch1(config-cmap)# class-map type inspect Other_HTTP
Branch1(config-cmap)# match protocol http
Branch1(config-cmap)# match access-group name LAN_Subnet
!
Branch1(config-cmap)# class-map type inspect ICMP
Branch1(config-cmap)# match protocol icmp
!
Branch1(config-cmap)# class-map type inspect Other_Traffic
Branch1(config-cmap)# match access-group name LAN_Subnet
```

In Step 4, the previously created class maps are associated with policy maps. ZFW policy maps can take the following actions under each class:

- **Drop:** Drop the packet
- **Inspect:** Use Context-Based Access Control Engine
- **Pass:** Pass the packet
- **Police:** Police the traffic

- **Service-policy:** Use Deep Packet Inspection Engine

- **Urlfilter:** Use URL Filtering Engine

Recall that the TCP and UDP timers needed to be reduced to 300 seconds for the general network traffic. This is done through a parameter map. A parameter map modifies the traffic inspection behavior for a specific class in a policy map. In Example 9-18, the parameter map Timeouts sets the TCP and UDP idle timeouts to 300 seconds. Parameter maps can also set alerts and audit trails, and they control other session parameters such as number of half-open sessions. The policy map LAN2WAN associates all the class maps created so far, and applies the parameter map to the Other_Traffic class. It also polices Other_HTTP traffic to 1 Mbps with a burst rate of 8 KBps. Note that policy map configuration also uses the **type inspect** keywords.

**Example 9-18**  *Configuring ZFW Parameter Maps and Policy Maps*

```
Branch1(config)# parameter-map type inspect Timeouts
Branch1(config-profile)# tcp idle-time 300
Branch1(config-profile)# udp idle-time 300
!
Branch1(config-profile)# policy-map type inspect LAN2WAN
Branch1(config-pmap)# class type inspect Corp_Servers
Branch1(config-pmap-c)# inspect
!
Branch1(config-pmap-c)# class type inspect Other_HTTP
Branch1(config-pmap-c)# inspect
Branch1(config-pmap-c)# police rate 1000000 burst 8000
!
Branch1(config-pmap-c)# class type inspect ICMP
Branch1(config-pmap-c)# drop
!
Branch1(config-pmap-c)# class type inspect Other_Traffic
Branch1(config-pmap-c)# inspect Timeouts
%No specific protocol configured in class Other_Traffic for inspection. All
   protocols will be inspected
```

In Step 5, now that the policy is created, it must be assigned to a zone pair. This is analogous to assigning a service policy to an interface in the MQC. The command is **service-policy type inspect** *policy-map-name*, given under the zone pair configuration mode.

The final step, Step 6, is to assign the router interfaces to their appropriate zones. To do this, issue the command **zone-member security** *zone-name* in interface configuration mode. Looking back at Figure 9-11, you see that interface FastEthernet 0/1 connects to the LAN and interface Serial 1/0/1 connects to the WAN. Example 9-19 shows how the service policy is assigned to a zone pair, and the two interfaces are assigned to zones.

**Example 9-19**  *Assigning ZFW Service Policies and Zones*

```
Branch1(config)# zone-pair security Internal source LAN destination WAN
Branch1(config-sec-zone-pair)# service-policy type inspect LAN2WAN
Branch1(config-sec-zone-pair)# exit
!
Branch1(config)# interface fa 0/1
Branch1(config-if)# zone-member security LAN
!
Branch1(config-if)# interface s1/0/1
Branch1(config-if)# zone-member security WAN
!
!Verify the configuration
Branch1# show zone-pair security
Zone-pair name Internal
    Source-Zone LAN  Destination-Zone WAN
    service-policy LAN2WAN
Zone-pair name External
    Source-Zone WAN  Destination-Zone LAN
    service-policy not configured
```

So far you have seen some fairly complex firewall policies created and applied to traffic bound from the local LAN to the WAN. At this point, only responses can reach into the LAN. Another class map and service policy would need to be created to allow SSH sessions to be initiated from the WAN into the LAN. Then the policy map would be applied to the External zone pair. That configuration is not shown here, but would be a good exercise for you to do, to ensure that you understand the concepts behind ZFW.

## Control-Plane Policing

Firewalls and access lists affect traffic moving through the router, but what about traffic bound to the router itself? In the previous section, you saw that zone-based firewalls have a default "self-zone" that allows all traffic to it. You can apply an access list to the vty lines. But routers and switches must handle a variety of traffic, including BPDUs, routing updates, HSRP, CDP, CEF, process-switched packets, ARP, and management traffic such as SSH, SNMP, and RADIUS. All of these are processed by the router or switch's *control plane*. This raises the possibility that excessive traffic from any of these sources could overload the control plane and prevent the processing of other traffic. Whether that overload is caused by a malicious attacker or by accident, the result is still the same.

Control-plane policing (CoPP) addresses this problem by leveraging the MQC to rate-limit or drop control-plane traffic. Grouping types of traffic into class maps and then applying policies through a policy map allows you much greater control over the amounts and types of traffic processed by the control plane. As of this writing, CoPP is supported on most Cisco routers and multilayer switches.

**NOTE**    The MQC, class maps, and policy maps are explained in Chapter 3, "Classification and Marking."

## Preparing for CoPP Implementation

Planning is the key to a successful CoPP implementation. You don't want to set the allowed rate for a class so low that important traffic is dropped, or so high that the processor is overworked. You also need to be careful in the way that you group traffic types to form classes. For example, perhaps you put all management traffic together in one class. Then an excess amount of one type of traffic could prevent you from using SSH to the router. On the other hand, placing each type of traffic into its own class would be unwieldy and very complex.

A typical procedure is to configure the class maps and then initially allow all traffic to be transmitted in the policy map. You would then monitor the traffic until you had a good idea of typical amounts for each class. It is important that you have an accurate picture of the expected router control-plane traffic. Otherwise you might, for example, configure CoPP on a Layer 3 switch, which then starts dropping BPDUs and creates a spanning-tree loop in the network.

As with a QoS implementation, you should carefully consider the number of classes, the types of traffic that will be grouped into each class, and the bandwidth allowed per class. Each network is different, but a typical grouping might be as follows:

- Malicious traffic, which is dropped. This is usually fragmented packets or packets using ports associated with known malicious programs.

- Routing protocols class, which is not limited.

- SSH and Telnet, limited to a small amount but enough to ensure connectivity when needed.

- Other management protocols such as SNMP, FTP, and TFTP.

- Network applications such as HSRP, DHCP, IGMP, and so on, if used.

- All other IP traffic.

- Default class, which would include Layer 2 protocols. The only Layer 2 protocol that can be explicitly assigned to a class in CoPP is ARP. All other Layer 2 protocols fall under the default class.

The only **match** options that can be used with CoPP class maps are IP precedence, DSCP, and access lists. You will likely configure a series of access lists to use in classifying traffic. Keep in mind that most routers only support policing of inbound traffic, so configure your access lists accordingly.

## Implementing CoPP

After you have planned the classes to use and the initial amount of bandwidth to allow for each, use the following steps to implement CoPP:

**Step 1.** Create the access lists to classify traffic. A **permit** statement allows matching traffic to be placed into the class. A **deny** statement causes matching traffic to be evaluated by the next class map.

**Step 2.** Create the class maps and match the appropriate access lists, or either IP Precedence or DSCP values.

**Step 3.** Create a policy map and associate the class maps with it. Be aware that the class map statements in a policy map are evaluated from the top down. For this reason, you will likely place the malicious class at the top of the policy map to drop that traffic immediately.

**Step 4.** Under each class in the policy map, assign an allowed bandwidth amount and then specify a conform action and an exceed action. When you first implement CoPP, both of these actions will often be set to **transmit**. After monitoring for a period of time, the bandwidth amounts can be tuned and then the exceed action can be set to **drop** (except for the routing protocols.)

**Step 5.** Assign the policy map to the router or switch's control plane as a service policy.

Example 9-20 shows a CoPP implementation and a command to verify the actions of CoPP. In the interest of space, this is just a simple example showing three classes and simple access lists. Your implementation will likely be much more complex.

**Example 9-20**   *Implementing Control-Plane Policing*

```
!
!Access lists to classify the traffic
Extended IP access list BAD_STUFF
    10 permit tcp any any eq 5554 !Sasser worm port
    20 permit tcp any any eq 9996 !Sasser worm port
    30 permit ip any any fragments
!
Extended IP access list INTERACTIVE
    10 permit tcp 10.17.4.0 0.0.3.255 host 10.17.3.1 eq 22
    20 permit tcp 10.17.4.0 0.0.3.255 eq 22 host 10.17.3.1 established
!
Extended IP access list ROUTING
    10 permit tcp host 172.20.1.1 gt 1024 host 10.17.3.1 eq bgp
    20 permit tcp host 172.20.1.1 eq bgp host 10.17.3.1 gt 1024 established
    30 permit eigrp 10.17.4.0 0.0.3.255 host 10.17.3.1
!
!CoPP class maps
```

```
Class Map match-all CoPP_ROUTING (id 0)
   Match access-group name ROUTING

 Class Map match-all CoPP_BAD_STUFF (id 1)
   Match access-group name BAD_STUFF

 Class Map match-all CoPP_INTERACTIVE (id 2)
   Match access-group name INTERACTIVE
!
!CoPP policy map. Note that both the conform and the exceed actions
!are "transmit" for all classes except CoPP_BAD_STUFF. The class
!CoPP_ROUTING will continue to be "transmit" but after sufficient
!monitoring the CoPP_INTERACTIVE and default classess will be tuned
!and then "drop" will be configured as the exceed action
Policy Map CoPP
    Class CoPP_BAD_STUFF
     police cir 8000 bc 1500
       conform-action drop
       exceed-action drop
    Class CoPP_ROUTING
     police cir 200000 bc 6250
       conform-action transmit
       exceed-action transmit
    Class CoPP_INTERACTIVE
     police cir 10000 bc 1500
       conform-action transmit
       exceed-action transmit
    Class class-default
     police cir 10000 bc 1500
       conform-action transmit
       exceed-action transmit
  !
!The CoPP policy applied to the device control plane
control-plane
 service-policy input CoPP
 !
!Verify the policy and its effects
R1# show policy-map control-plane
 Control Plane

   Service-policy input: CoPP

    Class-map: CoPP_BAD_STUFF (match-all)
continues
      14 packets, 832 bytes
      5 minute offered rate 0 bps, drop rate 0 bps
```

```
          Match: access-group name BAD_STUFF
          police:
               cir 8000 bps, bc 1500 bytes
             conformed 14 packets, 832 bytes; actions:
               drop
             exceeded 0 packets, 0 bytes; actions:
               drop
             conformed 0 bps, exceed 0 bps

      Class-map: CoPP_ROUTING (match-all)
        0 packets, 0 bytes
        5 minute offered rate 0 bps, drop rate 0 bps
        Match: access-group name ROUTING
        police:
             cir 200000 bps, bc 6250 bytes
           conformed 0 packets, 0 bytes; actions:
             transmit
           exceeded 0 packets, 0 bytes; actions:
             transmit
           conformed 0 bps, exceed 0 bps

      Class-map: CoPP_INTERACTIVE (match-all)
        0 packets, 0 bytes
        5 minute offered rate 0 bps, drop rate 0 bps
        Match: access-group name INTERACTIVE
        police:
             cir 10000 bps, bc 1500 bytes
           conformed 0 packets, 0 bytes; actions:
             transmit
           exceeded 0 packets, 0 bytes; actions:
             transmit
           conformed 0 bps, exceed 0 bps

      Class-map: class-default (match-any)
        0 packets, 0 bytes
        5 minute offered rate 0 bps, drop rate 0 bps
        Match: any
        police:
             cir 10000 bps, bc 1500 bytes
           conformed 0 packets, 0 bytes; actions:
             transmit
           exceeded 0 packets, 0 bytes; actions:
             transmit
           conformed 0 bps, exceed 0 bps
```

## Dynamic Multipoint VPN

IPsec is a commonly implemented method of forming secure tunnels from site to site or from remote users to a central site. However, it has limitations. In a site-to-site, hub-and-spoke environment, for example, all VPN traffic from spoke to spoke must traverse the hub site, where it must be unencrypted, routed, and then encrypted again. This is a lot of work for a VPN Concentrator, especially in a large environment with many spoke sites where a lot of traffic must flow between spokes. One result is additional network overhead and memory and CPU requirements at the central site. Another is significant configuration complexity at the hub router.

Dynamic Multipoint VPN (DMVPN) takes advantage of IPsec, GRE tunnels, and Next Hop Resolution Protocol (NHRP) to make IPsec scale better in a hub-and-spoke environment. DMVPN also supports traffic segmentation across VPNs and is VRF aware.

In a typical hub-and-spoke IPsec VPN environment, the hub router must have separate, statically configured crypto maps, crypto access lists, GRE tunnels, and **isakmp peer** statements for each spoke router. This is one of the limits of traditional hub-and-spoke VPN scalability that DMVPN eliminates. In a DMVPN environment, the spoke router connection information is not explicitly configured on the hub router. Instead, the hub router is configured for a single multipoint GRE (mGRE) tunnel interface and a set of profiles that apply to the spoke routers. Each spoke router points to one or more hubs, facilitating redundancy and load sharing. DMVPN additionally supports multicast traffic from hub to spoke routers.

The benefits of DMVPN compared to a traditional IPsec hub-and-spoke VPN environment include these:

**Key Topic**

- Simpler hub router configuration. A DMVPN hub router requires only one multipoint GRE tunnel interface, one IPsec profile, and no crypto access lists.

- Zero touch at the hub router for provisioning spoke routers. The hub router does not require configuration when new spoke routers are brought online.

- Automatically initiated IPsec encryption, facilitated by NHRP.

- Dynamic addressing support for spoke routers. Instead of static configuration, the hub learns spoke router addresses when they register to the network.

- Dynamically created spoke-to-spoke tunnels. Spoke routers learn about each other using NHRP so that they can form tunnels between each other automatically instead of requiring spoke-to-spoke traffic to be encrypted, unencrypted, and routed at the hub router.

- VRF integration for MPLS environments.

A dynamic routing protocol (EIGRP, OSPF, BGP, RIP, or even ODR for small deployments) is required between the hub and the spokes. (Cisco recommends a distance vector protocol and therefore prefers EIGRP for large-scale deployments.) This is how spoke routers learn about the networks at other spoke routers. In a DMVPN environment, the next-hop IP address for a spoke network is the tunnel interface for that spoke.

Figure 9-12 shows a DMVPN network with one hub and three spoke routers. In this network, each spoke router has a permanent IPsec tunnel to the hub router. Each of the spokes, which are NHRP clients, registers with the NHRP server (the hub router). When a spoke router needs to send traffic to a private network on another spoke router, which it has learned about by using the dynamic routing protocol running between the hub and the spokes, that spoke router queries the NHRP server in the hub router for the outside IP address of the destination spoke router. When the NHRP server returns that information, the originating spoke router initiates a dynamic IPsec tunnel to the other spoke router over the mGRE tunnel. After the required traffic has passed and the connection has been idle for a preconfigured time, the dynamic IPsec tunnel is torn down to save router resources (IPsec security associations, or SAs).

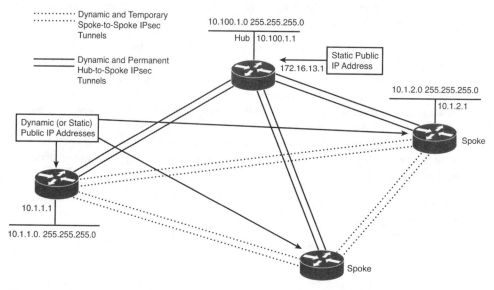

**Figure 9-12**   *Basic DMVPN Network*

Now that we have a working understanding of the concept behind DMVPNs, we need to explore the configuration necessary to deploy them. First, we must recognize that the configuration is broken up into a series of steps:

**Step 1.**   Basic configuration of IP addresses.

**Step 2.**   GRE Multipoint Tunnel configuration on all routers (for spoke-to-spoke connectivity).

**Step 3.**   Configure IPsec to encrypt mGRE tunnels.

**Step 4.**   DMVPN routing configuration.

## Step 1: Basic Configuration of IP Addresses

As the configuration in Example 9-21 demonstrates, the IP addresses of the physical interfaces will be used to create the tunnels that are necessary to deploy a DMVPN.

**Example 9-21**  *DMVPN Configuration: Step 1*

```
R1(config)# interface fa 0/0
R1(config-if)# no shutdown
R1(config-if)# ip address 192.168.123.1 255.255.255.0
R1(config)# interface loopback 0
R1(config-if)# ip address 1.1.1.1 255.255.255.255
!!!!
R2(config)# interface fa 0/0
R2(config-if)# no shutdown
R2(config-if)# ip address 192.168.123.2 255.255.255.0
R2(config)# interface loopback 0
R2(config-if)# ip address 2.2.2.2 255.255.255.255
!!!!!
R3(config)# interface fa 0/0
R3(config-if)# no shutdown
R3(config-if)# ip address 192.168.123.3 255.255.255.0
R3(config)# interface loopback 0
R3(config-if)# ip address 3.3.3.3 255.255.255.255
```

## Step 2: GRE Multipoint Tunnel Configuration on All Routers (for Spoke-to-Spoke Connectivity)

Now that Step 1 is complete, we will create the necessary tunnel interfaces, as illustrated in Example 9-22. Note that we configure an IP address on the tunnel 0 interface, but instead of defining a destination IP address, we will configure it as GRE multipoint. If we want to use a routing protocol like RIP, OSPF, or EIGRP, it will be necessary to define an **ip nhrp map multicast dynamic** command to allow multicast traffic to support those protocols. Additionally, for each DMVPN configured, we will require a unique network ID that is configured through the **ip nhrp network-id** command. If we choose to do so, we can specify a password for our NHRP process through the **ip nhrp authentication** command.

**Example 9-22**  *GRE Multipoint Tunnel Configuration*

```
!!!!!!!!!!First we will start with the hub.
!!!!!!!!!!!!!!!!!!!!!!!!!!!!!!!!!!!!!!!!!!!!!!
R1(config)# interface tunnel 0
R1(config-if)# ip address 172.16.123.1 255.255.255.0
R1(config-if)# tunnel mode gre multipoint
R1(config-if)# tunnel source fastEthernet 0/0
R1(config-if)# ip nhrp map multicast dynamic
R1(config-if)# ip nhrp network-id 1
R1(config-if)# ip nhrp authentication CISCO
!!!!!!!!!!!!!!!!!!!!!!!
!!Now let's configure our spoke routers
!!!!!!!!!!!!!!!!!!!!!!!
```

```
R2(config)# interface tunnel 0
R2(config-if)# ip address 172.16.123.2 255.255.255.0
R2(config-if)# tunnel mode gre multipoint
R2(config-if)# ip nhrp authentication CISCO
R2(config-if)# ip nhrp map multicast dynamic
R2(config-if)# ip nhrp map 172.16.123.1 192.168.123.1
R2(config-if)# ip nhrp map multicast 192.168.123.1
R2(config-if)# ip nhrp network-id 1
R2(config-if)# ip nhrp nhs 172.16.123.1
R2(config-if)# tunnel source fastEthernet 0/0
!!!!!!!!!!!!!!!!!!!!!!!!!!
R3(config)# interface tunnel 0
R3(config-if)# ip address 172.16.123.3 255.255.255.0
R3(config-if)# tunnel mode gre multipoint
R3(config-if)# ip nhrp authentication CISCO
R3(config-if)# ip nhrp map multicast dynamic
R3(config-if)# ip nhrp map 172.16.123.1 192.168.123.1
R3(config-if)# ip nhrp map multicast 192.168.123.1
R3(config-if)# ip nhrp network-id 1
R3(config-if)# ip nhrp nhs 172.16.123.1
R3(config-if)# tunnel source fastEthernet 0/0
```

Observe that it was not necessary to apply many commands on the hub router. This means that the majority of the configuration will be assigned to the spokes where we use the **ip nhrp map** command to map the IP address of the Next Hop Server (NHS) to the outside IP address of the hub. In this particular deployment, 172.16.123.1 is the IP address on the tunnel interface of R1 and 192.168.123.1 is the outside IP address of R1. We need to use the **ip nhrp nhs** command to define exactly how to reach the IP address of the NHS.

The **ip nhrp map multicast** command configures the spoke router to send multicast traffic only to the hub router, not to other spoke routers.

As stated in Step 1, we are using the Fast Ethernet 0/0 interface as the source of the tunnels, and this is accomplished with the **tunnel source** command.

With this accomplished, we need to do some verification. The verification of our current DMVPN configuration is pretty straightforward, as demonstrated in Example 9-23.

**Example 9-23**  *Multipoint GRE Verification on the "Hub"*

```
!!!!!!!!!!First we will start with the hub.
!!!!!!!!!!!!!!!!!!!!!!!!!!!!!!!!!!!!!!!!!!!!!!!
R1# show dmvpn
Legend: Attrb --> S - Static, D - Dynamic, I - Incomplete
        N - NATed, L - Local, X - No Socket
        # Ent --> Number of NHRP entries with same NBMA peer
```

```
Tunnel0, Type:Hub, NHRP Peers:2,
 # Ent   Peer NBMA Addr Peer Tunnel Add State  UpDn Tm Attrb
 ----- --------------- --------------- ----- -------- -----
     1   192.168.123.2    172.16.123.2    UP     never D
     1   192.168.123.3    172.16.123.3    UP     never D
```

Example 9-23 shows us that R1 has two peers. There are a number of very useful fields in this output, as outlined in Table 9-11.

**Table 9-11**   *Useful Fields from the* **show dmvpn** *Command Output*

| Header | Description |
|---|---|
| Ent | Represents the number of entries in the NHRP database for this spoke router. |
| Peer NBMA Addr | The IP address on the outside interface of the spoke router, in our example 192.168.123.2 and 192.168.123.3. |
| Peer Tunnel Add | The IP address on the tunnel interface of the spoke router. |
| State | Shows whether the tunnel is up or down. |
| UpDn Tm | Up or down time of the current state (up or down). Populated after the tunnels are in service. |

We need to repeat this **show** command on the spokes and look at the output in Example 9-24.

**Example 9-24**   *Multipoint GRE Verification on the "Spokes"*

```
!!!!!!!!!!!!!!!!!!!!!!!!!!!!!!!!!!!!!!!!!!!!!!
R2# show dmvpn
Legend: Attrb --> S - Static, D - Dynamic, I - Incompletea
        N - NATed, L - Local, X - No Socket
        # Ent --> Number of NHRP entries with same NBMA peer


Tunnel0, Type:Spoke, NHRP Peers:1,
 # Ent   Peer NBMA Addr Peer Tunnel Add State  UpDn Tm Attrb
 ----- --------------- --------------- ----- -------- -----
     1   192.168.123.1    172.16.123.1    UP 00:43:44 S
!!!!!!!!!!!!!!!!!!!!!!!!!!!!!!!!!!!!!!!!!!!!!!!!!!!!!!!!!!
R3# show dmvpn
Legend: Attrb --> S - Static, D - Dynamic, I - Incompletea
        N - NATed, L - Local, X - No Socket
        # Ent --> Number of NHRP entries with same NBMA peer


Tunnel0, Type:Spoke, NHRP Peers:1,
 # Ent   Peer NBMA Addr Peer Tunnel Add State  UpDn Tm Attrb
 ----- --------------- --------------- ----- -------- -----
     1   192.168.123.1    172.16.123.1    UP 00:46:58 S
```

At this juncture of our configuration, the spoke routers only have a tunnel that connects to the hub router. Now we need to test the "Dynamic" aspect of this configuration. We will do that by executing a series of ping tests. First, we will test reachability between the spokes and the hub and, finally, hub-to-hub reachability. This can all be seen in Example 9-25.

**Example 9-25**   *Testing the Dynamic Multipoint VPN Configuration Through* ping

```
!!!!!!!!!!!!!!!!!!!!!!!!!!!!!!!!!!!!!!!!!!!!!!
R2# ping 172.16.123.1

Type escape sequence to abort.
Sending 5, 100-byte ICMP Echos to 172.16.123.1, timeout is 2 seconds:
!!!!!
Success rate is 100 percent (5/5), round-trip min/avg/max = 4/4/8 ms
R3# ping 172.16.123.1

Type escape sequence to abort.
Sending 5, 100-byte ICMP Echos to 172.16.123.1, timeout is 2 seconds:
!!!!!
Success rate is 100 percent (5/5), round-trip min/avg/max = 4/4/8 ms
Both spoke routers are able to reach the hub. Now let's try to ping between the two
spoke routers:

R2# ping 172.16.123.3

Type escape sequence to abort.
Sending 5, 100-byte ICMP Echos to 172.16.123.3, timeout is 2 seconds:
!!!!!
Success rate is 100 percent (5/5), round-trip min/avg/max = 4/6/12 ms
!!!!!!!!!!!!!!!!!!!!!!!!!!!!!!!!!!!!!!!!!!!!!!!!!!!!!!!!!!!!!!!!!!!!!!!!!!!!!!!!!!!
!! The ping is working and this is the interesting part of multipoint GRE. The
!! spoke
!! routers will dynamically create a tunnel between each other as you can see below
!!!!!!!!!!!!!!!!!!!!!!!!!!!!!!!!!!!!!!!!!!!!!!!!!!!!!!!!!!!!!!!!!!!!!!!!!!!!!!!!!!!
!!
R2# show dmvpn
Legend: Attrb --> S - Static, D - Dynamic, I - Incompletea
          N - NATed, L - Local, X - No Socket
          # Ent --> Number of NHRP entries with same NBMA peer

Tunnel0, Type:Spoke, NHRP Peers:2,
 # Ent  Peer NBMA Addr Peer Tunnel Add State  UpDn Tm Attrb
 ----- --------------- --------------- ----- -------- -----
     1   192.168.123.1    172.16.123.1     UP 00:01:41 S
     1   192.168.123.3    172.16.123.3     UP    never D
R3# show dmvpn
```

```
Legend: Attrb --> S - Static, D - Dynamic, I - Incompletea
          N - NATed, L - Local, X - No Socket
          # Ent --> Number of NHRP entries with same NBMA peer


Tunnel0, Type:Spoke, NHRP Peers:2,
  # Ent  Peer NBMA Addr Peer Tunnel Add State  UpDn Tm Attrb
  ----- --------------- --------------- ----- -------- -----
      1  192.168.123.1    172.16.123.1     UP 00:01:42 S
      1  192.168.123.2    172.16.123.2     UP    never D S
```

Example 9-25 clearly illustrates that new tunnels have been dynamically established between R2 and R3. This means that the multipoint GRE is working.

However, this type of deployment would be very risky in a live environment because the default operation of DMVPN is to send traffic in clear text, and that is simply unacceptable.

### Step 3: Configure IPsec to Encrypt mGRE Tunnels

To protect our deployment, we will apply IPsec to the DMVPN configuration. The process is illustrated in Example 9-26.

**Example 9-26**  *IPsec Configuration Through DMVPN*

```
!!!!!!!!!!!!!!!!!!!!!!!!!!!!!!!!!!!!!!!!!!!!
!!!!! All Devices in the DMVPN Configuration
!!!!!!!!!!!!!!!!!!!!!!!!!!!!!!!!!!!!!!!!!!!!
(config)# crypto isakmp policy 1
(config-isakmp)# encryption aes
(config-isakmp)# hash md5
(config-isakmp)# authentication pre-share
(config-isakmp)# group 2
(config-isakmp)# lifetime 86400
!
(config)# crypto isakmp key 0 NETWORKLESSONS address 0.0.0.0
(config)# crypto ipsec transform-set MYSET esp-aes esp-md5-hmac
!
(config)# crypto ipsec profile MGRE
(ipsec-profile)# set security-association lifetime seconds 86400
(ipsec-profile)# set transform-set MYSET
!
(config)# interface tunnel 0
(config-if)# tunnel protection ipsec profile MGRE
```

**Key Topic**

If the DMVPN configuration relies on a dynamic IP address on the spoke routers, be sure to use IP address 0.0.0.0 when configuring the crypto isakmp key.

We need to verify whether our tunnels are now encrypted. Best practice at this point would be to shut and no shut our tunnel interfaces. This will ensure that the crypto configuration has been applied and that the tunnel interfaces come up as we hope. This process is described in Example 9-27.

**Example 9-27** *Verification of IPsec-Encrypted Tunnels*

```
!!!!!!!!!!!!!!!!!!!!!!!!!!!!!!!!!!!!!!!!!!!!!!
!!!!! All Devices in the DMVPN Configuration
!!!!!!!!!!!!!!!!!!!!!!!!!!!!!!!!!!!!!!!!!!!!!!
(config)# interface tunnel 0
(config-if)# shutdown
(config-if)# no shutdown
!!!!!!!!!!!!!!!!!!!!!!!!!!
!!!! Next step is to check if IPSEC is active!!!!!!
!!!! From the HUB!!!!!!!!
R1# show crypto session
Crypto session current status

Interface: Tunnel0
Session status: UP-ACTIVE
Peer: 192.168.123.2 port 500
  IKE SA: local 192.168.123.1/500 remote 192.168.123.2/500 Active
  IPSEC FLOW: permit 47 host 192.168.123.1 host 192.168.123.2
       Active SAs: 2, origin: crypto map

Interface: Tunnel0
Session status: UP-ACTIVE
Peer: 192.168.123.3 port 500
  IKE SA: local 192.168.123.1/500 remote 192.168.123.3/500 Active
  IPSEC FLOW: permit 47 host 192.168.123.1 host 192.168.123.3
       Active SAs: 2, origin: crypto map
!!!!!!!!!!!!!!!!!!!!!!!!!!!!!!!!!!!!!
!!! As you can see IPSEC is active for both peers. We will test rechability via
!!! sending some pings
!!!!!!!!!!!!!!!!!!!!!!!!!!!!!!!!!!!!!!!!!!!!!!
R2# ping 172.16.123.1

Type escape sequence to abort.
Sending 5, 100-byte ICMP Echos to 172.16.123.1, timeout is 2 seconds:
!!!!!
Success rate is 100 percent (5/5), round-trip min/avg/max = 4/4/4 ms
R3# ping 172.16.123.1
```

```
Type escape sequence to abort.
Sending 5, 100-byte ICMP Echos to 172.16.123.1, timeout is 2 seconds:
!!!!!
Success rate is 100 percent (5/5), round-trip min/avg/max = 4/4/4 ms
!!!!!!!!!!!!!!!!!!!
!! Now we will verify that the packets are encrypted
!!!!!!!!!!!!!!!!!!!
R1# show crypto ipsec sa

interface: Tunnel0
    Crypto map tag: Tunnel0-head-0, local addr 192.168.123.1

  protected vrf: (none)
  local  ident (addr/mask/prot/port): (192.168.123.1/255.255.255.255/47/0)
  remote ident (addr/mask/prot/port): (192.168.123.2/255.255.255.255/47/0)
  current_peer 192.168.123.2 port 500
    PERMIT, flags={origin_is_acl,}
    #pkts encaps: 26, #pkts encrypt: 26, #pkts digest: 26
    #pkts decaps: 26, #pkts decrypt: 26, #pkts verify: 26
!!!!!!!!!!!!!!!!!!!!!!
!!! Packets in the tunnel are encrypted.
!!!!!!!!!!!!!!!!!!!!!!
```

## Step 4: DMVPN Routing Configuration

The tunnels are up and running and encrypted; however, there is no reachability between the loopbacks of any of the devices. To remedy this situation, we have two options. We could use static routing or one of our dynamic routing protocols.

In Example 9-28, we will illustrate how to run Open Shortest Path First (OSPF) across the mGRE tunnel interfaces.

**Example 9-28**  *OSPF Across MGRE Tunnel Interfaces*

```
!!!!!!!!!!!!!!!!!!!!!!!!!!!!!!!!!!!!!!!!!!!!!!!!!
!!!!! All Devices in the DMVPN Configuration
!!!!!!!!!!!!!!!!!!!!!!!!!!!!!!!!!!!!!!!!!!!!!!!!!
R1(config)# router ospf 1
R1(config-router)# network 1.1.1.1 0.0.0.0 area 0
R1(config-router)# network 172.16.123.0 0.0.0.255 area 0

R1(config)# interface tunnel 0
R1(config-if)# ip ospf network broadcast
R2(config)# router ospf 1
R2(config-router)# network 2.2.2.2 0.0.0.0 area 0
R2(config-router)# network 172.16.123.0 0.0.0.255 area 0
```

```
R2(config)# interface tunnel 0
R2(config-if)# ip ospf priority 0
R2(config-if)# ip ospf network broadcast
R3(config)# router ospf 1
R3(config-router)# network 3.3.3.3 0.0.0.0 area 0
R3(config-router)# network 172.16.123.0 0.0.0.255 area 0

R3(config)# interface tunnel 0
R3(config-if)# ip ospf priority 0
R3(config-if)# ip ospf network broadcast
!!!!!!!!!!!!!!!!!!!!!!!!!!
```

**Key Topic**

Previously we used the **ip nhrp map multicast** command on the spoke routers, which means that the spoke routers can only send OSPF hellos to the hub router. This means that we'll have an OSPF hub-and-spoke topology, and the spoke routers should never become the designated router (DR) or backup designated router (BDR).

As shown in Example 9-28, we used the OSPF broadcast network type so that the spoke routers will use each other's IP addresses as the next hop.

Now that this configuration is completed, we will do the verification necessary to check it all out. At this juncture, we are using OSPF verification commands, as illustrated in Example 9-29.

**Example 9-29**  *Verification of DMVPN Routing*

```
!!!!!!!!!!!!!!!!!!!!!!!!!!!!!!!!!!!!!!!!!!!!!!!!!!
R1# show ip ospf neighbor


Neighbor ID     Pri   State          Dead Time   Address          Interface
2.2.2.2           0   FULL/DROTHER   00:00:33    172.16.123.2     Tunnel0
3.3.3.3           0   FULL/DROTHER   00:00:33    172.16.123.3     Tunnel0
R2# show ip ospf neighbor


Neighbor ID     Pri   State          Dead Time   Address          Interface
1.1.1.1           1   FULL/DR        00:00:31    172.16.123.1     Tunnel0
R3# show ip ospf neighbor


Neighbor ID     Pri   State          Dead Time   Address          Interface
1.1.1.1           1   FULL/DR        00:00:31    172.16.123.1     Tunnel0
The spoke routers have formed an OSPF neighbor adjacency with the hub router. Let's
check the routing tables:


R2# show ip route ospf
      1.0.0.0/32 is subnetted, 1 subnets
O        1.1.1.1 [110/11112] via 172.16.123.1, 00:04:16, Tunnel0
      3.0.0.0/32 is subnetted, 1 subnets
O        3.3.3.3 [110/11112] via 172.16.123.3, 00:04:16, Tunnel0
```

```
R3# show ip route ospf
     1.0.0.0/32 is subnetted, 1 subnets
O       1.1.1.1 [110/11112] via 172.16.123.1, 00:04:10, Tunnel0
     2.0.0.0/32 is subnetted, 1 subnets
O       2.2.2.2 [110/11112] via 172.16.123.2, 00:04:09, Tunnel0
!!!!!!!!!!!!!!!!!
!!!! R2 and R3 have learned about the other networks. Note that R2 and R3 are using
!!!! each other's IP address as the next hop for each other's networks.
!!!! Now to test via the ping utility
!!!!!!!!!!!!!!!!!

R2# ping 1.1.1.1 source loopback 0

Type escape sequence to abort.
Sending 5, 100-byte ICMP Echos to 1.1.1.1, timeout is 2 seconds:
Packet sent with a source address of 2.2.2.2
!!!!!
Success rate is 100 percent (5/5), round-trip min/avg/max = 4/4/4 ms
R2# ping 3.3.3.3 source loopback 0

Type escape sequence to abort.
Sending 5, 100-byte ICMP Echos to 3.3.3.3, timeout is 2 seconds:
Packet sent with a source address of 2.2.2.2
!!!!!
Success rate is 100 percent (5/5), round-trip min/avg/max = 4/4/4 ms
!!!!!!!!!!!!!!!!!!!!!!!!
!!!! R2 is able to reach the loopback interfaces of R1 and R3
!!!!!!!!!!!!!!!!!!!!!!!!
```

# IPv6 First Hop Security

In this section, we take a look at several common security threats on IPv6 campus access networks and explain the value of using first hop security (FHS) technology in mitigating these threats.

## First Hop Security for IPv6

Anyone working in the network engineering market today has to recognize that there are a growing number of large-scale IPv6 deployments in enterprise, university, and government networks. To guarantee the success of each of these networks, we need to ensure that the IPv6 deployments are secure and are of a service quality that equals or exceeds that of the existing IPv4 infrastructure.

Network users must be comfortable that regardless of what type of network they are working on—IPv4 or IPv6—each shares the same levels of security and serviceability. From the network administrator's point of view, there also needs to be a similar assumption: that both IPv4 and IPv6 networks are secure environments with a high degree of traceability and quality assurance, thus allowing us to both avoid and trace any level of possible network incursion.

This situation is made somewhat more complicated in IPv6 environments as a direct result of the sheer size of these deployments as well as the advent of a number of new technology paradigms that were created to support the protocol. Thus it is a fair assumption that the majority of threats that impact an IPv6 enterprise are very much tied to the topology and nature of the given network itself. This means that security considerations for IPv6 environments are considerably different in that they have

- More end nodes allowed on individual links (up to $2^{64}$)

- Larger neighbor cache on end nodes

- Larger neighbor cache on the default router

Each of these elements actually serves to provide attackers with greater opportunities for denial of service (DoS) attacks. The security risks associated with IPv6 deployments, however, are not specifically limited to the topological aspects of the protocol. There are other threats associated with the protocols that might or might not be in use on that network. A few of these protocols include

- Neighbor Discovery Protocol (NDP) integrates all link operations in charge of determining address assignment, router discovery, and associated tasks like redirect.

- Dynamic Host Configuration Protocol (DHCP) has a smaller role in address assignment compared to IPv4.

- Noncentralized address assignment creates true challenges for controlling address misusage.

Thanks to an ever-increasing level of IPv6 deployments and the intrinsic differences between IPv4 and IPv6 outlined previously, it is very important to have both a secure IPv4 environment and a secure IPv6 environment. It will be useful to understand where IPv6 is used for the various aspects and how best to secure the IPv6 infrastructure when connecting systems and devices to a network link. This will involve taking a closer look at areas where opportunities might arise in the IPv6 topology. In this section, we will focus on the different links found in the network. Before we can discuss the method of securing these links, we first need to look at the fundamentals of link operations, because understanding the basic operation of links in an IPv6 deployment will better allow us to secure them.

## Link Operations

When determining where we can secure link operations, we find that there are basically three different locations within the network where operations can be secured. These locations where security enforcement can take place are

- The end nodes

- The first hop within the network

- The last hop

Figure 9-13 illustrates these three locations by illustrating a very simple network.

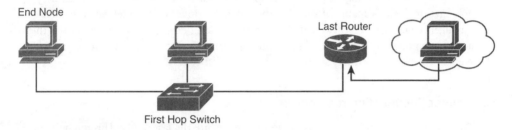

**Figure 9-13**  *Link Operation Security Enforcement*

We will look at each of the three locations more in depth now that we have identified where they are in a very small topology.

### End Node Security Enforcement

This security model, a distributed model where the end nodes take care of themselves, does not provide any link operation with bottlenecks or single points of failure. This security model does not need central administration or operation as it is assumed that each node takes care of itself. To read more about this process of Secure Neighbor Discovery, consult RFC 3971. The ultimate level of security in this model is accomplished by what is referred to as a Secure Neighbor Discovery (SeND) deployment. We will discuss SeND in a later section because to understand how SeND helps us, we need to know a bit more about another protocol used for neighbor discovery. Suffice it to say that this model is especially good for threats coming directly from the link; however, it provides poor protection against threats from offlink devices. Another consideration for this model is that because of its distributed nature, a degree of complexity and heavy provisioning of end nodes is involved that spreads over the complete networking domain that is being secured. So this solution is good but has its limitations; plus based on our new understanding of its operation, we can easily see that it is not scalable. So now we need to look at the next security enforcement point in our topology.

### First Hop Switch Security Enforcement

The first hop switch security model is based upon a centralized model. It is maintained and run by a centralized security administration and, as such, differs significantly from the end node method. In the end node method, we saw that the burden of security enforcement is pushed toward the first-hop device. Because the first hop switch security enforcement uses a centralized model, it has better scalability in that fewer devices are affected by the security tasks involved. This model makes the transition from a nonsecure link operation to a secure network easier as fewer components will have to be touched, monitored, and reconfigured.

Although this is a very convenient model for the network operator and the actual end user, it will be useful only in certain topologies in which all end users go through an aggregation device capable of securing the link operations. This model increases the intelligence and the awareness that first-hop networking devices need to have about the actual end nodes attached, thus also adding significantly to the required processing and memory resources on the first-hop switch.

### Last Router Security Enforcement

We have only one option available if we want to secure the last router. This method, like the previous one, will be a centralized model, which is good for securing against threats coming from outside of the link that is being protected. A property of this model is that the attached link is protected as well as all the downstream network elements. This provides a significant enhancement over the previous security enforcement methods that we have discussed. But it is not an either/or scenario. The last router security enforcement model needs to combine with the first-hop switch model. Together these solutions can defeat threats that might originate from the inside the network. This is a necessity because it is possible that a device has been compromised and might be used by an assailant to affect the network infrastructure.

To operate effectively, this enforcement method requires the last-hop router to discover all the end nodes on the operational segment where the security process is being enforced. This is accomplished through the next protocol set that we have to discuss.

## ICMPv6 and Neighbor Discovery Protocol

This section introduces the Internet Control Message Protocol version 6 (ICMPv6). In comparison with IPv4, IPv6 has an increased set of capabilities to simplify end-system autoconfiguration while at the same time running service detection by means of ICMP. Because of these new ICMP capabilities, the importance of ICMP for IPv6 is much higher than it ever was for IPv4.

One of the new functionalities within ICMPv6 is the Neighbor Discovery Protocol (NDP), which in its base specification is a nonauthenticated protocol. NDP is an application and operates on top of ICMPv6. NDP makes heavy usage of multicast packets for link efficiency.

The functional applications of NDP include

- Router discovery

- Autoconfiguration of addresses (stateless address autoconfiguration [SLAAC])

- IPv6 address resolution (replaces Address Resolution Protocol [ARP])

- Neighbor reachability (neighbor unreachability detection [NUD])

- Duplicate address detection (DAD)

- Redirection

### Secure Neighbor Discovery (SeND)

We mentioned SeND in a previous section where we discussed end node security enforcement, but we deferred to mention exactly what the protocol was until now. In that we have a basic understanding of how ICMPv6 and NDP work, we need to also point out that their operation processes are not secure. It is SeND that adds security to the NDP and its operation; however, we will note later that this security enhancement has its limitations. So the best working definition of Secure Neighbor Discovery is a protocol that enhances NDP. It enhances the operation of NDP by providing three critical capabilities:

- Proof of address ownership

  - Makes stealing IPv6 addresses "impossible"

  - Used in router discovery, DAD, and address resolution

  - Based upon Cryptographically Generated Addresses (CGA)

  - Alternatively also provides non-CGAs with certificates

- Message protection

  - Message integrity protection

  - Replay protection

  - Request/response correlation

  - Used in all NDP messages

- Router authorization

  - Authorizes routers to act as default gateways

  - Specifies prefixes that routers are authorized to announce "on-link"

While SeND provides a significant security enhancement to the IPv6 neighbor discovery technology by introducing the enhancements we pointed out previously, it does not provide any end-to-end security and provides no actual packet confidentiality. Plus we need to recognize that that SeND is not a new protocol and still remains a protocol operating on the link. Secure Neighbor Discovery is just an "extension" to NDP and defines a set of new attributes by defining new network discovery options, new network discovery messages, and new attributes that describe the preferred behavior when a SeND node receives a message supported by SeND or not supported by SeND.

SeND technology works by having a pair of private and public keys for each IPv6 node in combination with new options like Cryptographically Generated Addresses (CGA) and RSA, which all work to provide a security shield against replay attacks.

Nodes that are using SeND cannot choose their own interface identifier because the interface identifier is cryptographically generated based upon the current IPv6 network prefix and the "public" key. However, the CGA interface identifier alone is not sufficient to guarantee that the CGA address is used by the appropriate node.

For this purpose, SeND messages are signed by using the RSA public and private key pair. For example, if node 1 wants to know the MAC address of node 2, it will tradition-ally send a neighbor solicitation request to the node 2 solicited node multicast address. Node 2 will respond with a corresponding neighbor advertisement containing the MAC address–to–IPv6 address mapping. In addition, node 2 will add the CGA parameters (which include among others the public key) and a private key signature of all neighbor advertisement fields. When node 1 receives this neighbor advertisement, it uses the public key to verify with the CGA address the private key signature of node 2. After this last step has been successfully completed, the binding on node 1 of the MAC address and CGA address of node 2 can be successfully finalized.

Note that this mechanism is simply an explanation to verify the correct relationship between a node MAC address and its CGA IPv6 address. SeND does not check any of the node's privileges to be allowed, or not allowed, on the network. If this is required, other means of infrastructure protection will be required, such as 802.1X (discussed ear-lier in this chapter).

## Securing at the First Hop

The first hop for an end node is very often a Layer 2 switch. By implementing the right set of security features, this switch has the potential to solve many of the caveats attached to a SeND deployment and increase the link security model. The first-hop switch is strategically located to learn about all its neighbors, and hence the switch can easily either allow or deny certain types of traffic, end-node roles, and claims. In its central position, the first-hop switch can fulfill a number of functions. It will inspect the neighbor discovery (ND) traffic and provide information about Layer 2/Layer 3 binding and monitor the use of ND by host to spot potentially abnormal behaviors. Ultimately, the switch can block undesired traffic such as a rogue Router Advertisement (RA), rogue DHCP server advertisement, and data traffic coming from undesired IP addresses or pre-fixes.

Securing the IPv6 link is a cooperative effort, and all concerned parties or sites should be involved. Experience proves, however, that the first-hop switch is a key piece of this puz-zle and certainly plays a central role in link security, just like it did for IPv4. Compared to IPv4, IPv6 offers a number of technologies, such as SeND, that make security more flex-ible to deploy and more efficient at catching malicious behavior, paving the way for more secure deployments.

We can see the configuration of this feature in Example 9-30.

**Example 9-30**   *Securing the First Hop*

```
!!!!!!!!!!!!!!!!!!!!!!!!!!!!!!!!!!!!!!!!!!!!!!!!
CAT2(config)# ipv6 access-list ACCESS_PORT
CAT2(config-ipv6-acl)# remark Block all traffic DHCP server -> client
CAT2(config-ipv6-acl)# deny udp any eq 547 any eq 546
CAT2(config-ipv6-acl)# remark Block Router Advertisements
CAT2(config-ipv6-acl)# deny icmp any any router-advertisement
CAT2(config-ipv6-acl)# permit any any
CAT2(config-ipv6-acl)# !
CAT2(config-ipv6-acl)# interface gigabitethernet 1/0/1
CAT2(config-if)# switchport
CAT2(config-if)# ipv6 traffic-filter ACCESS_PORT in
```

## RA Guard

In typical IPv6 deployments, the majority of networks have a common attribute. That attribute is that their nodes are on a link layer bonded by some intermediary device. This device is typically a switch and describes a scenario where devices are not directly connected. This configuration makes it possible to use a mechanism called RA snooping. This concept of snooping has been present in computer networks for decades, in the form of features such as IGMP snooping or DHCP snooping. Furthermore, it is common knowledge that switches use only information provided by the link-layer header of received frames to forward those packets through the correct interface on a given device. The concept of snooping exceeds this behavior in that the switch will additionally inspect upper-layer information embedded in the packet. Based on that upper protocol layer information, the switch will take defined actions. These actions are either optimizing (IGMP) or security (DHCP, RA) in nature.

RA Guard is a mechanism designed against rogue RA attacks that uses an idea called RA Snooping as its foundation. The key condition that must be met prior to RA Guard deployment is that there must be some intermediary device in a network that all traffic will pass through. The switch in our analogy is where RA Guard is implemented. The core functionality of RA Guard is that it inspects Router Advertisements, and based on the information provided, it decides whether to drop or forward them. Note that RA Guard is not any particular protocol or strictly defined mechanism. It is an umbrella term describing a set of recommendations and a general description of prevention mechanisms that have been implemented by various vendors.

Example 9-31 outlines how RA Guard is implemented on a Catalyst switch.

**Example 9-31**   *RA Guard*

```
!!!!!!!!!!!!!!!!!!!!!!!!!!!!!!!!!!!!!!!!!!!!!!!!
Switch(config)# ipv6 nd raguard policy POLICY-NAME
! Defines the RA Guard policy name
```

```
Switch(config-ra-guard)# device-role {host | router}
!Specifies the role of the device attached to the port.
!!!!!!!!!!!!!!!!!!!!!!!!!!!!!!!!!!!!!!!!!!!
!The RA Guard policy can have several other optional options checking the hop limit,
!router preference etc. After the policy is configured, it has to be applied to
!appropriate interfaces.
!!!!!!!!!!!!!!!!!!!!!!!!!!!!!!!!!!!!!!!!!!!
Switch(config)# interface INTERFACE
Switch(config-if)# ipv6 nd raguard attach-policy POLICY-NAME
! Applies the RA Guard policy
```

If a policy is configured with a device-role host, a switch will drop any RA messages received on an interface where the policy is applied, thus eliminating the RA attack. Interfaces toward a router should be configured with a policy where device-role is set to **router**.

## DHCPv6 Guard

The DHCPv6 Guard feature blocks reply and advertisement messages that come from unauthorized DHCP servers and relay agents. This configuration is illustrated in Example 9-32.

Packets are classified into one of the three DHCP type messages. All client messages are always switched regardless of device role. DHCP server messages are only processed further if the device role is set to server. Further processing of server messages includes DHCP server advertisements (for source validation and server preference) and DHCP server replies (for permitted prefixes).

If the device is configured as a DHCP server, all the messages need to be switched, regardless of the device role configuration.

**Example 9-32**  *DHCPv6 Guard*

```
!!!!!!!!!!!!!!!!!!!!!!!!!!!!!!!!!!!!!!!!!!!!!!!!
CAT1# enable
CAT1# configure terminal
Enter configuration commands, one per line.  End with CNTL/Z.
CAT1(config)# ipv6 access-list acl1
CAT1(config-ipv6-acl)# permit host FE80::A8BB:CCFF:FE01:F700 any
CAT1(config-ipv6-acl)# ipv6 prefix-list abc permit 2001:0DB8::/64 le 128
CAT1(config-ipv6-acl)# ipv6 prefix-list abc permit 2001:0DB8::/64 le 128
CAT1(config)# ipv6 dhcp guard policy pol1
CAT1(config-dhcp-guard)# device-role server
CAT1(config-dhcp-guard)# match server access-list acl1
CAT1(config-dhcp-guard)# match reply prefix-list abc
CAT1(config-dhcp-guard)# preference min 0
CAT1(config-dhcp-guard)# preference max 255
```

```
CAT1(config-dhcp-guard)# trusted-port
CAT1(config-dhcp-guard)# interface GigabitEthernet 1/0/1
CAT1(config-if)# switchport
CAT1(config-if)# ipv6 dhcp guard attach-policy pol1 vlan add 1
!!!!!!!!!!!!!!!!!!!!!!!!!!!!
CAT1# show ipv6 dhcp guard policy pol1
Dhcp guard policy: pol1
        Trusted Port
        Target: Gi1/0/1

CAT1#
```

## DHCPv6 Guard and the Binding Database

IPv6 Snooping is not a security feature in its own right. It builds a database table of IPv6 neighbors connected to the device created from information sources like DHCPv6, which we discussed in the previous section. This database, or binding table, is used by various IPv6 FHS features to validate the link-layer address (LLA), the IPv6 address, and the prefix binding of the neighbors to prevent spoofing and redirect attacks. This binding table will get automatically populated after IPv6 Snooping is enabled. The following output in Example 9-33 shows a sample content of an IPv6 binding table.

**Example 9-33**   *IPv6 Binding Table*

```
!!!!!!!!!!!!!!!!!!!!!!!!!!!!!!!!!!!!!!!!!!!!!!!!
CAT1(config
Switch# show ipv6 neighbors binding
Binding Table has 4 entries, 4 dynamic
Codes: L - Local, S - Static, ND - Neighbor Discovery, DH - DHCP, PKT - Other
  Packet, API - API created
IPv6 address             Link-Layer addr Interface vlan prlvl  age    state
  Time left
ND  FE80::81E2:1562:E5A0:43EE  28D2.4448.E276  Gi1/15         1   0005     3mn  REACHABLE
  94 s
ND  FE80::3AEA:A7FF:FE85:C926  38EA.A785.C926  Gi1/2          1   0005    26mn  STALE
  86999 s
ND  FE80::10                   38EA.A785.C926  Gi1/2          1   0005    26mn  STALE
  85533 s
ND  FE80::1                    E4C7.228B.F180  Gi1/7          1   0005     35s  REACHABLE
  272 s
```

As we can see, the binding table has four entries beginning with "ND," which means that these associations were learned from snooping NDP packets. When a new entry is appended to the database, the following log message is generated on the switch (when "IPv6 snooping logging" is enabled).

```
%SISF-6-ENTRY_CREATED: Entry created A=2001:DB8:1:0:C04D:ABA:A783:2FBE V=1
  I=Gi1/15 P=0024 M=28D2.4448.E276
```

IPv6 Snooping is tightly integrated in the various IPv6 Guard features like DHCPv6 Guard and RA Guard. To allow those packets, you have to configure, for example, DHCPv6 Guard so that the switch knows that these DHCPv6 packets are legitimate and must not be filtered. The complete configuration for DHCPv6 Guard is done with the commands outlined in Example 9-34.

**Example 9-34**  *DHCPv6 Address Integrated with the IPv6 Binding Database*

```
!!!!!!!!!!!!!!!!!!!!!!!!!!!!!!!!!!!!!!!!!!!!!!
CAT1(config)# ipv6 access-list dhcpv6_server
CAT1(config-ipv6-acl)# permit host FE80::1 any
CAT1(config-ipv6-acl)# $-list dhcpv6_prefix permit 2001:DB8:1::/64 le 128
CAT1(config)# ipv6 dhcp guard policy dhcpv6guard_pol
CAT1(config-dhcp-guard)# device-role server
CAT1(config-dhcp-guard)# match server access-list dhcpv6_server
CAT1(config-dhcp-guard)# match reply prefix-list dhcpv6_prefix
CAT1(config-dhcp-guard)# vlan configuration 1
CAT1(config-vlan-config)# ipv6 dhcp guard attach-policy dhcpv6guard_pol
CAT1(config-vlan-config)#
```

Essentially, Example 9-34 illustrates how we instruct the switch that DHCPv6 packets from FE80::1 (specified in the ACL) with a prefix of 2001:db8:1::/64 (specified in the prefix list) shall not be dropped. We combine these "elements" in a DHCPv6 Guard policy, which is then bound to VLAN 1. After the configuration is done, DHCPv6 is working again as intended and the DHCPv6 addresses are populated in the binding table indicated by the following log message:

```
%SISF-6-ENTRY_CREATED: Entry created A=2001:DB8:1:0:BCC1:41C0:D904:E1B9 V=1
  I=Gi1/15 P=0024 M=28D2.4448.E276
```

Looking into the binding table again, the IPv6 address now appears as shown in Example 9-35.

**Example 9-35**  *IPv6 Binding Database*

```
!!!!!!!!!!!!!!!!!!!!!!!!!!!!!!!!!!!!!!!!!!!!!
Switch# show ipv6 neighbors binding
Binding Table has 6 entries, 6 dynamic
Codes: L - Local, S - Static, ND - Neighbor Discovery, DH - DHCP, PKT - Other
  Packet, API - API created
Preflevel flags (prlvl):
0001:MAC and LLA match     0002:Orig trunk           0004:Orig access
0008:Orig trusted trunk    0010:Orig trusted access  0020:DHCP assigned
0040:Cga authenticated     0080:Cert authenticated   0100:Statically assigned
IPv6 address                    Link-Layer addr Interface vlan prlvl  age    state
  Time left
ND  FE80::81E2:1562:E5A0:43EE        28D2.4448.E276  Gi1/15      1  0005     3mn
  REACHABLE  94 s
ND  FE80::3AEA:A7FF:FE85:C926        38EA.A785.C926  Gi1/2       1  0005    26mn
  STALE      86999 s
```

```
ND   FE80::10                                38EA.A785.C926   Gi1/2        1   0005   26mn
     STALE        85533
ND   FE80::1                                 E4C7.228B.F180   Gi1/7        1   0005   35s
     REACHABLE    272 s
DH   2001:DB8:1:0:BCC1:41C0:D904:E1B9        28D2.4448.E276   Gi1/15       1   0024   3mn
     REACHABLE    87 s(166161s
```

Now we see an new entry starting with "DH," indicating that this binding was learned by snooping the DHCPv6 packet.

Now that DHCPv6 is working again, we have to configure an RA Guard policy to allow the router advertisements of our legitimate router. We will just configure the system so that the port (where our router is connected) is a "trusted port," which means that RAs are allowed regardless of the configuration in the policy. We will do this as illustrated in Example 9-36.

**Example 9-36**   *Trusting the Port*

```
!!!!!!!!!!!!!!!!!!!!!!!!!!!!!!!!!!!!!!!!!!!!!!!
CAT1(config)# ipv6 nd raguard policy ra_pol
CAT1(config-nd-raguard)# device-role router
CAT1(config-nd-raguard)# trusted-port
CAT1(config-nd-raguard)# exit
CAT1(config)# int g1/0/1
CAT1(config-if)# ipv6 nd raguard attach-policy ra_pol
```

After the configuration is applied to g1/0/1, RAs will not be dropped by the switch.

## IPv6 Device Tracking

The IPv6 device tracking feature provides IPv6 host tracking so that a neighbor table can be immediately updated when an IPv6 host disappears. The feature tracks the reachability of the neighbors connected through the Layer 2 switch on a regular basis to revoke network access privileges as they become inactive. We can see the configuration and verification of this feature in Example 9-37.

**Example 9-37**   *IPv6 Device Tracking*

```
!!!!!!!!!!!!!!!!!!!!!!!!!!!!!!!!!!!!!!!!!!!!!!!!!
CAT1(config)# ipv6 neighbor binding vlan 100 interface Gi 1/0/1 reachable-lifetime
   100
CAT1(config)# ipv6 neighbor binding max-entries 100
CAT1(config)# ipv6 neighbor binding logging
!!!!!!!!!!!!!!!!!!!!!!!!!!!!
!!!   Verification
!!!!!!!!!!!!!!!!!!!!!!!!!!!!
CAT1# show ipv6 neighbor tracking
```

```
        IPv6 address              Link-Layer addr Interface vlan prlvl age    state
     Time left
ND  FE80::A8BB:CCFF:FE01:F500   AABB.CC01.F500   Et0/0      100  0002    0   REACHABLE
    8850
L   FE80::21D:71FF:FE99:4900    001D.7199.4900   Vl100      100  0080  7203   DOWN
    N/A
ND  2001:600::1                 AABB.CC01.F500   Et0/0      100  0003    0   REACHABLE
    3181
ND  2001:300::1                 AABB.CC01.F500   Et0/0      100  0007    0   REACHABLE
    9559
L   2001:400::1                 001D.7199.4900   Vl100      100  0080  7188   DOWN
    N/A
```

## IPv6 Neighbor Discovery Inspection

IPv6 ND inspection learns and secures bindings for stateless autoconfiguration addresses in L2 neighbor tables. IPv6 ND inspection analyzes neighbor discovery messages to build a trusted binding table database, and IPv6 neighbor discovery messages that do not conform are dropped. An ND message is considered trustworthy if its IPv6–to–Media Access Control (MAC) mapping is verifiable. Example 9-38 demonstrates the basic configuration of this feature.

**Example 9-38**  *IPv6 Device Tracking*

```
!!!!!!!!!!!!!!!!!!!!!!!!!!!!!!!!!!!!!!!!!!!!!!
CAT1(config)# ipv6 nd inspection policy example_policy
CAT1(config-nd-inspection)# device-role switch
CAT1(config-nd-inspection)# drop-unsecure
CAT1(config-nd-inspection)# limit address-count 1000
CAT1(config-nd-inspection)# tracking disable stale-lifetime infinite
CAT1(config-nd-inspection)# trusted-port
CAT1(config-nd-inspection)# validate source-mac
CAT1(config-nd-inspection)# no validate source-mac
CAT1(config-nd-inspection)# default limit address-count
CAT1(config-nd-inspection)#
!!!!!!!!!!!!!!!!!!!!!!!
!! Now to verify the configuration
!!!!!!!!!!!!!!!!!!!!!!!
CAT1# show ipv6 nd inspection policy example_policy
Policy example_policy configuration:
  trusted-port
  device-role switch
  drop-unsecure
  tracking disable stale-lifetime infinite
Policy example_policy is applied on the following targets:
Target              Type  Policy           Feature       Target range
CAT1#
```

We see the policy but we do not see that it has been applied. The step is to ensure that we apply it to an interface, as shown in Example 9-39.

**Example 9-39**  *Applying IPv6 ND Inspection Policy*

```
!!!!!!!!!!!!!!!!!!!!!!!!!!!!!!!!!!!!!!!!!!!!!!
CAT1(config)# int gi1/0/2
CAT1(config-if)# ipv6 nd inspection attach-policy example_policy
CAT1(config-if)# exit
CAT1(config)# exit
!!!!!!!!!!!
!!! Now to verify the configuration again
!!!!!!!!!!!
CAT1# show ipv6 nd inspection policy example_policy
*Mar  1 00:56:30.423: %SYS-5-CONFIG_I: Configured from console by console
Policy example_policy configuration:
  trusted-port
  device-role switch
  drop-unsecure
  tracking disable stale-lifetime infinite
Policy example_policy is applied on the following targets:
Target             Type  Policy          Feature          Target range
Gi1/0/2            PORT  example_policy  NDP inspection   vlan all
CAT1#
```

We can see now that the policy is applied to interface Gi1/0/2.

## IPv6 Source Guard

IPv6 Source Guard is an interface feature between the populated binding table and data traffic filtering. This feature enables the device to deny traffic when it is originated from an address that is not stored in the binding table. IPv6 Source Guard does not inspect ND or DHCP packets; rather, it works in conjunction with IPv6 neighbor discovery (ND) inspection or IPv6 address glean, both of which detect existing addresses on the link and store them in the binding table. IPv6 Source Guard is an interface between the populated binding table and data traffic filtering, and the binding table must be populated with IPv6 prefixes for IPv6 Source Guard to work.

IPv6 Source Guard can deny traffic from unknown sources or unallocated addresses, such as traffic from sources not assigned by a DHCP server. When traffic is denied, the IPv6 address glean feature is notified so that it can try to recover the traffic by querying the DHCP server or by using IPv6 ND. The data-glean function prevents the device and end user from getting deadlocked, whereupon a valid address fails to be stored in the binding table, there is no recovery path, and the end user is unable to connect.

Figure 9-14 provides an overview of how IPv6 Source Guard works with IPv6 address glean.

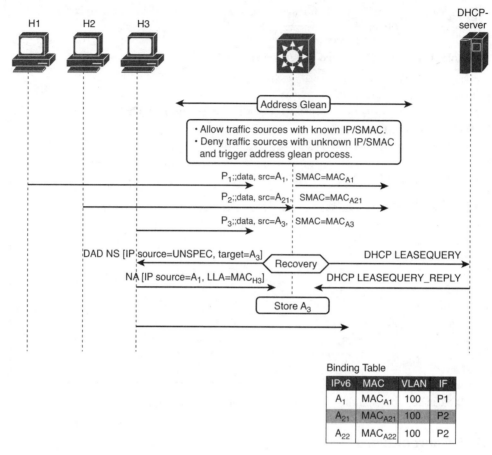

**Figure 9-14** *IPv6 Source Guard and Address Glean*

Example 9-40 demonstrates how to configure IPv6 Source Guard and confirm the configuration.

**Example 9-40** *IPv6 Source Guard Configuration and Verification*

```
!!!!!!!!!!!!!!!!!!!!!!!!!!!!!!!!!!!!!!!!!!!!!!!!!!!!!
CAT2(config)# ipv6 access-list acl1
CAT2(config-ipv6-acl)# permit host FE80::A8BB:CCFF:FE01:F700 any
CAT2(config-ipv6-acl)# ipv6 prefix-list abc permit 2001:0DB8::/64 le 128
CAT2(config)# ipv6 dhcp guard policy pol1
CAT2(config-dhcp-guard)# device-role server
CAT2(config-dhcp-guard)# match server access-list acl1
CAT2(config-dhcp-guard)# match reply prefix-list abc
CAT2(config-dhcp-guard)# trusted-port
CAT2(config-dhcp-guard)# interface GigabitEthernet 1/0/1
CAT2(config-if)# switchport
CAT2(config-if)# ipv6 dhcp guard attach-policy pol1 vlan add 10
```

```
!!!!!!!!!!!!!!
!!!! Now that the config is applied we will verify
!!!!!!!!!!!!!!
CAT2(config-if)# do show ipv6 dhcp guard policy pol1
Dhcp guard policy: pol1
        Trusted Port
        Target: Gi1/0/1

CAT2#
```

## Port Access Control Lists (PACL)

Another method that can be used to protect devices is the Port Access Control List (PACL). This switching feature is very similar to the Router ACLs. These access lists are applied to switch ports and can be configured to operate in ingress or egress with regard to traffic flows. PACL should not be confused with VLAN Access Lists (VACL). In fact, if a PACL and a VACL are applied simultaneously, the PACL will be processed first by the switch IOS. In this situation, let's say that inbound traffic was permitted by the PACL; it will then be tested by the VACL. This process affords administrators more granular control over "interesting" traffic when it comes to transit devices like switches.

Example 9-41 illustrates both the basic configuration and the directional nature of these configuration tools.

**Example 9-41**  *PACL Configuration*

```
!!!!!!!!!!!!!!!!!!!!!!!!!!!!!!!!!!!!!!!!!!!!!!
CAT2(config)# int g1/0/1
CAT2(config-if)# ip access-group PACLIPList in
CAT2(config if)# mac access-group PACLMACList in
CAT2(config-if)#
```

# Foundation Summary

This section lists additional details and facts to round out the coverage of the topics in this chapter. Unlike most of the Cisco Press Exam Certification Guides, this "Foundation Summary" does not repeat information presented in the "Foundation Topics" section of the chapter. Please take the time to read and study the details in the "Foundation Topics" section of the chapter, as well as review items noted with a Key Topic icon.

Table 9-12 lists some of the key protocols covered in this chapter.

**Table 9-12** *Protocols and Standards for Chapter 9*

| Name | Standard |
|---|---|
| RADIUS | RFC 2865 |
| Port-Based Network Access Control | IEEE 802.1X |
| EAP | RFC 3748 |
| One-Time Password System | RFC 2289 |
| Router Security | RFCs 2827 and 3704 |
| Next Hop Resolution Protocol (NHRP) | RFC 2332 |
| Secure Neighbor Discovery (SeND) | RFC 3971 |

Table 9-13 lists some of the most popular router IOS commands related to the topics in this chapter.

**Table 9-13** *Router IOS Commands Related to Chapter 9*

| Command | Description |
|---|---|
| **service password-encryption** | Global command to enable simple encryption of passwords |
| **aaa group server radius \| tacacs+** *group-name* | Global command to create the name of a group of AAA servers |
| **aaa group server ldap** | Defines the AAA server group with a group name and enters LDAP server group configuration mode |
| **server** *ip-address* [**auth-port** *port-number*] [**acct-port** *port-number*] | AAA group mode; defines a RADIUS server and ports used |
| **radius-server host** {*hostname* \| *ip-address*} [**auth-port** *port-number*] [**acct-port** *port-number*] [**timeout** *seconds*] [**retransmit** *retries*] [**key** *string*] [**alias**{*hostname* \| *ip-address*}] | Global mode; defines details regarding a single RADIUS server |

| Command | Description |
| --- | --- |
| **radius-server key** {0 *string* | 7 *string* | *string*} | Global mode; defines the key used to encrypt RADIUS passwords |
| **tacacs-server host** {*host-name* | *host-ip-address*} [**key** *string*] [**nat**] [**port** [*integer*]] [**single-connection**] [**timeout** [*integer*]] | Global mode; defines details regarding a single TACACS+ server |
| **tacacs-server key** *key* | Global mode; defines the key used to encrypt the TACACS+ payload |
| **aaa authentication enable default** *method1* [*method2...*] | Global mode; defines the default authentication methods used by the **enable** command |
| **aaa authentication login** {**default** | *list-name*} *method1* [*method2...*] | Global mode; defines the default authentication methods used by console, vty, and aux logins |
| **aaa authentication ppp** {**default** | *list-name*} *method1* [*method2...*] | Global mode; defines the default authentication methods used by PPP |
| **aaa new-model** | Global mode; enables AAA globally in a router/switch |
| **login authentication** {**default** | *list-name*} | Line mode; defines the AAA group to use for authentication |
| **ppp authentication** {*protocol1* [*protocol2...*]} [**if-needed**] [*list-name* | **default**] [**callin**] [**one-time**] [**optional**] | Interface mode; defines the type of AAA authentication used by PPP |
| **auto secure** [**management** | **forwarding**] [**no-interact**] | Global mode; automatically configures IOS with the Cisco-recommended device security configuration |
| **enable password** [**level** *level*] {*password* | [*encryption-type*] *encrypted-password*} | Global mode; defines the enable password |
| **enable secret** [**level** *level*] {*password* | [*encryption-type*] *encrypted-password*} | Global mode; defines the enable password that is MD5 hashed |
| **ip verify unicast reverse-path** [*list*] | Interface subcommand; enables strict RPF |
| **ip verify unicast source reachable-via** {**rx** | **any**} [**allow-default**] [**allow-self-ping**] [*list*] | Interface subcommand; enables strict or loose RPF |
| **username** *name* {**nopassword** | **password** *password*} | Global mode; defines local usernames and passwords |
| **username** *name* **secret** {[**0**] *password* | **5** *encrypted-secret*} | Global mode; defines local usernames and MD5-hashed passwords |
| **ip tcp intercept list** *access-list-number* | Global mode; identifies an ACL to be used by TCP intercept |

| Command | Description |
| --- | --- |
| ip tcp intercept mode {intercept \| watch} | Global mode; defines the mode used by TCP intercept |
| ip tcp intercept watch-timeout *seconds* | Global mode; defines the timeout used before acting to clean up an incomplete TCP connection |
| ip inspect name inspection-name protocol [timeout seconds] | Global mode; configures inspection rules for CBAC |
| ip inspect inspection-name {in \| out} | Interface mode; applies a CBAC inspection rule to an interface |
| zone security *name* | Global mode; creates an IOS ZFW security zone |
| zone-pair security *name* source *source-zone-name* destination *destination-zone-name* | Global mode; creates IOS ZFW zone pairs |
| class-map type inspect *name* | Global mode; creates a ZFW class map |
| parameter-map type inspect *name* | Global mode; creates a ZFW parameter map |
| policy-map type inspect | Global mode; creates a ZFW service policy |
| service-policy type inspect *name* | Zone-pair configuration mode; assigns a policy map to a zone pair |
| zone-member security *zone-name* | Interface mode; associates an interface with a ZFW zone |
| show ip ips configuration | Displays detailed IOS IPS configuration information |
| crypto key pubkey-chain rsa | Global mode; creates an IOS IPS crypto key |
| ip ips signature-category | Global mode; load or make changes to an IPS signature package |
| ip ips *name* | Global mode; creates an IOS IPS signature rule |
| ip ips *name* [outbound \| inbound] | Interface mode; assigns an IOS IPS rule to an interface |
| show ip ips configuration | Displays the IOS IPS configuration |
| ip nhrp authentication *password* | Configures password authentication for NHRP traffic |
| ip nhrp nhs *ip* | Identifies the IP address of the NHS server ("Hub") |

| Command | Description |
|---|---|
| ip nhrp map multicast | Identifies the IP address of the "Hub" such that multicast and broadcast traffic can be passed between DMVPN members. Additionally, this could be configured as dynamic rather than statically configured |
| ip nhrp map *nbma ip dmvpn ip* | Provides one-to-one mapping for reachability to the NBMA address of the hub |
| ip nhrp network-id *number* | Specifies the network number to be shared between devices participating in the same DMVPN cloud |
| ipv6 dhcp guard policy name | Defines the DHCPv6 Guard policy name and enters DHCP Guard configuration mode |

Table 9-14 lists some of the Catalyst IOS switch commands used in this chapter.

**Table 9-14**  *Catalyst IOS Commands Related to Chapter 9*

| Command | Description |
|---|---|
| spanning-tree guard root | Interface mode; enables Root Guard. |
| aaa authentication dot1x {default} *method1* | Global mode; defines the default authentication method for 802.1X. Only one method is available, because only RADIUS is supported. |
| arp access-list *acl-name* | Global mode; creates an ARP ACL with the stated name. |
| dot1x system-auth-control | Global mode; enables 802.1X. |
| dot1x port-control {auto \| force-authorized \| force-unauthorized} | Interface mode; defines 802.1X actions on the interface. |
| dot1x timeout {quiet-period *seconds* \| reauth-period *seconds* \| server-timeout *seconds* \| supp-timeout *seconds* \| tx-period *seconds*} | Global mode; sets 802.1X timers. |
| control plane | Global mode; accesses the router or switch control-plane configuration mode |
| service-policy input *name* | Control plane configuration mode; applies a policy map to the control plane |
| show policy-map control-plane | Displays the CoPP policy actions |

# Memory Builders

The CCIE Routing and Switching written exam, like all Cisco CCIE written exams, covers a fairly broad set of topics. This section provides some basic tools to help you exercise your memory about some of the broader topics covered in this chapter.

## Fill In Key Tables from Memory

Appendix E, "Key Tables for CCIE Study," on the CD in the back of this book, contains empty sets of some of the key summary tables in each chapter. Print Appendix E, refer to this chapter's tables in it, and fill in the tables from memory. Refer to Appendix F, "Solutions for Key Tables for CCIE Study," on the CD, to check your answers.

## Definitions

Next, take a few moments to write down the definitions for the following terms:

AAA, authentication method, RADIUS, TACACS+, MD5 hash, enable password, enable secret, ACS, SAFE Blueprint, DAI, port security, IEEE 802.1X, DHCP snooping, IP Source Guard, man-in-the-middle attack, sticky learning, fraggle attack, DHCP snooping binding database, EAP, EAPoL, OTP, supplicant, authenticator, authentication server, smurf attack, TCP SYN flood, TCP intercept, ACE, storm control, CBAC, classic IOS firewall, zone-based IOS firewall, IOS IPS, inspection rule, DMVPN, CoPP

Refer to the glossary to check your answers.

## Further Reading

*Network Security Principles and Practices*, by Saadat Malik

*Network Security Architectures*, by Sean Convery

*Router Security Strategies*, by Gregg Schudel and David Smith

*LAN Switch Security: What Hackers Know About Your Switches*, by Eric Vyncke and Christopher Paggen

Cisco SAFE Blueprint Introduction: www.cisco.com/go/safe

Cisco IOS Security Configuration Guide: Securing the Data Plane, Release 12.4, www.cisco.com/en/US/docs/ios/sec_data_plane/configuration/guide/12_4/sec_data_plane_12_4_book.html

"IPv6 First Hop Security—Protecting Your IPv6 Access Network": www.cisco.com/c/en/us/products/collateral/ios-nx-os-software/enterprise-ipv6-solution/whitepaper_c11-602135.html

"Dynamic Multipoint VPN (DMVPN)," www.cisco.com/en/US/docs/ios/sec_secure_connectivity/configuration/guide/sec_DMVPN_ps6350_TSD_Products_Configuration_Guide_Chapter.html

**Blueprint topics covered in this chapter:**

This chapter covers the following subtopics from the Cisco CCIE Routing and Switching written exam blueprint. Refer to the full blueprint in Table I-1 in the Introduction for more details on the topics covered in each chapter and their context within the blueprint.

- Generic Routing Encapsulation (GRE) Tunnels

- Dynamic Multipoint VPN (DMVPN) Tunnels

- IPv6 Tunneling and Related Techniques

- Layer 2 VPNs

- IP Security (IPsec) with Preshared Keys

- Group Encrypted Transport VPNs (GET VPN)

# Tunneling Technologies

Chapter 10 discusses the independent Virtual Private Network technologies that need to be mastered as part of the CCIE Routing and Switching exam. These technologies come in many forms and varieties, and mastering each of them will involve working with many different authentication or encryption features. This chapter will focus on all the necessary skills to implement each of the basic features that are part of the lab exam.

Note that our involvement with aspects of this technology that extend to more specific security studies will be kept to a minimum.

## "Do I Know This Already?" Quiz

Table 10-1 outlines the major headings in this chapter and the corresponding "Do I Know This Already?" quiz questions.

**Table 10-1** *"Do I Know This Already?" Foundation Topics Section-to-Question Mapping*

| Foundation Topics Section | Questions Covered in This Section | Score |
|---|---|---|
| DMVPN | 1–3 | |
| IPv6 Tunnels | 4 | |
| Layer 2 VPNs | 5–7 | |
| GET VPNs | 8, 9 | |
| Total Score | | |

To best use this pre-chapter assessment, remember to score yourself strictly. You can find the answers in Appendix A, "Answers to the 'Do I Know This Already?' Quizzes."

1. The main benefit of DMVPN is that it allows the traditional hub-and-spoke network design to better support what feature?

   a. Packet transmission

   b. Scalability

   c. Quality of service

   d. Traffic shaping

**2.** Several protocols combine to support the idea of a DMVPN solution, but foundationally a stable working DMVPN environment relies heavily on a number of Cisco-enhanced technologies. Choose the correct technologies.

   **a.** Generic Routing Encapsulation (GRE) Protocol

   **b.** First-Hop Redundancy Protocol (FHRP)

   **c.** Next-Hop Resolution Protocol (NHRP)

   **d.** Dynamic Routing Protocol

   **e.** Secure DMVPN

   **f.** IPsec encryption protocols

**3.** What new message type is sent from the hub to the spoke to let the spoke know that there is a better path to the other spoke than through the hub?

   **a.** ICMP Redirect

   **b.** Proxy ARP

   **c.** NHRP Redirect

   **d.** Local Proxy ARP

**4.** In an ipv6ip auto-tunnel, the destination for an IPv4-compatible tunnel is automatically determined by what portion of the tunnel interface address?

   **a.** Upper-order 32 bits

   **b.** Lower-order 16 bits

   **c.** Upper-order 16 bits

   **d.** Lower-order 32 bits

**5.** L2VPN is the simplest solution available to allow clients to manage network features that include which of the following?

   **a.** Routing protocols

   **b.** Policing policies

   **c.** QoS mechanisms

   **d.** IOS management protocols

   **e.** IP management

**6.** The output of the following command indicates what status associated with the DMVPN configuration?

```
R2# show xconnect all

Legend: XC ST=Xconnect State, S1=Segment1 State, S2=Segment2 State
UP=Up, DN=Down, AD=Admin Down, IA=Inactive, NH=No Hardware
XC ST Segment 1 S1 Segment 2 S2
------+-------------------------------+--+--------------------------------
+--
DN ac Fa0/0(Ethernet) AD mpls 4.4.4.4:204 DN
```

   **a.** The pseudowire link is up.

   **b.** The pseudowire link is administratively down.

   **c.** The pseudowire link is down.

   **d.** The pseudowire link is operating normally.

**7.** What are the two primary segments used in an MPLS Layer 2 pseudowire?

   **a.** Segment 1

   **b.** Segment A

   **c.** Segment B

   **d.** Segment 1-2

   **e.** Segment 2

**8.** In any DMVPN solution, the most important function of the key server is the generation of encryption keys. What two keys are created as a result of this process?

   **a.** RSA

   **b.** TEK

   **c.** SHA1

   **d.** TLS

   **e.** KEK

**9.** When configuring DMVPN group members, the encryption policy is created through an IPsec profile. What tool is used to identify what packets require encryption?

   **a.** ip prefix-list

   **b.** PACL

   **c.** ACL

   **d.** VACL

## Foundation Topics

# GRE Tunnels

Generic Routing Encapsulation (GRE) defines a method of tunneling data from one router to another. To tunnel the traffic, the sending router encapsulates packets of one networking protocol, called the passenger protocol, inside packets of another protocol, called the transport protocol, transporting these packets to another router. The receiving router deencapsulates and forwards the original passenger protocol packets. This process allows the routers in the network to forward traffic that might not be natively supported by the intervening routers. For example, if some routers did not support IP multicast, the IP multicast traffic could be tunneled from one router to another using IP unicast packets.

GRE tunnels are useful for a variety of tasks. From the network standpoint, GRE tunnel traffic is considered GRE; that is, it's not IP unicast or multicast or IPsec or whatever else is being encapsulated. Therefore, you can use GRE to tunnel traffic that might not otherwise be able to traverse the network. An example of this is encapsulating multicast IP traffic within a GRE tunnel to allow it to pass across a network that does not support multicast.

GRE tunnels can also be used to encapsulate traffic so that the traffic inside the tunnel is unaware of the network topology. Regardless of the number of network hops between the source and destination, the traffic passing over the tunnel sees it as a single hop. Because tunnels hide the network topology, the actual traffic path across a network is also unimportant to the traffic inside the tunnel. If loopback addresses are used for source and destination addresses, the tunnel provides connectivity between the source and destination as long as there is any available route between the loopbacks. Even if the normal egress interface were to go down, traffic across the tunnel could continue to flow.

IPsec virtual tunnel interfaces (VTI) are routable interfaces used for terminating IPsec tunnels and are often an easy way to define protection between sites. VTIs simplify configuration of IPsec for protection of remote links, simplify network management, and support multicast. The IPsec VTI enables flexibility of sending and receiving both IP unicast and multicast encrypted traffic on any physical interface. For the purposes of the CCIE Exam, it's important to understand the benefits of virtual tunnel interfaces and how to configure a VTI using the various tunneling mechanisms including GRE, Layer 2 Virtual Private Networks (L2VPN), and Multiprotocol Label Switching (MPLS).

The router must be configured to pass the desired traffic across the tunnel. This is often accomplished using a static route to point traffic to the tunnel interface.

Example 10-1 shows a typical tunnel configuration on two routers. Both routers source traffic from a loopback interface and point to the corresponding loopback interface. IP addresses in a new subnet on these routers are assigned to the loopback interfaces.

**Example 10-1**  *GRE Tunnel Configuration*

```
R2# show run int lo0
interface Loopback0
 ip address 150.1.2.2 255.255.255.0
R2# show run int tun0
interface Tunnel0
   ip address 192.168.201.2 255.255.255.0
   tunnel source Loopback0
   tunnel destination 150.1.3.3
! Now on to R3:
R3# show run int lo0
interface Loopback0
 ip address 150.1.3.3 255.255.255.128
R3# show run int tun0
interface Tunnel0
 ip address 192.168.201.3 255.255.255.0
 tunnel source Loopback0
 tunnel destination 150.1.2.2
R3# show ip interface brief
Interface              IP-Address       OK? Method Status        Protocol
Serial0/2              144.254.254.3    YES TFTP   up            up
Serial0/3              unassigned       YES NVRAM  up            down
Virtual-Access1        unassigned       YES unset  up            up
Loopback0              150.1.3.3        YES NVRAM  up            up
Tunnel0                192.168.201.3    YES manual up            up
```

## Dynamic Multipoint VPN Tunnels

There is no escaping the fact that VPN-based security architectures are proving their worth in modern distributed infrastructures. The ever-changing landscape of our networks demands that sensitive data be sent from point to point through different mediums, many of which, like the Internet, are insecure. So it should come as no surprise that tools to protect that data are also expanding and evolving.

Evolution is not the only external force acting on our network architectures. As network engineers, we find ourselves constantly looking at how things have been traditionally done, and asking ourselves whether those methods are going to be efficient and scalable for our individual organizational needs. Take the typical IPsec-based hub-and-spoke deployment model. This solution has been used for decades to provide interconnectivity for site-to-site networks, but looking at how our needs are constantly expanding, it becomes evident that what was traditional yesterday is rapidly become less and less adequate for larger or enterprise-size networks. These "enterprise" networks need a scalable and more dynamic solution that will provide secure transport of information across wide-area network topology through the application of dynamic features, like IPsec, that will optimize network performance by decreasing latency and maximizing bandwidth utilization.

Dynamic Multipoint VPN (DMVPN) technology is one such feature. DMVPN provides much-needed scalability to distributed infrastructures; scalability can help virtually any network expand simply and easily to its full potential.

## DMVPN Operation

The main benefit of DMVPN is that it allows the tradition hub-and-spoke network design to better support scalability. This enhanced ability to service more capacity means reduced latency and optimized performance for traffic exchange between multiple sites. This one simple enhancement translates directly to a number of immediate benefits:

- Dynamic tunnels across hub-and-spoke topologies

- Increased network performance

- Reduced latency, which provides immediate optimization for "real-time" applications

- Reduced router configuration

- Ability to dynamically add more tunnels to new sites without modifying the hub router configuration ("zero-touch")

- Dynamic IPsec encryption that eliminates packet loss

- Dynamic "spoke-to-spoke" tunnels between sites (intersite communication) that bypasses the hub

- Support for routing protocols over individual or all tunnels

- Support for multicast traffic

- Virtual Routing and Forwarding (VRF) awareness

- Supports MPLS

- Supports load balancing

- Automatically reroutes traffic during network outages

Geographic site isolation and the "slow" internetwork connections used to transport traffic between them have long plagued the distributed network deployment model, but keep in mind that other factors are also contributors, to include network availability and secure communications options. DMVPN is the perfect solution to the problem; it is secure, it is scalable, and it is self-healing.

## DMVPN Components

Several protocols combine to support the idea of a DMVPN solution, but foundationally a stable working DMVPN environment relies heavily on a number of Cisco-enhanced technologies:

- Generic Routing Encapsulation (GRE) Protocol

- Next-Hop Resolution Protocol (NHRP)

- Dynamic routing protocols

- IPsec encryption protocols

## DMVPN Operation

DMVPN primarily distills down to one clear-cut operation the creation of dynamic tunnel overlay networks. In this design, each spoke becomes a persistent IPsec tunnel to the hub. Keep in mind that spokes in this scenario will not build tunnels with other spokes. For this process to function reliably, the address of the hub must be known by all the spokes in the topology. Using this information, each spoke will register its actual address as a client to the NHRP server process running on the hub. It is this NHRP server that is responsible for maintaining a database of all the public interface addresses used by each spoke during its registration process. In situations where a spoke requires packets to be sent to a destination (in this case, a private address) on another spoke, it will solicit the NHRP server for the public (outside) address of the other spoke device so that it can create a direct tunnel. The reliance on the NHRP server eliminates the need for dynamic routing protocols to discover routes to spokes. We mentioned dynamic routing protocols in the previous list, but those protocols only create adjacencies between spoke devices and the hub.

After the spoke is informed of the peer address of the destination device (spoke), it will initiate a dynamic IPsec tunnel to that target, thus creating a dynamic spoke-to-spoke tunnel over the DMVPN topology. These tunnels are going to be established on demand, meaning whenever traffic is forwarded between spokes but after they have been created, packets can bypass the hub and use the tunnel directly.

To illustrate this process, we will pursue the implementation of the technology on the command line by taking an analytical look at the feature following the recommended three-phase implementation.

DMVPN Phase 1 introduces a simple hub-and-spoke topology where dynamic IP addresses on the spokes are used, as shown in Example 10-2.

**Example 10-2**  *Simple Hub-and-Spoke Topology with Dynamic IP Addresses*

```
!First we need ISAKMP Policy with pre-shared key configured. Note that in DMVPN we
!need to configure so-called "wildcard PSK" because there may be many peers. This
!is why a more common solution in DMVPN is to use certificates and PKI.


R1(config)# crypto isakmp policy 1
R1(config-isakmp)# encr 3des
R1(config-isakmp)# authentication pre-share
R1(config-isakmp)# group 2
```

```
R1(config-isakmp)# crypto isakmp key cisco123 address 0.0.0.0 0.0.0.0
R1(config)# crypto ipsec transform-set TSET esp-3des esp-sha-hmac
R1(cfg-crypto-trans)# mode transport

!The "mode transport" is used for decreasing IPSec packet size (an outer IP header
!which is present in tunnel mode is not added in the transport mode).

R1(cfg-crypto-trans)# crypto ipsec profile DMVPN
R1(ipsec-profile)# set transform-set TSET
R1(ipsec-profile)# exi

!There is only one interface Tunnel on every DMVPN router. This is because we use
!GRE \ multipoint type of the tunnel.

R1(config)# interface Tunnel0
R1(config-if)# ip address 172.16.145.1 255.255.255.0
R1(config-if)# ip mtu 1400

!Maximum Transmission Unit is decreased to ensure that DMVPN packet would not
!exceed IP MTU set on non-tunnel IP interfaces - usually a 1500 bytes (When
!"transport mode" isused then DMVPN packet consists of original IP Packet, GRE
!header, ESP header and outer IPSec IP header. If original IP packet size is close
!to the IP MTU set on real IP interface then adding GRE and IPSec headers may lead
!to exceeding that value)

R1(config-if)# ip nhrp authentication cisco123
R1(config-if)# ip nhrp map multicast dynamic
R1(config-if)# ip nhrp network-id 12345

!The Hub works as NHS (Next Hop Server). The NHRP configuration on the Hub is
!straight forward. First, we need NHRP network ID to identify the instance and
!authenticate key to secure NHRP registration. There is a need for NHRP static
!mapping on the Hub. The Hub must be able to send down all multicast traffic so
!that dynamic routing protocols can distribute routes between spokes. The line "ip
!nhrp map multicast dynamic" simply tells the NHRP server to replicate all multi
!cast traffic to all dynamic entries in the NHRP table (entries with flag
!"dynamic").

R1(config-if)# no ip split-horizon eigrp 145
```

```
!Since we use EIGRP between the Hub and the Spokes, we need to disable Split Horizon
!for that protocol to be able to send routes gathered from one Spoke to the other
!Spoke. The Split Horizon rule says: "information about the routing is never sent
!back in the direction from which it was received". This is basic rule for loop
!prevention.

R1(config-if)# tunnel source FastEthernet0/0
R1(config-if)# tunnel mode gre multipoint
R1(config-if)# tunnel key 12345
R1(config-if)# tunnel protection ipsec profile DMVPN

!A regular GRE tunnel usually needs source and destination of the tunnel to be
!specified. However in the GRE multipoint tunnel type, there is no need for a
!destination. This is because there may be many destinations, as many Spokes are
!out there. The actual tunnel destination is derived form NHRP database. The tunnel
!has a key for identification purposes, as there may be many tunnels on one
!router and the router must know what tunnel the packet is destined to.
```

DMVPN Phase 2 introduces a new feature, which is direct spoke-to-spoke communication through the DMVPN network. It is useful for companies that have communication between branches and want to reduce the hub's overhead. Example 10-3 describes DMVPN Phase 2 when Enhanced Interior Gateway Routing Protocol (EIGRP) is in use. This is important to understand the difference between routing protocols used in the DMVPN solution. They must be especially configured or tuned to work in the most scalable and efficient way. However, there are some disadvantages of using one protocol or another.

**Example 10-3**  *Hub-and-Spoke Topology with Spoke-to-Spoke Connection*

```
R1(config)# crypto isakmp policy 1
R1(config-isakmp)# encr 3des
R1(config-isakmp)# authentication pre-share
R1(config-isakmp)# group 2
R1(config-isakmp)# crypto isakmp key cisco123 address 0.0.0.0 0.0.0.0
R1(config)# crypto ipsec transform-set TSET esp-3des esp-sha-hmac
R1(cfg-crypto-trans)# mode transport
R1(cfg-crypto-trans)# crypto ipsec profile DMVPN
R1(ipsec-profile)# set transform-set TSET
R1(ipsec-profile)# exi
R1(config)# interface Tunnel0
R1(config-if)# ip address 172.16.145.1 255.255.255.0
R1(config-if)# ip mtu 1400
R1(config-if)# ip nhrp authentication cisco123
R1(config-if)# ip nhrp map multicast dynamic
R1(config-if)# ip nhrp network-id 12345
```

```
R1(config-if)# no ip split-horizon eigrp 145
R1(config-if)# no ip next-hop-self eigrp 145


!The difference is in routing protocol behavior. The DMVPN Phase 2 allows for
!direct Spoke to Spoke communication. Hence, one spoke must send the traffic to the
!other spoke using its routing table information. In DMVPN Phase 1 the spoke sends
!all traffic up to the Hub and uses the Hub for Spoke to Spoke communication. How
!ever,in DMVPN Phase 2 a spoke must point to the other spoke directly.


!This is achieved by changing the routing protocol behavior. The EIGRP changes next
!hop in the routing update when sending it further so that, the Hub changes the
!next hop to itself when sending down the routing updates to the Spokes. This
!behavior can be changed by the command "no ip next-hop-self eigrp AS".


R1(config-if)# tunnel source FastEthernet0/0
R1(config-if)# tunnel mode gre multipoint


!Note that in DMVPN Phase 2 the Hub is in GRE Multipoint mode as it was in Phase 1.


R1(config-if)# tunnel key 12345
R1(config-if)# tunnel protection ipsec profile DMVPN
R1(config-if)# exi
%LINEPROTO-5-UPDOWN: Line protocol on Interface Tunnel0, changed state to up
%CRYPTO-6-ISAKMP_ON_OFF: ISAKMP is ON
R1(config)# router eigrp 145
R1(config-router)# network 172.16.145.0 0.0.0.255
R1(config-router)# network 192.168.1.0
R1(config-router)# no auto-summary
R1(config-router)# exi
```

After this procedure is completed, we can verify the configuration through a number of commands, a few of which can be seen in Example 10-4.

**Example 10-4**  *DMVPN Verification*

```
R1# sh crypto ipsec sa
interface: Tunnel0
Crypto map tag: Tunnel0-head-0, local addr 10.1.12.1
protected vrf: (none)
local  ident (addr/mask/prot/port): (10.1.12.1/255.255.255.255/47/0)
remote ident (addr/mask/prot/port): (10.1.24.4/255.255.255.255/47/0)
current_peer 10.1.24.4 port 500
PERMIT, flags={origin_is_acl,}
#pkts encaps: 19, #pkts encrypt: 19, #pkts digest: 19
#pkts decaps: 18, #pkts decrypt: 18, #pkts verify: 18
#pkts compressed: 0, #pkts decompressed: 0
```

```
#pkts not compressed: 0, #pkts compr. failed: 0
#pkts not decompressed: 0, #pkts decompress failed: 0
#send errors 0, #recv errors 0

!The traffic is going through the tunnel between the Hub and the Spoke. This traffic
!is an EIGRP updates as we have not initiated any traffic yet.

local crypto endpt.: 10.1.12.1, remote crypto endpt.: 10.1.24.4
path mtu 1500, ip mtu 1500, ip mtu idb FastEthernet0/0
current outbound spi: 0x49DC5EAF(1239178927)
inbound esp sas:
spi: 0xF483377E(4102240126)
transform: esp-3des esp-sha-hmac ,
in use settings ={Transport, }
conn id: 2003, flow_id: NETGX:3, crypto map: Tunnel0-head-0
sa timing: remaining key lifetime (k/sec): (4524624/3565)
IV size: 8 bytes
replay detection support: Y
Status: ACTIVE
inbound ah sas:
inbound pcp sas:
outbound esp sas:
spi: 0x49DC5EAF(1239178927)
transform: esp-3des esp-sha-hmac ,
in use settings ={Transport, }
conn id: 2004, flow_id: NETGX:4, crypto map: Tunnel0-head-0
sa timing: remaining key lifetime (k/sec): (4524622/3565)
IV size: 8 bytes
replay detection support: Y
Status: ACTIVE
outbound ah sas:
outbound pcp sas:
protected vrf: (none)
local  ident (addr/mask/prot/port): (10.1.12.1/255.255.255.255/47/0)
remote ident (addr/mask/prot/port): (10.1.25.5/255.255.255.255/47/0)
current_peer 10.1.25.5 port 500
PERMIT, flags={origin_is_acl,}
#pkts encaps: 17, #pkts encrypt: 17, #pkts digest: 17
#pkts decaps: 15, #pkts decrypt: 15, #pkts verify: 15
#pkts compressed: 0, #pkts decompressed: 0
#pkts not compressed: 0, #pkts compr. failed: 0
#pkts not decompressed: 0, #pkts decompress failed: 0
#send errors 0, #recv errors 0

!The traffic is going through the tunnel between the Hub and the Spoke. This traffic
```

```
!is an EIGRP update as we have not initiated any traffic yet.

local crypto endpt.: 10.1.12.1, remote crypto endpt.: 10.1.25.5
path mtu 1500, ip mtu 1500, ip mtu idb FastEthernet0/0
current outbound spi: 0x1FB68E8D(532057741)
inbound esp sas:
spi: 0xE487940A(3834090506)
transform: esp-3des esp-sha-hmac ,
in use settings ={Transport, }
conn id: 2001, flow_id: NETGX:1, crypto map: Tunnel0-head-0
sa timing: remaining key lifetime (k/sec): (4411380/3563)
IV size: 8 bytes
replay detection support: Y
Status: ACTIVE
inbound ah sas:
inbound pcp sas:
outbound esp sas:
spi: 0x1FB68E8D(532057741)
transform: esp-3des esp-sha-hmac ,
in use settings ={Transport, }
conn id: 2002, flow_id: NETGX:2, crypto map: Tunnel0-head-0
sa timing: remaining key lifetime (k/sec): (4411379/3563)
IV size: 8 bytes
replay detection support: Y
Status: ACTIVE
outbound ah sas:
outbound pcp sas:
```

DMVPN Phase 3 was introduced by Cisco to fix some disadvantages found in Phase 2. Specifically, these issues include scalability and performance issues. Example 10-5 illustrates how the DMVPN process is implemented:

■ Phase 2 allows hub daisy-chaining, Open Shortest Path First (OSPF) single area, and a limited number of hubs because of OSPF DR/DBR election.

■ Scalability: Phase 2 does not allow route summarization on the hub; all prefixes must be distributed to all spokes to be able to set up direct spoke-to-spoke tunnels.

■ Performance: Phase 2 sends first packets through the hub using process switching (not Cisco Express Forwarding [CEF]), causing CPU spikes.

■ DMVPN Phase 3 uses two NHRP enhancements to remedy the Phase 2 disadvantages outlined above:

   ■ **NHRP Redirect:** A new message is sent from the hub to the spoke to let the spoke know that there is a better path to the other spoke than through the hub.

   ■ **NHRP Shortcut:** A new way of changing (overwriting) CEF information on the spoke.

**Example 10-5**  *DMVPN Phase 3*

```
R2(config)# crypto isakmp policy 10
R2(config-isakmp)# encr 3des
R2(config-isakmp)# authentication pre-share
R2(config-isakmp)# group 2
R2(config-isakmp)# crypto isakmp key cisco123 address 0.0.0.0 0.0.0.0
R2(config)# crypto ipsec transform-set TSET esp-3des esp-sha-hmac
R2(cfg-crypto-trans)# mode transport
R2(cfg-crypto-trans)# crypto ipsec profile DMVPN
R2(ipsec-profile)# set transform-set TSET
R2(ipsec-profile)# exi
R2(config)# int Tunnel0
R2(config-if)# ip address 172.16.245.2 255.255.255.0
R2(config-if)# ip mtu 1400
R2(config-if)# ip nhrp authentication cisco123
R2(config-if)# ip nhrp map multicast dynamic
R2(config-if)# ip nhrp network-id 123
R2(config-if)# ip nhrp redirect

!NHRP Redirect is a special NHRP message sent by the Hub to the spoke to tell the
!spoke that there is a better path to the remote spoke than through the Hub. All
!it does is enforces the spoke to trigger an NHRP resolution request to IP
!destination. The "ip nhrp redirect" command should be configured on the Hub only.

R2(config-if)# tunnel source s0/1/0
R2(config-if)# tunnel mode gre multipoint
R2(config-if)# tunnel key 123
R2(config-if)# tunnel protection ipsec profile DMVPN
R2(config-if)# no ip split-horizon eigrp 245
Note that we do not need "no ip next-hop-self eigrp" command in the DMVPN Pahse 3.
R2(config-if)# exi
%CRYPTO-6-ISAKMP_ON_OFF: ISAKMP is ON
R2(config)# router eigrp 245
R2(config-router)# no auto
R2(config-router)# net 172.16.245.2 0.0.0.0
R2(config-router)# net 192.168.2.2 0.0.0.0
R2(config-router)# exi
```

## IPv6 Tunneling and Related Techniques

When IPv6 development and initial deployment began in the 1990s, most of the world's networks were already built on an IPv4 infrastructure. As a result, several groups recognized that there was going to be a need for ways to transport IPv6 over IPv4 networks and, as some people anticipated, vice versa.

One of the key reasons for tunneling is that today's Internet is IPv4 based, yet at least two major academic and research networks use IPv6 natively, and it is desirable to provide mechanisms for hosts on those networks to reach each other over the IPv4 Internet. Tunneling is one of the ways to support that communication.

As you might gather, tunneling meets a number of needs in a mixed IPv4 and IPv6 world; as a result, several kinds of tunneling methods and techniques have emerged. This section looks at several of them and examines one in detail.

## Tunneling Overview

Tunneling, in a general sense, is encapsulating traffic. More specifically, the term usually refers to the process of encapsulating traffic at a given layer of the OSI seven-layer model *within another protocol running at the same layer*. Therefore, encapsulating IPv6 packets within IPv4 packets and encapsulating IPv4 packets within IPv6 packets are both considered tunneling.

For the purposes of this book, which is to meet the CCIE Routing and Switching blueprint requirements, in this section, we are mostly interested in methods of carrying IPv6 over IPv4 networks, not the other way around. This chapter also does not explore methods of tunneling IPv6 inside IPv6. However, you should be aware that both of these types of tunneling exist, in addition to the ones covered here. With that in mind, consider some of the more common tunneling methods, starting with a summary shown in Table 10-2.

Key
Topic

**Table 10-2**  *Summary of Tunneling Methods*

| Tunnel Mode | Topology and Address Space | Applications |
|---|---|---|
| Automatic 6to4 | Point-to-multipoint; 2002::/16 addresses | Connecting isolated IPv6 island networks. |
| Manually configured | Point-to-point; any address space; requires dual-stack support at both ends | Carries only IPv6 packets across IPv4 networks. |
| IPv6 over IPv4 GRE | Point-to-point; unicast addresses; requires dual-stack support at both ends | Carries IPv6, CLNS, and other traffic. |
| ISATAP | Point-to-multipoint; any multicast addresses | Intended for connecting IPv6 hosts within a single site. |
| Automatic IPv4-compatible | Point-to-multipoint; ::/96 address space; requires dual-stack support at both ends | Deprecated. Cisco recommends using Intra-Site Automatic Tunnel Addressing Protocol (ISATAP) tunnels instead. Coverage in this book is limited. |

In case you are not familiar with implementing tunnels based on IPv4, take a moment to cover the basic steps involved:

**Step 1.**    Ensure end-to-end IPv4 reachability between the tunnel endpoints.

**Step 2.**    Create the tunnel interface using the **interface tunnel** *n* command.

**Step 3.**    Select a tunnel source interface and configure it using the **tunnel source inter-face** {*interface-type-number* | *ip-address*} command.

**Step 4.**    For nonautomatic tunnel types, configure the tunnel destination using the **tunnel destination** {*ip-address* | *ipv6-address* | *hostname*} command. To use the **hostname** argument, Domain Name System (DNS) or local host name–to–IP address mapping is required.

**Step 5.**    Configure the tunnel IPv6 address (or prefix, depending on tunnel type).

**Step 6.**    Configure the tunnel mode using the **tunnel mode** *mode* command.

Table 10-3 shows the Cisco IOS tunnel modes and the destinations for the tunnel types covered in this section.

**Table 10-3**    *Cisco IOS Tunnel Modes and Destinations*

| Tunnel Type | Tunnel Mode | Destination |
|---|---|---|
| Manual | **ipv6ip** | An IPv4 address |
| GRE over IPv4 | **gre ip** | An IPv4 address |
| Automatic 6to4 | **ipv6ip 6to4** | Automatically determined |
| ISATAP | **ipv6ip isatap** | Automatically determined |
| Automatic IPv4-compatible | **ipv6ip auto-tunnel** | Automatically determined |

Let's take a closer look at the methods of carrying IPv6 traffic over an IPv4 network.

## Manually Configured Tunnels

This tunnel type is point-to-point in nature. Cisco IOS requires statically configuring the destination addresses of these tunnels. Configuring a manual IPv6-over-IPv4 tunnel is almost identical to configuring an IPv4 GRE tunnel; the only difference is setting the tunnel mode. Example 10-6 and Figure 10-1 show a manually configured tunnel. IPv4 reachability has already been configured and verified, but is not shown.

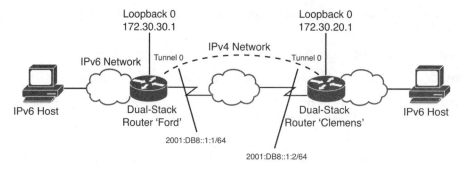

**Figure 10-1**    *Manually Configured Tunnel*

**Example 10-6**    *Manual Tunnel Configuration*

```
! In this example, Clemens and Ford are running IPv4 and OSPFv2 on their
! loopback 0 interfaces and the link that connects the two routers. This provides
! the IPv4 connectivity required for these tunnels to work.
!Configuration on the Ford router:
Ford# show run interface tunnel0
interface Tunnel0
 no ip address
 ipv6 address 2001:DB8::1:1/64
 tunnel source Loopback0
! In the tunnel destination, 172.30.20.1 is Clemens's Loopback0 interface:
 tunnel destination 172.30.20.1
 tunnel mode ipv6ip
Ford#
! Configuration on the Clemens router:
Clemens# show run interface tunnel0
interface Tunnel0
 no ip address
 ipv6 address 2001:DB8::1:2/64
 tunnel source Loopback0
! In the tunnel destination, 172.30.30.1 is Ford's Loopback0 interface:
 tunnel destination 172.30.30.1
 tunnel mode ipv6ip
! Demonstrating reachability across the tunnel:
Clemens# ping 2001:DB8::1:1
Type escape sequence to abort.
Sending 5, 100-byte ICMP Echos to 2001:DB8::1:1, timeout is 2 seconds:
!!!!!
Success rate is 100 percent (5/5), round-trip min/avg/max = 36/36/40 ms
Clemens#
```

## Automatic IPv4-Compatible Tunnels

This type of tunnel uses IPv4-compatible IPv6 addresses for the tunnel interfaces. These addresses are taken from the ::/96 address space. That is, the first 96 bits of the tunnel interface addresses are all 0s, and the remaining 32 bits are derived from an IPv4 address. These addresses are written as 0:0:0:0:0:0:A.B.C.D, or ::A.B.C.D, where A.B.C.D represents the IPv4 address.

The tunnel destination for an IPv4-compatible tunnel is automatically determined from the low-order 32 bits of the tunnel interface address. To implement this tunnel type, use the **tunnel mode ipv6ip auto-tunnel** command in tunnel interface configuration mode.

IPv4-compatible IPv6 addressing is not widely deployed and does not conform to current global usage of the IPv6 address space. Furthermore, this tunneling method does not scale well. Therefore, Cisco recommends using ISATAP tunnels instead of this method, and for these reasons, this book does not explore this tunnel type further.

## IPv6-over-IPv4 GRE Tunnels

GRE tunnels provide two options that the other tunnel types do not—namely, encapsulating traffic other than IPv6 and support for IPsec. Like the manually configured variety, GRE tunnels are designed for point-to-point operation. With IPv6 as the passenger protocol, typically these tunnels are deployed between edge routers to provide connectivity between two IPv6 "islands" across an IPv4 cloud.

Configuring GRE tunnels for transporting IPv6 packets over an IPv4 network is straightforward. The only difference between GRE and the manual tunneling example shown in Example 10-6 is the syntax of the **tunnel mode** command, which for GRE is **tunnel mode gre ipv6**.

## Automatic 6to4 Tunnels

Unlike the previous two tunnel types that we have discussed, automatic 6to4 tunnels are inherently point-to-multipoint in nature. These tunnels treat the underlying IPv4 network as an NBMA cloud.

In automatic 6to4 tunnels, the tunnel operates on a per-packet basis to encapsulate traffic to the correct destination—thus its point-to-multipoint nature. These tunnels determine the appropriate destination address by combining the IPv6 prefix with the globally unique destination 6to4 border router's IPv4 address, beginning with the 2002::/16 prefix, in this format:

> 2002:*border-router-IPv4-address*::/48

This prefix-generation method leaves another 16 bits in the 64-bit prefix for numbering networks within a given site.

Cisco IOS supports configuring only one automatic 6to4 tunnel on a given router. Configuring these tunnels is similar to configuring the other tunnels previously discussed, except that the tunnel mode is configured using the **tunnel mode ipv6ip 6to4** command. Also, the tunnel destination is not explicitly configured for 6to4 tunnels because of the automatic nature of the per-packet destination prefix determination method that 6to4 uses.

In addition to the basic tunnel configuration, the extra step of providing for routing the desired packets over the tunnel is also required. This is usually done using a static route. For example, to route packets destined for prefix 2002::/16 over the tunnel0 6to4 tunnel interface, configure this static route:

```
ipv6 route 2002::/16 tunnel 0
```

Example 10-7 and Figure 10-2 show a sample of a 6to4 tunnel and the routers' other relevant interfaces to tie together the concepts of 6to4 tunneling. In the example, note that the Fast Ethernet interfaces and the tunnel interface get the bold portion of the prefix 2002:**0a01:6401**:: from the Ethernet 0 interface's IPv4 address, 10.1.100.1. For this type of tunnel to work, the tunnel source interface must be the connection to the outside world, in this case the Ethernet 2/0 interface. Furthermore, each Fast Ethernet interface where hosts connect is (and must be) a different IPv6 subnet with the 2002:**0a01:6401** prefix.

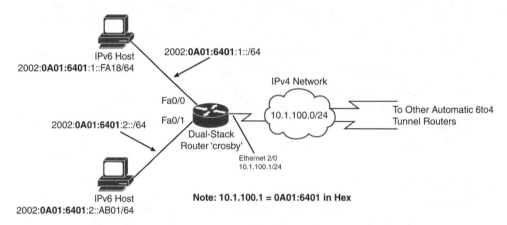

**Figure 10-2** *Automatic 6to4 Tunnel Topology*

**Example 10-7** *Automatic 6to4 Tunnel Configuration*

```
crosby# show running-config
! output omitted for brevity
interface FastEthernet0/0
 description IPv6 local host network interface 1 of 2
 ipv6 address 2002:0a01:6401:1::1/64
!
interface FastEthernet0/1
 description IPv6 local host network interface 2 of 2
 ipv6 address 2002:0a01:6401:2::1/64
!
interface Ethernet2/0
```

```
 description Ethernet link to the outside world
 ip address 10.1.100.1 255.255.255.0
 !
interface Tunnel0
 no ip address
 ipv6 address 2002:0a01:6401::1/64
 tunnel source Ethernet 2/0
 tunnel mode ipv6ip 6to4
 !
ipv6 route 2002::/16 tunnel 0
```

### ISATAP Tunnels

ISATAP, short for Intra-Site Automatic Tunnel Addressing Protocol, is defined in RFC 4214. Like 6to4, ISATAP tunnels treat the underlying IPv4 network as a nonbroadcast multiaccess (NBMA) cloud. Therefore, like 6to4, ISATAP tunnels support point-to-multipoint operation natively and determine destination on a per-packet basis. However, the method they use for determining the addressing for hosts and the tunnel interface differs from 6to4 tunnels. Otherwise, ISATAP and automatic 6to4 tunneling are similar.

ISATAP develops its addressing scheme using this format:

*[64-bit link-local or global unicast prefix]:0000:5EFE:[IPv4 address of the ISATAP link]*

The ISATAP interface identifier is the middle part of the address, 0000:5EFE.

For example, let's say that the IPv6 prefix in use is 2001:0DB8:0ABC:0DEF::/64 and the IPv4 tunnel destination address is 172.20.20.1. The IPv4 address, converted to hex, is AC14:1401. Therefore the ISATAP address is

2001:0DB8:0ABC:0DEF:0000:5EFE:AC14:1401

Configuring an ISATAP tunnel on a router differs slightly from configuring the previous tunnel types in that it uses a different tunnel mode (**ipv6ip isatap**) and in that it must be configured to derive the IPv6 address using the EUI-64 method. EUI-64 addressing in a tunnel interface differs from EUI-64 on a nontunnel interface in that it derives the last 32 bits of the interface ID from the tunnel source interface's IPv4 address. This method is necessary for ISATAP tunnels to provide a mechanism for other tunnel routers to independently know how to reach this router.

One other key difference in ISATAP tunnels is important to know. By default, tunnel interfaces disable router advertisements (RA). However, RAs must be enabled on ISATAP tunnels to support client autoconfiguration. Enable RAs on an ISATAP tunnel using the **no ipv6 nd suppress-ra** command.

## SLAAC and DHCPv6

Dynamic Host Configuration Protocol for IPv6, known as DHCPv6, is an upper-layer protocol that encompasses IPv6 address assignment dynamically. IPv6 is more complicated and provides more options than IPv4. DHCPv6 provides stateful DHCP services similarly to IPv6, but it also provides Stateless Address Autoconfiguration, or SLAAC. SLAAC is defined in RFC 4862, IPv6 Stateless Address Autoconfiguration. Stateless Address Autoconfiguration does not require the services of a DHCP server. In some cases, SLAAC only involves the router and the router advertisement messages, while in other cases, both the router advertisement (RA) message and other configuration parameters from a DHCP server are involved. SLAAC provides dynamic addressing without the services of DHCP.

## NAT-PT

Although it is not technically a tunneling protocol, one of the methods of interconnecting IPv6 and IPv4 networks is a mechanism known as Network Address Translation–Protocol Translation (NAT-PT), defined in RFCs 2765 and 2766 (obsoleted by 4966). NAT-PT works by performing a sort of gateway function at the IPv4/IPv6 boundary. At that boundary, NAT-PT translates between IPv4 and IPv6. This method permits IPv4 hosts to communicate with IPv6 hosts and vice versa without the need for those hosts to run dual protocol stacks.

Much like NAT and PAT (NAT overloading) for IPv4, NAT-PT supports static and dynamic translations, as well as port translation.

## NAT ALG

Network Address Translation–Protocol Translation is designed to communicate at the network layer, performing translation from IPv6 to IPv4 networks. Application Level Gateways (ALG) operate at the application layer of the OSI model while NAT-PT does not look at the payload. Thus an ALG allows communications at an application level from two disparate networks—one being IPv6 and another IPv4.

## NAT64

Two advantages that network translation offers over tunneling include the following:

■ Transparent services delivered to IPv6 Internet users by providers

■ A seamless migration to IPv6

Network Address Translation IPv6 to IPv4, also known as NAT64, replaces NAT-PT as documented in RFC 6144 (Framework for IPv4/IPv6 Translation). NAT64 together with DNS64 was created to allow an IPv6-only client to initiate communications to an IPv4-only server. This can be done using manual or static bindings. NAT64 is also described in RFC 6146 (Stateful NAT64). Translation in NAT64 is performed using IP header translation and IP address translation between IPv6 and IPv4 using algorithms defined in RFC

6145 (IP/ICMP Translation Algorithm) and RFC 6052 (IPv6 Addressing of IPv4/IPv6 Translators). Three components to NAT64 include NAT64 prefix, NAT64 router, and DNS64 server.

## Layer 2 VPNs

Market demand combined with modern high-bandwidth services and applications that use IP for transport necessitate that service providers modify the customary approach paradigm that they have used for years. One change that has been adopted in the service provider industry at large is the use of MPLS VPNs to satisfying bandwidth issues. However, note that service providers have two choices for VPN services: Layer 2 or Layer 3 VPNs. We will focus on Layer 2 VPNs in this section because it is the Layer 2 VPN that allows the service provider to simultaneously address high-bandwidth needs while providing "Layer 2" adjacency between physically isolated networks through the IP/MPLS-enabled service provider cloud. This particular service, L2VPN, is typically extended to customers who want to be responsible for their own networks. L2VPN is the simplest solution where a client wants to manage his own routing protocols, IP management, and QoS mechanisms; this means that the service provider only focuses on providing high-throughput Layer 2 connections. Many times these L2VPN connectivity solutions are described as "pseudowire" connections.

Specifically, Ethernet pseudowire (PW) allows Ethernet frames to traverse an operational MPLS cloud. Using this solution, the service provider extends Layer 2 adjacency between sites. This implies that spanning tree will run on the links, and devices connected through these connections will use the same subnet. This service has its own field name, Emulated Service, and operates over pseudowire. In addition to this, it is necessary to have an operational packet label switched network (MPLS network).

Ethernet pseudowire has two modes: raw mode and tagged mode.

### Tagged Mode

The "tagged" in tagged mode makes reference to the 802.1Q tag. In the context of pseudowire, this has significance to the local and end-point devices. But we also need to point out that if the VLAN identifier is modified by the egress provider edge (PE), the Ethernet Spanning Tree Protocol might fail to work properly. This identifier is required to match on the attachment circuits at both ends of the connection. The identifier or the VLAN tag should match on each end of the link. The tagged mode of operation uses the pseudowire type 0x0004. Every frame sent on the PW must have a different VLAN for each customer; this is referred to as a "service-delimiting" VLAN tag. If a frame as received by a PE from the attachment circuit is missing a service-delimiting VLAN tag, the PE must prepend the frame with a dummy VLAN tag before sending the frame on the PW.

### Raw Mode

If the pseudowire is operating in raw mode, the service-delimiting tag might or might not be added in the frame and has no significance to the end points. This mode uses pseudowire type 0x0005. If an Ethernet pseudowire is operating in raw mode, service-delimiting tags are never through the attachment circuit by the PE; it is mandatory that they are stripped from the frame before the frame is transmitted.

## Layer 2 Tunneling Protocol (L2TPv3)

The Layer 2 Tunneling Protocol version 3 feature is an expansion of Layer 2 VPNs. As outlined in an IETF working group (RFC 3931 and RFC 4719), L2TPv3 provides several enhancements to L2TP to tunnel any Layer 2 payload over L2TP, by defining how the L2TP protocol tunnels Layer 2 payloads over an IP core network by using Layer 2 VPNs. L2TPv3 utilizes IP protocol ID 115. To configure L2TPv3 on a Cisco IOS device, two prerequisites are important to know. The first prerequisite is that the Cisco Express Forwarding (CEF) feature must be enabled using the **ip cef** or **ip cef distributed** command. The second prerequisite is that the loopback interface must have a valid IP address that is reachable from the remote PE device at the other end of an L2TPv3 control channel.

## AToM (Any Transport over MPLS)

Example 10-8 illustrates how to configure a typical AToM configuration for the purpose of establishing Layer 2 adjacency between geographically isolated sites.

**Example 10-8** *AToM Configuration*

```
!First we will create the xconnect configuration on routers.


R2(config)# int f0/0
R2(config-if)# xconnect 4.4.4.4 204 encapsulation mpls
R2(config-if-xconn)# end


!Now we do the matching configuration on the other device.


R4(config)# int f0/0
R4(config-if)# xconnect 2.2.2.2 204 encapsulation mpls
R4(config-if-xconn)# end
```

The **xconnect** command used on the F0/0 interface on both routers is used to create a bridged connection with the destination specified. The command is broken down with an **xconnect** keyword followed by the peering router address and the unique virtual circuit ID (VCID). The VCID must match on both ends of the connection. The encapsulation can be L2TPv2, L2TPv3, or MPLS. Never lose sight of the fact that there must be a unique address per router for each xconnect. Example 10-9 shows how to verify the pseudowire that we just created.

**Example 10-9**  *Pseudowire Verification*

```
R2# show xconnect all

Legend: XC ST=Xconnect State, S1=Segment1 State, S2=Segment2 State
UP=Up, DN=Down, AD=Admin Down, IA=Inactive, NH=No Hardware
XC ST Segment 1 S1 Segment 2 S2
------+-------------------------------+--+-------------------------------+--
DN ac Fa0/0(Ethernet) AD mpls 4.4.4.4:204 DN
```

An MPLS Layer 2 pseudowire has two segments. Segment 1 (S1) is for the customer-facing port. Segment 2 (S2) relates to the core configuration. The output of the **show** command reveals that Segment 1 of the connection is administratively shut down. We can correct this by bringing up each end of the remaining links, as illustrated in Example 10-10, and then repeat the verification.

**Example 10-10**  *Link Turn-Up and Verification*

```
!On all devices in the configuration bring up the interfaces on the media.

int f0/0
no shut

!Now we will verify the configuration.

R4# show xconnect peer 2.2.2.2 vcid 204

Legend: XC ST=Xconnect State, S1=Segment1 State, S2=Segment2 State
UP=Up, DN=Down, AD=Admin Down, IA=Inactive, NH=No Hardware
XC ST Segment 1 S1 Segment 2 S2
------+-------------------------------+--+-------------------------------+--
UP ac Fa0/0(Ethernet) UP mpls 2.2.2.2:204 UP

!The S2 section has now been configured and verified to be working properly with
!state !(ST) of active(ac).
```

## Virtual Private LAN Services (VPLS)

VPLS is a Layer 2 VPN service that enables geographically separate LAN segments to be interconnected as a single bridged domain over an MPLS network. VPLS over GRE enables VPLS across an IP network. The provider edge (PE) routers for VPLS over GRE must support VPLS and additional GRE encapsulation and decapsulation. An instance of VPLS must be configured on each PE router.

### Overlay Transport Virtualization (OTV)

OTV looks like VPLS without the MPLS transport and multicast support similar to those used in Layer 3 VPNs. A technology typically deployed at the customer edge (CE), unlike VPLS, OTV is configured on each CE router or switch. OTV provides Layer 2 LAN extension over Layer 3-, Layer 2-, or MPLS-based networks. As of this publication, OTV is supported on Cisco IOS XE Software Release 3.5 or later and Cisco NX-OS Release 6.2(2) or later. One of the significant benefits or advantages of OTV is the fault-domain isolation feature; thus spanning-tree root does not change. With each CE having its own root, there is no intervention or planning required by the provider. OTV supports automatic detection of multihoming and ARP optimization.

## GET VPN

Group Encrypted Transport (GET) VPN is a technology used to encrypt traffic going through unsecured networks. It leverages the IPsec protocol suite to enforce the integrity and confidentiality of data. Typical GET deployment consists of a router called Key Server (KS) and a couple of routers called Group Members (GM). The KS is used to create, maintain, and send a "policy" to GMs. The policy provides information as to what traffic should be encrypted by the GM and what encryption algorithms must be used. The most important function of KS is the generation of encryption keys. Two keys are used:

- **Transport Encryption Key (TEK):** Used by the GM to encrypt the data

- **Key Encryption Key (KEK):** Used to encrypt information between the KS and GM

A very important aspect of GET is that it does not set up any IPsec tunnels between GMs. It is not like DMVPN. Every GM has the policy (what to encrypt, what encryption algorithm to use, and what key is used by the encryption algorithm) and just encrypts every packet that conforms to its specific policy and sends it to the network using ESP (Encapsulated Security Payload). Note that it uses original IP addresses to route the packet out (this is called the IP Header Preservation mechanism); hence the packet can be routed toward every other router in the network as long as the routing table has such information.

Example 10-11 illustrates the initial stages used to create a functional GET VPN configuration. First we need Rivest, Shamir, and Adelman (RSA) keys to be used by our KS for the Rekey process. The KS must send out a new TEK (and KEK) before the TEK expires (default is 3600 seconds). It does this in a so-called Rekey phase. This phase is authenticated and secured by an ISAKMP SA, which is established between the KS and GM. This ISAKMP uses GDOI (Group Domain of Interpretation) messages (think of this as a mutation of Internet Key Exchange [IKE]) to build an SA and encrypt the GM registration. The GDOI uses UDP/848 instead of UDP/500, as IKE does.

The RSA keys are used to authenticate the KS to GM in the Rekey process.

**Example 10-11**  *GET VPN Basic Configuration*

```
!Remember that to generate new RSA keys you must have Hostname and Domain-name
!configured on the router.

R1(config)# ip domain-name cisco.com
R1(config)# crypto key generate rsa modulus 1024
The name for the keys will be: R1.cisco.com
% The key modulus size is 1024 bits
% Generating 1024 bit RSA keys, keys will be non-exportable...[OK]
R1(config)#
%SSH-5-ENABLED: SSH 1.99 has been enabled
Then we need ISAKMP paramaters, just like in regular IPSec configuration. Pre-shared
key must be specified on both KS and GM to be able to authenticate. This will be
used to establish ISAKMP SA to secure further GDOI messages.
R1(config)# crypto isakmp policy 10
R1(config-isakmp)# authentication pre-share
R1(config-isakmp)# exi
R1(config)# crypto isakmp key GETVPN-R5 address 10.1.25.5
R1(config)# crypto isakmp key GETVPN-R4 address 10.1.24.4

!The IPSec parameters must be configured on KS. These parameters are not used by KS
!itself. They are part of policy that will be sent down to the GMs. The IPSec
!profile tells the GM what encryption algorithm use.

R1(config)# crypto ipsec transform-set TSET esp-aes esp-sha-hmac
R1(cfg-crypto-trans)# crypto ipsec profile GETVPN-PROF
R1(ipsec-profile)# set transform-set TSET

!Now it's time to configure KS. To do that we need to specify The Group. One KS
!may have many groups and each group may have different security policy.

R1(ipsec-profile)# crypto gdoi group GETVPN
R1(config-gdoi-group)# identity number 1
R1(config-gdoi-group)# server local
%CRYPTO-6-GDOI_ON_OFF: GDOI is ON
```

**Key Topic**

Here we need to specify Rekey parameters. The Rekey phase can be performed in two ways:

■ **Unicast Rekey:** When we do not have multicast support in our infrastructure (might be the case when the ISP does not support multicast in its IP VPN cloud). The KS sends down a Rekey packet to every GM it knows of.

■ **Multicast Rekey:** When we have a multicast-ready infrastructure, we can enable multicast Rekey and the KS generates only one packet and sends it down to all GMs at one time.

Example 10-12 demonstrates specifying the Rekey parameters.

**Example 10-12**   *Rekey Parameters*

```
R1(gdoi-local-server)# rekey authentication mypubkey rsa R1.cisco.com
R1(gdoi-local-server)# rekey retransmit 10 number 2
R1(gdoi-local-server)# rekey transport unicast

!By default every GM can register to KS as long as it has correct PSK configured (or
!valid Certificate in case of PKI). To authorize GMs to be able to register in this
!group on KS, you need to specify a standard ACL with GM's IP addresses. Our ACL is
!named GM-LIST.

R1(gdoi-local-server)# authorization address ipv4 GM-LIST
```

Now it's time to configure a policy for our GMs. The encryption policy is created by the IPsec profile configured earlier. To tell the GMs what packets they should encrypt, we need another ACL (extended this time). Our ACL is named LAN-LIST. We can also specify a window size for time-based antireplay protection. The last important parameter is KS's IP address. This parameter must also be sent down to the GMs as the KS can be run on different IP addresses (such as loopback).

Example 10-13 demonstrates configuring a GET VPN policy.

**Example 10-13**   *GET VPN Policy*

```
R1(gdoi-local-server)# sa ipsec 1
R1(gdoi-sa-ipsec)# profile GETVPN-PROF
R1(gdoi-sa-ipsec)# match address ipv4 LAN-LIST
R1(gdoi-sa-ipsec)# replay counter window-size 64
R1(gdoi-sa-ipsec)# address ipv4 10.1.12.1
R1(gdoi-local-server)#
%GDOI-5-KS_REKEY_TRANS_2_UNI: Group GETVPN transitioned to Unicast Rekey.
R1(gdoi-local-server)# exi
R1(config-gdoi-group)# exi
R1(config)# ip access-list standard GM-LIST
R1(config-std-nacl)# permit 10.1.25.5
R1(config-std-nacl)# permit 10.1.24.4
R1(config-std-nacl)# exi

!Here's our "policy ACL". Note that we must exclude GDOI (UDP/848) from this policy
!as there is not much sense to encrypt something already encrypted.
```

```
R1(config)# ip access-list extended LAN-LIST
R1(config-ext-nacl)# deny udp any eq 848 any eq 848
R1(config-ext-nacl)# permit ip 192.168.0.0 0.0.255.255 192.168.0.0 0.0.255.255
R1(config-ext-nacl)# exi
```

Now we will configure the Group Members. The configuration in Example 10-14 would need to be performed on every Group Member.

**Example 10-14** *GM Configuration*

```
R5(config)# crypto isakmp policy 10
R5(config-isakmp)# authentication pre-share
R5(config-isakmp)# exi
R5(config)# crypto isakmp key GETVPN-R5 address 10.1.12.1
R5(config)# crypto gdoi group GETVPN
R5(config-gdoi-group)# identity number 1
R5(config-gdoi-group)# server address ipv4 10.1.12.1
R5(config-gdoi-group)# exi

!This ACL is optional. In general we should configure our policy on KS only, but
!there are some situations when we need to exclude some flows from encryption. Like
!here, we were asked for excluding SSH traffic between 192.168.4.0/24 AND
!192.168.5.0/24 networks.

R5(config)# ip access-list extended DO-NOT-ENCRYPT
R5(config-ext-nacl)# deny tcp 192.168.4.0 0.0.0.255 eq 22 192.168.5.0 0.0.0.255
R5(config-ext-nacl)# deny tcp 192.168.5.0 0.0.0.255 192.168.4.0 0.0.0.255 eq 22
R5(config-ext-nacl)# deny tcp 192.168.4.0 0.0.0.255 192.168.5.0 0.0.0.255 eq 22
R5(config-ext-nacl)# deny tcp 192.168.5.0 0.0.0.255 eq 22 192.168.4.0 0.0.0.255
R5(config-ext-nacl)# exi
R5(config)# crypto map CMAP-GETVPN 10 gdoi
% NOTE: This new crypto map will remain disabled until a valid
group has been configured.
R5(config-crypto-map)# set group GETVPN
R5(config-crypto-map)# match address DO-NOT-ENCRYPT
R5(config-crypto-map)# exi
R5(config)# int s0/1/0.52
R5(config-subif)# crypto map CMAP-GETVPN
R5(config-subif)# exi
R5(config)#
%CRYPTO-5-GM_REGSTER: Start registration to KS 10.1.12.1 for group GETVPN using
  addr
10.1.25.5
R5(config)#
%CRYPTO-6-GDOI_ON_OFF: GDOI is ON
R5(config)#
```

```
%GDOI-5-GM_REKEY_TRANS_2_UNI: Group GETVPN transitioned to Unicast Rekey.
%GDOI-5-GM_REGS_COMPL: Registration to KS 10.1.12.1 complete for group GETVPN using
address 10.1.25.5


!See above SYSLOG messages. They indicate that GM has started registration process
!with KS and registered successfully.
```

Finally, we can verify the GET VPN configuration, as illustrated in Example 10-15.

**Example 10-15** *Final GET VPN Verification*

```
R1# sh crypto gdoi group GETVPN
Group Name              : GETVPN (Unicast)
Group Identity          : 1
Group Members           : 2
IPSec SA Direction      : Both
Active Group Server     : Local
Group Rekey Lifetime    : 86400 secs
Group Rekey
Remaining Lifetime   : 86361 secs
Rekey Retransmit Period  : 10 secs
Rekey Retransmit Attempts: 2
Group Retransmit
Remaining Lifetime   : 0 secs
IPSec SA Number      : 1
IPSec SA Rekey Lifetime: 3600 secs
Profile Name            : GETVPN-PROF
Replay method           : Count Based
Replay Window Size      : 64
SA Rekey
Remaining Lifetime   : 3562 secs
ACL Configured          : access-list LAN-LIST
Group Server list       : Local


R1# sh crypto gdoi ks policy
Key Server Policy:
For group GETVPN (handle: 2147483650) server 10.1.12.1 (handle: 2147483650):
# of teks : 1  Seq num : 0
KEK POLICY (transport type : Unicast)
spi : 0x76749A6D99B3C0A3827FA26F1558ED63
management alg    : disabled  encrypt alg     : 3DES
crypto iv length  : 8          key size        : 24
orig life(sec): 86400      remaining life(sec): 86355
sig hash algorithm : enabled    sig key length    : 162
sig size          : 128
sig key name      : R1.micronicstraining.com
```

```
TEK POLICY (encaps : ENCAPS_TUNNEL)
spi               : 0xAF4FA6F8  access-list          : LAN-LIST
# of transforms   : 0  transform            : ESP_AES
hmac alg          : HMAC_AUTH_SHA
alg key size      : 16           sig key size        : 20
orig life(sec)    : 3600         remaining life(sec) : 3556
tek life(sec)     : 3600         elapsed time(sec)   : 44


R1# sh crypto gdoi ks acl
Group Name: GETVPN
Configured ACL:
access-list LAN-LIST deny udp any port = 848 any port = 848
access-list LAN-LIST permit ip 192.168.0.0 0.0.255.255 192.168.0.0 0.0.255.255


!Here's the ACL which tells the GMs what traffic they should encrypt.


R1# sh crypto gdoi ks members
Group Member Information :
Number of rekeys sent for group GETVPN : 1
Group Member ID   : 10.1.24.4
Group ID          : 1
Group Name        : GETVPN
Key Server ID     : 10.1.12.1
Rekeys sent       : 0
Rekeys retries    : 0
Rekey Acks Rcvd   : 0
Rekey Acks missed : 0
Sent seq num :     0     0     0     0
Rcvd seq num :     0     0     0     0
Group Member ID   : 10.1.25.5
Group ID          : 1
Group Name        : GETVPN
Key Server ID     : 10.1.12.1
Rekeys sent       : 0
Rekeys retries    : 0
Rekey Acks Rcvd   : 0
Rekey Acks missed : 0
Sent seq num :     0     0     0     0
Rcvd seq num :     0     0     0     0
```

# Foundation Summary

This section lists additional details and facts to round out the coverage of the topics in this chapter. Unlike most of the Cisco Press Exam Certification Guides, this "Foundation Summary" does not repeat information presented in the "Foundation Topics" section of the chapter. Please take the time to read and study the details in the "Foundation Topics" section of the chapter, as well as review items noted with a Key Topic icon.

Table 10-4 lists the protocols mentioned in or pertinent to this chapter and their respective standards documents.

**Table 10-4**   *Protocols and Standards for Chapter 10*

| Name | Standardized in |
|---|---|
| Generic Routing Encapsulation | RFC 2784 |
| NHRP (Next-Hop Resolution Protocol) | RFC 2332 |
| Basic Transition Mechanisms for IPv6 Hosts and Routers | RFC 4213 |
| The Group Domain of Interpretation | RFC 3547 |
| Layer 2 Virtual Private Network (L2VPN) | RFC 6136 |
| Layer 2 Tunnel Protocol version 3 | RFC 3931 and RFC 4719 |
| IPv6 Stateless Address Autoconfiguration | RFC 4862 |
| Stateful NAT64: Network Address and Protocol Translation | RFC 6146 |
| Framework for IPv4/IPv6 Translation | RFC 6144 |

# Memory Builders

The CCIE Routing and Switching written exam, like all Cisco CCIE written exams, covers a fairly broad set of topics. This section provides some basic tools to help you exercise your memory about some of the broader topics covered in this chapter.

## Definitions

Next, take a few moments to write down the definitions for the following terms:

GRE, ISATAP, 6to4, L2VPN, AToM, Tagged mode, Raw mode, DMVPN, GDOI, NHRP, Key Server, Group Members, IPsec profile, TEK, KEK, Unicast-Rekey, Multicast-Rekey

Refer to the glossary to check your answers.

**Blueprint topics covered in this chapter:**

This chapter covers the following subtopics from the Cisco CCIE Routing and Switching written exam blueprint. Refer to the full blueprint in Table I-1 in the Introduction for more details on the topics covered in each chapter and their context within the blueprint.

- Implement MPLS Layer 3 VPNs

- Implement Multiprotocol Label Switching (MPLS)

- Implement MPLS VPNs on PE, P, and CE routers

- Implement Virtual Routing and Forwarding (VRF)

- Implement Multi-VRF Customer Edge (VRF Lite)

## CHAPTER 11

# Multiprotocol Label Switching

Multiprotocol Label Switching (MPLS) remains a vitally important part of many service provider (SP) networks. MPLS is still growing in popularity in enterprise networks as well, particularly in larger enterprise internetworks. This chapter introduces the core concepts with MPLS, particularly its use for unicast IP forwarding and for MPLS VPNs.

## "Do I Know This Already?" Quiz

Table 11-1 outlines the major headings in this chapter and the corresponding "Do I Know This Already?" quiz questions.

**Table 11-1** *"Do I Know This Already?" Foundation Topics Section-to-Question Mapping*

| Foundation Topics Section | Questions Covered in This Section | Score |
|---|---|---|
| MPLS Unicast IP Forwarding | 1–4 | |
| MPLS VPNs | 5–9 | |
| Other MPLS Applications | 10 | |
| VRF Lite | 11 | |
| Total Score | | |

To best use this pre-chapter assessment, remember to score yourself strictly. You can find the answers in Appendix A, "Answers to the 'Do I Know This Already?' Quizzes."

1. Imagine a frame-based MPLS network configured for simple unicast IP forwarding, with four routers, R1, R2, R3, and R4. The routers connect in a mesh of links so that they are all directly connected to the other routers. R1 uses LDP to advertise prefix 1.1.1.0/24, label 30, to the other three routers. What must be true for R2 to advertise a label for 1.1.1.0/24 to R1 using LDP?

   a. R2 must learn an IGP route to 1.1.1.0/24.

   b. R2 will not advertise a label to R1 because of Split Horizon rules.

   c. R2 can advertise a label back to R1 before learning an IGP route to 1.1.1.0/24.

   d. R2 must learn a route to 1.1.1.0/24 using MP-BGP before advertising a label.

2.  In a frame-based MPLS network configured for unicast IP forwarding, LSR R1 receives a labeled packet, with a label value of 55. Which of the following could be true?

    a.  R1 makes its forwarding decision by comparing the packet to the IPv4 prefixes found in the FIB.

    b.  R1 makes its forwarding decision by comparing the packet to the IPv4 prefixes found in the LFIB.

    c.  R1 makes its forwarding decision by comparing the packet to the MPLS labels found in the FIB.

    d.  R1 makes its forwarding decision by comparing the packet to the MPLS labels found in the LFIB.

3.  R1, R2, and R3 are all MPLS LSRs that use LDP and connect to the same LAN. None of the three LSRs advertise a transport IP address. Which of the following could be true regarding LDP operation?

    a.  The LSRs discover the other two routers using LDP Hellos sent to IP address 224.0.0.20.

    b.  Each pair of LSRs forms a TCP connection before advertising MPLS labels.

    c.  The three LSRs must use their LAN interface IP addresses for any LDP TCP connections.

    d.  The LDP Hellos use port 646, with the TCP connections using port 721.

4.  In a frame-based MPLS network configured for simple unicast IP forwarding, MPLS TTL propagation has been enabled for all traffic. Which of the following could be true?

    a.  A traceroute command issued from outside the MPLS network will list IP addresses of the LSRs inside the MPLS network.

    b.  A traceroute command issued from outside the MPLS network will not list IP addresses of the LSRs inside the MPLS network.

    c.  Any IP packet with a TCP header, entering the MPLS network from outside the MPLS network, would not have its IP TTL field copied into the MPLS TTL field.

5.  An ICMP echo sent into the MPLS network from outside the MPLS network would have its IP TTL field copied into the MPLS TTL field. Which of the following is an extension to the BGP NLRI field?

    a.  VRF

    b.  Route Distinguisher

    c.  Route Target

    d.  BGP Extended Community

6. Which of the following controls into which VRFs a PE adds routes when receiving an IBGP update from another PE?

   a. Route Distinguisher

   b. Route Target

   c. IGP metric

   d. AS Path length

7. An ingress PE router in an internetwork configured for MPLS VPN receives an unlabeled packet. Which of the following is true?

   a. It injects a single MPLS header.

   b. It injects at least two MPLS headers.

   c. It injects (at least) a VPN label, which is used by any intermediate P routers.

   d. It uses both the FIB and LFIB to find all the required labels to inject before the IP header.

8. An internetwork configured to support MPLS VPNs uses PHP. An ingress PE receives an unlabeled packet and then injects the appropriate label(s) to the packet before sending the packet into the MPLS network. Which of the following is/are true about this packet?

   a. The number of MPLS labels in the packet will only change when the packet reaches the egress PE router, which extracts the entire MPLS header.

   b. The number of MPLS labels in the packet will change before the packet reaches the egress PE.

   c. The PHP feature will cause the egress PE to act differently than it would without PHP enabled.

   d. None of the other answers is correct.

9. Which of the following are true regarding a typical MPLS VPN PE BGP configuration, assuming that the PE-CE routing protocol is not BGP?

   a. It includes an **address-family vpnv4** command for each VRF.

   b. It includes an **address-family ipv4** command for each VRF.

   c. At least one BGP subcommand must list the value of the exported Route Target (RT) of each VRF.

   d. Peer connections to other PEs must be enabled with the **neighbor activate** command under the VPNv4 address family.

**10.** Which of the following answers help define which packets are in the same MPLS FEC when using MPLS VPNs?

   **a.** IPv4 prefix

   **b.** ToS byte

   **c.** The MPLS VRF

   **d.** The TE tunnel

**11.** Which of the following are true about the VRF Lite (Multi-VRF CE) feature?

   **a.** It provides logical separation at Layer 3.

   **b.** It requires the use of LDP or TDP.

   **c.** It uses VRFs, but requires static routing.

   **d.** It can be used on CE routers only when those routers have a link to a PE in MPLS VPN.

   **e.** It creates separate routing table instances on a router by creating multiple VRFs.

## Foundation Topics

MPLS defines protocols that create a different paradigm for how routers forward packets. Instead of forwarding packets based on the packets' destination IP address, MPLS defines how routers can forward packets based on an MPLS label. By disassociating the forwarding decision from the destination IP address, MPLS allows forwarding decisions based on other factors, such as traffic engineering, QoS requirements, and the privacy requirements for multiple customers connected to the same MPLS network, while still considering the traditional information learned using routing protocols.

MPLS includes a wide variety of applications, with each application considering one or more of the possible factors that influence the MPLS forwarding decisions. For the purposes of the CCIE Routing and Switching written exam, this book covers two such applications in the first two major sections of this chapter:

- MPLS unicast IP

- MPLS VPNs

This chapter also includes a brief introduction to many of the other MPLS applications and to the VRF Lite (Multi-VRF CE) feature. Also, as usual, please take the time to check www.ciscopress.com/title/9781587144912 for the latest version of Appendix B, "CCIE Exam Updates," to find out whether you should read further about any of the MPLS topics.

**Note**  MPLS includes frame-mode MPLS and cell-mode MPLS, while this chapter only covers frame-mode MPLS. The generalized comments in this chapter might not apply to cell-mode MPLS.

## MPLS Unicast IP Forwarding

MPLS can be used for simple unicast IP forwarding. With MPLS unicast IP forwarding, the MPLS forwarding logic forwards packets based on labels. However, when choosing the interfaces out which to forward the packets, MPLS considers only the routes in the unicast IP routing table, so the end result of using MPLS is that the packet flows over the same path as it would have if MPLS were not used, but all other factors were unchanged.

MPLS unicast IP forwarding does not provide any significant advantages by itself. However, many of the more helpful MPLS applications, such as MPLS Virtual Private Networks (VPN) and MPLS traffic engineering (TE), use MPLS unicast IP forwarding as one part of the MPLS network. So to understand MPLS as you would typically implement it, you need a solid understanding of MPLS in its most basic form: MPLS unicast IP forwarding.

MPLS requires the use of control plane protocols (for example, Open Shortest Path First [OSPF] and Label Distribution Protocol [LDP]) to learn labels, correlate those labels to particular destination prefixes, and build the correct forwarding tables. MPLS also requires a fundamental change to the data plane's core forwarding logic. This section begins by examining the data plane, which defines the packet-forwarding logic. Following that, this section examines the control plane protocols, particularly LDP, which MPLS routers use to exchange labels for unicast IP prefixes.

## MPLS IP Forwarding: Data Plane

MPLS defines a completely different packet-forwarding paradigm. However, hosts do not and should not send and receive labeled packets, so at some point, some router will need to add a label to the packet and, later, another router will remove the label. The MPLS routers—the routers that inject (push), remove (pop), or forward packets based on their labels—use MPLS forwarding logic.

MPLS relies on the underlying structure and logic of Cisco Express Forwarding (CEF) while expanding the logic and data structures as well. First, a review of CEF is in order, followed by details about a new data structure called the MPLS *Label Forwarding Information Base (LFIB)*.

### CEF Review

A router's unicast IP forwarding control plane uses routing protocols, static routes, and connected routes to create a *Routing Information Base (RIB)*. With CEF enabled, a router's control plane processing goes a step further, creating the CEF *Forwarding Information Base (FIB)*, adding a FIB entry for each destination IP prefix in the routing table. The FIB entry details the information needed for forwarding: the next-hop router and the outgoing interface. Additionally, the CEF *adjacency table* lists the new data-link header that the router will then copy in front of the packet before forwarding.

For the data plane, a CEF router compares the packet's destination IP address to the CEF FIB, ignoring the IP routing table. CEF optimizes the organization of the FIB so that the router spends very little time to find the correct FIB entry, resulting in a smaller forwarding delay and a higher volume of packets per second through a router. For each packet, the router finds the matching FIB entry, then finds the adjacency table entry referenced by the matching FIB entry, and forwards the packet. Figure 11-1 shows the overall process.

With this backdrop in mind, the text next looks at how MPLS changes the forwarding process using labels.

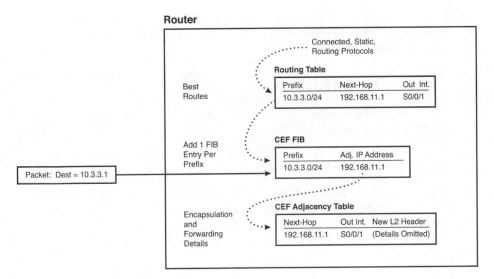

**Figure 11-1**   *IP Routing Table and CEF FIB—No MPLS*

## Overview of MPLS Unicast IP Forwarding

**Key Topic**

The MPLS forwarding paradigm assumes that hosts generate packets without an MPLS label. Then, some router imposes an MPLS label, other routers forward the packet based on that label, and then other routers remove the label. The end result is that the host computers have no awareness of the existence of MPLS. To appreciate this overall forwarding process, Figure 11-2 shows an example, with steps showing how a packet is forwarded using MPLS.

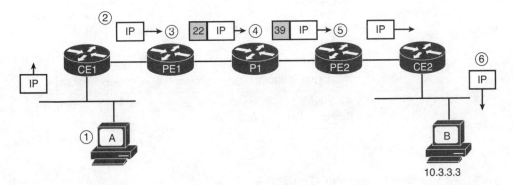

**Figure 11-2**   *MPLS Packet Forwarding—End to End*

The steps from the figure are explained as follows:

1. Host A generates and sends an unlabeled packet destined to host 10.3.3.3.

2. Router CE1, with no MPLS features configured, forwards the unlabeled packet based on the destination IP address, as normal, without any labels. (Router CE1 might or might not use CEF.)

3.  MPLS Router PE1 receives the unlabeled packet and decides, as part of the MPLS forwarding process, to impose (push) a new label (value 22) into the packet and forwards the packet.

4.  MPLS Router P1 receives the labeled packet. P1 swaps the label for a new label value (39) and then forwards the packet.

5.  MPLS Router PE2 receives the labeled packet, removes (pops) the label, and forwards the packet toward CE2.

6.  Non-MPLS Router CE2 forwards the unlabeled packet based on the destination IP address, as normal. (CE2 might or might not use CEF.)

The steps in Figure 11-2 show a relatively simple process and provide a great backdrop from which to introduce a few terms. The term *Label Switch Router (LSR)* refers to any router that has awareness of MPLS labels, for example, Routers PE1, P1, and PE2 in Figure 11-2. Table 11-2 lists the variations of the term LSR, and a few comments about the meaning of each term.

Key Topic

**Table 11-2**   *MPLS LSR Terminology Reference*

| LSR Type | Actions Performed by This LSR Type |
| --- | --- |
| Label Switch Router (LSR) | Any router that pushes labels onto packets, pops labels from packets, or simply forwards labeled packets. |
| Edge LSR (E-LSR) | An LSR at the edge of the MPLS network, meaning that this router processes both labeled and unlabeled packets. |
| Ingress E-LSR | For a particular packet, the router that receives an unlabeled packet and then inserts a label stack in front of the IP header. |
| Egress E-LSR | For a particular packet, the router that receives a labeled packet and then removes all MPLS labels, forwarding an unlabeled packet. |
| ATM-LSR | An LSR that runs MPLS protocols in the control plane to set up ATM virtual circuits. Forwards labeled packets as ATM cells. |
| ATM E-LSR | An E-edge LSR that also performs the ATM Segmentation and Reassembly (SAR) function. |

## MPLS Forwarding Using the FIB and LFIB

To forward packets as shown in Figure 11-2, LSRs use both the CEF FIB and the MPLS LFIB when forwarding packets. Both the FIB and LFIB hold any necessary label information, as well as the outgoing interface and next-hop information.

The FIB and LFIB differ in that routers use one table to forward incoming unlabeled packets and the other to forward incoming labeled packets, as follows:

- **FIB:** Used for incoming unlabeled packets. Cisco IOS matches the packet's destination IP address to the best prefix in the FIB and forwards the packet based on that entry.

- **LFIB:** Used for incoming labeled packets. Cisco IOS compares the label in the incoming packet to the LFIB's list of labels and forwards the packet based on that LFIB entry.

Figure 11-3 shows how the three LSRs in Figure 11-2 use their respective FIBs and LFIB. Note that Figure 11-3 just shows the FIB on the LSR that forwards the packet using the FIB and the LFIB on the two LSRs that use the LFIB, although all LSRs have both a FIB and an LFIB.

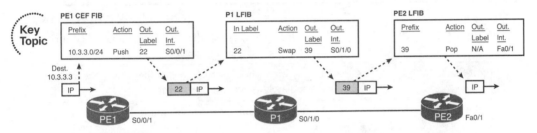

**Figure 11-3**  *Use of the CEF FIB and MPLS LFIB for Forwarding Packets*

The figure shows the use of the FIB and LFIB, as follows:

- **PE1:** When the unlabeled packet arrives at PE1, PE1 uses the FIB. PE1 finds the FIB entry that matches the packet's destination address of 10.3.3.1—namely, the entry for 10.3.3.0/24 in this case. Among other things, the FIB entry includes the instructions to push the correct MPLS label in front of the packet.

- **P1:** Because P1 receives a labeled packet, P1 uses its LFIB, finding the label value of 22 in the LFIB, with that entry stating that P1 should swap the label value to 39.

- **PE2:** PE2 uses the LFIB as well, because PE2 receives a labeled packet. The matching LFIB entry lists a pop action, so PE2 removes the label, forwarding an unlabeled packet to CE2.

Note that P1 and PE2 in this example never examined the packet's destination IP address as part of the forwarding process. Because the forwarding process does not rely on the destination IP address, MPLS can then enable forwarding processes based on something other than the destination IP address, such as forwarding based on the VPN from which the packet originated, forwarding to balance traffic with traffic engineering, and forwarding over different links based on QoS goals.

### The MPLS Header and Label

The MPLS header is a 4-byte header, located immediately before the IP header. Many people simply refer to the MPLS header as the MPLS label, but the label is actually a 20-bit field in the MPLS header. You might also see this header referenced as an MPLS *shim header*. Figure 11-4 shows the entire label, and Table 11-3 defines the fields.

| 20 | 3 | 1 | 8 |
|----|-----|---|-----|
| Label | EXP | S | TTL |

**Figure 11-4** *MPLS Header*

**Table 11-3** *MPLS Header Fields*

| Field | Length (Bits) | Purpose |
|-------|---------------|---------|
| Label | 20 | Identifies the portion of a label switched path (LSP). |
| Experimental (EXP) | 3 | Used for QoS marking; the field is no longer used for truly experimental purposes. |
| Bottom-of-Stack (S) | 1 | Flag, which when set to 1, means that this is the label immediately preceding the IP header. |
| Time-to-Live (TTL) | 8 | Used for the same purposes as the IP header's TTL field. |

Of the four fields in the MPLS header, the first two, Label and EXP, should already be familiar. The 20-bit Label is usually listed as a decimal value in **show** commands. The MPLS EXP bits allow for QoS marking, which can be done using CB Marking, as covered in Chapter 3, "Classification and Marking." The S bit will make more sense after you examine how MPLS VPNs work, but in short, when packets hold multiple MPLS headers, this bit allows an LSR to recognize the last MPLS header before the IP header. Finally, the TTL field requires a little more examination, as covered in the next section.

### The MPLS TTL Field and MPLS TTL Propagation

The IP header's TTL field supports two important features: a mechanism to identify looping packets and a method for the **traceroute** command to find the IP address of each router in a particular end-to-end route. The MPLS header's TTL field supplies the same features. In fact, using all defaults, the presence or absence of MPLS LSRs in a network has no impact on the end results of either of the TTL-related processes.

MPLS needs a TTL field so that LSRs can completely ignore the encapsulated IP header when forwarding IP packets. Essentially, the LSRs will decrement the MPLS TTL field, and not the IP TTL field, as the packet passes through the MPLS network. To make the entire process work, using all default settings, ingress E-LSRs, LSRs, and egress E-LSRs work as follows:

- **Ingress E-LSRs:** After an ingress E-LSR decrements the IP TTL field, it pushes a label into an unlabeled packet and then copies the packet's IP TTL field into the new MPLS header's TTL field.

- **LSRs:** When an LSR swaps a label, the router decrements the MPLS header's TTL field and always ignores the IP header's TTL field.

- **Egress E-LSRs:** After an egress E-LSR decrements the MPLS TTL field, it pops the final MPLS header and then copies the MPLS TTL field into the IP header TTL field.

Figure 11-5 shows an example in which a packet arrives at PE1, unlabeled, with IP TTL 4. The callouts in the figure list the main actions for the three roles of the LSRs as described in the previous list.

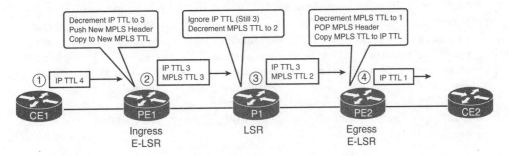

**Figure 11-5**  *Example of MPLS TTL Propagation*

The term *MPLS TTL propagation* refers to the combined logic as shown in the figure. In effect, the MPLS routers propagate the same TTL value across the MPLS network—the same TTL values that would have occurred if MPLS was not used at all. As you might expect, a truly looping packet would eventually decrement to TTL 0 and be discarded. Additionally, a **traceroute** command would receive ICMP Time Exceeded messages from each of the routers in the figure, including the LSRs.

However, many engineers do not want hosts outside the MPLS network to have visibility into the MPLS network with the **traceroute** command. SPs typically implement MPLS networks to create Layer 3 WAN services, and the SP's customers sit outside the MPLS network. If the SP's customers can find the IP addresses of the MPLS LSRs, it can annoy the customer who wants to see only customer routers, and it can create a security exposure for the SP.

Cisco routers can be configured to disable MPLS TTL propagation. When disabled, the ingress E-LSR sets the MPLS header's TTL field to 255, and the egress E-LSR leaves the original IP header's TTL field unchanged. As a result, the entire MPLS network appears to be a single router hop from a TTL perspective, and the routers inside the MPLS network are not seen from the customer's **traceroute** command. Figure 11-6 shows the same example as in Figure 11-5 but now with MPLS TTL propagation disabled.

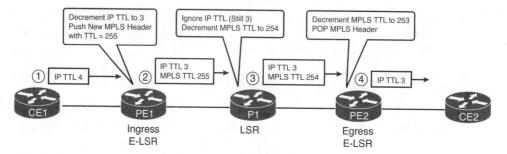

**Figure 11-6**   *Example with MPLS TTL Propagation Disabled*

Cisco supports the ability to disable MPLS TTL propagation for two classes of packets. Most MPLS SPs might want to disable TTL propagation for packets forwarded by customers, but allow TTL propagation for packets created by the SP's routers. Using Figure 11-5 again for an example, an SP engineer might be logged in to Router PE1 to issue a **traceroute** command. PE1 can be configured to use TTL propagation for locally created packets, which allows the **traceroute** command issued from PE1 to list all the routers in the MPLS cloud. At the same time, PE1 can be configured to disable TTL propagation for "forwarded" packets (packets received from customers), preventing the customer from learning router IP addresses inside the MPLS network. (The command is **no mpls ip propagate-ttl**.)

**Note**   Although the PE1 router has TTL-Propagation disabled, *all* routers in the MPLS domain should also have TTL disabled for consistent output of the TTL propagation.

## MPLS IP Forwarding: Control Plane

For pure IP routing to work using the FIB, routers must use control plane protocols, like routing protocols, to first populate the IP routing table and then populate the CEF FIB. Similarly, for MPLS forwarding to work, MPLS relies on control plane protocols to learn which MPLS labels to use to reach each IP prefix, and then populate both the FIB and the LFIB with the correct labels.

MPLS supports many different control plane protocols. However, an engineer's choice of which control plane protocol to use is mainly related to the MPLS application used, rather than any detailed comparison of the features of each control plane protocol. For example, MPLS VPNs use two control plane protocols: LDP and multiprotocol BGP (MP-BGP).

While multiple control plane protocols can be used for some MPLS applications, MPLS unicast IP forwarding uses an IGP and one MPLS-specific control protocol: LDP. This section, still focused on unicast IP forwarding, examines the details of label distribution using LDP.

**Note**    The earliest pre-standard version of LDP was called *Tag Distribution Protocol (TDP)*. The term *tag switching* was also often used instead of label switching.

## MPLS LDP Basics

For unicast IP routing, LDP simply advertises labels for each prefix listed in the IP routing table. To do so, LSRs use LDP to send messages to their neighbors, with the messages listing an IP prefix and corresponding label. By advertising an IP prefix and label, the LSR is essentially saying, "If you want to send packets to this IP prefix, send them to me with the MPLS label listed in the LDP update."

The LDP advertisement is triggered by a new IP route appearing in the unicast IP routing table. Upon learning a new route, the LSR allocates a label called a local label. The local label is the label that, on this one LSR, is used to represent the IP prefix just added to the routing table. An example makes the concept much clearer. Figure 11-7 shows a slightly expanded version of the MPLS network shown earlier in this chapter. The figure shows the basic process of what occurs when an LSR (PE2) learns about a new route (10.3.3.0/24), triggering the process of advertising a new local label (39) using LDP.

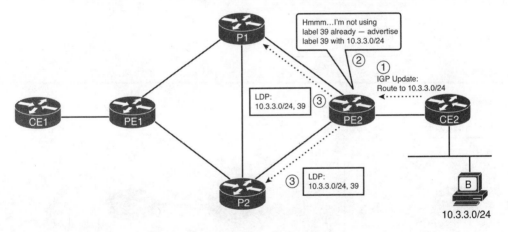

**Figure 11-7**    *LDP Process Triggered by New Unicast IP Route*

The figure shows the following simple three-step process on PE2:

1. PE2 learns a new unicast IP route, which appears in the IP routing table.

2. PE2 allocates a new *local label*, which is a label not currently advertised by that LSR.

3. PE2 uses LDP to advertise to neighbors the mapping between the IP prefix and label to all LDP neighbors.

Although the process itself is simple, it is important to note that PE2 must now be ready to process labeled packets that arrive with the new local label value in it. For example, in Figure 11-7, PE2 needs to be ready to forward packets received with label 39. PE2 will forward the packets with the same next-hop and outgoing interface information learned in the IGP Update at Step 1 in the figure.

Although interesting, the process shown in Figure 11-7 shows only the advertisement of one segment of the full label switched path (LSP). An MPLS LSP is the combined set of labels that can be used to forward the packets correctly to the destination. For example, Figures 11-2 and 11-3 show a short LSP with label values 22 and 39, over which packets to subnet 10.3.3.0/24 were sent. Figure 11-7 shows the advertisement of one part, or segment, of the LSP.

**Note**    LSPs are unidirectional.

The routers in the MPLS cloud must use some IP routing protocol to learn IP routes to trigger the LDP process of advertising labels. Typically, for MPLS unicast IP routing, you would use an interior gateway protocol (IGP) to learn all the IP routes, triggering the process of advertising the corresponding labels. For example, Figure 11-8 picks up the process where Figure 11-7 ended, with PE2 advertising a route for 10.3.3.0/24 using EIGRP, causing other routers to then use LDP to advertise labels.

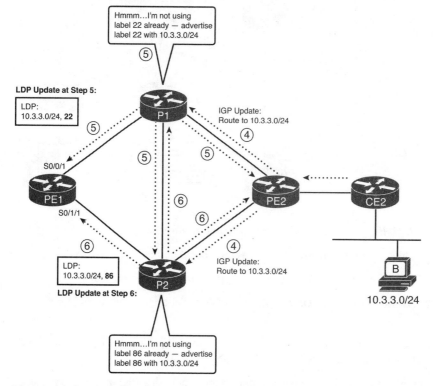

**Figure 11-8**    *Completed Process of Advertising an Entire LSP*

The steps in the figure are as follows, using numbers that continue the numbering from Figure 11-7:

4.   PE2 uses EIGRP to advertise the route for 10.3.3.0/24 to both P1 and P2.

5.   P1 reacts to the newly learned route by allocating a new local label (22) and using LDP to advertise the new prefix (10.3.3.0/24) to label (22) mapping. Note that P1 advertises this label to all its neighbors.

6.   P2 also reacts to the newly learned route by allocating a new local label (86) and using LDP to advertise the new prefix (10.3.3.0/24) to label (86) mapping. P2 advertises this label to all its neighbors.

This same process occurs on each LSR, for each route in the LSR's routing table: Each time an LSR learns a new route, the LSR allocates a new local label and then advertises the label and prefix mapping to all its neighbors—even when it is obvious that advertising the label might not be useful. For example, in Figure 11-8, P2 advertises a label for 10.3.3.0/24 back to router PE2—not terribly useful, but it is how frame-mode MPLS LSRs work.

After the routers have all learned about a prefix using the IGP protocol, and LDP has advertised label/prefix mappings (bindings) to all other neighboring LSRs, each LSR has enough information with which to label-switch packets from ingress E-LSR to egress E-LSR. For example, the same data plane process shown in Figures 11-2 and 11-3 could occur when PE1 receives an unlabeled packet destined to an address in 10.3.3.0/24. In fact, the labels advertised in Figures 11-7 and 11-8 purposefully match the earlier MPLS data plane figures (11-2 and 11-3). However, to complete the full process, you need to understand a bit more about what occurs inside an individual router, in particular, a data structure called the MPLS Label Information Base (LIB).

### The MPLS Label Information Base Feeding the FIB and LFIB

**Key Topic**

LSRs store labels and related information inside a data structure called LIB. The LIB essentially holds all the labels and associated information that could possibly be used to forward packets. However, each LSR must choose the best label and outgoing interface to actually use and then populate that information into the FIB and the LFIB. As a result, the FIB and LFIB contain labels only for the currently used best LSP segment, while the LIB contains all labels known to the LSR, whether the label is currently used for forwarding or not.

To make a decision about the best label to use, LSRs rely on the routing protocol's decision about the best route. By relying on the routing protocol, the LSRs can take advantage of the routing protocol's loop-prevention features and react to the routing protocol's choice for new routes when convergence occurs. In short, an LSR makes the following decision:

> For each route in the routing table, find the corresponding label information in the LIB, based on the outgoing interface and next-hop router listed in the route. Add the corresponding label information to the FIB and LFIB.

To better understand how an LSR adds information to the FIB and LFIB, this section continues the same example as used throughout the chapter so far. At this point, it is useful to examine the output of some **show** commands, but first, you need a little more detail about the sample network and the configuration. Figure 11-9 repeats the same sample network used in earlier figures in this chapter, with IP address and interface details included. The figure also notes on which interfaces MPLS has been enabled (dashed lines) and on which interfaces MPLS has not been enabled (solid lines).

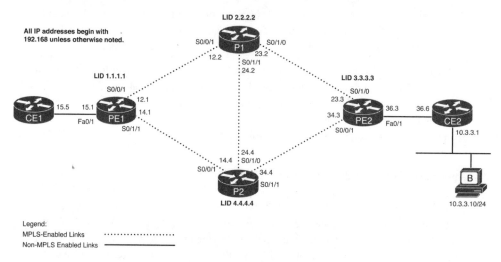

**Figure 11-9** *Sample Network for Seeing the LIB, FIB, and LFIB*

The configuration of MPLS unicast IP routing is relatively simple. In this case, all six routers use EIGRP, advertising all subnets. The four LSRs enable MPLS globally and on the links noted with dashed lines in the figure. To enable MPLS for simple unicast IP forwarding, as has been described so far in this chapter, an LSR simply needs to enable CEF, globally enable MPLS, and enable MPLS on each desired interface. Also, IOS uses LDP by default. Example 11-1 shows a sample generic configuration.

**Example 11-1** *MPLS Configuration on LSRs for Unicast IP Support*

```
! The first three commands enable CEF and MPLS globally, and
! use LDP instead of TDP
ip cef
! Repeat the next two lines for each MPLS-enabled interface
interface type x/y/z
 mpls ip
! Normal EIGRP configuration next - would be configured for all interfaces
router eigrp 1
 network ...
```

To see how LSRs populate the FIB and LFIB, consider subnet 10.3.3.0/24 again, and think about MPLS from Router PE1's perspective. PE1 has learned a route for 10.3.3.0/24 with EIGRP. PE1 has also learned (using LDP) about two labels that PE1 can use when forwarding packets destined for 10.3.3.0/24—one label learned from neighboring LSR P1 and the other from neighboring LSR P2. Example 11-2 highlights these details. Note that the labels do match the figures and examples used earlier in this chapter.

**Example 11-2**   *PE1's IP Routing Table and LIB*

```
PE1# show ip route 10.0.0.0
Routing entry for 10.0.0.0/24, 1 known subnets
  Redistributing via eigrp 1
D      10.3.3.0 [90/2812416] via 192.168.12.2,  00:44:16,  Serial0/0/1
PE1# show mpls ldp bindings 10.3.3.0 24
  lib entry: 10.3.3.0/24, rev 2
        local binding:  label: imp-null
        remote binding: lsr: 2.2.2.2:0, tag: 22
        remote binding: lsr: 4.4.4.4:0, tag: 86
```

Example 11-2 shows some mundane information and a few particularly interesting points. First, the **show ip route** command does not list any new or different information for MPLS, but it is useful to note that PE1's best route to 10.3.3.0/24 is through P1. The **show mpls ldp bindings 10.3.3.0 24** command lists the LIB entries from 10.3.3.0/24. Note that two remote bindings are listed—one from P1 (LDP ID 2.2.2.2) and one from P2 (LDP ID 4.4.4.4). This command also lists the local binding, which is the label that PE1 allocated and advertised to its neighbors.

**Note**   The term *remote binding* refers to a label-prefix binding learned through LDP from some LDP neighbor.

From Example 11-2, you could anticipate that PE1 will use a label value of 22, and an outgoing interface of S0/0/1, when forwarding packets to 10.3.3.0/24. To see the details of how PE1 arrives at that conclusion, consider the linkages shown in Figure 11-10.

The figure shows the following steps:

1.  The routing table entry to 10.3.3.0/24 lists a next-hop IP address of 192.168.12.2. PE1 compares that next-hop information to the list of interface IP addresses on each LDP peer and finds the LDP neighbor who has the IP address 192.168.12.2.

2.  That same stanza of the **show mpls ldp neighbor** command output identifies the LDP ID (LID) of this peer, namely, 2.2.2.2.

3.  PE1 notes that for that same prefix (10.3.3.0/24), the LIB contains one local label and two remote labels.

4.  Among the known labels listed for prefix 10.3.3.0/24, one was learned from a neighbor whose LID is 2.2.2.2, with label (tag) value of 22.

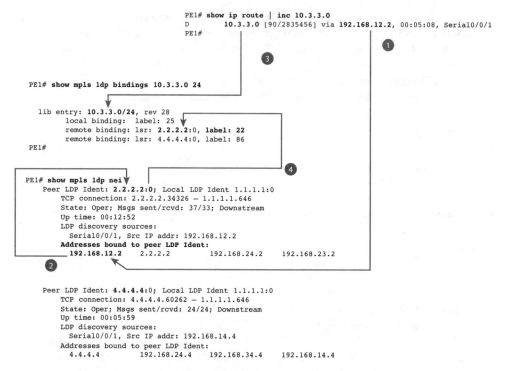

**Figure 11-10**  *PE1's Process to Determine the Outgoing Label*

As a result of these steps, PE1 knows it should use outgoing interface S0/0/1, with label 22, when forwarding packets to subnet 10.3.3.0/24.

## Examples of FIB and LFIB Entries

As mentioned earlier in the chapter, the actual packet-forwarding process does not use the IP routing table (RIB) or the LIB. Instead, the FIB is used to forward packets that arrived unlabeled, and the LFIB is used to forward packets that arrived already labeled. This section correlates the information in **show** commands to the conceptual view of the FIB and LFIB data structures shown back in Figure 11-3.

First, again focusing on PE1, PE1 simply adds information to the FIB stating that PE1 should impose an MPLS header, with label value 22. PE1 also populates the LFIB, with an entry for 10.3.3.0/24, using that same label value of 22 and an outgoing interface of S0/0/1. Example 11-3 shows the contents of the two tables.

**Example 11-3**  *FIB and LFIB Entries for 10.3.3.0/24 on PE1*

```
! This next command shows the FIB entry, which includes the local tag (24), the
! tags (label) imposed, and outgoing interface.
R7# show ip cef 10.1.78.0 internal
10.1.78.0/32, epoch 0, flags receive, refcount 5, per-destination sharing
  sources: I/F
```

```
  subblocks:
   gsb Connected receive chain(0): 0x314E47F4
   Interface source: Serial0/0/0 flags: none
   Dependent covered prefix type cover need deagg, cover 10.1.78.0/24
  ifnums: (none)
  path 2C69F91C, path list 32278664, share 1/1, type receive, for IPv4
  receive for Serial0/0/0
  output chain: receive
! The next command lists the LFIB entry for 10.3.3.0/24, listing the same basic
! information-the local tag, the outgoing tag (label), and outgoing interface.
PE1# show mpls forwarding-table 10.3.3.0 24
Local   Outgoing    Prefix        Bytes tag  Outgoing    Next Hop
tag     tag or VC   or Tunnel Id  switched   interface
24      22          10.3.3.0/24   0          Se0/0/1     point2point
```

In the data plane example of Figure 11-3, PE1 received an unlabeled packet and forwarded the packet to P1, with label 22. The information in the top part of Example 11-3, showing the FIB, matches that same logic, stating that a tag (label) value of 22 will be imposed by PE1.

Next, examine the LFIB at P1, as shown in Example 11-4. As shown in Figure 11-3, P1 swaps the incoming label of 22 with outgoing label 39. For perspective, the example also includes the LIB entries for 10.3.3.0/24.

**Example 11-4**   *LFIB and LIB Entries for 10.3.3.0/24 on P1*

```
P1# show mpls forwarding-table 10.3.3.0 24
Local   Outgoing    Prefix        Bytes tag  Outgoing    Next Hop
tag     tag or VC   or Tunnel Id  switched   interface
22      39          10.3.3.0/24   0          Se0/1/0     point2point
P1# show mpls ldp bindings 10.3.3.0 24
  tib entry: 10.3.3.0/24, rev 30
        local binding:  tag: 22
        remote binding: tsr: 1.1.1.1:0, tag: 24
        remote binding: tsr: 4.4.4.4:0, tag: 86
        remote binding: tsr: 3.3.3.3:0, tag: 39
```

The highlighted line in the output of the **show mpls forwarding-table** command lists the incoming label (22 in this case) and the outgoing label (39). Note that the incoming label is shown under the heading "local tag," meaning that label (tag) 22 was locally allocated by this router (P1) and advertised to other routers using LDP, as shown in Figure 11-8. P1 originally allocated and advertised label 22 to tell neighboring routers to forward packets destined to 10.3.3.0/24 to P1, with a label of 22. P1 knows that if it receives a packet with label 22, P1 should indeed swap the labels, forwarding the packet out S0/1/0 with a label of 39.

The LIB entries in Example 11-4 also reinforce the concept that (frame-mode) MPLS LSRs retain all learned labels in their LIBs, but only the currently used labels in the LFIB.

The LIB lists P1's local label (22) and the three remote labels learned from P1's three LDP neighbors. To create the LFIB entry, P1 used the same kind of logic shown in Figure 11-10 to correlate the information in the routing table and LIB and choose a label value of 39 and outgoing interface S0/1/0 to forward packets to 10.3.3.0/24.

To see an example of the pop action, consider the LFIB for PE2, as shown in Example 11-5. When PE2 receives a labeled packet from P1 (label 39), PE2 will try to use its LFIB to forward the packet. When populating the LFIB, PE2 can easily realize that PE2 should pop the label and forward an unlabeled packet out its Fa0/1 interface. Those reasons include the fact that PE2 did not enable MPLS on Fa0/1 and that PE2 has not learned any labels from CE2. Example 11-5 shows the outgoing tag as "pop label."

**Example 11-5**   *LFIB Entries for 10.3.3.0/24 on PE2*

```
PE2# show mpls forwarding-table 10.3.3.0 24
Local   Outgoing     Prefix          Bytes tag  Outgoing    Next Hop
tag     tag or VC    or Tunnel Id    switched   interface
39      Pop Label    10.3.3.0 24        0        Fa0/1      192.168.36.6
```

Note that while the text in Example 11-5 only showed LFIB entries, every LSR builds the appropriate FIB and LFIB entries for each prefix, in anticipation of receiving both unlabeled and labeled packets.

## Label Distribution Protocol Reference

Before wrapping up the coverage of basic MPLS unicast IP forwarding, you should know a few more details about LDP itself. So far, this chapter has shown what LDP does, but it has not provided much information about how LDP accomplishes its tasks. This section hits the main concepts and summarizes the rest.

LDP uses a Hello feature to discover LDP neighbors and to determine to what IP address the ensuing TCP connection should be made. LDP multicasts the Hellos to IP address 224.0.0.2, using UDP port number 646 for LDP (TDP uses UDP port 711). The Hellos list each LSR's LDP ID (LID), which consists of a 32-bit dotted-decimal number and a 2-byte label space number. (For frame-based MPLS, the label space number is 0.) An LSR can optionally list a *transport address* in the Hello message, which is the IP address that the LSR wants to use for any LDP TCP connections. If a router does not advertise a transport address, other routers will use the IP address that is the first 4 bytes of the LDP ID for the TCP connections.

After discovering neighbors through an LDP Hello message, LDP neighbors form a TCP connection to each neighbor, again using port 646 (TDP 711). Because the TCP connection uses unicast addresses—either the neighbor's advertised transport address or the address in the LID—these addresses must be reachable according to the IP routing table. After the TCP connection is up, each router advertises all its bindings of local labels and prefixes.

Cisco routers choose the IP address in the LDP ID just like the OSPF router ID. LDP chooses the IP address to use as part of its LID based on the exact same logic as OSPF, as summarized in Table 11-4, along with other details.

**Table 11-4** *LDP Reference*

| LDP Feature | LDP Implementation |
|---|---|
| Transport protocols | UDP (Hellos), TCP (updates) |
| Port numbers | 646 (LDP), 711 (TDP) |
| Hello destination address | 224.0.0.2 |
| Who initiates TCP connection | Highest LDP ID |
| TCP connection uses this address | Transport IP address (if configured), or LDP ID if no transport address is configured |
| LDP ID determined by these rules, in order of precedence | Configuration |
| | Highest IP address of an up/up loopback when LDP comes up |
| | Highest IP address of an up/up nonloopback when LDP comes up |

This concludes the coverage of MPLS unicast IP forwarding for this chapter. Next, the chapter examines one of the more popular uses of MPLS, which happens to use unicast IP forwarding: MPLS VPNs.

# MPLS VPNs

One of the most popular MPLS applications is called *MPLS Virtual Private Networks (VPN)*. MPLS VPNs allow a service provider, or even a large enterprise, to offer Layer 3 VPN services. In particular, SPs oftentimes replace older Layer 2 WAN services such as Frame Relay and ATM with an MPLS VPN service. MPLS VPN services enable the possibility for the SP to provide a wide variety of additional services to its customers because MPLS VPNs are aware of the Layer 3 addresses at the customer locations. Additionally, MPLS VPNs can still provide the privacy inherent in Layer 2 WAN services.

MPLS VPNs use MPLS unicast IP forwarding inside the SP's network, with additional MPLS-aware features at the edge between the provider and the customer. Additionally, MPLS VPNs use MP-BGP to overcome some of the challenges when connecting an IP network to a large number of customer IP internetworks—problems that include the issue of dealing with duplicate IP address spaces with many customers.

This section begins by examining some of the problems with providing Layer 3 services and then shows the core features of MPLS that solve those problems.

## The Problem: Duplicate Customer Address Ranges

When an SP connects to a wide variety of customers using a Layer 2 WAN service such as Frame Relay or ATM, the SP does not care about the IP addressing and subnets used by those customers. However, to migrate those same customers to a Layer 3 WAN service, the SP must learn address ranges from the various customers and then advertise those routes into the SP's network. However, even if the SP wanted to know about all subnets from all its customers, many enterprises use the same address ranges—namely, the private IP network numbers, including the ever-popular network 10.0.0.0.

If you tried to support multiple customers using MPLS unicast IP routing alone, the routers would be confused by the overlapping prefixes, as shown in Figure 11-11. In this case, the network shows five of the SP's routers inside a cloud. Three customers (A, B, and C) are shown, with multiple customer routers connected to the SP's network. All three customers use network 10.0.0.0, with the three customer sites on the right all using subnet 10.3.3.0/24.

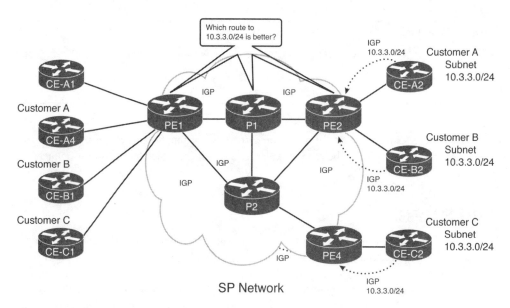

**Figure 11-11** *Main Challenge with Supporting Layer 3 VPNs*

The first and most basic goal for a Layer 3 VPN service is to allow customer A sites to communicate with customer A sites—and only customer A sites. However, the network in Figure 11-11 fails to meet this goal for several reasons. Because of the overlapping address spaces, several routers would be faced with the dilemma of choosing one customer's route to 10.3.3.0/24 as the best route, and ignoring the route to 10.3.3.0/24 learned from another customer. For example, PE2 would learn about two different 10.3.3.0/24 prefixes. If PE2 chooses one of the two possible routes—for example, if PE2 picked the route to CE-A2 as best—PE2 could not forward packets to customer B's 10.3.3.0/24 off Router CE-B2. Also, a possibly worse effect is that hosts in one customer site might be able to send and receive packets with hosts in another customer's network. Following this same example, hosts in customer B and C sites could forward packets to subnet 10.3.3.0/24, and the routers might forward these packets to customer A's CE-A2 router.

## The Solution: MPLS VPNs

The protocols and standards defined by MPLS VPNs solve the problems shown in Figure 11-11 and provide a much larger set of features. In particular, the MPLS VPN RFCs define the concept of using multiple routing tables, called *Virtual Routing and Forwarding (VRF) tables*, which separate customer routes to avoid the duplicate address range issue. This section defines some key terminology and introduces the basics of MPLS VPN mechanics.

MPLS uses three terms to describe the role of a router when building MPLS VPNs. Note that the names used for the routers in most of the figures in this chapter have followed the convention of identifying the type of router as CE, PE, or P, as listed here:

- **Customer edge (CE):** A router that has no knowledge of MPLS protocols and does not send any labeled packets but is directly connected to an LSR (PE) in the MPLS VPN.

- **Provider edge (PE):** An LSR that shares a link with at least one CE router, thereby providing a function particular to the edge of the MPLS VPN, including internal BGP (iBGP) and VRF tables.

- **Provider (P):** An LSR that does not have a direct link to a CE router, which allows the router to just forward labeled packets, and allows the LSR to ignore customer VPNs' routes.

The key to understanding the general idea of how MPLS VPNs work is to focus on the control plane distinctions between PE routers and P routers. Both P and PE routers run LDP and an IGP to support unicast IP routing—just as was described in the first half of this chapter. However, the IGP advertises routes only for subnets inside the MPLS network, with no customer routes included. As a result, the P and PE routers can together label-switch packets from the ingress PE to the egress PE.

PEs have several other duties as well, all geared toward the issue of learning customer routes and keeping track of which routes belong to which customers. PEs exchange routes with the connected CE routers from various customers, using either external BGP (eBGP), RIPv2, OSPF, or EIGRP, noting which routes are learned from which customers. To keep track of the possibly overlapping prefixes, PE routers do not put the routes in the normal IP routing table—instead, PEs store those routes in separate per-customer routing tables, called VRFs. Then the PEs use IBGP to exchange these customer routes with other PEs—never advertising the routes to the P routers. Figure 11-12 shows the control plane concepts.

> **Note**  The term *global routing table* is used to refer to the IP routing table normally used for forwarding packets, as compared with the VRF routing tables.

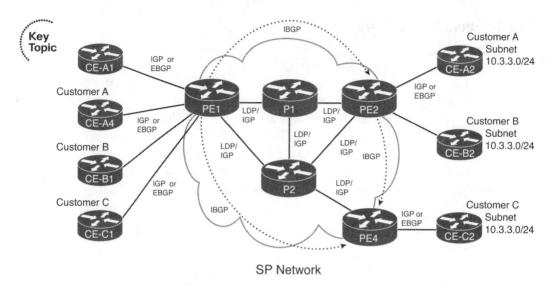

**Figure 11-12**   *Overview of the MPLS VPN Control Plane*

The MPLS VPN data plane also requires more work and thought by the PE routers. The PE routers do not have any additional work to do, with one small exception, as compared with simple unicast IP routing. The extra work for the PE relates to the fact that the MPLS VPN data plane causes the ingress PE to place two labels on the packet, as follows:

- An outer MPLS header (S-bit = 0), with a label value that causes the packet to be label switched to the egress PE

- An inner MPLS header (S-bit = 1), with a label that identifies the egress VRF on which to base the forwarding decision

Figure 11-13 shows a general conceptual view of the two labels and the forwarding process. The figure shows a subset of Figure 11-12, with parts removed to reduce clutter. In this case, a host in customer A on the left side of the figure sends a packet to host 10.3.3.3, located on the right side of the figure.

The figure shows the following steps:

1. CE1 forwards an unlabeled packet to PE1.

2. PE1, having received the packet in an interface assigned to VRF-A, compares the packet's destination (10.3.3.3) to the VRF-A CEF FIB, which is based on VRF-A's routing table. PE1 adds two labels based on the FIB and forwards the labeled packet.

3. P1, acting just the same as with unicast IP routing, processes the received labeled packet using its LFIB, which simply causes a label swap. P1 forwards the packet to PE2.

4. PE2's LFIB entry for label 2222 lists a pop action, causing PE2 to remove the outer label. PE2's LFIB entry for label 3333, populated based on the VRF for customer A's VPN, also lists a pop action and the outgoing interface. As a result, PE2 forwards the unlabeled packet to CE2.

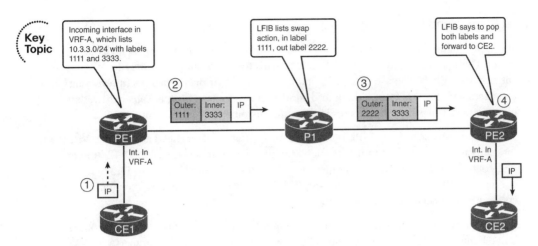

**Figure 11-13** *Overview of the MPLS VPN Data Plane*

**Note** In actual practice, Steps 3 and 4 differ slightly from the descriptions listed here, because of a feature called penultimate hop popping (PHP). This example is meant to show the core concepts. Figure 11-25, toward the end of this chapter, refines this logic when the router uses the PHP feature, which is on by default in MPLS VPNs.

The control plane and data plane processes described around Figures 11-12 and 11-13 outline the basics of how MPLS VPNs work. Next, the chapter takes the explanations a little deeper with a closer look at the new data structures and control plane processes that support MPLS VPNs.

## MPLS VPN Control Plane

The MPLS VPN control plane defines protocols and mechanisms to overcome the problems created by overlapping customer IP address spaces, while adding mechanisms to add more functionality to an MPLS VPN, particularly as compared to traditional Layer 2 WAN services. To understand the mechanics, you need a good understanding of BGP, IGPs, and several new concepts created by both MP-BGP RFCs and MPLS RFCs. In particular, this section introduces and explains the concepts behind three new concepts created for MPLS VPNs:

- VRFs
- Route Distinguishers (RD)
- Route Targets (RT)

The next several pages of text examine these topics in order. While reading the rest of the MPLS VPN coverage in this chapter, note that the text will keep expanding a single example. The example focuses on how the control plane learns about routes to the duplicate customer subnets 10.3.3.0/24 on the right side of Figure 11-12, puts the routes into the VRFs on PE2, and advertises the routes with RDs over to PE1 and then how RTs then dictate how PE1 adds the routes to its VRFs.

## Virtual Routing and Forwarding Tables

To support multiple customers, MPLS VPN standards include the concept of a virtual router. This feature, called a VRF table, can be used to store routes separately for different customer VPNs. The use of separate tables solves part of the problems of preventing one customer's packets from leaking into another customer's network because of overlapping prefixes, while allowing all sites in the same customer VPN to communicate.

A VRF exists inside a single MPLS-aware router. Typically, routers need at least one VRF for each customer attached to that particular router. For example, in Figure 11-12, Router PE2 connects to CE routers in customers A and B but not in customer C, so PE2 would not need a VRF for customer C. However, PE1 connects to CE routers for three customers, so PE1 will need three different VRFs.

For more complex designs, a PE might need multiple VRFs to support a single customer. Using Figure 11-12 again as an example, PE1 connects to two CEs of customer A (CE-A1 and CE-A4). If hosts near CE-A1 were allowed to access a centralized shared service (not shown in the figure) and hosts near CE-A4 were not allowed access, PE1 would need two VRFs for customer A—one with routes for the shared service's subnets and one without those routes.

Each VRF has three main components, as follows:

**Key Topic**

- An IP routing table (RIB)

- A CEF FIB, populated based on that VRF's RIB

- A separate instance or process of the routing protocol used to exchange routes with the CEs that need to be supported by the VRF

For example, Figure 11-14 shows more detail about Router PE2 from Figure 11-12, now with MPLS VPNs implemented. In this case, PE2 will use RIP-2 as the IGP to both customer A (Router CE-A2) and customer B (Router CE-B2). (The choice of routing protocol used from PE-CE is unimportant to the depth of explanations shown here.)

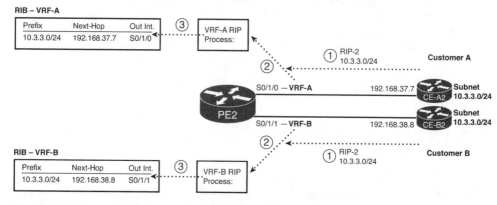

**Figure 11-14**  *Adding Routes Learned from a CE to VRFs on Router PE2*

The figure shows three parallel steps that occur with each of the two customers. Note that Step 1 for each customer does not occur at the same instant in time, nor does Step 2 or Step 3; the figure lists these steps with the same numbers because the same function occurs at each step. The explanation of the steps is as follows:

1. The CE router, which has no knowledge of MPLS, advertises a route for 10.3.3.0/24 as normal—in this case with RIP-2.

2. In the top instance of Step 2, the RIP-2 update arrives on PE2's S0/1/0, which has been assigned to customer A's VRF, VRF-A. PE2 uses a separate RIP process for each VRF, so PE2's VRF-A RIP process interprets the update. Similarly, the VRF-B RIP process analyzes the update received on S0/1/1 from CE-B2.

3. In the top instance of Step 3, the VRF-A RIP process adds an entry for 10.3.3.0/24 to the RIB for VRF-A. Similarly, the bottom instance of Step 3 shows the RIP process for VRF-B adding a route to prefix 10.3.3.0/24 to the VRF-B RIB.

**Note**   Each VRF also has a FIB, which was not included in the figure. IOS would add an appropriate FIB entry for each RIB entry.

## MP-BGP and Route Distinguishers

Now that PE2 has learned routes from both CE-A2 and CE-B2, PE2 needs to advertise those routes to the other PEs, in order for the other PEs to know how to forward packets to the newly learned subnets. MPLS VPN protocols define the use of IBGP to advertise the routes—all the routes, from all the different VRFs. However, the original BGP specifications did not provide a way to deal with the fact that different customers might use overlapping prefixes.

MPLS deals with the overlapping prefix problem by adding another number in front of the original BGP network layer reachability information (NLRI) (prefix). Each different number can represent a different customer, making the NLRI values unique. To do this, MPLS took advantage of a BGP RFC, called MP-BGP (RFC 4760), which allows for the redefinition of the NLRI field in BGP Updates. This redefinition allows for an additional variable-length number, called an *address family*, to be added in front of the prefix. MPLS RFC 4364, "BGP/MPLS IP Virtual Private Networks (VPNs)," defines a specific new address family to support IPv4 MPLS VPNs—namely, an MP-BGP address family called *Route Distinguishers (RD)*.

RDs allow BGP to advertise and distinguish between duplicate IPv4 prefixes. The concept is simple: Advertise each NLRI (prefix) as the traditional IPv4 prefix, but add another number (the RD) that uniquely identifies the route. In particular, the new NLRI format, called VPN-V4, has the following two parts:

■ A 64-bit RD

■ A 32-bit IPv4 prefix

For example, Figure 11-15 continues the story from Figure 11-14, with Router PE2 using MP-BGP to advertise its two routes for IPv4 prefix 10.3.3.0/24 to PE1—one from VRF-A and one from VRF-B. The BGP Update shows the new VPN-V4 address family format for the NLRI information, using RD 1:111 to represent VPN-A and 2:222 to represent VPN-B.

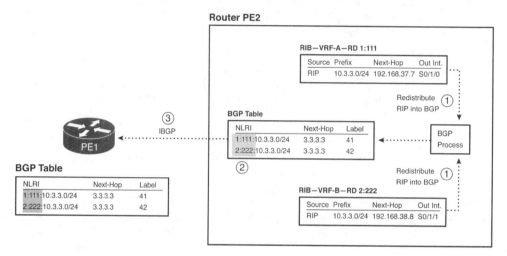

**Figure 11-15**  *Making Prefixes Unique Using an RD*

---

**Note**  PE2 uses next-hop-self, and an update source of a loopback interface with IP address 3.3.3.3.

---

Without the RD as part of the VPN-V4 NLRI, PE1 would have learned about two identical BGP prefixes (10.3.3.0/24) and would have had to choose one of the two as the best route—giving PE1 reachability to only one of the two customer 10.3.3.0/24 subnets. With VPN-V4 NLRI, IBGP advertises two unique NLRI—a 1:111:10.3.3.0 (from VRF-A) and 2:222:10.3.3.0 (from VRF-B). As a result, PE1 keeps both NLRI in its BGP table. The specific steps shown in the figure are explained as follows:

1. PE2 redistributes from each of the respective per-VRF routing protocol instances (RIP-2 in this case) into BGP.

2. The redistribution process pulls the RD from each respective VRF and includes that RD with all routes redistributed from the VRF's routing table.

3. PE2 uses IBGP to advertise these routes to PE1, causing PE1 to know both routes for 10.3.3.0/24, each with the differing RD values.

---

**Note**  Every VRF must be configured with an RD; the IOS **rd** VRF subcommand configures the value.

---

The RD itself is 8 bytes with some required formatting conventions. The first 2 bytes identify which of the three formats is followed. Incidentally, because IOS can tell which of the three formats is used based on the value, the IOS **rd** VRF subcommand only requires that you type the integer values for the last 6 bytes, with IOS inferring the first 2 bytes (the type) based on the value. The last 6 bytes, as typed in the **rd** command and seen in **show** commands, follow one of these formats:

- 2-byte-integer:4-byte-integer

- 4-byte-integer:2-byte-integer

- 4-byte-dotted-decimal:2-byte-integer

In all three cases, the first value (before the colon) should be either an Autonomous System Number (ASN) or an IPv4 address. The second value, after the colon, can be any value you want. For example, you might choose an RD that lists an LSR's BGP ID using the third format, like 3.3.3.3:100, or you can use the BGP ASN, for example, 432:1.

At this point in the ongoing example, PE1 has learned about the two routes for 10.3.3.0/24—one for VPN-A and one for VPN-B—and the routes are in the BGP table. The next section describes how PE1 then chooses the VRFs into which to add these routes, based on the concept of a Route Target.

## Route Targets

One of the most perplexing concepts for engineers, when first learning about MPLS VPNs, is the concept of Route Targets (RT). Understanding the basic question of what RTs do is relatively easy, but understanding why MPLS needs RTs and how to best choose the actual values to use for RTs can be a topic for long conversation when building an MPLS VPN. In fact, MPLS RTs enable MPLS to support all sorts of complex VPN topologies—for example, allowing some sites to be reachable from multiple VPNs, a concept called overlapping VPNs.

PEs advertise RTs in BGP Updates as BGP Extended Community path attributes (PA). Generally speaking, BGP extended communities are 8 bytes in length, with the flexibility to be used for a wide variety of purposes. More specifically, MPLS defines the use of the BGP Extended Community PA to encode one or more RT values.

RT values follow the same basic format as the values of an RD. However, note that while a particular prefix can have only one RD, that same prefix can have one or more RTs assigned to it.

To best understand how MPLS uses RTs, first consider a more general definition of the purpose of RTs, followed by an example of the mechanics by which PEs use the RT:

MPLS uses Route Targets to determine into which VRFs a PE places IBGP-learned routes.

Figure 11-16 shows a continuation of the same example in Figures 11-14 and 11-15, now focusing on how the PEs use the RTs to determine into which VRFs a route is added. In this case, the figure shows an *export RT*—a configuration setting in VRF configuration mode—with a different value configured for VRF-A and VRF-B, respectively. PE1 shows its import RT for each VRF—again, a configuration setting in VRF configuration mode—which allows PE1 to choose which BGP table entries it pulls into each VRF's RIB.

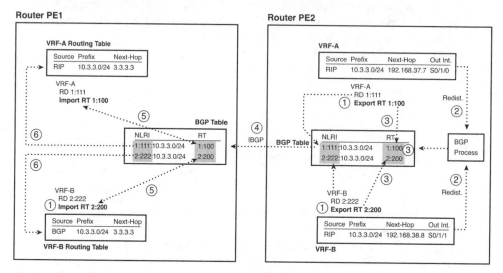

**Figure 11-16**  *Mechanics of the MPLS Route Target*

The figure has a lot of details, but the overall flow of concepts is not terribly difficult. Pay particular attention to the last two steps. Following the steps in the figure:

1. The two VRFs on PE2 are configured with an export RT value.

2. Redistribution out of the VRF into BGP occurs.

3. This step simply notes that the export process—the redistribution out of the VRF into BGP—sets the appropriate RT values in PE2's BGP table.

4. PE2 advertises the routes with IBGP.

5. PE1 examines the new BGP table entries and compares the RT values to the configured import RT values, which identifies which BGP table entries should go into which VRF.

6. PE1 redistributes routes into the respective VRFs, specifically the routes whose RTs match the import RT configured in the VRFs, respectively.

**Note**  It is sometimes helpful to think of the term *export* to mean "redistribute out of the VRF into BGP" and the term *import* to mean "redistribute into the VRF from BGP."

Each VRF needs to export and import at least one RT. The example in Figure 11-16 shows only one direction: exporting on the right (PE2) and importing on the left (PE1). However, PE2 needs to know the routes for the subnets connected to CE-A1 and CE-B1, so PE1 needs to learn those routes from the CEs, redistribute them into BGP with some exported RT value, and advertise them to PE2 using IBGP, with PE2 then importing the correct routes (based on PE2's import RTs) into PE2's VRFs.

In fact, for simple VPN implementations, in which each VPN consists of all sites for a single customer, most configurations simply use a single RT value, with each VRF for a customer both importing and exporting that RT value.

**Note**   The examples in this chapter show different numbers for the RD and RT values so that it is clear what each number represents. In practice, you can set a VRF's RD and one of its RTs to the same value.

## Overlapping VPNs

MPLS can support overlapping VPNs by virtue of the RT concept. An overlapping VPN occurs when at least one CE site needs to be reachable by CEs in different VPNs.

Many variations of overlapping VPNs exist. An SP can provide services to many customers, so the SP actually implements CE sites that need to be reached by a subset of customers. Some SP customers might want connectivity to one of their partners through the MPLS network. For example, customer A might want some of its sites to be able to send packets to some of customer B's sites.

Regardless of the business goals, the RT concept allows an MPLS network to leak routes from multiple VPNs into a particular VRF. BGP supports the addition of multiple Extended Community PAs to each BGP table entry. By doing so, a single prefix can be exported with one RT that essentially means "make sure that all VRFs in VPN-A have this route," while assigning another RT value to that same prefix—an RT that means "leak this route into the VRFs of some overlapping VPN."

Figure 11-17 shows an example of the concepts behind overlapping MPLS VPNs, in particular, a design called a central services VPN. As usual, all customer A sites can send packets to all other customer A sites, and all customer B sites can send packets to all other customer B sites. Also, none of the customer A sites can communicate with the customer B sites. However, in addition to these usual conventions, CE-A1 and CE-B2 can communicate with CE-Serv, which connects to a set of centralized servers.

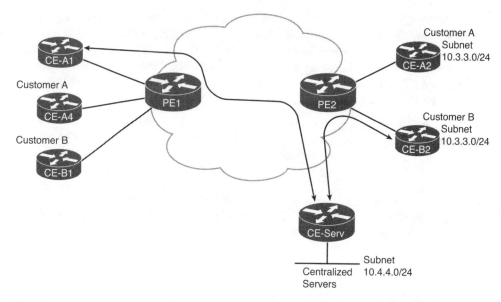

**Figure 11-17** *Central Services VPN*

To accomplish these design goals, each PE needs several VRFs, with several VRFs export-ing and importing multiple RTs. For example, PE1 needs two VRFs to support customer A—one VRF that just imports routes for customer A and a second VRF that imports cus-tomer A routes as well as routes to reach the central services VPN. Similarly, PE2 needs a VRF for the central services VPN, which needs to import some of the routes in VPN-A and VPN-B.

## MPLS VPN Configuration

MPLS VPN configuration focuses primarily on control plane functions: creating the VRF and associated RDs and RTs, configuring MP-BGP, and redistributing between the IGP used with the customer and BGP used inside the MPLS cloud. Given this focus on con-trol plane features, this section explains MPLS VPN configuration, leaving the data plane details for the later section "MPLS VPN Data Plane."

MPLS VPN configuration requires a fairly large number of commands. For the sake of learning the details of a straightforward MPLS VPN configuration, which still has a lot of commands, this section builds a sample configuration using the internetwork shown in Figure 11-18.

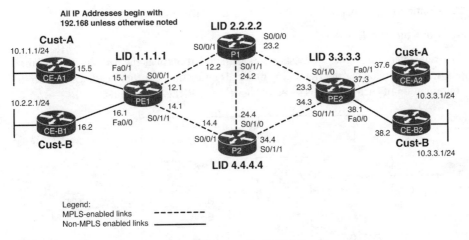

**Figure 11-18** *Sample Internetwork for MPLS VPN Configuration*

The MPLS VPN design for this internetwork, whose configuration is demonstrated in the coming pages, uses the same RD and RT values seen throughout the earlier section "MPLS VPN Control Plane." Before moving into the configuration specific to MPLS VPNs, keep in mind that the internetwork of Figure 11-18 has already been configured with some commands, specifically the following:

- All links between P and PE routers are configured with IP addresses, the IP address on the other end of each link is pingable, and these interfaces have been enabled for frame-mode MPLS with the **mpls ip** interface subcommand.

- All P and PE routers use a common IGP (EIGRP with ASN 200 in this case), with all loopbacks and subnets between the P and PE routers being advertised. As a result, all P and PE routers can ping IP addresses of all interfaces on those routers, including the loopback interfaces on those routers.

- Between each PE and CE, IP addresses have been configured, and the links work, but these subnets are not currently advertised by any routing protocol.

- The PE router interfaces that connect to the CE routers do not have the **mpls ip** interface subcommand, because these interfaces do not need to be MPLS enabled. (The **mpls ip** command tells IOS that IP packets should be forwarded and received with an MPLS label.)

- None of the features specific to MPLS VPNs have yet been configured.

MPLS VPN configuration requires many new commands and several instances of some of those commands. To help make sense of the various steps, the configuration in this section has been broken into the following four major areas:

**Key Topic**

1. Creating each VRF, RD, and RT, plus associating the customer-facing PE interfaces with the correct VRF

2. Configuring the IGP between PE and CE

**3.** Configuring mutual redistribution between the IGP and BGP

**4.** Configuring MP-BGP between PEs

For visual reference, Figure 11-19 shows a diagram that outlines the four major configuration sections. Following the figure, the materials under the next four headings explain the configuration of each area, plus some of the relevant EXEC commands.

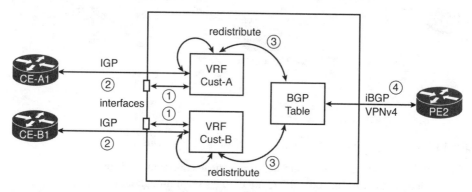

**Figure 11-19**  *Four Major Configuration Topics for MPLS VPNs*

## Configuring the VRF and Associated Interfaces

After you understand the concept of a VRF, RD, and RT, as explained in the earlier section "MPLS VPN Control Plane," the configuration can be straightforward. Certainly, the simpler the design, like the basic nonoverlapping MPLS VPN design used in this section, the easier the configuration. To give you a taste of MPLS VPN configuration, this section uses the same RD and RT values as shown in Figure 11-15 and Figure 11-16, but with slightly different VRF names, as follows:

- VRF Cust-A, RD 1:111, RT 1:100

- VRF Cust-B, RD 2:222, RT 2:200

The configuration for each item occurs on the PE routers only. The customer router has no awareness of MPLS, and the P routers have no awareness of MPLS VPN features. The configuration uses these four commands:

**Key Topic**

- Configuring the VRF with the **ip vrf** *vrf-name* command

- Configuring the RD with the **rd** *rd-value* VRF subcommand

- Configuring the RT with the **route-target {import|export}** *rt-value* VRF subcommand

- Associating an interface with the VRF using the **ip vrf forwarding** *vrf-name* interface subcommand

The moment that the **ip vrf forwarding** command is applied to the interface, the IP address of the interface will be removed, necessitating its reapplication.

Example 11-6 shows the configuration, with additional comments following the example.

**Example 11-6**  *VRF Configuration on PE1 and PE2*

```
! Configuration on PE1
! The next command creates the VRF with its case-sensitive name, followed by
! the definition of the RD for this VRF, and both the import (from MP-BGP)
! and export (to MP-BGP) route targets.
ip vrf Cust-A
 rd 1:111
 route-target import 1:100
 route-target export 1:100

ip vrf Cust-B
 rd 2:222
 route-target import 2:200
 route-target export 2:200

! The next highlighted command associates the interface (Fa0/1) with a VRF
! (Cust-A)
interface fastethernet0/1
 ip vrf forwarding Cust-A
 ip address 192.168.15.1 255.255.255.0

! The next highlighted command associates the interface (Fa0/0) with a VRF
! (Cust-B)
interface fastethernet0/0
 ip vrf forwarding Cust-B
 ip address 192.168.16.1 255.255.255.0

! Configuration on PE2
ip vrf Cust-A
 rd 1:111
 route-target import 1:100
 route-target export 1:100

ip vrf Cust-B
 rd 2:222
 route-target import 2:200
 route-target export 2:200

interface fastethernet0/1
 ip vrf forwarding Cust-A
 ip address 192.168.37.3 255.255.255.0

interface fastethernet0/0
 ip vrf forwarding Cust-B
 ip address 192.168.38.3 255.255.255.0
```

The configuration on both PE1 and PE2 shows two VRFs, one for each customer. Each VRF has the required RD, and at least one import and export route tag. The planning process must match the exported RT on one PE router to the imported RT on the remote PE, and vice versa, for the two routers to exchange routes with MP-BGP. In this case, because no overlapping VPN sites are expected, the engineer planned a consistent single RT value per customer, configured on every PE, to avoid confusion.

In addition to the obvious parts of the configuration, Example 11-6 unfortunately hides a couple of small items. First, the **route-target both** command could be used when using the same value as both an import and export RT. IOS then splits this single command into a **route-target import** and **route-target export** command, as shown. In addition, the **ip vrf forwarding** interface subcommand actually removes the IP address from the interface and displays an informational message to that effect. To complete the configuration, Example 11-6 shows the reconfiguration of the same IP address on each interface, expecting that the address was automatically removed.

### Configuring the IGP Between PE and CE

The second major configuration step requires adding the configuration of a routing protocol between the PE and CE. This routing protocol allows the PE router to learn the customer routes, and the customer routers to learn customer routes learned by the PE from other PEs in the MPLS cloud.

Any IGP, or even BGP, can be used as the routing protocol. Often, the customer continues to use its favorite IGP, and the MPLS provider accommodates that choice. In other cases, the provider might require a specific routing protocol, often BGP in that case. The example in this section makes use of EIGRP as the PE-CE routing protocol.

Regardless of the routing protocol used between the PE and CE, the new and interesting configuration resides on the PE router. The engineer configures the CE router so that it becomes a peer with the PE router, using the same familiar IGP or BGP commands (nothing new there). The PE, however, must be VRF-aware, so the PE must be told the VRF name and what interfaces to consider when discovering neighbors inside that VRF context.

**Note**  The rest of this section refers generally to the PE-CE routing protocol as an IGP, because EIGRP is used in these examples. However, remember that BGP is also allowed.

The configuration for EIGRP as the PE-CE routing protocol requires these steps:

- Configuring the EIGRP process, with an ASN that does not need to match the CE router, using the **router eigrp** *asn* global command.

- Identifying the VRF for which additional commands apply, using the **address-family ipv4 vrf** *vrf-name* **autonomous-system** *asn* router subcommand.

- From VRF configuration submode (reached with the **address-family ipv4 vrf** command), we can still configure the ASN to match the CE router's **router eigrp** *asn* global command. This is accomplished through the **autonomous-system** *asn* command. Note that this command is being deprecated.

- From VRF configuration submode, configure the **network** command. This command only matches interfaces that include an **ip vrf forwarding** *vrf-name* interface subcommand, with a VRF name that matches the **address-family ipv4 vrf** command.

- From VRF configuration submode, configure any other traditional IGP router subcommands (for example, **no auto-summary** and **redistribute**).

Continuing the same example, both Customer A and Customer B use EIGRP, and both use EIGRP ASN 1 on the **router eigrp** command. PE1 will become EIGRP neighbors with both CE-A1 and CE-B1, but only in the context of the corresponding VRFs Cust-A and Cust-B. Example 11-7 shows the configuration on these three routers.

**Example 11-7**  *EIGRP Configuration: CE-A1, CE-B1, and PE1*

```
! Configuration on CE-A1
router eigrp 1
 network 192.168.15.0
 network 10.0.0.0


! Configuration on CE-B1
router eigrp 1
 network 192.168.16.0
 network 10.0.0.0
! Configuration on PE1
! Pay close attention to the command prompts and modes
PE1#conf t
Enter configuration commands, one per line.  End with CNTL/Z.
PE1(config)# router eigrp 65001
PE1(config-router)# address-family ipv4 vrf Cust-A
PE1(config-router-af)# autonomous-system 1
PE1(config-router-af)# network 192.168.15.1 0.0.0.0
PE1(config-router-af)# address-family ipv4 vrf Cust-B
PE1(config-router-af)# autonomous-system 1
PE1(config-router-af)# network 192.168.16.1 0.0.0.0
PE1(config-router-af)# no auto-summary
```

The configuration in Example 11-7 has two potential surprises. The first is that the **router eigrp 65001** command's ASN (65,001) does not need to match the CE routers' ASN values. Instead, the ASN listed on the **autonomous-system** subcommand inside the address family submode must match (keep in mind that this command is hidden inside context-sensitive help). In this case, both Customer A and B use the same EIGRP ASN (1), just to show that the values do not have to be unique.

The second potential surprise is that the commands that follow the **address-family ipv4 vrf Cust-A** command apply to only the Cust-A VRF and interfaces. For example, the **network 192.168.15.1 0.0.0.0** command tells IOS to search only interfaces assigned to VRF Cust-A—namely, Fa0/1 in this case—and only attempt to match those interfaces using this **network** command.

Note that similar configuration is required between PE2 and the two CE routers on the right side of Figure 11-19, but that configuration is not listed in Example 11-7.

At this point in the configuration, the VRFs exist on each PE, the PE-CE interfaces are assigned to the VRFs, and the PE routers should have learned some routes from the CE routers. As a result, the PE should have EIGRP neighborships with the CE routers, and the PE should have learned some customer routes in each VRF. Example 11-8 lists a few **show** commands for PE1's Cust-A VRF that demonstrate the per-VRF nature of the PEs.

**Example 11-8**   *show Commands on PE1 Related to VRF Cust-A*

```
! The next command shows the EIGRP topology table, just for VRF Cust-A
PE1# show ip eigrp vrf Cust-A topology

IP-EIGRP Topology Table for AS(1)/ID(192.168.15.1) Routing Table: Cust-A
Codes: P - Passive, A - Active, U - Update, Q - Query, R - Reply,
       r - reply Status, s - sia Status

P 10.1.1.0/24, 1 successors, FD is 156160
        via 192.168.15.5 (156160/128256), FastEthernet0/1
P 192.168.15.0/24, 1 successors, FD is 28160
        via Connected, FastEthernet0/1
! The next command shows EIGRP neighbors, just for VRF Cust-A. Note that PE1
! actually has 4 EIGRP neighbors: 1 for VRF Cust-A, 1 for VRF Cust-B, and two for
! the EIGRP instance used to exchange routes inside the MPLS cloud.

PE1# show ip eigrp vrf Cust-A neighbors
IP-EIGRP neighbors for process 1
H   Address           Interface        Hold Uptime    SRTT    RTO  Q  Seq
                                       (sec)          (ms)         Cnt Num
0   192.168.15.5      Fa0/1            12 00:21:40      1     200  0  3

! the next command lists IP routes for VRF Cust-A
PE1# show ip route vrf Cust-A

! lines omitted for brevity

C   192.168.15.0/24 is directly connected, FastEthernet0/1
    10.0.0.0/24 is subnetted, 1 subnets
D      10.1.1.0 [90/156160] via 192.168.15.5, 00:21:56, FastEthernet0/1
PE1#
```

```
! Finally, the last command shows that the normal routing table does not have
! any routes for customer route 10.1.1.0/24, nor for the connected subnet
! between PE1 and CE-A1 (192.168.15.0/24).
PE1# show ip route | include 10.1.1
PE1#
PE1# show ip route | include 192.168.15
PE1#
```

Most of the output from the **show** commands in Example 11-8 should look familiar, but the commands themselves differ. These commands mostly list a parameter that identifies the VRF by name.

For those completely new to VRFs and MPLS VPNs, pay close attention to the output of the **show ip route vrf Cust-A** and **show ip route** commands. The first of these commands lists the connected route on PE1's Fa0/1 (192.168.15.0/24) and one EIGRP-learned route (10.1.1.0/24, learned from CE-A1). However, the final two **show ip route** commands, which display routes from the normal IP routing table, do not contain either route seen in the Cust-A VRF, because interface Fa0/1 and the EIGRP configuration associates those routes with VRF Cust-A.

## Configuring Redistribution Between PE-CE IGP and MP-BGP

After the completion of configuration Steps 1 and 2 (per Figure 11-19), the PE routers have IGP-learned customer routes in each VRF, but they have no ability to advertise these routes across the MPLS VPN cloud. The next step takes those IGP-learned routes and injects them into the BGP table using redistribution. At the same time, the PE routers also need to use redistribution to pull the BGP-learned routes into the IGP, for the appropriate VRFs.

For BGP to advertise routes between the PE routers, IP prefixes must first be injected into a router's BGP table. As discussed back in Chapter 1, "Fundamentals of BGP Operations," the two most common methods to inject new routes into the BGP table are redistribution and the BGP **network** command. The BGP **network** command works well when injecting a small number of predictable prefixes (for example, when injecting the public IP address prefix used by a company). The redistribution process works best when the prefixes are not predictable, there might be many, and when the routes are not destined for the Internet core routers' routing tables (all true when using MP-BGP for MPLS). So, MPLS VPN BGP configurations typically use redistribution.

The mechanics of the MPLS VPN mutual redistribution configuration requires that both the IGP and BGP be told the specific VRF for which redistribution occurs. Redistribution takes routes from the IP routing table. When configured specific to a particular VRF, that redistribution acts on the VRF IP routing table.

**Key Topic**

The configuration of the **redistribute** command, under both the BGP and IGP process, uses the **address-family ipv4 vrf** *vrf-name* command to set the VRF context as shown in Example 11-7. The **redistribute** command then acts on that VRF. Other than this new detail, the redistribution configuration is no different than before we introduced the concept of VRFs. Example 11-9 shows the redistribution configuration on Router PE1.

**Example 11-9**   *PE1 EIGRP and BGP Mutual Redistribution Configuration*

```
PE1# conf t
Enter configuration commands, one per line.  End with CNTL/Z.


! The next command moves the user to BGP config mode. The following
! command identifies the VRF, and the third command in sequence tells
! IOS to take EIGRP routes from the VRF routing table.


PE1(config)# router bgp 65001
PE1(config-router)# address-family ipv4 vrf Cust-A
PE1(config-router-af)# redistribute eigrp 1


! Next, the same concept is configured for VRF Cust-B.
PE1(config-router-af)# address-family ipv4 vrf Cust-B
PE1(config-router-af)# redistribute eigrp 1


! Next, EIGRP is configured, with the redistribute command being issued
! inside the context of the respective VRFs due to the address-family commands.


PE1(config-router-af)# router eigrp 65001
PE1(config-router)# address-family ipv4 vrf Cust-A
PE1(config-router-af)# redistribute bgp 65001 metric 10000 1000 255 1 1500


! next, the same concept is configured, this time for VRF Cust-B.


PE1(config-router-af)# address-family ipv4 vrf Cust-B
PE1(config-router-af)# redistribute bgp 65001 metric 5000 500 255 1 1500
```

The metrics used at redistribution can be set with the **redistribute** command, the **default-metric** command, or a **route-map**. In Example 11-9, the **redistribute bgp** command sets the EIGRP metric components because EIGRP does not have an inherent default metric when redistributing into EIGRP. However, BGP uses a default metric (BGP MED) of using the integer metric to the redistributed route, so the **redistribute eigrp** command did not require a default metric setting.

**Note**   The metric values are required, but the values chosen have no particular significance.

Assuming a similar (if not identical) configuration on the other PE routers, the PE routers should all now have customer routes in their BGP tables, as shown in Example 11-10.

**Example 11-10**  *PE1 BGP Table with Prefixes of Customers A and B*

```
! The BGP table for all VRFs, in succession, are listed next. Note that only
! locally injected routes are listed, but no routes for the prefixes on the
! other side of the MPLS cloud.


PE1# show ip bgp vpnv4 all
BGP table version is 21, local router ID is 1.1.1.1
Status codes: s suppressed, d damped, h history, * valid, > best, i - internal,
              r RIB-failure, S Stale
Origin codes: i - IGP, e - EGP, ? - incomplete
   Network          Next Hop          Metric LocPrf Weight Path
Route Distinguisher: 1:111 (default for vrf Cust-A)
*> 10.1.1.0/24      192.168.15.5         156160        32768 ?
*> 192.168.15.0     0.0.0.0                   0        32768 ?
Route Distinguisher: 2:222 (default for vrf Cust-B)
*> 10.2.2.0/24      192.168.16.2         156160        32768 ?
*> 192.168.16.0     0.0.0.0                   0        32768 ?


! Next, note that show ip bgp does not list the BGP table entries for
! either VRF.


PE1# show ip bgp
PE1#


! Next, an example of how to display BGP table entries per VRF.


PE1# show ip bgp vpnv4 rd 1:111
BGP table version is 21, local router ID is 1.1.1.1
Status codes: s suppressed, d damped, h history, * valid, > best, i - internal,
              r RIB-failure, S Stale
Origin codes: i - IGP, e - EGP, ? - incomplete


   Network          Next Hop          Metric LocPrf Weight Path
Route Distinguisher: 1:111 (default for vrf Cust-A)
*> 10.1.1.0/24      192.168.15.5         156160        32768 ?
*> 192.168.15.0     0.0.0.0                   0        32768 ?
```

## Configuring MP-BGP Between PEs

The fourth and final configuration step in this section defines the MP-BGP connections between PEs. After being configured, PEs can exchange prefixes in VPNv4 (VPN for IPv4) format. In other words, BGP prepends the RD in front of the IPv4 prefix to make each prefix unique.

To configure each peer, some commands appear as normal with BGP in non-MPLS configurations, and others occur inside a new VPNv4 address family context. Comparing this MPLS VPN BGP configuration to traditional BGP configuration:

**Key Topic**

- The PE neighbors are defined under the main BGP process, not for a particular address family.

- Commonly, MPLS VPN designs use a loopback as update source on the PE routers; in such cases, the **neighbor update-source** command is also under the main BGP process.

- The PE neighbors are then activated, using the **neighbor activate** command, under the VPNv4 address family (**address-family vpnv4**).

- BGP must be told to send the community PA (**neighbor send-community** command, under the **address-family vpnv4** command).

- The VPNv4 address family does not refer to any particular VRF.

- Only one iBGP neighbor relationship is needed to each remote PE; there is no need for a neighbor per VRF on each remote PE.

Example 11-11 shows the configuration for Step 4 on both PE1 and PE2.

**Example 11-11** *BGP Configuration on PE Routers PE1 and PE2*

```
!PE1 - BGP config for VPNv4
! note the new configuration sub-mode for the address family, with the
! suffix of "-af" at the end of the command prompt.


PE1# conf t
Enter configuration commands, one per line.  End with CNTL/Z.
PE1(config)# router bgp 65001
PE1(config-router)# neighbor 3.3.3.3 remote-as 65001
PE1(config-router)# neighbor 3.3.3.3 update-source loop0
PE1(config-router)# address-family vpnv4
PE1(config-router-af)# neighbor 3.3.3.3 activate
PE1(config-router-af)# neighbor 3.3.3.3 send-community

!PE2 - BGP config for VPNv4
PE2(config)#router bgp 65001
PE2(config-router)# neighbor 1.1.1.1 remote-as 65001
PE2(config-router)# neighbor 1.1.1.1 update-source loop0
PE2(config-router)#
PE2(config-router)#address-family vpnv4
PE2(config-router-af)# neighbor 1.1.1.1 activate
PE2(config-router-af)# neighbor 1.1.1.1 send-community
```

At this point, the BGP neighbor relationships can form, and the configuration process is complete, at least for this example. However, although this sample configuration uses many configuration commands—roughly 35 commands just for the PE1 MPLS configuration for the example in this section—many additional configuration options exist, and a wide variety of **show** and **debug** options, too. Example 11-12 lists some **show** command output that confirms the current state of the control plane.

**Example 11-12**   *Current BGP Status After the Completed Configuration*

```
! The next command confirms that the MP-BGP prefixes are not displayed by
! the show ip bgp command.
PE1# show ip bgp

PE1#

! The next command shows the per-RD BGP table. The highlighted lines shows the
! overlapping 10.3.3.0/24 part of the two customers' address spaces.

PE1# show ip bgp vpnv4 all
BGP table version is 33, local router ID is 1.1.1.1
Status codes: s suppressed, d damped, h history, * valid, > best, i - internal,
              r RIB-failure, S Stale
Origin codes: i - IGP, e - EGP, ? - incomplete

   Network          Next Hop         Metric LocPrf Weight Path
Route Distinguisher: 1:111 (default for vrf Cust-A)
*> 10.1.1.0/24      192.168.15.5      156160         32768 ?
*>i10.3.3.0/24      3.3.3.3           156160    100      0 ?
*> 192.168.15.0     0.0.0.0                0         32768 ?
*>i192.168.37.0     3.3.3.3                0    100      0 ?
Route Distinguisher: 2:222 (default for vrf Cust-B)
*> 10.2.2.0/24      192.168.16.2      156160         32768 ?
*>i10.3.3.0/24      3.3.3.3           156160    100      0 ?
*> 192.168.16.0     0.0.0.0                0         32768 ?
*>i192.168.38.0     3.3.3.3                0    100      0 ?

! The next command lists the per-VRF routing table for Cust-A.


PE1# show ip route vrf Cust-A
! lines omitted for brevity
C    192.168.15.0/24 is directly connected, FastEthernet0/1
     10.0.0.0/24 is subnetted, 2 subnets
B       10.3.3.0 [200/156160] via 3.3.3.3, 01:33:49
D       10.1.1.0 [90/156160] via 192.168.15.5, 02:02:31, FastEthernet0/1
B    192.168.37.0/24 [200/0] via 3.3.3.3, 01:33:49


! Now on router CE-A1
! The next command confirms that the customer router (CE-A1) has learned
```

```
! the route for 10.3.3.0/24, as advertised by CE-A2.


CE-A1# show ip route
! lines omitted for brevity
C    192.168.15.0/24 is directly connected, Vlan111
     10.0.0.0/24 is subnetted, 2 subnets
D       10.3.3.0 [90/156416] via 192.168.15.1, 01:34:12, Vlan111
C       10.1.1.0 is directly connected, Loopback1
D    192.168.37.0/24 [90/28416] via 192.168.15.1, 01:34:12, Vlan111
```

## MPLS VPN Data Plane

The explanations of the VRF, RD, and RT features explain most of the details of the MPLS VPN control plane. VRFs allow PEs to store routes learned from various CEs, even if the prefixes overlap. The RD allows PEs to advertise routes as unique prefixes, even if the IPv4 prefixes happen to overlap. Finally, the RT tells the PEs which routes should be added to each VRF, which provides greater control and the ability to allow sites to be reachable from multiple VPNs.

At the end of the process, however, to support the forwarding of packets, ingress PEs need appropriate FIB entries, with Ps and PEs needing appropriate LFIB entries. This section focuses on explaining how LSRs fill the FIB and LFIB when using MPLS VPNs.

As usual for this chapter, this section focuses on how to forward packets to subnet 10.3.3.0/24 in the customer A VPN. To begin this examination of the MPLS VPN data plane, consider Figure 11-20. This figure repeats the same forwarding example shown in Figure 11-13 but now shows a few details about the FIB in the ingress PE and the LFIB entries in the P and egress PE routers.

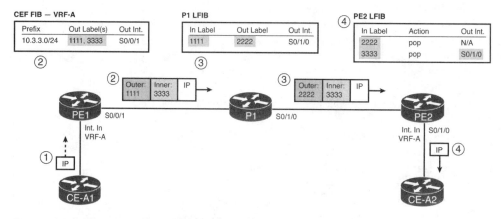

**Figure 11-20**  *Ingress PE FIB and Other Routers' LFIBs*

The numbered steps in the figure are as follows:

1.  An unlabeled packet arrives on an interface assigned to VRF-A, which will cause ingress PE1 to use VRF-A's FIB to make a forwarding decision.

2. Ingress PE1's VRF-A FIB entry for 10.3.3.0/24 lists an outgoing interface of S0/0/1 and a label stack with two labels—an inner label of 3333 and an outer label of 1111. So PE1 forwards the packet with these two labels pushed in front of the IP header.

3. P1 uses the LFIB entry for incoming (local) label 1111, swapping this outer label value to 2222.

4. PE2 does two LFIB lookups. PE2 finds label 2222 in the table and pops that label, leaving the inner label. Then PE2 looks up the inner label 3333 in the LFIB, noting the pop action as well, along with the outgoing interface. So PE2 forwards the unlabeled packet out interface S0/1/0.

**Note**   As was the case with the example shown in Figure 11-13, the details at Steps 3 and 4 will differ slightly in practice, as a result of the PHP feature, which is explained around Figure 11-25 at the end of this chapter.

The example shows the mechanics of what happens in the data plane after the correct FIB and LFIB entries have been added. The rest of this topic about the MPLS VPN data plane examines how MPLS VPN LSRs build these correct entries. While you read this section, it is helpful to keep in mind a couple of details about the purpose of the inner and outer label used for MPLS VPNs:

- The outer label identifies the segments of the LSP between the ingress PE and the egress PE, but it does not identify how the egress PE should forward the packet.

- The inner label identifies the egress PE's forwarding details, in particular the outgoing interface for the unlabeled packet.

## Building the (Inner) VPN Label

The inner label identifies the outgoing interface out which the egress PE should forward the unlabeled packet. This inner label, called the *VPN label*, must be allocated for each route added to each customer VRF. More specifically, a customer CE will advertise routes to the PE, with the PE storing those routes in that customer's VRF. To prepare to forward packets to those customer subnets, the PE needs to allocate a new local label, associate the label with the prefix (and the route's next-hop IP address and outgoing interface), and store that information in the LFIB.

Figure 11-21 shows PE2's routes for 10.3.3.0/24 in both VRF-A and VRF-B and the resulting LFIB entries. The figure shows the results of PE2's process of allocating a local label for each of the two routes and then also advertising those labels using BGP. (Note that the LFIB is not a per-VRF table; the LFIB is the one and only LFIB for PE2.)

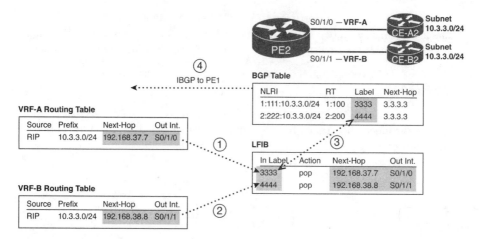

**Figure 11-21** *Creating the VPN Label LFIB Entry on the Egress PE*

The steps shown in the figure are as follows:

1.  After adding a route for 10.3.3.0/24 to VRF-A, PE2 allocates a local label (3333) to associate with the route. PE2 then stores the local label and corresponding next hop and outgoing interface from VRF-A's route for 10.3.3.0/24 into the LIB (not shown) and LFIB.

2.  PE2 repeats the logic in Step 1 for each route in each VRF, including the route in VRF-B shown at Step 2. After learning a route for 10.3.3.0/24 in VRF-B, PE2 allocates a different label value (4444), associates that route's next-hop IP address and outgoing interface with the new label, and adds the information to a new LFIB entry.

3.  PE2 adds the local labels to the BGP table entry for the routes, respectively, when redistributing routes into BGP.

4.  PE2 uses IBGP to advertise the routes to PE1, with the BGP Update including the VPN label.

As a result of the first two steps in the figure, if PE2 receives a labeled packet and ana-lyzes a label value of 3333, PE2 would be able to forward the packet correctly to CE-A2. Similarly, PE2 could correctly forward a received labeled packet with label 4444 to CE-B2.

> **Note** Steps 3 and 4 in Figure 11-21 do nothing to aid PE2 to forward packets; these steps were included to be referenced at an upcoming step later in this section.

### Creating LFIB Entries to Forward Packets to the Egress PE

The outer label defines the LSP from the ingress PE to the egress PE. More specifically, it defines an LSP used to forward packets to the BGP next-hop address as advertised in BGP Updates. In concept, the ingress PE adds the outer label to make a request of the core of the MPLS network to "deliver this packet to the egress PE—which advertised this particu-lar BGP next-hop address."

MPLS VPNs use an IGP and LDP to learn routes and labels, specifically to learn the label values to use in the outer label. To link the concepts together, it can be helpful to think of the full control plane process related to the LSP used for the outer label, particularly Step 4 onward:

1. A PE, which will be an egress PE for this particular route, learns routes from some CE.

2. The egress PE uses IBGP to advertise the routes to an ingress PE.

3. The learned IBGP routes list some next-hop IP address.

4. For MPLS VPNs to work, the PE and P routers must have advertised a route to reach the BGP next-hop addresses.

5. Likewise, for MPLS VPNs to work, the PE and P routers must have advertised labels with LDP for the routes to reach the BGP next-hop addresses.

6. Each P and PE router adds its part of the full end-to-end LSP into its LFIB, supporting the ingress PE's ability to send a packet to the egress PE.

For example, Figure 11-21 shows PE2 advertising two routes to PE1, both with BGP next-hop IP address 3.3.3.3. For MPLS to work, the collective PE and P routers need to advertise an IGP route to reach 3.3.3.3, with LDP advertising the labels, so that packets can be label-switched toward the egress PE. Figure 11-22 shows the basic process. However, note that this part of the process works exactly like the simple IGP and LDP process shown for unicast IP forwarding in the first half of this chapter.

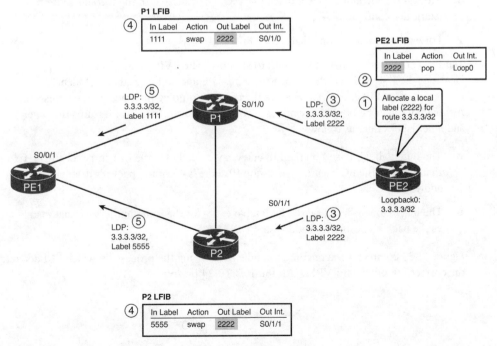

**Figure 11-22** *Creating the LFIB Entries to Reach the Egress PE's BGP Next Hop*

The steps in the figure focus on the LFIB entries for prefix 3.3.3.3/32, which matches PE2's BGP next-hop IP address, as follows. Note that the figure does not show all LDP advertisements but only those that are particularly interesting to the example.

1. PE2, upon learning a route for prefix 3.3.3.3/32, allocates a local label of 2222.

2. PE2 updates its LFIB for the local label, listing a pop action.

3. As normal, PE2 advertises to its LDP neighbors the label binding of prefix 3.3.3.3/32 with label 2222.

4. P1 and P2 both independently learn about prefix 3.3.3.3/32 with the IGP, allocate a local label (1111 on P1 and 5555 on P2), and update their LFIBs.

5. P1 and P2 advertise the binding of 3.3.3.3/32, along with their respective local labels, to their peers.

Figure 11-20 showed the FIB and LFIB entries required for forwarding a packet from CE-A1 to CE-A2, specifically into subnet 10.3.3.0/24. Figures 11-21 and 11-22, and their associated text, explained how all the LFIB entries were created. Next, the focus turns to the FIB entry required on PE1.

### Creating VRF FIB Entries for the Ingress PE

The last part of the data plane analysis focuses on the ingress PE. In particular, the ingress PE uses the following logic when processing an incoming unlabeled packet:

1. Process the incoming packet using the VRF associated with the incoming interface (statically configured).

2. Forward the packet using that VRF's FIB.

The FIB entry needs to have two labels to support MPLS VPNs: an outer label that identifies the LSP with which to reach the egress PE and an inner label that identifies the egress PE's LFIB entry that includes the correct outgoing interface on the egress PE. Although it might be obvious by now, for completeness, the ingress PE learns the outer and inner label values as follows:

■ The outer label is based on the LIB entry, specifically for the LIB entry for the prefix that matches the BGP-learned next-hop IP address—not the packet's destination IP address.

■ The inner label is based on the BGP table entry for the route in the VRF that matches the packet's destination address.

Figure 11-23 completes the ongoing example by showing the process by which PE1 adds the correct FIB entry into VRF-A for the 10.3.3.0/24 prefix.

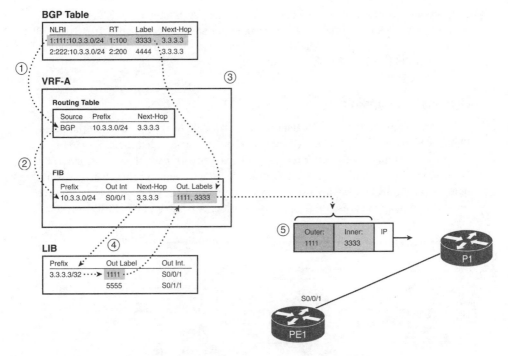

**Figure 11-23**  *Creating the Ingress PE (PE1) FIB Entry for VRF-A*

The figure picks up the story at the point at which PE1 has learned all required BGP and LDP information, and it is ready to populate the VRF routing table and FIB.

PE1's BGP table holds the VPN label (3333), while PE1's LIB holds the two labels learned from PE1's two LDP neighbors (P1 and P2, labels 1111 and 5555, respectively). In this case, PE1's best route that matches BGP next-hop 3.3.3.3 happens to point to P1 instead of P2, so this example uses label 1111, learned from P1.

The steps in the figure are explained as follows:

1.  PE1 redistributes the route from BGP into the VRF-A routing table (based on the import RT).

2.  PE1 builds a VRF-A FIB entry for the route just added to the VRF-A routing table.

3.  This new FIB entry needs to include the VPN-label, which PE1 finds in the associated BGP table entry.

4.  This new FIB entry also needs to include the outer label, the one used to reach the BGP next-hop IP address (3.3.3.3), so PE1 looks in the LIB for the best LIB entry that matches 3.3.3.3 and extracts the label (1111).

5.  Ingress PE1 inserts the MPLS header, including the two-label label stack.

At this point, when PE1 receives a packet in an interface assigned to VRF-A, PE1 will look in the VRF-A FIB. If the packet is destined for an address in prefix 10.3.3.0/24, PE1 will match the entry shown in the figure, and PE1 will forward the packet out S0/0/1, with labels 1111 and 3333.

## Penultimate Hop Popping

The operation of the MPLS VPN data plane works well, but the process on the egress PE can be a bit inefficient. The inefficiency relates to the fact that the egress PE must do two lookups in the LFIB after receiving the packet with two labels in the label stack. For example, the data plane forwarding example used throughout this chapter has been repeated in Figure 11-24, with a summary description of the processing logic on each router. Note that the egress PE (PE2) must consider two entries in its LFIB.

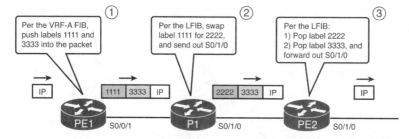

**Figure 11-24**   *Two LFIB Lookups Required on the Egress PE*

To avoid this extra work on the very last (ultimate) LSR, MPLS uses a feature called *penultimate hop popping (PHP)*. (*Penultimate* simply means "1 less than the ultimate.") So the penultimate hop is not the very last LSR to process a labeled packet, but the second-to-last LSR to process a labeled packet. PHP causes the penultimate-hop LSR to pop the outer label, so that the last LSR—the ultimate hop if you will—receives a packet that only has the VPN label in it. With only this single label, the egress PE needs to look up only one entry in the LFIB. Figure 11-25 shows the revised data plane flow with PHP enabled.

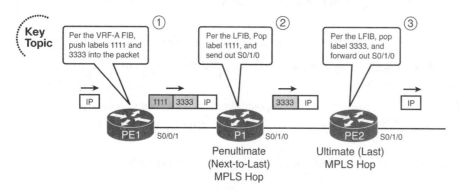

**Figure 11-25**   *Single LFIB Lookup on Egress PE Because of PHP*

# Other MPLS Applications

This last relatively short section of the chapter introduces the general idea about the protocols used by several other MPLS applications. To that end, this section introduces and explains the concept of a *Forwarding Equivalence Class (FEC)* and summarizes the concept of an FEC as used by various MPLS applications.

**Key Topic**

Frankly, this chapter has already covered all the concepts surrounding the term FEC. However, it is helpful to know the term and the FEC concept as an end to itself, because it helps when comparing various MPLS applications.

Generally speaking, an FEC is a set of packets that receives the same forwarding treatment by a single LSR. For simple MPLS unicast IP forwarding, each IPv4 prefix is an FEC. For MPLS VPNs, each prefix in each VRF is an FEC—making the prefix 10.3.3.0/24 in VRF-A a different FEC from the 10.3.3.0/24 prefix in VRF-B. Alternately, with QoS implemented, one FEC might be the set of packets in VRF-A, destined to 10.3.3.0/24, with DSCP EF in the packet, and another FEC might be packets in the same VPN, to the same subnet, but with a different DSCP value.

For each FEC, each LSR needs a label, or label stack, to use when forwarding packets in that FEC. By using a unique label or set of labels for each FEC, a router has the ability to assign different forwarding details (outgoing interface and next-hop router.)

Each of the MPLS applications can be compared by focusing on the information used to determine an FEC. For example, MPLS traffic engineering (TE) allows MPLS networks to choose to send some packets over one LSP and other packets over another LSP, based on traffic loading—even though the true end destination might be in the same location. By doing so, SPs can manage the flow of data over their high-speed core networks and prevent the problem of overloading the best route as determined by a routing protocol, while barely using alternate routes. To achieve this function, MPLS TE bases the FEC concept in part on the definition of an MPLS TE tunnel.

You can also compare different MPLS applications by listing the control plane protocols used to learn label information. For example, this chapter explained how MPLS VPN uses both LDP and MP-BGP to exchange label information, whereas other MPLS applications use LDP and something else—or do not even use LDP. Table 11-5 lists many of the common MPLS applications, the information that determines an FEC, and the control plane protocol that is used to advertise FEC-to-label bindings.

**Key Topic**

**Table 11-5**  *Control Protocols Used in Various MPLS Applications*

| Application | FEC | Control Protocol Used to Exchange FEC-to-Label Binding |
|---|---|---|
| Unicast IP routing | Unicast IP routes in the global IP routing table | Tag Distribution Protocol (TDP) or Label Distribution Protocol (LDP) |
| Multicast IP routing | Multicast routes in the global multicast IP routing table | PIM version 2 extensions |

| Application | FEC | Control Protocol Used to Exchange FEC-to-Label Binding |
|---|---|---|
| VPN | Unicast IP routes in the per-VRF routing table | MP-BGP |
| Traffic engineering | MPLS TE tunnels (configured) | RSVP or CR-LDP |
| MPLS QoS | IP routing table and the ToS byte | Extensions to TDP and LDP |

# Implement Multi-VRF Customer Edge (VRF Lite)

VRF Lite, also known as Multi-VRF CE, provides multiple instances of IP routing tables in a single router. By associating each interface/subinterface with one of the several VRF instances, a router can create Layer 3 separation, much like Layer 2 VLANs separate a Layer 2 LAN domain. With VRF Lite, engineers can create internetworks that allow overlapping IP address spaces without requiring Network Address Translation (NAT), enforce better security by preventing packets from crossing into other VRFs, and provide some convenient features to extend the MPLS VPN concept to the CE router.

VRF Lite uses the same configuration commands already covered earlier in the section "MPLS VPN Configuration." The rest of this short section introduces VRF Lite, first by explaining how it can be configured as an end to itself (without MPLS). Following that, the use of VRF Lite to extend MPLS VPN services to the CE is explained.

## VRF Lite, Without MPLS

As an end to itself, VRF Lite allows the engineer to separate IP internetworks into different domains or groupings without requiring separate routers and without requiring separate physical connections. Normally, to provide separation of Layer 3 domains, several tools might be used: ACLs to filter packets, route filters to filter routes, NAT to deal with overlapping IP address spaces, and separate physical links between sites. With only a single IP routing table in a router, some problems present a bigger challenge that might have been best solved using a separate router.

The mechanics of VRF Lite configuration match the configuration listed as Steps 1 and 2 from the "MPLS VPN Configuration" section, earlier in this chapter. The router configuration begins with multiple VRFs. Then, the interfaces are associated with a single VRF, so the router will choose the VRF to use when forwarding packets based on the VRF association of the incoming interface. Finally, any routing protocols operate on specific VRFs.

For example, consider Figure 11-26, which shows a simple design of a small portion of an internetwork. In this case, two companies merged. They had offices in the same pair of cities, so they migrated the users to one building in each city. To keep the users separate, the users from each former company sit inside a company-specific VLAN.

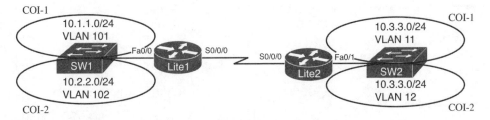

**Figure 11-26**  *Design Used for VRF Lite*

The design shows the overlapping subnets on the right side of Figure 11-26 (10.3.3.0/24). The engineers could have such reassigned IP addresses in one of the subnets and ignored VRF Lite. However, because of other security considerations, the design also calls for preventing packets from hosts in one former company from flowing into subnets of the other former company. One solution then is to create two VRFs per router.

Beyond the configuration already shown for MPLS VPNs, as Steps 1 and 2 from the "MPLS VPN Configuration" section, the only other new configuration step is to ensure that the routers use subinterfaces on links that support traffic for multiple VRFs. VRF Lite requires that each interface or subinterface be associated with one VRF, so to share a physical link among VRFs, the configuration must include subinterfaces. For example, a design might use Ethernet, with trunking, and the associated subinterface configuration.

In the case of a leased line, however, the typical High-Level Data Link Control (HDLC) and PPP configuration does not allow for subinterfaces. In such cases, most configurations use Frame Relay encapsulation, which does allow for subinterfaces. However, an actual Frame Relay network is not necessary; instead, the engineer chooses a Data-Link Connection Identifier (DLCI) to use for each VC—the same DLCI on each end—and configures a point-to-point subinterface for each such DLCI.

Example 11-13 shows the complete configuration for VRF Lite for the design shown in Figure 11-26, including the Frame Relay configuration on the serial link.

**Example 11-13**  *VRF Lite Configuration on Router Lite-1*

```
! CEF is required. The VRF configuration still requires both an RD and
! an import/export RT. Without MPLS however, the values remain local.
ip cef

ip vrf COI-1
 rd 11:11
 route-target both 11:11

ip vrf COI-2
 rd 22:22
 route-target both 22:22


! Next, the user chose DLCI 101 and 102 for the two Frame Relay subinterfaces.
! Note that the other router must match these DLCI values. Also, note that each
```

```
! Frame Relay subinterface is associated with a different VRF.

int s0/0/0
 encapsulation frame-relay
 clock rate 1536000
 no shut
 description to Lite-2

int s0/0/0.101 point-to-point
 frame-relay interface-dlci 101
 ip address 192.168.4.1 255.255.255.252
 no shutdown
 ip vrf forwarding COI-1

int s0/0/0.102 point-to-point
 frame-relay interface-dlci 102
 ip address 192.168.4.5 255.255.255.252
 no shutdown
 ip vrf forwarding COI-2

! Next, the usual 802.1Q router config is listed, matching the VLANs
! shown in Figure 11-26. Note that each subinterface is also associated
! with one VRF.

int fa0/0
 no ip address
 no shut
 description to C-1
int fa0/0.1
 encapsulation dot1q 101
 ip vrf forwarding COI-1
 ip addr 10.1.1.100 255.255.255.0

int fa0/0.2
 encapsulation dot1q 102
 ip vrf forwarding COI-2
 ip addr 10.2.2.100 255.255.255.0

! Finally, the EIGRP configuration, per VRF - nothing new here compared
! to the MPLS VPN configuration. Note that router Lite-2 would also need
! to configure the same autonomous-system 1 commands, but the router
! eigrp asn command would not need to match.

router eigrp 65001
 address-family ipv4 vrf COI-1
  autonomous-system 1
```

```
network 10.0.0.0
no auto-summary
address-family ipv4 vrf COI-2
 autonomous-system 1
 network 10.0.0.0
 no auto-summary
```

## VRF Lite with MPLS

The other name for VRF Lite, *Multi-VRF CE*, practically defines its use with MPLS VPNs. From a technical perspective, this feature allows a CE router to have VRF aware-ness, but it remains in the role of CE. As such, a CE using Multi-VRF CE can use multiple VRFs, but it does not have the burden of implementing LDP, pushing/popping labels, or acting as an LSR.

From a design perspective, the Multi-VRF CE feature gives the provider better choices about platforms and where to put the relatively large workload required by a PE. A multi-tenant unit (MTU) design is a classic example, where the SP puts a single Layer 3 device in a building with multiple customers. The SP engineers could just make the CPE device act as PE. However, by making the CPE router act as CE, but with using Multi-VRF CE, the SP can easily separate customers at Layer 3, while avoiding the investment in a more powerful Layer 3 CPE platform to support full PE functionality. Figure 11-27 shows such a case.

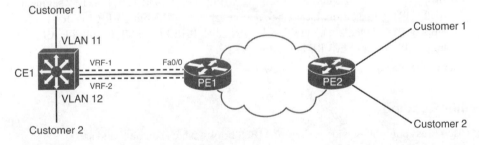

**Figure 11-27**   *Design Used for VRF Lite*

## Foundation Summary

Please take the time to read and study the details in the "Foundation Topics" section of the chapter, as well as review the items noted with a Key Topic icon.

## Memory Builders

The CCIE Routing and Switching written exam, like all Cisco CCIE written exams, covers a fairly broad set of topics. This section provides some basic tools to help you exercise your memory about some of the broader topics covered in this chapter.

### Fill In Key Tables from Memory

Appendix E, "Key Tables for CCIE Study," on the CD in the back of this book, contains empty sets of some of the key summary tables in each chapter. Print Appendix E, refer to this chapter's tables in it, and fill in the tables from memory. Refer to Appendix F, "Solutions for Key Tables for CCIE Study," on the CD, to check your answers.

### Definitions

Next, take a few moments to write down the definitions for the following terms:

FIB, LIB, LFIB, MPLS unicast IP routing, MPLS VPNs, LDP, TDP, LSP, LSP segment, MPLS TTL propagation, local label, remote label, label binding, VRF, RD, RT, overlapping VPN, inner label, outer label, VPN label, PHP, FEC, LSR, E-LSR, PE, CE, P, ingress PE, egress PE, VRF Lite, Multi-VRF CE

Refer to the glossary to check your answers.

### Further Reading

Cisco Press publishes a wide variety of MPLS books, which can be found at www.ciscopress.com. Additionally, you can see a variety of MPLS pages from www.cisco.com/go/mpls.

## CHAPTER 12

# Final Preparation

The first 11 chapters of this book cover the portion of technologies, protocols, and considerations required to be prepared to pass the 400-101 CCIE Routing and Switching written exam. While these chapters supply the detailed information, most people need more preparation than simply reading the first 11 chapters of this book. This chapter details a set of tools and a study plan to help you complete your preparation for the exams.

This short chapter has two main sections. The first section lists the exam preparation tools useful at this point in the study process. The second section lists a suggested study plan now that you have completed all the earlier chapters in this book.

**Note** Note that Appendixes E and F exist as soft-copy appendices on the CD included in the back of this book.

## Tools for Final Preparation

This section lists some information about the available tools and how to access the tools.

## Pearson Cert Practice Test Engine and Questions on the CD

The CD in the back of the book includes the Pearson Cert Practice Test engine—software that displays and grades a set of exam-realistic multiple-choice questions. Using the Pearson Cert Practice Test engine, you can either study by going through the questions in Study Mode or take a simulated (timed) CCNA Security exam.

The installation process requires two major steps. The CD in the back of this book has a recent copy of the Pearson Cert Practice Test engine. The practice exam—the database of CCIE Routing and Switching exam questions—is not on the CD.

**Note** The cardboard CD case in the back of this book includes the CD and a piece of paper. The paper lists the activation key for the practice exam associated with this book. *Do not lose the activation key.*

## Install the Software from the CD

The software installation process is pretty routine as compared with other software installation processes. To be complete, the following steps outline the installation process:

**Step 1.**    Insert the CD into your PC.

**Step 2.**    The software that automatically runs is the Cisco Press software to access and use all CD-based features, including the exam engine and the CD-only appendices. From the main menu, click the option to **Install the Exam Engine**.

**Step 3.**    Respond to Windows prompts as with any typical software installation process.

The installation process will give you the option to activate your exam with the activation code supplied on the paper in the CD sleeve. This process requires that you establish a Pearson website login. You will need this login to activate the exam, so please register when prompted. If you already have a Pearson website login, there is no need to register again. Just use your existing login.

## Activate and Download the Practice Exam

After the exam engine is installed, you should then activate the exam associated with this book (if you did not do so during the installation process) as follows:

**Step 1.**    Start the Pearson Cert Practice Test (PCPT) software from the Windows **Start** menu or from your desktop shortcut icon.

**Step 2.**    To activate and download the exam associated with this book, from the **My Products** or **Tools** tab, click the **Activate** button.

**Step 3.**    At the next screen, enter the activation key from the paper inside the cardboard CD holder in the back of the book. After it is entered, click the **Activate** button.

**Step 4.**    The activation process will download the practice exam. Click **Next**, and then click **Finish**.

When the activation process is completed, the **My Products** tab should list your new exam. If you do not see the exam, make sure that you have selected the **My Products** tab on the menu. At this point, the software and practice exam are ready to use. Simply select the exam and click the **Use** button.

To update a particular exam that you have already activated and downloaded, simply select the **Tools** tab and click the **Update Products** button. Updating your exams will ensure that you have the latest changes and updates to the exam data.

If you want to check for updates to the Pearson Cert Practice Test exam engine software, simply select the **Tools** tab and click the **Update Application** button. This will ensure that you are running the latest version of the software engine.

## Activating Other Exams

The exam software installation process, and the registration process, only has to happen once. Then, for each new exam, only a few steps are required. For example, if you buy another new Cisco Press Official Cert Guide or Pearson IT Certification Cert Guide, extract the activation code from the CD sleeve in the back of that book; you don't even need the CD at this point. From there, all you have to do is start the exam engine (if it is not still up and running) and perform Steps 2 through 4 from the previous list.

## Premium Edition

In addition to the free practice exam provided on the CD-ROM, you can purchase additional exams with expanded functionality directly from Pearson IT Certification. The Premium Edition of this title contains an additional two full practice exams as well as an eBook (in both PDF and ePub format). In addition, the Premium Edition title also has remediation for each question to the specific part of the eBook that relates to that question.

Because you have purchased the print version of this title, you can purchase the Premium Edition at a deep discount. There is a coupon code in the CD sleeve that contains a one-time-use code as well as instructions for where you can purchase the Premium Edition.

To view the Premium Edition product page, go to www.informit.com/title/9780133591057.

# The Cisco Learning Network

Cisco provides a wide variety of CCIE Routing and Switching preparation tools at a Cisco Systems website called the Cisco Learning Network. This site includes a large variety of exam preparation tools, including sample questions, forums on each Cisco exam, learning video games, and information about each exam.

To reach the Cisco Learning Network, go to www.cisco.com/go/learningnetwork or just search for "Cisco Learning Network." You will need to use the login you created at www.cisco.com. If you don't have such a login, you can register for free. To register, simply go to www.cisco.com, click **Register** at the top of the page, and supply the requested information.

# Memory Tables

Like most Official Cert Guides from Cisco Press, this book purposefully organizes information into tables and lists for easier study and review. Rereading these tables can be very useful before the exam. However, it is easy to skim over the tables without paying attention to every detail, especially when you remember having seen the table's contents when reading the chapter.

Instead of simply reading the tables in the various chapters, this book's Appendices E and F give you another review tool. Appendix E lists partially completed versions of many of the tables from the book. You can open Appendix F (a PDF file on the CD that comes with this book) and print the appendix. For review, you can attempt to complete the tables. This exercise can help you focus on the review. It also exercises the memory connectors in your brain; plus it makes you think about the information without as much information, which forces a little more contemplation about the facts.

Appendix F, also a PDF file located on the CD, lists the completed tables to check your work. You can also just refer to the tables as printed in the book.

## Chapter-Ending Review Tools

Chapters 1–11 have several features in the Exam Preparation Tasks sections at the end of the chapter. You might have already worked through these in each chapter. It can also be useful to use these tools again as you make your final preparations for the exam.

## Suggested Plan for Final Review/Study

This section lists a suggested study plan until you take the 400-101 CCIE Routing and Switching written exam. Certainly, you can ignore this plan, use it as is, or just take suggestions from it.

The plan uses three steps:

**Step 1.** **Review Key Topics and DIKTA Questions:** You can use the table that lists the key topics in each chapter, or just flip the pages looking for key topics. Also, reviewing the "Do I Know This Already" (DIKTA) questions from the beginning of the chapter can be helpful for review.

**Step 2.** **Complete Memory Tables:** Open Appendix E on the CD, and print the entire appendix, or print the tables by major part. Then complete the tables.

**Step 3.** **Use the Pearson Cert Practice Test Engine to Practice:** The Pearson Cert Practice Test engine on the CD can be used to study using a bank of unique exam-realistic questions available only with this book.

## Using the Exam Engine

The Pearson Cert Practice Test engine on the CD includes a database of questions created specifically for this book. The Pearson Cert Practice Test engine can be used either in study mode or practice exam mode, as follows:

- **Study mode:** Study mode is most useful when you want to use the questions for learning and practicing. In study mode, you can select options like randomizing the order of the questions and answers, automatically viewing answers to the questions as you go, testing on specific topics, and many other options.

- **Practice Exam mode:** This mode presents questions in a timed environment, providing you with a more exam-realistic experience. It also restricts your ability to see your score as you progress through the exam and view answers to questions as you are taking the exam. These timed exams not only allow you to study for the actual 400-101 CCIE Routing and Switching written exam, but they also help you simulate the time pressure that can occur on the actual exam.

When doing your final preparation, you can use study mode, practice exam mode, or both. However, after you have seen each question a couple of times, you will likely start to remember the questions, and the usefulness of the exam database might go down. So, consider the following options when using the exam engine:

- Use this question database for review. Use study mode to study the questions by chapter, just as with the other final review steps listed in this chapter. Plan on getting another exam (possibly from the Premium Edition) if you want to take additional simulated exams.

- Save the question database, not using it during your review of each book part. Save it until the end, so you will not have seen the questions before. Then, use practice exam mode to simulate the exam.

Picking the correct mode from the exam engine's user interface is pretty obvious. The following steps show how to move to the screen from which to select study or practice exam mode:

**Step 1.**   Click the **My Products** tab if you are not already in that screen.

**Step 2.**   Select the exam that you want to use from the list of available exams.

**Step 3.**   Click the **Use** button.

When you take these actions, the engine should display a window from which you can choose **Study Mode** or **Practice Exam Mode**. When in study mode, you can further choose the book chapters, limiting the questions to those explained in the specified chapters of the book.

## Summary

The tools and suggestions listed in this chapter have been designed with one goal in mind: to help you develop the skills required to pass the 400-101 CCIE Routing and Switching written exam. This book has been developed from the beginning to not just tell you the facts but also to help you learn how to apply the facts. No matter what your experience level is leading up to taking the exams, it is our hope that the broad range of preparation tools, and even the structure of the book, will help you pass the exam with ease. We hope you do well on the exam.

# Answers to the "Do I Know This Already?" Quizzes

## Chapter 1

1. D
2. C
3. A and D
4. D
5. A and B
6. C
7. A and C
8. A, D, and E
9. D
10. A and B
11. A, C, and E
12. C

## Chapter 2

1. B and D
2. C
3. A
4. A and B
5. B
6. A and C
7. B and C
8. A
9. E
10. A
11. C

12. D
13. A and D
14. C

## Chapter 3

1. C
2. A and D
3. A, B, and E
4. B and D
5. A
6. A and B
7. D
8. B and E
9. A
10. A and B
11. C and D

## Chapter 4

1. C
2. A and B
3. E
4. B
5. A and B
6. A
7. C
8. D
9. A

## Chapter 5

1. C
2. C
3. B, C, and D
4. A
5. B
6. C
7. A and C
8. A

## Chapter 6

1. B
2. D
3. C and D
4. B
5. C
6. D

## Chapter 7

1. B, C, and D
2. C
3. A and D
4. D
5. D
6. D
7. E

## Chapter 8

1. C
2. D
3. D

4. C and E
5. A and C
6. C and D
7. B
8. C and D
9. A, C, and D
10. C

## Chapter 9

1. D
2. A
3. C
4. A, B, and E
5. D
6. B
7. D
8. A and B
9. B

## Chapter 10

1. B
2. A, C, D, and F
3. C
4. D
5. A, C, and E
6. C
7. A and E
8. B and E
9. C

# Chapter 11

1. A

2. D

3. B

4. A

5. A

6. B

7. B

8. B and C

9. B and D

10. A and C

11. A and E

# CCIE Exam Updates

Over time, reader feedback allows Cisco Press to gauge which topics give our readers the most problems when taking the exams. Additionally, Cisco might make small changes in the breadth of exam topics or in the emphasis of certain topics. To assist readers with those topics, the authors create new materials clarifying and expanding upon those troublesome exam topics.

The document you are viewing is Version 1.0 of this appendix and there are no updates. You can check for an updated version at www.ciscopress.com/title/9781587144912.

# Index

# C

# D

# E

# J-K

# L

# M

# N

# O

# Q

# S

# T

# X-Y-Z

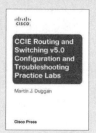